Love Letters
to Africa

Love Letters to Africa

Don Pinnock

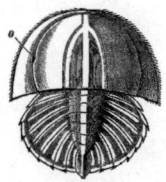

DOUBLE
STOREY
a juta company

in association with *Getaway* magazine

First published 2005 by Double Storey Books,
a division of Juta & Co. Ltd,
Mercury Crescent, Wetton, Cape Town,
in association with *Getaway* magazine

© 2005 Don Pinnock

ISBN 1 919930 68 X

All rights reserved. No part of this book may be reproduced
or utilised in any form and by any means, electronic or
mechanical, including photocopying, without permission
in writing from the publisher.

Typesetting by Christabel Hardacre
Printing by CTP Book Printers, Cape
24509

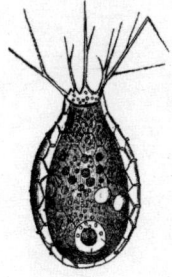

Also by Don Pinnock:
African Journeys (2003)
Natural Selections (2002)

contents

PREFACE IX

THE BIG PICTURE
The trouble with shooting stars 2
An ill-advised road and silver ghosts from the edge of time 10
Living kingdoms of the clouds 16
The long haul of the bath ducks 23
The strange history of a fix 31

OUR PEOPLED WORLD
Why zebras never went to war and sheep ended up stupid 42
Dying islands in the sun 52
Uneasy rumblings down in the swamp 59
Birds of heaven 66
Kiss those sweet red lips goodbye 73
Donkey wars and the Green Revolution 79
Deadly lost rivers of the urban sprawl 87

ODD ADVENTURERS
The trek to Copper Mountain   98
A brief history of clouds   104
Thank God for Skukuza   115
St Barbe and the Incredible Journey   124
Michael Fay and the human footprint   131

BIG AND HAIRY
Mythical monsters of the ancient forest   140
Vermin hunting   148

SMALL AND SPINELESS
Brilliant bees that waggle with intent   158
In defence of worms   165

GREEN AND GRACIOUS
*Sugar highs and water lows in the death-defying drama
    of desiccation*   176
The wasp that cares a fig   182

DR DON
Dr Don's sex advice for the spineless and distressed   192
Dr Don's advice for vexed vertebrates   201

A FINAL WORD
The way of wilderness   210

BIBLIOGRAPHY OF A SORT   219

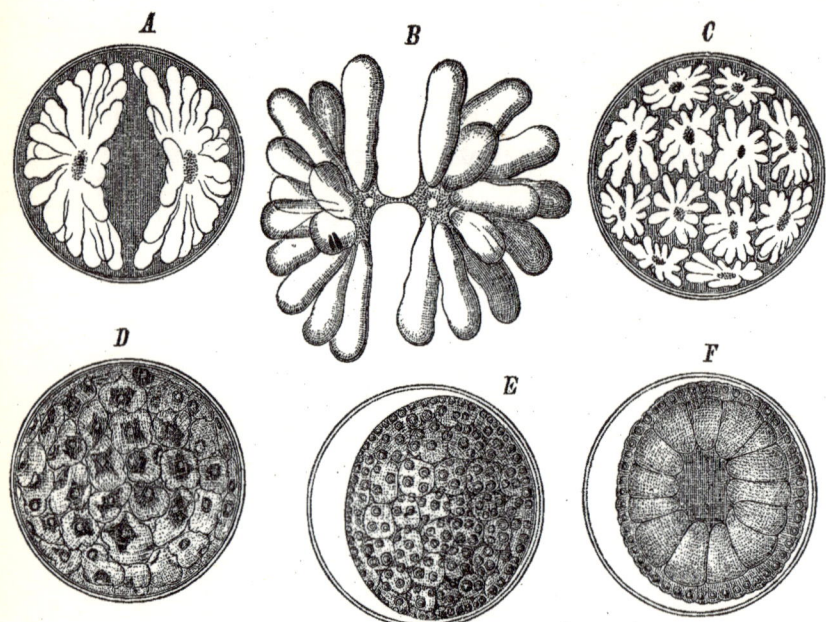

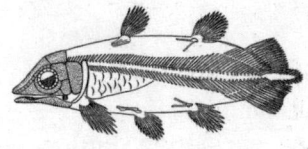

Preface

There are places in Africa so close to dreams it takes effort to imagine they're real. Take Kibale Forest in Uganda, for example. Even locals generally avoid it. But there's something so uncanny in there it gives me goosebumps. The forest is ancient and enfolding, huge yet accommodating: it's like strolling into a great medieval castle and realising it feels … like home.

I hopped off a bus one day (the driver thought I was mad) and simply walked into the arms of a million trees. Ebony, mahogany, teak and countless other species, buttressed on wide, fluted root systems, soared upwards through the canopy some 40 metres above. Brightly coloured bracket fungi step-laddered up dark, rotting stumps, lurid mosses lurked in gloomy wooden root crotches and – in shockingly bright shafts of sunlight – butterflies of many kinds pirouetted and played. The whole space seemed to be bound together by lianas and threaded with birdsong.

Kibale consists of 750 square kilometres of rainforest and has the highest density of primate species in Africa, including around 600 chimps. I soon found them – atop a fig tree nesting, copulating, peeing and stuffing themselves on sweet fruit. Occasionally a barking argument broke out, and the forest rang with their whoops and yells.

A storm in one of these forests is something to behold: I experienced one in Bwindi Impenetrable Forest, a bit further south. It was a commanding performance: with an ear-numbing crack, lightning slammed into a giant mahogany towering above the rainforest, unleashing a tropical deluge which bent the giant trees, sending leaves spinning to the ground. Huge, tightly packed drops seemed to squeeze the breath out of the sweaty air and left me drenched, gasping and enraptured.

Half an hour later it was gone, trailing wraiths of sun-flared mist which billowed from the dripping canopy. A black-and-white colobus monkey began its frog-like *gwaar*, *gwaar*, *gwir*, *gwir* call. Drinking it all in, I realised that I had stood, just so, in many places in Africa, enraptured by the continent's sounds and beauty, humbled by its grandeur.

It is, of course, a great privilege to be able to have such adventures and call it a profession. Working for *Getaway* magazine, I have been to places on the continent few people see in a lifetime, as well as to a number few would wish to visit. The further I travel the more I become fascinated by the ancient skein of life that today makes the continent so multi-textured – and shocked by the cavalier way we treat it. Lowly earthworms, tiny fig wasps, huge elephants, intuitive bees, sand-blasting steenbras, Okavango crocodiles, biting zebras, declining cranes and many more creatures that have taken millions of years to perfect are heading for the evolutionary dustbin unless we do something about it. A writer can but write and hope to influence, and hope some more.

It was something greater than concern that prompted these stories, though. In compiling this book I realised that the common thread running through them was love – they're love letters to a continent.

I owe much thanks for support, planning and suggestions to my adventurous colleagues at *Getaway*, and to my extraordinary family, Gaelen, Romaney-Rose and Patricia Schonstein, who bear (and share) my odd enthusiasms and put up with my frequent absences. And great tribute is due to my publishers at Double Storey, Bridget Impey and Russell Martin. We have established a relationship so casual and comfortable that it often comes as a surprise to find the outcome is a book.

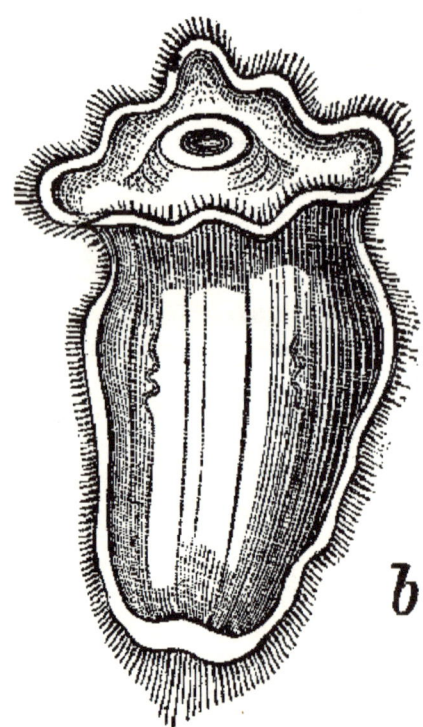

The big picture

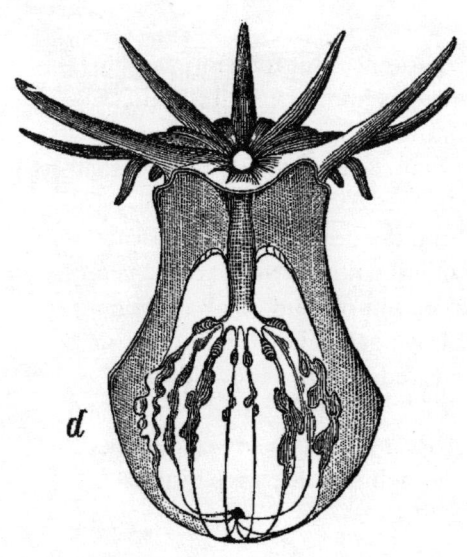

The trouble with shooting stars

There were parallels, naturally. But for Tintin and his dog, Snowy, the day ended as hot as ... well ... blue blistering barnacles. For me it closed cold and rainy.

We were both, it turns out, awed by a fiery object that had fallen from space. In Hergé's comic *Shooting Star*, Tintin's meteorite fell into the North Sea with a deafening boom, melting tar and wilting startled citizens on the way. Mine was planted in my hand one wet evening by University of Cape Town geologist Duncan Miller. As he did so, Duncan cleared his throat and did the dramatic: 'That's the oldest object ever held by a human being. At 4.56 billion years it pre-dates any earth rocks. It was formed in the solar nebulae that gave birth to our planets.'

I stared at the lump, which suddenly seemed heavy with portent.

'If you look at the polished surface,' he continued, knowing he'd hooked me, 'you'll see little spots, about half a millimetre across. They're chondrules – space dust from supernovas, star-death explosions, captured in the meteorite. The rock looks like nothing. But you must admit it's …. evocative.'

That was my introduction to Korra Korrabes, a chondrite meteorite recently discovered in Namibia, where it was helping to prop up a wall. It's a magical thing – quite as spectacular as Tintin's shooting star – and a lens into time so deep it makes all recorded history seem like the brief flick of a butterfly's wing. The space rock was tracked down by a Tintinesque meteorite hunter who probably required less whiskey than Tintin's friend, Captain Haddock, and a good deal more knowledge. For reasons mysterious, he wishes to remain anonymous.

Exactly why Korra Korrabes had been floating around for billions of years requires a rather circuitous explanation. Stars are elemental cookers, and they've been at it for a time. The Big Bang produced only hydrogen, helium and lithium-7, great clouds of which, through gravitational attraction, whirled together and ignited to give birth to huge, unstable stars. In the hearts of these stars, oxygen and carbon were produced, and when the stars exploded – as most stars eventually do – they ejected gas and dust across space. This eventually formed daughter stars which brewed up still newer, ever heavier, elements. By the time our sun was formed, 4.5 billion years ago, generations of stars had been succeeding one another for around ten billion years. By then there were nearly 100 elements to choose from – a very good soup in which to spark life.

The real star performers, however, are supernovas. When the hydrogen of a massive star – maybe ten times the size of the sun – is used up, it collapses. Under unthinkable gravitational forces, atoms are crushed to a hard neutron core which suddenly halts the collapse. The effect is like a jet of water hitting a brick wall. The rebound causes a massive explosion which ejects the outer layers of the star, producing an immense shock wave. The flash can outshine an entire galaxy. This wave, passing through the hurtling material of the dying star, causes what is described as nucleosynthesis, creating new elements and causing them to merge and condense to form sand-sized droplets of matter. These are the seeds of new stars.

How we know this is described rather well by Tintin's friend, Professor Phostle: 'You've heard of the spectroscope? It's the instrument that breaks up light and enables us to discover elements in stars, elements not yet isolated here on earth. Each of these lines is characteristic of a metal. These lines in the centre represent an unknown metal which exists in the meteor …'

In galactic terms our local star, the sun, is a mere speck. If you filled a fair-sized cathedral with rice grains it would give you an approximation of the number of stars in the Milky Way. To get their distribution proportionally right, you'd have to scatter them from earth to the moon.

The sun was formed by space dust which spiralled as it fell inwards. This left a disc of circling matter – dust, ice-encrusted comets, asteroids and larger 'planetesimals' – millions of which collided with each other, eventually forming planets.

The earth itself, comparatively speaking, is little more than stardust. While the sun makes up something like 99.8 per cent of the solar system's mass and Jupiter two thirds of what's left, earth weighs in at around 0.05 per cent – basically leftover material.

However, not all the matter was claimed in the great spiral dust-gathering. Between Mars and Jupiter is a dangerous, swarming asteroid belt and out beyond Jupiter there's a strange zone known as the Oort Cloud, consisting of billions of restless comets – affectionately referred to by astronomers as cosmic snowballs.

There are basically three sources of meteorites: ancient accumulations of stardust, the iron cores and rocky crusts of asteroids or destroyed planets, and chunks ejected into space from other planets or the moon by meteorite impact. They rain down on earth in astounding numbers. It's estimated that around 100 tons a day hit the upper atmosphere, generally as space dust. Most meteorites explode when they encounter the atmosphere, but some are big enough to survive. Most splash into the oceans – which cover two thirds of the planet – but occasionally they make the news.

In 1911 a meteorite killed a dog in Egypt, in 1991 a roof in Japan was holed and in 1992 a meteorite slammed through the boot of a car in Kentucky, New Jersey. In

1994 one thumped through the roof of a warehouse in George. More recently a herder in Namibia was hit on the head by a chunk which first bounced off the branch of a tree, and a girl in North Yorkshire was struck on the foot by a small space rock.

Generally, meteorites are not troublesome, but there's a lot of stuff flying round up there, some of it frighteningly big. The Shoemaker-Levy 9 comet, which hit Jupiter in July 1994, left a crater the size of the earth in the giant planet.

There's also strong evidence that the moon was created from flying debris when the earth collided with an object about the size of Mars somewhere round four billion years ago. This Big Splat re-melted and thinned the earth's crust, tilted the planet and increased its spin speed, giving us a short (in planetary terms) 24-hour day. Another 'splat' could have led to the demise of the dinosaurs some 65 million years ago, when a space object is thought to have hammered a 200-kilometre diameter crater into Yucatan province in Mexico. Dust from the impact and smoke from runaway forest fires would have blanketed the earth, preventing photosynthesis in plants and so killing off giant herbivores and their predators.

On average, a collision between earth and a big meteorite or comet seems to occur about every 100 000 years. We're a little overdue. You'd think *Homo sapiens* would take steps to avoid being dinosaured. But no, they have other interests. The budget for the film *Deep Impact*, about a meteorite collision with earth, far exceeded the amount of money spent on detecting dangerous incoming space missiles.

If this seems to be a long, wild ramble, it's the only way to describe Korra Korrabes. The scrap of meteorite in my hand was a grainy amalgam of captured supernova dust.

Meteorites look much like ordinary rocks and generally only experts can recognise them. But in deserts like the Namib or on the icefields of Antarctica they're out of character and easier to spot, which is why these areas attract meteorite hunters. Herein lies the problem. To astrophysicists, meteorites are dipsticks into deep time and a potential source of new and exciting elements. For collectors they're fascinating treasures. Kilo for kilo, some types of meteorite are far rarer than almost any precious mineral on earth. This has ensured some of them a high price tag.

Meteorites are damnably hard to find. If you were to traverse, say, every 2.5 square metres in a ten-square-kilometre site you'd have to walk 20 000 kilometres.

There are marketing sites on the web with names from the seriously scientific to the pure whimsical: International Meteorite Brokerage, Southwest Meteorite Laboratory, Meteorite.com, Cosmic Matter, Dinocom ...

'Whether it's your first meteorite purchase or you're looking for that extraordinary show piece,' warbles Meteorite.com, 'these fine dealers are here to serve you!'

With a growing market for space objects, there's little doubt market forces are leading to theft of meteorites from museum and possibly from university collections. On www.meteorite.com there are some sad appeals for lost or stolen rocks:

Arkansas Planetarium: 'We have a missing Mundrabilla meteorite. If someone should contact you from Arkansas with a meteorite for sale, would you please work with us on it? Thanks.'

Transvaal Museum: 'The only known sample of the Namibian Itzawisis pallasite has disappeared from the collection. This meteorite is of profound interest to a research programme being run at the University of Cape Town, and we beg anyone with information about it to please contact us urgently.'

American Meteorite Survey: 'A 444.5-gram complete slice of Glorieta Mountain meteorite was lifted at the Tucson Show. This is a very valuable piece.'

Casper Meteorites: 'Our 0.016-gram slice of lunar meteorite DAG 400 has been stolen.'

In South Africa and Namibia ownership of meteorites found in those countries is effectively illegal for private collectors.

'My position', commented Mary Leslie of the South African Heritage Resources Agency, 'is that legislation disallows private ownership of meteorites as they are considered to provide information on cosmic matters which all people need to be able to share in.'

The head of the Namibian Geological Survey, Gabi Schneider, has much the same view. 'The Monuments Council will not issue a permit to a private collector,' she says, 'since this rare material should not be on someone's coffee table, but rather available for science and education.'

Not all scientists agree. Marian Tredaux of the University of Cape Town's Geological Sciences considers such legislation to be a death warrant for meteorite research. 'Most people won't come forward with their samples, nor go to find others, if they fear the state will take them away without reward.'

Duncan Miller considers the South African and Namibian laws to be flawed. 'In reality, they're unimplementable,' he commented. 'No customs officer would be able to distinguish between a meteorite and an innocuous stone or lump of rusty iron. The result is that collectors can smuggle meteorites out of the country with ease.'

A South African meteorite dealer, who asked not to be named, said nobody was going to hand in a meteorite to the state when there was no incentive and they could sell it overseas. The legislation just scared them away.

'The law should encourage people to find meteorites and also make them accessible to science and the state,' he said. 'My suggestion is that they should be handed to an academic institution for classification, then half should be handed back to the finder with a certificate of authenticity allowing them to keep or sell it. That way the state gains a meteorite and the finder has value added to their treasure.'

Tintin, of course, found his treasure in true adventurer style with no messy paperwork. He parachuted onto the teetering meteorite and leapt off as it sank, clinging to a precious lump of the stuff wrapped in a flag. He returned home, of course, to a hero's welcome.

Snowy, on the other hand, merely got himself into nasty scrapes and wondered why there was so much fuss about a silly rock. Until Duncan Miller parked a 4.56-billion-year-old space rock in my hand, I would have voted with Snowy.

An ill-advised road and silver ghosts from the edge of time

A breeze rippled the surface of the sheltered coastal lagoon. Nothing else was familiar. No insects buzzed through the strange undergrowth, no flowers grew up the banks, no creatures foraged in the woods, no birds settled in the scaly, mop-haired trees. They were not yet part of the grand adventure of life on earth.

Below the water surface, however, experimentation was in full swing: great armour-plated fish with jointed paddles, spike-backed sharks and leg-finned coelacanths hunted lungfish and each other, lunging into the weedy shallows after shoals of juvenile fish. Water scorpions up to a metre long scavenged the bones.

The shallows – with thick mats of seaweeds, stonewort weeds and the fallen leaves from the lagoon banks –

were compelling hunting grounds. Certain fish with gill covers developed the ability to haul themselves across shallow mud flats on leg-like fins to reach them. This was the Devonian Period and these creatures were our ancestors.

Pity for some about the great extinction which was to follow. Around 345 million years ago something unimaginable occurred – we do not yet know what – and life's successes were cut back to a fortunate few. Not for the first time, and not for the last either. In the mud of the lagoon, however, time's patient layering had preserved leaves, branches and bones. Cavities left during the decay of these remains were filled with minerals. These were slowly replaced by silvery white kaolin. And there they lay, for millions of years, until the outcome of a ridiculous political decision.

Few townspeople wanted the bypass. Grahamstown's traders talked of lost revenue, hotels of lost guests, romantics of a lost town along the N2. There were predictions of horrendous car accidents along the new speedway (eventually, they proved correct). But this was the mid-1980s and the apartheid government wanted a fast road that didn't go through poor townships where youths burned tyres, threw stones and worse.

So, in time-honoured style, the city fathers decided to hold a meeting. It was a farce. Hundreds of people turned up to oppose the bypass, but only those who owned property were allowed in. The rest milled and shouted outside. The bypass would be good for the town, those eventually assembled were told. The reasons were unclear. The people objected. But this wasn't democracy, it was a lesson in self-interest.

The plans for the bypass were approved. The mayor, a dentist, bought a cement works and construction began. Because the army base was on the best, flattest northern route for the road, it was built instead on the deep-valleyed southern side of town. Huge graders were soon hacking a massive scar through once-beautiful farms and the much-loved Mountain Drive. Towering gantries supported cladding into which prodigious amounts of cement were poured. People were furious but the country was under virtual military rule, so what could they do?

Zoology professor Roy Lubke, who owned one of the desecrated farms, was having a braai with friends one day. One of the party, Mark Aken, wandered over to survey the damage and soon returned with the news that there were fossil plant fragments in the black shale of the new cutting. One thing led to another and soon Rhodes University palaeontologist Rob Gess was poking round the cutting with mounting excitement. It turned out the graders had sliced into the shale bed of an ancient lagoon. What he would unearth over the next 15 years would be a Devonian treasure trove. Almost every species he and other researchers came across would be new to science.

So while shopkeepers and garage owners watched their revenues dwindle, Gess's pile of fossils grew. It was painstaking labour. Working carefully with a pocketknife, he prised away layers of the soft, brittle shale, sometimes only a few millimetres thick, across several square metres of excavation. This allowed him 'snapshots' of the lagoon floor over time. Old time.

Back at his laboratory he worked round delicate fossils with a scalpel, a needle, an artist's brush and even a fingernail. Sometimes all it needed was a puff of breath to reveal a trace of plant or fish scale. Hundreds of photographs of the fossils were taken, which Gess enlarged and used to sketch three-dimensional views. From the sketches came beautiful watercolour pictures. What emerged were strange new creatures with no comfortable, easy-to-remember common names. Gess collected nearly a thousand specimens, representing some 50 taxa, including at least eight new species of fish and many new plants.

Discovering how the pieces fitted together and what they implied was like putting together a jigsaw puzzle cut by nature and time. It was a job requiring collaboration, intuition, comparison with overseas species and some educated guesswork.

Black mud meant still water. Complete leaf fossils meant slow decay, which indicated oxygen-poor water – a backwater. Leaves of some simple plants were compared to European ones which had stomata, proving they had grown out of the water. Whole branches were unbattered, proving that trees grew nearby. Some fish had proto-legs which may have permitted them to leave the lagoon to forage ...

Like silver pinholes of light in a camera of time, the patterns in the shale began to illuminate the existence of a quiet and almost unthinkably ancient lagoon. Scientific papers with arcane titles began to appear, with Gess's name among the authors: 'A new species of *Diplacanthus* from the Late Devonian'; 'The first *Bothriolepis*-associated Devonian fish fauna from Africa'; 'Late Devonian *charophytes*'; 'Devonian *Archaeopteris*'; 'Marine algal remains from the Upper Devonian'; 'New *placoderm* fishes'; 'An Unusual New Fossil Shark'. And a massive work with the paragraph-length title: *A Preliminary Catalogue of Fossil Algal, Plant, Anthropod and Fish Remains from a Late Devonian Black Shale near Grahamstown, South Africa.*

The road builders, meanwhile, were in trouble. The shale was weathering rapidly, exposing more and more Devonian treasure to Gess, but slowly destroying the road barrier and threatening motorists. In 1999 the cutting slumped, causing the closure of one lane of traffic.

The National Roads Agency cast about for a solution and a private company tendered, proposing to cut back deeply into the shale wall. Gess, alarmed, contacted them and they agreed to preserve some of the shale by creating wide terraces for the material to slump onto, while capping other areas with soil and vegetation. Still, there would be a great loss of valuable material, so Gess chiselled out about 30 cubic metres, loaded it onto a flat-bed truck and transported it, bit by bit, to his smallholding in Bathurst.

As such things often do, the bypass shale-bed project ran out of funding. I tracked down Rob Gess at his smallholding in the picturesque Eastern Cape village.

He and his wife were growing herbs and vegetables for the local market, running a small shop, doing other things.

He led me down a worn path through the long grass to a low roof on gumpoles under which was a large pile of shale pieces, carefully stacked, then offered me a chunk and showed me how to prise apart the layers with a pocket knife. It was like a lucky packet: who could know what would be inside? It was easy to understand how you could get obsessive about this.

Gess picked up a piece and began carefully unlayering it. After a while I'd done enough splitting to satisfy my curiosity. I watched him for a while, chatted to his young daughter, then bade him farewell. I had other appointments.

At the far end of the path I glanced back and he was still at it, chipping away, his body in the 21st century, his head in a shallow Devonian lagoon 360 million years old. Beyond the vegetable beds, lost in thought, he was busy peeling back time, layer by layer.

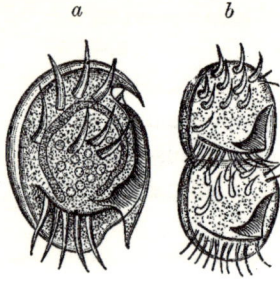
a *b*

Living kingdoms of the clouds

The idea was preposterous, but also simple and obvious. And like all simple, brilliant ideas you've never thought of, you go: 'Oh yeah, why not?' when you hear it.

I first came across it in *Trawler*, an intriguing book by Redmond O'Hanlon about fishing at the edge of the continental shelf north of the Orkney Islands. A gale was fluctuating between force nine and twelve, the seas were hideous, it was freezing and nobody was getting any sleep – maybe one or two hours a night – and they were already a week deep into the expedition. With all the bashing about they were dead beat but unable to drop off and suffering from sleep deprivation, so they'd lie in their bunks and rave on. Stream-of-consciousness stuff.

But I digress.

O'Hanlon, while rambling on to a companion on the trawler, recounts a story about Bill Hamilton whom he met while he (O'Hanlon) was editing the science pages for the *Times Literary Supplement*. Hamilton, he insists, was one of the great theoretical biology geniuses of all time, a specialist on kin selection who solved, among many other evolutionary puzzles, all the key problems Darwin failed to solve in *The Origin of Species*.

At one point before his early demise Hamilton got interested in clouds. This O'Hanlon discovered while having dinner with him; a dinner, incidentally, during which Hamilton's wife announced that she was divorcing him. Undeterred by this, he evidently broke his discussion for half a second, glanced at her and carried on (which might explain his wife's problem).

The reason we have clouds, he explained to O'Hanlon, is because water vapour condenses into puffy white stuff (and, ultimately, becomes rain) if it has a particle to condense around. Dust. That's the usual explanation. On closer investigation, he said, that dust would turn out to be bacteria. Clouds are therefore biological. They're servant-agents, sustained, created if you like, by bacteria to distribute themselves. Every time it rains, down they come: flu, pneumonia, TB and God knows what else, plus all sorts of useful bacteria. Biology. Life. Thundering down on our heads.

As far as O'Hanlon knew, only one experiment had been done to test this theory and it found clouds to be *pullulating* with bacteria. Was this possible? Had anything more been done? If it's true it will change our whole view of infection – and of life on earth. I simply had to find out.

That didn't turn out to be easy. Quiet, reclusive Hamilton had a way of coming to conclusions seemingly so odd and so many steps ahead of fellow academics that he gained a reputation as something of a crank. So while he was lauded for his kin selection work and awarded important prizes, pursuit of his wilder-seeming ideas has clearly not been the recommended path for aspiring young doctoral researchers. A journal and web search came up with remarkably few references to what must be one of the most interesting directions in astrobiology (the study of the atmosphere's biology). The few, however, are worth recounting.

Until recently nobody believed bacteria and viruses spent much time in the atmosphere between sneezes. If they were caught up in winds, it was thought they would be quickly killed by ultraviolet radiation from the sun. As I write, Bruce Moffett, a researcher from the University of East London, is gathering cloud samples over Britain with a giant 'vacuum cleaner' attached to an aircraft and analysing them. He is evidently finding whole colonies up there.

Russell Schnell from the University of Colorado, doing research on why there were so many hailstorms in western Kenya, stumbled on the fact that at the heart of each hailstone was the plant pathogen *Pseudomonas syringae* (can't they invent short names for these tiny things?). Gene Shinn of the US Geological Survey has come across more than 130 species of African bacteria and fungal spores over the Caribbean, one of which, *Aspergillus sybowii*, killed nearly all the region's sea fans.

Bridgitt Sattler of the University of Innsbruck, who sampled clouds over the Alps, was startled to find she had scooped around 1500 bacteria in each millilitre of cloud meltwater. As the lifetime of a cloud far exceeds the lifespan of a bacterium, she was forced to assume that they not only lived in clouds but bred there as well. 'We have proved that there is life up there and it can reproduce,' she wrote. 'Clouds should be considered as a microbal habitat.'

Now it's one thing to find bacteria in clouds, but quite another to suggest that they make the clouds. How could they do it? One way may be inferred from algal blooms at sea. During warm spells sea algae increase massively and minute spores of phytoplankton (plants) drift upward on the wind and, at a certain height, form the nuclei of water droplets which condense around them.

A second theory is more interesting. Many species, such as *P. syringae*, can grow ice crystals around themselves by exuding chemicals that encourage supercooled water to freeze. These plant pathogens may have developed this ability to promote frost damage on leaves, the better to consume them, but colonies living in clouds could do the same. And a cloud is what results when airborne water forms ice crystals. Bacteria could therefore 'seed' clouds and cause them to grow. Why, though, would they do this? To breed and travel. Rain may merely be bacteria's way of greening the earth and ensuring an abundant food supply – which includes us.

The idea that clouds might be biological colonies didn't simply pop into Bill Hamilton's head. As a brilliant evolutionary biologist, he puzzled most of his life about why creatures which were supposed to compete – according to Darwin's theory of natural selection – should cooperate, and particularly why they developed the precarious practice of sex in order to procreate.

He concluded that sex was a defence against parasites; an invention of metazoans and large plants to counteract the pressure of coevolving parasites (succession by simple division – cloning – would pass on the pathogens). So the movement of bacteria and diseases interested him, be it by way of clouds, clones or vaccines. For the same reason he grew deeply concerned about organ transplants between animals and humans, predicting the inadvertent transfer of a virus that could wipe out humanity.

The idea of living clouds raises the curtain on a larger issue. Without clouds, earth would, millions of years ago, have become a wasteland like Pluto or Mars. Clouds reflect enough sunlight to keep the earth cool, distribute water from the sea to the land and purify it along the way. It is not hyperbole to suggest that they make life possible. But the idea that they make it possible for their own ends suggests that we should give more thought to the interconnection of all things.

Conventional thinking, for many years following Darwin, was that animals and plants are the result of adaptation to their environment and that they depended on it. In the late 1960s atmospheric scientist James Lovelock first suggested that earth was a self-regulating system, that living creatures on the planet had made life possible by altering the environment to suit their needs. He named the concept the Gaia Theory. It was hooted out of court by most scientists at the time.

Some years later he went even further, suggesting that the earth was and still is managed largely by its microbal ecosystem – run, if you like, by its microscopic creatures. The biologist Richard Dawkins, a friend of Hamilton, went beyond even that: all plants and creatures, he speculated, are merely the various forms in which genes ensure their survival through space and time. We are, in other words, merely gene taxis. And inside your genes live organisms that are, genetically speaking, not you.

As with all radical new theories, the first response to these ideas was rejection, then argument, followed by partial acceptance. But here's the problem. Lovelock and Dawkins are alive and able to defend their ideas. Bill Hamilton is dead. The reason has to do with another wild but plausible idea.

In the early 1990s Hamilton came across two papers, one a work in progress, the other in *Rolling Stone*, suggesting that the HIV virus was introduced to humans through the Salk 11 anti-polio vaccine administered to Africans by the League of Nations. Pathogens being his passion, he decided to investigate.

On his first trip to the Congo he discovered that in the West, polio vaccine had been cultured on the livers of cows. But there are no cows in the tropics because of tsetse flies, so in the lower latitudes it had been cultured on the livers of green monkeys and chimps, which carried

Living kingdoms of the clouds 21

the HIV virus but were immune to it. The vision of caring nurses dutifully injecting thousands – maybe millions – of unsuspecting Africans with HIV is … well, it's explosive stuff.

On Hamilton's second trip to the Congo in 2000 he became critically ill and died. The official cause was given as malaria, but there were suggestions about poison and the desire of certain world bodies to curtail his investigation. The jury is still out on that one.

In serious journals and the popular press Hamilton was thereafter targeted as something of a crank, causing what his partner, Maria Luisa Bozzi, described as 'an embarrassed avoidance of the topic by his peers and the refusal of the editors of *Science*, *Nature* and *Lancet* to publish his ideas and their implications.'

His notion of living clouds was quietly buried. But, like all Hamilton's ideas, it may merely take a while for the rest of science to catch up. Meanwhile, just in case, keep your head out of the clouds.

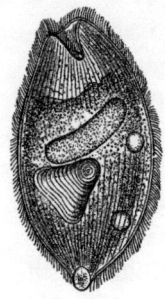

The long haul of the bath ducks

It began with yellow, plastic bath ducks – thousands of them – and ended somewhere quite different. I picked up the duck story from some wayward report and it led me to …

Wait! I need to begin with a warning: if you are prone to anxiety then read some other tale because you're not going to like this one. It's not about travel or the wonders of nature or something you can forget about after you've finished reading. It's going to stick.

The lure into the story was irresistible. In May 1990 the container vessel *Hansa Carrier* hit a severe storm in the north Pacific on its way from Korea and lost 21 shipping containers. Four of these spilled 60 000 new Nike shoes into the sea. Some time later they began appearing on beaches.

This, so the story went, alerted a retired Seattle oceanographer, Curtis Ebbesmeyer, who figured that their drift might tell him something about ocean currents. He and a colleague set up a computer drift model to plot them. Then in 1992, serendipitously, a storm near the International Date Line in the Pacific relieved a ship of 12 containers, one of which was carrying 29 000 bathtub toys. 'They're nice little critters,' Ebbesmeyer commented at the time. 'They're green frogs, little blue turtles, red beavers and yellow ducks. They're made to float in a bathtub.'

(A small side issue here is that around 10 000 containers evidently fall off container ships every year and quite a number of these big steel boxes are out there floating about. It's a sobering thought.)

Anyway, Ebbesmeyer began tracking ducks in the vast Pacific bathtub, gleaning reports from beachcombers, lighthouse keepers and his own sightings. Part of the bobbing flotilla headed for Hawaii, another got itself into the Gulf of Alaska gyre – a great spiralling current – and fetched up on the Queen Charlotte Islands and the coast of Alaska. Still more headed for the Bering Sea, bobbing through the Bering Strait and into the Arctic Ocean. That trip took about five years.

They should have stopped there, but because of global warming the Arctic ice was cracking up. According to Ebbesmeyer's computer model, they had a good chance of getting to the North Atlantic, and he put out a notice offering a US$100 reward for the first recovery there. A few weeks before writing this, several ducks, now faded to white but still going, beached in Nova Scotia: they'd made it through the legendary Northwest Passage, past Greenland and down the Labrador Sea. Next stop New York.

That got me interested in sea currents, so I visited the University of Cape Town's Oceanography Department in search of Frank Shillington, who runs it. He hadn't heard of the bath ducks, but he offered me the use of the oceanography library to see what I could dredge up. After a few days of reading I discovered there was a lot more to currents than moving water.

It works like this: wind pushes the upper layers of the sea, which flow as currents. That's the easy part. This is happening, however, on a spinning sphere which, at the equator, is travelling at 1675 kilometres an hour. The earth goes one way and – rather like pulling the carpet out from under someone who's standing on it – the main streams of wind and water go the other. Oceans slop west and pile up against the eastern shores of continents. Sea level is clearly a relative term. As you know, water flows downhill. These piled waters create currents along eastern Asia, the Atlantic coast of the Americas and East Africa, which push north or south at really impressive speeds, seeking equilibrium. The Agulhas current is an example.

Rather more interestingly, though, ocean currents also prowl the abyssal plains at depths of up to ten kilometres (deeper than Mount Everest is high). By a process known as thermohaline circulation cooling (or more commonly Global Conveyor Belt cooling), salt-saturated (and therefore heavy) waters of the Gulf

Stream cascade to the bed of the north Atlantic between Norway and Greenland. It's been estimated that this water mass plunges at a rate of 17 million cubic metres a second – rather more water than all the rivers in the world combined.

For maybe the next 1000 years the icy, abyssal water snakes south through the depths of the Atlantic – unaffected by currents and storms above – until it is caught in the Antarctic Circumpolar Current, which circles the frozen continent. As this water slowly rises it feeds into the upper levels of the Pacific, Atlantic and Indian oceans – it's the mother of all oceanic surface currents. To say the least, thermohaline circulation is a neat system.

These ever-moving waters do us several favours. They distribute heat around the globe – ensuring, for example, that Europe is warmer than Siberia. They also soak up tremendous volumes of carbon and provide a means for it to be safely locked away.

Zillions of little marine creatures with unpronounceable names such as *foraminiferans* and *coccoliths* and *calcareous* algae capture atmospheric carbon to make their shells. When they die, thermohaline circulation drags them to the ocean floor where they eventually become limestone, preventing oxygen from combining with the carbon to create the greenhouse gas carbon dioxide. (A ten-centimetre cube of limestone – chalk – contains more than a thousand litres of compressed CO_2.)

One problem is that a little change in the earth's dynamics is likely to have repercussions beyond imagination. Another is that currents and weather are so closely linked, they're virtually a single system. And while the seas, covering 71 per cent of the globe, are rather difficult for humans to mess with, the atmosphere is a far more fragile fabric. There's not much of it.

The troposphere – the bit that contains most of the air and all of the clouds – is only about 10 to 16 kilometres high. To quote Bill Bryson in *A Short History of Nearly Everything*, 'If you reduced earth to the size of a school globe, our atmosphere would be about as thick as a few layers of varnish … there's not much between us and oblivion.'

Since the Industrial Revolution we've been generating carbon dioxide, chlorofluorocarbons (CFCs) and other nasty gases in increasing amounts. It has been estimated that since 1850 humans have lofted into the sky an average of seven billion tonnes of these a year. Volcanoes and decaying plants put out nearly 30 times as much, but it may not take much to tip the balance. It's rather like shoving one of those old light switches: it takes a few pushes but the mechanism finally goes snap.

There are now strong indications that it was not a giant meteor at the end of the Cretaceous Period that wiped out the dinosaurs (and much else on earth) but a runaway greenhouse event triggered by an over-enthusiastic volcano. During the Permian Period, a little over a hundred million years earlier, the fossil record of this wonderfully biologically diverse period stops dead. Its total biological mass, even in the seas, apparently simply collapsed. The verdict? Yep: global warming.

Some ominous papers in the oceanography library spelled out how this could happen today. An increase of only a few degrees could cause the Arctic ice cap and Greenland's vast glaciers to melt, pouring fresh water into the north Atlantic. Even a modest amount of ice melt could desalinate the Gulf Stream, preventing its waters from sinking. This would stop it in its tracks. If the Global Conveyor Belt halted, it would liberate all the suspended CO_2 and possibly huge beds of methane hydrate, an even more damaging greenhouse gas present in vast quantities round the fringes of the polar seas.

Without the Gulf Stream, much of the North Sea would eventually freeze over, bouncing back the heat of the sun and kicking off an ice age. Before that, as the temperature rose elsewhere, the boundless ice deserts of the Antarctic would begin to melt – there's enough water locked up there to raise sea levels by 65 metres. Believe me, your coastal property investments would become liabilities.

Not only would world economies collapse, but a runaway greenhouse could destabilise the atmosphere to a point where little would survive. Evidently, it would take a warming of a mere 6°C to begin the process.

The good news is that runaway greenhouse events appear to have happened in the past and life has bounced back. Nature is resourceful. The carbon cycle reasserts itself and the situation re-stabilises. The last time it occurred the recovery took only sixty thousand years. Recovery from the Permian collapse took a bit longer … oh, about 150 million. But here we are.

All this information was unnerving, so I fled the oceanography library and hoped it was all simply academic. But my habit of trawling the world's media denied me that refuge. The reports were cold comfort.

Carbon dioxide in the atmosphere is now 375 parts per million, the highest level for at least half a million years. Europe's winters are now 11 days shorter than they were 35 years ago. Europe's biggest glacier, the Breidhamerkurjökull in Iceland, is expected to slide into the Atlantic within five years – right into the teeth of the Gulf Stream. The Arctic ice cover is definitely shrinking by an area the size of Lesotho each year and now averages only five metres thick. One estimate puts the Arctic temperature increase in the last 30 years as … oops … 6°C.

These facts are not from eco-agitators but from serious researchers and worried writers like Bill Bryson. Just a few months ago the World Meteorological Organisation, an august United Nations body not given to hyperbole, issued an unprecedented report warning that the land and sea temperatures in May 2003 were the second highest since the records began in 1880 and, on land, the highest on record. It records the hottest-yet temperatures in Switzerland and France, a record number of tornadoes in the United States and unseasonably heavy rainfalls in Sri Lanka. The year 2003, it said, would be likely to end as the warmest ever recorded. They were wrong. 2004 was hotter

Earlier that year Britain's environment minister, Michael Meacher, urged people to ignore the optimists. The global warming horror stories, he said, were all true.

And 2003 may, in future history, be seen as the year the crisis began.

So what are we doing about it? Research suggests that to stabilise the situation industrialised nations must decrease emissions immediately by 60 per cent. That means, as a start, a cutback of the use of vehicles, aircraft and factories.

And who are the big spenders? All of Africa produces just three per cent of the world's greenhouse gases. Britain alone produces that amount. The United States pumps out a whopping 23 per cent. The United States signed the Kyoto Protocol on emission reductions but President Bush repudiated it, claiming it would damage the US economy. Based on 1990 levels, therefore, global emissions by the year 2020 will probably *increase* by 75 per cent.

Meanwhile, let's not forget about the bath ducks – which I do not thank for provoking this exploration. There's a slight chance that some may have rounded Cape Horn and are heading for Africa's beaches. If so, and the currents keep going for a while, the plastic quackers and their friends should be here any day now. If you find one you can e-mail Curtis Ebbesmeyer on curtisebbesmeyer@msn.com. If it's the right kind of duck, turtle, frog or beaver, you can claim your US$100 reward. You'll know it by the words 'The First Years' on its chest.

I can't quite put my finger on why, but I find that phrase disconcerting.

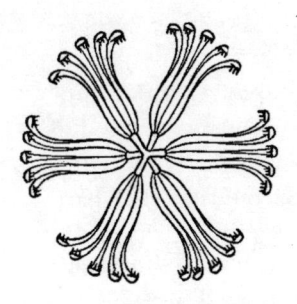

The strange history of a fix

If you'd like to drop in for a visit, my desk is at S33°56′037″ and E21°32′747″.

Peering at these numbers on my hand-held GPS, I swear I can hear generations of sextant-clutching land surveyors weeping. The device has done to them what the motorcar did to wheelwrights and farriers.

It got me wondering, though, what I was 33° south of and 21° east of – and who figured it all out. Some digging led me to a story about a well in Syene (now drowned by the Nile's High Aswan Dam) and a brilliant Greek librarian and mathematician with the grand name of Eratosthenes. The year was around 200 BC, the date 21 June. At noon that day the sun shone straight down the deep well, leaving no shadows. Nothing so odd had ever been seen in the Egyptian city of Alexandria where Eratosthenes lived.

In those days it was generally accepted that the earth was flat, and that the moon, sun and stars were fixed to the underside of a celestial sphere which rotated round the motionless earth. Who, indeed, could say they had felt the earth move?

The Greeks knew, however, that the sun inexplicably migrated north in summer and south in winter, and named the extremes of this migration 'tropics', after the word *tropos*, meaning 'turn'. The midpoint between the turns they termed 'equator'.

Eratosthenes was fascinated by the story of the well, which a traveller had told him. It meant that at that time and place the sun was directly overhead, on what we know today as the Tropic of Cancer. But he had another idea: maybe the earth was round and somehow wobbled. After all, Socrates had noticed that ships sailing out to sea disappeared hull first, and had suggested the possibility that the earth was on a celestial ball.

If the sun's rays were parallel and the earth was a sphere, thought Eratosthenes, sunlight would hit different parts of the earth's surface at different angles. If he could discover the distance between Syene and Alexandria, then measure the angle of the shadow on the same midsummer day in Alexandria, he could use the triangle theorem of another Greek, Pythagoras, to measure the size of the earth.

Travellers gave him the rough distance between the well and his library in Alexandria, and the shadow gave him two sides of a triangle. He found the angle between the top of a pole in Alexandria and the tip of its shadow to be about one fiftieth of a circle, so he simply multiplied the distance between Syene and Alexandria by 50 and declared the circumference of the earth to be the Greek equivalent of 46 250 kilometres. He was only 6000 kilometres out – and one must remember this was around 200 BC. Eratosthenes is rightly considered the father of modern cartography, the science of mapmaking.

For about 400 years, this information lay in the great library of Alexandra, awaiting another genius who could comprehend its implications. That person was Claudius Ptolemy. His interests ran from biography and music to mathematics and optics, but his influence has come down through the centuries from two monumental books, one on astronomy and the other on geography.

He got many things wrong – it was AD 200 after all – but what he gave to the world was the subdivision of the degrees of a circle into minutes and seconds, and the notion that maps should be drawn with reference to these sub-divisions as measurable coordinates. The task of the cartographer, he said, was to 'survey the whole in its just proportions'.

There is a parallel claim to this notion. The Chinese cartographer Chang Heng – a near-contemporary of Ptolemy – wrote that a cartographer's job was to 'cast a network of coordinates about heaven and earth, and reckon on the basis of it'. The source of his inspiration, it seems, came from a girl who was employed to embroider one of his maps on silk. When he looked at the intersecting lines of warp and weft, he was struck by the way they bisected his map.

Eratosthenes had established three lines of longitude: the equator and the tropics of Cancer and Capricorn (named after star signs which coincided with the summer and winter equinoxes). Ptolemy divided the circle of the planet as viewed from one of the poles into degrees, each of which was a line of longitude. It was he who originated the practice of placing north at the top, simply because most of the known world at the time was in the northern hemisphere and maps were easier to study with the land on top and all the writing and fanciful sketches below.

In the 500-year-old library of Alexandria, where both men had laboured, lay all the basic tools of modern cartography for the mapping of the planet. Then disaster struck. In the year 391 Christian zealots sacked the library of Alexandria and burned its irreplaceable contents, converting the now-empty library into a church – a symbolic triumph of faith over reason. We today cannot know what knowledge the world lost that day. Some works were hastily smuggled out, but most went up in flames, including much of the formulations of Eratosthenes and Ptolemy. Cartography was dealt a deadly blow. The earth, once again, became flat, the sun and stars were reattached to their ever-circling heavenly sphere, and science died.

During the thousand-year slough of intellectual stagnation which followed – some of it, for good reason, named the Dark Ages – surviving copies of the ancient cartographic texts were hidden by scholars and monks and handed down in secrecy. Maps reverted to being wildly speculative – more ecclesiastical than cartographic – and mostly dead wrong. They sported the demons of the time: horse-footed men with ears so long they covered their bodies, savages who gulped mead from human skulls, griffons with savage beaks, pythons which sucked on the udders of cows, a cockatrice with crocodile forequarters and hindquarters suspended from lateral fins. It was thought that at the equator the seas would boil a boat to pieces.

The Renaissance and brave Portuguese mariners would change all that, dragging a slumbering Europe into a confrontation with the ideas of Greece's Golden Age and the exotic wonders of the New World.

Early in the 15th century Ferdinand Magellan circumnavigated the planet and it could never again be thought flat. The Portuguese drew maps; not good ones, but with usable information for adventurers to follow. And follow they did.

During the next century Eratosthenes' writing on triangulation – one of the texts which survived – was dusted off and reinstated in the universities of Lisbon, while Ptolemy's notion of grids and degrees was widely debated in the salons and shipping offices of the great ports of Europe. But the problem of how to fix a point on the earth remained elusive. By what method could you know exactly how far you were from the equator, the pole or the nearest shore? Sailors died in the absence of this information. Explorers became hopelessly lost. The problem was that, since the size of the earth was not known, the exact distance that a degree of latitude or longitude covered at any point was mere guesswork.

Enter Jean Picard. In 1669 this Frenchman – laboriously laying end on end well-seasoned, varnished wooden rods – measured an 11.4-kilometre baseline from Paris to Fontainebleau. Then, by Pythagorean triangulation, he sighted an arc from Paris to a clock tower in the village of Sourdon. Several other triangulations later he calculated – I will not tax you with his mathematics – that a degree of latitude measured 110.46 kilometres, a remarkably accurate result.

There was, however, a problem. Picard's measurement would be fine if the earth was a perfect sphere. But was it? Isaac Newton in England suggested that, because of centrifugal force, the earth bulged at the equator and flattened at the poles. The French Royal Academy of Sciences, for some reason, thought it was flatter round its waist and pointy at the poles.

To solve the problem, the Academy laid plans for two geodetic expeditions, one to Peru on the equator, the other to the Arctic Circle. They were to be terrible trips.

In 1736 French Academy member Pierre Louis Moreau de Maupertuis set off for Lapland with three other Academy members, a priest and a good deal of equipment. The Swedish king tried to dissuade them from 'so desperate an undertaking'. But the party pressed on to the icy northern end of the Gulf of Bothnia where they made a base. Then they proceeded up the Torne River, braving cataracts and 'great flies with green heads that fetch blood wherever they fix'.

Using methods pioneered by long-dead Eratosthenes, they triangulated their way across the Arctic Circle, laying base lines with chains and taking sightings on mountain peaks and known stars. To get accurate fixes they would climb peaks, strip the bark off trees to make them more visible and build log pyramids. The effort amid the snow and ice was unthinkable. Fog and a forest fire they had started by accident delayed them.

After nearly two months of sightings they headed south, winter freezing the river behind them as they travelled. When it was all over, Maupertius made his calculations. A degree, he found, was 111.094 kilometres, different by more than half a kilometre from a degree measured in France. The earth was definitely not a perfect sphere.

Lapland was almost a walk in the park compared to Peru. The other expedition, led by Pierre Bouguer and Charles Marie de La Condamine, encountered (as Bouguer wrote) 'difficulties not to be imagined'. The Peruvians and Spanish were suspicious: who could believe the ridiculous story about measuring arcs and fixing meridians? The party persevered amid hostilities, triangulating from Quito near the equator to a place named Cuenca in the Andes Mountains. Every angle measured tested their endurance to the utmost.

They hacked their way up the Andes, where members fainted from the altitude and had 'little haemorrhages' of the lungs. Clouds prevented sightings, rain fell for weeks on end. They lived on bad cheese and biscuits made from hard maize. One of the party, a surgeon, was killed in an argument in a village; a botanist suffered a mental breakdown and never recovered. The expedition took nine-and-a-half years. La Codamine became the first foreigner to raft down the Amazon River.

His calculations showed that a degree of latitude at the equator was 109.92 kilometres, shorter than in Europe. The earth was definitely more curved at the equator and flatter at the Arctic Circle. Given that the Arctic party had returned many years earlier, La Codamine arrived in Paris with incredible tales of the Andes and Amazon, but no startling news. His weary lament: 'We returned seven years too late to inform Europe of anything new concerning the figure of the earth.'

In order to fix the imaginary planetary grid in place only one line remained to be settled. The equator is where it is because that position is halfway between the poles. It is the line of zero latitude, the prime parallel, and it could run nowhere else. But the line of zero longitude, the prime meridian, is another matter. It is arbitrarily designated and could be almost anywhere – and at one time or another it has been. Ptolemy chose the Fortunate Islands, the westernmost extremity of his known world. Depending on the origin of the map, it has also run through Toledo, Cadiz, Madrid, Cracow, Copenhagen, Pisa, Naples, Rome, Augsburg, Ulm, Tübingen, Peking, St Petersburg, Washington, Philadelphia and Greenwich.

This caused immense confusion when pinpointing coordinates on maps so, in 1884, the United States government called an International Meridian Conference.

At that meeting, with few dissenting votes, the Royal Observatory at Greenwich was chosen to be zero longitude. The grid was complete.

There is a sequel to this story which has to do with the GPS on my desk. Satellites in space are now used as points for geodetic triangulation. Their use in global positioning systems makes cartographic calculations startlingly accurate. It has been confirmed that the earth is flattened, but not by much. Its equatorial diameter exceeds the polar diameter by a mere 42.77 kilometres.

But GPS accuracy has turned up something even more surprising which would have got those old surveyors with their rods and chains really excited. It is also strangely charming. Using instruments capable of measuring distances to within a couple of centimetres, plus 27 satellites and more than half a million optical, radio and laser sightings, the US Goddard Space Flight Centre recently found that the southern hemisphere is larger than the northern hemisphere.

The earth is pear-shaped.

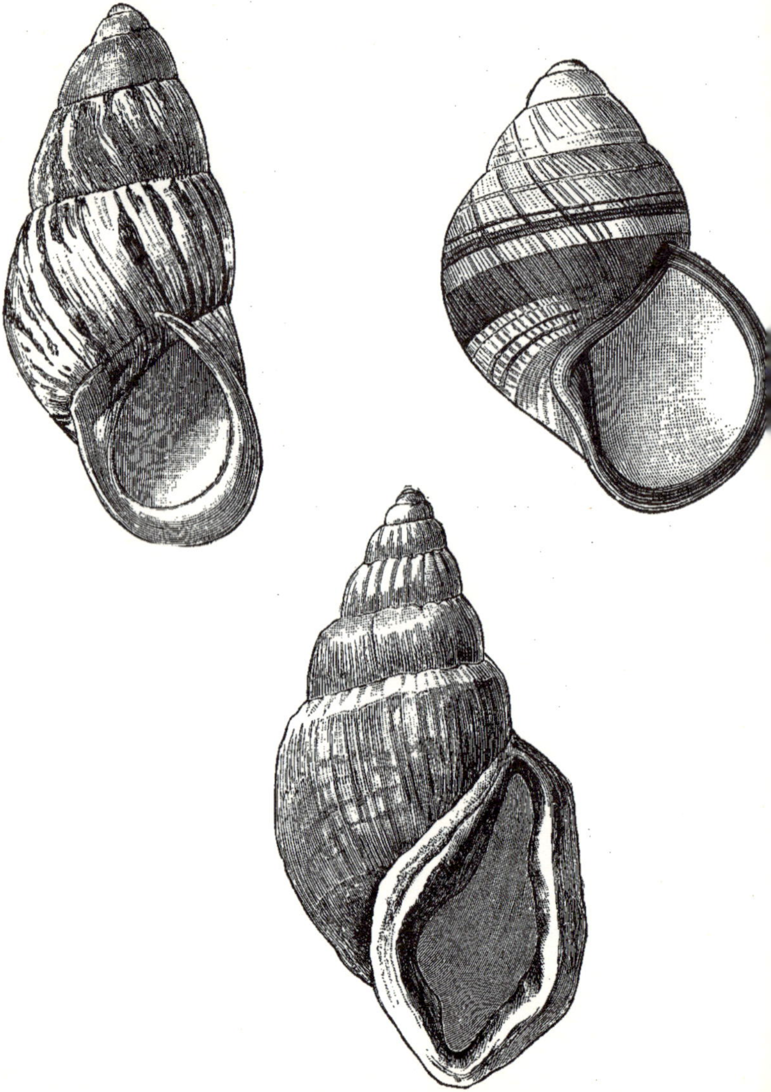

Our peopled world

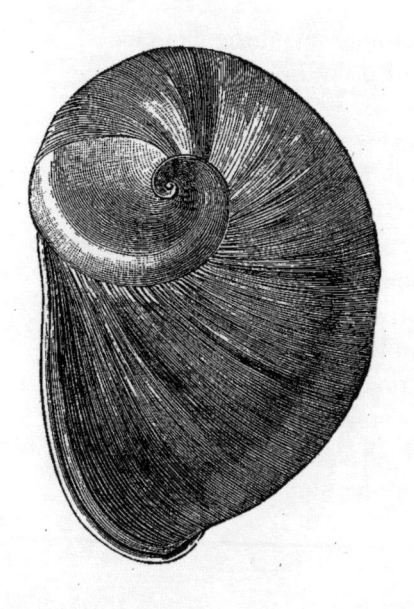

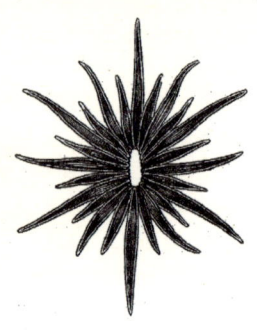

Why zebras never went to war and sheep ended up stupid

Between school history sermons about the glorious and simultaneous advance of European might and culture into Africa and the inevitable Great Trek, the question was raised about why Africans never invented the trappings of higher civilisation. I don't remember our history teacher, a certain Mr Grey, ever directly explaining why they failed in this necessary enterprise, other than a nudge-wink implication that they were way too dumb to invent anything worthwhile.

In those days South African history had more to do with justification than education but, in the absence of any other explanation, Grey's legacy was a feeling I had all through high school that he had a point. On such foundations racism finds a firm footing.

A welcome antidote to school history came in the form of a marvellous historian named Robin Hallett, who enthralled me at university with descriptions about the many African kingdoms which rose and fell within the past 2000 years. But a puzzle remained: kingdoms are one thing, but what of writing, the wheel, cities and technology? Why, if *Homo sapiens* arose in Africa, did the Yoruba not build sailing ships, Zulus not invent gunpowder or Bushmen fail to domesticate a single animal? Why, by the 19th century, were Europeans able to colonise and control most of the peoples of Africa?

This lacuna is surprising, because Africa was the cradle of human evolution for millions of years and the probable homeland of modern *Homo sapiens*. To the advantages of Africa's enormous head start were added those of wonderfully diverse climates and habitats and the world's highest human density in prehistory. An extraterrestrial visiting Earth 10 000 years ago might have been forgiven for predicting that Europe would end up as a set of vassal states of a sub-Saharan African empire. Quite the opposite occurred. Why?

Crude history views human progress as a march from savagery to civilisation. The first steps along this noble path are deemed to be the development of sophisticated social organisation, technology, and writing.

But that view begs the question – why did some societies develop these elements of civilisation while others failed to? Writing, it appears, was invented only twice – in Sumeria (now Iraq) and Mexico – and the alphabet once, in the area of Syria and Israel (derived from Egyptian hieroglyphs). All other scripts, even Chinese pictograms, have been found to be derived from these sources.

Why invent it at all? Because writing – like technology and complex social organisation – were outcomes of an earlier phase of human development, a period when agricultural systems began replacing hunter-gathering practices in certain areas of the world. So the question we need to ask is not why some people were smarter than others and invented things, but why some cultures, in certain places at certain times, settled down, raised crops and domesticated animals; because by the 19th century the peoples who benefited from these developments were dominating the world.

One would imagine these first steps on the road to civilisation would have been taken in an area of lush growth and abundant animals, maybe Africa's Great Rift Valley. Instead they occurred, around 11 000 years ago, in an area of deserts and climatic extremes known as the Fertile Crescent: now the countries of Iraq, Syria, Jordan, Israel, Lebanon and southern Turkey.

Why there? The answer, it seems, is amazing good fortune – a subject to which Jared Diamond, an evolutionary biologist from the University of California, has given a good deal of thought.

'The first farmers could not have chosen farming consciously,' he writes in *Guns, Germs and Steel*, 'because there were no other farmers for them to observe.' Farming began, says Diamond, as an alternative strategy to hunter-gathering, and its success had nothing to do with the people and everything to do with the environment.

Judging from the few remaining groups today, hunter-gatherers had a sophisticated knowledge of food plants and many commonly kept pets. They would have discovered which wild plants were good to eat and which animals were pliable enough to breed in captivity. They would also have noticed plant foods they'd eaten growing round their latrine pits (the seeds having passed through them). The possibility of consciously sowing such plants would surely have occurred to people throughout the world.

In the Fertile Crescent, however, there was a suite of plants and animals unlike anywhere else on earth. The early success of food growing in that area was a matter of selection, size and some fortunate mutations.

As an early gatherer, Diamond says, you would prefer large berries over small, large grass seeds over tiny ones, simply because you'd get more food for less effort. The Fertile Crescent had large-seeded plants in abundance: the cereals emmer wheat, einkorn wheat and barley, and the pulses peas, chickpeas and lentils – all large-seeded and high in calories. Because of the area's winter rains and dry summers, these plants tended to be self-seeding annuals with durable seeds to last through the hot, dry months: ideal for storage. Self-seeding was of course essential, because plants requiring fertilisation from other plants would have prevented farmers from isolating and developing useful mutant strains.

By constantly selecting the largest seeds when gathering these plants and replanting them, people would, over hundreds of years, have unconsciously altered genetic tendencies in the direction of ever larger seeds.

Of the some 200 000 wild plant species, a paltry dozen today account for more than 80 per cent of the world's tonnage of crops. The heavyweights are the cereals wheat, corn, barley and rice, the pulse sorghum and the roots potato, sweet potato and manioc. West Africa had a few good starters: sorghum and pearl millet plus the pulses cowpeas and groundnuts. Africa south of the equator had none of these early crop types and, today, all the major food crops grown there are from elsewhere.

The Fertile Crescent, though, had a double fortune: large-seeded crops *and* eminently domesticable animals. Domestication is the process whereby a species is selected and its genetic form (consciously or unconsciously) is changed to make it more useful to humans. The five major mammals in this category are cows, sheep, goats, pigs and horses, all of which were found in the Fertile Crescent or were introduced into it from nearby Asia. Dogs, bred from wolves, were the first animals to be domesticated, but never became a food source.

Diamond studied a range of animals he considered candidates for domestication (any terrestrial mammal weighing more than an arbitary 45 kilograms) and found that in the Fertile Crescent, 18 per cent of the available indigenous animals ended up domesticated, four per cent in the Americas and none in Australia or Sub-Saharan Africa. Of the 14 species of big domesticated herbivores, 13 came from Eurasia. By the time the Roman Empire was at its height – some 2000 years ago – all the major domestic animal species had been established and very few have been added since then. Was there something special about the handful that made it onto our farms? Apparently there was.

There are certain characteristics required of an animal for domestication, Diamond insists, the absence of any one disqualifying its selection. One is diet. Here's an example. It takes around 4500 kilograms of fodder to raise a 400-kilogram cow. If you want to raise a carnivore that big and feed a 400-kilogram herbivore to it, that will take 45 000 kilograms of fodder. So raising carnivores would be a very uneconomical farming strategy.

A domestic animal's growth rate needs to be fast. It's not worth a gorilla or elephant rancher waiting around for a decade or more for a usable beast. A good domestic animal must also be happy to breed in captivity – something cheetahs, for example, refuse to do – and it needs a good disposition. Most large mammals can kill a human, and a tendency to do so disqualified virtually all African candidates.

The African buffalo, hippo or rhino would all have provided good meat for early pastoralists, as well as useful transport. The vision of an army of Bantu warriors mounted on rhinos flattening the legions of the Roman Empire is compelling, as is their rout of slavers from the backs of zebras. But it never occurred. Rhinos are simply too dangerous; zebras, when they bite, refuse to let go; buffalos have a vindictive disposition and hippos kill more people than any other African land animal.

Suitable species also need to have low panic levels – they must be creatures that stand when threatened and don't bolt. These tend to be herd animals, which is the final requirement for domestication. Herd animals maintain a well-developed hierarchy with overlapping home ranges rather than exclusive territories. Creatures with these tendencies follow leaders, and are pliable when humans take over as head of the hierarchy. They are tolerant and lend themselves to herding. That is why a dog is attached to you, its pack leader, while a cat (a solitary hunter by nature) is attached to where it lives.

Along the way, domestic animals were changed to suit human needs. Cows, pigs and sheep became smaller; guinea pigs, bred by the Incas, became larger. Sheep and alpacas (Andean cameloids) were selected for retention of wool and loss of hair, while cows were selected for high milk yields. Several species, such as sheep, have smaller brains and less developed sense organs than their wild ancestors, because they no longer need to protect themselves from wild predators. The Pekinese is a long way from the wolf.

So the Fertile Crescent had crops and animals that made it the breadbasket of civilisation. But there is still more to it than that, it appears. Food production led to inventions such as flint-bladed sickles for harvesting, baskets for grain, mortars and pestles for grinding, ploughs, storage pits and the techniques of grain roasting and bread making.

In addition to food, animals were used for milk, wool, ploughing and transport, giving rise to cheese production, weaving, farm technologies, distance travel and, in the case of the horse, mobile armies.

Food production also led to larger, denser populations and (the deadly side of animal husbandry) disease. The major killers throughout history – smallpox, flu, tuberculosis, malaria, plague, measles, cholera and now Aids – are all infectious diseases that evolved from animals.

Farming, then cities, were a bonanza for microbes. Over the millennia farmers, and then urban dwellers of the Old World, either died of these animal-linked 'crowd diseases' or built up immunities. When production led to trade, trade to exploration and exploration to conquest, far more hapless victims in Africa and the New World died of imported germs against which they had no defense than were gunned down by European weapons.

This, then, begins to explain the nature of Africa's disadvantage. It was a matter of environment and timing. Around 3000 BC, Bantu farmers began migrating from an area around the present Cameroon. With them they brought domesticated auroch cattle (from North Africa), sorghum and pearl millet. They had far fewer crops than the Fertile Crescent, however, which meant a much later start in food production.

Emerging from the forests into the plains of East Africa around 2000 BC, they encountered tsetse flies, which radically culled their herds. By about AD 500 Bantu farmers had reached the Fish River in South Africa, but there they stopped. The climate further south was Mediterranean, which meant winter rainfall. Sorghum and pearl millet are summer rainfall crops.

The other peoples of sub-Saharan Africa, Pygmies and San, remained hunter-gatherers because they lived in an area where neither wild plants nor animals provided them with the possibility of organised food production. There was one exception. The Khoi kept cattle, but this was probably a late acquisition.

For all these reasons, those African kingdoms which did arise depended on food production that required great effort for low gains in calories and protein. Slight changes in the environment such as drought or cattle disease often brought them down. The Maya, Aztec and Inca kingdoms of South America were fragile for the same reasons.

The arrival of Europeans, therefore, was almost always a disaster for them. In South America a surprisingly small number of Spanish conquistadors brought about the downfall of the Mesoamerican and Amazonian cultures. In 1652 Dutch sailors arrived at the Cape bearing winter-rainfall crops and Fertile Crescent animals. They brought technologies, weapons, diseases and, later, standing armies. With these they decimated the Khoisan and fought protracted wars with the Bantu along South Africa's eastern seaboard. And won. In the business of colonisation, there's nothing like a few thousand years' head start.

Europe's colonisation of Africa, therefore, had little to do with differences between European and African people themselves, as my school teacher Mr Grey would have had us believe. It was due, it seems, to accidents of geography and to the varied types of wild plants and animals which different peoples inherited from the earth. Proof of this is that when crops such as Mexican maize and Mesopotamian wheat, and animals such as West Asian sheep and goats, were introduced to African society, their advantages were immediately realised and rapidly incorporated. So were the plough and other farming implements. The different historical trajectories of Africa and Europe, Diamond concludes, stem ultimately from differences in real estate.

On the matter of civilisation, though, here is something to ponder. Since the early 20th century, civilisation's engines have run on oil. The countries of the ever-bountiful Fertile Crescent have huge reserves of it. These are much coveted by those who benefited most from the advantages of civilisation which that area bequeathed them. For this reason, the cradle of civilisation is now the cockpit of war. By what, one needs ask, does one measure civilisation? History certainly has its ironies.

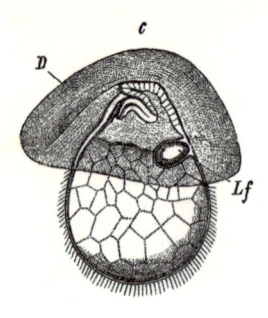

Dying islands in the sun

'Grape vines are bloody weeds,' said Justin Basson, scowling at the vineyards rolling away beyond the fence of Clara Ana Fontein, his farm in the Durbanville Hills. 'Wheat too – weeds.'

Spoken in the Tygerberg at the heart of the Western Cape's enormously profitable wheat and wine farms, these words were heretical. But Justin has his reasons to go to war on bread and wine. With around 8500 plant species, the Western Cape fynbos is one of the richest floristic regions on earth. Within this biome is a veld type with the curious name of renosterveld (nobody's quite sure why it was named after rhinoceroses). As spring shoulders the rain clouds over the horizon the land explodes into colour.

Our peopled world

Bulbous plants called geophytes, having stored desire in their underground bulbs for a year, burst out of the ground and drive bees and other insects moggy with their scent. Daisies, hyacinths, wild rosemary, kooigoed, oxalis, wild asparagus and even the grey renosterbos turn the hillsides into colour-speckled scenes which Monet and Renoir could have used to vindicate Impressionism.

Justin's problem is that it didn't take European settlers long to discover that the renosterveld was the best place to plant wheat and grapes. And plant they did – unchecked for 300 years. Today only four per cent of the West Coast renosterveld is left, desperate islands clinging to hilltops and the bottoms of deep valleys where ploughs cannot go. The Red Data listing of endangered species in the area goes on and on, page after page. Renosterveld is a treasure on the road to oblivion.

Concern about whether or not the battle among the Cape koppies is already lost raises the question about just when to chuck in the towel on a species or its surroundings. Why waste time on a mere four per cent? Of course it's only worth conserving something that has a chance of sustaining itself in the end. So the issue is: how big does an ecosystem have to be to ensure its integrity into the future? When do we abandon hope? In Southern Africa, where trans-frontier parks are blossoming like Namaqualand daisies, yet local reserves are falling to housing and neglect, these are important questions.

They were first raised in another context by biologists studying islands. Charles Darwin was an island biogeographer before he was a Darwinist, his contemporary Alfred Russel Wallace spent eight years collecting specimens in the Malay Archipelago, and – at about the same time – the biologist Joseph Hooker went to ground on the Pacific islands of Tasmania, New Zealand and the Kerguelens. They alerted the world to the uniqueness of isolated biomes. Islands are instructive – they're limited in size, far from anywhere, have fewer species than mainlands and are more easily disrupted. Things become extinct easily.

Nearly a century later, in 1967, two American biologists, Robert MacArthur and Edward O Wilson, published *The Theory of Island Biogeography*, possibly the most important work on islands since Darwin's *The Origin of Species*. Their central quest was to discover the patterns which shape biological communities. What, they wondered, caused populations to increase, reach equilibrium or fall? And just how many species could a certain size and type of land support?

They found that islands without humans are ecosystems in balance – species would vanish at about the same rate as others would fly or drift in from the great beyond. Earlier research had indicated that an island ten times as small as another had two fewer species – a useful benchmark (later bitterly contested). What MacArthur and Wilson showed, however, was that there were patterns, and knowing them allowed scientific predictions.

What was obvious, though, was that when you added humans to island systems the result was species meltdown and environmental decay. They could now see where it would lead. The predictions were gloomy. Ask the dodo.

It was subsequently realised that island biogeography could be applied to continents as well, because human activities such as farming, city building and road building prevented plants, reptiles, mammals and even birds from accessing the areas they required for survival. From an environmental point of view, the humanised, chopped-up world was a speckle of islands. This raised more and urgent questions. What impact did isolation have on the rate of extinction? How large should an 'island' be to ensure equilibrium? Which was better for conservation: one big reserve or many small ones?

A flurry of research produced worrying results. Blocked by human activity, wandering creatures could no longer reach neighbouring populations. The gene pool was reduced; pollinators often couldn't make it across the gaps between isolates. More questions arose: species were lost, yes, but which species? Were the losses random or were they dictated by the structure of the ecosystem? Was there a quantifiable, and therefore predictable, relationship between isolation and doom?

A big problem for such areas, cut off from each other, is what biologists term genetic maiming. Small populations contain only a meagre sample of the larger population's genetic diversity. Small populations are also vulnerable to natural catastrophe. Take the Cape's endangered riverine rabbit. Imagine the last two colonies, one dug in on a hillside and another near a river – 80 rabbits in all. Comes a catastrophic flood, a once-in-a-century event, and half are drowned. Forty are left, but two droughts and a tough winter reduces the numbers to 20.

Now you're worried. Several females, lacking other options, breed with their sons; some males breed with their daughters. As a result, a few of the offspring are sterile, which brings down the overall birth rate. Disease hits the now genetically fragile colony, and the rabbits that surivive are victims of inbreeding depression – a general lack of vigour. Somehow they're just not robust.

Another winter and these languid bunnies die. Now you've got eight rabbits, but only two are female. One is too old to breed, the other one has a litter but it is eaten by a jackal. The final tally? Seven males and a non-breeding female. The species is history. Take a photo and kiss it goodbye.

That's not conjecture. It's the probable future of both the riverine rabbit and that beautiful symbol of the renosterveld, the geometric tortoise. The reason? Human fragmentation of their habitats.

Extinctions, of course, are normal. Before the human explosion, it is estimated that the background extinction level was a few bird species, a few fish species, some mammals and a few insect species every million years. Such losses were counterbalanced by gains of new species. Since the arrival of *Homo sapiens*, however, things have changed. Conservation biologist Paul Ehrlich has estimated the current extinction rate among birds and mammals at roughly a hundred times that background rate. Edward Wilson calculates the loss of rainforest species to be far higher: at least a thousand times above normal. Since Neolithic times 20 per cent of bird species have become extinct.

Surveying humanity's role as planetary killer from his vantage point of more than half a century of research, Wilson clamed to have learned three lessons:

- The noble savage never existed;
- Eden occupied was a slaughterhouse; and
- Paradise found is paradise lost.

The biological world, it seems, is falling to pieces. Can something be done about it? According to ecologist Michael Soulé, 'there are no hopeless cases, only people without hope, and expensive cases'.

We have formulae for viable population sizes, we can make educated guesses at the numerical thresholds for viability, we can – as is being done spectacularly in Southern Africa – link reserves into ever-greater areas of wilderness. The key question is: how much do we care? How badly do we want to preserve the geometric tortoise, the riverine rabbit, the elephant or the black rhino? How long they survive is now in human hands.

In the Durbanville Hills, Justin Basson is negotiating corridors. He sits down with local farmers and discusses the importance of saving the renosterveld. That patch on the hilltop: would they consider preserving it? Would they possibly not plant vines along a corridor linking it to that patch of renosterveld over there on the next farm? Would they bring down some fences, avoid spraying poisons, help spread the message? It's hard work, but he's making headway.

Clara Anna Fontein is given over entirely to renosterveld. Justin has brought back, zebra, wildebeest, eland and other antelope. He cherishes porcupines.

'They spread seeds,' he enthuses. 'The antelope open up thickets. Look at how the natural veld is bouncing back. It's slow ... I can wait. But we need corridors. In Africa we don't have hedgerows, but if we restored roadsides they'd work just as well.

'Just think of the bees. They're essential for pollination, but maybe their hive is over on that far hill. From there to here to pollinate my flowers they'd have to fly over urban sprawl and vine desert. They must get so tired, if they get here at all. And in a howling southeaster ...'

A jackal buzzard sails over a vineyard, surveying the poisoned plants between the vines, and beats a swooping retreat to Clara Anna's tangle of flowers and renosterbos.

'Look, isn't that beautiful?' Justin asks. I follow his gaze which is not fixed on the buzzard, but directed at the ground. 'It's called kukumakranka, *Gethyllis afra*. It's highly endangered. What an extraordinary plant. Just look at those delicate flowers.'

So is the renosterveld worth saving? There's an eerie symbolism about its demise. At the Last Supper, before his death, Christ told his disciples: 'Eat of my body and drink of my blood, and do this in remembrance of me.' This is the injunction behind the bread and wine of Holy Communion. In the Western Cape that bread and wine comes from the renosterveld and is also the product of a supreme sacrifice. Only this time we have a chance to alter the outcome.

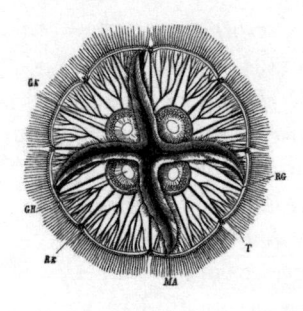

Uneasy rumblings down in the swamp

In summer, tropical storms rumble and flash across the high Bei Plateau in Angola from Huambo to Cuito Cuanavale. Water pours off steep slopes, gathering sand, leeching salts from the sodden earth and picking up speed as it gutters down long, straight valleys. If you look at a map you'll see these rivers as parallel blue lines, like human fingers or the feathers of a bird's wing, gradually drawing together as they head south. Their names have the musicality of the local languages: Cuebe, Longa, Cuatir, Cichi, Cubango.

A thousand kilometres from Huambo the river – for it is now a single river – turns east, becoming for a while the border between Angola and Namibia, then it dives southeast across the Caprivi Strip. At the Popa Falls in western Caprivi the river widens across a rocky shelf, dropping four metres, then channels into the Okavango Panhandle. Ahead is a great geological fault which spreads the waters like a fan, slowly unfolding them into the burning sands of the Kalahari. Beyond the fault a miracle occurs.

The Okavango River once flowed elsewhere, possibly into the Zambezi, but tectonic stresses in the East African Rift Valley system millions of years ago caused a section of the earth's crust in northwestern Botswana to collapse. This depression would probably have been filled by the waters of the suddenly diverted Okavango, but sand from the river's long run would gradually have filled the lake.

The Kalahari is exceptionally flat: across 250 kilometres of the delta the elevation drops a mere 61 metres. Water which falls in the Angolan highlands in December, and which pours into the Panhandle at a staggering 11 million cubic kilometres a year, takes six months to fill the Okavango's furthermost channels.

Unlike most rivers, this water carries very little mud, salts and nutrients – about one tenth of what is found in Johannesburg's tap water. Most of the sediment is sand. But everything the water brings remains behind, because the Okavango River has no outlet. Almost every drop is pumped into the atmosphere by plant transpiration or sucked up by the sun through evaporation. So despite low nutrient loads, salt is accumulating at the rate of about 450 000 tonnes a year. This should have killed the delta ages ago, but it hasn't. The reason is astounding: swamp trees quarantine it.

Terence McCarthy from the School of Geosciences at the University of the Witwatersrand has found that the plant communities of the Okavango are not mere spectators to the passing seasons, but co-operate in orchestrating it like the organs of your body.

Papyrus and hippo grass dominate the channels of the upper swamp, allowing water to escape slowly into back-swamp areas but confining the sandy sediment. These back-swamp communities – grasses, sedges and other aquatic species – transpire water into the atmosphere and produce peat, while bacteria fix dissolved salts. Lower downstream are hummocky islands which support a large variety of trees; the master-pumps of transpiration. They release more water into the atmosphere than grasses and sedges do – so much, in fact, that they cause the water table beneath the islands to fall below the level of the surrounding swamp.

As a result, ground water from beneath flooded areas, where most of the salts congregate, flows towards the islands, taking dissolved chemicals with it. This material causes the islands to grow, with less soluble salts forming a ridge round the outer edge and more soluble (and damaging) salts accumulating in the centre. Eventually the ground water in the centre of these islands becomes so saline it is toxic to plants, leaving barren interiors dotted with a few hardy palms. Even when it rains the salts cannot escape over the island ridge and trees on the island edge continue to pump salinity out of the swamp system.

McCarthy has found that after about 150 years the toxic salts will destroy all plants on the island. At this point the floodwaters should erode it and release salts into the swamp. But, with perfect timing, papyrus and hippo grass upstream will have encroached into their channels, causing sand levels to rise and blocking their flow. The water is diverted elsewhere and the old islands dry out.

Then, in that mysterious way it does, the peat in these dry areas catches fire, creating a mosaic of burning fronts up to 15 centimetres deep. These wild fires can burn for decades, destroying all life growing above them. After the fires have passed, summer rains flush saline poisons deep below ground. Nutrients from the fires combine with sand to form fertile soils which produce lush grasslands. Because the area is so flat, the loss of peat causes the level of the land to drop, and swamp water gradually reclaims the grasslands. In this way the flow of water and the creation of islands are constantly changing, the toxicity is controlled and the entire organism named Okavango renews itself.

There is, however, a problem against which the living swamp has not had time to develop a defence: humans.

In 1969 a plan was drawn up to dam the Okavango River at Popa Falls, providing Caprivi with water and hydroelectricity. It was shelved, but in 2002 the Namibian government requested a pre-feasibility study to rethink the plan. The project's leader, John Langford of NamPower, said he hoped construction of a weir near the falls would begin in 2005. And there's another problem. The recent decline in hostilities in Angola is good news for the war-weary people of the southern regions, but bad news for the region's rivers. The

International Rivers Network has discovered that at least ten dams are being planned for the headwaters of the Okavango. It has described plans for both these dams and a weir at Popa Falls as alarming.

NamPower, Namibia's power provider, is understandably approaching the issue with some sensitivity. It has given assurances that if 'fatal flaws' in the plan are detected by the pre-feasibility study the project will be rethought, that only two per cent of the annual flow will be extracted and that the hydro-electric turbine will be a run-of-the-river system in a low weir.

Langford has, however, pointed out that the Popa Falls project 'is probably one of the most viable projects to be investigated by NamPower lately'. He said the falls area was the only potential hydroelectric site situated within Namibia. When he put these views to a meeting consisting mainly of representatives of safari companies and lodge owners in Botswana in February, they were unconvinced, claiming that the project could ruin the delta.

Scientists are inclined to agree with them. An intensive study done by McCarthy, together with Fred Ellery from the School of Life and Environmental Sciences at the University of Natal, found that the extraction of two per cent of the river's inflow would have little effect on the delta, but the way in which it was extracted could have a large impact. Most rivers carry their sediment in the water column. But the Okavango is unusual in that its sediment, being mainly sand, rolls along the bottom. So the amount of sand transported depends on the volume and speed of the river's flow. Virtually any dam or weir will slow the flow. According to Ellery, 'the moment the water enters the head of the impoundment all bedload sediment will be deposited. Because of this the river will become erosional downstream of the weir, with disastrous consequences for the delta.'

Habitat diversity would decrease. Channels would not fill over time and would be cut more deeply. Water would not be distributed across the system.

An upstream dam could also lead to higher levels of evaporation and therefore greater salt levels flowing into the Panhandle. Scoured channels would lead to more salt accumulating in the lower swamps. This could kill off the vital papyrus and exceed the ability of islands to neutralise the dangers of excess salinity. If the Angolan or Namibian governments decide to dam rivers within their own borders, who is there to stop them?

The delta has long been recognised by scientists as unique on earth. This means that engineers and designers have no precedents from which to work. They would have to use computer modelling, with all its attendant unknowns. And even the tiniest unknowns could bring about disastrous consequences downstream. Ellery's worry is that, because of enormous momentum being gained by the Popa Falls project, NamPower might be forced to proceed despite flaws. 'There's widespread concern that the project has gained enormous momentum,' he commented. 'This suggests that other agendas are being served by the construction of the impoundment. In such a case it's difficult to work out what environmentalists are up against.'

As Terence McCarthy has observed, the Okavango has been around a long time and is pretty robust. But it, too, has its jugular. The delta could die.

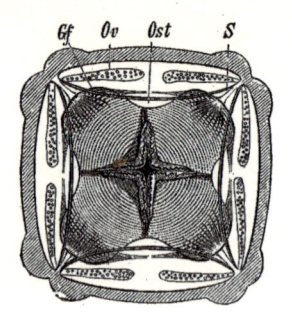

Birds of heaven

So here we are, clinging to the skin of our planet during a temporary thaw. How are we doing? If human numbers are anything to go by – six billion and climbing – pretty impressively. About our housekeeping, though, 'appallingly' is a word that comes to mind.

I'll level with you: writing about natural history in the 21st century is not balm for the soul. Scratch the surface and you end up with global warming, the great apes running out of time, mounting extinctions, corals dying back, virus-sickened marine mammals, declining numbers of sea turtles and much more. It has often occurred to me it'd be saner to write a baking column – or maybe the history of spaniel breeding. But then …

Here are two stories, one about hope, the other about despair. That the hope was unfulfilled and the despair bore some fruit is irrelevant, because they are synecdoches for a larger issue concerning our stewardship of the earth. Both are about cranes.

The first concerns Sadako Sasaki, who was two years old and living on the outskirts of Nagasaki when the American B52 Superfortress bomber *Enola Gay* dropped an atomic bomb on the city. Sadako escaped visible injury, though thousands of buildings and people were vaporised.

Ten years later the bomb came back to haunt her in the form of leukemia, a blood cancer caused by the radiation. Sadako had, until then, been a healthy, fun-loving girl and didn't want to die. She knew that cranes were symbols of good luck and that if you ever saw a thousand cranes your greatest wish would be granted. But where could she find so many cranes? She decided to make them out of paper.

Sadako managed to fold 650 before she died, but her classmates and friends continued making origami cranes in her honour, then dedicated them as a prayer for peace. Out of this initiative, in Hiroshima's Peace Park, a Children's Peace Memorial was erected to the hundreds of child victims of the atomic bombs and as a symbol of a future peaceful world. Its central motif is a statue of a folded paper crane.

It is a strange irony that some 60 years after the flight of the *Enola Gay*, cranes are desperately in need of the same wish for survival that so motivated Sadako Sasaki.

The second story is about a crowned crane named Beautiful. He had been an unfortunate egg. Snatched from his parents' nest somewhere in East Africa –

probably Uganda – and transported to the Netherlands in a small incubator, he hatched on the estate of a wealthy Dutchman who thought some crowned cranes would add elegance to his gardens. They undoubtedly did, but keeping protected birds in Holland, as in many countries, is illegal.

Dutch authorities confiscated Beautiful and another crane named Baldy (because his crest was damaged), identified them as African grey crowned *Balearica regulorum*, and began hunting for an appropriate home. The Hlatikulu Crane and Wetland Sanctuary in KawZulu-Natal was contacted and agreed to take the two. They were shipped south to join some young blue cranes and two large wattled cranes in the Drakensberg foothills.

Beautiful's troubles were not yet over. In South Africa he developed bumblefoot, an odd condition that required two toes to be amputated. Baldy found a mate named Nibbler, who was of a different species, so their eggs were removed before they could hatch. But at least they had each other. Beautiful was alone, though why Nibbler chose Baldy is unfathomable. Having met Beautiful, I think she made a mistake: he really is beautiful. But then I'm not a crane. It's a tangle that's positively Shakespearian.

A visit to Kamberg had alerted me to cranes, which is why I came upon the story about Sadako Sasaki. All around the sanctuary, wild cranes were landing with their graceful hop-skip steps, or taking off with evocative bugling calls. It was like being at a small airport for feathered craft. Close up they have startling presence: big, elegant, colourful and remarkably attractive.

At his full height Beautiful was almost as tall as I am. He was watchful but clearly not afraid of the approaching human with a camera – a wild and powerful creature with a family tree that made mine look proletarian. When I raised my arms he extended his wings. We danced a little. I became an instant crane devotee.

Southern Africa is the only region where three crane species overlap. Crowned cranes (*Balearica regulorum*) share their habitat with South Africa's national bird, the blue crane (*Anthropoides paradisea*) and the wattled crane (*Bugeranus carunculatus*). There are 15 species of living cranes in the world, making up the avian family Gruidae. The first crane-like birds were around at the time of the dinosaurs in the late Palaeocene period, about 55 million years ago. The fossil record suggests they were strong flyers, radiating across Europe, Asia, North America and Africa, though where they began nobody knows for sure.

Their expansion would have coincided with the epoch of worldwide cooling and drying of the mid-Tertiary period around 30 million years ago. It brought a great expansion of grassland and standing water, an ecosystem most hospitable to cranes. And it is in these habitats that they have been found ever since.

Early humans marvelled at their grace, their ancient ancestry, their mating dances and the fact that they pair for life. Tributes to cranes can be found in the prehistoric art of Africa and Europe. They appear in Roman and

Greek myths, in Aborigine dances, in Egyptian tombs and on Native American totems. In Asia cranes are still sacred symbols of peace, happiness and long life. They are above all a symbol of the great beyond. The pioneering American conservationist Aldo Leopold described the crane as 'no mere bird' but 'wilderness incarnate'.

Someone – I forget who it was – once said that we can best be judged by our treatment of that which we revere. Reverence, unfortunately, has not spared cranes from destruction, and in those terms we stand poorly judged. They are presently among the most endangered avian families, struggling to survive hunters, habitat loss, predation, agricultural poisons and power-line collisions.

In South Africa the blue crane is faring best, though being the country's national bird has not saved it from persecution. Farmers resent its taste for seed and it has suffered from widespread intentional as well as indirect poisoning of croplands. Not long ago 675 blue cranes were killed in a single field by grain soaked in commercial insecticides. In the last 20 years the blue crane population has declined by about 90 per cent in the grassland biome. The blue and crowned cranes are now listed as vulnerable in the Red Data Book, and the wattled crane as critical, the only large South African bird to be so listed.

All this got me thinking about the virtues of a baking column; then I met Donella Young of the University of Cape Town's Avian Demography Unit. She introduced me to Coordinated Avifaunal Roadcounts (Car) and the

International Crane Foundation. They are organisations of people in whose presence it is possible to get enthusiastic about human stewardship of wildlife. Antidotes, you might say, to terminal depression.

All over the world affiliate crane organisations, like the South African Crane Working Group, are out there batting for their birds: raising popular awareness, assisting with breeding programmes, helping to change laws, supporting research and generally gaining acceptance of cranes as the flagship species which reflects the health of an ecosystem. And where they work crane numbers are stabilising or rising. Their message is loud and clear: if we put our hearts and minds to it, we can bring species back from the brink.

The roadcounts in South Africa are part of this initiative, though they include counts of other large terrestrial birds such as korhaans, bustards, storks, herons and guineafowl. Twice a year around 750 volunteer birdwatchers from many backgrounds bump along 18 000 kilometres of country roads for a day, counting birds. The information they collect is fed into the Avian Demography Unit, which comes up with findings and ideas about species conservation.

Reserves, evidently, aren't the answer for cranes. Around 80 per cent of the land they use is privately owned. Farmers or forestry have taken over most of the grasslands and wetlands that provided cranes with a sustainable habitat for millions of years. And although some farmers have been part of the problem, others are increasingly part of the solution – many even taking part in the roadcounts and implementing bird-friendly management practices. They are undertaking to use poisons responsibly, flag overhead cables, protect wetlands, natural veld and breeding sites, create habitat corridors and control dogs and cats, which raid nests and can devastate bird populations. Farmers are learning – from organisations such as the South African Crane Working Group and Car – that though they own land, they also hold it in sacred trust for species far older than our own.

So how are we doing? In truth, not well. Often we do too little too late. But what social action around cranes (and rhinos and Brenton blue butterflies) proves, is that we can do something positive about stewardship. And if you've ever danced with a crane, you'll know why we should.

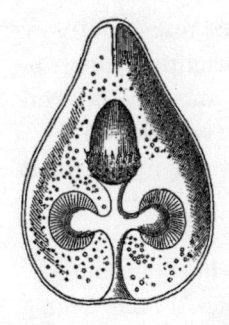

Kiss those sweet red lips goodbye

As spring warms the southern seas in August, white steenbras begin to spawn along the coasts of South Africa. They're beautiful fish, silvery white with large eyes, prominent red lips, rakish, swept-back fins and fetching flecks of gold on their upper scales. In holes and on sandbanks near estuaries females lay clouds of eggs which – as their kind have done for millions of years – attendant males dutifully fertilise. Now and then they feed in their endearing way: floating tail up and blasting crustaceans out of the sand with their fleshy lips.

Once they were part of the great steenbras migrations; today they'll be lucky to find a mate. Pignose grunters, as they are more appropriately known (they grunt), are on the edge of an abyss.

'They're critically at risk,' commented researcher Steve Lamberth, pushing over a handful of scientific papers to prove it. 'We estimate they're down to about six per cent of their pre-exploited numbers. Maybe even less. We might be seeing our first biological extinction of marine fishes in the not too distant future.'

It's not only marine scientists who have a passion for fish documentation and measurement. From the meticulous records of the Liesbeek Park Angling Club the decline of the white steenbras can be best seen. The club's entries go back to 1938, but the steenbras suddenly made its appearance in 1960. Within a year one in three of all fish caught by club anglers was a white steenbras. By mid-1970 the catch was up to 43 per cent, then came the crash. By 1991 it was down to a mere eight per cent. By the end of the century it was almost zero.

What happened? Steve and other marine biologists have been putting together a picture that is both controversial and sobering. People are quick to blame others for their misfortunes. If you ask recreational anglers where the steenbras went, they're apt to tell you the fish were taken by sein or gill netters, or maybe skiboat fishermen or trawlers. Netters blame the anglers, and fishermen who get their living or pleasure in estuaries blame the surf types. None are entirely wrong, but the truth is greater than they imagine.

White steenbras spawn near the shore and close to estuaries for good reason. Their young – tasty to almost everything in the sea – can smell fresh estuarine water and make for it as hard as their little tails can drive them.

They are entirely dependent on the availability of these 'nursery' waters. Estuaries are calm, warm and seething with edibles: perfect neighbourhoods to grow up in. Here a young steenbras can thrive, alongside countless other marine fingerlings marking time before they're big enough to take on the sea. There is, however, a problem.

Until recently, estuaries were thought of as those annoying, soggy swamps sprawling precisely where humans like to build houses. Too often they were filled in or canalised – 'killed' seems a better word. The rivers that fed them were useful to swell dams, or convenient drains for all manner of nasty substances humans wanted to get rid of. That estuaries happened to be the nurseries of maybe 70 per cent of coastal marine fish wasn't factored in when their use was considered.

The thing about rivers in Africa is that they pulse, flooding when there are storms and often drying up in rain-lean months. This throbbing opens sand-clogged estuary mouths, spewing fresh water into the sea and signalling estuarine availability. Dams stop this, creating stagnating inland waterways behind permanent sandbars. White steenbras can live as long as 40 years and they are territorial. Like salmon, they remember their birth rivers. Fingerlings may be born along the shore their parents know to be the right place, but a blocked estuary means they just mill about on the sandbar and end up as something's lunch. No future there.

So if the problems are in the sandbar, what's that got to do with fishermen? Can hauling a fish out for fun be that bad? Yep, bad news: anglers are the other half of the problem. Let's begin with the estuaries: South Africa has 255 of them.

Research done by Steve and University of Cape Town biologist Jane Turpie suggests that around 67 000 anglers use South African estuaries, as do 5700 cast netters and 1200 gill netters. These 73 000-odd fishermen haul out a staggering 2500 tons of fish a year from aquatic systems that are near-sacred in terms of global biodiversity.

And that's not where most people fish. The majority are shore anglers – around 400 000 of them. Calculated against the number of days each angler actually stands throwing sinkers at the sea, this translates into 3.2 million angler days a year. That adds another 2800 tons to the tally. If you add the 12 000 or so skiboat fishes, toss in another 1700 tons. We're talking here about a mainly recreational annual fish catch of 7000 tons.

Before about 1950 recreational catches were insignificant. Since then, improved tackle, echo sounders, more access to the seashore and greater leisure time among an increasingly affluent angler population have shifted catches from a pre-breakfast vigil to mass tonnage. Commercial fishing is another whole ball game: you don't want to know about *their* catch rate.

The stark truth is that, in the face of this assault, many estuarine and surf fish populations have crashed in the past two decades – and the writing is on the wall for many species. Of the 80 estuary-associated fish in South Africa, 14 are considered over-exploited and six of these – including steenbras and cob – have collapsed. Among the rest, 27 species – including spotted grunter and leervis – are exploited to their limits and will soon decline.

These species are extremely dependent on particular niches – niches which humans are hacking into. Estuarine dependence creates a life-history bottleneck for these fish and has a major impact on their surf and deep-sea adult populations.

Of the ten top fish favoured by shore anglers, the populations of four – galjoen, bronze bream, cob and white steenbras – are officially listed as collapsed and two others – elf and Cape stumpnose – are deemed overexploited. The populations of those skiboat favourites out beyond the breaker line, geelbek, silver cob and rock cod, have also collapsed.

Could recreational fishing be stopped? It's not that easy. Most sports fishermen are in the upper income bracket, which means they have economic and, at mainly local level, political clout. They feel it's their God-given right to fish and they're very vociferous.

Since the 1980s the government has attempted to reduce the impact of anglers by setting minimum size limits, daily bag limits, closed seasons, commercial bans, gear restrictions, marine protected areas or moratoria on the capture of certain species. These measures have failed to provide a reasonable measure of resource protection. New linefish protocols are being considered, but between the promulgation of a regulation and its enforcement falls the shadow. South Africa has more than 3000 kilometres of coastline and it's almost impossible to police.

Steve and Jane estimate the value of the estuarine catch, taken at commercial fish values, to be around R400 million, most of that being from anglers. Add in the surf fishers and you have a billion-rand pleasure industry which supports a host of tackle shops, 4x4 salesmen, clothing shops, holiday accommodation and countless gillies. Anglers and their dependent industries aren't about to roll over and go away.

And the white steenbras? Those few that are left will continue to stand on their heads, blast crustaceans out of the sand and spawn hopefully on sandbanks and in holes near estuaries. The steenbras could be made a cause célèbre of marine conservation. But it probably won't. So, if you ever see one, just kiss it goodbye on its big red lips. Extinction is forever.

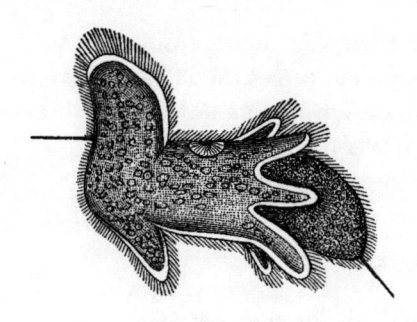

Donkey wars and the Green Revolution

A war suggests an opposition, so the events that took place in Bophuthatswana in 1983 are more accurately described as a massacre. Given that the shoot-up – in which more than 20 000 died – occurred only a few hundred kilometres from Johannesburg, the virtual absence of reportage about it is remarkable. But then, depredations affecting dirt-poor peasants seldom make headlines anywhere in the world.

For one old man, the massacre began while he was on his way to collect building sand in his cart pulled by four donkeys. A troop carrier roared towards him and soldiers opened up at his donkeys with automatic weapons, killing them in their harnesses. In the little village of Ncweng people had gathered their donkeys together for counting. Soldiers arrived and shot the lot from their vehicles. They then fanned out across the veld, searching river valleys and grazing areas, pumping bullets into every donkey they found. People who resisted were threatened. A few, realising the danger, hid donkeys in their houses. The soldiers then moved to the next village, then the next …

'They didn't take aim,' one person told researcher Nancy Jacobs. 'They shot animals anywhere, as often as it took to kill them. They were not put to death, they were savaged. Others were shot in the eye, or different parts of the body and the feet. This made killing gruesome because they had to suffer too much pain.'

The reasons for the Great Donkey Massacre are obscure. One story was that the Bantustan's president, Lucas Mangope, nearly collided with some donkeys on a highway and had turned against the species. Others said that, given opposition to apartheid's Bantustan system, it was an attempt to terrorise people and pre-empt opposition. Some speculated the slaughter was a move by the cattle-keeping class to reduce pressure on grazing.

The official decree simply announced that 'surplus' donkeys were to be exterminated, but trigger-happy soldiers soon turned the cull into mass slaughter. The estimate of 20 000 dead donkeys is probably conservative. Those who suffered most were the subject gender of a subject class, and the massacre hardly made a headline in the daily press.

Coming across this story by chance, I began trawling for more donkey information, and discovered that a jihad seems to have been declared against the humble ass. A report from Brazil spoke of donkey-catching units which round up thousands of the animals for deportation. In some regions donkeys have been banned entirely. In Western Australia elimination is high-tech: 'Judas' donkeys have radio collars attached to them and are released to find herds which 'infest' the scrublands. These are then blasted from a helicopter. Since 1978 the Department of Agriculture has killed more than half a million this way.

Given the Biblical reverence for the donkey, its hardiness, longevity, intelligence and gentleness, this is an odd war of man against beast. I put the problem to Bruce Joubert, who runs the Animal Traction Unit at Fort Hare University, and discovered that donkey wars were part of a much larger issue: the march of the Green Revolution.

The throbbing engine at the heart of this revolution – which was to feed the world's burgeoning population – was the tractor. This gawky machine was undoubtedly one of the finest developments of the 20th century, allowing millions of hectares of land to be opened up for agriculture. It quadrupled production and underpinned the growth of megacities.

By about the 1930s governments, agricultural educators and extension officers had fallen in love with modernisation. Using oxen to plough, they told peasants, was primitive. Cattle were for eating and not for traction. Donkeys, well ... they were good at feeding time in lion parks and crocodile farms. But, otherwise, they were a damn nuisance. Moreover, they were a sign of poverty

There was another reason officials and industry distrusted animal traction. Back in the 19th century most transport not on rails was animal-drawn. In the last decade of that century, however, the deadly bovine disease, rinderpest, followed by horse sickness and East Coast fever, decimated working animals. Commerce in Southern Africa was brought to a standstill.

Before the memory of that disaster had faded, there was a massive demand for equids – horses, mules and donkeys – occasioned by the outbreak of the First World War. In that conflict more than six million perished on the battlefields. A worldwide shortage of working animals followed. By the time the internal combustion engine went into mass production in the 1930s it was hailed as the final solution to these woes. And so it was. After the Second World War, agricultural extension officers, trained in modern farming methods, encouraged peasants to sell their oxen, cull their donkeys and stand by for the Massey Ferguson marvel. The Green Revolution was about to begin.

Bruce Joubert used to be into tractors. As a trained agricultural engineer he knew a good deal about them and enjoyed working with them. When he graduated around 30 years ago he landed a job with the government, testing tractors for peasant ploughing schemes. He was in heaven. But it slowly dawned on him that something was wrong, very wrong. Tractors did the job, but the economy of their use was flawed.

While South Africa's 60 000 or so commercial farmers raised loans from an agreeable Land Bank, bought tractors and implements, and got on with the business of feeding the nation, the 500 000 small-scale and mainly black farmers weren't candidates for loans. The government, keen to increase production in the Bantustans in order to feed the masses cooped up there by decree (and ensure they stayed there), created tractor schemes. But its officials forgot to ask small-scale farmers how they went about their business. The new dynamic, Bruce discovered, was throwing centuries of communal support systems out of kilter. Somehow, whenever a tractor was needed, it was elsewhere (maybe if a goat was offered as payment, it would arrive). Control over farming seeped out of the community and into the hands of tractor drivers. If the tractor broke, that control shifted to mechanics in the towns, far away. If parts were needed it shifted even further, to city agents. For farmers who'd eaten their trek oxen and sold their donkeys (or had them shot), there was nothing to do but wait, watch the skies and hope. Some fields were ploughed, many weren't. Then the government, plagued by the mismanagement of the schemes, decided to lease tractors to their drivers, who were expected to run their own businesses.

The plan spawned problems. Farmers paid the drivers to plough, but only what they could afford, and often in kind. The drivers weren't good at calculating overheads, so when implements broke or the tractor needed servicing, they had no ready cash. You can't pay a mechanic in goats or donkeys. Tractors were left in fields, quietly rusting. One after another, the tractor schemes collapsed. In many parts of southern Africa you can still see dead tractors all over the countryside – peeling monuments to questionable intentions.

The tractor debacle took around 20 years to play itself out. In that time a generation of newly 'modern' farmers had learned to depend on machines. Vital animal-handling skills had been lost, along with the animals. Instead of booming, peasant agriculture was falling apart, with families depending on wages remitted from relatives in urban areas. Following the 1994 elections, legislation which bottled people up in the Bantustans was eventually repealed, and people from these areas flooded the cities. The squatter camps around South Africa's towns bear testament to a failed agricultural policy.

Bruce, watching all this rural decay, was horrified by the social and financial implications of the loss of skills in animal traction. In poor areas, tractors just didn't make sense. Of every R100 spent on tractor hire, he found, most was exported from the rural area. Of every R100 spent on the hire of draft animals, however, most remained in the community.

'I'm not a Luddite harking back to a machine-free world,' he commented as we watched a perfectly matched team of oxen working a field. 'But small farmers using tractors is a no-win situation. Animals appreciate but tractors depreciate. You can buy an ox for R1800, work it for three years and sell it for R8000. What are you going to get from an old tractor? Nothing but trouble.'

In the early 1990s he created the Animal Traction Unit at Fort Hare University, which trains farmers in animal use and holds workshops for traction enthusiasts from all over the world. If you yearn to see a team of eight drawing a hand-held plough, hear the crack of a driver's whip or watch two snow-white percheron horses drawing a harrow, that's the place to go.

'If we can change perceptions,' Bruce reflected, gazing at the rich soil curling off a plough shear, 'we'll change the future of farming in this country.'

And the humble ass? It's tempting to view the Bophuthatswana Donkey Massacre as a metaphor – the bootprint of the mechanical age in the face of its older, animal-using predecessor. Well here's a prediction, for what it's worth: the donkey will outlive modernism – and the postmodern age as well.

The rabbit-eared equine was probably the next creature to be domesticated after the dog – around 8000 years ago. It would have been the first draught animal in human history, and there is good reason for its long and continuing association with our species.

We live in a world where population growth is outpacing the ability of governments to ensure overall human prosperity. Contrary to the dreams of modernism, living standards in marginalised countries are falling while rain, increasingly often, isn't. Attempts to mechanise small-scale farming in these areas have failed. As men beat a path to the cities to earn what they can, marginal farming has become woman's business. And the donkey is a woman's best friend. Donkeys seem to like human company. They're small enough to handle easily, can survive in drought-stricken areas (they need little water), eat less food than an ox but can work as hard, are remarkably long-lived (up to 50 years), are inexpensive to buy, produce drinkable milk, seldom become ill, make friends for life and are remarkably intelligent. They can carry water and firewood all day, plough and protect flocks (they have an ingrained dislike for dogs and jackals and will kill them if they threaten).

Apart from its annoying tendency to ignore oncoming motor vehicles, the donkey remains, after thousands of years, the perfect farming companion. There's a side of its character that infuriates men but delights women. You can beat an ox and command a horse. But with a donkey it is necessary to negotiate. And women are good negotiators. So as long as there are women on the land in developing countries, there'll be donkeys trotting along behind them.

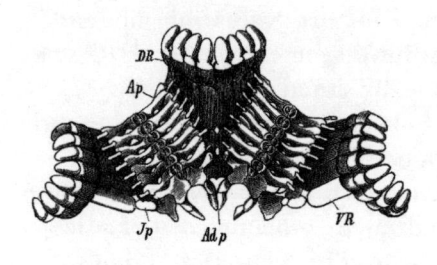

Deadly lost rivers of the urban sprawl

One lazy spring day, while staring idly into a stream on Table Mountain, I made the acquaintance of a worm. It was hanging off a rock, its mouth and anus wide open, taking a chance on whatever passed through its half-a-centimetre-long, high-speed intestine.

Well, I could have been wrong about that. No biologist I talked to had heard of such a beastie. Maybe it was just a blackfly larvae yawning. Maybe a new species. But it certainly looked like a tube with foot hooks.

Some years later, as I dug my paddle into one of the most dangerous rivers in Africa, it struck me that it was rather like passing through that worm: I stood to be digested at any moment. I had been advised against the trip by both ecologists and my wife, who predicted dire consequences. In my line of work I've gone down some wild rivers: the Orange, Zambezi, Nile, Urubamba and Amazon among them. But I'll confess: the Black River in suburban Cape Town really scared me.

One is not, however, always guided by caution. So early one morning on a high tide Leon Franken of Coastal Kayaks and I dropped our craft into the river at its mouth in Table Bay. As we did, another mouth – that of a sleepy, worker hanging over the road bridge – slacked into an incredulous 'O'. It stayed that way as we donned our protective gear: wetsuits, gumboots, industrial-strength rubber gloves and gas masks. I appreciated the incongruity. From his perspective we were about to paddle up a sewer. The only floating objects he'd ever seen in it were probably polystyrene jetsam, rotting weed and flotillas of turds. Shiny kayaks and men in fancy dress were a bit out of the ordinary.

The surging tide and, we hoped, relatively clean sea water carried us under the first few bridges. Industrial backyards provided a sombre backdrop to dozens of seagulls and a few egrets scrimmaging in the shallows, their snowy plumage flashing in the rising sun. A bit further inland the industrial stuff backed off a bit, opening up glorious views of Devil's Peak and Table Mountain. The vista from the sewer was spectacular.

Then my kayak grounded under a bridge and I had to get out to haul it through. As my boots sunk into the sludge a profoundly awful smell assailed us: something between a sulphurous stink bomb and diahorrea. As I eased my way back into the kayak some water spilled into the top of my boot. When I sat down it spilled back out and slushed round my seat. My defences had been breached by the enemy.

When Cape Town was little more than a scruffy village, the Salt River catchment system, of which the Black River is a part, fingered its way through a fynbos type known as renosterveld. Seventeenth-century maps suggest that most of the area was a series of marshy wetlands connected by a few seasonal rivers lined by reed beds. Hippos still galumphed in pools and the area would have been a magnet for migratory birds. Elephants were seen (and, like everything else, shot) among the channels.

In the area where the rivers entered Table Bay were large mudflats, esturine wetlands and islands. For early European settlers the wetlands were messy and dangerous. Many were drained and filled in for farming. By the late 1800s the area had changed from agricultural to suburban land, and by the early 20th century the reed beds were burned off and many parts of the rivers canalised, transforming them into drains. Blomvlei became Athlone, Tiervlei became Ravensmead and Paarden Island ended up an industrial estate.

Rivers were perfect for sluicing storm water out of the city and were irresistible receptors for sewage-processing plants, now more delicately known as wastewater treatment works. Step by step, year by year, the urban rivers died a little more. From sources of sustenance, they became areas of leisure, then dumping grounds, and finally distasteful places upon which the city turned its back. Very often, they stank.

Their management was left to city engineers who saw them, understandably, in terms of drainage. A natural river is far more than a drain, however. It's a self-cleansing system with intricate food webs of micro-organisms, plants and animals feeding on each other and processing nutrients through diverse communities of bacteria, fungi, plants, invertebrates, fish, frogs, birds and mammals. But only to a certain point. Yank out the indigenous plants, straightjacket rivers in concrete and they're no longer rivers at all. Their only use to the city is the same as that of the flush system in your toilet.

Up the Black River are the Athlone and Borcherds Quarry wastewater treatment works. South Africa has very strict regulations about what such plants can discharge into a river. 'The waste water or effluent,' reads Regulation 991 of 1984, 'shall contain no constituents in concentrations which are poisonous or injurious to humans, animals, fish other than trout [poor trout] or other forms of aquatic life, or which are deleterious to agricultural use.'

There are no end of 'constituents' which are potentially injurious, high on the list being faecal *E. coli*.

E. coli is bad news. It's full name is *Escherichia coli*, the first word being derived from the name of the man who isolated the virus back in 1885, the second being the species. We all have millions of *E.coli* in our intestines – in fact we depend on them to help digest food. The Darth Vader of the family – the bad bug – is *E. coli* 0157:H7. It attacks intestine walls, causes lots of bleeding, and can kill if the victim is weak or a child. A mere ten of these microscopic bacteria can lay you low.

In 2000 Justine Fowler and Cate Brown of Southern Waters Ecological Research tested the waters of the Cape Flats rivers and came up with some worrying results. By then a regulation had raised the allowed faecal *E. coli* count per 100 millilitres to 1000. But the Black River had 6000, the Salt River 9000 and the Vygekraal just below the Athlone Waste Water Works 200 000.

Cape Town, though, is not the country's prime river-fouler. Some other cities have rivers that range from nasty to deadly. The Buffalo River, flowing through East London, is virtually dead, the Klipspruit in Soweto is a dumping ground for dead animals and wrecked cars, the Jukskei in Johannesburg is mostly full of litter, dangerous cocktails of industrial effluent and the overspill of sewage blockages, and the Swartkops in Port Elizabeth carries hazardous levels of heavy metal pollutants.

A quote from a report by Free State researchers Griesel and Jagals on the Modder-Riet river catchment in Bloemfontein is a fine study in understatement: 'These surface water bodies receive faecally polluted urban discharges that contain pathogenic micro-organisms in such high numbers that the assimilation capacity of the receiving water body is overcome.' Not a good place for children to swim.

At Keiskammahoek in the Eastern Cape it's the pumping station that gets overcome, spewing raw sewage into the Gulu River, causing spectacular blooms of algae overjoyed at all that nutritious fallout.

A survey by the Umgeni Water Board in KwaZulu-Natal of rivers round Pietermaritzburg and Durban came up with surreal figures: 720 000 *E. coli* per 100 millilitres in the Umlaas, one million in the Umgeni and ten million in the Isipingo. Veritable bug paradise. The Plankenbrug River in Stellenbosch, which flows through picturesque wine estates (does it water them?) was recently found to contain more than 12 million. The Mooi River, which runs through the town of the same name in KwaZulu-Natal, though, takes line honours. It's radioactive. The probable culprit: upstream mining.

At the confluence of the Liesbeek we were stopped short by a mass of alien water hyacinth (*Eichhorina crassipes*). We changed tack and hammered through the weed into the Liesbeek and paddled up a filthy canal past the River Club to a weir which forms the so-called Liesbeek Lake. Peering over the weir, we discovered a bubbling, putrid mess, and beat a hasty retreat.

To continue up the Black River you have to haul your kayak out and re-enter the river half a kilometre upstream, where it's crossed by the N2. From there it is an attractive paddle (if you ignore the highway noise) past the Rondebosch Golf Course and towards Athlone Power Station: reeds, ducks, green grass, trees and unwary caddies fishing for golf balls in the unwholesome faecal soup. Beyond the golf course there's a full stop at the Athlone Waste Water Treatment Plant. The stench is overpowering.

Just beyond the works is the confluence of the Vygekraal and Jakkalsvlei rivers. The latter runs, as a canal, beside the Joe Slovo informal settlement. All along the river, facing away from it, is the longest row of toilets

I have ever seen. Their positioning is convenient: if the buckets overflow, as they do, the muck trickles into the canal to join piles of garbage which regularly collect there. Long before that we gave up, phoned Leon Franken's partner, Rowena, who soon rolled up in the bright little Coastal Kayaks van to transport us and our nose-wrinkling kayaks to an urgent scrub-down.

Later I asked Cape Town Unicity's water catchment manager, Mark Obree, how he felt about the urban rivers the law entrusts him to manage.

'What gets done is a balance between political priorities and the need to deal with absolute necessities,' he explained. 'Then there's the infrastructure. Much of it in Cape Town is more than 100 years old. Canals were built to drain the wetlands and tame the floods for agriculture. 'In the 1950s and 1960s, the imperative was to develop the urban fabric for the growing city. Now city dwellers need green breathing spaces for relaxation and recreation but some rivers are canalised and many have disappeared.'

The logistics of the city's storm water and river management is scary, and Obree's task is not an enviable one. Cape Town has 1500 kilometres of rivers, streams and canals, and a nightmare 5000 kilometres of underground storm water pipes and culverts to maintain. There can be any number of blockages a day, and when one occurs the sewage generally flows into the storm water system, then into the rivers. Manhole covers get stolen and people use the dark holes as convenient dustbins. Workers even find dead dogs and shopping trolleys down there.

The underlying problem is the burgeoning population. There are around 3.5 million people in Cape Town and perhaps 100 000 informal dwellings. More than half of these have no access to sanitation at all. One can only guess at the size of the dung heaps that eventually get washed into rivers when it rains.

Apart from the health problem, there's a good political imperative for a clean-up, as Obree pointed out. 'The poor can't take a drive to the beach or the bushveld for their recreation. But city rivers are often within walking distance of their homes. We owe it to these families to make them safe and beautiful.'

It's just possible, though, that the filth of urban rivers may be a blessing in disguise. In the race for more buildings and roads, developers have shunned these forgotten waterways, allowing them, in many cities, to go wild. Riverside properties face the other way, leaving the banks to compost heaps, scrap heaps and the backs of garden sheds.

Only when you dare their befouled waters do you realise the potential beauty of these natural arteries, and the unusual views of the cities they afford. If the water is cleaned, as the law says it must be, alien vegetation cleared and the bases of the canals bulldozed to allow indigenous river plants to take hold, they could become green jewels at the heart of urban sprawl.

It has taken us hundreds of years to throttle our urban rivers. Even with the political will and sufficient funds, how long would it take to rehabilitate those that are not yet underground drains? That's a hard question to answer.

Cape Town, at least, has begun this process. The city has earmarked R100 million for water management and R300 million for upgrades to the Athlone wastewater works. The city's 'soft engineering' approach has seen permeable walls, natural edges and indigenous plants replacing hard-edged canalisation – the wetland at Fish Hoek being a fine example.

Fortunately, sick rivers – even those that are victims of urban pollution and neglect – have a remarkable ability to re-establish themselves. All they need is a little help from their friends.

A few days after my paddle, *my* friends were no help at all, wagging their fingers and saying predictable things like 'I told you so' as I lay sweating and groaning. There was no escape for the foolhardy: I had fallen victim of the contents of my boot.

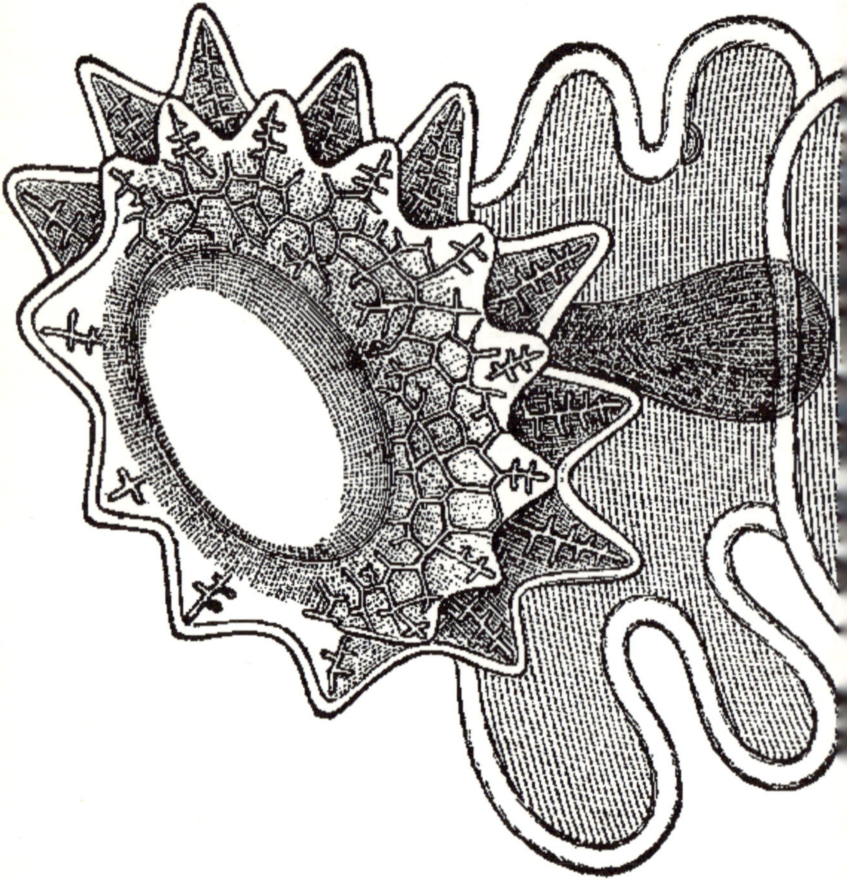

Odd adventurers

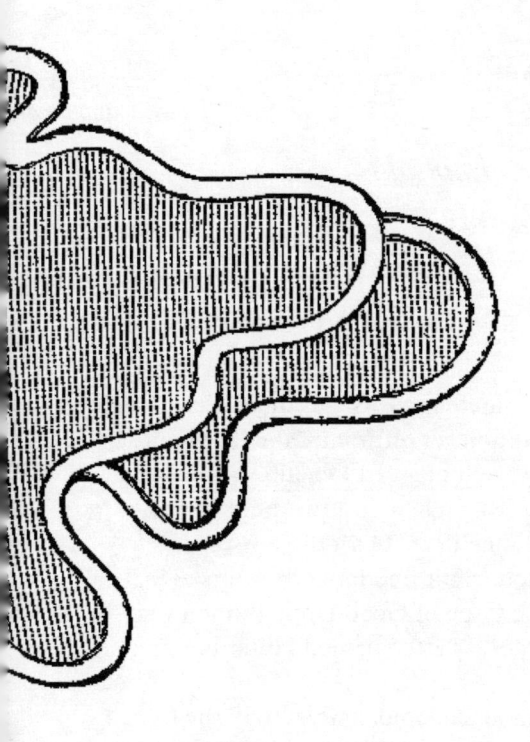

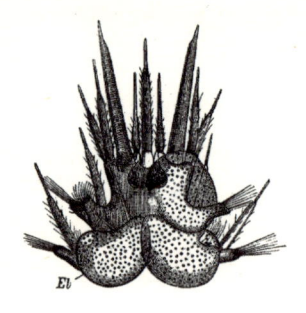

The trek to Copper Mountain

Three hundred and nineteen years ago, at 10 o'clock in the morning, an expedition set off from Cape Town into unknown territory in search of an El Dorado. It consisted of a coach and five horses, eight asses, two field pieces, eight carts, 15 wagons, one boat, 14 saddle horses, 353 oxen for draft or burden, eight free farmers, four slaves, the Commander of the Cape of Good Hope (Simon van der Stel), and an apothecary artist named Hendrik Claudius.

There had been rumours of gold, and in 1659 the Cape Council authorised the search for 'Chobona [Shona] gold and pearls &c ... in the city of Monomotapa.' No less than seven expeditions headed north from the Cape over the next four years but none were successful in their quest for gold – or anything of value. They did, however, make contact with the Namaqua people.

Interest in 'commodities of value to the VOC (Dutch East India Company)' waned until some Namas visited the Fort on Table Bay with lumps of copper ore. Van der Stel thought it to be of good quality and sent an expedition under Ensign Oloff Bergh to investigate. Bergh found it impossible to locate a way through the jumble of broken land and dunes to the north and returned empty-handed.

Then in 1685 a VOC commissioner, Hendrik van Rheede, arrived at the Cape to investigate trading. He shared with Van der Stel a passion for natural history (he described Van der Stel as 'a distinguished botanophile'), and this, together with the possibility of copper, got them talking about yet another expedition. Van Rheede records that Van der Stel was anxious to take personal command, which he permitted. The commander was instructed to 'give a description of the country, mountains, rivers, roads, forests … likewise everything that is perceived worthwhile to be noted.' A meticulous logbook of the trip was to be kept.

The apothecary Hendrik Claudius happened to be in the right place at the right time. He was born in Breslau, Germany, but nothing more is known of him until he was sent to the Cape by Andreas Cleyer, an influential doctor and botanist in Batavia, to collect medicinal herbs and draw anything of interest. By the time Claudius arrived in Cape Town, Cleyer had been transferred to China and no longer needed his services. Instead, the apothecary was employed by Van der Stel as recorder and artist on the Oloff Bergh expedition. Van Rheede saw his drawings and was impressed – 'he draws and paints animals and plants to perfection' – and suggested Claudius accompany Van der Stel.

His instructions were 'to keep a record and to make accurate notes of passing daily occurrences, especially of what may be met with in the nature of plants and animals, all distinct and perfect as is practicable'.

Five days after leaving Cape Town, the expedition reached Riebeek Kasteel and explored that mountain. Along the way they met some San hunters and gave them a sheep 'which they skinned and roasted on the spot'. After leaving their camp at Trompeters Drift near the Piketberg massif, they were attacked by a rhinoceros, which narrowly missed Van der Stel when his blunderbuss misfired.

They shot an eland, and while the men skinned it Claudius sketched plants, snakes and lizards previously unknown to science. They crossed the Olifants River and camped at a place which would in future be called Vredendal. After that it was a hard slog across the dry Knersvlakte to the Groen River and on to a camp which would become Garies. With the help of the San – whom they befriended with gifts of liquor and an ox – the expedition lumbered on to the present Kamieskroon, where they met some Namaquas. Claudius sketched them.

'They wear the skins of dassies, jackals and wild cats,' he wrote, 'and the men wear an iron plate on front of the forehead which they polish. They are very untruthful and eat rats, dogs, cats, caterpillars ...' He painted a 'sweet and loveable little beast [meerkat] which cannot keep still'. Into his sketchbooks went 'a frightening lizard covered with thick scales', a 'graceful bird that produces a lovely sound when flying ... and never alights', a snake 'with powerful venom [puffadder] with which the San poison their arrows', a 'hairy spider called by the Namaquas *hoeb* ...'.

Because he was an apothecary, plants interested Claudius and he went to great lengths to find out their uses to the local people. One was a purgative, another was good to eat, a third relieved flatulence. He drew a tree 'from which the inhabitants make quivers', a shrub called *thou* (obnoxious to the stomach), and bulbs which caused constipation ...

With the Namaquas as guides, the expedition reached the Koperberge (Copper Mountains) where they dug out copper ore which would be sent to the Netherlands for essay (and declared low-grade and not worth mining). Claudius drew the mountains and the camp, noting that one of the mountains 'consist(ed) wholly of copper ore from top to bottom.'

Searching for a suitable harbour to ship out ore, the expedition headed for the coast – it was a terrible, waterless trip on which some oxen died – and after much wandering up and down the beaches found no suitable harbour.

Six weeks later the expedition was back in Cape Town with the first paintings and descriptions of an area which is now known to have more than 9000 species of plants, nearly 70 per cent of them endemic. The low grade of the ore, the scarce water and the lack of a harbour would delay mining operations in Namaqualand for some 200 years.

Claudius's paintings, together with a detailed description of the journey, possibly written by Van der Stel himself, were sent to the VOC offices in Holland and eventually lost. A copy of the paintings found its way to Holland and it, too, disappeared. It seemed to be an expedition destined to fade completely from history. Nearly a century was to elapse before botanists and naturalists such as the Swedes Carl Thunberg and Anders Sparrman, the Scots William Paterson and Francis Masson and the Frenchman François le Vaillant were to pick up the baton of natural history in South Africa again.

Two hundred and sixty three years after the expedition, Gilbert Waterhouse, a professor of German at Trinity College in Dublin, asked the librarian, on a whim, if he had any archived documents in Dutch. The man dug up a dusty old journal, and when Waterhouse read its title he couldn't believe his eyes: *Dagh Register Gehouden op de Voiagie gedoen naar der E Heer Symon van der Stil.*

What was it doing in Dublin? Waterhouse began to dig. It had evidently been removed from the VOC archives (probably stolen: its document number was obliterated), and had ended up in the possession of Baron Hendrik Fagel. In 1794 Holland was invaded by the French revolutionary army under Pichegru, and Fagel obviously considered the report valuable enough to remove to England. In 1802 it went on sale at Christie's Auctioneers with a batch lot of other Dutch manuscripts. They were bought by a Trinity College archivist and simply buried in the university library.

With Claudius's paintings in hand it was possible to identify another set. It seems these were copied from the originals in 1692 for Nicholaas Witsen, a leading citizen of Amsterdam and a director of the VOC. By an extraordinary number of chances, they ended up in the hands of Sir Johannes Truter, chief justice of the Cape Colony, who presented them to the South African Literary Society. It is not known how they came into his possession, but they lay on dusty shelves until Waterhouse's discovery. They are now a treasured holding of the South African Museum and copies have recently been published in a fine book, *Codex Witsenii*.

Claudius's paintings and the descriptions appended to them are undoubtedly the foundation documents of biology, zoology and herpetology (the study of reptiles) in South Africa. They are not the most accurate of paintings, but they were the first, and for that reason they are a treasure.

By the mid-19th century the richest worked copper deposits in the world were to be found, not many metres from the site where Van der Stel had prospected.

But there is another matter worth mentioning: a massive oversight which, had it not occurred, would have changed the course of South African history. The beaches along which the men tramped between the Groen and Orange rivers were strewn with diamonds, and nobody noticed.

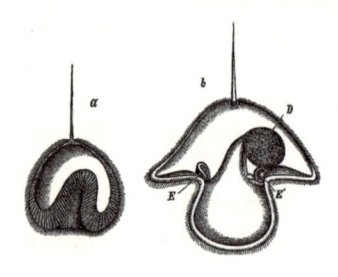

A *brief history of clouds*

At six o'clock one evening in December 1802 clouds ceased to be the exclusive domain of poets and lovers. A young man named Luke Howard untied his bundle of notes in the basement of Plough Court, London, and began to speak. The skies were never to appear the same again. It was a startling performance, and when he finished speaking the place was in uproar.

In a way almost unimaginable today, the middle classes of cities in early 19th-century Europe and North America had a thirst for new knowledge. In halls, basements and clubs anyone with something new to tell and the confidence to tell it would draw crowds of paying spectators. Plough Court was one such venue.

The speaker that day had been born to a Quaker family in Red Cross Street, London: honest, hardworking people who placed a high value on technical education. Theirs was a household in which luxury and idleness were held to be entirely against God's wishes. Young Luke's habit of staring at clouds for hours must have seemed a grievous waste of time to his stern Quaker father. The boy's interest was quickened when, in 1773, a sickly haze from volcanic eruptions as far away as Japan and Iceland cloaked Britain for months and caused wild thunderstorms. Weather was on the front page of every newspaper and on everyone's lips.

When Luke completed his secondary schooling, Howard senior decided that the best remedy for his son's dreaminess would be to apprentice him to a chemist in London. As religious dissenters, Quakers were denied admission to higher institutions of learning. In the basements of London he joined other young dissenting scientists in endless, intense discussions which would produce some of the finest minds of the century. Retail chemistry would ever after provide Luke with his income, but meteorology would be his life.

Clouds write, erase and rewrite themselves with endless fluidity, showing clearly that there is no moment in nature when nothing can be said to be happening. To the poetic imagination they stood as ciphers of a desolate beauty, gathering randomly and dispersing with the wind. By their nature, they are self-ruining and fragmentary. They flee upwards or over the horizon to a forgotten end. To quote Richard Hamblyn in *The Invention of Clouds*, 'every cloud is a small catastrophe, a vapour that dies as we watch it. When it is gone, without a trace, how could it be registered as anything but a brief sign in the sky?'

Until the moment Howard gave his Plough Court lecture, clouds had – for countless millennia – been the domain of words but not measurement. They were, as Samuel Johnson complained, 'always available, always with us and always unclear'. How could they be imagined as part of nature's continuous scheme? What could there be to a cloud in the sky but vague metaphorical allure?

There had always been those, however, who attempted a more scientific understanding of them. Three-thousand-year-old Chaldean clay tablets from southern Babylonia observed that 'when a cloud grows dark in heaven, wind will blow'. During the Shang dynasty, Chinese scholars kept weather journals, recording wind direction, rainbows, snowfalls and cloud movements. A few centuries later the Taoists developed a whole pantheon of weather (from which the modern ideas of feng shui, 'wind and water' are derived). This pantheon included the gods of Thunder and Lightning, the Earl of Wind, the Master of Rain and his young apprentice, the Little Boy of Clouds.

By 600 BC the Greek Thales – probably Western civilisation's first scientist – was conversant with astronomy, brontology (the study of thunder), ceraunics (the study of lightning) and nephrology (the study of clouds). He discovered the fundamental truth that we do not live on the summit of solid earth but at the bottom of an ocean of air. Some 200 years later his fellow countryman, Aristophanes, was droller about clouds, claiming them to be the patron goddesses of the layabout, from which we derive our intelligence and reason.

Aristotle, in around 340 BC, viewed them with a far more critical eye. Clouds, he said, depended on the mingling of the stratified elements: the heat of the sun rearranging cold water on the surface of the earth to form a new, warmer substance – similar to air – which rises. This, he said, was the substance from which clouds were formed. They did not gather at the 'top' of the sky, as the fire of the sun burned them, he reasoned, and were not too close to the earth because of heat from reflected sunlight. As theories go, it wasn't bad.

By AD 79 the Roman scholar Pliny the Elder was attributing the meterological lifecycle to the attractive power of the stars: 'rain falls, clouds rise, rivers dry up, hailstorms sweep down, rays scorch ... then are broken and recoil and carry with them moisture they have drunk up. Steam falls from on high and again returns on high. The stars attract and repel.'

With the coming of the early Christian era these views sank from view, weather being attributed to divine and moral intervention. 'The Lord hath his way with the whirlwind, and in the storm,' says the Book of Nahum, 'and the clouds are the dust of His feet.'

There meteorological matters rested, until the Jesuit philosopher René Descartes turned his mind to them in the early 17th century. Clouds, he argued, most likely consisted of water droplets or small particles of ice formed by compressed vapours given off by objects on

A brief history of clouds ⌒ 107

the ground. These droplets coalesce, rise up in little heaps and, gathered together, 'compose vast Bulks so loose and spongy that they cannot by their weight overcome the Resistance of the Air'. Then, too large to stay aloft, they fall as rain, snow or hail. It was a fair description, but exactly why clouds formed the shapes they did eluded him and those who followed.

One early proposal was that acids in the air corroded water into cloud shapes (the *menstruum* theory); another was that particles of fire became detached from sunbeams and adhered to particles of water, creating lighter-than-air molecules which rose to create clouds.

The most persistent theory against which Howard had to do battle was the 'bubble' theory. This held that particles of water, through the action of the sun, formed hollow spherules filled with an 'aura' of rarefied air which rose like balloons until they burst, the water falling as rain.

When Luke Howard had been speaking for nearly an hour his audience found itself in a state of mounting excitement. Most people in the room would have understood that clouds were staging posts in the rise and fall of water. Howard had gone way beyond that. Not only did clouds have fixed properties of their own, he said, but their form and their action could be described in a few types 'as distinguishable from each other as a tree from a hill, or the latter from a lake'. They could be understood as families and species.

Clouds, claimed Howard, came in three basic types: cirrus (from the Latin for fibre or hair), cumulus (from the Latin for heap or pile) and stratus (from the Latin for layer or sheet). A fourth form, nimbus (from the Latin for cloud) was a rainy combination of all three types. He described their creation, their action, their transformation and dissolution.

What galvanised the Plough Court audience was the elegant and powerful fittingness of Howard's descriptions. He had reduced the ever-changing vaporous masses overhead to just four easily identifiable types. What they had heard seemed so simple and self-evident – as path-breaking ideas often are. Many must have wondered why it had taken so long for someone to understand the form of clouds. As the lecture ended, the excited audience could see clouds for what they were: the visible signs of the otherwise hidden movements of the atmosphere. Howard had opened up the clouds to view.

He would battle those who initially objected to his descriptions (and one who tried to claim them as his own). His essay *On the Modification of Clouds* was translated and discussed, and its fame spread. Within ten years Howard was regarded as meteorology's greatest living exponent, cited wherever the subject was discussed. His reputation would grow until he became an ever-shy but often-present member of gatherings of England's celebrated sons. His descriptions overcame contenders on the Continent and in America, altering, elaborated upon but remaining essentially unmistakable.

Howard's way of seeing clouds profoundly influenced the work of English landscape artists Constable and

Turner, and captivated the great German philosopher Goethe, who penned a poem in his honour, part of which reads (in translation):

> *Howard gives us with clearer mind*
> *The gain of lessons new to all mankind;*
> *That which no hand can reach, no hand can clasp,*
> *He first has gain'd, first held with mental grasp.*

He became the only Englishman Goethe ever addressed as 'Master'.

Luke Howard died in Tottenham at eleven o'clock in the evening of 21 March 1864. There were high, feathery cirrus clouds in the sky.

There the understanding of cloud forms rested, virtually unchanged, until 1960. In that year a Polish mathematician, Benoit Mandelbrot, had the ghost of an idea.

Mandelbrot was born in Warsaw in 1924 to a Lithuanian Jewish family, and moved to Paris in 1936. When the Nazis invaded France he went to ground in the southern town of Tulle, working as an apprentice toolmaker. After the war he gained entrance to the elite Ecole Polytechnique.

A decade later, irritated with the formalism of French mathematical teaching, he headed for the United States and took refuge in the research centre of the computer giant, IBM. He described himself as a nomad by choice and a pioneer by necessity. Whatever he did seemed to be off the radar of mainstream science. IBM tolerated his obscure endeavours, as only a large, wealthy corporation could do. According to a brief biography of the mathematician by James Gleick in his book *Chaos*,

Mandelbrot began looking at problems other mathematicians and scientists put aside and hoped would go away: transmission errors on telephone lines, long-range pattern anomalies in cotton prices, the randomness of the Nile flooding since Biblical times, anomalies in heartbeats, the random branching of trees, the shape of coastlines, the outlines of clouds. Randomness interested him.

He found existing geometry of no use in all this. 'Clouds are not spheres,' he was fond of saying. 'Mountains are not cones. Lightning does not travel in a straight line.' A real geometry of nature's complexity – pitted, pocked, broken up, tangled and intertwined – would have to agree that odd shapes carry meaning. The pits and tangles are not just blemishes, as Euclidian geometry would have it, he insisted, but are often the keys to the essence of the thing.

In 1960 Mandelbrot wrote a paper which marked the turning point of his thinking. It was titled *How Long is the Coast of Britain?* It would be a benchmark work in a field which was to become known as chaos theory.

If a surveyor walked round the entire coast marking it off with a one-yard divider, he argued, they would arrive at a certain distance. If they used a one-foot divider, the distance would be greater because the divider would capture more detail. If the divider was, say, four inches, it would be longer again. If they followed a snail negotiating every pebble, the distance would be vast.

Mandelbrot found that as the measurement became smaller, the distance rose without limit. Down at atomic levels the coastline was, for all practical purposes, infinite. It was all a matter of scale.

Above other things, Mandelbrot mistrusted formal analysis, but he had an unfailing intuition about patterns and shapes. His work led him to a profound conclusion: the degree of irregularity remains constant over different scales. The unit of measurement for this irregularity he named 'fractal' (a word he coined from fracture and fraction). It was, in the mind's eye, a way of seeing infinity.

For example, imagine a triangle ten centimetres across. Add a triangle one-third the length of one side to each side and you have a Star of David. Keep doing this to each triangle and the outline becomes more detailed, resembling a snowflake. You could keep adding triangles forever and their edges would never intersect. But they would all be contained within a circle the size of your original ten-centimetre triangle. Connecting their sides, you would get an infinite, zigzagging line within finite space. It would be possible to hold an infinity of triangular fractals in your hand. Mathematically speaking, it's a conceptual monster.

With IBM as his working environment, it was obvious that Mandelbrot would devise mathematical equations to feed chaos onto a computer screen. The results were startling. Before his eyes, randomness organised itself into dynamic but recognisable forms, which repeated themselves in beautiful spirals to infinity. Each point, magnified, carried a pattern not quite identical, but recognisable from the previous magnification – whatever the scale. And these alluring patterns repeated themselves across disciplines, whether it was cotton sales you were measuring or the movements of stars. All existence it seemed, was written in the fractalated codes of chaos.

Chaotically forming clouds were perfect material for his fractal geometry. Their characteristic irregularity, Mandelbrot found, changes not at all as they are observed at different scales. That is why, according to Gleick, air travellers lose all perspective on how far away a cloud is. Without help from cues such as birds or aeroplanes, a cloud 50 metres away is indistinguishable from one 5000 metres away. Indeed, analysis of satellite pictures has shown an invariant fractal dimension in clouds observed from hundreds of kilometres. Mountain ranges will obey the same rule. So will coastlines, tree branches and almost everything else you look at.

Far from being merely 'desolate beauty, gathering randomly and dispersing with the wind', it appears that clouds are, indeed, part of nature's continuous scheme. From such discoveries was to develop the mathematical notion of 'self-similarity', a component of chaos theory, which is a field presently revolutionising natural science.

Until recently, most formal science saw life as the triumph of order and regularity over randomness and entropy. Chaos theory is changing that notion. In diverse fields, from human anatomy and biology to pure mathematics and astrophysics, researchers are finding that the information which informs the natural world is contained in ghostly, beautiful envelopes of unfolding pattern which contain and embrace chaos. Disorder, it seems, is the messenger of life. And it is beautiful.

This is something anyone looking at the branches of a winter tree or the forming and reforming of a cloud knows intuitively. In the end, it seems, the poets were right. Clouds, like trees, mountains and much else that pleases our eyes, have form and meaning beyond their mere existence. As a man who created a language of the seemingly unknowable, Luke Howard would surely have delighted in that bit of information.

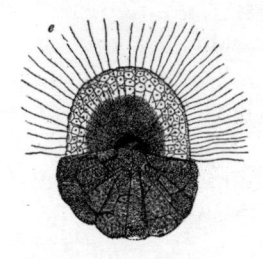

Thank God for Skukuza

At a place named Kamberg in the foothills of the Drakensberg there's a path which leads to Game Pass Shelter. Under a rock overhang is a panel of startlingly clear, polychrome San paintings. The centrepiece shows a man with an antelope's head holding an eland's tail. Both are surrounded by the sort of lines children draw around the sun, giving them a rather hedgehog appearance – or maybe a shimmer.

This panel has been dubbed the Rosetta Stone of San rock art, a visual syntax from which other paintings have been interpreted. It is the depiction of a shamanistic ritual, with the man taking on the energy of the eland and in the process of being transformed into it. There's also a wider interpretation: that of a human energised and transformed by contact with the spirit of a creature from the natural world.

In a sense, the way to Game Pass Shelter is a symbolic path, but one that was not well trodden in the colonial states of Southern Africa. There has been precious little shelter for the great herds of game that once roamed the subcontinent, and even less for creatures which hunted them. Guns, traps and poison felled them in their hundreds of thousands.

There have also been a few who felt the spirit of untouched wilderness and, in feeling it, fought for its survival. Those who did, however, are exceptional people; one of them was a man nicknamed Skukuza, 'he who turns everything upside down', James Stevenson-Hamilton. Arriving in the Transvaal Lowveld when he did, he just happened to be the right man in the right place at the right time, and he would end up changing forever the face of conservation in South Africa.

Many Europeans who poured into the Cape in the 17th century were fascinated by the flora, fauna and geology of this new-found land. They explored, collected and wrote while their fellows hacked, hunted and impoverished the soil with their alien flocks and food crops. In terms of environmental impact, the latter crowd won hands down, turning large parts of the Karoo from verdant grasslands into semi-desert with the help, by 1865, of some ten million sheep.

There were, among the early amateur naturalists, scientifically minded travellers who found and described plants, animals, reptiles and birds. Some complained about the disappearance of these species in the face of Boer and British colonisation. But few had the vision to see where it might end. The Swedish botanist Anders Sparrman was one. Faced with the almost hysterical slaughter of 'vermin' around the Cape, he pleaded for an understanding of the balance of nature.

Predators, he wrote in 1772, 'serve, in conjunction with mankind, to keep in a just equilibrium the increase of the animal kingdom, so that it may not exceed the supplies afforded it by the vegetable part of creation [and] lay it waste'. The idea of a balance of nature was taken up some years later by the English naturalist William Burchell, who travelled in South Africa from 1810.

'Nothing more bespeaks a littleness of mind and a narrowness of ideas,' he wrote, 'than the admiring of a production of Nature merely for its magnitude, or the despising of one merely for its minuteness. Nothing is more erroneous than to regard as useless all that does not visibly tend to the benefit of man. Nothing is superfluous. Each has its peculiar part to perform, conducive to the well-being of all.'

The early views of men such as Sparrman and Burchell were, however, isolated shouts in the dusty avalanche of colonial expansion. Those hunting and game protection laws which were passed to curb the slaughter of wildlife, first in the Cape, then in the Transvaal and Natal, were simply ignored.

The great herds evaporated in gunsmoke and any predators that competed were declared vermin and shot on sight. Lions took a liking to horses and jackals to sheep. Lions were too conspicuous to survive for long on the open plains and by the mid 19th century they'd disappeared from the Cape, as had Cape hunting dogs. Jackals, leopards and caracals proved far wilier, so war was declared and a price put on their heads. Poisoning clubs were established in the 1880s. In Vryburg, in 1892, a single bounty hunter named Jan claimed for five leopards, 32 wild dogs, 62 red cats, 17 baboons and 655 jackals. In the six years from 1917 to 1922, more than a quarter of a million Cape jackals were killed for reward.

The Transvaal fared little better. By the end of the 19th century sport and subsistence hunting were still in full swing. Landowners refused to accept self-discipline in wildlife exploitation and any measures of enforcement were simply ignored. At the end of the 1890s, rinderpest reduced still further what was left of the great herds. All the wildlife of the Transvaal was threatened with extinction.

In 1895 the Volksraad, prodded into concern by members from the Lowveld – and aware that the area was a malarial death trap for humans and no good for farming – proclaimed a reserve in the Sabi area. The idea was to preserve game animals for future hunters by curbing poaching – and shooting all predators. The proclamation, however, was acted on only in 1898 when funds were allocated for the employment of a warden. Then the Anglo Boer War intervened. In 1902, amid post-war turbulence and an over-abundance of lawless guns, Colonel James Stevenson-Hamilton was appointed to the post.

In his book, *South African Eden*, he records his moment of arrival: 'It is the afternoon of July 25, 1902. On the edge of the last escarpment of the Drakensberg, overlooking the huddled welter of bush-clad ravines and rocky terraces which compose the foothills, my little caravan has come to a halt that I may for a while absorb the wonderful panorama of mountain and forest which has disclosed itself.

'Francolins are calling all around, and from a nearby donga comes the sudden clatter of a guinea fowl. Bush babblers are chatting among the trees ... It is the voice of Africa, and with it comes to me a sense of boundless peace and contentment.'

Unbeknown to the Volksraad or Stevenson-Hamilton at the time, it was in this area and under his steady hand that the future relationship between humans and the wilderness in Southern Africa was to be hammered out.

A Scot who was heir to large estates near Glasgow, educated at Rugby and Sandhurst, Stevenson-Hamilton was a man sure of his abilities and as tough as they come. He was, furthermore, intelligent, unmarried, and administratively efficient, and he loved the wilderness. He also had two Celtic qualities that were to serve the future Kruger National Park well: gritty tenacity and charm.

His first battle was against hunters. 'There were no hunting ethics whatever,' he was to observe. 'Their main consideration was the largest number [of animals] shot in the shortest time.' His parallel action was to begin the removal of all human inhabitants from the new reserve.

And in line with his brief, he and his assistants began shooting all predators in order to 'bring up' the antelope herds – action he was later to regret.

Inevitably, Stevenson-Hamilton soon looked to the vast, empty areas to the north of the little Sabi reserve and began to dream: a park from Komatipoort to the Limpopo River – was it possible? Taking time off from the bush, he made the rounds of all the land-owning companies with property between the Letaba and Pafuri rivers and extracted agreements to hand over control of their areas for five years, adding 10 000 square kilometres to the reserve. This northern section became the Shingwidzi Game Reserve and was eventually incorporated into the Kruger Park.

It is difficult today to imagine the incomprehension with which Stevenson-Hamilton's attitude to wildlife was regarded among all sections of the population. While in Pretoria, someone once exclaimed that they envied him for the wonderful shooting he must be having down in Sabi. When he replied that neither he nor his staff ever shot an animal, the man stared at him, speechless, for a moment, then blurted out, 'Why? Can't you hit them?'

One of his African attendants once remarked to somebody: 'Never have I travelled with such a white man; when he saw a zebra standing so close that I could hit it with a stone, he only looked at it. Truly, he is quite mad!'

Painfully slowly, Stevenson-Hamilton's iron control of the reserve together with his non-hunting approach bore fruit. Each year on his epic travels through what was to become the Kruger National Park – on foot with pack donkeys, on horseback or in an ox wagon – he would enthuse over a single sable or a waterbuck, and be delighted the following year to see several more.

He fought Pretoria for more funds to appoint rangers, one of them being the stalwart Harry Wolhuter, who was to become a legend for killing a lion with his sheath knife while it dragged him by his shoulder. He argued for and obtained control over all policemen and border officials in the park area, in this way adding to his anti-poaching force. When he caught several white policemen from Komatipoort poaching, he refused to let it pass and prosecuted them, creating an outcry in the district, but making a powerful point about wildlife protection.

For a while, Stevenson-Hamilton was to be vilified by many Lowvelders who objected to this 'foreigner' throwing his weight around. Local papers bristled with anonymous letters about 'pampered officials' and claimed the park was merely a government breeding ground for lions, crocodiles and wild dogs. There were calls for him to be fired. His response was characteristic. 'I began to develop,' he wrote, 'a certain hitherto unsuspected strain of obstinacy.'

The fracas got him thinking, though. Why waste all this time and money simply to build up a future hunting reserve? Why not, instead, turn it into a national park held in trust for perpetuity? Was there possibly a future in that? The seed had been sown. Stevenson-Hamilton began to agitate, something he proved remarkably good at. 'I would talk at great length about national parks – when I could get anyone to listen to me.'

When a railway line was routed through the park in 1912, he got trains to stop for a bush lunch so passengers could admire the wildlife. It proved a runaway success with tourists. In 1916 a commission was appointed to assess the future of the reserves and its members were taken on tour by Stevenson-Hamilton. They were bowled over by the beauty of the Lowveld. 'The Spirit of the Wild is quick to assert her supremacy,' he would write, 'every member of the commission soon became a confirmed game protectionist.' In its report the commission insisted that the park should be more than a preservation of fauna – it should become a wilderness for all to enjoy. The seed had taken root.

As the legislative wheels began to turn, slowly as ever, Stevenson-Hamilton and his friend, the South African Railways publicity officer Stratford Caldecott, hit on an idea that was pure marketing genius. As an act of conciliation by the British administration, why not call it the Kruger National Park? And that, when the National Parks Act was passed in 1926, is what it became.

The name was purely political. The Volksraad minutes clearly show that President Kruger had never given much support to wildlife protection and, Stevenson-Hamilton wrote, never in his life thought of wild animals except as biltong. 'I wonder what he would say could he see himself depicted as the Saviour of the South African Game!?'

In the years which followed, as people streamed into the new park, Stevenson-Hamilton watched in wonder as what he called his Cinderella became a princess and part of the country's national identity. Having long ceased to hunt predators in favour of his 'balance of nature' principles, he was delighted to note that lions, instead of being considered a menace, 'suddenly acquired immense popularity with the sightseeing public and became [the park's] greatest asset'. Growing up unthreatened by hunters, they quit their nocturnal ways and lay round by day beside (and often on) the growing network of roads – to the delight of tourists.

In 1927, the year it was opened to the public, only 10 carloads braved it, but by 1935 some 26 000 people had made the pilgrimage. Today the number is around a million a year. Stevenson-Hamilton retired in 1946 after nearly half a century as park warden, and settled down to pen his memoirs.

'Nature, left entirely alone,' he would write, 'manages her own affairs. Lion, leopard, wild dog, jackal and other predatory creatures, great and small, and whether of the earth, air or water, have their full place in nature, just as much as the animals on which they are accustomed to prey, and are entitled to equal respect.' Understand this, he said, and nature will transform you. 'Ignore it and she will return armed with a pitchfork.'

Up in Game Pass Shelter is evidence that this necessary accord with nature is an idea with ancient origins. It is also the foundation of modern ecology. And in the Kruger National Park, by virtue of one man's tenacity and his feel for the spirit of nature, wild lions still roar in the Lowveld.

St Barbe and the Incredible Journey

Once upon a time there was a man named Richard St Barbe Baker. He was not an ordinary man, this St Barbe, and his journey was not an ordinary journey. His goal was in the realm of fantasy: to protect the planet's existing trees, to reforest the Sahara and to save earth from environmental destruction. He took this goal very seriously. He is no longer with us, and his story has become lost to all but a few who cherish his name. So I will tell a part of it here, particularly about his Incredible Journey. For he was a man way ahead of his time and he should not be forgotten.

St Barbe was born in a country house in Hampshire, England, in 1889 and at some point, while wandering in the Hampshire forests, it came to him that he loved trees.

In the years that followed, trees had to make a bit of space in his heart for horses, but were never displaced. As a teenager he went to study science at the University of Saskatchewan in Canada, and spent a good deal of time thundering around on horseback with Amerindians. Back in England he followed a loftier path for a while, studying divinity at Cambridge, but when the First World War broke out he signed up and went to France, where he won a Military Cross. Back at Cambridge, having been injured and discharged, he studied forestry and, after graduating in 1920, was posted to Kenya as a forester with the Colonial Service. For a young country gentleman of the time his trajectory thus far was fairly normal. What followed was not.

He arrived in northern Kenya to find forests being decimated and the desert closing in. 'I was driven to the conclusion,' he wrote, 'that it was essential to obtain the co-operation of the people to stem the tide of destruction.'

He discovered that the Kikuyu, when they cut down a portion of forest, left giant fig trees to collect the spirits of their felled companions. He also discovered that anything meaningful began with a dance. So he dispatched runners all over the country, inviting warriors to a dance of the tree spirits. Thousands came, all decked in war paint, and filed past his forest station, clan by clan.

What followed became the stuff of legend. He told them they needed to replace the trees they cut. They told him they thought planting trees was God's business. He told them the spirit of the trees lived in the seeds and these could not make new forests without their help. There was, it seems, a collective 'aaha!' and, right there and then, *Watu wa Miti* (Men of the Trees) was born. It was an organisation that required people to protect and plant trees.

It caught on like wildfire. Within a year his *Watu wa Miti* had nurtured and raised 80 000 trees. Then, under St Barbe's guidance, the idea began to spread like the arms of an oak. At last count (and I am the victim of my sources here) the organisation had branches in eight countries and these had planted more than a billion trees. That is an achievement worthy of admiration, without doubt. This story, though, is not about tree planting but about the Incredible Journey undertaken in the name of trees.

St Barbe had seen the effects of desertification. In 1953 he decided that the best way to fight the desert was to understand it. And to do that he needed to travel through the greatest one on earth, the Sahara. It must be remembered that in the 1950s the Sahara was pretty much still *terra incognita* to Westerners – a place where people ventured and were never seen again. Travelling there was like going to Mars.

St Barbe and two other Brits, in a vehicle that looked like a cross between a Model T Ford and a shoebox, planned to travel from Algiers (without French permission) across the Sahara to northern Nigeria, east through the Sahel, then southeast through the Congo, across the Ruwenzori Mountains to Uganda, then through Kenya to Mount Kilimanjaro. No radio, no backup plans. They left

London with bags of peach pips donated by eager crowds in order to turn the desert into a Garden of Eden.

St Barbe listed their supplies as 'cans of pineapple juice, soup powders, hard biscuits, fig preserve, lots of fresh citrus fruits, dry tablets of Horlicks malted milk and seven jerry cans of petrol given to us by the Shell Company.' Water was carried in goatskins. He wore a 'Bombay bowler', which he soon lost, after which he reverted to Arab headgear. He also lost his sunglasses.

St Barbe was nothing if not thorough. At the edge of the Sahara he felled a eucalyptus tree and counted every leaf. From this he calculated the transpiration per leaf, then per tree. He multiplied this by the number of possible trees per hectare and concluded that each day a hectare of these trees pumped 36 cubic metres of water into the atmosphere. No trees = no clouds = no rain = Sahara. Simple.

Before the travellers lay a vast, barren landscape with not a tree in sight. They plunged into it. At the oasis of Djelfa they found goats nibbling the bushes. At Laghouat they found goats browsing up in trees. At In Salah they found goats nibbling at stumps. 'They eat everything, trees, bushes, olives and tufts of grass,' St Barbe complained. He developed an abiding hatred for goats.

He chewed Horlicks tablets to stay awake at the wheel when they travelled at night, which is when they mostly did travel. Old Arab camelmen told them stories of forests that had existed in the central Sahara in their lifetime; all cut for fodder and firewood. They followed dry watercourses, and St Barbe dreamed of drawing up underground water to raise millions of trees to push back the desert. At one point they traversed 1000 kilometres of desert without seeing an oasis or a person. They nearly lost their vehicle in quicksand. In the middle of all that they found a solitary thorn tree and nearly overturned in their excitement.

Heaven knows how, they got across the Sahara, rolled along the Sahel and plunged into the Congolese rainforests, marvelling at their verdancy and aghast at the effects of slash-and-burn agriculture.

They climbed through the foothills of the Ruwenzoris, barrelled through Uganda and into Kenya. In these two countries they were shocked to see Sahara-like conditions advancing at speed. Finally they pulled up on the slopes of Mount Kilimanjaro.

Back in England, St Barbe sat down and puzzled through what he'd achieved. 'I wondered what to do,' he wrote in what was to become a book, *Sahara Challenge*. 'How to begin to tackle such a stupendous task, as to fight seven million square miles of desert? How could I, one man, reclaim the Sahara? It's not even a project for one nation.'

He began reasoning. The goats had to go. Then the oases had to be assisted to expand their tree cover and eventually link up, creating microclimates to stimulate rain. Then what about all those dry riverbeds? The water must have gone somewhere. Was it in vast, underground aquifers waiting to be tapped?

St Barbe's Incredible Journey would be the rudder which set the course for the rest of his life. 'The Sahara affords a challenge not only to Africa alone, but to the world,' he wrote. 'It offers a glorious opportunity to sink the political differences and past exploitations of our planet into a new creative economy, a new way of living, a biologically correct way of life bringing health and security.'

He worked tirelessly to get governments and organisations to work together to plant trees and halt the march of deserts. He befriended presidents and royalty, gaining their support for his projects. At his suggestion, Franklin D Roosevelt established a forest 'shelter belt' from the Canadian border one thousand miles long and a hundred wide, and formed the Civilian Conservation Corps, which provided six million people with conservation work.

He sat with peasants and warriors, urging them to sow seeds. He badgered the State of California into creating a forest reserve and he set up a Save the Redwoods Fund. 'The Ancients believed that the earth was a sentient being,' he wrote. 'They believed that the film of growth around the earth was its protecting skin and that the earth felt the treatment afforded to it. Geological observation certainly points to this.'

In England, at the age of 74, he rode 530 kilometres on horseback, giving talks about forests to schoolchildren. He took flying lessons so he could see forests from the air. He wrote 20 books dealing mainly with trees. All are now out of print and virtually unobtainable.

In June 1982 St Barbe was in Canada to place in the earth the last of the million trees he personally planted during his lifetime. It was a poplar. A few days later he died. His gravestone in Saskatoon reads:

> *Richard St Barbe Baker, OBE*
> *9 October 1899 – 9 June 1982*
> *Founder of Men of the Trees*
> *Pioneer of desert reclamation*
> *through tree planting*
> *Crusader of virgin forests worldwide*

Since his death, two important discoveries have been made in the Sahara. As he had predicted, huge fossil aquifers have been found under the sands, one of them thought to be about the size of France.

The other discovery was the result of satellite studies by meteorologist Jules Charney. He found that green-covered areas absorb more solar radiation and therefore give off more heat. Warm air carries more moisture, which increases the likelihood of rain. Overgrazed or deforested areas are lighter in colour, absorb less radiation and therefore create cooler, less-moist conditions: potentially deserts. The conclusion is that deserts do not cause droughts; people do.

We now have much of the information needed to halt the spread of the Sahara. What we require, urgently, is the political will and a Richard St Barbe Baker – a man of the trees ahead of his time.

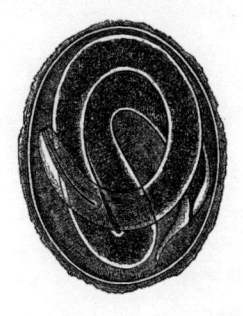

Michael Fay and the human footprint

Michael Fay is looking distinctly out of place in the lounge of a huge Westcliff Ridge house surrounded by beautiful objects of high Western culture. He's dressed in a slightly misshapen red jumper, khaki shorts and sandals. Turns out he's been sleeping on the lawn. It's midwinter, this is Johannesburg, and there are still traces of frost on the grass.

'I could hear the lions at the zoo roaring,' he comments, by way of explanation. 'And the air is fresh.'

This house of generous proportions belongs to Nora Kreher, the *grande dame* of the Bateleurs, a group of enthusiastic private pilots who fly missions of mercy for the environment. It's a good launching pad for Michael's next adventure, the Africa MegaFlyover.

I know Michael by reputation: anyone who reads *National Geographic* could hardly have missed the buzz of articles about him as he walked with a team of Pygmies clear across Africa's wild jungle heart, compiling a painstaking inventory of its biodiversity and the threats to its future.

The day before, I'd downloaded his curriculum vitae – eight closely typed pages. Under 'skills' are listed 'commercial and bush pilot, exploration and reconnaissance, survival, firearms, climbing, biological and human survey, reserve establishment, leadership, videography, photography, fund-raising, community relations, scientific and popular writing, computers, construction, mechanics and public speaking' (he speaks seven languages).

He's been awarded six research fellowships and I count 53 research grants, but run out of patience scanning the endless list of scientific publications. Michael's also been consultant to a slew of organisations, including the World Bank, USAID, National Geographic, the BBC, the US Peace Corps and the National Cancer Institute of America. Most of his fieldwork has been in Kenya, the Congo and Gabon.

'I'm an African conservationist,' he explains when I tax him on his outrageous CV, which seems to have needed three lifetimes to achieve. 'And I'm good at getting people to believe in what I'm doing. Africa is perceived as one of the last frontiers of wilderness. People in the West say, 'It's okay if we turn our wild places into food crops because Africa's still there.' I'm not sure I go with that. We may be losing this last frontier. That's what MegaFlyover is all about.'

The easiest way to describe Michael's new adventure is to say that he is following – and at the same time making – a map. But if by map you think of something on paper with lines and colours which you carry in order not to get lost, the description is misleading. It would be like comparing a game of chequers to three-dimensional chess. This is a map, in short, of the human footprint on the planet.

Until recently such a map was not possible because detailed information on human activities at a global level simply wasn't available. But in the 1990s and with the thawing of the Cold War, Nasa's satellite images were released to the public by the US National Imagery and Mapping Agency.

For the first time, non-military cartographers and geographers could get access to global maps of startling accuracy. Using colour, temperature, elevation and other satellite-produced indicators, a team of scientists from the New York-based Wildlife Conservation Society and Columbia University's Center for International Earth Science Information Network produced a multi-layered map showing population, land cover, roads, railways, rivers, coastlines, the electrical power infrastructure (grading light use at night) and entire terrestrial biomes. From this information were extracted figures about biome transformation, land accessibility and human influence: the sum total of our planetary footprint. And, most compelling of all, was that this could be shown on a single global information system (GIS) map.

From this digitalised wonder they created a human disturbance index, which showed that nearly three quarters of the habitable surface of the planet has been transformed by human use.

'That's what my walk in Central Africa was all about,' said Michael, negotiating a large omelette – which seemed more cheese than egg – that had appeared from Nora's kitchen. 'We looked at the GIS map and asked: "Where are the wildest places on earth?" We called them the Last of the Wild, and selected 568 last-of-the-wild areas representing all biomes in all the realms on earth.

'In the Afrotropical realm, all ten of these areas fall in Central Africa. I worked out a route through the wildest places in these forests and walked it – about 3200 kilometres in 15 months. We called it The Last Place on Earth, a place where the human habitation is lightest. It's an absolute treasure.'

Some probing reveals that there are dangers in heaven: he was attacked by a forest elephant which put a tusk into his side. He saved his life by hanging onto its tusks so it couldn't continue to gore him.

To describe the outcome of Michael's walk as spectacular would be an understatement. He convinced the president of Gabon, Omar Bongo Ondimba, to declare 13 national parks, and raised around $120 million to support development in the Congo Basin. Ondimba has become something of a hero, the World Bank has rolled over his country's foreign debt and huge chunks of pristine forest are now protected.

'I thought,' (Michael says): 'Let's do across the whole of Africa what we did in Gabon. This time we would mostly fly. Go from areas of the highest to the lowest human footprint in all the biomes.

'You see things from a plane that you just don't recognise when you're on the ground. That's what the MegaFlyover is. We're going to be taking high-resolution digital photographs every 16 seconds. Then we'll stitch them together and the human impact will be right there for everyone to see. We'll be filling in the GIS map to its finest detail.'

'You'll be able to see if the wildest of the wild places are protected in parks or are outside them. You'll be able to assess habitability, land use, biodiversity soil type … This way you can find out how far along the path of destruction an ecosystem is. We'll have the information; we can then take action.'

Michael answers a call. He's needed at Lanseria Airport. Urgently. Something to do with a Cessna. He sits down again, seemingly unperturbed by urgency, switches on his laptop and the GIS map appears. He starts layering on information.

'There's something more here than merely protecting the environment. Look at red, that's human density. See how it's stacked up against political boundaries. On the other side there's no red. Empty of humans. That's a danger signal. People without land will move into such land. People in Central Africa are moving west whether you like it or not. That's behind all the conflicts in the Congo, Rwanda, Uganda. That's the message of Darfur, the Sudanese genocide, Kisangani. With maps like this we can pinpoint potential flash points, almost to the month. This is a whole new science of conservation: futures prediction ecology. We can say: "These people are going to kill each other in 2.3 years."

'It's not about politics, it's about resource management. We have huge scope for improving how well we live on this planet, how we manage food production, energy consumption, soil and forest management. About 99 per cent of the timber cut in Central Africa is wasted, burned or left to rot. Think about that. If we don't get our planetary management right in this century, we will cease to exist as a species in any kind of way that humans would want to exist.'

I'm more worried about Michael's urgent call from Lenasia than he seems to be, but I have to ask one last question.

'Why Africa?'

'It's the place I've lived for the past 30 years. I consider Africa my home. But also it's the place on the planet where people are living closer to the ground than anywhere else, where they survive on the resources around them with little import from anywhere else. The rest of the world thinks Africa is where wilderness is intact. It isn't and hasn't been for a long time. Even so, humans here are doing a much better job of living with nature. We need to understand what lessons this has for the world.

'The United States is consuming 20 million barrels of oil a day. Twenty million! We preserve our forests by burning fossil fuel instead of wood, but they're dying off anyway because they're weakened by pollution and are being killed off by bark beetles. Fossil fuel, fossil water, it can't last.'

Michael unwinds himself from the couch when Norah comes in, tapping her watch, and I give him a ride to the airport. Next day I drive through the rampant new urbanism and pollution north of Johannesburg to Swartkop Air Force Base where two red Cessnas packed with equipment are being prepared for takeoff. There's a farewell breakfast at which Michael displays one of his many talents: public speaking. Then he and his co-pilot, Austrian Peter Ragg, head for their aircraft.

'How long will the MegaFlyover take?' I ask as he hauls himself onboard.

'Oh, about 15 months. Maybe more. As long as it takes …'

Soon the two Cessnas are little receding red dots in the blue Highveld sky.

P

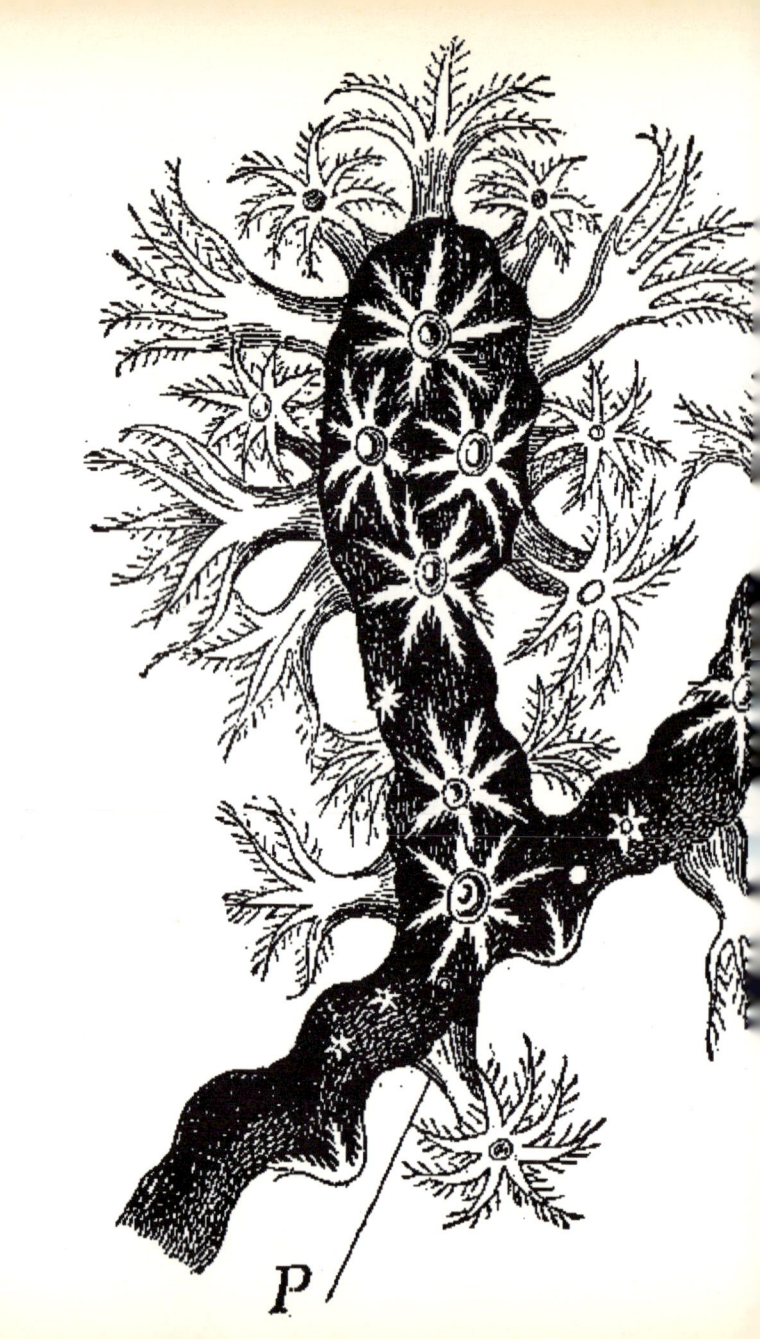

Big and hairy

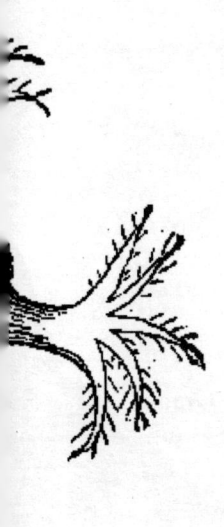

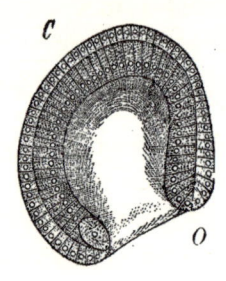

Mythical monsters of the ancient forest

A forest without the possibility of a monster is empty. It's always been like that.

The most fearsome of monsters was probably Grendel, who appeared one day at the great mead hall of Hrothgar, a Danish king, ripping the limbs and heads from poets and pages as he entered. Those were the days when warriors wore helmets of gold and chain-mail suits – and annealed their broadswords in the blood of their enemies. But nothing stopped the steel-taloned beast – until the arrival of Beowulf from the land of Geat, across the sea.

He, so the legend goes, was the strongest man alive, mighty and noble. But he also knew a thing or two about monsters. They were difficult to find by day, deadly at night, cloaked in magic and therefore impervious to sword strokes.

Beowulf waited in the mead hall, pretending to sleep. 'Came then,' to quote the legend, 'striding in the night, the walker of darkness; a horrible light like fire in his eyes.' When Grendel reached for the hero, Beowulf grabbed the monster by its hand and crushed its bones. The monster wrenched so hard in fright, its arm was ripped from its body, and it ran, screaming into the night to die in a swamp.

When Grendel's mother, a huge matriarch, came out of the gloomy forest to avenge her son's death, Beowulf dispatched her as well. Somehow dark forests and dangerous things attracted him.

That was but the start of an illustrious career in which Beowulf ended up as king, only to die towards the end of his long life in mortal battle with a dragon. He just couldn't leave the monster business alone.

The tale gives some interesting facts about the monster's habitat. He left large footprints, which, if one dared to follow them, led to a secret land of windy mountains and perilous fens, where waterfalls plunged over bluffs and ran, at times, underground. Here were dark groves of deep-rooted trees, dangerous to man and beast.

In fairy tales and folklore people invariably find their way into the forest. It is there that they lose and find themselves and where they gain a sense of what is to be done.

When Gareth Patterson – a far gentler warrior than Beowulf – entered the Knysna forests, there were tales of those who had done likewise and never returned. There was also a monster far larger than Grendel – only one, and that intrigued Gareth. He knew what had to be done.

The Tsitsikamma (the name means 'the water that speaks' in Khoi) is a relic of the temperate forests that once carpeted the eastern parts of Africa from Kenya to the Cape Peninsula. Today the tree cover is much reduced, stretching along the coast from Robinson's Pass west of George to the Tsitsikamma River near Humansdorp – a little over 600 square kilometres.

Within the forest edge, away from the disturbance of human enterprise, a deep gloom envelopes you, even in daylight. You enter a world that transcends human understanding, a place for veneration – and uneasiness. Sometimes you sense the forest trusts you, sometimes not. It has a tangible presence, drawing in elements from air and water and the sun, and weaving them into life.

High above, out of sight and in the sunlight, spread the branches of forest giants: Outeniqua yellowwoods (*Podocarpus falcatus*) up to 45 metres tall, white pear (*Apodytes dimidiata*), black stinkwood (*Ocotea bullata*), ironwood (*Olea capensis*) and African holly (*Ilex mitis*), with their leaves arranged in a light-trapping mosaic. Below them, dark groves huddle, and beneath them other species stand, waiting their turn for a giant to fall, providing sunlight and a chance to grow. From them hang orchids, ferns, lichens, mosses, herbs and succulents in profusion, and down in the shadows crouch smaller ferns, wild pomegranate, black witch hazel and grasses. Under them, if you care to look, is a dank, sweet-smelling world of dismemberment and decay: gaudy-coloured bracket fungi, puffballs and mushrooms whose filaments and chemicals devour the forest from below.

Four years ago Gareth was on a chance visit to the Knysna area. He walked into the forest and felt uneasy. Something worrying was going on and he couldn't put his finger on it.

He is, it needs to be said, an unusual environmentalist, using sophisticated science where necessary, but leading with his heart and intuition. Gareth spent his childhood in Nigeria and Malawi and worked in Kenya with George Adamson of *Born Free* fame. When George was murdered by poachers, Gareth got permission to reintroduce his lions to the wilds in Botswana. In doing so he ran with lions, becoming part of the pride in the process and earning the name Rraditau, father of lions.

In South Africa he came across canned lion hunting and exposed it, causing a furore in the hunting fraternity. When he discovered maltreatment of young elephants in the Tuli Block, he exposed that too, which resulted in death threats. 'I'm not an activist,' he said, 'but I can't abide cruelty. Someone has to make it known.'

In Knysna he heard tales of the Matriarch, a huge, mysterious elephant that ruled the great forests but was never seen. 'When I asked locals about her it was like talking about the Loch Ness Monster. It was a myth, many told me. They said the last Knysna elephants died out in the 1990s.

'I didn't want to believe that. I had a sort of intuition that I had something that needed to be done there. I felt strongly compelled to learn what I could about these elephants.'

He moved to Knysna and began walking the forests, deeper and deeper, covering hundreds of kilometres. Almost immediately he found traces: footprints, dung, broken branches and scrape marks on trees …

'There was quite a lot of evidence of elephants. I couldn't believe people thought they'd entirely disappeared. Early one morning I suddenly found fresh tracks of two elephants moving together. These were elephants, barely in their teens, that had not been known about before, and to this day have not been seen, let alone photographed.

'That morning I even heard the elephants feeding. It was a great moment, and I sensed there was hope, not doom, for the Knysna elephants.

'A few months later the forest guards discovered, and even filmed, a young but fully adult cow elephant. They found her lying fast asleep. With this discovery, I wondered when the footprints of a baby would be seen, and not long ago came across what looked like the footprints of a calf. But I need clearer prints for a positive ID on this. That day will come, I'm sure.'

The widest part of an elephant is its flanks. When elephants have rolled in mud, it rubs off onto trees as they walk. Their flanks are three quarters the height of their shoulders, so it is possible to estimate elephant size from these marks.

'Look at this,' Gareth enthused as we wandered down a forest path. 'High marks, medium marks, low marks.

Three elephants passed here. People just aren't looking for the right signs in the right places. They think these are forest elephants, so they look in the forest and find very little. I arrived with no preconceptions and instead explored surrounding fynbos areas and plantations and found plenty of evidence of elephants. That's where they feed at times, there's not much nutrition in the forest. Of the 162 dung samples I've collected, only 32 were in the forest.'

Gareth later discovered the reason for his unease when he first entered the forest. In 1994 three young elephant cows had been brought in from the Kruger Park. The youngest female died and the two others spent their time in the fynbos. It was presumed they'd failed as 'forest' elephants, and that there was no hope of their breeding. They were caught and translocated to Shamwari Game Reserve. The transfer took place on the very day Gareth first entered the forest.

'I was picking up their distress, he commented. 'What else could it have been? And what a shame. Now we know there's a bull in the forest and I've discovered they feed in the fynbos. A big chance to introduce new blood into the population was missed.'

Gareth found it was possible to identify elephants by taking DNA samples of the mucus around their dung. He linked up with a conservation geneticist at the Smithsonian Institute in the United States, then set about collecting 35 fresh droppings. It took a few months and now he's waiting for the results.

'I've found positive proof of at least *three* elephants so far,' he said, 'but there's an excellent chance there are others. In fact, I know in my heart there have to be others that I don't know about. This forest covers hundreds of square kilometres. I've only searched a small part of it.'

Since European settlers came to South Africa, it's estimated that ivory hunters and sportsmen have wiped out around 100 000 elephants. In the 1870s a conservator reckoned that perhaps 400 to 600 elephants existed in the narrow 200-kilometre coastal belt between the Outeniqua/Tsitsikamma Mountains and the shores of the Indian Ocean.

'They were hunted ruthlessly,' Gareth commented, picking over a piece of dung to identify the plants within it. 'The fact that these few have survived is amazing. They should be declared living monuments or national treasures.

These are the southernmost elephants in Africa and the only truly wild and unfenced of their kind in South Africa. People might not realise it, but they're a good lesson in the art of co-existence between humans and wild animals.'

One day, deep in an ancient part of the forest, Gareth came upon a pool which indicated that elephants came there regularly to drink. He named it The Secret Place of Elephants. Sitting up the hill from the pool, he heard them feeding, then the blast of a full trumpet. 'I remembered there was an elephant path nearby straight down to where they were. Here was a chance to get something nobody had managed before: a photo of two Knysna elephants together.

'But I sat there and thought: "I'm not going to do that." I just watched and listened for half an hour, then walked away from the rarest elephants in the world. According to the odds they shouldn't exist at all. Humans have persecuted them for so long, yet they're such enormous survivors. I wasn't going to compromise them.'

As we ambled back through the forest two tourists strode up, looking expectant. 'Have you seen the elephant?' they asked. 'We're from England and we'll be really disappointed if we don't see it.' Gareth smiled and said maybe they'd see it back there. We didn't rate their chances, but it was good to see there were some believers left.

'I sleep well at night because I know there are wild and dangerous elephants out there in the forest,' Gareth mused as we got back to the road, 'and that they exist and that nobody can really interfere with them. They're elephants of inspiration.'

Would Beowulf understand?

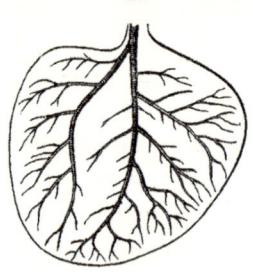

Vermin hunting

THE WAR, THE WEAPONS,
THE VICTIMS AND THE SURVIVORS

The big male looked me over with wise, hazel-coloured eyes, then yawned toothily and rolled on his back to snooze. The female glanced shyly and continued breast-feeding her tiny infant. I was grinning like a chacma with a bag of bananas. I'd been accepted into the baboon troop.

After a while the male rolled off his boulder and sat next to the female, his arm protectively round her waist. They gazed at the bright-eyed baboonlet, both making soft sucking noises. All round were more than 30 baboons, foraging, arguing, dozing or simply gazing over the flower-cloaked Cape Peninsula mountains.

Vermin! At least according to legislation first promulgated in the 17th century. For 350 years in South Africa baboons have been treated as mortal enemies in a horrific, legally declared, unpublicised war of attrition, which has left hundreds of thousands dead – without the loss of a single human life. A very unequal conflict.

The word vermin, curiously, comes from the Latin *vermis*, meaning worm. Collins Dictionary describes vermin as 'animals or insects that are troublesome to man'. Leaving aside the probability that humans are troublesome to almost everything else on the planet, being declared vermin is bad news. It's a death warrant. Your extermination becomes compulsory.

Before Europeans dropped anchor in Table Bay, the Khoisan foraged and hunted, but hardly dented the abundant herds of game roaming the Peninsula. The new, pale settlers picked off the top predators – as settlers with cattle, sheep and gardens generally do. A mere four years after the Dutch formerly settled in the Cape in 1652, the first vermin laws were issued. Reward for shooting a lion was set at six *realen*, a tiger (big leopard) or wolf (hyena) bagged you four *realen* and a small leopard three.

That gave all those formerly persecuted second-rankers a welcome break. They obligingly proliferated. So much so, in fact, that in 1740 it became necessary, for public safety, to forbid hunting on horseback 'between the Castle and the last house in Cape Town'. The colonists continued to blaze away at anything wild, decimating the antelope herds, shooting the last hippo on the Cape Flats and, further north, gunning the quagga and bluebuck into extinction.

But, some years later, they felt the need for protection from the teeming, dangerous animals beyond the Cape Folded Mountains, so bounty was offered for elephants (three *rixdalers*), rhino, giraffes or elands (two *rixdalers*) and lions or zebras (one *rixdaler*).

Farmers reserved a particular hatred for hyenas. If one was caught in a baited 'wolf trap' they would get hold of a hind leg through the bars, cut a hole through the sinew above the joint and fix a heavy wagon chain to it. Then they would raise the door, turn it out and set hunting dogs on the tethered creature, finishing it off with bayonets and knives.

When game became scarce, predators were blamed. In 1822 Cape Governor Lord Charles Somerset obligingly placed a bounty on leopards, Cape hunting dogs, wildcats, polecats and hawks. A bit later it was extended to include lynx, cerval, jackal, badger and hyena.

Some years later 'poisoning clubs' were set up under a Cape parliamentary grant. The rewards paid were: lynxes 3/6d, jackals 3/6d, baboons 2/6d, badgers 2/-, porcupines 2/6d, polecats 2/-, wildcats 2/- golden vultures (probably lammergeiers) 2/-, crocodiles 1/- per foot, caracals 5/-, secretary birds 5/- and hawks 2/-.

Around the beginning of the 20th century, trout were introduced to many streams. Riverine predators couldn't believe their luck until, in 1909, a bounty was set on 'trout vermin': otters 10/-, water mongooses 5/-, large kingfishers 2/- and small kingfishers 1/-.

If anything, the persecution got even worse in the 20th century. In terms of National Ordinance 26 of 1957, dassies, genets and springhares were added to the list, and state-funded 'Wildlife Problem Animal Hunt Clubs' were established. In an Orwellian shift to placate the squeamish, the new ordinance replaced 'exterminate', 'destroy' and 'vermin' with 'control', 'combat' and 'problem animal'.

The enabling legislation creating a hunt club – still in existence – is both racist and despotic: 'Six or more persons who are not Blacks and who are owners of land in a region may establish a club for the combating of problem animals in such region. Every person who is not a Black ... shall be entitled to become a member.' (Well, at least 'blacks' are spared the necessity of killing to order).

The club may maintain a pack of 'vermin' hounds, anyone in the region not cooperating with the hunt can be fined, and no legal action can be taken against club members if they damage property or kill livestock as they bay through the countryside in hot pursuit. To exterminate is compulsory and all-consuming.

A considerate side clause prohibited the shooting of wild animals on Sundays. But it was to be an only brief respite for vermin. A later ruling made it lawful to shoot them on sight on Sundays, 'even though not actually apprehended in doing damage'.

The state stopped fully subsidising hunt clubs only recently, but they continue nonetheless. Today, though, the vermin lists are shorter – mainly because most things on the earlier lists have been exterminated – and go by province. In the Free State, until very recently, baboons, vervet monkeys, black-backed jackals, hunting dogs and bushpigs were still vermin ... excuse me, problem animals. In Gauteng it's baboons, vervets, jackals, caracals and bush pigs.

Fortunately, in the Western Cape, baboons are no longer on the list, because the cheeky chacmas of the Cape Peninsula are probably the most photographed primates in the world. But they are still being persecuted. In fact, most primates are in trouble: at least 90 species worldwide are endangered and, together, they would hardly fill the seats of a football stadium.

Charles Darwin, that thoughtful old Victorian, suggested why humans might verminise primates so heavily. 'Competition will generally be most severe,' he wrote in *The Origin of Species*, 'between the forms which are most like each other in all respects. The improved and modified descendents of a species will generally cause the extermination of the parent-species, i.e. the species of the same genus will be the most liable to extermination.' If chimps, gorillas and baboons could read, they'd see the writing on the wall.

There are people, however, who find the sordid history of vermin control abhorrent and are doing something about it – good people with strong convictions that tend to get them into trouble.

Chris Mercer and Beverly Pervan of the Kalahari Raptor Centre had three caracals in their care forcibly removed by nature conservation officers because, the officers told them, the 1957 Problem Animal Control Ordinance forbade keeping problem animals. They have fought the removal and, with it, the ordinance all the way to the High Court in Kimberley, and are preparing to take it to the Constitutional Court. They want all vermin laws set aside.

Arthur Hunt, a Tzaneen bee farmer, took up the cudgels for grey vervet monkeys after a newborn monkey was handed to him. Its mother had been shot and he raised it, illegally. Searching for information, he came across the 1957 ordinance and was horrified. 'It read like something out of *Mein Kampf*,' he later wrote. 'Before the white man came there were millions of vervets in South Africa. Today it is estimated that there are less than 250 000.'

He formed the Vervet Monkey Foundation, which has become the advocate for this primate species. It provides sanctuary and protection for orphaned monkeys countrywide.

In Cape Town, Wally Peterson and Jenny Trethowan head up Baboon Matters, which was formed when it came to light that angry Peninsula residents, invaded by foraging baboons, were shooting and poisoning members of the dwindling troops in the area. There are about 360 baboons in some ten troops roaming the Table Mountain chain – and they often have bad press. Tourists feed them, then get chased. They get into cars, where they have learned food can be found. They raid orchards and occasionally get through windows left open and make an awful mess in houses. They're big, scary and unafraid of humans – they've been known to walk through the door into the Comfort Zone Tea Shop in Kommetjie.

The Peninsula baboons are a relict population, cut off from the rest of the province by Cape Flats urbanisation. Occasionally a frustrated, solitary male makes a dash for the distant Hottentots Holland Mountains and ends up in big trouble among suburban houses. Before Baboon Matters was founded, he generally ended up dead. The baboons' status, to say the least, is precarious.

A survey carried out by Ruth Kansky and Dave Gaynor found that while more than 140 000 tourists a year see baboons for the first time on the Peninsula, 28 000 have items stolen by them. Something of a mixed blessing. Still, they're a great tourist attraction.

Living close to humans, though, is stressful for baboons. At 13 per cent, their mortality rate is abnormally high and more than half of all youngsters die soon after birth. Apart from being directly killed by people, baboons are also hit by vehicles and are prevented from foraging for essential protein along the shoreline by human presence.

Baboon Matters tries to keep baboons away from human habitation areas and so ensure their survival. With the help of former game guard Thembela Jantjies, baboon monitors have been trained to follow troops from their sleeping places each day and prevent them from heading down to villages or roads.

So far it's working well. As is so often the case with conservation, though, the funds are often unequal to the dedication. It's hard work for low pay.

As we sat among the Da Gama Park troop in the mountains above Kommetjie, Thembela looked thoughtful for a moment, then chuckled.

'You know, when we began,' he told me, 'we saw our job as protecting houses and people by chasing away the baboons. But we spend every day with them, it's like we're part of the troop. So now the way we think is we have to protect the baboons from people. Baboons were here before us. People don't want to understand that this place belongs to them. We build houses all over this place, but who really owns these mountains?'

There is a hopeful postscript. I phoned Cape Nature Conservation to check if Ordinance 26 was for real. It is. I ended up talking to Hannes Stadler, a conservation officer who's done extensive work on the history and effect of legislation on problem animals. He's no friend of vermin laws and is appalled at the slaughter they've engendered.

Stadler served on a National Problem Animal Control Committee which drafted regulations that do not target any problem animal for destruction. These regulations may soon become law. After 350 years of wanton bloodletting, South Africa's war on demonised wildlife might then, eventually, come to an end.

d

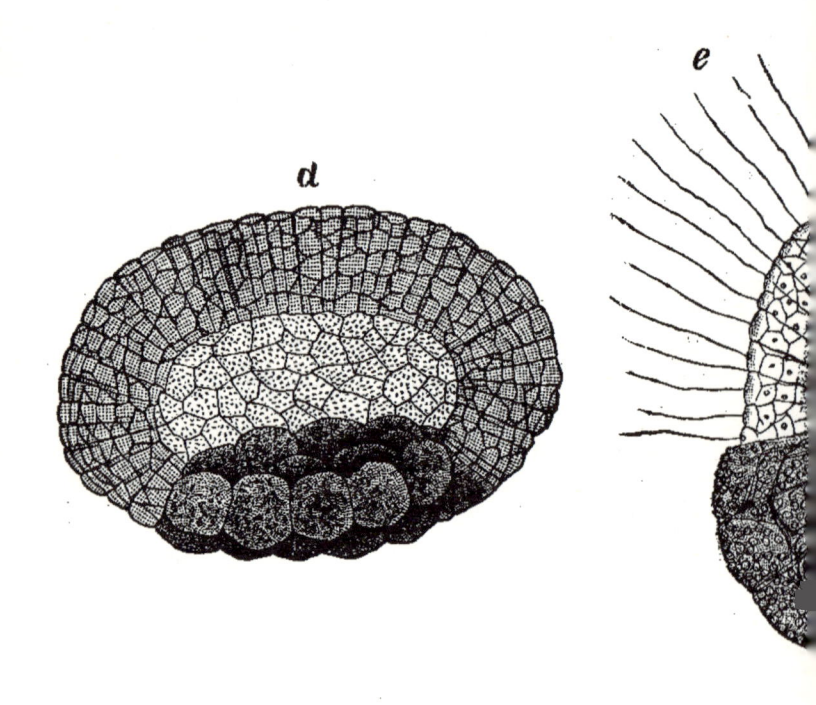

e

Small and spineless

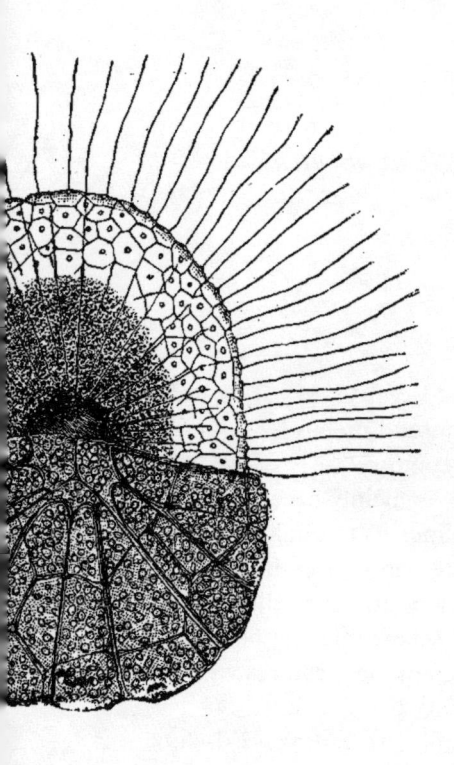

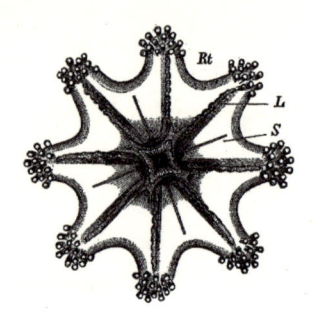

Brilliant bees that waggle with intent

Bees pose a problem. Not because they sting – all creatures have the right to defend themselves – but because they do spherical geometry.

This may be hard to believe, mainly because the arrogance of our species inclines us to think that those creatures most like us – vertebrates – top the intelligence list. Insect intelligence is apparently unsettling, even for scientists. In really scary science fiction movies, the horrors always seem to be scheming creatures with exoskeletons – or no skeletons at all.

Fortunately an Austrian biologist, Karl von Frisch, was too focused on his work to worry about whom he unsettled. While the First World War loomed in Europe, Von Frisch was at the University of Munich studying the colour adaptation of fishes. When war was declared he retreated to his country home in Brunnwinkl.

Strolling in spring fields, he got to wondering whether bees could see colour. The more he watched the little insects, the more they charmed him, so he set up some hives.

'How do they know where the best flowers are?' he wondered. He constructed a glass-fronted hive. Watching this, he noticed that returning bees generated excitement among their neighbours on the comb.

'It appears,' he wrote, 'that in some way or another the firstcomer must not only have announced her rich find to the other bees in the hive, but must also have led some of them to it so they might exploit it for themselves. What we should like to know is *how* they do it.'

By marking certain bees with a spot of colour, he could keep his eye on them in the melee of creatures on a comb. What he saw excited him. They danced. Not randomly but in very specific patterns. What did the patterns mean?

He put out feeding trays, marked some bees that arrived at them, then watched them when they returned to the hive. Not long afterwards, the feeding tray would be buzzing with bees. Some communication was clearly taking place.

A scout bee encountering a tray near the hive would return and do a circular dance, closely trailed by other bees with their feelers on her abdomen. After a few rounds these other bees would fly off, scout round and find the tray. If the tray was beyond a certain distance, however, the scout bee would change her dance (worker bees are all female – the drones just drone about). She would circle first left then right, doing a little straight run in the middle while waggling her tail.

Other bees would watch and follow, occasionally making little 'weeping' noises, whereupon the dancing scout would stop and share her food with them. Then they would fly off in the direction of the 'straight' run of her dance to exactly the tray the scout had come from. Von Frisch was astounded.

How did the scouts indicate direction and distance? Herein lay the biologist's genius. He timed the rotation of the scouts and the number of tail waggles. The slower they rotated and the fewer times they waggled, the further was the tray from the hive. Eventually Von Frisch could predict exactly where the bees would go by counting and timing. He had learned bee language.

His next conclusion was to give rise to massive controversy in the scientific world for several decades. The earth is, of course, horizontal to a bee, but the combs upon which they dance are vertical and, generally, are kept in pitch darkness.

Scout bees, he said, transpose the solar angle into a gravitational angle. Up represents the sun, and the angle of the straight part of the waggle dance to the vertical is the angle between the sun and the food source. If they dance facing down, the worker bees 'read' that as meaning 'fly with the sun at your back, but angle from it according to my waggle line.'

In 1927 he published his findings in a book, *The Dancing Bees*. 'So little is known about the mental capacity of the honey bee,' he concluded, 'it is better not to say too much about it. But without doubt they can learn. And what they learn they remember – for many weeks, perhaps for the rest of their lives.'

The book caused a storm. Many scientists at the time believed that Von Frisch was suffering from delusions. One university refused to publish the book, others refused to use it in the teaching of entomology.

In the United States two eminent biologists set up elaborate experiments attempting to disprove the dancing bee theory. They failed: Von Frisch was right. He would later win a Nobel Prize for his work. Writing in a recent *Scientific American Journal* publication, biologists James and Carol Gould, looking back at the debate, concluded that 'the assumption that insects were, by virtue of their size or their lack of an internal skeleton, necessarily simple had frequently beguiled researchers into overly reductionist hypotheses'.

Building on Von Frisch's legacy, researchers continued to discover abilities in bees that astonished them. Institutes for research into honey bees were set up in several countries and facts from open-minded observers mounted fast.

Bee ancestry dates back at least 40 million years and they have been socially organised into swarms for around 30 million of those. So they've had time to practice their communication techniques.

A single honey bee, it was estimated, flies about 900 kilometres in her life. That's equivalent to about 100 000 human kilometres or more than twice round the earth. They are born with magnetite (lodestone) in their lower abdomens and therefore are virtually flying compasses.

Although they were once thought to be deaf, highly directional ears have been discovered in their feelers. When a scout bee waggles, it also emits low sounds rather like a small motorboat. It has been speculated that the frequency of these sounds communicates distance.

The most extraordinary findings, however, remain the sophistication of honeybee navigation. It is all very well to navigate by the sun but, as we all know, the sun moves. How does a bee take that into account when communicating direction? Even more puzzling is that, in terms of how a bee's compound eyes work, it is unlikely that the bee can even see the sun. Researchers found that bees use polarised light. In space, the sun's light is not polarised. But on hitting the earth's atmosphere rays are scattered, and by the time they hit the ground, the shorter ultraviolet rays have been forced into a single plane of vibration. They are polarised, but in a certain way – perpendicular to the line linking that point to the sun. So the polarised light pattern in the sky will encircle the sun, like concentric fences – the further from the sun, the more it will be polarised.

Bees see this ultraviolet light. They can look at any part of the sky, see the angle of polarisation, drop a line from that point to the horizon, estimate the sun's azimuth and know exactly where they are. They can do this if it's cloudy or even after the sun has set. When humans do this, it's known as spherical geometry. There are two other skills they need to get their geometry right: a good speedometer and an absolutely acute sense of time.

If this all sounds complicated, it is. But bees do it with an ease and accuracy that is astonishing. This information, plus the scents and tastes they gather, they communicate in their waggle dance; and they can direct their sister bees accurately for up to five kilometres.

They're even democratic. When they swarm, scouts will go ahead to check for suitable places to settle, returning to dance directions. After a number of bees visit the various suggested places, a 'voting' process takes place until one site (generally the best) wins out by having more bees dance for it.

It appears that all species of honeybees speak some variant of the dance language, but with slightly different dialects.

Intelligence is usually measured in terms of a creature's ability to learn. Anything else is instinct or luck. If all this navigation were hard-wired into a bee's brain it would be startling enough. But bees have to learn it.

Around 20 per cent of all young bees that leave the hive for the first time get lost. Elaborate experiments have shown that bees scout their terrain – a building, a tall tree, a pool of water – and memorise these positions in terms of their polarised sun grid, rather like a GPS logging position against satellites. Once they have done this they remember the positions and never get lost. If they're blown off course they just shoot the sun, check their GPS, set a new course and fly home. If you move the hives they build up a new map, and they do this quite quickly.

Japanese researchers have found that bees use learned knowledge to detect poorly visible or camouflaged objects, and that they're pretty good at memorising mazes. They even have associative recall: a whiff of scent can trigger the recall of an associated colour.

In 1965 Von Frisch took his findings through another quantum leap and raised another storm. In *The Dance Language and Orientation of Bees* he pointed out that bees use symbolic representation to communicate. Their dance shapes are graphic representations of their intentions, and are designed to communicate with others. Though they have a brain only the size of a pinhead they can create and understand abstract forms which have social meaning. The only other creatures on earth able to do that, as far as we know, are ourselves.

This raises all sorts of thorny questions, such as: What is the relation between brain size and abstract thought? What is abstract thought? And if we put as much effort into studying other insects as we have into studying bees, would we find they're far smarter than we imagined?

Until we find out, perhaps we should go easy on that bug spray. The beetle in the corner may be pondering particle physics.

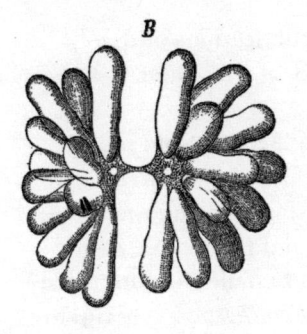

In defence of worms

Of the great worm hunt which began in the early 1850s, history has retained only the faintest traces.

We know there was a book, *Ludwig K Schmarda's Reise um die Erde* (Ludwig K Schmarda's Journeys Around the Earth) published in 1861, and a copy or two are undoubtedly in some German university library. For all but the most dogged researcher, however, details of the journey are today inaccessible.

We are left to speculate. Contemplating another long, dreary German winter, Professor Ludwig Karl Schmarda, a university biologist, chose instead to take an extended sabbatical and set sail in pursuit of his strange passion: worms. Today they are still regarded as slimy, distasteful things. In his day, they suffered added associations with death and serpents. Of the few publications of that period which survive, almost all deal with their eradication.

Undeterred by the inevitable bad jokes from his colleagues, Schmarda set sail for Ceylon, where he found yet-to-be-named worms in profusion. He dug them out, dusted them off, sketched them and moved on. South Africa attracted him next, though he failed to find there the world's biggest earthworm, *Microchaetus rappi* (up to four metres, found in the Eastern Cape). Then he braved the southern oceans to dig up worms in Australia, New Zealand and, finally, the Americas.

He returned triumphant, bearing the sketches and remains of 191 new species of leech and worm, wrote a two-volume monograph in which were included his illustrations, then drifted into scientific obscurity. He was mentioned in a few biographies, but a recent book on the history of earthworm ecology doesn't even footnote him.

Apart from his sketches, however, the interesting question about Professor Schmarda's travels is: who fired his interest in this obscure branch of science, now known as invertebrate ethology? The answer raised even more questions about strange biological fascinations. It was Charles Darwin, that Victorian champion of revolutionary ideas concerning natural selection and the origin of species, who found it.

Between 1831 and 1836 Darwin sailed around the world in the *Beagle*. In those five years he gathered experiences, material and notes which were eventually to lead him to the notion of natural selection – the idea that chance mutations over great lengths of time lead to the evolution of species from lower to higher forms, including us.

The trip, however, exhausted him and caused his health to deteriorate. He had contracted Chagas disease, a prolonged and debilitating ailment similar to African sleeping sickness, though it was never diagnosed in his lifetime. His doctor strongly urged him to 'knock off all work and go live in the country for a few weeks'. He went to ground at the country seat of his uncle, Josiah Wedgwood (of pottery fame). While he and his uncle were strolling the fields, Wedgwood suggested that, by bringing earth to the surface in their castings (faeces), earthworms must undermine any objects on that surface.

The young Darwin, eager of mind but with a disinclination ever again to travel further than he could walk, seized on the idea. He sat on his uncle's wide veranda drinking tea and watching worms – for weeks. On hand was JC Loudon's *Encyclopaedia of Gardening*, which listed earthworms, along with snails, caterpillars and other insects, as noxious animals, and listed poisons for eradicating them.

Darwin disagreed with Loudon. In 1837 he wrote a paper which he read at the Geological Society of London. In essence, it stated that earthworms created essential vegetable mould, aerated the soil and, over time, raised the surface levels of the earth. The paper was translated into German and had piqued Schmarda's interest. His destiny was to go on a long journey and remain obscure.

Darwin was never to leave the countryside again. Being of the wealthier classes (and marrying into the Wedgwood empire), he bought himself a small estate in Kent and, in the following decades, focused his attention on his other publications, which established his fame. He hadn't saved earthworms from a bad press and horticultural literature continued to devise methods for their extermination. As far as worms went, that seemed to be that.

By 1877, after 40 years of battling against an often hostile church and general public over his evolutionary theories, Darwin – then famous beyond his humble imaginings – considered himself to be a spent force. In a letter to an old friend, the Reverend Jenyns Blomefield, he wrote:

'My dear Jenyns, You ask about my future work; I doubt whether I shall be able to do much more that is new. I suppose that I shall go on as long as I can without obviously making a fool of myself.

'I have a great mass of matter with respect to variation under nature; but so much has been published since the appearance of the *Origin of Species*, that I very much doubt whether I retain power of mind and strength to reduce the mass into a digested whole.'

About that he was correct – no more writing about evolution was ever again to flow from his pen. For the next six years, until his death in 1882, Darwin disappeared into profound contemplation of his lawn and the paths surrounding it. Beneath them were an unimaginable number of worms.

History was to show, however, that they had never been far from his attention. In his letters, now housed in Cambridge University Library, are notes from academics and relations which suggest that Darwin, glued to his estate like a barnacle, had been cautiously enlisting aid in worm work.

'My worms have not turned up any earth since I enclosed them,' stated one note from his niece, Lucy Wedgwood. Another brief correspondence, from Archibald Gerkie of Edinburgh University, was headed 'Some notes on the action of the earthworm'. It turned out that three of Darwin's sons (he sired ten children) had been raising earthworms in pots and reporting the results to their father.

In October 1881, to the astonishment of those who thought Darwin was a spent force, he brought to press a book with the rambling title *The Formation of Vegetable Mould through the Action of Worms with Observations on their Habits*. It was to be the foundation of modern soil science and much more. To write it, he had hardly moved from his lawn and adjoining field, sending his sons and friends poking round fields, woods and ancient ruins all over the world. His conclusions were, as usual, controversial.

Earthworms, he discovered (by shouting at them) are deaf, but (by breathing on them) extremely sensitive to touch, and have enough perception of light to distinguish between night and day. They're hermaphrodites, but share sperm by entwining, have five hearts and can live in air or water. Without moisture they die.

To make holes, they shove sand aside when they can, and consume it when they can't, grinding rock particles to smaller pieces in their gizzards and extracting nutrients as soil passes through their gut. They line their tunnels and any open spaces under the ground with their castings and also stack them above their holes. At night they close their holes by dragging leaves down them or rolling small stones over them.

Though most of this is fairly basic, little of it was known at the time. The combined effect of these actions and what they implied, however, turned Darwin's final book into an overnight success.

By painstakingly observing (at night – earthworms are nocturnal), Darwin discovered that, in seizing leaves to close their holes, the worms always grabbed the pointed end, which permitted easy passage down the hole. This occurred even when he cleared all leaves and 'strewed' small paper triangles – the earthworms always attached themselves to the sharpest point. This, wrote Darwin, implied intelligence.

By counting and averaging the number of worms in various soils, he calculated that in temperate zones there were around 133 000 worms a hectare (some recent estimates run at more than two million). Weighing their castings brought to the surface, he discovered that earthworms were the planet's prime earth-moving equipment, bringing an annual average of up to 30 tons of soil to the surface across each hectare. In a million years, 'not very long in a geological sense', they'd covered Britain in around 320 billion tons of earth.

The planet's entire soil, he speculated, had passed through the alimentary canals of worms. To it they'd added useful intestinal chemicals, broken-down vegetable matter and ground-down sand. Without this process, almost nothing on earth would grow – and life as we know it wouldn't have existed at all.

From forays by his sons to Beaulieu Abbey in Hampshire, a Roman villa in Gloucestershire, the remains of a Roman town at Silchester, Stonehenge, and other similar sites, Darwin assembled information suggesting that ancient walls and pillars (such as Stonehenge) could be toppled by the action of worms beneath them. Entire ruins, he found, were quite soon covered over by the castings of earthworms.

'Archaeologists,' he wrote, 'are probably not aware how much they owe to worms for the preservation of many ancient objects.'

In an attention to detail which would surely have driven a less pedantic mind crazy, Darwin measured the volume of dry castings which rolled down slopes, wet castings washed down by rain and 'castings blown to leeward by wind'.

He could write: 'In a day of rain, for every 100 yards in length in a valley with sides sloping six degrees, 480 cubic inches of damp earth, weighing above 23 pounds, will annually reach the bottom. On the same slope annually, nearly seven pounds of dry castings will cross a horizontal line, 100 yards in length.' These are merely statistics until you realise that Darwin was out there with ruler and scales measuring entire hillsides.

'When we behold a wide, turf-covered expanse,' he wrote in the conclusion to his book, 'we should remember that its smoothness, on which so much of its beauty depends, is mainly due to all the inequalities having been slowly levelled by worms.

'It may be doubted whether there are many other animals which have played so important a part in the history of the world, as have these lowly organised creatures.'

It may be doubted, one could add, that so much important scientific speculation had ever taken place on the evidence of a small field and a single front lawn.

A year after the book's publication, Darwin had joined his beloved worms beneath the ground. His study is today considered to be the first work in a then-unnamed branch of biology – ecology – and the foundation of both invertebrate ethology and soil science.

As the English editions were prepared, German, French, Italian and Russian versions were being translated. Ludwig Schmarda, then 61, would undoubtedly have read the German translation. If any colleagues were still around who had doubted the sanity of his great worm hunt, he would have felt well vindicated.

Darwin, it seems, never read *Ludwig K. Schmarda's Reise um die Erde* or he would surely have referred to the monographs in his study. It's a pity. He would have enjoyed them.

Nb

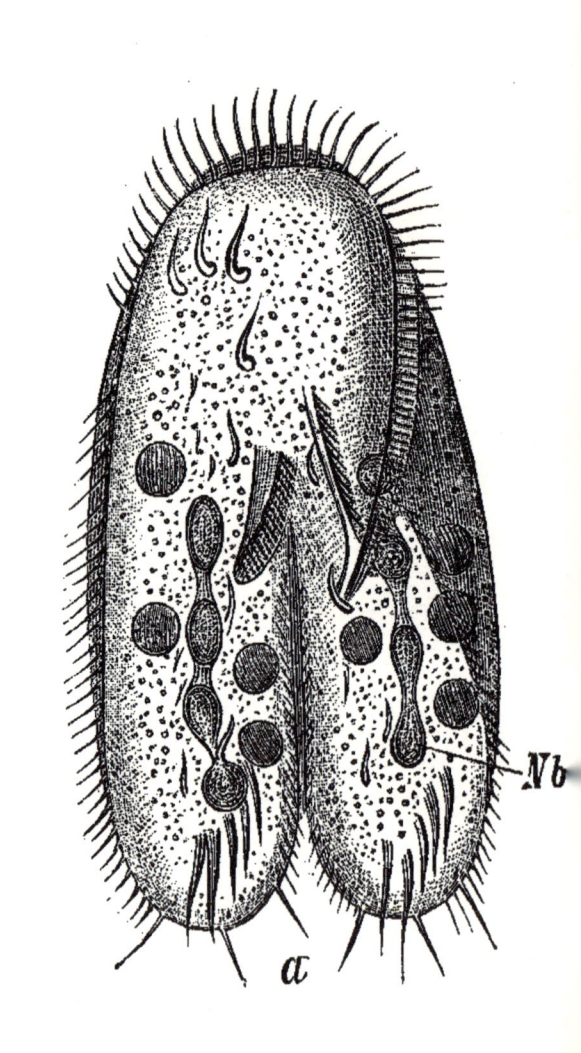

a

Green and gracious

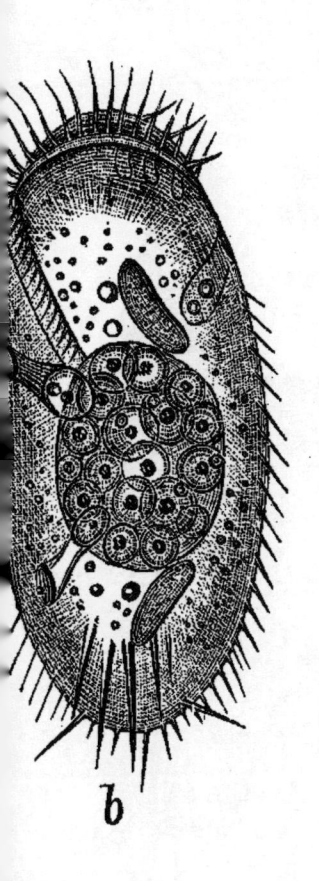

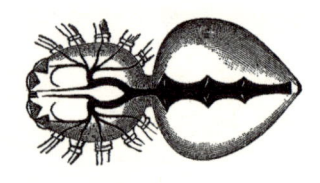

Sugar highs and water lows in the death-defying drama of desiccation

On African inselbergs there are things engaging in poikilochlorophylly. Honestly, there are. The creatures die, and come back to life in biological ceremonies of resurrection.

In case you have visions of warped creatures engaging in necrophilia, let me hasten to add that poikilochlorophylls are plants with a special affinity for those weird mounds of granite (and sometimes sandstone) you see in Zimbabwe and northern Mozambique, among other places. And they don't actually die, though what happens to them when the rains don't arrive forces a re-evaluation of the notion of death.

I once found one on a rocky dome in Zimbabwe's Matobo Hills. My guide pointed to the hard, shrivelled, sun-blackened thing and said: 'This is magic plant.' On his instructions I stuck a piece in a glass of water and next morning it was a happy little plant with green leaves doing all the right things with chlorophyll and oxygen. I was amazed.

This led me on a trail to Jill Farrant, a molecular physiologist at the University of Cape Town, who has a special affinity for plants with a taste for extreme desiccation.

'Resurrection plants are incredible things,' she enthused. 'They can dry to only five per cent of their original water content – suspended animation really – then come right back up and continue functioning after a shower.'

The ones she'd been starving to near death in little transparent boxes looked seriously deceased. A discarded autumn leaf had more life in it. But no, they were okay, just waiting for a drink.

For some odd reason almost all angiosperm resurrection plants are to be found in Southern Africa. Most live on inselbergs, where almost nothing else but lichen survives. These rather spooky mountains heat up during the day and dry out any soil clinging to cracks and crinkles. When it rains the cracks become natural drainpipes with way too much water for comfort. This is where poikilo-hydropylls have made their niche.

Their name's a real mouthful, the sort of thing biologists drop casually into conversation at dinner parties to check if there are any of their kind around. Poikilo-hydrous plants are those whose water content follows the fluctuations of humidity in their environment.

Homoiohydrous ones hang on to their water at all costs, come drought or deluge.

Because poikilohydrous plants have never made it into gardens or flower pots, they haven't been awarded common names. So they trade under awful Latin names such as *Myrothamnus flabellifolius* and *Eragrostis nindensis*. There's a creeper with a love of shallow depressions from a family named *Scrophulariaceae*. I defy you to get that one right first time off.

Never mind their names, it's how they got there and learned to desiccate that's important. Conquering the land is all about how you hold your water. All plants started in some seaweedy state, slopping round in the shallows of ancient seas. Eventually, there would have been those that made a go of it in freshwater lakes. Unlike the sea, however, lakes can dry up, leaving all their previously contented green stuff to crisp like overcooked bacon.

Most of these plants probably simply snuffed it, though some learned to skulk in swampy puddles while others found a way to survive dry-outs and hang in for rain. The survivors were the ancestors of every plant we can see without goggles and flippers. In those far-off days, probably all land plants had resurrection abilities inscribed, by trial and error, in their genes. It was a crucial step in the colonisation of land.

While plants may look like dumb vegetables, their DNA is as smart as yours. It figured out how to make plants hang on to water, choose places where water was constantly renewed, increase growth rates and complexity, and pump enough water vapour into the atmosphere to start cycles of rainfall. In biospeak, the plants internalised water relationships and became homoiohydrous. In so doing they changed the face of the planet.

Their genetic coding for handling dessication, however, didn't get hacked off the end of the DNA on the way to the tap. It was merely switched off in the plants but is still at work in seeds, which can survive, in some cases, for hundreds of years without water.

Up on inselbergs, life was a lot harder. Maybe the plants that hiked up onto them never forgot how to successfully desiccate. Maybe they relearned the skill in response to the challenges. Either way, they became pretty good at it.

To survive water loss, resurrection plants have to limit the damage of drying to a repairable level, hold their physical form when they're dry and not fall to dust, and have ready a nifty repair kit to put them back in order when the rains come. Some species are better at damage control, others are good at repair, but all undergo startling physical changes that would be the envy of anyone who's watched their skin wrinkle and the bald patch creep up their cranium. It's all to do with that remarkable but dangerous process, photosynthesis.

Why dangerous? It's standard high-school science litany that chlorophyll in leaves converts the energy of sunlight into organic food which plants scoff in order to give us that wonderful choice on supermarket shelves. But what we were seldom told is that if chlorophyll – the green in leaves – gets energised by sunlight and, if it can't get rid of the energy because there's no water around, it combines with oxygen to create free radicals. These are not good news. They scoot around looking for something to link up with – including your genes – and cause all manner of problems, such as ageing and cancer.

For a plant losing water, chlorophyll is not something you want to excite; so high on the list of tasks for a drying resurrection plant is the prevention of photosynthesis. One species folds its leaves against its stem to keep them out of the sun, another uses outer leaves to cover its inner leaves, and there's even a plant that manufactures purple sunscreen which covers its leaves. The real masters of the game, however, boot out their chlorophyll (they're the ones termed poikilochlorophyllous).

In the symphony of life and death, it's not the much-lauded DNA that's the show stopper, it's proteins. If DNA's the musical score, proteins are the music. In the first two hours of being freeze-dried in a laboratory, a plant under study, *Tortula ruralis*, stopped the production of 25 proteins and began synthesising or radically upping the production of 74 others. In the process it completely broke down its chlorophyll. On rehydration the new proteins proved to be the toolkit which restored the plant to its happy, blooming self within 16 hours.

When normal plants dry out they fall apart, as you'd know if you've picked up a bit of rotting wood and had it crumble in your hands. Resurrection plants can't afford to let that happen, so they do something which is, in nature, simply astounding. As the plant begins drying, proteins manufacture massive amounts of sugars, which pack tightly around the plant's cells, preventing free radical damage and quite literally turning the plant into crystallised fudge. Tough stuff, fudge.

When the cells of more normal plants dry, their outer walls are breached and bacteria enter and chew the plant to destruction. The sugars and 'chaperone' proteins curb this in resurrection plants and hold cell walls in place, preventing them from unravelling. When water returns to the plant, the sugars dissolve and the clutch of dehydration proteins disappears. Cells get back to business and begin hastily manufacturing chlorophyll for the great post-sleep sun and water binge.

So what's all this seriously marginal information got to do with life more abundant and an academic salary?

'What interests me,' said Jill Farrant, as she pulled out dangerously Latin-littered papers for me to read, 'is how resurrection plants switch on the desiccation-tolerance protection mechanisims that most plants have in only their seeds. All plants have the DNA coding necessary to do it, but only these did.

'Imagine the boon to the human population if we could find out how to switch on this ability in, say, maize or wheat? Or any dry-land food crop? It's not genetic engineering I'm involved in here. I'm looking for the switch.'

The wasp that cares a fig

There were chimpanzees all over the fig tree looking like fat brown fruit ripe for the picking. They were eating, arguing, posturing, and playing; and one couple, unconcerned with a cluster of admiring youngsters, were copulating.

Bits of discarded fig and the occasional scat or stream of pee were raining down and, given the massive spread of the tree's branches and the closeness of the surrounding forest, it was hard both to see chimps and avoid being splodged.

I had hiked to the huge fig at the heart of the Kibale Forest in Uganda with a guide and a small group of primate enthusiasts. We stared at the *Pan troglodytes*' performance for a while, as one would, but I gradually became aware of the sideshows – countless birds and periodic raids by nervous red-tailed monkeys. The tree was aswarm with life. Down below, the ground was covered in rotting, marinating figs and buzzing with all manner of intoxicated insects. After the silent, confidential forest it was like entering a supermarket with a sale on.

There's just something about fig trees that, like baobabs, sets them apart. Strangler figs spiralling their way up forest giants and looking like Jack's beanstalk, rock figs clawing their way up cliff faces and here, a Zanzibar fig (*Ficus sansibarica*), crawling with chimps. They have presence.

Because they fruit all year round, fig trees – all 750 species of them – are the very foundations of life. They're more than mere trees: they're whole ecosystems. Depending on its size and type, a tree can yield up to 100 000 figs twice a year (we're talking tonnage here) and each fruit can contain up to 1000 tiny seeds. This all makes for some serious eating by an extraordinary range of creatures.

Naturalist Duncan Butchart, who staked out a large Stuhlmann fig in Maputaland, ticked off 16 trumpeter hornbills, ten African green pigeons, eight purple-crested turacos, eight white-eared barbets, seven black-bellied starlings, six speckled mousebirds, six yellow white-eyes, four black-eyed bulbuls, two black-collared barbets, a golden-rumped tinkerbird and a solitary sombre greenbul, all of which visited the tree within 30 minutes. This definitely beat counting partridges in a pear tree.

The wasp that cares a fig

But that hardly scratches the surface of fig society. While the parrot-like green pigeons are the standard rent-a-crowd in fruiting fig trees, you will invariably also find several species of turaco and hornbill. Patient observation might also turn up African pygmy geese, white-backed ducks, twinspots, canaries, fire finches, francolins, guineafowls, geckos, agamas, arboreal snakes, tree frogs, dragonflies, wasps, damsel flies, fig tree moths, spiders, ants, termites and the beautiful fig tree blue butterfly.

Then of course, depending on the tree's location, there are fruit bats (Whalberg's epauletted, Peter's epauletted, straw-coloured and Egyptian), samango and vervet monkeys, galagos, baboons, chimps, gorillas and humans.

At ground level you may find elephants, several species of duiker, bushpigs, African civets, dassies, squirrels, mice and other rodents, tortoises (which love munching fermenting fruit) and, if the tree overhangs water, banded tilapia and silver catfish which snap up floating fruit. Under the mulch and fallen figs are no end of sap-sucking beetles, weevils and bugs.

I guess you get the picture. But here's the amazing bit.

At the base of this extraordinary balancing act of interdependence is a creature the size of the head of a pin and a fraction of its weight: the fig wasp of the family *Agaonidae*. Each of the hundreds of *Ficus* species has its own, private and personal pollinator wasp. Without a fig, the wasp is toast; without the wasp the only evidence of the genus *Ficus* would be in coal or fossil deposits.

The fig wasp is involved with figs the way fish are involved with the sea: they live and have their meaning within its enfoldment. It's one of the most extraordinary examples of co-evolution. In fact it has been suggested that the tree and the insect have co-speciated: when new species of fig evolved, the wasp evolved to meet its needs.

If you've ever eaten a fig, you'll know that it's an enclosed sphere which, when you break it open, contains what looks like a deep-pile carpet of edible stuff. The 'pile' is not flesh but flowers, hundreds of them. To breed, the tiny female wasps have to squeeze their way through a tightly closed opening (the ostiole) at the apex of the fig to get into this sphere, and to do this they have developed what entomologist Simon van Noort of Iziko Museums in Cape Town described to me as 'quite bizarre morphology'. On his desk was a display case of several hundred wasps and a microscope. 'This is the only way you can appreciate them,' he commented as he adjusted the scope's focus.

Suitably magnified, the wasp certainly was bizarre – but beautiful. She had an elongated head and a flattened thorax, delicate mandibles and backward-pointing teeth to prevent her slipping backwards while boring, a few teeth on her legs for good measure and two delicate, fan-like antennae. With this equipment she has to squeeze and labour her way into the fruit before some predator comes along.

'It's tough getting into a fig if you're the pollinator,' Simon observed. 'Her wings and antennae usually break off. But she doesn't need them once she's inside.'

Within the protective fruit, which seals the hole she's made, the wasp lays her eggs in some of the flowers and pollinates others with pollen she's conveniently stuffed into pockets on her legs or which has stuck to her body. Then, in her tomb blossom, she dies. A lifespan of but a few days.

When her offspring are mature they hatch into the enclosed world of the fig. The generally wingless males – runty little things – have what from a non-wasp perspective seems a short, unenviable life measured in mere hours. They chew holes in the galls containing the young females, mate, dig exit tunnels through the fig wall, from which the females escape, then die.

The females see a bit more of the world. Some trees have figs that perform both the male (pollen production) and female (seed production) functions, but others (dioecious species – around half of all figs) have separate male and female trees. In this case the female trees produce figs that only have seeds and the male trees figs that only produce wasps (you may be relieved to know that the edible fig we enjoy comes from a female tree.)

Once the female wasps have left the fig, it ripens, changes colour and smell, and becomes attractive to fruit-eating creatures which dutifully disperse the seeds.

For a tiny wasp on a mission, the problem of finding the right fig is solved by the tree, which emits a perfume cocktail attractive to only that special wasp which pollinates it. Just to make it more challenging, the tree remains receptive to wasps for only a few days, but it makes sure it presents its pollen on exactly the day the adults emerge from the fig.

It can be pretty rough outside the protective fruit, which may explain why the males stay put. As the females emerge, ants, birds, geckos and even flies snap them up. But, luckily, the fig only ripens after the wasps have left and so fruit-eaters don't chomp the pollinators of the next fig crop.

Once out, the females sniff their way up the scented trail, regularly clocking up to ten kilometres. The record, though, presently stands at 450 kilometres – and this is an insect around a millimetre long. You try figuring that one out.

So the wasp locates a fig to ensure the continuation of her species, and the tree makes sure that its pollen reaches future generations in the only way that it can – in the knee pockets of a near-microscopic insect. Neither could survive without the other.

You might wonder how the tree got all this orchestration just right, but recent research suggests that fig trees and wasps have been refining their mutualism for around 90 million years. If the wasps fail to find their goal and pollination doesn't take place, a tree (almost as an act of chagrin) will commonly abort its entire crop.

Just in case you think that's the end of the story, you need to know there are hundreds of species of parasitic, non-pollinating fig wasps that the tree does its best to ignore, and countless mites and nematode worms that live in the figs and travel and propagate by way of fig wasps.

There are layers upon layers of mutualism and co-evolution out there which we're only beginning to get a handle on. A British mathematician, Augustus de Morgan, seemed to get it just right when, after puzzling over life's interconnections, he wrote:

> *'Great fleas have little fleas upon their backs to bite 'em,*
> *And little fleas have lesser fleas, and so ad infinitum,*
> *And the great fleas themselves, in turn,*
>   *have greater fleas to go on,*
> *While these again have greater still, and greater still,*
>   *and so on.'*

I'd love to know what he'd think about fig wasps and that tree full of chimps in Uganda. Probably he'd nod and say: 'Just so.'

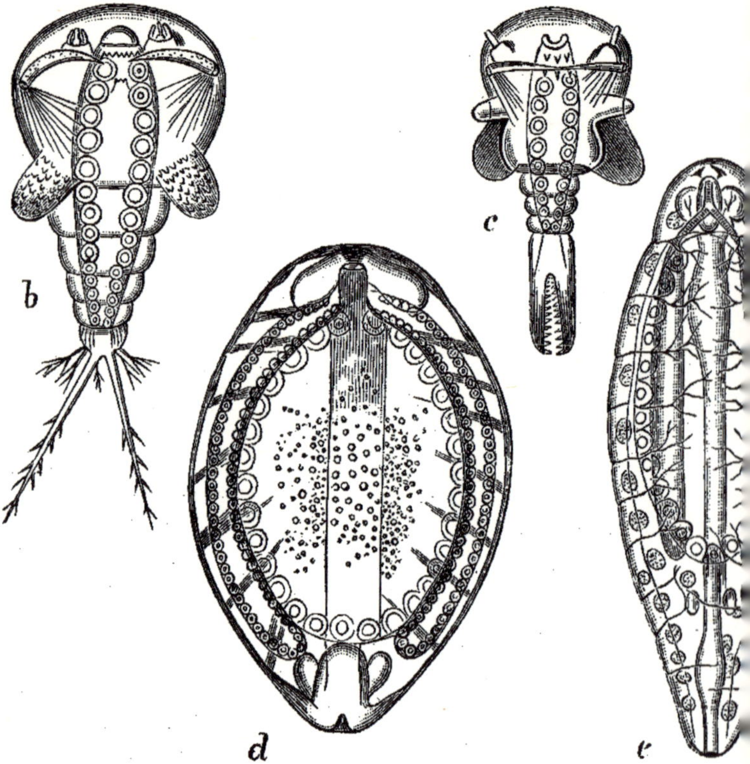
b
c
d
e

Dr Don

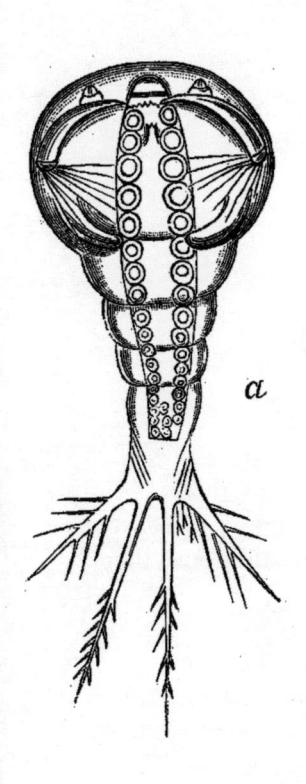

a

Dr Don's sex advice for the spineless and distressed

We don't hear much about invertebrates, those creatures that hang together without a spine. It's a shame, they're fascinating beasties. But, like us, they have their problems.

Dear Dr Don,
The breeding season is coming soon and I have heard that when I have some fun with a partner my penis will drop off. Is this true? Oh, I'm a nautilus named *Argonauta*.

Dear Argo,
The rumours, I'm afraid, are true. Research suggests that it won't be painful and your penis will go on living inside

your chosen gal. Consider it as a sort of Valentine card to your love.

When scientists first spotted the wiggling thing in the female cavity they thought it was a parasitic worm and even gave it a name – *Hectocotylus*. These days that's the title given to the penis of all cephalopods. It does a lot of good work, even without you, and your offspring will soon be in egg strings all over the sea floor.

Dear Dr Don,
What is sex? I'm a *Bryozoa*, part of a sea mat.

Dear Bryo,
That's a good question and it's far from solved. It's a process of replication – or reproduction if you like – through the exchange of genetic material between males and females of a species.

It is not self-evident why it's necessary to reproduce sexually, and the process has been described as an enigma within a mystery. On one hand, copulation creates diversity and reduces potentially harmful genes by diluting their effect on the species. But having half the genome in another creature reduces sexual efficiency, raises the energy costs in tiresome displays of courtship and increases mortality, with partners stumbling round looking for a mate. It also wastes sperm if no mate is found.

So, though sex is almost universal, it's costly. It may have a long-term benefit for the group, but it carries only a very short-term advantage for the individual.

In your case, though, this discussion is merely academic. You're a hermaphrodite – you have ovaries and testes and fertilise yourself. In terms of evolutionary survival, you're onto a good thing.

Dear Dr Don,
I'm a polychaete worm named *Syllidae* and my family members tell me my mother died so I could be born. This is a heavy burden to me. Is this common?

Dear Syllidae,
Her death was not only common, but essential for your arrival in the water column. Shimmy worms and bloodworms – your family – have no way for fertilised eggs to leave their bodies. So when the time is right, they simply explode, releasing their gametes like seeds bursting from a milkwood pod. It's tough, but there you are. Have you considered therapy?

Dear Dr Don,
Every time I get the hots for a chick she lunges at me. She's a scorpion like me, so what's the problem?

Dear Arachno,
Change your dance, stroke her. If you don't, she'll think you're lunch.

Dear Dr Don,
I am so distressed. A huge, nasty grouper grabbed me by an arm and, my dear, the thing came right off. Is there anything I can do about it? It looks so awful.

Dear Starre,
You are one of the lucky ones. Your arm will soon grow back. That's the blessing of being a starfish.

You have a very clever system. The joints between the plates of your skeleton where your arms emerge are weak points. By having these joints opposite each other you could easily break right in half if a fish grabbed you. So, by having five arms instead of four or six, you're a much stronger sea star (*echinoderm*). So take heart.

Dear Dr Don,
I am a *Neopilina* – I guess you'd call me a shellfish – and I've heard of this thing called sex. My problem is that though no male ever comes near me, I keep laying eggs that do rather well, though I say so myself. Am I being compromised in my sleep or is there something I don't know about sex?

Dear Neopilina,
The good news is that you're not being compromised. The bad news, I'm sorry to tell you, is that there's no copulation in the offing.

Because you live in water, the males of your species are lazy. They have very active testicles which release sperm in great clouds. This gets under your shell and fertilises your eggs.

Dear Dr Don,
I'm a *Tardigrada*, though we're better known as water bears or slow walkers. People consider us cute because we evidently look like things I've never seen called

Dr Don's sex advice

teddy bears – though they're big and we're only a few millimetres long.

It's taken a lot of courage to write to you, so I hope you can help. I really enjoy sex, but all the females I copulate with are so boring. They never even move and just float away afterwards without even a 'thank you'.

Dear Tardi,
The reason your gals are boring is that they're dead. The only time you find sex exciting is when they're moulting. They deposit their eggs in their moulted skin and that's what you're having fun with. Maybe if you're quick and find a female in early moult you might get a bit more action.

Dear Dr Don,
I'm a male spider and I find female spiders really scary. When I want a date I do all the dancing and there's a good chance she thinks I'm food and eats me. And I can never find a lady my size: they're all huge.

Then I drop my packet of sperm in front of her and have to run like hell. Where's the pleasure in that?

Dear Spi,
When we all lived in the sea it was a hospitable environment. Squirting loads of sperm into the water meant that there was a good chance that some of it would find its mark.

Dry land is very inhospitable to sperm and eggs, which is why so many creatures grew penises and purses so they could plop sperm right where it was needed.

Your method, if you'll excuse my being direct, is an example of a rather primitive approach to the problem. That packet you deposit smells good to your beloved, so she'll pop your present into her gonopore and you'll soon be a daddy. Just watch your back.

Dear Dr Don,
I'm a girl horseshoe crab and I just want to tell you that sex is such fun. I can't wait for the next spring tide!

Dear Horsenella,
Good for you! May your ardour never dim in your long life. I had to read up on why you were such an enthusiast – and I now see why. At spring tide that little man of yours climbs right into your shell and snuggles up to your tummy, hanging on while you dig a hole and lay your eggs. Phew, 30 000 eggs a go; you're quite prolific! Then your beau sprays your clutch with sperm before you cover the hole. Next spring tide you welcome the family. At that rate you'll soon be the empress of a dynasty.

Dear Dr Don,
I'm a lobster and I just can't leave the ladies alone. I grab one and hang on, sometimes for days, but she just ignores me. Then, just when I'm getting really excited, she sheds the skin that I'm hanging onto and just buggers off.

Dear Claw,
You're missing your cue. When she moults it's a come-on. You need to let go of the skin, scoot over to her and get

on with it. You see, her exoskeleton's far too hard to get your penis into at any other time.

Dear Dr Don,
I'm a dragonfly and the guys are always clutching at me. They have really nasty claspers.

Dear Dragona,
Yeah, guys get like that. They want to mate with you, I'm sure you've guessed that. It's not so bad. Find a nice beau and just go for it.

He'll have so much sperm your body will store it and you'll never need to mate again, ever. Afterwards the guys will leave you alone.

Dear Dr Don,
I have an uncontrollable sexual urge, but nothing much comes of it. Is this normal? I'm a *Branchiostoma*.

Dear Bran,
Well, you have 26 pairs of gonads, whereas most males have only one pair, so it's hardly surprising. The reason is that at sunset you fertilise your females by pumping sperm into the water column from your burrow on the seabed. It has to fight its way through zillions of planktonic creatures to reach your wives near the surface. It's pretty hit-and-miss, so you need to generate a lot of sperm. All those little tadpole-looking creatures shooting round in the plankton: they're your children.

Dear Dr Don,
I'm a teenage hawk moth and my feelers are getting very hairy. Is there something I should do about it?

Dear Hawk,
I bet you've been feeling very sexy lately. Those hairs are for picking up airborne pheromones – perfumes – from female moths. Try tracking the smell: there could be a nice surprise waiting for you. Be warned, though, it could be a good few kilometres away.

Dear Dr Don,
My man is so romantic. When he wants it he sits at the edge of my web and plucks the threads, making the most delightful vibrations. I just thought I'd let you know. You don't have to publish this letter.

Dear Orb Weaver,
Some men just have the touch, don't they? But be sure not to mistake him for a struggling insect. It isn't good form to eat fellow spiders, especially mates. It's often best to respond to your man just after a moult when your jaws haven't hardened. That way you won't be tempted to consume him.

Dear Dr Don,
I am a clam named *Glochidium* and I really worry about my larvae. When I release them where do they go?

Dear Glo,
They sink to the bottom of the sea, not too deep, because you live in the intertidal zone. You do have cause for concern, though, because most of them die there or are eaten. If one touches a fish, however, it attaches itself pretty smartly and begins to feed on its host. The fish's body forms a cyst around it, protecting it. After a while each larva becomes a tiny clam, falls off the fish and attaches itself to a rock. Quite possibly, it becomes your neighbour.

Dear Dr Don,
I'm a Namibian toktokkie and this mating business is really hurting my backside.

Dear Tok,
That's the price of passion, fellah. Seriously, though, you'll probably find you've ended up on some human-made slab of concrete or tiles, and tapping it is bound to hurt your bum if you keep at it. Try moving round a bit to locate a softer surface. Here's a tip: if you find a wooden floor it'll be like advertising on television. You'll get responses from miles around. Happy hunting.

Dr Don's advice for vexed vertebrates

Dear Dr Don,
I am a young spotted hyena and though I'm a female I think I may be growing a penis. Am I changing sex?

Dear Spot,
If you look carefully at your mother you'll see she's got one too – bigger than yours. And *she* hasn't changed sex. So don't worry. The reason's in your history. Your species is very aggressive and in the past it was only females with high levels of testosterone who could compete successfully against males for food and survive.

The result of several million years of selection is that many female hyenas are larger and more aggressive than males and have even higher levels of testosterone. That's why females usually lead a hunt and why a male will always give way to a female.

An incidental spin-off of your male-like vooma is the presence of a sort of ghost phallus. The upside of it is that you're top dog. That's not common among females in the animal kingdom, so enjoy it.

Dear Dr Don,
My dad's gone mad. We were out hunting the other day when he just flipped. He chased his tail, rolled over, whined, and bounced round like a nutter. Then he reared up, moaned and fell over backwards and just lay there like he was dead.

What was seriously embarrassing was that a hare was watching. It just stared and stared. Only when I went up to my dad did the hare run away. Then he yelled at me for being so stupid. Me stupid! You should have seen *him*. Oh, I'm an ichneumon. I think you'd call me an Egyptian mongoose.

Dear Ich,
Well, I hate to tell you this, but your dad was right. Not that you're stupid, you just have a lot to learn about how your species hunts. You see creatures that are hunted expect to be stalked and chased – they're hard-wired that way. When your dad does crazy, unexpected things, hares and other creatures (especially guinea fowls) become confused, even interested.

Hares, especially, seem to get hypnotised by the antics and your old man will be able to go right up and grab them. Next time you see him go 'crazy', don't move, just watch – he's obviously a fine hunter. I bet you never go hungry.

Dear Dr Don,
I'm a blue duiker and I just hate rotting fruit. Fruit, fruit, ugh! That's all there ever is. If I eat anything else will I get sick?

Dear Bluey,
I understand your problem – it's the result of being hyper-specialised. You're from an ancient family that has left no traces in the archaeological record, but we can guess at the cause of your ancestors' fruit fetish. For protection they colonised Africa's deep forests; being small they could whiz through the underbrush and hide by 'freezing'. But the only things to eat on forest floors are fallen leaves and fruit, and there's not much nutrition in brown leaves.

Suggesting a new diet is difficult, because your molars just aren't made to get the best out of leaves. And unless you know your leaves, you could get a bellyache. Fruit made your species successful, but perhaps you should be more assertive under fruit trees. On the other hand, rotting fruit has a higher alcohol content. It could add spring to your ducking and diving. Which is how you got your name.

Dear Dr Don,
I have no complaints about my boar. I just thought I'd share something with you. My bushpig has the most beautiful white mane, but best of all, he sings to me. Isn't that sweet?

Dear Porcus,
It is very dear. The men of your species are extremely romantic and, having heard their song, I must say the *chant de coeur* is appealing.

Actually your boar's probably quite a lover, too, going on for hours like that. You may like to know that his huge testes produce up to 600 millilitres of semen, containing perhaps 290 million sperm in each ejaculation. It's rather odd that his member is shaped like a corkscrew, though.

Dear Dr Don,
I'm really distressed. I'm a golden jackal and when my new mate and I first had sex we got stuck. Even when he dismounted we couldn't part. We were like that for nearly half an hour. There were hyenas around and it was really dangerous, not to mention embarrassing. If they'd chased us, I don't know what we would have done.

Dear Goldie,
Getting stuck is quite common for your species. It's caused by the large swelling of a sort of bulb at the base of his member. It only happens in the canid (dog) species and nobody's quite sure why. It has been suggested that it's to ensure you are thoroughly fertilised and it may explain why your species can have such large litters.

One jackal mum gave birth to 19 pups, and eight or ten is not uncommon. I don't know what you do about the hyenas. Maybe make sure you're in a private place next time.

Dear Don,

I'm a tree hyrax and I want to protest about the appalling behaviour of leopards. One chased me up a tree, and when I jumped out another one was waiting below and grabbed me. It bit me quite hard then put its paw on me. When it lifted its paw, which was very heavy, I ran, but it batted me like a ball and jumped on me.

Then the other one came and took me in its mouth to a rock. I pretended to be dead and when it looked away I dived into a bayonet bush. It jumped after me but got some nasty spikes in its face. Good thing too. What's to be done about these bullying creatures? They make the neighbourhood unsafe.

Dear Dassie,

You're very lucky to be alive. Next time remember: never, ever, jump out of a tree. A leopard can't get to the topmost branches and you can. Also remember, many predators hunt in pairs.

Dear Dr Don,

I'm a forest shrew and am suffering from stress. Really, it's killing me. I get so hungry and have to hunt almost all the time, then I get terribly thirsty and have to find water, then I've hardly had any sleep and I'm hungry again. It wakes me up. I see other creatures relaxing and snoozing, especially mice, but I just can't manage that. Is there anything I can do?

Dear Myosorex,
Speed, I'm afraid, is in your genes. You are tiny, don't have much body fat, and get hungry and thirsty because you move so fast. But you move fast because you get hungry. It's all to do with your metabolism – and a cycle I'm not sure I can help you out of.

If you don't eat or drink almost constantly you could die. In fact you eat up to two thirds your body weight each day. That takes a lot of hunting. In your lifetime you'll eat a whopping four kilograms of food; quite a lot, considering you're only about ten centimetres long and weigh only a few grams.

All this puts a strain on your body and your lifespan is only about 16 months. But take heart: you pack into those months more activity than any other mammal on this planet.

Dear Dr Don,
I'm a hyrax residing in a good neighbourhood near the Augrabies Falls. Recently a dassie rat family moved onto the hill, and they have completely lowered the tone of the area.

The male sits in full view of everybody and burps the contents of his stomach back into his mouth and eats it all over again. To do this he jack-knifes, then sort of throws up. And that's not the worst. Sometimes he bends over and plucks his own turds out of his bum and eats them. I mean, really! Is he a bad egg, or are all dassie rats like that? I've never seen one before. They're definitely foreigners.

Dear Hyromere,

Well, I can't exactly come up there and evict your dassie rats. But they do do those sorts of things, I'm afraid. However, if we're considering who got there first, in species terms you're the foreigners. *Petromus*, as they're called, are the oldest rodent inhabitants of the Namib Desert.

What they do may look disgusting, but having had to cope with desert conditions for millions of years, they've learned to use every bit of food and moisture they can get. Very often they find it in poorly chewed food, including in their own faeces. It's called coprophagy. Just be tolerant, or look the other way. They're not going to change their habits for the sake of the neighbourhood.

Dear Dr Don,

I'm a klipspringer in the Kruger Park and this guy keeps walking round me humming. It got so bad I bit him, but he wouldn't go away. What can I do to get rid of him?

Dear Klipette,

You're being naive. He's trying to mate with you and humming is how he tells you. Biting him is no good, he'll just consider that a come-on – and he'll hum even more. Mating isn't all that bad. Give it a try.

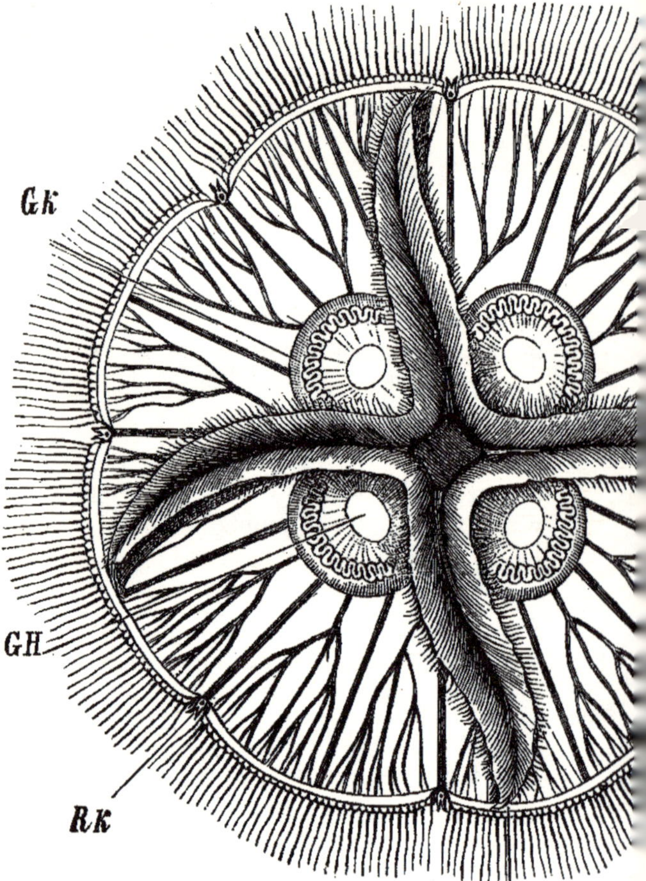
GK
GH
RK
MA

A final word

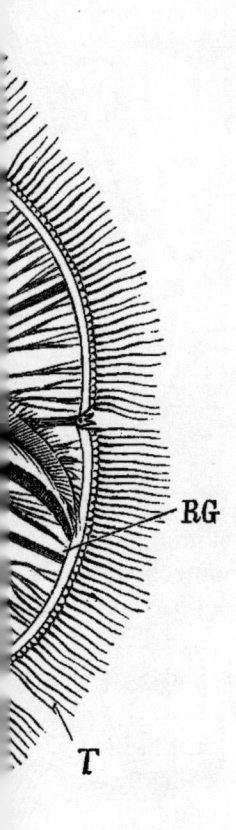

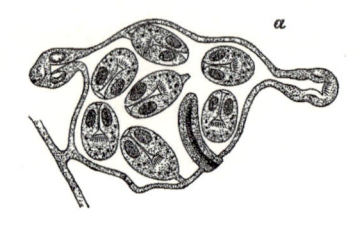

The way of wilderness

Not sure why I am here, now that I'm here. As city traffic swirled round and phones rang, the idea of spending time alone in a tent in the wilds was alluring, so I gave myself good reasons. I was on holiday and needed wilderness detail for a book I'm writing. The area is beautiful and empty. The weather was holding.

But sitting here as the sun hauls down the day and alien, old-gold rocks loom monstrously about, I'm no longer so sure. What was it, exactly, that I was pursuing?

The silence, but for the occasional zip of a prowling fly, is utter. Are these crickets or just the sound of empty ears? Warmth is being leeched out of the air and the little blue tent looks unbelievably lonely against the towering cliff wall. My head's throbbing from the four-hour drive and the heat of the day – no headache yet, but pressure that could become one. I've no inclination to do anything, which is vaguely disturbing.

Earlier a baboon barked. Just round the corner are painted caves that must have been used by the /Xam for thousands of years. They brood and seem to want understanding, but I cannot fathom their message.

The baboon barks again, closer. I hope he shows himself. It's curious how we calibrate our life by doing. I'm sitting thinking 'what is about to happen?' Waiting for it. My eyes scan the rocks and fynbos for movement and my ears strain for sound. But here there's nothing to do and no continuous sound. Heat's legacy has rendered even reverie an effort. I'm just being, a point of view in this rock jumble, waiting.

Slowly, alarmingly, the coordinates of my self-perception begin collapsing and I grasp at sensual minutiae. Small things – the *prrp* of a bird's bounding flight as it cuts across my vision, too fast to identify; a small yellow butterfly doing service among the spiky restios flowers; the slight bending of the grass as a zephyr drifts through and dies; the slow lengthening of a shadow as the earth turns. As organised thought deserts me, an assurance insinuates itself: this place is ancient, gentle, incorporating, tolerant. Where did that voice come from? I have no idea.

Perhaps what we fear in solitude is merely solitude itself; of being turned inside out because we rely on others to create our boundaries. We are herd animals. Alone, we were easy meat. The /Xam say the mind is outside the body, that we are merely the place where

The way of wilderness

thought expresses itself. Here it's not difficult to imagine that as being true. In the wilderness, mind leaks.

Supper is less than interesting. The Cadac stove also leaks as I screw in the new tank – angrily hissing away all its gas while I try to figure out what's wrong. I eat cold soya mush with tomatoes and rye bread. And some garlic to keep away unfriendly spirits. Not too bad, really. The baboon troop shows up while I prepare it: a magnificent male, still in his winter coat, with a sizeable community, including a yammer of youngsters. He warns me of his approach with a resonating *bahoo*, then, after a few minutes' surveillance, leads his family to their cave somewhere up the valley. Brown movement.

The evening has become beautiful beyond measure. I watch the shadow of a distant mountain sundialing up the nearby cliffs, swallowing the gold and unrolling sandy brown below it. The heat has gone but the ground's still warm and the rocks reflect the psychedelic underside of ruddy, roiling clouds against a polarising sky. A sunbird is making gentle nesting noises: the only sound.

To celebrate, I break open a succulent nectarine and eat each yellow smile slowly, savouring the pale sweetness and the soft pop as the sap sacks break. As the sky turns milky, a confiding dove takes over from the peeping sunbird, an altogether more appropriate sound in the cusp of night. Then a pair of Egyptian geese hiss-quack across the glowing western rim of a rapidly light-emptying sky.

The first stars appear, too eager to wait for night: the Pointers hauling a reluctant, madly angled Southern

Cross up from the rock-ragged horizon. A waxing moon is going to ensure they don't steal the sky show for long, though. When earth's gleaming satellite appears, the surrounding cliffs assume fantastic shapes: long cubist faces and drop-jawed nightmare beasts picked out from adamantine shadow.

An insect chitters incessantly until my ears cancel it out in desperation; then it stops suddenly, tearing a startling hole in the fabric of its cacophony. A nightjar begins calling 'poor Will', a poignant sound which is batted between the rock walls in ever softer but perfect replication: poor Will … poor Will … poor Will.

In the dead hours I ease myself out of my bag to recycle nutrients. The moon has set and the sky is a jewelled wonder – a magnificent tumult of stars with the Magellanic Clouds shimmering in their solitude. The horizon is glowing strangely, backlighting the granulated circular frame of the surrounding mountains. So much going on in such utter silence.

Our instinctive need for quick movement deludes us into seeing stillness as immobility. How wrong, I realise. Countless stars are flaming into life or collapsing, exhausted. All around the rocks are being corroded by the acid water of a recent rainstorm – mountains being dismembered grain by grain. Thirsty plants are thrusting downwards into the sand of melted mountains and reaching up, capturing life-giving carbon leaf by leaf. Trillions of beetles, worms and small reptiles are skittering to and fro, terra-forming surfaces and turning fallen leaves into soil.

The way of wilderness

In a hundred years the space between the rocks will have widened perhaps a centimetre, in a million the pieces of cliff will stand apart like the well-worn molars of a pensioned carthorse. We are too brief to perceive such movement. Years, days, hours and minutes are calibrations too minute to measure the dismounting of a mountain or a river filling a valley with its granulated bones.

I snuggle back into my sleeping bag and notice a rumble, soft and at the very edge of hearing like a faraway Boeing taking off endlessly. I realise it has been there since I arrived. Is it the turning of the earth or the blood in my veins? George Eliot termed it 'the roar which lies on the other side of silence'. In *Middlemarch* she wrote that it was like hearing the grass grow or a squirrel's heartbeat, but our ears generally don't pick it up because we walk about 'well-wadded in stupidity'.

The stars fade to a feather-soft dawn. Suddenly, between one minute and the next, the clear sky is sprinkled with clouds, each with a bright pink glow along its eastern rim. Cotton-wooled morning. I drag on some clothes and go looking for signs. A black-backed jackal passed only metres from the tent; a bat-eared fox hunted near the track, digging out tasty insects detected by its over-sized ears. A mongoose has inspected my food box, and up the track are the human-like footprints of last night's troop.

The Egyptian geese do a return flypast and a love-sick clapper lark begins his aerobatics – flying vertically, clapping his wings, then dropping suddenly with a drawn-out *peeeeuw*. A pair of showy bulbuls skitter in to compete noisily with some Cape canaries feeding in the bush beside the tent – to be screeched at from the clifftop by some irritable red-wing starlings.

The sandstone cliffs are stratified horizontally and split vertically, giving them an urban orderliness but for the rubble of their constant collapse. The ruin looks precarious, as though their maker shouted 'freeze' in mid-earthquake. I undress and wash myself with a facecloth from a cup – water is scarce here – and see no reason to re-dress. I go exploring the caves, wondering what someone seeing me would make of a man wearing nothing but boots.

There are paintings on the cave walls – a herd of eland, stretched figures, some with antelope heads, a row of dancers, a bulbous red rain animal and webs of black trance lines and dots. As I clamber past rock pillars and into smaller caves, each obvious handhold is shiny from thousands of years of use, like the worn handrails of a lost city. There's a long tunnel – I think of a birthing canal – its floor polished and slippery, but I back away from it. Sitting high above the valley, I'm drawn away from my outer life, loosened from its cultural moorings. Between the silence and the birdsong something else is hovering, needing words, just off the edge of perception. 'Nature's text' the Antarctic explorer Ernest Shackleton called it, and complained that 'the roughness of human speech cannot tell it'.

The wind is sighing fitfully through the bushes and fluting through the pocked rocks, booming softly. If wind is air moving from high to low pressure, why does it rise and fall so? In the heat of the afternoon I pull my mattress under a tree with branches curving to the ground, forming a bower, and sleep. I feel no guilt, have left no tasks undone. My noisy neighbours, the bulbuls, provide the alarm clock for cold supper.

On the second day I climb up onto a high, cool ledge offering a fine view over the jumbled fission of rocky outcrops. This distresses a pair of swallows building their nest in a niche above my head. They do several urgent chittering flypasts before I realise what the problem is, then they cling to the cliff a little along and scold me soundly. After a while they decide I'm not threatening and continue building, one mud spit ball at a time.

Two starlings must have a nest nearby. Each time a raptor drifts overhead, they mob it raucously, launching themselves from their watchtower, chukking angrily. The tactic is to dive at the intruder in a pincer movement from above and behind. A hawk fares badly and is hit. It weaves desperately and, when it's out of range, screeches angrily. Crows are much smarter. They flip upside down with a *woosh* of wings and lash at the starlings with claws and beak, forcing them to pull up. The raptors are all eventually routed through sheer persistence, though, and the starlings whistle in triumph and return to their watchtower.

I detect a nagging sentiment, like an itch you forget you're scratching until it hurts. It's the tunnel. Its entrance is on a high ledge behind the cave near me and it ends in a hole about ten metres above the cave floor –

an extraordinary piece of natural architecture. I push myself into the entrance face down, but slide back alarmingly on the glassy floor. Then I try on my back, bracing my feet against the roof and pushing. My hips jam temporarily and I can taste ancient mammalian panic in my mouth. Air! Life! Who would find me here if I became stuck? Then I'm through. I turn over and peer out the hole. The view is glorious.

In the dawn of the last morning I sit reflecting again on why I came here. The reasons I told myself before are not what I found. Those were merely what logic offered up to excuse a more visceral, inarticulate desire. Something deeper and more simple happened here.

I slowed down to wind and rock speed, gazed aimlessly, listened to birdsong. I watched the moon rise, marvelled at our galaxy, slept at ground level, walked naked, felt the wind and heard the earth spinning. I pushed myself through a birth canal and saw the world from a different perspective. And I wrote this down so I'd remember it.

As I dismantle my tent, it comes to me in one of those flashes you have to hold onto or they disappear like dreams in the morning: the wilderness is where our souls go to live when we forget.

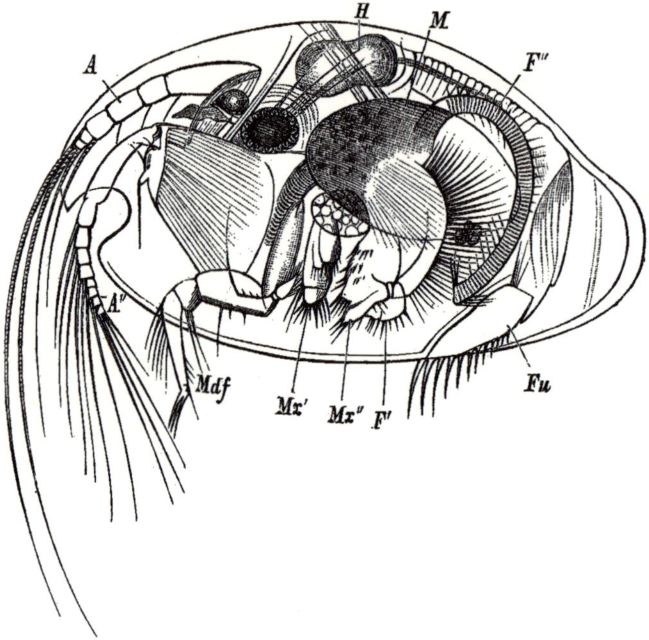

A
H
M
F''
A''
Mdf
Mx'
Mx''
F'
Fu

Bibliography of a sort

Most of these chapters first appeared as Natural Selections columns in *Getaway* magazine. Not being a scientist, I have had to gather facts from others far better versed in their subjects than I, and therefore drew on the work of many writers and researchers for ideas and information. To them I owe considerable debt: their help was invaluable. The books cited here are those I have used and from which, if at all, I have quoted while researching and writing particular chapters of *Loveletters*. There were, in addition, many theses and research papers which have been omitted for the sake of brevity.

Living kingdoms of the clouds
Trawler by Redmond O'Hanlon (Penguin, London, 2003) is destined to become one of the great classics of wild,

gung-ho travellers' tales. Redmond's ability to immerse himself in chaos and render it into such hilarious prose is simply amazing.

The long haul of the bath ducks
A Short History of Nearly Everything by Bill Bryson (Doubleday, London, 2003) is a feast of worldly wonders by a writer who can make even potentially dull topics un-put-downable.

The strange history of a fix
The Mapmakers by John Noble Wilford (Pimlico, London 2002) is an excellent resource for anyone interested in the history of cartography from its origins to the space age.

Why zebras never went to war and sheep ended up stupid
Guns, Germs and Steel: The Fates of Human Societies by Jared Diamond (Vintage, London, 1998) – from which the ideas for this chapter were largely drawn – is a startlingly relevant book for the 21st century and is a must-read for anyone interested in the future of the human race.

Dying islands in the sun
The Song of the Dodo by David Quammen (Pimico, London, 1996) is one of the classics of science writing by a master craftsman. It's about island biogeography and extinctions – weighty subjects – but the book is a delightful, if worrying, read. *The Future of Life* (Barnes & Knoble, New York, 2003), from one of the world's most influential scientists and Pulitzer prizewinner Edward O

Wilson, is an impassioned call for quick and decisive action to save Earth's biological heritage, and a plan to achieve that rescue. *The Tygerberg* by Neil du Plessis (Tafelberg, Cape Town, 1998) is a fine-grained study of the impact of urbanisation on an area near Cape Town once covered in now-endangered renosterveld.

Donkey wars and the green revolution
Animal Traction in South Africa by Paul Starkey (Development Bank of Southern Africa, Halfway House, 1995) is everything you need to know about animals pulling things in the old way. *Donkeys for Development* by Peta Jones is a pamphlet that's not easy to get hold of but makes you love the humble ass. *Environment, Power and Injustice* by Nancy Jacobs (Cambridge University Press, Cambridge, 2003) is a scholarly work about the relationship between people, creatures and their environment in the Kuruman area of South Africa. She researched the Great Donkey War of 1983.

The trek to Copper Mountain
Codex Witsenii (Iziko Museums, Cape Town, 2002) is a reprint of documents and paintings by Cape governor Simon van der Stel's artist on the journey to find copper up the Cape west coast in the 17th century.

A brief history of clouds
The Invention of Clouds by Richard Hamblyn (Picador, London, 2001) is an excellent biography of Luke Howard from which details of his life were sourced. *Chaos* by

James Gleick (Vintage, London, 1998) from which information about Mandelbrot was drawn, is a far more challenging work which cuts across traditional scientific disciplines and reveals some strange and intriguing ideas.

Thank God for Skukuza
South African Eden: the Kruger National Park by James Stevenson-Hamilton is a South African classic from a man without whom the Kruger Park may not have happened. For a more critical look at his 'rule' of the park there's *The Kruger National Park: A Social and Political History* by Jane Carruthers. *The Rise of Conservation in South Africa* by William Beinart (Oxford University Press, Oxford, 2003) is a scholarly but highly readable book about the impact of settlers and livestock on the South African environment from 1770 to 1950.

St Barbe and the incredible journey
Sahara Challenge by Richard St Barbe Baker (Lutterworth Press, London, 1954) is a rollicking travel adventure with some prescient thinking by the man who founded the worldwide Men of the Trees movement.

Brilliant bees that waggle with intent
The Dancing Bees by Karl von Frisch (Belknap, Cambridge, 1927) is the classic on the subject by the man who discovered that bees dance. *Beekeeping: a Practical Guide for Southern Africa*, written and published by Dominique & Jenny Marchand, is an excellent handbook for anyone who is bee-inclined.

Birds of heaven
The Birds of Heaven by Peter Matthiessen (Vintage, London, 2002) is a sensitive, elegantly crafted work by a master naturalist.

The wasp that does care a fig
Figs of Southern and South Central Africa by John and Sandra Burrows (Umdaus Press, Pretoria, 2003) is *the* comprehensive study of these leafy monsters of the forest.

In defence of worms
Ludwig K Schmarda's Reise um die Erde by Ludwig K Schmarda (Wilhelm Engelmann, 1861) is almost impossible to get one's hands on, but has some of the finest colour drawings ever done of earthworms. Plates can be viewed on the website
http://biodiversity.uno.edu/~worms/docs/schmarda.html.
The Formation of Vegetable Mould through the Action of Worms with Observations on their Habits by Charles Darwin (John Murray, London, 1883) is Darwin's last work and is as wacky as it is wonderful.

Dr Don's sex advice for the spineless and distressed
These answers were assembled with the help of Prof. Charles Griffiths of the University of Cape Town. The column was inspired by Dr Tatiana's *Sex Advice for All Creation by Olivia Judson* (Chatto & Windus, London). It's great fun.

Dr Don's advice for vexed vertebrates
The Behavior Guide to African Mammals by Richard Despard Estes (Russel Friedman, Halfway House, 1991) is a book that seems to have needed several lifetimes to assemble. To quote the biologist EO Wilson (who wrote the Foreword) 'if you know an animal's behaviour well, you know its essence.' This is a book for the connoisseur of animal behaviour.

THE AUSTRALIAN ALMANAC
& BOOK OF FACTS
1989

Compiled by
Belinda Henwood

ANGUS & ROBERTSON PUBLISHERS

ANGUS & ROBERTSON PUBLISHERS

Unit 4, Eden Park, 31 Waterloo Road,
North Ryde, NSW, Australia 2113;
94 Newton Road, Auckland 1,
New Zealand; and
16 Golden Square, London W1R 4BN,
United Kingdom

This book is copyright.
Apart from any fair dealing for the
purposes of private study, research,
criticism or review, as permitted
under the Copyright Act, no part may
be reproduced by any process without
written permission. Inquiries should
be addressed to the publishers.

First published in Australia
by Angus & Robertson Publishers in 1988
First published in New Zealand
by Angus & Robertson NZ Ltd in 1988

Copyright © Angus & Robertson Publishers 1988

ISBN 0 207 15918 1

Typeset in Plantin by Midland Typesetters
Printed in Australia by The Book Printer

CONTRIBUTORS

Jan Brazier
Warren Fahey
Graham Greenleaf
Sally Harper
Louise Kelaher
John Morton
Andrew Mowbray
Michael Niblett
Tasker Ryrie
Jim Shepherd
Anne Skinner
Phillip Tardif
Alan Tyree
Hazel Vickers
Clinton Walker
Trevor Whitehead
Robert Wills

Illustrations by Patrice Guilbert
Index by Diane Regtop
Maps by Liz Seymour and Gail Hill
Flags by Diana Wells

CONTENTS

CHRONOLOGIES
Australian Events 3
International Events 21

SPORT
ABC Sports Award 52
Australian Football 53
Basketball 67
Boxing 68
Commonwealth Games 82
Cricket 83
Cycling 92
Equestrian 95
Golf 97
Greyhound Racing 107
Horseracing 109
Lawn Bowls 135
Motorcycling 137
Motor Racing 139
Netball 152
Olympic Games 153
Powerboating 157
Rowing and Sculling 158
Rugby League 161
Rugby Union 172
Sailboarding 175
Sailing and Yachting 176
Soccer 182
Speedway Racing 186
Surfing 193
Surf Lifesaving 195
Tennis 197
Track and Field 208
Trotting and Pacing 215
Wrestling 221
Milestones in Sport 223
Top Earners in Sport 227
Sporting Obituaries 228

FACTS AND FIGURES
Calendars 232
Public Holidays 237
School Terms 238
Births, Marriages, Divorces
  and Deaths 240
Population 261
Migrants 268
Religions 274
Housing 276
Climate 277
AIDS Cases 280
Geographical Features 282
Insurance Statistics 283
Advance Australia Fair 287
Important Dates in Australian
  History 288
Obituaries 298
Australians of the Year 301
Royal Visits 303
Australian Flags 309
Pseudonyms 310
Most Popular Names 312
Convict Women of Tasmania ... 314
Semaphore 320
Beginnings 321
Morse Code and Braille 327
Proofreader's Marks 328
Food Preservation 332
How the Economy Works 333
Currency 347
Volume of Money 349
Industry Sectors 350
Cost of Living 350
Top Companies 352
Labour Force 356
Occupations 364
Income 368
Industrial Disputes 369
Average Weekly Earnings 373
Imports and Exports 376
Wine Sales 384
Who Owns What 388
Computers and the Law 392
Aboriginal Sacred Sites and
  Land Claims 401
Poisonous Plants 411
Endangered Species
  Regulations 416
Imported Pests 417
Aviation 426
Aircraft Movements 433
Air Distances 434
Tourists 435
Method of Travel to Work 444
Education 444
Government 450
Elections 460
Defunct Political Parties 462
Prime Ministers 465
Women in Parliament 478

Top Films and Videos..........489	Antarctic Program.............541
Bestsellers....................494	Astronomy 544
Newspaper and Magazine Circulation 505	**INTERNATIONAL**
Top Albums, Singles and CD's 516	Countries A to Z 564
	External Territories............713
Oz Rock 517	Diplomatic Missions 738
Folk Music...................525	Climates around the World 749
History and Languages of the Pacific.....................531	INDEX 764

PART ONE
CHRONOLOGIES

AUSTRALIAN EVENTS 1987

JANUARY

The elephants in Sydney's Taronga Park Zoo were moved into their new enclosure on **2 January**, giving them five times more space.

The Most Reverend Desmond Tutu, Archbishop of South Africa, arrived in Australia on **2 January** for a twelve-day visit.

A pavement artist was arrested at Sydney's Circular Quay on **4 January** and charged with giving an unlawful display and disobeying a direction. He was the first artist to be arrested under the Maritime Services Board Waters and Waterside Land Regulations in an attempt to eradicate the buskers and pavement artists of Circular Quay.

Official visits to Australia by the French Foreign Ministry were suspended on **6 January** for an indefinite period after Australia supported New Caledonian independence in the United Nations.

British singer Elton John underwent an exploratory throat operation at Sydney's St Vincent's Hospital on **6 January**. He had been suffering problems with his throat which had affected his singing.

Bruce Ruxton, the Victorian President of the Returned Services League, had a televised confrontation with two members of Melbourne's African Community Centre on **7 January** after making comments about the visit of Archbishop Desmond Tutu to Australia. The men, who challenged Ruxton's statement that Desmond Tutu was a 'witchdoctor in archbishop's clothing', were ejected from his office after a twenty-minute argument.

On **9 January** the Australian Consul-General in Noumea, John Dauth, was ordered to leave New Caledonia by the French government.

Violence erupted in Goondiwindi on the Queensland-New South Wales border on **10 January** between Aboriginal and white residents. Ten people were reported to be seriously hurt while several others were injured.

It was reported on **10 January** that the new Parliament House 81 metre flagpole, which cost $4.4 million, would have to be cut down and re-welded because it was out of alignment with the flag-raising mechanism.

Two men who had been held by French authorities on the Indian Ocean island of Reunion since October 1986 after convictions of illegal fishing, escaped on **16 January**. They made their way on a fishing boat to nearby Mauritius and, later, to Singapore. The men were originally suspected of gun-running, drug smuggling and spying.

It was reported on **16 January** that a Japanese entrepreneur had successfully introduced the Aussie meat pie to the Japanese market. In his first month of business he had to supplement his initial shipment of 43,000 pies with a further 100,000 and had calls from other businesses interested in buying franchise rights.

The tenth anniversary of the Granville train disaster in Sydney occurred on **18 January**. Eighty-three people died in the crash.

A special investigation of Australian Embassy staff members in Indonesia was announced on **19 January** after allegations of involvement in an illegal car sales racket in Jakarta. Allegedly, large profits were made on duty-free imported vehicles which were sold before the regulatory two-year waiting period.

The Australian Broadcasting Tribunal announced an inquiry on **22 January** into Rupert Murdoch's bid for the Herald and Weekly Times. Under the tribunal's regulations, the bid would not be allowed to proceed if it was shown that Murdoch, an American citizen, controlled News Ltd.

A Darwin couple was convicted on **22 January** of offensive behaviour for having sex in their home in view of the public. The couple were arrested by an off duty policeman who looked through their living-room window.

The skeleton of a young Aboriginal woman, buried between 200 and 2000 years ago, was found in the grounds of a waterfront home in the Sydney suburb of Abbotsford on **28 January** by workers excavating for a swimming pool. The owners of the property shortened the length of the pool so that the burial site could remain intact.

A successful three-week expedition which uncovered 600 important artefacts from the First Fleet's flagship, HMS *Sirius*, began on **29 January**.

On **30 January** there was an outbreak of bushfires near Hobart which was to become the worst for five years. The fires took several days to control.

Scientists from the United States and Australia met in Darwin in January to conduct a month-long meteorological experiment into tropical weather patterns. It was the largest project of its type in the world. The scientists looked at the way thunderclouds interacted with the summer monsoon system.

FEBRUARY

A riot occurred at Goulburn Gaol in New South Wales on **2 February** after prisoners held a meeting to discuss grievances. Tear gas was used to quell the riot although a spokesperson for the Minister for Corrective Services said that there had been no violence between prisoners and prison officers.

The New South Wales Minister for Transport, Ron Mulock, announced on **3 February** that drivers' licences carrying photographs would be introduced gradually over the next three years.

The word 'incentivation' was introduced by the federal Liberal Party as a key element of their election campaign on **4 February**. The word received amused attention in parliament and the media. Eight high school students died and others were injured on **4 February** when a chartered school bus went over a cliff after its brakes failed on a sharp bend on Gillies Highway, south of Cairns. The students were returning from a camp at Tinaroo Dam.

Chief Justice Harry Gibbs retired from the High Court Bench on **5 February**, after seventeen years of service.

John Dauth, Australia's Consul-General in New Caledonia, was accused on **6 February** of establishing contacts and giving aid to the Kanak separatist movement. His expulsion was due to breach of normal diplomatic activity according to France's Minister for Overseas Territories, Bernard Pons.

On **6 February** the Herald and Weekly Times auctioned their television and radio assets in a $490 million deal.

The New South Wales Industrial Supplies Office revealed on **11 February** that Australia pays approximately $4 billion per year in import costs for items as far ranging as bicycle pumps and chalk.

On **14 February** it was reported that a University of Queensland researcher, Professor Charles Mitchell, had developed the world's first dictionary of chest sounds for doctors.

The Australian Institute of Fund Raising on **16 February** awarded the Liberal Party a prize for the most cost-effective direct mailing campaign.

The development of a new solar cooker by researchers at Sydney University was reported on **17 February**. Interest in it was shown by developing countries which have a serious fuel shortage.

The prominent Perth horse trainer, George Way jnr, was disqualified from racing for fifteen years on **17 February**. He was accused of doping the winning horse in races at Ascot, Perth, on 26 and 31 January with the drug etorphine, or 'elephant juice'.

Work on Sydney's controversial monorail began on **18 February**, with the erection of the first of 120 steel columns.

On **19 February** it was reported that a marriage celebrant in Adelaide had watched a man walk in from the street and steal her handbag while she was in the middle of a wedding ceremony. The woman chose to continue the ceremony rather than chase the thief.

Robert Hughes's book *The Fatal Shore* entered American best-seller lists in February, only one week after publication.

The labelling of Queensland's XXXX Beer was changed in February. The hometown of XXXX, Castlemaine, was deleted and replaced with 'Bond Corporation Holdings Ltd'.

MARCH

In early March Australian astronomers identified what they believed to be the star that exploded to become a new supernova. It was the first time that a precursor star had been identified.

Sir Joh Bjelke-Petersen announced on **1 March** his intention of campaigning to become Prime Minister in the next federal election.

An Anglican priest performed an exorcism at a Queensland gaol on **1 March**. Local Aboriginal residents believed that evil spirits were responsible for two suicides and one attempted suicide in the previous three months.

From **2 March**, all Commonwealth public service offices were declared smoke free zones.

The Soviet Foreign Minister, Mr Eduard Shevardnadze, arrived for an Australian visit on **3 March**.

Sir Joh Bjelke-Petersen broke political convention on **4 March** by campaigning on his trip to Japan. He told the Japanese media of his campaign to defeat Prime Minister Hawke in the next federal election. The convention is that, whilst overseas, Australians in public office should not represent partisan interests.

The Anglican Church's Appellate Tribunal, their highest legal body, announced their decision on **5 March** to favour the ordination of women.

On **5 March** the New South Wales Minister for Public Works, Laurie Brereton, announced the government's decision to close the Newcastle State Dockyard.

The Northern Territory held an election on **7 March**. The Country-Liberal Party, led by Chief Minister Steve Hatton, was returned with a comfortable majority.

The Arbitration Commission introduced the two-tier wage system on **10 March**. The new system would allow employees to negotiate pay rises of up to 4 per cent above the Arbitration Commission's $10 a week rise, but was dependent on productivity agreements with employers.

Prominent Sydney businessman Abe Saffron appeared in court on two bribery charges on **12 March**.

On **12 March** Neville Wran, former Premier of New South Wales, was fined $25,000 for contempt of court. The fine was in regard to comments he made to the media in 1985 in which he asserted his conviction that Justice Lionel Murphy, on a charge of attempting to pervert the course of justice, was innocent.

The author of *Spycatcher*, former MI5 agent Peter Wright, was able to have his book released in Australia after the Supreme Court dismissed the British government's application for an injunction to suppress publication on **14 March**.

On **17 March** Sir Nicholas Shehadie, chairman of the Special Broadcasting Service (SBS), told a Senate Standing Committee conducting a hearing into a proposed amalgamation of the SBS and the ABC that the multicultural philosophy of SBS would be under threat if the two merged. On 26 April the Prime Minister announced that the merger would not proceed.

A member of the May Gibbs Foundation, Marion Shand, expressed fears on **17 March** that Nutcote, the home of the late May Gibbs in the Sydney suburb of Neutral Bay, would be developed into townhouses. The foundation lobbied successfully for the house of the famous children's author to be saved.

The Sydney Harbour Bridge celebrated its fifty-fifth birthday on **19 March**.

On **19 March** 1000 passengers were cleared from the international terminal at Sydney Airport after Customs X-rayed a travelling case which they believed contained a bomb. The items producing the image turned out to be a Stanley knife, a book, batteries and an electric razor.

The Queensland government announced its plan on **21 March** to sell off the major islands of the Great Barrier Reef to tourist developers.

Andrew Peacock, Deputy Leader of the Opposition and Shadow Treasurer, was sacked from the Shadow Ministry on **23 March** after the release of a tape of a tapped car telephone conversation between Peacock and Jeff Kennett, the Leader of the Victorian Liberal Party.

On **26 March** the New South Wales government sacked the Sydney City Council and replaced it with a specially appointed commission. The council had suffered internal conflict as well as conflict with the state government.

A young American tourist, Ginger Meadows, was taken by a crocodile on **28 March** at the mouth of the Prince Regent River, on the far north-west coast of Western Australia.

Yiannos Kouros won the Sydney to Melbourne 1050 kilometre footrace on **31 March**. The Greek runner, who completed the course in five and a half days, twenty-four hours ahead of his nearest rival, established a world record.

APRIL

The French newspaper *Le Figaro* published a story early in April about Aboriginal people living in the Sydney suburb of Redfern which angered Australian officials. The report made claims that Aboriginal people throw stones and pieces of concrete at white passers-by, that buses and taxis will not go there and that Aborigines call whites 'skinned pigs'.

On **1 April** the OECD praised Australia's economic policies and predicted an optimistic economic outlook for 1987 and 1988.

It was reported on **1 April** that an acute shortage of rabbit fur had forced the famous Australian Akubra hat company to import rabbit skins from Europe.

The $3 million Safe Sex Campaign was launched on **5 April**, the work of the National Advisory Committee on AIDS (NACAIDS). The 'Grim Reaper' television advertisement which alerted Australian viewers to the dangers of AIDS was cancelled on 17 April because of its sensationalist approach. Professor David Pennington, chairman of the AIDS taskforce, claimed that widespread panic caused by the advertisement had led to large numbers of low risk people attending hospitals and pathologists for blood tests.

On **7 April** the New South Wales government lost an appeal against the Equal Opportunity Tribunal which supported the claims of high school student Melinda Leves in an anti-discrimination claim. The loss of the appeal enabled Melinda to study the same high school subjects as her brother. The case arose three years earlier when Melinda discovered that her twin brother was able to study technics and technical drawing while she would only be offered domestic science and textiles.

On **11 April** Sir Joh Bjelke-Petersen announced the New National Party, after calling for federal National Party members to leave the Coalition on 10 April. This led to the dissolution of the Liberal-National Coalition on 28 April, before the July election.

Australia's sixth annual Palm Sunday Peace March was held on **12 April**. Rallies across Australia drew hundreds of thousands of people.

A Sydney man, Samuel Movizio, bought Elvis Presley's gold Cadillac at a Sotheby's auction for $99,000 on **12 April**. It was the highest price paid for a vehicle at the auction. The car had a bullet hole in the side where Elvis had shot it one morning because it would not start.

In Brisbane on **22 April** a team of surgeons transplanted part of an adult liver into an eight-month-old baby, suffering from a rare liver disease. Ashleigh, from Perth, was the youngest Australian to have received a cut down liver. She was discharged from hospital at the end of April.

Russ Hinze, Queensland Minister for Main Roads, Local Government and Racing, attacked Police Minister Bill Gunn at a press conference on **24 April** over a drug raid by police at the house of Hinze's niece. Gunn found that it was not possible to authorise an apology from the police.

The sixty-sixth Anzac Day celebration took place on **25 April**.

A Melbourne midwife, aged thirty, was admitted to Bendigo Base Hospital on **25 April** suffering what she believed were stomach cramps from injuries she received in a car accident five years earlier. She gave birth to a baby, totally unaware that she was pregnant. The woman and her husband believed that the injuries she had sustained in the car accident would make normal pregnancy unlikely.

Jan Murray, wife of the federal Minister

for Tourism, John Brown, confessed on **26 April** that she and her husband had made love on his ministerial desk on the day that he received his portfolio.

The skeletal remains of James Annetts and Simon Amos were found in the Great Sandy Desert, Western Australia, on **27 April**. The sixteen- and seventeen-year-old youths had disappeared in December from a remote cattle station where they were working. Some months later an inquest into the boys' deaths was opened following suggestions of suspicious circumstances.

The New South Wales Minister for Education, Rod Cavalier, introduced a new code of behaviour for school sports on **30 April**. Under the new guidelines, teachers would be able to send badly behaved parents off the sidelines. Some parents had been criticised for their barracking behaviour.

The president of the Royal Australian College of General Practitioners announced on **30 April** that one-quarter of Australia's general medical practices were financially non-viable.

The Northern Territory's Minister for Labour and Administrative Services was sacked on **30 April** after making remarks in parliament that Indonesia was a virtual dictatorship dominated by armed forces. Michael Talbot, a sheep farmer turned novelist, visited Sydney on **30 April** promoting his book *To the Ends of the Earth*. Talbot, disillusioned and impoverished by sheep farming, went to New York in 1986 to sell his novel and sold 15,000 hardback copies in the first few months after publication.

Two Australian diplomats were asked to leave Tehran at the end of April because Iranian officials were offended by the portrayal of the Ayatollah in a sketch on the television comedy show, *The Dingo Principle*.

A schoolteacher was dismissed from a Catholic school in Wodonga, Victoria, in April because her lifestyle was said to place students in moral danger. She was dismissed when the school found out that she had a child from a ten-year de facto relationship.

MAY

The appointment of Robert Somerville as chairman of the ABC was announced on **1 May**.

Queensland's first in-vitro quads were born on **2 May** by caesarian section. The two boys and two girls were Australia's third in-vitro quads.

A man in Broken Hill was charged with stealing a vinyl jacket from a German shepherd pup on **2 May**. The dog was left wearing only a T-shirt.

Sydney celebrated its twenty-fifth anniversary of the Clean Air Act on **4 May**. Bob Carr, Minister for the Environment, said that in fifteen years Sydney had gone from being one of the dirtiest to being one of the cleanest large cities in the world.

The First Fleet re-enactment left Portsmouth on **14 May**, bound for Australia. A demonstration was held by Aboriginal supporters who saw no cause for celebration of the arrival of the First Fleet in Australia.

The body of Robert Trimbole, organised-crime boss, was brought from Spain to Australia on **15 May**. Trimbole, who was wanted in Australia on numerous charges including conspiracy to murder, had been a fugitive since 1981.

Cricketer Kim Hughes was invited back to cricket on **16 May** after a court decision overturned the decision of the West Australian Cricket Association to ban him after his controversial tour of South Africa.

After clinging to a 1 metre square buoy for five days, three fishermen were rescued from sea waters near Point Sampson, Western Australia, on **17 May**. Their prawning trawler had sunk in half a minute, leaving them no time to send a distress signal. The search was about to be called off when the men were found by an RAAF pilot.

Sydney doctor Geoffrey Edelsten and his wife Leanne were summonsed to the New South Wales Supreme Court on **18 May** over a $1.2 million debt to the Taxation Office.

The twentieth anniversary of the referendum which put the welfare of Aboriginal people in the hands of the federal government occurred on **27 May**. On **27 May** Prime Minister Hawke announced the federal election would be held on 11 July.

The announcement that candidates for

Sir Joh Bjelke-Petersen's party would be selected from respondents to newspaper advertisements was made on **29 May**. Members of the Sydney Citizens Against the Monorail (SCAM) held a protest rally in Sydney on **30 May**. This was one of a series of demonstrations that failed to stop construction of the $40 million project.

Paul Keating, federal Treasurer, announced a $2.6 million cutback in public spending in the May mini-budget. It was claimed to be the biggest cutback for thirty years.

The Australian film *Palisade*, directed by Laurie McInnes, won the prize for the best short film at the Cannes Film Festival in May. This was the second consecutive year that an Australian film-maker won the award.

An outbreak of Legionnaire's disease in the city of Wollongong, New South Wales, was first confirmed in early May. By the end of the month thirty-five people had been confirmed as having the disease. A hospital air-conditioner was found to be contaminated with the Legionella bacteria.

JUNE

The Sydney Harbour Bridge toll rose from twenty cents to one dollar on **1 June**. On the first day of the new toll, forty-four motorists refused to pay. The increase in toll was introduced to pay for the proposed Harbour Tunnel.

Lindy Chamberlain was given a full pardon on **2 June**. Mrs Chamberlain had been convicted of the murder of her six-week-old daughter Azaria in 1980. It was estimated that the cost of the trial, two High Court appeals and a Commission of Inquiry was $23 million.

On **3 June** Sir Joh Bjelke-Petersen withdrew his plan to stand for Prime Minister at the July election.

A computer fault in the Westpac bank's new software for international and automatic teller transactions was detected on **4 June** which enabled customers across Australia to withdraw unauthorised money from automatic teller machines. The bank was thought to have lost potentially millions of dollars.

On **9 June** a team of Sydney medical researchers announced the development of a technique to detect the presence of a substance released by a human embryo within hours of conception. This would enable detection of pregnancy 'the morning after'.

Five men were convicted on **10 June** of the brutal murder of the Sydney nurse Anita Cobby in February 1986. The men were sentenced to life imprisonment, with the judge's recommendation that they should never be released.

A team of archaeologists from the Australian National University were led by Aborigines to 5000-year-old footprints on the Nullarbor Plain in May. The leader of the ANU team, Dr Scott Cane, said on **11 June** that the area was very rich in Aboriginal sites.

Thirty men, members of the Comanchero and Bandido bike gangs, were convicted of murder and manslaughter charges on **12 June** after a 332-day trial in Sydney. The men faced multiple murder charges after the 'Father's Day Massacre' of 1984, when the two rival gangs had a gunfight in a hotel car park during a bike swap attended by over 1000 people. Seven people were killed and another twenty-one were injured.

Japanese pop star Hirimi Go married Yurie Nitani in Sydney on **16 June**. The marriage was sponsored by Australian companies who hoped to increase the number of Japanese honeymooners visiting Australia.

A central Queensland farmer announced on **17 June** that he had struck oil when a contractor put down for bore water. The farmer was more concerned for the survival of his cattle.

On **18 June** it was reported that two sculptors from the Sepik region of Papua New Guinea had been lost in Sydney for four hours when visiting the New South Wales Institute of Technology in November. Nawi and Apkwini, who speak very little English, suffered a series of mishaps as they attempted to gain access to the institute, including being sent to Sydney University's Anthropology Department and the Papua New Guinea Consulate. They were almost put on a flight back to Port Moresby because officials were unable to understand their problem. Fortunately, inquiries were made which established their rightful whereabouts.

The tenth anniversary of the inauguration of the Uniting Church was celebrated on **21 June**.

On **22 June** two cleaners at the Crows Nest branch of the Commonwealth Bank in Sydney, found $22,000 in a garbage bin in one of the offices. The money had been left there by accident by two bank workers who had gone home. The cleaners, who had decided to keep the money, were later charged.

The twentieth anniversary of East-West Airlines' inaugural flight was celebrated on **23 June**. The 1947 flight was from Tamworth to Sydney and took approximately one and a half hours.

Douglas Beane, the American marine who deserted to Australia during the Vietnam War, was discharged without penalty on **23 June**.

On **25 June** English newspapers reported the legal action of a group of parents whose children had been removed from their care by an Australian doctor practising at the Middlesborough General Hospital in north-east England. Over 200 children had been diagnosed as victims of sexual abuse in the previous month, in contrast to thirty reports for the entire year before the doctor's appointment to the hospital.

On **29 June** the Maralinga-Tjarutja Aborigines of South Australia refused access to Department of Science officials to their traditional lands near Woomera. The department was wanting to make their visit in regard to proposed rocket flights to be launched by West German and United States agencies later in the year.

JULY

Cigarette packets were required to display a selection of four new warning labels from **1 July**. The tobacco lobby does not accept the warnings about the health risks associated with smoking but agreed to print them nevertheless. They are: 'smoking causes lung cancer', 'smoking causes heart disease', 'smoking damages your lungs' and 'smoking reduces your fitness'.

Australia's oldest man died on **4 July** at the age of 110, three months before his 111th birthday. Mr Louey Hay had lived in Australia for eighty-eight years. He emigrated from Canton in 1899 and became an Australian citizen in 1964. He stopped working in Melbourne's Victoria Markets at the age of ninety-five.

On **5 July** tennis player Pat Cash became the first Australian since 1971 to win the men's championship at Wimbledon. Cash beat Ivan Lendl in three sets.

It was reported on **6 July** that an Australian psychic would lead divers to the remains of the Colossus of Rhodes, one of the seven wonders of the world. The clairvoyant, Ann Dankbaar, believed that she had located the exact spot where the bronze statue was submerged. A subsequent search by divers did not recover the Colossus.

On **8 July** Justice Jane Hamilton Mathews became the first New South Wales woman to be appointed to the Supreme Court Bench. Justice Mathews was also the first woman to be appointed New South Wales Crown Prosecutor in 1968 and the first woman New South Wales District Court Judge in 1980.

Holly McDonnell became the youngest child in Australia to hear through a 'bionic ear' on **8 July**. Holly, who was five years old, became deaf after contracting meningitis. She was the twenty-seventh person in Sydney to receive the implant.

It was revealed on **9 July** that the United States has documented plans for dealing with a nuclear weapons emergency in Australia. The documents were released under the US Freedom of Information Act and recommended that if a nuclear accident occurred in a Pacific port, it should be described as non-nuclear.

Three men who were awarded the Order of Australia for their climb of Mt Everest's North Face, climbed 200 metres to the top of Sydney Tower on **9 July** as part of a Greenpeace protest against naval nuclear weapons. They attached a 30 metre-long Greenpeace banner to the tower after an operation that involved scrambling across the tops of city buildings, bypassing rooftop security systems, and an ascent of the tower which took six hours. The men were arrested and charged with trespassing when they descended.

On **11 July** the Labor Party was led to an historic third term victory by Prime Minister Bob Hawke. The government was returned with an increased majority, including a 1.3 per cent swing to Labor in Queensland attributed to a backlash against the campaign of Sir Joh Bjelke-Petersen.

On **14 July** plans for a Bicentennial birthday cake which would sit on the top of the Kings Cross tunnel were announced. The cake was to be one of a number of decorations and illuminations to be bestowed on the city of Sydney in the Bicentennial year. After extensive public comment and controversy over the cake concept, a competition for an alternative idea was funded by Sydney developer Sid Londish. The winner was nine-year-old Louise Johnson who suggested an echidna spiked with 200 birthday candles. Finally the idea was scrapped altogether and it was decided to donate the $200,000 needed to build the monument, to a charity.

Australia's earliest known convict industrial site was uncovered at Newcastle Harbour on **19 July** when archaeologists and volunteers discovered a kiln during an excavation. The site has been retained as part of an historic park.

The last episode of the national music program *Countdown* was shown on **19 July** after thirteen years on ABC television. It was made at the Sydney Entertainment Centre where the annual Countdown awards were being held. Host Molly Meldrum, characterised by his Akubra hat, stole the show when he removed the hat to reveal a shaved head.

On **20 July** the Queensland state cabinet ordered that crocodiles be removed from the most populated areas in the state and put in zoos. The program was aimed at reducing the number of human fatalities.

It was reported on **20 July** that a number of previously unknown species of trees and an unknown bird had been discovered in the Kimberleys in Western Australia. It was part of an ecological survey of Australia which also found populations of rare reptiles and birds.

It was announced on **22 July** by three Supreme Court judges that a Human Rights Commission would hold an inquiry into the deaths of Aboriginal people in police custody. At this date there had been fifteen Aboriginal deaths in custody in the previous seven months.

A man whose novel had been rejected by fifty-seven publishers, thus earning him a place in the *Guinness Book of Records* as the world's least successful author, announced the publication of his book *One Best-seller* on **25 July**. The author, William Gold, finally published the novel himself. It tells the story of a chronically rejected novelist.

When the First Fleet Re-enactment vessels arrived in Rio de Janeiro on **26 July** the organisers announced the possibility of abandoning the voyage due to financial difficulties. An application to the Australian Bicentennial Authority for increased funding of $900,000 failed but funds were raised in the corporate and private sectors.

Melbourne and Perth both suffered flooding at the end of July. In Melbourne on **30 July** the State Emergency Service evacuated thirty-five people after the Maribyrnong River broke its banks during the worst rains for thirteen years. At the same time in Perth, thirty homes were evacuated in the heaviest rain reported in ninety-six years.

The Kings Cross Wax Works closed on **31 July**. The Wax Works had been a popular Sydney attraction for twenty years, housing dummies of famous people such as Ned Kelly, Adolf Hitler and Prince Charles.

East-West Airlines was bought by Ansett Transport Industries on **31 July**. Ansett at the time was jointly controlled by Rupert Murdoch's News Corporation and Sir Peter Abele's TNT Ltd.

The famous Sydney city fruit shop where Dame Nellie Melba used to buy her peaches, De Luca's, closed on **31 July** after 101 years of business. The shop, in King Street, was closed to make way for a forty-five-storey office block.

AUGUST

On **4 August** two crew members of the submarine HMAS *Otama* drowned when the vessel dived with them stranded in the fin area, or conning tower. It was more than an hour before the crew realised that the sailors were missing. The Royal Australian Navy conceded that a deficiency in safety procedures was the cause of the accident.

Archaeologists of the Sydney Cove Redevelopment Authority announced on

6 August that they had found a well full of 1850s artefacts behind a house in The Rocks in Sydney. The house had been built in 1831.

The federal Liberal and National parties announced that their coalition would be reformed on **7 August**. The previous coalition split had been in April when the Queensland National Party ordered its federal members of parliament to leave as part of Sir Joh Bjelke-Petersen's unsuccessful election campaign.

Nineteen-year-old Julian Knight opened fire in the Melbourne suburb of Clifton Hill on **9 August**, killing six people and injuring ten others. Knight, who shot randomly at passing traffic on Hoddle Road, was arrested about an hour after the shooting started.

An auction of nineteenth century ornithologist John Gould's rare lithographs of Australian birds was held in Melbourne at Sotheby's on **9 August**. It was the largest auction of its kind in Australia and the lithographs fetched over a million dollars.

On **10 August** Lecki Ord was elected Melbourne's first woman Lord Mayor. The federal government announced a Royal Commission of Inquiry into Aboriginal deaths in custody on **11 August**—the Muirhead Royal Commission.

Racial tensions exploded in the northern New South Wales town of Brewarrina on **15 August** when white and Aboriginal people clashed at a local hotel. The Aboriginal community had attended the funeral of Lloyd Boney, an Aborigine who had died while in police custody. In response, the secretary of the federal Department of Aboriginal Affairs, Charles Perkins, called for a treaty to be incorporated into the Constitution which would acknowledge Aborigines as the original owners of Australia.

At dawn on **16 August** over 600 people joined hands in meditation at Bronte Beach in Sydney for an event called the Harmonic Convergence. It was part of worldwide celebrations of the alignment of the planets—for the first time in 23,412 years. Using satellite links with San Francisco and New York, the meditators joined with millions around the world who hoped to bring about a fundamental change in human consciousness.

The *Business Daily*, the first new national newspaper for twenty-three years, closed down on **19 August** after only five weeks of operation. Michael Gill, editor and managing director, announced that low circulation and lack of funds were the reasons for the closure.

The largest non-nuclear explosion on Australian soil occurred on **19 August** at Woomera in South Australia. The Defence Science and Technology Organisation and the RAAF detonated a stockpile of thirty-six bombs, a total of 8000 kilograms of TNT, as part of a program to improve RAAF safety standards. The explosion, which cost half a million dollars, was to test materials for blast walls.

On **23 August** a demonstration organised by the Movement for the Ordination of Women (MOW) was held outside St Andrew's Cathedral in Sydney. Dignitaries were attending the opening service of the Anglican General Synod while the women sang psalms and held lit candles as a way of publicising their cause.

A Norwegian seaman drowned when he fell overboard from the First Fleet Re-enactment vessel the *Anna Kristina* on **23 August**.

The former New South Wales Minister for Corrective Services, Rex Jackson, was found guilty on **28 August** of conspiring to accept bribes for the release of prisoners. He was sentenced to seven and a half years imprisonment.

On **31 August** a lottery prize was paid to the family of a woman who bought a winning ticket thirty-seven years earlier. In 1950 the woman bought the ticket with a threepenny piece she found on the footpath in Newtown, Sydney. The Lotteries Office was unable to trace her because she had given her address as 'c/-GPO'. Before her death in 1985, the woman told a family member that she had won a prize but had not collected it because she had lost the ticket. Samples of her handwriting were sent to the Police Scientific Investigation Section which helped to verify the claim.

Student unions of three universities and colleges of advanced education in Queensland faced prosecution over the installation of condom vending machines in August. The machines were installed as part of the campaign against the spread of AIDS. A state Health Act which classified condoms under drugs and poisons makes it illegal to dispense them from vending machines. While the state cabinet decided not to prosecute the unions, Premier Sir Joh Bjelke-Petersen was concerned for the grave moral issue posed by their installation.

SEPTEMBER

Members of People for Nuclear Disarmament protested when the American warship USS *Constellation* visited Fremantle in early September. They also distributed condoms to women who attended a ball held by the US navy, as a safeguard against the AIDS virus which may have been carried by some of the 6900 sailors on board.

On **1 September** the Australian Privacy Foundation launched a national campaign against the introduction of the proposed Australia Card. Rock singer Peter Garrett, Senator Janine Haines of the Democrats and yacht designer Ben Lexcen helped publicise the campaign.

On **3 September** two journalists from the ABC's *Four Corners* program were committed for trial on two counts of criminal defamation against bookmaker Bill Waterhouse.

The national parachuting record was broken on **6 September** by a Brisbane man who made seventy jumps in a day.

It was announced on **7 September** that the updated edition of the government *Style Manual* would allow the official dropping of the apostrophe in certain circumstances.

Australia's first $2 coin was struck at the Mint on **7 September** by the federal Treasurer, Paul Keating. The new coins were expected to be released by April 1988.

An Australian missionary was killed in a shooting in Sri Lanka on **7 September**. A team of masked gunman had opened fire on the streets of a northern town, killing four people.

A plan for an Australian Studies program at the National University of Singapore was launched by the Governor-General, Sir Ninian Stephen, on **7 September**. The program will focus on arts, social sciences, science and engineering science.

Actress Meryl Streep arrived in Australia on **8 September** to play the role of Lindy Chamberlain in the film *Evil Angels*.

The seizure of 16 tonnes of herbs contaminated by radioactivity by food inspectors in Sydney was reported on **10 September**. The herbs came from areas of Europe that had been contaminated by fallout from the nuclear accident at Chernobyl.

Fifteen people died in the year up to **10 September** as a result of climbing Uluru (Ayer's Rock). This makes it a more dangerous tourist attraction than crocodiles which had only killed two people in the same period.

A 2 tonne circus elephant, Abu, of Ashton's Circus, crushed a trainer to death on **14 September**. The man was Abu's third victim.

On **15 September** federal Treasurer Paul Keating brought down a balanced budget. It was the first time in seventeen years that a federal government had been able to present a balanced budget.

Aussat 3, the third and final stage of Australia's broadcast satellite system, was launched from French Guiana in South America on **16 September**. Aussat allows people living in remote areas of Australia to receive television broadcasts.

The New South Wales government announced the intended sale of nine of the state's mental hospitals on **17 September**. Patients from the hospitals would be moved to community-based accommodation, in line with recommendations of the Richmond Report.

Schoolboy James Ferguson, from Tamworth in New South Wales, became the first Australian to win a scholarship to NASA's international summer student program on **17 September**.

The Australian Broadcasting Tribunal lifted restrictions on television advertisements on **24 September**. For a two-year trial period commercial television broadcasters are allowed any number of advertising breaks where they had previously been limited to four an hour.

Sydney's entrepreneurial doctor, Geoffrey Edelsten, filed a petition for bankruptcy and claimed debts of more than $2 million on **27 September**. Dr Edelsten was being investigated by the Taxation Office and the Medical Tribunal.

Manly defeated Canberra in an historic Rugby League Final on **27 September**. It was the last Grand Final to be played at the Sydney Cricket Ground. After 1987, the match will be held at the new Sydney Football Stadium.

Warwick Fairfax succeeded in taking over the John Fairfax Ltd media group on **28 September** and thus privatising the Fairfax family empire. Warwick, twenty-six, is the great-great-grandson of the original founder of the company.

Motorcycle rider Wayne Gardner won the Brazilian Grand Prix on **28 September**, making him the world 500cc champion. On his return to Australia and his home town of Wollongong in New South Wales he received a hero's welcome.

Former Sydney detective Roger Rogerson was arrested and charged with conspiracy to pervert the course of justice on **29 September**. The charge was related to money deposited in bank accounts under false names.

On **29 September** Prime Minister Hawke announced that the federal government had abandoned the introduction of the Australia Card. Forces opposed to the ID card had combined in the Senate to block the passage of the legislation.

Several up-market restaurants in Adelaide began serving freshwater crocodile in September. Diners paid between $25 and $30 for a main course.

In September a world record was set by the sale of a mature merino ram in Adelaide for $215,000.

The Japanese Ministry for International Trade and Industry presented a feasibility study to the New South Wales government in September on a proposed 'technopolis' – a technology city which would be built in Sydney's west. The government responded positively to the study in March 1988.

OCTOBER

On **2 October** BHP announced that 2,600 jobs would be cut from the Port Kembla Steelworks.

Fitzroy Crossing in Western Australia set a new record on **2 October** for the number of drunks locked up in cells on the first night of the annual three-day rodeo event. One hundred and sixty-nine people were crammed into the cells.

Australian Vietnam Veterans numbering 25,000 marched in a 'welcome home' parade in Sydney on **3 October**, fifteen years after their return from the Vietnam War.

For the first time a transsexual woman from New South Wales, Estella Esta, was granted the right, on **3 October,** to have a birth certificate proclaiming her to be a female.

On **6 October** the federal government announced the end of the two-airline agreement, which has regulated the aviation industry since the 1950s. Deregulation allows other airlines to compete with Ansett and Australian Airlines.

Legislation was introduced into the Victorian parliament on **7 October** which bans tobacco advertising in cinemas and on billboards, and which will cut sporting and cultural sponsorship by tobacco companies.

The New South Wales government announced on **8 October** that the New South Wales Institute of Technology would become the University of Technology, Sydney, in 1988. This would enable the institution to gain federal funding.

Pat Cash, Australian Wimbledon champion, moved out of his Kings Cross hotel room on **12 October** because he feared it was haunted by a ghost.

On **12 October** the Anglican Archbishop of Sydney, the Most Reverend Donald Robinson, asserted his opposition to the ordination of women priests at the opening of the Diocesan Synod. At the same time, Melbourne's Archbishop, Dr David Penman, met church advisers to try to set a date to begin the ordination of women.

Police raided the Builders Labourers' Federation (BLF) union offices in Melbourne on **13 October** and seized truckloads of their files and documents. The BLF was investigated for illegal financial dealings.

Melbourne radio personality Derryn Hinch was imprisoned on **15 October** for contempt of court. The one month sentence was imposed for comments that

Hinch made on air regarding the case of a Catholic priest charged with sex offences. Hinch served four days of the sentence.

More than 100 demonstrators were arrested at the Pine Gap American military base near Alice Springs on **18 October**. They were protesting against the renewal of the base's lease. Democrat Senator Jo Vallentine was among those arrested.

Australia's stock market crash was reported on **19 October**, after $9 billion was lost in the day's trading. The All Ordinaries index showed a record slump of 79.9 points. The crash reflected similar activity in major world trading centres.

Sydney businessman Abe Saffron was convicted on **23 October** of tax fraud. He was sentenced to three years' imprisonment but he appealed.

Four people died in floods in Sydney on the weekend of **24 and 25 October**. The Bureau of Meteorology recorded 145 millimetres of rain over the two-day period, which is four times the average total rainfall for October.

Residents of New South Wales saw a spectacular light display in the night sky on **27 October** when a piece of 'space junk' burnt in the atmosphere. The burning debris was the remains of a satellite which had re-entered the earth's atmosphere.

John Elliot, chairman of Elders IXL, was elected president of the federal Liberal Party on **30 October**.

On **31 October** it was reported that prison officers at Bathurst Gaol refused to distribute condoms to prisoners. The gaol was the first in New South Wales to be issued with condoms as part of a government program to prevent the spread of AIDS.

In October a Brisbane man was fined $250 for riding a horse while under the influence of alcohol.

NOVEMBER

Australia's first Solar Car Race started in Darwin on **1 November**. Within an hour Sunraycer, the General Motors' entry, had taken a definitive lead in the 36,000 kilometre race to Adelaide. Sunraycer won the race on 6 November after five and a half days, two days ahead of other competitors.

The *Young Endeavour*, Britain's Bicentennial gift to Australia, arrived in Fremantle on **1 November**.

An Australian Assemblies of God missionary in Mozambique was arrested on **2 November** on charges of serving an organisation of anti-government terrorists.

On **3 November** the federal government sacked the Christmas Island Assembly only two weeks after its election. The sacking was due to a failure to meet economic objectives set by the Minister for Territories.

In an operation at Sydney's Westmead Hospital on **4 November**, two patients each received a pancreas in Australia's first successful pancreas transplants.

On **5 November** a Queensland shark fisherman caught what he believed to be a world record 2 tonne shark near Phillip Island in Victoria.

Australia's cricket team won the World Cup in India on **8 November**. They won by seven runs.

Sir John Kerr, the Governor-General who sacked Prime Minister Gough Whitlam in 1975, said in a rare television interview on **9 November** that he had no regrets over the sacking. The twelfth anniversary of the event was on 11 November.

A photograph of Ned Kelly sold at a Melbourne auction for $19,800 on **12 November**.

A ten-year-old German girl flew from Frankfurt to Melbourne's Tullamarine Airport on **14 November** without a ticket, passport or baggage. The girl stowed away on the flight in the hope of going to Turkey where her father lives.

Gerhard Berger led Ferrari to victory on **15 November** in the Australian Grand Prix in Adelaide.

Non-members were admitted to the Members Stand at the Sydney Cricket Ground on **15 November** for the first time in its 110 year history. The move was hoped to increase flagging attendances.

Pat Cash arrived in Johannesburg on **17 November** to play tennis in the South African Open tournament despite opposition from the Australian Anti-Apartheid Movement.

Saboteurs caused massive damage to

Telecom cables in Sydney on **20 November**. Telephone lines, computer data lines, automatic bank teller machines, facsimile services and telex lines were severely affected in the central business district and thiry-six surrounding suburbs. The saboteurs, who gained access to tunnels beneath the city, were believed to be employees or ex-employees of Telecom.

A cyclist arrived in Sydney on **23 November** after spending two years on a 42,000 kilometre ride around the world. The Adelaide man, Paul McManus, set out to raise money for the Freedom from Hunger Campaign.

On **24 November** the Premier of Queensland, Sir Joh Bjelke-Petersen, attempted to sack five cabinet ministers. The Governor, Sir Walter Campbell, refused to endorse Sir Joh's request to remove their commissions and the ministers refused to stand down. On 26 November, the National Party's management committee called a parliamentary meeting at which Sir Joh was replaced by Mike Ahern as leader. Sir Joh initially refused to resign, placing the Queensland government in a constitutional crisis. Sir Walter Campbell refused to exercise his powers to dismiss Sir Joh, calling for the party to persuade him to resign which he finally did on 1 December.

Laurie Brereton, New South Wales Minister for Public Works, resigned on **25 November** after a fight with the Premier, Barrie Unsworth, who had plans to demote him.

Australia's first corporate child care centre was opened on **25 November** at Observatory Hill in Sydney. The centre was funded and established by Esso Australia and Lend Lease Corporation.

A horse which won a race at Rosehill in New South Wales on **28 November** was found to be under the influence of the illegal drug etorphine or 'elephant juice'. It was the first positive test-result of the drug found in New South Wales.

A fisherman who had been stranded for a month on an isolated beach north of Cooktown in Queensland was rescued on **30 November**. An Aviation Department aircraft spotted a distress signal that he had written in the sand.

On **30 November** the sale to China of the Australian television mini-series *The Shiralee* was announced by the South Australian Film Corporation. It is amongst the first Australian mini-series to be seen in China.

DECEMBER

A fifteen-year-old Queensland boy who arrived in Britain to visit an uncle on 27 November left on **1 December** after being refused an entry visa. Entry was refused when he told immigration officials that he intended to work for his uncle.

On **1 December** it was reported that the AIDS virus had killed 347 people in Australia in the five years since it was first diagnosed in November 1982.

Sir Joh Bjelke-Petersen, Premier of Queensland, announced his resignation on **1 December** on a live television broadcast.

Smoking was banned on domestic airline flights on **1 December**. Smokers' Rights demonstrators protested at Sydney airport on the first day of the ban.

At Brisbane's Boggo Road Gaol on **2 December**, 250 prisoners rioted in protest against the famous 'Black Hole' cells.

On **3 December** the Soviet leader, Mikhail Gorbachev, gave assurances to Prime Minister Hawke that two Jewish families could emigrate from the USSR. Hawke had originally negotiated on behalf of one of the families in 1979 when he was in Moscow with the ACTU.

Sir Frank Renouf announced the end of his marriage to Lady Susan on **3 December**.

On **4 December** a report confirmed that a ten-year-old Queensland boy had died of rabies five months previously. Tests conducted overseas had recently ascertained the cause of death.

A gunman entered a Melbourne city office block on **8 December** and shot nine workers before jumping from the eleventh floor window. The shooting became known as the 'Queen Street Massacre'.

The Tall Ships made their first entry into Australia on **8 December**, sailing into Fremantle Harbour in Western Australia. The personalised numberplates of Sydney doctor Geoffrey Edelsten were auctioned on **9 December**. One, 'SPUNKY', sold for a record price of $3800. Others auctioned were 'FOXY', 'SEXY' and 'CLASSY'.

A sixteen-year-old Sydney boy claimed on **10 December** that a statue of the Virgin Mary that he bought had wept and had powers of healing. He reported that over 4000 people had visited the family home to see the statue in the past month.

The federal government announced on **11 December** that it would be officially documented that the Aboriginal people were the first owners of Australia.

On **14 December** it was reported that Dr William McBride, founder and chairman of the medical research organisation Foundation 41, may have altered data in an experiment on the pregnancy sickness drug Debendox, thus committing fraud in his campaign against the drug. Dr McBride's research into the drug Thalidomide in the 1960s made him one of the world's best-known medical researchers.

Senator Susan Ryan, Special Minister of State, announced her retirement from politics on **16 December**. She was later to become the publishing editor of Penguin.

Aboriginal poet Kath Walker changed her name to Oodgerooo Noonuccal, her tribal name, on **16 December** as a protest against the Bicentenary.

On **17 December** the federal Minister for Tourism, John Brown, resigned after admitting that he had misled parliament over his role in the tendering process for the Expo contract.

1988

JANUARY

Fifteen thousand Scouts from around the world arrived in Sydney in January to celebrate the sixteenth World Jamboree.

The pewter plate which Dutch explorer Dirk Hartog used to record his arrival on the shores of Australia in 1616 was loaned to Australia by the Rijksmuseum in Amsterdam for the Bicentenary. It arrived in Perth in early January.

On **2 January** it was reported that sex education would be taught in Queensland schools for the first time.

Gerry Hand, the federal Minister for Aboriginal Affairs, announced his intention on **3 January** to boycott all official Bicentennial functions thereby backing black protests over the Bicentenary. The Prime Minister, Bob Hawke, supported his decision. The New South Wales Minister for Aboriginal Affairs, Ken Gabb, also chose to boycott.

A $5 arrival tax was introduced on **3 January** for all passengers arriving in Australia. The fee was supposed to be paid on departure along with the existing $20 departure tax.

On **9 January** a man living in Sydney's Kirribilli, opposite the Opera House, offered his unit for rent on Australia Day for $10,000. Property owners in waterfront residences with a ringside view of the Australia Day celebrations were reportedly asking up to $15,000 rental for the day.

On **17 January** it was announced that several boxes of explosives were stolen from a federal police munitions store in Canberra. There were fears that the explosives would be used in violent Bicentennial protests.

On **22 January** the first group of Aborigines to join a mass anti-Bicentennial protest at Sydney's La Perouse arrived from Queensland. Aboriginal activist Burnum Burnum arrived in London and on 26 January he claimed Britain on behalf of the Aboriginal people.

On **25 January** it was announced that the shortage of doctors in New South Wales had led the Medical Board to introduce new legislation allowing foreign doctors to treat patients without taking the board's clinical examination.

After Torres Strait Island leaders voted to secede from the Commonwealth, Prime Minister Bob Hawke announced on **25 January** the government's intention to grant them rights for greater autonomy.

More than one million people visited the

Tall Ships during their stay in Sydney's Darling Harbour in the week leading up to Australia Day.

A documentary claiming that the CIA was involved in the dismissal of the Whitlam government was screened in Britain on **26 January**. Part of a series made by John Pilger, the program was shown in Australia in February.

Australia celebrated its two hundredth anniversary of European settlement on **26 January**. Prince Charles and Princess Diana were in Sydney for the celebrations on the harbour, which featured the arrival of the First Fleet Re-enactment, a parade of sail by visiting Tall Ships, an air force flyover and a fireworks display. There was also a demonstration held by Aboriginal people and supporters who mourned the 200 years of European domination.

On **27 January** a team of researchers from Sydney University announced their discovery that echidnas living in the Snowy Mountains hibernate in winter. The New South Wales government decided on **28 January** to protect 80,000 hectares of forest in the logging region near Eden in the south-east of the state. Sir William Knox, Queensland's Liberal Leader, resigned on **30 January**.

On **30 January** it was reported that Aboriginal leaders intended to ask the Anglican Church for the return of the remains of the first Aborigine to die on British soil. The man, Yemmerrawanyea Kebbarah, was taken to England by Governor Phillip in 1792 but was unable to adapt to life in Britain and died two years later. He was buried in an Anglican Church cemetery in South London.

A series of earthquakes occurred in and around the Northern Territory town of Tennant Creek in the third week of January. The area does not have a history of earthquake activity.

The New South Wales government held a gun amnesty in January in an attempt to recover banned semi-automatic weapons.

FEBRUARY

From **1 February** companies were required to begin to submit reports to the federal government about their implementation of equal employment opportunity policies. Under the Affirmative Action Act of 1986 the government aims to provide women with equal employment and advancement prospects.

A sixteen-year-old Australian schoolboy became the youngest International Master of Chess on **1 February**. There are only nine Australian International Masters.

On **2 February** it was revealed that the federal Minister for Immigration, Mick Young, was at the centre of a controversy over the donation by a woodchip manufacturer of $10,000 for an election campaign. The Labor Party had failed to publicly disclose the donation. Stephen Loosely, the New South Wales ALP Secretary, claimed the responsibility on 4 February, but Young resigned over the affair on 8 February.

On **6 February** the medical research organisation Foundation 41 announced that it would hold an inquiry into allegations that Dr William McBride had falsified data relating to the drug Debendox.

The state seat of Adelaide was lost by Labor to the Liberal Party on **6 February**. It had been an ALP seat since 1966.

On **7 February** there was a national twenty-four hour strike by coalminers over changes to award conditions.

On **8 February** a Melbourne man attempted to pay the Taxation Office with trees. It was his fifth year of protest against taxes being spent on armaments. The previous year he attempted to pay his taxes with shovels.

A burst water main at Sydney's International Airport on **9 February** caused 10,000 passengers to be delayed for several hours as workers tried to clear up the flood.

It was reported on **15 February** that in the first month since the introduction of the $5 arrival tax, 96,000 people had failed to pay. The airline carrying the defaulter was obliged to pay.

A tribute to Dame Joan Sutherland was unveiled at Sydney Town Hall on **15 February**. It was a giant ear, sculpted in marble and weighing more than 1 tonne.

A new Queensland afternoon newspaper, the *Sun*, was published for the first time on **15 February**. This followed the closure of the *Telegraph* the week before. James Finch, the man convicted of the 1973 fire-bomb attack on Brisbane's Whisky Au Go-Go in which fifteen people were killed, was released on **16 February**. After fifteen years in prison he was deported to Britain where he sought an inquiry into his conviction.

The twenty-ninth International Youth Skill Olympics opened in Sydney on **18 February**. Over four days 400 apprentices from around the world competed in such categories as mechanics, cookery and hairdressing.

On **19 February** twenty-one Australians left on the Bicentennial Mount Everest expedition. It was to be the first attempt without the use of Nepalese porters.

Premier Brian Burke of Western Australia retired from politics after five years in the position and Peter Dowding was named Premier-elect on **23 February**.

Former Sydney detective Roger Rogerson was charged on **24 February** with conspiring to murder drug squad detective Michael Drury.

Sydney's tenth Gay Mardi Gras was held on **27 February**. For the first time there was an Aboriginal float in the parade, which featured an Aboriginal Captain Cook and Sir Joseph Banks.

MARCH

A delegation of Japanese officials arrived in Sydney on **3 March** to discuss plans for the proposed 'technopolis' to be established in Sydney's west.

On **3 March** a seventy-one-year-old banana farmer from northern New South Wales met a Yorkshire woman with whom he had a romantic attachment in 1945 when stationed in Lincolnshire with the RAAF. The couple, still in love after more than forty years, decided to marry.

The establishment of a new problem-solving unit set up by the Taxation Office was announced on **4 March**. The office is to look at complaints from the taxpayer's point of view, and one of the methods they envisage using to apologise for mistakes is to send the taxpayer flowers.

French winegrowers have prevented Australian wines being sold to the European Economic Community on the basis of the names of the wines. A report on **6 March** stated that the French have taken exception to Australian adaptations of French styles, such as Beaujolais, Champagne and Hermitage, which represent specific areas of France.

On **7 March** Jeff Fenech won the World Boxing Featherweight Championship for the third time.

A magistrate dismissed charges on **7 March** against a Sydney woman who had failed to pay the Harbour Bridge toll sixty times. The magistrate, Lillian Austin, said that she sympathised with the woman.

On **8 March** a proposal to establish a nuclear waste industry in Australia was announced. While former New South Wales Premier and current chairman of the CSIRO, Neville Wran, supported the proposal, Prime Minister Hawke rejected it on the same day.

The 'Woolworths Bomber', Larry Burton Danielson, who was convicted and sentenced to twenty years' gaol in 1982 for placing bombs in three Sydney stores, was released and deported to New Zealand on **9 March**.

The OECD (Organisation for Economic Cooperation and Development) reported on 10 March that Australia was the fastest growing tourist attraction of 1987.

A survey of salary levels in twenty-four countries which was reported on **10 March** found that Australian executives are among the worst paid in the world.

A man reported seeing a crocodile on the banks of Adelaide's suburban West Lakes on **10 March**.

On **10 March** the High Court passed down a judgement supporting Commonwealth legislation to make the Lemonthyme and Southern Forest of Tasmania eligible for the World Heritage List. The Tasmanian government had challenged the federal government legislation.

The New South Wales Teachers' Federation launched a Bicentennial program on **11 March** which takes an Aboriginal perspective of European settlement. They aim to have the program formally adopted by the Education Department.

The federal government announced on **11 March** that part of the Australian

Embassy in Tokyo had been sold to a Japanese business enterprise. In return, the buyers are to buy 1.5 million tonnes of coal from New South Wales.

On **12 March** a 'killer' cassowary, the bird indigenous to north Queensland and Papua New Guinea, was reported to have been terrorising visitors on a walking trail near Cairns.

Former federal Minister for Immigration, Mick Young, was the centre of a new controversy on **12 March** when it was discovered that Prime Minister Bob Hawke had lobbied on his behalf to secure his appointment as a consultant for Qantas.

On **12 March** the Chinese gift to Australia for the Bicentenary, the loan of two giant pandas, was prevented from boarding the flight that was to bring it to Australia. Officials of the Chinese airline, CAAC, refused to allow them to travel in the passenger cabin, while forestry officials did not want them held with cargo.

Archaeologists released reports of a recently discovered ice age campsite in central Australia on **12 March**. The discovery may lead to a change in the theory of how Australia was originally colonised. Currently it is believed that the coast was colonised first, followed by migration to the centre. The campsite suggests that people may have travelled along inland waterways to reach the centre of the country during initial colonisation.

The Australian Institute of Sport awarded its first scholarship to a disabled athlete, Russell Short, on **13 March**. He is a visually impaired thrower.

Jon Sanders, a West Australian, became the first person to sail single-handed around the world three times on **13 March** when he completed his third circumnavigation.

Leaders of trade unions representing 100 countries met in Melbourne on **14 March** for the fourteenth World Congress of International Confederation of Free Trade Unions.

On **14 March** Warwick Fairfax closed the *Sun* and the *Times on Sunday*, and announced plans to sell his equity in the *Age* in Melbourne.

The federal Minister for Finance, Senator Peter Walsh, announced on **15 March** the sale of Commonwealth Accommodation and Catering Services Ltd. The service, which provides the Commonwealth public service with tea ladies, would now be privatised.

On **19 March** the New South Wales Liberal Party, under the leadership of Nick Greiner, was elected to office. With a swing of about 10 per cent, the election marked the end of twelve years of Labor government.

The Australian missionary Ian Grey, who was arrested in Mozambique in November on charges of working for anti-government guerillas, went to trial on **21 March**. He was sentenced to ten years' imprisonment.

Australian Bureau of Statistics figures released in March showed that February's unemployment rate was the lowest for six years.

A. S.

INTERNATIONAL EVENTS 1987

JANUARY

PUERTO RICO
A fire which swept through the twenty-one storey Dupont Plaza Hotel on **1 January** claimed at least ninety-five lives and injured a further 140 people. Most of the victims were tourists from the United States and Canada holidaying in Puerto Rico. A maintenance worker later admitted to starting the fire.

JAPAN
A Japanese National Railways official hanged himself on **2 January**, believing he was responsible for the deaths of six people when a train fell from Asia's highest railway bridge.

CHAD
In a protracted territorial dispute with Libya, government forces in Chad captured the Libyan-held base at Fada on **2 January** and French aircraft raided Libyan installations at Ouadi-Doum on **7 January**.

PHILIPPINES
On **2 January** security forces killed at least fifteen people during a march by 10,000 farmers pressing for land reforms. Rebel troops led by Colonel Oscar Canlas seized a television station and other government installations on **27 January** to protest alleged communist influence within the government. President Aquino ordered court martial proceedings against those responsible after the last of the troops surrendered on **29 January**.

COOK ISLANDS
Cyclone Sally devastated the waterfront administrative and commercial centre of the main Rarotonga island on **4 January** and left 1000 people homeless. It was the worst storm to hit the Cook Islands this century.

CÔTE D'IVOIRE
Two survivors from the wreckage of a Brazilian airliner were rescued by French troops on **4 January**. The plane crashed 40 kilometres from Abidjan, en route to Rio de Janeiro, killing all the other forty-nine passengers and crew.

INDIA
On **6 January** former Finance Minister Pranab Mukherjee and other 'Indira loyalists' formed the National Socialist Congress Party.

MACAO
Portugal agreed on **6 January** to the transfer of Macao to China before the year 2000.

VIETNAM
Vietnam claimed on **7 January** that it had forced back Chinese incursions in the Vi Xuyen area of the Ha Tuyen border province.

IRAN—IRAQ
A major offensive was started by Iran on **9 January** near the Iraqi city of Basra while Iraq claimed to have bombed the Iranian holy city of Qom on **10** and **11 January**.

GREAT BRITAIN
A lorry, one of a convoy believed to be carrying nuclear weapons, slid off an icy road and overturned near Dean Hill, Wiltshire, on **11 January**. A Ministry of Defence spokesman would neither confirm nor deny whether the convoy was carrying nuclear weapons.

On **12 January** Buckingham Palace announced that Prince Edward had decided to leave the Royal Marines.

LEBANON
Terry Waite, the Archbishop of Canterbury's personal envoy, who arrived in Beirut on **12 January**, was not seen in public after **20 January**. Waite, who went to Lebanon to negotiate the release of Westerners already held hostage, disappeared after walking alone to a night rendezvous.

UNITED STATES
Seven Mafia leaders who coordinated the activities of the city's major crime families were each sentenced to 100-year gaol

terms on **14 January** after they were found guilty of conspiracy in usury, gambling, drug trafficking and extortion. President Reagan delivered his annual televised State of the Union address to Congress on **27 January**. It was widely noted by political commentators that the President's legislative position had been weakened by the combined effects of Democrat control of the Senate, continuing controversy over the administration's arms sales to Iran and the diversion of proceeds from these sales to Contra rebels in Nicaragua, as well as doubts about the health of the seventy-five-year-old President. The address was President Reagan's first public appearance since a prostate operation and tests for cancer in early January.

The deposed Philippines President Ferdinand Marcos and his wife Imelda were reported to have spent $A3000 in a Honululu store on combat boots and camouflage outfits and on **28 January** were prevented from returning to the Philippines by US government officials.

SOUTH KOREA
Following the death on **15 January** of a student under police torture, Kim Chong Hoh was replaced as Interior Minister by General Chung Ho Yong.

CHINA
In a significant display of dissent several thousand students staged marches in some eleven cities, including Beijing. Denouncing 'conservatives' and 'reactionaries' in the Communist Party the students claimed they were attempting to inhibit China's modernisation program. The marches took place in defiance of a newly introduced ban.

On **16 January** Hu Yaobang, China's second most powerful man, resigned as general secretary of the Communist Party, after admitting he violated party principles. He was replaced by Zhao Ziyang, the Prime Minister.

EUROPE
By **16 January** the death toll in Europe's worst winter for decades reached 200.

HONG KONG
Sir David Wilson was appointed Governor of Hong Kong on **16 January**, succeeding the late Sir Edward Youde.

WEST GERMANY
Following a general election on **25 January** the Christian Democrat-Free Democrat governing coalition was returned under the chancellorship of Helmut Kohl.

NICARAGUA
On **28 January** the Nicaraguan government released Sam Hall 'on humanitarian grounds'. The brother of a US congressman, Hall had been arrested in a restricted military zone on 12 December 1986.

USSR
On **29 January**, in a series of senior personnel changes, Alexander Yakovlev, a key adviser to Mikhail Gorbachev during the Reykjavik meetings, was elected to the Politburo. Western diplomats believe the election of Yakovlev could greatly affect the Kremlin's policies towards the West and towards the United States in particular.

SOUTH AFRICA
President Botha, opening the 1987 session of parliament in Pretoria on **30 January**, announced that elections – the first since 1981 – would be held to the (white) House of Assembly on 6 May. The President faced a mounting rebellion within the ruling National Party as Dennis Worrall, formerly one of its most articulate supporters, resigned as Ambassador to Britain.

Exxon, reputed to be the world's largest corporation, announced its withdrawal from South Africa.

SRI LANKA
Tamil paramilitary groups merged to form the Liberation Tigers of Tamil Eelam (LTTE) and took control of the northern Jaffna peninsula. The LTTE are fighting for a separate Tamil homeland in the north and east of Sri Lanka.

FEBRUARY

NEW ZEALAND
On **2 February** the United States announced it would not renew nor renegotiate a five-year-old memorandum of understanding on logistical support because of the New Zealand government's continued ban on visits by US nuclear warships.

PHILIPPINES
In a referendum on **2 February** the electorate approved the country's new constitution, which was accordingly promulgated on **11 February**. Although the result of the referendum was seen as confirmation of Aquino's presidency, the ratification of the constitution significantly reduced the President's power and extended the role of the Congress and the Senate.

UNITED STATES
On **3 February** William Casey, Director of the CIA and a leading figure in the Iran-Contra arms scandal resigned. The Tower Commission report released on **27 January** found that diplomatic initiatives conducted by the National Security Council subverted US policies toward a number of Middle Eastern countries. White House Chief of Staff, Donald Regan, immediately announced his resignation and was replaced by former Republican Senator Howard Baker.

The flamboyant entertainer Liberace died in Los Angeles on **4 February** from an 'opportunistic infection' triggered by the AIDS virus, the Riverside County Coroner said.

GREAT BRITAIN
Alistair Maclean, the best-selling writer of gripping thrillers such as *HMS Ulysses*, *The Guns of Navarone* and *Ice Station Zebra* died on **3 February** aged sixty-four.

On **24 February** a High Court judge made legal history by ruling that a woman was entitled to proceed with an abortion despite the opposition of the unmarried father.

Meanwhile, a controversy broke out this month in the tabloid press over the true height of US film star Paul Newman.

IRAN—IRAQ
On **5 February** Iran launched a missile attack on the Iraqi capital Baghdad while Iraq, on **6 February**, carried out bombing raids as part of the continuing 'war of the cities'.

NEW DELHI
An accord signed by India and Pakistan on **5 February** eased tensions which had brought the two neighbours to the brink of war in the preceeding fortnight.

SRI LANKA
At least 153 Tamil civilians were killed near Batticaloa by government troops and on **7 February** Tamils took revenge by killing twenty-nine Sinhalese.

USSR
On **8 February** two Soviet cosmonauts, Yuri Romanenko and Alexander Laveikin, on board Soyuz TM-2, completed the first automatic docking with orbiting space station Mir.

Signalling a new tolerance and openness in the Soviet Union the Gorbachev administration released 140 political prisoners and announced on **10 February** that a similar number of cases were being reviewed.

On **28 February** Mikhail Gorbachev proposed the removal of both Soviet and US intermediate-range nuclear missiles from Europe over a five-year period.

FRANCE
Dr Abraham Behar, a biophysicist at the Curie Institute of the University of Paris, predicted on **10 February** that France would move its nuclear test site from Mururoa Atoll to another isolated Polynesian atoll or to the sub-Antarctic Kerguelen Islands, south-west of Western Australia. The move would take place within three years due to the deterioration in the volcanic base caused by the explosion of 119 bombs at Mururoa since 1966.

Four militant members of the illegal Direct Action organisation were arrested in Vitry-aux-Loges, 90 kilometres south of Paris. Direct Action was formed in 1979 from an assemblage of several extremist factions and is believed to be responsible for about eighty bomb attacks and several murders and attempts on the lives of public figures.

MALTA
President Agatha Barbara relinquished office at the end of her five-year term on **15 February**. Earlier on the same day she dissolved the parliament (last elected in December 1981) and a general election was called for 14 May.

IRELAND
Following a general election on **17 February** the Fianna Fail, led by Charles Haughey, formed a minority government which replaced the out-going Fine Gael–Labour coalition.

VIETNAM
Following a reorganisation, the ruling

Communist Party announced on **17 February** that officials known to be economic reformists had been placed in key party positions. This would seem to open the way for new policies of modernising economic reforms.

THAILAND

On **19 February** Khun Sa, reputed to be the largest opium trader in the so-called Golden Triangle region where the borders of Burma, Laos and Thailand converge, was under siege by some 2000 troops near the Thai–Burmese border. The fifty-four-year-old warlord affronted officials in Burma and Thailand in January by holding a news conference in rebel-held territory in Burma, during which he announced a bumper opium crop.

CANADA

New immigration laws which were designed to curb abuses of political refugee status were introduced on **20 February**.

VATICAN

A warrant was issued in Milan for the arrest of the president of the Vatican Bank and two other senior Vatican officials on **25 February** on charges relating to fraudulent bankruptcy leading to the collapse of Banco Ambrosiano in 1982.

CHINA—USSR

Talks between Chinese and Soviet officials opened in Moscow this month on the settlement of the two countries' mutual border, the first such talks since November 1979.

MARCH

NEW ZEALAND

On **2 March** a series of strong earthquakes destroyed buildings, roads, bridges and railways in northern New Zealand, and a civil defence emergency was declared in the Bay of Plenty region where some 200,000 people live.

ITALY

Amidst fears that Italy would be plunged into political crisis after its longest period of political stability since World War II, Bettino Craxi submitted the resignation of his coalition government on **3 March**. On **20 March** Air Force General Licio Giorgieri was shot dead in Rome. The Red Brigade claimed responsibility.

PHILIPPINES

On **3 March** President Aquino announced a land reform program for which $A1.5 billion would be allocated. Land reform is considered to be crucial to effective social change in the Philippines and to quashing communist insurgency in rural areas.

Four people were killed on **18 March** when a bomb exploded at the Philippines Military Academy in Baguio, and nineteen soldiers were killed by a land-mine explosion in Quezon province.

UNITED STATES

In an historic televised speech to the nation on **5 March**, President Reagan accepted responsibility for the Iran arms debacle. The speech was his formal response to the report of the Tower Commission, which had been appointed to investigate the secret Iran-Contra arms deals.

On **6 March** a US Federal Court judge ordered Alabama state schools to withdraw thirty-six textbooks on home economics, history and social studies on the basis of a US statute which forbids the teaching of religion in government schools. Judge Brevard Hand ruled that school textbooks which did not mention God were promoting a religion called 'secular humanism'.

On **30 March** the United States closed sensitive communication links with its Moscow Embassy following the arrest of two marine guards who were accused of allowing Soviet spies access to restricted areas of the embassy.

A team of Harvard researchers who examined decisions made by government agencies in enforcing regulations on chemical pollution over the past ten years concluded that a human life was worth $A3 million to US government officials.

ECUADOR

Between **5** and **13 March** earthquakes registering up to 6.6 on the Richter scale caused mudslides resulting in the deaths of at least 2000 people.

BELGIUM

A cross-channel ferry, the *Herald of Free Enterprise*, capsized on **6 March** soon after leaving the Belgian port of Zeebrugge. Some 200 people were estimated to have lost their lives as a result of the disaster.

SINGAPORE

On **7 March**, in a reversal of its population policy, the Singapore government offered financial and other inducements to encourage people to 'go forth and multiply'. The declining birth rate had led to concern over the future of its defence capability and the size of its workforce.

GREENLAND

The coalition government of Greenland collapsed on **11 March** over the issue of modernisation of the US military base at Thule. A premature general election was called for 26 May.

HUNGARY

In a rally marking the anniversary of Hungary's 1848 rebellion against Austrian rule more than 2000 Hungarians marched through the centre of Budapest on **15 March** calling for freedom and democracy. It was the first time for more than thirty years that Hungarian authorities had permitted such an open expression of dissent.

WEST GERMANY

A bomb exploded at the British military base at Rheindahlen, west of Dusseldorf in the Federal Republic of Germany, on **23 March** injuring thirty-one people. Responsibility was claimed by the Provisional Irish Republican Army and also by a previously unknown group, the National Democratic Front for the Liberation of West Germany.

Also on **23 March** Willy Brandt, the former Federal Chancellor, resigned as chairman of the Social Democratic Party amid controversy over his appointment of Margarita Mathiopoulosa as party press officer; a Greek journalist who was not a member of the SPD.

TUNISIA—IRAN

Tunisia severed diplomatic relations with Iran on **26 March** following the alleged discovery of evidence linking the Iranian Embassy in Tunis with terrorist activities in Tunisia and abroad.

GREECE—TURKEY

Tension rose between Greece and Turkey when the Greek oil exploration ship *Sismik 1*, accompanied by Turkish warships, sailed to the Dardanelles on **26 March** in preparation for its departure on **28 March** to disputed waters in the northern Aegean. The ships turned back on the same day after the Greek authorities indicated that they would not carry out exploration in the disputed area at that time.

ISRAEL

Iraeli Prime Minister Yitzhak Shamir said after his re-election as Herut party chairman on **30 March** that the West Bank and Gaza Strip would forever remain under Israeli control. The territories have been occupied by Israel since the 1967 Middle East War.

VATICAN

Pope John Paul began a two-week trip to South America on **31 March** which was highlighted by a visit to Chile. There the Roman Catholic Church, openly challenging military rule and charging it with human rights offences, had come under fierce attack from the government for being too political.

SPAIN

The largest trial in Spanish history opened on **31 March** with thirty-eight people charged with being responsible for nearly 600 deaths and about 25,000 injuries from the sale of contaminated cooking oil in 1981.

CHILE

Astronomers continued to study the supernova which was first detected in Santiago at the end of February. The star is in the Greater Magellanic Cloud, a large circular patch of luminescence near the arc of the Milky Way, some 160,000 light-years from earth. It was the closest supernova to have become visible since 1604, appearing as a glittering jewel in the night skies over the Andes.

SIERRA LEONE

An apparent attempt to seize power by senior police and junior army officers in Sierra Leone was suppressed by forces loyal to President Joseph Momoh.

APRIL

EL SALVADOR

On **1 April** guerilas attacked one of El Salvador's most highly defended military bases at El Paraiso, 60 kilometres north of San Salvador, killing at least forty-three Salvadoran soldiers and a US military adviser. Eight rebels died. Normally housing a garrison of 1000 troops, the base was left a smoking ruin.

GREAT BRITAIN

Six scientists – five dead and one missing – were named on **2 April** by members of parliament calling for a government enquiry into the mystery surrounding their deaths. All the scientists had worked on sensitive defence projects. On **6 April** it was disclosed that a sixth scientist involved in secret defence work had died in mysterious circumstances in February.

Prime Minister Margaret Thatcher said on her return on **3 April** from a five-day visit to the Soviet Union that Europe must retain nuclear weapons for at least another thirty years. This view contradicted claims by both the United States and the Soviet Union that all nuclear weapons could be eliminated by the year 2000.

The disclosure that Sir Maurice Oldfield – a major figure in post-war British intelligence and head of MI6 from 1972 to 1978 – had concealed his homosexuality for thirty years re-opened the issue of parliamentary responsibility for the British security and intelligence services.

Northern Ireland's second most senior judge Justice Maurice Gibson and his wife Cecily were killed by a car bomb near Newry, just over the border from the Irish Republic.

PAKISTAN

Afghan guerillas rejected Kabul's calls for national reconciliation and claimed on **2 April** that Soviet and Afghan troops were about to launch a major offensive on the Afghan Pakistani border. Afghan refugees fleeing the border zone to escape the fighting continued to arrive in Pakistan at a rate of about 8000 a month, according to local officials.

CHILE

In the cities of Santiago, Punta Arenas and Concepcion Chilean riot police fired tear gas and water-cannon into crowds who were welcoming the Pope and protesting against human rights abuses. President Augusto Pinochet, who has led Chile's military government since heading a violent coup thirteen years ago, told the Pope that Chile was a victim of a foreign campaign of 'hate, lies, and the culture of death'. On **3 April** half a million people gathered to hear the Pope speak on the outskirts of Santiago.

EGYPT

The ruling National Democratic Party of President Hosni Mubarak won a majority in the election to the Egyptian People's Assembly on **8 April**. The assembly election was regarded as an important test of the strength of Muslim fundamentalism in Egypt.

PARAGUAY

On **8 April** President Alfredo Stroessner lifted a state of siege which had been in force since the 1947 civil war saying he no longer needed the special powers to maintain peace in Paraguay.

ITALY

Italy's five-party government collapsed on **9 April** with the resignation of the caretaker Prime Minister, Bettino Craxi. The collapse was the forty-fifth Italian government to fall since World War II.

FIJI

In a general election concluding on **12 April** the Alliance Party government of Ratu Sir Kamisese Mara was toppled by a coalition of the National Federation Party and the Labour Party. Dr Timoci Bavadra of the Labour Party took office as Prime Minister on **13 April**. The new government's platform included a ban on visits by nuclear ships, support for independence of Irian Jaya and membership of the Non-Aligned Movement.

USSR—AFGHANISTAN

Accounts of a rocket attack by Afghan rebels on a Soviet textile factory near the Afghan-Soviet border were publicised on **13 April**. Hundreds of Afghans were killed during fierce Soviet retaliation. American-backed Afghan rebels operating from bases in Pakistan have been attempting to force the overthrow of the Soviet-supported government in Kabul.

SOUTH AFRICA

The South African President, P. W. Botha, claimed on **13 April** that a reformist revolt in his National Party would fail. The rebels, including the former ambassador to London, Dr Dennis Worrall, left the National Party to stand as Independents in the May whites-only general election.

Six striking railway workers were shot dead near Johannesburg by police on **22 April**, while the state-owned South

African Transport Service sacked 16,000 black railway men in one of the biggest mass dismissals in South Africa's history.

SOUTH KOREA

President Chun Doo Hwan put police on emergency alert on **15 April** to guard against civil disturbance following the government's decision to set aside constitutional reform until after the 1988 Olympics. This indicated that the President's successor would be chosen by way of the existing electoral procedure.

ARGENTINA

In what was considered to be the gravest crisis of President Raul Alfonsin's civilian government, an army rebellion broke out on **16 April** near the western city of Cordoba. Unrest within the military had been increasing following several successful prosecutions of army officers accused of human rights violations. The rebellion collapsed on **19 April**.

SRI LANKA

There were several violent attacks in Sri Lanka between **17** and **22 April**, with the number of people killed in incidents connected with the Tamil civil war rising to more than 350. Sinhalese outrage following the terrorist bombing of Colombo's main bus station, in which 106 people were killed, fuelled popular resentment about the haven offered to separatist groups in the South Indian state of Tamil Nadu. President Junius Jayewardene said on **26 April** that his government would not hold a general election scheduled for 1989 unless Tamil terrorism was quashed.

ALGERIA

At a meeting of the Palestine National Council, often called the parliament-in-exile of the Palestinians, rival factions of the Palestinian Liberation Organisation agreed upon a new political platform on **20 April**. The new platform is aligned with efforts by the Soviet Union to convene an international peace conference on the Middle East, under terms that have been rejected by the United States and Israel.

UNITED STATES

After biologists captured the last Californian condor on **20 April** the foothills of southern California were without the bird for the first time in 15,000 years.

It was announced by US health officials on **22 April** that AIDS had been reported in 102 of the 131 countries which report to the World Health Organisation. Also, the number of cases worldwide had probably reached 100,000, with as many as ten million people already infected with the virus.

JAPAN

A Japanese man became the first person to ride a motorcycle to the North Pole on **21 April**. Mr Shinji Kazama rode and pushed his 200cc motorcycle for forty-four days through 2000 kilometres of snow and freezing temperatures from Canada's Ward Hunt Island.

MALAYSIA

Following his re-election by a narrow margin to the presidency of the ruling United Malays National Organisation (UMNO) on **24 April**, the Malaysian Prime Minister, Dr Mahathir Mohamad, was faced with unprecedented divisions in the party. On **30 April** he terminated the commissions of three ministers and accepted the resignations of three others, including the Trade and Industry Minister, Tengku Razaleigh Hamzah, who lost the ballot for the UMNO presidency by forty-three votes.

INDONESIA

In a general election for 400 of the 500 seats in the Indonesian House of Representatives (the remaining 100 being reserved for military appointees) President Soeharto's ruling Golka Party had taken 72 per cent of the vote by **25 April**. The victory delivered a major blow to Indonesia's main Muslim-backed party, the United Development Party.

AUSTRIA

The US Justice Department announced on **28 April** that the Austrian President, Dr Kurt Waldheim, would be prevented from entering the United States as a private individual because of evidence emerging that he was involved in war crimes perpetrated by Hitler's army in the Balkans.

MAY

JAPAN

It was disclosed on **1 May** that Japanese police and the US Defence Department were investigating a subsidiary of the giant Toshiba Corporation which illegally sold the Soviet Union technology which enables submarines to move with a minimal risk of detection.

A journalist was killed on **7 May** in a shotgun attack on a bureau of *Asahi Shimbun*, a mainstream Japanese newspaper with a circulation of eight million. The ultra-nationalist Japan Volunteer Army for National Independence claimed responsibility, accusing the newspaper of nurturing anti-Japanese sentiment by questioning government policy.

PHILIPPINES

President Aquino approved on **3 May** the sale of 113 state-run enterprises, including Philippine Airlines, the Manila Hotel, several banks and subsidiaries of the national oil company.

UNITED STATES

After negotiations finishing on **3 May** the Japanese Prime Minister, Yasuhiro Nakasone, failed to secure American guarantees to lift tariffs imposed on Japanese electronic imports. The tariffs were imposed in retaliation for alleged Japanese dumping of semi-conductors on US markets.

The *Miami Herald* reported on **4 May** that it had discovered a relationship between Gary Hart, a Democrat Party presidential nominee, and a part-time model, Donna Rice. Innuendo about Hart's marital fidelity had become an issue in his campaign because it raised questions concerning his judgement and integrity, the newspaper said.

A new immigration law which came into effect on **5 May** provided for an unprecedented amnesty for the expected 3.9 million illegal aliens who can prove they have lived in the United States since 1981. While giving legal status to established aliens more will be deterred from entering the United States by the imposition of criminal penalties against employers.

Democrat nominee Gary Hart announced his withdrawal from the presidential race on **9 May** following a revelation regarding a further assignation with a woman in December 1986.

Rita Hayworth, the red-haired love goddess of 1940s cinema, died on **14 May** at the age of sixty-nine after years of suffering Alzheimer's disease. A photo of Miss Hayworth kneeling on a bed in a negligee was a favourite pin-up during World War II, and her picture was pasted on the first atom bomb exploded in peacetime in 1946. During her thirty-seven-year career she made sixty-one films, achieving stardom in 1941 in *You'll Never Get Rich* with Fred Astaire.

Under the terms of a Federal Court verdict in March, Beulah Mae Donald, a sixty-seven-year-old black woman from Alabama, was given the property deed to the headquarters of one of America's largest Ku Klux Klan organisations. The building was turned over to her as part of a settlement arising from the conviction of two Klansmen for the murder of her teenage son in 1981.

FRANCE

Former Nazi Gestapo chief Klaus Barbie claimed on **3 May** that he obtained intelligence information from French collaborators belonging to all sections of French society during World War II. There was widespread speculation that his trial for war crimes had been delayed because of French embarrassment at the possibility of revelations about the extent of collaboration. Barbie, sought for eleven years by authorities, has twice been sentenced to death in his absence by military courts for executing 4000 people during the war.

LEBANON

The Lebanese Prime Minister, Rashid Karami, announced the resignation of his government on **4 May**. Karami, a Sunni Muslim, had boycotted President Amin Gemayel, a Maronite Christian, since January 1986 because of the President's failure to act upon a Syrian-mediated plan to end Lebanon's civil war.

ITALY

It was announced on **4 May** that the ashes of the fourteenth century poet and moral philosopher Dante Alighieri, which were last displayed in 1929, were found in the Senate building in Rome after being reported missing from the National Library in Florence. Envelopes containing other relics belonging to the poet were still missing.

SOUTH AFRICA

Gavin Relly, chairman of the Anglo-American Corporation, South Africa's most powerful mining and banking conglomerate, urged white voters in a newspaper column on **4 May** to support candidates committed to racial equality in the forthcoming elections.

Contrary to many predictions, President Botha and his National Party won South Africa's whites-only election on **6 May** with an increased majority, thereby sealing Nationalist dominance of white South African politics. In a general swing to the right, the far-right Conservative Party made significant gains and replaced the liberal Progressive Federal Party as the official opposition.

INDONESIA
About 175 people were feared to have died in a landslide which buried a limestone mining village in West Sumatra on **4 May**.

MURUROA ATOLL
On **5 May** France resumed its underground nuclear testing in the South Pacific with a blast registered at an estimated 5 kilotons, an explosive force equivalent to 5000 tonnes of TNT. The test was condemned by New Zealand and Australia.

GREAT BRITAIN
The IRA was dealt a severe blow on **8 May** when eight of its masked gunmen were shot dead in an ambush set by commandos of the Special Air Service Regiment.

On **11 May** Prime Minister Margaret Thatcher announced general elections would be held on 11 June. The date for the poll was decided in a mood of great optimism in the Conservative Party, which had a majority of 136 in the 650-member House of Commons and commanded an eleven point lead in opinion polls.

POLAND
In Poland's worst air disaster, on **9 May** 172 passengers and eleven crew died instantly when a Soviet-built Ilyushin 62 owned by the LOT state airline crashed and exploded in a pine forest in a Warsaw suburb.

MALTA
The leader of Malta's Nationalist Party, Dr Edward Fenech Adami, was sworn in as the country's new Prime Minister on **12 May** after sixteen years of Labour Party rule. Dr Fenech Adami favoured retaining economic links with Libya while moderating the political relationship established by the previous government, and continuing with an application for membership in the European Community.

FIJI
On **14 May** a dramatic but bloodless military coup, led by Lieutenant Colonel Sitiveni Rabuka, wrested power from the newly elected government of Dr Timoci Bavadra. The new regime, which included former Prime Minister Ratu Sir Kamisese Mara, detained the entire Bavadra government as well as potential opponents (including foreign journalists) of the newly formed Council of Ministers. Colonel Rabuka stated that he organised the coup to pre-empt the government calling out the army to move against Fijians plotting against the government.

PERSIAN GULF
Twenty-five American crewmen were killed aboard the frigate USS *Stark* when it was hit by an Exocet missile fired by an Iraqi aircraft on **17 May**.

SOUTH KOREA
The South Korean President, Chun Doo Hwan, sacked his Prime Minister and five other ministers on **26 May** in an effort to put an end to public anger over the death of a student activist under police torture.

CHINA
China's biggest forest fire for nearly forty years was brought under control by rain and the efforts of tens of thousands of people on **26 May**. Since 6 May the fire had killed over 200 people and made 50,000 homeless.

AFGHANISTAN
It was reported on **27 May** that Soviet and Afghan government planes and artillery reduced the north-western Afghan city of Baghlan to rubble after the defection of up to 800 Afghan troops to opposition Muslim guerillas.

USSR
Soviet leader Mikhail Gorbachev dismissed Defence Minister Marshal Sergei Sokolov and Chief of Air Defences Marshal Aleksandr Koldunov for 'negligence and disorganisation' following the penetration of Soviet air-space by a light plane which flew unimpeded for 700

kilometres before landing outside the Kremlin on **28 May**. The West German pilot was arrested by Soviet militiamen.

JUNE
LEBANON
On **1 June** Lebanon's Prime Minister, Rashid Karami, was assassinated when a bomb exploded under his seat on an army helicopter flying him from his home in Tripoli to his office in Beirut. Karami was serving his ninth term as Prime Minister in a thirty-seven-year political career. Selim Hoss, an American-educated economist and Prime Minister from 1976 to 1980, was named as Karami's successor.

SRI LANKA
Tamil guerillas stopped a bus in eastern Sri Lanka and killed thirty-three passengers including twenty-nine Buddhist monks on **2 June**. The killings occurred as troops in the northern Jaffna peninsula were mopping up resistance from Tamil separatists after a week-long government offensive. A flotilla of Indian ships carrying supplies to Tamil areas of northern Sri Lanka was turned back by Sri Lankan naval forces on **3 June**, but supplies were successfully dropped into Tamil areas by Indian Air Force aircraft on **4 June**. The airdrop was described by Colombo as an outrage.

UNITED STATES
A former president of the International Brotherhood of Teamsters, Roy Williams, admitted at a federal trial on **3 June** to being controlled by the Mafia when he was trustee of a major Teamster pension fund.

Also on **3 June** the US Senate voted overwhelmingly that all immigrants be required to be tested for the AIDS virus.

On **17 June** a New York jury of ten whites and two blacks found that Bernhard Goetz acted in self-defence when he shot four unarmed black men who asked him for $5 on a subway train in December 1984.

Figures released by the Commerce Department on **23 June** revealed that the US foreign debt had more than doubled in 1986 to $US263.3 billion ($A368.78 billion).

The former White House aides Lieutenant-Colonel Oliver North, Rear-Admiral John Poindexter, Mr Robert McFarlane and the late CIA director, Mr William Casey, all concurred in a cover-up after US arms sales to Iran became publicly known in November 1986 according to testimony given by Charles Cooper, an assistant Attorney General, on **25 June**.

Meanwhile, diplomats, intelligence specialists and congressmen revealed that Saudi Arabia had been regularly financing US foreign policy and had assisted pro-Western movements or governments in Afghanistan, Yemen, Somalia, Sudan, Pakistan, Zaire and Nicaragua.

SPAIN
Andre Segovia, the Spanish musician acclaimed as the world's greatest classical guitarist, died at his home from an unspecified illness on **3 June**. He was ninety-four.

On **10 June** Spain's ruling Socialist Party suffered a setback in local and European elections as months of protests against the austerity policies of the government took their toll. The Socialists lost their overall majority in Madrid and Valencia as well as in Seville which is the hometown of the Prime Minister, Felipe González Márquez.

BARBADOS
Errol Barrow, Prime Minister of Barbados, who led his island nation to independence in 1966, died of a heart attack at his home in Bridgetown on **3 June**. He was sixty-seven.

NEW ZEALAND
New Zealand officially became nuclear free on **4 June** when the Nuclear Free Zone, Disarmament and Arms Control Bill was approved by parliament. The legislation formalised a policy which forced the end of Wellington's thirty-five-year-old ANZUS alliance with Washington.

On **30 June** a general election was called for 15 August.

ITALY
The leaders of the seven most highly industrialised Western nations—the United States, Japan, Britain, France, Italy, West Germany and Canada—broke up on **11 June** after three days of talks which decided little, if anything, of

discernible value. The conference agreed in theory on the need to cure economic ills, such as slowing down economic growth and ending the subsidies war, but no practical solutions were adopted to overcome them.

Italy's Socialist Party, led by Bettino Craxi, scored its best result in a general election in forty years when the final outcome was announced on **16 June**.

CENTRAL AFRICAN REPUBLIC

Former Central African dictator Jean-Bedel Bokassa was sentenced to death on **12 June** after being found guilty of gruesome crimes during his thirteen-year period in power up to 1979.

GREAT BRITAIN

In a general election on **12 June** the Conservatives were returned to office with an overall majority of 102. Margaret Thatcher became the first British Prime Minister in 150 years to win three consecutive terms in Downing Street. The election result was seen as a clear endorsement of Conservative economic policies, which included curbs on trade union power, privatisation of state-owned enterprises and deregulation.

It was announced on **30 June** that a genetic probe which can determine the sex carried by a single sperm cell had been developed in Edinburgh. For the first time the sex of a baby can be chosen before its mother's egg is fertilised by its father's sperm.

INDIA

State Assembly elections in Haryana on **17 June** resulted in one of the most humiliating defeats for the Congress Party of the Prime Minister, Rajiv Gandhi. The elections were won by a coalition between the Lok Dal (People's Party) and the Hindu-revivalist Bharatiya Janata Party.

SOUTH KOREA

About 7000 students fought running street battles with police just hours after a five-day siege of Seoul's Roman Catholic cathedral ended peacefully. The students were demanding free elections and the resignation of President Chun Doo Hwan's government. On **18 June**, the centre of Seoul was seized by thousands of charging students who overwhelmed riot police units. The violent clashes between civilians and police, the worst since President Chun came to power in 1979, indicated that there would be no popular acceptance of his plan to prolong effective military rule in South Korea.

VIETNAM

Premier Pham Van Dong and President Truong Chinh, the only surviving founders of the Vietnamese Communist Party still in power, were removed by vote of the National Assembly on **18 June**. Their departure ended more than fifty years of government leadership by contemporaries and colleagues of Ho Chi Minh.

HONDURAS

Nicaraguan Miskito Indians who oppose the Sandinista government concluded an assembly in a remote part of eastern Honduras with an agreement to forge a unified organisation allied with the main army of the Nicaraguan rebels on **19 June**. The assembly was sponsored by the United States.

NIGERIA

An international economic conference on Africa called on **23 June** for the creation of an Africa Club to deal collectively with Western countries over the continent's debt crisis, estimated at $US200 billion ($A260 billion). The conference meeting in Nigeria was organised by the United Nations Economic Commission for Africa.

ALGERIA

The Libyan leader Colonel Muammer al Gaddafi visited Algiers on **28 June** for talks with President Chadli Bendjedid on a federation between their two countries. Colonel Gaddafi has been keen for political union among Arab states.

JULY

UNITED STATES

On **1 July** the pilots of a Delta Air Lines jet 'inadvertently' switched off both engines during take-off from Los Angeles but were able to restart them in time to avoid crashing into the Pacific Ocean, air traffic controllers reported.

According to the United Nations the world's population reached five billion on **11 July**, double that of 1950.

An eight-year-old boy, born with deformed arms and hands after his mother was prescribed the common anti-nausea drug Benectin during pregnancy, was awarded $US95 million ($A135.91 million) in damages on **15 July**. The judgement was issued against the manufacturer of the drug, Merrill Dow Pharmaceuticals, a subsidiary of the Dow Chemical Company.

After a week of dramatic testimony by Lieutenant-Colonel Oliver North, during which he said that he assumed President Reagan knew of the diversion of profits from arms sales to Iran to Contra rebels in Nicaragua (when such aid was banned by Congress), Rear-Admiral John Poindexter took responsibility for the affair. On **15 July** Poindexter told the US congressional committee investigating the scandal that he did not brief the President on the issue.

NIGERIA
President Babangida of Nigeria announced on **1 July** a return to civilian rule by 1992, after supervising a phased handover to civilians this year.

PAPUA NEW GUINEA
Thousands of mourning Highlanders lined Goroka's flower-strewn streets on **2 July** in tribute to the memory of Jim Taylor, who had died the previous week aged eighty-six. Taylor was regarded as one of the country's greatest patrol officers in the 1930s. The most important expedition associated with Taylor was the 1933 patrol into the Waghi Valley which led to the discovery of huge New Guinea populations — well over 200,000 — thriving in high, malaria-free valleys.

FRANCE
After hearing 190 hours of evidence from 105 witnesses the trial of former Nazi Gestapo chief Klaus Barbie, aged seventy-three, ended on **4 July** with his conviction of multiple crimes against humanity and sentence of life imprisonment. In a final plea of innocence Barbie — whose atrocities included savaging his victims with dogs, electrocuting and even skinning them alive — said: 'It was the war but the war is over'.

The French government on **17 July** broke off diplomatic relations with Iran after the Iranian authorities at Tehran's Paris Embassy had refused to release Vahid Gordji, an interpreter wanted for questioning over bomb attacks in Paris that left thirteen people dead. French police had sealed off the Iranian Embassy on 30 June.

INDIA
Sikh extremists killed forty Hindu bus passengers, including pilgrims, in the north Indian state of Punjab on **6 July**. It was the worst single act of violence by Sikhs during their five-year fight for a separate Sikh homeland in Punjab. A further thirty-two Hindus were killed in a similar attack the next day in Haryana state. In a Hindu backlash over the following days at least a dozen people were killed amid arson, looting and stone-throwing in several towns across Haryana and Uttar Pradesh.

USSR
Nearly fifteen months after the world's worst nuclear accident, the trial of a manager and two senior engineers from the Chernobyl nuclear power plant opened in the Ukraine on **7 July**. They were charged with wilful negligence leading to the nuclear disaster on 26 August 1986.

PANAMA
Tens of thousands of people defied a government ban on protests and took to the streets on **8 July** in the biggest display of public discontent since Panama plunged into crisis in early June. On **27 July** security forces armed with machine guns and tear gas and supported by helicopters launched a dawn raid on the home of retired Colonel Roberto Diaz Herrera, and arrested him after a two-hour battle. Herrera, a leading critic of strongman General Manuel Noriega, had charged Noriega on 7 June with election rigging in 1984 and with planning the death of Panama's leader General Omar Torrijos Herrera in a plane accident in 1981. The charges set off a train of unrest and violence in Panama.

SOUTH KOREA
Civil rights were restored to 2335 people including opposition leader Kim Dae Jung on **10 July**.

Also on **10 July** President Chun Doo Hwan resigned his post as chief of South Korea's ruling Democratic Justice Party in favour of Roh Tae Woo, and on **13 July** removed the Prime Minister and eight other ministers.

CHINA

On **12 July** the West German Chancellor, Dr Helmut Kohl, became the first foreign leader to visit Tibet since Chinese troops occupied the region in 1950.

BOLIVIA

Bolivia signed an agreement on **14 July** whereby millions of hectares of threatened tropical rainforests in the Amazon basin would be protected in return for a reduction of its foreign debt. The agreement involved the bank Citicorp buying outstanding Bolivian debt at a discounted market price and selling it to Conservation International, an environmental protection organisation.

PAKISTAN

Pakistani government officials reportedly blamed Afghanistan for two car-bomb explosions which killed seventy-two people in Karachi on **14 July**. It was the most devastating bomb attack in Pakistan's recent history.

WEST GERMANY

The only Jewish citizen of the small West German town of Gedern was finally forced to leave the community of 7000 people on **17 July** after enduring five years of racist and anti-Semitic humiliation. Anonymous telephone calls, death threats, smashed windows and swastikas daubed on his house characterised the persecution of Dan Kiesal, a forty-nine-year-old chiropractor of German Jewish descent, who had to give up his medical practice and move elsewhere.

GREAT BRITAIN

On **18 July** a bomb exploded in a car driven by Amir-Hussein Amir Parviz, head of the National Resistance Movement of Iran, and leading opponent of the Ayatollah Khomeini. Parviz was seriously injured and a previously unknown group calling itself the Guardians of the Islamic Revolution claimed responsibility.

PERSIAN GULF

On **22 July** a Kuwaiti supertanker, the *Bridgeton*, entered the Gulf, the first of eleven Kuwaiti oil tankers to be registered under the US flag and placed under the escort of three US warships. On **24 July** the *Bridgeton* was damaged by a mine believed to have been sown by Iranian Revolutionary Guards in a direct challenge to US pledges to protect the free navigation of Kuwaiti ships in the region.

PHILIPPINES

Before surrendering to Congress her power to legislate by executive decree, President Aquino signed a presidential order on **22 July** which initiated the program of land reform drafted in February 1987. The timetable and the extent of the program remained to be decided by the newly elected Congress.

MEXICO

At least forty-one people were killed and thirty-six injured when a Boeing 377 Stratocruiser built in the late 1940s crashed on a highway crowded with bumper-to-bumper traffic on **31 July**.

SAUDI ARABIA

On **31 July** at least 402 people – including 275 Iranian pilgrims, 85 Saudi citizens and security personnel and 42 people of other nationalities – died when Iranians staged a mass political demonstration at the holiest shrine of the world's one billion Muslims. Saudi Arabia and Iran issued sharply conflicting versions of the incident.

MOZAMBIQUE

The Mozambique government accused rebels of the Mozambique National Resistance Movement of responsibility for a raid at Homoine in Inhambane province which lead to the deaths of at least 380 villagers.

AUGUST

IRAN

On **1 August** Iranian protesters attacked the embassies of Saudi Arabia, Kuwait, France and Iraq in retaliation for Iranian deaths during violent rioting in Mecca on 31 July, while the Ayatollah Khomeini urged his people to hold a 'unity rally' in Mecca and seek deliverance from infidels.

PHILIPPINES

Jaime Ferrer, Minister for Local Government and a prominent supporter of the activities of anti-communist vigilantes, was shot dead in Manila on **2 August**. While suspicion was centred on the communist New People's Army, Ferrer had many political enemies, including a Muslim organisation called Holy War of Allah.

On **28 August** an attempted right-wing coup led by Colonel Gregorio Honasan and dissident junior army officers resulted in fifty deaths before troops loyal to President Aquino defeated the rebel military faction. The coup attempt was the fifth failed revolt by army officers attempting to overthrow the government in the eighteen months since the ousting of Ferdinand Marcos.

SRI LANKA

Vellupillai Prabakharan, leader of the Liberation Tigers of Tamil Eelam, formally declared on **4 August** that his guerillas would surrender their weapons to Indian peace-keeping forces, ending Sri Lanka's four-year ethnic conflict which has claimed 6000 lives.

President Junius Jayewardene escaped unhurt on **18 August** when two grenades were thrown into a parliamentary committee room where the ruling United National Party was meeting. The District Minister, Keerthi Abeywickrema, died from injuries he received in the attack and five other ministers and fifteen members of parliament were wounded. The Janatha Vimukthi Peramuna (People's Liberation Front), which has been waging an unceasing guerilla war against the government in southern Sri Lanka, was blamed for the attack.

PALAU

Voters in the tiny Western Pacific island state of Palau, 800 kilometres east of the Philippines, decided to surrender their anti-nuclear status in exchange for what their president called economic survival. Following a referendum on **4 August** the Palauans endorsed on **7 August** a proposed Compact of Free Association with the United States, allowing US nuclear-armed and nuclear-powered ships and aircraft in Palau territory, and providing Palau with $US1 billion in aid over fifty years. At the same time other Pacific island states were adopting or considering nuclear-free zones.

PERSIAN GULF

Amid intensified Iranian threats against the United States and Saudi Arabia Iran banned all foreign ships from its waters on **4 August** for its 'Operation Martyrdom' military manoeuvres. Mines damaged the supertanker *Texas Carribean* near Fujairah on **10 August** and destroyed the British-mastered supply ship *Anita* on **15 August**. In a reversal of Persian Gulf naval policy, Britain and France decided to send minesweepers to the Gulf on **11 August** after earlier refusing to enter the US-Iran naval confrontation in the region. Italy and the Netherlands also announced their willingness to send patrols. The 'tanker war' escalated on **29 August** with large-scale attacks by Iraq on ships and the Kharg Island oil terminal.

Meanwhile, a Stockholm-based international arms trade expert disclosed that sixteen countries were delivering arms to Iran, which had imported more than $US5 billion worth of arms since 1979.

PAPUA NEW GUINEA

On **5 August** Papua New Guinea's parliament elected Paias Wingti as Prime Minister for a five-year term, defeating Michael Somare by fifty-four votes to fifty-one. The parliament was formed after elections which ended on 4 July.

GUATEMALA

A Central American summit attended by Costa Rica, El Salvador, Guatêmala, Honduras and Nicaragua on **7 August** endorsed a regional peace accord which had been first proposed by President Arias of Costa Rica. The agreement called for a simultaneous cease-fire throughout Central America within ninety days, as well as an end to foreign aid to all rebel forces, an amnesty for unarmed political opposition groups and a ban on the use of any country's territory for fighting against another. A further meeting of foreign ministers in El Salvador on **19** and **20 August** devised mechanisms for implementing the peace initiatives.

USSR

Tass, the official Soviet press agency, announced on **7 August** that the Soviet Union had offered to ship Iranian oil across the Caspian Sea, thereby reducing the Khomeini regime's dependence on the Persian Gulf.

On **26 August** the Soviet government announced a decree which required the testing of both Soviet citizens and foreigners suspected of carrying the AIDS virus. The law provides for gaol sentences of up to eight years for people who knowingly transmit the virus or infect another person.

BURMA
At an extraordinary meeting of the Burma Socialist Program Party on **10 August** party chairman U Ne Win spoke for the first time of failures in the country's path to socialism and hinted at possible changes to the constitution.

SOUTH AFRICA
On **10 August** 340,000 black workers in South Africa's forty-six crucial gold and coal mines went on strike demanding a 30 per cent wage increase and improved working conditions. The strike ended on **30 August** after widespread violence, eleven deaths and the sacking of 40,000 workers. However, the South African parliament repealed legislation which had discriminated against blacks rising above the most menial positions and, theoretically, the new system allowed for the advancement of blacks to positions of managerial status. The strike had developed into the most significant trial of strength between white-led industry and black labour in South Africa.

UNITED STATES
President Ronald Reagan, addressing the nation on **12 August** on the Iran-Contra affair, said that he had been 'as mad as a hornet' over what he called 'the Iran-Contra mess'. He said 'no President should ever be protected from the truth' and that he was 'ultimately accountable to the American people', but he had not been told about the diversion of funds to the Contras.

A Northwest Airlines McDonnell Douglas MD-80, an updated version of the DC-9, clipped a building and skidded under three overpasses as it crashed on a busy freeway in Romulus, a Detroit suburb, on **16 August**. One hundred and sixty people were killed.

Lee Marvin, the consummate 'tough guy' both in movies and in life, died of a heart attack on **29 August** at the age of sixty-three. Marvin starred in the movies *Cat Ballou*, *The Dirty Dozen*, *The Caine Mutiny*, and *The Iceman Cometh*.

NEW ZEALAND
On **15 August** Prime Minister David Lange's Labour government was returned to office with a fifteen-seat majority in the ninety-seven member New Zealand parliament.

EAST GERMANY
Adolf Hitler's former deputy, Rudolf Hess, aged ninety-three, was found dead with an electric cord around his neck in Spandau Prison on **18 August**. He had spent the last forty years of his life in the rambling West Berlin gaol after being sentenced to life imprisonment at the Nuremburg Trials.

LEBANON
In the early hours of **18 August** kidnapped US journalist Charles Glass sneaked out of a seventh-floor apartment in Beirut's southern suburbs and walked to the Summerland Hotel on the outskirts of Syrian-controlled Muslim West Beirut. Glass had been kidnapped by pro-Iranian Shi'ite Muslim activists on 17 June, the first foreigner to be abducted since thousands of Syrian troops were deployed in West Beirut in February.

GREAT BRITAIN
Former British paratrooper Michael Ryan, aged twenty-seven, ran amok on **19 August** with an AK-47 assault rifle in Hungerford, Berkshire, and shot dead fifteen people, including his own mother. Ryan injured another sixteen before shooting himself. His rampage prompted the government to re-examine British gun laws.

SOUTH KOREA
South Korea's largest labour dispute ended on **20 August** when officials at Hyundai agreed to recognise an independent union formed by employees. Hundreds of factories still remained closed, however, as the worst labour strife in Korean history continued for the fourth consecutive week.

On **31 August** South Korea's two main political parties agreed on the draft charter for a new, more democratic constitution. Talks on revising the controversial 1980 constitution, drawn up a few months after President Chun declared martial law, were a major demand of tens of thousands of protesters who thronged city streets across the nation in June.

NEW CALEDONIA
Tension mounted in New Caledonia as the 13 September referendum on independence from France approached.

On **22 August** twenty-three people were injured, several seriously, when police with riot shields, batons and tear gas charged into a peaceful demonstration of 300 supporters of the Kanak Socialist National Liberation Front (FLNKS) sitting in the main square of Noumea. The FLNKS opposes the referendum on independence, saying it is designed to perpetuate 154 years of French rule. The clubbing of cowering Kanak men and women sitting in the square provoked criticism of the French government in Paris and abroad.

FIJI

It was reported on **27 August** that France was prepared to provide $A18.4 million ($US13 million) towards the construction of a naval base at Uduya Point, west of the Suva suburb of Lami. The offer to the interim government is believed to have been made during a visit to Fiji on **14 August** by the French Minister of State for the South Pacific, Gaston Flosse.

THAILAND

A Thai Airways 737 jet crashed into the sea off Thailand's southern island province of Phuket, killing all eighty-three people aboard, on **31 August**. The plane apparently veered off course on its final approach to the airport to avoid another aircraft.

JAPAN

After decades of debate the Japanese government was preparing itself this month for legislation lifting the ban on the contraceptive pill. The pill became available in most Western countries in the 1960s but was not introduced in Japan because of moral and medical concerns.

SEPTEMBER

PERSIAN GULF

On **1 September** Iraq rejected a US plea to stop attacking Iranian oil facilities in the Gulf. The renewed Iraqi air attacks on Gulf oil facilities continued for the fourth consecutive day, Iraq citing as its reason Iranian statements that Iran would not accept a United Nations Security Council resolution demanding a halt to the seven-year war.

Iran's Revolutionary Guards attacked a Spanish-registered oil tanker 80 kilometres north of Bahrain on **1 September** and followed with attacks on three other tankers and a cargo ship within sixteen hours.

Four Iranian sailors were killed and four wounded after a US helicopter attack set their ship ablaze, the US Defence Department announced on **22 September**. The incident marked another threshold in the steady escalation of military forces in the Gulf.

BURMA

On **1 September** Burma lifted a twenty-one-year ban on private dealing in rice, maize and other agricultural products in recognition of problems in the state-controlled food supply system. Widespread anger at a government decision to eliminate much of Burma's currency sparked the first street protests in Burma for thirteen years. On **5 September** about 1000 students from Rangoon University stoned buses on campus routes and in Mandalay, unconfirmed reports stated the house of the Home Affairs Minister was burned. The government did not disclose the reason for the demonetisation, however speculation centred on black marketeering and on counterfeiting operations by anti-government guerilla organisations.

BURUNDI

President Jean-Baptiste Bagaza of Burundi was overthrown on **3 September** by the military leadership while absent from the country attending a summit of francophone countries in Canada. Major Pierre Buyoya, the leader of the coup, was elected to succeed him on **9 September** by the newly formed Military Committee of National Salvation.

PAPUA NEW GUINEA

Papua New Guinea announced its intention to join the Non-Aligned Movement on **4 September**, as part of what officials called an 'independent commitment to international co-operation'.

TURKEY

The Turkish Prime Minister, Turgut Ozal, announced on **6 September** that a general election would be held in November. A referendum on the same day narrowly approved the early return of fifty-five former leaders banned from active politics for ten years from 1982 following political turmoil in the late 1970s which resulted in 5000 deaths. The group included former prime ministers Suleyman Demirel and Bulent Ecevit.

ARGENTINA
In mid-term elections on **6 September** the Radical Party of President Raul Alfonsin lost the majority it had maintained in the House of Deputies since taking power in 1983. The labour-based Peronist Party increased its strength in the lower house of Congress as well as winning the elections for governors in at least two-thirds of the twenty-two provinces.

CHAD
Two Libyan Tupolev bombers were shot down over the Chadian capital on **7 September**. The intended target of the bombers seemed to be either the Franco-Chadian air base near the airport or the residence of Chadian President, Hissene Habre.

ITALY
One of Italy's leading industrialists, Ferdinando Borletti, was interrogated by police on **7 September** over his role in the unauthorised sale of arms to Iran. The Borletti company owns Italy's leading business daily newspaper, *Il Sole—24 ore*.

DENMARK
Denmark's Conservative Prime Minister, Poul Schlueter, resigned on **9 September** after failing to secure a working majority in a general election.

PHILIPPINES
All twenty-six members of President Aquino's Cabinet submitted their resignations on **9 September** in order to allow her to reorganise her government. On **16 September** the Vice President, Salvador Laurel, resigned as Foreign Secretary but stayed on as Vice President in an apparent attempt to undermine President Aquino, with whom he differed over the handling of the communist insurgency.

On **17 September** President Aquino accepted the resignation of Joker Arroyo whom the military accused of being a communist sympathiser.

Leandro Alejandro, aged twenty-seven, Secretary-General of the leftwing Bayan organisation of peasants and urban poor and executive member of the Partivo Ny Bayan (People's Party) was ambushed and killed in Manila on **19 September**.

JAMAICA
The reggae star Peter Tosh was shot dead on **11 September** after he refused a demand for money by three robbers who invaded his home. A guest at the house was also killed and five others were wounded. The killing sent shock waves through Kingston, the birthplace of reggae music which Tosh had used to condemn injustice and poverty.

NEW CALEDONIA
On **13 September** the French government claimed a victory in New Caledonia's referendum on independence in which 58 per cent of registered voters turned out to vote and which was boycotted by many indigenous Kanaks. Foreign ministers from Papua New Guinea, Vanuatu and the Solomon Islands in a joint statement called for international pressure to end French rule in New Caledonia and condemned the referendum. The New Zealand Foreign Minister, Russell Marshall, said the result of the referendum had done nothing to solve the problems facing the French territory.

GREAT BRITAIN
It was revealed on **15 September** that young West German computer hacks had successfully broken into a top-secret worldwide computer network which connected National Aeronautics and Space Administration (NASA) scientific centres with their counterparts in Britain, France, Germany, Switzerland and Japan. The hackers reportedly gained access by asking NASA computers for information stored under key words such as 'shuttle', 'Challenger' and 'secret'.

UNITED STATES
An agreement signed by US Secretary of State George Schultz and Soviet Foreign Minister Eduard Shevardnadze on **16 September** provided for the establishment of special 'nuclear risk reduction centres' in each capital to exchange information on military activities. In principle, the centres would serve to generate mutual trust and to avoid crises arising from misinterpretations of each country's intentions. On **18**

September the two envoys reached a 'tentative agreement' to abolish medium- and short-range (483 km to 5471 km) nuclear missiles. However, both sides faced tough negotiations on how to reduce weapons with a range of more than 5470 kilometres, including intercontinental ballistic missiles, which are central to each side's nuclear strategy.

CANADA
Twenty-four United Nations member countries ratified an agreement on **17 September** intended to protect the earth's ozone layer by restricting production of chemicals used in aerosol sprays. Many scientists have argued that emissions of the chemicals — chlorofluorocarbons, which are inert, odourless and non-toxic compounds — must be significantly reduced in order to prevent a doubling of the predicted 'greenhouse' warming of the atmosphere caused by the burning of fossil fuels.

FRANCE
President Francois Mitterand called on **17 September** for far-reaching economic reforms in New Caledonia to end what he described as profound colonial-style inequalities in the French Pacific territory. His criticism of the right-wing government's policy in New Caledonia coincided with a visit to the territory by Prime Minister Jacques Chirac.

LEBANON
The first contingent of 800 Lebanese Druze and Communist Party fighters left Lebanon on **21 September** for Tripoli to fight in Libya's army in the Chad conflict.

FIJI
Following the announcement on **22 September** of an agreement in principle to form an interim government by representatives of both the coalition, led by Dr Timoci Bavadra, and the Alliance Party, led by Ratu Sir Kamisese Mara, a second military coup was staged by Brigadier Sitiveni Rabuka on **25 September**. The following day Rabuka stated he had reassumed executive authority over the government headed by the Governor-General Ratu Sir Penaia Ganilau. He promised swift implementation of the original coup's aims of guaranteeing ethnic Fijian control of the parliament and the country, which he said the Governor General had failed to do.

POLAND
On **27 September** Poland's leader General Jaruzelski rebuffed appeals from US Vice President George Bush for political changes sought by the banned Solidarity trade union.

CHINA
Tibetan monks on **30 September** led a march through the streets of Lhasa in protest against their Chinese rulers and in support of Tibetan independence. The demonstration was the first confirmed display of major dissent since an abortive Tibetan uprising twenty-eight years ago during which hundreds of Buddhist monks were killed and thousands were imprisoned. The protest coincided with the thirty-seventh anniversary of the Chinese military occupation of Tibet and followed the execution of three Tibetans in the previous week for alleged murder and robbery.

PERU
The Peruvian Congress approved a bill on **30 September** to allow the state to take control of private banks. The proposal to takeover ten private banks and twenty-three finance and insurance houses had dominated Peruvian politics since President Alan Garcia announced it on 28 July. The measure was designed to wrest control of private banks from Peru's wealthiest families and, in President Garcia's words, to 'democratise credit'.

OCTOBER

FIJI
Brigadier Sitiveni Rabuka announced on **1 October** that Fiji's 1970 constitution had been revoked. On **6 October** he declared Fiji to be a republic and appointed a twenty-two member interim Cabinet. Queen Elizabeth II accepted the resignation of Ratu Sir Penaia Ganilau as Governor-General on **15 September**, effectively bringing to an end Fiji's membership of the Commonwealth.

UNITED STATES
An earthquake in Los Angeles which measured 6.1 on the Richter scale left six people dead and started several fires on **1 October**. The city lies less than 50

kilometres from the San Andreas Fault where seismologists say there is a 50 per cent chance of an earthquake measuring 8.0 on the Richter scale occurring before the end of the century.

New regulations announced on **2 October** in Miami virtually grant anyone the right to carry concealed weapons and removed restrictions on carrying guns in plain view. Over 130,000 people were expected to apply for the new concealed weapons permit.

The Senate Judiciary Committee voted 9 to 5 on **6 October** against the nomination of Judge Robert Bork to the Supreme Court. Judge Bork has in the past criticised Supreme Court rulings on civil rights and privacy laws. His nomination was seen by many as an attempt by President Reagan to establish a Conservative influence that would remain within the court after Reagan had left office.

Share prices dropped US$500 billion in seven hours as the Dow Jones industrial average plummeted 508 points on **19 October**, sending shock waves through world stock markets. The 23 per cent slump in the value of the share market was almost twice the size of the crash in 1929 when a market fall of 13 per cent ushered in the Great Depression.

VANUATU

The French ambassador, Henri Crepin-Leblond, and an embassy attache were expelled from Vanuatu on **1 October** for providing substantial financial aid to the French-speaking opposition Union of Moderate Parties. Relations between Vanuatu and France had been tense since the former condominium of the New Hebrides, jointly administered by Britain and France, achieved independence in 1980.

GREAT BRITAIN

Confidential notes left by Sir Melville Macnaghten who was head of Scotland Yard detectives revealed that Jack the Ripper, the Victorian murderer who terrorised London ninety-nine years ago and was never caught, was a failed barrister and schoolmaster named Montague John Druitt. Investigators claimed on **1 October** that the Home Office knew of Druitt's activities but remained quiet because of his friendship with Queen Victoria's grandson the Duke of Clarence.

UGANDA

At least 130 hymn-singing followers of a rebel priestess were killed in attacks on Ugandan troops on **5 October**. The followers belonged to the Acholi, a northern tribe whose members headed the short-lived military government that Yoweri Museveni's National Resistance Army drove from power in Kampala in 1986.

SOUTH AFRICA

On **6 October** President P. W. Botha rejected a recommendation by his own advisory council that the law providing for segregation of public facilities should be repealed.

SWEDEN

The Swedish government announced on **6 October** that it would commence closing down its twelve nuclear reactors by 1995 as a step towards dismantling the entire network. Swedes voted in a referendum in 1980 to scrap all twelve reactors at Sweden's four nuclear power stations by the year 2010. Sweden was one of the countries worst affected by the 1986 Chernobyl disaster.

SPAIN

Spain struck a blow at the Basque separatist guerilla organisation ETA (standing for Basque Homeland and Freedom) with a Madrid court sentencing seven members to long gaol terms on **9 October**. ETA guerillas have killed nearly 600 people in their nineteen-year war for Basque independence.

IRAN

Iran said on **11 October** that it had obtained US Stinger missiles and that it was manufacturing copies of the portable anti-aircraft weapons which its forces had fired at US helicopters in the Persian Gulf. The infra-red guided missiles have a range of 8 kilometres and are designed to attack helicopters and low-flying aircraft.

TONGA

Tonga broke with the South Pacific Forum countries and recognised the Rabuka regime as the legitimate government of Fiji on **11 October**. The recognition of the Rabuka republic by Tonga came at a time when all other Forum states still recognised Fiji's

Governor-General Ratu Sir Penaia Ganilau as the legitimate head of state.

BRAZIL

Experts rushed to Brazil on **11 October** to assist in a radiation accident which was the worst of its kind in the western hemisphere. A broken capsule of caesium-137 from a discarded radiotherapy machine contaminated at least 243 people, ten of whom were in a critical condition in Goiania, 200 kilometres south-west of Brasilia. Caesium-137 was one of the lethal substances that escaped during the Chernobyl nuclear accident.

NORWAY

On **13 October** it was announced that Costa Rica's President, Oscar Arias Sanchez, had won the 1987 Nobel peace prize for his work for peace in Central America.

BURKINA FASO

The President of Burkina Faso, Captain Thomas Sankara, was overthrown in a coup led by his deputy, Captain Blaise Compaore, on **15 October**. Captain Sankara, who changed the name of the West African state from Upper Volta to Burkina Faso—'land of upright men'— was killed with another 100 people in fighting in the capital.

PERSIAN GULF

An Iranian missile strike on the US-flagged tanker *Sea Isle City* in which several Americans were injured on **16 October** was the most serious Iranian provocation against US interests in the Gulf since the United States built up its naval force in the region. In retaliation US vessels destroyed an Iranian oil rig on **19 October**. Iran struck back by firing a Silkworm missile into Kuwait's main offshore oil-loading terminal, setting it ablaze.

INDONESIA

Eighty-six people died and 305 others were injured when two packed commuter trains crashed head-on on **18 October** near the southern Jakarta suburb of Kebayoran.

SRI LANKA

On **25 October** Indian troops claimed full control of the northern town of Jaffna. The troops had been sent to enforce the Indo-Sri Lankan pact of 29 July aimed at ending four years of fighting between the island's minority Tamils and Sinhalese.

TAHITI

The French High Commissioner in Tahiti declared a state of emergency on **26 October** in the wake of confrontations between police and rioting dock workers. Hundreds of paramilitary police and Foreign Legion troops patrolled the streets of Papeete to maintain order after ten people were injured, scores of shops were smashed and burned and vehicles were gutted in clashes on **23 October** triggered by a police move to end the occupation of the port by striking workers.

NEW CALEDONIA

Kanak separatists marched peacefully through the capital of New Caledonia on **31 October** to protest against the freeing of pro-French loyalists who shot dead ten Kanaks in 1984.

CANADA

The Commonwealth Heads of Government Meeting (CHOGM) discussed principally the political question of Fiji, sanctions against South Africa and issues of world trade when it convened in Vancouver.

MALAYSIA

Sixty-three people, including the leader of the parliamentary opposition and other prominent critics of the government of Dr Mahathir Mohammed were arrested under a law allowing detention without trial. Three newspapers were also ordered to stop publishing in the wide-ranging crackdown on dissidents.

NOVEMBER

CHINA

Deng Xiaoping, 83, Li Xiannian, 82 and Peng Zhen, 85, were among more than ninety Long March generation veterans who retired from the Central Committee of the Communist Party on **1 November**. On **2 November** China's Premier, Zhao Ziyang, formally became the party's most powerful official as general secretary. Deng Xiaoping would continue to be regarded as China's 'paramount leader' despite retiring from his party posts.

SYRIA

Alois Brunner, one of the most notorious

Nazi war criminals still at large, stated on **1 November** that he regretted nothing he did in World War II and would do it all over again. Brunner, aged seventy-five, lives in Damascus where he is protected by the Syrian government in exchange for service to Syria in 'security matters'.

USSR
On **2 November**, in an historic marathon speech to 5800 Communist Party delegates and the nation, live on television, Mikhail Gorbachev conceded that Josef Stalin had been responsible for 'gross political mistakes' and announced that a new commission had been established to study rehabilitation of the dictator's victims. Dr Andrei Sakharov, in an unprecedented interview published in Moscow on **4 November** said 'the whole terrible truth about the rule of Josef Stalin remained to be told'.

WEST GERMANY
Demonstrators protesting against Frankfurt Airport's controversial third runway shot dead two policemen and injured nine others on **2 November** in the worst incident of its kind reported in post-war West Germany.

UNITED STATES
On **5 November** Caspar Weinberger became the third Cabinet member to resign in the past month and the sixth member of the Reagan administration to leave office in twelve months. Weinberger had often counterbalanced the advice of key administration moderates, including Secretary of State George Schultz and White House Chief of Staff Howard Baker. He was replaced by the National Security Adviser, Frank Carlucci.

On **7 November** President Reagan suffered yet another blow as his second nominee to the Supreme Court withdrew after admitting he had smoked marijuana. On **15 November** a Continental Airlines DC-10 jet flipped over and tore into three pieces while taking off in a blinding snowstorm in Denver, Colorado, killing twenty-six of the eighty-one people aboard.

The Congressional report on the Iran-Contra scandal released on **18 November** questioned President Reagan's denial of prior knowledge of the affair and was trenchantly critical of him. The report added little that was not already in the public domain.

MURUROA ATOLL
Trade union officials announced on **5 November** that Polynesian workers at France's most highly guarded defence site had staged at least two strikes in the previous fortnight to protest about working conditions.

SOUTH AFRICA
The unconditional release on **6 November** of Govan Mbeki, a stalwart of the outlawed African National Congress (ANC), raised hopes that South Africa would also release the ANC leader Nelson Mandela. Govan Mbeki, aged seventy-seven, a former national chairman of the ANC and leading member of the South African Communist Party, had been gaoled for life for sabotage with Nelson Mandela and six co-saboteurs at the Rivonia trial in 1964.

JAPAN
Yasuhiro Nakasone retired as Prime Minister on **6 November** and was succeeded by Noboru Takeshita.

TUNISIA
The Tunisian Prime Minister, Zine Abidine Benali, took power in Tunisia on **7 November** on the grounds that Habib Bourguiba, President for life, was too ill and senile to govern any longer. Mr Bourguiba had ruled for thirty-one years, since independence was gained from France.

PAPUA NEW GUINEA
Mr Ted Diro, the former commander of the Papua New Guinea Defence Force, resigned from Cabinet on **8 November** after it was revealed that Indonesia's armed forces commander General Benny Murdani had contributed $A203,000 to campaign funds of the People's Action Party headed by Mr Diro.

SRI LANKA
Troops sealed off parliament and armoured cars patrolled Colombo's streets after a bomb blast in a suburb in the capital on **9 November** killed at least thirty-two people and wounded 106. Police suspected the outlawed Marxist group Janatha Vimukthi Peramuna (People's Liberation Front) was responsible for the blast.

BANGLADESH
President Hossain Mohammad Ershad proclaimed a state of emergency and strict press restrictions during a fortnight of strikes and often violent demonstrations. The opposition accused President Ershad of election-rigging, oppression and corruption and said arrests would not stop its campaign. On **11 November** Sheikh Hasina, leader of the main opposition, the Awami League, and Begum Zia, head of the Bangladesh Nationalist Party, were arrested by police.

ITALY
The fifteen-week-old government of Prime Minister Giovanni Goria resigned on **14 November** after the Liberal Party withdrew from the governing coalition in a dispute over measures to reduce the huge budget deficit. Italy has the largest official budget deficit in proportion to the size of its economy of any major Western nation.

ROMANIA
Several thousand rioting workers ransacked the city hall in the industrial city of Brasov on **16 November** in the first major industrial violence since coalminers went on strike ten years ago.

GREAT BRITAIN
Terrified commuters were carried screaming to their deaths as an escalator descended into a fire in Kings Cross tube station in London on **18 November**. The worst fire in the history of the London Underground, which killed thirty-four people and injured more than twenty, started in a machine room under a wooden escalator on the Piccadilly line.

NICARAGUA
On **22 November** in an act described as part of a regional peace plan, the Nicaraguan government released 985 pardoned political prisoners in what was by far the largest single-day release in eight years of Sandinista rule. All had been pardoned on 5 November by President Daniel Ortega in a speech marking ninety days since the signing of a peace accord on 7 August by five Central American countries—Costa Rica, El Salvador, Guatemala, Honduras and Nicaragua—in Guatemala City.

SWITZERLAND
On **25 November** the United States and the Soviet Union announced that they had resolved their differences over a treaty banning medium- and short-range nuclear missiles and that signing of the treaty in Washington would proceed in a fortnight.

ISRAEL
Arab guerillas landed in a light aircraft just outside an Israeli army base in northern Israel on **25 November** and killed six Israeli soldiers before being shot dead. The Popular Front for the Liberation of Palestine-General Command (PFLP-GC), a pro-Syrian Palestinian guerilla group, claimed responsibility for the assault.

PHILIPPINES
Right-wing opponents of President Aquino joined forces under one party to challenge her ruling coalition in local elections in January. The newly unified party included Senator Juan Ponce Enrile, Marcos's former Foreign Minister, Aturo Tolentino and former Aquino allies who defected to the opposition.

On **27 November** 361 people were killed when Typhoon Nina roared across the Philippines, 275 of them swept to their deaths by a giant tidal wave that smashed into a coastal town. Nearly 90,000 people had been made homeless.

MEXICO
The presidents of eight Latin-American countries agreed on **28 November** that Cuba should be invited to rejoin regional organisations from which it was expelled more than two decades ago. The decision was made at a summit conference in Mexico, the first held without the participation of the United States.

SOUTH KOREA
In the worst outbreak of violence yet in South Korea's presidential campaign the ruling party candidate Roh Tae Woo was pelted with rocks, eggs, and tear gas cannisters on **29 November** as he faced hostile crowds in Kwangju.

HAITI
Elections scheduled for **29 November** were cancelled after at least twenty-seven people had died during widespread political violence, allegedly instigated by supporters of former President Jean-Claude Duvalier. The election was to have been the first round in a process to produce a civilian president and

legislature by February. Haiti's military government announced that elections were now to be held in January.

VANUATU
Prime Minister Father Walter Lini and his Vanua'aku Party were re-elected on **30 November** after the second election since Vanuatu achieved independence in 1980.

THAILAND
What appeared to be the wreckage of a South Korean airliner carrying 115 people which disappeared on 29 November was found on **30 November** close to a remote Thai village near the Burmese border. KAL flight 858, en route from Baghdad to Seoul, had been scheduled to refuel in Bangkok but contact was lost with the plane after it made a routine report to the control tower in Rangoon.

TURKEY
Turkey's pro-Western Prime Minister, Turgut Ozal, and his Motherland Party won a general election on **30 November** in the country's most open election for a decade. Mr Ozal had campaigned on a record of political calm and economic liberalisation since taking office in 1983, three years after a military coup which crushed extremist violence.

DECEMBER

FRANCE
American author James Baldwin, aged sixty-three, died in the south of France from stomach cancer on **1 December**. In his novels and essays Baldwin angrily portrayed the suffering of his fellow black Americans. His first novel, *Go Tell It on the Mountain*, was published in 1953.

On **4 December** the Kampuchean resistance leader, Prince Norodom Sihanouk, and the Prime Minister of Kampuchea, Hun Sen, signed a four-point agreement aimed at accelerating efforts to end nine years of civil war in Kampuchea. It was the first indication that Phnom Penh's Vietnamese-installed government was ready to negotiate with the Chinese-backed Khmer Rouge, ousted by Vietnam in 1978 and blamed for hundreds of thousands of deaths.

UNITED STATES
The Indian government filed criminal charges, including culpable homicide, on **2 December** against Union Carbide Corporation for the 1984 gas leak in Bhopal that killed 2800 people. The government acted as public opinion in India became aroused by an anticipated civil settlement with Union Carbide that many considered to be unfair to the accident victims.

Cuban inmates in Atlanta freed their eighty-nine hostages on **4 December** and peacefully ended an eleven-day prison uprising under an agreement providing for a moratorium on the deportations of 3800 detainees held in the United States. The seige, one of the longest prison revolts in US history, left one prisoner dead and three buildings gutted.

The Soviet leader, Mikhail Gorbachev, arrived in Washington on **7 December** and immediately challenged President Reagan to offer 'some new words' that would lead to a treaty dramatically reducing the Soviet and US strategic nuclear arsenals. A treaty eliminating both countries' land-based medium- and short-range nuclear missiles was signed by the leaders on **7 December**.

The US administration was angered when France made a $US330 million ($A470 million) payment on a thirteen-year debt to Iran as part of an apparent deal leading to the release of two Fench hostages in Beirut.

CANADA
It was announced on **4 December** that under new Canadian laws tobacco advertisements were to be banned from newspapers as of New Year's Day. Also, from 1 January 1989, all tobacco advertising on billboards and magazines and sponsorship of televised or non-televised sports and cultural events would cease.

DENMARK
A European Community summit meeting collapsed in disagreement on **6 December** as leaders failed for the second time in 1987 to adopt a financial package to avert bankruptcy in the next five years. The meeting broke down as several shifting factions fought over the extent of EC cuts in agricultural subsidies, increases in aid to the EC's poorer members and how to decide each member's contribution to the EC budget.

SOUTH AFRICA

It was reported on **6 December** that South Africa had commenced troop withdrawals from southern Angola where it had been helping pro-Western rebels in a civil war against government forces backed by Cuba. South Africa has provided covert military and logistic support to the Union for the Total Independence of Angola (UNITA), led by Dr Jonas Savimbi, throughout its seven-year war with the government in Luanda.

PERSIAN GULF

On **7 December** an Iranian gunboat fired rocket-propelled grenades into the Singapore-flagged *Norman Atlantic*, setting it ablaze at the entrance to the Gulf. The Danish-flagged tanker *Estelle Maersk* was hit, possibly by the same boat, in the southern Gulf.

BANGLADESH

In an effort to seek reconciliation with his opponents President Hossain Mohammad Ershad stated on **8 December** his intention to lift the state of emergency. An eight-hour general strike called by opposition parties in a new attempt to topple the President on **29 December** was the sixteenth since the opposition began a united campaign on 10 November to force the President to resign.

NICARAGUA

Nicaragua announced on **8 December** that an American pilot flying a Cessna 172 had been shot down over Nicaragua on 6 December while 'engaging in enemy activity against our country'. James Jordon Denby was in custody and being interrogated in Managua.

ISRAEL

Israel held more than 1000 Palestinians arrested since a wave of violent disturbances began in the occupied West Bank and Gaza Strip on **9 December**. Twenty-two people had been killed and over 170 wounded, many seriously, during the two weeks of riots which UN officials said were the worst since Israel's occupation of the areas in 1967. Israel drew condemnation from around the world for its handling of the disturbances.

FIJI

Almost half of Fiji's new Cabinet announced on **9 December** by the Prime Minister, Ratu Sir Kamisese Mara, consisted of ministers of the former Rabuka military government.

PHILIPPINES

Colonel Gregorio Honasan, who led an August coup attempt, was captured on **9 December** in a Manila townhouse. He offered no resistance and no shots were fired.

More than 2000 people were feared dead after a ferry crammed with Christmas travellers sank in flames on **20 December** in what was perhaps the worst peacetime shipping disaster. The 2215 tonne ferry *Dona Paz* collided with the Philippines tanker *Victor* in darkness off Mindoro Island, 170 kilometres south of Manila.

USSR

The Soviet leader, Mikhail Gorbachev, speaking to the nation on **14 December** about his talks in Washington with President Reagan, said that important differences over US plans for a space-based missile defence system still divided their two governments.

SOUTH KOREA

South Korea went to the polls on **16 December** amid numerous reports of voting irregularities in the first presidential election since 1971. After the announcement of the victory of the government candidate, Roh Tae Woo, more than 2000 demonstrators clashed with police in Kwangju on 17 December. Opposition leaders called for nationwide protests to prevent Roh taking power, accusing the government of massive fraud.

South Korea said it would cease talks with North Korea on sharing the 1988 Olympic Games if Pyongyang proved to be implicated in the crash of a Korean Air Line Boeing 707 which vanished from radar screens on 29 November over Burma.

PAPUA NEW GUINEA

The commander of Papua New Guinea's Defence Force, Brigadier-General Tony Huai, was dismissed on **17 December** following his alleged leaking of details of bilateral defence negotiations with Australia to the Indonesian military.

CZECHOSLOVAKIA

President Gustav Husak stepped down as Communist Party leader on **17**

December. He was succeeded by a staunch ally in the policy-making presidium, Milos Jakes.

NEW CALEDONIA
Police fired tear gas at protesters in the Loyalty Islands. The protesters threw incendiary devices at police and tried to block roads and a runway after the arrest of the Melanesian separatist leader Mr Yeiwene Yeiwene on **25 December**. Mr Yeiwene was released on 28 December when an appeals court rejected his detention on charges of inciting to murder.

HARARE
Zimbabwe marked the beginning of a new political era on **31 December** with the swearing in of former guerilla leader Robert Mugabe as its first executive President. Mr Mugabe, who had been Prime Minister since 1980, said the change would mark the end of the 'constitutional shackles from Britain'.

1988

JANUARY

ISRAEL
After a week of relative calm protests flared again in the West Bank and Gaza Strip coinciding with the anniversary of Fatah, the Palestinian Liberation Organisation's main guerilla group, on **1 January**. On **6 January** Israel deplored a United Nations resolution condemning its handling of disturbances in the occupied territories.

A diplomatic rift occurred between Israel and Britain over remarks made by David Mellor, Minister of State for Foreign Affairs, on a visit to a Palestinian refugee settlement. Mr Mellor denounced conditions in the camp as an 'affront to civilised values' and warned Israel it could not continue to ignore the plight of Palestinians living under Israeli occupation.

UNITED STATES
On **2 January** President Reagan and Canadian Prime Minister Brian Mulroney signed a landmark agreement whereby all tariffs on bilateral trade would be eliminated within ten years and non-tariff trade barriers between the world's two largest trading partners would be reduced.

A group of private scientists reported on **16 January** that the United States had concealed 117 nuclear explosions at its underground test site in the Nevada desert over the past twenty-five years. The tests constitute 20 per cent of all American nuclear explosions in that period.

According to an annual study released in Washington by a former economic chief of the US Arms Control Agency, the nations of the world spent almost $US1.8 million ($A2.6 million) per minute in 1987 on their military forces.

INDONESIA
President Suharto announced on **5 January** increased spending on the controversial mass resettlement scheme needed to ease overcrowding on Java where 100 million people live, and to develop the other main islands of Sumatra, Borneo, and Celebes as well as Irian Jaya.

GREAT BRITAIN
Trevor Howard, the stalwart British actor, died in his sleep in a London hospital on **7 January** after suffering influenza complicated by jaundice. He was seventy-one. Howard's films included *Brief Encounter, Mutiny on the Bounty, Sons and Lovers* and *Gandhi*.

CANADA
On **11 January** a Canadian Indian couple were considering a lawsuit against the Canadian government after airport security guards put their infant daughter through an X-ray scanner prior to boarding their flight.

KUWAIT
A diplomatic row broke out on **11 January** between Egypt and Israel when the Egyptian leader, Mr Mubarak, while on a tour of the Gulf States, accused Israel of breaching the 1978 Camp David peace accords. Egypt has repeatedly denounced Israel's management of the unrest in the occupied territories.

NORTH KOREA
North Korea announced on **11 January**

that it would not attend the Seoul Olympic Games only hours after the Soviet Union said it would take part.

TAIWAN
The President of Taiwan, Chiang Ching-kuo, aged seventy-seven, died on **12 January**. Mr Chiang inherited the leadership from Generalissimo Chiang Kai-shek, his father, and had been responsible for relaxing some long-standing Nationalist Party policies regarding China, including restrictions on travel by residents of Taiwan to China.

IRAQ
The leader of the Palestinian Liberation Organisation (PLO), Yasser Arafat, said on **14 January** that he would recognise Israel's right to exist if Israel and the United States agreed to an international conference on Middle East peace. The PLO has traditionally refused to recognise Israel's right to exist and Israel has for years refused to negotiate with the PLO.

USSR
The Soviet Politburo disclosed on **14 January** that the 1986 Chernobyl nuclear disaster had cost the Soviet Union almost $US14 billion ($A20 billion).

Soviet cosmonaut Yuri Romanenko, who set an endurance record by staying in orbit for 326 days in 1987, said on **20 January** that he saw no limit to how long humans could stay in space.

SOUTH KOREA
Hours after announcing on **15 January** that it was holding North Korea responsible for the loss of the Korean Air Lines plane in November, the South Korean government placed the country's 600,000 troops on full alert and ordered all officers to their stations. 'All forms of retaliation' against North Korea were discussed at a meeting of military chiefs called by the Defence Minister, Mr Chung Ho Yong. A self-avowed North Korean female agent was put on television to confess to the bombing of KAL flight 858.

HAITI
Diplomatic sources reported that more than 90 per cent of Haiti's registered voters stayed away from the polls on **17 January** in an opposition-organised boycott of the presidential election. The election, postponed from November after widespread violence, was called by Haiti's military junta to choose a civilian president. On **24 January** the government appointed electoral council declared Mr Leslie Manigat, aged fifty-seven, Haiti's next President.

PAPUA NEW GUINEA
On **18 January** Prime Minister Wingti conducted his first state visit to Indonesia and issued a public denial of having any common ground with Melanesian 'freedom fighters' of the adjoining Indonesian province of Irian Jaya. He drew strong protest from their supporters in Papua New Guinea.

ARGENTINA
On **19 January** Argentina's President Raul Alfonsin crushed the second military rebellion in a year, using force of arms to restore authority. Afterwards he stated his intention to purge the army of extremist middle-ranking officers who opposed charges of human rights abuses directed at the military.

LEBANON
As Shi'ite Muslim Amal forces ended their seige on **21 January**, Palestinians from two refugee camps became free for the first time in three years.

COLOMBIA
Colombia's Attorney-General was kidnapped and shot dead on **25 January** on his way to the airport at Medellin. In a communique the kidnappers declared 'total war' against Colombians who supported the extradition of Colombian citizens to the United States to face drug-trafficking charges. The government responded by announcing wide-ranging 'anti- terrorist' measures.

POLAND
The Polish government announced sweeping price rises on **30 January**, including a 40 per cent rise in retail food prices. Rail fares were to rise by 50 per cent and petrol by 60 per cent. The government said the increases were crucial to 'limit state subsidies and to accelerate the transition to a market economy'. In protest at the rises a crowd marched on Communist Party headquarters in Gdansk.

INDIA
The Indian Prime Minister, Mr Rajiv Gandhi, dissolved the government of the

southern state of Tamil Nadu on **31 January** after violent brawling on the floor of the State Assembly had to be broken up by police. The fighting was a consequence of the political turmoil resulting from the death on 24 December of Mr M. G. Ramachandran, a former film star who had been Chief Minister for the past decade.

FEBRUARY

INDONESIA
According to the French Secretary of State for Defence, Jacques Boyon, who was visiting Indonesia on **1 February**, France was offering to sell Indonesia naval frigates and MM-30 and MM-40 sea-to-sea missiles and had expressed a wish to conduct joint naval exercises.

PAPUA NEW GUINEA
Sacked defence force commander Brigadier-General Tony Huai said on **1 February** that Papua New Guinea's new defence pact with Australia was a 'thorn' in PNG's relations with Indonesia.

ZAMBIA
The President of Zambia, Kenneth Kuanda, opened the two-day Commonwealth Foreign Minister's meeting on **1 February** by denouncing South Africa's regional aggression and criticising countries such as Britain which reject demands for stronger sanctions.

NEW ZEALAND
A political crisis within the New Zealand government ended on **1 February** with Prime Minister David Lange and his Finance Minister, Roger Douglas, agreeing to proceed with the introduction of a flat income tax rate and other sweeping economic reforms.

ANGOLA
On **2 February** Angola's Marxist government for the first time agreed that Cuban troops had to leave Angolan territory as part of a regional peace settlement.

FINLAND
President Mauno Koivisto was assured of a new six-year term on **2 February**. The result was seen as an endorsement of his 'political stability' campaign theme.

PHILIPPINES
The 10,000 winners in Manila's local elections on 18 January took office on **2 February**. The ceremonies around the country marked the first time in fifteen years that the country was to be governed at the provincial and town levels by people chosen in free elections.

UNITED STATES
The House of Representatives narrowly defeated President Reagan's aid package for the Nicaraguan Contra rebels on **3 February**. The defeat followed last-minute lobbying by Secretary of State George Schultz in favour of the $US43 million aid request. The Contras stated afterwards that they would fight on to overthrow the Sandinista government despite the vote.

A federal grand jury indicted the Panamanian leader, General Antonio Noriega, on **5 February** on charges of aiding international cocaine traffickers. President Reagan's last budget presented to Congress on **18 February** made massive cuts in defence spending and optimistic projections for the US economy. Meanwhile, the US Defence Department added China to its list of nations hostile to the United States. The move was prompted by Pentagon charges that Beijing had sold Silkworm missiles to Iran.

GREAT BRITAIN
It was revealed on **3 February** that John Lennon's assassin, Mark Chapman, told investigators he was playing out the role of Holden Caulfield when he murdered the musician on 8 December 1980. Caulfield is the hero of *The Catcher in the Rye*, J. D. Salinger's classic 1951 novel about adolescence.

AFGHANISTAN
After nine years of vicious guerilla warfare which devastated Afghanistan and cost more than a million lives, Afghan rebels were sceptical of Soviet intentions following Moscow's announcement on **9 February** that it could withdraw its troops in ten months starting on 15 May.

ANTARCTICA
It was reported on **9 February** that an iceberg, 144 kilometres long and 32 kilometres wide, known as 'B9', was drifting slowly towards shipping lanes after breaking off from the Ross Ice Shelf in October.

EGYPT

On **10 February** two limestone slabs with a combined weight of about 320 kilograms fell from the right shoulder of the Sphinx. The Sphinx, 20 metres high and more than 70 metres long, was built around 2600 BC. A rising water table is eroding the Sphinx's limestone and recent rains and sandstorms had battered its surface.

PARAGUAY

General Alfredo Stroessner's Colorado Party claimed on **14 February** a victory in Paraguayan elections which were marred by widespread claims of electoral fraud. General Stroessner, Paraguay's President for thirty-three years, won another five-year term.

BELGIUM

On **14 February** the twelve nation European Community approved a financial package, ending months of financial crisis, after major concessions were made by Britain. The agreement to control the community's agricultural surplus meant that virtual bankruptcy for the trade bloc in 1989 was averted.

THAILAND

In what was perhaps the world's biggest heroin seizure, authorities said on **14 February** that they had intercepted 1.4 tonnes of no. 4 grade heroin at Klong Toey Port on a freighter bound for New York.

After months of fighting an undeclared border war that claimed hundreds of casualties on both sides, Thailand and Laos agreed to a cease-fire and a withdrawal of troops from the disputed area on **17 February**.

BRAZIL

A savage tropical storm hit Rio de Janiero on **21 February** causing floods and rockslides that killed at least 251 people and left several thousand injured or homeless.

NAMIBIA

South African aircraft attacked guerilla bases in Angola on **21 February** in retaliation for a bomb blast which killed eighteen people in the Pretoria-run territory of Namibia.

CYPRUS

Mr George Vassiliou, aged fifty-six, became President of Cyprus on **22 February**. The separation of Cyprus was the dominant issue in the election campaign. Cyprus has been divided since Turkish troops occupied the northern third of the island after a short-lived coup in Nicosia backed by the military junta ruling Greece at the time.

ISRAEL

Palestinians continued to protest and be killed under Israeli occupation on the West Bank where military authorities in early February closed all educational institutions. On **23 February** the Israeli Attorney-General, Yosef Harish, announced that Israeli troops were to be given strict guidelines prohibiting the use of force against Palestinians. His remarks reflected the widespread unease in Israel over measures used to suppress the Palestinian uprising, in which at least sixty Arabs had been killed.

NEW CALEDONIA

On **23 February** New Caledonia separatists released unharmed nine Paris-based gendarmes whom they had held hostage for more than twelve hours. Three gendarmes were in a serious condition after about 100 Melanesians wielding sticks ambushed a squad of approximately fifty policemen guarding a remote hospital building site claimed as tribal ground.

PANAMA

President Eric Arturo Delvalle, speaking on television, ordered the dismissal of the de facto leader, General Manuel Noriega, on **25 February**. General Noriega responded by sending troops to surround the President's home and the American Embassy. On **26 February** the President was ousted and Noriega installed Manuel Solis Palma. The whereabouts of President Delvalle were unknown.

NAURU

The tiny Pacific island of Nauru established diplomatic relations with the Soviet Union but President Hammer DeRoburt said his country would remain non-aligned.

MARCH

USSR

On **1 March** Soviet troops and tanks were sent to Sumgait in Azerbaijan, the republic bordering Armenia, to restore order after people were injured in violent anti-Armenian demonstrations. The reported violence followed deaths of two Azerbaijanis in large-scale clashes with Armenians in the previous week in Nagorny Karanakh, a disputed border region which Armenians want returned.

INDONESIA
Mr Sudharmono, chairman of the ruling Golka Party and one of President Suharto's most trusted allies, was named the party's vice-president on **2 March**. President Suharto took the oath of office before the 1000-member National Assembly on **11 March** for his fifth consecutive term.

NASA reported on **30 March** that Indonesia had launched three experimental solid fuel rockets and had hopes of putting a satellite in orbit by the year 1993.

GIBRALTAR
On **6 March** British undercover police shot dead three suspected Irish Republican Army guerillas after they left a parked car thought to be containing an explosive device.

AUSTRIA
The Austrian President, Dr Kurt Waldheim, publicly apologised on behalf of his country on **10 March** for Nazi crimes committed by Austrians.

SWITZERLAND
The heir to the British throne, Prince Charles, escaped death by a few metres in an avalanche in the Swiss Alps on **10 March**. He helped dig out the body of Major Hugh Lindsay, a former equerry to the Queen and a close personal friend, who was killed instantly.

NEPAL
In the worst such incident in Nepal for decades, sixty-nine people died and ninety-seven were injured on **12 March** during a stampede at a football match at the national stadium. The tragedy occurred as people rushed for exits in panic when a violent hailstorm hit the largely uncovered stadium.

SPRATLY ISLANDS
On **14 March** Chinese and Vietnamese forces clashed in the disputed Spratly Islands in the South China Sea. Both countries are determined to exercise their territorial claims over the islands, which are also claimed by Taiwan, Brunei, the Philippines and Malaysia.

PANAMA
Dock workers went on strike at Panama's three major ports on **14 March** after the cash-starved government of General Noriega failed to pay them. Panama had been moving towards economic collapse since 3 March when the government ordered all banks to close because of a cash flow crisis. Shop-owners kept their stores closed on **29 March**, the ninth day of a general strike, despite a violent crackdown by troops against opponents of the government on 28 March. Also on **29 March** the Roman Catholic Church called for the resignation of General Noriega.

GREAT BRITAIN
Three people were killed and dozens injured in Belfast on **16 March** when a man threw grenades into a huge funeral crowd and then fled from the enraged mourners. Thousands of people had gathered to bury three IRA guerillas who were killed on 6 March by British undercover agents in Gibraltar.

UNITED STATES
Lieutenant-Colonel Oliver North, Rear-Admiral John Poindexter and two key participants in the Iran-Contra affair were indicted on **16 March** on charges of conspiracy to defraud the United States government by allegedly providing Nicaraguan rebels with profits from the sale of American weapons to Iran. On **17 March** President Reagan ordered the deployment of four battalions of troops (about 3200 men) to Honduras as a sign of support for their government amid accusations in Congress that the administration had manufactured a crisis to distract public attention from the Iran-Contra scandal.

On **23 March** the President announced that he would visit Moscow from 29 May to 2 June for his fourth meeting with Soviet leader Mikhail Gorbachev. It will be the first time a US President has been to Moscow for fourteen years.

BURMA
On **17 March** troops fired tear gas to quell student protests sparked by the death of a student who was shot during earlier unrest.

A fire devastated the remote Burmese town of Lahio on **22 March**, killing 113 people and making 20,000 homeless.

SOUTH AFRICA
The Pretoria Supreme Court on **18 March** ordered a postponement of the execution of six black South Africans due to be hanged at dawn the next day. The six were to have been executed because the Supreme Court found they had 'common purpose' with a mob which stoned and burnt a Sharpeville town councillor. There was no evidence they had been responsible for the actual killing.

Tens of thousands of black workers staged a national one-day strike on **21 March** to commemorate the twenty-eighth anniversary of the Sharpeville Massacre when sixty-nine protesters were killed by police.

NICARAGUA
Honduran Air Force jets bombed suspected troop positions on **20 March** for the second time in three days. The bombing took place in the border region where Sandinista government troops had been attacking US-backed Contra rebels. A peace accord between the Sandinista government and Contra rebels was signed by President Daniel Ortega and the Contra leader, Adolfo Calero, on **23 March**. A sixty-day cease-fire was to be declared on 1 April. The signing ceremony was the biggest advance in efforts to pacify Central America and was unprecedented in Nicaragua's turbulent political history.

HUNGARY
More than 10,000 people chanting 'democracy' marched through Budapest on **22 March** in Hungary's largest independent demonstration since the anti-communist uprising of 1956. Police did not obstruct the marchers, many of whom were wearing cockades in the Hungarian national colours.

CHINA
China announced on **22 March** that as many as 300,000 people in the city of Shanghai had contracted hepatitis since January. The epidemic was caused by contaminated hairy clams, which 90 per cent of sufferers were said to have eaten.

ISRAEL
After talks in Washington the Israeli Prime Minister, Yitzhak Shamir, on **22 March** refused to countenance proposals by US Secretary of State George Schultz for resuming peace efforts. In the three months of unrest in the Gaza Strip and the West Bank, over 100 Palestinians had died at the hands of Israeli soldiers and settlers.

MOZAMBIQUE
Australian missionary Ian Grey was sentenced to ten years imprisonment for aiding the rebel Mozambican National Resistance on **23 March**. Grey was acquitted of espionage by Mozambique's Revolutionary Military Tribunal but was convicted on charges of illegal association with a clandestine organisation, encouraging people to commit crimes against the state, illegal entry and inciting rebellion.

BANGLADESH
Bangladeshi opposition leaders dismissed President Hossain Mohammad Ershad's Cabinet re-shuffle on **27 March** as a cosmetic exercise, saying it would not cause any major political or administrative changes sought by the opposition groups. The opposition parties demanded that the President resign by 8 April or face an indefinite general strike.

COLOMBIA
Colombia's acting Attorney-General, Alfredo Gutierrez Marquez, resigned on **28 March** after the revelation of his family's dealings with the Medellin Cartel cocaine smuggling ring.

SOUTH KOREA
The brother of the former South Korean President, Chun Doo Hwan, was summoned for questioning on **28 March** on allegations involving the embezzlement of millions of dollars from government programs.

PHILIPPINES
On **30 March** Philippine troops captured the commander-in-chief of the communist rebel army in a raid on a hideout in Manila. The New People's Army leader, Romulo Kintanar, was one of the country's most wanted guerillas.

M. N.

Part Two
SPORT

ABC SPORTS AWARD

The ABC Sports Award (formerly known as the ABC Sportsman of the Year Award) is Australia's oldest and still most respected sporting honour. The name change to the ABC Sports Award was made in 1983, partly to avoid possible charges of discrimination by female sporting organisations and partly to overcome the problem of a team winning the award. In 1980 the Confederation of Australian Sport launched the Sport Australia Awards and introduced separate awards for the male athlete of the year, female athlete of the year and the team of the year and other awards for such categories as the junior male and female athletes of the year, best junior team, administrator of the year and coach of the year.

ABC SPORTS AWARD WINNERS

Year	Winner
1951	Frank Sedgman (Vic.) Tennis
1952	Marjorie Jackson (now Nelson) (NSW) Athletics
1953	Jimmy Carruthers (NSW) Boxing
1954	John Landy (Vic.) Athletics
1955	Peter Thomson (Vic.) Golf
1956	Betty Cuthbert (NSW) Athletics
1957	Stuart Mackenzie (NSW) Sculling
1958	Herb Elliott (Vic.) Athletics
1959	Jack Brabham (now Sir John) (NSW) Motor Racing
1960	Herb Elliott (Vic.) Athletics
1961	Richie Benaud (NSW) Cricket
1962	Dawn Fraser (NSW) Swimming
1963	Margaret Smith (now Court) (WA) Tennis
1964	Dawn Fraser (NSW) Swimming
1965	Ron Clarke (Vic.) Athletics
1966	Jack Brabham (NSW) Motor Racing
1967	Heather McKay (ACT) Squash
1968	Lionel Rose (Vic.) Boxing
1969	Rod Laver (Qld) Tennis
1970	Margaret Court (WA) Tennis
1971	Shane Gould (NSW) Swimming
1972	Shane Gould (NSW) Swimming
1973	Stephen Holland (Qld) Swimming
1974	Raelene Boyle (Vic.) Athletics
1975	Bart Cummings (SA) Horse Racing
1976	Greg Chappell (SA) Cricket
1977	Graham Marsh (WA) Golf
1978	Tracey Wickham (Qld) Swimming
1979	David Graham (NSW) Golf
1980	Alan Jones (Vic.) Motor Racing
1981	Geoff Hunt (Vic.) Squash
1982	Robert de Castella (Vic.) Athletics
1983	Robert de Castella (Vic.) Athletics
1984	Jon Sieben (Qld) Swimming
1985	Jeff Fenech (NSW) Boxing

Year	Winner
1986	Greg Norman (Qld) Golf
1987	Wayne Gardner (NSW) Motor Cycling

SPORT AUSTRALIA AWARDS (Major)

Male Athlete of the Year

Year	Winner
1980	Alan Jones (Vic.) Motor Racing
1981	Geoff Hunt (Vic.) Squash
1982	Robert de Castella (Vic.) Athletics
1983	Robert de Castella (Vic.) Athletics
1984	Jon Sieben (Qld) Swimming
1985	Jeff Fenech (NSW) Boxing
1986	Greg Norman (Qld) Golf
1987	Wayne Gardner (NSW) Motor Cycling

Female Athlete of the Year

Year	Winner
1980	Michelle Ford (NSW) Swimming
1981	Vicki Hoffman (SA) Squash
1982	Lisa Curry (Qld) Swimming
1983	Jan Stephenson (NSW) Golf
1984	Glynis Nunn (SA) Athletics
1985	Adair Ferguson (Qld) Sculling
1986	Debbie Flintoff (Vic.) Athletics
1987	Kerry Saxby (Vic.) Athletics

Team of the Year

Year	Winner
1980	Australian Men's 4 x 100 m Medley Relay (Swimming)
1981	Australian Men's Hockey Team
1982	National Youth Soccer Team
1983	Crew, Australia II (Yachting)
1984	Australian 400 m pursuit team (Cycling)
1985	Australian Rugby Union Team
1986	Australian eight-oar crew (Rowing)
1987	Australian Men's Hockey Team

AUSTRALIAN FOOTBALL

BEGINNINGS IN AUSTRALIA

Australian Football (previously known as 'Australian Rules Football') had its beginnings in Ballarat, Victoria, in the 1840s, when Irish miners in the goldfields played Gaelic football in their spare time. Evidence exists that by 1853, the miners had streamlined the Gaelic rules and placed more accent on passing skills. Matches were played purely on a social basis, but news of the 'new' football game trickled into Sydney and Melbourne and began to arouse interest.

First organisers:

Thomas Wentworth Wills (b. Molonglo, near Canberra, 1835) and his cousin, Henry Colden Harrison. Wills, a top cricketer, had been Captain of Rugby School in England and had played cricket for Kent, UK. When he returned to Australia in 1856 he asked Harrison to help him devise a new code of football, to enable cricketers to maintain their fitness in the winter months. Harrison (later to become Secretary of the Melbourne Cricket Club) and Wills studied the football developments on the Ballarat goldfields, borrowed the new rules and added a touch of hurling to formulate their game.

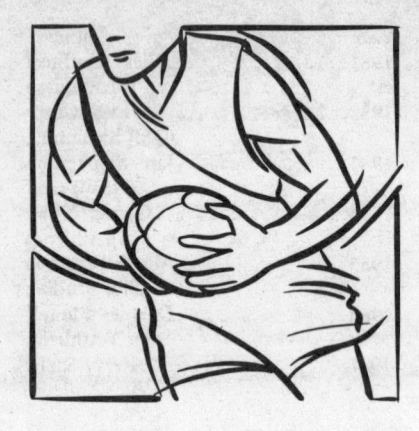

First match in Australia:
Discounting the early matches at Ballarat, the first game staged by Wills and Harrison was between Scotch College and Melbourne Grammar School at Yarra Park, Melbourne, Vic., on 7 August 1858. Both teams fielded 40 players on a paddock more than 1.6 km in length, with one set of posts on Jolimont Hill (close to the future site of VFL headquarters) and the other at Punt Road, Richmond. The first game was something of a farce, with players making up the rules as they went and no field umpire or referee present. The game lasted from noon to dusk and Scotch scored the only goal. A fortnight later the two schools played again (this time Melbourne Grammar scored the only goal) and in a third game a week later, no goals were scored. A year later, the two teams met again, and this time Scotch scored a goal and were declared winners. In this fourth game, Wills acted as 'field umpire'. The Melbourne Cricket Ground stands on part of the site used for the games.

First clubs:
The Melbourne Football Club was formed in 1858. Wills and Harrison were the instigators, assisted by Messrs W. J. Hammersley and J. N. Thompson. The second club formed was Geelong (1859), followed by South Yarra and Richmond (1860).

First name for new code:
Just after the first school matches and probably in 1859, Wills and Harrison christened the new football code 'Victorian Rules', a title which was to seriously slow the progress of the game in NSW.

First controlling body:
The Victorian Football Association (VFA), formed in 1877.

First night game:
On 5 August 1879, at the Melbourne Cricket Ground, between Collingwood Artillery and East Melbourne. The Melbourne *Argus* reported that 12,000 attended the game which was illuminated by clear glass lamps suspended from poles around the fence. A white ball was used for the first time but as the field was muddy there were frequent stoppages to clean the ball. The experiment was not voted a success.

First VFA premiers:
Carlton won the first premiership competition anywhere in Australia.

Formation of Victorian Football League (VFL):
In 1897, when eight clubs broke away from the VFA and formed the new body. Essendon won the first premiership competition staged by the VFL.

First 'international' match:
Theoretically in 1888, when a touring British Isles Rugby Union team outclassed Melbourne and accepted a challenge from the Carlton club to play what was still known as 'Victorian Rules'. Carlton easily defeated a bewildered British Isles side by 14 goals, 17 behinds to 3 goals, 7 behinds.

First 'Victorian Rules' played in each State:
Victoria 1858, South Australia 1860, New South Wales 1864, Queensland 1866, Tasmania 1875 and Western Australia 1883.

First use of the name 'Australian Rules':
In 1908, Jubilee Year of the game and the occasion of the first interstate carnival at the MCG. The Prime Minister, Mr Alfred Deakin (possibly mistakenly)

proposed a toast to 'Australian Rules football' and the name stuck, much to the relief of NSW officials who had found it almost impossible to interest anybody in a game called 'Victorian Rules'.

First matches against New Zealand:
At the 1908 interstate carnival. New Zealand had been introduced to the game in 1876 and surprisingly, defeated New South Wales and Queensland.

First Brownlow Medal winner:
Edward Goodrich 'Cargie' Greeves, a Geelong centreman, who received the award in 1924. The Medal award honours the memory of Charles Brownlow, a cricket and football stalwart from the Geelong area. It has been awarded every year, except the World War II years.

First interstate match:
In 1879, when Victoria played South Australia in Melbourne.

Historic 'double century match':
It took from 1877 (first year of the VFA competition) until 1924 before opposing teams each scored 100 points in a match. The game saw Fitzroy (16.9–105) defeat Carlton (15.13–103).

AUSTRALIAN RECORDS

Highest attendance:
121,696 for the 1970 VFL Grand Final, Carlton v. Collingwood at the MCG, won by Carlton.

Most, best and fairest medals in a senior career:
Six by Haydn Bunton Snr (1911-56) who won three Brownlow Medals (VFL, Vic.) and three Sandover Medals in the WANFL competition.

Most goals in a senior match:
28 by Bill Wood, (South Sydney) against Sydney in NSW AFL competition, 21 August 1943.

Most goals in career:
1,419 by Ken Farmer (North Adelaide, SA) in 224 matches over 13 seasons, plus interstate games.

Most goals in a season:
220 by Bill Pearson (Melbourne Amateurs) in 1934.

Most goals in a VFA season:
188 by Ron Todd (Williamstown) in 1945.

Most goals in a VFL season:
150 each by Bob Pratt (South Melbourne) in 1934 and Peter Hudson (Hawthorn) in 1971.

Most goals in a Tasmanian season:
202 by Peter Hudson (then with Glenorchy) in 1979.

Most goals in an interstate game:
23 by Bonnie Campbell (WA) against Queensland in 1924.

Record senior game score:
In the Sydney first-grade competition, Newtown (49.26–320) d. Liverpool (6.8–44), on 20 April 1981.

Lowest senior game score:
A single point from one behind scored by St Kilda v. Geelong in 1899. Sydney first-grade club Liverpool failed to score in a match against St George in 1962 and, in 1912, West Perth scored only three behinds against Subiaco (6.9–45).

Most premierships of any State:
28 by Port Adelaide, SA, including six in succession 1954–59. The club was undefeated in winning the 1914 premiership.

MEDAL FIRSTS:

First player to win two Brownlow Medals:
Ivor Warne-Smith (Melbourne), in 1926 and 1928.

First player to win successive Brownlow Medals:
Haydn Bunton Snr (Fitzroy), 1931 and 1932. (The feat was repeated in later years by Dick Reynolds (Essendon), Ian Stewart (St Kilda) and Keith Greig (North Melbourne).

Winners of the most Brownlow Medals:
Haydn Bunton Snr (Fitzroy), Dick Reynolds (Essendon), Bob Skilton (South Melbourne) and Ian Stewart (St Kilda) have each won three medals.

Youngest Brownlow Medal winner:
Dinny Ryan (Fitzroy) in 1936, aged 19.

First player to win four Magarey Medals in SANFL competition:
Russell Ebert (Port Adelaide) in 1971, '74, '76 and '80.

First player to win three successive Sandover Medals in competition:
Bill Walker (Swan District) in 1965, '66 and '67 (when he tied with J. Parkinson (Claremont)).

Youngest Sandover Medal winner:
John Todd (South Fremantle) in 1955, aged 16 years 10 months—in his first senior season.

First father-son combination to win the Sandover Medal:
Haydn Bunton Snr (1938, '39 and '41) for Subiaco and son Haydn Jnr in 1962 for Swan District.

VFL RECORDS

Most goals in career:
1,299 by Gordon Coventry (1902-68) of Collingwood, between 1920 and 1937. Coventry averaged 4.24 goals in his 306 games.

Most senior matches:
The record is held by Kevin Bartlett (b. 6 March 1947), of Richmond. Bartlett bettered Kevin Murray's (Fitzroy) mark of 333 in the 1980 season, before retiring at the end of the 1983 season, with a record 403 games. His total includes VFL premiership matches, night and interstate games.

Most goals in a match:
18 by Fred Fanning (Melbourne) against St Kilda in 1947.

First player to kick 100 goals in a season:
Gordon Coventry (Collingwood) with 124 goals in 1929.

Most successive games:
204 by Jack Titus (1908-78) in his 294-game career for Richmond, between 1924 and 1947.

First drawn grand final:
In 1948, between Melbourne and Essendon. Melbourne won the replay.

Record grand final winning margin:
83 points, when Hawthorn defeated Essendon in 1983 (20.20-140 to 8.9-57). The previous record had been 81 points, when Richmond defeated Collingwood in 1980.

Most senior wins in succession:
23 by Geelong, from July 1952 to August 1953. Geelong drew in their 24th and 25th matches, then won two more, making 27 matches in succession without a loss.

Most premiership wins:
15 by Carlton.

VFA RECORDS

After a breakaway movement in 1896, the Victorian Football Association became a virtual second division of Victorian football, but has maintained a strong and enthusiastic following.

Attendance record:
48,238 at the MCG for the Williamstown v. Brunswick Grand Final in 1939.

Most goals in a season:
188 by Rod Todd (Williamstown), in 1945.

Most goals in a match:
25 by George Gough (Northcote) against Prahran in 1924.

AUSTRALIAN FOOTBALL IN NEW SOUTH WALES

First club competition:
In 1880, when five teams played social games. The game virtually ceased in 1898 due to opposition from Rugby, and the unacceptable name of the southern game (Victorian Rules).

First controlling body:
In 1902 Victorian officials and influence helped form the NSW Australian National Football League.

First club premiership competition:
In 1903. East Sydney were the first Sydney club premiers.

First NSW win over Victoria:
In 1923. NSW defeated Victoria again in 1925. The wins did little to boost the popularity of the game at basic club level in and around Sydney.

AUSTRALIAN FOOTBALL IN SOUTH AUSTRALIA

The first (friendly) matches were played in 1860 between members of the Adelaide Football Club.

Largest crowd:
66,897 for the 1976 Port Adelaide v. Sturt Grand Final at Football Park, West Lakes, Adelaide.

First premiership:
Held in 1877 and won by South Adelaide.

Only player in history to kick over 100 goals for 11 straight seasons:
Ken Farmer of North Adelaide, who kicked 105, 126, 102, 112, 106, 128, 134,

108, 112, 113 and 123 (1931–40). Farmer's feat remains a national record.

AUSTRALIAN FOOTBALL IN WESTERN AUSTRALIA
First game:
On 21 May 1885, a pre-season match between 'West Australia' and 'The World', won by the former.
First premiership match:
On 6 June 1885, Rovers (later to become Perth) v. Victorians (later West Perth) at the Esplanade, Perth. Rovers won the match, but Fremantle won the first premiership.
WA's greatest success:
In 1961 in Brisbane, when WA won the Australian Championship carnival – their first in 40 years.
Most goals in a season:
162, scored by Austin Robertson Jnr (Subiaco). His total included 5 in the finals. Robertson was eight times leading goal kicker.

AUSTRALIAN FOOTBALL IN TASMANIA
First association:
The Southern Tasmanian Football Association, inaugurated in Hobart in 1879. The present controlling body, the Tasmanian Football League, was formed in April 1886. In recent years the name of the body has been changed to the Tasmanian National Football League.
First premiership:
1879, won by City, a Hobart club.
Interstate record:
Tasmania has defeated every State except Victoria in annual interstate carnivals. In 1960, the Tasmanian State side defeated a select Victorian VFL club (not representing Victoria) for the first time.
Largest crowd:
24,968 for the 1979 Grand Final at North Hobart Oval. Clarence defeated Glenorchy to win only its second premiership since 1947.

AUSTRALIAN FOOTBALL IN QUEENSLAND
First association:
The Queensland Football Association, inaugurated in 1879.

First premiership:
Played in 1926 and won by Brisbane.
First player to play 300 games:
Syd Guildford (b. 1945) played his 300th game, a State record, in May 1979. Guildford played all of his matches in first grade.

AUSTRALIAN FOOTBALL IN ACT
First premiership:
Played in 1924 and won by Acton.

VFL CLUBS 1988
Carlton.
  Formed 1864. Premiers 1906-07-08-14-15-38-45-47-68-70-72-79-81-82-87. Nickname—The Blues. Home ground, Prince's Park.
Collingwood.
  Formed 1892. Premiers 1902-03-10-17-19-27-28-29-30-35-36-53-58. Nickname—The Magpies. Home ground, Victoria Park Oval.
Essendon.
  Formed 1873. Premiers 1897-1901-11-12-23-24-42-46-49-50-62-65-84-85. Nickname—The Bombers. Home ground, Essendon Reserve.
Fitzroy.
  Formed 1884. Premiers 1898-99-1904-05-13-16-22-44. Nickname—The Lions. Home ground, Prince's Park.
Footscray.
  Formed 1883. Premiers 1954. Nickname—The Bulldogs. Home ground, Western Oval.
Geelong.
  Formed 1859. Premiers 1925-31-37-51-52-63. Nickname—The Cats. Home ground, Kardinia Park.
Hawthorn.
  Formed 1873. Premiers 1961-71-76-78-83-86. Nickname—The Hawks. Home ground, Prince's Park.
Melbourne.
  Formed 1859. Premiers 1900-26-39-40-41-55-56-59-60-64. Nickname—The Demons. Home ground, Melbourne Cricket Ground.
North Melbourne.
  Formed 1874. Premiers 1975–77. Nickname—The Kangaroos. Home ground, Melbourne Cricket Ground.

Richmond.
Formed 1885. Premiers 1920-21-32-34-43-67-69-73-74-80-82. Nickname – The Tigers. Home ground, Melbourne Cricket Ground.

St Kilda.
Formed 1873. Premiers 1966. Nickname – The Saints. Home ground, Moorabbin Oval.

Sydney Swans (Formerly *South Melbourne*).
Formed 1874. Premiers 1909-18-33. Nickname – The Swans. Home ground, Sydney Cricket Ground.

Brisbane.
Formed 1987. Premierships nil. Nickname – The Bears. Home ground, Carrara Oval, Gold Coast, Qld.

West Coast.
Formed 1987. Premierships nil. Nickname — The Eagles. Home ground, Subiaco Oval and the WACA, Perth.

VFL PREMIERSHIP WINNERS

Year	Winning Team
1897	Essendon
1898	Fitzroy
1899	Fitzroy
1900	Melbourne
1901	Essendon
1902	Collingwood
1903	Collingwood
1904	Fitzroy
1905	Fitzroy
1906	Carlton
1907	Carlton
1908	Carlton
1909	South Melbourne
1910	Collingwood
1911	Essendon
1912	Essendon
1913	Fitzroy
1914	Carlton
1915	Carlton
1916	Fitzroy
1917	Collingwood
1918	South Melbourne
1919	Collingwood
1920	Richmond
1921	Richmond
1922	Fitzroy
1923	Essendon
1924	Essendon
1925	Geelong
1926	Melbourne
1927	Collingwood
1928	Collingwood
1929	Collingwood
1930	Collingwood
1931	Geelong
1932	Richmond
1933	South Melbourne
1934	Richmond
1935	Collingwood
1936	Collingwood
1937	Geelong
1938	Carlton
1939	Melbourne
1940	Melbourne
1941	Melbourne
1942	Essendon
1943	Richmond
1944	Fitzroy
1945	Carlton
1946	Essendon
1947	Carlton
1948	Melbourne**
1949	Essendon
1950	Essendon
1951	Geelong
1952	Geelong
1953	Collingwood
1954	Footscray
1955	Melbourne
1956	Melbourne
1957	Melbourne
1958	Collingwood
1959	Melbourne
1960	Melbourne
1961	Hawthorn
1962	Essendon
1963	Geelong
1964	Melbourne
1965	Essendon
1966	St Kilda
1967	Richmond
1968	Carlton
1969	Richmond
1970	Carlton*
1971	Hawthorn
1972	Carlton
1973	Richmond
1974	Richmond
1975	North Melbourne
1976	Hawthorn
1977	North Melbourne**
1978	Hawthorn

Year	Winning Team
1979	Carlton
1980	Richmond
1981	Carlton
1982	Carlton
1983	Hawthorn
1984	Essendon
1985	Essendon
1986	Hawthorn
1987	Carlton

* Record crowd—121,696
** Won in replay after draw in grand final

BROWNLOW MEDAL WINNERS (VFL)

Year	Winner
1924	Edward 'Cargie' Greeves (Geelong)
1925	Colin Watson (St Kilda)
1926	Ivor Warne-Smith (Melbourne)
1927	Syd Coventry (Collingwood)
1928	Ivor Warne-Smith (Melbourne)
1929	Albert Collier (Collingwood)
1930	Stan Judkins (Richmond)
1931	Haydn Bunton Snr (Fitzroy)
1932	Haydn Bunton Snr (Fitzroy)
1933	Wilfred Smallhorn (Fitzroy)
1934	Dick Reynolds (Essendon)
1935	Haydn Bunton Snr (Fitzroy)
1936	Dennis Ryan (Fitzroy)
1937	Dick Reynolds (Essendon)
1938	Dick Reynolds (Essendon)
1939	Marcus Whelan (Collingwood)
1940	tied—Des Fothergill (Collingwood) Herb Matthews (South Melbourne)
1941	Norman Ware (Footscray)

1942–45 *Not awarded* (WW II)

Year	Winner
1946	Dr Don Cordner (Melbourne)
1947	Bert Deacon (Carlton)
1948	Bill Morris (Richmond)
1949	Ron Clegg (South Melbourne)
1950	Allan Ruthven (Fitzroy)
1951	Bernie Smith (Geelong)
1952	Roy Wright (Richmond)
1953	Bill Hutchison (Essendon)
1954	Roy Wright (Richmond)
1955	Fred Goldsmith (South Melbourne)
1956	Peter Box (Footscray)
1957	Brian Gleeson (St Kilda)
1958	Neil Roberts (St Kilda)
1959	Bob Skilton (South Melbourne)
1960	John Schultz (Footscray)
1961	John James (Carlton)
1962	Alastair Lord (Geelong)
1963	Bob Skilton (South Melbourne)
1964	Gordon Collis (Carlton)
1965	Ian Stewart (St Kilda)
1966	Ian Stewart (St Kilda)
1967	Ross Smith (St Kilda)
1968	Bob Skilton (South Melbourne)
1969	Kevin Murray (Fitzroy)
1970	Peter Bedford (South Melbourne)
1971	Ian Stewart (Richmond)
1972	Len Thompson (Collingwood)

Year	Winner
1973	Keith Greig (North Melbourne)
1974	Keith Greig (North Melbourne)
1975	Gary Dempsey (Footscray)
1976	Graham Moss (Essendon)
1977	Graeme Teasdale (South Melbourne)
1978	Malcolm Blight (North Melbourne)
1979	Peter Moore (Collingwood)
1980	Kelvin Templeton (Footscray)
1981	tied—Bernie Quinlan (Fitzroy) Barry Round (South Melbourne)
1982	Brian Wilson (Melbourne)
1983	Ross Glendinning (North Melbourne)
1984	Peter Moore (Melbourne)
1985	Bradley Hardie (Footscray)
1986	tied—Greg Williams (Sydney Swans) Robert Dipierdomenico (Hawthorn)
1987	tied—Tony Lockett (St Kilda) John Platten (Hawthorn)

WAFA (Western Australian Football Association) CLUBS—1987

Claremont.
Entered 1926 (as *Claremont-Cottesloe*. Club renamed *Claremont* in 1935). Premiers 1938-39-40-64-81-87. Nickname—The Tigers. Home ground, Claremont Oval.

East Fremantle.
Entered 1885 (as *Fremantle*. Club renamed *East Fremantle* in 1900). Premiers 1885-87-88-89-90-91-92-93-94-95-96-98-1900-02-03-04-06-08-09-10-11-14-18-25-28-29-30-31-33-37-43-45-46-57-65-74-79-85. Nickname—Old Easts. Home ground, East Fremantle Oval.

East Perth.
Entered 1885. Premiers 1919-20-21-22-23-26-27-36-44-56-58-59-72-78. Nickname—The Royals. Home ground, Perth Oval.

Perth.
Entered 1899. Premiers 1907-55-66-67-68-76-77. Nickname—The Demons. Home ground, Lathlain Oval.

South Fremantle.
Entered 1900. Premiers 1916-17-47-48-50-52-53-54-70-80. Nickname—Souths. Home ground, Fremantle Oval.

Subiaco.
Entered 1900. Premiers 1912-13-15-24-73. Nickname—Subi's. Home ground, Subiaco Oval.

Swan Districts.
Entered 1934. Premiers 1961-62-63-82-83-84. Nickname—The Swans. Home ground, Bassendean Oval.

West Perth.
Entered 1891. (Originally formed in 1885 as *The Victorians*, changed to *Metropolitans* in 1889 and to *West Perth* in 1891.) Premiers 1897-1905-32-34-36-41-42-49-51-60-69-71-75. Nickname—The Cardinals. Home ground, Leederville Oval.

WANFL (Western Australian National Football League) PREMIERS

Year	Winning Team
1885	Fremantle
1886	Unions
1887	Fremantle
1888	Fremantle
1889	Fremantle
1890	Fremantle
1891	Fremantle
1892	Fremantle
1893	Fremantle
1894	Fremantle
1895	Fremantle
1896	Fremantle
1897	West Perth
1898	Fremantle
1899	West Perth
1900	East Fremantle
1901	West Perth
1902	East Fremantle
1903	East Fremantle
1904	East Fremantle
1905	West Perth

Year	Winning Team	Year	Winning Team
1906	East Fremantle	1960	West Perth
1907	Perth	1961	Swan Districts
1908	East Fremantle	1962	Swan Districts
1909	East Fremantle	1963	Swan Districts
1910	East Fremantle	1964	Claremont
1911	East Fremantle	1965	East Fremantle
1912	Subiaco	1966	Perth
1913	Subiaco	1967	Perth
1914	East Fremantle	1968	Perth
1915	Subiaco	1969	West Perth
1916	South Fremantle	1970	South Fremantle
1917	South Fremantle	1971	West Perth
1918	East Fremantle	1972	East Perth
1919	East Perth	1973	Subiaco
1920	East Perth	1974	East Fremantle
1921	East Perth	1975	West Perth
1922	East Perth	1976	Perth
1923	East Perth	1977	Perth
1924	Subiaco	1978	East Perth
1925	East Fremantle	1979	East Fremantle
1926	East Perth	1980	South Fremantle
1927	East Perth	1981	Claremont
1928	East Fremantle	1982	Swan Districts
1929	East Fremantle	1983	Swan Districts
1930	East Fremantle	1984	Swan Districts
1931	East Fremantle	1985	East Fremantle
1932	West Perth	1986	Subiaco
1933	East Fremantle	1987	Claremont
1934	West Perth		
1935	West Perth		
1936	East Perth		
1937	East Fremantle		
1938	Claremont		
1939	Claremont		
1940	Claremont		
1941	West Perth		
1942	West Perth		
1943	East Fremantle		
1944	East Perth		
1945	East Fremantle		
1946	East Fremantle		
1947	South Fremantle		
1948	South Fremantle		
1949	West Perth		
1950	South Fremantle		
1951	West Perth		
1952	South Fremantle		
1953	South Fremantle		
1954	South Fremantle		
1955	Perth		
1956	East Perth		
1957	East Fremantle		
1958	East Perth		
1959	East Perth		

SANDOVER MEDAL
The Sandover Medal is the official award of the WANFL to the season's best and fairest player.

Year	Player
1921	T. Outridge (Subiaco)
1922	H. Boys (West Perth)
1923	W. Thomas (East Perth)
1924	J. Gosnell (West Perth)
1925	G. Owens (East Perth)
1926	J. Leonard (Subiaco)
1927	J. Craig (West Perth)
1928	J. Rocchi (South Fremantle)
1929	W. Thomas (East Perth)*
1930	E. Fleming (East Perth)

Year	Player	Year	Player
1931	L. Richards (East Fremantle)	1957	Jack Clarke (East Fremantle)
1932	K. Hough (Claremont)	1958	Ted Kilmurray (East Perth)
1933	S. Clarke (Claremont)	1959	Brian Foley (West Perth)
1934	S. Clarke (Claremont)	1960	Graham Farmer (East Perth)
1935	tied—L. Daily (Subiaco) G. Krepp (Swan Districts)	1961	Neville Beard (Perth)
		1962	Haydn Bunton Jnr (Swan Districts)***
1936	G. Moloney (Claremont)	1963	Ray Sorrell (East Fremantle)
1937	F. Jenkins (South Fremantle)	1964	Barry Cable (Perth)
1938	Haydn Bunton Snr (Subiaco)	1965	Bill Walker (Swan Districts)
1939	Haydn Bunton Snr (Subiaco)	1966	Bill Walker (Swan Districts)
1940	E. O'Keefe (West Perth)	1967	tied—Bill Walker (Swan Districts)**** John Parkinson (Claremont)
1941	Haydn Bunton Snr (Subiaco)		
1942	L. Bowen (West Perth)	1968	Barry Cable (Perth)
1943	T. Moriarty (Perth)	1969	Mal Brown (East Perth)
1944	J. Davies (Swan Districts)	1970	Pat Dalton (Perth)
1945	G. Bailey (Perth)	1971	David Hollins (East Fremantle)
1946	J. Loughridge (West Perth)	1972	Ian Miller (Perth)
1947	G. Lewington (South Fremantle)	1973	Barry Cable (Perth)
1948	Merv McIntosh (Perth)	1974	Graham Melrose (East Fremantle)
1949	G. Maffina (Claremont)	1975	Alan Quartermaine (East Perth)
1950	J. Conway (East Fremantle)	1976	Peter Spencer (East Perth)
1951	Fred Buttsworth (West Perth)	1977	Brian Peake (East Fremantle)
1952	Steve Marsh (South Fremantle)	1978	Phil Kelly (East Perth)
1953	Merv McIntosh (Perth)	1979	Phil Kelly (East Perth)
1954	Merv McIntosh (Perth)	1980	Stephen Michael (South Fremantle)
1955	John Todd (South Fremantle)**	1981	Stephen Michael (South Fremantle)
1956	Graham Farmer (East Perth)	1982	Phil Narkle (Swan Districts)

Year	Player
1983	John Ironmonger (East Perth)
1984	three-way tie – Steve Malaxos (Claremont) Michael Mitchell (Claremont) Peter Spencer (East Perth)
1985	Murray Wrensted (East Fremantle)
1986	Mark Bairstow (South Fremantle)
1987	Mark Watson (Perth)

* No relation to 1923 winner.
** Youngest winner, 16 yrs 10 mths at start of the season.
*** Son of 1938-39-41 winner.
**** First player to win three successive medals.

SANFL (South Australian National Football League) CLUBS—1987

Central District.
Entered 1964. Premierships nil. Nickname – The Bulldogs. Home ground, Elizabeth Oval.
Glenelg.
Entered 1921. Premiers 1934-73-85-86. Nickname – The Tigers. Home ground, Glenelg Oval.
North Adelaide.
Entered 1907. Premiers 1902-05-20-30-31-49-52-60-71-72-87. Nickname – The Roosters. Home ground, Prospect Oval.
Norwood.
Entered 1877. Premiers 1878-79-80-81-82-83-87-88-89-91-94-1901-04-07-22-23-25-29-41-43 (combined with *North Adelaide*)-44 (combined with *North Adelaide*)-46-48-50-75-78-82-84. Nickname – The Redlegs. Home ground, Norwood Oval.
Port Adelaide.
Entered 1877. Premiers 1884-90-97-1903-06-10-13-14-21-28-36-37-39-42 (combined with *West Torrens*) -51-54-55-56-57-58-59-62-63-65-77-79-80-81. Nickname – The Magpies. Home ground, Alberton Oval.
South Adelaide.
Entered 1877. Premiers 1877-85-92-93-95-96-98-99-1938-64. Nickname – The Panthers. Home ground, Adelaide Oval.
Sturt.
Entered 1901. Premiers 1915-26-29-32-40-66-67-68-69-70-74-76. Nickname – The Blues. Home ground, Adelaide Oval.
West Adelaide.
Entered 1897. Premiers 1908-09-11-12-27-47-61-83. Nickname – The Bloods. Home ground, Richmond Oval.
West Torrens.
Entered 1897. Premiers 1924-33-42 (with *Port Adelaide*)-45-53. Nickname – The Eagles. Home ground, Thebarton Oval.
Woodville.
Entered 1964. Premierships nil. Nickname – The Warriors. Home ground, Woodville Oval.

SANFL PREMIERS

Year	Winning Team
1877	South Adelaide
1878	Norwood
1879	Norwood
1880	Norwood
1881	Norwood
1882	Norwood
1883	Norwood
1884	South Adelaide
1885	South Adelaide
1886	Adelaide
1887	Norwood
1888	Norwood
1889	Norwood
1890	Port Adelaide
1891	Norwood
1892	South Adelaide
1893	South Adelaide
1894	Norwood
1895	South Adelaide
1896	South Adelaide
1897	Port Adelaide
1898	South Adelaide
1899	South Adelaide
1900	North Adelaide
1901	Norwood
1902	North Adelaide
1903	Port Adelaide
1904	Norwood
1905	North Adelaide
1906	Port Adelaide
1907	Norwood

Year	Winning Team	Year	Winning Team
1908	West Adelaide	1964	South Adelaide
1909	West Adelaide	1965	Port Adelaide
1910	Port Adelaide	1966	Sturt
1911	West Adelaide	1967	Sturt
1912	West Adelaide	1968	Sturt
1913	Port Adelaide	1969	Sturt
1914	Port Adelaide	1970	Sturt
1915	Sturt	1971	North Adelaide
1916-18	*No competition* (WW I)	1972	North Adelaide
1919	Sturt	1973	Glenelg
1920	North Adelaide	1974	Sturt
1921	Port Adelaide	1975	Norwood
1922	Norwood	1976	Sturt
1923	Norwood	1977	Port Adelaide
1924	West Torrens	1978	Norwood
1925	Norwood	1979	Port Adelaide
1926	Sturt	1980	Port Adelaide
1927	West Adelaide	1981	Port Adelaide
1928	Port Adelaide	1982	Norwood
1929	Norwood	1983	West Adelaide
1930	North Adelaide	1984	Norwood
1931	North Adelaide	1985	Glenelg
1932	Sturt	1986	Glenelg
1933	West Torrens	1987	North Adelaide
1934	Glenelg		
1935	South Adelaide		
1936	Port Adelaide		
1937	Port Adelaide		
1938	South Adelaide		
1939	Port Adelaide		
1940	Sturt		
1941	Norwood		
1942	Port/Torrens*		
1943	Norwood/North Adelaide*		
1944	Norwood/North Adelaide*		
1945	West Torrens		
1946	Norwood		
1947	West Adelaide		
1948	Norwood		
1949	North Adelaide		
1950	Norwood		
1951	Port Adelaide		
1952	North Adelaide		
1953	West Torrens		
1954	Port Adelaide		
1955	Port Adelaide		
1956	Port Adelaide		
1957	Port Adelaide		
1958	Port Adelaide		
1959	Port Adelaide		
1960	North Adelaide		
1961	West Adelaide		
1962	Port Adelaide		
1963	Port Adelaide		

* Combined teams during WWII

MAGAREY MEDAL

Official award of the South Australian National Football League.

The basis for the award of the Magarey Medal is slightly different from all other football awards in Australia: the Magarey Medal is awarded to the fairest and most brilliant player of the season, whereas all other medal awards are to the best and fairest player. The idea of the South Australian award came from early supporter Mr W. A. Magarey, who donated the first medal in 1898.

Year	Player
1898	A. Green (Norwood)
1899	S. Malin (Port Adelaide)
1900	*Not awarded*
1901	P. Sandland (North Adelaide)
1902	Tom McKenzie (West Torrens)
1903	S. Waye (Sturt)
1904	*Not awarded*
1905	Tom McKenzie (North Adelaide)

AUSTRALIAN FOOTBALL • 65

Year	Player	Year	Player
1906	Tom McKenzie (North Adelaide)	1935	J. Cockburn (South Adelaide)
1907	J. Mack (Port Adelaide)	1936	W. B. McCallum (Norwood)
1908	J. Tierney (West Adelaide)	1937	H. J. Hawke (North Adelaide)
1909	Dick Head (West Adelaide)	1938	Bob Quinn (Port Adelaide)
1910	Shine Hosking (Port Adelaide)	1939	J. Pash (North Adelaide)
1911	H. V. Cumberland (Sturt)	1940	M. Brock (Glenelg)
1912	D. Lowe (West Torrens)	1941	Marcus Boyall (Glenelg)
1913	Tom Leahy (North Adelaide)	1942-44	*Not awarded* (WW II)
1914	Jack Ashley (Port Adelaide)	1945	Bob Quinn (Port Adelaide)
1915	F. M. Barry (South Adelaide)	1946	Bob Hank (West Torrens)
1916-18	*Not awarded* (WW I)	1947	Bob Hank (West Torrens)
1919	Dan Moriarty (South Adelaide)	1948	Ron Phillips (North Adelaide)
1920	Dan Moriarty (South Adelaide)	1949	Ron Phillips (North Adelaide)
1921	Dan Moriarty (South Adelaide)	1950	Ian McKay (North Adelaide)
1922	R. Barnes (West Adelaide)	1951	John Marriott (Norwood)
1923	Horace Riley (Sturt)	1952	Len Fitzgerald (Sturt)
1924	W. Scott (Norwood)	1953	Jim Deane (South Adelaide)
1925	Alec Lill (Norwood)	1954	Len Fitzgerald (Sturt)
1926	Bruce McGregor (West Adelaide)	1955	Lindsay Head (West Torrens)
1927	Bruce McGregor (West Adelaide)	1956	David Boyd (Port Adelaide)
1928	Jim Handby (Glenelg)	1957	Ron Benton (West Adelaide)
1929	R. Snell (West Adelaide)	1958	Lindsay Head (West Torrens)
1930	W. Scott (Norwood)	1959	Len Fitzgerald (Sturt)
1931	Bob Snell (West Adelaide)	1960	Barrie Barbary (North Adelaide)
1932	Max Pontifex (West Torrens)	1961	John Halbert (Sturt)
1933	W. K. Dunn (Sturt)	1962	Ken Eustice (West Adelaide)
1934	G. B. Johnston (Glenelg)	1963	Lindsay Head (West Torrens)

Year	Player
1964	Geoff Motley (Port Adelaide)
1965	Gary Window (Central District)
1966	Ron Kneebone (Norwood)
1967	Trevor Obst (Port Adelaide)
1968	Barry Robran (North Adelaide)
1969	Fred Phillis (Glenelg)
1970	Barry Robran (North Adelaide)
1971	Russell Ebert (Port Adelaide)
1972	Malcolm Blight (Woodville)
1973	Barry Robran (North Adelaide)
1974	Russell Ebert (Port Adelaide)
1975	Peter Woite (Port Adelaide)
1976	Russell Ebert (Port Adelaide)
1977	Trevor Grimwood (West Adelaide)
1978	Kym Hodgeman (Glenelg)
1979	John Duckworth (Central District)
1980	Russell Ebert* (Port Adelaide)
1981	Michael Aisch (Norwood)
1982	Tony McGuinness (Glenelg)
1983	Tony Antrobus (North Adelaide)
1984	John Platten (Central District)
1985	Grant Fielke (West Adelaide)
1986	Greg Anderson (Port Adelaide)
1987	Andrew Jarman (North Adelaide)

* First player to win four times.

TFL (Tasmanian Football League) PREMIERS

Year	Winning Team
1879	City
1880	Cricketers
1881	Railway
1882	Railway
1883	Railway
1884	Holebrook
1885	Holebrook
1886	City
1887	Railway
1888	City
1889	Railway
1890	Holebrook
1891	Holebrook
1892	City
1893	Railway
1894	Railway
1895	tied – Railway/City
1896	Railway
1897	Hobart
1898	Lefroy
1899	Lefroy
1900	Wellington
1901	Lefroy
1902	North Hobart
1903	Wellington
1904	Wellington
1905	North Hobart
1906	Derwent
1907	Lefroy
1908	North Hobart
1909	Cananore
1910	Cananore
1911	Cananore
1912	Lefroy
1913	Cananore
1914	North Hobart
1915	Lefroy
1916-18	*Not held* (WW I)
1919	*Not held* (flu outbreak)
1920	North Hobart
1921	Cananore
1922	Cananore
1923	North Hobart
1924	Lefroy
1925	Cananore
1926	Cananore
1927	Cananore
1928	North Hobart
1929	North Hobart
1930	Lefroy
1931	Cananore
1932	North Hobart
1933	Cananore
1934	North Hobart
1935	New Town

Year	Winning Team	Year	Winning Team
1936	North Hobart	1963	Hobart
1937	Lefroy	1964	Sandy Bay
1938	North Hobart	1965	Glenorchy
1939	North Hobart	1966	Hobart
1940	North Hobart	1967	North Hobart
1941	North Hobart	1968	New Norfolk
1942–44	*Not held* (WW II)	1969	North Hobart
1945	North Hobart	1970	Clarence
1946	Sandy Bay	1971	Sandy Bay
1947	North Hobart	1972	Sandy Bay
1948	New Town	1973	Hobart
1949	New Town	1974	North Hobart
1950	Hobart	1975	Glenorchy
1951	New Town	1976	Sandy Bay
1952	Sandy Bay	1977	Sandy Bay
1953	New Town	1978	Sandy Bay
1954	Hobart	1979	Clarence
1955	New Town	1980	Hobart
1956	New Town	1981	Clarence
1957	North Hobart	1982	New Norfolk
1958	Glenorchy	1983	Glenorchy
1959	Hobart	1984	Glenorchy
1960	Hobart	1985	Glenorchy
1961	North Hobart	1986	Glenorchy
1962	North Hobart	1987	North Hobart

BASKETBALL

The fastest-growing professional team sport in Australia, basketball dates back to 1905, but remained an obscure amateur pastime until after World War II. The first Australian championship was staged in 1946 when New South Wales defeated Victoria 50–44 in the final.

First international appearance:
At the 1956 Melbourne Olympic Games. As host nation at Melbourne Australia did not have to qualify and finished 12th of 15 competing nations, defeating Thailand and Singapore and losing to Chile, Canada, Brazil and Formosa–China. Australia has competed at all subsequent Olympic Games with a best result of sixth place at Los Angeles in 1984.

Establishment of National League:
Australian basketball went completely professional in 1979 with the establishment of the National Basketball League. To the surprise of the sceptics, the National League was an instant success with capacity crowds at most matches, blanket sponsorship and television coverage.

National Basketball champions

Year	Winning Team
1979	St Kilda (Vic.)
1980	St Kilda (Vic.)
1981	Launceston (Tas.)

Year	Winning Team	Year	Winning Team
1982	West Adelaide (SA)	1985	Brisbane (Qld)
1983	Canberra (ACT)	1986	Adelaide 36ers (SA)
1984	Canberra (ACT)	1987	Brisbane Bullets (Qld)

BOXING

BEGINNINGS IN AUSTRALIA
Bare-knuckle boxing, although discouraged and later outlawed, can be traced back to the arrival of the First Fleet in 1788.

First recorded bare-knuckle fight:
On 7 January 1814, at the southern end of the (then) Sydney Racecourse (now Hyde Park). Australian-born John Berringer knocked out Englishman Charles Lifton in the 56th round, after a two-hour battle.

Last bare-knuckle fight:
On 17 April 1844, at Randwick Racecourse, Sydney, NSW, when American negro Jimmy Lawson knocked out Alex Agar (Vic.). Boxing was illegal in the Colony and when Agar died without regaining consciousness, Lawson was arrested and gaoled for six months.

Longest bare-knuckle fight on record:
On 3 December 1856 James Kelly and Jonathon Smith (Vic.) fought for 6 hrs 15 mins at Fiery Creek, near Daylesford, Vic. Only a knockdown terminated a round and the first round lasted almost two hours. The authoritative *Ring Record Book* (USA) lists the duration of the fight as a world record for bare-knuckle contests.

First recognised bare-knuckle champions:
Young Kable of Windsor, NSW, was only a middleweight (approx. 11 st 6 lbs) when he was recognised as champion of the Colony. Izaac Gorrick, who fought as 'Bungaree', and Bill Sparkes (NSW) were early champions who ran out of opponents in Australia. They continued their careers in England in 1842 and 1847 respectively. Larry Foley, only a welterweight (67 kg), was never beaten in bare-knuckle and, later, gloved fights, despite accepting challenges from heavyweights. Taught by famous English bare-knuckle champion Jem Mace, Foley became a trainer after his retirement in 1879 and developed two world champions: Bob Fitzsimmons (b. Cornwall, England) and Albert Griffiths (b. Sofala, NSW, 15 April 1869) and other great fighters such as Frank Slavin.

Last-known bare-knuckle championship fight:
In 1879, when Larry Foley retained his welterweight title against Englishman Abe Hickin at Dead Horse Point, NSW, just across the Murray River from Wharparilla.

Australia's most infamous bare-knuckle fighter:
Bushranger Ned Kelly, who had at least a dozen fights and one outstanding win over 20 rounds against Wild Wright at Beechworth, Vic., on 8 August 1871.

First use of and first fight with gloves:
Gloves were first used in an exhibition on 8 November 1834, when pupils of boxing tutor Abraham (Alby) Davis boxed exhibitions at the Dolphin Inn in Elizabeth Street, Sydney, NSW. The first recorded fight with gloves took place on 25 July 1849, when William Thompson, athletics champion of the Colony, knocked out Bill Sparkes in five rounds at the Tennis Court Inn in Sussex Street, Sydney.

First championship fight with gloves:
On 26 July 1884, when Bill Farnan knocked out Peter Jackson at the Victoria Hall, Melbourne, Vic., to win the Australian Heavyweight Championship.

First world championship fight in Australia:
On 3 September 1890 at Larry Foley's White Horse Hotel in Sydney, when Australia's Albert Griffiths (Young Griffo) stopped New Zealand's 'Torpedo' Billy Murphy in 15 rounds to win the Featherweight Championship. Despite the fact that Murphy, who had won the title in the USA on 13 January 1890, had remained undefeated and the Australian contest was staged under full championship conditions, Young Griffo was not recognised as champion in the USA.

First internationally recognised world championship fight in Australia:
On 24 August 1908, when heavyweight champion Tommy Burns (b. Noah Brusso) of Canada retained his title with a 13th round knockout of Australian Bill Squires at Rushcutters Bay Stadium in Sydney (later known as Sydney Stadium). Including the Griffiths-Murphy fight, 22 recognised world title fights have been held in Australia, the last being in March 1988 when Australia's Jeff Fenech stopped Puerto Rico's Victor Callejas. He won the vacant WBC featherweight title and became the first Australian to have won three world championships. More than 50 contests have been billed as being for 'world titles' but less than half have gained even partial international recognition.

Australian world champions:
Young Griffo won the featherweight title, 3 September 1890, KO 15 rds Billy Murphy (NZ), holder, at the White Horse Hotel, Sydney. Jimmy Carruthers (NSW) won the bantamweight title, 15 November 1952, KO 1 Vic Toweel (South Africa), holder, at Johannesburg, South Africa. Lionel Rose (Vic.) won the bantamweight title, 27 February 1968, pts 15 rds v. Fighting Harada (Japan), holder, at Tokyo, Japan. Johnny Famechon (Vic.) won the featherweight title, 21 January 1969, pts 15 rds v. Jose Legra (Cuba), for vacant title, at London, UK. Rocky Mattioli (Vic.) won the junior middleweight title (World Boxing Council version) 6 August 1977, KO 7 Eckhardt Dagge (Germany), holder, at Berlin, West Germany. Lester Ellis (Vic.) won the junior lightweight title (IBF version), 15 February 1985, pts 15 rds v. Hwan Kil Yuh (Korea), holder at Melbourne. Jeff Fenech (NSW) won the bantamweight title (IBF version), 26 April 1985, KO 9 v. Satoshi Shingaki (Japan), at Sydney and later won the world WBC junior featherweight and WBC featherweight titles. Barry Michael (Vic.) won the junior lightweight title (IBF version), 12 July 1985, pts 15 rds v. Lester Ellis (Vic.), holder, at Melbourne.

Mattioli (b. Rocco Mattioli, at Ripa Teatine, Chata, Italy, 20 July 1953 and raised in Melbourne where he became an Australian citizen) won only the WBC version of the junior middleweight title. Mattioli never fought another title claimant, Eddie Gazo of Nicaragua, who won a separate version of the same title in 1977 and was still 'champion' when Mattioli won his 'title'. Les Darcy (b. Stradbroke, NSW, 31 October 1895 – d. Memphis, Tennessee, USA, 24 May 1917) won an Australian version of the world middleweight title when he defeated Jeff Smith (USA) at Baker's Stadium (Sydney Stadium) on 22 May 1915. Darcy's claim was not recognised in the USA at the time, but as the title was vacant and so many claims existed, the *Ring Record Book*, 1984 edition, lists the Darcy-Smith fight as being for the championship. Mick King of Australia had earlier defeated Smith in a fight advertised as being for the world title (28 November 1914), but even King did not press claims to the championship.

Though some early doubt existed about the universal recognition of Famechon's title, it is now accepted that the win was legitimate. When Famechon defeated Jose Legra for the vacant title, every international boxing organisation except the World Boxing Association recognised him as champion. The WBA was ignored throughout the world.

A number of contests have been billed in Australia at various times as being for a 'World Championship'. The most recent was staged in Perth, Western Australia on 21 January 1987 between Perth boxer Tony Jones and Yodkwan Donjadee of Thailand for the 'World Boxing Council Superlightweight' title. Jones, who won the 'title' with a five round knockout of Canadian Laurie Mann on 17 December 1986, retained the 'title' by stopping the Thailander in the first round. For understandable reasons, the 'title' is not recognised by any body other than the WBC, and even that 'recognition' is confusing. The WBC did not sanction the Jones-Mann contest and did not, as is its custom, appoint officials or send a supervisor. Yet the contest was still staged as being for a 'world title'. To compound the confusion, the WBC *did* sanction the Jones-Donjadee bout and appointed the referee and judges. No body other than the WBC recognises Jones as a legitimate champion.

Australians who have fought in a world championship:
Excluding the acknowledged champions, plus Darcy and King, the following have participated in accepted world title fights. All lost.
Heavyweight: Bill Squires (Vic.) v. Tommy Burns, 1907 and twice in 1908. Bill Lang (Vic.) v. Tommy Burns, 1908, 1909
Middleweight: Tony Mundine (NSW) v. Carlos Monzon, 1974
Welterweight: Tom Williams (NSW) v. Mysterious Billy Smith, 1893
Junior welterweight: Hector Thompson (Qld) v. Antonio Cervantes, 1975
Lightweight: Hector Thompson (Qld) v. Roberto Duran, 1973
Junior lightweight: Lionel Rose (Vic.) v. Yoshiaki Numata, 1970
Featherweight: George Powell (NSW) v. Young Griffo, 1891
Bantamweight: Paul Ferreri (Vic.) v. Carlos Zarate, 1976
Junior bantamweight: Wayne Mulholland (NSW) v. Elly Pical, 1985
Flyweight: Rocky Gattellari v. Salvatore Burruni, 1965

Largest attendance in Australia:
32,500, for Jimmy Carruthers' successful defence of his world bantamweight title, against Henry 'Pappy' Gault (USA) outdoors at the Sydney Sports Ground, 13 November 1953.

Largest total gate:
Although gate takings were not released, receipts for the Fenech v. Coffee world bantamweight title fight at the Sydney Entertainment Centre on 2 December 1985 were clearly an Australian record. A capacity crowd of 12,074 paid up to $150 a seat and conservative estimates have placed the gross takings at around $400,000. The previous record was $300,000 for Lionel Rose's successful defence of his world bantamweight title against Alan Rudkin (UK) outdoors at the Kooyong Tennis Stadium, Melbourne, on 8 March 1969.

First Australian to win three world championships:
Jeff Fenech (b. Sydney, NSW, 28 May 1964), after winning the world IBF bantamweight title from Japanese title holder, Satoshi Shingaki on 26 April 1985, made two successful defences. He then resigned the title late in 1986 to step up a division. At the Sydney Entertainment Centre on 8 May 1987 he made boxing history by becoming the first Australian to win two world titles when he knocked out title holder Samart Payakarun of Thailand in four rounds to win the world WBC super-bantamweight championship. Fenech made two successful defences before resigning the title to step up to the featherweight division. In March 1988,

Title fights by all-Australian world champions:

Boxer	Title	Date/Venue	Defeated/Result
Young Griffo	Featherweight	3.9.1890 Sydney	Billy Murphy (NZ) KO 15 rds
Young Griffo	Featherweight	12.3.1891 Sydney	George Powell disqu. 20 rd
Jimmy Carruthers	Bantamweight	15.11.1952 Johannesburg	Vic Toweel (Sth Africa) KO 1
Jimmy Carruthers	Bantamweight	21.3.1953 Johannesburg	Vic Toweel KO 10
Jimmy Carruthers	Bantamweight	2.5.1954 Bangkok	Chamrern Songitrat w pts 12
Jimmy Carruthers	Bantamweight	13.11.1963 Sydney	Henry 'Pappy' Gault (USA) w pts 15
Lionel Rose	Bantamweight	27.2.1968 Tokyo	'Fighting' Harada (Japan) pts 15
Lionel Rose	Bantamweight	2.7.1968 Tokyo	Takao Sakuri (Japan) w pts 15
Lionel Rose	Bantamweight	8.3.1969 Kooyong	Alan Rudkin (UK) w pts 15
Ruben Olivares (Mexico)	Bantamweight	22.8.1969 Los Angeles	Lionel Rose KO 5
Yoshiaki Numata (Japan)	Jnr Lightweight	30.5.1970 Hiroshima	Lionel Rose lost pts 15
Johnny Famechon	Featherweight	21.1.1969 London	José Legra (Cuba) pts 15
Johnny Famechon	Featherweight	28.7.1969 Sydney	'Fighting' Harada (Japan) w pts 15
Johnny Famechon	Featherweight	6.1.1970 Tokyo	'Fighting Harada' (Japan) w KO 14
Vicente Saldivar (Mexico)	Featherweight	9.5.1970 Rome	Johnny Famechon pts 15
Rocky Mattioli	WBC Jnr Middleweight	6.8.1977 Berlin	Eckhardt Dagge (Germany) KO 5
Rocky Mattioli	WBC Jnr. Middleweight	11.3.1978 Melbourne	Elisha Obed (Bahamas) KO 7
Rocky Mattioli	WBC Jnr. Middleweight	14.5.1978 Pescara, Italy	José Duran (Spain) KO 5
Maurice Hope (Antigua)	WBC Jnr Middleweight	4.3.1979 San Remo, Italy	Rocky Mattioli KO 8
Maurice Hope	WBC Jnr Middleweight	12.7.1980 Wembley, UK	Rocky Mattioli KO 11
Lester Ellis	IBF Jnr Lightweight	15.2.1985 Melbourne	Hwan Kil Yuh (Korea) pts 15

Boxer	Title	Date/Venue	Defeated/Result
Lester Ellis	IBF Jnr Lightweight	26.4.1985 Melbourne	Rod Sequenan, Phillipines KO 13
Barry Michael	IBF Jnr Lightweight	12.7.1985 Melbourne	Lester Ellis pts 15
Jeff Fenech	IBF Bantamweight	26.4.1985 Sydney	Satoshi Shingaki (Japan) KO 9
Jeff Fenech	IBF Bantamweight	23.8.1985 Sydney	Satoshi Shingaki KO 3
Barry Michael	IBF Jnr Lightweight	19.10.1985 Darwin	Jin Sick Choi (Korea) KO 4
Jeff Fenech	IBF Bantamweight	2.12.1985 Sydney	Jerome Coffee (USA) w pts 15
Barry Michael	IBF Jnr Lightweight	23.5.1986 Melbourne	Mark Fernandez (USA) KO 4
Jeff Fenech*	IBF Bantamweight	18.7.1986 Sydney	Steve McCrory (USA) KO 14
Barry Michael	IBF Jnr Lightweight	23.8.1986 Manchester, UK	Najib Daho (Morocco/England) w pts 12
Jeff Fenech	WBC Jnr Featherweight	8.5.1987 Sydney	Samart Payakarun (Thailand) KO 4
Rocky Lockridge (USA)	IBF Jnr Lightweight	9.8.1987 London, UK	Barry Michael KO 9
Jeff Fenech	WBC Jnr Featherweight	10.7.1987 Sydney	Greg Richardson (USA) KO 5
Jeff Fenech	WBC Jnr Featherweight	16.10.1987 Sydney	Carlos Zarate (Mexico) W 4**
Jeff Fenech	WBC Featherweight	7.3.1988 Sydney	Victor Callejas (Puerto Rico) KO 14

*Fenech resigned the championship in late 1986 to seek a contest for the world IBF Super Bantamweight title (referred to by other organisations as Junior Featherweight).

**A technical points decision. Fenech could not continue on doctor's orders after suffering a severe eye cut in the fourth round. Under WBC rules the boxer ahead on points at the end of the fourth round, but unable to continue due to an eye cut, is declared the winner. Fenech was ahead on all judges' scorecards, 40-34, 40-34, 40-34.

Fenech again made history by winning a third world title, stopping Puerto Rico's Victor Callejas at Sydney to win the vacant world WBC featherweight championship.

Australian Commonwealth championship winners:

First winner: Hughie Mehegan (NSW) won the Empire (now Commonwealth) lightweight title on 16 September 1912 on a foul in the 14th round against Matt Wells of England at London, UK.

Empire or Commonwealth title wins following Mehegan:
Jimmy Kelso.......lightweight (1933)
Ron Richards.....middleweight (1940)
Dave Sands.......middleweight (1949)

Jimmy Carruthers....... bantamweight (1952)
Pat Ford..... lightweight (1953, 1954)
George Barnes........... welterweight (1954, 1956, 1958)
Darby Brown...... welterweight (1956)
Johnny Famechon....... featherweight (1967)
Bob Dunlop........ light-heavyweight (1968)
Lionel Rose...... bantamweight (1969)
Henry Nissen........ flyweight (1971)
Tony Mundine.... middleweight (1972)
Charkey Ramon... junior middleweight (1972)
Paul Ferreri............ bantamweight (1972, 1980)
Bobby Dunne..... featherweight (1972)
Hector Thompson... light-welterweight (1973, 1977)
Big Jim West........ flyweight (1974)
Steve Aczel... light-heavyweight (1975)
Tony Mundine...... light-heavyweight (1975)
Billy Moeller....... junior lightweight (1975)
Baby Cassius Austin . light-welterweight (1977, 1978)
Al Korovou...... middleweight (1978)
Jeff Malcolm........ light-welterweight (1978)
Barry Michael...... lightweight (1981)
Ken Salisbury..... junior middleweight (1984)
Graeme Brooke..... lightweight (1984)
Lester Ellis......... junior lightweight (1984)
Barry˙ Michael...... lightweight (1985)
Brian Janssen....... welterweight (1987)
Wilf Gentzen....... welterweight (1987)
Troy Waters.. light middleweight (1987)

Multiple Australian titles:
Five boxers have held three Australian titles simultaneously: Billy Grime (NSW) featherweight, lightweight and welterweight; Ron Richards (Qld) middleweight, light-heavyweight and heavyweight; Dave Sands (NSW) middleweight, light-heavyweight and heavyweight; Paul Ferreri (Vic.) bantamweight, featherweight and junior lightweight; Tony Mundine (NSW) light-heavyweight, cruiserweight, heavyweight.

Three separate titles:
Twelve boxers have held Australian titles at three different weight limits, but not simultaneously: Jack McGowan (Vic.) bantamweight, featherweight and lightweight; Tommy Jones (NSW) bantamweight, featherweight and lightweight; Frank Thorn (SA) featherweight, lightweight and welterweight; Dave Smith (NZ) middleweight, light-heavyweight and heavyweight; Jimmy Clabby (USA) welterweight, middleweight and heavyweight; Tommy Uren (NSW) lightweight, welterweight and middleweight; Jackie Green (NSW) flyweight, bantamweight and featherweight; Hughie Dwyer (NSW) lightweight, welterweight and middleweight; Ambrose Palmer (Vic.) middleweight, light-heavyweight and heavyweight; Jeff White (Qld) junior lightweight, lightweight and welterweight; Lawrence Austin (Vic.) lightweight, junior welter and welterweight; Wally Carr (NSW) junior, middleweight and light-heavyweight.

Most titles won:
Eight, by Tony Mundine (b. Baryulgil, NSW, 9 June 1951). Mundine won the Commonwealth middleweight and light-heavyweight, Australian middleweight, light-heavyweight, cruiserweight and heavyweight, Australasian light-heavyweight and Pacific heavyweight titles in a career which spanned 1969–84.

Mundine's great record:
Mundine scored more KO victories than any other Australian boxer – 65 in 96 fights. He is the only Australian to achieve a world ranking in three divisions and the only Australian to win a Commonwealth title in two divisions. He held the Australian heavyweight title for a record six years 10 months and would have held it longer but for an ill-advised retirement. He held the light-heavyweight title for a record eight years five months and is the only Australian to contest an official bout for the World Middleweight Championship. Mundine was never beaten by an Australian boxer.

Oldest Australian champion:
Aboriginal Jerry Jerome (b. Queensland, 24 May 1874) was almost 39 when he

won the middleweight title on 12 February 1913. He defeated Arthur Cripps on a foul in the 12th round.

Youngest Australian champion:
Jackie Green (b. Wellington NSW, 12 November 1901) was 15 years 4 months when he outpointed Al White to win the Australian flyweight title at Sydney. (His title win was not recognised in Victoria.)

Australian title in first fight:
The only boxer to win an Australian title in his first professional fight is Harold Hardwick (NSW), who outpointed Les O'Donnell in what was advertised as an elimination match on 6 March 1915 for the vacant Australian heavyweight title. No more elimination fights were held and Hardwick received recognition as champion. Hardwick, who had won the heavyweight title at the 1911 Festival of Empire Games in London, UK, lost his professional title on a seventh round knockout to Les Darcy on 19 February 1916. Hardwick put up a great fight and knocked out one of Darcy's teeth. The tooth was replaced, but is now believed to have led to blood poisoning, one of the factors which caused Darcy's death in the USA in 1917.

Quick championship wins:
Six boxers have won Australian professional championships in three or fewer fights:
One fight – Harold Hardwick (NSW) heavyweight title, 1915.
Two fights – Tony Barber (NSW) junior middleweight title, 1965. Junior Thompson (Qld) junior flyweight title, 1978.
Three fights – Fred Casey (Qld) heavyweight title, 1965. Dave Cullen (Vic.) heavyweight title, 1967.*
Henry Nissen (Vic.) flyweight title, 1970.
*Not recognised in all States.

Fathers and sons who won national titles:
There have been three such instances: Eric Barnes, who fought as 'Frank Burns', won the Australian middleweight title in 1921. His son George (George Barnes) won the Australian welterweight title in 1953, the first time in the world history of boxing that a father-son combination had won national championships. On 21 April 1982, Jim Bowen (NSW) won the vacant Australian junior featherweight title. His father, Cliff, had won the Australian Middleweight Championship in 1944. Russell Sands won the Australian welterweight title in 1984. His father, Alfie, won a version of the Australian middleweight title in 1954.

Champion brothers:
Seven sets of brothers have won Australian championships and one pair of brothers won a national title and *claimed* a title. The legitimate brother champions have been:
1. Jackie and Teddy Green. Jackie Green received partial recognition as Australian flyweight champion in 1917, was nationally recognised as bantamweight champion on 17 January 1920 when he defeated Vince Blackburn and as featherweight champion on 5 April 1920 when he defeated Sid Godfrey. Teddy Green defeated Patsy Kelly to win the flyweight title on 24 September 1926, lost the title to Vic White on 14 August 1929 and regained it from White on 16 July 1930.
2. Dave Sands won the Australian middleweight title from Jack Kirkham on 11 May 1946, the heavyweight title from Jack Johnson on 24 August 1946 and the vacant heavyweight title on 4 September 1950 by outpointing Alf Gallagher. His youngest of five brothers, Russell, won the vacant Australian featherweight title on 10 December 1954 with a second round KO of Young Layton. Another of the Sands brothers, Alfie, won a version of the Australian middleweight title on 25 February 1954 when he knocked out Harry Hayes in a fight billed as being for the vacant title. His title was recognised only by the Leichhardt Stadium (Sydney) promoters, the Australian Boxing Club.
3. Rocky Gattellari became Australian flyweight champion on 26 February 1962 by knocking out defending titleholder Jackie Bruce in 6 rounds. His younger brother, Fortunato ('Lucky') won the Australian featherweight title from Ken Bradley on 7 June 1971.
4. Matt Ropis became Australian lightweight champion on 13 March 1975 when he stopped Blakeney Matthews in 9 rounds. (Ropis had won an unofficial 'title' on 4 December 1974.) His younger

brother Frank won the welterweight title on 16 April 1980 with a points decision over Lawrence Austin.

5. Billy Mulholland won the vacant Australian lightweight title when he outpointed Frank Gibilisco on 7 October 1977. His younger brother Wayne won the Australian flyweight title on 8 April 1982 with a cut eye-points decision over Steve Bell.

6. The Janssen brothers, Brian and Mark, were the first brothers to hold Australian titles simultaneously. Brian won the Australian junior welterweight title on 14 February 1983 with a first round knockout of defending titleholder Peter Berrigan. When he out-grew the division, he became Australian welterweight champion on Anzac Day, 25 April 1985 with a points win over defending champion Russell Sands. While Brian still held the title, his younger brother Mark won the vacant Australian middleweight championship on 4 August 1986 with a points win over Paul James.

7. The Waters brothers, Dean and Guy, in 1986 and 1987 respectively became the second brothers to hold Australian titles simultaneously. Dean won the heavyweight title on 15 March 1986 with a 10 round knockout of defending champion Dave Russell. Guy became Australian light-heavyweight champion on 5 February 1987 when he outpointed defending champion Garry Hubble.

Claimants

1. The Moore brothers, Alan and Paul respectively won a national title and laid claims to a national title. Alan won the undisputed Australian welterweight championship on 29 September 1969 with a points win over defending champion Carmen Rotolo. Paul won the same (welterweight) title in a bout billed for the championship on 7 March 1973 when he stopped Dave Clarke in 8 rounds. The title 'win' was never seriously regarded because Queensland's Jeff White was still the official champion. To add to the confusion, Stadiums Ltd promoted a contest on 19 March 1973 between Alan Aldenhoven and Michael Karparney for the same welterweight title. Aldenhoven won and received Stadiums Ltd recognition. White, who had been the official champion since 2 October 1970, finally lost his championship when he was stopped by Rocky Mattioli on 17 May 1973.

2. A third member of the Waters family, junior middleweight Troy, outpointed Paul Toweel on 26 November 1986 in a contest promoted by his father Cec at the Cardiff Workers Club, NSW, and billed as being for the vacant Australian championship. Troy's title 'win' cannot be seriously regarded, because New Zealander Steve Renwick had defeated Toweel for the vacant Australian and Australasian junior middleweight titles on 29 August 1986. Had Troy Waters won a legitimate title, it would have meant that three brothers held Australian championships simultaneously – a situation unique in the world history of boxing.

Fastest knockout wins:
Australian title fight defence – *35 secs* by defending Australian Featherweight Champion Lucky Gattellari against Neville Williams at the Apia Club, Sydney, on 18 April 1972. To win Australian title – *25 secs* by Herb Narvo to win the heavyweight title from holder Billy Britt at Newcastle Stadium, NSW, on 3 April 1943. Any fight – *7 secs* by preliminary boxer Ian Gordon against Frank Brooks at the Brisbane Stadium, Qld, on 2 November 1951.

Boxer who packed Sydney Stadium most times:
Tommy Burns (b. Mullumbimby, NSW, 19 May 1922) helped attract a capacity crowd to Sydney Stadium (approx. capacity 13,000) on 10 occasions. Burns, who won the Australian welterweight title on a fourth round KO of Hockey Bennell (NSW) on 3 February 1947, drew his first capacity crowd on 2 February 1946 when he challenged Vic Patrick (NSW) for the welterweight title. Patrick won by a knockout in the ninth round, but Burns' popularity remained unimpaired.

Famous serial fights:
Ron Richards (Qld) and Fred Henneberry (NSW) at various times Australian Middleweight Champions 1933-42, met in 10 brutal battles. Richards won five on foul, one on knockout. Henneberry

won one on knockout and two on points. One fight was drawn.

Most famous boxing family:
The Sands brothers of Newcastle (NSW). All six brothers became main-event fighters. Born to George and Lillian Ritchie at Burnt Bridge, near Kempsey, NSW, the brothers adopted the ring name 'Sands' after Percival, the first of the brothers to start a professional career, was helped to success by a train guard named Snowy Sands. Newcastle trainer Tom Maguire decided that 'Percival' or even a shortened 'Percy' was unsuitable for a fighter and decided on the ring name of Ritchie Sands for Percival. All following brothers used the name 'Sands'. Most famous of the brothers was Dave Sands who became Empire Middleweight Champion, Australian Middleweight, Light-heavyweight and Heavyweight, and Australian Light-heavyweight Champion, and won 97 of 110 fights (1942-52). Sands twice defeated future World Middleweight Champion Carl Olson (USA), but was unable to secure a world title fight. Clem Sands, a welterweight, won 45 of 100 fights (1938-51), Ritchie Sands, a welterweight/middleweight won 45 of 89 fights (1938-56), George Sands, a welterweight, won 54 of 101 (1939-52), Alfie Sands, who won a version of the Australian middleweight title, won 87 of 148 fights (1944-59) and the youngest, Russell, became Australian Featherweight Champion and won 34 of 57 fights (1952-59). Alfie's son, Russell, became Australian Welterweight Champion in 1984 but was forced to retire after being injured in a motorcycle accident. After making a successful comeback he was killed in a car accident in 1987.

AUSTRALIAN OLYMPIANS WHO WON NATIONAL PROFESSIONAL TITLES:
(No winners before World War II)

Boxer	Olympics	Professional Title
Harold Hardwick	Stockholm, 1912	Heavyweight, 1916
Jimmy Carruthers	London, 1948	Bantamweight, 1952
Warner Batchelor	Melbourne, 1956	Flyweight, 1957
Max Carlos	Melbourne, 1956	Lightweight, 1959
Peter Read	Melbourne, 1956	Middleweight, 1963
Rocky Gattellari	Rome, 1960	Flyweight, 1962
Sid Prior	Rome, 1960	Welterweight, 1962
Tony Barber	Tokyo, 1964	Light-middleweight, 1965
Fred Casey	Tokyo, 1964	Heavyweight, 1965
Jeff Fenech	Los Angeles, 1984	Junior bantamweight, 1984
Wilf Gentzen	Los Angeles, 1984	Welterweight, 1987

AMATEUR BOXING
No Australian has won an Olympic gold medal for boxing, but many have won gold medals at Empire and Commonwealth Games or won major international tournaments.

Olympic medallists:
Silver – Reginald 'Snowy' Baker (NSW), middleweight, London, 1908.
Bronze – Kevin Hogarth (Vic.), welterweight, Melbourne, 1956. Ollie Taylor (Qld), bantamweight, Rome, 1960. Tony Madigan (NSW), light-heavyweight, Rome, 1960.

Most successful amateur:
Tony Madigan (NSW) won a bronze medal at the 1960 Rome Olympics, gold medals at the 1958 and 1962 Commonwealth Games, won the 1958 and 1959 International Diamond Belt

(recognised then as the unofficial World Amateur Championship), a silver medal at the 1954 Vancouver Empire Games, the 1954 British Championship, the Australian middleweight title in 1951 and the Australian Light-heavyweight Championship in 1957 and 1962. Madigan missed many Australian championships because of overseas business commitments. As a light-heavyweight, Madigan became the only Australian to fight Cassius Clay (Muhammad Ali), losing in the 1959 US Golden Gloves final at Chicago and in a quarter-final of the 1960 Rome Olympic Games.

'Snowy' Baker's 1908 Olympic medal: Baker was possibly a shade unlucky to miss out on a gold medal in the middleweight final at London. Opposed to J. W. H. T. (Johnny) Douglas (later to captain England at cricket), Baker suffered an early knockdown, but recovered to finish strongly. Unlike in professional boxing, knockdowns in Olympic matches do not necessarily carry points and contests are judged on aggression and the most scoring punches landed. One legend persists that Douglas' father refereed the fight and influenced the judges, but although Baker claimed in a magazine article in later years that Douglas Snr was the referee, the official Olympic Games records make no reference to the fact.

Longest career:
Fifteen years, by Tasmanian light-welterweight Wayne Devlin. Devlin was Australian champion eight times.

Unluckiest Australian Olympian:
Jeff Fenech (NSW), who was awarded victory in the quarter-finals of the 1984 flyweight competition at the Los Angeles Olympics and then had the decision overruled by the international jury. The second decision cost Fenech at least a bronze medal. Fenech, who was given the first decision by three of the five ringside judges, saw his opponent Redzep Redsepovski (Yugoslavia) go into the final and lose on points to win a silver medal.

The gold medal was won by American negro Steve McCrory. After both had become professionals and Fenech won the IBF World Bantamweight title, Fenech stopped McCrory in the 14th round in defence of his championship at the Sydney Entertainment Centre, 18 July 1986.

At the same 1984 Olympics, lightweight representative Renato Cornett (NSW) suffered the same fate as Fenech, winning his second-round fight against Chin Chil-Sung (Korea) and having the verdict overruled by the international jury.

CHAMPIONS
The emergence of rival international boxing organisations during the 1970s created intense confusion, with three (four in the mid-1980s) such bodies recognising different 'champions' in many divisions. The three major organisations—WBA (World Boxing Association), WBC (World Boxing Council) and IBF (International Boxing Federation)—often failed to rate rival organisations' 'champions' in their lists of the top 10 boxers in a number of divisions. No such confusion exists with holders of Commonwealth championships, but the existence of two bodies in Australia—the ABF (Australian Boxing Federation) and PBAAI (Professional Boxing Association of Australia International)—has occasionally led to some degree of confusion, mainly at State championship level.

Australian champions
(as at April 1988):
Heavyweight......Dean Waters (NSW)
 —won title 15 March 1986
Cruiserweight ....Dave Russell (Vic.)
 —won title 30 April 1987
Light-heavyweight...Guy Waters (NSW)
 —won title 5 February 1987
Junior light-heavyweight ......Doug Sam
 (Qld)—won title 2 August 1985
Middleweight ....Mark Janssen (Qld)
 —won title 4 August 1986
Junior-middleweight ....Steve Peel
 (NSW)—won title 30 April 1988
Welterweight ....Brian Janssen (Qld)
 —won title 25 April 1985
Junior-welterweight..Pat Leglise (NSW)
 —won title 26 July 1984
Lightweight............Lester Ellis (Vic.)
 —won title 30 April 1987
Junior-lightweight.........Tony Miller
 (Vic.)—won title 24 March 1985
Featherweight......Jeff Fenech (NSW)
 —won title 3 April 1987

Title	Winner
Junior-featherweight	Title vacant
Bantamweight	Peter Mitrevski (NSW) —won title 18 July 1988
Junior-bantamweight	Peter Mitrevski (NSW)—won title 6 December 1986
Flyweight	Wayne Mulholland (NSW) —won title 8 April 1982
Junior-flyweight	Junior Thompson (Qld)—won title 26 October 1985

WORLD CHAMPIONS
(as at April 1988):

Division	Organisation	Boxer	Country
Heavyweight (over 190 lbs)	IBF champion	Mike Tyson	USA
	WBA champion	Mike Tyson	USA
	WBC champion	Mike Tyson	USA
Cruiserweight (190 lbs)	IBF champion	Evander Holyfield	USA
	WBA champion	Evander Holyfield	USA
	WBC champion	Carlos De Leon	Panama
Light-heavyweight (175 lbs)	IBF champion	Bobby Czyz	USA
	WBA champion	Marvin Johnson	USA
	WBC champion	Thomas Hearns	USA
Junior light-heavyweight (168 lbs)	IBF champion	Chong-Pal Park	Korea
	WBA champion	Not recognised	
	WBC champion	Not recognised	
Middleweight (160 lbs)	IBF champion	Sugar Ray Leonard	USA
	WBA champion	Sugar Ray Leonard	USA
	WBC champion	Sugar Ray Leonard	USA
Junior middleweight (154 lbs)	IBF champion	Buster Drayton	USA
	WBA champion	Mike McCallum	Jamaica/USA
	WBC champion	Duane Thomas	USA
Welterweight (147 lbs)	IBF champion	Lloyd Honeyghan	England
	WBA champion	Vacant	
	WBC champion	Lloyd Honeyghan	England
Junior welterweight (140 lbs)	IBF champion	Joe Manley	USA
	WBA champion	Patrizio Oliva	Italy
	WBC champion	Tsuyoshi Hamada	Japan
Lightweight (135 lbs)	IBF Champion	Greg Haugen	USA
	WBA champion	Hector Comacho	USA
	WBC champion	Edwin Rosario	Panama
Junior lightweight (130 lbs)	IBF champion	Rocky Lockridge	USA
	WBA champion	Brian Mitchell	Sth Africa
	WBC champion	Julio Cesar Chavez	Mexico
Featherweight (126 lbs)	IBF champion	Antonio Rivera	Panama
	WBA champion	Antonio Esparragoza	Venezuela
	WBC champion	Jeff Fenech	Australia
Junior featherweight (122 lbs)	IBF champion	Seung Hoon Lee	Korea
	WBA champion	Louie Espinosa	USA
	WBC champion	Jeff Fenech	Australia
Bantamweight (118 lbs)	IBF champion	Vacant	
	WBA champion	Miguel Lora	Colombia
	WBC champion	Miguel Lora	Colombia

Division	Organisation	Boxer	Country
Junior bantamweight (115 lbs)	IBF champion	Elly Pical	Indonesia
	WBA champion	Kaosai Galaxy	Thailand
	WBC champion:	Gilberto Roman	Mexico
Flyweight (112 lbs)	IBF champion	Hi-Sup Chin	Korea
	WBA champion	Hilario Zapata	Panama
	WBC champion	Sot Chitalada	Thailand
Junior flyweight (108 lbs)	IBF champion	Jun Hwan Choi	Korea
	WBA champion	Fidel Bassa	Colombia
	WBC champion	Jung Koo Chang	Korea

WORLD HEAVYWEIGHT CHAMPIONSHIP

In recent years, the emergence of many rival 'controlling' bodies has resulted in up to four boxers being recognised as 'champion'. The 'controlling' bodies are: WBC (World Boxing Council), WBA (World Boxing Association) and IBF (International Boxing Federation).

Year	Venue	Boxers	Result
1892	New Orleans	James J. Corbett d John L. Sullivan	KO 21
1897	Nevada	Bob Fitzsimmons d James J. Corbett	KO 14
1899	New York	James Jeffries d Bob Fitzsimmons	KO 11
1905		James Jeffries retired as reigning champion. Title declared vacant.	
1905	Nevada	Marvin Hart d Jack Root	KO 12
1906	Los Angeles	Tommy Burns d Marvin Hart	Ret. 20
1908	Sydney	Jack Johnson d Tommy Burns	TKO 14
1915	Havana	Jess Willard d Jack Johnson	KO 26
1919	Toledo	Jack Dempsey d Jess Willard	TKO 4
1926	Philadelphia	Gene Tunney d Jack Dempsey	pts 10
1928		Gene Tunney retired as reigning champion. Title declared vacant.	
1930	New York	Max Schmeling d Jack Sharkey	Foul 4
1932	Long Island	Jack Sharkey d Max Schmeling	pts 15
1933	Long Island	Primo Carnera d Jack Sharkey	KO 6
1934	Long Island	Max Baer d Primo Carnera	TKO 11
1935	Long Island	James J. Braddock d Max Baer	pts 15
1937	Chicago	Joe Louis d James J. Braddock	KO 8
1949		Joe Louis retired as reigning champion. Title declared vacant.	
1949	Chicago	Ezzard Charles d Joe Walcott	pts 15
1951	Pittsburgh	Joe Walcott d Ezzard Charles	KO 7

Year	Venue	Boxers	Result
1952	Philadelphia	Rocky Marciano d Joe Walcott	KO 13
1956		Rocky Marciano retired as reigning and first undefeated world heavyweight champion. Title declared vacant.	
1956	Chicago	Floyd Patterson d Archie Moore	KO 5
1959	New York	Ingemar Johansson d Floyd Patterson	TKO 3
1960	New York	Floyd Patterson d Ingemar Johansson First man to regain heavyweight title.	KO 5
1962	Chicago	Sonny Liston d Floyd Patterson	KO 1
1964	Miami Beach	Cassius Clay d Sonny Liston	TKO 7
1965	Chicago	Ernie Terrell d Eddie Machen NBA (later the WBA) withdrew recognition of Clay when he contracted to fight Liston and instead recognised Terrell as champion. No other body in the world supported the NBA/WBA.	pts 15
1967		Clay, by now known as Muhammad Ali, refused to take the Oath of Allegiance to join the US Armed Forces. The NBA/WBA and the New York State Athletic Commission refused to recognise him as champion, a view not shared by all other international commissions.	
1968	New York	Joe Frazier d Buster Mathis Title recognised only by the NYSAC.	KO 11
1968	Oakland	Jimmy Ellis d Jerry Quarry Title recognised only by the WBA.	pts 15
1970		Muhammad Ali announced retirement.	
1970	New York	Joe Frazier d Jimmy Ellis Bout received general international recognition as a legitimate world title contest.	KO 5
1973	Kingston	George Foreman d Joe Frazier	KO 2
1974	Kinshasa, Zaire	Muhammad Ali d George Foreman	KO 8
1978	Las Vegas	Leon Spinks d Muhammad Ali On 17 March 1978 the WBC withdrew recognition of Leon Spinks as champion when he failed to comply with an order to sign for a title defence against Ken Norton and announced its recognition of Norton as champion. Because titles can only be won in the ring, no other world commission recognised Norton.	pts 15
1978	Las Vegas	Larry Holmes d Ken Norton Recognised only by the WBC.	pts 15

Year	Venue	Boxers	Result
1978	New Orleans	Muhammad Ali d Leon Spinks Muhammad Ali announced retirement.	pts 15
1979	Pretoria	John Tate d Gerrie Coetzee Recognised by the WBA as being for the vacant title.	pts 15
1980	Knoxville, USA	Mike Weaver d John Tate Recognised by the WBA but *Ring* magazine gave recognition to Larry Holmes because he had knocked out Weaver in a 1979 WBC title fight.	KO 15
1982	Las Vegas	Michael Dokes d Mike Weaver Recognised only by the WBA.	KO 1
1983	Richfield, USA	Gerrie Coetzee d Michael Dokes Recognised only by the WBA.	KO 10
1983		Larry Holmes resigned his WBC title and was recognised by the IBF as the world champion.	
1984	Las Vegas	Tim Witherspoon d Greg Page Recognised only by the WBC as being for the vacant title.	pts 12
1984	Las Vegas	Pinklon Thomas d Tim Witherspoon Recognised only by the WBC.	pts 12
1984	Sun City, Africa	Greg Page d Gerrie Coetzee Recognised only by the WBA.	KO 8
1985	Buffalo	Tony Tubbs d Greg Page Recognised only by the WBA.	pts 15
1985	Las Vegas	Michael Spinks d Larry Holmes Recognised by the IBF.	Pts 15
1986	Atlantic City	Tim Witherspoon d Tony Tubbs Recognised by the WBA.	pts 15
1986	Las Vegas	Trevor Berbick d Pinklon Thomas Recognised by the WBC.	pts 12
1986	Las Vegas	Mike Tyson d Trevor Berbick Recognised by the WBC.	KO 2
1986	New York	James Smith d Tim Witherspoon Recognised by the WBA.	KO 1
1987	Las Vegas	Mike Tyson d James Smith Recognised by both the WBA and WBC.	pts 12
1987	Las Vegas	Mike Tyson d Tony Tucker Recognised by IBF.	pts 12
1988	Atlantic City	Mike Tyson d Michael Spinks For undisputed world championship.	KO 1

COMMONWEALTH GAMES

Australia has been represented at all Commonwealth Games since the inaugural carnival held at Hamilton, Canada, in 1930. The event was known as the Empire Games until 1954, when the staging at Vancouver, Canada, became the Empire and Commonwealth Games. The ninth Games, staged at Edinburgh, Scotland, were the first to be officially described as the Commonwealth Games. An Australasian team participated in London in 1911, at an event called the Festival of Empire. Harold Hardwick (Australia) won the 100 yards freestyle swimming event plus the heavyweight boxing title, but no medals were awarded and the Festival of Empire has never been included as part of the history of the Empire and Commonwealth Games.

Australia as Games host:
Australia has staged three Commonwealth Games: at Sydney in 1938, Perth in 1962 and Brisbane in 1982.

Australia's most successful Games:
The Perth Games in 1962, when the large Australian team won 105 medals—38 gold, 36 silver and 31 bronze—a total not bettered until the Canadian team won 109 medals at Edmonton, Canada in 1978.

AUSTRALIA'S RECORD—EMPIRE AND COMMONWEALTH GAMES

Games	Team Members	Gold	Silver	Bronze	Total
1930	9	3	4	1	8
1934	26	8	4	2	14
1938	158	24	19	22	65
1950	148	34	27	19	80
1954	73	20	11	17	48
1958	106	27	22	17	66
1962	208	38	36	38	105
1966	101	23	28	22	73
1970	107	36	24	22	82
1974	168	29	28	25	82
1978	148	24	33	27	84
1982	212	39	39	29	107
1986	237	40	46	34	120

Notes: (1) Figures given for team members do not include officials.
(2) Medal tallies include only a single medal for success in team events.

Venues:
1930—Hamilton, Canada, 1934—London, England, 1938—Sydney, Australia, 1950—Auckland, New Zealand, 1954—Vancouver, Canada, 1958—Cardiff, Wales,

1962–Perth, Australia, 1966–Kingston, Jamaica, 1970–Edinburgh, Scotland, 1974–Christchurch, New Zealand, 1978–Edmonton, Canada, 1982–Brisbane, Australia, 1986–Edinburgh, Scotland. The 1990 Games will be held at Auckland, New Zealand.

After the 1938 Games in Sydney, the British Empire Games Federation allocated the 1942 Games to Montreal, Canada. The Games were officially abandoned following the outbreak of World War II. Canada was given first option on the 1950 Games but declined.

CRICKET

BEGINNINGS IN AUSTRALIA

Some sketchy evidence exists that cricket may have developed in France. It has been established that Prince Edward played a game called *creag* about 1300, a Decretal by Pope Gregory IX (about 1230) contains an illumination showing a young man with a straight club and a ball, and other illustrations from the 13th and 14th centuries depict what appears to be a game similar to modern cricket. Definite evidence from 1598 exists of pupils of the Royal Grammar School at Guildford, UK, playing a game referred to as *creckett*. By 1677 cricket (or *creckitt*) was played in many parts of England.

There is a similar haziness of origins of the game in Australia, but evidence indicates that British settlers introduced the game and that the first match was played in Sydney in December 1803. The game was played almost exclusively in the first few years at what is now Hyde Park, Sydney, and clubs were formed in Sydney in 1826. Cricket was introduced in Tasmania in the 1820s and the Hobart Town Cricket Club was formed in 1832. The game was first played in Perth about 1835, Melbourne about 1838, Adelaide about 1839 and Brisbane about 1840.

One of the most important matches in Australian cricket history took place in May 1834, when 11 British-born military officers played a team of 'natives' (Australian-born sons of free settlers). Almost certainly, 'first class' cricket took place in 1855–56, when NSW played Victoria for the first time. The standard of cricket at the time lagged well behind that of England and in 1862, when the Melbourne catering firm of Spiers and Pond brought H. H. Stephenson's English team to Australia, the gap between the English professionals and the Australian amateurs was dramatically underlined. The first match played by the English side (not an official English touring squad) was at the Melbourne Cricket Ground on 1-4 January and the Englishmen agreed to play against 18 men representing 'Melbourne'. The tourists won by 95 runs; Spiers and Pond made a small fortune (more than 45,000 spectators attended) and the seeds for Australia v. England Test matches were sown. The English team played 13 matches and only one was against a local XI ('Surrey' v. 'The World'). Eleven of the games were against teams of 22 players and the Englishmen won five, lost two and drew four. They won their first match (against the 18-strong 'Melbourne' team) and drew the game against 'The World'.

English influence on Australian cricket:

Following the visit of Stephenson's team in 1862, English professional teams were eagerly pursued by private promoters and cricket associations. The second English team, captained by George Parr, toured in 1864, and in 1873–74 W. G. Grace captained a tour side sponsored by a group of Melbourne enthusiasts. The tour was enveloped in controversy, partly because of Grace's excessive financial demands, but was a towering success in most respects. The tourists became the first English team to play at the Adelaide Oval.

First England-Australia Test matches:
In 1876-77, when James Lillywhite Jnr captained the fourth English team to tour Australia. The first Australia v. England Test began at the Melbourne Cricket Ground on 15 March 1877 and Charles Bannerman (Australia) scored a single off the second ball of Alfred Shaw's historic opening Test over. Bannerman went on to score 165 (retired hurt) and Australia entered the record books as the winner of the first Test match in cricket history. Australia (245 and 104) defeated England (196 and 108) by 45 runs. Bannerman's century (the first in Test cricket) remained the highest score in Test cricket until 12 August 1884, when William Murdoch of Australia scored 211 against England in the third Test of the series against England at Kennington Oval, London, UK.

Aboriginal teams in England:
The first Australian cricket team to tour England was an Aboriginal side which played more than 30 matches in 1868. The second Aboriginal team began a tour of England in 1988 and played the first of a 28 one-day games schedule against Surrey at the famous London ground, The Oval, on 14 May.

FIRST AUSTRALIAN TESTS v. ALL NATIONS:
v. South Africa 1902-03 in South Africa. Australia won the series 2-0 (1 drawn).
v. West Indies 1930-31 in Australia. Australia won the series 4-1.
v. New Zealand 1945-46 in New Zealand. Australia won the only Test played.
v. India 1947-48 in Australia. Australia won the series 4-0 (1 drawn).
v. Pakistan 1956-57 in Pakistan. Pakistan won the only Test played.
v. Sri Lanka 1983 in Sri Lanka. Australia won the only Test played.

Tied Tests:
Only two Test matches have resulted in a tie. The first occurred in the First Test, Australia v. the West Indies at the Woolloongabba ground, Brisbane, on 9-14 December 1960. The West Indies scored 453 in its first innings and Australia replied with 505. The West Indies then scored 284, leaving Australia the task of scoring 233 runs in 312 minutes on the final day to win the match. Australia tied the scores with two balls remaining, one wicket to fall and one run needed for victory. Tail-end batsmen Lindsay Kline and Ian Meckiff began the winning run off the second last ball and Meckiff was run out by fieldsman Joe Solomons who broke the wicket with a magnificent throw from 12 metres. The first ever tied Test came after 3,142 balls had been bowled, with one ball remaining and after a total of 1,474 runs had been scored.

The second tied Test also involved Australia. In the first Test against India at Madras on 19-23 September 1986, Australia closed its first innings at 7-574. India replied with 397 and Australia declared at 5-170 in its second innings, leaving India the task of scoring 348 runs to win. Amazingly, like the tied Test against the West Indies, the match was also tied off the second last delivery of the game when NSW off-spinner Greg Matthews trapped India's Maninder Singh leg before wicket for no score. India was dismissed for 347 runs and the Test ended in a tie with both sides scoring a total of 744 runs off 2,416 deliveries.

First England v. Australia Test in England:
The fourth Test between the two

AUSTRALIA'S TEST RECORD v. ALL NATIONS

v.	Played	Won	Drawn	Lost	Tied	Abandoned
England	268*	98	79	90	–	1
South Africa	53	29	13	11	–	–
West Indies	62	27	15	19	1	–
New Zealand	24	11	8	5	–	–
India	45	20	16	8	1	–
Pakistan	28	11	9	8	–	–
Sri Lanka**	4	4	–	–	–	–
Totals	484	226	140	141	2	1

* Wisden's Almanack and all other English record books show the total number of Tests between England and Australia as 262. The difference in statistics stems from the Test scheduled to be played at the Melbourne Cricket Ground from 31 December 1970 to 5 January 1971. After the toss was made and the players took the field, rain made play impossible and the match was finally abandoned on the third day, without a ball being bowled. The Australian Cricket Board ruled that, because the toss had been made, all members of the Australian team should be credited with a Test appearance. The MCC did not agree with the ACB and none of the English players was similarly credited.
** A match played against Sri Lanka in May 1981 was officially described as an 'unofficial Test'. Rain washed out play when Sri Lanka needed only 127 runs to win with all their second innings wickets intact. The match was played at Colombo.

countries, played on 6-9 September 1880 at Kennington Oval, London. England won by five wickets and in England's first innings W. G. Grace became the second batsman to score a century in a Test match (152).

OTHER FIRST TEST MATCHES PLAYED OVERSEAS BY AUSTRALIA:
v. South Africa, 11-14 October 1902, Johannesburg, South Africa. Match drawn.
v. New Zealand, 29-30 March 1946, Wellington, NZ. Australia won by an innings and 103 runs.
v. West Indies, 26-31 March 1955, Kingston, Jamaica. Australia won by nine wickets.
v. Pakistan, 11-17 October 1956, at Karachi, Pakistan. Pakistan won by nine wickets.
v. India, 19-23 October 1956, at Madras, India. Australia won by an innings and five runs.

Australians who played Test cricket for two countries:
John Ferris (NSW) for Australia in 1886-90 and for England in 1891-92; William (Billy) Midwinter (Vic.*) for Australia in 1876-77 and for England in 1881-82; William Murdoch (NSW**) for Australia in 1876-90 and for England in 1891-92; Albert Trott (Vic.) for Australia in 1894-95 and for England in 1898-99; Samuel (Sammy) Woods (NSW) for Australia in 1888 and for England in 1895-96.

* Midwinter was born in England and came to Australia at the age of nine. He is the only player to have appeared for and against Australia.
** Murdoch was born in Victoria but played his first cricket in NSW.

MOST FAMOUS TEST MATCHES
Not necessarily among the most exciting, best attended or historically important, three Test matches rank as the most discussed and best remembered in Australian cricket history:
1. 1932-33—The Bodyline Series:
The English team, captained by Douglas Jardine, came to Australia for a five-Test series which became known as the 'Bodyline Series'. The entire series, and

one Test in particular, prompted the publishing of at least 22 books and, in recent times, a television series on the subject. The key Test was the third, at Adelaide Oval, SA, 13-19 January 1933. In this Test, the English bowling attack maintained such a short-pitched assault on the leg stump that Australian batsmen played in fear of serious injury. (The 'Bodyline' technique was not new and had actually been employed in England the previous year.) During the Test, the Australian Board of Control sent a cable of protest to the Marylebone Cricket Club (MCC) in England. The MCC cabled a furious reply in which they hinted at cancelling the rest of the Australian tour and the Australian Control Board shied away from prolonging a controversy which could easily have caused at least a temporary cessation of Tests between the two countries. England won the gory Adelaide Test by 338 runs after successfully curbing brilliant Australian batsman Don Bradman, inflicting painful injuries on most of the Australian team and sending Bert Oldfield to hospital with a fractured skull. Spectator feelings were at such fever pitch that 400 foot policemen were sent to Adelaide Oval to line the fence and an astounding 400 mounted policemen were stationed at a nearby oval in case the crowd got out of control.

2. 1960-61—The Tied Test:

The first test of the series between Australia and the third West Indies team to tour Australia resulted in the first tie in the history of Test cricket between all nations. The West Indies scored 453 in their first innings and Australia, with a magnificent 181 from Norman O'Neill, replied with 505. In their second innings, the West Indies scored 284, leaving Australia to score 233 in their second innings to win the match. Australia began its second innings on the last day, 14 December 1960, after captain Richie Benaud had been unsuccessful with his request for the outfield to be mown. As the match turned out, Australia would almost certainly have won comfortably had the outer turf, which was far too thick and high, been trimmed as requested. Australia suffered an early collapse and were 3-32 after 70 minutes and, following the quick dismissals of Colin McDonald and Les Favell, were in a desperate situation at 5-57 with 176 runs needed in 176 minutes. Alan Davidson and Ken Mackay rallied to score 35 runs in an hour before Mackay was dismissed with the score 6-92. Benaud then joined Davidson and pushed the score to 100, but at tea, Australia still needed to score 123 runs in 120 minutes to win. Benaud decided against playing for a draw and announced Australia would take any reasonable risk to win. At drinks, Australia needed 60 runs in 60 minutes. With 10 minutes remaining and Davidson and Benaud still at the wicket, Australia needed a bare nine runs. Disaster struck when Benaud called for a suicide single and Davidson was run out for 80, his highest-ever Test score. Wicket-keeper Wally Grout sprinted from the dressing room to the wicket to save valuable seconds with Australia needing seven runs in six minutes and three wickets remaining. Grout scored a single but when Benaud was unable to steal a run Grout was left to face speedster Wes Hall, who threw down a fearful bouncer which struck Grout in the groin but bounced away from fieldsmen. Grout hobbled through for a single and Australia required five runs to win from the seven balls remaining. Benaud was then caught behind off a Hall bouncer and Australia needed to score five runs off six balls. Ian Meckiff came to the wicket and stole a single off the second ball he faced—four runs to win off four balls. Grout then skied a ball, which Hall fumbled and dropped, and Australia needed three runs off the remaining three balls. Australia almost won the Test off the next ball, when Meckiff swung Hall to the boundary. The ball was slowed by the thick outfield clover and Meckiff and Grout, having run two, turned for the third and winning run but were beaten by a brilliant return from Conrad Hunte to wicket-keeper 'Gerry' Alexander who ran out Grout. The two runs scored levelled the scores—737 runs each with one run required for victory off the two remaining balls. The Gabba ground was hushed. Australia's last batsman, Lindsay Kline, came to the wicket, pushed his first delivery to leg and set off on what he hoped would be the winning run. Joe Solomons fielded from 12 m away and whipped the ball at the stumps at the batsman's end. From his fielding angle, he could sight only a single stump, but his aim was immaculate and Meckiff was run out with the scores tied and Australia all out, needing only one run to win with one ball remaining.

3. **1977—The Centenary Test:**
Held at the MCG, 12-17 March 1977, the Centenary Test between Australia and England ranks in the opinion of many veteran observers as the most exciting Test match ever played between two countries in Australia. Incredibly, Australia won the Test by 45 runs— exactly the same margin by which they won the inaugural Test on the same ground on 15-17 March 1877. Australia looked set for an easy win after batting first and scoring 138, dismissing England for 95 and then scoring 9-419 in their second innings to leave England the task of scoring 462 to win. England staged a remarkable recovery in their second innings on the fourth day and at stumps were 2-191. On the fifth and final day, a capacity crowd was kept in continual excitement as Dennis Amiss and Derek Randall added 166 before Amiss was bowled by Greg Chappell for 64. Randall was later felled by a Dennis Lillee bouncer and then given out caught behind when he was 161, but was recalled by Australian wicket-keeper Rodney Marsh who advised the umpire he had not taken the catch cleanly. Alan Knott and English captain Tony Greig almost won the Test for England, but all hopes vanished when Knott was given out lbw to Lillee for 42. The English tail-enders were not up to the task and England was all out for 417, losing the Test by 45 runs.

The Test was remarkable for many record achievements:
• On the fourth day Rodney Marsh became the first Australian wicket-keeper to score a Test century (110 not out in Australia's second innings) against England.
• On the second day Marsh passed Wally Grout's record of 187 Test dismissals by an Australian wicket-keeper.
• In Australia's first innings, Derek Underwood captured his 250th Test wicket when he bowled Greg Chappell for 40.
• Derek Randall scored his maiden Test century for England with 174 in the second innings.

A second Centenary Test was played three years later to celebrate the first Test played in England against Australia. Diehards were disappointed that the Test was staged not at The Oval (venue for the first England v. Australia Test in England), but at Lord's, which could accommodate a much larger crowd. The match ended tamely in a draw.

AUSTRALIAN TEST CRICKET RECORDS: BATTING
First century:
165 (retired hurt), by Charles Bannerman against England in the inaugural Test at the MCG, 1877.

First Test century partnership:
107, for the fifth wicket by Tom Horan (124) and George Giffen (30) against England at the MCG, 1881-82.

Highest individual score in a Test:
334, by Donald Bradman (b. Cootamundra, NSW, 27 August 1908) against England at Leeds, UK, 1930.

Most runs in Test career (against all nations):
7,110, at an innings average of 53.86 by Greg Chappell (b. Adelaide, 7 August 1948) in 87 Tests. Chappell broke Sir Donald Bradman's record of 6,996 runs (scored in 52 Tests, innings average 99.94), at the Sydney Cricket Ground on 4 January 1984 in his final Test appearance against Pakistan. Chappell scored 182 and became the third Australian to score centuries in his first (108) and last Test matches.

Sir Donald Bradman's records:
Tests played: 52. Runs: 6,996 at 99.94. Wickets: two at 36.00. Bradman's first class career record: 28,067 runs at 95.14 and 36 wickets at 37.97. He still holds the world record as the only batsman to score six triple centuries in first-class

cricket. He scored his 100th first-class century on 15 November 1947–172 for an Australian XI against India at Sydney, hit eight successive centuries against England in 1936–37 and 1938 and holds the record for the highest Test innings score by an Australian–334 against England at Leeds, UK, 1930. His highest score in first class cricket was 452 not out, for NSW v. Qld at Sydney in 1929–30. This remained a world record until bettered by Hanif Mohammad of Pakistan–499 for Karachi v. Bahawalpur in 1958–59.

Highest Test innings by Australia:
8-758 (dec.) against the West Indies in the fifth Test at Kingston, Jamaica, 1954–55.

Lowest Test innings by Australia:
36, against England in the first Test at Edgbaston, UK, 1902.

Highest Test innings against Australia:
7-903 (dec.), by England in the fourth Test at The Oval, UK, 1938.

Lowest Test innings against Australia:
36, by South Africa in the fifth Test at the MCG, 1931–32.

Highest Test innings score by an Australian in Australia:
307, by Bob Cowper against England in the fifth Test at the MCG, 1965–66. *Note:* The only other Australian apart from Bradman and Cowper to score 300 in a Test match innings is Bob Simpson–311 against England in the fourth Test at Old Trafford, UK, 1964.

Centuries by Australians in Test debut:
Charles Bannerman (165 retired hurt) against England at the MCG, 1877; Henry Graham (107) against England at Lord's, UK, 1893; Reginald Duff (104) against England at the MCG, 1902; Roger Hartigan (116) against England at Adelaide, 1908; Herbert Collins (104) against England at the SCG, 1920; Bill Ponsford (110) against England at the SCG, 1924; Archie Jackson (164) against England at Adelaide, 1929; Jim Burke (101 not out) against England at Adelaide, 1951; Doug Walters (155) against England at Brisbane, 1965; Greg Chappell (108) against England at Perth, 1970; Gary Cosier (109) against West Indies at the MCG, 1975; Dirk Wellham (103) against England at The Oval, UK, 1981; Kepler Wessels (162) against England at Brisbane, 1982; Wayne Phillips (159) against Pakistan at Perth, 1983. (*Note:* Many record books include Neil Harvey in the above list. Harvey scored 100 in his first Test against *England*–the third Test of his career.)

AUSTRALIAN TEST CRICKET RECORDS: BOWLING

Most wickets in a Test match:
Bob Massie (16-137) against England in the second Test at Lord's, UK, 1972. Next best: Fred Spofforth (14-90) against England at The Oval, UK, 1882; Clarrie Grimmett (14-119) against South Africa at Adelaide, 1932.

Most wickets in Test career:
355–then a world record by Dennis Lillee in 70 Tests spanning 1971-84. Lillee's average was 23.92. He captured a wicket (Sarfraz Nawaz of Pakistan) with the last ball he bowled in his Test career (fifth Test against Pakistan at the SCG, 9 January 1984). Lillee's record has since been exceeded by Ian Botham of England. Richie Benaud (248), Graham McKenzie (246), Ray Lindwall (228), and Clarrie Grimmett (216) are the only other Australians to capture more than 200 wickets in Test cricket.

Most wickets in a Test innings:
9-121, by Arthur Mailey against England at the MCG, 1921.

Test hat-tricks by Australians (final figures in brackets):
Fred Spofforth (6-48) against England at the MCG, 1879.
Hugh Trumble (4-49) against England at the MCG, 1901.
Hugh Trumble (7-28) against England at the MCG, 1904.
Thomas Matthews* (3-16) against South Africa at Old Trafford, UK, 1912.
Thomas Matthews* (3-38) against South Africa at Old Trafford, UK, 1912.
Lindsay Kline (3-18) against South Africa, at Cape Town, 1958.

*Matthews is the only bowler in the history of Test cricket to take a hat-trick in each innings. Both were achieved on the same day and without a fieldsman. He clean bowled two batsmen, caught and bowled two and captured two wickets lbw during a triangular Test series (Australia v. England v. South Africa) in England in 1912.

Most wickets by an Australian in Test series v. England:
42, in six Tests by Terry Alderman, 1981.

Most wickets by an Australian in Test series v. West Indies:
33, by Clarrie Grimmett, 1930-31 and by Alan Davidson, 1960-61.

Most wickets by an Australian in Test series v. South Africa:
44, by Clarrie Grimmett, 1935-36.

Most wickets in Test series v. India:
29, by Alan Davidson and by Richie Benaud, same season—1959-60.

AUSTRALIAN TEST CRICKET RECORDS: FIELDING

Most Test career catches:
122, by Greg Chappell, who broke Colin Cowdrey's (England) world record of 120, in his last Test appearance against Pakistan at the SCG, 1984.

Chappell set a world record with seven catches in the second Test against England at Perth in 1974-75. The record was equalled in 1977 by India's Yajurvindra Singh in a Test against England.

AUSTRALIAN TEST CRICKET RECORDS: WICKET-KEEPING

Most Test wickets taken:
A world record 355 by Rodney Marsh in 96 Tests (an Australian appearance record). In his final Test series against Pakistan in 1983-84, Marsh held 21 catches in 21 matches. His combination with fast bowler Dennis Lillee (b. Subiaco, WA, 18 July 1949) is the most famous in the history of Test cricket and his record of taking 95 (or almost 40 per cent) of the 239 Test catches off Lillee's bowling will probably never be equalled.

Most dismissals in a Test:
9 (8 caught, 1 stumped), against England at Lord's in 1956 by Gil Langley.

Only Australian wicketkeepers to score a Test century:
Rodney Marsh (3)—118 against Pakistan at Adelaide, 1972-73; 132 against New Zealand at Adelaide, 1973-74; 110 not out against England in the Centenary Test at the MCG, 1977. Wayne Phillips (1)—159 against Pakistan at Perth, 1983-84.

YOUNGEST AND OLDEST

Youngest Australian Test cricketer:
Ian Craig (b. Yass, NSW, 12 June 1935), who was 17 years 329 days old when he made his Australian debut against South Africa at the MCG, 1953.

Youngest Australian Test captain:
Ian Craig, who was 22 years 188 days old when he captained Australia in South Africa in 1957-58.

Oldest Australian captain:
Sydney Edward Gregory (b. Sydney, NSW, 14 April 1870), who was 42 years 130 days old when he captained Australia in England in 1912.

Oldest Australian Test player:
D. D. (Don) Blackie, who was 46 years 253 days old when he made his debut against England in 1928.

Highest attendance (any match) in Australia:
Highest single day attendance for a Test: 90,800 for the second day of the fifth Test Australia v. the West Indies at the MCG, 1961 (world record).

Highest attendance for one-day game:
78,142 for Australia v. the West Indies at the MCG, 10 January 1982.

Highest aggregate crowd for a Test match:
350,534 for the third Test Australia v. England at the MCG, 1-7 January 1937. On the third day of the Test, a then world record crowd of 87,798 attended the ground.

Record ground attendances:
SCG: 58,446 England v. Australia second day, second Test, 15 December 1928. **MCG:** 90,800 for the second day of the fifth Test, Australia v. the West Indies, 11 February 1961. **Adelaide Oval:** 50,962 on the second day of the third Test, Australia v. England, 14 January 1933. (This was the most publicised Test of the 'Bodyline' series.) **WACA ground, Perth:** 24,151 for the third day of the second Test, Australia v. England, 15 December 1974. **Brisbane (Woolloongabba ground):** 23,647 for the Australia v. the West Indies World Series Cup match, 17 January 1982. **Hobart:** 11,001 for the third day of a match between Tasmania and the West Indies, 1951-52.

WORLD SERIES CRICKET

International Test cricket was severely disrupted in May 1977 when Sydney media tycoon, Kerry Packer, announced that he had contracted 36 of the world's leading players to take part in a promotion he later called World Series Cricket. Australians who signed contracts were Ian Chappell, Greg Chappell, Rodney Marsh, Ray Bright, Doug Walters, David Hookes, Ian Davis, Jeff Thomson (who was later released from his contract), Rick McCosker, Kerry O'Keeffe, Len Pascoe, Max Walker, Richie Robinson, Ian Redpath, Mick Malone, Dennis Lillee, Gary Gilmour and Ross Edwards. WSC staged its first matches in 1977-78 and the Australian Cricket Board advised that even though Packer was willing to release his players for Test matches (provided they did not clash with his own promotions) none would be considered for Australian teams. Packer and the Board finally reached an agreement after the 1978-79 WSC season and all players returned to 'legitimate' cricket—in return for Packer's National Nine TV network gaining exclusive international and representative television rights. The costly and messy affair was a near-disaster in the first WSC season, but turned the corner when Packer introduced night cricket (first match at VFL Park) and attracted huge crowds.

First night match at the MCG:

On 17 February 1985, when $4,600,000 worth of equipment lit the ground for the opening round of the World Championship of Cricket match between Australia and England. Construction of the six towers and fitting of 844, 2,000-watt floodlights was delayed by industrial action by the Builders Labourers' Federation. The installation was finally completed by members of the Australian Workers' Union and the Federated Ironworkers' Association. Attendance at the match was 83,494.

SHEFFIELD SHIELD

The competition and the perpetual trophy was named in honour of Lord Sheffield of England who brought the 1891-92 English team to Australia and donated funds to help develop Australian cricket. Australian authorities instituted the first Sheffield Shield competition (for a series of matches between all States) in 1892-93, when entries came from NSW, Vic. and SA. Qld entered in 1926-27, WA in 1947-48 and Tas. in 1977-78. NSW has been the most successful state, while Qld and Tas. have never won.

Miscellaneous records:

Highest team score: 1,107, by Vic. against NSW at the SCG, 1926-27.

Lowest team score:

27, by SA against NSW at the SCG, 1955-56.

Highest individual score:

452 not out, by Don Bradman for NSW against Qld at the SCG, 1929-30.

SHEFFIELD SHIELD WINNERS

Season	Winner
1892-93	Victoria
1893-94	South Australia
1894-95	Victoria
1895-96	New South Wales
1896-97	New South Wales
1897-98	Victoria
1898-99	Victoria
1899-1900	New South Wales
1900-01	Victoria
1901-02	New South Wales
1902-03	New South Wales
1903-04	New South Wales
1904-05	New South Wales
1905-06	New South Wales
1906-07	New South Wales
1907-08	Victoria
1908-09	New South Wales
1909-10	South Australia
1910-11	New South Wales
1911-12	New South Wales
1912-13	South Australia
1913-14	New South Wales
1914-15	Victoria
1915-19	*Not Held*
1919-20	New South Wales
1920-21	New South Wales
1921-22	Victoria
1922-23	New South Wales
1923-24	Victoria
1924-25	Victoria
1925-26	New South Wales
1926-27	South Australia
1927-28	Victoria
1928-29	New South Wales
1929-30	Victoria
1930-31	Victoria

Season	Winner
1931-32	New South Wales*
1932-33	New South Wales
1933-34	Victoria
1934-35	Victoria
1935-36	South Australia
1936-37	Victoria
1937-38	New South Wales
1938-39	South Australia
1939-40	New South Wales
1940-46	Not Held
1946-47	Victoria
1947-48	Western Australia**
1948-49	New South Wales
1949-50	New South Wales
1950-51	Victoria
1951-52	New South Wales
1952-53	South Australia
1953-54	New South Wales
1954-55	New South Wales
1955-56	New South Wales
1956-57	New South Wales
1957-58	New South Wales
1958-59	New South Wales
1959-60	New South Wales
1960-61	New South Wales
1961-62	New South Wales
1962-63	Victoria
1963-64	South Australia
1964-65	New South Wales
1965-66	New South Wales
1966-67	Victoria
1967-68	Western Australia
1968-69	South Australia
1969-70	Victoria
1970-71	South Australia
1971-72	Western Australia
1972-73	Western Australia
1973-74	Victoria
1974-75	Western Australia
1975-76	South Australia
1976-77	Western Australia
1977-78	Western Australia
1978-79	Victoria
1979-80	Victoria
1980-81	Western Australia
1981-82	South Australia
1982-83	New South Wales
1983-84	Western Australia
1984-85	New South Wales
1985-86	New South Wales
1986-87	Western Australia
1987-88	Western Australia

* Won position by averages
** Won position by percentages

WOMEN'S CRICKET

Women's cricket is believed to have been first played at Bendigo (Vic.) in 1874, but some evidence has since been unearthed which indicates that women may have played in Sydney before that date.

First interstate match:
In 1890, between NSW and Vic., in Sydney.

Formation of the first national body:
1931 when the Australian Women's Cricket Council was established comprising delegates from NSW, Vic. and Qld.

First Test matches:
In 1934-35, when England, captained by Betty Archdale (later a leading Australian educationalist), toured Australia and NZ. England defeated Australia 2-0 (one Test drawn) and won 14 and drew 6 matches of 21 played in Australia.

First Australian team overseas:
In 1937, when Australia, captained by Margaret Peden, made a 19-match tour of the UK and lost only one match, the second Test. Australia drew the Test series with a win, a loss and a draw.

First century in a Test:
119, by Myrtle Maclagan of England in the second Test at Sydney in 1935.

First double century:
200, by Pat Holes of Australia against West of England at Basingstoke, England in 1937.

World Cup competition:
The World Cup was instituted in England in 1973 and Australia was runner-up to England. Australia won the Cup in 1978 in India.

Historic match at Lord's:
History was made in August 1976 when the MCG agreed to make the famous Lord's ground available for a non-Test match between Australia and England. It was won by England, before a crowd of 3,500.

World record crowd:
35,000, for the 1978 World Cup match between Australia and India at Patna, India, on 8 January 1978.

Greatest Australian all-rounder:
Betty Rebecca Wilson (b. Melbourne, Vic. 1921), who began her Test career against NZ in 1948 and in her first match set a fourth wicket partnership of 163

with Una Paisley. She became the first Australian to score a century in a Test in 1948–49 (111 against England). In 16 Test innings she scored 862 runs, including three centuries, and took 66 wickets at 11.56, including, in 1957–58, the remarkable Test figures of 7–7 which included a hat-trick.

Highest grade score:
298, by Jan Molyneux (later Mrs Jan Wilkinson) for Olympic v. Northcote in the 1967 Melbourne A-grade final at Mayor's Park, Clifton Hill, Vic. In 1975 Molyneux scored 252 not out for Olympic and shared in a first wicket partnership of 278 with Dawn Rae (228). Olympic declared at 2–532.

CYCLING

BEGINNINGS IN AUSTRALIA

Cycling became a national recreational passion following the appearance of the first bicycles (velocipedes) in Australia in 1868. The first club was formed in the same year and one of the enthusiasts who laid down the foundations for competitive cycling was R. C. Bagot, Secretary of the Victoria Racing Club and design consultant on the construction of the Melbourne Cricket Ground and Flemington Racecourse.

First races:
The earliest-known race was staged on grass at the MCG on 10 July 1869 and drew an estimated 12,000 spectators. J. Finlay of Fitzroy won the historic event from R. Warnock of Emerald Hill.

First championship:
The NSW Championship held on the grassed Association Cricket Ground (now the Sydney Cricket Ground) at Moore Park, Sydney, on 26 August 1882. The meeting was organised by the Sydney Bicycle Club, formed in 1879 and still in existence.

First interstate distance record:
On 23 May 1884 Mr A. Edwards, of the Sydney Bicycle Club, left Sydney to ride a 'boneshaker' (penny-farthing) to Melbourne. Edwards took eight and a half days to cover the 856 km of cattle trails, sandy tracks and open paddocks. The machine he rode is still on display at the Sydney Bicycle Club premises in Carrington Street, Sydney.

First professional races:
In 1890, when the Melbourne Bicycle Club broke away from the Victorian Bicycle Association and staged an unofficial version of the Austral Wheelrace (first held on 30 January 1886), at the Melbourne Cricket Ground. The promotion attracted more than 40,000 spectators and the rebel riders received prize money for the first time (Con Dwyer (Vic.), winner of the inaugural Austral Wheelrace, received a grand piano as his prize).

First major road race:
Held on 6 October 1895. The event was the Dunlop Road Race, over 165 miles (265.5 km) from Warrnambool to Melbourne. The winner was A. Calder, off a two-hour handicap, who covered the distance in 11 hrs 44 mins 30 secs. The race, which is still held, became world famous within 20 years.

First major track race in Sydney:
The 'Sydney Thousand', staged by colourful promoter Hugh D. McIntosh at the Sydney Cricket Ground in 1903. McIntosh decided to upstage the famous Austral Wheelrace and offered 750 pounds – 350 pounds more prize money than the Melbourne classic – to make the Sydney event the richest in the world. To

ensure a good crowd, McIntosh imported a team of champion American riders headed by negroes Major Taylor and Floyd McFarland and spent a small fortune installing track lighting. The race drew an estimated 60,000 spectators and N. C. Hopper (USA) won off a handicap of 75 yds (68.5 m), clocking 1 min 53.4 secs for the 1 mile (1.6 km) race.

First Australian to win a world championship:
Bob Spears (1893-1950) of Dubbo, NSW, who won the World Professional Sprint Championship in Paris in 1920.

First Australian Olympic gold medallist:
Edgar L. 'Dunc' Gray (b. Goulburn, NSW, 1907), who won the 1,000 m time trial at the Los Angeles Games in 1932.

First Empire or Commonwealth Games gold medallist:
Edgar L. 'Dunc' Gray, who won the 1,000 m time trial at the Empire Games (now Commonwealth Games) in 1934, in a Games record of 1 min 16.4 secs.

First winner of a world amateur championship:
Sid Patterson (b. Melbourne, 1927), who won the World Amateur Sprint Championship at Copenhagen, Denmark, in 1949.

First Australians to compete at the Olympic Games:
Jack King and Jerry Halpin, represented Australia in the 1,000 m sprint at Antwerp in 1920. Halpin fared best to be placed third in his semi-final. King was eliminated in the third heat of the sprint and was injured in a fall early in the 50 km track race.

First Australians at the Empire or Commonwealth Games:
Edgar L. 'Dunc' Gray (NSW) and Horace Pethybridge (NSW), at the London Empire Games in 1934. Gray won the gold medal in the time trial and Pethybridge won a silver medal in the 1,000 yds (914.4 m) track sprint. Both had punctures and retired in the 10 mile (16 km) track race.

First six-day race:
In 1881, for amateur riders, at the Melbourne Cricket Ground.

First races for women:
A tricycle event held in Adelaide by the South Australian Bicycle Club in 1885. The winner was a Miss Wills, who covered 3 miles (4,828 m) in 9 mins 43 secs and won a trophy valued at four guineas.

Greatest women riders:
Doreen Middleton, daughter of early champion A. C. (Albert) Middleton, who, in May 1931, set a record for women by riding from Adelaide to Melbourne in 4 days 20 hrs 30 mins. The following month she lowered her own record, arriving at the Melbourne GPO on 28 June 1931 in 3 days, 23 hrs, 56 mins.

In the modern era, Julie Speight (NSW), aged 19, has remained unbeatable in track and road cycling since she won the Australian Sprint (1,000 m) and Road Championships in 1983 at the age of 16. She retained both titles in 1984 and added the NSW sprint, 5 km and Road Race titles. In 1984 she won the Yu King Cup road race over 54 km in China. Speight was a surprise omission from the Australian team at the 1984 Los Angeles Olympic Games, after being advised she would be chosen for the women's road race. The Japanese riders she defeated in China all finished in the top 20 at Los Angeles and experts were convinced that Speight could have placed as high as sixth and perhaps have won at least a bronze medal.

First Australians to contest the Tour de France:
Hubert (later Sir Hubert) Opperman (b. Melbourne, 1904), O. Bainbridge, A. Watson and H. Osborne. The four made up an official Australian team captained by Opperman. All except Opperman failed to finish the world's most gruelling road race. Opperman battled on to finish a remarkable 17th.

First Australian to win a major overseas road race:
Hubert Opperman, who in 1931 became the first non-European to win the classic 726 mile non-stop Paris–Brest–Paris event.

First Australian to win a national title of another country:
Alf Goullet of Gippsland, Vic. became the American all-round champion in 1912, when he won 22 races of a season-long point-score competition covering a wide variety of track events.

Australian world championship winners:

- 1920: Bob Spears (NSW), professional sprint title at Paris, France
- 1949: Sid Patterson (Vic.), amateur sprint title at Copenhagen, Denmark
- 1950: Sid Patterson (Vic.), amateur pursuit title
- 1950: Jack Hoobin (Vic.), amateur road title at Moorslede, Belgium
- 1952: Sid Patterson (Vic.), professional pursuit title
- 1953: Sid Patterson (Vic.), professional sprint title
- 1956: Graeme French (Tas.), professional motor-paced title
- 1970: Gordon Johnson (Vic.), professional sprint title
- 1975: John Nicholson (Vic.), professional sprint title
- 1976: John Nicholson (Vic.), professional sprint title
- 1980: Danny Clark (Tas.), professional Keirin title
- 1980: Gary Sutton (NSW), amateur 50-pointscore
- 1983: Steele Bishop (WA), world professional pursuit title
- 1987: Martin Vinnicombe (NSW), world amateur time trial.

MARATHON CHAMPIONS AND RECORD BREAKERS

The most successful long distance and city-to-city record breakers have been Hubert Opperman (Vic.), Vic Browne (Vic.), and Murray Walker (NSW).

At the peak of his career, Opperman held every major city-to-city record in Australia plus the world record for 24 hrs unpaced on a track and 1,000 miles (1,609 km) track motor-paced. His three most famous long-distance road records in Australia were: 1937 – Perth to Sydney (13 days, 10 hrs, 11 mins); 1936 – Brisbane to Sydney (47 hrs 10 mins); 1929 – Melbourne to Sydney (39 hrs 42 mins). He also once held the record for the famous length of Scotland and England (Lands End to John O'Groats) course.

In April 1969, Vic Browne bettered Opperman's Perth to Sydney record with 11 days, 6 hrs, 47 mins, but rode a far superior cycle with modern gears, on greatly improved roads.

In 1957, Browne also bettered Opperman's Melbourne to Sydney record with a time of 32 hrs 57 mins 9 secs. Again, he had the advantage of superior equipment and road conditions.

In 1970, Murray Walker broke Opperman's 32-year-old Newcastle (NSW) to Sydney and return record, taking 4 mins, 37.4 secs off the record with a time of 10 hrs 6 mins 22.6 secs.

In 1972, Walker bettered Opperman's record from Brisbane to Sydney by 1 hr 33 mins, with a time of 45 hrs 37 mins. Walker announced plans to attack every major road distance and city-to-city record, but a few months later was killed in a car accident.

World record prize money—modern era:

In 1973, the Lavington (NSW) Sports Club staged what was then the world's richest track handicap race over 3,219 metres. Frank Atkins (Tas.), won the race and collected A$3,500 in prize money. The single race carried A$5,300.

Only national championship clean sweep:

In 1973, Danny Clark (Tas.) won every track title at the National Amateur Championship carnival – the 1,000 m time trial, 1,000 m sprint, 16 km track race and 4,000 m individual pursuit.

Youngest major race winner:

Stephen McGlede, 16, of Kingswood, NSW, became the youngest winner of a major track race in Australian cycling history when he won the Sydney Thousand (1,000 m handicap) at Sydney's Camperdown Velodrome on 8 December 1985. McGlede, the Australian track and road juvenile champion, started only 80 m ahead of the Commonwealth Games sprint champion, Kenrick Tucker, and Los Angeles Olympic sprint silver medallist, Nelson Vails of the United States.

Most six-day wins:
Australians have always shone in six-day track races on the rich overseas circuits. Danny Clark (Tas.) won 36 such events between 1974 and 1987, often with fellow Australian Don Allen (Vic.) as partner. Behind Clark, the best record is held by Reg McNamara (NSW, 1887–1971), with 19 wins, nearly all achieved in the USA. Next best are Don Allen (Vic.) – 18; Reg Arnold (NSW) and Sid Patterson (Vic.) – 16; and Alfred Goullet (Vic.) – 15.

Most versatile rider:
Many experts consider Victorian Russell Mockridge (1928–58), the most adaptable rider in the history of Australian cycling. Though handicapped by poor eyesight, he rode a standard touring bike to victory in 1946 in the first race he ever contested, and less than two years later won the Australian Amateur Road Championship. He represented Australia in the road race at the 1948 Olympic Games and then switched to track events. In 1950 he won the Empire Games 1,000 m sprint and the time trial, and in 1952 the World Open Grand Prix (a sprint event open to professionals), before competing at the Helsinki Olympic Games where he won two gold medals: in the 1,000 m time trial and the 2,000 m tandem race with Lionel Cox (NSW). A year later, Mockridge turned professional and in 1955, after many major track wins, teamed with fellow Australians Reg Arnold and Sid Patterson to win the Paris Six-Day Classic. That same year he entered the Tour de France road marathon and, despite riding solo against teams of 10 riders who protected each other, finished well up in the 60 riders who completed the exhausting 4,466 km event. Mockridge then returned to Australia, set a world record average of 44 km/h for the Melbourne to Warrnambool road race, won the Australian road title for the second successive year (it was his third successive Victorian Road Championship), and a string of major tour events besides many major races on the track. Mockridge was killed when he swerved to avoid a fallen rider in the Tour of Gippsland event and was hit by a passing bus.

EQUESTRIAN

BEGINNINGS IN AUSTRALIA
Although competition was widespread and dates back to at least 1830, organised equestrian sport did not emerge until the Equestrian Federation of Australia was formed in 1949. Prior to this, competitions were largely confined to country areas and city dwellers usually only became aware of the sport when attending events such as the Sydney, Melbourne and Brisbane Royal Shows.

First Australian team at the Olympic Games:
1956 when the events were held in Stockholm, Sweden. Although Australia hosted the Games that year in Melbourne strict quarantine laws made it impossible for equestrian events to form part of the Melbourne competitions. Australia's team was David Wood, Brian Crago, B. Jacobs, J. Winchester, E. Barker and W.

Thompson. Australia finished fourth in the three-day teams event with Crago placing eleventh in the individual section.

First Olympic success:
1960 in Rome where the Australian team won the three-day teams event. Laurie Morgan, who was a shock omission from the 1956 team, took out the individual section with the lowest (best) score ever recorded at an Olympics. The other team members were Neale Lavis and veteran Bill Roycroft, who signed himself out of hospital after a fall on the second day and rode with a broken collarbone.

First World Champion:
Greg Eurell, 19, the son of former Tumut (NSW) jockey Laurie. He won the 1979 World Equestrian Championship with an unmatched six clear rounds riding Johnny Mac.

First woman Olympic competitor:
Bridget McIntyre (NSW) who represented Australia at the 1964 Tokyo Games.

First overseas success by a woman competitor:
1978 when Sally Horner (WA), aged 17, won the women's National Show Jumping Championship at the Royal Windsor Horse Show (UK).

Australians to win Badminton Trial (UK)
Bill Roycroft (Vic.) 1960 and Laurie Morgan (NSW) 1961. Morgan finished runner-up to Roycroft in 1960. The Badminton is an individual three-day event inaugurated in 1949.

Most famous Olympic competitor:
Bill Roycroft (Vic.) who won a gold medal at Rome in 1960 and made five successive Games appearances through to Montreal in 1976. Roycroft was 61 when he rode at Montreal with two of his sons, Barry, 32, and Wayne, 30, joining him in the team. He carried the Australian flag at the Opening Ceremony of the 1968 Mexico City Olympics and won bronze medals at Mexico and at Montreal in the three-day teams event. Two more Roycroft sons have represented Australia—Bill jnr at Mexico City and Clarke at Munich in 1972.

Most famous competitor:
Kevin Bacon (b. Dungog, NSW) who represented Australia at three Olympics (1968, '72, '76). Bacon was leading rider at the Sydney Royal Easter Show for 18 successive years; champion rider at Melbourne on 10 occasions; and champion rider at Brisbane 15 times. He later settled permanently in Paris, France, and became a full-time professional show rider. Among his major successes have been wins in the Madison Square Garden International (USA)—4 times; the Berlin International Prize (acknowledged as the unofficial world professional championship); and in the national championships of Canada, France, USA and New Zealand.

Most versatile competitor:
Laurie Morgan (Vic.), who won the individual gold medal at the 1960 Rome Olympic Games three-day teams event and became the first (and to date only) competitor to record a plus score. Morgan mixed equestrian with VFL football for Fitzroy and represented Victoria; rowed for the state in the King's Cup eight; won the 1934 Victorian amateur heavyweight boxing championship; and played polo for Victoria.

Australia's Olympic boycott:
In response to a general request from Prime Minister Malcolm Fraser, the Australian Equestrian Federation boycotted the 1980 Moscow Olympics following the Russian invasion of Afghanistan. The decision probably cost veteran Bill Roycroft the chance to represent Australia a record six times. Roycroft had already been chosen as team manager and as the team had not been finalised and Roycroft had announced his availability, there was every possibility he would have been chosen as a competitor—at the age of 65.

Australia's greatest-ever team performance:
10-11 January 1981 at the Benson and Hedges International held at Wentworth Park, Sydney. Competing against official teams from England, Ireland, New Zealand and the USA,

Australian riders made a clean sweep of major events. Shelley Kelly (NSW) won the Grand Prix final from Greg Eurell (NSW) and Kevin Bourke (NSW). Vicki Roycroft (NSW) (daughter-in-law of the famous Bill snr) won the incorporated British Airways Championship from Glen Bolger (Vic.) and Andrew Inglis (NSW). Peter Mullins (Qld) won the NSW Show Jumping Association Power Stakes from Eric Musgrove (Vic.) and Kerry Langbecker (Qld) and the Australian team easily defeated Ireland in the final of the team show jumping after faultless rounds by captain Guy Creighton (NSW), Gavin Chester (Vic.) and Jeff McVean (Vic.). To ensure fairness, all competitors drew for mounts from a pool of horses leased from Australian owners.

GOLF

BEGINNINGS IN AUSTRALIA
Although only scant documentation exists, it seems reasonably certain that a Scottish immigrant named Alex Reid was the first man to play golf in Australia on a surveyed course. According to most golf historians, Reid pegged out a short course at Ratho, Bothwell, near Hobart, Tasmania, in the late 1820s and played golf with friends who shared his small supply of clubs and 'featheries' (feather-packed sewn leather balls). Reid's rough course is now part of the Bothwell Golf Club.

The first man to play golf on the mainland was another Scotsman, the Hon. James Graham, who designed his own course at Flagstaff Gardens, Melbourne, Vic., in 1847.

First Australian club:
Flagstaff Hill (see above) was the first course in Australia to boast a clubhouse, a membership list and a properly constituted committee. The course stretched from the present site of Flagstaff Gardens in Melbourne to near the Flemington Bridge.

First Australian championship:
The Australian Ladies' Championship, played at Geelong on 29-30 August 1894 and won by Miss C. B. McKenzie of Victoria. The event was officially the Victorian Ladies' Championship, but Australian golfing records have always listed the result under the heading 'Australian Championship'.

First men's Australian championship:
L. A. Whyte of Geelong, Vic., won the Australian Amateur Championship at Caulfield, Melbourne, on 9 November 1894.

First Australian Open champion:
The Hon. Michael Scott of England, at the Australian Golf Club, Botany, near Sydney, on 3 September 1904. Entrants from all States, England, Scotland and New Zealand, played 36 holes for two successive days; Scott won with an aggregate of 315 with scores of 77, 74, 80 and 84. Scott was runner-up the following year and won the Open again in 1907. He also won the Australian Amateur Championship in 1905, '07, '09 and '10 before returning to England where he became England's captain, finished runner-up in the British Open and won the French Championship.

Australian Open:
The Open has been held every year since 1904, with the exception of the war years of 1914-19 and 1940-45. Especially in post-World War II years, many of the world's greatest golfers have attempted to win the event. Winners include Gene Sarazen, Jack Nicklaus, Arnold Palmer, Jerry Snead, Bill Rogers and Tom Watson (USA), and South Africans

Bobby Locke and Gary Player.
Most Open wins:
Seven, by Gary Player (South Africa) in 1958, '62, '63, '65, '69, '70 and '74. Player finished runner-up (tied with Ossie Pickworth) in 1957 and in 1968.
Most wins by an Australian:
Five, by amateur Ivo Whitton in 1912, '13, '26, '29 and '31.
Amateurs who have won the Open:
1904 .... Hon. M. Scott
1907 .... Hon. M. Scott
1908 .... C. Pearce
1909 .... C. Felstead

Year	Winner
1912	I. Whitton
1913	I. Whitton
1924	A. Russell
1926	I. Whitton
1929	I. Whitton
1931	I. Whitton
1932	M. Ryan
1938	J. Ferrier
1939	J. Ferrier
1960	B. Devlin

Most wins in succession:
Three, by Ossie Pickworth (Vic.) in 1946, '47 and '48.

AUSTRALIAN OPEN WINNERS

Year	Venue	Winner	Score
1904	The Australian (Botany)	Hon. Michael Scott (UK) (a)	315
1905	Royal Melbourne	Dan Soutar	330
1906	Royal Sydney	Carnegie Clark	322
1907	Royal Melbourne	Hon. Michael Scott (UK) (a)	318
1908	The Australian (Kensington)	Clyde Pearce (a)	311
1909	Royal Melbourne	Clyde Felstead (a)	316
1910	Royal Adelaide	Carnegie Clark	306
1911	Royal Sydney	Carnegie Clark	321
1912	Royal Melbourne	Ivo Whitton (a)	321
1913	Royal Melbourne	Ivo Whitton (a)	302
1914-19	Not played		
1920	The Australian (Kensington)	Joe Kirkwood	290
1921	Royal Melbourne	A. Le Fevre	295
1922	Royal Sydney	C. Campbell	307
1923	Royal Adelaide	Tommy Howard	301
1924	Royal Melbourne	Alex Russell (a)	303
1925	The Australian (Kensington)	Fred Popplewell	295
1926	Royal Adelaide	Ivo Whitton (a)	297
1927	Royal Melbourne	Rufus Stewart	297
1928	Royal Sydney	Fred Popplewell	295
1929	Royal Adelaide	Ivo Whitton (a)	309
1930	The Metropolitan (Melbourne)	Frank Eyre	306
1931	The Australian (Kensington)	Ivo Whitton (a)	301
1932	Royal Adelaide	Mick Ryan (a)	296
1933	Royal Melbourne	Mick Kelly	302
1934	Royal Sydney	Bill Bolger	283
1935	Royal Adelaide	F. McMahon	293

Year	Venue	Winner	Score
1936	The Metropolitan (Melbourne)	Gene Sarazen (USA)	282
1937	The Australian (Kensington)	George Naismith	299
1938	Royal Adelaide	Jim Ferrier (a)	283
1939	Royal Melbourne	Jim Ferrier (a)	285
1940-45	Not played		
1946	Royal Sydney	Ossie Pickworth	289
1947	Royal Queensland	Ossie Pickworth	285
1948	Kingston Heath, Vic.	Ossie Pickworth*	289
1949	The Australian (Kensington)	Eric Cremin	287
1950	Kooyonga, SA	Norman Von Nida	286
1951	The Metropolitan (Melbourne)	Peter Thomson	283
1952	Lake Karrinyup, WA	Norman Von Nida	278
1953	Royal Melbourne	Norman Von Nida	278
1954	Kooyonga, SA	Ossie Pickworth	280
1955	Gailes (Brisbane)	Bobby Locke (S. Africa)	290
1956	Royal Sydney	Bruce Crampton	289
1957	Kingston Heath, Vic.	Frank Phillips	287
1958	Kooyonga, SA	Gary Player (S. Africa)	271
1959	The Australian (Kensington)	Kel Nagle	284
1960	Lake Karrinyup, WA	Bruce Devlin (a)	282
1961	Victoria (Melbourne)	Frank Phillips	275
1962	Royal Adelaide	Gary Player (S. Africa)	281
1963	Royal Melbourne	Gary Player (S. Africa)	278
1964	The Lakes, NSW	Jack Nicklaus (USA)**	287
1965	Kooyonga, SA	Gary Player (S. Africa)	264****
1966	Royal Queensland	Arnold Palmer (USA)	276
1967	Commonwealth (Melbourne)	Peter Thomson	281
1968	Lake Karrinyup, WA	Jack Nicklaus (USA)	270
1969	Royal Sydney	Gary Player (S. Africa)	288
1970	Kingston Heath, Vic.	Gary Player (S. Africa)	280
1971	Royal Hobart	Jack Nicklaus (USA)	269
1972	Kooyonga, SA	Peter Thomson***	281
1973	Royal Queensland	J. C. Snead (USA)	280
1974	Lake Karrinyup, WA	Gary Player (S. Africa)	277
1975	The Australian (Kensington)	Jack Nicklaus (USA)	279
1976	The Australian (Kensington)	Jack Nicklaus (USA)	286
1977	The Australian (Kensington)	David Graham	284
1978	The Australian (Kensington)	Jack Nicklaus (USA)	284
1979	The Metropolitan (Melbourne)	Jack Newton	288

Year	Venue	Winner	Score
1980	The Lakes, NSW	Greg Norman	284
1981	Victoria (Melbourne)	Bill Rogers (USA)	282
1982	The Australian (Kensington)	Bob Shearer	287
1983	Kingston Heath, Vic.	Peter Fowler	285
1984	Royal Melbourne	Tom Watson (USA)	281
1985	Royal Melbourne	Greg Norman	212[1]
1986	The Metropolitan (Melbourne)	Rodger Davis	278
1987	Royal Melbourne	Greg Norman	273

* After play-off with Jim Ferrier. Pickworth 71, Ferrier 74.
** After play-off with Bruce Devlin. Nicklaus 67, Devlin 70.
*** After play-off with David Graham. Thomson 68, Graham 74.
**** Record score
(a) Amateur
(1) Reduced to 54 holes by heavy rain
Note: Carnegie Clark was born in Scotland but did not return to that country after arriving in Australia in 1902, and has never been regarded as an 'overseas' winner of the Australian Open (1906, '10 and '11).

Australian Masters:

First staged in 1979, the Australian Masters is now recognised as the second most important local event behind the Australian Open.

1979 .... Barry Vivian
1980 .... Gene Littler (USA)
1981 .... Greg Norman
1982 .... Graham Marsh
1983 .... Greg Norman
1984 .... Greg Norman
1985 .... Bernardt Langer (W.Germany)
1986 .... Mark O'Meara (USA)
1987 .... Greg Norman
1988 .... Ian Baker-Finch

Major overseas wins by Australian professionals:

British Open: Peter Thomson (Vic.) 1954, '55, '56, '58 and '65; Kel Nagle (NSW) 1960; Greg Norman (Qld) 1986.
US Open: David Graham (NSW–resident USA) 1981.
US PGA Championship: Jim Ferrier (NSW–resident USA) 1947. David Graham (NSW–resident USA) 1979.
World Match Play Championship: David Graham (NSW–resident USA) 1976. Graham Marsh (WA) 1977. Greg Norman (Qld) 1980, 1986.
Canadian Open: Joe Kirkwood (NSW–resident USA) 1933. Jim Ferrier (NSW–resident USA) 1950 and '51. Kel Nagle (NSW) 1964. Greg Norman (Qld) 1984.
French Open: Kel Nagle (NSW) 1961. Alan Murray (NSW) 1962. Bruce Devlin (NSW) 1963. Greg Norman (Qld) 1980.
Japan Open: David Graham (NSW–resident USA) 1972.
European Open: Greg Norman (Qld) 1986.

Australians have also largely dominated the New Zealand Open in post-World War II years and have won semi-major events such as the Philippines Open, Hong Kong Open, Malaysian Open, Cannes Open and a small number of US PGA Championship events.

Australia in the World Cup:

Australian teams have been regular entrants in the World Cup (instituted as the Canada Cup at Montreal in 1953 and re-named the World Cup in 1967). The World Cup is the only major event on the international calendar in which professional players receive expenses only.

Australian successes:

1954: Montreal, Canada. 1st–Peter Thomson (Vic.) and Kel Nagle (NSW). Thomson equal second in individual International Trophy.
1959: Melbourne, Australia. 1st–Peter Thomson (Vic.) and Kel Nagle (NSW). Thomson tied for first place in the individual International Trophy and lost the play-off to Stan Leonard (Canada).
1970: Buenos Aires, Argentina. 1st–David Graham (NSW) and Bruce Devlin

(NSW). Graham finished second and Devlin third in the individual.

Australia in the Dunhill Cup:
The Australian team of Greg Norman, David Graham and Graham Marsh won the inaugural event with a 3-0 defeat of the United States at St Andrews, Scotland on 20 October 1985. The event, scheduled to be played annually, was the first US$1,000,000 teams tournament in the history of golf. The three Australians each received A$142,490. Australia's team of Greg Norman, David Graham and Rodger Davis won again in 1986.

First Australian golf 'millionaire':
Bruce Crampton (NSW) became the first Australian to win US$1,000,000 in prize money, on 1 July 1973, when he took his career earnings to US$1,002,885 by finishing fourth in the Western Open at Chicago, USA. He was the fifth player in the history of the game to earn more than US$1,000,000 (after Arnold Palmer, Jack Nicklaus, Billy Casper and Lee Trevino) and when he retired in May 1977, had taken his career earnings to US$1,374,294.

Most course records set in Australia:
75 — believed to be a world record — set by Billy Dunk (NSW) between 1959 and 1976. His lowest score in tournament play was a course-record 60 (out in 33, in with 27) in the NBN-3 Newcastle Ten Thousand Professional Tournament at the Merewether Golf Course, NSW, on 15 November 1970. Dunk finished with seven straight birdies to be 10 under par. His score is still the lowest recorded in a major Australian tournament.

Australian PGA Championship:
First held as a match-play event in 1906 and won by D. G. (Dan) Soutar at Royal Sydney. The Championship was changed to a 72-hole stroke-play competition in 1964.

Most PGA Championship wins:
Four each by Norman Von Nida (1946, '48, '50 and '51), Kel Nagle (1949, '54, '58 and '59) and Billy Dunk (1967, '71, '74 and '76).

Seniors golf:
An ever-increasing number of former Australian Champions have entered the rich US PGA Seniors Championship tour. On 10 December 1984, Peter Thomson (Vic.), five times winner of the British Open 1954-65, became the first Australian to win the US PGA Seniors Championship, earning US$40,000 – the biggest purse of his career. In 1985, Thomson almost dominated the rich Seniors circuit in the United States, winning an unprecedented nine major championships and more than US$500,000 prize money, to take his total earnings on the Seniors circuit well over US$1,000,000. Thomson's earnings for the 1985 season were a new record, easily bettering the previous best of US$328,597, earned in 1984 by American Don January.

Bruce Crampton took over from Thomson as the most successful Australian on the Seniors tour in 1986. Crampton topped the tour prize money list with US$454,299 with seven tournament wins, a second, and three third placings. In 1987 Crampton returned to Australia and on 1 March won the inaugural World Senior Matchplay Championship at Coolangatta-Tweed Heads. Crampton, who defeated American Miller Barber 1-up in the final, received $60,000.

AUSTRALIAN PGA CHAMPIONSHIP

Year	Player
1906	Dan Soutar
1907	Dan Soutar
1908	Carnegie Clark
1909-1921	Unknown*
1922	C. Campbell

Year	Player	Year	Player
1923	Fred Popplewell	1983	Bob Shearer
1924	Tom Howard	1984	Greg Norman
1925	Tom Howard	1985	Greg Norman
1926	F. Eyre	1986	Mike Harwood
1927–28	*Not held*	1987	Roger Mackay
1929	Rufus Stewart		
1930	J. Robertson		
1931	J. D. Spence		
1932	F. McMahon		
1933	Vic Richardson		
1934	M. L. Kelly		
1935	Vic Richardson		
1936	W. J. Clifford		
1937	Eric Cremin		
1938	Eric Cremin		
1939	E. Naismith		
1940–1945	*Not held*		
1946	Norman Von Nida		
1947	Ossie Pickworth		
1948	Norman Von Nida		
1949	Kel Nagle		
1950	Norman Von Nida		
1951	Norman Von Nida		
1952	Bill Holder		
1953	Ossie Pickworth		
1954	Kel Nagle		
1955	Ossie Pickworth		
1956	Len Wilson		
1957	Gary Player (S. Africa)		
1958	Kel Nagle		
1959	Kel Nagle		
1960	J. Sullivan		
1961	Alan Murray		
1962	Bill Dunk		
1963	Col Johnston		
1964**	Col Johnston		
1965	Kel Nagle		
1966	Peter Thompson		
1967	Bill Dunk		
1968	Kel Nagle		
1969	Bruce Devlin		
1970	Bruce Devlin		
1971	Bill Dunk		
1972	Randall Vines		
1973***	Randall Vines		
1974	Bill Dunk****		
1975	Vic Bennetts		
1976	Bill Dunk****		
1977	Mike Cahill		
1978	Hale Irwin (USA)		
1979	Stewart Ginn		
1980	Sam Torrance (Scotland)		
1981	Seve Ballesteros (Spain)		
1982	Graham Marsh		

*No records were kept in this period and it is likely the championship was not held for many years.

**Event changed from match play to 72 hole stroke competition.

***Event reverted to match play over 18 holes.

****In 1974 Dunk defeated Ian Stanley 71–72 in a play-off and in 1976 Dunk defeated Peter Croker 71–75 in a play-off.

WOMEN'S GOLF

First Australian championship:

In 1894, at Geelong, Victoria. Won by Miss C. B. McKenzie of Victoria. The title has been contested every year since, with the exception of the war years of 1914–19 and 1940–45.

Most Australian Championship wins:

Four each by Miss C. B. McKenzie (Vic.) (1894, '95, '96 and '98), Mona McLeod (Vic.) (1921, '26, '27 and '32), Pat Borthwick (NSW) (1948, '49, '53 and '56) and Sandra McCaw (Vic.) (1972, '74, '82 and '84).

History of professional golf:

Due to lack of sponsorship support, professional golf has never succeeded in Australia. The first Australian Women's Open Championship was held in 1974 at the Victoria Golf Club. Australia's Penny Pulz finished runner-up to Japan's Chako Higuchi. The Open ceased after the 1978 event won by Debbie Austin (USA).

Most successful professionals:

Margaret Masters (b. Swan Hill, Vic., 1934) turned professional in 1965 after a brilliant amateur career. She was named Rookie of the Year in her first (1965) US professional season and set a course record of 67 in her first US Open. Masters won her first US tournament in 1967 and topped the US$100,000 mark in career earnings in 1974.

Jan Stephenson (b. Sydney 1952) turned professional in 1972 and in 1973 won the Australian Ladies PGA title and two other professional events in three weeks in Australia. She was named US Rookie of the Year in 1974, won the 1975 King Hassan Trophy in Morocco in 1975, the Birmingham and Sarah Coventry-Naples Classics in the USA in 1976, the

Australian Open in 1977 and, following a win in the US Open in 1983, took her career earnings to US$850,960. Stephenson, who also won the LPGA championship in 1982, earned US$165,238 on the American tour in 1986 to take her American career earnings to US$1,265,443, easily the most by any Australian woman professional. Next best to the end of 1985 is Penny Pulz (b. Melbourne 1954) with career earnings of US$487,660. She turned professional in 1974.

Jane Lock (b. Melbourne 1954) turned professional in 1982 and had won US$58,234 on the US circuit by the end of 1983.

Major overseas wins by Australian amateurs:

In 1978, Edwina Kennedy (NSW) became the first Australian woman to win the British Amateur Championship and in 1980 won the Canadian Amateur Championship.

Margaret Masters (Vic.) won the national championships of three countries—New Zealand 1956, South Africa 1957 and Canada 1964.

Marea Parsons (nee Hickey) (NSW) won the 1964 New Zealand Championship on her 19th birthday, and the South African Championship in 1969.

Jane Lock (Vic.) won the 1975 New Zealand Open title and the 1981 Canadian Amateur Championship.

Most remarkable Australian Championship win:

Australian Champion in 1907 and 1908, Leonora Wray (1886-1979) was stricken with typhoid fever in 1919 and retired from golf for 10 years. In 1929, at the age of 43, she made a comeback and within a few months of resuming the game, won her third Australian title.

International record of Australian women's teams:

Australia has competed every year in the Espirito Santo world amateur teams title since the inaugural competition at St Germain, Paris in 1964. Australia's team of Edwina Kennedy, Jane Lock and Lindy Goggin won for the first time at Pacific Harbour, Fiji, in 1978. Australia's previous best was second place, behind the USA at the Victoria Club, Melbourne, in 1968. The team that year was Marea Parsons, Elizabeth Blackmore and Diana Thomas.

Commonwealth Teams Championship:

Australia has sent a team every year since the event commenced in 1959. The first success was achieved at Edmonton, Canada in 1983 by Lindy Goggin, Corinne Dibnah, Edwina Kennedy and Louise Briers. The team edged out five-time champions Great Britain.

MISCELLANY

Youngest winner of a major Australian championship:

Harry Llewellyn Williams (1915-61), who was 16 when he won the Australian Amateur Championship at The Australian, NSW, in 1931.

Five rounds under 70:

Peter Thomson became the first Australian to play five tournament rounds under 70, when he won the 1959 Pelaco Tournament at Victoria Park, Melbourne. Thomson shot 68, 68, 67, 67 and 69, on a par 73 course.

Brothers in championship final:

The only recorded instance of two brothers contesting the final of a national championship occurred in 1954, when Peter Toogood (Tasmania) defeated his younger brother John five and four in the final of the Australian amateur title at Royal Adelaide.

Lowest score for 72 holes by an Australian:

260 (64, 65, 66, 65) by Kel Nagle (NSW), when he won the Irish Hospitals Tournament at Woodbrook, Ireland, in 1961, and 260 (including a 62) by Nagle, when he won the Hong Kong Open the same year.

Oldest to shoot age:

Legh Winser, Australian Amateur Champion in 1921, who shot 76 at Barwood Heads course, Victoria, at the age of 88.

HOLE-IN-ONE RECORDS

Youngest:

Justin Gibson, who set a world record at the age of six years and 22 days, when he aced the 64 m sixth hole at Albert Park, Melbourne, Vic., on 21 January 1979.

Oldest:
Legh Winser, who was 10 days away from his 91st birthday when he holed-in-one with a five iron on the 146 m eighth hole at Barwon Heads, Victoria, on 17 November 1975.

First to score consecutive aces:
Sydney's Sue Prell became the first woman in the world and the 16th player in the history of golf to score consecutive aces. Prell holed out with a six iron on the 122 m 13th and a four wood on the 167 m 14th at the Chatswood Golf Club, Sydney, NSW, on 29 May 1977.

Most holes-in-one by an Australian:
29, by Sydney-born Joe Kirkwood (1899-1970), a top professional (Canadian Open Champion 1933) and trick shot exponent. Other leading Australian players include Jim Ferrier with 10 (including two scored in the 1946 San Francisco Open, California, USA), Frank Phillips (NSW) with nine and Harry Hattersley (NSW) with eight.

BRITISH OPEN GOLF CHAMPIONSHIP

Year	Venue	Winner	Score
1860	Prestwick	Willie Park Snr	174
1861	Prestwick	Tom Morris Snr	163
1862	Prestwick	Tom Morris Snr	163
1863	Prestwick	Willie Park Snr	168
1864	Prestwick	Tom Morris Snr	160
1865	Prestwick	Andrew Strath	162
1866	Prestwick	Willie Park Snr	169
1867	Prestwick	Tom Morris Snr	170
1868	Prestwick	Tom Morris Jnr	154
1869	Prestwick	Tom Morris Jnr	157
1870	Prestwick	Tom Morris Jnr	149
1871	Prestwick	Tom Morris Jnr	166
1872	Prestwick	Tom Morris Jnr	166
1873	St Andrews	Tom Kipp	179
1874	Musselburgh	Mungo Park	159
1875	Prestwick	Willie Park Snr	166
1876	St Andrews	Robert Martin	176
1877	Musselburgh	Jamie Anderson	160
1878	Prestwick	Jamie Anderson	157
1879	St Andrews	Jamie Anderson	169
1880	Musselburgh	Robert Ferguson	162
1881	Prestwick	Robert Ferguson	170
1882	St Andrews	Robert Ferguson	171
1883	Musselburgh	Willie Fernie*	159
1884	Prestwick	Jack Simpson	160
1885	St Andrews	Robert Martin	171

Year	Venue	Winner	Score
1886	Musselburgh	David Brown	157
1887	Prestwick	Willie Park Jnr	161
1888	St Andrews	Jack Burns	171
1889	Musselburgh	Willie Park Jnr*	155
1890	Prestwick	John Ball (a)	164
1891	St Andrews	Hugh Kirkaldy	166
1892**	Muirfield	Harold H. Hilton (a)	305
1893	Prestwick	William Auchterlonie	322
1894	Sandwich	John H. Taylor	326
1895	St Andrews	John H. Taylor	322
1896	Muirfield	Harry Vardon*	316
1897	Hoylake	Harold H. Hilton (a)	314
1898	Prestwick	Harry Vardon	307
1899	Sandwich	Harry Vardon	310
1900	St Andrews	John H. Taylor	309
1901	Muirfield	James Braid	309
1902	Hoylake	Alexander Herd	307
1903	Prestwick	Harry Vardon	300
1904	Sandwich	Jack White	296
1905	St Andrews	James Braid	318
1906	Muirfield	James Braid	300
1907	Hoylake	Arnaud Massy	312
1908	Prestwick	James Braid	291
1909	Deal	John H. Taylor	295
1910	St Andrews	James Braid	299
1911	Sandwich	Harry Vardon	303
1912	Muirfield	Edward Ray	295
1913	Hoylake	John H. Taylor	304
1914	Prestwick	Harry Vardon	306
1915–1919 *Not held* (WWI)			
1920	Deal	George Duncan	303
1921	St Andrews	Jock Hutchison*	296
1922	Sandwich	Walter Hagen	300
1923	Troon	Arthur Havers	295
1924	Hoylake	Walter Hagen	301
1925	Prestwick	James Barnes	300

106 • SPORT

Year	Venue	Winner	Score
1926	Royal Lytham & St Annes	Bobby Jones Jnr (a)	291
1927	St Andrews	Bobby Jones Jnr (a)	285
1928	Sandwich	Walter Hagen	292
1929	Muirfield	Walter Hagen	292
1930	Hoylake	Bobby Jones Jnr (a)	291
1931	Carnoustie	Tommy Armour	296
1932	Princes	Gene Sarazen	283
1933	St Andrews	Denny Shute*	292
1934	Sandwich	Henry Cotton	283
1935	Muirfield	Alfred Perry	283
1936	Hoylake	Alfred Padgham	287
1937	Carnoustie	Henry Cotton	290
1938	Sandwich	R. A. Whitcombe	295
1939	St Andrews	Richard Burton	290
1940–1945 *Not held* (WWII)			
1946	St Andrews	Sam Snead	290
1947	Hoylake	Fred Daly	293
1948	Muirfield	Henry Cotton	298
1949	Sandwich	Bobby Locke*	283
1950	Troon	Bobby Locke	279
1951	Portrush	Max Faulkner	285
1952	Royal Lytham & St Annes	Bobby Locke	287
1953	Carnoustie	Ben Hogan	282
1954	**Royal Birkdale**	**Peter Thomson (Aust.)**	**283**
1955	**St Andrews**	**Peter Thomson (Aust.)**	**281**
1956	**Hoylake**	**Peter Thomson (Aust.)**	**286**
1957	St Andrews	Bobby Locke	279
1958	**Royal Lytham & St Annes**	**Peter Thomson* (Aust.)**	**279**
1959	Muirfield	Gary Player	284
1960	**St Andrews**	**Kel Nagle (Aust.)**	**278**
1961	Royal Birkdale	Arnold Palmer	284
1962	Troon	Arnold Palmer	276
1963	Royal Lytham & St Annes	Bob Charles*	277
1964	St Andrews	Tony Lema	279
1965	**Royal Birkdale**	**Peter Thomson (Aust.)**	**285**
1966	Muirfield	Jack Nicklaus	282

Year	Venue	Winner	Score
1967	Hoylake	Roberto de Vicenzo	278
1968	Carnoustie	Gary Player	289
1969	Royal Lytham & St Annes	Tony Jacklin	280
1970	St Andrews	Jack Nicklaus*	283
1971	Royal Birkdale	Lee Trevino	278
1972	Muirfield	Lee Trevino	278
1973	Troon	Tom Weiskopf	276
1974	Royal Lytham & St Annes	Gary Player	282
1975	Carnoustie	Tom Watson*	279
1976	Royal Birkdale	John Miller	279
1977	Turnberry	Tom Watson	268+
1978	St Andrews	Jack Nicklaus	281
1979	Royal Lytham & St Annes	Seve Ballesteros	283
1980	Muirfield	Tom Watson	271
1981	Royal St Georges	Bill Rogers	276
1982	Troon	Tom Watson	284
1983	Royal Birkdale	Tom Watson	275
1984	St Andrews	Seve Ballesteros	276
1985	Royal St Georges	Sandy Lyle	282
1986	**Turnberry**	**Greg Norman (Aust.)**	**280**
1987	Muirfield	Nick Faldo	279
1988	Royal Lytham & St Annes	Seve Ballesteros	273

* Winner in playoff
** Prior to 1892 36 holes were played and from 1892 on 72 holes
\+ Tournament record
(a) Amateur

GREYHOUND RACING

BEGINNINGS IN AUSTRALIA
Greyhounds first stood on Australian soil in 1770 when they were brought ashore by Captain James Cook and his party. Greyhound racing was the natural development from live hare coursing which was first staged as a sporting 'attraction' in the early 1870s. The most famous live hare coursing event was the Australian Waterloo Cup first held in 1873 and won by Mr W. Watson's Miss Heller. The barbarous sport of coursing,

which was eventually banned by all state governments, virtually faded from existence in the 1920s, but many illegal events were staged in and near Sydney as late as the early 1950s.

First greyhound racing:
28 May 1927 when American 'Judge' Frederick Swindell came to Australia, formed a company called the Greyhound Coursing Association and staged what was first known as Electric Hare Racing at the Epping racecourse (now Harold Park) in Sydney. Greyhounds chased an artificial lure powered by electricity which was dragged along the outside fence of the track. (All lures in modern racing follow the inside fence.)

Two years earlier, Sydney boxing promoter Jack Munro failed to attract sufficient financial backing to launch the sport but after the success of the Swindell promotions, he had no difficulty finding support and started racing at a track known as Shepherd's Bush oval in the Sydney suburb of Mascot.

First control of racing:
Both Swindell and Munro were forced out in 1933 when the NSW government granted sole control and promotional rights to the NSW Trotting Club. Later a new body, the NSW Greyhound Breeders', Owners' and Trainers' Association took over. Another body, the National Coursing Association, was formed to conduct racing at Wentworth Park and tracks near Sydney such as Penrith.

First racing all states:
NSW: 28 May 1927 at Epping racecourse (now Harold Park).
Vic.: 1 January 1956 at Sandown Park, Melbourne. (Racing was held much earlier than this date, but Sandown hosted the first legal meeting. The Sandown meeting coincided with the Olympic year in Melbourne and the controlling association celebrated by staging the inaugural Melbourne Cup—still the most prestigious greyhound race in Australia.)
NT: 1969 at Darwin.
Qld: 6 April 1972 at the Brisbane Cricket Ground.
WA: 1973 at Cannington Central, Perth.
SA: 1973 at Angle Park, Adelaide.
Tas. June 1978 at Quamby, near Hagley.

First Australian championships:
1965 when the National Sprint Championship was held at Harold Park, Sydney, and won by Best Sun (NSW). Other semi-official championship races were held even earlier—the Australian Cup in 1960, and the National Derby in 1963. The National Sprint Championship was held at Sandown, Melbourne, the following year and held on a rotating basis in all states in subsequent years. The first National Distance Championship was staged in 1969 at Wentworth Park, Sydney, and won by Amerigo Lady (Vic.).

Richest match race:
8 July 1978 when Aaron King (Vic.) and Just Biddy (SA) met at Angle Park, SA, for $27,000 in stakes and side bets. Aaron King won by ¾ length over 512 m—0.18 secs outside the course record held by the South Australian bitch.

Australian attendance record:
18,600 (almost capacity) at Wentworth Park, Sydney, on 3 December 1949 when the track re-opened after massive reconstruction. On 24 May 1944, an estimated 17,000 attended Sydney's Harold Park to watch champion dog Chief Havoc successfully attack a series of track records.

Richest race in Australia:
The annual Melbourne Cup, now held at Olympic Park, Melbourne. The race was first held at Sandown in 1956 with an almost token $6,000 prize money. By 1978 the prize money pool had grown to $75,000 with the winner collecting $35,000 and by the mid-1980s, the prize money pool had exceeded $100,000.

Greatest Australian greyhound:
Champion NSW sprinter Black Top who was retired while still a two-year-old after winning 17 of 20 starts and amassing a then Australian record of prize money earnings of $11,000. Black Top made a fortune at stud, earning a then record of $250,000 in fees in only nine years and mating with 1,400 bitches. He sired a world record 9,000 puppies who between them have won over 600 races and more than $600,000

prize money. Black Top died in 1972 was embalmed and given the unique honour of being displayed at the Australian Museum in Sydney.

First $100 million betting turnover: 1968-69 when the turnover from on-course betting on the totalisator and with bookmakers and off-course on the TAB exceeded $100 million. By the 1976-77 season, with more tracks operating and thousands of dogs being syndicated, the betting boom reached incredible proportions. In NSW alone, turnover for the season exceeded $256 million. Turnover figures dropped nationally in the early 1980s but the national figure in 1986-87 was still in excess of $500 million.

HORSERACING

BEGINNINGS IN AUSTRALIA

A stallion, three mares and three yearlings arrived with the First Fleet on 28 January 1788 and by 1798 regular importations of horses from the Cape of Good Hope, South Africa, had increased the total to 44 horses and 73 mares. In 1799 the English-bred stallion Rockingham was imported from Cape Colony, and in October 1802 the stallion Northumberland, together with a mare, was brought from England, followed a short time later by the American stallion Washington. From 1803 a great many Arabian horses were imported, among them a government-owned stallion named Satellite. This mixed bunch set Australia's 'thoroughbred' breeding industry off to a tottering start. Early breeding records were not meticulously kept, nor were details of the very first race meetings.

First horseracing in Australia:
Turf historian Douglas M. Barrie claims in his book *Turf Cavalcade*, published in 1960, that the earliest racing of any significance was probably held in 1805 at a racecourse on Ham Common, near the present-day Hawkesbury Racecourse, in the Richmond-Windsor area of NSW.

First recorded racing:
On 5 April 1810, when the celebrated horse Parramatta defeated a bay stallion called Belfast in a match race at Parramatta, NSW. The match race was part of a mixed sporting day which featured trotting, footraces and wheelbarrow races. It was promoted by James Larra who had arrived as a convict with the Second Fleet but was pardoned in 1794. He was to become the leading auctioneer in Parramatta and that town's most successful publican and prominent citizen. Races (mainly match races) were held around the Sydney area on a regular basis until late 1810.

First recognised race meeting:
On 15, 17 and 18 October 1810, at the former Sydney Racecourse (now Hyde Park). The race meeting was organised by officers of the 73rd Regiment, on a clockwise course which had the finishing straight running north along the present line of Elizabeth Street. Racing continued at Hyde Park until November 1821, when the Governor, Sir Thomas Brisbane, acting on reports that some meetings 'had degenerated into a system of low gambling and dissipation subversive of order and good morals', implemented such restrictions that racing was made impossible for the next three years.

Revival of racing:
After some picnic-style racing in the Hawkesbury district of NSW, racing returned to Sydney on 3 March 1825 at a course situated in the eastern suburbs.

Known as either the Woollahra Course, the Bellevue Course (it was situated close to present day Bellevue Hill) or Captain Piper's Racecourse (after Captain John Piper, one of the organisers), the racecourse incorporated the land on which the Bondi Bowling Club and Barracluff Park now stand.

Australia's first racing club:
At a meeting held on 18 March 1825 the Sydney Turf Club (the existing STC has no connection with the original) was established and Mr George Mills elected its Secretary. Some lapses in concentration by the taker of minutes at later meetings have resulted in the body being referred to, mistakenly, as the Australian Turf Club. The STC began staging race meetings at the Woollahra (or Bellevue) Course on 25 April 1825.

First meetings in other States:
Tas.: On 3 September 1814, at Newtown (now New Town) near Hobart. The 'meeting' was in fact a series of match races between two horses.
Vic.: On 6 March 1838, at Batman's Hill Racecourse located on the present site of Spencer St Railway Station, Melbourne.
SA: On 1 January 1838, on a paddock owned by breeder Mr Hurtle Fisher and believed to be in the vicinity of the present Victoria Park Racecourse.
Qld: On 17 July 1843, in a paddock at Cooper's Plains, Brisbane.
WA: Believed to have been staged in Fremantle in October 1833.

Opening of major racecourses:
Randwick, NSW: 17 April 1833. The track was not then known as Randwick because the surrounding municipality was not declared and named until 1858. 'Randwick' had been in use for some time as a sand track and was first known as the 'sandy course on the Botany Road'. Then, for a short time, when it opened as a fully grassed track, with grandstands and other amenities, it became the 'Subscription Track', so named because many enthusiasts had subscribed towards its funding.
Flemington, Vic.: 3 March 1840. Flemington was initially known simply as 'The Racecourse', but was later named Flemington after, legend persists, a local butcher named Fleming.
Ascot, WA: 18 April 1848.
Eagle Farm, Qld: 14 August 1865.
Elwick, Tas.: 11 February 1875.
Caulfield, Vic.: 5 August 1876. Early races were held on a rough bush track on the site in 1859.
Moonee Valley, Vic.: 15 September 1883.
Canterbury, NSW: 19 January 1884.
Rosehill, NSW: 18 April 1885.
Warwick Farm, NSW: 16 March 1889.
Cheltenham, SA: 26 December 1895.
Albion Park, Qld: 12 May 1923.
Doomben, Qld: 20 May 1933.
Sandown, Vic.: 19 June 1965.

First major upheaval in racing control:
On 9 November 1827 the Sydney Turf Club held an anniversary dinner to celebrate the occasion on which the club's first Patron, His Excellency Sir Thomas Brisbane, then Governor of NSW, had first dined with the members. The new Governor, Sir Ralph Darling, an aloof figure on poor terms with STC members William Charles Wentworth and Robert Wardell, declined an invitation to attend. When a toast to Governor Darling received no applause and was followed by the band of the 57th Regiment playing the air 'Over the Hills and Far Away', Governor Darling, who preferred to live out of Sydney (hence 'far away') at Parramatta, was furious and STC members who tried to explain that no insult was intended found him unapproachable. Governor Darling then dismissed from his position the Sheriff of the colony, John Mackaness, for his part in chairing the anniversary dinner. The Crown Solicitor, Mr W. H. Moore, who was also at the dinner, was suspended from office and the STC Secretary, Mr C. D. Moore, was dismissed from his post as Assistant Clerk of the Supreme Court. All persons employed by the Government were warned that it would be 'inconsistent with their duty' if they remained members of the STC. In May 1828 a new club was formed by the fearful STC members and friends of the Governor, and the Australian Racing and Jockey Club came into being. The STC lingered barely another 18 months. The 'Jockey Club' staged its inaugural meeting on the site of the

future Randwick Racecourse and prior to that staged meetings at a new track at Homebush, where the present Sydney abattoirs now stand.

The 1830s expansion:
Horseracing in and around Sydney flourished from the late 1820s through the early 1830s. New tracks opened at Camperdown, near the present site of Sydney University, the outer suburbs of Campbelltown and Liverpool, at centres such as Parramatta and the Hawkesbury district and near country areas such as Maitland, Bathurst, Wollongong, Yass and Braidwood.

Establishment of the Australian Jockey Club:
In 1840 a body known as the Australian Race Committee was formed in Sydney with the intention of standardising the sport throughout NSW and eventually Australia, laying down new rules and injecting strict control of what was, even then, a sporting industry. On 5 January the Australian Race Committee was formed into the Australian Jockey Club (Australia's oldest still-operating racing club) and the AJC staged its first meeting at the Homebush track, on the future site of Sydney's abattoirs, on 29 March.

Oldest classic race:
The AJC St Leger, first run at the Homebush Racecourse (known at the time as Home Bush) in 1841 and won by James Rouse's filly Eleanor. The St Leger was held at Homebush from 1841 to 1859 and was officially called the Homebush (or Home Bush) St Leger. The St Leger was not staged in 1860 and resumed at Randwick in 1861.

MELBOURNE CUP
The First Cup:
Held on Thursday 7 November 1861 and won by the Sydney horse Archer owned by Mr Etienne De Mestre and ridden by John Cutts. Archer started at 6/1 in a field of 17 and won easily in 3 mins 52 secs — the slowest time ever recorded. The following year, Archer, again ridden by Cutts and carrying 10 st 2 lbs, became the first horse to win successive Cups.

The Victoria Turf Club staged the inaugural race, attracting a crowd of 4,000, but gained little publicity for a race that was to become the greatest all-age handicap in the world. Archer's owner collected approximately 710 pounds for the first win but did not receive a Cup trophy. The VTC presented only a gold watch as a memento.

First postponement of the Cup:
In 1870, when the Flemington track was soaked with 6 inches (150 mm) of rain in September and 4 1/2 inches (112.5 mm) in October, and the Victoria Racing Club, which had taken over from the VTC in 1864, postponed the Cup for a week. The Cup was again postponed in 1916, after torrential rain, and was held for the first time on a Saturday.

NOTABLE CUP FIRSTS
First 100,000 crowd:
In 1880, when the VRC announced an exact 100,000 as the official attendance for the clash between champion three-year-olds Grand Flaneur and Progress. Grand Flaneur won by a length.

First film coverage:
In 1896, when French cameraman Walter Sestier filmed highlights of the race as part of a general sporting documentary produced for Sydney entrepreneur Walter Barnett. The original print of the Cup film was taken to France and it was not until 1969 that the French Government agreed, somewhat reluctantly, to present a print of it to the National Library in Canberra, ACT.

First radio broadcast:
In 1925, when the Australian Broadcasting Commission had racing journalist Bill

Priestley describe the race won by Windbag.

First same-night showing of Cup film:
In 1933, when Fox-Movietone News had Sir Charles Kingsford Smith fly a film of the Cup from Essendon Airport to Mascot in Sydney. The film was processed and edited within an hour and shown at Sydney's Regent Theatre six hours after the Cup was run.

CUP ODDITIES
Smallest field:
There were only seven runners in the 1863 Cup won by the 10/1 outsider Banker which set the current record as the lightest-weighted horse (5 st 4 lbs (33.6 kg)) to win the race.

Heaviest weight allotted and most heavily weighted horse to win:
In 1869 The Barb was allotted 11 st 7 lbs (73 kg) and was withdrawn by connections. The Barb had won in 1866 carrying only 6 st 11 lbs (38.5 kg). The heaviest weight carried to victory was 10 st 5 lbs (66 kg) by Carbine in 1890.

Youngest jockey to win:
Peter St Albans, who was only 13 when he won the 1876 Cup on Briseis. Racing historians are still unsure whether 'St Albans' was the rider's real name. The horse was entered by the St Albans stables and the coincidence appears to be too strong.

Biggest winning bet:
Almost certainly the 10,000 pounds won by the Hon. James White, owner of Chester which won the Cup in 1877. White invested 400 pounds with Melbourne bookmaker Joe Thompson, who settled in 100 pound notes. Allowing for inflation, the win would represent about $750,000 today.

Jockeys to win successive Cups:
John Cutts on Archer in 1861 and 1862; W. H. 'Midge' McLachlan on Prince Foote in 1909 and Comedy King in 1910; Albert Shanahan on Piastre in 1912 and Posinatus in 1913; A. 'Toch' Wilson on King Ingoda in 1922 and Bitalli in 1923; Jack Purtell on Wodalla in 1953 and Rising Fast in 1954; Jim Johnson on Rain Lover in 1968 and 1969; Harry White on Think Big in 1974 and 1975, and again on Arwon in 1978 and Hyperno in 1979.

Most successful jockeys:
Bobby Lewis and Harry White have each ridden four winners. Darby Munro, W. H. 'Midge' McLachlan, Jack Purtell and Jim Johnson have each ridden three winners.

Most memorable win by any jockey:
Apprentice Ray Neville scored an upset win in 1948 on the 80/1 outsider Rimfire. Neville had never ridden a metropolitan winner before, was having his first ride in the Cup and had never won another race. He was forced into early retirement with weight problems and although he rode briefly as a hurdle and steeplechase jockey, failed to ride another winner. Rimfire's win was notable for a second reason: Jack Thompson, who rode the second-placed horse, Dark Marne, was convinced he had won, despite the photo-finish camera being in use. Although the VRC did not admit the possibility of an error, the position of the camera at Flemington was changed after the 1948 Cup.

Only 100/1 winners:
Three horses have won at the punter's dream odds – The Pearl in 1871, Wotan in 1936 and Old Rowley in 1940. The longest priced winner since 1940 has been Rimfire at 80/1 in 1948.

Most famous winning 'tips':
The 1934 VRC racebook front cover carried an illustration of a racehorse carrying No. 1 saddlecloth and thousands of punters backed No. 1, Peter Pan, which duly won at odds of 14/1. In 1980, the NSW TAB how-to-bet card listed No. 15 in the winning square. Beldale Ball, carrying No. 15 saddlecloth, was an easy winner at 11/1.

Trained most winners:
Bart Cummings, who has trained seven winners. Cummings broke a 98-year-old record held by Etienne De Mestre, when his charge Gold and Black won him his sixth Cup. His seventh winner was Hyperno in 1979.

Controversial finishes:
In 1871 The Pearl won from the favourite Romula and Irish King. Because it was obvious that the grey,

Saladin, had finished third, a length clear of Irish King, Saladin's owner, Mr J. R. Crooke, protested about the result. The judge dismissed the protest, claiming he 'had not been looking' and that a steward had been appointed to judge the third placing. The 'steward' was never identified or produced.

In 1866 the judge, Mr J. D. Dougharty, correctly signalled that The Barb had won by a head from Exile, but refused to signal the third placegetter because Falcon, which had finished a clear third, had raced in colours different from those in the official colours sheet. There were no saddlecloth numbers that year. When the judge suggested that the stewards could grant third place to Falcon 'if they wished', bookmakers correctly protested and said that only the judge was empowered to nominate the placegetters. Judge Dougharty was unmoved and was quoted as saying that 'no horse has run third'. The following day, the VRC announced that it had 'decided' that Falcon had placed third. Bookmakers still refused to pay out successful place bets because the judge would not alter his stand.

Classic Melbourne Cup lead-up:
In 1906 Poseidon won, in succession, the AJC Derby, the Caulfield Cup, the Victoria Derby and the Melbourne Cup — a feat never repeated. The winnings helped his owner Hugh (later Sir Hugh) Denison amass sufficient capital to establish the Sydney publishing company Associated Newspapers, later taken over by John Fairfax & Sons Limited.

Phar Lap's record:
Phar Lap, Australia's greatest racehorse in the 'modern' era, had three starts in the Melbourne Cup. In 1929, as a champion three-year-old, he started favourite and finished third, four lengths behind the winner, Nightmarch. Critics were scathing about the tactics adopted by champion jockey Bobby Lewis who allowed Phar Lap to lead at the six furlongs and lead the field around the home turn. Phar Lap's second start was in 1930 with Jim Pike as jockey. Pike timed his run from the home turn to such perfection that the champion galloper won, going away by three lengths, carrying 9 st 12 lbs and starting favourite at 11/8 on. His last start was in 1931, when he was asked to carry a massive 10 st 10 lbs – 22 lbs over weight-for-age. Jockey Pike realised the weight had beaten Phar Lap well before the home turn and eased the champion home into eighth place. Despite his weight, Phar Lap was again sent out favourite at 3/1.

Infamous nobbling attempts:
In 1930 an attempt was made to shoot Phar Lap before the running of the Cup. Two shots were fired at the champion in a lane off Manchester Grove near Caulfield Racecourse, but handler Tommy Woodcock managed to steer the pony he used to lead Phar Lap between the gunmen and the Cup favourite. Both shots missed. In 1940, another attempt was made to shoot the favourite, when a gunman fired into a stall he thought housed Beau Vite and wounded El Golea. In 1969 a nobbler doped the second favourite, Big Philou. The horse was scratched at the order of the stewards barely 30 minutes before the start of the Cup, when the great galloper scoured and became badly distressed. An analysis showed that Big Philou had been nobbled with a purgative called Canthron. All money invested on the horse on Cup Day was refunded but other punters lost thousands on the pre-post market plunges. Despite the later arrest of a stablehand who worked for the horse's trainer, Bart Cummings, and a conspiracy trial in Melbourne, the culprits were never apprehended.

MELBOURNE CUP RESULTS 1861–1987

Year	Winner	Jockey	S/P	Field
1861	Archer	J. Cutts	6/1	17
1862	Archer	J. Cutts	2/1	20
1863	Banker	H. Chifney	10/1	7

Year	Winner	Jockey	S/P	Field
1864	Lantern	S. Davis	15/1	19
1865	Tory Boy	E. Cavanagh	20/1	23
1866	The Barb	W. Davis	6/1	28
1867	Tim Whiffler	I. Driscoll	5/2	27
1868	Glencoe	C. Stanley	10/1	25
1869	Warrior	J. Morrison	10/1	26
1870	Nimblefoot	J. Day	12/1	28
1871	The Pearl	J. Cavanagh	100/1	23
1872	The Quack	W. Enderson	5/1	22
1873	Don Juan	W. Wilson	3/1	24
1874	Haricot	P. Piggot	15/1	18
1875	Wollomai	R. Batty	16/1	20
1876	Briseis	P. St Albans	7/1	33
1877	Chester	P. Piggot	5/1	33
1878	Calamia	T. Brown	10/1	30
1879	Darriwell	S. Cracknell	33/1	27
1880	Grand Flaneur	T. Hales	4/1	22
1881	Zulu	J. Gough	33/1	33
1882	The Assyrian	C. Hutchins	33/1	25
1883	Martini Henri	J. Williamson	3/1	29
1884	Malua	A. Robertson	6/1	24
1885	Sheet Anchor	M. O'Brien	14/1	35
1886	Arsenal	W. English	20/1	28
1887	Dunlop	T. Sanders	20/1	18
1888	Mentor	M. O'Brien	7/1	28
1889	Bravo	J. Anwin	8/1	20
1890	Carbine	R. Ramage	4/1	39
1891	Malvolio	G. Redfern	14/1	34
1892	Glenloth	G. Robson	50/1	35
1893	Tarcoola	H. Cripps	40/1	30
1894	Patron	H. G. Dawes	33/1	28
1895	Auraria	J. Stevenson	33/1	36
1896	Newhaven	H. Gardiner	4/1	25
1897	Gaulus	S. Callinan	14/1	29
1898	The Grafter	J. Gough	8/1	28
1899	Meriwee	V. Turner	7/1	28
1900	Clean Sweep	R. Richardson	20/1	29
1901	Revenue	F. Dunn	7/4	19
1902	The Victory	R. Lewis	25/1	22
1903	Lord Cardigan	N. Godby	5/1	24
1904	Acrasia	T. Clayton	14/1	34
1905	Blue Spec	F. Bullock	10/1	27
1906	Poseidon	T. Clayton	4/1	21
1907	Apologue	W. Evans	3/1	19

Year	Winner	Jockey	S/P	Field
1908	Lord Nolan	J. R. Flynn	16/1	22
1909	Prince Foote	W. H. McLachlan	4/1	26
1910	Comedy King	W. H. McLachlan	10/1	30
1911	The Parisian	R. Cameron	5/1	33
1912	Piastre	A. Shanahan	7/1	23
1913	Posinatus	A. Shanahan	15/1	20
1914	Kingsburgh	G. Meddick	20/1	28
1915	Patrobus	R. Lewis	8/1	24
1916	Sasanof	F. Foley	12/1	28
1917	Westcourt	W. H. McLachlan	4/1	20
1918	Nightwatch	W. Duncan	12/1	27
1919	Artilleryman	R. Lewis	10/1	20
1920	Poitrel	K. Bracken	8/1	23
1921	Sister Olive	E. O'Sullivan	16/1	25
1922	King Ingoda	A. Wilson	8/1	32
1923	Bitalli	A. Wilson	4/1	26
1924	Backwood	P. Brown	8/1	18
1925	Windbag	J. Munro	5/1	28
1926	Spearfelt	H. Cairns	10/1	21
1927	Trivalve	R. Lewis	6/1	26
1928	Statesman	J. Munro	7/2	17
1929	Nightmarch	R. Reed	6/1	14
1930	Phar Lap	J. E. Pike	8/11	15
1931	White Nose	N. Percival	8/1	14
1932	Peter Pan	W. Duncan	4/1	27
1933	Hall Mark	J. O'Sullivan	4/1	18
1934	Peter Pan	D. Munro	14/1	22
1935	Marabou	K. Voitre	9/2	22
1936	Wotan	O. Philips	100/1	20
1937	The Trump	A. Reed	11/2	28
1938	Catalogue	F. Shean	25/1	22
1939	Rivette	E. Preston	5/1	26
1940	Old Rowley	A. Knox	100/1	20
1941	Skipton	W. Cook	8/1	23
1942	Colonus	H. McCloud	33/1	24
1943	Dark Felt	V. Hartney	7/2	24
1944	Sirius	D. Munro	3/1	23
1945	Rainbird	W. Cook	12/1	26
1946	Russia	D. Munro	16/1	35
1947	Hiraji	J. Purtell	12/1	30
1948	Rimfire	R. Neville	80/1	30
1949	Foxzami	W. Fellows	16/1	31
1950	Comic Court	P. Glennon	25/1	26
1951	Delta	N. Sellwood	10/1	28

Year	Winner	Jockey	S/P	Field
1952	Dalray	W. Williamson	5/1	30
1953	Wodalla	J. Purtell	14/1	21
1954	Rising Fast	J. Purtell	5/2	25
1955	Toparoa	N. Sellwood	6/1	24
1956	Evening Peal	G. Podmore	15/1	22
1957	Straight Draw	N. McGrowdie	13/1	19
1958	Baystone	M. Schumacher	10/1	29
1959	Macdougal	P. Glennon	8/1	28
1960	Hi Jinx	W. A. Smith	50/1	32
1961	Lord Fury	R. Selkrig	20/1	25
1962	Even Stevens	L. Coles	3/1	26
1963	Gatum Gatum	J. Johnson	25/1	26
1964	Polo Prince	R. Taylor	12/1	26
1965	Light Fingers	R. Higgins	15/1	26
1966	Galilee	J. Miller	11/2	22
1967	Red Handed	R. Higgins	4/1	22
1968	Rain Lover	J. Johnson	7/1	26
1969	Rain Lover	J. Johnson	8/1	23
1970	Baghdad Note	E. Didman	25/1	23
1971	Silver Knight	R. Marsh	10/1	21
1972	Piping Lane	J. Letts	40/1	22
1973	Gala Supreme	F. Reys	9/1	24
1974	Think Big	H. White	12/1	22
1975	Think Big	H. White	33/1	21
1976	Van Der Hum	R. Skelton	9/2	23
1977	Gold & Black	J. Duggan	7/2	24
1978	Arwon	H. White	5/1	22
1979	Hyperno	H. White	7/1	22
1980	Beldale Ball	J. Letts	11/1	22
1981	Just A Dash	P. Cook	15/1	22
1982	Gurner's Lane	L. Dittman	8/1	23
1983	Kiwi	J. A. Cassidy	9/1	24
1984	Black Knight	P. Cook	10/1	19
1985	What a Nuisance	P. Hyland	15/1	23
1986	At Talaq	M. Clarke	10/1	22
1987	Kensei	L. Olsen	12/1	21

MELBOURNE CUP SECOND AND THIRD PLACEGETTERS

Year	Horse	S/P	Place
1861	Mormon	3/1f	2nd
	Prince	20/1	3rd
1862	Mormon	4/1	2nd
	Camden	4/1	3rd

Year	Horse	S/P	Place
1863	Musidora	2/1ef	2nd
	Rose of Denmark	2/1ef	3rd

Year	Horse	S/P	Place	Year	Horse	S/P	Place
1864	Poet	20/1	2nd	1887	Silvermine	14/1	2nd
	Rose of Denmark	10/1	3rd		The Australian Peer	6/1	3rd
1865	Panic	7/1	2nd	1888	Tradition	8/1	2nd
	Riverina	16/1	3rd		The Yeoman	15/1	3rd
1866	Exile	20/1	2nd				
	Falcon	7/1	3rd	1889	Carbine	7/1	2nd
1867	Queen of Hearts	20/1	2nd		Melos	4/1f	3rd
				1890	Highborn	33/1	2nd
	Exile	50/1	3rd		Correze	100/1	3rd
1868	Strop	20/1	2nd	1891	Sir William	16/1	2nd
	Shenandoah	15/1	3rd		Strathmore	6/1	3rd
1869	The Monk	200/1	2nd	1892	Ronda	50/1	2nd
	Phoebe	20/1	3rd		Penance	33/1	3rd
1870	Lapdog	5/1ef	2nd	1893	Carnage	9/1	2nd
	Valentine	20/1	3rd		Jeweller	15/1	3rd
1871	Romula	3/1f	2nd	1894	Devon	14/1	2nd
	Irish King	50/1	3rd		Nada	14/1	3rd
1872	The Ace	5/1	2nd	1895	Hova	5/1f	2nd
	Dagworth	7/1	3rd		Burrabari	50/1	3rd
1873	Dagworth	25/1	2nd	1896	Bloodshot	33/1	2nd
	Horatio	6/1	3rd		The Skipper	33/1	3rd
1874	Protos	12/1	2nd				
	The Diver	6/1	3rd	1897	The Grafter	33/1	2nd
1875	Richmond	16/1	2nd		Aurum	20/1	3rd
	Goldsbrough	10/1	3rd	1898	Wait-a-Bit	15/1	2nd
1876	Sibyl	25/1	2nd		Cocos	15/1	3rd
	Timothy	10/1	3rd	1899	Voyou	20/1	2nd
1877	Savanaka	5/1ef	2nd		Dewey	10/1	3rd
	The Vagabond	15/1	3rd	1900	Malster	20/1	2nd
1878	Tom Kirk	33/1	2nd		Alix	25/1	3rd
	Waxy	16/1	3rd	1901	San Fran	4/1	2nd
1879	Sweetmeat	8/1	2nd		Khaki	25/1	3rd
	Suwarrow	4/1ef	3rd	1902	Vanity Fair	33/1	2nd
1880	Progress	3/1f	2nd		Abundance	4/1ef	3rd
	Lord Burghley	4/1	3rd	1903	Wakeful	12/1	2nd
1881	The Czar	20/1	2nd		Seaport	50/1	3rd
	Sweetmeat	7/1	3rd	1904	Lord Cardigan	12/1	2nd
1882	Stockwell	15/1	2nd		Blinker	16/1	3rd
	Gudarz	30/1	3rd	1905	Scot Free	7/1	2nd
1883	First Water	33/1	2nd		Tartan	7/2f	3rd
	Commotion	20/1	3rd	1906	Antonius	50/1	2nd
1884	Commotion	20/1	2nd		Proceed	12/1	3rd
	Plausible	10/1	3rd	1907	Mooltan	7/1	2nd
1885	Grace Darling	20/1	2nd		Mountain King	7/1	3rd
	Trenton	6/1	3rd				
1886	Trenton	12/1	2nd	1908	Tulkeroo	25/1	2nd
	Silvermine	14/1	3rd		Delawere	40/1	3rd

Year	Horse	S/P	Place
1909	Alawa	8/1	2nd
	Aberdeen	100/1	3rd
1910	Trafalgar	9/2f	2nd
	Apple Pie	16/1	3rd
1911	Flavian	16/1	2nd
	Didus	25/1	3rd
1912	Hallowmas	33/1	2nd
	Uncle Sam	5/1	3rd
1913	Belove	33/1	2nd
	Ulva's Isle	12/1	3rd
1914	Sir Alwynton	25/1	2nd
	Moonbria	25/1	3rd
1915	Westcourt	50/1	2nd
	Carlita	7/1	3rd
1916	Shepherd King	4/1f	2nd
	St Spasa	50/1	3rd
1917	Lingle Wallace	7/1	2nd
	Isinglass	25/1	3rd
1918	Kennaquhair	14/1	2nd
	Gadabout	33/1	3rd
1919	Richmond Main	11/1	2nd
	Two Blues	33/1	3rd
1920	Erasmus	33/1	2nd
	Queen Comedy	12/1	3rd
1921	The Rover	10/1	2nd
	Amazonia	12/1	3rd
1922	The Cypher	6/1f	2nd
	Mufti	25/1	3rd
1923	Rivoli	7/1	2nd
	Accarak	100/1	3rd
1924	Stand By	10/1	2nd
	Spearfelt	9/4f	3rd
1925	Manfred	7/4f	2nd
	Pilliewinkie	5/1	3rd
1926	Naos	33/1	2nd
	Pantheon	9/4f	3rd
1927	Silvius	3/1f	2nd
	Son O'Mine	12/1	3rd
1928	Strephon	9/4f	2nd
	Demost	40/1	3rd
1929	Paquito	33/1	2nd
	Phar Lap	evensf	3rd
1930	Second Wind	50/1	2nd
	Shadow King	50/1	3rd

Year	Horse	S/P	Place
1931	Shadow King	25/1	2nd
	Concentrate	4/1	3rd
1932	Yarramba	20/1	2nd
	Shadow King	25/1	3rd
1933	Shadow King	33/1	2nd
	Topical/Gauine	8/1	dead heat
	Carring	20/1	3rd
1934	Sarcherie	50/1	2nd
	Latrobe	25/1	3rd
1935	Sarcherie	6/1	2nd
	Sylvandale	15/1	3rd
1936	Silver Strand	7/1	2nd
	Balkan Prince	15/1	3rd
1937	Willie Win	40/1	2nd
	Sarcherie	40/1	3rd
1938	Bourbon	9/1	2nd
	Ortelle's Star	40/1	3rd
1939	Maikai	9/1	2nd
	Pantler	14/1	3rd
1940	Maikai	20/1	2nd
	Tidal Wave	40/1	3rd
1941	Son of Aurous	7/1	2nd
	Beau Vite	11/2 f	3rd
1942	Phocion	50/1	2nd
	Heart's Desire	33/1	3rd
1943	Counsel	8/1	2nd
	Claudette	12/1	3rd
1944	Peter	12/1	2nd
	Cellini	66/1	3rd
1945	Silver Link	7/1f	2nd
	Leonard	14/1	3rd
1946	On Target	8/1	2nd
	Carey	15/1	3rd
1947	Fresh Boy	11/2f	2nd
	Red Fury	14/1	3rd
1948	Dark Marne	12/1	2nd
	Saxony	40/1	3rd
1949	Hoyle	20/1	2nd
	Benvolo	12/1	3rd

Year	Horse	S/P	Place
1950	Chicquita	9/1	2nd
	Morse Code	14/1	3rd
1951	Akbar	7/1	2nd
	Double Blank	50/1	3rd
1952	Welkin Sun	200/1	2nd
	Reformed	25/1	3rd
1953	Most Regal	33/1	2nd
	My Hero	5/1	3rd
1954	Hellion	7/1	2nd
	Gay Helios	200/1	3rd
1955	Rising Fast	2/1f	2nd
	Sir William	66/1	3rd
1956	Redcraze	7/4f	2nd
	Caranna	12/1	3rd
1957	Prince Darius	12/1	2nd
	Pandie Sun	7/1	3rd
1958	Monte Carlo	11/2	2nd
	Red Pine	10/1	3rd
1959	Nether Gold	20/1	2nd
	White Hills	50/1	3rd
1960	Howsie	20/1	2nd
	Ilumquh	7/2	3rd
1961	Grand Print	20/1	2nd
	Dhaulagiri	7/1	3rd
1962	Comicquita	40/1	2nd
	Aquanita	9/2	3rd
1963	Ilumquh	16/1	2nd
	Grand Print	5/1	3rd
1964	Elkayel	10/1	2nd
	Welltown	14/1	3rd
1965	Ziema	10/1	2nd
	Midlander	20/1	3rd
1966	Light Fingers	12/1	2nd
	Duo	10/1	3rd
1967	Red Crest	20/1	2nd
	Floodbird	80/1	3rd
1968	Fileur	20/1	2nd
	Fans	12/1	3rd

Year	Horse	S/P	Place
1969	Alsop	8/1	2nd
	Ben Lamond	9/1	3rd
1970	Vansittart	9/1	2nd
	Clear Prince	10/1	3rd
1971	Igloo	12/1	2nd
	Tails	15/1	3rd
1972	Magnifique	7/2f	2nd
	Gunsynd	4/1	3rd
1973	Glengowan	5/2	2nd
	Daneson	16/1	3rd
1974	Leilani	7/2	2nd
	Captain Peri	14/1	3rd
1975	Holiday Waggon	7/1	2nd
	Medici	125/1	3rd
1976	Gold and Black	5/1	2nd
	Kythera	9/1	3rd
1977	Reckless	11/2	2nd
	Hyperno	66/1	3rd
1978	Dandaleith	20/1	2nd
	Karu	40/1	3rd
1979	Salamander	10/1	2nd
	Red Nose	16/1	3rd
1980	My Blue Denim	16/1	2nd
	Love Bandit	33/1	3rd
1981	El Laurena	25/1	2nd
	Flashing Light	20/1	3rd
1982	Kingston Town	6/1	2nd
	Noble Comment	20/1	3rd
1983	Noble Comment	16/1	2nd
	Mr Jazz	10/1	3rd
1984	Chagemar	25/1	2nd
	Mapperley Heights	10/1	3rd
1985	Koiro Corrie May	10/1	2nd
	Tripsacum	33/1	3rd
1986	Rising Fear	50/1	2nd
	Sea Legend	20/1	3rd
1987	Empire Rose	25/1	2nd
	Rosedale	5/1	3rd

RACING GENERAL

Most wins in succession:
21, on country tracks, by Queensland gelding Picnic in the Park. Next-best winning sequences *on metropolitan courses* are: 19 – Desert Gold and Gloaming; 18 – Ajax; 17 – Mainbrace; 16 – Carbine and Bernborough; 14 – Phar Lap; 13 – Limerick; 12 – Firestick and Tulloch.

Unbeaten horses:
Four horses have retired with unbeaten records after a minimum of nine starts: Boniform, Malt Queen, Grand Flaneur and Lecturer.

First horse to win four Derbies in a season:
Dayana, the South Australian galloper, which won the South Australian, Victorian, Western Australian and Australian Derbies in 1972. In 1977 Stormy Rex won the first three Derbies and was beaten into second place in the Australian Derby.

Most popular horse since Phar Lap:
Probably Gunsynd, the 'Goondiwindi Grey', bred at Goondiwindi, Qld. Gunsynd was the first Australian horse to win a quarter of a million dollars and to be sold for almost the same amount – $280,455 stakes, $270,618 sale price. Gunsynd had 54 starts for 29 wins, 7 seconds and 8 thirds and was only once beaten over the mile distance (1,500 m) – by Triton in the 1972 Epsom Handicap at Randwick. In 1970-71, Gunsynd won the mile-distance Grand Slam – the Epsom, Toorak, George Adams and Doncaster Handicaps. A crowd of 55,022 at Randwick saw Gunsynd win his farewell race on 21 April 1973 and such was his popularity that racegoers petitioned racing clubs for Gunsynd to make farewell appearances at Flemington and Doomben.

First horse to win $200,000 in Australia:
Tulloch, with earnings of $220,247. Sailor's Guide won $132,088 in Australia and $104,088 in the USA – a total of $236,176.

Highest stakeswinner bred in Australia:
Strawberry Road, which bettered Kingston Town's record of $1,605,790 when he finished second in the $2,600,000 Breeders' Cup at the Aqueduct Racecourse, New York, USA, on 3 November 1985. Strawberry Road's second-place prize money was $585,000, taking his career earnings to $1,913,853. Of that amount, $680,000 was won in Australia before his syndicate owners took him to Europe, Japan and the United States.

Longest-priced winner of a major race:
Murray King won the 1926 Sydney Cup at 200/1 after opening at 250/1.

Most horses in dead heat:
Four in the pre-photo-finish camera days. Blucher, Lord Roseberry, Minister Melle and Cornet were declared by the judge to have dead-heated for first at Toowoomba, Qld, in 1897. Stewards ordered a re-run and the race was won by Cornet. The chances of a judge calling a four-horse dead heat with the naked eye are incalculable.

First triple dead heat with photo-finish camera in operation:
Ark Royal, Fighting Force and Pandie Sun, in the Hotham Handicap at Flemington, on 3 November 1956.

Shortest-priced winner of major race:
Valerius won the 1961 Chipping Norton Stakes at Warwick Farm, Sydney, at 33/1 on.

Shortest-priced losing favourite:
Ajax, which was sent to the post at 40/1 on and was beaten by Spear Chief at Rosehill, NSW, in 1939.

Australian jockeys overseas:
Many Australian jockeys have had brilliant careers overseas, especially in England and Europe. Most successful in England has been Arthur 'Scobie' Breasley who rode 2,161 winners from 9,716 rides between 1950 and 1968 when he retired to become a trainer. He rode two English Derby winners and was premier English jockey four times. Breasley (b. Wagga, NSW, 1914) had compiled a brilliant riding record in Australia before leaving for England but like so many champion jockeys (among them George Moore, George Mulley, Harold Badger, Jack McCarten and Geoff Lane) never won a Melbourne Cup.

Rae 'Togo' Johnstone (1905-64) probably ranks second to Breasley as the most successful Australian jockey in England and Europe. Sydney-born Johnstone is the only Australian to win every English classic race, including three Derbies. He won well over 2,000 races.

Most successful Australians overseas:
Russell Maddock (SA), Bill Williamson (Vic.), Edgar Britt, Bernard 'Brownie' Carslake, Neville Sellwood, George Moore, Bill Cook, Frank Wootton and Bill McLachlan (NSW) head the list of Australian jockeys who achieved outstanding success in Great Britain and Europe. McLachlan, Sellwood, Cooke, Breasley, Moore and Maddock all rode for royalty.

Australian jockeys to win the English Derby:
Rae Johnstone, Scobie Breasley, Neville Sellwood, Pat Glennon and George Moore. Wins by Breasley in 1964-65, Glennon in 1966 and Moore in 1967 made four wins in a row for Australia.

AUSTRALIAN RIDING RECORDS

First jockey to 'ride the card' at a metropolitan meeting:
Tasmanian Geoff Prouse, who rode all seven winners at Elwick, Hobart, Tas., on 22 January 1972. His feat is yet to be equalled.

First to ride all winners (any meeting):
Bill Thomas (Qld), who rode all seven winners at Townsville, Qld, on 27 July 1929.

Most successive wins:
In Australia: John Naughton (NSW), who rode 11 successive winners at Sydney and provincial meetings during December 1951.
Overseas: John Taylor, who rode in Mauritius 1935-39 and is reported to have ridden 19 successive winners.

Jockey who rode five race winners at metropolitan meeting:
Sydney jockey Jack Toohey rode all of the five race winners at Canterbury Park, Sydney, on 12 May 1923. Two other races on the program were jumping events. Toohey rode the winners of his first two races at Randwick on 19 May 1923. His feat is almost comparable to that of Geoff Prouse at Elwick, Tas., in 1972.

First woman jockey to ride against men in open meetings:
New Zealand-born Linda Jones, in Sydney, in 1979.

First Australian woman jockey:
Pam O'Neill of Brisbane, Qld, made history on 19 May 1979 when she became the first Australian jockey to ride against men at a non-restricted meeting at Southport, Qld. She won three races.

First Australian woman jockey in a jumping race:
Tracey Byrnes (SA), at Mt Gambier, SA, in August 1979. She finished unplaced on her father's horse, Bravado Star, in a 14-jump steeplechase.

Most winners in a season:
126.5 (including three dead heats), by Bill Cook (NSW), in the Sydney season of 1939-40.

Most winners in a season by an apprentice:
107.5 (one dead heat), by Malcolm Johnston (NSW), in the Sydney season of 1975-76. Johnston broke Jack Thompson's 1940-41 apprentice record by one win.

Most wins by a trainer:
200, by South Australian Colin Hayes, in the 1979-80 season. Hayes' winners were shared between Vic. and SA.

First bookmaker in Australia:
Englishman Robert Siever, who began his Australian career when he arrived in Melbourne in 1882. Siever was the first to sport the traditional bookies' bag and to call out the odds. Prior to his arrival, on-course bookmakers worked almost in private and waited for punters to approach them and ask the odds. Siever was also the first bookmaker to print betting tickets.

Jockey fatalities:
No accurate records exist of the total number of jockey fatalities since the first days of racing. Among the top riders to lose their lives on the track have been Billy Duncan, Billy Lappin, Keith Voitre, Reg Heather, Stan Cassidy (in a training accident) and famous Victorian steeplechase rider Tommy Corrigan.

Champion NSW rider Neville Sellwood was killed in a fall in France on 7 November 1962.

The Phar Lap tragedy:
Probably Australia's greatest racehorse, New Zealand-bred Phar Lap, died in mysterious circumstances at Menlo Park, near San Francisco, USA, on 5 April 1932, a few days after he had won his only start on a planned national tour. Phar Lap won the Agua Caliente Handicap at Tijuana, just over the Mexican border. The exact cause of Phar Lap's death has never been satisfactorily explained. An autopsy was inconclusive and after vague explanations ranging from Phar Lap eating damp lucerne to fodder brought over from Australia being tainted, many people close to the champion believed Phar Lap had been deliberately poisoned. Melbourne journalist Bert Wolfe 'Cardigan', the only Australian media man to accompany Phar Lap to the USA, claimed in his book *My 50 Years on the Turf*, published in 1960, that evidence pointed to Phar Lap being poisoned after eating arsenic pellets mixed with his feed. Phar Lap is the only Australian racehorse to be honoured by museum displays. The champion's body was mounted by American taxidermists and brought back to Melbourne where it has been on display ever since.

The super champions:
The first great champion of the Australian turf was Carbine, which was bred in New Zealand. Carbine won the 1890 Melbourne Cup carrying a still-standing record 10 st 5 lbs (66 kg) and scored 33 wins in 43 starts, only once finishing out of a place. In the immediate post-war years, Bernborough, a Qld entire, became the nation's idol, winning 16 races in succession. His great sequence ended when he finished fifth in the 1946 Caulfield Cup carrying 10 st 10 lbs. Bernborough's owner Mr A. O. Romano sacked jockey George Mulley and signed Qld rider Billy Briscoe to ride the champion in the LKS Mackinnon Stakes. Bernborough had to be pulled up in the race after fracturing a sesamoid bone but was saved for the stud and sold to American interests for a price reported to be US$50,000. The history of Australian racing is studded with super champions from the Carbine era through to 1980s stars such as Kingston Town. So great has been the ability of horses such as Ajax, Peter Pan, Tulloch, Delta, Dalray, Carioca, Comic Court, Dulcify, Flight, Galilee, Gloaming, Gunsynd, Heroic, Light Fingers, Manfred, Mollison, Poseidon, Rain Lover, Redcraze, Red Handed, Rising Fast, Sailor's Guide, Sobar, Sky High, Think Big, Wakeful and Windbag, that it is impossible to draw any realistic comparisons.

Caulfield Cup—Melbourne Cup double winners:
The first horse to achieve the double was Poseidon in 1906. Other dual winners have been: The Trump 1937, Rivette 1939, Rising Fast 1954, Even Stevens 1962, Galilee 1966 and Gurner's Lane 1982.

Record attendances:
The largest crowd for a Melbourne Cup was 103,170 in 1973. The largest Sydney crowd was 93,500 at Randwick for the 1948 Doncaster Handicap.

ADELAIDE CUP
Run over 3,200 m, the Adelaide Cup was first staged over two miles and from 1884–1944 over one mile, five furlongs. It reverted to two miles in 1945 and the metric distance of 3,200 m in 1973. It is run at Morphettville each May.

Year	Winner	Time
1864	Falcon	3.50
1865	Ebor	3.55.5
1866	Cowra	3.50
1867	Cowra	3.55
1868	Cupbearer	3.46
1869	Norma	3.47.5
1870–71	*Not held*	
1872	Australian Buck	3.51
1873	Dolphin	3.49
1874	Ace of Trumps	3.44
1875	Lurline	3.41
1876	Impudence	3.37
1877	Aldinga	3.58.5
1878	Glenormiston	3.43
1879	Banter	3.35
1880	First Water	3.59
1881	Totalizator	3.37.3
1882	Euclid	3.36.5

Year	Winner	Time
1883	Sting	3.35.8
1884	Malua	2.55.8
1885	Lord Wilton	2.53.8
1886-88	Not held	
1889	The Lawyer	2.56.3
1890	Shootover	2.53
1891	Stanley	2.54
1892	Jericho	2.55
1893	Vakeel	2.54.5
1894	Port Admiral	2.52.5
1895	Elswick	2.53
1896	War Paint	2.51.3
1897	Mora	2.52
1898	Paul Pry	2.51.8
1899	Contrast	2.51.3
1900	Tarquin	2.54.3
1901	Gunga Din	2.52.8
1902	The Idler	2.51.5
1903	Sojourner	2.51
1904	Sport Royal	2.49
1905	Troytown	2.52.8
1906	Dynamite	2.50
1907	Spinaway	2.50
1908	Destinist	2.54
1909	Kooringa	2.50.8
1910	Medaglia	2.51.3
1911	Eye Glass	2.50.3
1912	Eye Glass	2.50.3
1913	Midnight Sun	2.50
1914	Hamburg Belle	2.50
1915	Naxbery	2.49
1916	St Spasa	2.49.3
1917	Green Cap	2.48.3
1918	Elsdon	2.46
1919	Dependence	2.49
1920	Wee Gun	2.53.8
1921	Sir Marco	2.47.8
1922	Repique	2.49.3
1923	King Ingoda	2.51.5
1924	Wynette	2.45
1925	Stralia	2.47.5
1926	Spearer	2.47.5
1927	Three Kings	2.45.3
1928	Altimeter	2.44
1929	Parallance	2.49
1930	Temptation	2.46.5
1931	Suzumi	2.45.3
1932	Romany Eye	2.44.5
1933	Infirmiere	2.46
1934	Sir Roseland	2.46
1935	Mellion	2.45
1936	Cape York	2.51.5
1937	Donaster	2.43.5
1938	Dartford	2.48.5
1939	Son of Aurous	2.46
1940	Apostrophe	2.44.8
1941	Yodvara	2.46.5
1942-43	Not held (WW II)	
1944	Chief Watchman	2.49
1945	Blankenburg	3.26.5
1946	Little Tich	3.31
1947	Beau Cheval	3.23.5
1948	Sanctus	3.25
1949	Colin	3.23
1950	Peerless Fox	3.23
1951	Peerless Fox	3.30
1952	Aldershot	3.25.8
1953	Royal Pageant	3.24.8
1954	Spearfolio	3.27
1955	Storm Glow	3.29
1956	Pushover	3.31.8
1957	Borgia	3.29.6
1958	Star Aim	3.34
1959	Mac	3.24
1960	Lourdale	3.35.8
1961	Far Away Places	3.26.4
1962	Cheong Sam	3.23.8
1963	Woolstar	3.24
1964	Jamagne	3.24
1965	Hunting Horn	3.23.5
1966	Prince Camillo	3.29.7
1967	Fulmen	3.25.3
1968	Rain Lover	3.31
1969	Gnapur	3.21
1970	Tavel	3.23.2
1971	Laelia	3.25.5
1972	Wine Taster	3.27.2
1973	Tavel	3.28.2
1974	Phar Ace	3.30.2
1975	Soulman	3.29.4
1976	Grand Scale	3.20.5(r)
1977	Reckless	3.25.8
1978	Hyperno	3.32.7
1979	Panamint	3.25.1
1980	Yasmak	3.22.4
1981	Just A Dash	3.23.2
1982	Dealer's Choice	3.29
1983	Amarant	3.27.5
1984	Moss Kingdom	3.21.6
1985	Toujours Mio	3.28.8
1986	Mr Lomondy	3.25.3
1987	Mr Lomondy	3.25.3
1988	Lord Reims	3.30.9

(r) Race record (for 3,200 m)

BRISBANE CUP
Run over 3,200 metres (originally two miles), the Brisbane Cup is held at Eagle

Farm each June. It was first staged on 25 May 1866 and won by T. F. Ryan's Forester. Statistics prior to 1879 are unavailable.

Year	Winner	Time
1879	Sydney	3.41
1880	Major	3.49
1881	Lord Clifden	3.37
1882	Proctor	3.38
1883*	Mozart	3.12
1884	Legacy	3.52
1885	Lancer	3.36
1886	Bonnie Bee	3.40.5
1887	Wetherondale	3.37.5
1888*	Sirius	3.07
1889	Quicksilver	3.38.8
1890	Lyndhurst	3.37.5
1891	Lurline	3.39
1892	Splendide	3.41.8
1893	Tridentate	3.34.5
1894	Yelverton	3.34
1895	Orville	3.41
1896	Tornado	3.34.3
1897	Battalion	3.35.8
1898	Ruby d'Or	3.34.8
1899	Dundonald	3.36
1900	Boreas II	3.39
1901	Rabato	3.34
1902	Palmer	3.32.5
1903	Jessie	3.35.3
1904	Fitz Grafton	3.29
1905	Fitz Grafton	3.32
1906	Scorcher	3.34
1907	Haidee	3.34.3
1908	Plunder	3.33.5
1909	Fightaway	3.32
1910	Curve	3.32.8
1911	Black Paint	3.30
1912	Goard	3.30
1913	Rosard	3.32.5
1914	Cagou	3.28
1915	Rue Victoria	3.27.8
1916	Demeranthus	3.30
1917	Bunting	3.28.5
1918	Irish Princess	3.24.8
1919	Venerable	3.26.8
1920	Golden Sunset	3.26.3
1921	Impeyan	3.24
1922	Grichka	3.26.3
1923	Seremite	3.35
1924	Balaton	3.38.5
1925	Te Kara	3.26.5
1926	Plastoon	3.27
1927	Kentle	3.29.8
1928	Canning Queen	3.22.5

Year	Winner	Time
1929	In Petto	3.23.5
1930	Trainer	3.27
1931	Royal Smile	3.26.5
1932	St Valorey	3.24.8
1933	Herolage	3.24.3
1934	St Valorey	3.24.8
1935	Rivalli	3.25.3
1936	Lough Neagh	3.25.8
1937	Glen Spear	3.23
1938	Spear Chief	3.28.8
1939	Spear Chief	3.19.8
1940	Tragopan	3.25.5
1941	Lady Buzzard	3.25
1942-46	Not held (WW II)(t)	
1947	Blue Boots	3.22
1948	Secarda	3.24.8
1949	Sanctus	3.24
1950	Silver Buzz	3.28.5
1951	Prince of Fairies	3.23.5
1952	Putoko	3.27.3
1953	Hydrogen	3.22
1954	Lancaster	3.21.5
1955	The Wash	3.23.3
1956	Redcraze	3.22
1957	Cambridge	3.21.5
1958	Timor	3.20.9
1959	Macdougal	3.22.4
1960	Valerius	3.21.2
1961	Tulloch	3.22.7
1962	Kamikaze	3.21.7
1963	Campo	3.22.8
1964	Fair Patton	3.23.1
1965	Fair Patton	3.24.1
1966	Apa	3.28.7
1967	Fulmen	3.21.7
1968	Prominence	3.18.6
1969	Galleon King	3.20.7
1970	Cachondeo	3.22.9
1971	Royal Shah	3.22.4
1972	Mode	3.21.9
1973	Irish Whip**	3.18.5 (r)
1974	Igloo	3.22.1
1975	Herminia	3.18.9
1976	Balmerino	4.24.2
1977	Reckless	3.19.6
1978	Muros	3.22.5
1979	Grey Affair	3.19.6
1980	Love Bandit	3.27
1981	Four Crowns	3.24.9
1982	Queen's Road	3.19.7
1983	Amarant	3.23
1984	Chiamare	3.22.5
1985	Foxseal	3.24
1986	Marlon	3.21.6

Year	Winner	Time
1987	Limitless	3.30.8
1988	Lord Hybrow	3.26.2

* Run over one mile.
** Won on protest. The Developer was first past the post.
(r) Race Record.
(t) One-mile race held on the traditional date in 1946 and called the Victory Cup.

CAULFIELD CUP

The Caulfield Cup was run over a 1.5 mile distance from its inception until the introduction of metric distances in 1972. The distance was then officially announced as 2,400 metres. The Cups of 1880 and 1881 were run over 1.25 miles 'and a distance'.

Year	Winner	Time
1879	Newminster	2.45.5
1880	Tom Kirk	2.28.5
1881	Blue Ribbon	2.30
1882	Little Jack	2.29.5
1883	Calma	2.41.5
1884	Blink Bonny	2.42
1885	Grace Darling	2.40
1886	Ben Bolt	2.42
1887	Oakleigh	2.41.8
1888	Chicago	2.38.3
1889	Boz	2.43
1890	Vengeance	2.38
1891	G'Naroo	2.36
1892	Paris	2.38.3
1893	Sainfoin	2.38*
1894	Paris	2.38.3
1895	Waterfall	2.36.8
1896	Cremorne	2.38.5
1897	Amberite	2.37
1898	Hymettus	2.36.8
1899	Dewey	2.38.3
1900	Ingliston	2.36.8
1901	Hymettus	2.35.3
1902	Lieutenant Bill	2.36
1903	Sweet Nell	2.35.3
1904	Murmur	2.37.5
1905	Marvel Loch	2.35.8
1906	Poseidon	2.34.8
1907	Poseidon	2.35.5
1908	Maranui	2.35.8
1909	Aborigine/ Blue Book (dead heat)	2.35
1910	Flavinius	2.34.5
1911	Lady Medallist	2.34.5
1912	Uncle Sam	2.34.3
1913	Aurifer	2.34
1914	Uncle Sam	2.34.3
1915	Lavendo	2.34
1916	Shepherd King	2.33.3
1917	Bronzetti	2.39.5
1918	King Offa	2.33.3
1919	Lucknow	2.32
1920	Eurythmic	2.33.3
1921	Violoncello	2.35.8
1922	Whittier	2.32
1923	Wynette	2.33
1924	Purser	2.33
1925	Whittier	2.34
1926	Manfred	2.32.5
1927	Textile	2.32.5
1928	Maple	2.33.3
1929	High Syce	2.30.5
1930	Amounis	2.34.3
1931	Denis Boy	2.31.3
1932	Rogilla	2.34.3
1933	Gaine Carrington	2.28.5
1934	Journal	2.29
1935	Palfresco	2.27.8
1936	Northwind	2.28.8
1937	The Trump	2.28.8
1938	Buzalong	2.29.8
1939	Rivette	2.29.3
1940	Beaulivre	2.29
1941	Velocity	2.29.5
1942	Tranquil Star	2.32.8
1943	St Warden	2.30.8**
	Skipton	2.29.5**
1944	Counsel	2.29.5
1945	St Fairy	2.30.3
1946	Royal Gem	2.30.3
1947	Columnist	2.28.3
1948	Red Fury	2.32
1949	Lincoln	2.36.3
1950	Grey Boots	2.31
1951	Basha Felika	2.30
1952	Peshawar	2.30.3
1953	My Hero	2.28.8
1954	Rising Fast	2.30
1955	Rising Fast	2.29.3
1956	Redcraze	2.33.8
1957	Tulloch	2.26.9 (r)
1958	Sir Blink	2.28.8
1959	Regal Wench	2.28.7
1960	Ilumquh	2.27.9
1961	Summer Fair	2.34.1
1962	Even Stevens	2.34.1
1963	Sometime	2.28.1
1964	Yangtze	2.36.2
1965	Bore Head	2.28.3
1966	Galilee	2.27.8
1967	Tobin Bronze	2.31.1

Year	Winner	Time
1968	Bunratty Castle	2.29.7
1969	Big Philou	2.28.3***
1970	Beer Street	2.31.2
1971	Gay Icarus	2.28
1972	Sobar	2.27.1 (mr)
1973	Swell Time	2.35.9
1974	Leilani	2.38.3
1975	Analight	2.30
1976	How Now	2.36.7
1977	Ming Dynasty	2.28.5
1978	Taksan	2.27.5
1979	Mighty Kingdom	2.29.9
1980	Ming Dynasty	2.28.7
1981	Silver Bounty	2.27.1(emr)
1982	Gurner's Lane	2.32.5
1983	Hayai	2.38.8
1984	Affinity	2.29.7
1985	Trisarc	2.30.9
1986	Mr Lomondy	2.30.1
1987	Lord Reims	2.36.3

* Tim Swiveller was first past the post but was disqualified for interference.
** Run in two divisions.
*** Nausori was first past the post but was relegated to second following a protest by Roy Higgins (Big Philou).
(emr) Equalled metric distance record.
(r) Race, track and Australian record.
(mr) Metric distance record.

GOLDEN SLIPPER

The AJC Golden Slipper Stakes is run over 1,200 m and is the richest race in Australia for two-year-olds. The 1985 prize money was a record $600,000. The race is run each March at Rosehill Racecourse near Sydney.

Year	Winner	Time
1957	Todman (N. Sellwood)	1.11.4
1958	Skyline (A. Mulley)	1.12.7
1959	Fine and Dandy (J. Thompson)	1.12.8
1960	Sky High (A. Mulley)	1.11.9
1961	Magic Night (M. Schumacher)	1.11.9
1962	Birthday Card (R. Greenwood)	1.11.4
1963	Pago Pago (W. Pyers)	1.15.5
1964	Eskimo Prince (A. Mulley)	1.11.9
1965	Reisling (L. Billett)	1.11.1
1966	Storm Queen (R. Higgins)	1.12.9
1967	Sweet Embrace (C. Clare)	1.13.2
1968	Royal Parma (N. Campton)	1.11.9
1969	Vain (P. Hyland)	1.12.1
1970	Baguette (G. Moore)	1.12.7
1971	Fairy Walk (G. Moore)	1.12.6
1972	John's Hope (K. Langby)	1.11.1
1973	Tontonian (R. Higgins)	1.11.7
1974	Hartshill (K. Langby)	1.13
1975	Toy Show (K. Langby)	1.12
1976	Vivarchi (J. Duggan)	1.11.7
1977	Luskin Star (J. Wade)	1.10
1978	Manikato (G. Willetts)	1.10.7
1979	Century Miss (W. Harris)	1.10.7
1980	Dark Eclipse (K. Moses)	1.10.4
1981	Full on Aces (L. Dittman)	1.13.1
1982	Marscay (R. Quinton)	1.10.6
1983	Sir Dapper (R. Quinton)	1.9.9 (r)
1984*	Inspired (D. Beadman)	1.11.6
1985	Rory's Jester (R. Quinton)	1.10.3
1986	Bounding Away (L. Dittman)	1.9.9 **
1987	Marauding (R. Quinton)	1.10.6
1988	Star Watch (L. Olsen)	1.13.0

* Run in April.
** Equalled race record.
(r) Race record.

PERTH CUP

The Perth Cup is run over a distance of 3,200 m (originally two miles) at Ascot in early January. Two races were held in 1901, '21, '25, '38, '42 and '49.

HORSERACING • 127

Year	Winner	Time
1888	Telephone	3.40.3
1889	Aim	3.46
1890	Wandering Willie	3.44.3
1891	The Duke	3.44
1892	Wandering Willie	3.45
1893	Scarpia	3.43
1894	Scarpia	3.43.5
1895	Durable	3.48
1896	Inverary	3.37.5
1897	Snapshot	3.40
1898	Le Var	3.38.5
1899	Mural	3.38.3
1900	Carbineer	3.37
1901	Flintlock*	3.38.8
1901	Australian**	3.42.8
1902	Novitiate	3.37.8
1903	Cypher	3.35
1904	Blue Spec	3.35
1905	Czarovitch	3.33.8
1906	May King	3.33
1907	Post Town	3.29
1908	Scorcher	3.30.8
1909	Loch Shiel	3.30
1910	Jolly Beggar	3.39.5
1911	Artesian	3.30
1912	Sparkle	3.32.2
1913	Artesian	3.30.2
1914	Dollar Dictator	3.31.2
1915	Irish Knight	3.28.4
1916	Lucky Escape	3.28.8
1917	Downing Street	3.27.4
1918	Macadam	3.26.4
1919	Eurythmic/ Rivose (dead heat)	3.25.8
1920	Not held	
1921	Seigneur*	3.30.6
1921	Earl of Seafield**	3.26.8
1922	Jolly Cosy	3.27.8
1923	Not held	
1924	Lilypond	3.27.4
1925	Mercato*	3.27.2
1925	Great Applause**	3.28.4
1926	Au Fait	3.26.2
1927	Phoenix Park	3.25.6
1928	Not held	
1929	Jemidar	3.25.5
1930	Coolbarro	3.25.8
1931	The Dimmer	3.29.8
1932	Bonny Note	3.29.8
1933	Alienist	3.26.3
1934	Cueesun	3.33
1935	Cueesun	3.28
1936	Picaro	3.29.3
1937	Manolive	3.25.3
1938	Maikai*	3.26.3

Year	Winner	Time
1938	Gay Balkan**	3.30.8
1939	Tomito	3.38.5
1940	Not held	
1941	Fernridge	3.24.3
1942	Ragtime*	3.28
1942	Temple Chief**	3.27.5
1943	Not held	
1944	Loyalist	3.26
1945	Gay Parade	3.26
1946	Maddington	3.23.8
1947	Sydney James	3.22.5
1948	Kingscote	3.24
1949	Gurkha*	3.24.5
1949	Beau Vasse**	3.28
1950	Azennis	3.26.3
1951	Avarna	3.26.8
1952	Not held	
1953	Raconteur	3.24.5
1954	Beau Scot	3.29
1955	Lenarc	3.29
1956	Yabaroo	3.25.5
1957	Elmsfield	3.27
1958	Fairetha	3.28.3
1959	Fairetha	3.28
1960	England's Dust	3.25.3
1961	Royal Khora	3.22
1962	Bay Court	3.24
1963	Resolution	3.23.3
1964	Fair's Print	3.22
1965	Royal Coral	3.22
1966	Special Reward	3.22
1967	Not held	
1968	Lintonmare	3.23
1969	Jenark	3.20
1970	Fait Accompli	3.21.5
1971	Artello Bay	3.23.8
1972	Fait Accompli	3.21.5
1973	Dayana	3.18.2 (r)
1974	Allegation	3.20.82
1975	Runyon	3.21.17
1976	Philomel	3.18.83
1977	Muros	3.21.26
1978	Golden Centre	3.20.15
1979	Meliador	3.18.93
1980	Rothschild	3.22.81
1981	Magistrate	3.21.01
1982	Magistrate	3.21.92
1983	Bianco Lady	3.23.84
1984	Moss Kingdom	3.23.14
1985	Phizam	3.20.10
1986	Ullyatt	3.20.14
1987	Rocket Racer	3.21.01
1988	Linc the Leopard	3.24.39

* Race held New Year's Day.
** Race held December same year.
(r) Race record.

SYDNEY CUP

The AJC Sydney Cup is run over a distance of 3,200 m (originally two miles) at Randwick during the Easter Carnival. The 1985 prize money was a record $262,000.

Year	Winner	Time
1866	Yattendon	3.43
1867	Fishhook	3.41.5
1868	The Barb	3.40
1869	The Barb	3.40
1870	Barbelle	3.43
1871	Mermaid	3.40
1872	The Prophet	3.36.8
1873	Vixen	3.40
1874	Speculation	3.39
1875	Imperial	3.36
1876	A. T.	3.37.8
1877	Kingfisher	3.36.3
1878	Democrat	3.36.5
1879	Savanaka	3.33.8
1880	Petrea	3.37.5
1881	Progress	3.36.8
1882	Cunnamulla	3.34
1883	Darebin	3.33.5
1884	Favo	3.36
1885	Normanby	3.35
1886	Cerise and Blue	3.33.3
1887	Frisco	3.39.8
1888	The Australian Peer	3.32.5
1889	Carbine	3.31
1890	Carbine	3.37
1891	Highborn	3.37.5
1892	Stromboli	3.31.5
1893	Realm*	3.39
1894	Lady Trenton	3.34
1895	Patroness	3.38.5
1896	Wallace	3.31
1897	Tricolor	3.31.5
1898	Merloolas	3.31
1899	Diffidence	3.31
1900	La Carabine	3.31.5
1901	San Fran	3.32
1902	Wakeful	3.28.8
1903	Street Arab	3.31.8
1904	Lord Cardigan	3.31
1905	Tartan	3.27
1906	Noreen	3.29.5
1907	Realm**	3.29
1908	Dyed Garments	3.34
1909	Trafalgar	3.29.5
1910	Vavasor	3.29.5
1911	Moorilla	3.36.5
1912	Saxonite	3.29
1913	Cadonia	3.28.3
1914	Lilyveil	3.26.5
1915	Scotch Artillery	3.36.5
1916	Prince Bardolph	3.24.8
1917	The Fortune Hunter	3.26
1918	Rebus	3.26.5
1919	Ian 'Or	3.31.5
1920	Kennaquhair	3.22.8
1921	Eurythmic	3.24.8
1922	Prince Charles	3.26.3
1923	David	3.26.3
1924	Scarlet	3.28.3
1925	Lilypond	3.26.8
1926	Murray King	3.26
1927	Piastoon	3.33.8
1928	Winalot	3.32.3
1929	Crucis	3.23.3
1930	Gwilliam	3.22.5
1931	The Dimmer	3.35.3
1932	Johnnie Jason	3.32
1933	Rogilla	3.23
1934	Broad Arrow	3.28
1935	Akuna	3.27.8
1936	Contact	3.24.8
1937	Mestoravon	3.21.8
1938	L'Aigion	3.23
1939	Mosaic	3.21.5
1940	Mosaic	3.25.5
1941	Lucrative	3.20.8
1942	Veiled Threat***	3.25.5
1943	Abspear	3.26
1944	Veiled Threat	3.27
1945	Craigie	3.25.5
1946	Cordale	3.28.5
1947	Proctor	3.27.5
1948	Dark Marne	3.26.3
1949	Carbon Copy	3.23.5
1950	Sir Falcon	3.26.8
1951	Bankstream	3.22
1952	Opulent	3.37.3
1953	Carioca	3.22.5
1954	Gold Scheme	3.21.8
1955	Talisman	3.29.5
1956	Sailor's Guide	3.30.6
1957	Electro	3.22.6
1958	Straight Draw	3.22
1959	On Line	3.30.9
1960	Grand Garry	3.20.7
1961	Sharply	3.24.9
1962	Grand Print	3.33.7
1963	Maidenhead	3.33.1
1964	Zinga Lee	3.23.3
1965	River Seine	3.25.1
1966	Prince Grant	3.24
1967	Galilee	3.21.1

Year	Winner	Time
1968	General Command	3.26.4
1969	Lowland	3.24.4
1970	Arctic Symbol	3.35.8
1971	Gallic Temple	3.20.6
1972	Dark Suit	3.30.3
1973	Apollo Eleven	3.19 (r)
1974	Battle Heights	3.37.1
1975	Gay Master	3.22.6
1976	Oopik	3.23.6
1977	Reckless	3.19.4
1978	My Good Man	3.27.9
1979	Double Century	3.20.8
1980	Kingston Town	3.28.2
1981	Our Paddy Boy	3.21.7
1982	Azaway	3.22.8
1983	Veloso	3.23.4
1984	Trissaro	3.22.4
1985	Late Show	3.26.7
1986	Marooned	3.27
1987	Major Drive	3.21.2
1988	Banderol	3.34.1

* By Archie.
** By Majestic.
*** Run at Rosehill.
(r) Race record.

HOBART CUP

The Hobart Cup is run over 2,380 metres on the second day of the Tasmanian Racing Club January–February carnival. First run in 1875 over two miles, the Cup was staged over 1¾ miles from 1878 to 1885 and 1½ miles from 1886 until the introduction of metric distances in 1972.

Year	Winner	Time
1875	Ella	3.45
1876	Strop	3.45
1877	Spark	3.41
1878	Swiveller	3.21
1879	Lord Harry	3.10.5
1880	Avernus	3.14.5
1881	Monarque	3.14
1882	The Marchioness	3.13.5
1883	The Assyrian	3.12
1884	King of the Vale	3.16.8
1885	Ringwood	3.9.3
1886	Duration	2.44
1887	Maori Chief	2.43
1888	Ballarat	2.46
1889	Chaldean	2.47
1890	Macquarie	2.42
1891	Lapstone	2.43.5
1892	Hopetoun	2.46.3
1893	Pauline	2.51
1894	Amadeus	2.42.5

Year	Winner	Time
1895	Music	2.40.5
1896	Lena	2.43.8
1897	Benedict	2.42.5
1898	Rosella	2.41.5
1899	Flintlock	2.42.8
1900	Eirisdale	2.41.3
1901	Timbrel	2.43.8
1902	Progredior	2.38
1903	Chesterfield	2.41.5
1904	Proceedor	2.40.5
1905	Newmarket	2.44.3
1906	Postulate	2.40
1907	Viola	2.40.8
1908	Admirer	2.39.3
1909	Jack Smith	2.39.5
1910	Eighteen Carat	2.39.3
1911	Bolan	2.35.8
1912	Flavel	2.39.8
1913	Belove	2.39.8
1914	Delphic	2.42
1915	Defence	2.40
1916	Polska	2.43.4
1917	Sea Pink	2.37.8
1918	Ladino	2.38
1919	Prince Moeraki	2.37.8
1920	Nadir Shah/ Trusty Blade (*dead heat*)	2.38.8
1921	Talisman	2.38.2
1922	Ouverte	2.37.2
1923	Binbi	2.38.4
1924	Llanthony	2.36.2
1925	Pukka	2.36.2
1926	Royal Simon	2.36
1927	Roonsleigh	2.33
1928	Roonsleigh	2.38.8
1929	Prince Viol	2.36.4
1930	Tarapunga	2.35.4
1931	Royal Simon	2.37.4
1932	Billy Barton	2.34.4
1933	Air Favorite	2.37
1934	Song of Solomon	2.37.2
1935	Sunbronze	2.36.2
1936	Coolart	2.38.2
1937	Royalty	2.38.4
1938	Stylish Lady	2.36.6
1939	Mac O'Roni	2.35
1940	El Nene	2.35.6
1941	Mercator	2.38.5
1942	Mac O'Roni	2.34.6
1943	Lord Saltash	2.34.8
1944	Thurso Bay	2.36
1945	Gaelane	2.34.2
1946	Paramente	2.36.2
1947	Wingfire	2.34.6

Year	Winner	Time
1948	Evade	2.36
1949	The Artist	2.33.8
1950	English	2.32.8
1951	Tarcombe	2.34
1952	Royal Release	2.32.2
1953	Sir Legis	2.33.4
1954	Sea Wolf	2.34.4
1955	Seriki	2.33.8
1956	Seriki	2.34.2
1957	Buzzie	2.35
1958	Legismars	2.32.8
1959	King Thane	2.32.6
1960	Orden	2.30.2
1961	Welton	2.30.6
1962	Great Singer	2.31.6
1963	Volterra	2.30
1964	Macdalla*	2.30.4
1965	Macdalla	2.30.4
1966	Sailing Prince	2.29.6
1967	Haughty Boy	2.30
1968	Bounteous	2.31
1969	Dalarus	2.34.6
1970	Dark Purple	2.27.8**
1971	Trial and Error	2.29
1972	Piping Lane	2.29
1973	Sir Trutone	2.31.6
1974	Knee High	2.34.1
1975	Lord Pascoe	2.29.1
1976	Brailos	2.29
1977	Brailos	2.28
1978	Clean Heels	2.28.6
1979	Kubla Khan	2.29.4
1980	Strident King	2.28.6
1981	Andrias	2.30
1982	Powerful Prince	2.30.1
1983	Palomine	2.30.6
1984	Viscount Geoffrey	2.27.7***
1985	Macbyrne	2.29.5
1986	Dark Intruder	2.30.7
1987	Cylai	2.29.8****
1988	Brisque	2.27.8

*Wangle finished first but was disqualified after a positive swab.
**Race record 1½ miles distance.
***Race record 2,380 metres.
****First $100,000 race run in Tasmania.

AJC DERBY

The AJC Derby was run in the spring until 1977 and has been in the autumn since 1979. It was held over 1½ miles until 1972 when, with the introduction of metrication, it became 2,400 metres.

Year	Winner	Time
1861	Kyogle	*
1862	Regno	*
1863	Remornic	*
1864	Yattendon	*†
1865	Clove	2.51
1866	The Barb	2.48
1867	Fireworks	2.48
1868	The Duke	2.50
1869	Charon	2.47
1870	Florence	2.51
1871	Javelin	2.47
1872	Loup Garou	2.46.3
1873	Benvolio	2.48.5
1874	Kingsborough	2.50
1875	Richmond	2.55
1876	Robinson Crusoe	2.43.5
1877	Woodlands	2.49.3
1878	His Lordship	2.55
1879	Nellie	2.51
1880	Grand Flaneur	2.45.5
1881	Wheatear	2.52.3
1882	Navigator	2.48.8
1883	Le Grand	2.46
1884	Bargo	2.42
1885	Nordenfeldt	2.47
1886	Trident	2.38
1887	Abercorn	2.39
1888	Melos	2.46
1889	Singapore	2.44
1890	Gibraltar	2.39
1891	Stromboli	2.41
1892	Camoola	2.40
1893	Trenchant	2.54.5
1894	Bonnie Scotland	2.44.3
1895	Bob Ray	2.41.5
1896	Charge	3.14
1897	Amberite	2.45.2
1898	Picture	2.46.5
1899	Cranberry	2.39
1900	Malster	2.39
1901	Hautvillers	2.37.5
1902	Abundance	2.45
1903	Belah	2.39.5
1904	Sylvanite	2.37
1905	Noctuiform	2.32.5
1906	Poseidon	2.38
1907	Mountain King	2.41.7
1908	Parsee	2.38.2
1909	Prince Foote	2.37.5
1910	Tanami	2.36.2
1911	Cisco	2.37.5
1912	Cider	2.38
1913	Beragoon	2.35.7
1914	Mountain King	2.35.2
1915	Cetigne	2.37

Year	Winner	Time
1916	Kilboy	2.39.7
1917	Biplane	2.34.7
1918	Gloaming	2.33.5
1919	Artilleryman	
	Richmond Main (dead heat)	2.35
1920	Salitros	2.32
1921	Cupidon	2.33.7
1922	Rivoli	2.35.5
1923	Ballymena	2.33.5
1924	Heroic	2.34.2
1925	Manfred	2.35
1926	Rampion 2	2.33
1927	Trivalve	2.33
1928	Prince Humphrey	2.32.7
1929	Phar Lap	2.31.2
1930	Tregilla	2.33.2
1931	Ammon Ra	2.34.7
1932	Peter Pan	2.34
1933	Hall Mark	2.37.5
1934	Theo	2.32.7
1935	Allunga	
	Homer (dead heat)	2.33.7
1936	Talking	2.32.5
1937	Avenger	2.36.5
1938	Nuffield	2.32
1939	Reading	2.34
1940	Pandect	2.37
1941	Laureate	2.32
1942	Main Topic	2.31.5
1943	Moorland	2.37.7
1944	Tea Rose	2.33.5
1945	Magnificent	2.36.7
1946	Concerto	2.34.5
1947	Valiant Crown	2.35
1948	Carbon Copy	2.33.5
1949	Playboy	2.34
1950	Alister	2.32.2
1951	Channel Rise	2.33.7
1952	Deep River	2.38.2
1953	Prince Morvi	2.31.2
1954	Prince Delville	2.33
1955	Caranna	2.33.2
1956	Monte Carlo	2.31.3
1957	Tulloch	2.29.1
1958	Skyline	2.28.8
1959	Martello Towers	2.32.4
1960	Persian Lyric	2.30.6
1961	Summer Fair	2.32.2**
1962	Summer Prince	2.29.2
1963	Summer Fiesta	2.32.3
1964	Royal Sovereign	2.33.5
1965	Prince Grant	2.29.9
1966	El Gordo	2.34.5
1967	Swift Peter	2.30.3
1968	Wilton Park	2.31.2
1969	Divide and Rule	2.33.5
1970	Silver Sharpe	2.31.9
1971	Classic Mission	2.36.1
1972	Gold Brick	2.36.5
1973	Imagele	2.32.1
1974	Taras Bulba	2.33.6
1975	Battle Sign	2.33.9
1976	Great Lover	2.33.9
1977	Belmura Lad	2.33
1978	Not held	
1979	Dulcify	2.30.7
1980	Kingston Town	2.34.2
1981	Our Paddy Boy	2.31.2
1982	Rose of Kingston	2.31
1983	Strawberry Road	2.41.8
1984	Prolific	2.34.8
1985	Tristarc	2.31.3
1986	Bonecrusher	2.35.6
1987	Myocard	2.32.6

* No time recorded
† Won on protest
** Two starters

VRC DERBY

The VRC Derby is run in the spring at Flemington. It was 1½ miles until 1972 when the distance was set at 2,400 metres. Since 1972 it has been 2,500 metres.

Year	Winner	Time
1855	Rose of May	2.59
1856	Flying Doe	3.01
1857	Tricolor	3.03.3
1858	Brownlock	2.45
1859	Buzzard	2.52.5
1860	Flying Colors	3.02
1861	Camden	2.53
1862	Barwon	2.59
1863	Oriflamme	3.03
1864	Lantern	3.05
1865	Angler	2.51
1866	Seagull	3.04
1867	Fireworks	2.56
1868	Fireworks	2.53*
1869	My Dream	2.48*
1869	Charon	2.55
1870	Florence	3.00
1871	Miss Jessie	2.49
1872	Loup Garou	2.46
1873	Lapidist	2.51
1874	Melbourne	2.46.5
1875	Robin Hood	2.48
1876	Briseis	2.43.2
1877	Chester	2.43
1878	Wellington	2.47

Year	Winner	Time	Year	Winner	Time
1879	Suwarrow	2.43	1934	Theo	2.35.7
1880	Grand Flaneur	2.44	1935	Feldspar	2.31.2
1881	Darebin	2.41.5	1936	Talking	2.33
1882	Navigator	2.41.5	1937	Hua	2.32.7
1883	Martini-Henry	2.39	1938	Nuffield	2.34.7
1884	Rufus	2.41.7	1939	Reading	2.33
1885	Nordenfelt	2.38.7	1940	Lucrative	2.32
1886	Trident	2.38.7	1941	Skipton	2.34.5
1887	The Australian Peer	2.40	1942	Great Britain	2.31.2
1888	Ensign	2.45.5	1943	Precept	2.34.2
1889	Dreadnought	2.41	1944	San Martin	2.33.5
1890	The Admiral	2.47.6	1945	Magnificent	2.33
1891	Strathmore	2.41.5	1946	Prince Standard	2.33
1892	Camoola	2.42	1947	Beau Gem	2.30.5
1893	Carnage	2.39	1948	Comic Court	2.35.2
1894	The Harvester	2.40	1949	Delta	2.32.7
1895	Wallace	2.46	1950	Alister	2.35.7
1896	Newhaven	2.39.5	1951	Hydrogen	2.31
1897	Amberite	2.39.5	1952	Advocate	2.30
1898	Cocos	2.41.2	1953	Prince Morvi	2.31.5
1899	Merriwee	2.41.2	1954	Pride of Egypt	2.32.5
1900	Malster	2.48	1955	Sailor's Guide	2.31.5
1901	Hautvillers	2.37	1956	Monte Carlo	2.34.5
1902	Abundance	2.36.2	1957	Tulloch	2.33.5
1903	FJA	2.36.2	1958	Sir Blink	2.30.2
1904	Sylvanite	2.49	1959	Travel Boy	2.34
1905	Lady Wallace	2.40	1960	Sky High	2.32
1906	Poseidon	2.40.5	1961	New Statesman	2.30.7
1907	Mountain King	2.39	1962	Coppelius	2.31.4
1908	Alawa	2.35.5	1963	Craftsman	2.30.4
1909	Prince Foote	2.37	1964	Royal Sovereign	2.28.2
1910	Beverage	2.37.5	1965	Tobin Bronze	2.34
1911	Wilari	2.38.7	1966	Khalif	2.30.1
1912	Wolowa	2.39.5	1967	Savoy	2.30
1913	Beragoon	2.35.5	1968	Always There	2.31
1914	Carlita	2.37.5	1969	Daryl's Joy	2.33.3
1915	Patrobas	2.37	1970	Silver Sharpe	2.30.5
1916	Wolorai	2.42.5	1971	Classic Mission	2.32.5
1917	Biplane	2.35.5	1972	Dayana	2.29.9
1918	Eusebius	2.47.7	1973	Taj Rossi	2.39.4
1919	Richmond Main	2.35.7	1974	Haymaker	2.44.4
1920	Salitros	2.37.7	1975	Galena Boy	2.44.4
1921	Furious	2.35	1976	Unaware	2.36.1
1922	Whittier	2.34	1977	Stormy Rex	2.35.5
1923	Frances Tressady	2.38.2	1978	Dulcify	2.37.5
1924	Spearfelt	2.35	1979	Big Print	2.35
1925	Manfred	2.31.5	1980	Sovereign Red	2.38.4
1926	Rampion	2.32.5	1981	Brewery Boy	2.36.2
1927	Trivalve	2.33	1982	Grosvenor	2.35.9
1928	Strephon	2.33	1983	Bounty Hawk	2.38.5
1929	Phar Lap	2.31.2	1984	Red Anchor	2.35.9
1930	Balloon King	2.33.5	1985	Handy Proverb	2.36.4
1931	Johnny Jason	2.33.5	1986	Raveneaux	2.35.1
1932	Liberal	2.34.2	1987	Omnicort	2.38.9
1933	Hall Mark	2.31.2			

*Run on New Year's Day

ENGLISH DERBY

Officially known as the Epsom Derby, the blue riband event of the English turf was first held more than 200 years ago and was named after the twelfth Earl of Derby who was among a small group of racing enthusiasts who organised the race.

Year	Winner	S/P
1780	Diomed (S. Arnull)	6/4f
1781	Young Eclipse (C. Hindley)	10/1
1782	Assassin (S. Arnull)	5/1
1783	Saltram (C. Hindley)	5/2f
1784	Sergeant (J. Arnull)	3/1
1785	Aimwell (C. Hindley)	7/1
1786	Noble (J. White)	30/1
1787	Sir Peter Teazle (S. Arnull)	2/1f
1788	Sir Thomas (W. South)	5/6f
1789	Skyscraper (S. Chifney Snr)	4/7f
1790	Rhadamanthus (J. Arnull)	5/4f
1791	Eager (M. Stephenson)	5/2
1792	John Bull (J. Buckle)	4/6f
1793	Waxy (W. Clift)	12/1
1794	Daedalus (F. Buckle)	6/1
1795	Spread Eagle (A. Wheatley)	5/2f
1796	Didelot (J. Arnull)	*
1797	(Colt by Fidget) (J. Singleton)	10/1
1798	Sir Harry (S. Arnull)	7/4f
1799	Archduke (J. Arnull)	12/1
1800	Champion (W. Clift)	7/4
1801	Eleanor (J. Saunders)	5/4f
1802	Tyrant (F. Buckle)	7/1
1803	Ditto (W. Clift)	7/2
1804	Hannibal (W. Arnull)	3/1f
1805	Cardinal Beaufort (D. Fitzpatrick)	20/1
1806	Paris (J. Shepherd)	5/1
1807	Election (J. Arnull)	3/1
1808	Pan (F. Collinson)	25/1
1809	Pope (T. Goodison)	20/1
1810	Whalebone (W. Clift)	2/1f
1811	Phantom (F. Buckle)	5/1
1812	Octavius (W. Arnull)	7/1
1813	Smolensko (T. Goodison)	evens f
1814	Blucher (W. Arnull)	5/2
1815	Whisker (T. Goodison)	8/1
1816	Prince Leopold (W. Wheatley)	20/1
1817	Azor (J. Robinson)	50/1
1818	Sam (S. Chifney Jnr)	7/2
1819	Tiresias (W. Clift)	5/2
1820	Sailor (S. Chifney Jnr)	7/2
1821	Gustavus (S. Day)	2/1f
1822	Moses (T. Goodison)	6/1
1823	Emilius (F. Buckle)	11/8
1824	Cedric (J. Robinson)	9/2
1825	Middleton (J. Robinson)	7/4
1826	Lapdog (G. Dockeray)	50/1
1827	Mameluke (J. Robinson)	9/1
1828	Cadland (J. Robinson)	4/1
1829	Frederick (J. Forth)	40/1
1830	Priam (S. Day)	4/1
1831	Spaniel (W. Wheatley)	50/1
1832	St Giles (W. Scott)	3/1
1833	Dangerous (J. Chapple)	30/1
1834	Plenipotentiary (P. Conolly)	9/4
1835	Mundig (W. Scott)	6/1
1836	Bay Middleton (J. Robinson)	7/4f
1837	Phosphorus (G. Edwards)	40/1
1838	Amato (J. Chapple)	30/1
1839	Bloomsbury (S. Templeman)	25/1
1840	Little Wonder (W. Macdonald)	50/1
1841	Coronation (P. Conolly)	5/2f
1842	Attila (W. Scott)	5/1
1843	Cotherstone (W. Scott)	13/8f
1844	Orlando (E. Flatman)	20/1
1845	The Merry Monarch (F. Bell)	15/1
1846	Pyrrhus the First (S. Day)	8/1
1847	Cossack (S. Templeman)	5/1
1848	Surplice (S. Templeman)	evens f
1849	The Flying Dutchman (C. Marlow)	2/1f
1850	Voltigeur (J. Marson)	16/1
1851	Teddington (J. Marson)	3/1
1852	Daniel O'Rourke (F. Butler)	25/1
1853	West Australian (F. Butler)	6/4f
1854	Andover (A. Day)	7/2
1855	**Wild Dayrell** (R. Sherwood)	evens f
1856	Ellington (T. Aldcroft)	20/1
1857	Blink Bonny (J. Charlton)	20/1
1858	Beadsman (J. Wells)	10/1
1859	Musjid (J. Wells)	9/4f
1860	Thormanby (H. Custance)	4/1
1861	Kettledrum (R. Bullock)	16/1
1862	Caractacus (J. Parsons)	40/1
1863	Macaroni (T. Challoner)	10/1
1864	Blair Athol (J. Snowden)	14/1
1865	Gladiateur (H. Grimshaw)	5/2f
1866	Lord Lyon (H. Custance)	5/6f
1867	Hermit (J. Daley)	100/15
1868	Blue Gown (J. Wells)	7/2f
1869	Pretender (J. Osborne)	11/8f
1870	Kingcraft (T. French)	20/1
1871	Favonius (T. French)	9/1

Year	Winner	S/P	Year	Winner	S/P
1872	Cremorne (C. Maidment)	3/1f	1921	Humorist (S. Donoghue)	6/1
1873	Doncaster (F. Webb)	45/1	1922	Captain Cuttle (S. Donoghue)	10/1
1874	George Frederick (H. Custance)	9/1	1923	Papyrus (S. Donoghue)	100/15
1875	Galopin (J. Morris)	2/1f	1924	Sansovino (T. Weston)	9/2f
1876	Kisber (C. Maidment)	4/1f	1925	Manna (S. Donoghue)	9/1
1877	Silvio (F. Archer)	100/9	1926	Coronach (J. Childs)	11/2
1878	Sefton (H. Constable)	100/12	1927	Call Boy (E. C. Elliott)	4/1f
1879	Sir Bevys (G. Fordham)	20/1	1928	Felstead (H. Wragg)	33/1
1880	Bend Or (F. Archer)	2/1f	1929	Trigo (J. Marshall)	33/1
1881	Iroquois (F. Archer)	11/2	1930	Blenheim (H. Wragg)	18/1
1882	Shotover (T. Cannon)	11/2	1931	Cameronian (F. Fox)	7/2f
1883	St Blaise (C. Wood)	11/2	1932	April the Fifth (F. Lane)	100/6
1884	d.h. St Gatien (C. Wood)	100/8	1933	Hyperion (T. Weston)	6/1f
	Harvester (S. Loates)	100/7	1934	Windsor Lad (C. Smirke)	15/2
1885	Melton (F. Archer)	75/40	1935	Bahram (F. Fox)	5/4f
1886	Ormonde (F. Archer)	4/9f	1936	Mahmoud (C. Smirke)	100/8
1887	Merry Hampton (J. Watts)	100/9	1937	Mid-day Sun (M. Beary)	100/7
1888	Ayrshire (F. Barrett)	5/6f	1938	Bois Roussel (E. C. Elliott)	20/1
1889	Donovan (T. Loates)	8/11f	1939	Blue Peter (E. Smith)	7/2f
1890	Sainfoin (J. Watts)	100/15	1940	Pont l'Eveque (S. Wragg)	10/1+
1891	Common (G. Barrett)	10/11	1941	Owen Tudor (W. Nevett)	25/1+
1892	Sir Hugo (F. Allsopp)	40/1	1942	Watling Street (H. Wragg)	6/1+
1893	Isinglass (T. Loates)	4/9f	1943	Straight Deal (T. Carey)	100/6+
1894	Ladas (J. Watts)	2/9f	1944	Ocean Swell (W. Nevett)	28/1+
1895	Sir Visto (S. Loates)	9/1	1945	Dante (W. Nevett)	100/30+
1896	Persimmon (J. Watts)	5/1	1946	Airborne (T. Lowrey)	50/1
1897	Galtee More (C. Wood)	1/4f	1947	Pearl Diver (G. Bridgland)	40/1
1898	Jeddah (O. Madden)	100/1	1948	My Love (W. Johnstone)	100/9
1899	Flying Fox (M. Cannon)	2/5f	1949	Nimbus (E. C. Elliott)	7/1
1900	Diamond Jubilee (H. Jones)	6/4f	1950	Galcador (W. Johnstone)	100/9
1901	Volodyovski (L. Reiff)	5/2f	1951	Arctic Prince (C. Spares)	28/1
1902	Ard Patrick (J. H. Martin)	100/14	1952	Tulyar (C. Smirke)	11/2f
1903	Rock Sand (D. Maher)	4/6f	1953	Pinza (G. Richards)	5/1f
1904	St Amant (K. Cannon)	5/1	1954	Never Say Die (L. Piggott)	33/1
1905	Cicero (D. Maher)	4/11f	1955	Phil Drake (F. Palmer)	100/8
1906	Spearmint (D. Maher)	6/1	1956	Lavandin (W. Johnstone)	7/1f
1907	Orby (J. Reiff)	100/9	1957	Crepello (L. Piggott)	6/4f
1908	Signorinetta (W. Bullock)	100/1	1958	Hard Ridden (C. Smirke)	18/1
1909	Minoru (H. Jones)	7/2	1959	Parthia (W. H. Carr)	10/1
1910	Lemberg (B. Dillon)	7/4f	1960	St Paddy (L. Piggott)	7/1
1911	Sunstar (G. Stern)	13/8f	1961	Psidium (R. Poincelet)	66/1
1912	Tagalie (J. Reiff)	100/8	1962	Larkspur (N. Sellwood)	22/1‡
1913	Aboyeur (E. Piper)	100/1**	1963	Relko (Y. Saint-Martin)	5/1f
1914	Durbar II (M. MacGee)	20/1	1964	Santa Claus (A. Breasley)	15/8f‡
1915	Pommern (S. Donoghue)	11/10f+	1965	Sea Bird II (P. Glennon)	7/4f‡
1916	Fifinella (J. Childs)	11/2+	1966	Charlottown (A. Breasley)	5/1‡
1917	Gay Crusader (S. Donoghue)	7/4+f	1967	Royal Palace (G. Moore)	7/4f‡
1918	Gainsborough (J. Childs)	33/1	1968	Sir Ivor (L. Piggott)	4/5f
1919	Grand Parade (F. Templeman)	33/1	1969	Blakeney (E. Johnson)	15/2
			1970	Nijinsky (L. Piggott)	11/8f
			1971	Mill Reef (G. Lewis)	3/1f
1920	Spion Kop (F. O'Neill)	100/6	1972	Roberto (L. Piggott)	3/1f
			1973	Morston (E. Hide)	25/1

Year	Winner	S/P
1974	Snow Knight (B. Taylor)	50/1
1975	Grundy (P. Eddery)	5/1
1976	Empery (L. Piggott)	10/1
1977	The Minstrel (L. Piggott)	5/1
1978	Shirley Heights (G. Starkey)	8/1
1979	Troy (W. Carson)	6/1
1980	Henbit (W. Carson)	7/1
1981	Shergar (W. Swinburn)	7/2
1982	Golden Fleece (P. Eddery)	5/1
1983	Teenoso (L. Piggott)	9/2f
1984	Secreto (C. Roche)	11/1
1985	Slip Anchor (S. Cauthen)	5/4
1986	Shahrastani (W. Swinburn)	3/1
1987	Reference Point (S. Cauthen)	6/4f
1988	Kahyasi (R. Cochrane)	11/1

* Price not known
** Craganour defeated Aboyeur by a head but was disqualified for interference. Race was marred by a sensational incident when suffragette Miss Emily Davison was killed when she ran onto the course and caused King George V's colt Anmer to fall on Tattenham Corner.
+ Race transferred from Epsom to Newmarket.
‡ Australian jockey.

LAWN BOWLS

BEGINNINGS IN AUSTRALIA
It is generally accepted that the first game was played on 1 January 1845 when English migrant Fred Liscombe played another Englishman, T. Burgess, on a green Liscombe had laid down at his hotel, the Beach Tavern, in Sandy Bay Road, Hobart. Almost certainly the game was played earlier than that date because Liscombe had advertised the availability of his green the previous year.

First games in Sydney:
August 1845 when Thomas Shaw opened a green at his Woolpack Inn on Parramatta Road, Petersham, Sydney.

First official club:
The first semi-private club was opened on 28 October 1846 at William Turner's Bowling Green Hotel in Fitzroy Place, Hobart. Instead of players paying a few pence for a game, Turner charged enthusiasts an annual subscription of ten shillings payable in advance.

First clubs all states:
Tas.: Turner's Bowling Green Hotel, Hobart, 28 October 1846
Vic.: Melbourne Bowling Club, 22 October 1864
NSW: The Woolpack Club, Petersham, Sydney, circa 1870
Qld: Brisbane Bowling Club, September 1878
WA: Perth Esplanade Club, 1895
SA: Adelaide Bowling Club, September 1897
ACT: Canberra Bowling Club, 24 December 1925.

First inter-club competition:
1867 when the then existing Victorian clubs of Melbourne, Fitzroy, Prahran, St Kilda, Ballarat and West Melbourne (now City of Melbourne) played under a new set of laws governing team competitions.

First interstate games:
14 April 1880 when NSW opposed Victoria in Sydney.

First state body:
The NSW Bowling Association, formed on 22 May 1880, was the first anywhere in the world to control the game on an area basis. The Victorian Bowling Association was formed two months later.

First Australian championship:
1900 at the Melbourne Cricket Ground. J. H. Sheedy of the Richmond Club in Melbourne won the inaugural singles title. The title has yet to be recognised by the Australian Bowling Council,

formed in 1911. ABC national championship statistics commence from the 1912-13 titles held in Melbourne.

First Australian team overseas:
1901 when a team comprising Australians and New Zealanders representing Australasia toured Great Britain and Ireland. Thirty Australians and 12 New Zealanders made the trip and after a token number of appearances as a combined side, split into separate teams. Australia won 11 matches and lost 10 with 1 tied and New Zealand won 9 and lost 10.

First official Australian titles:
1912-13 in Melbourne when the ABC was in existence (formed 1911). W. E. Sayers of Ballarat, Vic., won the singles title. At the age of 38, Sayers remained the youngest winner of the title until Ellis Crew won in 1961, also at the age of 38.

First world championships in Australia:
October 1966 when the inaugural championships were staged at the NSW Leagues' Club Bowling Club at Kyeemagh, Sydney. Eighty bowlers from 16 countries competed.

Australian winners of world championships:
Australians won two championships at the inaugural world titles. Winners were:
Triples: Don Collins (SA), Athol Johnson (NSW) and John Dobbie (Vic.).
Pairs: Bert Palm (Qld) and Geoff Kelly (NSW).
(Collins, Palm, Johnson and Dobbie finished runners-up in the Fours, Geoff Kelly finished eighth in the singles and Australia won the W. M. Leonard Trophy as the world champion nation.)

Australia finished ninth in the 1972 world championships in England and ninth again in 1976 at Johannesburg, South Africa. In 1980, the championships were again held in Australia—at the City of Frankston Bowling Club in Melbourne where Australia won another gold medal:
Pairs: Peter Rheuben (NSW) and Alf Sandercock (SA).

The 1984 world titles were held at Aberdeen, Scotland.

First women's bowls in Australia:
1881 at Stawell, Victoria.

First women's Australian championships:
1949 in Sydney, NSW. Mrs R. Cranley (Qld) won the singles, Mesdames Ness and Barker (NSW) the Pairs, and Mesdames Gray, Williams, Cox and McKibbin (Vic.) the Fours.

Bowls on television:
The Australian Broadcasting Commission made bowls history in 1980 by producing a weekly program *Jack High* which loosely followed the lines of televised snooker. The program achieved very high ratings and the initial title was won by Keith Poole (Qld).

Professionalism in bowls:
The way was opened for professionals on 21 January 1981 when the Australian Bowls Council met in Melbourne and agreed to abolish the strict concept of amateurism and adopt the infrastructure of a new organisation to include both professionals and amateurs. All affiliated Australian clubs became free to stage professional events and offer cash prizes.

Australia at the Commonwealth Games:
Lawn Bowls has been included at all Games except Kingston, Jamaica, in 1966. Medal winners have been:
1938 Sydney: Fours team—A. Murray, H. F. Murray, C. H. McNeill, T. Kinder—Bronze (3rd)
1950 Auckland, NZ: Fours team—James Cobley, L. Knight, C. Cordaly, John Cobley—Silver (2nd)
Singles—Albert Newton—Silver (2nd)
1974 Christchurch, NZ: Fours team—R. King, E. Bungey, C. Stewart, K. Poole—Silver (2nd)
Singles—C. White—Silver (2nd)
1978 Edmonton, Canada: J. Snell—Singles—Silver (2nd)
1982 Brisbane: Fours team—R. Dobbins, D. Sherman, B. Sharp, K. Poole—Gold (1st)
Singles—R. Parella—Silver (2nd)
Pairs—D. Dalton, P. Rheuben—Silver (2nd)
1986 Edinburgh, Scotland: Men's singles—I. Schuback—Silver (2nd)

Women's fours—Pat Smith, Clarice Power, Betty Schenke, Audrey Hefford—Silver (2nd)

Note: Women played lawn bowls for the first time at Brisbane in 1982. Australia's best result was a fourth placing by the Triples team.

MOTORCYCLING

BEGINNINGS IN AUSTRALIA
The first recorded race (as distinct from short reliability trials in Sydney and Melbourne) was a three-heat competition for motorised De Dion tricycles on 1 January 1901 around the concrete cycling track which once ringed the Sydney Cricket Ground. Jack Green won all three races with a fastest race average of 37.7 km/h.

First club:
The Pioneer Motor Cycle Club established in Sydney in 1904. The Victorian Motor Cycle Club and the Perth Motor Cycle club were both formed later the same year.

First road racing:
About 1908-09 on a public road circuit known as Campbellfield in the shire of Broadmeadows in Victoria. Races were conducted by the Victorian Motor Cycle Club.

First Australian Grand Prix:
23 June 1924 on a 34 km 'road' course (largely unsealed) south of Goulburn, NSW. The Grand Prix was restricted to motorcycles of 500 cc capacity and was held over a distance of 136 km.

First racing at Mt Panorama, Bathurst:
Easter 1938 on an unsealed circuit. Winner of the first race held on the famous circuit was Les Sherrin (Qld) who won the combined Lightweight/Junior Tourist Trophy on a 350 cc Norton. The meeting was officially called the Bathurst Centenary Tourist Trophy and the feature race for machines up to 500 cc was won by Les Tobin (NSW) who averaged 99.8 km/h for the 161/km distance on a Norton. (From 1931-37, prior to the first Bathurst races, meetings were held on a series of public roads nearby known as the Vale circuit.)

First Australian world champion:
Keith Campbell (1931-58) (Vic.) who won the world 350 cc championship in 1957 on a works Moto-Guzzi.

Australians who have won official world road racing championships:
1957 . . . . Keith Campbell (Vic.)
350 cc title
1961 . . . . Tom Phillis (NSW)
125 cc title
1969 . . . . Kel Carruthers (NSW)
250 cc title
1987 . . . . Wayne Gardner (NSW)
500 cc title

First Australian 'international':
Les Bailey (NSW) who visited England in 1911 and was signed by the Douglas team. Bailey rode a Douglas in the 1912 junior (up to 350 cc) and senior (up to 500 cc) races at the famous Isle of Man Tourist Trophy meeting.

First Australian successes at the Isle of Man:
Ken Kavanagh (Vic.) was the first Australian to win a Tourist Trophy race on the IOM (1956 Junior TT on a Moto-Guzzi works machine). The next Australian win was not until 1969 when Kel Carruthers (NSW) won the 250 cc lightweight title, an event he won again the following year. No Australian has ever won the Blue Riband event, the Senior TT.

Most successful Australian rider:
In financial terms, Wayne Gardner (b. Corrimal, NSW), whose contracts with Rothmans International and the giant Japanese Honda organisation, make him the richest in the sport. Gardner's 1987 world 500 cc championship win has been estimated to be worth more than $1.5 million in guarantees, appearance and starting money and associated advertising contracts.

Most successful in domestic racing:
Until recent years, motorcycle road racing in Australia remained largely an amateur sport. The late Harry Hinton (NSW) left one of the most outstanding records in domestic racing, including winning the Senior TT at Bathurst 5 times, the Junior TT 6 times and being one of only four riders ever to have won the Lightweight, Junior and Senior TTs at the same Bathurst meeting. Hinton accomplished the feat in 1953. The others to win the triple are: Jack Ahearn (NSW) 1957; Kel Carruthers (NSW) 1963, 1964 and 1965; and Ron Toombs (NSW) 1966.

Interstate record attempts:
The first city-to-city record attempt was made in 1912 when John Fair of the Sydney Bicycle and Motor Cycle Club set a record for the ride from Sydney to Melbourne when he clocked 29 hrs 43 mins on his 2.6 kW (500 cc) Speedwell. On 16 February 1913 James Bolger of Sydney became the first man to better 24 hrs for the ride with a time of 23 hrs 41 mins on a 4.5 kW NSU V-twin. (He collected a 20-guinea gold watch as a prize from the Dunlop Company.) The last official record for the ride before NSW and Victorian police banned such attempts was set in February 1933 by Don Bain (NSW) who covered the distance in 11 hrs 27 mins on a Velocette.

The Speed Bowl era:
Australia has had two high-banked American-style racing bowls especially built for car and motorcycle racing prior to the opening of Bob Jane's Calder 'Thunderdome' in 1988. First was the Melbourne Motordrome which opened in 1924. When the 508.4 m bowl was closed in 1931, the outright motorcycle lap record was held by Swiss rider Louis Geisler who averaged 149.7 km/h in 1928 on an English Chater-Lea. The second bowl to open was the Olympia Speedway (better known as the Maroubra Speedway) in Sydney in 1925. Fastest known motorcycle average lap speed on the larger Sydney circuit was set on 8 January 1928 when Harry Peel (NSW) was timed at 165.9 km/h on a track-racing special based on Velocette components.

MOTO-CROSS
Australia was slow to follow the European and later American fad for what was first known as Moto-Cross and became Super-Cross racing—a competition in which large fields of riders race on artificial loose-surfaced circuits incorporating high jumps, right and left corners, banked turns and 'roller coaster' sections. When the sport finally arrived in Australia in the early 1970s it was an instant success. It was later staged on major city arenas such as the Sydney and Melbourne Showgrounds and in more recent times, indoors at the Sydney Entertainment Centre.

First Stadium Super-Cross:
1980 at the Sydney Showground. Attendance was a near-capacity 30,000.

First indoors Super-Cross:
1985 at the Sydney Entertainment Centre. Attendance was a capacity 9,000 for three successive nights.

Most successful riders:
First Australian champions were Trevor Flood (Vic.), Jim Scaysbrook (NSW) and Laurie Alderton (NSW). In more recent years riders such as Stephen Gall (NSW) and Les Leisk (WA) rose to international stardom. In 1984, Leisk won a virtual world championship staged at the Chelsea football ground in London.

MOTOR RACING

BEGINNINGS IN AUSTRALIA

Unlike the vast majority of Western countries, Australia took slowly to all forms of motor sport. Pioneer racing was restricted to dirt and concrete oval tracks and the first 'road' racing, the inaugural Australian Grand Prix of 1928, was actually staged on a rough square of dirt and gravel roads near the township of Cowes on Phillip Island, Victoria.

The first official motor race on a sealed road circuit was not held until 26 December 1936 when the Australian Grand Prix took place on public roads near Victor Harbor, South Australia.

First recorded motor sport event:
Races for motorised tricycles on the concrete cycling track which encircled the Sydney Cricket Ground, on 1 January 1901.

First reliability run and racing demonstration for four-wheeled vehicles:
On 31 January 1904, when 20 cars driven by members of the Automobile Club of Victoria toured from Melbourne to Aspendale and took part in 'speed demonstrations' on the local racecourse.

First organised car and motorcycle races:
On 12 March 1904, at the Sandown racecourse, Melbourne, Victoria.

First long-distance reliability trial:
The Dunlop-sponsored event from Sydney to Melbourne (572 miles (920 km)) which started on 21 February 1905 and ended on 26 February. Seventeen of the 23 entries reached Melbourne and when a winner could not be decided, the organisers dispatched the survivors on a 'tie-breaker' run of approximately 140 miles (225 km) to Ballarat and return. Captain Harley Tarrant driving a 10–12 hp (7.5–9 kW) Argyll was finally declared the winner from J. H. Craven and Sydney Day, both in De Dions. The trial was the fourth longest to be staged anywhere in the world.

Longest race:
The first – and to date, only – 24-hour race held in Australia at the old Mt Druitt circuit, in Sydney's western suburbs on 31 January – 1 February 1954. The winners (Mrs Geordie Anderson, Charles Whatmore and Bill Pitt of Queensland) covered 2,028 km in their XK120 Jaguar closed coupe.

Closest finish in major race:
$\frac{1}{20}$ sec, when Alec Mildren (Cooper-Maserati) won the Australian Grand Prix from Lex Davison (Aston Martin) at Lowood, Qld, on 12 June 1960.

First Australian Grand Prix:
On 31 March 1928, at Cowes, Phillip Island, Victoria. The race was won by South Australian-born Captain Arthur Waite in a supercharged Austin Seven at an average speed of 56.25 mph.

First meetings at other major circuits:

Mt Panorama (NSW)	18 April 1938
Warwick Farm (NSW)	18 December 1960
Calder (Vic.)	14 January 1962
Oran Park (NSW)	18 February 1962
Sandown (Vic.)	11 March 1962
Lakeside (Qld)	19 March 1964
Surfers Paradise Raceway (Qld)	22 May 1966
Wanneroo (WA)	2 March 1969
Amaroo Park (NSW)	31 May 1970
Adelaide International Raceway (SA)	9 January 1972

Fastest track:
The 7.2 km public-road Longford circuit near Launceston, Tasmania. When the circuit closed in 1968, the lap record stood at 2 mins 13.3 secs (195.6 km/h).

First 100 mph (160.9 km/h) lap on a road circuit:
Almost certainly achieved by Stirling Moss (UK) when he won the 1956 Australian Grand Prix at Albert Park, Melbourne. Moss' fastest lap was announced at 1 min 52.2 secs (100.25 mph) (161.3 km/h).

First driver to reach 100 mph:
Don Harkness (NSW) recorded 107.75

mph (172.4 km/h) in a speed record attempt at Gerringong Beach (NSW) in 1925, driving an Overland powered by an aero engine.

First to lap at 100 mph in a race:
Peter White (NSW), at the Olympia Speedway (1,500-yd high-banked concrete oval), Maroubra, NSW, in 1925, driving a Fronty Ford.

First to break 100 mph lap barrier at Bathurst:
1968 and 1969 Australian Drivers Champion Kevin Bartlett, who broke the barrier in a Repco Brabham Climax with a time of 2 mins 17.4 secs (163.3 km/h) on 27 March 1969.

First Australian Championship:
Oddly, the first official national title event was not for circuit racing, but for hill climbing. Arthur Wylie (Vic.), then editor and publisher of *Australian Motor Sports* magazine, won the title at Rob Roy (Vic.) on 2 November 1947, driving a Ford A Special.

First Australian Championship—road racing:
The Australian Tourist Trophy for sports cars held at Albert Park, Melbourne, on 25 November 1956 and won by Stirling Moss (UK) in a Maserati 300S.

Largest attendance:
Officially, 120,000 for the World Championship Formula One Grand Prix held on a city-street circuit in Adelaide, South Australia, on 26 October 1986. The race, Australia's third World Championship event, was an all-ticket promotion and organisers were able to audit every detail of the gate takings. It is still believed that a larger attendance, generally referred to as an 'estimated 125,000', attended Albert Park, Melbourne, for the 1956 Australian Grand Prix which was won by Stirling Moss (UK) in a Maserati 250F. The Albert Park promotion was, however, plagued by lack of turnstiles, forged tickets and gate-crashers.

World Championship races in Australia:
The first event for an official World Championship was the final round of the World Endurance Championship for Le Mans-type sports cars, staged at Sandown, Melbourne, on 2 December 1984. The race was won by Stefan Bellof and Derek Bell in a works Porsche 956. Bellof had already clinched the WEC Drivers Championship before the Sandown race. The Light Car Club of Australia, promoters of the race, incurred a huge financial loss when the attendance failed even to approach the hoped-for 30,000 mark. The LCCA issued a vague attendance figure and many experienced Sandown observers estimated the crowd to be as low as 6,000.

Australia's second official World Championship race was the Adelaide Grand Prix, final round of the World Drivers Championship, held on a street circuit on 3 November 1985. The race was won by Keke Rosberg of Finland driving a Williams Honda, but the overall championship was won by Frenchman Alain Prost. The event was backed by the South Australian State Government with further financial support from the Federal Government and, although failing to show a profit, achieved its purpose of having the city of Adelaide promoted via the world-wide telecast.

GREATEST DRIVERS

Two Australians have won the World Drivers Championship—Jack Brabham (now Sir John Brabham, b. Sydney, 1926) in 1959, '60 and '66 and Alan Jones (b. Melbourne, 1947) in 1980.

Sir Jack Brabham graduated to hill climbing and road racing from dirt track speedway, was the first man to win the World Championship (1966) in a car he designed and constructed and in 1967 was runner-up in the title to teammate Dennis Hulme (NZ). Brabham again won the coveted Constructors' Championship in 1967. He won the Australian Grand Prix in 1955, '63 and '64 and in 1961 became the first Australian to drive in the Indianapolis 500 — he finished ninth. (Brabham was not the first Australian to *compete* at Indianapolis. That honour fell to Rupert Jeffkins who competed in the 1912 Indianapolis 500 as riding mechanic for American, Ralph de Palma.)

Alan Jones began his racing career in Go-Karts, went to England and worked his way into Grand Prix racing via Formula Three and Two cars and was runner-up in the 1979 World Championship before clinching his first title in 1980. Jones won the rich USA Can Am Championship in 1978 and '79 and the Australian Grand Prix in 1980. He retired from Grand Prix racing in 1981 but announced a comeback attempt in January 1985. Jones finally returned to racing mid-way through the 1985 Grand Prix season, as No. 1 driver for the Beatrice FORCE team, in a Hart-engined Lola. He again retired from Formula One racing at the end of 1986.

Vern Schuppan (b. near Whyalla, SA, 1942) shared the drive in the winning car at the 1983 Le Mans 24-hour race and is the only Australian to be successful in the classic. Like Jones, Schuppan began driving go-carts and broke into Formula One racing after proving his ability in a variety of open-wheeler classes in England and Europe. A versatile driver, he is the only Australian to fill a major placing in the Indianapolis 500 and has been a champion endurance sports car driver for five years.

Oldest Australian champion:
Lex Davison (Vic.), who was 37 when he won the last of his four Australian Grand Prix in 1961.

Youngest champion:
Geoffrey Brabham (NSW), son of former World Champion Jack, who was barely 23 when he won the Australian Formula Two Championship in 1976.

Oldest driver:
Tom Sulman (NSW), who was 69 when he died in a racing accident at Bathurst on Easter Monday 1970.

First Australian to succeed overseas:
Selwyn Edge (1868-1940), who went to Europe around 1892 as a racing cyclist and, among many other wins, took out the Paris-Bordeaux road race. Switching to car racing, Edge set a world 24-hour record at Brooklands in 1907 (2,545 kilometres in a Napier) and later won Britain's first 24-hour race, averaging 65.4 mph (104.6 km/h).

First great woman racing driver:
Miss Joan Richmond of Melbourne, Vic., the first Australian to compete in the Le Mans 24-hour race. Miss Richmond drove as a member of Captain George Eyston's MG PB Midget team in the 1936 classic. Earlier, in 1931, she competed in the Monte Carlo Rally and in 1932 shared the winning drive with English competitor Elsie Wisdom in a 1,610 km race at Brooklands, becoming the first woman to win a major overseas race and probably the third Australian (after Selwyn Edge in 1907 and Captain Arthur Waite in 1923) to win.

TRIALS AND RALLIES
First reliability trial:
From Sydney to Melbourne on 21-26 February 1905.

First 1,000 km trial:
In November 1905, when the Dunlop Rubber Company sponsored a second trial, this time from Melbourne to Sydney (920 km). When a winner could not be decided in Sydney, the field was sent on a return run to Medlow Bath in the Blue Mountains. Officials still could not find a winner so the survivors were dispatched back to Melbourne — a total distance of 1,384 miles (2,227.3 km). Captain Harley Tarrant, in his own creation, a Tarrant, was finally declared the winner.

First partial 'round-Australia' trial:
The inaugural Redex Trial in 1953, which covered 6,500 miles (10,458 km) but avoided large areas of Western Australia. The second Redex Trial, staged in 1954 was close to being 'round Australia', covering a distance of 9,600 miles (15,446 km).

Longest trial in Australia:
The 1979 Repco Reliability Trial which

covered almost 20,000 km.

London to Sydney Rallies:
Sydney has twice hosted the finish of London–Sydney Marathon Rallies: in 1968 (won by Andrew Cowan, Brian Coyle and Colin Malkin (UK) in a Hillman Hunter) and in 1977 (won by Andrew Cowan, Colin Malkin and Mike Broad (UK) in a Mercedes 280SE).

Australians in international rally success:
The most important – and famous – victory was achieved by Ken Tubman, Andre Welinski and Jim Reddiex (NSW) when they drove a Citroen to win the 1974 World Cup Rally over 17,700 km through England, the Sahara Desert and Europe.

SPEED RECORDS
Fastest speed recorded in Australia:
652.5 km/h, by the late Donald Campbell at Lake Eyre, SA, on 17 July 1964. Campbell, driving his *Bluebird* powered by a Bristol Siddeley Proteus 755 gas turbine, set a new world land-speed record for cars driven directly through the wheels.

'Wizard' Smith's records:
Sydney-born Norman 'Wizard' Smith (1897–1958) set a world land speed record for 10 miles at Ninety Mile Beach, North Island, NZ, in 1932 when he averaged 164 mph in atrocious conditions. Smith, who set many Australian and Australasian speed records, including a 24-hour solo effort of 1710.6 miles (2,737.5 km) at Lake Perkolilli (WA) in 1928, is the only Australian ever to hold any world land speed record. He also won 44 major reliability trials and hill climbs and set 30 city-to-city records in an era when daredevils defied police restrictions and risked their lives to set fastest times for inter-city dashes, Sydney to Melbourne being the greatest challenge.

City-to-City records:
From 1908 until 1924 the Royal Automobile Club officially timed record attempts between major cities, but succumbed to the protests of police and public after 1924 and ceased official timing and supervision. The first officially recorded dash from Melbourne to Sydney (approx. 619 miles) was 25 hrs 40 mins by Charles Kellow and Harry James (Vic.) in 1908, driving a 25 hp Talbot. The last officially timed run took 12 hrs 34 mins (A. V. Tutner and Ossie O'Connor (NSW)) for the Sydney to Melbourne run in 1924.

The last accurately timed (but not by the RAC) run from Sydney to Melbourne was 10 hrs 5 mins set by Don Robertson in a Graham-Paige in 1930. Later the same year, Victorian drivers Reg Brearly and Albert Elliot were killed attempting to lower Robertson's record, when their Bugatti crashed near Gunning, NSW. Record attempts ceased from that time.

AUSTRALIAN GRAND PRIX

Year	Venue	Winners	Vehicle
1928	Phillip Is. (Vic.)*	**Captain Arthur Waite** (SA)	Austin 750 cc
1929	Phillip Is. (Vic.)	**Arthur Terdich** (Vic.)	Type 37A Bugatti
1930	Phillip Is. (Vic.)	**Bill Thompson** (Vic.)	Type 37A Bugatti
1931	Phillip Is. (Vic.)	**Carl Junker** (Vic.)	Type 39 Bugatti
1932	Phillip Is. (Vic.)	**Bill Thompson** (Vic.)	Type 37A Bugatti
1933	Phillip Is. (Vic.)	**Bill Thompson** (Vic.)	Brooklands Riley
1934	Phillip Is. (Vic)	**Bob Lea-Wright** (Vic.)	Singer 9
1935	Phillip Is. (Vic)	**Les Murphy** (Vic.)	MG P Type
1936	Victor Harbor (SA)**	**Les Murphy** (Vic.)	MG P Type
1937	*Not held*		
1938	Bathurst (NSW)	**Peter Whitehead** (UK)	ERA S/C

Year	Venue	Winners	Vehicle
1939	Lobethal (SA)	Allan Tomlinson (WA)	MG Special
1940-46	*Not held*		
1947	Bathurst (NSW)	Bill Murray (NSW)	MG TC Special
1948	Point Cook (Vic.)	Frank Pratt (Vic.)	BMW Sports
1949	Leyburn (Qld) ***	John Crouch (NSW)	Delahaye
1950	Nuriootpa (SA)	Doug Whiteford (Vic.)	Ford V8 Special
1951	Narrogin (WA)	Warwick Pratley (Vic.)	Ford V8 Special
1952	Bathurst (NSW)	Doug Whiteford (Vic.)	Lago Talbot
1953	Albert Park (Vic.)	Doug Whiteford (Vic.)	Lago Talbot
1954	Southport (Qld)	Lex Davison (Vic.)	HWM Jaguar
1955	Port Wakefield (SA)	Jack Brabham (NSW)	Cooper Bristol
1956	Albert Park (Vic.)	Stirling Moss (UK)	Maserati 250F
1957	Caversham (WA)	Lex Davison (Vic.)	Ferrari 3.0
1958	Bathurst (NSW)	Lex Davison (Vic.)	Ferrari 3.0
1959	Longford (Tas.)	Stan Jones (Vic.)	Maserati 250F
1960	Lowood (Qld)	Alec Mildren (NSW)	Cooper Maserati
1961	Mallala (SA)	Lex Davison (Vic.)	Cooper Climax 2.2
1962	Caversham (WA)	Bruce McLaren (NZ)	Cooper Climax
1963	Warwick Farm (NSW)	Jack Brabham (NSW)	Repco Brabham Climax
1964	Sandown (Vic.)	Jack Brabham (NSW)	Repco Brabham Climax
1965	Longford (Tas.)	Bruce McLaren (NZ)	Cooper Climax
1966	Lakeside (Qld)	Graham Hill (UK)	BRM V8
1967	Warwick Farm (NSW)	Jackie Stewart (Scot)	BRM V8
1968	Sandown (Vic.)	Jim Clark (UK)	Lotus 49 Ford V8
1969	Lakeside (Qld)	Chris Amon (NZ)	Ferrari Dino V6
1970	Warwick Farm (NSW)	Frank Matich (NSW)	McLaren M10B Repco
1971	Warwick Farm (NSW)	Frank Matich (NSW)	Repco Matich A50
1972	Sandown (Vic.)	Graham McRae (NZ)	Leda GM1
1973	Sandown (Vic.)	Graham McRae (NZ)	McRae GM2
1974	Oran Park (NSW)	Max Stewart (NSW)	Lolo T332
1975	Surfers Paradise (Qld)	Max Stewart (NSW)	Lola T400
1976	Sandown (Vic.)	John Goss (NSW)	Repco Matich A53
1977	Oran Park (NSW)	Warwick Brown (NSW)	Lola T430
1978	Sandown (Vic.)	Graham McRae (NZ)	McRae GM3
1979	Wanneroo (WA)	John Walker (SA)	Lola T332
1980	Calder (Vic.)	Alan Jones (Vic.)	Williams Ford
1981	Calder (Vic.)	Roberto Moreno (Brazil)	Ralt RT4 Ford
1982	Calder (Vic.)	Alain Prost (France)	Ralt RT4 Ford

Year	Venue	Winners	Vehicle
1983	Calder (Vic.)	**Roberto Moreno** (Brazil)	Ralt RT4 Ford
1984	Calder (Vic.)	**Roberto Moreno** (Brazil)	Ralt RT4 Ford
1985	Adelaide (SA)****	**Keke Rosberg** (Finland)	Williams FW-10 Honda
1986	Adelaide (SA)****	**Alain Prost** (France)	McLaren MP4-TAG
1987	Adelaide (SA)*****	**Gerhard Berger** (W. Germany)	Ferrari

* Inaugural race (1928) run as two separate heats, each catering for two different classes based on engine capacity. Fastest time recorded over 16 laps (approximately 104 miles) decided the winner. The 1928 winner, Captain A. C. R. (Arthur) Waite, was born in Adelaide, South Australia on 9 April 1894 and became an engineering apprentice. He enlisted in the Army in World War I, landed at Gallipoli and later served in Africa and France, and was awarded the Military Cross in 1916. In October 1918, he married Irene, the elder daughter of Sir Herbert (later Lord) Austin and joined the Austin Motor Company. Captain Waite was deeply involved in the design, testing and racing of the first Austin Seven models, set a number of world 750 cc class speed records and in 1923 won the first Italian Grand Prix for Light Cars. He returned to Australia in 1927 to represent the Austin Company, went back to England after the Australian Grand Prix and retired from racing after being injured in the Tourist Trophy race in Ireland.
** The 1936 race was never officially advertised or promoted as the Australian Grand Prix. Organisers called it the South Australian Centenary Grand Prix, but motor sport historians have always considered it as an official race.
*** First year run as a scratch race. Until 1949, all Grand Prix (with the exception of those of 1928, '29 and '30 when different classes were started at intervals) were run on a handicap basis with the winner being the first car to finish.
**** The final round of the World Drivers Championship, restricted to international Formula One entrants. No Australian-based cars or drivers were eligible.
***** Final round of world championship pointscore won by Nelson Piquet (Brazil).

AUSTRALIAN TOURING CAR CHAMPIONSHIP

Now decided by a season-long series of races in all States, the Touring Car Championship had humble beginnings. The inaugural title—and the eight that followed—were decided by a single race and such were the reservations about the importance of the class that the inaugural title race was tucked away at the old Gnoo Blas circuit at Orange, NSW. Touring car racing and the national championship series in particular are now the most popular branch of racing in Australian motor sport.

Year	Venue	Winners	Vehicle
1960	Gnoo Blas (NSW)	**David McKay** (NSW)	Jaguar 3.4
1961	Lowood (Qld)	**Bill Pitt** (Qld)	Jaguar 3.4
1962	Longford (Tas.)	**Bob Jane** (Vic.)	Jaguar 3.8
1963	Mallala (SA)	**Bob Jane** (Vic.)	Jaguar 3.4
1964	Lakeside (Qld)	**Ian Geoghegan** (NSW)	Cortina GT
1965	Sandown (Vic.)	**Norm Beechey** (Vic.)	Ford Mustang
1966	Bathurst (NSW)	**Ian Geoghegan** (NSW)	Ford Mustang
1967	Lakeside (Qld)	**Ian Geoghegan** (NSW)	Ford Mustang
1968	Warwick Farm (NSW)	**Ian Geoghegan** (NSW)	Ford Mustang
1969	National series	**Ian Geoghegan** (NSW)	Ford Mustang
1970	National series	**Norm Beechey** (Vic.)	Holden Monaro
1971	National series	**Bob Jane** (Vic.)	Chevrolet Camaro
1972	National series	**Bob Jane** (Vic.)	Chevrolet Camaro
1973	National series	**Allan Moffat** (Vic.)	Ford GTHO
1974	National series	**Peter Brock** (Vic.)	Torana XU1

MOTOR RACING • 145

Year	Venue	Winners	Vehicle
1975	National series	Colin Bond (NSW)	Torana L34
1976	National series	Allan Moffat (Vic.)	Falcon GT
1977	National series	Allan Moffat (Vic.)	Falcon GT
1978	National series	Peter Brock (Vic.)	Torana A9X
1979	National series	Bob Morris (NSW)	Torana A9X
1980	National series	Peter Brock (Vic.)	Holden Commodore
1981	National series	Dick Johnson (Qld)	Ford Falcon XD
1982	National series	Dick Johnson (Qld)	Ford Falcon XD
1983	National series	Allan Moffat (Vic.)	Mazda RX-7
1984	National series	Dick Johnson (Qld)	Ford Falcon
1985	National series	Jim Richards (Vic.)	BMW 635
1986	National series	Robbie Francevic (NZ)	Volvo 240 Turbo
1987	National series	Jim Richards (Vic.)	BMW 635

AUSTRALIAN DRIVERS CHAMPIONSHIP

The Australian Drivers Championship was first held in 1957 when the Confederation of Australian Motor Sport (CAMS) introduced a Gold Star award for Australia's champion racing driver. The inaugural championship consisted of nine races, and points were awarded for first down to fifth place. The number of races and the point score system has varied considerably from year to year.

Year	Winner	
1957	Lex Davison	(Vic.)
1958	Stan Jones	(Vic.)
1959	Len Lukey	(Vic.)
1960	Alec Mildren	(NSW)
1961	Bill Patterson	(Vic.)
1962	Bib Stillwell	(Vic.)
1963	Bib Stillwell	(Vic.)
1964	Bib Stillwell	(Vic.)
1965	Bib Stillwell	(Vic.)
1966	Spencer Martin	(NSW)
1967	Spencer Martin	(NSW)
1968	Kevin Bartlett	(NSW)
1969	Kevin Bartlett	(NSW)
1970	Leo Geoghegan	(NSW)
1971	Max Stewart	(NSW)
1972	Frank Matich	(NSW)
1973	John McCormack	(SA)
1974	Max Stewart	(NSW)
1975	John McCormack	(SA)
1976	John Leffler	(NSW)
1977	John McCormack	(SA)
1978	Graham McRae	(NZ/Vic.)
1979	John Walker	(SA)
1980	Alfredo Costanzo	(Vic.)
1981	Alfredo Costanzo	(Vic.)
1982	Alfredo Costanzo	(Vic.)
1983	Alfredo Costanzo	(Vic.)
1984	John Bowe	(Vic.)
1985	John Bowe	(Vic.)
1986	Graham Watson	(NSW)
1987	David Brabham	(NSW)*

* CAMS caused a major controversy by allocating the title to a single race staged as a supporting event to the 1987 Australian Grand Prix in Adelaide. Brabham, son of Sir John, world champion in 1959, '60, '66, won the (Formula Two) race driving a Ralt RT-30. The race was held two days prior to the AGP and was not even televised.

JAMES HARDIE 1000

Australia's most prestigious motor race had its beginnings in 1960 at the old Phillip Island circuit in Victoria when Armstrong York Engineering, shock absorber manufacturers, agreed to sponsor a 500 mile race for standard touring cars. The race had no official outright winner, but was divided into five classes with all class winners being decided when the first car finished 500 miles. For purposes of historical continuity, motor sport statisticians have always listed 'outright' winners as being the first driver(s) and car to finish. The Armstrong 500 was staged again at Phillip Island in 1961 and 1962, but damage to the circuit was so severe after the latter race that the Armstrong organisation decided to move the event to the Mt Panorama circuit at Bathurst, NSW, for 1963. The race continued as the Armstrong 500 at Bathurst until 1966 when the UK tobacco company Gallaher International, then attempting to launch itself on the Australian market, took over the sponsorship. Gallaher withdrew after the 1967 race and the Sydney-based Hardie-Ferodo company (then involved in producing friction materials for railway locomotives and rolling stock — not motor vehicles) agreed to take over the sponsorship.

As the Hardie-Ferodo 500, the race continued until 1973, when the organisers, the Australian Racing Drivers Club, lengthened the race from 500 miles to 1,000 kilometres and the race was re-named the Hardie-Ferodo 1000. The 1,000 kilometre distance has remained unchanged, but in 1981, the sponsors, having expanded into a multitude of widely varying business enterprises, decided to rename the race the James Hardie 1000.

For many years telecast nationally and in recent years televised on a delayed basis to the United States, Japan and many other countries, the James Hardie 1000 attracts a viewing audience of millions and, weather permitting, an average attendance at Bathurst of 35,000–40,000. From the original race in 1960, the James Hardie 1000 has been as controversial as it is important, due mainly to the ever-changing rules and regulations.

As long ago as 1966, the importance of the event prompted overseas companies to enter teams of works cars driven by international stars.

In March 1988, the James Hardie organisation announced that it would no longer sponsor Australia's most important motor race. The organisers, the Australian Racing Drivers Club, reacted by offering the event to a number of prospective sponsors.

JAMES HARDIE 1000 RESULTS: (outright winners)

Year	Venue	Winners	Vehicle
1960	Phillip Is. (Vic.)	**John Roxburgh** (Vic.) **Frank Coad** (Vic.)	Vauxhall Cresta
1961	Phillip Is. (Vic.)	**Bob Jane** (Vic.) **Harry Firth** (Vic.)	Mercedes 220SE
1962	Phillip Is. (Vic.)	**Bob Jane** (Vic.) **Harry Firth** (Vic.)	Ford Falcon
1963	Bathurst (NSW)	**Harry Firth** (Vic.) **Bob Jane** (Vic.)	Ford Cortina GT
1964	Bathurst (NSW)	**Bob Jane** (Vic.) **George Reynolds** (Vic.)	Ford Cortina GT
1965	Bathurst (NSW)	**Barry Seton** (NSW) **Midge Bosworth** (NSW)	Ford Cortina GT 500
1966	Bathurst (NSW)	**Rauno Aaltonen** (Finland) **Bob Holden** (NSW)	Morris Cooper S
1967	Bathurst (NSW)	**Harry Firth** (Vic.) **Fred Gibson** (NSW)	Falcon GT
1968	Bathurst (NSW)	**Bruce McPhee** (NSW) **Barry Mulholland** (NSW)	Monaro GTS
1969	Bathurst (NSW)	**Colin Bond** (NSW) **Tony Roberts** (NSW)	Holden GTS 350
1970	Bathurst (NSW)	**Allan Moffat** (Vic.)	Falcon GTHO
1971	Bathurst (NSW)	**Allan Moffat** (Vic.)	Falcon GTHO

Year	Venue	Winners	Vehicle
1972	Bathurst (NSW)	Peter Brock (Vic.)	Torana XU1
1973	Bathurst (NSW)	Allan Moffat (Vic.) Ian Geoghegan (NSW)	Falcon GT
1974	Bathurst (NSW)	John Goss (NSW) Kevin Bartlett (NSW)	Falcon GT
1975	Bathurst (NSW)	Peter Brock (Vic.) Brian Sampson (Vic.)	Torana SLR
1976	Bathurst (NSW)	Bob Morris (NSW) John Fitzpatrick (UK)	Torana L34
1977	Bathurst (NSW)	Allan Moffat (Vic.) Jackie Ickx (Belgium)	Falcon GT
1978	Bathurst (NSW)	Peter Brock (Vic.) Jim Richards (Vic.)	Torana A9X
1979	Bathurst (NSW)	Peter Brock (Vic.) Jim Richards (Vic.)	Torana A9X
1980	Bathurst (NSW)	Peter Brock (Vic.) Jim Richards (Vic.)	Holden Commodore
1981	Bathurst (NSW)	Dick Johnson (Qld) John French (Qld)	Ford Falcon XD
1982	Bathurst (NSW)	Peter Brock (Vic.) Larry Perkins (Vic.)	Holden Commodore
1983	Bathurst (NSW)	Peter Brock (Vic.) John Harvey (Vic.) Larry Perkins (Vic.)	Holden Commodore
1984	Bathurst (NSW)	Peter Brock (Vic.) Larry Perkins (Vic.)	Holden Commodore
1985	Bathurst (NSW)	Armin Hahne (Germany) John Goss (NSW)	Jaguar XJS
1986	Bathurst (NSW)	Alan Grice (NSW) Graeme Bailey (NSW)	Holden Commodore
1987	Bathurst (NSW)	Peter Brock (Vic.) Peter McLeod (Vic.) David Parsons (Tas.)	Holden Commodore

Notes:
1. 1960-65 races known as the Armstrong 500.
2. 1966-67 races known as the Gallaher 500.
3. 1968-72 races known as the Hardie-Ferodo 500.
4. 1973-80 races known as the Hardie-Ferodo 1000.
5. 1981-onwards races known as the James Hardie 1000.
6. Allan Moffat in 1970 and 1971 and Peter Brock in 1972 did not use a co-driver.
7. In 1983, Peter Brock was forced out of the race with engine trouble. The rules permitted him to take over the second of the Marlboro Holden Dealers Team Commodores driven by his brother Phil Brock and John Harvey. As Harvey had driven his car from the start of the race, he was officially credited with being one of the three successful drivers. Phil Brock, who had not taken part in the race before Peter Brock took over the No. 2 car was unable to claim credit for the win.
8. In 1987, the Brock team actually crossed the line in third position behind the Ford Texaco Ford Sierra Racing Team cars of Steve Soper (GB)/Pierre Dieudonne (Belgium) and Klaus Ludwig (Denmark)/Klaus Niedzwiedz (Denmark). The first two cars were later disqualified by Bathurst officials because they did not fully comply with the rules governing modifications. An appeal by the Ford Sierra team was dismissed at a full-scale motor sport court hearing at the headquarters of FISA in Paris, in late March 1988.

AUSTRALIAN SPORTS CAR CHAMPIONSHIP

First staged as the Australian Tourist Trophy in 1956, this championship continued as a single race until 1968 when the Confederation of Australian Motor Sport instituted a race series point score for the 1969 championship. Lack of competitors and public interest resulted in the championship reverting to a single race in 1975, but the race series point score was revived in 1976.

Year	Winner	
1956	Stirling Moss	(UK)
1957	Not held	
1958	David McKay	(NSW)
1959	Ron Phillips	(Vic.)
1960	Derek Jolly	(SA)
1961	Bib Stillwell	(Vic.)
1962	Bib Stillwell	(Vic.)
1963	Ian Geoghegan	(NSW)
1964	Frank Matich	(NSW)
1965	Ian Geoghegan	(NSW)
1966	Frank Matich	(NSW)
1967	Frank Matich	(NSW)
1968	Frank Matich	(NSW)
1969	Frank Matich	(NSW)
1970	Peter Woodward	(Vic.)
1971	John Harvey	(Vic.)
1972	John Harvey	(Vic.)
1973	Phil Moore	(SA)
1974	Henry Mitchell	(SA)
1975	Garrie Cooper	(SA)
1976	Ian Goeghegan	(NSW)
1977	Alan Hamilton & John Latham	(Vic.) (Vic.) tie
1978	Ross Mathieson	(Vic.)
1979	Ross Mathieson	(Vic.)
1980	Allan Moffat	(Vic.)
1981	John Latham	(Vic.)
1982	Chris Clearihan	(ACT)
1983	Peter Hopwood	(Vic.)
1984	Bap Romano	(Qld.)
1985	Chris Clearihan	(ACT)
1986	John Bowe	(Tas.)
1987	John Bowe	(Tas.)

AUSTRALIAN RALLY CHAMPIONSHIP

Although major reliability trials and rallies were held in Australia as early as 1905, the Confederation of Australian Motor Sport did not institute a national championship until 1968. The inaugural championship consisted of six events in Victoria, NSW, Queensland, South Australia and the ACT with the winner being decided on a point score basis. Rounds of the national championship are quite separate from classic international events such as the Southern Cross Rally.

Year	Winners	
1968	Harry Firth	(Vic.),
	Graeme Hoinville	(Vic.)
1969	Frank Kilfoyle	(Vic.),
	Doug Rutherford	(Vic.)
1970	Bob Watson	(Vic.),
	Jim McAuliffe	(Vic.)
1971	Colin Bond	(NSW),
	George Shepheard	(NSW)
1972	Colin Bond	(NSW),
	George Shepheard	(NSW)
1973	Peter Lang	(ACT),
	Warwick Smith	(ACT)
1974	Colin Bond	(NSW),
	George Shepheard	(NSW)
1975	Ross Dunkerton	(WA),
	John Large	(WA)
1976	Ross Dunkerton	(WA),
	Jeff Beaumont	(Vic.)
1977	Ross Dunkerton	(WA),
	Alan Mortimer	(SA) &
	George Fury	(NSW),
	Monty Suffern	(Vic.) tie
1978	Greg Carr	(ACT),
	John Dawson-Damer	(NSW)
1979	Ross Dunkerton	(WA),
	Jeff Beaumont	(Tas.)
1980	George Fury	(Vic.),
	Monty Suffern	(Vic.)
1981	Geoff Portman	(Vic.),
	Ross Runnalls	(Vic.)
1982	Geoff Portman	(Vic.),
	Ross Runnalls	(Vic.)
1983	Ross Dunkerton	(WA),
	Geoff Jones	(WA)
1984	David Officer	(Vic.),
	Kate Officer	(Vic.)
1985	Barry Lowe	(SA),
	Mark Stacey	(SA)
1986	Barry Lowe	(SA),
	Mark Stacey	(SA)
1987	Greg Carr	(ACT),
	Fred Gocentas	(NSW)

INDIANAPOLIS 500

The world's most famous oval track race is staged each year in May. The circuit was originally paved with bricks (hence the still-used nickname 'The Brickyard') and was finally sealed in 1932.

Year	Driver	Vehicle	Race speed (mph)
1911	Ray Harroun	Marmon Wasp	74.59
1912	Joe Dawson	National	78.72
1913	Jules Goux	Peugeot	75.933
1914	Rene Thomas	Delage	82.47
1915	Ralph DePalma	Mercedes	89.84
1916	Dario Resta	Peugeot	84.00*
1917–18	*Not held* (WWI)		
1919	Howdy Wilcox	Peugeot	88.05
1920	Gaston Chevrolet	Monroe	88.16
1921	Tommy Milton	Frontenac	89.62
1922	Jimmy Murphy	Murphy Special	94.48
1923	Tommy Milton	HCS	90.95
1924	L. L. Corum-Joe Boyer	Duesenberg	98.23
1925	Pete DePaulo	Duesenberg	101.13
1926	Frank Lockhart	Miller	95.904**
1927	George Souders	Duesenberg	97.545
1928	Louis Meyer	Miller	99.482
1929	Ray Keech	Simplex	97.585
1930	Billy Arnold	Miller-Hartz	100.448
1931	Louis Schneider	Bowes Seal Fast	96.629
1932	Fred Frame	Miller-Hartz	104.144
1933	Louis Meyer	Tydol	104.162
1934	Bill Cummings	Boyle Special	104.683
1935	Kelly Petillo	Gilmore Special	106.240
1936	Louis Meyer	Ring Free Special	109.069
1937	Wilbur Shaw	Shaw-Gilmore Special	113.580
1938	Floyd Roberts	Burd Special	117.200
1939	Wilbur Shaw	Boyle Special	115.035
1940	Wilbur Shaw	Boyle Special	114.277
1941	Floyd Davis-Mauri Rose	KO Special	115.117
1942–45	*Not held* (WWII)		
1946	George Robson	Thorne Engineering	114.820
1947	Mauri Rose	Blue Crown Special	116.338
1948	Mauri Rose	Blue Crown Special	119.814

Year	Driver	Vehicle	Race speed (mph)
1949	Bill Holland	Blue Crown Special	121.327
1950	Johnny Parsons	Wynn Kurtis Kraft	124.002***
1951	Lee Wallard	Belanger	126.224
1952	Troy Ruttman	Agajanian Special	128.922
1953	Bill Vukovich	Fuel Injection Special	128.740
1954	Bill Vukovich	Fuel Injection Special	130.840
1955	Bob Sweikert	John Zink Special	128.209
1956	Pat Flaherty	John Zink Special	128.490
1957	Sam Hanks	Belond Special	135.601
1958	Jimmy Bryan	Belond Special	133.791
1959	Rodger Ward	Leader Card Special	135.857
1960	Jim Rathmann	Ken-Paul Special	138.767
1961	A. J. Foyt	Bowes Seal Fast Special	139.130
1962	Rodger Ward	Leader Card Special	140.293
1963	Parnelli Jones	Agajanian Special	143.137
1964	A. J. Foyt	Sheraton-Thompson Special	147.350
1965	Jim Clark (Scot.)	Lotus-Ford	150.686
1966	Graham Hill (Eng.)	Red Ball	144.317
1967	A. J. Foyt	Sheraton-Thompson Special	151.207
1968	Bobby Unser	Rilstone Special	152.882
1969	Mario Andretti	STP Special	156.867
1970	Al Unser	Johnny Lightning Special	155.749
1971	Al Unser	Johnny Lightning Special	157.735
1972	Mark Donohue	McLaren	162.962
1973	Gordon Johncock	STP Special	159.036****
1974	Johnny Rutherford	McLaren	158.589
1975	Bobby Unser	Jorgensen Eagle	149.213*****
1976	Johnny Rutherford	McLaren	148.725******
1977	A. J. Foyt	Coyote-Foyt	161.331
1978	Al Unser	Lola	161.363
1979	Rick Mears	Penske-Cosworth	158.889
1980	Johnny Rutherford	Chapparal Cosworth	142.862
1981	Bobby Unser	Norton Penske	139.08
1982	Gordon Johncock	STP Wildcat	162.02
1983	Tom Sneva	March 83C	162.11
1984	Rick Mears	Penzoil March	163.61
1985	Danny Sullivan	March-Cosworth	152.98

Year	Driver	Vehicle	Race speed (mph)
1986	**Bobby Rahal**	March-Cosworth	170.722
1987	Al Unser	March-Cosworth	169.63
1988	Rick Mears	Penske-Chevrolet	144.809

* In 1916 the race was shortened to 300 miles because of WWI fuel restrictions.
** In 1926 rain shortened the race to 400 miles.
*** In 1950 rain shortened the race to 345 miles.
**** In 1973 rain shortened the race to 332.5 miles.
***** In 1975 rain shortened the race to 435 miles.
****** In 1976 rain shortened the race to 255 miles.

WORLD DRIVERS CHAMPIONSHIP

Since the inaugural year, the championship has been conducted on a points system involving an international schedule of races. Australia first hosted a round of the championship in 1985 and the final race of the series was staged on a street circuit in Adelaide, SA.

Year	Winner	Vehicle
1950	Giuseppe Farina *(Italy)*	Alfa-Romeo
1951	Juan Fangio *(Argentina)*	Alfa-Romeo
1952	Alberto Ascari *(Italy)*	Ferrari
1953	Alberto Ascari *(Italy)*	Ferrari
1954	Juan Fangio *(Argentina)*	Mercedes & Maserati
1955	Juan Fangio *(Argentina)*	Mercedes
1956	Juan Fangio *(Argentina)*	Lancia-Ferrari
1957	Juan Fangio *(Argentina)*	Maserati
1958	Mike Hawthorn *(England)*	Ferrari
1959	**Jack Brabham *(Australia)***	**Cooper**
1960	**Jack Brabham *(Australia)***	**Cooper**
1961	Phil Hill *(USA)*	Ferrari
1962	Graham Hill *(England)*	BRM
1963	Jim Clark *(Scotland)*	Lotus Climax
1964	John Surtees *(England)*	Ferrari
1965	Jim Clark *(Scotland)*	Lotus Climax
1966	**Jack Brabham *(Australia)***	**Repco Brabham**
1967	Dennis Hulme *(New Zealand)*	Repco Brabham
1968	Graham Hill *(England)*	Lotus Ford
1969	Jackie Stewart *(Scotland)*	Matra Ford
1970	Jochen Rindt *(Austria)**	Lotus Ford
1971	Jackie Stewart *(Scotland)*	Tyrrell Ford
1972	Emerson Fittipaldi *(Brazil)*	John Player Special
1973	Jackie Stewart *(Scotland)*	Tyrrell Ford
1974	Emerson Fittipaldi *(Brazil)*	McLaren Ford

Year	Winner	Vehicle
1975	Niki Lauda *(Austria)*	Ferrari
1976	James Hunt *(England)*	McLaren Ford
1977	Niki Lauda *(Austria)*	Ferrari
1978	Mario Andretti *(USA)*	Lotus Ford
1979	Jody Scheckter *(South Africa)*	Ferrari
1980	**Alan Jones *(Australia)***	**Williams Ford**
1981	Nelson Piquet *(Brazil)*	Brabham Ford
1982	Keke Rosberg *(Finland)*	Williams Ford
1983	Nelson Piquet *(Brazil)*	Brabham BMW
1984	Niki Lauda *(Austria)*	McLaren Porsche
1985	Alain Prost *(France)*	McLaren Porsche
1986	Alain Prost *(France)*	McLaren Porsche
1987	Nelson Piquet *(Brazil)*	Williams Ford

* Awarded posthumously.

NETBALL

BEGINNINGS IN AUSTRALIA
One of the fastest-growing international sports, netball developed from basketball when English women in the Victorian era found it difficult to play basketball in their long skirts. They divided the court into thirds, decided on nine players to a team, restricted the movement of players and introduced a small ball. Although the game of netball was introduced in Australia around the turn of the century, it was confusingly referred to as basketball until August 1970 when the All Australian Women's Basket Ball Association was renamed the All Australian Netball Association.

Australian growth:
Since 1970, netball in Australia has expanded at such a rate that Australia is now regarded as the world headquarters of the game. The game's administrators estimate the number of active participants is 750,000 in Australia with a growth rate of 15,000 each year; figures which suggest that one in seven Australian women under the age of 40 are regular players. In 1984-85 the total sponsorship support was $300,000. By the 1985-86 financial year, that support had risen to $1.3 million.

World championships:
Australian teams have won five of the seven world championships held since 1963. In the 1987 world titles held in Glasgow, Scotland, Australia suffered its worst-ever result, managing only a tie for second place with Trinidad. New Zealand became the new world champions.

The next World Championship carnival will be held in Sydney in July 1991 and until that time Australia will administer the international body, the International Federation of Netball

Associations (IFNA).
Australia's World Championship record:

Year	Venue	Place
1963	London, UK	1st
1967	Perth, WA	Runner-up to New Zealand
1971	Kingston, Jamaica	1st
1975	Auckland, NZ	1st
1979	Trinidad, Jamaica	1st
1983	Melbourne, Vic.	1st
1987	Glasgow, Scotland	Tied, 2nd with Trinidad

AUSTRALIA AT THE OLYMPIC GAMES

AUSTRALIA'S PARTICIPATION RECORD:
Australia is one of only three countries (with Great Britain and Greece) to have appeared in every modern Olympic Games. Twice—in 1908 and 1912—the team represented Australasia and included New Zealand competitors. Twice—at the inaugural Modern Olympic Games at Athens, Greece, in 1896 and at St Louis, USA, in 1904—Australia's 'team' consisted of a single athlete. In 1896, Australia's sole representative was Edwin H. Flack, then resident in London, who won gold medals in the 800 m and 1,500 m track events. In 1904, the representative was athlete Corrie H. Gardner, from Melbourne, who competed without success in the 110 m hurdles. The next smallest team representing Australia went to Paris in 1900 and consisted of athlete Stanley Rowley and swimmer Freddy C. V. Lane. Lane won 2 gold and Rowley 3 bronze medals for Australia. Under the highly elastic rules then in force, Rowley competed for Great Britain in a cross-country teams event and won a gold medal. (Edwin H. Flack represented Australia in 1896 in athletics and at singles tennis, but also played for Great Britain in the tennis doubles event.)

Australia as Olympic Games host:
Australia has only once been selected as host nation for the Games. In 1956, the Olympics were staged at Melbourne, Vic., and the Melbourne Cricket Ground was used as the main venue.

Australia's most successful Games:
Melbourne, Vic., in 1956, when Australia's team of 314 competitors (the largest in Australian Olympic history) won 35 medals, comprising 13 gold, 8 silver and 14 bronze.

Australia's worst performances:
Discounting the early years, when Australian teams were small, Australia's worst performance was at Montreal in 1976. The team of 184 competitors failed to win a gold medal for the first time since 1936 and returned with only 1 silver and 4 bronze medals.

Most successful competitor:
Swimmer Dawn Fraser, who won 8 medals (4 gold, 4 silver) at three successive Games (1956, '60, '64) and became the first swimmer, male or female, to win the same event, the 100 m freestyle, at consecutive Olympics (Melbourne 1956, Rome 1960, Tokyo 1964). Sprint and hurdles champion Shirley Strickland (Mrs de la Hunty), won 7 medals (3 gold, 1 silver and 3 bronze) in three Olympics (1948, '52, '56). Her medal tally would have been 8, equalling Dawn Fraser's record, but at London in 1948 the judges did not bother to inspect the print of a photo-finish in the final of the 200 m track event and placed American Audrey Patterson third,

ahead of Strickland. Almost 32 years later, the photo-finish print was unearthed in London. It showed clearly that Strickland had finished third and should have been awarded the bronze medal.

Most gold medals won:
Four each by Dawn Fraser (swimming: 1956, '60, '64), Betty Cuthbert (athletics: 1956, '60, '64) and Murray Rose (swimming: 1956 and 1960).

Represented at most Olympics:
Canoeist Dennis Green (NSW) created the record of five appearances at the 1972 Munich Games. It was later equalled by another canoeist, Adrian Powell (NSW), pentathlon competitor Peter Macken (NSW) and veteran equestrian Bill Roycroft (NSW) — all at the 1976 Montreal Games.

Oldest gold medal winner:
Bill Northam (NSW), who was 60 years of age when he won a gold medal in the 5.5 m yachting class at the 1964 Tokyo Olympics.

Youngest gold medal winner:
Shane Gould (NSW), who was 15 years and 9 months old when she won 3 gold medals in swimming events at the 1972 Munich Olympics.

Australia at the Winter Olympics:
Australia was first represented at the Winter Olympics when Sydney speed skater Kenneth Kennedy competed at the 1936 Games at the Bavarian town of Garmisch-Partenkirchen. Australian-born F. J. McEvoy also competed at the 1936 Winter Olympics, but represented Great Britain and won a bronze medal in the four-man bobsleigh event. Australia is yet to win a medal at the Winter Olympics.

Most appearances at a Winter Olympics:
Four, by speed skater Colin Coates (1968, '72, '76 and '80).

Olympic Games Venues:
1896 – Athens, Greece; 1900 – Paris, France; 1904 – St Louis, USA; 1908 – London, UK; 1912 – Stockholm, Sweden; 1920 – Antwerp, Belgium; 1924 – Paris, France; 1928 – Amsterdam, Holland; 1932 – Los Angeles, USA; 1936 – Berlin, Germany; 1948 – London, UK; 1952 – Helsinki, Finland; 1956 – Melbourne, Australia; 1960 – Rome, Italy; 1964 – Tokyo, Japan; 1968 – Mexico City, Mexico; 1972 – Munich, West Germany; 1976 – Montreal, Canada; 1980 – Moscow, USSR; 1984 – Los Angeles, USA. The 1988 Games are scheduled for Seoul, South Korea.

Olympic Games cancelled because of World Wars I and II were scheduled for Berlin, Germany (1916) and Tokyo, Japan (1940). Japan was awarded both the Summer and Winter Olympics but following the Japanese invasion of China the Games were withdrawn. The Winter Olympics were then awarded to Germany and the Summer Games to Helsinki, Finland. The outbreak of World War II resulted in both Games being abandoned. The 1944 Summer Games allocated to London, UK, were also abandoned.

AUSTRALIAN GOLD MEDAL WINNERS
1896—Athens
Edwin H. Flack – 800 metres
Edwin H. Flack – 1,500 metres
1900—Paris
Gold Medals – nil
1904—St. Louis
Gold Medals – nil.
1906—Interim Games—Athens
Gold Medals – nil
1908—London*
Australian Rugby Union team
1912—Stockholm**
Sarah 'Fanny' Durack – 100 metres freestyle swimming
Men's 4 × 200 metres freestyle swimming relay (Leslie Boardman, Malcolm Champion (NZ), Harold Hardwick, Cecil Healy)

1920—Antwerp
Gold Medals—nil

1924—Paris
Anthony 'Nick' Winter—hop, step and jump (now known as triple jump)
Richmond 'Dick' Eve—plain high diving
Andrew 'Boy' Charlton—1,500 metres freestyle swimming

1928—Amsterdam
Henry 'Bobby' Pearce—single sculls

1932—Los Angeles
Edgar 'Dunc' Gray—1,000 metres time trial cycling
Henry 'Bobby' Pearce—single sculls
Clare Dennis—200 metres breaststroke swimming

1936—Berlin
Gold Medals—nil

1948—London
John Winter—high jump
Mervyn Wood—single sculls

1952—Helsinki
Marjorie Jackson—100 metres track
Marjorie Jackson—200 metres track
Shirley Strickland—80 metres hurdles
Russell Mockridge—1,000 metres cycling sprint
Russell Mockridge and Lionel Cox—2,000 metres tandem cycling

1956—Melbourne
Betty Cuthbert—100 metres track
Betty Cuthbert—200 metres track
Women's 4 × 100 metres track relay (Norma Croker, Betty Cuthbert, Fleur Mellor, Shirley Strickland)
Shirley Strickland—80 metres hurdles
Ian Browne and Tony Marchant—2,000 metres tandem cycling
John Henricks—100 metres freestyle swimming
Murray Rose—400 metres freestyle swimming
Murray Rose—1,500 metres freestyle swimming
David Theile—100 metres backstroke swimming
Men's 4 x 200 metres freestyle swimming relay (Kevin O'Halloran, John Devitt, Murray Rose, Jon Henricks)
Lorraine Crapp—400 metres freestyle swimming
Dawn Fraser—100 metres freestyle swimming
Women's 4 × 200 metres freestyle relay (Dawn Fraser, Sandra Morgan, Faith Leech, Lorraine Crapp)

1960—Rome
Herb Elliott—1,500 metres track
Three day equestrian team (Laurence Morgan, Bill Roycroft, Neale Lavis)
Laurence Morgan—three day equestrian individual
John Devitt—100 metres freestyle swimming
John Konrads—1,500 metres freestyle swimming
Murray Rose—400 metres freestyle swimming
David Theile—100 metres backstroke swimming
Dawn Fraser—100 metres freestyle swimming

1964—Tokyo
Betty Cuthbert—400 metres track
Kevin Berry—200 metres butterfly swimming
Ian O'Brien—200 metres breaststroke swimming
Bob Windle—1,500 metres freestyle swimming
Dawn Fraser—100 metres freestyle swimming
5.5 metre class yachting crew (Bill Northam, Peter O'Donnell, James Sargeant)

1968—Mexico City
Ralph Doubell—800 metres track
Maureen Caird—80 metres hurdles
Michael Wenden—100 metres freestyle swimming
Michael Wenden—200 metres freestyle swimming
Lynne McClements—100 metres butterfly swimming

1972—Munich
Brad Cooper—400 metres freestyle swimming
Shane Gould—200 metres freestyle swimming
Shane Gould—400 metres freestyle swimming
Shane Gould—200 metres individual medley swimming
Gail Neall—400 metres individual medley swimming
Beverley Whitfield—200 metres breaststroke swimming
Star class yachting crew (John Anderson, David Forbes)
Dragon class yachting crew (Thomas Anderson, John Cuneo, John Shaw)

1976—Montreal
Gold medals—nil
1980—Moscow
Michelle Ford—800 metres freestyle swimming
Men's 4 × 100 metres medley swimming relay (Mark Kerry, Neil Brooks, Peter Evans, Mark Tonelli)
1984—Los Angeles
Glynis Nunn—women's heptathlon (track and field)

Dean Lukin—super-heavyweight weightlifting
Jon Sieben—200 metres butterfly swimming
4,000 metres cycling pursuit team (Michael Grenda, Kevin Nichols, Michael Turtur, Dean Woods)

*Represented as Australasia. Rugby Union team all Australians.
**Represented as Australasia.

AUSTRALIA'S RECORD—SUMMER OLYMPIC GAMES

Games	Team Members	Gold	Silver	Bronze	Total
1896	1	2	—	—	2
1900	2	2	—	3	5
1904	1	—	—	—	—
1906*					
1908**	27	1	2	1	4
1912**	28	2	2	2	6
1920	13	—	2	1	3
1924	37	3	1	2	6
1928	18	1	2	1	4
1932	12	3	1	1	5
1936	33	—	—	1	1
1948	76	2	6	5	13
1952	82	6	2	3	11
1956	314	13	8	14	35
1960	188	8	8	6	22
1964	234	6	2	10	18
1968	143	5	7	5	17
1972	170	8	7	2	17
1976	184	—	1	4	5
1980	123	2	2	5	9
1984	249	4	8	12	24

* The Interim, or Intercalated, Games held at Athens in 1906 are not officially recognised by the International Olympic Committee and related statistics have been deliberately omitted from the above figures. (Australia was represented by four athletes and one swimmer, and won 1 silver and 3 bronze medals).
** Medals won by New Zealand competitors participating in the 1908 and 1912 'Australasian' teams have not been included.
Notes: (1) Figures given for team members do not include officials.
(2) Team successes involving more than one competitor are shown as a single medal in the medal tally for each Games.
(3) As many Australians have represented at more than one Olympic Games, the combined total of each team does not provide an accurate total of Australia's Olympians.

AUSTRALIA'S RECORD—WINTER OLYMPIC GAMES

Year	Venue	Team Members
1936	Garmisch-Partenkirchen, Germany	1
1948	St Moritz, Switzerland	—*
1952	Oslo, Norway	7
1956	Cortina d'Ampezzo, Italy	10

Year	Venue	Team Members
1960	Squaw Valley, USA	32**
1964	Innsbruck, Austria	6***
1968	Grenoble, France	3
1972	Sapporo, Japan	4
1976	Innsbruck, Austria	8
1980	Lake Placid, USA	9
1984	Sarajevo, Yugoslavia	11
1988	Calgary, Canada	18

* Australia was not represented in 1948.
** The 1960 team was the largest in Australian history because for the first (and until the 1984 Winter Olympics, only) time, an ice hockey squad comprising 18 players and a coach represented.
*** Only five Australians actually competed at Innsbruck in 1964. Ross Milne was fatally injured while practising for the downhill race before the Games were opened.

POWERBOATING

BEGINNINGS IN AUSTRALIA
The first organised powerboat racing took place in Sydney and Melbourne around 1909, prompted to a large degree by the excitement produced by powerboat competition at the 1908 Olympic Games in London. Powerboat racing, along with other 'offbeat' sports such as polo, royal tennis (as distinct from lawn tennis) and racquets, was a popular sport at the Games. Australians came back from the Games enthusiastic for the 'new' sport. The first major event to be staged in Australia was an ambitious Sydney to Newcastle (NSW) and return reliability trial.

First Australian (still water) Championships:
Held in 1909-10, when Sydney enthusiast Ernest Griffiths presented a trophy which is still competed for at national championship carnivals.
Another early trophy donor was Frank Albert, Commodore of the Motor Yacht Club at Rose Bay, Sydney.

First Australian controlling body:
The Australian Powerboat Association, formed in 1927.

Australian powerboating landmark:
A new world water-speed record of 464.457 km/h, set on 20 November 1977 by Ken Warby (NSW), at Blowering Dam, Tumut, NSW. Warby designed and built his boat, *Spirit of Australia*, and purchased a second-hand jet aircraft engine for it from the RAAF. Handicapped by lack of finance and unable to attract more than token sponsorship, Warby assembled the boat in his backyard, aided by RAAF engineers who helped rebuild the engine. Warby's record speed was the average of two runs, the second of which was staged on water made choppy by uncooperative drivers of pleasure boats. Warby's feat was one of the great Australian sporting stories of the year and almost won him the coveted ABC Sportsman of the Year Award. In 1980 he was given a Federal Government grant to take *Spirit of Australia* on a tour of the USA. Despite several multi-million dollar attempts in the United States to better his record, Warby's still stood in early 1986. Warby, a former small powerboat racing champion of NSW, 'retired' from the water-speed record field when it was obvious that his record was safe and took up jet car drag racing in the USA and Australia.

First Australian world record:
Established on 14 January 1950, when Keith Barry (NSW) bettered the world

91 cubic inch record in *Firefly II* with 72.289 mph (116.34 km/h) at Kogarah Bay, NSW. On 11 November 1950, Barry loaned *Firefly II* to the much lighter Bill McLachlan, who raised the record to 78.003 mph (125.53 km/h) on the same one-mile course at Kogarah Bay. Later the same day, the 1250 cc MG TA engine in *Firefly II* blew up as McLachlan was making an attempt on the Australian unlimited record.

Other Australian world records:
In 1973 John Toyer (Vic.) set a world record of 73.4 km/h driving *Oscar IV* in the SB outboard class. During the 1968-69 season, Tom Watts (Vic.) set a series of world records for 1,200 kg Reactor boats in his hydroplane *Exciter* powered by a Rolls-Royce engine. Watts raised the record from 221.1 km/h to 261.7 km/h in less than a year.

First woman to better 100 mph (160.9 km/h):
Mrs Grace Walker, in the hydroplane *Dianne* in 1950.

First driver to better 250 km/h:
Bob Saniga (Vic.) set an Australasian record for unlimited hydroplanes in *Stampede II* in May 1973 at the Eppalock Reservoir, Vic. Saniga's record still stood after Ken Warby's world record, because he drove a screw-driven boat. Warby's record was achieved with jet power.

Donald Campbell's world record in Australia:
The late Donald Campbell (UK) set a new world water-speed record of 444.71 km/h in December 1964 at Lake Dumbleyung, WA, to become the first man to simultaneously hold the world land- and water-speed records. Campbell was killed trying to raise his own water-speed record when his boat *Bluebird* crashed at Lake Coniston, England, in 1967.

Most famous offshore race:
The Sydney to Newcastle (NSW) and return race, first staged in 1964. The race resulted in a double tragedy in 1972, with brothers Val and Paul Carr losing their lives when their boat *Cigarette* (imported from the USA) was overturned by a freak wave near Wedding Cake Island, off Coogee Beach, near Sydney. From 1977 the race organisers deleted the compulsory stop at Newcastle. Fastest time for the non-stop 281.6 km race was set by Brian Stevens (Vic.) at 2 hrs 32 mins 45 secs in *Whiplash*.

ROWING AND SCULLING

BEGINNINGS IN AUSTRALIA
The sport of rowing is easily linked with challenge races on Sydney Harbour between ships' crews in four-oar gigs in the period 1818-1922. Such races were half in fun, and really intended to give crews exercise. Organised competition also has links with a Foundation Day regatta held in Sydney on 26 January 1837 and an earlier regatta on the Derwent River, Hobart, on 5 January 1827.

First serious rowing club:
The Melbourne University Boat Club, founded by Professor M. H. Irving who

came from England to take up a chair at Melbourne University. The club was formed in 1859 and is still in existence.

First Sydney club:
The Australian Subscription Boat Club, founded slightly later in the same year (1859).

First interstate competition:
In 1863, when a Sydney representative crew defeated Victoria on the Parramatta River, Sydney, in a four-oar race.

First State champion:
Quarton Levitt Deloitte of Sydney, NSW, who won the NSW Amateur Sculling Championship on the Parramatta River in 1864.

First Australian sculling 'championship':
In 1868, when Arthur Nicholls (Vic.) defeated Henry Freeman (NSW) on the Yarra River, Melbourne. (The 'championship' has never been seriously regarded.)

First grading of rowers:
In the early 1860s, when the Sydney rowing establishment, anxious to keep out the 'riff raff', announced three classes of competition—Professionals, Bona Fide Amateurs (anybody who did not earn a living from manual labour, but was allowed to accept cash prizes) and Manual Labourers, who were allowed to compete for cash prizes, but *not* in competition with the Bona Fide Amateurs.

First association of rowing clubs:
In October 1876, when the Victorian Rowing Association—the first of its kind in the world—was formed with 18 member clubs.

First interstate eight-oar race:
On 6 March 1878, when Victoria defeated Sydney on the Lower Yarra. The Sydney crew was a second-rate eight and included only one member of the premier Sydney Rowing Club—the result of a dispute over the Bona Fide Amateur and Manual Labourer ruling.

First official Australian sculling champion:
Dick Green of Sydney, who defeated A. Candlish of England for a stake of 400 pounds, on the Parramatta River championship course in 1858. Green went to England in 1863 and unsuccessfully challenged for Robert Chambers' world title.

First Australian world sculling champion:
Edward Trickett (1851–1916), who took the world title from England's Joseph Sadler on the River Thames, UK, on 27 June 1876.

First world championship sculling race in Australia:
On 30 June 1877, when Trickett retained his title against Australian Michael Rush on the Parramatta River.

First undefeated world sculling champion:
William Beach (1850–1935), who was born in England and settled at Dapto, NSW, as a blacksmith. Beach won the title from Edward Hanlan (Canada) on 16 August 1884 and retired undefeated, after seven defences, in 1888. Under the strange rules of the sport, he 'bequeathed' his title to his trainer Peter Kemp, who made several successful defences.

First Australian international crew win:
In 1912, when an Australian Olympic eight crew, en route to the Stockholm Olympic Games, won the Grand Challenge Cup at Henley, England.

First Olympic Games gold medal:
In 1928, when Henry 'Bobby' Pearce (1905–76) won the single sculls at Amsterdam.

First Australian Olympic Games entries:
In 1912, when an eight-oar crew and individual sculler Cecil McVilly (Tas.) competed at Stockholm. Though the Australian eight was entirely composed of NSW and Victorian rowers, they

competed as 'Australasia'. The crew easily won their heat and were unlucky to be beaten by an English club, Leander, in the semi-final. McVilly won his heat, but was disqualified for causing interference to his German opponent.

First Australian at Empire or Commonwealth Games:
H. R. 'Bobby' Pearce, who won the gold medal in the single sculls at Hamilton, Canada, in 1930.

First King's Cup race:
On 5 July 1919 at Henley, England. His Majesty King George V presented a trophy for the winner of an eight-oared competition between crews from the Allied forces. One of two AIF crews entered defeated Oxford (a crew of returned servicemen) in the final. The trophy, which later became known as the King's Cup, was taken back to Australia and placed in the Australian War Museum. A petition to the King for its release resulted in the King commanding that the trophy be released and competed for annually in Australia.

First King's Cup race in Australia:
In 1920, when interstate eight-oar races were revived after World War I. The race, held on Brisbane Water (Qld), was won by the Murray Bridge crew (SA).

Greatest scullers—amateur:
H. R. 'Bobby' Pearce, son of Australian professional champion Harry Pearce. Australian Champion 1927, '28 and '29, Pearce won the Diamond Sculls at Henley in 1930, the Commonwealth Games gold medal at Hamilton, Canada, in 1930 and the Olympic gold medal in 1928 and 1932. He turned professional in 1933, retiring undefeated in 1948. Pearce settled in Toronto, Canada, where he died in 1976.

Merv Wood (b. Sydney, NSW, 30 April 1917) represented Australia at four Olympic Games (1936, '48, '52 and '56). He won the single sculls gold medal in 1948 and the silver in 1952, the Diamond Sculls at Henley in 1948 and 1952, the Philadelphia Cup in 1948, gold medals for the single and double sculls at the 1950 Commonwealth Games, gold medals for the double sculls and coxed four at the 1954 Commonwealth Games and, although considered 'over the hill', entered and won a bronze medal in the double sculls at the 1956 Melbourne Olympic Games.

Stuart Mackenzie, the most colourful sculler the world has seen, won a record six Diamond Sculls at Henley in succession from 1957 to 1962, and a silver medal at the 1956 Olympics, a gold medal at the 1958 Commonwealth Games, three straight European Championships and the South African Championship.

Australia's first official world champion:
Adair Ferguson of Queensland, who, in September 1985, became the first Australian to win a gold medal at an official world rowing championship. Ferguson, who had been rowing for only two years, won the women's lightweight sculls in Belgium, defeating Romanian Maria Macoviciuc in the final.

Australians captured two more titles at the world championships held immediately after the 1986 Commonwealth Games. The men's eight-oar crew, which had won a gold medal at the Games at Edinburgh, became the first Australian crew to win a world championship and Peter Antonie won the lightweight sculls title.

PROFESSIONAL SCULLING

Australia produced a string of world champions from 1876 until the 1940s, when interest in professional rowing waned. The last Australian holder of the title was George Cook, in the late 1940s.

Henry Searle tragedy:
On 10 December 1889, Henry Searle (b. Maclean, NSW, 12 July 1866) died of typhoid fever in a Melbourne sanatorium after returning from successfully defending his world title in London. Searle was accorded what was then the biggest funeral—actually a series of funerals—in Australian history. Such was the interest in sculling at the time that an estimated 170,000 fans crowded the shores of Sydney Harbour to farewell the steamer *Thetis*, which carried his remains back to his home town of Grafton, NSW.

RUGBY LEAGUE

BEGINNINGS IN AUSTRALIA

Rugby League became established in Australia for precisely the same reasons that professional Rugby football was established in England. In 1893, several Yorkshire Rugby Union clubs asked the Rugby Football Union to consider compensating players for loss of wages resulting from being injured in games. The RFU opposed the motion and some clubs which began paying their players for lost work time were suspended. On 29 August 1895, 20 out of 22 original breakaway clubs formed the Northern Rugby Football Union and instituted a competition aimed at making the code more attractive to spectators and, ultimately, profitable enough to ensure that all players received match fees.

In Australia the switch to semi-professional Rugby followed a similar pattern. In 1907 top-line Rugby forward Alex Burdon incurred heavy medical expenses after sustaining a shoulder injury playing for NSW, and several clubs decided to use the incident as a test case for the NSW Rugby Union to agree to compensate representative players financially. The Rugby Union rejected the idea and the seeds of a breakaway movement were sown. Former Australian Test cricketer Victor Trumper, and other notable Sydney sportsmen and businessmen, met to discuss the possibilities of establishing professional Rugby. When it was learned that a similar breakaway movement had already succeeded in New Zealand and that a semi-professional team of New Zealand Rugby players was to leave for England, the decision was taken to invite the New Zealanders to play in Sydney *en route* to England. Trumper and his associates discovered a reticence on the part of many players to leave the security of the amateur code and decided that if they could lure champion Australian player Herbert Henry 'Dally' Messenger (1883-1959) away from amateur Rugby, many other stars would follow. It is believed that Messenger, after much negotiation, agreed to accept the sum of 180 pounds to leave the amateurs and play three matches against the New Zealand side. The Messenger theory proved correct and Trumper and associates had no trouble contracting 21 other players.

First professional Rugby matches in Australia:

On 17, 21 and 24 August 1907, at the Sydney Showground, between the New Zealand All Golds and the Australian 'Pioneers'. All three matches (won by New Zealand 12-8, 19-5 and 5-3) were played under existing Rugby rules by the normal teams of 15 players. The New Zealand team was guaranteed 500 pounds for the three matches and all of the Australian players except Messenger received one pound per match plus travelling expenses. The three matches returned a profit of 180 pounds and James J. Giltinan, who had then taken over as leader of the push towards professional Rugby, received the agreement of other enthusiasts to invest the money in establishing professional Rugby at club level.

First Australian professional players:

H. H. Messenger, C. Hedley, J. Stuntz, E. Fry, F. B. Cheadle, W. A. Cann, J. Devereaux, D. Brown, A. Rosenberg, L. d'Alpuget, R. Graves, H. L. Brackenregg, A. Halloway, P. Moir, S. Pearce, R. Mable, A. S. Hennessy, H. C. Hamill, A. Dobbs, H. Glanville, E. Courtney and J. Abercrombie.

Messenger first overseas:

'Dally' Messenger was the first Australian to play the professional code overseas. He accepted an invitation to tour with the New Zealand All Golds on their 1907-08 tour of England. Messenger was the star of the New Zealand side, scoring 146 points (101 points more than any other member of the team) and under his contract arrangements, arrived home the richer by 200 pounds. According to many sources and verified by Messenger's grandson, Dally R. Messenger, in his book *The Master*, published in 1982, Messenger received at least two offers to join English soccer clubs. Manchester United offered him 3,000 pounds per season (a vast sum in those days) and this offer was matched by Tottenham Hotspur. Messenger, on the advice of his mother whom he cabled in Sydney, rejected the offers.

Establishment of the NSW Rugby League:
Early in 1908, when H. Hoyle was elected President, Victor Trumper Hon. Treasurer and J. J. Giltinan Hon. Secretary.

Establishment of the first Sydney clubs:
Though some doubt now exists about the identity of the first club to be inaugurated, it appears that Newtown was formed on 8 January 1908, Glebe on 9 January, South Sydney on 17 January, Balmain on 24 January, Eastern Suburbs on 25 January, Western Suburbs on 4 February and Northern Suburbs on 7 February. Another club (Cumberland) was also formed in 1908, but subsequently amalgamated with Western Suburbs. Newtown and Glebe are no longer involved in the Sydney competition. Northern Suburbs eventually became North Sydney.

First club premiership competition:
Played in 1908 and won by South Sydney. (During this inaugural season, a club from Newcastle, NSW, played several games in the competition.)

First Rugby League in Queensland:
In 1907, when the Queensland Rugby League was formed and a small number of clubs played friendly matches. The first premiership-style matches were not played until 1909.

First NSW v. Queensland matches:
In 1908. NSW won all three matches 43-0, 37-8 and 12-3.

First Australian team overseas:
In 1908-09, when the original Kangaroos sailed to England on the S.S. *Macedonia*. Dinny Lutge of the North Sydney (NSW) club was captain, Dally Messenger (Eastern Suburbs, NSW) vice-captain and J. J. Giltinan was manager. The touring party comprised 34 players, one of whom was Alex Burdon, whose rejected compensation claim had led to the establishment of professional Rugby in 1907. The team played 45 matches, won 18, lost 21 and drew 6, scoring 561 points against 467. The tour was a financial failure, with a net loss of some 383 pounds, 9 shillings and 11 pence, but was a success on another front: the Kangaroo tour coincided with a Wallaby (Australian Rugby Union) tour and Giltinan and Messenger were able to convince many of the amateurs to turn professional on their return to Australia.

Major triumph over Rugby Union:
After the 1908-09 Wallaby (Rugby Union) tour of the British Isles, 14 of the tourists and two non-tourists agreed to turn professional at the end of the 1909 domestic Rugby season. In September, four matches were staged under the professional Rugby League rules (which specified 13 men to a side) between the Kangaroos and the Ex-Wallabies, and with lavish sponsorship from Sydney business magnate Sir James Joynton Smith. All matches were played at the Sydney Showground, with the following results: 4 September, Kangaroos 29 d. Ex-Wallabies 26; 8 September, Ex-Wallabies 34 d. Kangaroos 21; 11 September, Ex-Wallabies 15 d. Kangaroos 6; 18 September, Kangaroos

8 d. Ex-Wallabies 6, before respective attendances of 18,000, 10,000, 16,000 and 15,000. Although rumours began that the games had been played with a final match decider in mind, the gate takings put NSW Rugby League in a powerful financial situation.

First Australia v. England Test matches:
The first such Test was played during the 1908-09 tour at Royal Park, London, on 12 December 1908. Messenger captained Australia and the Test resulted in a 22-all draw. England scored five tries to four and Australia was saved by Messenger who kicked five goals. England won the other two Tests—15-5 at Newcastle Upon Tyne on 23 January 1909 and 6-5 at Birmingham on 10 February 1909. Injury caused Messenger to miss the third Test; Australia undoubtedly would have won had he been fit.

TESTS AGAINST OTHER COUNTRIES
Australia v. France:
First Test played at Paris, 2 January 1938. Australia d. France 35-6. Tests played to end of 1986: 41. Won by Australia 27; won by France 12. Drawn 2.

Australia v. New Zealand:
First Test played at Sydney, 9 May 1908. New Zealand d. Australia 11-10. Tests played to end of 1986: 59. Won by Australia 40; won by New Zealand 19. No draws.

Australia v. South Africa:
First Test played Brisbane, 20 July 1963. Won by Australia 34-6. Tests played to end of 1984: 2. Won by Australia 2.

Australia v. Wales:
First Test played EbbwVale, 1911. Won by Australia 28-20. Tests played to end of 1982: 7. Won by Australia 7.

Australia v. Papua New Guinea:
First Test played, 1982. Won by Australia 38-2. Second Test played, 1986. Won by Australia.

Australia in World Series Championship:
Staged in an effort to interest more countries in the professional Rugby game, the first World Series was held at various venues in France in 1954. Teams involved (Great Britain, France, Australia and New Zealand) played a series of round-robin matches with the two top teams playing off in the final.

1954: Australia placed third. Final won by Great Britain.

1957: Played in Australia. Competing teams: Australia, Great Britain, New Zealand and France. Australia placed first and no final played because of unbeaten record in competition.

1960: Played in Great Britain. Competing teams: Great Britain, Australia, New Zealand and France. Australia placed second. No final played because Great Britain was unbeaten and declared winners.

1968: Played in Australia and New Zealand. Competing teams: Australia, France, Great Britain and New Zealand. Australia d. France 20-2 in the final at Sydney, NSW.

1970: Played in Great Britain. Competing teams: Great Britain, Australia, France and New Zealand. Australia d. Great Britain 12-7 in the final at Leeds.

1972: Played in France. Competing teams: Great Britain, Australia, France and New Zealand. Great Britain drew with Australia 10-10 in the final at Lyons

AUSTRALIA v. GREAT BRITAIN TEST STATISTICS

Series	Venue	Result	Won by Aust.*	Won by GB	Drawn
1908-09	G. Britain	G. Britain	—	2	1
1910**	Australia	Drawn	1	1	1
1911-12	G. Britain	Australasia	2	—	1
1914	Australia	G. Britain	1	2	—
1920	Australia	Australia	2	1	—

Series	Venue	Result	Won by Aust.*	Won by GB	Drawn
1921-22	G. Britain	G. Britain	1	2	–
1924	Australia	G. Britain	1	2	–
1928	Australia	G. Britain	1	2	–
1929–30***	G. Britain	G. Britain	1	2	1
1932	Australia	G. Britain	1	2	–
1933	G. Britain	G. Britain	–	3	–
1936	Australia	G. Britain	1	2	–
1937	G. Britain	G. Britain	1	2	–
1946	Australia	G. Britain	–	1	1
1948	G. Britain	G. Britain	–	3	–
1950	Australia	Australia	2	–	–
1952	G. Britain	G. Britain	1	2	–
1954	Australia	Australia	2	1	–
1956	G. Britain	G. Britain	1	2	–
1958	Australia	G. Britain	1	2	–
1959	G. Britain	G. Britain	1	2	–
1962	Australia	G. Britain	1	2	–
1963	G. Britain	Australia	2	1	–
1966	Australia	Australia	2	1	–
1967	G. Britain	Australia	2	1	–
1970	Australia	G. Britain	1	2	–
1973	G. Britain	Australia	2	1	–
1974	Australia	Australia	2	1	–
1978	G. Britain	Australia	2	1	–
1979	Australia	Australia	3	–	–
1982****	G. Britain	Australia	3	–	–
1984	Australia	Australia	3	–	–
1986*****	G. Britain	Australia	3	–	–
	Totals		47	46	5

* The 1911–12 Australian side to Great Britain included four New Zealand players and was represented as Australasia.
** On the 1910 tour of Australia, Great Britain played four 'internationals'. Statisticians agree that one (a 'Test' played at Brisbane, Qld), should be deleted because the side was officially a combined NSW–Queensland team and did not (officially) represent Australia.
*** Four Tests were played on the 1929–30 Australian tour of Great Britain, the only time this has happened in the history of Tests between the two countries. Australia won the first Test 31–8, lost the second 3–9 and drew 0–0 in the third. In this Test, Australia was not awarded one clearly fair try, because an unsighted touch judge wrongly claimed Australian half Joe 'Chimpy' Busch had knocked over the corner post before grounding the ball. The equally unsighted referee was powerless to overrule the touch judge. The English Rugby League, undoubtedly prompted by thoughts of a huge gate for a deciding Test, offered to stage a history-making fourth Test. England won this Test at Rochdale 3–0 to clinch the series.
**** First Australian team to win all three Tests in Great Britain and remain unbeaten in all matches in Great Britain and France (including two Test matches).
***** Second Australian team to win all three Tests in Great Britain and remain unbeaten in all matches in Great Britain and France.

and when no further score was added after extra time, Great Britain was declared the winner because of their better for and against points scoring in preliminary matches.

1975: Played in Great Britain, France, New Zealand and Australia. Competing teams: Australia, England, Wales, New Zealand and France. Decided on a pointscore basis with no final. Australia placed first with six wins and a draw in eight matches.

1977: Played in New Zealand and Australia. Competing teams: Australia, Great Britain, New Zealand and France. Australia d. Great Britain 13-12 in the final at Sydney.

Series abandoned.

First British tour of Australia:
In 1910. The tourists played their first match in Australia at the Sydney Showground on 4 June and lost 14-28 to NSW. Three internationals were played, but only one against Australia. The matches (all at the Sydney Showground) yielded the following results: 18 June, England 27 d. Australia 20; 9 July, Australasia 13 drew England 13; 13 July, Australasia 32 d. England 15.

First Rugby League on the Sydney Cricket Ground:
Coronation Day 20 June 1911, NSW d. New Zealand 35-10. The tour was an important milestone for Rugby League because the code had finally broken the Rugby Union stranglehold on Sydney's premier ground.

MISCELLANEOUS TEST STATISTICS

Record crowd in Australia:
70,204, for Australia v. Great Britain at the SCG, 6 June 1932.

First Australian Test team to win the Ashes in England:
The 1963-64 Kangaroos defeated Great Britain by a record 50-12 at Swinton, UK, on 9 November 1963 to clinch the series (having won the first Test 28-2). The 50 points was a record total against Great Britain.

First undefeated Kangaroo team in Great Britain and France:
The 1982 side captained by Max Krilich of Manly-Warringah, NSW, which won 23 games and scored 752 points at an average of 33 per game and scored 176 tries against nine. The side scored a record 99 points in three Tests against Great Britain (won 40-4, 27-6 and 32-8).

Second undefeated Kangaroo team in Great Britain and France:
The 1986 side captained by Wally Lewis of Wynnum-Manly, Brisbane, which won 20 matches and scored 738 points at an average of 36.9 per game and scored 139 tries against 16. This team set a long list of new records, including:
• An Anglo-Australian Test record crowd of 50,583 in the First Test at Old Trafford, Manchester.
• The three Test series against Great Britain produced gate receipts of $1 million for the first time.
• A 52-0 victory over France in the Second Test at Carcassonne – the widest winning margin in the history of Rugby League Test football.

State of Origin matches, NSW v. Queensland:
After NSW had defeated Queensland in 15 successive interstate matches between 1975 and 1980, NSW and Queensland authorities agreed to change the format for the last of the annual three-match series in 1980. The two teams were selected on the basis of State of origin and Queensland was strengthened by the 'return' of seven top players who were then playing in Sydney: Arthur Beetson, Kerry Boustead, John Lang, Rod Morris, Greg Oliphant, Rod Reddy and Alan Smith. Queensland defeated NSW 20-10 before a crowd of 28,000 at Lang Park, Brisbane.

The success of that experiment led to the old NSW v. Queensland matches being abandoned in favour of the State of Origin clashes as from the end of the second old-version State game of 1981.

Results of all State of Origin matches:
1980: Qld d. NSW 20-10 at Brisbane

1981: Qld d. NSW 22-15 at Brisbane

1982: NSW d. Qld 20-16 at Brisbane
1982: Qld d. NSW 11-7 at Brisbane
1982: Qld d. NSW 10-5 at Sydney

1983: Qld d. NSW 24-12 at Brisbane
1983: NSW d. Qld 10-6 at Sydney
1983: Qld d. NSW 43-22 at Brisbane

1984: Qld d. NSW 29-12 at Brisbane
1984: NSW d. Qld 14-12 at Sydney
1984: NSW d. Qld 22-12 at Brisbane

1985: NSW d. Qld 18-2 at Brisbane
1985: NSW d. Qld 21-14 at Sydney
1985: Qld d. NSW 20-6 at Brisbane

1986: NSW d. Qld 12-16 at Brisbane
1986: NSW d. Qld 24-20 at Sydney
1986: NSW d. Qld 18-16 at Brisbane

The crowd for the first 1984 match at Lang Park, Brisbane, on 29 May was 33,000. The record crowd for a State of Origin match in Sydney is 40,707, for the second match of the 1986 series played under lights at the SCG on 10 June.

STATE PREMIERSHIPS
First Sydney premiership:
Held in 1908 and won by South Sydney.
First Brisbane premiership:
Held in 1909 and won by Valleys. (Not all teams competing came from the Brisbane metropolitan area. The first all-Brisbane premiership was not staged until 1922. It was won by Western Suburbs.)
Most premierships—Sydney:
South Sydney 20 (1908-71).
Most successive premierships—Sydney:
11, by St George (then a world record for senior football of any code) between 1956 and 1966.
Largest crowd—Sydney:
Officially, 78,056 for the 1965 Grand Final at the SCG between St George and South Sydney. The crowd was, in fact, much larger because thousands gatecrashed their way into the ground. St George defeated South Sydney 12-8. Following construction of new grandstands and other alterations at the SCG, the maximum possible crowd is now nearer 55,000.
Most premierships—Brisbane (including premierships played 1909-21 when non-Brisbane teams competed):
Valleys 22 (1909-79).

Most successive premierships—Brisbane:
6, by Northern Suburbs 1959-64.
Largest crowd—Brisbane:
38,950, for the 1973 Brisbane Grand Final between Valleys and Redcliffe at Lang Park. Valleys won.
Most points in a city premiership season:
282 (16 tries, 117 goals), by Michael Cronin for Parramatta in the 1978 Sydney competition. The previous record was 265 (1 try, 112 goals and 19 field goals) by Eric Simms for South Sydney in 1969. Field goals were then worth two points (now only one). An earlier record of 244 points was established by Dave Brown for Eastern Suburbs in 1935.

INTERNATIONAL SCORING
Most points in Australia v. Great Britain Tests:
104, by Graeme Langlands (St George, NSW) from 6 tries and 43 goals in 12 Tests, 1963-74.
Most points in Test career (against all countries):
199, by Mick Cronin (Parramatta, NSW) with 5 tries and 92 goals in 22 Tests.
Most famous Australian club side:
Undoubtedly the St George team of 1956-66 when they won 11 successive premierships. In 1963, the club won the premiership in all three grades, the club championship and the pre-season competition (the first time this had happened at senior level anywhere in Australia) and became the first club side to defeat a visiting international team (New Zealand by 22-7).
Dual Rugby Union/Rugby League Internationals:
To the end of 1985, 36 Australian Rugby Union Test players have represented Australia after switching to Rugby League. In the post-World War II era, the players have been: John Brass, Mike Cleary, Phil Hawthorne, Bob Honan, Ken Kearney, Stephen Knight, Jim Lisle, Rex Mossop, Michael O'Connor, Ray Price, Geoff Richardson, Kevin Ryan, Arthur Summons and Dick Thornett.

The most famous capture from Rugby Union in the 1980s has been Queenslander Wally Lewis, who toured with the undefeated 1977-78 Australian Schoolboys Rugby Union team to Japan, Great Britain and Europe and switched to Rugby League on his return. After touring with the Kangaroos to Great Britain and France in 1982, Lewis rose to become Australian and Queensland captain in 1984.

Test tries by fullbacks:
Until the 1960s the role of fullbacks was mainly that of a last line of defence. Fullbacks began scoring tries in Rugby League Test matches when more accent was placed on attacking play in 1961.

First fullback (any country) to score a Test try:
Don Parish (Aust.), in the first Test against New Zealand at Carlaw Park, Auckland, NZ, on 1 July 1961.

First fullback to score a Test try in Australia:
Frank Drake (Aust.), in the third Test against Great Britain at the SCG, on 14 July 1962.

First fullback to score a Test try in Great Britain:
Ken Thornett (Aust.), in the first Test against Great Britain at Wembley, London, on 16 October 1963.

Most tries by fullback in a Test:
Three by Gary Jack (Aust.) in the Second Test against France at Carcassonne, France, on 14 December 1986.

Most tries by any player in a Test match:
Four—by John Ribot (Aust.) against Papua New Guinea, 1982 and by Dale Shearer (Aust.) against France at Carcassonne, France, on 14 December 1986. Both Ribot and Shearer played on the wing.

Most points in a Test match:
22 by Michael O'Connor (Aust.) from three tries and five goals in the First Test against Great Britain at Old Trafford, Manchester on 25 October 1986.

AUSTRALIAN TEST MATCH RECORDS 1908-87

Australia v.	Wins	Draws	Losses	Total
Great Britain	47	5	48	100
France	27	2	12	41
New Zealand	40	–	20	60
PNG	2	–	–	2

MOST INDIVIDUAL POINTS IN A TEST MATCH

Player	Tx4	Tx3	G	FG	Total	Versus
Michael O'Connor	3	–	5	–	22	GB, *Manchester 25.10.86*
Les Johns	–	1	9	–	21	South Africa, *Sydney 27.7.63*
Keith Barnes	–	–	10	–	20	France, *Brisbane 2.7.60*
Michael Cronin	–	–	10	–	20	GB, *Brisbane 16.6.79*
Ken Irvine	–	2	7	–	20	France, *Sydney 18.7.64*
Graeme Langlands	–	2	7	–	20	GB, *Swinton 9.11.63*
Mal Meninga	–	1	8	–	19	GB, *Hull 30.10.82*
Noel Pidding	–	1	8	–	19	GB, *Sydney 12.6.54*
Michael Cronin	–	–	9	–	18	New Zealand, *Sydney 22.7.78*
Michael Cronin	–	2	6	–	18	GB, *Sydney 30.6.79*
Graeme Langlands	–	–	9	–	18	GB, *Brisbane 6.6.70*
John McDonald	–	2	6	–	18	New Zealand, *Brisbane 1.7.67*

Australia v.	Wins	Draws	Losses	Total
South Africa	2	–	–	2
Wales*	7	–	–	7
Total	**125**	**7**	**79**	**211**

* No series involved. Single matches between 1911 and 1982.

Ashes v. Great Britain:
33 held (first in 1908). Australia won 14: 1911, 1920, 1950, 1954, 1963, 1966, 1967, 1973, 1974, 1978, 1979, 1982, 1984, 1986.

NSWRL CLUBS 1988

Balmain. Formed 1908. Premiers 1915-16-17-19-20-24-39-44-46-47-69. Nickname–The Tigers. Home ground, Leichhardt Oval.
Brisbane. Formed 1988. Premierships nil. Nickname–The Broncos. Home ground, Lang Park.
Canberra. Formed 1982. Premierships nil. Nickname–The Raiders. Home ground, Seiffert Sports Ground.
Canterbury-Bankstown. Formed 1935. Premiers 1938-42-80-84-85. Nickname–The Bulldogs. Home ground, Belmore Sports Ground.
Cronulla-Sutherland. Formed 1967. Premierships nil. Nickname–The Sharks. Home ground, Endeavour Field.
Eastern Suburbs. Formed 1908. Premiers 1911-12-13-23-35-36-37-40-45-74-75. Nickname–The Roosters. Home ground, Sydney Football Stadium (formerly Sydney Sports Ground).
Gold Coast. Formed 1988. Premierships nil. Nickname–The Giants. Home ground, Seagulls Stadium, Tweed Heads.
Illawarra. Formed 1982. Premierships nil. Nickname–The Steelers. Home ground, Wollongong Showground.
Manly-Warringah. Formed 1947. Premiers 1972-73-76-78-87. Nickname–The Sea Eagles. Home ground, Brookvale Oval.
Newcastle. Formed 1988. Premierships nil. Nickname–The Knights. Home ground, Newcastle International Sports Centre.
North Sydney. Formed 1908. Premiers 1921-22. Nickname–The Bears. Home ground, North Sydney Oval.
Parramatta. Formed 1947. Premiers 1981-82-83-86. Nickname–The Eels. Home ground, Parramatta Stadium.
Penrith. Formed 1967. Premierships nil. Nickname–The Panthers. Home ground, Penrith Park.
South Sydney. Formed 1908. Premiers 1908-09-14-18-25-26-27-28-29-31-32-50-53-54-55-67-68-70-71. Nickname–The Rabbitos. Home ground, Sydney Football Stadium (formerly Sydney Sports Ground).
St George. Formed 1921. Premiers 1941-49-56-57-58-59-60-61-62-63-64-65-66-77-79. Nickname–The Dragons. Home ground, Belmore Sports Ground.
Western Suburbs. Formed 1908. Premiers 1930-34-48-52. Nickname–The Magpies. Home ground, Orana Park.

SYDNEY PREMIERSHIP

Year	Team
1908	South Sydney
1909	South Sydney
1910	Newtown
1911	Eastern Suburbs
1912	Eastern Suburbs
1913	Eastern Suburbs
1914	South Sydney
1915	Balmain
1916	Balmain
1917	Balmain
1918	South Sydney
1919	Balmain
1920	Balmain
1921	North Sydney
1922	North Sydney
1923	Eastern Suburbs
1924	Balmain
1925	South Sydney
1926	South Sydney
1927	South Sydney
1928	South Sydney
1929	South Sydney
1930	Western Suburbs
1931	South Sydney
1932	South Sydney
1933	Newtown
1934	Western Suburbs
1935	Eastern Suburbs
1936	Eastern Suburbs
1937	Eastern Suburbs
1938	Canterbury-Bankstown

Year	Team
1939	Balmain
1940	Eastern Suburbs
1941	St George
1942	Canterbury-Bankstown
1943	Newtown
1944	Balmain
1945	Eastern Suburbs
1946	Balmain
1947	Balmain
1948	Western Suburbs
1949	St George
1950	South Sydney
1951	South Sydney
1952	Western Suburbs
1953	South Sydney
1954	South Sydney
1955	South Sydney
1956	St George
1957	St George
1958	St George
1959	St George
1960	St George
1961	St George
1962	St George
1963	St George
1964	St George
1965	St George*
1966	St George
1967	South Sydney
1968	South Sydney
1969	Balmain
1970	South Sydney
1971	South Sydney
1972	Manly-Warringah
1973	Manly-Warringah
1974	Eastern Suburbs
1975	Eastern Suburbs
1976	Manly-Warringah
1977	St George**
1978	Manly-Warringah**
1979	St George
1980	Canterbury-Bankstown
1981	Parramatta
1982	Parramatta
1983	Parramatta
1984	Canterbury-Bankstown
1985	Canterbury-Bankstown
1986	Parramatta
1987	Manly-Warringah

*Record attendance—78,056.
** Won replay after draw in Grand Final.

BRL CLUBS 1988

Brothers. Entered 1922. Premiers 1926-35-39-42-43-56-58-67-68-87. Nickname—The Leprechauns. Home ground, Corbett Park, Stafford.
Eastern Suburbs. Entered 1918. Premiers 1923-47-50-72-77-78-83. Nickname—The Tigers. Home ground, Langlands Park.
Northern Suburbs. Entered 1933. Premiers 1934-38-40-59-60-61-62-63-64-66-69-80. Nickname—The Devils. Home ground, Bishop Park, Nundah.
Redcliffe. Entered 1960. Premiers 1965. Nickname—The Dolphins. Home ground, Dolphin Oval, Redcliffe.
Southern Suburbs. Entered 1933. Premiers 1945-49-51-53-81-85. Nickname—The Magpies. Home ground, Davies Park, West End.
Valleys. Entered 1909. Premiers 1909-11-14-15-17-18-19-24-31-33-37-41-44-46-55-57-70-71-73-74-79. Nickname—The Diehards. Home ground, Neumann Oval, Albion.
Western Suburbs. Entered 1915. Premiers 1916-20-22-32-36-48-52-54-75-76. Nickname—The Panthers. Home ground, Purtell Park, Bardon.
Wynnum-Manly. Entered 1951. Premiers 1982-84-86. Nickname—The Seagulls. Home ground, Kougari Oval, Wynnum.

BRISBANE PREMIERSHIP

Year	Team
1909	Valleys
1910	Ipswich
1911	Valleys
1912	Natives
1913	West End
1914	Valleys
1915	Valleys
1916	Western Suburbs
1917	Valleys
1918	Valleys
1919	Valleys
1920	Western Suburbs
1921	Carltons
1922	Western Suburbs*
1923	Coorparoo
1924	Valleys
1925	Carltons
1926	Brothers
1927	Grammars
1928	University
1929	University
1930	Carltons

Year	Team
1931	Valleys
1932	Western Suburbs
1933	Valleys
1934	Northern Suburbs
1935	Brothers
1936	Western Suburbs
1937	Valleys
1938	Northern Suburbs
1939	Brothers
1940	Northern Suburbs
1941	Valleys
1942	Brothers
1943	Brothers
1944	Valleys
1945	Southern Suburbs
1946	Valleys
1947	Eastern Suburbs
1948	Western Suburbs
1949	Southern Suburbs
1950	Eastern Suburbs
1951	Southern Suburbs
1952	Western Suburbs
1953	Southern Suburbs
1954	Western Suburbs
1955	Valleys
1956	Brothers
1957	Valleys
1958	Brothers
1959	Northern Suburbs
1960	Northern Suburbs
1961	Northern Suburbs
1962	Northern Suburbs
1963	Northern Suburbs
1964	Northern Suburbs
1965	Redcliffe
1966	Northern Suburbs
1967	Brothers
1968	Brothers
1969	Northern Suburbs
1970	Valleys
1971	Valleys
1972	Eastern Suburbs
1973	Valleys
1974	Valleys
1975	Western Suburbs
1976	Western Suburbs
1977	Eastern Suburbs
1978	Eastern Suburbs
1979	Valleys
1980	Northern Suburbs
1981	Southern Suburbs
1982	Wynnum-Manly
1983	Eastern Suburbs
1984	Wynnum-Manly
1985	Southern Suburbs
1986	Wynnum-Manly
1987	Brothers

* First all-Brisbane premiership.

PLAYER OF THE YEAR—NSW

The official award to the best and fairest player in the Sydney premiership competition is the Rothmans Medal inaugurated in 1968. Prior to that year the nearest thing to an official award was the nomination by the late Ernie Christensen, editor of the official *NSW Rugby League Yearbook*. Christensen made his first nomination in 1946.

Year	Player
1946	Lionel Cooper (Eastern Suburbs)
1947	Bob Lulham (Balmain)
1948	Len Smith (Newtown)
1949	Clive Churchill (South Sydney)
1950	Clive Churchill (South Sydney)
1951	Keith Holman (Western Suburbs)
1952	Clive Churchill (South Sydney)
1953	Jack Rayner (South Sydney)
1954	Roy Bull (Manly-Warringah)
1955	Ken Kearney (St George)
1956	Keith Holman (Western Suburbs)
1957	Norm Provan (St George)
1958	Keith Holman (Western Suburbs)
1959	Reg Gasnier (St George)
1960	John Raper (St George)
1961	Reg Gasnier (St George)
1962	Arthur Summons (Western Suburbs)
1963	Ian Walsh (St George)
1964	Reg Gasnier and John Raper (St George) tie

Year	Team
1965	Ken Thornett (Parramatta)
1966	Billy Smith (St George)
1967	Les Johns (Canterbury-Bankstown)
*1968	Terry Hughes (Cronulla-Sutherland)
1969	Denis Pittard (South Sydney)
1970	Kevin Junee (Eastern Suburbs)
1971	Denis Pittard (South Sydney)
1972	Tom Raudonikis (Western Suburbs)
1973	Ken Maddison (Cronulla-Sutherland)
1974	Graham Eadie (Manly-Warringah)
1975	Steve Rogers (Cronulla-Sutherland)
1976	Ray Higgs (Parramatta)
1977	Mick Cronin (Parramatta)
1978	Mick Cronin (Parramatta)
1979	Ray Price (Parramatta)
1980	Geoff Bugden (Newtown)
1981	Kevin Hastings (Eastern Suburbs)
1982	Greg Brentnall (Canterbury-Bankstown)
1983	Mike Eden (Eastern Suburbs)
1984	Terry Lamb (Canterbury-Bankstown)
1985	Wayne Pearce (Balmain)
1986	Mal Cochrane (Manly-Warringah)
1987	Peter Sterling (Parramatta)

*(The player of the year from 1968 onwards has been awarded the Rothmans Medal. The medal format is based on the VFL's Brownlow Medal, with first grade referees allocating points on a 3-2-1 basis after every premiership match.)

PLAYER OF THE YEAR— QUEENSLAND

Though many awards have been made by newspapers and radio stations from 1946, none has been given even partial official recognition by either the Queensland Rugby League or the Brisbane Rugby League. The first award officially approved by the BRL was the Rothmans Medal introduced in 1968. Winners have been:

Year	Player
1968	Wayne Head (Southern Suburbs)
1969	John Brown (Northern Suburbs)
1970	Graeme Atherton (Southern Suburbs)
1971	Len Brunner (Wynnum-Manly)
1972	Marty Scanlan (Valleys)
1973	Jim Eales (Eastern Suburbs)
1974	Jeff Fyffe (Eastern Suburbs)
1975	Steve Calder (Northern Suburbs)
1976	Daryl Brohman (Northern Suburbs)
1977	Alan Currie (Eastern Suburbs)
1978	Ian Pearce (Redcliffe)
1979	Neville Draper (Northern Suburbs)
1980	Tony Obst (Redcliffe)
1981	Chris Phelan (Southern Suburbs)
1982	Tony Currie (Western Suburbs)
1983	Trevor Paterson (Eastern Suburbs)
1984	Cavill Heigh (Eastern Suburbs)
1985	Ian French (Wynnum-Manly)
1986	Bryan Niebling (Redcliffe)*
1987	Gene Miles (Wynnum-Manly))

*On countback from Scott Tronc (Southern Suburbs)

RUGBY UNION

BEGINNINGS IN AUSTRALIA
Rugby of a sort was played in Sydney not long after William Webb Ellis made history by picking up the ball and running at Rugby School, England, in 1823. The first matches in Australia, like the English matches, were rough and tumble affairs with few rules, played almost exclusively by soldiers stationed at or near Victoria Barracks.

As of 1984-85, Australia was recognised as one of the top three Rugby nations in the world, a position the country has occasionally held in the long history of the game. It is a remarkable achievement, considering that the game is still an amateur one and so many top internationals have been lured to the professional Rugby League code, especially in post World War II years. Since 1948, players of the calibre of Rex Mossop, Trevor Allan, John Brass, Mike Cleary, Phil Hawthorne, Bob Honan, Ken Kearney, Stephen Knight, Jim Lisle, John McLean, Ray Price, Geoff Richardson, Kevin Ryan, Arthur Summons, Dick Thornett and Michael O'Connor have transferred, as have dozens more — among them Ken Wright, Tony Melrose, Don Price, George Reubner, Phil Smith, Alan Cardy, Jim Hindmarsh, Dave Shepherd and Bob Sullivan. The vast majority became dual internationals by playing Rugby League for Australia, and Kearney, Hawthorne and Summons all captained Australia at Rugby League.

Wally Lewis of Brisbane, a recruit from the 1977-78 Australian Schoolboys Rugby Union team which toured overseas, has also captained Australia at Rugby League.

First club:
Sydney University, established in 1864. Teams from the University played matches against teams from visiting British warships in 1864-65. The matches (often between teams of up to 25 players) were so brutal that Eldred Harmer, a prominent member of the NSW Parliament, introduced a bill to stamp out the game. Harmer's motion lapsed for want of a seconder.

First 'serious' club:
The Wallaroo Club, formed in 1870 in Sydney by Montague Arnold, a NSW pastoralist, his brother Richard, Septimus Stephen, Tom Brown and George Deas-Thompson.

First controlling body:
The Southern Rugby Football Union, formed in June 1874. The Union controlled organised matches between the Wallaroo, The King's School, Newington College, Goulburn, Waratah, Balmain, North Shore, Sydney University and Camden College teams.

First Rugby in Queensland:
Rugby commenced in Queensland in 1880, at a time when Sydney boasted more than 100 clubs.

First interstate match:
In 1882, when Queensland, captained by Jim Brodie, played NSW, captained by A. J. Hickson, at the Association Ground (now the SCG). Richard Arnold refereed the game, which was won by NSW 28-4. A second match was played shortly after and NSW won 18-0.

First Australian team overseas:
In 1882 a NSW side led by Ted Raper of Sydney University made a short tour of New Zealand. Only 16 players travelled to New Zealand and when one became ill and returned home, NSW was left with a bare playing strength of 15 men and no reserves. Despite this disadvantage, NSW won four matches and lost three.

First overseas team in Australia:
In 1884, when New Zealand, captained by W. V. Milton of Canterbury, toured NSW and won all eight matches.

First British Isles team in Australia:
In 1888. The team was not an official touring side and ended up playing more matches of Australian Rules (then known

as Victorian Rules) than Rugby. The side won 14 out of 16 Rugby matches but, remarkably, could not defeat two school teams—The King's School and Sydney Grammar School. Grammar fielded 16 men, among them several old boys who were current first grade players, and held the tourists to a 3-3 draw. The King's School, with seven pupils and masters and eight old boys, among them C. C. G. Wade, later Sir Charles Wade, Premier of NSW and Chief Justice, held the British Isles to a 10-10 draw.

First NSW 'international' win:
In 1894, when NSW defeated New Zealand at Christchurch, NZ, 8-6. Until 1899 and from 1919 to 1928 inclusive, New Zealand gave Test status to matches against NSW, claiming this team to be the best available side in Australia. Australian bodies have never recognised these matches as Tests.

First Test played by Australia:
On 24 June 1899, when Australia defeated the British Isles 13-3 at the SCG. Two more Tests played on the tour were both won by the British Isles.

First overseas tour by Australia:
In 1908-09, when a side captained by Dr H. Moran of Newcastle, NSW, toured the UK and won 25 out of 31 matches.

Olympic success:
One of the overseas tour matches resulted in a win in the Olympic Games competition at London. Australia defeated UK County champions Cornwall 32-3 and won a 'gold medal' (no medals were awarded—all 15 Australian players received inscribed certificates).

Most international appearances:
50 tests against all countries, by Simon Poidevin (NSW). Australia, unlike the International Rugby Board, grants Test status to matches against Fiji, Tonga, Japan, Argentina, Italy and the United States. Peter Johnson, who played 42 Tests, still holds the record for the most Tests against Board-recognised countries (England, Ireland, Scotland, Wales, the British Isles, France, New Zealand, and south Africa) of 39, a total equalled by New Zealand-born Greg Davis (1939-79) who represented Australia 1963-72.

Only Australian team to win all four Tests on a tour of the UK:
The 1984 team captained by Andrew Slack (Qld). During the tour, former Australian captain Mark Ella became the first Australian to score a try in each of the Tests (v. England, Ireland, Scotland and Wales).

Most individual Test points:
263, by Paul McLean (Qld) in 30 Tests between 1974 and 1982.

Most individual points in a Test:
23 by Michael Lynagh (Qld) against Canada in 1985 and 21 against Scotland in 1984; 21 by Paul McLean (Qld) against Japan in 1975 and Scotland in 1982; and 21 by David Knox (NSW) against Fiji in 1985.

Most tries in a Test:
Four each by Greg Cornelsen (NSW) against New Zealand in 1978 and David Campese (ACT) against the USA in 1983.

STATE RECORDS
First Rugby played in each State (Organised club competition):
New South Wales 1870; Queensland 1880; Western Australia 1881; Victoria 1889; South Australia 1932; Tasmania 1956.

Most points in a senior club season:
302, by Rod Cann of the Perth (WA) club in 23 matches in 1969. Cann scored 18 tries and kicked 43 goals, 53 penalty goals and 1 field goal.

FIRST TEST AGAINST OVERSEAS TEAMS

Australia v.	Date	Venue	Result
British Isles	24.6.1899	Sydney	Australia won 13-3
New Zealand	15.8.1903	Sydney	New Zealand won 22-3
Wales	12.12.1908	Cardiff, Wales	Wales won 9-6
England	9.1.1909	Blackheath, UK	Australia won 9-3
New Zealand Maoris	9.9.1931	Palmerston North, NZ	Australia won 14-3
South Africa	8.7.1933	Cape Town, South Africa	South Africa won 17-3
Scotland	24.11.1947	Murrayfield, Scotland	Australia won 16-7
Ireland	6.12.1947	Dublin, Ireland	Australia won 16-3
France	11.1.1948	Paris, France	France won 13-6
Fiji	26.7.1952	Sydney	Australia won 15-9
Tonga	23.6.1973	Sydney	Australia won 30-12
Japan	2.8.1975	Sydney	Australia won 37-7
USA	31.1.1976	Anaheim, USA	Australia won 24-12
Argentina	27.10.1979	Buenos Aires, Argentina	Argentina won 24-13
Italy	22.10.1983	Padova, Italy	Australia won 29-7
Canada	15.6.1985	Sydney	Australia won 59-3

Note: Australia defeated 'USA' on 16 November 1912 at Berkeley, California, by 12-8. The Australian Rugby Union has never recognised this match as an official Test.

Most first grade matches:
346, by Tony Miller of the Manly Club (NSW). Drummoyne (NSW) player Ken Williams holds the record for the most matches played in all grades. On 22 May 1982 he played his 500th match for the club, at the age of 44.

Refereed most first grade matches:
Dr Roger Vanderfield (NSW) with 302. He retired at the end of the 1976 season (his 25th as a senior referee) and in his last season became the first referee to have controlled 300 first-grade games.

Most club premiership wins:
30, by the University Club (NSW), including one tied in 1901.

State sides to defeat touring international teams:
New South Wales has defeated national teams representing New Zealand, British Isles, New Zealand Maoris, South Africa, Fiji, Ireland, Scotland, Tonga, Japan and Canada.
Queensland has defeated New Zealand, British Isles, New Zealand Maoris, Fiji, Maoris to Central West of NSW (1958); British Isles to Sydney (1899) and Scotland, Tonga, Japan, Italy and the USA.
ACT has defeated Wales, Tonga, Italy and Argentina.
Victoria has defeated Tonga.
Western Australia has defeated Canada.
Note: New Zealand has also lost to a NSW Second XV (1925); New Zealand Western Districts of NSW (1908); Fiji to Southern Harbour of Sydney (1961) and Southern NSW (1961); England to NSW Country (1975); Tonga to NSW Country (1973); Japan to NSW Country (1975); and Canada to NSW Country (1985).

AUSTRALIA'S TEST RECORD AGAINST OVERSEAS TEAMS

Team	Played	Won	Lost	Drawn
British Isles	14	2	12	—
England	12	7	5	—

Team	Played	Won	Lost	Drawn
Ireland	11	5	6	–
Scotland	11	4	7	–
Wales	12	5	7	–
France	16	5	9	2
New Zealand	85	22	58	5
South Africa	28	7	21	–
Fiji	17	14	2	1
Japan	2	2	–	–
Tonga	2	1	1	–
Argentina	9	4	4	1
United States	2	2	–	–
Italy	1	1	–	–
NZ Maoris	9	4	3	2
Canada	2	2	–	–
Totals	**233**	**87**	**137**	**11**

RECORDS GENERAL
Australian attendance record:
52,000, for New South Wales v. the New Zealand All Blacks at the SCG in 1907.

Test attendance record:
48,698, for Australia v. New Zealand at the SCG in 1980.

SAILBOARDING

BEGINNINGS IN AUSTRALIA
Sailboarding – or windsurfing as it is also known – is one of the more recent sports introduced into Australia. The first equipment was imported in 1976 from California, where the sport originated in 1967. Under a licensing agreement with American manufacturers, two young Sydney enthusiasts, Roger Dulhunty and Greg Kelly, began manufacturing boards in 1977 using the brand name Windsurfer. From small sales of some 400 sailboards in 1976, the Australian manufacture and sales of equipment in the mid-1980s has now reached the mini-industry level.

Equipment:
Sailboards are made from polystyrene foam covered by either Conben fibre, Kevlar or S-glass. Sails are made from either mylar or kevlar, both high-strength materials with a very low stretch quality.

First Australian championships:
Held in 1977 at Belmont, NSW. A field of 89 competitors contested five different titles, including one for women.

First Australian world champion:
1979-80 Australian heavyweight class titleholder Grant Long of NSW, who won the heavyweight competition at the 1980 world titles at Freeport in the Bahamas.

Most successful woman competitor:
Sarah Kenny of Sydney, NSW, who won the Australian Windsurfer Pentathlon Championship in 1982, '83, '84 and '85,

was second in the national Funboard title in 1985, fourth in the World Windsurfer Championship in 1985, won the Western Hemisphere Windsurfer Championship in 1984 and the World University Windsurfer Championship in Malta in the same year.

Successful Australian male competitors at international level:
Arthur Brett, who was judged overall winner of the 1984 Canadian Windsurfer Regatta, finished third in the 1984 Dufor Wing World Championship and second in the 1985 World Marathon Championship. Bruce Wylie, who won the Olympic Boardsailing Exhibition at Los Angeles in 1984, is ranked the world's No. 1 Windsurfer racer. Other past and present stars include Robert Wilmot, Greg Butchard, Lachlan Gilbert, Greg Hyde, Grant Long, Tom Luedecke, Stuart Gilbert, Greg Johns, Luke Hargraves and Paul Ivshenko.

General competitions:
Sailboarding competitions are held under strict international rules and include weight divisions from lightweight to heavyweight, a marathon, surf slalom racing, course racing, Windsurfer racing and open racing (any type of board and any type of sail).

Professional competitions:
In recent years competition sponsorship has risen dramatically and the 1985 Sony Surflite event, held at Long Reef Beach, Sydney, was the world's richest sailboarding competition at the time. The Peter Jackson Bluewater Classic, held in Queensland, Western Australia, South Australia, Victoria and New South Wales from January to March 1986, carried $60,000 prize money.

SAILING AND YACHTING

BEGINNINGS IN AUSTRALIA
Sailing and (later) yachting in blue water began in Australia with friendly competitions on harbours and rivers. From the 1920s onwards, pictorial evidence exists of skiffs equipped with sails in such close formation as to suggest some form of competition. The first serious competition appears to have taken place in Tasmania on the Derwent River in 1827. Little evidence exists of serious competition in Sydney until 1837, when the Anniversary Regatta was held on the harbour. The main race at the Regatta was won by James Milson after whom Sydney's harbourside suburb of Milsons Point is named. The first yacht clubs were established in Sydney and Melbourne during the 1830s and the first 'Royal' club was the Royal Sydney Yacht Squadron (originally the Australian Yacht Squadron), inaugurated in 1863.

First attempt to design a serious racing yacht:
In 1858 Richard Hayes Hartnett drew up plans for a yacht which was built in Sydney by Dan Sheehy and named *Australians*. The timber used came from the Aberdeen clipper *Catherine Anderson*

which had been wrecked on Middle Head, Sydney Harbour, in 1857. Hartnett claimed his design was inspired by the shape of a mackerel and the hull was so revolutionary that cynics named it 'Beaky' and 'Soda Water Bottle'. *Australians* proved to be almost unbeatable and won races for the next 27 years. She entered Australia's first recorded (1861) offshore race (Sydney Harbour to Botany Bay and return) and, after spread-eagling the field to Botany Bay, retired with damaged rigging.

Australian racing classes:
Australia has given the sailing world a long list of internationally accepted classes and designs. They include 18-footers, 16-footers, Sabots, Vee Jays (a design created for junior members of the Vaucluse club in Sydney—hence VJs), Vee Ess's, Contenders, Moths, Gwen 12s, and a range of catamarans, one of which was selected by the International Yacht Racing Union as the international design for A Class Catamaran racing.

SYDNEY-HOBART OCEAN RACE
First race planned as a pleasure cruise:
In 1945 the first Sydney-Hobart race, now a world-famous ocean classic, was originally planned by the Cruising Yacht Club of Australia as a pleasure cruise. However, on the recommendation of committeeman Commander John Illingworth the 'cruise' became a serious race and started, as have all subsequent races, on Boxing Day. The field for the inaugural race was a record low of nine yachts and the race line and handicap honours were won by Commander Illingworth's *Rani* in 6 days, 14 hrs 22 mins (corrected time on handicap was 4 days 9 hrs 38 mins).

By 1980 only three other boats had achieved the feat of winning both line and handicap honours—R. Turner's *American Eagle* in 1972, J. B. Kilroy's *Kialoa* in 1977 and the syndicate-owned *New Zealand*, skippered by Peter Blake, in 1980.

First hat-trick:
Freya won three years in succession (1963, '64, '65) and the owners, well-known Sydney boat-builders Trygve and Magnus Halvorsen, continued to compile one of the greatest records in the history of the race.

Most famous winning skipper:
The Hon. Edward Heath, later Prime Minister of England, took race and handicap honours with *Morning Cloud* in 1969.

Race tragedies:
In 1984 veteran crewman Wal Russell was washed overboard in huge seas from *Yahoo II* on the second day of the race. Conditions were the worst recorded in the history of the race and more than half the fleet had retired by the third day. The worst previous conditions were encountered in 1977, when 56 yachts from a record field of 131 retired. The only other tragedy linked to the race is the disappearance of the 37-foot Tasmanian yacht *Charleston* en route from Hobart to Sydney for the start of the 1979 event. *Charleston* was skippered by Charles Davies and had a crew of four. No trace was ever found of yacht or crew.

Safety precautions for the 630 nautical miles (1,014 km) race are among the most stringent in the world.

SYDNEY TO HOBART RACE RESULTS (see over)
Times are in days, hours, minutes and seconds to 1974 and in days, hours, minutes and decimals of minutes from 1975. The outright winner is the yacht with the fastest corrected time (after deduction of handicap from elapsed time).

SYDNEY TO HOBART RACE RESULTS

Year	Starters	Handicap	Owner/Skipper	Elapsed Time
1945	9	Rani	J. Illingworth	6.14.22
1946	19	Christina	J. R. Bull	6.18.51.15
1947	28	Westward	G. D. Gibson	5.13.19.04
1948	18	Westward	G. D. Gibson	4.14.17.32
1949	15	Trade Winds	M. E. Davey	5.11.15.34
1950	16	Nerida	C. P. Haselgrove	5.06.15.49
1951	14	Struen Marie	T. Williamson	4.03.38.35
1952	17	Ingrid	J. S. Taylor	6.17.07.22
1953	23	Ripple	R. C. Hobson	5.12.58.36
1954	17	Solveig	T.& M. Halvorsen	5.07.38.56
1955	17	Moonbi	H. S. Evans	5.01.28.24
1956	28	Solo	V. Meyer	4.05.03.33
1957	20	Anitra V	T. & M. Halvorsen	4.06.38.30
1958	22	Siandra	G. P. Newland	5.10.02.37
1959	30	Cherana	R. T. Williams	5.02.13.53
1960	32	Siandra	G. P. Newland	5.00.59.03
1961	35	Rival	A. Burgin/N. Rundle	4.17.28.21
1962	42	Solo	V. Meyer	3.04.29.15
1963	44	Freya	T. & M. Halvorsen	4.15.17.03
1964	37	Freya	T. & M. Halvorsen	4.01.17.35
1965	49	Freya	T. & M. Halvorsen	4.06.23.32
1966	44	Cadence	H. S. Mason	5.13.25.24
1967	67	Rainbow II	C. Bouzaid	4.19.59.38
1968	67	Koomooloo	D. O'Neil	4.10.26.52
1969	79	Morning Cloud	E. Heath**	4.05.59.53
1970	61	Pacha	R. Crichton-Brown***	3.17.41.18
1971	61	Pathfinder	B. Wilson	4.00.02.04
1972	79	American Eagle	R. Turner	3.04.42.39
1973	90	Ceil III	W. Turnbull	3.12.05.34
1974	63	Love and War	P. Kurts	4.04.27.33
1975	102	Rampage	P. Packer	3.04.43.03
1976	85	Piccolo	J. Pickles	4.05.30.15
1977	131	Kialoa	J. B. Kilroy	3.10.14.09
1978	97	Love and War	P. Kurts	4.04.45.72
1979	147	Bumblebee IV	J. Kahlbetzer	3.01.45.87
1980	102	New Zealand	P. Blake	2.18.45.68
1981	159	Zeus II	J. Dunstan	5.13.48.41
1982	118	Scallywag	R. Johnston	3.13.56.44
1983	171	Challenge	L. Abrahams	3.12.37.28
1984++	152	Indian Pacific	J. Eyles/G. Heuchmer	4.04.03.49
1985	179	No winner****		
1986	123	Ex Tension	A. Dunn	3.23.22.00
1987	142	Sovereign	D. Kellett	2.21.58.08

* Formerly *Morna*.
** The Honourable Edward Heath, later Prime Minister of Great Britain.
*** Later Sir Robert Crichton-Brown.

Corrected Time	Line Honours	Skipper	Elapsed Time
4.09.38	Rani		
4.11.53.27	Morna	C. Plowman	5.02.53.33
4.00.24.56	Morna	C. Plowman	5.03.03.54
3.07.45.48	Morna	C. Plowman	4.05.01.21
3.23.39.43	Waltzing Matilda	P. Davenport	5.10.33.10
2.30.17.13	Margaret Rintoul	A. W. Edwards	5.05.28.35
2.19.48.26	Margaret Rintoul	A. W. Edwards	4.02.29.01
4.09.56.18	Nocturne	J. R. Bull	6.02.34.47
3.16.12.12	Solveig	T. & M. Halvorsen	5.07.12.50
3.17.58.01	Kurrewa IV*	F. & J. Livingston	5.06.09.47
3.09.21.05	Even	F. J. Palmer	4.18.13.14
3.08.33.52	Kurrewa IV	F. & J. Livingston	4.04.31.14
3.00.55.37	Kurrewa IV	F. & J. Livingston	3.18.30.39
3.13.46.35	Solo	V. Meyer	5.02.32.52
3.08.33.02	Solo	V. Meyer	4.13.33.12
3.07.48.04	Kurrewa IV	F. & J. Livingston	4.08.11.15
3.03.57.31	Astor	P. R. Warner	4.04.42.11
2.12.45.14	Ondine	S. A. Long	3.03.46.16
3.06.03.17	Astor	P. R. Warner	4.10.53.00
3.05.58.14	Astor	P. R. Warner	3.20.05.05
3.10.03.26	Stormvogel	C. Bruynzeel	3.20.30.09
4.02.46.24	Fidelis	J. V. Davern	4.08.39.43
3.16.39.15	Pen-Duick II	E. Tabarly	4.04.10.31
3.13.38.52	Ondine II	S. A. Long	4.03.20.02
3.04.25.57	Crusade	M. Aitken	3.15.07.40
3.10.07.39	Buccaneer	T. E. Clark	3.14.06.12
3.03.14.34	Kialoa II	J. B. Kilroy	3.12.46.21
3.02.15.49	American Eagle		
2.17.28.28	Helsal	A. Fisher	3.01.32.9
3.13.25.04	Ondine	S. A. Long	3.13.51.93
2.13.16.56	Kialoa +	J. B. Kilroy	2.14.36.56
3.07.45.07	Ballyhoo	J. Rooklyn	3.07.59.26
3.13.58.10	Kialoa		
3.12.13.00	Apollo	J. Rooklyn	4.02.23.40
3.06.23.08	Bumblebee IV		
2.21.13.48	New Zealand		
3.19.25.59	Vengeance	B. Lewis	3.22.30.00
2.19.19.16	Condor of Bermuda	R. A. Bell	3.00.59.17
2.23.07.42	Condor	R. A. Bell	3.00.50.29
3.07.45.03	New Zealand	P. Blake	3.11.21.21
	Apollo	W. Rooklyn	3.4.32.28
3.01.14.30	Condor	R. Bell	2.23.26.25
3.01.58.41	Sovereign		

**** The Cruising Yacht Club of Australia was unable to award any yacht with outright victory following protests over collisions at the start. The matter may be subject to an international appeal.
+ Race record.
++ Record number of retirements due to storm—106.

AMERICA'S CUP

The America's Cup had its beginning on 22 August 1851 when John Cox Stevens sailed his 102 foot yacht, *America*, to Cowes on the Isle of Wight and challenged skippers from the Royal Yacht Squadron to a 53 mile race around the island. *America* won easily and Stevens received a trophy known as the Hundred Guinea Cup (because that was the price charged by Garrard, the London jeweller, to make it). Stevens later handed the trophy to the New York Yacht Club with instructions for it to become a perpetual challenge cup for competition against overseas yacht clubs. The first challenge came in 1870 from Britain's James Ashbury and his schooner *Cambria*.

AUSTRALIA AND THE AMERICA'S CUP

One of the greatest Australian sporting victories in modern times was achieved on 26 September 1983, when Australia wrested the America's Cup from the USA.

Australia II, skippered by John Bertrand, defeated the American entry, *Liberty*, in the deciding race at Newport, USA, to end 132 years of American domination.

Australia II was designed by Ben Lexcen and sported the ultimate yachting 'secret weapon' – a revolutionary winged keel. The challenge was masterminded by Western Australian business magnate Alan Bond, who had mounted three previous challenges – in 1974, '77 and '80 with *Southern Cross* (1974) and *Australia*.

Prior to the historic win in 1983, Australian challenges had been made in 1962 (*Gretel*), 1967 (*Dame Pattie*), 1970 (*Gretel II*), and Bond's challenges of 1974, '77 and '80. During that period, Australian yachts had won only three races. *Gretel* lost to *Weatherly* 1–4, *Dame Pattie* lost to *Intrepid* 0–4, *Gretel II* lost to *Intrepid* 1–4, *Southern Cross* lost to *Courageous* 0–4, *Australia* lost to *Courageous* 0–4 and then lost to *Freedom* 1–4.

In the 1983 challenge, the American defender, *Liberty*, won the first race after the initial attempt to sail the race was called off by the American committee in controversial circumstances, with *Australia II* holding a distinct advantage as the two yachts approached the starting line.

Liberty won the second race, again in controversial circumstances, the jury dismissing an Australian protest that *Australia II* had been forced to alter course to avoid a collision. USA 2 – Australia 0.

Australia II was a clear (3 mins 14 secs) winner in the third race. USA 2 – Australia 1.

Liberty won the fourth race after *Australia II* made a poor start and was out-manoeuvred. USA 3 – Australia 1. At this stage, *Liberty* needed to win only one more race to retain the Cup.

Australia II lost the start, but won the race in the fifth meeting, crossing the line 1 min 47 secs ahead. USA 3 – Australia 2.

The sixth race was a must-win situation for Australia and *Australia II*. Skipper John Bertrand again lost the start, but out-sailed American skipper Dennis Conner to win the race and tie the series, forcing the Americans into an unprecedented seventh race.

Australia II duly won the seventh and deciding race.

Australia lost in the first defence of the Cup off Fremantle, WA, in 1987. The United States' challenger, *Stars and Stripes*, skippered by Dennis Conner, defeated *Kookaburra*, skippered by Iain Murray 4–0. The Alan Bond syndicate entry, *Australia III*, was eliminated in the finals of the preliminary races to decide the defending yacht.

AUSTRALIA AND THE ADMIRAL'S CUP
First Australian challenge:

In 1965, when four yachts – *Camille*, *Caprice of Huon*, *Freya* and *Lorita Marie* (reserve) – entered for the tough series of races held every two years on the south coast of England. Four races are incorporated in the Admiral's Cup, the longest being the 605 nautical mile (874 km) Fastnet Race. *Caprice of Huon* won the 225 mile (362 km) Channel Race, the 30 mile (48.3 km) Britannia Cup Race around the Solent, a third Solent race for the New York Challenge Cup and finished fourth in the Fastnet, with *Camille* third and *Freya* sixth in the Fastnet. Great Britain was overall team winner from Australia.

America's Cup results:

Year	Defender	Challenger	Result
1870	Magic	Cambria (GB)	USA 1-0
1871	Columbia/Sappho*	Livonia (GB)	USA 4-1
1876	Madelaine	Countess of Dufferin (Canada)	USA 2-0
1881	Mischief	Atalanta (Canada)	USA 2-0
1885	Puritan	Genesta (GB)	USA 2-0
1886	Mayflower	Galatea (GB)	USA 2-0
1887	Volunteer	Thistle (GB)	USA 2-0
1893	Vigilant	Valkyrie II (GB)	USA 3-0
1895	Defender	Valkyrie III (GB)	USA 3-0
1899	Columbia	Shamrock I (GB)	USA 3-0
1901	Columbia	Shamrock II (GB)	USA 3-0
1903	Reliance	Shamrock III (GB)	USA 3-0
1920	Resolute	Shamrock IV (GB)	USA 3-2
1930	Enterprise	Shamrock V (GB)	USA 4-0
1934	Rainbow	Endeavour (GB)	USA 4-2
1937	Ranger	Endeavour II (GB)	USA 4-0
1958	Columbia	Sceptre (GB)	USA 4-0
1962	Weatherly	**Gretel (Australia)**	USA 4-1
1964	Constellation	Sovereign (GB)	USA 4-0
1967	Intrepid	**Dame Pattie (Australia)**	USA 4-0
1970	Intrepid	**Gretel II (Australia)**	USA 4-1
1974	Courageous	**Southern Cross (Australia)**	USA 4-0
1977	Courageous	**Australia (Australia)**	USA 4-0
1980	Freedom	**Australia (Australia)**	USA 4-1
1983	Liberty	**Australia II (Australia)**	Aust. 4-3
1987**	**Kookaburra**	Stars and Stripes (USA)	USA 4-0

* *Columbia* won the first two races, but after *Livonia* won the third, the NYYC replaced *Columbia* with *Sappho*, which won the next two racese. This prompted *Livonia*'s skipper John Ashbury to return home complaining about the 'cunning, unfair and unsportsmanlike proceedings'.

** Sailed for the first time outside of the United States (off Fremantle, Western Australia).

First Australian success:
In 1967, when Australian yachts *Balandra*, *Mercedes II* and *Caprice of Huon* amassed sufficient points to win from Great Britain and the USA.

Australia's second win:
In 1979, the year in which the Fastnet race was run in mountainous seas. Fifteen yachtsmen lost their lives when an unexpected storm hit the fleet. Australia's entries were *Ragamuffin*, *Police Car* and *Impetuous*.

AUSTRALIA AT THE OLYMPICS

First Australian appearance:
In 1948, when Jock Sturrock and crewman L. Fenton Jnr finished seventh in the Star class and Bob French (Vic.) was 20th in the 12 footer (3.6 m) Firefly class. (Yachting was first held at the Olympic Games at Paris in 1900.)

First Australian medals:
At the 1956 Melbourne Games, when Rolly Tasker and John Scott won a silver medal in the 12 m class but were deprived

of a gold medal when disqualified after a French protest in the final heat. At the same Games Jock Sturrock, Douglas Buxton and Devereaux Mytton won a bronze medal in the 5.5 m class.

First Olympic gold medal:
At the 1964 Tokyo Games, when veteran Bill Northam skippered to victory in the 5.5 m class with crewmen Peter O'Donnell and James Sargeant.

18-footer racing:
18-footers first appeared on Sydney Harbour in the summer of 1894 and instantly attracted interest. As the class developed, designers aimed at creating hulls and masts capable of carrying enormous areas of sail and while the boats were incredibly fast, they were also prone to capsizing in high winds. As the class developed further, crews were whittled down from the original 12 or more to three, and more accent was placed on reducing weight and streamlining hulls.

First official Australian 18-footer champion:
Bill Dunn (NSW), who skippered *Kismet* at Sydney in 1912-13. (Claims concerning 'championship wins' go back to the last century.)

First 'World Championship' for 18-footers:
In 1938, in Sydney, when the Secretary of the NSW 18-Footer Sailing League, James J. Giltinan (one of the founders of Rugby League in Australia), issued invitations throughout the world. Acceptances (later withdrawn) were received from England, the USA and Hong Kong, and the first 'world title' (a championship few take seriously) was contested by four New Zealand and 23 Australian boats. The winner was *Taree*, skippered by Bert Swinbourne of NSW. The event drew huge crowds of spectators on shore and in chartered ferries, because it coincided with Sydney's 150th anniversary.

Most successful 18-footer skippers:
Bob Holmes and Iain Murray of NSW who dominated 'World' and Australian Championships from 1965 to 1982.

SOCCER

BEGINNINGS IN AUSTRALIA
Historians have never been able accurately to establish when football (or soccer as it is commonly known throughout Australia) was first played in the Colony. The game, as it is known today, was widely played in the UK in the mid-1850s and the Football Association was formed in 1863. It is therefore logical to assume that new settlers brought the game to Australia from that year onwards and that versions of the game would have been played in Australia in 1864 or 1865. For some unaccountable reason, the origin of Australian soccer is officially dated many years later.

Acknowledged first recorded game:
On 14 August 1880, when a team called the Wanderers, organised by two resident English schoolteachers, played The King's School at Parramatta, NSW, and won 5-0. The date (which must be many years too late), is officially recognised, by the Australian and NSW Soccer Federations, as the start of the code in Australia.

First club competitions and controlling body in NSW:
In 1882 a body called the South British Football Soccer Association was formed in Sydney and a loose competition was

established between clubs from Sydney, the NSW South Coast and the Greater Newcastle area.

First interstate matches:
In 1883, when NSW sent an official team to Victoria and played that State at Melbourne in a 2-2 draw. A second Victorian side was selected for a further match and the two teams drew 0-0. Queensland sent a team to Sydney in 1890 and won two games against two different NSW sides.

First international match:
In 1922, when an Australian team toured New Zealand, lost the first Test 1-3, drew the second 1-1 and lost the third 1-3. Earlier, in 1904, a NSW team toured New Zealand and in one match played a 3-3 draw with the New Zealand 'national' side.

First national controlling body:
The Football Association (Australia) was formed on 12 October 1923. It was based in Sydney and all States were affiliated with it.

First English team to come to Australia:
In 1925. The tourists played and won 26 matches including five Tests. England won the inaugural Test at Brisbane 5-1 and the others 2-1 (at Sydney), 8-2 (at Maitland, NSW), 5-0 (at Sydney) and 2-0 (at Melbourne).

Council of the English Football Association assistance:
In 1929 the Council gave the Australian Association a lavish trophy for interstate competition and in 1931 made a large cash grant to assist in the development of the game in NSW and Queensland.

Second English tour:
In 1937 the Australian Association invited an English amateur side to play an eight-match tour, including three Tests. Surprisingly Australia won the first and third Tests, the first at Sydney on 10 July when a crowd claimed to number 37,295 saw Australia win 5-4. The tour was an immense financial success.

Record English win over Australia:
During an Australian tour in 1951, an English professional team defeated Australia at the SCG by 17-0 (on 30 June), before a crowd of 14,146. The score still stands as the biggest winning margin in recorded international soccer history. Australia's demoralising loss did not help the game in NSW. When the English team returned to Sydney for the fourth Test on 14 July, the attendance was only 7,894.

Black years of Australian soccer:
In 1957 dissatisfied clubs began a breakaway movement from the then controlling body, the Australian Soccer Association Limited, and by 1961 the Association had lost complete control and was superseded by the Australian Soccer Federation. The breakaway hindered the progress of Australian soccer because all State amateur associations lost affiliation with the various State Olympic bodies. Australia had competed at the 1956 Olympic Games for the first time. In 1959, FIFA, the world controlling body, suspended Australia after proving that many European players had been illegally (under international rules) 'poached' from their European clubs. The Australian Soccer Federation was forced to pay FIFA $A50,000 and wait until 1963 before being reinstated as an affiliated body. It took until 1977 before the Australian Olympic Federation agreed to re-admit the soccer code as an affiliated member.

Establishment of the National Soccer League (NSL):
The first fully national football league in the history of Australian sport was established in April 1977 when Philips Industries launched the Philips Soccer

League. The 14 clubs in the inaugural season (won by the Sydney club Hakoah), were Hakoah-Eastern Suburbs, Marconi-Fairfield, St George-Budapest, Sydney Olympic and Western Suburbs (all Sydney clubs), Fitzroy United, Footscray, Mooroolbark and South Melbourne-Hellas (all Melbourne clubs), West Adelaide-Hellas and Adelaide City (SA), Brisbane City and Brisbane Lions (Qld) and Canberra City (ACT). Despite many critics predicting disaster, the first season was a success with total attendances of 650,524. Mooroolbark dropped out of the second (1978) season and was replaced by Newcastle United (NSW) and the 182-match competition, won by West Adelaide, drew an aggregate of 780,524 spectators.

Switch to summer soccer:
Late in 1980 the Philips League Council of Clubs decided to switch the Philips Soccer League season to summer months after the 1981 schedule. This move entailed programming matches from November 1981 through to May 1982. When all State Associations decided to continue with their traditional winter club competitions, Australia became the only major soccer nation in the world to run a 12-month season.

NSL champions since inception:
The National Soccer League has had three major sponsors since its inception—Philips Industries, Olympic Airways and in 1987, the South Australian Brewing Company which christened the competition the West End National League. The 1987 competition was based on a top-of-the-table point score to decide the National League Championship and a Grand Final competition between the top four teams on the ladder. The 1988 National League Championship will be decided on only a Grand Final system.

Year	Club
1977	Hakoah-Eastern Suburbs (NSW)
1978	West Adelaide Hellas (SA)
1979	Marconi-Fairfield (NSW)
1980	Sydney City (NSW)
1981	Sydney City-Hakoah (NSW)
1982	Sydney City-Hakoah (NSW)
1983	St George-Budapest (NSW)

Year	Club
1984	
Southern Div	South Melbourne-Hellas (Vic.)
Northern Div	Sydney Olympics (NSW)
NSL Final:	South Melbourne-Hellas (Vic.)
1985	
Southern Div	Brunswick Juventus (Vic.)
Northern Div	Sydney City (NSW)
NSL Final:	Brunswick Juventus (Vic.)
1986	
Southern Div	Brunswick Juventus (Vic.)
Northern Div	Sydney Croatia (NSW)
NSL Final:	Adelaide City (SA)
National League Championship	Apia-Leichhardt (NSW)
NSL Grand Final	St George (NSW)

Rothmans Medal Winners:
Inaugurated in 1985 to honour the best and fairest player in the National Soccer League.

Year	Player
1985	Jim Patikas Sydney Croatia (NSW)
1986	Bobby Russell South Melbourne (Vic.)
1987:	Andrew Zinni Brunswick Juventus (Vic.)

First Victorian club to win the National Soccer League Championship:
South Melbourne-Hellas in 1984. Hellas defeated Sydney Olympic 2-1 in both rounds of the final played at Olympic Park, Melbourne (crowd approx. 10,000), and St George Stadium, Sydney (crowd 11,221).

Represented Australia most times:
English-born Peter Wilson has played 63 full internationals and 51 non-internationals for a total of 114 matches for Australia. As of November 1987, the top ten players who have represented in full internationals are: Peter Wilson (NSW)—63; Atti Abonyi (NSW)—56; Jim Rooney (NSW)—54; John Kosmina (NSW)—51; Manfred Schaefer (NSW)—49; Ray Baartz (NSW)—48; John Warren (NSW)—44; Adrian Alston (NSW)—40; Doug Utjesenovic (NSW)—34 and Gary Byrne (Vic.)—33.

Top goal scorer in internationals:
Atti Abonyi, who played club soccer with Melbourne-Hungaria, St George-Buda-

pest and Sydney Croatia. Abonyi, who played his last game for Australia in 1977, scored 25 goals for Australia in full internationals and 36 for Australia in all matches.

NATIONAL RECORDS
Largest crowd:
Probably the 1956 Olympic Games Final at the MCG, played before the Closing Ceremony. Over 100,000 tickets had been sold or issued for the final day, but no accurate count was possible to ascertain the actual number of spectators who came to watch the soccer final in which the USSR defeated Yugoslavia 1-0.

Largest crowd for a non-Olympic match:
An official 51,566 at the Sydney Cricket Ground in 1965, to see English club side Everton defeat NSW 4-1.

Olympic record:
Australia has only once (in 1956) been represented at the Olympic Games. In that year, Australia, as host nation, did not have to qualify and was seeded into the final 11 teams. Australia won its first round match against Japan 2-0, but lost its second round match 2-4 to India and was eliminated.

Australia in the World Cup:
Australia made its first attempt to qualify for the World Cup Final in 1965 by entering the Pacific Zone Group 16 eliminations, and was quickly eliminated with 0-6 and 1-3 losses to North Korea.

Australia was again eliminated in 1969, but in 1973, under coach Rale Rasic, battled though 11 qualifying matches to reach the World Cup Final for the first time. In the finals in West Germany, Australia lost 0-2 to East Germany at Hamburg, 0-3 to West Germany at Hamburg and drew 0-0 with Chile at West Berlin, to be placed 14th.

To the end of 1986 (the World Cup is played every four years), Australia has failed to qualify for another Final and apart from players, coaches Rale Rasic, Rudi Gutendorf and Les Scheinflug have all been replaced.

INTERNATIONAL RECORD
Australia's record against international teams and visiting overseas clubs dates back to 1922 and matches against New Zealand. To the end of the 1987 season, Australia has played full internationals against New Zealand, Singapore, South Korea, South Vietnam, Scotland, Japan, Greece, Zimbabwe, Israel, Mexico, Indonesia, Philippines, Bulgaria, Iraq, Iran, Uruguay, East Germany, West Germany, Chile, USSR, Hong Kong, Taiwan, Fiji, Kuwait, Czechoslovakia, England, Northern Ireland, Thailand and China. Australia was host to the 1988 Bicentennial Gold Cup which included matches against reigning World Cup champions Argentina, Brazil and Saudi Arabia. Australia's surprise win, defeating World Cup champions Argentina 4-1, took the team to the final against Brazil. Brazil won 2-0 after a scoreless first half before a near-capacity crowd at the Sydney Football Stadium. Australian soccer teams have played more full internationals than Rugby League and Rugby Union combined.

MOST INDIVIDUAL GOALS
Australia's most prolific goal scorer:
Reg Date (b. Wallsend, NSW, 26 July 1921) scored 664 goals in his career and, in an era when Australia played few internationals, gained national selection nine times and scored eight goals. His best scoring efforts were nine goals in a club match for Wallsend v. Weston, NSW, on 10 April 1943, and eight for NSW against Queensland. His career spanned from 1930 to 1954 and included 1,616 junior and schoolboy, and senior matches.

Australian captaincy record:
English-born Peter Wilson came from the Middlesborough Club to Australia and captained Australia 51 times in 63 internationals.

Nine-goal players at senior level:
Apart from Reg Date, Trevor Rumley of the Woonona-Bulli Club on the NSW South Coast is the only player to score nine goals (against North Shore (Sydney), at Woonona, 24 April 1945).

Most first grade matches in Australia:
Believed to be 552, by Jim Wilkinson with the Weston and Mayfield United clubs in the NSW competition.

Pele in Australia:
The champion Brazilian player Pele appeared in Australia as a member of the Santos team in 1972. Santos, which was guaranteed A$40,000 by the Australian Soccer Federation, refused to take the field at the Sydney Sports Ground to play an Australian select side unless they received the money in cash in advance. The game was held up for almost 45 minutes. The match was drawn 2-2 before a crowd of 28,755.

AUSTRALIA'S 1987 INTERNATIONAL RECORD

Australia v.	Venue	Result
New Zealand	Melbourne	1-1
New Zealand	Wellington, NZ	NZ 2-1
Taiwan	Taipei	Aust. 3-0*

* Olympic Games qualifying match

WORLD CUP

Year	Venue	Winner
1930	Uruguay	Uruguay d. Argentina 4-2
1934	Italy	Italy d. Czechoslovakia 2-1
1938	France	Italy d. Hungary 4-2
1939-49	Not held (WWII)	
1950	Brazil	Uruguay d. Brazil 2-1
1954	Switzerland	West Germany d. Hungary 3-2
1958	Sweden	Brazil d. Sweden 5-2
1962	Chile	Brazil d. Czechoslovakia 3-1
1966	England	England d. West Germany 4-2
1970	Mexico	Brazil d. Italy 4-1
1974*	West Germany	West Germany d. Holland 2-1
1978	Argentina	Argentina d. Holland 3-1
1982	Spain	Italy d. West Germany 3-1
1986	Mexico	Argentina d. West Germany 3-2

* Australia qualified for the Finals for the first time.

SPEEDWAY RACING

BEGINNINGS IN AUSTRALIA
Sporting historians have perpetuated the myth that dirt track motorcycle racing—speedway—was an Australian invention, first staged at the West Maitland Showground, NSW, in 1923. Such motorcycle racing had been held for many years before in the United States and also, by some accounts, in South Africa. Apart from the fact that the first racing at West

Maitland was on grass, not dirt, many other forms of small oval track racing, the perfect description for 'speedway', were staged in Australia as early as the turn of the century.

First speedway style race:
On 1 January 1901, when motorised tricycles raced on the cycling track which then ringed the Association Ground (now the Sydney Cricket Ground).

First car and motorcycle racing on a dirt track:
On 12 March 1904, at Sandown racecourse, Melbourne. (This meeting followed a motoring exhibition at Aspendale racecourse, near Melbourne.)

First professionally constructed speedway:
At Aspendale, Vic. It opened on 28 January 1906 as a one-mile crushed-gravel circuit, similar in design to existing American fairground circuits.

First speedway in Sydney:
A nine-furlong clay and cinder American fairground-style circuit laid down at Victoria Park racecourse, Rosebery, Sydney, and opened on 6 October 1908.

Early speedways and speedway-style racing at other centres:
Motorcycles on Sydney Sports Ground cycling track, 1908; motorcycles on Richmond, Vic., banked cycling track, 1908; motorcycles on Sydney Showground dirt track, 1911; motorcycles and 'baby' cars on Claremont Showground, Perth, WA, 1914. Opening of one-mile (1.6 km) dirt track for cars and motorcycles at Penrith, NSW, 1920; similar-sized dirt track at Northfield, near Adelaide, SA, 1920.

First illuminated commercial speedway:
Thebarton Oval, Adelaide, SA, which opened for night racing on a grassed surface in 1922.

First motorcycle racing at West Maitland:
In October 1923, as more of a sideshow event at a carnival called 'The Greatest Sporting Event of the Year'. The showground was then fully grassed but after a dirt track was laid down in November, Sydney promoters, Messrs Campbell and Du Froq, took over the lease for night motorcycle racing and staged their first meeting in December 1923.

Major professional speedways in the 1920s:
New Zealand-born John S. Hoskins, who staged the first motorcycle exhibition at West Maitland in 1923, was appointed manager of a half-mile, high-banked car-and motorcycle-speedway at Hamilton, NSW, in November 1925. A. J. Hunting of Sydney staged the first short-track motorcycle racing in Brisbane, Qld, on the grassed Brisbane Exhibition Ground on 16 October 1926 and the following year constructed a quarter-mile dirt track at Davies Park, Brisbane. John S. Hoskins relaunched speedway racing at the Sydney Showground on 31 July 1927 and in the next year took over the promotion of the Claremont Showground in Perth, WA. The Wayville Showground, Adelaide, SA, opened in late 1926 and operated until 1934. Messrs Gene Cowley and Jack Hede launched dirt-track speedway at the Exhibition Oval, in the Exhibition Gardens, Melbourne, in 1927-28.

First American-style 'speed-dromes' in Australia:
The Melbourne Motordrome (high-banked concrete oval, 536 m to the lap) opened on the present site of Olympic Park on 29 November 1924. The circuit drew huge crowds, but was found to be unsuitable for car racing and after a spate of fatal accidents was demolished in the early 1930s.

Australia's second high-banked speed-drome:
The Olympia Speedway at the southern Sydney suburb of Maroubra. The

Olympia measured 1,372 m to the lap and was egg-shaped, with the tighter bend banked to 37 degrees. Cars and motorcycles were able to lap in excess of 100 mph (160.9 km/h) and the opening meeting on 2 December 1925 attracted a crowd of 75,000. Opposition from the Sydney Showground, lack of public transport and police complaints about the high number of accidents (five fatal), caused the circuit to close in the early 1930s.

First Australian riders overseas:
In October 1927 Keith McKay and Geoff Meredith (NSW) went to England to pioneer the sport. They were joined later the same year by Billy Galloway (NSW), Peter Smith and 'Digger' Pugh (Qld) and Stewart St George (NZ). Galloway and McKay competed at Britain's first serious speedway meeting at King's Oak, Epping Forest, near London, on 18 February 1928.

First organised Australian teams in England:
In 1928 promoters A. J. Hunting (Qld) and John S. Hoskins (WA) took Vic Huxley, Frank Arthur, Charlie Spinks, Ben Unwin, Noel Johnson, Jack Bishop, Hilary Brown (USA), Ron Johnson, Sig Schlam and Charlie Datsun (WA) to cash in on the boom in England. They were joined later by freelance riders Paddy Dean, Irvine Jones and Frank Duckett (NSW).

First Australian overseas champions:
Vic Huxley, Frank Arthur and Billy Lamont dominated the first years of racing in England and Huxley and Lamont won unofficial 'World Championships'.

First matches—Australia v. England:
The first motorcycle-teams speedway Test match was staged at Wimbledon, London, UK, in 1930. Australia won the nine-heat match 35–17. Four other Tests were held in the series over 16 heats and England won all four. The 50th anniversary of England v. Australia Test Matches was celebrated in 1980.

The World Championship:
Australian and New Zealand riders have won 16 of the 40 official World Solo Motorcycle Speedway Championships held between 1936 and 1985. The 1939 Championship final was abandoned after the outbreak of World War II and the Championship was revived in 1949.

Australian winners:
1936........Lionel Van Praag (NSW) Wembley, London
1939. Arthur 'Bluey' Wilkinson (NSW) Wembley, London
1951...............Jack Young (SA) Wembley, London
1952...............Jack Young (SA) Wembley, London

Aub Lawson (NSW and WA) (1913–77) rode in more World Championship finals (nine) than any other Australian and was placed third in 1958. Lawson also holds the record for appearing in the most Test matches (84) and scoring the most points (680).

Most remarkable season by an Australian:
Vic Duggan (b.West Maitland, NSW, 1915) in the 1947 season. Duggan rode in 348 races for the London first-division league team Harringay, won 297, finished second 39 times and third three times. Engine problems caused him to finish last (fourth) only once and he retired only eight times. At one stage of the season he had won 55 out of 59 races. In the major individual event of the year, the British Riders' Championship, Duggan was considered a certainty, but after winning two of his first three races, fell and retired with minor injuries. He won the Championship the next year.

First Australian Championship:
In 1927–28, at Davies Park, Brisbane, Qld. The winners were: up to 3½ hp, Max Grosskreutz (Qld); up to 2½ hp, Frank Pearce (Qld).

Most Championship wins:
Billy Sanders (NSW), who had seven wins between 1977 and 1985.

Speedway fatalities:
More deaths have occurred in speedway racing than in any other professional sport in Australia. Since the sport began on a semi-professional basis in 1906, the total number of fatalities (excluding spectators) has exceeded 136. Ken le Breton (NSW) has been the only rider to have lost his life in an official Test match (at the Sydney Sports Ground on 5

January 1951). The first double fatality in the modern history of the sport occurred at the Sydney Sports Ground on 20 January 1950, when Australian Test riders Ray Duggan (younger brother of Vic) and Norm Clay (NSW) lost their lives.

First World Championship event in Australia:
The World Speedway Pairs Championship, held at Liverpool City Raceway, NSW, on 11 December 1982. The event was won by the USA.

AUSTRALIAN CHAMPIONSHIP WINNERS:
Solos

Year	Rider
1929	Max Grosskreutz (Qld)*
1930	Jack Chapman (SA)*
1931	Ray Tauser (USA)
1932	Harold Hastings (England)
1933	Vic Huxley (Qld)
1934	Bluey Wilkinson (NSW)
1935	Bluey Wilkinson (NSW)
1936	Max Grosskreutz (Qld)
1937	Jack Milne (USA)
1938	Bluey Wilkinson (NSW)
1939	Jack Milne (USA)
1940	Cordy Milne (USA)
1941–44	*Not held* (WWII)
1945	Vic Duggan (NSW)
1946	Frank Dolan (NSW)
1947	Vic Duggan (NSW)*
1948	Vic Duggan (NSW)
1949	Aub Lawson (NSW)*
1950	Aub Lawson (NSW)*
1951	Jack Parker (England)*
1952	Keith Ryan (NSW)*
1953	Aub Lawson (NSW)
1954	Aub Lawson (NSW)
1955	Aub Lawson (NSW)
1956	Ulf Eriksson (Sweden)
1957–59	*Not held*
1960	Bob Sharp (NSW)
1961	*Not held*
1962	Mike Broadbanks (England)
1963	*Not held*
1964	Ken McKinlay (Scotland)
1965	Bob Sharp (NSW)
1966	Chum Taylor (WA)
1967	Jack Scott (SA)
1968	Jim Airey (NSW)
1969	Jim Airey (NSW)
1970	Jim Airey (NSW)
1971	John Boulger (SA)
1972	Jim Airey (NSW)
1973	John Boulger (SA)
1974	Steve Reinke (Qld)
1975	Phil Crump (Vic.)
1976	Ole Olsen (Denmark)
1977	Billy Sanders (NSW)
1978	Billy Sanders (NSW)
1979	Phil Crump (Vic.)
1980	Billy Sanders (NSW)
1981	Billy Sanders (NSW)
1982	Billy Sanders (NSW)
1983	Billy Sanders (NSW)
1984	Phil Crump (Vic.)
1985	Billy Sanders (NSW)
1986	Troy Butler (Qld)
1987	Steve Regeling (Qld)
1988	Phil Crump (Vic.)

* In each of these years, the championship was split either into two divisions (1929) or staged as up to four different races, a situation which has long confused historians. In the 1928–29 season, Grosskreutz won the title for machine up to 3½ hp and at the same meeting, Frank Pearce (Qld) won a 'junior' national title in the up to 2¾ hp class. In the 1929–30 season, Jack Chapman won the South Australian version of the title at the Wayville Showground and Max Grosskreutz the Queensland version at Davies Park, Brisbane. Chapman is generally recognised as the true champion. In 1947, Bill Rogers (Vic.) and Andy Menzies (Vic.) each won Victorian and Queensland versions respectively, but Vic Duggan won by far the most important version at Sydney. In 1949-50-51-52 three different versions of the championship were staged and a 'Champion of Champions' run-off was held to decide the overall winner. Some doubt exists about the recognition given Keith Ryan as 1952 champion. Ryan won two of the three 'championship' races held but finished third behind Aub Lawson and Lionel Levy in the 'Champion of Champions' run-off held at Brisbane. Ryan is generally regarded as champion because Lawson did not win any of the three 'championship' races held prior to the run-off. As the Australian speedway season runs through the summer months (i.e.: 1986–87), the years listed represent the actual year in which the championship final was held.

SIDECAR RACING
Though motorcycle sidecar racing (three-wheeled machine for rider and passenger) was popular in the USA in the early 1900s, Australia is recognised as establishing the sport in its modern form. Australians have taken the sport to England and New Zealand. Organised racing (always clockwise in Australia) has been traced back to 1912.

Greatest Australian rider:
Jim Davies (b. Victoria, 1917), who won a record six national titles, two New Zealand national titles and seven Australian Championships between 1936 and 1961. Davies, with Peter Speerin

(NSW), pioneered the sport in England in 1953.

AUSTRALIAN CHAMPIONSHIP WINNERS:
Solo

Year	Winner
1940	Jack Carruthers (NSW)
1941-46	*Not held* (WWII)
1947	Jim Davies (NSW)
1948	Jim Davies (NSW)
1949	Jim Davies (NSW)
1950	Jim Davies (NSW)
1951	Jack Carruthers (NSW)
1952	'Chook' Hodgekiss (NSW)
1953-54	*Not held*
1955	Jim Davies (NSW)
1956	Jim Davies (NSW)
1957	*Not held*
1958	Bill Sullivan (Vic.)*
1959	Don Willison (SA)*
1960	Bruce Kelley (SA)
1961	Allan Chance (Qld)
1962	Bill Bingham (NSW)
1963	Ron Johnson (Qld)
1964	Bruce Kelley (SA)
1965	Bruce Kelley (SA)*
1966	Bob Levy (NSW)
1967	Doug Robson (NSW)
1968	Len Bowes (SA)
1969	Graham Young (NSW)
1970	*Not held*
1971	Gary Innes (NSW)
1972	Geoff Grocott (NSW)
1973	Neil Munro (SA)
1974	Doug Robson (NSW)
1975	Doug Robson (NSW)
1976	Dennis Nash (WA)
1977	Ken l'Anson (SA)
1978	Keith Sewell (Qld)
1979	Keith Sewell (Qld)
1980	Ken Walker (Vic.)
1981	Dennis Nash (WA)
1982	Clarrie Jones (Vic.)
1983	Dennis Nash (WA)
1984	Phil McCurtayne (NSW)
1985	Phil McCurtayne (NSW)
1986	Phil McCurtayne (NSW)
1987	Andrew Cleave (Vic.)
1988	Dennis Nash (WA)

* South Australian version.

SPEEDCAR RACING
Australia did not lag far behind the USA in introducing car racing on short dirt and sealed oval tracks. The first such racing dates back to Sandown in 1904 and the first appearance of modified cycle cars to at least 1914.

First racing with modern-era speedcars:
In 1933, at Olympic Park, Melbourne, and the Granville Showground, Sydney (both dirt tracks).

Most famous driver:
Arguably, Jack (now Sir John) Brabham (b. Sydney, 1926). Brabham commenced his motor-racing career in a dirt track speedcar in 1947 and was one of Australia's leading drivers before switching to hill climbs and road racing in 1952.

First Australian Championship:
In 1933, at Olympic Park, Melbourne, and won by Les Gough (Vic.).

Most Australian Championship wins:
Pre-1940, Les Gough (Vic.) – five. Post-1945, Ray Revell (NSW) – five.

Largest attendance for speedcar racing:
Discounting large-track crowds of more than 60,000 at the Olympia Speedway, Maroubra, NSW, in the mid-1920s, the largest attendance for modern-style dirt track speedcar racing is 40,000-plus for the reopening of the Brisbane Exhibition track in March 1946.

Australian Championship winners:
Rivalry between interstate promoters and lack of control in many years has resulted in speedcar racing being plagued with an abundance of races being staged as 'Australian championships'. In one season in the 1950s, no less than eight separate races were held in four states and were advertised as being for an 'Australian championship'. The vast majority of these events have been disregarded. In the 1938-39, 1939-40, 1940-41 and 1941-42 seasons when no 'championship' races were staged some licence has been taken and the winner of the *major* semi-international race has been recognised as the national champion to achieve a form of continuity. Further confusion arose in 1964-65 and 1965-66 when top drivers competed in the 'Craven Filter National Speedcar Pointscore' and also competed in separate races billed as being for the 'Australian Championship'. Because the

Craven Filter series was by far the most important, the winners of that series have been accepted as the true champions.

Year	Driver
1933	Les Gough (Vic.)
1934	Les Gough (Vic.)
1935	Les Gough (Vic.)
1936	Les Gough (Vic.)
1937	Les Gough (Vic.)
1938	Paul Swedeberg (USA)
1939	Bill Reynolds (England)
1940	Paul Swedeberg (USA)
1941	Bill Reynolds (England)
1942	Ray Revell (NSW)
1943–46	*Not held* (WWII)
1947	Ray Revell (NSW)*
1948	Cal Niday (USA)
1949	Frank Brewer (USA)
1950	Frank Brewer (USA)
1951	Ray Revell (NSW)
1952	Ray Revell (NSW)
1953	Ray Revell (NSW)
1954	Andy McGavin (NSW)
1955	Andy McGavin (NSW)
1956	Bill Reynolds (NSW)**
1957	Dick Brown (USA)***
1958	Len Brock (NSW)
1959	Andy McGavin (NSW)
1960	Bob Tattersall (USA)
1961	Andy McGavin (NSW)
1962	Bob Tattersall (USA)
1963	Jim Davies (USA)
1964	Jeff Freeman (NSW)****
1965	Peter Cunneen (NSW)
1966	Johnny Stewart (NSW)
1967	Johnny Stewart (NSW)
1968	Johnny Stewart (NSW)
1969	Blair Shepherd (Qld)
1970	Bob Morgan (Qld)
1971	Ronald Mackay (NSW)
1972	Ronald Mackay (NSW)
1973	George Tatnell (NSW)
1974	George Tatnell (NSW)
1975	John Fenton (WA)
1976	John Fenton (WA)
1977	George Tatnell (NSW)
1978	Ron Wanless (Qld)
1979	Ron Wanless (Qld)
1980	Barry Pinchbeck (NSW)
1981	Keith Mann (WA)
1982	Keith Mann (WA)
1983	Geoff Pilgrim (WA)
1984	Keith Mann (WA)
1985	Jim Holden (Qld)
1986	Phil March (SA)
1987	Tom Watson (WA)
1988	Stephen Gall (NSW)

* American Perry Grimm was first to finish but was not recognised as champion under a residential rule, later lifted.
** Reynolds settled in Sydney after his first appearance in Australia in 1939.
*** Andy McGavin (NSW) won another version of the title and deserves some recognition.
**** Ken Morton (NSW) won another version in Sydney. Freeman won his 'title' at Brisbane and is generally recognised as having won the more important race.

SPRINT CAR RACING

Now the most popular division of the sport in Australia, sprint car racing evolved from hot rod racing, which in turn evolved from the bash and crash days of 'stock car racing'. The first national title was held in 1963 at Sydney's old Windsor Speedway and was won by Bill Willis of Victoria. Modern sprint car racing is now based entirely on the American concept with the cars resembling the old Indianapolis-style roadster racing cars, festooned with wings and aerofoils designed to improve downforce and provide maximum traction. Easily Australia's most successful driver has been Sydney's Garry Rush who drove the first fully-imported American car seen in Australia. On 7 February 1987 Rush won an event promoted as the World Championship at Perth's Claremont Speedway. Although the 'championship' did not gain acceptance in the United States, the home of world sprint car racing, Rush's win over a field which included eight American, two New Zealand and Australia's leading 27 drivers stamped him as one of the top 10 drivers in the world.

Australian Championship winners

Year	Driver
1963	Billy Willis (Vic.)
1964	Dick Briton (NSW)
1965	Bill Warner (NSW)
1966	Bill Warner (NSW)
1967	Dick Briton (NSW)
1968	Bob Tunks (NSW)
1969	Jim Winterbottom (NSW)
1970	Bill Wigzell (SA)
1971	Dick Briton (NSW)
1972	Graeme McCubbin (Vic.)
1973	John Moyle (SA)
1974	Jim Winterbottom (NSW)
1975	Dick Briton (NSW)
1976	Noel Bradford (WA)
1977	Garry Rush (NSW)

Year	Driver	Year	Driver
1978	Garry Rush (NSW)	1985	Ron Krikke (WA)
1979	Steve Brazier (NSW)	1986	Garry Rush (NSW)
1980	Steve Brazier (NSW)	1987	Brett Lacey (Vic.)
1981	Garry Rush (NSW)	1988	George Tatnell (NSW)*
1982	Garry Rush (NSW)		
1983	Garry Rush (NSW)		
1984	Garry Rush (NSW)		

* First driver to win the national speedcar (1973, '74, '77) and sprint car championships.

WORLD CHAMPIONSHIP

Several competitions were staged in the late 1920s and early 1930s which carried a 'world championship' claim. Most notable were a series of events sponsored by the *London Star* newspaper. The world body controlling motorcycle sport (FIM) does not recognise any events staged prior to 1936.

Year	Venue	Winner
1936	Wembley, UK	**Lionel Van Praag** (Australia)
1937	Wembley, UK	**Jack Milne** (USA)
1938	Wembley, UK	**Arthur Wilkinson** (Australia)
1939	*Final abandoned* (WWII)	
1949	Wembley, UK	**Tommy Price** (England)
1950	Wembley, UK	**Freddy Williams** (Wales)
1951	Wembley, UK	**Jack Young** (Australia)
1952	Wembley, UK	**Jack Young** (Australia)
1953	Wembley, UK	**Freddy Williams** (Wales)
1954	Wembley, UK	**Ronnie Moore** (New Zealand)
1955	Wembley, UK	**Peter Craven** (England)
1956	Wembley, UK	**Ove Fundin** (Sweden)
1957	Wembley, UK	**Barry Briggs** (New Zealand)
1958	Wembley, UK	**Barry Briggs** (New Zealand)
1959	Wembley, UK	**Ronnie Moore** (New Zealand)
1960	Wembley, UK	**Ove Fundin** (Sweden)
1961	Malmo, Sweden	**Ove Fundin** (Sweden)
1962	Wembley, UK	**Peter Craven** (England)
1963	Wembley, UK	**Ove Fundin** (Sweden)
1964	Ullevi, Sweden	**Barry Briggs** (New Zealand)
1965	Wembley, UK	**Bjorn Knutsson** (Sweden)
1966	Ullevi, Sweden	**Barry Briggs** (New Zealand)
1967	Wembley, UK	**Ove Fundin** (Sweden)
1968	Ullevi, Sweden	**Ivan Mauger** (New Zealand)
1969	Wembley, UK	**Ivan Mauger** (New Zealand)
1970	Wroclaw, Poland	**Ivan Mauger** (New Zealand)
1971	Ullevi, Sweden	**Ole Olsen** (Denmark)
1972	Wembley, UK	**Ivan Mauger** (New Zealand)

Year	Venue	Winner
1973	Slaski, Poland	**Jerzy Szczakiel** (Poland)
1974	Ullevi, Sweden	**Anders Michanek** (Sweden)
1975	Wembley, UK	**Ole Olsen** (Denmark)
1976	Slaski, Poland	**Peter Collins** (England)
1977	Ullevi, Sweden	**Ivan Mauger** (New Zealand)
1978	Wembley, UK	**Ole Olsen** (Denmark)
1979	Wroclaw, Poland	**Ivan Mauger** (New Zealand)
1980	Ullevi, Sweden	**Michael Lee** (England)
1981	Wembley, UK	**Bruce Penhall** (USA)
1982	Los Angeles, USA	**Bruce Penhall** (USA)
1983	Norden, W. Germany	**Egon Muller** (W. Germany)
1984	Ullevi, Sweden	**Erik Gundersen** (Denmark)
1985	Bradford, UK	**Erik Gundersen** (Denmark)
1986	Slaski, Poland	**Hans Nielsen** (Denmark)
1987	Amsterdam, Netherlands	**Hans Nielsen** (Denmark)

SURFING

BEGINNINGS IN AUSTRALIA

The establishment of the sport of surfboard riding in Australia has been submerged in a mass of semi-truths. Popular belief has it that Australian surfers were introduced to the art of surfboard riding by Hawaiian Duke (his actual Christian name) Kahanamoku who brought a Hawaiian board to Sydney when he arrived for swimming engagements in 1915. While Kahanamoku was the first man to ride a surfboard successfully off Sydney beaches, the sport was well known to many Australians who had visited Hawaii, and experiments had been made well before 1915.

First recorded attempt to ride a surfboard:

In 1908, when Solomon Islander Alick Wickham, who had come to Sydney in 1898, fashioned a crude board and attempted to ride waves at Curl Curl Beach, north of Sydney. In the same year (1908), Frank and Charlie Bell of Manly, NSW, constructed an equally crude board and tried the surf at Freshwater Beach, Sydney. Fred Notting of Collaroy, who had surfed in Hawaii, shaped a number of solid planks and named two of them 'Honolulu Queen' and 'Fiji Flyer'. Notting had limited success.

First Hawaiian board in Australia:

In 1912 C. D. Paterson of North Steyne, Sydney, returned from an overseas trip with a genuine Hawaiian board. Neither Paterson nor other surfing enthusiasts, such as Notting, Jack Reynolds, Steve McKelvey and Fred None, could master the board and it appears that none realised that the heavy, solid plank design was most manoeuvrable in deep water and not in the shallow, broken water near the beach.

Duke Kahanamoku's visit:
When the Hawaiian swimming and surfing star Duke Kahanamoku (Kahanamoku won the 100 m freestyle at the 1912 Olympic Games at Stockholm) visited Sydney in 1915 to take part in a series of swimming carnivals, local surfers quizzed him about the mysteries of the surfboard. Kahanamoku obligingly had a board fashioned and gave demonstrations at Freshwater (now Harbord) Beach. In one demonstration, he invited 15-year-old Isabel Letham to climb on the board and finished the day by holding Isabel upright as he caught a large wave to the beach. Isabel Letham, aged 86, now lives at Harbord, Sydney. At the age of 15 she was the first Australian woman to 'solo' on a surfboard and was acknowledged to be the greatest woman body surfer of the time. At 16 she was the first Australian woman to take up aquaplaning, forerunner of modern water-skiing, and is now Patron of the Women Surfriders' Association.

First Australian surfboard expert:
Claude West, who watched Kahanamoku's demonstrations in 1915 and asked for lessons. When Kahanamoku returned to Hawaii he gave West his board. West won an unofficial Australian 'Championship' in 1915 and reigned supreme as the finest board rider on the NSW coast until 1925, when he retired from surf-club activities and presented the board to the Freshwater Club.

First surfboards in Victoria:
In the early 1920s, when Geelong businessman Lew Whyte brought back a 34-kg, 2.74 m x 61 cm x 76 mm redwood plank he had purchased and ridden in Hawaii, and successfully caught waves at Lorne Point, Vic. The board is now owned by veteran Melbourne surfer Vic Tauntau.

Early board developments:
Claude West is believed to have been the first surfer to experiment with hollowed-out boards covered with crude laminations. West's first hollow board was made in 1918. 'Snowy' McAllister, who won an unofficial Australian 'title' in 1925, made similar experiments and revolutionised the design of the tail.

First Australian rider overseas:
Keightly 'Blue' Russell of Palm Beach, NSW, won the Hawaiian Championship in 1939 as a member of the Australian surf team competing at the Pacific Games.

First 'Malibu' boards in Australia:
In 1954, when American film actor, the late Peter Lawford, brought a board to Australia. The boards were called 'Malibu' because it is believed the first such models were used at Malibu Beach, near Los Angeles, USA. The boards revolutionised surfing because they were extremely light—Lawford's board was reported to have been 8 ft 6 ins long, and to have weighed only 25 lbs (11.33 kg). With its fin and curved and shaped 'walls' (sides), it was easy to manoeuvre.

Lawford's board created intense interest, but the real surfboarding popularity surge came in 1956 when a group of American surfers took part in an international carnival at Bells Beach, Vic., during the Olympic Games festivities. Overnight, surfboard riding was established as a true sport and the first moves were made by many surfers to break away from traditional surf-lifesaving clubs and associated carnival competition and establish surfboarding as an individual sport.

First Australian association:
The Australian Surfriders' Association, which staged the inaugural Australian titles in 1964.

First major overseas win by an Australian:
In 1964, when Bernard 'Midget' Farrelly won the Makaha Open International in Hawaii. The event was then the most important open event on the international surfing calendar.

First official Australian Championship:
In 1964, when Bernard Farrelly won the Men's Open Championship, Robert Coneeley the Junior Men's title and Phyllis O'Donnell the Women's Open title.

First World Championship in Australia:
The inaugural world titles were held at Manly Beach, Sydney, in 1964. Bernard Farrelly won the Men's Open and Australia scored a double when Phyllis O'Donnell won the Women's Open. Australia's Jenny Gill won the Women's World Amateur Championship in 1982.

Australia's World Champions:
Bernard Farrelly (1964 winner) came close to a second title in 1968 at Puerto Rico when he finished runner-up, only two points behind winner Fred Hemmings of the USA. Controversy raged about the scoring method and many changes were made the following year.

Year	Winner
1964	Bernard 'Midget' Farrelly (NSW)
1966	Robert 'Nat' Young (NSW)
1973	Ian Cairns (WA)
1975	Mark Andrews (NSW)
1976	Peter Townend (Qld)
1978	Wayne Bartholomew (Qld)
1979	Mark Richards (NSW)
1980	Mark Richards (NSW)
1981	Mark Richards (NSW)
1982	Mark Richards (NSW)
1983-84	Tom Carroll (NSW)*
1984-85	Tom Carroll (NSW)
1987-88	Damien Hardman (NSW)

* First of new split-year championship series.

SURF LIFESAVING

BEGINNINGS IN AUSTRALIA
The first recognised Australian surf club was formed at Bondi, NSW, in 1906 though claims still exist that the surf lifesaving movement began with the formation of a club at Manly, NSW, in 1902 and, at about the same time, one at Bronte, NSW. Only the Bondi club has documented evidence of formation.

First surf club controlling body:
The Surf Swimming and Open Sea Lifesaving Association of NSW, formed in 1907. The same year the organisation became the Surf Bathers' Association of NSW. The Surf Life Saving Association of Australia was formed in 1908.

First inter-club carnival:
February 1908 at Manly Beach, Sydney, with clubs from Wollongong, NSW, competing against Sydney clubs.

First state titles:
The NSW Championships held at Bondi, NSW, in 1915. The first title events were for swimming and rescue and resuscitation events.

First Australian Championships:
20 March 1915. Winner of the inaugural senior surf race was Bondi club member J. G. Brown, the only entrant to master the huge seas and complete the course. The only other championship contested was the Rescue and Resuscitation (R and R) event, won by the Bondi club.

First surf boat races:
January 1908 at Manly, NSW, when boats from ships berthed in Sydney Harbour were tried out. The first modified surf boat was constructed in 1910.

First Iron Man Championship:
1965-66 at Alexandra Headlands Beach, Qld. The event was won by Hayden Kenny of the local club. Kenny's son Grant later won the same championship. (See the great champions.)

First World Championship:
2-3 May 1981 in Bali, Indonesia. Competing nations included Australia, New Zealand, Indonesia, Hong Kong, the United States and Great Britain.

First female to win open surf race:
Ann Bender, 13, of the Newcastle club, NSW, on 5 October 1980 when she won the cadet race at Forster Beach, NSW. On 31 July 1980, the SLSA voted to allow girls to join surf clubs and compete in open events. The Forster carnival was the first of the 1980-81 season.

THE GREAT CHAMPIONS:
Surf swimming:
Bob Newbiggen (NSW) Australian open surf champion 5 times 1939-40, 1940-41, 1945-46, 1946-47 and 1947-48.
Noel Ryan (NSW) Australian open surf champion 3 times 1929-30, 1931-32 and 1933-34.
Brian Hutchings (NSW) won 2 national surf belt titles and 3 open surf titles 1953-54, 1955-56 and 1958-59.
Jon Donohoe (NSW) won 3 national open surf titles 1957-58, 1959-60 and 1960-61.
Graham White (Vic.) won 4 national open surf titles 1968-69, 1969-70, 1971-72 and 1972-73. He was also open belt champion in 1969-70 and in 1968-69 took out the junior and open surf title double.

Iron Man competition:
Outstanding competitors have been:
Grant Kenny (Qld), who took out the junior and open double in the 1979-80 national titles, the junior and open titles at the national open carnival in December 1980 and in 1981 won the New Zealand junior and open championships at New Plymouth, NZ, the same day.
Barry Rodgers (NSW) won the national Iron Man title 3 times, 1966-67, 1967-68 and 1968-69. He also won the national open surf championship in 1962-63.

Belt swimming:
Easily the standout competitor has been Don Morrison (WA) who won the national open title 4 times, 1947-48, 1949-50, 1951-52 and 1952-53 and was twice runner-up.

Double ski:
Dennis Green (NSW) shared in winning the national title a record 8 times between 1953-54 and 1966-67 with different partners: Wally Brown, Barry Stuart and Dennis Maguire.

Single ski:
Phil Coles (NSW), who like Green, represented Australia as a canoeist at the Olympic Games, won 3 national titles **1955-56, 1958-59 and 1960-61 and also won 2 national double ski** championships. He shared with Ken Vidler of the Scarborough club, WA, the honour of winning the most ski titles. Vidler won the national single ski title 3 times and also won 3 Iron Man titles.

Long boards:
Dennis Huessner (NSW) won the national title 6 times, the last in 1970-71, and his Maroubra clubmate Ross Hazelton won three titles between 1952-53 and 1955-56.

Rescue and Resuscitation:
The Bondi club dominated the event at national titles until the late 1940s, after which Queensland clubs came to the fore. Since 1961-62 Queensland clubs have won 21 national titles with the most successful clubs being Alexandra Headlands, Southport and Kirra.

Surf boats:
First national title event was won by the Freshwater (NSW) club in 1919-20. North Steyne (NSW) won 7 national titles between 1920-21 and 1929-30, the Cronulla (NSW) club was the first to score a hat-trick of wins (1933-34, 1934-35 and 1935-36) and the first club outside NSW to win the title was Mollymook (Qld) in 1959-60.

Beach sprinting:
The Manly (NSW) club has produced

a steady stream of competitors who have largely dominated this event. Rex Phillips won 4 years in a row and Rugby League footballer Johnny Bliss (5) and Nick Yakich (4) reigned for the club in the 1950s and 1960s.

Most versatile surf champion:
Arguably Fitz Lough of the North Steyne (NSW) club. The winner of the inaugural national surf belt title in 1919-20, Lough was a first-grade cricketer, field hockey player, Rugby Union footballer, lacrosse player, an A-grade tennis player, A-grade pennant golfer, a NSW cross-country snow-skiing champion, a NSW table tennis champion, NSW croquet champion and he won senior competitons at inter-club level in swimming, diving, athletics, ice and roller skating.

Most famous rescue:
The 'Black Sunday' tragedy at Bondi Beach (NSW) on 6 February 1938 when a series of freak waves washed more than 100 bathers off a sandbank. Seventy had to be rescued and at one stage 40 were unconscious on the beach. The final death toll was 5, but in the circumstances, the Bondi club members performed magnificently to save so many. To the end of the 1987-88 summer surfing season, affiliated members of the SLSA have rescued an estimated 275,000 swimmers since statistics were recorded in 1908. Rescue equipment now includes helicopters, jet rescue boats and special rescue boards. Such equipment is not always available and in 1979-80 a recorded 2,750 rescues were made by club members striking out unaided.

TENNIS

BEGINNINGS IN AUSTRALIA
Early in 1878, when enthusiasts who had seen the game played in England laid a rectangular asphalt court at the Warehousemen's Cricket Ground in St Kilda Road, Melbourne, a small oval behind one of the grandstands at the then headquarters of the Melbourne Cricket Club.

First lawn court:
Laid down in 1879, on or near the original asphalt court.

First men's championship:
In January 1880, at the original lawn court. A. F. Robinson won the Victorian singles title and also won the doubles title with C. Trench. In November of the same year, a second Victorian Singles Championship was staged. It was won by F. Highett.

First women's championship:
In 1884, at the St Kilda Road lawn court. Miss E. McKenzie won the Victorian singles title, and Misses Riddell and Ross, the doubles championship.

First mixed doubles championship:
In 1884, at the Victorian Championships. The winners were W. J. C. Riddell and his sister Elizabeth.

First Australian Championships:
In 1905, in Melbourne and officially called the Australasian Championships, incorporating the Victorian Championships. Rodney Heath (Vic.), won the singles and T. Tatchell and R. Lycett (Vic.), the doubles titles.

First Sydney club:
The Association Lawn Tennis Club (now the Sydney Lawn Tennis Club), formed

in 1878 with courts at the Association Ground (now the Sydney Cricket Ground).

First controlling body:
The Lawn Tennis Association of Australasia, formed in 1904 in Sydney, with Mr W. H. Forrest as President. Australasia was a foundation member of the International Lawn Tennis Federation when that body was formed in 1913. After New Zealand withdrew affiliation from the ITA of Australasia in 1922, the Association, for obscure reasons, continued to operate under that title until 1926, when its headquarters were moved to Melbourne and the name changed to the Lawn Tennis Federation of Australia. Norman E. Brookes (later Sir Norman) was elected President, a post he held until 1955.

First Australasian entry in the Davis Cup:
In 1905, when Norman Brookes (Vic.) and Anthony Wilding (NZ) were selected as the singles players and Brookes and A. W. Dunlop (Vic.) as the doubles pair. H. A. Parker (NZ) was also selected for the team.

The team went to England, defeated Austria 5-0 in the first round and was then eliminated by the United States 5-0. Dunlop acted as captain and manager. No record exists of Parker playing in either match.

First Davis Cup win by Australasia:
In 1907, when Australasia (Norman Brookes of Australia and Anthony Wilding of NZ), defeated the British Isles (A. W. Gore and H. Roper Barrett), 3-2 at Wimbledon, UK.

Last Australasian entry in the Davis Cup:
In 1922. The team comprised only Australians: James O. Anderson (NSW), Gerald L. Patterson (Vic.) and Patrick O'Hara Wood (Vic.). They lost 4-1 to the United States in the Challenge Round at Forest Hills, New York, USA. Australia and New Zealand entered separate teams from 1923 onwards.

First win by Australia:
In 1939. Australia (John Bromwich and Adrian Quist of NSW) defeated the USA (Bobby Riggs, Frank Parker, Jack Kramer, and Joseph R. Hunt) 3-2 in the Challenge Round at Forest Hills. It was the first time in Davis Cup history that any country had won the Challenge Round after losing the first two singles. Bromwich lost to Riggs and Quist to Parker on the first day, but defeated Kramer-Hunt in the doubles on the second day. Quist outlasted Riggs in a five-set battle on the final day and in the deciding singles, Bromwich outclassed Parker 6-0, 6-3, 6-1.

Australia's first 'World Champion':
Norman E. Brookes (Vic.), who won the tournament officially titled the 'World Championship and the Renshaw Cup' immediately after playing in the 1905 Davis Cup Challenge at the Queen's Club, London, UK. Brookes won this (unofficial) 'World Championship' in 1907 and the same year won an equally unofficial world doubles 'championship' with Anthony Wilding at Wimbledon, UK.

First Australasian Wimbledon men's singles winner:
Norman E. Brookes, who defeated A. W. Gore (GB) 6-4, 6-2, 6-2, in 1907.

First Australasian Wimbledon men's doubles winners:
Norman E. Brookes and Anthony Wilding (NZ), who defeated B. C. Wright and K. Behr (USA), 6-4, 6-4, 6-2, in 1907.

First Australian woman to win the Wimbledon singles:
Margaret Court (nee Smith) (WA), who defeated Billy Jean King (nee Moffit) (USA), 6-3, 6-4, in 1963.

First Australian to win an overseas national championship:
Jack Crawford (NSW), who won the 1933 French singles title, defeating Henri Cochet (France), 8-6, 6-1, 6-3.

WIMBLEDON CHAMPIONSHIP
The world's most important and famous championship tournament. Restricted to amateur players until 1968 when it was renamed the Wimbledon Open Championships and made open to professionals.

Men's singles:

Year	Winner
1877	Spence Gore (GB)
1878	P. Frank Hadow (GB)
1879	Canon John Hartley (GB)*
1880	Canon John Hartley (GB)
1881	William Renshaw (GB)
1882	William Renshaw (GB)
1883	William Renshaw (GB)
1884	William Renshaw (GB)
1885	William Renshaw (GB)
1886	William Renshaw (GB)
1887	Herbert Lawford (GB)
1888	J. Ernest Renshaw (GB)
1889	William Renshaw (GB)
1890	William Hamilton (GB)
1891	Wilfred Baddeley (GB)
1892	Wilfred Baddeley (GB)
1893	Joshua Pym (GB)
1894	Joshua Pym (GB)
1895	Wilfred Baddeley (GB)
1896	Harold Mahony (Ireland)
1897	Reginald Doherty (GB)
1898	Reginald Doherty (GB)
1899	Reginald Doherty (GB)
1900	Reginald Doherty (GB)
1901	Arthur W. Gore (GB)
1902	Hugh Doherty (GB)
1903	Hugh Doherty (GB)
1904	Hugh Doherty (GB)
1905	Hugh Doherty (GB)
1906	Hugh Doherty (GB)
1907	**Norman Brookes (Aust.)**
1908	Arthur W. Gore (GB)
1909	Arthur W. Gore (GB)
1910	Anthony Wilding (NZ)
1911	Anthony Wilding (NZ)
1912	Anthony Wilding (NZ)
1913	Anthony Wilding (NZ)
1914	**Norman Brookes (Aust.)**
1915-18	*Not held* (WWI)
1919	**Gerald Patterson (Aust.)**
1920	Bill Tilden (USA)
1921	Bill Tilden (USA)
1922	**Gerald Patterson (Aust.)**
1923	Bill Johnston (USA)
1924	Jean Borotra (France)
1925	Jean-Rene Lacoste (France)
1926	Jean Borotra (France)
1927	Henri Cochet (France)
1928	Jean-Rene Lacoste (France)
1929	Henri Cochet (France)
1930	Bill Tilden (USA)
1931	Sidney Wood (USA)
1932	Ellsworth Vines (USA)
1933	**Jack Crawford (Aust.)**
1934	Fred Perry (GB)
1935	Fred Perry (GB)
1936	Fred Perry (GB)
1937	Donald Budge (USA)
1938	Donald Budge (USA)
1939	Bobby Riggs (USA)
1940-45	*Not held* (WWII)
1946	Yvon Petra (France)
1947	Jack Kramer (USA)
1948	Bob Falkenburg (USA)
1949	Ted Schroeder (USA)
1950	Budge Patty (USA)
1951	Dick Savitt (USA)
1952	**Frank Sedgman (Aust.)**
1953	Vic Seixas (USA)
1954	Jan Drobny (Egypt)*
1955	Tony Trabert (USA)
1956	**Lew Hoad (Aust.)**
1957	**Lew Hoad (Aust.)**
1958	**Ashley Cooper (Aust.)**
1959	Alex Olmedo (USA)
1960	**Neale Fraser (Aust.)**
1961	**Rod Laver (Aust.)**
1962	**Rod Laver (Aust.)**
1963	Chuck McKinley (USA)
1964	**Roy Emerson (Aust.)**
1965	**Roy Emerson (Aust.)**
1966	Manuel Santana (Spain)
1967	**John Newcombe (Aust.)**
1968	**Rod Laver (Aust.)****
1969	**Rod Laver (Aust.)**
1970	**John Newcombe (Aust.)**
1971	**John Newcombe (Aust.)**
1972	Stan Smith (USA)
1973	Jan Kodes (Czech.)
1974	Jimmy Connors (USA)
1975	Arthur Ashe (USA)
1976	Bjorn Borg (Sweden)
1977	Bjorn Borg (Sweden)
1978	Bjorn Borg (Sweden)

Year	Winner	Year	Winner
1979	Bjorn Borg (Sweden)	1924	Kitty McKane (GB)
1980	Bjorn Borg (Sweden)	1925	Suzanne Lenglen (France)
1981	John McEnroe (USA)	1926	Kitty Godfree + (GB)
1982	Jimmy Connors (USA)	1927	Helen Wills (USA)
1983	John McEnroe (USA)	1928	Helen Wills (USA)
1984	John McEnroe (USA)	1929	Helen Wills (USA)
1985	Boris Becker (W. Germany)	1930	Helen Moody ++ (USA)
1986	Boris Becker (W. Germany)	1931	Cilly Aussem (Germany)
1987	**Pat Cash (Aust.)**	1932	Helen Moody (USA)
1988	Stefan Edberg (Sweden)	1933	Helen Moody (USA)

* Drobny was born in Prague, Czechoslovakia, but left that country as a refugee in 1948. He took up residence in Egypt and technically represented that country at Wimbledon. In 1959 he adopted British nationality.
** First Open Wimbledon.

Year	Winner
1934	Dorothy Round (GB)
1935	Helen Moody (USA)
1936	Helen Jacobs (USA)
1937	Dorothy Round (GB)
1938	Helen Moody (USA)
1939	Alice Marble (USA)
1940-45	*Not held* (WWII)
1946	Pauline Betz (USA)
1947	Margaret Osborne (USA)
1948	Louise Brough (USA)
1949	Louise Brough (USA)
1950	Louise Brough (USA)
1951	Doris Hart (USA)
1952	Maureen Connolly (USA)
1953	Maureen Connolly (USA)
1954	Maureen Connolly (USA)
1955	Louise Brough (USA)
1956	Shirley Fry (USA)
1957	Althea Gibson (USA)
1958	Althea Gibson (USA)
1959	Maria Bueno (Brazil)
1960	Maria Bueno (Brazil)
1961	Angela Mortimer (GB)
1962	Karen Susman (USA)
1963	**Margaret Smith (Aust.)**
1964	Maria Bueno (Brazil)
1965	**Margaret Smith (Aust.)**
1966	Billie Jean King (USA)
1967	Billie Jean King (USA)
1968	Billie Jean King (USA)
1969	Ann Jones (GB)
1970	**Margaret Court +++ (Aust.)**
1971	**Evonne Goolagong (Aust.)**
1972	Billie Jean King (USA)
1973	Billie Jean King (USA)
1974	Chris Evert (USA)
1975	Billie Jean King (USA)
1976	Chris Evert (USA)
1977	Virginia Wade (GB)
1978	Martina Navratilova (Czech./USA)
1979	Martina Navratilova (USA)
1980	**Evonne Cawley ‡ (Aust.)**
1981	Chris Lloyd ‡‡ (USA)

Women's Singles:

Year	Winner
1884	Maud Watson (GB)
1885	Maud Watson (GB)
1886	Blanche Bingley (GB)
1887	Lottie Dod (GB)
1888	Lottie Dod (GB)
1889	Blanche Hillyard * (GB)
1890	L. Rice (GB)
1891	Lottie Dod (GB)
1892	Lottie Dod (GB)
1893	Lottie Dod (GB)
1894	Blanche Hillyard (GB)
1895	Charlotte Cooper (GB)
1896	Charlotte Cooper (GB)
1897	Blanche Hillyard (GB)
1898	Charlotte Cooper (GB)
1899	Blanche Hillyard (GB)
1900	Blanche Hillyard (GB)
1901	Charlotte Sterry** (GB)
1902	Muriel Robb (GB)
1903	Dorothea Douglas (GB)
1904	Dorothea Douglas (GB)
1905	May Sutton (USA)
1906	Dorothea Douglas (GB)
1907	May Sutton (USA)
1908	Charlotte Sterry (GB)
1909	Dora Boothby (GB)
1910	Dorothea Chambers *** (GB)
1911	Dorothea Chambers (GB)
1912	Ethel Larcombe (GB)
1913	Dorothea Chambers (GB)
1914	Dorothea Chambers (GB)
1915-18	*Not held* (WWI)
1919	Suzanne Lenglen (France)
1920	Suzanne Lenglen (France)
1921	Suzanne Lenglen (France)
1922	Suzanne Lenglen (France)
1923	Suzanne Lenglen (France)

Year	Winner
1982	Martina Navratilova (USA)
1983	Martina Navratilova (USA)
1984	Martina Navratilova (USA)
1985	Martina Navratilova (USA)
1986	Martina Navratilova (USA)
1987	Martina Navratilova (USA)
1988	Steffi Graf (W. Germany)

* Nee Bingley
** Nee Cooper (1895, '96, '98)
*** Nee Douglas (1903, '04, '06)
+ Nee McKane (1924)
++ Nee Wills (1927, '28, 29)
+++ Nee Smith (1963, '65)
‡ Nee Goolagong (1971)
‡‡ Nee Evert (1976)

AUSTRALIA'S WIMBLEDON RECORD

Most wins—men's singles:
Four by Rod Laver (Qld), 1961, '62, '68 and '69, the last two after the event became an Open Championship in 1968.

Most wins—women's singles:
Three by Margaret Court (nee Smith) (WA) 1963, '65 and '70.

Most wins—men's doubles:
Most successful combination, John Newcombe (NSW)–Tony Roche (NSW), with five wins (1965, '68, '69, '70 and '74). Newcombe won a sixth title with Ken Fletcher (Qld) in 1966.

Most wins—women's doubles:
No Australian pair has ever won more than one title.

Most wins—mixed doubles:
Four by Ken Fletcher (Qld)–Margaret Smith (WA), 1963, '65, '66 and '68 and Owen Davidson (Vic.)–Billie Jean King (USA) 1967, '71, '73 and '74.

THE GRAND SLAM

Grand Slam is the traditional description of a win in the Wimbledon, French, US and Australian Singles Championships or, in recent years, Opens. The first man to achieve the feat was Donald Budge (USA), in 1938. The first woman to do so was Maureen Connolly (USA), in 1983.

First Australian man to win the Grand Slam:
Rod Laver (Qld), in 1962. In this year, Laver also won the Italian Championship. Laver won a second Grand Slam in 1969, when all events were Opens.

First Australian woman to win the Grand Slam:
Margaret Court (WA), in 1970.

First doubles Grand Slam:
In 1951 Frank Sedgman (Vic.) and Ken McGregor (SA), became the first pair in the world to win the Grand Slam.

First mixed doubles Grand Slam:
Won in 1963 for the first time in the history of tennis by Ken Fletcher (Qld) and Margaret Smith (WA).

AUSTRALIAN OPEN CHAMPIONSHIP

Originally the Australasian Championship for amateurs, the competition became the Australian Championship in 1915 and the Australian Open Championship in January 1969, to fall in line with the international switch to open championships in 1968. In 1972 the Open was permanently sited at Kooyong, Melbourne, but this venue will be discarded when the National Tennis Stadium is completed. In 1977, two Australian Opens were staged—in January and December—to overcome the problem of top international players being committed to overseas events.

Men's singles:

Year	Winner & Venue
1905	R. W. Heath (Vic.) Melbourne
1906	A. F. Wilding (NZ) Christchurch
1907	H. M. Rice (NSW) Brisbane
1908	F. B. Alexander (USA) Sydney
1909	A. F. Wilding (NZ) Perth
1910	R. W. Heath (Vic.) Adelaide
1911	N. E. Brookes (Vic.) Melbourne
1912	J. C. Parke (UK) Hastings, NZ
1913	E. F. Parker (WA) Perth
1914	A. H. O'Hara Wood (Vic.) Melbourne
1915	F. Gordon Lowe (UK) Brisbane
1916-18	*Not held* (WW I)
1919	A. R. F. Kingscote (UK) Sydney

1920..........P. O'Hara Wood (Vic.)
          Adelaide
1921...........R. H. Gemmel (WA)
          Perth
1922..........J. O. Anderson (NSW)
          Sydney
1923..........P. O'Hara Wood (Vic.)
          Brisbane
1924..........J. O. Anderson (NSW)
          Melbourne
1925..........J. O. Anderson (NSW)
          Sydney
1926.............J. B. Hawkes (Vic.)
          Adelaide
1927.............G. Patterson (Vic.)
          Melbourne
1928.............J. Borotra (France)
          Sydney
1929............J. C. Gregory (UK)
          Adelaide
1930.................E. Moon (Qld)
          Melbourne
1931.............J. Crawford (NSW)
          Sydney
1932.............J. Crawford (NSW)
          Adelaide
1933.............J. Crawford (NSW)
          Melbourne
1934...............F. J. Perry (UK)
          Sydney
1935.............J. Crawford (NSW)
          Melbourne
1936.............A. K. Quist (NSW)
          Adelaide
1937.............V. McGrath (NSW)
          Sydney
1938.............J. D. Budge (USA)
          Adelaide
1939............J. Bromwich (NSW)
          Melbourne
1940.............A. K. Quist (NSW)
          Sydney
1941–45 *Not held* (WW II)
1946............J. Bromwich (NSW)
          Adelaide
1947................D. Pails (NSW)
          Sydney
1948.............A. K. Quist (NSW)
          Melbourne
1949..............F. Sedgman (Vic.)
          Adelaide
1950..............F. Sedgman (Vic.)
          Melbourne
1951................R. Savitt (USA)
          Sydney

1952.............K. McGregor (SA)
          Adelaide
1953.............K. Rosewall (NSW)
          Melbourne
1954.................M. Rose (NSW)
          Sydney
1955.............K. Rosewall (NSW)
          Adelaide
1956.................L. Hoad (NSW)
          Brisbane
1957................A. Cooper (Vic.)
          Melbourne
1958................A. Cooper (Vic.)
          Sydney
1959..............A. Olmedo (USA)
          Adelaide
1960.................R. Laver (Qld)
          Brisbane
1961................R. Emerson (Qld)
          Melbourne
1962.................R. Laver (Qld)
          Sydney
1963................R. Emerson (Qld)
          Adelaide
1964................R. Emerson (Qld)
          Brisbane
1965................R. Emerson (Qld)
          Melbourne
1966................R. Emerson (Qld)
          Sydney
1967................R. Emerson (Qld)
          Adelaide
1968..............W. Bowery (NSW)
          Melbourne
1969.................R. Laver (Qld)
          Brisbane
1970..................A. Ashe (USA)
          Sydney
1971.............K. Rosewall (NSW)
          Sydney
1972.............K. Rosewall (NSW)
          Melbourne
1973............J. Newcombe (NSW)
          Melbourne
1974...............J. Connors (USA)
          Melbourne
1975............J. Newcombe (NSW)
          Melbourne
1976..........M. Edmondson* (NSW)
          Melbourne
1977......R. Tanner (USA) (January)
          Melbourne
1977..V. Gerulaitis (USA) (December)
          Melbourne

1978............G. Vilas (Argentina) Melbourne
1979............G. Vilas (Argentina) Melbourne
1980..............B. Teacher (USA) Melbourne
1981................J. Kriek (USA)** Melbourne
1982.................J. Kriek (USA) Melbourne
1983..........M. Wilander (Sweden) Melbourne
1984..........M. Wilander (Sweden) Melbourne
1985.............S. Edberg (Sweden) Melbourne
1986.............S. Edberg (Sweden) Melbourne
1987...........M. Wilander (Sweden) Melbourne

* Edmondson was the first unseeded player to win the Open.
** Born South Africa

Women's singles:

Although some evidence exists that an Australian 'championship' was held as early as 1908, it is more likely that it and subsequent 'title' events up to 1922 were State championships.

Year　　　　　　　Winner & Venue
1922...........M. Molesworth (Qld) Sydney
1923...........M. Molesworth (Qld) Brisbane
1924 ....S. Lance (NSW) Melbourne
1925 ....D. Akhurst (NSW) Sydney
1926.............D. Akhurst (NSW) Adelaide
1927..................E. Boyd (Vic.) Melbourne
1928..............D. Akhurst (NSW) Sydney
1929..............D. Akhurst (NSW) Adelaide
1930..............D. Akhurst (NSW) Melbourne
1931...........C. Buttsworth (NSW) Sydney
1932...........C. Buttsworth (NSW) Adelaide
1933..............J. Hartigan (NSW) Melbourne
1934..............J. Hartigan (NSW) Sydney
1935.................D. Round (UK) Melbourne
1936..............J. Hartigan (NSW) Adelaide
1937............Nancye Wynne (Vic.) Sydney
1938............D. M. Bundy (USA) Adelaide
1939..............V. Westacott (Qld) Melbourne
1940...........Nancye Wynne (Vic.) Sydney
1941-45 *Not held* (WW II)
1946 ....Nancy Bolton* (Vic.) Adelaide
1947............Nancye Bolton (Vic.) Sydney
1948............Nancye Bolton (Vic.) Melbourne
1949..................D. Hart (USA) Adelaide
1950................L. Brough (USA) Melbourne
1951............Nancye Bolton (Vic.) Sydney
1952..................T. Long (Vic.) Adelaide
1953.............M. Connolly (USA) Melbourne
1954...................T. Long (Vic.) Sydney
1955...............B. Penrose (NSW) Adelaide
1956 ....M. Carter (NSW) Brisbane
1957....................S. Fry (USA) Melbourne
1958...............A. Mortimer (UK) Sydney
1959 ....M. Reitano** (NSW) Adelaide
1960 ....M. Smith (NSW) Brisbane
1961................M. Smith (NSW) Melbourne
1962................M. Smith (NSW) Sydney
1963................M. Smith (NSW) Adelaide
1964................M. Smith (NSW) Brisbane
1965................M. Smith (NSW) Melbourne
1966................M. Smith (NSW) Sydney

1967...............N. Richey (USA)
                          Adelaide
1968.............B. J. King (USA)
                          Melbourne
1969...............M. Court*** (WA)
                          Brisbane
1970................M. Court (WA)
                          Sydney
1971................M. Court (WA)
                          Sydney
1972.................V. Wade (UK)
                          Melbourne
1973................M. Court (WA)
                          Melbourne
1974............E. Goolagong (NSW)
                          Melbourne
1975............E. Goolagong (NSW)
                          Melbourne
1976............E. Goolagong (NSW)
                          Melbourne
1977................K. Reid (NSW)
                          Melbourne
1978...............C. O'Neil (NSW)
                          Melbourne
1979...........Barbara Jordon (USA)
                          Melbourne
1980.........H. Mandlikova (Czech.)
                          Melbourne
1981............M. Navratilova (USA)
                          Melbourne
1982............C. Evert-Lloyd (USA)
                          Melbourne
1983............M. Navratilova (USA)
                          Melbourne
1984............C. Evert-Lloyd (USA)
                          Melbourne
1985............M. Navratilova (USA)
                          Melbourne
1986.........H. Mandlikova (Czech.)
                          Melbourne
1987............S. Graf (W. Germany)
                          Melbourne

* nee Wynne
** nee Carter
*** nee Smith

Most wins by Australians:
Men's singles: Six by Roy Emerson (Qld), between 1961 and 1967. But for a loss to Rod Laver (Qld) in 1962, Emerson would have won seven consecutive titles.
Women's singles: Eleven by Margaret Court (nee Smith) (WA), between 1960 and 1973.
Men's doubles: Eight by John Bromwich (NSW)–Adrian Quist (NSW), between 1938 and 1950. Quist won two earlier titles in 1936 and 1937 with Don Turnbull (NSW).
Women's doubles: Ten by Thelma Coyne (later Thelma Long) and Nancye Wynne (later Nancye Bolton). The pair won five titles in successive years 1936–40 and five more in 1947, '48, '49, '51 and '52. Thelma Long won two more titles with Mary Hawton in 1956 and 1958.

YOUNGEST CHAMPIONS
Australian men's singles:
Ken Rosewall (NSW) was 18 when he won in 1953.
Wimbledon singles:
Lew Hoad (NSW) was 22 when he won in 1956.
Australian women's singles:
Margaret Smith (WA) was 18 when she won in 1960.
Wimbledon singles:
Evonne Goolagong (NSW) was 20 when she won in 1971.

OLDEST CHAMPIONS
Australian men's singles:
Ken Rosewall was 37 when he won in 1972.
Wimbledon singles:
Norman E. Brookes was 37 when he won in 1914.
Australian men's doubles:
Norman E. Brookes was 47 when he partnered James O. Anderson to win in 1924.

OLYMPIC GAMES TENNIS
Four players have represented Australia in the Olympic Games, which included tennis on the program from 1896 to 1924. Edwin H. Flack (Vic.) represented Australia in the singles at the 1896 Games. He was eliminated in the first round. R. V. Thomas (SA), who won the Wimbledon doubles title with Pat O'Hara Wood in 1919, played in the singles at the Antwerp Olympics in 1920 but was eliminated in the first round. James Willard (NSW) and J. M. Bayley (NSW) played in the 1924 Paris Games. Both were eliminated in the third round of the singles and after winning their first round, were beaten in the second round of the doubles.

DAVIS CUP

The Davis Cup competition was inaugurated in 1900 at the suggestion of American patron and player Dwight F. Davis, after whom the event was named. Two nations participated in the first year.

DAVIS CUP RESULTS

Year	Venue	Result
1900	Boston, USA	USA d. GB 3-0
1901	*Not held*	No challenger
1902	Brooklyn, USA	USA d. GB 3-2
1903	Boston, USA	GB d. USA 4-1
1904	Wimbledon	GB d. Belgium 5-0
1905	Wimbledon	GB d. USA 5-0
1906	Wimbledon	GB d. USA 5-0
1907	**Wimbledon**	**Australasia d. GB 3-2**
1908	**Melbourne**	**Australasia d. USA 3-2**
1909	**Sydney**	**Australasia d. USA 5-0**
1910	*Not held*	No challenger
1911	**Christchurch, NZ**	**Australasia d. USA 5-0**
1912	Melbourne	GB d. Australasia 3-2
1913	Wimbledon	USA d. GB 3-2
1914	**New York**	**Australasia d. USA 3-2**
1915–18	*Not held* (WWI)	
1919	**Sydney**	**Australasia d. GB 4-1**
1920	Auckland, NZ	USA d. Australasia 5-0
1921	New York	USA d. Japan 5-0
1922	New York	USA d. Australasia 4-1
1923	New York	USA d. Australia 4-1
1924	Philadelphia	USA d. Australia 5-0
1925	Philadelphia	USA d. France 5-0
1926	Philadelphia	USA d. France 4-1
1927	Philadelphia	France d. USA 3-2
1928	Paris	France d. USA 4-1
1929	Paris	France d. USA 3-2
1930	Paris	France d. USA 4-1
1931	Paris	France d. GB 3-2
1932	Paris	France d. USA 3-2
1933	Paris	GB d. France 3-2
1934	Wimbledon	GB d. USA 4-1
1935	Wimbledon	GB d. USA 5-0
1936	Wimbledon	GB d. Australia 3-2
1937	Wimbledon	USA d. GB 4-1

Year	Venue	Result
1938	Philadelphia	USA d. Australia 3-2
1939	**Philadelphia**	**Australia d. USA 3-2**
1940–45	*Not held* (WWII)	
1946	Melbourne	USA d. Australia 5-0
1947	New York	USA d. Australia 4-1
1948	New York	USA d. Australia 5-0
1949	New York	USA d. Australia 4-1
1950	**New York**	**Australia d. USA 4-1**
1951	**Sydney**	**Australia d. USA 3-2**
1952	**Adelaide**	**Australia d. USA 4-1**
1953	**Melbourne**	**Australia d. USA 3-2**
1954	Sydney	USA d. Australia 3-2
1955	**New York**	**Australia d. USA 5-0**
1956	**Adelaide**	**Australia d. USA 3-2**
1957	**Melbourne**	**Australia d. USA 3-2**
1958	Brisbane	USA d. Australia 3-2
1959	**New York**	**Australia d. USA 3-2**
1960	**Sydney**	**Australia d. Italy 4-1**
1961	**Melbourne**	**Australia d. Italy 5-0**
1962	**Brisbane**	**Australia d. Mexico 5-0**
1963	Adelaide	USA d. Australia 3-2
1964	**Cleveland, USA**	**Australia d. USA 3-2**
1965	**Sydney**	**Australia d. Spain 4-1**
1966	**Melbourne**	**Australia d. India 4-1**
1967	**Brisbane**	**Australia d. Spain 4-1**
1968	Adelaide	USA d. Australia 4-1
1969	Cleveland, USA	USA d. Romania 5-0
1970	Cleveland, USA	USA d. W. Germany 5-0
1971	Charlotte, USA	USA d. Romania 3-2
1972	Bucharest, Romania	USA d. Romania 3-2
1973	**Cleveland, USA**	**Australia d. USA 5-0**
1974	*Not held*	S. Africa won by default*
1975	Stockholm	Sweden d. Czechoslovakia 3-2
1976	Santiago, Chile	Italy d. Chile 3-2
1977	**Sydney**	**Australia d. Italy 3-1**
1978	Palm Springs, USA	USA d. GB 4-1
1979	San Francisco	USA d. Italy 5-0
1980	Rome	Czechoslovakia d. Italy 4-1

Year	Venue	Result
1981	Cincinnati (USA)	USA d. Argentina 3-1
1982	Grenoble, France	USA d. France 4-1
1983	**Melbourne**	**Australia d. Sweden 3-2**
1984	Gothenburg, Sweden	Sweden d. USA 4-1
1985	Munich, W. Germany	Sweden d. West Germany 3-2
1986	Gothenburg, Sweden	Sweden d. West Germany 4-1
1987	Gothenburg, Sweden	Sweden d. India 5-0

* As a protest against apartheid, India refused to play South Africa in the Final.

MISCELLANY

Largest attendance in Australia:
25,578 – at Sydney's White City Stadium for the Davis Cup Challenge Round between Australia and the USA, on 27 December 1954. It remained a world record for a single-day attendance until 1973.

Australia's first official world champion:
Ken Rosewall (NSW), when he won the inaugural World Championship of Tennis at Dallas, Texas, USA in 1970. Rosewall defeated fellow Australian Rod Laver (Qld), 6-4, 1-6, 7-6, 7-6.

Biggest prize won by an Australian:
A$222,000 won by John Newcombe (NSW), when he lost to Jimmy Connors (USA) in a A$592,000 match sponsored by the CBS TV network at Caesar's Palace, Las Vegas, in 1975. Winner Connors received A$370,000 after winning 6-3, 4-6, 6-2, 6-4.

First overseas tour by official Australian women's team:
In 1925, when Daphne Ackhurst (NSW), Esme Boyd (Vic.), R. Harper (Vic.) and F. St George (NSW) toured England, Wales, Scotland, Ireland, Belgium, Holland, France and the USA, winning five 'Tests' and losing four – to England, France, East America and West America.

Only unseeded player to win the Australian Singles Championship or Open:
Mark Edmondson (NSW), who upset defending champion John Newcombe (NSW) at Kooyong, Vic. in 1976, 6-7, 6-3, 7-6, 6-1.

Two Australian singles titles in one year:
In 1977 the LTAA was forced to rearrange the championship circuit to fit in with overseas countries and could not avoid scheduling two Australian Men's Singles Championships within 12 months. In January, traditionally the month for the national singles title, Roscoe Tanner (USA) defeated Guillermo Vilas (Argentina) and in December of the same year, Vitas Gerulaitis (USA) defeated John Lloyd (USA).

TRACK AND FIELD

BEGINNINGS IN AUSTRALIA
The first track competition centred on solo long-distance record attempts and runs for bets by such memorable characters as 'The Flying Pieman', who thought nothing of challenging horse-drawn coaches to races between Sydney and Parramatta. The first track and road races were completely professional, and organised amateur competition did not commence until early 1872.

First Australian Championships (amateur):
Staged, as so many other sports were at the time, as the 'Australasian Championships', at Melbourne, in 1893. Two outstanding winners at the inaugural titles were Edwin H. Flack of Melbourne (later to win two gold medals at the inaugural Modern Olympics in 1896), who won the one mile (1.6 km) event in 4 mins 44 secs, and sprinter Billy MacPherson (NSW), who won the 100 yds, 220 yds and 440 yds (91.4 m, 201 m and 402.3 m) titles.

First controlling body:
The Amateur Athletics Association of Australasia formed in 1897 (later, after the withdrawal of New Zealand in 1927, to become the Australian Amateur Athletic Union).

First Australian Olympian—men:
E. H. (Edwin) Flack (1874–1935), who represented Australia and the London Athletic Club at the 1896 inaugural Modern Olympics in Athens and won the 800 m in 2 mins 11.0 secs, the 1,500 m in 4 mins 33.2 secs and led the marathon until he collapsed at the 37 km mark. Flack was not an official Australian entry. He was practising accountancy in London and competing with the London Athletic Club when he decided to pay his own way to Athens. Flack, who it is believed competed in the singlet of his London club, also entered as an Australian for the singles tennis and represented Great Britain in tennis at doubles at the same Games.

First Olympian—women:
Miss Edie Robinson (Mrs Edie Payne) who, in 1926, in Amsterdam, competed in the 100 m and 800 m events. She finished third behind American Elizabeth Robinson in the semi-final of the 100 m and just missed qualifying for the final, won by the American. Reports of her performance in the 800 m vary from finishing fifth to retiring in her heat.

Australia's Olympic Games gold medal winners:

Men

800 m	Albert Flack (Vic.) Athens 1896
	Ralph Doubell (Vic.) Mexico City 1968
1,500 m	Albert Flack (Vic.) Athens 1896
	Herb Elliott (Vic.) Rome 1960
High Jump	John Winter (WA) London 1948
Triple Jump	A. W. (Nick) Winter (NSW) Paris 1924

Note: At the 1900 Paris Olympic Games, Stanley Rowley (NSW) won a gold medal representing England in the 5,000 m cross country teams event.

Women

100 m	Marjorie Jackson (NSW) Helsinki 1952
	Betty Cuthbert (NSW) Melbourne 1956
200 m	Marjorie Jackson (NSW) Helsinki 1952
	Betty Cuthbert (NSW) Melbourne 1956

400 m	....	Betty Cuthbert (NSW) Tokyo 1964
80 m hurdles	...	Shirley Strickland (WA) Helsinki 1952 Shirley Strickland (WA) Melbourne 1956 Maureen Caird (NSW) Mexico City 1968
4 x 100 m relay	....	Australian team (Shirley Strickland, Fleur Mellor, Norma Croker, Betty Cuthbert) Melbourne 1956
Heptathlon	....	Glynis Nunn (SA) Los Angeles 1984

First Australian world record holder:
Nigel Barker (NSW, 1883-1948), who clocked 48.5 secs for 440 yds (402.3 m) at the Sydney Cricket Ground on 11 November 1905. The time was universally accepted and stood as the world record until 1916, and as the Australian record until 1930. In 1891, Billy MacPherson (NSW, 1866-1922), was clocked at 9.8 secs for 100 yds (91.4 m) and this time stood as an Australian amateur record until bettered by Jimmy Carlton (NSW) in 1930.

First to break four minutes for the mile:
John Landy (Vic.), who set a new world mile (1,609.3 m) record of 3 mins 57.9 secs at Turku, Finland, on 21 June 1954 — just 46 days after Roger Bannister of England became the first man to break the four-minute barrier with 3 mins 59.4 secs at Oxford, England, on 6 May 1954.

First Australian woman to hold a world record:
Marjorie Jackson (b. Coffs Harbour, NSW, 13 September 1931), later Mrs Marjorie Nelson, equalled the world 100 yds (91.4 m) record held by Fanny Blankers-Koen (Holland), when she was clocked at 10.8 secs in Sydney in 1950. Later the same year she equalled Fanny Blankers-Koen's world record for 220 yds (201 m), when she clocked 24.3 secs to win the Empire Games gold medal in Auckland and again equalled the world 100 yds record in her heat and final.

First Australian sprinter to reach an Olympic sprint final:
Stan Rowley (b. Sydney, NSW, 1877), who won the bronze medal (third place) in the 60 m, 100 m and 200 m at the Paris Olympic Games of 1900. Rowley also won a (long-forgotten) gold medal at the same Olympics. Competing (as the rules of the time allowed) for Great Britain in the 5,000 m cross country teams event, he was classed as an official finisher.

First Australian to win a field games gold medal at an Olympic Games:
A. W. 'Nick' Winter (1884-1955), all-round sportsman, who won the hop, step and jump (now known as the triple jump) at the 1924 Paris Games.

First woman to win an Olympic track gold medal:
Marjorie Jackson, who won the 100 m sprint at the 1952 Helsinki Olympics, equalling the world record of 11.5 secs despite a headwind.

Most gold medals at an Olympic Games—men:
Two: for the 800 m and 1,500 m, won by Edwin Flack at the Athens Games in 1896.

Most gold medals at an Olympic Games—women:
Four: for the 100 m, 200 m and 4 × 100 m relays at the Melbourne Games in 1956 and the 400 m relay at the Tokyo Games in 1964, by Betty Cuthbert (b. Sydney, NSW, 20 April 1938).

Most famous record breakers:
Ron Clarke (b. Melbourne, Vic., 1937), who set 17 world records in a four-year span (1963-68), for distances ranging from two miles (3.2 km) to the maximum distance coverable in one hour (12 miles, 1,006 yds). Despite his towering ability, Clarke never won an Olympic gold medal, his only medal coming at the 1964 Tokyo Games when he finished third in the 10,000 m after leading into the final 200 m. Nor was he able to win a gold medal at the Commonwealth Games. He was placed second three times (three miles at Perth, 1962, and three and six miles at Kingston, Jamaica, in 1966).

Herb Elliott (b. Perth, WA, 25 February 1938), was never beaten at senior level over the mile or 1,500 m and lost only one race over either distance in his entire career. Elliott won the 1,500 m at the 1960 Rome Olympic Games in a world record 3 mins 35.6 secs and won gold medals for the 880 yds and one mile at the 1958 British Commonwealth Games at Cardiff, Wales. Elliott broke four minutes for the mile 17 times, and in Dublin on 6 August 1958, set a world mile record of 3 mins 54.5 secs.

Only Australian gold medallist at consecutive Olympic Games:
Shirley Strickland (gold: 80 m hurdles 1952 and 1956, 4 × 100 m relay 1956; silver: 4 × 100 m relay 1948; bronze: 100 m and 80 m hurdles 1948, 80 m hurdles 1952).

Note: Strickland's total should, in all fairness, be eight. She appeared to have finished third in the 200 m at London in 1948, but the judge did not call for the photo finish and awarded third place to American Audrey Patterson. No Australian protest was made. Much later, when the photographic evidence was examined, it was obvious she should have been awarded a bronze medal.

The marathon:
Easily Australia's greatest marathon runner is Robert de Castella (b. Melbourne, Vic., 27 May 1957). De Castella won the 1982 Commonwealth Games event at Brisbane and after that the unofficial 'World Championship' at Helsinki, Finland. Lack of judgement resulted in him finishing out of a place at the 1984 Olympics at Los Angeles, USA. He made a comeback to win the famous Boston Marathon in the USA in April 1986 and clocked the third fastest time on record for the distance. He also retained his Commonwealth title at Edinburgh in 1986. Before De Castella's rise to fame Derek Clayton (b. Ireland, arrived Melbourne 1963), was Australia's outstanding marathon runner. On 30 May 1969, Clayton ran the distance (26 miles 385 yards — 42,195 m) in 2 hrs 8 mins 33.6 secs at Antwerp, Belgium, to clock the fastest time ever by an Australian and the fastest ever recorded for the race. Because the terrain of marathon courses varies from race to race, 'record' times are not accepted.

Best woman marathon runner:
Lisa Martin of South Australia who won the gold medal at the inaugural Commonwealth Games marathon for women at Edinburgh on 1 August 1986. (Robert de Castella won the men's marathon the same day.) She finished 7th in the inaugural women's marathon at the 1984 Olympic Games at Los Angeles. She set her first Australian national record at Chicago, USA, on 24 October 1984 with a time of 2 hrs 27 mins 40 secs.

COMMONWEALTH GAMES

Australians have won almost every event on the Commonwealth Games schedule since the first (Empire) Games were staged at Hamilton, Canada, in 1930 and before that at the Festival of Empire competition at London in 1911. Australia has hosted the Games on three occasions — Sydney in 1938, Perth in 1962 and Brisbane in 1982.

First Games track winner:
Decima Norman (1914-83), won the women's 100 yds at the Sydney Cricket Ground in 1938.

First Games field winner:
Jack Metcalfe (b. Sydney, NSW, 3 February 1912), who won the triple jump at London in 1934.

Most Australian gold medals:
The Australian team won 39 gold, 39 silver and 29 bronze (total 107) at the 1982 Games in Brisbane, Qld.

Most individual gold medals at a single Games:
Five by Decima Norman at Sydney in

1938 – 100 yds, 220 yds, 440 yds medley relay, 660 yds medley relay, long jump.

Most gold medals all Games:
Seven by Marjorie Jackson – 100 yds, 220 yds, 440 yds medley relay, 600 yds medley relay at Auckland, NZ, 1950; 100 yds, 220 yds, 4 × 100 yds relay at Vancouver, Canada, 1954.

PROFESSIONAL ATHLETICS

The first recorded professional footrace took place early in the 1830s and the first fully documented races in 1868, when Victorian Tom Cusack of Wangaratta clashed with Irish-born star Mat Higgins, at a number of different venues in and around Melbourne.

First Stawell Gift:
Synonymous with professional athletics in Australia and famous throughout the world, the first Stawell Gift (at Stawell, Vic.) was held in 1878 and won by W. J. Millard off a handicap of 8 yds (7.3 m). The Stawell Gift was first held over 130 yds (118.9 m) and remained unchanged until 1973 when the organisers decided to use the metric system and changed the distance to 120 m.

First overseas winner:
Edward S. Skinner (USA), who, in 1899, won the Gift in 12 secs from a 9 yd (8.2 m) handicap.

First to win from scratch:
Jean-Louis Ravelomanantsoa of

STAWELL GIFT WINNERS

Year	Winner	Hcp yds/metres	Time secs
1878	W. J. Millard	8.0	12.75
1879	T. Grose	6.5	13.0
1880	C. G. Whiteney	7.5	12.7
1881	J. Rogers	9.0	12.0
1882	A. Parkinson	11.0	12.75
1883	R. Kinnear	14.0	12.5
1884	W. Smith	7.5	12.0
1885	W. Mummery	10.0	12.25
1886	W. Clarke	7.0	11.75
1887	J. Brown	12.0	11.75
1888	C. Bingham	10.5	11.25
1889	E. S. Skinner	9.0	12.0
1890	J. Midson	11.0	11.9
1891	H. Martin	13.0	11.75
1892	A. Hepner	12.0	12.0
1893	F. J. Hough	12.5	11.5
1894	P. J. Breen	11.0	11.75
1895	W. E. Joy	5.0	12.25
1896	R. G. Nesbitt	11.5	12.25
1897	G. S. Tuckey	12.0	12.25
1898	U. S. Lewis	14.0	11.8
1899	N. C. Clarke	14.5	11.8
1900	D. Strickland	10.0	12.0
1901	E. T. Kenny	14.0	12.0
1902	A. Tredinnick	11.5	12.2
1903	H. Dew	12.0	12.2

Year	Winner	Hcp yds/metres	Time secs
1904	J. F. Flannagan	10.0	12.2
1905	C. N. McKenzie	10.0	12.0
1906	E. W. Thompson	10.0	12.2
1907	C. W. Knox	12.5	12.4
1908	C. King	12.0	11.8
1909	H. Rigby	11.5	11.8
1910	T. Dancey	13.0	11.4
1911	D. H. Devine	13.0	11.4
1912	E. E. Carter	11.5	12.2
1913	E. A. George	12.5	12.2
1914	W. Robinson	12.0	11.8
1915	D. Fleming	10.0	11.4
1916	C. P. Cassidy	13.75	12.0
1917	F. C. Swindells	11.75	12.2
1918	A. Roach*	14.0	12.6
1919	H. W. Evans	10.5	12.2
1920	A. G. Cashmore	7.0	12.4
1921	L. J. Jennings	9.25	12.4
1922	P. L. Till	10.5	11.7
1923	J. E. Curran	9.0	12.0
1924	W. Twomey	8.5	12.1
1925	T. Banner	5.0	12.2
1926	W. G. Allen	9.5	12.25
1927	T. G. Miles	10.0	12.1
1928	L. Cooper	8.0	11.9
1929	C. H. Hearn	10.5	11.9
1930	R. K. Hodge	11.25	11.8
1931	F. J. Ralph	9.5	11.9
1932	R. Barker	11.75	12.1
1933	C. G. Heath	11.0	11.6
1934	T. L. Roberts	9.75	11.6
1935	M. M. Bishop	7.5	12.0
1936	R. McCann	6.5	12.25
1937	F. A. Bradley	10.0	12.0
1938	J. W. Grant	11.5	11.7
1939	L. W. Sprague	9.5	11.9
1940	A. J. Reid	8.5	12.2
1941	W. K. Hutton	6.25	12.4
1942–45	Not held (WWII)		
1946	V. T. Deane	7.0	11.9
1947	A. C. Martin	4.25	11.9
1948	T. F. Brudenhall	8.0	12.2
1949	J. E. Cann	8.25	11.8

Year	Winner	Hcp yds/metres	Time secs
1950	W. K. Trewick	10.0	11.9
1951	G. R. Hutchinson	8.0	11.8
1952	L. G. Mann	7.25	11.9
1953	R. J. Hart	5.75	12.0
1954	J. K. Hayes	9.0	11.8
1955	J. O'Donnell	8.75	12.0
1956	W. R. Williams	12.0	11.8
1957	J. R. Carr	10.5	11.8
1958	M. Durrant	8.5	11.8
1959	G. Treacey	11.25	11.8
1960	W. J. McCann	6.25	11.8
1961	C. Savage	6.25	12.2
1962	L. N. Beachley	8.25	12.1
1963	A. J. Bell	12.0	12.0
1964	N. Hussey	8.5	12.1
1965	B. Cox	7.5	12.5
1966	B. Howard	8.75	11.9
1967	B. Howard**	5.75	11.6
1968	I. Miller	9.75	11.6
1969	B. McLeod	7.75	12.0
1970	B. Foley	11.0	11.8
1971	J. McGregor	7.25	11.7
1972	B. Foley	7.5	11.8
1973	B. Moss***	10.75 m	12.1
1974	P. Durham	7.25	12.0
1975	J. Ravelomanantsoa****	Scratch	12.0
1976	A. Pollack	8.5	12.1
1977	W. Edmonson	1.25	12.0
1978	S. Proudlock	8.0	11.9
1979	N. McMahon	8.25	12.0
1980	J. Dinan	5.5	12.3
1981	G. McNeill	4.0	11.9
1982	C. Perry	7.0	12.19
1983	D. O'Brien	7.0	12.17
1984	P. Singleton	5.0	11.95
1985	P. Young	10.75	12.07
1986	G. Chapman	7.0	12.01
1987	R. Elliott	8.25	12.13
1988	S. Antonich	6.00	12.28

* First three placegetters 'disqualified' and prize-money withheld, but winner still recognised.
** First man to win the Gift twice (equalled in 1972 by B. Foley).
*** First man to win over metric distance (120 metres).
**** First man to win from scratch.

Malagasy, in 1975, with a time of 12.0 secs. No runner has won from scratch since. Prior to Ravelomanantsoa's victory, the winner from the lowest handicap was A. C. Martin from 4 1/4 yds (4.7985 m) in 1947 and in the metric era, Bill Edmonson (USA) won off 1.25 m in 1977 in 12.0 secs.

First man to win two Stawell Gifts:
Bruce Howard (Vic.) in 1966 off 8 3/4 yds (8 m) and in 1967 from 5 1/4 yds (4.8 m). The second man to win twice was Bob Foley (Vic.) in 1970 off 11 yds (10 m) and in 1972 off 7 1/2 yds (6.9 m).

First Australian international stars:
Arthur Postle (b. Qld, 1881) and Jack Donaldson (Vic., 1886-1933). Both dominated professional athletics in Australia and later competed with success in South Africa, England and Scotland. Donaldson, who later became an athletics coach in the United States and lost his life when he fell under a train in New York, set six world records and one of his records—for 130 yds (118.9 m)—stood from 1911 until 1951. After Donaldson set the record, the track was measured and found to be slightly uphill—and 132 yds 2 ins (120.8 m).

First professional to break four minutes for the mile:
Victorian Harold Downes, at Bendigo in March 1963. Downes started from scratch in a handicap, had to contend with a big field and clocked 3 mins 59.7 secs.

First professional World Championship in Australia:
In 1935, when 1932 Olympic champion Eddie Tolan (USA) and British champion Bill McFarlane came to Australia to race local champions Austin Robertson and T. L. Roberts at the Melbourne Exhibition Ground. Tolan won all events except the 130 yds (118.9 m), won by Robertson, and was acclaimed champion.

First professional to win amateur title:
On 29 March 1987, John Dinan became the first former professional runner to win an Australian amateur title. Dinan, who won the Stawell Gift in 1980 and later regained his amateur status, won the national 200 m sprint title in 20.69 secs. He was later omitted from the Australian team for the Seoul Olympic Games in controversial circumstances.

Notable long distance runners:
George Perdon (Vic.), whose greatest feat was running from Fremantle (WA) to Sydney (NSW), a distance of 2,897 miles (4,662.3 km) in 1973 in 47 days 1 hr 45 mins (11 August-27 September). En route he set world professional records for 1,000, 1,500, 2,000 and 2,600 miles (1,609.3, 2,414, 3,218.7 and 4,184.3 km).

Bill Emmerton of Tasmania became the first man (in 1968) to run the 125 mile (201.2 km) length of Death Valley, USA. Emmerton took 3 days 23 mins, in temperatures above 37°C.

Tony Rafferty of Victoria set a record (previously held by Emmerton) for the Adelaide to Melbourne distance, when he covered it in nine days exactly.

Far from the greatest runner, but easily the most publicised in recent times, is NSW farmer Cliff Young who won the inaugural Sydney-Melbourne road race. Young's age and his charisma gained him immense publicity, but his time was far short of George Perdon's 1978 record of 9 days 5 hrs for the 1,048 km.

TROTTING AND PACING

BEGINNINGS IN AUSTRALIA
Trotting, as distinct from pacing, was launched in Australia at exactly the same time as galloping races, and for exactly the same reasons. Rival owners enjoyed matching their horses in friendly competitions ranging from long-distance record attempts, such as the 15 miles or so between Sydney and the settlement at Parramatta, to match races on rough dirt or grass tracks.

First recorded race:
At James Latta's historic carnival at Parramatta on 10 April 1810. Added to the program of galloping match races and wheelbarrow races, sack races and athletic events, was a trotting race, won by Miss Kitty, described in *The History of NSW*, 2nd ed., 1818, as 'famous'. As author and trotting historian Greg Brown points out in his definitive work *One Hundred Years of Trotting 1877–1977*, the mention of Miss Kitty indicates that the mare and her deeds were well known and that, almost certainly, trotting races were held in some form prior to 1810. Following 1810, most trotting competitions took the form of match races on public roads, the stretch between Moore Park and Randwick in Sydney being especially popular.

First serious track racing:
In 1882 at Elsternwick Park, Vic., where Vermont Junior, a seven-year-old stallion imported from San Francisco, USA, was one of the early champions. Other tracks to operate after the opening of Elsternwick included Moonee Valley, Richmond and Ascot in Melbourne, Vic., and the Royal Agricultural Society's ground at Moore Park, Sydney.

Early racing in Sydney:
The RAS ground, known today as the Sydney Showground, included trotting events in equestrian exhibitions as early as 1882–83, and in August 1884 the Metropolitan Exhibition held at the ground featured 'show racing', similar to the events held at the Royal Easter Show.

First club in NSW:
The Sydney Driving Park Club, believed to have been formed in or about 1884. The club joined forces with the RAS in 1885 to stage regular meetings at the Sydney Showground and the first 'open' meeting was staged on 24 October 1885. Despite a lukewarm press and average crowds of only two to three thousand, racing continued at the Showground until 1892, when the Sydney Trotting Association was formed and began staging meetings at Canterbury Park Racecourse.

The Association lasted barely a year and was replaced on 13 September 1893 by the NSW Trotting Club which commenced racing at Kensington Racecourse. A combination of factors—public dissatisfaction with the control of the sport, too-obviously rigged races and disagreements between officials, owners and drivers—contributed to the downfall of the NSWTC in March 1894.

First trotting at Harold Park:
Prior to 1894, trotting was in a sorry state with few meetings in Sydney and enthusiasts forced to travel to outlying country centres to race their horses. The Sydney Showground, being a saucer track barely 556 yards to the lap, was too small and horse racing clubs were beginning to make it difficult for trotters to race at such tracks as Kensington and Canterbury Park. Enthusiasts began to look at the possibilities of the Lillie Bridge Athletic Ground in Glebe, Sydney, where promoter George Edgar regularly staged pony racing and athletic carnivals. Trotting was first held at the ground (later to be called Forest Lodge, then Epping Racecourse and finally, in 1929, Harold Park) on 16 February 1890. The occasion was historic because the trotters raced under lights.

Formation of the new NSW Trotting Club:

In October 1902, under the presidency of Mr John Moriarty, a Scotsman with wide business and sporting interests. The NSWTC staged its first meeting at Harold Park on 19 November 1902.

Expansion of trotting in NSW:

Between November 1902 and July 1904, the NSWTC encouraged the establishment of country zone associations and nine such controlling bodies were formed. By the 1913-14 season, no less than 116 affiliated associations were registered in NSW. Despite this expansion, trotting lagged well behind racing as a popular sport. In 1906 Sydney boasted 10 galloping tracks and conducted some 360 meetings a year, while trotting could only manage 26 meetings a year.

Expansion interstate:

The appeal of the original night meeting at Lillie Bridge (Harold Park) in 1890 was obviously lost on interstate trotting associations and promoters. The first night meeting at the Wayville Showground, Adelaide, SA, was held in 1920 and the first in Perth at the WA Cricket Association ground in 1914.

First totalisator meeting in Australia:

At Perth in 1916, the WA Trotting Club became the first racing club of any sort in Australia to use the automatic tote invented in 1913 by New Zealander Sir George Julius.

First 1,000-pound race:

Held in 1911, staged by colourful Melbourne business magnate John Wren who purchased the Richmond track in Melbourne and ran it as a proprietary course from 1905. Twenty horses (10 in harness and 10 saddle-ridden, as was normal in those days) started in the inaugural race which was won by the 7/4 favourite Delavan Chimes ridden by Gus Millsom. First prize was a huge (by the standards of the day) 750 pounds. Sydney's Australian Trotting Club copied the Wren promotion and staged a Sydney Thousand in 1914.

First Australian championship:

Held in 1925 in Perth, WA. This promotion paved the way for the staging of the now world-famous Inter-Dominion Championship, first staged in Perth in 1936.

Naming of Harold Park:

The original Lillie Bridge Athletic Ground was named Harold Park in 1929 after Childe Harold, son of the great American sire Harold, a son of the famous Hambletonian. Childe Harold (like his brothers Vancleve and Tuxedo) was the first great sire of many Australian trotting champions.

Establishment of the Inter-Dominion Championship:

In 1934, J. P. (James) Stratton, the President of the WATC, met in Sydney with New Zealand trotting chief H. F. (Harry) Nicoll to discuss the possibility of an Australasian trotting championship which would be held in the same esteem as galloping's Melbourne Cup. The meeting produced the idea of the Inter-Dominion carnival and Gloucester Park, Perth, was selected as the venue for the inaugural carnival held in 1936 and won by Evicus, a Tasmanian horse driven by Freeman Holmes Snr. The inaugural title was decided not on the result of the Grand Final (won by another Tasmanian horse, Logan Derby), which followed three qualifying rounds, but on a complex formula involving fastest times. Evicus spotted Logan Derby from a 24-yd start and emerged as the Grand Champion on points scored.

First horse to win successive Inter-Dominions:

Hondo Grattan, at Sydney in 1973 and Perth in 1974, driven by A. D. (Tony) Turnbull of NSW. The 1974 Grand

Final was marred by one of the worst pile-ups in the history of the race.

First horse to win two Inter-Dominions:
Captain Sandy, driven by J. D. (Jack) Watts in 1950 at Melbourne and by Bob Pollock at Perth in 1953.

New Zealand honours Inter-Dominion winner:
The New Zealand Government honoured the champion New Zealand pacer Cardigan Bay (first Australasian trotter or pacer to win more than $1,000,000 in prize money), following his win in the 1963 Inter-Dominion on the tight Wayville track in Adelaide, SA, by issuing a special postage stamp. It is believed to have been the first postage stamp issued in Australasia to honour a racehorse.

World record Inter-Dominion attendance:
An official crowd of 50,346 – a world record – attended the 1960 Grand Final at Sydney's Harold Park. The Grand Final was won by Caduceus (Jack Litten, NZ) and the attendance was actually higher than the official figure because thousands tore gaps in fences to gain admittance.

Youngest and oldest drivers to win the Inter-Dominion:
Chris Lewis (SA) was 20 when he won with Carclew at Adelaide in 1976. Freeman Holmes Snr (NZ) was 65 when he won the inaugural Grand Championship behind Evicus at Perth in 1936.

First $100,000-plus Inter-Dominion Grand Final:
Held in 1978 at Moonee Valley, when the race carried $105,000 and was won by Markovina driven by Brian Gath.

First Miracle Mile:
In March 1967, the W. D. & H. O. Wills tobacco company took over the previously named Lightning Stakes and sponsored the event as the Craven Filter Miracle Mile. It was the first major tobacco-product sponsored event in Australian trotting and was an instant success. The inaugural race at Harold Park drew a crowd of 20,000 and the winner, Robin Dundee, a champion New Zealand pony, flashed home the winner in less than two minutes, clocking 1 min 59 secs for the mile – the first time two minutes had been broken on the mainland. Two minutes has not always been broken for the mile sprint. Halwes (Tas.), Adaptor (Vic.), Lucky Creed (Qld) and Mount Eden (WA) all beat the clock in successive years 1968–71, but in 1972, winner Bay Foyle could clock 'only' 2.00.6. In the following year Reichman (Vic.) set a new race record with 1.58.4, equalled in 1976 by Paleface Adios (NSW).

First trotter or pacer to win $1,000,000 prize money in Australasia:
Gammalite (Vic.), which passed the million-dollar mark on 28 October 1983 when he won the Tatts Golden Mile at Harold Park and pushed his earnings to $1,007,000. By the end of the 1983–84 season Gammalite had increased this to $1,304,206 from 86 wins and 47 placings from 155 starts. At that stage only galloper Kingston Town (with $1,605,930) had earned more prize money in all forms of Australasian horseracing. New Zealand-bred Cardigan Bay was the first Australasian horse to earn more than $1,000,000 in prize money, but his total of $1,000,837 included prize money from 37 wins in the USA and Canada after he had been purchased for $100,000 by an American syndicate in 1964.

First use of a mobile barrier:
On 2 November 1956 at Harold Park, Sydney. The mobile barrier start was first used at an Inter-Dominion meeting at Moonee Valley, Vic., in 1978.

Greatest Australian-bred pacer:
Arguably, Popular Alm. In the 1983–84 Australian season, Popular Alm fractured a pastern in a back leg 10 days after winning the $50,000 Winfield Pacing Cup at Moonee Valley. The broken pastern was pinned together with compression screws in a five-hour operation in mid-December 1983 and by late February the champion was back in light training. Popular Alm was unbeaten in seven starts prior to his accident and won the $7,500 Navy Cup on 30 September 1983 by 10 m. He then won the $100,000 Craven Filter Sprint at the inaugural meeting of the rebuilt Albion Park track in Brisbane, Qld, and a week

INTER-DOMINION PACING CHAMPIONSHIP

Year	Venue	Winner (Driver)	Hcp	Dist.
1936	Perth (WA)*	**Logan Derby** (J. Agnew)	Fr	12 f
1937	Adelaide (SA)	**Dan's Son** (B. Coram)	Fr	12 f
1938	Christchurch (NZ)	**Pot Luck** (M. Holmes)	12 yds	13 f
1939	Launceston (Tas.)	**Springfield Globe** (W. A. O'Shea)	24 yds	12 f
1940	Perth (WA)	**Grand Mogul** (K. A. Anderson)	Fr	13 f
1941-46	*Not held* (WW II)			
1947	Perth (WA)	**Bandbox** (L. Moriarty)	12 yds	13 f
1948	Auckland (NZ)	**Emoleus** (K. Tatterson)	36 yds	16 f
1949	Adelaide (SA)	**Single Direct** (E. N. Kennerley)	36 yds	14 f
1950	Melbourne (Vic.)	**Captain Sandy** (J. D. Watts)	24 yds	14 f
1951	Christchurch (NZ)	**Vedette** (M. Holmes)	12 yds	13 f
1952	Sydney (NSW)	**Avian Derby** (G. D. Wilson)	24 yds	13 f
1953	Perth (WA)	**Captain Sandy** (R. Pollock)	24 yds	13 f
1954	Adelaide (SA)	**Tennessee Sky** (F. E. Kersley)	12 yds	13 f
1955	Auckland (NZ)	**Tactician** (M. C. McTigue)	18 yds	16 f
1956	Sydney (NSW)	**Gentleman John** (E. Rothacker)	12 yds	13½ f
1957	Perth (WA)	**Radiant Venture** (F. Connor)	Fr	13 f
1958	Adelaide (SA)	**Free Hall** (W. Shin)	Fr	12 f, 206 yds
1959	Melbourne (Vic.)	**Young Pedro** (L. P. Hunt)	Fr	14 f
1960	Sydney (NSW)	**Caduceus** (J. D. Litten)	36 yds	13 f, 98 yds
1961	Christchurch (NZ)	**Massacre** (D. C. Watts)	Fr	13 f
1962	Perth (WA)	**James Scott** (P. J. Hall)	24 yds	13 f
1963	Adelaide (SA)	**Cardigan Bay** (P. T. Wolfenden)	24 yds	12 f, 206 yds
1964	Melbourne (Vic.)	**Minuteman** (E. R. Hurley)	Fr	14 f
1965	Dunedin (NZ)**	**Robin Dundee** (D. J. Townley)	12 yds	13 f, 108 yds
		Jay Ar (G. B. Noble)	*(deadheat)*	
1966	Sydney (NSW)	**Chamfer's Star** (B. J. Forrester)	Fr	13 f, 98 yds

Year	Venue	Winner (Driver)	Hcp	Dist.
1967	Perth (WA)	**Binshaw** (P. Coulson)	Fr	13 f
1968	Auckland (NZ)	**First Lee** (K. Robinson)	Fr	13 f
1969	Adelaide (SA)	**Richmond Lass** (K. Brooks)	Fr	12 f, 206 yds
1970	Melbourne (Vic.)	**Bold David** (A. Simons)	Fr	14 f, 36 yds
1971	Christchurch (NZ)***	**Stella Frost** (D. J. Townley)	24 yds	13 f
1972	Brisbane (Qld)	**Welcome Advice** (A. Harpley)	12 yds	12 f
1973	Sydney (NSW)****	**Hondo Grattan** (A. D. Turnbull)	Fr	13 f, 98 yds
1974	Perth (WA)	**Hondo Grattan** (A. D. Turnbull)	15 m	2,600 m
1975	Auckland (NZ)	**Young Quinn** (J. Langdon)	15 m	2,700 m
1976	Adelaide (SA)	**Carclew** (C. Lewis)	Fr	2,660 m
1977	Brisbane (Qld)	**Stanley Rio** (J. Noble)	Fr	2,530 m
1978	Melbourne (Vic.)	**Markovina** (B. Gath)	Fr	2,900 m
1979	Christchurch (NZ)	**Rondel** (P. Wolfenden)	Fr	2,600 m
1980	Sydney (NSW)	**Koala King** (B. Hancock)	10 m	2,700 m
1981	Hobart (Tas.)	**San Simeon** (L. Austin)	Fr	2,750 m
1982	Perth (WA)	**Rhett's Law** (C. Warwick)	Fr	2,625 m
1983	Auckland (NZ)	**Gammalite** (B. Clarke)	Fr	2,700 m
1984	Adelaide (SA)	**Gammalite** (B. Clarke)	Fr	2,650 m
1985	Melbourne (Vic.)	**Preux Chevalier** (B. Perkins)	Fr	2,870 m
1986	Brisbane (Qld)	**Village Kid** (C. Lewis)	Fr	2,530 m
1987	Christchurch (NZ)	**My Lightning Blue** (J. O'Sullivan)	Fr	2,600 m
1988	Sydney (NSW)	**Our Maestro** (J. E. Binskin)	Fr	2,700 m

* Under the anomalous points system then in operation, Logan Derby, which won the Grand Final and was unbeaten throughout the inaugural Championship series in 1936, did not take out the title of 'Grand Champion'. This title was awarded to Grand Final runner-up Evicus. The unwieldy points system (based on times and handicaps) was abandoned after the 1947 Final. 'Grand Champion' awards were made to Evicus (1936), Parisienne (1938), Logan Derby (1940) and Bandbox (1947).
** This was the first — and to date only — dead heat in the Grand Final.
*** Junior's Image (WA), trained and driven by P. Coulson, was first past the post in 1971, but was disqualified after returning a positive swab.
**** 1973 was the first year in which total prize money exceeded $100,000. The total stakes were $155,000, with a first prize of $50,000.

MIRACLE MILE WINNERS

All Miracle Mile races have been staged at Harold Park, Sydney, held under free-for-all conditions and begun from a mobile start. The race was originally known as the Craven Filter Miracle Mile and in recent years has become the JPS (John Player Special) Miracle Mile at the request of sponsors, W. D. & H. O. Wills.

Year	Winner	Driver	Time
1967	Robin Dundee (NZ)	R. Cameron	1.59.0*
1968	Halwes (Tas.)	K. Newman	1.58.6
1969	Adaptor (Vic.)	J. Hargreaves	1.59.2
1970	Lucky Creed (Qld)	V. Frost	1.59.0
1971	Mount Eden (WA)	E. J. Miles	1.58.8
1972	Bay Foyle (NSW)	C. Parsons	2.00.6
1973	Reichman (Vic.)	R. Hocking	1.58.4
1974	Hondo Grattan (NSW)	A. Turnbull	1.59.0
1975	Young Quinn (NZ)	C. Hunter	1.58.8
1976	Paleface Adios (NSW)	C. Pike	1.58.4
1977	Royal Force (WA)	D. Anderson	1.59.5
1978	Pure Steel (WA)	T. Demmler	2.00.4
1979	The Scotsman (NSW)	G. W. Sparkes	2.00.7
1980	Lecarne (NZ)	R. D. Butt	2.00.4
1981	Friendly Footman (NSW)	K. Newman	1.59.2
1982	Gundary Flyer (NSW)	M. Day	1.56.9
1983	Popular Alm (Vic.)	V. Knight	1.57.7
1984	Double Agent (NSW)	J. Ilsley	1.59.6
1985	Preux Chevalier (WA)	B. Perkins	1.56.7
1986	Village Kid (WA)	C. Lewis	1.56.9
1986****	Master Mood (NZ)	K. Williams***	1.56.1**
1987	Village Kid (WA)	C. Lewis*****	1.57.7

* First time the two-minute barrier was broken in Australia under race conditions.
** Race record.
*** Record first-place prize money—$91,000.
**** Two races (January and December) were held in 1986.
***** First horse to win the race twice.

later on 2 October, set a world record 1 min 57 secs mile rate when he won over 2,100 m. A week later he set a new Australian race record, winning in an astounding 1.54.5, starting at 100/1 on, the shortest price in Australian racing history. On 19 November he won the $80,000 final of the Australian Pacing Championship at Brisbane and in his last race start prior to his accident set the fastest ever time for the final 800 m (55.7 secs), when he won the Winfield Cup. That win took Popular Alm's record to 47 wins from 60 starts and his earnings to $698,833, of which $174,512 was won in his unfortunately shortened 1983–84 season.

Most successive wins by a pacer or trotter:
29, by Perth pacer San Simeon, when he won the $5,000 Four-Year-Old Classic at Gloucester Park, Perth, on 12 December 1980. San Simeon, driven by trainer-driver Lou Austin, bettered the national record of 24 successive wins he shared with Maori's Idol and Lucky Creed.

Most wins by a driver in one season (all tracks):
174 by Kevin Thomas (Qld) in 1976–77. Thomas easily topped the century in three successive seasons (154 in 1974–75 and 161 in 1975–76) but in all those three seasons he had many wins on country tracks and at Brisbane's trotting headquarters of Albion Park.

Most Sydney (city) winners in a season:
52 by Kevin Newman at Harold Park in 1973–74 and by Vic Frost 1977–78.

First woman to drive against men (metropolitan track):
Mrs Margaret Frost, wife of champion trainer-driver Vic Frost, at Globe Derby Park, Adelaide, SA, on 3 June 1978. Mrs Frost, driving Juanita Belle, won the race from six men and three other women.

First metropolitan race with betting (all women drivers):
In May 1973 at Globe Derby Park, SA. Mrs Fran Donohoe (NSW) won the race driving Red Sky.

First woman to win a race against men (all tracks):
Miss Debbie Wicks, the first woman to drive against men at Nowra, NSW, on 12 November 1977, was the first to win such a race, driving the 6/4 favourite Darwin Boy at Hawkesbury, NSW, on 22 December 1977.

Licensing of women drivers:
Victoria was the first State to allow women to drive in trotting events. This rule came into effect in August 1977 and restricted women to country meetings. The NSW Labor Party approved the *Anti-Discrimination Bill* in 1977 and this Act literally forced the NSWTC to allow women to drive at registered meetings from September 1977.

First horse to win 100 races:
Paleface Adios, which won the Cranbourne Cup (Vic.) on 25 February 1980 to post his 100th win and become the first trotter, pacer or galloper in recorded Australian racing history to achieve the feat. Paleface Adios' century came in his 207th start.

Government takes control in NSW:
The NSW Government in 1978 appointed the NSW Trotting Authority to take over control of the sport in the State from the NSW Trotting Club. This move followed many years of administrative problems which led to an alarming slide in the popularity, attendances and TAB turnover of trotting.

WRESTLING

BEGINNINGS IN AUSTRALIA
As amateur wrestling was tremendously popular in England from the time of the Middle Ages, it has always been assumed that the sport began in Australia on an almost social basis not long after the arrival of the First Fleet. Few records exist and the first highly regarded wrestler was 'Professor' William Miller, who won what was described as the Australian wrestling 'championship' in 1874. The establishment of circus-like professional wrestling in

Australia, starting in the late 1920s, pushed amateur wrestling into the background and although many Australians have achieved international success, the sport is not a popular spectator attraction.

First (known) official Australian championships:
1946. Major tournaments, which must have included Australian title matches, date back to the 1930s but complete records cannot be located.

First Australian Olympic wrestlers:
C. Angelo represented Australia at the 1924 Olympic Games in Paris and was eliminated in his third match in the lightweight freestyle class. Australia was represented by three wrestlers at Amsterdam in 1928 and one of them, T. H. Morris, also competed in the fancy diving competition.

First Olympic success:
1932 at Los Angeles, USA, when Eddie Scarf won a bronze medal in the light-heavyweight division. Scarf represented Australia again at Berlin in 1936 and later turned professional.

Longest-serving Olympian:
Dick Garrard (b. Melbourne, 1914) who represented Australia at Berlin in 1936, London in 1948, Helsinki in 1952 and Melbourne in 1956. Garrard was eliminated in the second round of the lightweight class in 1936, won a silver medal as a welterweight in 1948, reached the third round of the lightweight competition in 1952, and in 1956, at the age of 42, was forced to retire before his first match, after sustaining an injury during training. Garrard was a superb all-rounder who represented Victoria in pistol-shooting and weightlifting, won the Yarra Endurance Swim race in 1928, and in 1946 took up surfboard riding, representing his State in Queensland. His son Richard became a rower and represented Australia at the 1964 Olympics and the 1966 World Championships.

Other Olympic medallist:
Jim Armstrong (NSW), who won a bronze medal in the heavyweight division in 1948.

Most successful Australian at the 1984 Los Angeles Olympics:
Zsigmond Kelevitz (Vic.), who was placed fifth in the lightweight freestyle (68kg) class.

AUSTRALIANS AT THE COMMONWEALTH GAMES:

Australians have compiled an admirable record and have participated at all Games other than the inaugural staging in 1930.
Gold Medallists:
London 1934:
Dick Garrard (Vic.), lightweight; Jack Knight (NSW), heavyweight.
Sydney 1938:
Ted Purcell (Vic.), bantamweight; Roy Purchase (NSW), featherweight; Dick Garrard (Vic.), lightweight; Tom Trevaskis (Vic.), welterweight; Eddie Scarf (NSW), light-heavyweight; Jack Knight (NSW), heavyweight.
Auckland 1950:
Bert Harris (NSW), flyweight; Dick Garrard (Vic.), lightweight; Jim Armstrong (NSW), heavyweight.
Vancouver 1954:
Geoffrey Jameson (NSW), bantamweight.
Cardiff 1958:
No gold medals.
Perth 1962:
No gold medals.
Jamaica 1966:
No gold medals.
Edinburgh 1970:
No gold medals.
Christchurch 1974:
No gold medals.
Edmonton 1978:
Zsigmond Kelevitz (Vic.), lightweight.
Brisbane 1982:
No gold medals.

Total medals won at the Commonwealth Games:
38 – gold 13, silver 14, bronze 11.

Most Olympic and Commonwealth Games medals:
Dick Garrard (Vic.) with five: one Olympic silver, three Commonwealth Games gold and one bronze.

PROFESSIONAL WRESTLING

Exhibitions by 'strong men' as far back as the 1880s created intense public interest and led to the importation of professional wrestlers from the USA, Turkey and India. Professional wrestling around the turn of the century was virtually 'straight', compared with the rehearsed and colourful presentations of the modern era. The first overseas star of any real significance to appear in Australia was Russian-born 'World Champion' George Hackenschmidt in 1904. The professional staging of wrestling reached its first peak shortly after World War I and invariably drew larger crowds than boxing.

First Australian international star:
Fred Atkins (b. Bundaberg, Qld, 1922) who became the number-one drawcard in Australia immediately after World War II. A match between Atkins and 'World Champion' Jim Londos at Sydney Stadium in 1946 drew a capacity 13,000 crowd. Atkins settled in the USA in 1948 and was a big drawcard there for the next 10 years.

Famous importations:
Londos, American Indian Chief Little Wolf, Rudy La Ditzi, 'Gorgeous George' (George Wagner), Dr Jerry Grahame, Laverne Baxter, Ted Thye, John Pesek, Ed 'Strangler' Lewis, Walter Browning, Dean Detton, Brother Jonathan, Dick Raines, 'Sliding' Billy Hansen, Danny Dusek, Joe Kopach, Don Noland, Lofty Blomfield, Earl McCready, and Lee Wycoff are representative of the many hundreds of American, British and NZ professionals who have appeared in Australia from the 1920s onwards. The vast majority were brought to Australia by John Wren's Stadiums Ltd.

The TV boom:
Professional wrestling lost its appeal in the late 1950s, but was revived in the late 1960s by American promoters who repackaged the 'sport' and sold it to the National Nine television network. TV exposure resulted in an upsurge of interest and twice-weekly programs in Sydney, Melbourne and Brisbane attracted near-capacity crowds until 1972-73, when the attraction again lost favour with the public. Crowd favourites among the regular fans included Killer Kowalski, Brute Bernard, Jimmy Golden, 'The Beast' (Pierre La Bell), Chief Billy White Wolf and The Great Togo, all from the USA.

The 'sport' made another comeback in early 1986, with the introduction of so-called 'Rock and Roll Wrestling', featuring a large troupe of American performers. Capacity crowds, paying up to $18 for ringside seats, flocked to promotions at the Festival Hall, Melbourne and Brisbane, and Sydney's Homebush Bay Sports Centre.

MILESTONES IN AUSTRALIAN SPORT

1803—Sydney was the venue for the first recorded cricket match played in Australia (in December).

1805—First horseraces were run on a paddock known as Ham Common in the Hawkesbury district west of Sydney.

1810—First recognised horserace meeting was held on 15-17-18 October. The venue was what is now known as Hyde Park in Sydney. In the same year, the first trotting races were held in Parramatta, Sydney.

1833—First official race meeting was held at what is now the Randwick racecourse (then known as the 'sandy course on the Botany road').

1848—First race meeting was held at what is now the Flemington racecourse in Melbourne.
1858—First game of what is now known as Australian Football (formerly 'Victorian Rules' and 'Aussie Rules') was played in Melbourne between teams from Scotch College and Melbourne Grammar School.
1861—Archer, ridden by John Cutts, won the inaugural Melbourne Cup at Flemington.
1877—First cricket Test was held at Melbourne and Australia defeated England. The Victorian Football Association was inaugurated in Melbourne.
1878—First recorded game of tennis was played in Melbourne. The world-famous professional footrace, the Stawell Gift was held for the first time.
1880—A crowd exceeding 100,000 set a new attendance record for the Melbourne Cup at Flemington. In Sydney the first recorded game of soccer was played.
1890—'Young Griffo' (Albert Griffiths) became the first Australian to win a world professional boxing championship when he stopped New Zealand titleholder 'Torpedo' Billy Murphy in Sydney. American promoters refused to recognise him as champion.
1893—First Sheffield Shield cricket competition was won by Victoria.
1896—Melbourne-born Edwin Flack was Australia's first (and sole) representative at the inaugural Modern Olympic Games at Athens, Greece. Flack won gold medals in the 800 m and 1,500 m track races.
1897—The Victorian Football League (VFL) was formed as a breakaway body from the VFA. The inaugural premiership was won by Essendon.
1899—Australia made its international debut as a Rugby Union nation and defeated the British Isles in Sydney.
1901—First recorded motor sport competition event was held when three motorised De Dion tricycles raced around the concrete cycling track which once ringed the Sydney Cricket Ground.
1904—The Hon. Michael Scott of England won the inaugural Australian Open golf championship staged at the original Australian Golf Club course at Botany, Sydney.
1905—Australia teamed with New Zealand and competed as Australasia in its Davis Cup tennis debut.
1906—Champion galloper Poseidon won (in order) the AJC Derby, Caulfield Cup, Victoria Derby and Melbourne Cup to become the first and only horse to accomplish this near-impossible feat.
1907—Professional Rugby League began in Sydney when a team of former (amateur) Rugby Union footballers played a team known as the New Zealand All Golds. Norman (later Sir Norman) Brookes became the first Australian to win the Wimbledon singles championship.
1908—First world heavyweight boxing championship contest was held in Australia. Canadian titleholder Tommy Burns retained his belt by stopping Australia's Bill Squires in Sydney. In one of the oddest Olympic Games gold medal victories, Australia's Rugby Union football team won the Olympic championship at London, defeating English county champions, Cornwall, in the only match played.
1908-09—An Australian Rugby League team made the first overseas tour and played a 22-all draw against Great Britain in the inaugural Test match between the two countries.
1912—Sydney's Fanny Durack was the first Australian to win an Olympic Games swimming gold medal when she won the 100 m freestyle at Stockholm.
1915—Australia's Les Darcy defeated American Jeff Smith in a bout advertised as the world middleweight boxing championship at Sydney Stadium, American promoters refused to recognise him as champion.
1920—First interstate competition for the King's Cup rowing title began. In Paris, France, Bob Spears became the first Australian to win a world cycling championship when he won the professional sprint title.
1924—Edward 'Carjie' Greeves of Geelong became the winner of the inaugural Brownlow Medal as best and fairest player in the VFL competition.
1928—Adelaide-born Captain Arthur Waite drove a supercharged Austin Seven to victory on Phillip Island to win the

1930—Jim Pike rode the immortal Phar Lap to win the Melbourne Cup.
1932—Shortly after winning the rich Agua Caliente Handicap at Tijuana, Mexico, Phar Lap died in mysterious circumstances at Menlo Park, near San Francisco. Edgar 'Dunc' Gray became the first Australian to win an Olympic Games gold medal for cycling when he took out the 1,000 m time-trial at Los Angeles.
1936—Sydney-born Lionel Van Praag won the inaugural world speedway motorcycle championship held at London's Wembley Stadium. The first Inter-Dominion trotting championship was run in Perth, WA. Sydney's Ken Kennedy was the first person to represent Australia at a Winter Olympics. The only team member, he competed in the speed skating in Germany.
1938—Sydney played host to the Empire (now Commonwealth) Games. The Australian team won a total of 65 medals, 24 of them gold. The first car races were held on the then unsealed Mt Panorama circuit at Bathurst, NSW.
1939—In Forest Hills in New York, the Australian team of John Bromwich and Adrian Quist won the Davis Cup competition for the first time. Previously, Australia had combined with New Zealand as 'Australasia'.
1945—*Rani* skippered by Captain John Illingworth, won the inaugural Sydney-Hobart blue water yachting classic. The race attracted only nine starters.
1947—Sydney-born Jim Ferrier was the first Australian to win the USPGA golf championship.
1948—Sir Donald Bradman's Test cricket career came to an end in unbelievable circumstances. Needing only four runs to achieve a Test career batting average of 100, he was bowled second ball for a duck. Bradman retired from the Test arena with an average of 99.94 (6,996 runs scored in 52 Tests).
1951—The inaugural ABC Sportsman of the Year Award (now known as the ABC Sports Award) was won by tennis star Frank Sedgman of Victoria.
1952—Jimmy Carruthers was the first Australian to win a universally recognised world boxing championship when he stopped world bantamweight titleholder Vic Toweel in the first round in Johannesburg, South Africa. Adelaide-born Jack Young was the first rider to win successive world speedway motorcycle championships.
1954—Victoria's Peter Thomson was the first Australian to win the British Open golf championship. A world record crowd of 25,578 packed into Sydney's White City to watch one day's play in a Davis Cup challenge round between Australia and the USA.
1956—For the first time, Australia hosted the Olympic Games in Melbourne. Australia's largest-ever team of 314 won 35 medals, a record 13 of them gold. Outstanding Australian was sprinter Betty Cuthbert who won three gold medals.
1959—Sydney-born Jack (now Sir John) Brabham was the first Australian to win the World Drivers Championship. Brabham, who was to win again in 1960 and 1966, drove for the Cooper team in England.
1960—For the first time in the history of Test cricket, a Test ended in a tie. The match was played at the Gabba ground in Brisbane between Australia and the West Indies.
1961—A world record cricket attendance of 90,800 for a single day's play was made on the second day of the fifth Test between Australia and the West Indies at the MCG.
1962—Australia, represented by *Gretel*, made its first challenge for the America's Cup. Rod Laver was the first Australian to take out the Grand Slam of tennis (singles championships of Australia, France, Wimbledon and the USA).
1963—Margaret Smith (later Mrs Margaret Court) was the first Australian woman to win the Wimbledon singles title.
1964—At the Tokyo Olympic Games, Dawn Fraser was the first swimmer, male or female, to win the same event (100 m freestyle) at three consecutive Games. Eight years after winning three gold medals at the Melbourne Olympic Games, Australia's 'Golden Girl' Betty Cuthbert made a dramatic Games comeback by winning the gold medal for

the 400 m at Tokyo. At Sydney's Manly Beach, Bernard 'Midget' Farrelly won the inaugural world surfing championship.

1968—In Tokyo, Victoria's Lionel Rose was the first Aborigine to win a world sporting championship when he defeated Japan's Fighting Harada to take out the world bantamweight boxing title.

1969—Victorian Johnny Famechon won the world featherweight boxing championship in London.

1970—A record VFL Grand Final crowd of 121,696 packed the MCG to see Carlton take the flag. Margaret Court made tennis history as the first Australian woman to win the Grand Slam.

1972—Tasmania's Geoff Prouse was the first jockey to win all races at an Australian metropolitan race meeting. Prouse rode the seven-race card at Elwick, Hobart.

1973—Against all the odds, Australia's soccer team, under coach Rale Rasic, made the finals of the World Cup in West Germany.

1975—For the first time since the inception of the event in 1878, a runner won the famous Stawell Gift professional footrace from scratch. History-maker was Jean-Louis Ravelomanantsoa of Malagasy.

1977—Ken Warby captured the outright world water speed record in his backyard-built *Spirit of Australia* jet boat with an average speed of 464.457 km/h at Blowering Dam, Tumut, NSW. The Centenary Test between Australia and England at the MCG ended with Australia winning by 45 runs—the same margin by which they had won the inaugural Test.

1980—Alan Jones was the first Australian since Jack Brabham in 1966 to win the World Drivers Championship.

1981—David Graham was the first Australian to win the US Open golf championship.

1983—*Australia II* skippered by John Bertrand captured the America's Cup from American defender *Liberty* in the deciding race at Newport, USA. South Australian-born Vern Schuppan was the first Australian to score an outright win in the famous Le Mans 24-hour motor racing classic when he co-drove with two Americans.

1984—The first official world championship motor race in Australia was held at Melbourne's Sandown circuit. The event was the final round of the world sports car endurance title. The event was a financial disaster for the promoters. Dennis Lillee retired from Test cricket after taking a wicket with the last ball he bowled in his Test career. Lillee's Test career wickets total (355) remained a world record until exceeded by England's Ian Botham.

1985—The first round of the World Drivers Championship was held in Australia on a public road circuit in the heart of the city of Adelaide. Finland's Keke Rosberg won the race in a Williams Honda, but the championship went to Frenchman Alain Prost. The race attracted a huge attendance estimated at 135,000.

1987—Melbourne's Pat Cash put Australian tennis back into international focus by winning the Wimbledon singles title. It was the first win by an Australian male since John Newcombe in 1971 and the first win by an Australian in a Wimbledon singles final since Evonne Cawley won the women's singles in 1980.

1988—Jeff Fenech was the first Australian to hold world boxing titles in three different divisions when he stopped Victor Callejas to win the vacant WBC featherweight championship. Previously Fenech had won world titles at bantamweight and junior featherweight. Melbourne entrepreneur Bob Jane opened the first NASCAR stock car track (the 'Thunderdome') outside America and drew a 45,000 crowd to the opening meeting. Australian cricket captain Allan Border emerged as Australia's highest scorer of runs (7,131) in Test cricket when he passed the previous record held by Greg Chappell (7,110).

TOP EARNERS IN SPORT

THE WORLD

Although it is common knowledge that many 'amateur' sports champions who contest events such as the Olympic Games are out-and-out professionals, one can only hazard a guess at their incomes. Competitors in this category include track and field athletes, tennis players, snow skiers (especially in Europe), cyclists (Japan, the USA and Europe), golfers (notably the USA) and boxers (in a few areas of Europe and South America).

In the United States an estimated 96 athletes earn more than US$1 million in annual earnings. Before his retirement from Grand Prix racing, Australia's Alan Jones was believed to be earning in the vicinity of $1.4 million per annum from driving and advertising contracts. Leading Australian racing trainers Tommy Smith, Bart Cummings and Brian Mayfield-Smith are all believed to be in the million-per-year category.

Top earnings for champion Rugby League and Australian Football players are reported as being around $100,000 per year.

Immediately after the top 10 Australian earners are competitors such as Vern Schuppan (motor racing), Craig Johnston (soccer), and Geoffrey Brabham (motor racing). Golfer David Graham has not been included in the list because the bulk of his income in 1987-88 came from endorsements and business activities associated with his sport.

The following list (current to mid-1988) concentrates on declared professionals. The annual earnings are approximate only and contain known sums earned from endorsements, testimonials and appearance fees. Figures are in US dollars.

1. **Mike Tyson** (USA)
   Boxing—$30 million
2. **Michael Spinks** (USA)
   Boxing—$12 million
3. **Thomas Hearns** (USA)
   Boxing—$5 million
4. **Greg Norman** (Aust.)
   Golf—$4 million
5. **Steve Young** (USA)
   Footballer—$3.2 million
6. **Moses Malone** (USA)
   Basketball—$2.4 million
7. **Jim Rice** (USA)
   Baseball—$2.4 million
8. **Alain Prost** (France)
   Motor racing—$2 million
9. **George Foster** (USA)
   Baseball—$2 million
10. **Ivan Lendl** (Czech.)
    Tennis—$2 million

AUSTRALIA

1. **Greg Norman**
   Golf—$4 million
2. **Wayne Gardner**
   Motorcycling—$1.7 million
3. **Pat Cash**
   Tennis—$1.6 million
4. **Eddie Krncevic**
   Soccer—$1 million
5. **Jan Stephenson**
   Golf—$750,000
6. **Rodger Davis**
   Golf—$500,000
7. **Robert de Castella**
   Athletics—$500,000
8. **Bruce Crampton**
   Golf—$450,000
9. **Ian Baker-Finch**
   Golf—$400,000
10. **Danny Clark**
    Cycling—$400,000

SPORTING OBITUARIES

Hoskins, Johnnie. At Herne Bay, Kent, England, 5 April 1987. Aged 94.

New Zealand-born Hoskins for many years was credited with being Australia's first professional speedway promoter. Although that honour was exaggerated, Hoskins did play a vital role in developing the sport in Australia and later, England, He was among the pioneers who introduced motorcycle speedway racing to England in 1928. Hoskins was the first promoter at London's famous Wembley Stadium and was the driving force behind the staging of the inaugural World Championship and Test matches between England and Australia. He was still active in promotion in England until the late 1970s.

Allen, Terry. At London, England, 8 April 1987. Aged 61.

A former holder of the world flyweight boxing championship, London-born Allen, whose real name was Edward Govier, had 76 professional bouts and lost only 11—9 of them in his last 15 fights. Allen became world champion on 25 April 1950 when he outpointed Frenchman Honoré Pratesi for the vacant title. He also held the British and European flyweight championships.

Hynes, Patrick (Pat). At Sydney, 12 April 1987. Aged 72.

A long-serving official of the Australian Amateur Boxing Association, Sydney-born Hynes served as president and secretary. He refereed and judged at Olympic and Commonwealth Games and Australian championships. He judged more fights than any other official at the 1976 Olympic Games in Montreal.

Van Praag, Lionel. At Brisbane, 19 May 1987. Aged 78.

Sydney-born Van Praag was the winner of the inaugural World Motorcycle Speedway Championship at Wembley, London, in 1936. A professional rider who competed all over the world from 1933-39, he became a RAAF pilot in World War II and was awarded the George Medal for bravery after his transport plane was shot down by Japanese Zeroes over the Arafura Sea. Van Praag mixed speedway racing with commercial flying until his retirement in the 1960s.

Favell, Les. At Adelaide, 14 June 1987. Aged 58.

Sydney-born Favell played 19 cricket Tests for Australia and made many records in South Australia where he transferred after finding it difficult making headway in his home state. At one stage he held the record for most Sheffield Shield runs scored by a South Australian; he played 143 games for the state and captained the side a record 95 times. Favell, who battled cancer in the last year of his life, averaged 27.03 as opening bat for Australia and also represented South Australia at baseball.

Pironi, Didier. At the Isle of Wight, UK, 23 August 1987. Aged 35.

French-born Pironi was a former Formula One Grand Prix driver who retired from car racing after suffering severe injuries in the 1982 German Grand Prix. Pironi, the leading world championship pointscorer prior to his accident, took up powerboat racing after recovering from his injuries. After reaching international fame with his San Tropez-based team, he lost his life in an offshore race near the Isle of Wight.

Young, Jack. At Adelaide, 28 August 1987. Aged 62.

The first rider to win two consecutive world motorcycle speedway championships, Adelaide-born Young captured the titles at Wembley, London, in 1951 and 1952, the first when he was attached to the second division British League team, Edinburgh. He came close to winning three titles in succession in 1953. Young reached the World Championship final on many other occasions and after a long stint with London first division team West Ham, finished his career with the Coventry club.

Cotton, Henry. At London, England, 22 December 1987. Aged 80.

One of the world's greatest golfers, England-born Cotton won the British Open championship in 1934, 1937 and 1948 and in 1937 was rated the world's No. 1 player. That year he held off champion Americans Gene Sarazen, Walter Hagen, Byron Nelson and Sam Snead to win the British Open, shooting a final round of 71 in gale-force wind and blinding rain. Cotton is recognised as the man who did most to help English professionals gain respect from the golfing fraternity.

Varey, Frank. At Sheffield, England, 8 February 1988. Aged 75.

One of England's greatest ever motorcycle speedway riders, Varey helped introduce the sport to South America. Until recent years he was promoter of the Sheffield track in England. He qualified for the final of the World Championship in 1937, 1938 and 1939 (when the final was abandoned following the declaration of war).

Locke, Arthur D'Arcy (Bobby). At Johannesburg, South Africa, 11 march 1988. Aged 69.

The first great South African golfer, Bobby Locke won the British Open in 1949, 1950, 1952 and 1957 and among a long list of major victories, the Australian Open in 1955. One of his most remarkable wins was in the 1947 Philadelphia Enquirer Open in the United States in which he trailed the great Ben Hogan by 5 strokes with 36 holes to play—and won by 4 shots. A year later he was banned from the US tour 'for life' for a trivial oversight with tournament entry forms. Locke served for 5 years in the South African Air Force in World War II, flying Liberators in the final year in the Middle East and Italy.

Thompson, Mickey. At Los Angeles, USA, 19 March 1988. Aged 59.

Mickey Thompson set 400 international and US speed and endurance motoring records in a 20-year period commencing in 1947. One of the pioneers of the American hot rod movement, Thompson, who became a multi-millionaire from his investments in the automobile industry and motor sporting promotions, was gunned down in front of his home. His wife Trudy was also killed.

Berwick, Harry. At Sydney, 3 April 1988. Aged 64.

One of Australia's greatest amateur golfers, Berwick turned professional in 1975 at the age of 52 to become the oldest Australian player to leave the amateur ranks. He won two Australian amateur titles in 1950 and 1956 and was a member of Australia's winning Eisenhower Cup team in 1966. Twice leading amateur in the Australian Open in 1949 and 1967, he won the 1956 Lakes Open from a hot field of professionals and was in the NSW amateur team every year from 1949 to 1963 except for 1954 when he went to England and won the St George Challenge Cup at the Royal St George Links at Sandwich. He made a first round record score of 67 and the lowest aggregate (141) recorded since the event was inaugurated in 1888. Berwick was awarded the MBE in 1977 for his services to golf.

Miller, Tony. At Manly, Sydney, 6 April 1988. Aged 58.

A long-serving Australian international Rugby Union Test forward, Tony Miller once held the national record for representing his country in 41 Tests. Business commitments forced him to miss several overseas tours and he was unlucky in not having reached 50 internationals. Miller made his debut for Australia against Fiji in 1952 and played his last Test against New Zealand in 1967. He played his entire career for the Manly club and coached the team for a while after retiring before accepting an offer to coach neighbouring Warringah.

Part Three
Facts
and
Figures

70 YEAR CALENDAR
1951 to 2020

Find the year required and note the letter below it. The column on the left hand side corresponding with the letter at the head will show the days of the week, and the figures in the same parallel line the days of the month for that year, all the Mondays etc., being in the same line.

In leap year use the first letter for January and February, and the second for the remaining months.

* Don't use both February 29 and March 1.

1951	1952	1953	1954	1955	1956	1957	1958	1959	1960	1961	1962	1963	1964
B	C-D	E	F	G	A-B	C	D	E	F-G	A	B	C	D-E
1965	1966	1967	1968	1969	1970	1971	1972	1973	1974	1975	1976	1977	1978
F	G	A	B-C	D	E	F	G-A	B	C	D	E-F	G	A
1979	1980	1981	1982	1983	1984	1985	1986	1987	1988	1989	1990	1991	1992
B	C-D	E	F	G	A-B	C	D	E	F-G	A	B	C	D-E
1993	1994	1995	1996	1997	1998	1999	2000	2001	2002	2003	2004	2005	2006
F	G	A	B-C	D	E	F	G-A	B	C	D	E-F	G	A
2007	2008	2009	2010	2011	2012	2013	2014	2015	2016	2017	2018	2019	2020
B	C-D	E	F	G	A-B	C	D	E	F-G	A	B	C	D-E

70 YEAR CALENDAR

B	C	D	E	F	G	A		January					February					March				
M	Tu	W	Th	F	S	S		1	8	15	22	29	–	5	12	19	26	–	5	12	19	26
Tu	W	Th	F	S	S	M		2	9	16	23	30	–	6	13	20	27	–	6	13	20	27
W	Th	F	S	S	M	Tu		3	10	17	24	31	–	7	14	21	28	–	7	14	21	28
Th	F	S	S	M	Tu	W		4	11	18	25	–	1	8	15	22	29*	1	8	15	22	29
F	S	S	M	Tu	W	Th		5	12	19	26	–	2	9	16	23	–	2	9	16	23	30
S	S	M	Tu	W	Th	F		6	13	20	27	–	3	10	17	24	–	3	10	17	24	31
S	M	Tu	W	Th	F	S		7	14	21	28	–	4	11	18	25	–	4	11	18	25	–

B	C	D	E	F	G	A		April					May					June				
M	Tu	W	Th	F	S	S		30	2	9	16	23	–	7	14	21	28	–	4	11	18	25
Tu	W	Th	F	S	S	M		–	3	10	17	24	1	8	15	22	29	–	5	12	19	26
W	Th	F	S	S	M	Tu		–	4	11	18	25	2	9	16	23	30	–	6	13	20	27
Th	F	S	S	M	Tu	W		–	5	12	19	26	3	10	17	24	31	–	7	14	21	28
F	S	S	M	Tu	W	Th		–	6	13	20	27	4	11	18	25	–	1	8	15	22	29
S	S	M	Tu	W	Th	F		–	7	14	21	28	5	12	19	26	–	2	9	16	23	30
S	M	Tu	W	Th	F	S		1	8	15	22	29	6	13	20	27	–	3	10	17	24	–

B	C	D	E	F	G	A		July					August					September				
M	Tu	W	Th	F	S	S		30	2	9	16	23	–	6	13	20	27	–	3	10	17	24
Tu	W	Th	F	S	S	M		31	3	10	17	24	–	7	14	21	28	–	4	11	18	25
W	Th	F	S	S	M	Tu		–	4	11	18	25	1	8	15	22	29	–	5	12	19	26
Th	F	S	S	M	Tu	W		–	5	12	19	26	2	9	16	23	30	–	6	13	20	27
F	S	S	M	Tu	W	Th		–	6	13	20	27	3	10	17	24	31	–	7	14	21	28
S	S	M	Tu	W	Th	F		–	7	14	21	28	4	11	18	25	–	1	8	15	22	29
S	M	Tu	W	Th	F	S		1	8	15	22	29	5	12	19	26	–	2	9	16	23	30

B	C	D	E	F	G	A		October					November					December				
M	Tu	W	Th	F	S	S		1	8	15	22	29	–	5	12	19	26	31	3	10	17	24
Tu	W	Th	F	S	S	M		2	9	16	23	30	–	6	13	20	27	–	4	11	18	25
W	Th	F	S	S	M	Tu		3	10	17	24	31	–	7	14	21	28	–	5	12	19	26
Th	F	S	S	M	Tu	W		4	11	18	25	–	1	8	15	22	29	–	6	13	20	27
F	S	S	M	Tu	W	Th		5	12	19	26	–	2	9	16	23	30	–	7	14	21	28
S	S	M	Tu	W	Th	F		6	13	20	27	–	3	10	17	24	–	1	8	15	22	29
S	M	Tu	W	Th	F	S		7	14	21	28	–	4	11	18	25	–	2	9	16	23	30

CALENDAR
1988

	January
Sun.	3 10 17 24 31
Mon.	4 11 18 25
Tue.	5 12 19 26
Wed.	6 13 20 27
Thu.	7 14 21 28
Fri.	1 8 15 22 29
Sat.	2 9 16 23 30

	February
Sun.	7 14 21 28
Mon.	1 8 15 22 29
Tue.	2 9 16 23
Wed.	3 10 17 24
Thu.	4 11 18 25
Fri.	5 12 19 26
Sat.	6 13 20 27

	March
Sun.	6 13 20 27
Mon.	7 14 21 28
Tue.	1 8 15 22 29
Wed.	2 9 16 23 30
Thu.	3 10 17 24 31
Fri.	4 11 18 25
Sat.	5 12 19 26

	April
Sun.	3 10 17 24
Mon.	4 11 18 25
Tue.	5 12 19 26
Wed.	6 13 20 27
Thu.	7 14 21 28
Fri.	1 8 15 22 29
Sat.	2 9 16 23 30

	May
Sun.	1 8 15 22 29
Mon.	2 9 16 23 30
Tue.	3 10 17 24 31
Wed.	4 11 18 25
Thu.	5 12 19 26
Fri.	6 13 20 27
Sat.	7 14 21 28

	June
Sun.	5 12 19 26
Mon.	6 13 20 27
Tue.	7 14 21 28
Wed.	1 8 15 22 29
Thu.	2 9 16 23 30
Fri.	3 10 17 24
Sat.	4 11 18 25

	July
Sun.	3 10 17 24 31
Mon.	4 11 18 25
Tue.	5 12 19 26
Wed.	6 13 20 27
Thu.	7 14 21 28
Fri.	1 8 15 22 29
Sat.	2 9 16 23 30

	August
Sun.	7 14 21 28
Mon.	1 8 15 22 29
Tue.	2 9 16 23 30
Wed.	3 10 17 24 31
Thu.	4 11 18 25
Fri.	5 12 19 26
Sat.	6 13 20 27

	September
Sun.	4 11 18 25
Mon.	5 12 19 26
Tue.	6 13 20 27
Wed.	7 14 21 28
Thu.	1 8 15 22 29
Fri.	2 9 16 23 30
Sat.	3 10 17 24

	October
Sun.	2 9 16 23 30
Mon.	3 10 17 24 31
Tue.	4 11 18 25
Wed.	5 12 19 26
Thu.	6 13 20 27
Fri.	7 14 21 28
Sat.	1 8 15 22 29

	November
Sun.	6 13 20 27
Mon.	7 14 21 28
Tue.	1 8 15 22 29
Wed.	2 9 16 23 30
Thu.	3 10 17 24
Fri.	4 11 18 25
Sat.	5 12 19 26

	December
Sun.	4 11 18 25
Mon.	5 12 19 26
Tue.	6 13 20 27
Wed.	7 14 21 28
Thu.	1 8 15 22 29
Fri.	2 9 16 23 30
Sat.	3 10 17 24 31

CALENDAR
1989

January
Sun.	1	8	15	22	29
Mon.	2	9	16	23	30
Tue.	3	10	17	24	31
Wed.	4	11	18	25	
Thu.	5	12	19	26	
Fri.	6	13	20	27	
Sat.	7	14	21	28	

February
Sun.	5	12	19	26
Mon.	6	13	20	27
Tue.	7	14	21	28
Wed.	1	8	15	22
Thu.	2	9	16	23
Fri.	3	10	17	24
Sat.	4	11	18	25

March
Sun.	5	12	19	26
Mon.	6	13	20	27
Tue.	7	14	21	28
Wed.	1	8	15	22	29
Thu.	2	9	16	23	30
Fri.	3	10	17	24	31
Sat.	4	11	18	25

April
Sun.	2	9	16	23	30
Mon.	3	10	17	24	
Tue.	4	11	18	25	
Wed.	5	12	19	26	
Thu.	6	13	20	27	
Fri.	7	14	21	28	
Sat.	1	8	15	22	29

May
Sun.	7	14	21	28
Mon.	1	8	15	22	29
Tue.	2	9	16	23	30
Wed.	3	10	17	24	31
Thu.	4	11	18	25
Fri.	5	12	19	26
Sat.	6	13	20	27

June
Sun.	4	11	18	25
Mon.	5	12	19	26
Tue.	6	13	20	27
Wed.	7	14	21	28
Thu.	1	8	15	22	29
Fri.	2	9	16	23	30
Sat.	3	10	17	24

July
Sun.	2	9	16	23	30
Mon.	3	10	17	24	31
Tue.	4	11	18	25
Wed.	5	12	19	26
Thu.	6	13	20	27
Fri.	7	14	21	28
Sat.	1	8	15	22	29

August
Sun.	6	13	20	27
Mon.	7	14	21	28
Tue.	1	8	15	22	29
Wed.	2	9	16	23	30
Thu.	3	10	17	24	31
Fri.	4	11	18	25
Sat.	5	12	19	26

September
Sun.	3	10	17	24
Mon.	4	11	18	25
Tue.	5	12	19	26
Wed.	6	13	20	27
Thu.	7	14	21	28
Fri.	1	8	15	22	29
Sat.	2	9	16	23	30

October
Sun.	1	8	15	22	29
Mon.	2	9	16	23	30
Tue.	3	10	17	24	31
Wed.	4	11	18	25
Thu.	5	12	19	26
Fri.	6	13	20	27
Sat.	7	14	21	28

November
Sun.	5	12	19	26
Mon.	6	13	20	27
Tue.	7	14	21	28
Wed.	1	8	15	22	29
Thu.	2	9	16	23	30
Fri.	3	10	17	24
Sat.	4	11	18	25

December
Sun.	3	10	17	24	31
Mon.	4	11	18	25
Tue.	5	12	19	26
Wed.	6	13	20	27
Thu.	7	14	21	28
Fri.	1	8	15	22	29
Sat.	2	9	16	23	30

CALENDAR
1990

January
Sun.		7	14	21	28
Mon.	1	8	15	22	29
Tue.	2	9	16	23	30
Wed.	3	10	17	24	31
Thu.	4	11	18	25	
Fri.	5	12	19	26	
Sat.	6	13	20	27	

February
Sun.		4	11	18	25
Mon.		5	12	19	26
Tue.		6	13	20	27
Wed.		7	14	21	28
Thu.	1	8	15	22	
Fri.	2	9	16	23	
Sat.	3	10	17	24	

March
Sun.		4	11	18	25
Mon.		5	12	19	26
Tue.		6	13	20	27
Wed.		7	14	21	28
Thu.	1	8	15	22	29
Fri.	2	9	16	23	30
Sat.	3	10	17	24	31

April
Sun.	1	8	15	22	29
Mon.	2	9	16	23	30
Tue.	3	10	17	24	
Wed.	4	11	18	25	
Thu.	5	12	19	26	
Fri.	6	13	20	27	
Sat.	7	14	21	28	

May
Sun.		6	13	20	27
Mon.		7	14	21	28
Tue.	1	8	15	22	29
Wed.	2	9	16	23	30
Thu.	3	10	17	24	31
Fri.	4	11	18	25	
Sat.	5	12	19	26	

June
Sun.		3	10	17	24
Mon.		4	11	18	25
Tue.		5	12	19	26
Wed.		6	13	20	27
Thu.		7	14	21	28
Fri.	1	8	15	22	29
Sat.	2	9	16	23	30

July
Sun.	1	8	15	22	29
Mon.	2	9	16	23	30
Tue.	3	10	17	24	31
Wed.	4	11	18	25	
Thu.	5	12	19	26	
Fri.	6	13	20	27	
Sat.	7	14	21	28	

August
Sun.		5	12	19	26
Mon.		6	13	20	27
Tue.		7	14	21	28
Wed.	1	8	15	22	29
Thu.	2	9	16	23	30
Fri.	3	10	17	24	31
Sat.	4	11	18	25	

September
Sun.		2	9	16	23	30
Mon.		3	10	17	24	
Tue.		4	11	18	25	
Wed.		5	12	19	26	
Thu.		6	13	20	27	
Fri.		7	14	21	28	
Sat.	1	8	15	22	29	

October
Sun.		7	14	21	28
Mon.	1	8	15	22	29
Tue.	2	9	16	23	30
Wed.	3	10	17	24	31
Thu.	4	11	18	25	
Fri.	5	12	19	26	
Sat.	6	13	20	27	

November
Sun.		4	11	18	25
Mon.		5	12	19	26
Tue.		6	13	20	27
Wed.		7	14	21	28
Thu.	1	8	15	22	29
Fri.	2	9	16	23	30
Sat.	3	10	17	24	

December
Sun.		2	9	16	23	30
Mon.		3	10	17	24	31
Tue.		4	11	18	25	
Wed.		5	12	19	26	
Thu.		6	13	20	27	
Fri.		7	14	21	28	
Sat.	1	8	15	22	29	

PUBLIC HOLIDAYS 1989

New Year's Day (*all States*)......................................2 January
Australia Day (*NSW, ACT and NT*).............................26 January
Australia Day (*Vic., Qld., SA, WA, Tas.*) ....30 January
Eight Hour Day (*Tas. only*)...6 March
Labour Day (*WA only*)..6 March
Labour Day (*Vic. only*)...13 March
Canberra Day (*ACT only*)...20 March
Good Friday (*all States*)...24 March
Easter Saturday (*all States except WA and Tas.*)....................25 March
Easter Monday (*all States*)...27 March
Easter Tuesday (*Vic. only*)...28 March
Bank Holiday (*Tas. only*)..28 March
Anzac Day (*all States*)...25 April
Labour Day (*Qld only*)..1 May
May Day (*NT only*)..2 May
Adelaide Cup Day (*SA only*).......................................15 May
Foundation Day (*WA only*)...5 June
Queen's Birthday Holiday (*all States except WA*)....................12 June
Alice Springs Show Day (*regional*)..................................7 July
Tennant Creek Show Day (*regional*)................................14 July
Katherine Show Day (*regional*)....................................21 July
Darwin Show Day (*Darwin only*)..................................28 July
Picnic Day (*NT only*)...7 August
Bank Holiday (*NSW and ACT*)....................................7 August
Melbourne Show Day (*Melbourne only*)........................28 September
Labour Day (*NSW and Act*)......................................2 October
Labour Day (*SA only*)..9 October
Melbourne Cup Day (*Melbourne only*)..........................1 November
Recreation Day (*northern Tas. only*)............................6 November
Christmas Day (*all States*).....................................25 December
Boxing Day (*all States*)..26 December
Proclamation Day (*SA only*)....................................28 December

SCHOOL TERMS 1989

ACT
Term 1 .... 31 January – 23 March
Term 2 .... 3 April – 23 June
Term 3 .... 10 July – 22 September
Term 4 .... 9 October – 15 December

NSW
Term 1 .... 31 January – 23 March
Term 2 .... 3 April – 23 June
Term 3 .... 10 July – 22 September
Term 4 .... 9 October – 15 December

NT
Term 1 .... 24 January – 17 March
Term 2 .... 28 March – 15 June
Term 3 .... 3 July – 8 September
Term 4 .... 25 September – 15 December

Qld
Term 1 .... 23 January – 17 March
Term 2 .... 28 March – 15 June
Term 3 .... 3 July – 8 September
Term 4 .... 25 September – 15 December

SA
Term 1 .... 31 January – 14 April
Term 2 .... 24 April – 30 June
Term 3 .... 17 July – 21 September
Term 4 .... 9 October – 14 December

Tas.
Term 1 .... 21 February – 26 May
Term 2 .... 12 June – 25 August
Term 3 .... 11 September – 20 December

Vic.
Term 1 .... 2 February – 23 March
Term 2 .... 3 April – 23 June
Term 3 .... 10 July – 22 September
Term 4 .... 9 October – 22 December

WA
Term 1 .... 1 February – 14 April
Term 2 .... 1 May – 7 July
Term 3 .... 25 July – 27 September
Term 4 .... 16 October – 20 December

MAP OF AUSTRALIA • 239

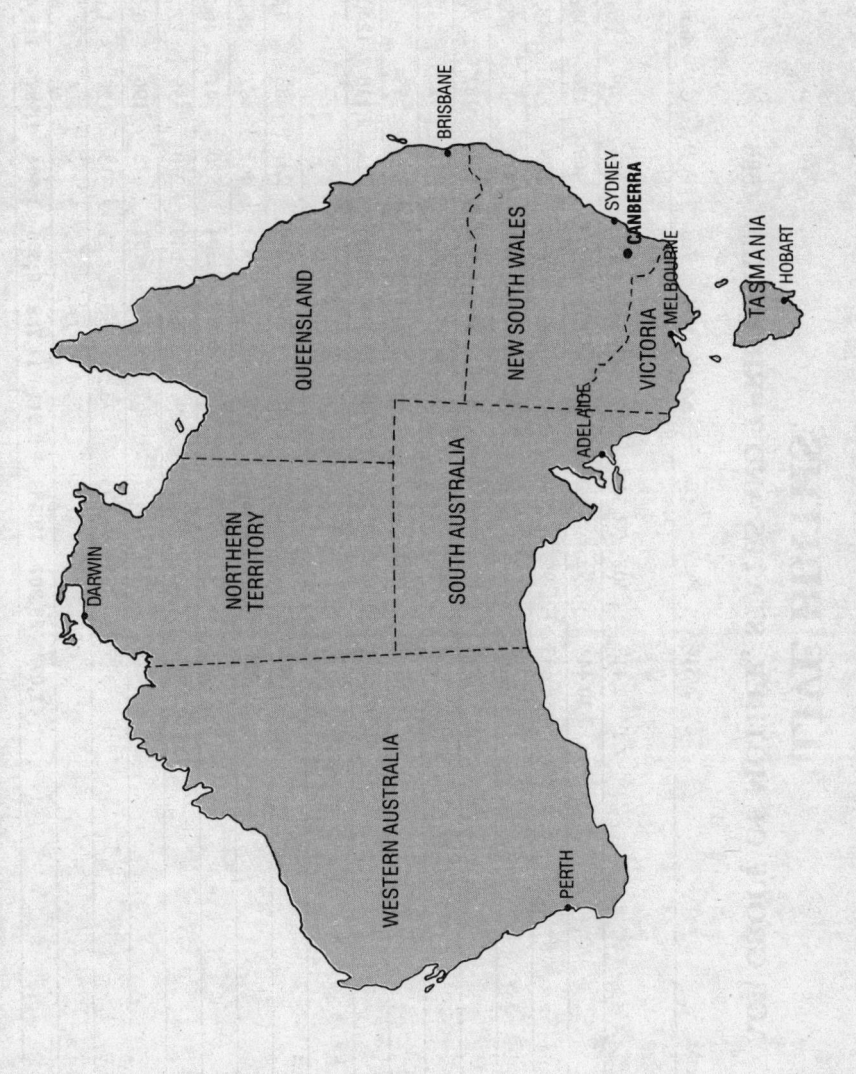

LIVE BIRTHS

AGE GROUP OF MOTHER, STATES AND TERRITORIES, 1986

Age group (years)	NSW	Vic.	Qld	SA	WA	Tas.	NT	ACT	Australia
Males									
Under 20	2,418	1,307	1,547	604	757	251	308	69	7,261
20–24	10,444	6,692	5,545	2,545	3,138	1,073	469	426	30,332
25–29	16,683	12,394	7,796	3,907	4,840	1,391	509	821	48,341
30–34	10,178	7,810	4,375	2,214	2,788	688	315	583	28,951
35–39	3,278	2,352	1,319	583	840	187	100	181	8,840
40 and over	456	296	200	76	85	25	10	22	1,170
Not stated	-	4	-	-	-	-	-	13	19
Total	43,458	30,855	20,782	9,930	12,448	3,615	1,711	2,115	124,914
Females									
Under 20	2,313	1,216	1,585	588	749	274	257	83	7,065
20–24	9,926	6,271	5,202	2,567	2,967	933	465	382	28,713
25–29	15,767	11,945	7,393	3,918	4,632	1,304	520	741	46,220
30–34	9,636	7,400	4,049	2,097	2,589	640	270	555	27,236
35–39	3,035	2,212	1,187	567	749	157	78	196	8,181
40 and over	395	261	173	73	96	27	13	25	1,063
Not stated	-	-	-	-	6	-	-	5	16
Total	41,073	29,307	19,589	9,811	11,788	3,335	1,604	1,987	118,494

Persons									
Under 20	4,731	2,523	3,132	1,192	1,506	525	565	152	14,326
20–24	20,370	12,963	10,747	5,112	6,105	2,006	934	808	59,045
25–29	32,450	24,339	15,189	7,825	9,472	2,695	1,029	1,562	94,561
30–34	19,814	15,210	8,424	4,311	5,377	1,328	585	1,138	56,187
35–39	6,313	4,564	2,506	1,150	1,589	344	178	377	17,021
40 and over	851	557	373	149	181	52	23	47	2,233
Not stated	-	6	-	-	6	-	-	18	35
Total births	**84,531**	**60,162**	**40,371**	**19,741**	**24,236**	**6,950**	**3,315**	**4,102**	**243,408**

These figures are based on the usual residence of the mother.

Adapted from: Births Australia 1986. *ABS Cat. no. 3301.0.*

CRUDE BIRTH RATES
STATES AND TERRITORIES, 1981 TO 1986

	NSW	Vic.	Qld	SA	WA	Tas.	NT	ACT	Australia
Annual rates-									
1981	15.7	15.0	16.6	14.6	16.8	16.9	25.2	18.2	15.8
1982	15.8	15.0	16.8	14.4	16.7	16.4	22.5	17.8	15.8
1983	15.5	14.8	17.0	14.8	16.9	16.3	23.3	17.5	15.8
1984	15.2	14.6	16.1	14.8	15.6	16.3	23.0	16.8	15.3
	(14.4)	(14.6)	(16.1)	(14.8)	(15.6)	(16.3)	(23.0)	(16.8)	(15.0)
1985	15.2	14.9	15.9	14.5	16.4	16.4	23.0	16.2	15.4
	(16.0)	(14.9)	(15.9)	(14.5)	(16.4)	(16.4)	(23.0)	(16.2)	(15.7)
1986	15.2	14.4	15.6	14.4	16.8	15.6	22.3	15.5	15.2

These figures are based on the usual residence of the mother. The 1984 and 1985 rates are adjusted for late registrations in NSW. The rates in brackets are based on the registered number of births.

Adapted from: Births Australia 1986. *ABS Cat. no. 3301.0.*

LIVE BIRTHS

NUPTIALITY AND PLURALITY, STATES AND TERRITORIES, 1986

	NSW	Vic.	Qld	SA	WA	Tas.	NT	ACT	Australia
Live Births									
Nuptial -									
Single	68,683	51,483	31,660	15,904	19,370	5,594	1,645	3,465	197,804
Twins	1,483	1,248	750	375	363	154	26	104	4,503
Triplets and quads	36	36	38	11	22	5	-	3	151
Total nuptial	70,202	52,767	32,448	16,290	19,755	5,753	1,671	3,572	202,458
Ex-nuptial -									
Single	14,072	7,232	7,780	3,384	4,408	1,189	1,620	522	40,207
Twins and triplets	257	163	143	67	73	8	24	8	743
Total ex-nuptial	14,329	7,395	7,923	3,451	4,481	1,197	1,644	530	40,950
Total births	**84,531**	**60,162**	**40,371**	**19,741**	**24,236**	**6,950**	**3,315**	**4,102**	**243,408**

These figures are based on the usual residence of the mother.

Adapted from: Births Australia 1986. *ABS Cat. no. 3301.0.*

MARRIAGES REGISTERED
STATES AND TERRITORIES, 1956 TO 1986

	NSW	Vic.	Qld	SA	WA	Tas.	NT	ACT	Australia
Annual averages									
1956–1960	28,432	20,422	10,254	6,517	5,145	2,573	190	321	73,854
1961–1965	31,788	23,262	11,437	7,514	5,768	2,700	248	533	83,250
1966–1970	39,216	29,481	14,714	9,920	8,147	3,330	394	983	106,188
1971–1975	40,313	30,262	16,082	10,616	9,185	3,442	492	1,411	111,803
1976–1980	37,284	27,648	16,222	10,134	9,563	3,296	590	1,560	106,297
1981–1985	39,550	29,043	18,545	10,506	10,281	3,592	767	1,754	114,038
Annual totals									
1981	40,679	28,648	18,305	10,252	10,111	3,515	719	1,676	113,905
1982	41,955	28,851	18,928	10,936	10,455	3,576	818	1,756	117,275
1983	39,995	28,974	18,645	10,550	10,519	3,644	776	1,757	114,860
1984	33,938	28,931	19,039	10,643	9,920	3,704	731	1,749	108,655
1985	41,183	29,810	17,810	10,148	10,398	3,520	791	1,833	115,493
1986	41,319	29,390	18,030	9,878	10,379	3,302	759	1,856	114,913

Figures for 1984–86 for NSW and Australia in this table have been affected by the late registrations in NSW.
Adapted from: Marriages Australia 1986. ABS Cat. no. 3306.0.

MARRIAGES

PREVIOUS MARITAL STATUS, AUSTRALIA, 1956 TO 1986

	Bridegroom					Bride				
	Never Married	Widowed	Divorced	Total		Never Married	Widowed	Divorced	Total
Annual average number									
1956–1960	66,364	3,086	4,404	73,854		65,579	3,305	4,970	73,854
1961–1965	75,384	3,063	4,803	83,250		74,962	3,218	5,070	83,250
1966–1970	96,438	3,320	6,430	106,188		96,341	3,568	6,279	106,188
1971–1975	99,203	3,473	9,126	111,803		99,287	3,810	8,705	111,803
1976–1980	82,344	3,394	20,559	106,297		82,987	4,022	19,288	106,297
1981–1985	86,900	2,948	24,178	114,038		88,069	3,498	22,471	114,038
Annual total number									
1981	87,460	3,152	23,293	113,905		88,308	3,727	21,870	113,905
1982	89,858	2,988	24,429	117,275		90,844	3,579	22,852	117,275
1983	87,568	2,959	24,333	114,860		89,029	3,457	22,374	114,860
1984	82,149	2,798	23,708	108,655		83,325	3,312	22,018	108,655
1985	87,521	2,843	25,129	115,493		88,839	3,414	23,240	115,493
1986	86,676	2,952	25,285	114,913		88,070	3,564	23,279	114,913

	Bridegroom				Bride			
	Never Married	Widowed	Divorced	Total	Never Married	Widowed	Divorced	Total
Average annual proportion percentage								
1956–1960	89.6	4.2	6.0	100.0	88.8	4.5	6.7	100.0
1961–1965	90.6	3.7	5.8	100.0	90.0	3.9	6.1	100.0
1966–1970	90.8	3.1	6.0	100.0	90.7	3.4	5.9	100.0
1971–1975	88.7	3.1	8.2	100.0	88.8	3.4	7.8	100.0
1976–1980	77.5	3.2	19.3	100.0	78.0	3.8	18.2	100.0
1981–1985	76.2	2.6	21.2	100.0	77.2	3.1	19.7	100.0
Annual proportion percentage								
1981	76.8	2.8	20.4	100.0	77.5	3.3	19.2	100.0
1982	76.6	2.6	20.8	100.0	77.5	3.1	19.5	100.0
1983	76.2	2.6	21.2	100.0	77.5	3.0	19.5	100.0
1984	75.6	2.6	21.8	100.0	76.7	3.0	20.3	100.0
1985	75.8	2.5	21.8	100.0	76.9	3.0	20.1	100.0
1986	75.4	2.6	22.0	100.0	76.6	3.1	20.3	100.0

Figures for 1984–1986 have been affected by the late registrations in NSW.
Adapted from: Marriages Australia 1986. *ABS Cat. no. 3306.0.*

MARRIAGES

CATEGORY OF CELEBRANT, STATES AND TERRITORIES, 1986

	NSW	Vic.	Qld	SA	WA	Tas.	NT	ACT	Australia
NUMBER									
Category of celebrant									
Ministers of religion of recognised denominations									
Roman Catholic Church	8,890	7,031	3,326	1,546	1,922	427	95	401	23,638
Church of England in Australia	6,677	3,699	2,333	814	1,279	765	26	274	15,867
Uniting Churches in Australia	4,268	3,315	2,237	1,719	807	302	57	145	12,850
Presbyterian Church of Australia	1,267	391	429	48	40	41	–	77	2,295
Orthodox Churches	911	923	104	249	86	11	12	36	2,332
Baptist Union of Australia	695	467	350	216	149	97	11	12	1,997
Lutheran Churches	111	201	427	455	49	3	10	26	1,282
Churches of Christ in Australia	184	488	217	181	169	24	–	16	1,280
Other Denominations	2,535	1,581	1,211	526	665	231	47	71	6,867
Total	25,538	18,096	10,634	5,754	5,166	1,901	261	1,058	68,408
Civil celebrants—									
Official registrars	4,476	1,730	1,217	1,852	881	284	310	572	11,322
Other civil celebrants	11,305	9,564	6,179	2,272	4,332	1,117	188	226	35,183
Total	15,781	11,294	7,396	4,124	5,213	1,401	498	798	46,505
All celebrants	41,319	29,390	18,030	9,878	10,379	3,302	759	1,856	114,913

PROPORTION (Per cent)	NSW	Vic.	Qld	SA	WA	Tas.	NT	ACT	Australia
Ministers of religion of recognised denominations									
Roman Catholic Church	21.5	23.9	18.4	15.7	18.5	12.9	12.5	21.6	20.6
Church of England in Australia	16.2	12.6	12.9	8.2	12.3	23.2	3.4	14.8	13.8
Uniting Churches in Australia	10.3	11.3	12.4	17.4	7.8	9.1	7.5	7.8	11.2
Presbyterian Church of Australia	3.1	1.3	2.4	0.5	0.3	1.2	0.3	4.1	2.0
Orthodox Churches	2.2	3.1	0.6	2.5	0.8	0.3	1.6	1.9	2.0
Baptist Union of Australia	1.7	1.6	1.9	2.2	1.4	2.9	1.4	0.6	1.7
Lutheran Churches	0.3	0.7	2.4	4.6	0.5	0.1	1.3	1.4	1.1
Churches of Christ in Australia	0.4	1.7	1.2	1.8	1.6	0.7	0.1	0.9	1.1
Other Denominations	6.1	5.4	6.7	5.3	6.4	7.0	6.2	3.8	6.0
Total	**61.8**	**61.6**	**59.0**	**58.3**	**49.8**	**57.6**	**34.4**	**57.0**	**59.5**
Civil celebrants—									
Official registrars	10.8	5.9	6.7	18.7	8.5	8.6	40.8	30.8	9.9
Other civil celebrants	27.4	32.5	34.3	23.0	41.7	33.8	24.8	12.2	30.6
Total	**38.2**	**38.4**	**41.0**	**41.7**	**50.2**	**42.4**	**65.6**	**43.0**	**40.5**
All celebrants	100.0	100.0	100.0	100.0	100.0	100.0	100.0	100.0	100.0

The figures in this table for NSW and Australia have been affected by late registrations in NSW. The proportions are unlikely to have been affected.
Adapted from: Marriages Australia 1986. *ABS Cat. no. 3306.0*

MARRIAGES

MONTH OF CELEBRATION OF MARRIAGE, AUSTRALIA, 1981 TO 1986

Month of celebration	1981	1982	1983	1984	1985	1986
Number						
January	11,533	11,942	11,400	10,840	10,185	10,199
February	9,751	9,917	9,599	9,656	9,668	9,430
March	10,152	10,797	11,731	12,853	13,589	13,845
April	9,530	11,048	11,645	11,285	10,051	10,088
May	10,097	9,724	8,257	8,243	8,145	8,654
June	6,968	6,911	6,630	7,426	7,442	6,232
July	6,084	6,708	6,623	5,469	5,017	4,850
August	8,296	7,253	6,902	6,627	7,378	7,470
September	9,555	9,682	9,635	11,736	9,658	9,249
October	11,680	12,396	12,230	9,455	10,588	10,403
November	10,247	10,490	10,426	7,464	12,246	12,005
December	9,589	9,573	10,425	5,299	9,229	5,053
Total	**113,482**	**116,441**	**115,503**	**106,353**	**113,196**	**107,478**
Per cent						
January	10.2	10.3	9.9	10.2	9.0	9.5
February	8.6	8.5	8.3	9.1	8.5	8.8
March	8.9	9.3	10.2	12.1	12.0	12.9
April	8.4	9.5	10.1	10.6	8.9	9.4
May	8.9	8.4	7.2	7.8	7.2	8.0
June	6.1	5.9	5.7	7.0	6.6	5.8
July	5.4	5.8	5.7	5.1	4.4	4.5
August	7.3	6.2	6.0	6.2	6.5	6.9
September	8.4	8.3	8.3	11.0	8.5	8.6
October	10.3	10.6	10.6	8.9	9.4	9.7
November	9.0	9.0	9.0	7.0	10.8	11.2
December	8.5	8.2	9.0	5.0	8.2	4.7
Total	**100**	**100**	**100**	**100**	**100**	**100**

Figures exclude marriages celebrated in the years shown but not registered by the end of 1986. Figures for 1984, 1985 and 1986 in this table have been affected by late registrations in NSW.
Adapted from: Marriages Australia 1986. *ABS Cat. no.. 3306.0.*

MARRIAGES

RELATIVE AGES OF BRIDEGROOM AND BRIDE, AUSTRALIA 1986

Age of bridegroom (years)	Under 17	17	18	19	20	21	22	23	24	25	26	27
Under 19	37	89	125	82	61	30	20	11	12	7	5	3
19	45	119	255	274	167	82	73	46	29	23	16	9
20	49	142	437	654	679	441	217	131	66	48	37	18
21	36	131	453	937	1,337	1,225	699	339	178	132	75	51
22	31	124	445	1,013	1,504	1,749	1,561	825	414	277	146	98
23	34	86	356	727	1,290	1,794	1,831	1,445	762	426	252	175
24	23	64	227	589	1,008	1,417	1,569	1,613	1,259	703	401	249
25	20	39	187	409	686	1,035	1,296	1,442	1,285	1,025	521	368
26	14	26	135	283	461	753	960	1,112	1,116	1,010	751	505
27	6	20	87	187	364	548	698	824	816	820	760	563
28	7	18	67	132	263	378	511	589	659	694	657	604
29	4	14	37	103	174	263	337	409	554	600	544	522
30-34	14	20	100	173	279	531	738	941	1,207	1,252	1,451	1,418
35-39	3	6	25	31	79	111	207	263	325	416	484	515
40-44	-	-	11	24	20	41	42	62	83	131	165	158

45-49	-	-	6	6	12	15	22	19	23	38	30	47
50-54	-	-	-	-	-	9	7	11	15	10	15	18
55-59	-	-	-	-	4	4	5	3	7	4	6	10
60 and over	-	-	-	-	-	-	-	6	5	6	10	4
Total brides	**324**	**902**	**2,955**	**5,628**	**8,392**	**10,427**	**10,793**	**10,091**	**8,815**	**7,622**	**6,326**	**5,335**
Percentage	0.8	0.8	2.6	4.9	7.3	9.1	9.4	8.8	7.7	6.6	5.5	4.6

Age of bridegroom (years)	**Age of Bride (years)**										
	28	*29*	*30-34*	*35-39*	*40-44*	*45-49*	*50-54*	*55-59*	*60 and over*	*Total bride-grooms*	*Percentage*
Under 19	3	-	5	-	-	-	-	-	-	492	0.4
19	5	4	8	-	-	-	-	-	-	1,157	1.0
20	13	13	26	13	-	-	-	-	-	2,985	2.6
21	47	25	42	16	-	-	-	-	-	5,724	5.0
22	74	30	95	31	7	-	-	-	-	8,246	7.3
23	112	94	153	33	4	3	-	-	-	9,577	8.3
24	147	101	204	68	13	3	-	-	-	9,658	8.4
25	232	164	329	70	22	5	-	-	-	9,137	8.0
26	256	187	408	84	17	4	-	-	-	8,082	7.0
27	405	236	477	123	23	7	-	-	-	6,965	6.1
28	444	301	600	147	31	4	-	-	-	6,107	5.3
29	474	344	671	180	45	9	-	-	-	5,288	4.6

Age of bridegroom (years)	Age of Bride (years)									Total bride-grooms	Percentage
	28	29	30-34	35-39	40-44	45-49	50-54	55-59	60 and over		
30-34	1,369	1,340	4,037	1,276	301	74	15	4	-	16,541	14.4
35-39	522	570	2,787	1,991	687	184	36	7	-	9,251	8.1
40-44	160	218	1,233	1,402	987	405	78	16	8	5,247	4.6
45-49	67	60	503	824	883	641	208	52	24	3,481	3.0
50-54	29	17	203	366	463	510	327	123	54	2,180	1.9
55-59	12	17	79	153	263	368	361	302	155	1,757	1.5
60 and over	9	9	62	98	174	256	341	494	1,379	2,858	2.5
Total Brides	**4,380**	**3,731**	**11,922**	**6,878**	**3,920**	**2,475**	**1,370**	**999**	**1,627**	**114,913**	**100**
Percentage	3.8	3.2	10.4	6.0	3.4	2.2	1.2	0.9	1.4	100.0	-

The figures in this table have been affected by late registrations in NSW.
Adapted from: Marriages Australia 1986. *ABS Cat. no. 3306.0.*

DIVORCES

AGE-SPECIFIC DIVORCE RATES PER 1,000 POPULATION, AUSTRALIA, 1981 TO 1986

Age group (years) at date of divorce

	Under 25(a)	25-29	30-34	35-39	40-44	45-49	50-54	55-59	60 and over	Total
Males										
1981	2.2	13.8	15.0	13.6	11.6	9.3	7.0	4.5	1.8	5.6
1982	2.1	13.6	16.0	14.4	12.7	9.9	7.0	4.9	1.8	5.8
1983	1.9	12.2	15.2	14.2	12.5	9.9	7.2	4.8	1.9	5.7
1984	1.8	11.7	14.6	14.1	12.3	10.0	7.1	5.0	1.9	5.6
1985	1.6	10.1	12.9	12.9	11.2	9.2	6.5	4.7	1.7	5.1
1986	1.4	9.8	12.2	11.9	11.2	9.4	7.0	4.5	1.7	5.0
Females										
1981	4.8	16.6	14.3	12.7	10.2	7.6	5.1	3.1	0.8	5.5
1982	4.5	16.7	15.4	13.5	11.1	8.2	5.2	3.0	0.8	5.8
1983	4.2	15.4	14.9	13.3	10.8	8.2	5.2	3.2	0.9	5.7
1984	3.9	15.1	14.5	13.1	11.3	8.2	5.0	3.1	0.9	5.5
1985	3.4	13.2	13.2	12.1	10.1	7.6	4.6	3.0	0.8	5.1
1986	3.3	12.6	12.6	11.4	10.0	7.9	4.9	2.8	0.7	4.9

(a) Males aged under 18 and females aged under 16 have been excluded from the population used in calculating these rates.
Source: Divorces Australia 1986. ABS Cat. no. 3307.0

DIVORCES

PERCENTAGE DISTRIBUTION AND MEDIAN DURATION, AUSTRALIA, 1981 TO 1986

Duration of marriage (years)

	Under 5	5-9	10-14	15-19	20-24	25-29	30 and over	Total number (a)	Median duration (years)
Interval between date of marriage and date decree made absolute
1981	20.8	28.5	19.6	11.9	8.6	5.6	5.0	41,412	10.2
1982	20.3	28.0	20.0	13.0	8.7	5.3	4.8	44,088	10.4
1983	20.8	26.8	20.3	13.2	8.6	5.3	5.0	43,525	10.5
1984	21.4	26.4	20.0	13.7	8.7	5.2	5.1	43,124	10.5
1985	21.7	26.2	18.7	14.0	9.2	5.1	5.0	39,830	10.5
1986	21.7	26.2	17.8	14.3	9.4	5.6	4.9	39,417	10.6
Interval between date of marriage and date of final separation
1981	36.4	24.9	15.9	10.2	7.0	3.5	2.1	41,412	7.5
1982	36.2	24.3	16.3	10.9	6.8	3.4	2.1	44,088	7.6
1983	36.3	23.3	16.9	11.0	6.9	3.3	2.2	43,525	7.7
1984	36.9	22.7	16.8	11.1	6.8	3.4	2.3	43,124	7.7
1985	37.1	22.1	16.5	11.5	6.8	3.4	2.4	39,830	7.6
1986	37.6	21.5	16.0	11.7	7.2	3.7	2.3	39,417	7.6

(a) Includes not stated duration of marriage.
Source: 1986. ABS Cat. no. 3307.0

DEATHS

NUMBER, RATE AND PROPORTION BY CAUSE AND SEX, AUSTRALIA, 1986

Cause of death	Number of deaths			Rate per million of mean population			Proportion of total deaths (per cent)		
	Males	Females	Persons	Males	Females	Persons	Males	Females	Persons
ALL CAUSES	62,210	52,771	114,981	7,777	6,581	7,178	100.0	100.0	100.0
Total infectious and parasitic diseases	340	258	598	43	32	37	0.5	0.5	0.5
Intestinal infectious diseases	24	23	47	3	3	3	(b)	(b)	(b)
Tuberculosis	45	16	61	6	2	4	0.1	(d)	0.1
Whooping cough	-	-	-	-	-	-	-	-	-
Meningococcal infection	5	4	9	1	(a)	1	(b)	(b)	(b)
Tetanus	3	2	5	(a)	(a)	(a)	(b)	(b)	(b)
Septicaemia	121	116	237	15	14	15	0.2	0.2	0.2
Smallpox	-	-	-	-	-	-	-	-	-
Measles	3	2	5	(a)	(a)	(a)	(b)	(b)	(b)
Malaria	1	-	1	(a)	—	(a)	(b)	—	(b)
All other infectious and parasitic diseases	138	95	233	17	12	15	0.2	0.2	0.2

Cause of death	Number of deaths			Rate per million of mean population			Proportion of total deaths (per cent)		
	Males	Females	Persons	Males	Females	Persons	Males	Females	Persons
Total malignant neoplasms	**15,701**	**12,194**	**27,895**	**1,963**	**1,521**	**1,742**	**25.2**	**23.1**	**24.3**
Stomach	874	508	1,382	109	63	86	1.4	1.0	1.2
Colon	1,492	1,600	3,092	187	200	193	2.4	3.0	2.7
Rectum, rectosigmoid junction and anus	603	437	1,040	75	54	65	1.0	0.8	0.9
Trachea, bronchus and lung	4,351	1,351	5,702	544	168	356	7.0	2.6	5.0
Female breast	-	2,230	2,230	-	278	139	-	4.2	1.9
Cervix uteri	-	350	350	-	44	22	-	0.7	0.3
Leukaemia	585	439	1,024	73	55	64	0.9	0.8	0.9
All other malignant neoplasms	7,796	5,279	13,075	975	658	816	12.5	10.0	11.4
Diabetes mellitus	906	1,052	1,958	113	131	122	1.5	2.0	1.7
Nutritional marasmus	2	2	4	(a)	(a)	(a)	(b)	(b)	(b)
Other protein-calorie malnutrition	21	21	42	3	3	3	(b)	(b)	(b)
Anaemias	115	137	252	14	17	16	0.2	0.3	0.2
Meningitis	22	22	44	3	3	3	(b)	(b)	(b)
Total diseases of the circulatory system	**27,949**	**27,316**	**55,265**	**3,494**	**3,407**	**3,450**	**44.9**	**51.8**	**48.1**
Acute rheumatic fever	1	5	6	(a)	1	(a)	(b)	(b)	(b)
Chronic rheumatic heart disease	130	264	394	16	33	25	0.2	0.5	0.3

Hypertensive disease	409	676	1,085	51	84	68	0.7	1.3	0.9
Ischaemic heart disease	18,057	13,946	32,003	2,257	1,739	1,998	29.0	26.4	27.8
Acute myocadial infarction	12,968	9,696	22,664	1,621	1,209	1,415	20.8	18.4	19.7
Other ischaemic heart disease	5,089	4,250	9,339	636	530	583	8.2	8.1	8.1
Cerebrovascular disease	5,000	7,491	12,491	625	934	780	8.0	14.2	10.9
Atherosclerosis	387	757	1,144	48	94	71	0.6	1.4	1.0
All other diseases of the circulatory system	3,965	4,177	8,142	496	521	508	6.4	7.9	7.1
Pneumonia	711	775	1,486	89	97	93	1.1	1.5	1.3
Influenza	14	32	46	2	4	3	(b)	0.1	(b)
Bronchitis, emphysema and asthma	1,367	777	2,144	171	97	134	2.2	1.5	1.9
Ulcer of stomach and duodenum	382	404	786	48	50	49	0.6	0.8	0.7
Appendicitis	18	10	28	2	1	2	(b)	(b)	(b)
Chronic liver disease and cirrhosis	852	318	1,170	107	40	73	1.4	0.6	1.0
Nephritis, nephrotic syndrome and nephrosis	454	652	1,106	57	81	69	0.7	1.2	1.0
Hyperplasia of prostate	83	-	83	10	-	5	0.1	-	0.1
Abortion	-	3	3	-	(a)	(a)	-	(b)	(b)
Direct obstetric deaths	-	12	12	-	1	1	-	(b)	(b)
Congenital anomalies	447	394	841	56	49	53	0.7	0.7	0.7

Cause of death	Number of deaths Males	Females	Persons	Rate per million of mean population Males	Females	Persons	Proportion of total deaths (per cent) Males	Females	Persons
Total conditions originating in the perinatal period	**507**	**357**	**864**	**63**	**45**	**54**	**0.8**	**0.7**	**0.8**
Birth trauma	22	8	30	3	1	2	(b)	(b)	(b)
Hypoxia, birth asphyxia and other respiratory conditions	243	162	405	30	20	25	0.4	0.3	0.4
Other conditions originating in the perinatal period	242	187	429	30	23	27	0.4	0.4	0.4
Signs, symptoms and ill-defined conditions	450	343	793	56	43	50	0.7	0.6	0.7
All other diseases	6,398	5,335	11,733	800	665	733	10.3	10.1	10.2
Total Accidents and adverse effects	**3,674**	**1,758**	**5,432**	**459**	**219**	**339**	**5.9**	**3.3**	**4.7**
Motor vehicle traffic accidents	2,132	855	2,987	267	107	186	3.4	1.6	2.6
Accidental falls	393	487	880	49	61	55	0.6	0.9	0.8
All other accidents and adverse effects	1,149	416	1,565	144	52	98	1.8	0.8	1.4
Suicide	1,531	451	1,982	191	56	124	2.5	0.9	1.7
Homicide	192	123	315	24	15	20	0.3	0.2	0.3
All other external causes	74	25	99	9	3	6	0.1	(b)	(b)

(a) Less than 0.5 (b) Less than 0.05.
Adapted from: Causes of Death Australia 1986. *ABS Cat. no. 3303.0*

SUMMARY OF PRINCIPAL CAUSES OF DEATH

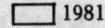

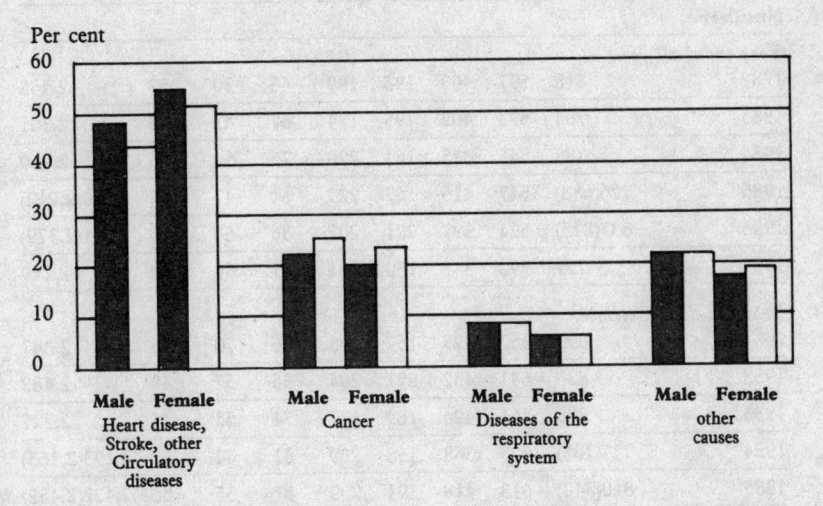

☐ 1981
■ 1986

Source: Deaths Australia 1986. *ABS Cat. No. 3302.0.*

INFANT DEATHS REGISTERED
STATE AND TERRITORY OF REGISTRATION

	NSW	Vic.	Qld	SA	WA	Tas.	NT	ACT	Australia
Number									
Year ended 30 June —									
1982	818	597	463	193	199	63	70	52	2,455
1983	784	593	402	195	174	67	43	43	2,301
1984	785	545	375	164	220	75	50	46	2,260
1985	726(688)	547	415	167	223	81	47	44	2,250(2,212)
1986	837(875)	524	397	201	202	86	54	40	2,341(2,379)
1987	727	592	343	150	204	67	56	30	2,169
Year ended 31 December —									
1981	809	562	425	157	193	86	70	45	2,347
1982	823	641	432	221	204	55	57	49	2,482
1983	805	561	426	189	177	74	52	43	2,327
1984	735(705)	525	368	158	230	81	44	52	2,193(2,163)
1985	810(840)	613	418	194	209	87	55	36	2,422(2,452)
1986	751	529	355	146	212	74	51	36	2,154
Quarter ended —									
1986 —									
March	203	94	91	35	37	17	13	8	498
June	172	84	98	42	62	22	9	11	500
September	203	215	95	35	59	26	14	12	659
December	173	136	71	34	54	9	15	5	497
1987 —									
March	176	100	92	35	53	20	9	7	492
June	175	141	85	46	38	12	18	6	521
Infant Mortality Rates (Per 1,000 Live Births)									
Year ended 31 December —									
1981	9.9	9.4	10.9	8.1	8.8	12.0	22.7	10.1	10.0
1982	9.9	10.7	10.7	11.5	9.2	7.9	19.8	10.9	10.3
1983	9.6	8.9	10.1	9.8	7.6	10.4	16.4	9.3	9.4
1984	9.0(9.1)	8.8	9.1	7.8	10.7	11.4	13.9	11.3	9.2(9.2)
1985	9.8(9.6)	9.9	10.4	9.8	9.1	12.1	16.7	7.8	10.0(9.9)
1986	8.9	8.8	8.8	7.1	8.8	10.7	15.4	7.8	8.8

The figures in brackets show numbers or rates of registered infant deaths prior to overcoming the 1984 backlog of unprocessed events in NSW. The Northern Territory infant death rate is affected, more than other states and the ACT, by the higher infant death rate among Aborigines. Figures for 1987 are subject to revision.
Adapted from: Australian Demographic Statistics. *ABS Cat. no. 3101.0.*

RATES OF RESIDENT POPULATION GROWTH
STATES AND TERRITORIES

Year ended 30 June	NSW	Vic.	Qld	SA	WA	Tas.	NT	ACT	Australia
Natural Increase									
1983	0.81	0.74	0.99	0.68	1.07	0.84	1.86	1.38	0.85
1984	0.77	0.76	0.97	0.77	1.02	0.85	1.86	1.37	0.84
1985	0.78	0.74	0.88	0.71	1.02	0.82	1.76	1.30	0.82
1986	0.72	0.71	0.85	0.67	1.01	0.75	1.88	1.24	0.78
1987	0.75	0.73	0.83	0.66	1.01	0.79	1.75	1.21	0.79
Net Overseas Migration									
1983	0.49	0.49	0.36	0.48	0.84	0.14	0.37	0.23	0.48
1984	0.39	0.36	0.13	0.29	0.31	0.15	0.61	0.28	0.32
1985	0.58	0.49	0.30	0.32	0.56	0.18	0.74	0.27	0.47
1986	0.75	0.64	0.44	0.37	0.92	0.20	0.81	0.56	0.64
1987	0.81	0.67	0.40	0.37	1.01	0.14	0.50	−0.29	0.65
Net Interstate Migration									
1983	−0.32	−0.13	0.86	−0.02	0.11	−0.28	0.41	0.42	—
1984	−0.19	−0.08	0.40	0.04	0.05	0.16	0.53	0.39	—
1985	−0.17	−0.14	0.51	−0.17	0.14	0.18	0.43	0.48	—
1986	−0.23	−0.32	0.64	−0.10	0.66	−0.03	−0.33	0.71	—
1987	−0.22	−0.28	0.70	−0.22	0.52	−0.34	0.32	0.72	—
Net Migration Gain									
1983	0.16	0.36	1.21	0.46	0.95	−0.14	0.78	0.66	0.48
1984	0.19	0.28	0.53	0.34	0.37	0.31	1.15	0.68	0.32
1985	0.41	0.35	0.82	0.15	0.70	0.35	1.17	0.75	0.47
1986	0.52	0.32	1.08	0.27	1.58	0.17	0.48	1.27	0.64
1987	0.59	0.39	1.10	0.15	1.53	−0.19	0.83	0.43	0.65
Total Population Growth (a)									
1983	0.93	1.07	2.38	1.10	2.25	0.69	4.30	2.55	1.38
1984	0.93	1.01	1.67	1.06	1.62	1.14	4.59	2.56	1.21
1985	1.14	1.07	1.88	0.82	1.96	1.16	4.49	2.56	1.34
1986	1.23	0.99	2.08	0.83	2.85	0.82	3.96	2.99	1.46
1987	1.33	1.13	1.93	0.81	2.54	0.60	2.58	1.64	1.44

(a) Discrepancies between the sum of natural increase and net migration rates and the rates of total growth are due to intercensal adjustment. 1987 figures are subject to revision.
Adapted from: Australian Demographic Statistics. *ABS Cat. no. 3101.0.*

ESTIMATED RESIDENT POPULATION

SEX, STATES AND TERRITORIES, 30 JUNE AND 31 DECEMBER ('000)

	NSW	Vic.	Qld	SA	WA	Tas.	NT	ACT	Australia
Males									
As at 30 June —									
1981(a)	2,608.4	1,958.7	1,178.4	653.9	657.2	212.6	65.4	113.6	7,448.3
1982	2,643.5	1,981.6	1,219.4	660.1	676.9	213.7	69.4	116.4	7,580.9
1983	2,668.0	2,003.1	1,248.7	667.9	691.7	215.1	72.3	119.4	7,686.3
1984	2,692.1	2,023.3	1,269.6	675.2	702.5	217.4	75.7	122.5	7,778.2
1985	2,723.3	2,045.0	1,293.2	681.2	715.6	219.8	79.0	125.5	7,882.7
1986 (a)	2,757.0	2,065.7	1,320.6	687.8	736.1	221.7	81.7	129.6	8,000.2
1987 (b)	2,792.9	2,088.7	1,345.1	693.1	754.4	222.9	83.6	131.8	8,112.6
Females									
1981(a)	2,626.5	1,988.2	1,166.8	664.8	642.8	214.7	57.2	114.0	7,475.0
1982	2,660.1	2,011.3	1,205.2	671.0	662.0	216.2	60.9	116.7	7,603.3
1983	2,684.9	2,032.6	1,233.6	677.8	677.4	217.7	63.6	119.5	7,707.1
1984	2,710.6	2,053.1	1,254.3	684.8	688.8	220.4	66.5	122.7	7,801.2
1985	2,741.3	2,075.0	1,278.0	690.0	702.9	223.0	69.5	125.8	7,905.6
1986 (a)	2,774.5	2,095.1	1,304.0	694.8	722.9	224.8	72.7	129.3	8,018.2
1987 (b)	2,812.4	2,119.0	1,330.2	700.7	741.7	226.2	74.8	131.3	8,136.2

Males

As at 31 December —

1981	2,624.6	1,969.3	1,200.5	657.0	667.4	212.9	68.0	114.6	7,514.3
1982	2,655.5	1,991.5	1,235.5	663.6	684.8	214.2	70.7	117.4	7,633.2
1983	2,678.3	2,012.4	1,259.1	671.7	697.6	216.1	74.2	120.9	7,730.4
1984	2,706.6	2,033.6	1,281.0	678.0	708.1	218.4	77.3	123.4	7,826.4
1985	2,739.3	2,055.4	1,306.3	684.4	725.0	220.7	80.9	128.0	7,940.0
1986	2,775.6	2,076.7	1,332.6	690.4	745.3	222.5	82.8	130.5	8,056.4

Females

1981	2,642.3	1,999.0	1,187.4	668.2	652.8	215.3	59.7	114.9	7,539.8
1982	2,672.7	2,021.2	1,220.9	674.1	670.2	216.8	62.1	117.6	7,655.7
1983	2,696.7	2,042.1	1,244.1	681.5	683.4	219.0	65.3	121.1	7,753.1
1984	2,725.2	2,064.0	1,266.0	687.4	695.0	221.7	68.0	123.7	7,850.9
1985	2,757.1	2,085.0	1,290.8	692.4	711.9	223.9	71.4	127.9	7,960.5
1986 (b)	2,794.4	2,106.8	1,317.0	697.7	732.4	225.7	73.9	130.2	8,078.2

(a) Census date. (b) These figures are subject to revision.
Adapted from: Australian Demographic Statistics. *ABS Cat. no. 3101.0.*

ESTIMATED RESIDENT POPULATION
CAPITAL CITIES AND OTHER MAJOR CITIES
30 JUNE 1976 TO 1986 ('000)

	1976	1981	1982 (a)	1983 (a)	1984 (a)	1985 (a)	1986 (a)
Sydney(b)	3,143.8	3,279.5	3,310.5	3,335.0	3,358.5	3,392.7	3,430.6
Melbourne(b)	2,723.7	2,806.3	2,836.8	2,865.7	2,890.7	2,917.2	2,942.0
Brisbane(b)	1,000.9	1,096.2	1,124.2	1,138.4	1,146.6	1,158.0	1,171.3
Adelaide(b)	924.1	(c)954.3	(c)961.0	(c)970.3	(c)980.0	985.9	993.1
Perth(b)	832.8	922.0	948.8	969.1	983.4	1,001.6	1,025.3
Hobart(b)	164.4	171.1	172.5	173.8	175.7	178.1	180.3
Darwin(b)	44.2	56.5	60.9	63.3	66.1	68.5	n.y.a.
Canberra(d)(e)	226.5	246.5	251.0	255.9	264.4	274.0	285.8
Newcastle(d)	380.0	402.7	410.3	414.7	419.1	424.7	429.3
Wollongong(d)	222.3	231.4	233.7	235.0	235.9	236.9	237.6
Gold Coast(d)(f)	110.9	162.7	178.8	189.1	198.4	208.4	219.3
Geelong(d)	138.3	142.0	143.0	143.9	145.4	147.1	148.3
Townsville(d)	90.5	96.3	98.0	99.6	100.5	101.8	103.7

(a) Subject to revision when 1986 Census-based estimates become available. (b) Capital City Statistical Division. (c) Estimate based on Statistical Division boundary as re-defined at 30 June 1985. (d) Statistical District of 100,000 or more. (e) Includes Queanbeyan in New South Wales. (f) Includes part of Tweed Shire in New South Wales.
Source: Australian Demographic Statistics. ABS Cat. no. 3101.0.

PRELIMINARY ESTIMATED RESIDENT POPULATION
BY AGE GROUPS, STATES AND TERRITORIES, 30 JUNE 1987

Age group (years)	NSW	Vic.	Qld	SA	WA	Tas.	NT	ACT	Australia
Males									
0–4	213,164	155,012	105,778	50,769	60,804	18,031	8,124	10,673	622,355
5–9	208,259	153,570	105,296	48,897	59,505	17,754	7,899	11,040	612,220
10–14	219,810	166,699	113,563	52,727	60,998	18,480	7,466	11,886	651,629
15–19	233,837	188,320	120,904	59,645	66,284	19,802	7,089	12,761	708,642
20–24	225,537	175,383	112,260	58,568	63,714	17,373	8,431	12,496	673,762
25–29	237,402	178,035	113,741	59,782	66,767	18,869	9,031	12,134	695,761
30–34	222,211	166,667	104,256	55,088	63,284	17,429	7,992	11,369	648,296
35–39	217,848	161,084	103,421	53,296	61,830	16,759	7,888	12,055	634,181
40–44	196,174	143,219	92,905	46,800	53,405	14,807	6,247	10,166	563,723
45–49	155,546	115,233	73,073	36,663	41,566	11,886	4,409	7,517	445,893
50–54	136,348	101,571	60,912	32,856	34,501	10,175	2,972	5,560	384,895
55–59	135,986	100,429	59,334	34,130	32,595	10,309	2,350	4,609	379,742
60–64	127,859	92,581	56,507	33,319	29,083	9,974	1,648	3,762	354,733
65–69	101,217	70,898	46,773	26,633	21,927	7,730	959	2,595	278,732
70–74	76,722	54,566	35,170	20,590	17,128	6,357	607	1,599	212,739
75–79	48,567	36,549	22,939	13,155	11,586	4,008	294	935	138,033

80–84	24,223	18,945	11,850	6,628	6,311	2,075	122	453	70,607
85 and over	12,207	9,923	6,441	3,602	3,099	1,077	77	222	36,648
All ages	2,792,917	2,088,684	1,345,123	693,148	754,387	222,895	83,605	131,832	8,112,591
Females									
0–4	203,544	147,937	99,933	48,598	57,965	17,459	7,835	10,326	593,597
5–9	198,582	146,891	98,891	46,532	55,798	17,054	7,249	10,705	581,702
10–14	209,611	158,102	107,797	49,385	57,869	17,618	6,814	11,481	618,677
15–19	223,141	180,702	115,653	56,690	63,255	19,264	6,775	12,370	677,850
20–24	216,878	171,714	107,212	55,713	61,387	17,382	7,865	12,164	650,315
25–29	232,657	176,252	110,059	57,973	64,524	18,693	8,556	11,865	680,579
30–34	220,672	167,831	102,858	54,827	62,557	17,566	7,591	11,696	645,598
35–39	212,520	161,726	101,052	53,017	59,388	16,564	6,796	12,337	623,400
40–44	185,862	138,490	88,692	45,674	48,776	14,175	4,856	9,965	536,490
45–49	147,331	109,664	67,771	35,737	38,681	11,467	3,263	7,025	420,939
50–54	130,201	97,975	57,726	32,167	32,555	10,026	2,190	5,140	367,980
55–59	132,104	96,652	57,417	33,149	30,452	10,060	1,643	4,208	365,685
60–64	134,121	97,635	57,150	34,890	28,999	10,210	1,318	3,996	368,319
65–69	115,833	81,753	50,680	30,351	24,434	9,046	871	2,935	315,903
70–74	97,364	70,182	42,538	25,481	21,303	7,795	566	2,186	267,415
75–79	72,481	53,647	30,608	19,101	16,263	5,774	300	1,474	199,648
80–84	44,556	34,441	18,884	11,760	10,077	3,383	174	818	124,093
85 and over	34,894	27,411	15,269	9,620	7,389	2,704	135	633	98,055

Age									
All ages	2,812,352	2,119,005	1,330,190	700,665	741,672	226,240	74,797	131,324	8,136,245
Persons									
0–4	416,708	302,949	205,711	99,367	118,769	35,490	15,959	20,999	1,215,952
5–9	406,841	300,461	204,187	95,429	115,303	34,808	15,148	21,745	1,193,922
10–14	429,421	324,801	221,360	102,112	118,867	36,098	14,280	23,367	1,270,306
15–19	456,978	369,022	236,557	116,335	129,539	39,066	13,864	25,131	1,386,492
20–24	442,415	347,097	219,472	114,281	125,101	34,755	16,296	24,660	1,324,077
25–29	470,059	354,287	223,800	117,755	131,291	37,562	17,587	23,999	1,376,340
30–34	442,883	334,498	207,114	109,915	125,841	34,995	15,583	23,065	1,293,894
35–39	430,368	322,810	204,473	106,313	121,218	33,323	14,684	24,392	1,257,581
40–44	382,036	281,709	181,597	92,474	102,181	28,982	11,103	20,131	1,100,213
45–49	302,877	224,897	140,844	72,400	80,247	23,353	7,672	14,542	866,832
50–54	266,549	199,546	118,638	65,023	67,056	20,201	5,162	10,700	752,875
55–59	268,090	197,081	116,751	67,279	63,047	20,369	3,993	8,817	745,427
60–64	261,980	190,216	113,657	68,209	58,082	20,184	2,966	7,758	723,052
65–69	217,050	152,651	97,453	56,984	46,361	16,776	1,830	5,530	594,635
70–74	174,086	124,748	77,708	46,071	38,431	14,152	1,173	3,785	480,154
75–79	121,048	90,196	53,547	32,256	27,849	9,782	594	2,409	337,681
80–84	68,779	53,386	30,734	18,388	16,388	5,458	296	1,271	194,700
85 and over	47,101	37,334	21,710	13,222	10,488	3,781	212	855	134,703
All ages	5,605,269	4,207,689	2,675,313	1,393,813	1,496,059	449,135	158,402	263,156	16,248,836

Source: Australian Demographic Statistics. ABS Cat. no. 3101.0.

SETTLER ARRIVALS
COUNTRY OF BIRTH

Country of birth	Year ended 30 June 1986	Year ended 30 June 1987	Year ended 31 December 1985	Year ended 31 December 1986	Quarter ended March 1986	Quarter ended June 1986	Quarter ended September 1986	Quarter ended December 1986	Quarter ended March 1987	Quarter ended June 1987
Africa—										
South Africa	3,130	4,670	2,060	4,180	930	930	230	1,210	1,490	860
Other	2,650	3,930	2,150	3,160	710	700	1,570	1,060	1,130	1,050
America—										
Canada	930	1,040	890	960	190	180	290	290	240	220
USA	1,670	1,800	1,540	1,790	420	360	490	520	390	400
Other	4,120	4,290	3,910	3,850	970	1,000	950	930	1,120	1,290
Asia—										
China	3,140	2,690	3,210	2,680	770	650	580	680	710	720
Hong Kong	3,120	3,400	2,940	3,260	940	680	910	740	1,000	760
India	2,140	2,540	2,030	2,140	530	540	570	500	690	780
Kampuchea	870	1,370	1,020	880	230	280	190	180	590	420
Lebanon	2,760	2,870	2,190	2,830	680	740	710	710	590	870
Malaysia	2,280	3,950	2,370	2,830	700	530	740	870	1,180	1,160
Philippines	4,130	6,410	3,750	4,850	1,040	1,060	1,220	1,530	1,510	2,150
Turkey (in Asia and Europe)	990	1,150	870	1,080	240	290	260	290	350	260

Vietnam	7,170	6,650	7,270	7,310	1,730	2,070	1,920	1,590	1,450	1,690
Other	10,050	14,100	8,820	11,910	2,510	2,900	3,230	3,270	3,620	3,970
Europe—										
Germany	1,030	1,390	950	1,260	240	300	340	380	340	330
Greece	880	950	800	890	220	170	210	280	220	230
Ireland	1,450	2,350	1,090	1,900	360	380	510	650	660	520
Italy	680	590	700	570	150	120	140	160	170	120
Netherlands	610	560	560	630	150	140	180	170	120	110
Poland	1,340	1,620	1,290	1,340	360	360	280	350	320	680
Portugal	1,000	1,170	930	1,070	290	250	290	240	360	280
United Kingdom	14,710	20,240	12,040	18,770	3,740	4,370	5,020	5,640	4,970	4,600
Yugoslavia	1,950	2,650	1,680	2,090	550	420	500	630	680	840
Other	4,100	4,570	3,600	4,330	1,040	990	1,010	1,300	1,200	1,060
Oceania—										
Australia	280	380	280	320	80	60	90	100	100	100
New Zealand	13,280	13,580	11,290	14,140	3,840	3,650	3,600	3,050	3,470	3,470
Other	2,140	2,640	1,760	2,300	650	460	610	580	740	710
Not stated	—	10	10	10	—	—	—	10	—	—
Total	**92,590**	**113,540**	**82,000**	**103,330**	**24,230**	**24,570**	**26,630**	**27,900**	**29,370**	**29,640**

Asia includes countries which are frequently regarded as 'Middle East' countries.
Adapted from: AUSTRALIAN DEMOGRAPHIC STATISTICS. *ABS Cat. no. 3101.0.*

BIRTHPLACE OF PARENTS OF AUSTRALIAN-BORN PERSONS

Father	Australia	Other Oceania	UK & Ireland	Southern Europe
Australia	9,070,739	50,896	363,980	28,202
Other Oceania	69,824	18,729	7,079	541
UK & Ireland	567,432	9,795	329,994	4,321
Southern Europe	120,371	1,864	11,336	411,259
Other Europe & USSR	147,904	3,501	21,179	7,455
Western Asia (Middle East)	9,868	415	1,158	2,360
Other Asia	32,814	1,422	5,499	683
South America	1,997	115	465	509
Other America	19,369	561	2,694	336
Africa	17,352	593	3,284	3,336
Total*	**10,135,070**	**89,026**	**752,666**	**461,865**

* including not stated
Source: ABS 1986 Census of Population and Housing.

Mother Other Europe & USSR	Western Asia	Other Asia	South America	Other America	Africa	Total*
64,983	3,425	26,631	1,614	11,881	11,017	9,663,956
1,409	118	1,311	66	371	345	100,241
13,846	576	7,139	602	2,735	3,619	943,452
14,768	2,715	2,151	1,273	704	4,012	572,838
147,848	1,233	5,569	466	858	1,679	339,049
1,239	64,314	400	200	170	862	81,363
3,009	283	53,841	98	227	441	98,702
244	71	124	6,723	68	75	10,454
811	88	341	65	2,518	167	27,049
1,420	848	575	98	157	16,104	43,934
251,775	**74,233**	**99,007**	**11,317**	**19,832**	**38,663**	**12,110,456**

LANGUAGE OTHER THAN ENGLISH SPOKEN AT HOME BY AGE

(Excludes Persons aged 0–4 Years)

	5–19 Years Males	5–19 Years Females	20–34 Years Males	20–34 Years Females
Arabic/Lebanese	19,638	19,071	14,922	16,183
Chinese	17,552	16,189	22,679	23,185
Dutch	2,447	2,538	5,071	5,810
French	4,332	5,523	7,306	7,510
German	6,041	7,031	10,023	10,417
Greek	40,234	38,540	30,678	30,676
Italian	43,801	43,078	49,511	49,511
Maltese	5,208	4,958	7,064	7,079
Polish	4,130	4,097	7,063	7,446
Serbian, Croatian	10,509	10,301	5,996	6,853
Spanish	10,645	10,442	8,391	9,106
Vietnamese	11,086	8,735	15,888	11,228
Other	60,726	58,644	70,858	74,318
Not Stated	6,394	5,836	6,021	5,384
Total	**242,743**	**234,983**	**261,471**	**264,706**

Source: ABS 1986 Census of Population and Housing.

35-64 Years Males	35-64 Years Females	65 Years and Over Males	65 Years and Over Females	Males	Total Females	Persons
18,961	13,883	1,631	1,749	55,152	50,886	106,038
21,640	21,681	3,312	4,531	65,183	65,586	130,769
16,380	17,353	5,500	6,336	29,398	32,037	61,435
11,079	10,832	2,047	2,768	24,764	26,633	51,397
30,135	30,401	6,664	8,734	52,863	56,583	109,446
58,067	55,674	6,208	6,991	135,187	131,881	267,068
93,774	87,484	18,925	18,954	206,011	199,027	405,038
15,240	13,860	2,164	2,264	29,676	28,161	57,837
14,121	16,832	7,315	5,181	32,629	33,556	66,185
16,559	13,681	1,334	1,376	34,398	32,211	66,609
15,325	13,992	805	1,369	35,166	34,909	70,075
6,724	4,770	449	528	34,147	25,261	59,408
107,069	99,211	20,552	23,177	259,205	255,350	514,555
11,908	10,656	4,256	6,516	28,579	28,392	56,971
436,982	**410,310**	**81,162**	**90,474**	**1,022,358**	**1,000,473**	**2,022,831**

RELIGIONS IN AUSTRALIA

	Males	Females	Persons	Prop %
Christian:				
Anglican	1,788,867	1,934,552	3,723,419	23.9
Baptist	92,328	104,454	196,782	1.3
Brethren	10,964	12,200	23,164	0.1
Catholic	1,988,013	2,076,400	4,064,413	26.1
Congregational	7,693	8,923	16,616	0.1
Churches of Christ	40,095	48,416	88,511	0.6
Jehovah's Witness	29,984	36,512	66,496	0.4
Latterday Saints	16,681	18,809	35,490	0.2
Lutheran	100,905	107,399	208,304	1.3
Oriental Christian	5,289	5,085	10,374	0.1
Orthodox	218,511	208,934	427,445	2.7
Pentecostal	50,333	56,674	107,007	0.7
Presbyterian	266,055	293,970	560,025	3.6
Salvation Army	35,449	42,322	77,771	0.5
Seventh Day Adventist	21,835	26,146	47,981	0.3
Uniting Church	550,535	631,775	1,182,310	7.6
Other Protestant	93,157	106,289	199,446	1.3
Other Christian	169,138	177,216	346,354	2.2

Total Christian	5,485,832	5,896,076	11,381,908	73.0
Other Religions:				
Buddhist	41,809	38,578	80,387	0.5
Hindu	11,493	9,961	21,454	0.1
Jewish	33,527	35,560	69,087	0.4
Muslim	58,229	51,294	109,523	0.7
Other non Christian	18,315	17,427	35,742	0.2
Total Other Religions	163,373	152,820	316,197	2.0
Other Groups:				
Non Theistic	3,069	1,840	4,909	0.0
Inadequately Described	33,125	24,915	58,040	0.4
No Religion	1,113,993	863,471	1,977,464	12.7
Not Stated	968,921	894,721	1,863,642	11.9
Total Persons	7,768,313	7,833,843	15,602,156	100.0

Source: ABS 1986 Census of Population and Housing.

HOUSING
(Excludes caravans etc. in parks)

	Separate House	Semi-Detached	Row/Terrace	Other Medium Density	Flats over 3 Storeys	Other	Not Stated	Total
Owned	1,750,160	27,417	13,223	130,485	20,943	18,976	20,715	1,981,919
Being purchased	1,471,328	18,890	10,951	69,396	8,709	6,845	18,286	1,604,405
Rented: Housing Authority	151,608	31,093	4,959	70,358	17,190	206	3,223	278,637
Other Govt Agency	52,826	1,373	751	10,289	1,027	1,095	1,190	68,551
Private	463,766	35,439	20,521	378,446	47,639	24,825	16,541	987,177
Other & Not Stated	192,162	5,341	3,409	32,213	7,258	10,464	15,886	266,733
Total	4,081,850	119,553	53,814	691,187	102,766	62,411	75,841	5,187,422

Source: ABS 1986 Census of Population and Housing.

EXTREME MINIMUM TEMPERATURES

(All years to September 1985)

Station	°C	Date
New South Wales		
Charlotte Pass	−22.2	14.7.1945
		22.8.1947
Kiandra	−20.6	2.8.1929
Perisher Valley	−19.5	23.7.1979
Victoria		
Mount Hotham	−12.8	13.8.1947
Omeo	−11.7	15.6.1965
Hotham Heights	−11.1	15.8.1968
Queensland		
Stanthorpe	−11.0	4.7.1895
Warwick	−10.6	12.7.1965
South Australia		
Yongala	−8.2	20.7.1976
Yunta	−7.7	16.7.1976
Ernabella	−7.6	19.7.1983
Western Australia		
Booylgoo	−6.7	12.7.1969
Tasmania		
Shannon	−13.0	30.6.1983
Butlers Gorge	−13.0	30.6.1983
Tarraleah	−13.0	30.6.1983
Northern Territory		
Alice Springs	−7.5	12.7.1976
Tempe Downs	−6.9	24.7.1971
Australian Capital Territory		
Canberra	−10.0	19.7.1924

Source: Year Book Australia 1986. *ABS Cat. no. 1300.0.*

EXTREME MAXIMUM TEMPERATURES

(All years to September 1985)

Station	°C	Date
New South Wales		
Bourke	52.8	17.1.1877
Walgett	50.1	2.1.1903
Wilcannia	50.0	11.1.1939

Station	°C	Date
Victoria		
Mildura	50.8	6.1.1906
Swan Hill	49.4	18.1.1906
Beulah	46.7	31.1.1968
Queensland		
Cloncurry	53.1	16.1.1889
Winton	50.7	14.12.1888
Birdsville	50.0	24.12.1972
South Australia		
Oodnadatta	50.7	2.1.1960
Marree	49.4	2.1.1960
Western Australia		
Eucla	50.7	22.1.1906
Mundrabilla	49.8	3.1.1979
Forrest	49.8	13.1.1979
Tasmania		
Bushy Park	40.8	26.12.1945
Hobart	40.8	4.1.1976
Northern Territory		
Finke	48.3	2.1.1960
Jervois	47.5	3.1.1978
Australian Capital Territory		
Canberra	42.8	11.1.1939

Source: Year Book Australia 1986. *ABS Cat. no. 1300.0.*

HIGHEST DAILY RAINFALLS

(All years to October 1984)

State	Station	Date	Amount (mm)
New South Wales	Dorrigo	21.2.1954	809
	Cordeaux River	14.2.1898	574
Victoria	Tanybryn	22.3.1983	375
	Balook	18.2.1951	275
	Hazel Park	1.12.1934	267
Queensland	Bellenden Ker (Top Station)	4.1.1979	1,140
	Crohamhurst	3.2.1893	907
	Finch Hatton	18.2.1958	878
	Mount Dangar	20.1.1970	869
South Australia	Stansbury	18.2.1946	222
	Stirling	17.4.1889	208
Western Australia	Whim Creek	3.4.1898	747
	Kilto	4.12.1970	635
	Fortescue	3.5.1890	593

State	Station	Date	Amount (mm)
Tasmania	Cullenswood	22.3.1974	352
	Mathinna	5.4.1929	337
Northern Territory	Roper Valley	15.4.1963	545
	Groote Eylandt	28.3.1953	513

Source: Year Book Australia 1986. *ABS Cat. no. 1300.0*

AVERAGE RELATIVE HUMIDITY
(%) AT 9 A.M.

Station	Period of record	Jan	Feb	Mar	Apr	May	Jun	Jul	Aug	Sep	Oct	Nov	Dec	Yr
Adelaide	1909-87	51	52	54	61	70	79	77	69	61	54	52	50	61
Alice Springs	1941-87	34	39	40	45	56	65	59	47	35	31	28	29	42
Armidale	1907-87	63	69	71	73	78	80	77	71	61	57	56	57	68
Brisbane	1936-87	66	70	71	69	70	70	68	64	61	60	60	62	66
Broome	1939-87	71	74	69	55	49	49	47	45	48	53	58	64	57
Canberra	1939-87	60	66	69	74	82	84	84	79	72	65	61	57	71
Carnarvon	1945-87	58	57	56	57	59	69	69	64	54	51	54	57	59
Ceduna	1939-87	53	59	61	66	76	81	80	75	64	54	51	51	60
Charleville	1942-87	47	53	52	53	63	71	66	56	44	40	37	39	52
Darwin	1941-87	82	84	83	75	67	63	64	68	71	71	74	77	73
Esperance	1969-87	58	60	64	70	74	77	77	74	68	61	60	57	67
Halls Creek	1944-87	51	56	44	34	34	34	31	25	22	25	30	39	35
Hobart	1944-87	59	63	66	70	76	79	78	74	66	62	60	59	67
Kalgoorlie	1939-87	45	51	53	59	68	74	74	67	54	48	44	43	57
Katanning	1957-87	57	64	66	75	83	88	88	86	80	68	59	56	73
Marble Bar	1937-87	44	47	40	33	39	42	39	32	27	26	26	33	36
Melbourne	1908-87	59	63	65	72	78	82	81	75	68	62	61	59	69
Mildura	1946-87	50	55	59	70	82	88	86	79	67	58	52	48	66
Perth	1942-87	50	52	56	65	72	78	78	74	68	59	54	51	63
Sydney	1958-87	69	72	72	71	72	74	69	66	62	61	63	65	68
Thursday Island	1950-87	84	86	85	82	82	81	80	78	75	73	73	77	80
Townsville	1940-87	72	76	74	69	68	67	67	63	60	61	63	66	67

Source: Commonwealth Bureau of Meteorology.

ACQUIRED IMMUNODEFICIENCY SYNDROME (AIDS)

CUMULATIVE ANALYSIS OF CASES IN AUSTRALIA
11 April 1988

State/Territory	Cases M	F	Total	(%)	Known Deaths M	F	Total	(%)
NSW	527	20	547	(67.2)	286	17	303	(55.3)
Vic.	147	3	150	(18.4)	57	2	59	(39.3)
Qld	52	4	56	(6.8)	34	3	37	(66.0)
WA	31	2	33	(4.0)	16	1	17	(51.5)
SA	17	1	18	(2.2)	4	1	5	(27.7)
NT	2	0	2	(0.2)	1	0	1	(50.0)
Tas.	1	1	2	(0.2)	1	0	1	(50.0)
ACT	5	0	5	(0.6)	3	0	3	(60.0)
Total	**782**	**31**	**813**	**(100)**	**402**	**24**	**426**	**(52.3)**

Age (Yrs)	Cases M	F	Total	(%)	Known Deaths M	F	Total	(%)
0–9	6	1	7	(0.8)	5	1	6	(85.7)
10–19	4	1	5	(0.6)	3	1	4	(80.0)
20–29	162	8	170	(20.9)	87	2	89	(52.3)
30–39	339	2	341	(41.9)	161	1	162	(47.5)
40–49	194	4	198	(24.3)	95	4	99	(50.0)
50–59	62	6	68	(8.3)	40	6	46	(67.6)
60+	15	9	24	(2.9)	11	9	20	(83.3)
Total	**782**	**31**	**813**	**(100)**	**402**	**24**	**426**	**(52.3)**

Transmission Category	Cases M	F	Total	(%)	Known Deaths M	F	Total	(%)
1. Homo-/Bisexual	711	0	711	(87.4)	357	0	357	(50.2)
2. IV drug users	3	1	4	(0.4)	1	1	2	(50.0)
3. Homo-/Bi. IV drug users	24	0	24	(2.9)	13	0	13	(54.1)
4. Blood transfusion	25	21	46	(5.6)	20	20	40	(86.9)

Transmission Category	Cases M	F	Total	(%)	Known Deaths M	F	Total	(%)
5. Haemophiliac	10	0	10	(1.2)	5	0	5	(50.0)
6. Heterosexual trans.	2	6	8	(0.9)	1	1	2	(25.0)
7. Under investigation	4	0	4	(0.4)	2	0	2	(50.0)
8. None of the above	3	3	6	(0.7)	3	2	5	(83.3)
Total	**782**	**31**	**813**	**(100)**	**402**	**24**	**426**	**(52.3)**

Source: NH & MRC AIDS Research Unit.

CUMULATIVE NUMBERS OF AIDS CASES

AUSTRALIA TO 6 NOVEMBER 1986 AND TO 31 DECEMBER 1987

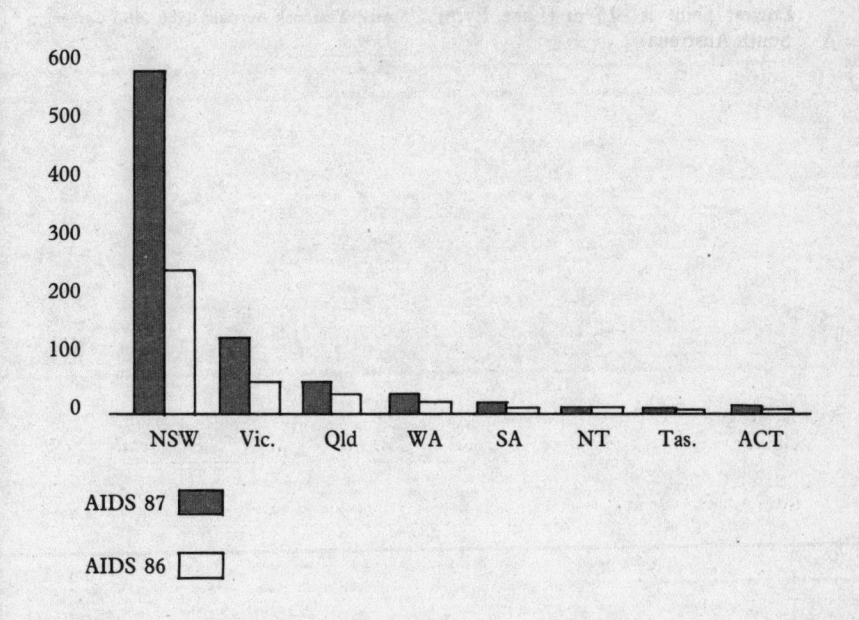

AIDS 87 ■

AIDS 86 □

Source: NH & MRC AIDS Research Unit.

GEOGRAPHICAL FEATURES OF AUSTRALIA

THE LAND
Land area is 7,682,300 sq. km
Land lies between latitudes 10° 41' S. (Cape York, Queensland) and 43° 39' S. (South Cape, Tasmania)
Latitudinal distance is 3,680 km approx.
Mainland's most southerly point is 39° 08' S. (South Point, Wilson's Promontory, Victoria)
Latitudinal distance is 3,180 km approx.
Land lies between longitudes 113° 09' E. (Steep Point, Western Australia) and 153° 39' E. (Cape Byron, New South Wales)
Longitudinal distance is 4,000 km approx.

ALTITUDES
Highest point is 2,230 m (Mount Kosciusko, New South Wales)
Lowest point is -15 m (Lake Eyre, South Australia)
Altitude of surface Australian land mass:
Average altitude is 300 m
Approx. 87% is less than 500 m
Approx. 99.5% is less than 1,000 m

RIVERS AND LAKES
The longest river system in Australia is the Murray-Darling which drains part of Queensland, the major part of New South Wales and a large part of Victoria.
The Murray is about 2,520 km long. The Darling and the Upper Darling together are just over 2,500 km long. The largest lakes are Lake Eyre, South Australia, 9,500 sq. km, Lake Torrens, South Australia 5,900 sq. km and Lake Gairdner, South Australia 4,300 sq. km.

Source: Yearbook Australia 1986. *ABS Cat. no. 1300.0.*

COMPLETE EXPECTATION OF LIFE

Life table	Age 0 M	F	Age 30 M	F	Age 65 M	F
1881–91	47.20	50.84	33.64	36.13	11.06	12.27
1891–00	51.08	54.76	35.11	37.86	11.25	12.75
1901–10	55.20	58.84	36.52	39.33	11.31	12.88
1920–22	59.15	63.31	38.44	41.48	12.01	13.60
1932–34	63.48	67.14	39.90	42.77	12.40	14.15
1946–48	66.07	70.63	40.40	44.08	12.25	14.44
1953–55	67.14	72.75	40.90	45.43	12.33	15.02
1960–62	67.92	74.18	41.12	46.49	12.47	15.68
1965–67	67.63	74.15	40.72	46.34	12.16	15.70
1970–72	68.10	74.80	41.10	46.86	12.37	16.09
1975–77	69.56	76.56	42.18	48.26	13.13	17.13
1980–82	71.23	78.27	43.51	49.67	13.80	18.00

Source: The Office of the Australian Government Actuary—Australian Life Tables 1980-82.

INSURANCE

OCCUPATIONS WHICH ARE NORMALLY DECLINED FOR DISABILITY INCOME INSURANCE

ABATTOIR WORKER
ACTOR/ACTRESS
ADVERTISING (FREELANCE)
AIR TRAFFIC CONTROLLER
ARMED FORCES
ARTIST (FREELANCE)
AUTHOR
BANK SECURITY STAFF
BOOKMAKER
CHEMICAL ENGINEER
  (EXPLOSIVES)
COMMERCIAL PILOT
COMPOSER (MUSIC)
DEMOLITION WORKER
DIVER
DOCKER
DRIVER (ARMOURED CAR)
ENTERTAINER
FASHION DESIGNER
  (FREELANCE)
FIREFIGHTER
FURNITURE REMOVALIST
GARBAGE COLLECTOR
HOUSEWIFE
INDUSTRIAL CHEMIST
  (EXPLOSIVES)
JOCKEY
LANDLORD
MARINE ENGINEER
MINING ENGINEER
MOTORCYCLE COURIER
PETROL TANKER DRIVER
POLICE
PROFESSIONAL SPORTSMEN

PUBLICAN
SERVICE STATION ATTENDANT
STUDENT
WILD ANIMAL TRAINER
WINDOW CLEANER

It may be difficult to work out why some of the above occupations are declined insurance. The essential criteria for disability income uninsurability are:
1. The occupation may be such that the person may not need to provide personal exertion in order to obtain income (eg. Landlord). Hence, there is no need for insurance.
2. The occupation may be subject to extreme fluctuations in income. Hence, during low income periods there may be a high risk of fraudulent claims.
3. The occupation may be such that the high risk of disability makes insurance prohibitively expensive.

AIDS AND INSURANCE

In the 1880s the life expectancy of an Australian male at birth was forty-seven years. By 1980 mortality had improved so much that this had increased to seventy-one years. Over time, life insurance companies have reflected such improvements in mortality by reducing premium rates charged to their policy holders.

The development of AIDS in the community places some doubt on the assumption of a continued improvement in mortality. In fact, life insurance companies have become so concerned about the possible financial consequences of AIDS that the following measures have been introduced:

UNDERWRITING MEASURES
Prospective policyholders will normally need to complete a declaration stating that:
- they or their spouse are not carrying the AIDS virus;
- they have not participated in anal sex since 1980;
- they are not IV drug users (except those drugs prescribed);
- they have not been a client of a prostitute in the recent past; and
- they have not been tattooed in the recent past.

If a prospective policyholder cannot fill out the declaration, they are asked why; they will normally then be sent for an AIDS antibody test. If the test is positive insurance will be declined. If negative, insurance may be accepted provided that the policyholder does not indulge in unsafe sexual practices.

It is interesting to note that life insurance in Australia is governed by federal legislation which gives insurers the right to underwrite various risks. This legislation overrides state anti-discrimination legislation. Hence, a life insurer is currently able to discriminate amongst risk groups when providing insurance.

For insurance in excess of $250,000 and up to $400,000 (depending on the insurer), an AIDS antibody test will be routinely requested.

OTHER MEASURES
Most insurers are removing guarantees from their premium rates in order to protect themselves from the possibility of high claims due to AIDS. It is likely that a number of insurers will increase premium rates to reflect the likely higher level of mortality.

Insurers have introduced strict measures in response to the AIDS epidemic in order to protect themselves. These types of measures, however, are likely to put insurers in the unenviable position of telling people that they have AIDS. One hopes that insurers are compassionate and discreet about this and refer the affected people to appropriate counselling services.

APPROXIMATE PROBABILITY OF STAYING IN THE PUBLIC SERVICE TO AGE 65

Starting Age	Probability	Starting Age	Probability
25	0.03%	45	2.80%
30	0.10%	50	5.90%
35	0.40%	55	10.20%
40	1.10%	60	25.40%

Source: Superannuation Fund Investment Trust—Annual Report 1986–87.

BREAKDOWN OF EXITS FROM SFIT* FOR 1986–87

Reason	% of exits
Voluntary retirement	11.1
Involuntary retirement	4.7
Ill-health	8.4
Death	1.6
Resignation	74.2
Total	**100.0**

* SFIT is the Commonwealth super scheme
Source: Superannuation Fund Investment Trust—Annual report 1986–87.

PROPORTION OF EMPLOYEES IN VARIOUS INDUSTRIES COVERED BY SUPERANNUATION

Industry Division	%
Agriculture, Forestry, Fishing & Hunting	28.2
Mining	78.3
Manufacturing	53.6
Electricity, Gas and Water	74.9
Construction	36.3
Wholesale & Retail Trade	43.6
Transport & Storage	61.2
Communication	93.2
Finance, Property & Business Services	67.4
Public Administration & Defence	86.0
Community Services	68.1
Recreation, Personal & Other Services	29.9

PROPORTION OF WORKERS COVERED BY SUPERANNUATION BY WORKFORCE SECTOR

Sector	%
Employers & Self-Employed	25.3
Private employees	39.1
Government employees	69.4
All Workers	45.5

Source: Superannuation Australia 1982.

ADVANCE AUSTRALIA FAIR

Words and Music by
P. D. McCORMICK

Maestoso

1. Australians all, let us rejoice, For we are young and free, We've golden soil and wealth for toil, Our home is girt by sea; Our land abounds in nature's gifts Of beauty rich and rare; In hist'ry's page, let ev'ry stage Advance Australia fair, In joyful strains then let us sing Advance Australia fair.

2. When gallant Cook from Albion sailed
   To trace wide oceans o'er,
   True British courage bore him on,
   Till he landed on our shore.
   Then here he raised Old England's flag,
   The standard of the brave,
   'With all her faults, we love her still,
   Britannia rules the wave'.
   In joyful strains then let us sing
   'Advance Australia fair'.

3. Beneath our radiant Southern Cross
   We'll toil with hearts and hands,
   To make this Commonwealth of ours
   Renowned of all the lands,
   For those who've come across the seas
   We've boundless plains to share,
   With courage let us all combine
   To advance Australia fair.
   In joyful strains then let us sing,
   'Advance Australia fair'.

IMPORTANT DATES IN AUSTRALIAN HISTORY

45 million years ago
Australia separated from Asia and Antarctica. Unique Australian flora and fauna began to develop.

2 million years ago
The last ice age began. Australia was the home of giant animals and birds.

40,000 years ago
Archaeological evidence suggests that towards the end of the Late Pleistocene period the first group of people, who have come to be known as Australian Aborigines, crossed from South-East Asia to Australia, spreading throughout the entire continent. There was still a land bridge to Tasmania.

12,000 years ago
With the rising of the seas, Bass Strait separated Tasmania from the mainland, isolating the Tasmanian Aborigines.

8000 years ago
Australia separated from New Guinea, with the flooding of the Gulf of Carpentaria, Torres Strait and the Arafura Sea.

1606
Dutch navigator Willem Jansz became the first European known to have made a landing on the Australian coast; he saw the coast near the present site of Weipa, on the Gulf of Carpentaria. Jansz charted about 320 kilometres of the coast, believing it to form part of New Guinea.
Luis Vaez de Torres sailed through the strait now bearing his name without realising its significance.

1616
Dutch sea captain Dirck Hartog, the first European known to have landed on the coast of Western Australia, came ashore on an island near the entrance to Shark Bay. He recorded the event by inscribing a pewter plate with the name of his ship and its officers.

1642
Dutch explorer Abel Tasman sailed around the western and eastern coasts of Tasmania, naming it Van Diemen's Land after the then Governor-General of the Dutch East Indies.

1688
William Dampier, English buccaneer, spent three months near King Sound, Western Australia. His book of his experiences aroused such interest that he was sent in 1699 to explore the western and northern coasts of Australia. He considered the region unfit for human habitation.

1770
April 20—Australia was sighted by Lt Zachary Hicks sailing with Captain James Cook on the *Endeavour*. Cook charted the east coast of Australia, landing at Botany Bay. In August on Possession Island, he proclaimed the whole of the eastern part of Australia a British possession, naming it New South Wales. His reports, together with those of Joseph Banks, influenced the decision to found a settlement there.

1786
The British government decided to make Botany Bay a penal colony.

1787
May 13—The First Fleet sailed from Portsmouth, carrying 756 convicts, about 450 crew and military personnel and 28 wives and 30 children.

1788
January 18—Captain Arthur Phillip, commander of the First Fleet, arrived in Botany Bay. Finding it unsuitable as a site for settlement, Phillip sailed on, locating the settlement at Sydney Cove. On 26 January he hoisted the British flag, taking possession of New South Wales.
February 3—The first Christian religious service was held by Rev. Johnson.
Over 250,000 Aborigines lived in Australia at this time, with possibly 500 tribes, each having its own language or dialect.

1789
June 4—The first play was performed

in the colony when convicts celebrated the King's birthday with a performance of Farquhar's comedy *The Recruiting Officer.*

1790
June—The Second Fleet arrived carrying the first detachment of 100 men of the New South Wales Corps.

1791
July-September—The Third Fleet arrived carrying the first Irish convicts.

1797
Australia's first merino sheep were imported from the Cape of Good Hope by captains Henry Waterhouse and William Kent. John Macarthur purchased two rams and one ewe to start his flock.

1798
October—Bass and Flinders in the *Norfolk* circumnavigated Van Diemen's Land, proving it to be an island.

1801-3
Matthew Flinders circumnavigated Australia in the *Investigator.*

1803
March 5—The first newspaper, the *Sydney Gazette and New South Wales Advertiser* was published. George Howe, a convict, was the editor.
September—A settlement was established in Tasmania at Risdon Cove. In 1804 it was moved to Sullivans Bay, the site of modern Hobart.

1804
March 4—Convicts rebelled at Castle Hill, the first and only convict uprising. Three hundred convicts rioted and marched on Parramatta. Troops killed nine rebels and the six leaders were hanged.

1807
John Macarthur shipped the first merino wool from the colony of New South Wales to England.

1808
January—The Rum Rebellion, the deposition of Governor Bligh by officers of the New South Wales Corps, took place. Bligh was held prisoner for more than a year before being released and returning to England.

1809
April 25—Australia's first post office opened in Sydney.

1810
January—The New South Wales Corps was recalled and Lachlan Macquarie was sworn in as Governor. A large program of public works was undertaken and extensive exploration encouraged.
October 15—Australia's first official horserace (i.e. with government approval) was organised by the 73rd Regiment at Hyde Park in Sydney. The horses allegedly raced clockwise, thus founding the New South Wales and Queensland traditions; in other states horses run anti-clockwise.

1811
April 10—A road from Sydney to Parramatta was opened to traffic.

1813
May—The Blue Mountains were crossed by Blaxland, Lawson and Wentworth.
November—George Evans entered the fertile Bathurst Plains, discovering the westward-flowing Lachlan and Macquarie rivers.

1814
July 17—Matthew Flinders in his book *A Voyage to Terra Australis*, published on the day of his death, suggested the continent be named 'Australia' instead of 'New Holland'.

1817
April 8—The Bank of New South Wales, Australia's first bank, was established by a group of Sydney businessmen. In 1982 the bank changed its name to Westpac.

1820
May 3—Australia's first officially appointed Roman Catholic priests, John Therry and Phillip Conolly, arrived from Ireland.

1823
The British Government, with the New South Wales Judicature Act, established the first Legislative Council, a nominated advisory body of five citizens, over whom the Governor had the power of veto.

1824
September—The penal settlement at

Moreton Bay in Queensland, then still part of New South Wales, was established.

1825

June 14—Van Diemen's Land became a separate colony under Lieutenant-Governor George Arthur.

1829

June—Captain James Stirling arrived as Lieutenant-Governor of the Swan River colony, with the first white settlers.

1830

October—In Van Diemen's Land, Lt-Governor Arthur attempted to round up the colony's remaining Aborigines to dispatch them to the islands to the north-east. Three thousand soldiers and settlers formed a line to force the Aborigines into the Tasman Peninsula area. Two Aborigines were shot, two were captured and 300 slipped through the net.

The first volume of Australia's first novel, *Quintus Servinton*, written by Henry Savery, was published.

1831

April 18—The *Sydney Herald*, from 1842 the *Sydney Morning Herald*, was first published. In 1841 John Fairfax and Charles Kemp purchased the paper, establishing the Fairfax publishing dynasty.

1835

June 6—John Batman 'bought' some 240,000 hectares of land near Melbourne from the local Aborigines for sundry items such as flour and blankets. Several months later he began a settlement and in August founded Melbourne. The treaty was disallowed by Governor Bourke, who declared that the land in question belonged to the Crown.

1836

December 28—South Australia became an independent colony.

1837

April 10—Governor Bourke, visiting from Sydney proclaimed the site of Melbourne, naming it after the British Prime Minister Lord Melbourne.

July 13—King William IV gave permission for the South Australian capital to be named after Queen Adelaide.

1838

June 9-10—The Myall Creek massacre occurred when twenty-eight Aborigines were murdered. Seven whites were found guilty and hanged. This was the first time in Australian history that whites had been punished for killing Aborigines.

1840

The British government agreed to cease sending convicts to New South Wales. By then over 80,000 convicts had landed.

1841

May 24—Sydney's streets were lit by gas for the first time. Gas lighting was used for the next eighty years.

During the 1840s the colonies experienced a serious economic slump, the worst years being 1841-43. Assisted immigration was stopped from 1841 to 1847.

1842

May 4—Moreton Bay in Queensland became a free settlement.

July 30—Representative government was granted to New South Wales with the Legislative Council comprising twenty-four elected and twelve appointed members.

1849

February 23—A public meeting in Perth decided to introduce convicts to aid the depressed economy. The first convicts landed in June 1850.

1850

June—The Australasian Anti-Transportation League was formed in the eastern states.

October 1—The University of Sydney, the first Australian university, was founded. Melbourne followed in 1855, and was the first to admit women in 1874. Adelaide opened in 1876, Tasmania in 1889, Queensland in 1910 and Western Australia in 1913.

1851

Goldrushes began after the discovery of gold near Bathurst in February. In July gold was discovered in Victoria and it overtook New South Wales as the principal gold state.

Victoria became a separate colony.
1853
Transportation to Van Diemen's Land ended, the last ship arriving in May.
1854
February—The first telegraph was opened between Melbourne and Williamstown, Victoria. By 1857 Melbourne, Sydney and Adelaide were joined.
October 17—The Melbourne *Age* was founded. In 1856 it was bought by David and Ebenezer Syme.
December 3—The Eureka Stockade uprising, under the leadership of Peter Lalor, occurred on the Ballarat goldfields. It was the culmination of protests by miners over the imposition of licence fees of 30 shillings per month and the manner in which licence hunts were conducted. Charges of high treason were laid against the miners but were later dismissed in court.
1855
November 26—Van Diemen's Land was officially renamed Tasmania.
Responsible government was granted to Tasmania and Victoria. It was granted to South Australia in 1857, Queensland in 1859 and Western Australia in 1890.
1856
The first intercolonial cricket match was played between New South Wales and Victoria in Melbourne. New South Wales won.
South Australia introduced universal male suffrage followed by Victoria in 1857, New South Wales in 1858, Queensland in 1859, Western Australia in 1893 and Tasmania in 1896. South Australia and Victoria introduced the secret ballot in 1856 followed by New South Wales and Tasmania in 1858, Queensland in 1859, Western Australia in 1877 and the Commonwealth in 1901.
1857
April 14—The first Torrens system of land conveyancing and registration came into operation in South Australia. It was adopted in Queensland in 1861, Victoria, New South Wales and Tasmania in 1862 and Western Australia in 1874.

1859
June 6—The Moreton Bay district separated from New South Wales to become Queensland.
December 25—Thomas Austin imported seventy-two partridges, twenty-four wild rabbits and five hares into Australia. He left a major agricultural pest as a legacy to the Australian farmer.
1861
June—Three thousand miners attacked a large Chinese encampment at Lambing Flat in New South Wales. As a result, the New South Wales government restricted Chinese immigration.
November 7—The first Melbourne Cup was run, organised by the Victorian Turf Club. The race was won by Archer.
The Acclimatisation Society of Victoria released dozens of canaries, blackbirds, thrushes, starlings and sparrows.
1863
May—The first indentured labourers from the Pacific islands were imported into Queensland. This quickly developed into blackbirding in kanakas to provide labour for the sugar industry. Between 1863 and 1904, when the trade ended, about 60,000 Pacific islanders came to Queensland, many coerced or tricked.
1868
January 9—Convict transportation to Western Australia ceased, after the arrival in Fremantle of the *Hougoumont* with a cargo of 279 prisoners.
1871
November 16—The telegraph cable between Port Darwin and Banjoewarji in Java was completed. Australia's first overseas telegram arrived in Palmerston, Darwin, four days later.
1872
August 2—The Overland Telegraph joining Port Augusta with Darwin was opened.
1873
September 1—The eight-hour working day was introduced in South Australia.

1877
March 15—The first Test cricket match between England and Australia took place at the Melbourne Cricket Ground. Australia won by 45 runs.

1879
April 28—Sutherland National Park (The Royal National Park), south of Sydney, was proclaimed. It was Australia's first national park and the second such in the world.

1880
January 31—The *Bulletin* was founded by J. F. Archibald and John Haynes.

April 16—New South Wales introduced compulsory state schooling for six to fourteen year olds.

June 28—The first telephone exchange was opened in Melbourne with forty-four subscribers.

November 11—Bushranger and folk hero Ned Kelly was hanged in Melbourne.

1881
April 3—Australia's first census put the white population at 2.25 million.

1883
June 14—The first train service between Sydney and Melbourne began.

The Ashes were created, when Ivo Bligh, captain of the successful English cricket team visiting Australia, was presented with an urn containing the ashes of the stumps and bails used in the 1882–83 match.

1884
South Australia introduced income tax followed by Tasmania in 1894, Victoria and New South Wales in 1895, Queensland in 1902 and Western Australia in 1907. The Commonwealth introduced income tax in 1915 as a wartime measure.

1885
March 3—A volunteer contingent of 732 officers and men and 200 horses left Sydney under the command of Colonel J. S. Richardson to assist the British in the Sudan. The Australians participated in little fighting: three were wounded in action and six died from fever contracted during the journey home.

Broken Hill Proprietary Limited was floated as a public company.

1890
During the 1890s the colonies experienced a severe economic depression, after the boom years of the 1880s. Long-running strikes ended in defeat for the unions: the maritime strike of 1890 and the shearers' strikes in Queensland in 1891 and 1894 were the most bitter and divisive.

1891
The Australian Labor Party was founded in New South Wales by trade unionists who, after the defeat of strike actions, hoped to gain advances through parliamentary action.

1892
Sheffield Shield cricket began.

Preferential voting was introduced in Queensland, followed by Tasmania and Western Australia in 1907, Victoria in 1911, the Commonwealth in 1918, New South Wales in 1926 and South Australia in 1929.

1894
December 18—Women were enfranchised in South Australia, the first in the British Empire to be so. Western Australia followed in 1899 and the Commonwealth in 1902.

1895
The words (by Banjo Paterson) and music of 'Waltzing Matilda' were performed in public for the first time at the North Gregory Hotel in Winton, Queensland.

1899–1902
Australians fought in the Boer War, having offered Britain troops in her fight against the Boers. Over 16,000 troops went; 251 were killed in action and 267 died of disease.

1900
Bubonic plague was reported in Adelaide and Sydney in January. Tonnes of garbage and sewage were cleared from slum areas and thousands of rats destroyed.

July 9—Queen Victoria gave her assent to the *Commonwealth of Australia Constitution Act*.

1901
January 1—The Commonwealth of Australia was inaugurated, with

Edmund Barton the first Prime Minister.
May 9—The first federal parliament opened in Melbourne.
1902
April 9—A uniform federal franchise was legislated, with Asians, Africans and Aborigines excluded.
1904
The Commonwealth Court of Conciliation and Arbitration was established.
1909
Invalid and old age pensions were introduced by the Commonwealth, with the maternity allowance or 'Baby Bonus' following in 1912.
1911
March 3—Palmerston was renamed Darwin by federal government decree. The name was chosen to honour the scientist Charles Darwin.
May 1—The federal government introduced standard postal rates and repealed all state rates and regulations.
July 10—The Royal Australian Navy was established.
1913
March 12—At a ceremony on Capital Hill, Lady Denman, the wife of the Governor-General, officially named Canberra. Suggested alternative names had been Marsupiala, Eucalypta and Kookemuroo.
1914
August 4—Britain declared war on Germany. Australia enthusiastically entered the war.
1915
April 25—The Anzacs landed at Gallipoli, to be withdrawn in December after the unsuccessful assault against Turkish positions on the peninsula.
Compulsory voting was introduced in Queensland, followed by the Commonwealth in 1924, Victoria in 1926, New South Wales and Tasmania in 1928 and Western Australia in 1939.
1916
October 28—The first conscription referendum, proposing conscription for overseas service, was held: it was rejected (with 51.61 per cent against and 48.39 per cent for). The ALP split over this issue, with pro-conscriptionists, led by Billy Hughes, leaving the party to form the National Labor Party.
1917
December 20—The second conscription referendum was held, defeated by a larger majority than the first (53.79 per cent against and 46.21 per cent for).
1918
November 11—World War I ended. 416,809 Australians had enlisted: 330,000 embarked; 59,258 died and 226,073 were wounded.
1919
December 10—The first flight from Britain to Australia ended, when Ross and Keith Smith touched down in Darwin in their Vickers Vimy. They had taken twenty-eight days to complete the journey and earned 10,000 pounds from the Australian government.
1920
November 16—Queensland and Northern Territory Aerial Services Ltd (Qantas) was established by P. J. McGinness and W. Hudson Fysh.
1921
The Royal Australian Air Force was established. The Australian Flying Corps, approved in 1912 and set up in 1914, evolved into the RAAF.
1922
The Labor government in Queensland abolished the Upper House of its parliament, the only state to do so. Victoria was the first state to have its Legislative Council elected by adult suffrage in 1950, with Western Australia following in 1963, Tasmania in 1969, South Australia in 1973 and New South Wales in 1978.
1923
June 13—Vegemite made its appearance.
Broadcasting began with the 'sealed set' system: licence fees went to the radio stations and sets were sealed so that they only received those stations for which they were licensed.
1927
May 3—The Australian Council of Trade Unions was set up to be the

national voice of the trade union movement. The biggest union, the Australian Workers Union, did not affiliate until 1967.
May 9—Federal parliament opened in Canberra.
1928
May 15—The world's first flying doctor service, the Australian Inland Mission Aerial Service, was inaugurated.
November—A referendum amended the constitution to allow the Commonwealth to take over and manage state debts and to set up the Loan Council.
1930
April 30—Prime Minister Scullin took part in the first overseas telephone call made between Australia and Britain. His call cost about 12 dollars for three minutes.
November 7—Phar Lap won the Melbourne Cup.
Unemployment stood at 19 per cent.
1931
April—The first airmail service between Australia and Britain took place.
Unemployment reached 28 per cent.
1932
March 19—The Sydney Harbour Bridge, designed by Sir Ralph Freeman, was opened. The opening ceremony was delayed when Captain Francis Edward de Groot, a member of the fascist New Guard organisation, slashed the ribbon before Premier Jack Lang was able to do so.
July 1—The Australian Broadcasting Commission (ABC) was established operating twelve radio stations.
1933
April 8—Western Australia held a referendum to secede, which was carried by 2:1 vote of the 90 per cent who participated. The result was declared constitutionally unacceptable by the British government.
The *Australian Women's Weekly* was established by Frank Packer and E. G. Theodore.
1934
December 10—A Qantas DH-86 flew the airline's inaugural overseas flight from Darwin to Singapore.
1936
Ansett Airlines Pty Ltd was founded to operate between Melbourne and Hamilton in Victoria. In 1957 the airline took over Australian National Airways (ANA).
1939
September 3—Britain and France declared war on Germany. Australia declared war on Germany forty-five minutes after Britain had done so.
1940
June—Menzies placed a ban on the Communist Party. This was removed in late 1941 when Herbert V. Evatt, Attorney-General in the Curtin Labor government, accepted Communist Party assurances of cooperation in the war effort.
1941
December 26—Prime Minister Curtin made his statement 'Australia looks to America', after the Japanese defeat of British naval power in South-East Asia.
1942
February 19—Japanese bombers carried out their first attack on Australian striking Darwin and killing 243 people, sinking twenty-one ships and destroying twenty-three aircraft.
February—Prime Minister Curtin insisted, against Churchill's wishes, on the withdrawal of the 6th and 8th Divisions of the AIF from the Middle East to defend Australia against Japan.
April 18—US General Douglas MacArthur set up headquarters to oversee the Pacific operations of Allied forces.
May 31—Three Japanese midget submarines entered Sydney Harbour. One hit the barracks ship *Kuttabul*. Two were destroyed and the third caught in the antisubmarine net.
1943
February—Limited conscription was introduced for service in the south-west Pacific zone.
August—The first women were elected to federal parliament: Enid Lyons and Senator Dorothy Tangney. Child endowment was introduced: 5 shillings per week was paid for each

child under sixteen, excluding the first child.

1944
October 13-16—The Liberal Party was born under Robert Menzies. It was built on Deakin's earlier Liberal Party, the Nationalists led by Hughes and the United Australia Party in the 1930s. The party was officially inaugurated on 28 August 1945.

1945
August 15—Japan surrendered, ending World War II. Australians who served totalled 993,000: 27,073 died or were killed in action, 23,477 were wounded, 22,376 were Japanese POWs (8031 died) and 8184 were German POWs (265 died).

1946
September—Trans Australia Airlines (TAA) was established.
October 30—The Commonwealth Arbitration Court agreed to the gradual implementation of the forty-hour working week, to be in force in all industries by January 1948.
The Australian National University in Canberra was founded as a research university with postgraduate courses.

1947
June 30—Qantas was bought by the Australian Government.

1948
November 28—The first Holden, aimed at postwar middle-class families, went on sale for 760 pounds.

1949
July—The Snowy Mountains Authority was established by the Chifley government. The scheme was completed in October 1972.

1950
October—The *Communist Party Dissolution Act* was passed. Its legality was challenged in the High Court which in 1951 ruled the act illegal.

1951
July 1—The New South Wales government introduced the first legislation in the world providing for paid sick leave and paid long-service leave.
September 1—Australia, New Zealand and the United States signed the ANZUS mutual defence pact.

September 22—The referendum on banning the Communist Party was narrowly defeated.

1954
September 8—The United States, the United Kingdom, France, Australia, New Zealand, the Philippines, Thailand and Pakistan formed the South-East Asia Treaty Organisation (SEATO) to resist communism in South-East Asia.

1956
September 16—The first television broadcast was made from TCN Channel 9 in Sydney. Melbourne went to air in November.
November 22-December 6—The XVI Olympiad, the first in the southern hemisphere, was held in Melbourne. Australia finished third, after the United States second, and the Soviet Union first.

1957
August—The Democratic Labor Party (DLP) was formed by state anti-communist Labor groups, except Queensland which joined later. The DLP played a significant role until 1972 keeping the ALP out of office by directing its preferences to the Liberal-Country Party coalition. It was disbanded in 1978.

1958
January 14—Qantas inaugurated its Australia-to-Britain service, using two aircraft—one flying to Britain via the United States and the other flying via Europe.
The National Institute for Dramatic Art (NIDA) was established.

1960
Social security benefits were made payable to all Aborigines on the same terms as the rest of the community.

1961
February 1—Uniform divorce laws came into operation.
Australia experienced a credit squeeze, the result of the fall in wool prices, drought, inflation and rising prices.
The contraceptive pill appeared in Australia.

1962
February—The Australian Ballet Company was established by the

Elizabethan Theatre Trust, under the direction of Peggy van Praagh. The company opened the next year with a performance of *Swan Lake*.

May 24—Australian army advisers were sent to Vietnam on training duties.

1964

November—National Service was introduced on the basis of two years full-time service. Conscripts were liable for service anywhere. Conscription was ended by the Whitlam government in 1972.

1965

April—Prime Minister Menzies announced his government's decision to send an Australian battalion to South Vietnam. The first contingent of regular army soldiers arrived in the war zone in May.

1966

January 20—Sir Robert Menzies retired as Prime Minister and leader of the Liberal Party after a record sixteen years in office.

February 14—Decimal currency was introduced.

March—The Arbitration Commission granted equal wages to Aboriginal pastoral workers to be effective by December 1968.

April 18—The first national service troops left for Vietnam.

1967

February 3—Ronald Ryan was the last man to be hanged in Australia at Melbourne's Pentridge Prison.

May 27—A referendum vote ended the constitutional discrimination against Aborigines and empowered the Commonwealth to legislate for Aborigines.

July—Four-digit postcodes were introduced for every place in Australia served by a post office, to facilitate the sorting of mail.

1968

October 23—Australia's first heart transplant operation was carried out at St Vincent's Hospital in Sydney. The patient survived for forty-five days.

1971

October—The term 'Green Ban' was coined for the first time by Jack Mundey, leader of the Builders Labourers' Federation, in support of conservation measures protecting heritage sites from redevelopment.

November 15—The 'R' (restricted) classification for films was introduced.

1972

December 2—The federal election swept Labor into office after twenty-three years in the wilderness. Under the leadership of Gough Whitlam the government quickly recognised the People's Republic of China and ended Australia's involvement in Vietnam.

1973

February 28—The age qualification under the *Electoral Act* for enrolment, voting and candidature, was changed from twenty-one to eighteen.

December 1—Papua New Guinea became self-governing. Independence was achieved on 6 September 1975.

Patrick White became the first Australian to be awarded the Nobel Prize for Literature.

Homosexuality was decriminalised in federal jurisdictions and by South Australia in 1975 and Victoria in 1980.

1974

October 9—Bankcard made its appearance in Australia.

December 25—Cyclone Tracy devastated Darwin: sixty-five people died and 90 per cent of the city's buildings were destroyed.

1975

March 1—Colour television was introduced.

July 8—Appeal from the Australian High Court in England was abolished with some limited exceptions.

October 1—The use of seat belts and child restraints in motor vehicles became law in New South Wales.

1976

January 5—The *Family Law Act* came into force. It provided for irretrievable breakdown of marriage as the only grounds for divorce.

April 26—The first Vietnamese boat people arrived. Between 1977 and 1981 fifty-one boats with 2011 people arrived.

1977
The *Aboriginal Land Rights Act* (NT) 1966 became operative. It allowed for Aboriginal claims to vacant or crown land where a traditional relationship could be demonstrated. Aborigines gained control of one-third of the Northern Territory under the act. South Australia introduced a land rights act in 1981.

1978
July 1—The Northern Territory was granted self-government.

1979
January—An act of parliament made it compulsory for Australian packaged-food products to carry a 'Use by . . .' date.

1980
August 17—The death of nine-week-old Azaria Chamberlain occurred at Ayers Rock. The child's mother, Lindy Chamberlain, claimed a dingo had taken her daughter but the body was never found. In February 1981 the coroner found the dingo had killed the child but in October 1982 Lindy Chamberlain was found guilty of murdering her daughter. In June 1987 Lindy Chamberlain was given a full pardon.
October 24—Multicultural television broadcasting began on channels 0 and 28 in Sydney and Melbourne.

1982
December 17—Random breath-testing of drivers for alcohol was introduced in New South Wales and the Australian Capital Territory.

1983
September—Australia won the America's Cup, after five unsuccessful challenges, the first contender to do so in 132 years. Alan Bond's yacht *Australia II* used a revolutionary winged keel designed by Ben Lexcen.
December 9—Federal Treasurer Paul Keating announced the Australian dollar would be allowed to float on the international money market.
December 15—The Canberra Mint began production of the dollar coin. The first $100 notes went into circulation in April.

1985
March 27—Unleaded petrol went on sale.
October 3—The first Australian Formula One Grand Prix was won in Adelaide by Keke Rosberg of Finland.

1986
March 2—Queen Elizabeth II signed the *Proclamation of Australia Act* in Canberra, severing the legal bond between Australia and Britain.
May 14—Treasurer Paul Keating made his reference to Australia being in danger of becoming a banana republic during a radio interview in Sydney.
August 4—Trans-Australia Airlines changed its name to Australian Airlines.
August 28—'Aussat 1', Australia's first communications satellite, was deployed by the US space shuttle *Discovery*.
November 8—The Pope arrived in Sydney at the start of his six-and-a-half-day tour.
December 8—New South Wales Solicitor-General Mary Gaudron became the first woman to be appointed to the High Court of Australia.

OBITUARIES
JANUARY 1987—JUNE 1988

Ahern, David, composer, aged 40—9 February 1988

Alley, Rewi, writer, aged 90—28 December 1987

Berg, Charles Josef, OBE, OAM, businessman and music patron, aged 70—6 February 1988

Blackburn, Sir Richard, distinguished jurist and chancellor of Australian National University, aged 69—2 October 1987

Both, Edward, OBE, inventor of the first portable iron lung and the electric tennis scoreboard, aged 79—November 1987

Bradfield, Alan, gynaecologist and pioneer in obstetrics, aged 61—19 September 1987

Burrell, Vice-Admiral Sir Henry Mackay, former navy chief of staff, aged 83—9 February 1988

Burrow, Kathleen Mary, MBE, Pro Ecclesia et Pontifice (a Papal Cross), United Nations Peace Medals 1975 and 1985, worker for peace, education, Unesco and women's affairs—20 May 1987

Campbell, Colin, OBE, film censor and public servant, aged 88—8 September 1987

Campbell-Craig, Lorayne, transsexual and socialite, 'queen of sleaze', aged 57—25 December 1987

Carey, Alex, senior lecturer in psychology at the University of New South Wales, anti-nuclear campaigner and founder of the Humanist Society, aged 64—7 December 1987

Chaffey, Bill, longest serving New South Wales MP, aged 82—11 March 1987

Cilento, Lady Phyllis, doctor, author and nutritionist, aged 93—26 July 1987

Clancy, Pat, trade union leader and communist, aged 68—24 July 1987

Clyne, Peter, controversial tax agent, aged 60—10 October 1987

Cook, Kenneth, author and filmmaker, aged 57—18 April 1987

Cowper, Sir Norman, lawyer, soldier and writer, aged 90—9 September 1987

Dark, Eric, medical practitioner and left-wing political activitist, aged 98—28 July 1987

David, Mary Edgeworth, conservationist and writer, aged 99—9 April 1987

Deegan, Allen Thomas, AM, chairman of Standard Telephones and Cables Pty Ltd, Australian Telecommunications Development Association, Commonwealth Government Electrical and Electronics Industry Advisory Council, aged 62—17 January 1987

Dufty, Kevin, leader of the Law Society of New South Wales, aged 57—30 November 1987

Fairfax, Sir Warwick, director of John Fairfax Ltd, aged 85 years—14 January 1987

Finey, George, artist and bohemian, aged 92—8 June 1987

FitzGerald, Robert D., poet, aged 85—24 May 1987

Foster, Reginald Tingey, political commentator and editor, aged 95—7 February 1987

Gow, Keith, cameraman, veteran screenwriter, director, aged 66—5 November 1987

Grant, Alan, gynaecologist and pioneer of infertility research, aged 82—29 April 1987

Hall, John Farnsworth, conductor and violinist, aged 87—15 June 1987

Halliday, Sir George, ear, nose and throat surgeon, aged 87—15 July 1987

Healy, Brother John Dominic, Christian Brother with teaching career spanning more than sixty years, aged 89—6 November 1987

Heinz, Henry John II, food mogul, aged 78—24 February 1987

Helpmann, Max, doctor, director and theatre-lover, brother of Robert, aged 72—6 April 1987

Hill, Edward Fowler, lawyer and communist, aged 73—1 February 1988

Hoffey, Frank, media lawyer, aged 43—21 May 1987

Hollis, Charlie, tennis coach, aged 77—24 December 1987

Isaacs, Simon, lawyer, aged 82—17 June 1987

Kearns, Billy, comedian, aged 81—12 February 1987

Kelly, Most Reverend John Anthony, Bishop of Melbourne, aged 72—24 July 1987

Kenna, Peter, actor, playwright, screenwriter and journalist, aged 57—29 November 1987

Kenny, Michael John Butler 'Jack', journalist and historian, aged 81—15 December 1987

Kenny, Sir Patrick, surgeon, aged 72—2 June 1987

Kerr, Bernard, former head of ABC sport department, aged 72—20 January 1987

Kripps, Henry, composer, pianist and conductor, aged 74—25 January 1987

Kyle, Sir Wallace, RAF air chief marshal and governor of Western Australia, aged 78—2 February 1988

Lawrence, Peter, cargo cult anthropologist, aged 65—12 February 1987

Lee, Bing, founder of the Chinese Christian Church and Bing Lee retail stores, lawn bowler, aged 79—4 July 1987

Lingiari, Vincent, pioneer of Aboriginal land rights—29 January 1988

McCarthy, Dudley, writer, historian, diplomat, soldier, aged 76—14 October 1987

McCusker, Neal, last New South Wales Rail Commissioner, aged 79—27 July 1987

McEwan, Brian, cancer specialist, aged 56—3 November 1987

Mackerras, Neil, lawyer, advocate for Aborigines, aged 57—12 August 1987

McKnight, Allan Duncan, inspector-general and deputy secretary of the International Atomic Energy Authority, aged 70—2 February 1987

MacMahon, Ted, CBE, general surgeon, aged 83—27 December 1987

McNeill, Sir James, AC, CBE, chairman of Broken Hill Proprietary Ltd, aged 70—13 March 1987

McNeilly, George, singer, musician, Changi veteran and YMCA officer, aged 84—11 February 1987

McNicoll, Sir Alan Wedel Ramsay, diplomat and high ranking naval officer, aged 79—15 October 1987

Mason, Peter, emeritus professor of physics, author and advocate of scientific responsibility, aged 65—20 March 1987

Meaney, Frank, teacher, aged 54—29 November 1987

Michaelis, Kevin William, pioneer welfare officer, aged 70—23 February 1987.

Mockridge, Carol, oldest Australian at time of death, infants teacher and pianist, aged 112—6 November 1987

Moore, Kevin, amateur historian of Vinegar Hill, Sydney, aged 66—8 April 1987

Moses, Sir Charles, general manager of ABC for three decades, aged 88—9 February 1988

O'Connor, William Paul, veteran Labor MP, aged 78—18 September 1987

O'Hagan, Jack Francis, MBE, composer whose works include 'God Bless Australia' and 'Along the Road to Gundagai', aged 88—16 July 1987

Peterson, George, pioneer of gas fuel development, aged 81—7 December 1987

Pettingell, Sir William, managing director of Australian Gas Light Co, chairman of Australian Consolidated Industries, deputy chairman of Foreign Investment Review Board and board member of the Reserve Bank, aged 72—27 January 1987

Pignolet, Josephine, chef and restaurateur, aged 31—21 December 1987

Renshaw, Hon. John Brophy 'Jack', former Labor premier of New South Wales, aged 77—28 July 1987

Ross, Lloyd, trade unionist, author, teacher and historian, aged 88—7 September 1987

Rossiter, Sir John Frederick, former Victorian agent-general in London, aged 74—18 January 1988

Rothwell, Geoffrey, arts administrator and patron, aged 57—31 October 1987

Russell, Julian, critic and pianist, aged 86—16 July 1987

Salisbury, Charles, gynaecologist and resident Fellow of St Paul's College, Sydney, aged 86—6 March 1987

Scott, Gordon, South Australian NFL player and coach, aged 71—8 November 1987

Seymour, Peter, OBE, music director and founder of the Australian Youth and Sydney Youth orchestras, aged 55—20 March 1987

Shaw, Albert Edward, former mayor and initiator of local government legislation, aged 85—2 October 1987

Sinclair, Marion, singer and songwriter, pioneer of the Australian Girl Guide Movement, composed 'Kookaburra Sits in the Old Gum Tree' in 1934—18 February 1988

Snedden, Rt Hon. Sir Billy Mackie, former federal Liberal MP, aged 61—26 June 1987

Sterns, Niels, principal of the Vogel organisation and patron of young writers and musicians, aged 64—19 November 1987

Tennant, Kylie, AO, award-winning author, aged 75—28 February 1988

Thompson, Patricia, historian, writer and arts supporter, aged 74—23 February 1987

Thorp, Roland, professor of pharmacology at the University of Sydney and founder of the Australian Consumers' Association, aged 72—8 May 1987

Townsend, Air Vice-Marshal William Edwin, CB, CBE, aged 70—23 April 1987

Trigg, Frank Elliot 'Sam', financial adviser and innovator aged 81—21 April 1987

Trimbole, Robert, 'organised crime' boss, aged 55—13 May 1987

Vizents, Allan, arts coordinator, aged 42—19 March 1987

Wainer, Bertram, medical practitioner and abortion law reformer, aged 58—19 January 1987

Walker, Johnnie, hotelier and restaurateur, aged 81—27 March 1987

Wallace, Sir Gordon, jurist, aged 87—14 December 1987

Wearne, Phillip, Liberal Party fundraiser, aged 55—18 November 1987

Weston, Robert, director of the Challenge Foundation and chief production manager for John Fairfax Ltd, aged 57—16 May 1987

White, Harold, former OTC chief, aged 73—4 August 1987

Windeyer, Sir Victor, soldier and High Court judge, aged 87—24 November 1987

Windsor, Harry, first heart transplant surgeon, aged 72—20 March 1987

Worrell, Eric, 'snakeman of Australia', world provider of antivenene for Australia, Papua New Guinea and Pacific island snakes and founder of the Australian Reptile Park, aged 63—15 July 1987

Wrigley, Air Vice-Marshal Henry, CBE, DFC, OAFC, RAAF pioneer, aged 95—14 September 1987

Young, Most Reverend Sir Guilford Clyde, KBE, Archbishop of Hobart, aged 71—16 March 1988

AUSTRALIANS OF THE YEAR

The Australian of the Year and Young Australian of the Year are awarded by the National Australia Day Council on Australia Day each year.

Year	Recipient	Occupation
1960	Sir Macfarlane Burnet	scientist
1961	Joan Sutherland	soprano
1962	Jock Sturrock	yachtsman
1963	Sir John Eccles	scientist
1964	Dawn Fraser	swimmer
1965	Sir Robert Helpmann	ballet dancer and choreographer
1966	Jack Brabham	racing car driver
1967	The Seekers	singing group
1968	Lionel Rose	boxer
1969	Lord Casey	statesman
1970	Cardinal Sir Norman Gilroy	prelate
1971	Evonne Cawley (nee Goolagong)	tennis player
1972	Shane Gould	swimmer
1973	Patrick White	novelist
1974	Sir Bernard Heinze	musician
1975	Professor John W. Cornforth	scientist
1976	Sir Edward Dunlop	surgeon
1977	Raigh Roe	Country Women's Association worker
1978	Galarrwuy Yunupingu	Aboriginal land rights leader
1979	Harry Butler	naturalist
1980	Professor Manning Clark	historian
1981	Sir John Crawford	economic adviser
1982	Sir Edward Williams	chairman, Commonwealth Games Foundation
1983	Robert de Castella	marathon runner
1984	Lois O'Donoghue	Aboriginal activist
1985	Paul Hogan	entertainer
1986	Dick Smith	businessman and adventurer
1987	John Farnham	singer

YOUNG AUSTRALIANS OF THE YEAR

Year	Recipient	Occupation
1979	Julie Sochacki	youth social worker
1980	Peter Hill	quadriplegic swimmer
1981	Paul Radley	novelist
1982	Mark Ella	footballer
1983	Michael Waldock	blind volunteer coastguard
1984	Jon Sieben	swimmer
1985	Deahnne McIntyre	spina bifida athlete
1986	Simone Young	conductor
1987	Marty Gauvin	computing innovator

ROYAL VISITS

1867-68 PRINCE ALFRED, DUKE OF EDINBURGH
31 October—6 April

The second son of Queen Victoria, Prince Alfred visited all the colonies except Western Australia. He arrived in Adelaide on 31 October, travelling on the HMS *Galatea*. At a picnic at Clontarf Beach near Sydney on 12 March 1868 an attempted assassination of the Prince was made when he was shot in the back by an Irishman, Henry James O'Farrell. He was saved when the bullet deflected off his braces. It was initially thought this was part of a Fenian plot; the mentally unstable O'Farrell was hanged on 21 April. After surgery and a short period of recovery the Prince left on 6 April. The Prince Alfred hospitals in Sydney and Melbourne were built as memorials to his visit.

1881 PRINCE ALBERT AND PRINCE GEORGE
17 May—10 August

Sons of the Prince of Wales (later King Edward VII), Prince Albert and Prince George, aged seventeen and fifteen, visited Australia in 1881 whilst serving on HMS *Bacchante* as midshipmen in training. They arrived at Albany, Western Australia, in May, crossed to South Australia in a passenger vessel, travelled overland to Melbourne, and from there sailed by a naval vessel to Sydney.

1901 DUKE AND DUCHESS OF CORNWALL AND YORK
3 May—July

The Duke (later King George V) and Duchess of Cornwall and York came to open the first Commonwealth parliament in the Exhibition Building in Melbourne on 9 May. Arriving at Albany on the *Ophir*, they sailed to Melbourne and later travelled by train to Sydney and Brisbane. On 6 June they left for New Zealand, calling at Hobart, Adelaide and Perth on their return voyage.

1920 EDWARD, PRINCE OF WALES
2 April—August

On an extensive three-month tour from April to August 1920, the Prince of Wales (later King Edward VIII) visited all states as the representative of his father to thank Australia for its part in World War I. He arrived at Melbourne on HMS *Renown* on 2 April and was greeted everywhere he travelled as 'Digger'—this being the greatest compliment the Australians could make. At Bridgetown, Western Australia, his train was derailed and the carriage overturned but the Prince was uninjured—he emerged from the wreckage with some important papers and a cocktail shaker.

1927 DUKE AND DUCHESS OF YORK
26 March—May

Prince Albert (later King George VI), with the Duchess of York (later Queen Elizabeth), visited all states and opened the first session of the new parliament in Canberra on 9 May, twenty-six years after his father had opened the first parliament in Melbourne. They travelled on HMS *Renown*, arriving at Sydney and leaving from Perth.

1934 PRINCE HENRY, DUKE OF GLOUCESTER
4 October—December

The third son of George V, the Duke of Gloucester visited for an extensive sixty-seven-day tour, the main purpose being to open the centenary celebrations of Victoria on 18 October. He arrived on HMS *Sussex* at Fremantle on 4 October, then travelled by train to Adelaide and ship to Melbourne. He also visited the Australian Capital Territory, Tasmania, New South Wales and Queensland. While in Melbourne the Duke dedicated the Shrine of Remembrance on 11 November. He sailed to England from Brisbane, to return in 1945 as Governor-General.

1945-47 PRINCE HENRY, DUKE OF GLOUCESTER

Prince Henry, the Duke of Gloucester, served as Governor-General from 30 January 1945 to 10 March 1947 as the first and only royal Governor-General.

1954 QUEEN ELIZABETH II AND DUKE OF EDINBURGH
3 February—1 April

After World War II King George VI and his family were invited to visit by the Chifley government. After the death of the King, the visit was made by Queen Elizabeth II and the Duke of Edinburgh. They visited all states and the Australian Capital Territory on a visit from 3 February to 1 April. Queen Elizabeth II was the first reigning monarch to set foot on Australian soil.

The tour was: New South Wales 3-13 February; Australian Capital Territory 13-18 February; Tasmania 20-24 February; Victoria 24 February-9 March; Queensland 9-18 March; South Australia 18-26 March and Western Australia 26 March-1 April. The Queen opened sessions of the Commonwealth, New South Wales, Victorian, South Australian and Tasmanian parliaments.

1956 PRINCE PHILIP, DUKE OF EDINBURGH
10 November—14 December

Prince Philip opened the Olympic Games in Melbourne on 22 November. He visited the Northern Territory, Australian Capital Territory, New South Wales and Victoria.

1958 QUEEN ELIZABETH, THE QUEEN MOTHER
14 February—7 March

The Queen Mother visited in February and March to attend the British Empire Service League conference in Canberra. She travelled to the Australian Capital Territory, Sydney, Melbourne, Tasmania, Adelaide and Perth as well as many provincial and country areas.

1959 PRINCESS ALEXANDRA OF KENT
14 August—26 September

Visiting for Queensland's centenary celebrations, Princess Alexandra arrived at Canberra and travelled to New South Wales, Victoria and the Northern Territory as well as Queensland.

1962 PRINCE PHILIP, DUKE OF EDINBURGH
20 November—2 December

The Duke of Edinburgh came out to open and attend the Commonwealth Games in Perth on 22 November. He visited Western Australia and made a brief visit to Canberra.

1963 QUEEN ELIZABETH II AND DUKE OF EDINBURGH
18 February—27 March

The Queen and Prince Philip visited Victoria, Tasmania, New South Wales and Queensland during a thirty-eight-day tour. Part of the visit was to celebrate the fiftieth anniversary of the naming of Canberra on 12 March.

1964 PRINCESS MARINA
26 September—8 October

The wife of the Duke of Kent, who died in 1942, Princess Marina arrived on 26 September for the British Exhibition in Sydney and to open the new Gladesville Bridge—the biggest bridge built in Sydney since the Sydney Harbour Bridge. She travelled in New South Wales and the Australian Capital Territory before leaving on 8 October, with a brief stop at Brisbane on the return flight.

1965 PRINCE PHILIP, DUKE OF EDINBURGH
20—26 February

Prince Philip visited to open the new Royal Australian Mint in Canberra and to deliver the inaugural Dunrossil lecture at the University of New South Wales.

DUKE AND DUCHESS OF GLOUCESTER
20 March—26 April
The Duke and Duchess of Gloucester visited the Australian Capital Territory, Victoria, Tasmania, New South Wales and Queensland. The new Tasman Bridge was opened by the Duke in Hobart, the Royal Easter Show in Sydney and a hydro-electric power station in the Snowy Mountains.

1966 CHARLES, PRINCE OF WALES
January—August
Prince Charles at the age of seventeen was a student at Timbertop, Geelong Grammar School, in Victoria.

QUEEN ELIZABETH, THE QUEEN MOTHER
22 March—7 April
The Queen Mother attended the Adelaide Festival of Arts as its patron and opened Flinders University. She also travelled to Western Australia, the Snowy Mountains and the Australian Capital Territory.

1967 PRINCE PHILIP, DUKE OF EDINBURGH
1—10 March
Prince Philip visited to work on organising the third Commonwealth Study Conference to be held in May 1968. He travelled in the Australian Capital Territory, Victoria and Tasmania, where he helped volunteer firefighters fight a local fire.

CHARLES, PRINCE OF WALES
22—23 December
Prince Charles attended the memorial service for Prime Minister Harold Holt who disappeared off Portsea Beach, Victoria, on 17 December.

1968 PRINCE PHILIP, DUKE OF EDINBURGH
10—20 May; 24 May—5 June
Flying in via Darwin, Mt Isa and Canberra, Prince Philip attended the Commonwealth Study Conference in Sydney and travelled in the Australian Capital Territory, Victoria and New South Wales. After visiting New Zealand, he travelled to Queensland, South Australia and Victoria.

1969 DUKE AND DUCHESS OF KENT
9 August—3 September
The Duke and Duchess of Kent arrived on 9 August for a twenty-five day tour of the Australian Capital Territory, South Australia, the Northern Territory, Western Australia and Queensland as well as Papua New Guinea. The Duke opened the South Pacific Games in Port Moresby on 13 August.

1970 QUEEN ELIZABETH II, DUKE OF EDINBURGH, PRINCE CHARLES AND PRINCESS ANNE
30 March—3 May
Travelling on the royal yacht *Britannia*, the royal family visited Sydney for the Captain Cook bicentenary. The tour included the Australian Capital Territory, Victoria, Queensland and Tasmania.

1971 PRINCE PHILIP, DUKE OF EDINBURGH
23 March—3 April
Prince Philip visited for the celebrations to mark the fiftieth anniversary of the RAAF. He attended many other functions, mostly associated with the Duke of Edinburgh Award Scheme and travelled in Western Australia, South Australia, the Australian Capital Territory and Sydney.

1972 PRINCESS MARGARET AND LORD SNOWDON
7—17 October
The Snowdons toured Western Australia on their first visit to Australia. Princess Margaret visited the children's hospital named after her in Perth.

1973 PRINCE PHILIP, DUKE OF EDINBURGH
12—29 March
Prince Philip visited as president of the Australian Conservation Foundation

to the Northern Territory, the Australian Capital Territory, New South Wales, Victoria and Tasmania.

QUEEN ELIZABETH II AND DUKE OF EDINBURGH
October—November

After a private visit to Queensland and the Northern Territory in early October, the Duke of Edinburgh attended the Duke of Edinburgh's Award Scheme Conference in Canberra on 14-17 October. He was joined by the Queen who came to open the Sydney Opera House on 20 October. After the departure of the Queen on 22 October, the Duke of Edinburgh travelled to Queensland, Tasmania, South Australia, New South Wales and Western Australia in connection with the Duke of Edinburgh's Award Schemes.

1974 QUEEN ELIZABETH II, DUKE OF EDINBURGH, PRINCESS ANNE AND CAPTAIN MARK PHILLIPS
27 February—March

The royal visitors arrived in Canberra after attending the Commonwealth Games in New Zealand. Princess Anne and Captain Mark Phillips attended the Equestrian Federation Ball in Sydney, and were unexpectedly accompanied by the Queen on their return to Britain on 28 February. The Queen had to break her tour because of the snap general elections called in Britain. Prince Philip continued the tour visiting South Australia, Western Australia and the Northern Territory.

CHARLES, PRINCE OF WALES
12—30 October

Prince Charles visited in October to open the Anglo-Australian Optical Telescope at Siding Spring in New South Wales. He also read a message from the Queen to mark the occasion of the first meeting of the Legislative Council in Sydney and of the inauguration of parliamentary institutions in Australia. He travelled to the Australian Capital Territory, New South Wales, Queensland, Tasmania and Victoria.

1975 PRINCESS ANNE AND CAPTAIN MARK PHILLIPS
23 April—6 May

The royal couple attended the International Equestrian Expo in Adelaide after a brief touchdown in Sydney. They then toured in the Australian Capital Territory, the Northern Territory and Western Australia.

PRINCESS MARGARET
22 October—3 November

Princess Margaret visited in October for the twenty-fifth anniversary of the Women's Royal Australian Army Corps, travelling in the Australian Capital Territory, New South Wales and Victoria.

1977 QUEEN ELIZABETH II AND DUKE OF EDINBURGH
7—30 March

The Queen and Prince Philip visited on their Silver Jubilee tour, visiting all the states, Australian Capital Territory and the Northern Territory.

CHARLES, PRINCE OF WALES
1—11 November

Prince Charles visited all the states, the Australian Capital Territory and the Northern Territory to present the Queen's Silver Jubilee Trust's special awards.

1978 CHARLES, PRINCE OF WALES
18—19 May

Prince Charles came to represent the Queen at the funeral of Sir Robert Menzies, Australia's longest serving Prime Minister, who died on 16 May.

PRINCESS ALEXANDRA AND HON. ANGUS OGILVY
20 September—3 October

Princess Alexandra came out to open the Royal Melbourne Show. The couple visited Victoria, the Australian Capital Territory, New South Wales, Queensland and the Northern Territory.

1979 DUKE AND DUCHESS OF GLOUCESTER
2—18 February

The Duke and Duchess of Gloucester visited the Australian Capital Territory, Tasmania, South Australia, Victoria, New South Wales and a brief touchdown in Perth. The Duke is the Grand Prior of the Order of St John of Jerusalem whose functions include the St John's Ambulance Brigade. The visit was in connection with this office.

CHARLES, PRINCE OF WALES
8 March—1 April

Prince Charles visited for Western Australia's one hundred and fiftieth anniversary celebrations. He travelled in Western Australia and the Australian Capital Territory and holidayed at the Great Barrier Reef in Queensland.

PRINCESS ANNE AND CAPTAIN MARK PHILLIPS
7—8 July; 19—23 July

Princess Anne and Captain Mark Phillips visited Sydney briefly before proceeding to Independence Day celebrations in the Gilbert Islands and to New Zealand. They returned to Australia travelling in New South Wales, South Australia and Western Australia, attending functions for the Save the Children Fund.

PRINCE PHILIP, DUKE OF EDINBURGH
25—30 September

Prince Philip visited Western Australia to open the Perth Agricultural Show and to present the Prince Philip Prize for Australian Design.

1980 QUEEN ELIZABETH II AND DUKE OF EDINBURGH
24—28 May

The Queen visited for five days to open the new High Court building in Canberra. They travelled to Canberra, New South Wales and Victoria where she opened the City Square in Melbourne.

PRINCESS ALEXANDRA AND HON. ANGUS OGILVY
28 September—15 October

Princess Alexandra and her husband arrived on 28 September for a seventeen-day visit to attend the Melbourne Centenary International Exhibition and to visit the Australian Capital Territory, South Australia, the Northern Territory and Western Australia.

1981 CHARLES, PRINCE OF WALES
12—28 April

Prince Charles visited for the Apex Club's Anniversary and toured in the Australian Capital Territory, New South Wales, Victoria, South Australia and Tasmania. While in Geelong, Victoria, he opened the National Jubilee Convention of Apex Clubs of Australia.

QUEEN ELIZABETH II AND DUKE OF EDINBURGH
26 September—7 October

The Queen and Prince Philip arrived on the royal yacht *Britannia* on 26 September to attend CHOGM, the Commonwealth Heads of Government Meeting, in Melbourne and to tour Tasmania, Adelaide and Perth. They had a brief stopover on 20-21 October travelling from New Zealand to Colombo.

PRINCE AND PRINCESS MICHAEL OF KENT
24—27 November

The Kents visited Sydney for the Variety Club.

1982 QUEEN ELIZABETH II AND DUKE OF EDINBURGH
27 September—13 October

Prince Philip arrived on 27 September to open the Commonwealth Games in Brisbane, with the Queen arriving to attend on 5 October. The Queen opened the National Gallery in Canberra.

1983 PRINCE AND PRINCESS OF WALES
20 March—17 April

The Prince and Princess of Wales, with their son Prince William, visited all states and the Northern Territory. Woomagarma, near Albury, was their base for the tour.

1985 DUKE AND DUCHESS OF KENT
17—25 April

The Duke and Duchess of Kent visited to open on 20 April the Performing Arts Complex, stage two of Brisbane's Cultural Centre. They also attended the inaugural Great Court Race at the Queensland University, which is modelled on Cambridge's famous race.

PRINCE PHILIP, DUKE OF EDINBURGH
13—15 October

Prince Philip visited Melbourne to attend the Conference of the Royal Agricultural Society of the Commonwealth of which he is the president.

PRINCE AND PRINCESS OF WALES
27 October—8 November

The Prince and Princess of Wales visited Victoria and the Australian Capital Territory on a thirteen-day tour, for Victoria's one hundred and fiftieth anniversary celebrations.

1986 QUEEN ELIZABETH II AND DUKE OF EDINBURGH
March

In the Queen's sixtieth year, she visited with Prince Philip on the *Britannia* for South Australia's sesquicentenary. They travelled to Sydney, Melbourne, Canberra and Adelaide during their twelve-day tour. While here the Queen signed the proclamation to bring the *Australia Act* 1986 into operation. The Act severed remaining constitutional links between Britain and Australia.

PRINCE PHILIP, DUKE OF EDINBURGH
10—28 May

Prince Philip visited in May to attend the sixth Commonwealth Study Conference in Sydney and the sixth World Three Day Event Championships in Adelaide. Captain Mark Phillips was commentator for Channel 9 for the championships. Prince Philip also visited Canberra and Brisbane.

DUKE OF KENT
May

The Duke of Kent arrived in Perth on 21 May to represent the Duke of Edinburgh at regional meetings of Commonwealth Study Groups in Perth, Bunbury and Karratha. He also travelled to New South Wales.

1988 PRINCE AND PRINCESS OF WALES
23 January—3 February

The Prince and Princess of Wales visited for Australia's Bicentennial celebrations, travelling in New South Wales, Victoria, South Australia and the Northern Territory.

PRINCESS ANNE AND CAPTAIN MARK PHILLIPS
28 March—1 April

The Princess Royal and her husband, Captain Mark Phillips, visited Sydney to attend the Royal Easter Show.

QUEEN ELIZABETH II AND DUKE OF EDINBURGH
19 April—10 May

The Queen and Duke of Edinburgh visited five states on a three-week tour including Western Australia, Tasmania, Victoria, Queensland, New South Wales and the Australian Capital Territory. The Queen opened the Stockman's Hall of Fame at Longreach, the Darling Harbour Project in Sydney and the new Parliament House in Canberra.

J. B.

THE HISTORY OF AUSTRALIAN FLAGS

THE AUSTRALIAN NATIONAL FLAG

Until Federation, the Australian colonies used for official purposes the flags of Great Britain—the Union Flag (popularly called the Union Jack) and the three ensigns (red, white and blue). The Union Flag is a composite flag with the cross of St George of England, the cornerwise cross of St Andrew of Scotland and the cross of the Order of St Patrick of Ireland. The flag raised by Governor Arthur Phillip on 26 January 1788 was an earlier form of the Union Flag: the red saltire of St Patrick was not added until 1801 when Ireland became a part of the United Kingdom of Great Britain and Ireland.

In the nineteenth century, various flags were devised in the Australian colonies, most of them incorporating in some way the Southern Cross. The flag of the Anti-Transportation League of 1851, showing the Union Jack and the five stars of the Southern Cross, resembles our present-day flag. The Eureka flag flown by the rebels of the Eureka Stockade in Victoria in 1854 was a broad white cross on blue, with five stars in the extremities of the cross and the centre symbolising the Southern Cross. This flag was taken up in the 1970s as a symbol of Australian nationalism. The Federation League flag at the end of the 1890s used a white ensign with a pale blue cross, with five white stars in the corners and the centre.

After Federation, action was taken to devise a national flag. A competition was held by the *Review of Reviews* and the Commonwealth government with a prize money of £200. A total of 32,823 designs was received. Five winners came up with the same design, which closely resembles the present flag. A flag of the design was flown from the Melbourne Exhibition Building in September 1901; it showed the Union Flag of the blue ensign with a large six-pointed star, representing the six states, and five stars of the Southern Cross (with nine- eight- seven- six- and five-pointed stars).

King Edward VII approved the flag in 1903 but no Commonwealth government formally adopted the flag. In 1908 the design was altered by the addition of a seventh point to the Commonwealth star, to represent the territories. It was not until the Flags Act of 1953 that the status and dimensions of the national flag were clarified in legislation. The design is a blue flag with a Union Jack in the upper quarter of the hoist. Below is a large seven-pointed white star—the Federation Star—with, on the fly, four smaller seven-pointed white stars and one with five points.

STATE FLAGS

All the state flags use the blue ensign with state badges.

New South Wales
In 1876 New South Wales adopted the badge of a golden lion on a red St. George's Cross within a white circle. At each extremity of the cross is a star.

Victoria
As the first colony to acquire a warship, Victoria became the first colony to have its own flag in 1856. The present-day badge shows the Southern Cross surmounted by a crown. The crown was not added until 1872.

Queensland
In 1876 Queensland adopted a blue Maltese cross on a white background with an imperial crown at the centre.

South Australia
South Australia adopted a piping shrike (white-backed magpie) with wings outstretched on a yellow ground in 1904.

Western Australia
The date of adoption of the flag is not known. The state badge is a black swan on a yellow ground. The swan emblem was adopted when the colony was founded in 1829.

Tasmania
In 1876 Tasmania adopted a red lion on a white ground.

J. B.

PSEUDONYMS

Patricia AINSWORTH
Patricia BIGG
writer

Peter ALLEN
Peter WOOLNOUGH
singer

Jennifer AMES
Maysie GREIG
writer of romantic fiction

Angry ANDERSON
Gary ANDERSON
singer with Rose Tattoo

Judith ANDERSON
Frances ANDERSON
Australian-born American actress

Dorothy AUCHTERLONIE
Dorothy GREEN
author

BADGERY
Suzanne HUNT
author

Margaret BARRY
Ida HIGMAN
author

Bullen BEAR
Augustine DONNELLY
writer on financial topics

Mona BRAND
Mona FOX
author

Jamieson BROWN
W. J. C. BROWN
author

Crash CRADDOCK
William James CRADDOCK
singer

Toby CRESWELL
William CRESWELL
music journalist and author

Fred DAGG
John CLARKE
comedian

Dick DALE
Richard MONSOUR
singer with the Deltones

Jack DANVERS
Camille Auguste Marie CASELEYR
author

Sonia DEAN
Gwendoline SOUTAR
author

Dick DIAMONDE
Dingeman VANDERSLUYS
singer with the Easybeats

Shane DOUGLAS
Richard WILKES-HUNTER
author

Charlie DRAKE
Charles SPRINGALL
singer

Slim DUSTY
David Gordon KIRKPATRICK
country and western singer

Sheena EASTON
Sheena Shirley ORR
singer

Dame Edna EVERAGE
Barry HUMPHRIES
comedian

Snowy FLEET
Gordon FLEET
member of the Easybeats

Florrie FORD
Florence FLANAGAN
singer who toured British music halls

Barry GIBB
Barry CROMPTON-GIBB
member of the BeeGees

Norman GUNSTON
Garry McDONALD
comedian

Bobby HARDY
Marjorie HARDY
author

Neville JACKSON
Gerald M. GLASKIN
author

Harvey JAMES
Harvey James HARRUP
member of Sherbet

KAMAHL
KAMALESVARAN, son of Kandiah
singer

Geordie LEACH
Gordon Everett LEACH
member of Rose Tattoo

Margaret LIVINGSTONE
Mary M. FLYNN
author

Gerry LONG
William F. LARKINS
author

Nellie MELBA
Helen MITCHELL
opera singer
Martin MILLS
Martin BOYD
author
MO or Roy RENE
Harry van der Sluice
comedian
Reg MOMBASSA
Christopher O'DOUGHERTY
member of Mental as Anything
Ruth MORRIS
Ruth WEBB
author
Tex MORTON
Robert LANE
country and western singer
Trisha NOBLE
Patsy Ann NOBLE
singer
Lyn PAUL
Lynda Susan BELCHER
member of the New Seekers
Josephine PLAIN
Isabel MITCHELL
author
Martin PLAZA
Martin Edward MURPHY
member of Mental as Anything
Snub POLLARD
Harold FRASER
comedian who acted in American silent films
Richard PRESTON
Jack LINDSAY
writer
John QUINLAN
Jack O'HAGAN
songwriter
Chips RAFFERTY
John GOFFAGE
actor
Henry Handel RICHARDSON
Ethel Henrietta RICHARDSON
novelist

Annie RIXON
Annie STUDDERT
author
Rodney RUDE
Rodney KEFT
comedian
Bon SCOTT
Ronald SCOTT
member of AC/DC
O. R. SCOTT
Ralph GOTTLIEBSEN
author
Victoria SHAW
Jeanette ELPHICK
actress who worked in Hollywood
Nevil SHUTE
Nevil Shute NORWAY
British novelist who emigrated to Australia
Greedy SMITH
Andrew SMITH
member of Mental as Anything
Bongo STARR
Robert STARKIE
member of Skyhooks
Austen TAYSHUS
Sandy GUTMAN
comedian
Harry VANDA
Johannes Jacob Hendrickus VANDENBERG
singer with the Easybeats
Victoria VETRI
Angela DORIAN
actress
John WARWICK
John McIntosh BEATTIE
Australian actor in British films
Wilbur WYLDE
Nicholas AITKEN
member of Jo Jo Zep and the Falcons
Jo Jo ZEP
Joseph CAMILLERI
singer

MOST POPULAR NAMES IN AUSTRALIA

1800–1830

William	Mary	Michael	Susan	Samuel	Maud
John	Sarah	Patrick	Eileen	Richard	Margaret
Thomas	Elizabeth	Benjamin	Charlotte	Reginald	Emily
George	Ann			Stanley	Rose
James	Maria	**1851–1870**		Cecil	Winifred
Henry	Hannah	William	Elizabeth	David	Patricia
Joseph	Emma	John	Mary	Clarence	Ivy
Charles	Phoebe	James	Margaret		
Robert	Harriet	George	Emily	**1891–1910**	
Edward	Ellen	Frederick	Sarah	John	Dorothy
Samuel	Margaret	Thomas	Annie	William	Jean
Richard	Martha	Henry	Emma	George	Mary
Alfred	Susannah	Robert	Ellen	James	Winifred
Frederick	Louisa	Charles	Florence	Ronald	Marjorie
Benjamin	Alice	Edward	Jane	Robert	Doris
David	Catherine	Stephen	Catherine	Kenneth	Kathleen
Daniel	Rachel	Michael	Violet	Frederick	Bridget
Walter	Emily	Ronald	Alice	Thomas	Elizabeth
Edwin	Susan	Daniel	Lily	Keith	Eileen
Isaac	Bridget	Benjamin	Agnes	Eric	Lilian
Andrew	Fanny	Edgar	Esther	Alfred	Daisy
Nicholas	Jane	Edwin	Bertha	Arthur	Vera
Patrick	Charlotte	Percy	Mabel	Charles	Margaret
Herbert	Rebecca	Horace	Bridget	Leslie	Edna
Horatio	Frances	David	Beatrice	Dennis	Gladys
		Patrick	Henrietta	Joseph	Florence
1831–1850		Matthew	Ada	Alan	Doreen
William	Mary	Richard	Effie	Stanley	Violet
John	Elizabeth	Ernest	Eva	Ernest	May
George	Sarah	Reginald	Rose	Harold	Joyce
Arthur	Annie			Norman	Phyllis
Thomas	Alice	**1871–1890**		Reginald	Erica
James	Nellie	William	Florence	David	Olive
Henry	Emily	John	Mary	Francis	Ivy
Charles	Edith	George	Alice		
Samuel	Ada	Thomas	Annie	**1911–1930**	
Edward	Margaret	Charles	Elsie	William	Joan
Alfred	Bridget	Frederick	Edith	John	Alice
Frederick	Emma	Arthur	Elizabeth	George	Annie
Walter	Jane	Albert	Doris	Ronald	Winifred
Richard	Louisa	James	Edna	James	Elsie
Albert	Clara	Ernest	Dorothy	Kenneth	Edith
Herbert	Harriet	Robert	Ethel	Keith	Irene
Edwin	Hannah	Alfred	Gladys	Peter	Lilian
David	Fanny	Sidney	Lilian	Michael	Dorothy
Daniel	Ethel	Joseph	Nellie	Brian	Beryl
Sidney	Martha	Harold	Lily	Alan	Betty
Horace	Ellen	Walter	Sarah	Paul	Doris
Robert	Agnes	Herbert	Gertrude	Donald	Mary
		Percy	Mabel	David	Amy

Robert	Violet	Richard	Joan	Patrick	Vicki
Richard	Jessie	Ian	Helen	Gregory	Lynnette
Frederick	Phyllis	Derek	Christine	Jason	Elizabeth
Hector	May	Ronald	Janet	Matthew	Joanne
Stephen	Diana	Christopher	Kathleen	Brett	Valerie
Reginald	Eileen	Paul	June		
Patrick	Elizabeth	Mark	Audrey	**1971-1980**	
Norman	Evelyn	Charles	Isobel	Andrew	Kylie
Ian	Nora			David	Michelle
Philip	Jean	**1951-1960**		Jason	Jennifer
Harold	Margaret	David	Christine	Mark	Julie
		Peter	Linda	Matthew	Fiona
1931-1940		John	Helen	Michael	Karen
Peter	Judith	Michael	Robyn	Christopher	Lisa
William	Patricia	Robert	Susan	Paul	Nicole
John	Maureen	Alan	Sandra	Peter	Melissa
Ronald	Shirley	Stephen	Valerie	Benjamin	Catherine
James	Joan	Paul	Margaret	Brett	Sarah
Michael	Margaret	Brian	Maureen	Craig	Elizabeth
Brian	Jean	Graham	Diane	James	Alison
Stephen	Doreen	Philip	Marilyn	Adam	Emma
Donald	Ruth	Anthony	Wendy	Nicholas	Alexandra
Neil	Barbara	Colin	Joan	Simon	Amanda
Dennis	Joyce	Barry	Elizabeth	Timothy	Jane
Kevin	Dorothy	Ian	Deborah	Sean	Joanne
David	Wendy	Raymond	Judith	Gregory	Belinda
Eric	Pamela	Trevor	Lynn	Stephen	Rebecca
Barry	Norma	Charles	Carol	Patrick	Vanessa
Joseph	Beryl	Thomas	Anne	Alexander	Justine
Robert	Marjorie	Patrick	Patricia	William	Kelly
Richard	Elizabeth	Christopher	Catherine	Stuart	Megan
Ian	June	James	Kerry	Scott	Melinda
Kenneth	Betty	Alexander	Lynnette		
Gordon	Sandra	Kevin	Janice	**Early 1980s**	
Philip	Eileen	Donald	Jennifer	Matthew	Sarah
Patrick	Mary			James	Rebecca
Alan	Yvonne	**1961-1970**		David	Amanda
Harold	Audrey	Stephen	Susan	Michael	Claire
		David	Deborah	Andrew	Alison
1941-1950		Paul	Karen	Christopher	Elizabeth
Peter	Linda	John	Carol	Benjamin	Kate
David	Judith	William	Linda	Daniel	Jennifer
John	Susan	Peter	Lisa	Nicholas	Lauren
Michael	Margaret	Michael	Jennifer	Timothy	Michelle
Alan	Carol	Alan	Marie	Luke	Catherine
Robert	Patricia	Robert	Julie	Robert	Amy
Stephen	Barbara	Brian	Jacqueline	Mark	Anna
Brian	Sandra	Anthony	Tracey	Alexander	Melissa
Graham	Jean	James	Anne	Stephen	Alexandra
Donald	Diana	Geoffrey	Kylie	Peter	Belinda
Patrick	Betty	Stuart	Jan	Jonathan	Erin
Anthony	Valerie	Donald	Christine	Adam	Emma
Philip	Elizabeth	Joseph	Amanda	Philip	Rachel
Roy	Wendy	Richard	Michelle	Simon	Katie
James	Gloria	Christopher	Megan	Paul	Lisa
Barry	Shirley	Andrew	Raelene	John	Natalie
Malcolm	Pamela	Mark	Narelle	Thomas	Emily

Anthony	Fiona	Timothy	Laura	Luke	Rachel
William	Nicole	John	Ashleigh	Mitchell	Hannah
		Benjamin	Sophie	Robert	Lucy
LATE 1980s		Alexander	Emma	Stephen	Melissa
James	Katherine	Michael	Lauren	Simon	Anna
Thomas	Sarah	David	Amy	Joshua	Madeleine
Nicholas	Rebecca	Daniel	Claire	Patrick	Hayley
Matthew	Jessica	Samuel	Stephanie	Ryan	Emily
Christopher	Alexandra	William	Samantha	Jonathan	Alison
Andrew	Elizabeth	Peter	Kate		

Source: Dynes, Cecily. *The Great Australian and New Zealand Book of Baby Names.* Angus & Robertson, Sydney, 1984.

SARAH BECKLEY and the CONVICT WOMEN of VAN DIEMEN'S LAND

On 26 January 1828, convict Sarah Beckley appeared before the magistrates of Hobart Town. She was charged with neglecting her duty, an offence for which she was sentenced to a week's solitary confinement at New Norfolk. What happened to Sarah Beckley was hardly an occurrence of much note and even to her, it was not a major event, being her third offence since arriving in Van Diemen's Land twelve months before.

Born in London around 1808, Sarah Beckley was a housemaid by trade but she could also wash and iron. She could not write, was almost five feet tall and had brown hair and brown eyes. On 6 April 1826 she was convicted at London's Old Bailey for stealing from a dwelling house and was sentenced to seven years' transportation. At the time she was aged eighteen years and was single. It was not her first offence—she had once served six months for a similar crime.

The voyage to Van Diemen's Land, on board the ship *Sir Charles Forbes*, was uneventful, and she arrived at Hobart Town on 3 January 1827. The ship's Surgeon-superintendent described her as 'a very quiet indolent girl'.

Within months of her arrival in the colony, Sarah Beckley appeared before the magistrates charged with absconding from her master, Mr Bent, and remaining absent for five days. For this she was ordered to be confined in a cell and fed on bread and water for four days, and then to be returned to her master.

Over the next three years she faced the magistrates on six occasions for a variety of minor offences. These included two more counts of absconding, one of neglect of duty and one of insolence and disobedience of orders. On 14 February 1829, while in the House of Correction, she was convicted of 'disobedience of orders and attempting to create a riot in the Crime Class Yard in the Female House of Correction'. Her last offence, nearly a year later, involved 'disorderly conduct in having a man secreted in her bed room in her Master's house on Saturday last, and also absconding from her service'. For this she was placed in a cell on bread and water for six days and sent to the House of Corrections.

In 1830 permission was granted for her to marry George Hopper, a free man who worked as a labourer. They were married in the same year at Hobart Town, after which she may have been assigned to him.

Finally, on 6 April 1833 Sarah Beckley's seven years' servitude ended and she once again became a free woman.

Eighteen months later her first child, Frederick William Hopper, was born at Hobart Town.

Such minor events made up the lives of the real women of early Tasmania. Too often, histories of our convict past have ignored these, and instead dwelled on the sensational and the bizarre, leaving us with a distorted picture of the convict's life. While recent works have helped create a more realistic picture, they have tended to concentrate on the male convicts—the popular image of the female convict remaining largely unchanged.

The reasons for this are threefold. Firstly, more men than women were transported—five out of every six—and thus they have commanded more attention. Secondly, most histories have been written by men, drawing on original records kept by men.

Thirdly, and perhaps most importantly, the society in which the convict woman lived placed severe constraints on her behaviour, for the most part excluding her from the more dramatic events that comprise the landmarks of history, and removing her from the extremes of the penal system.

With few exceptions, women were restricted to the roles of wife, mother, housekeeper or whore—sometimes to all four. Such 'domestic' occupations gave an impression that the women's lives were of less interest than their male counterparts and, in turn, that their behaviour was of such a uniform nature that it could be dismissed with a few sweeping generalisations.

In the eighty-one years that convicts were transported to Australia, some 162,000 were sent here from the British Isles. Of these, 25,000 were women— half of whom were sent to Sydney, and half to Van Diemen's Land.

The women were generally treated well on their four-month voyage to Australia. Removed from the debilitating effects of the urban slums from which many of them had been taken, they were adequately fed, clothed, and allowed liberal doses of fresh sea air. Medical attention, although primitive by today's standards, was effective in most cases. 'Purging' seemed the prevalent philosophy: blood-letting, the application of 'blisters', and other physical or medicinal methods, including opium, mercury, and various unguents, tinctures and pills. Robert Espie, for example, the Surgeon-superintendent on board the transport *Lord Sidmouth*, wrote that: 'Mary Sutton, a convict from Liverpool, has had a violent attack of giddiness which was relieved by profuse bloodletting [and] afterwards giving her a strong purgative.' Two days later, she was 'still very ill and has no recollection or sense of what occurs. [I] bled her most profusely and have shaved and Blister'd the whole of her head.'

Despite such treatments only a small number of those who left British shores failed to reach Australia. Christiana McDonald was one of the unlucky few. She was tragically drowned when she 'fell overboard in endeavouring to save her Cap, which was blown into [the] main channels'.

When a ship bearing convicts sailed into Port Jackson or the Derwent, the colonial administrations were sparked into a flurry of activity. In Van Diemen's Land that activity had become a well-regulated process by the time Lieutenant-Governor Arthur took office in 1824.

Once the ship was safely anchored, the women were issued with a new suit of clothing and paraded before the Lieutenant-Governor, who exhorted them to good behaviour. Then began a long period of induction into the colony's penal system. Full particulars of each woman's physical description were taken and each was questioned on details of her crime and the events surrounding it, the number and nature of previous offences, her marital status, trade, birthplace, next-of-kin and religion.

Thus, Elizabeth Broadway told how she was transported for 'stealing a parish blanket . . . from the poor house. My husband's brother killed my husband with a rake. I have three children. Mother at Islington. I went into the Poorhouse to Lye In [sic] . . . Protestant.' Hannah Maria Coe said she was transported for 'stealing a piece of bacon. I was once confined in the House of Correction for breaking a window while intoxicated. I lived last in Dillons Court, Petticoat Lane. I worked at my business as a dressmaker. Widow. Protestant.'

After all details were recorded, the women were ferried ashore and marched under guard up Macquarie Street to the Female House of Correction, or Factory. Large crowds normally gathered to enjoy this spectacle. In 1827, the *Hobart Town Gazette* reported that the people 'crowding on the Government Wharf while the female prisoners were landing ... being requested to stand back, not only rudely and insolently refused to comply, but pushed and abused the [police] officers ... using language too horrid to repeat.' For some of the women this must have been a bewildering introduction to the colony. For others, perhaps a source of reassurance at finding a society similar to the one they had left.

Soon after they arrived at the Female Factory, the women were collected by the master to whom they had been allocated under the *assignment system*. This system, which had developed in the very early years of settlement, involved the placement of convicts in the service of private settlers, usually as servants, cooks, dairymaids or nurserymaids.

The assignment system was rather loosely applied in the colony's first twenty years. For example, in 1816, it was said that 'two hundred female prisoners were brought down from Sydney ... proclamation was made, and the settlers were invited to receive them. There was little delicacy of choice: they landed, and vanished; and some carried into the bush, changed their destination before they reached their homes.'

In the north, conditions were particularly lax. J. B. Boothman stated that 'those that are not taken off by settlers are victualled from the stores and cohabit with the Male Convicts'. In fact all but two of the women at Launceston were said to live in this way.

From around 1818, though, a system of order began to emerge from this chaos, as a series of regulations were published which laid down the rules for master and servant alike. Each master had to furnish the convict servant with a minimum of 1½ lb of meat, 1½ lb of flour, 1 oz of sugar, ½ oz of soap and ¼ oz of salt per day, together with tea or tobacco, to be supplied at the discretion of the master. Convicts were supplied with a set amount of clothes each year, bedding, two blankets and a rug, comfortable lodgings and medicine in the event of illness. In return, they were forbidden to demand wages and the master 'strongly recommended' not to pay any.

Other regulations directed that masters could not return convicts to government without good reason, and that assigned convicts were not permitted to be 'on their own hands', hired-out or lent to other settlers, must reside on their master's premises, were not allowed out at night, had no set working hours, could not labour for themselves in their free time, and could not move off their master's property without a pass. Finally, to protect the convicts and to ensure a uniformity of discipline, masters were not allowed to punish their servants, but had to take any complaints to a magistrate, who would then decide on an appropriate punishment.

Generally speaking, the assignment system worked well, but even under this strictly codified system, it was open to abuse. Much of this stemmed from the sexual imbalance in Van Diemen's Land society—in 1820, for example, there were ten men to every three women and nine male convicts for every female convict. This resulted in a high demand for women as wives, servants and, no doubt, mistresses.

The women, aware that many masters would indulge them in the hope of retaining their services, often behaved as they wished. Mary Ann Laing, for example, faced the magistrates for 'disrespectful behaviour, violently abusing her Mistress, refusing to do any work, wilfully destroying earthenware and committing many disgusting nuisances in divers parts of the house'. It was said to be 'almost impossible for those families who study the quiet and morality of their children to endure Female Convicts', and that 'children learn the vilest expressions' from the convict women.

Cases of masters over-indulging their convict women servants are poorly documented, but the number charged with being out after hours or 'in Town without a pass' indicates the loose control often exercised. Catherine Flynn, for example, committed seventeen offences in the three years that she was assigned to J. Dunn, yet he always took her back; Mary Creed was removed from her master after she was found to be under 'very inefficient control'; while Mary Ann Anderson's master wished to retain her services despite her 'disobedience of orders, neglect of duty, insolence ... and threatening to knock her Master's brains out with a poker'.

The assignment system, however, did not always work to the benefit of the female convict. Although care was supposed to be taken not to place women in 'improper service', this was not always possible, and the settlers of Van Diemen's Land had never been known for their propriety. Arthur's predecessor, Sorell, thought a large proportion of them 'the most depraved and unprincipled people in the universe'.

Mary Miller's master was found to have assaulted her with a 'lewd intention', Lydia Hines' master beat and ill-treated her and Phoebe Allen, charged with refusing to do her work for Dr Ross, stated 'you may do what you like with me, I won't go back, and if you send me back I'll run away. I would rather be hanged than go back.' Elizabeth Smith, 'found in an indecent situation with a man in her Master's garden', pleaded that 'she was driven to do so to obtain clothing as her Mistress did not give her any'.

One way a woman could escape a bad master was by marrying, for a woman married to a free man could usually be assigned to him. With luck, this could mean an end to the pursuits, solicitations or worse from the various masters, policemen, soldiers and other convicts with whom they came into daily contact. As assigned servant to her husband, the woman's condition became little different from the normal state of marriage at that time.

The attractions of such an arrangement are shown by the fact that at least three-fifths of the women married. This figure is surprisingly high, considering that a large number were already married prior to being transported and were thus either prevented from remarrying, were disinclined to remarry, or were joined by their husbands soon after they arrived. Also, an unknown but possibly large number cohabited with the one partner for a long time, particularly in the earlier years, when society was less well ordered and clergymen were few and far between.

Marriage did not always improve the woman's situation. Any refusal to comply with her husband's wishes could lead to an appearance before the magistrates. The husbands, perhaps brutalised by the convict system themselves, could also be violent. In only a few cases were these roles reversed. Ann Margaret Wright, for example, attempted to murder her husband with a spade, after he returned from Hobart Town drunk.

Whether intentional or not, the transportation of women provided the colony with a population of prostitutes. The women's contemporaries had varying interpretations of what this entailed, ranging from women for whom it was their principal trade to women of 'loose morals'.

The first group were normally free or held a ticket-of-leave. In a society which offered women limited employment opportunities, prostitution was a relatively easy and profitable alternative, particularly given the undoubted demand from the predominantly male population. Women abandoned by their husbands, widowed or unable to marry, lacking tradeable skills or having been prostitutes before they were transported, must have been attracted to this type of employment. The second group might best be described as women who, having absconded from their service and lacking money of their own, used prostitution to purchase a night's entertainment, liquor or lodgings.

Absconding was only one of many misdemeanours for which a convict woman could be discplined. Others included being drunk and disorderly, insolence, assault, refusing to work, being out after hours, immoral conduct and pilfering. Examples are numerous, some of the more colourful including those of Keziah Paul, charged with 'assaulting Constable Birch ... by throwing a glass of beer on him and using abusive language'; and Mary Murphy, charged with being 'drunk and disorderly and indecently exposing her person as a number of prisoners were passing'.

The range of punishments ordered for these offences included a reprimand, up to a month's imprisonment in solitary confinement on bread and water, assignment to the 'interior', up to twelve months' imprisonment in the Female House of Correction, hard labour at the washtubs, shaving of the head, an extension of the sentence of transportation for up to three years, or a fine of five shillings for women holding a ticket-of-leave.

More 'physical' punishments were used less frequently. These included the stocks and the iron collar—a device weighing about 6¼ lb which gave the wearer the appearance of 'horned cattle'. Only one woman was flogged— Elizabeth Murphy received twenty-five lashes in 1806 for 'writing or causing to be wrote a letter directed to Francis Dring containing the most infamous language and accusing him of a most heinous crime'. Very few were hanged, the first being Mary McLauchlan, who was executed in 1830 for the murder of her infant child in the Female House of Correction. The *Hobart Town Gazette* reported that 'she died contrite and resigned. She was dressed in a white garment, with a black ribbon round her waist, and a very large concourse was assembled to witness her ignominious end. On the falling of the drop, the instant before her mortal scene was closed, she had just time to utter "Oh! My God!".'

Of the punishments meted out to convict women, the reprimand appears to have been quite useless—many women must have seen it as a bonus allowing them to repeat the offence. Reassignment after a period in the factory, on the other hand, may have allowed women inclined to 'reform' an escape from a particularly unpleasant master. Shaving of the head was universally detested and was probably an effective short-term deterrent. Perhaps the most effective punishment was assignment to the 'interior': the rigours of country life and the removal of the woman from the influence of her peers and the temptations of the public houses was thought very conducive to reform. At the very least, it reduced the opportunities for misconduct.

The principal instrument for carrying out these punishments was the Female House of Correction, or Factory, a building which also served as a maternity hospital and a clearing house for convicts awaiting assignment. Built in the late 1820s, it replaced the old Hobart Gaol as a place of internment for refractory females. The gaol had become totally inadequate for the purpose: the rooms were much too small and in want of proper ventilation; it was reported that the old and the young, the totally incorrigible and the less hardened convicts were thrown together without any attempt at classification; and communication with people outside and escape over the walls could be done with impunity.

The new House of Correction which opened in 1829, was substantial. By November 1832, it held 249 women and ninety-seven children. Construction of a new House of Correction at Launceston in 1834 further increased the numbers that could be accommodated— it held sixty-six women and thirteen children soon after opening.

The regulations of the factories reveal much of the transformation being worked on the convict society by Governor Arthur. Cleanliness, quietness, regularity, submission and industry were its fundamental objectives, proper observance of which would, it was hoped, lead to the appearance of 'patient industry' and 'reformation of character'. The inmates were grouped into three classes, according to the reason for their internment. All women were dressed in 'cheap and coarse materials', consisting of a 'cotton or stuff gown, a petticoat, a jacket and apron, with a common straw bonnet of strong texture'. Large yellow 'C's on their clothing distinguished the women of each class.

They were also distinguished by the type of work they were given and by their rations. The 1st Class were employed as cooks, task women and hospital attendants; the 2nd Class at making clothes for the establishment and 'getting up' linen; and the 3rd, or Crime Class, at carding wool, spinning and washing for the establishment, the orphan schools and the penitentiary. Daily rations were set at ½ lb meat, 1 lb bread, ½ oz salt, ½ oz soap, ½ lb vegetables, 1 oz sugar and 1 oz roasted wheat for coffee for the 1st and 2nd classes, while women in the Crime Class were deprived of these last two items. Prayer meetings were held twice-daily and women so inclined could be instructed to read and write.

Conditions in the factories, while initially good, deteriorated over time. Overcrowding in particular became a major problem. In 1841, it was reported that: 'The capacity of the building is so unequal to the number of the wretched inmates, that their working rooms resemble the hold of a slave ship . . . So foetid, so wholly unfitting for the human being is the atmosphere [of the sleeping rooms] after the night's halations, that if we are correctly informed, the turnkeys when they open the doors in the morning, make their escape from the passages with the utmost expedition to avoid semi-suffocation.'

As a balance to the punishments imposed for misconduct, the convicts were also offered a series of rewards to encourage their good behaviour. While they could regain their liberty simply by serving the full term of their sentence of transportation, this could be considerably shortened through the granting of a ticket-of-leave, a conditional pardon or a free pardon. These were of most importance to the women serving a fourteen-year or a life sentence, for whom liberation must otherwise have seemed an impossibly distant event.

The *ticket-of-leave* was the most common, but also the most tenuous form of liberty. It granted the holder exemption from public or assigned labour and permitted her to work for herself and choose her own place of residence. However, she had to remain in the one district or settlement, attend the monthly muster held by the police magistrate and, if living within two miles of a church, attend Sunday muster and Divine Service with the other convicts. Any offence could result in the ticket's removal and the return of the offender to gaol or assigned service. In most cases, however, a reprimand, a fine or a suspension of the ticket were deemed sufficient.

The second means by which a sentence could be shortened was by way of a *conditional pardon*. This granted the woman her freedom, but placed restrictions on her movements. A conditional pardon could be granted for Van Diemen's Land only, for the Australian colonies and New Zealand, or for all countries but Great Britain and Ireland. Both conditional pardons and tickets-of-leave were normally issued to women who had served minimum periods of time with good behaviour, depending on the length of their original sentence.

The *free pardon* involved a complete restoration of the convict's freedom, with no restrictions on her movements. These were granted sparingly.

One other way that a convict woman could regain her freedom was by absconding. This was difficult, particularly for women, whose fewer numbers and 'housebound' role made the absconding female a more easily identifiable target. The settlements in Van Diemen's Land were small and the movement of people closely watched.

Each week, lists of absconders' names and descriptions were circulated and rewards were offered for their capture. Shipping was strictly controlled and, until the mid- to late 1840s, Sydney was the nearest town into which an escaped convict could hope to disappear.

Most women who did abscond, therefore, did not attempt to leave the island but seemed content to evade capture for as long as possible, or sometimes to surrender themselves after a few days of freedom. A few women did manage to escape Van Diemen's Land, if only temporarily. Sarah O'Neil stowed-away on board the *Pilot*, only to be found 'in a most deplorable state' after the ship had sprung a leak and been forced to return to the Derwent. Jane Watt and Mary Ann Kirby reached Sydney, while Ann Margaret Wright got as far as Bombay. Some must have made good their escape. Ann Hogan, for example, disappeared in February 1828 and was never heard from again. For most, though, the balance of punishment and reward imposed by the convict system was such that the benefits of remaining in servitude far outweighed the risks inherent in flight.

P. T.

Sources:
Admiralty Papers, Medical Journals, Adm. 101. Public Record Office, London.
Conduct Register of Female Convicts Arriving in the Period of the Assignment System. 1803–43, CON 40. Archives Office of Tasmania.
Dixson, M. *The Real Matilda: Woman and Identity in Australia*. Penguin, Melbourne, 1976.
Historical Records of Australia. Series III, vol. 3, vol. 4.
Hobart Town Courier. 24 April 1830.
Hobart Town Gazette. 31 January 1818, 28 March 1818, 22 August 1818, 7 October 1826, 13 January 1827, 3 October 1829, 30 November 1832, 6 November 1834, 11 December 1834.
Hutchinson, R. C. 'Mrs Hutchinson and the Female Factories of Early Australia'. *Papers and Proceedings*. Tasmanian Historical Research Association, vol. 11 no. 2, December 1963.
Shaw, A. G. L. *Convicts and the Colonies*. Faber & Faber, London, 1966.
West, J. *The History of Tasmania*. Angus and Robertson, Sydney, 1971.

SEMAPHORE ALPHABET

BEGINNINGS

ACUPUNCTURE
The discovery of this type of pain relief is attributed to Shen Nung, Emperor of China circa 2700BC. It literally means to puncture with a needle and involves inserting fine needles into specific parts of the body.

ADELAIDE
In 1837 Colonel William Light named the settlement after Queen Adelaide, wife of King William IV, who had requested that it be named in her honour.

ANZAC DAY
This day commemorates the landing of the Australian and New Zealand Army Corps at Gallipoli on 25 April 1915. It was first observed as a public holiday in 1916 both in Australia and by Australian troops serving in Egypt in the safe defence zone on the Suez Canal.

AUSTRALIA DAY
The landing of Captain Arthur Phillip at Sydney Cove on 26 January 1788 was first celebrated as a public holiday in 1838. The name 'Australia Day' was used initially in Victoria in 1931 and later taken up by the other states.

BANTAMWEIGHT
A bantamweight boxer is one who weighs between 51 and 54 kilograms. The name derives from a fowl bred in the Banten district of West Java which is renowned for its tenacity and fearlessness as a fighter.

BARRACKING
It is an accepted aspect of a sporting match for spectators to shout their support and encouragement for one or more of the players. Several explanations exist concerning the derivation of this word. Some argue it comes from an Irish expression meaning to brag or boast about one's fighting prowess. Others see its derivation in English cockney and French expressions meaning gibberish or indiscernible sounds. Another source could be an Aboriginal word 'borak' meaning to make fun of someone. Barracking originally involved abusing the opposing team rather than shouting support for the favourite side.

BELL-BOTTOM TROUSERS
Sailors' duties included scrubbing decks and wading in shallow water to secure boats onto shore or to push away from shore. To keep the uniform dry, the bell-bottom trousers were developed with the flared design enabling them to be rolled up easily over the knees.

BIKINI
First modelled in Paris in 1946, the two-piece swimsuit was named after Bikini Island, part of the Marshall Islands. The United States had carried out atomic tests there and the emotive and visual impact of the bikini was likened to the devastation of the blasts and the resulting bareness of the island.

BILLYCAN
There are a number of explanations for the origin of the name given to the tin can with a wire handle and lid. One is that it comes from the Aboriginal word 'billa', meaning creek or river. Another suggests it comes from the Old Scottish 'billypot', meaning a cooking utensil. Some say it originates from 'boulli', a tinned soup consumed on the Victorian goldfields, where the empty cans were used in the same way as a billycan.

BOX OFFICE
Two theories have been suggested for the origins of box office. One suggests it comes from the time when theatre seats were not laid out in rows, but patrons sat in individual boxes. The other has it that the expression predates the time when admission tickets were sold and a box was passed around the audience to collect contributions. Later, it was left outside the entrance so that people could pay prior to taking their seats.

BRISBANE
While the explorer John Oxley named the Brisbane River in 1823, the name Brisbane, after Sir James Brisbane (Governor of New South Wales from 1821 to 1825), was not given to the settlement until 1827.

BUNKUM
Insincere talking and political speech-making has come to be called bunkum after

Buncombe County, North Carolina, USA. Buncombe County's representative in the US Congress, Felix Walker, was so intent on making his voice heard in the Congress that he rambled on and on in spite of the obvious unrest among his colleagues. He told them he was not speaking to them but was talking for Buncombe.

CANBERRA
Derived from an Aboriginal word, Canberra was announced as the name for Australia's capital city by Lady Denman when the city's foundation stones were laid on Capital Hill on 12 March 1913. Suggestions for the meaning of Canberra vary from a meeting place to a woman's breasts (referring to Mount Ainslie and Black Mountain).

CHAUVINISM
Meaning a blind enthusiasm or loyalty towards something it derives from Nicolas Chauvin, a soldier of Napoleon I who, in spite of constant injury and retirement on a miniscule pension, remained constantly loyal to and in awe of Napoleon.

CHRISTMAS CARDS
The first Christmas card was designed for Sir Henry Cole, director of the Victoria and Albert Museum in London, by the artist John Callcott Horsley in 1843. One thousand copies were printed. Louis Prang of Boston was the first to develop the idea in the United States.

COCKY
First used during the 1850s to distinguish between the small farmers and those who owned large tracts of land—the squatters. Cocky became more widely used after the Free Selection Act of 1861.

DARWIN
The site was named by the captain and crew of HMS *Beagle*, who explored the area in 1839. Charles Darwin, the naturalist, had been part of the ship's company on an earlier voyage to Australia but had not accompanied the 1839 expedition.

A DUCK (IN CRICKET)
This term for scoring no runs in cricket, is a shortening of 'duck's egg'. The shape of a duck's egg resembling zero.

DUTCH TREAT
The expression is used to describe a meal or entertainment where each person pays for him or herself. It originates in the seventeenth century when The Netherlands and Britain were bitter economic rivals, especially in the creation of overseas trading empires. This derogatory reference to what the British saw as the miserly greed of the Dutch, inferred there was no treat at all.

EASTER BUNNY
The association of Easter with rabbits comes from the tradition which considers rabbits as symbols of fertility and the abundance of life. Hence their link with a festival which celebrates dying and resurrection.

EYETEETH
Situated underneath the eyes with their roots extending towards them, these teeth are served by a network of nerves in common with the eyes. Alternatively called canine teeth, they have nothing to do with eyes or vision as such.

FATHER'S DAY
Celebrated in Australia on the first Sunday in September, Father's Day was started in the United States in 1910 by Sonora Louisa Smart Dodd.

GRANNY SMITH APPLES
The apple is named after Maria Ann Smith who cultivated it around 1868, probably by accident, on her family's land fronting the Great Northern Road in the Ryde district of Sydney. It is thought to be a crossbreed of the French crab-apple, cultivated in Tasmania around this time.

HAT TRICK
A bowler who managed to take three wickets with consecutive balls in a game of cricket was, in earlier times, rewarded with a new top hat from his club.

HAM ACTOR
This expression used to describe not very competent, amateurish performers comes from the time when actors in minstrel shows blackened their faces using ham fat and burnt cork. Nicknamed a 'ham', a minstrel was poorly regarded by colleagues. The name has evolved into the derogatory term known today.

HOBART
This name was chosen by Lieutenant John Bowen in 1803 when he was sent by Governor King to start a settlement on the

Derwent River. Robert Hobart, Earl of Buckinghamshire, was Secretary of State for War and the Colonies from 1801 to 1804. First known as Hobart Town, the name was officially shortened to Hobart in 1881.

JACKPOT
When playing cards the player who had at least a pair of jacks was entitled to all the money paid into the pot thus far. From this, jackpot has come to apply to the stakes which can be won in a whole range of games involving gambling.

KNOCK OFF WORK
Meaning the time to stop an activity, especially one's paid employment, this expression is explained by the practice of Roman galley slave overseers. To ensure uniform rowing, a rhythm was beaten out on wood. A special type of knock indicated when the slaves were permitted to stop for a break, thereby knocking off work.

LIFESAVING REEL AND LINE
Invented by Lyster Ormsby, first captain of the Bondi Club, the reel and line was first used in 1906. Ormsby developed his idea by using a cotton reel and hairpins to determine how the apparatus should work.

THE LOO
Two suggestions have been put forward for the origin of this euphemism for the lavatory, both of which are related to French expressions. One has it that it comes from the French for water, 'l'eau'. The other suggests that at one stage the lavatory was referred to as the place, or in the then French fashion as 'le lieu'. The loo is supposedly a British corruption of the French.

MAYDAY
This international radio telephonic distress signal used by ships and aircraft is an alteration of the French 'm'aidez', meaning 'help me'. A particular wavelength (2.182 kilohertz) is permanently reserved for it. Mayday is the voice-radio equivalent of the Morse code SOS signal.

MELBA TOAST
Supposedly created by accident, this thin dry toast was served to Dame Nellie Melba during a stay at the Savoy Hotel in London. In contrast to an expected complaint from Melba she praised the chef for his delicious toast. He, in turn, named this type of toast in her honour.

MELBOURNE
The settlement was named in 1837 by Governor Richard Bourke after the British Prime Minister Lord Melbourne.

MOTHERING SUNDAY
Observed on the fourth Sunday in Lent this English custom was the day when people in outlying villages visited their 'mother' cathedral. The idea spread to encompass a day for families to be together. Traditionally bunches of violets were given and a special simnel cake eaten.

MOTHER'S DAY
Celebrated in Australia on the second Sunday in May, Mother's Day was first observed in the United States in 1907 when Anna Jarvis of Philadelphia revived the earlier British concept of Mothering Sunday. Congress gave this day official standing in the American calendar in 1914.

MUD IN YOUR EYE
When this expression is used as somebody is about to take an alcoholic drink, the intent is that the drink should be consumed in one go. It probably originates from the resulting sediment left in the bottom of the glass which would presumably land in the drinker's eyes as the glass was tipped right up to down the drink.

OFFSIDER
Referring today to an assistant or helper, the expression comes from nineteenth century Australia when teams of bullocks were used as transports for goods and people. The driver's assistant attended to the bullocks on their offside when it was necessary to urge them on through difficult terrain and roads.

PACIFIC OCEAN
Meaning peaceful, this ocean was named by Ferdinand Magellan during his circumnavigation of the world from east to west in 1520-22. Although subject to storms and huge seas just as other oceans, at the time it seemed particularly peaceful to Magellan in contrast to the waters through which he had just sailed.

PEACH MELBA
This famous dessert was created by George Auguste Escoffier, chef at the Savoy Hotel in London, for Dame Nellie Melba during

a stay at the hotel in 1892-93. Fashioned to resemble a swan, it was comprised of ice-wings coated in icing sugar, peaches resting on vanilla ice-cream and raspberry sauce.

PERTH
The site for the city of Perth was chosen by Captain James Stirling who named it in honour of Sir George Murray, Secretary of State for War and Colonies at that time. Sir George's birthplace was Perthshire in Scotland.

PICNIC
The word picnic comes from the French 'piquer' (to pick) and 'pique-nique' (a coin or other small item). Originally a picnic was a meal where each guest contributed a favourite dish to a joint menu. The contribution was the guest's 'pick' and it was intended to be just a small part of the total menu, hence pique-nique. The meal could be held either indoors or outdoors.

PIN MONEY
This expression comes from the days when pins were handmade and therefore expensive. It was an old English custom for husbands to give wives money on New Year's Day to buy pins for the forthcoming year. From this it has come to mean an allowance or pocket-money.

PLIMSOLL LINE
This line painted onto the hull of a ship indicates the maximum level to which a ship may be loaded with cargo. To overfill, causing this line to be invisible, could lead to the ship capsizing. It was named after Samuel Plimsoll, a British member of Parliament, who fought for legislation to introduce the line after unscrupulous shipowners had caused loss of life by overfilling their ships.

PLONK
Used to refer to any cheap alcoholic liquor, especially wine, it may be a corruption of the French 'vin blanc' from the time when Australian soldiers served in France during World War I. Another suggestion links the word to the sound of a bottle being uncorked.

RAFFERTY'S RULES
A competition or organisation run in a slipshod manner is said to be run according to Rafferty's rules, that is, no rules at all. Its beginnings as an expression are unclear. Some think it may be a reflection on Irish convicts renowned for wild behaviour — Rafferty is a well-known Irish surname. Others suggest it comes from calling an out-of-hand game refractory and that rafferty is an Australian corruption of this word.

RAINING CATS AND DOGS
A variety of explanations have been put forward to explain this expression used to describe extremely heavy rainfall. One suggests it originated in the seventeenth century when heavy rain would result in many of the numerous wild cats and dogs being drowned. People imagined the corpses had actually come down from the sky with the rain. Another explanation suggest the expression is a corruption of the Greek 'catadupa' meaning 'waterfall'. Others link it with Norse mythology, where dogs were associates of Odin, god of thunder, and cats symbolised rain.

RED HERRING
This has come to mean something which is used to divert attention. Fox hunters used to train dogs by dragging a smoked herring across a fox's trail. Its smell was meant to cover up the fox's scent and lead the hounds off on a false trail.

RED TAPE
This expression originates from the pink-red tape used by public servants in England in the seventeenth century to tie up official documents. It now denotes delay and inaction.

RODEO
Many of the original cowboys were Mexican and part of their duties was to round up cattle. The Spanish word for surrounding and encircling is 'rodea' and competitions which allowed cowboys to display their prowess became known as rodeos.

SLEEPERS
The timber supports for railway lines laid at regular intervals were called sleeping timbers. At first they simply maintained the correct distance between the two parallel rails but as longitudinal rail supports were dispensed with, sleepers took over the function of rail supports. In spite of this active role, they retained their old passive name of sleepers.

SLOUCH HAT
Colonel Tom Price of the Victorian Mounted Rifles is thought to have instituted the upturned side of the military hat in 1885. The right side was turned up to allow free movement of the right hand and arm when saluting. In 1890 the Australian army adopted this hat but, after Federation, Commonwealth soldiers were issued with a hat which turned up on the left to allow for marching with rifles at the slope.

SON OF A GUN
On occasions women sailed on ships of the Royal Navy but were hidden from view in quarters between the guns. If a son of uncertain paternity was born he was listed as 'son of a gun' in the ship's log. The term became one of abuse and contempt. Another tradition links the term to the Hewbrew-Yiddish slang 'gunnef', meaning 'thief'.

STRIKES
When sailors wished to make their ship inoperative they lowered or 'struck' the sails. The word came to mean any stoppage by industrial action.

SYDNEY
Viscount Sydney submitted the original plan for a convict settlement at Botany Bay, hence Captain Arthur Phillip's choice of the name. After deciding that Botany Bay was unsuitable, Phillip moved north to Port Jackson and established the settlement at the place he named Sydney Cove.

TIPS
The derivation of tip is uncertain. It could be an acronym from eighteenth century England for to insure prompt service, supposedly written on special boxes placed in inns where customers could leave coins for waiters. Some say it is derived from stipend (which comes from the Latin 'stips') meaning a contribution or gift, or that it could come from an Old English word meaning a present.

TO BE FLAT OUT
To be flat out is to be extremely busy, sparing no effort in achieving a specific aim. The expression comes from car racing where the accelerator has to be fully depressed until it is flat out on the floor to achieve maximum speed.

TO GET THE SACK
Getting the sack is thought to have originated in England during the Industrial Revolution. Tradesmen were required to supply their own tools and if their services were no longer required they were given a sack by their employer in which to carry their tools home.

TO PULL THE LEG
The present-day meaning of this expression came from the practice of thieves. When attempting to rob a pedestrian, one would trip a passerby with a curved stick while the other removed valuables before the victim realised what was happening. The expression came to mean something to be laughed at rather than taken seriously, perhaps relating to the loss of dignity associated with the fall.

TO RUN AMOK
From the Malay word 'amuk', originally meaning to go beserk in battle, the word amok has come to refer to frenzied, uncontrollable state in which a person runs wild, often causing bloodshed.

TO SHOUT (A DRINK)
This derives from an English custom of shouting for the waiter in an inn to serve drinks to an individual's friends. It became widely used during the Australian goldrushes where those striking gold would celebrate by buying drinks for their mates. Pubs were crowded and noisy so it was necessary to shout the order. The act itself and the object of the act became one.

TOUCH AND GO
Deriving from Britain's past as a maritime nation, this expression refers to situations which are precarious. It comes from the occasion when a ship almost ran aground. The ship would 'touch' the bottom without sticking and be able to float clear (go) again.

WALTZING MATILDA
While a number of explanations exist about the origins of this song the one thought to be closest to the truth was first published by Sydney May in 1944 in a book *The Story of Waltzing Matilda*. Banjo Paterson, while staying at Winton in Queensland in 1885, heard a tune played on an autoharp which was later identified as a melody based on an old Scottish ballad. Taken with the tune, he looked for an Australian theme to write

words for it. He drew on a story of a swagman who, after stealing sheep, feared he would be arrested by two policeman and an Aborigine who came upon him by surprise. The swaggie jumped into deep water and drowned. Paterson coupled this story with an expression he heard from an overseer at Winton about seeing 'a couple of men waltzing Matilda down the billabong'. Waltzing Matilda meant to hump your swag (bundle of possessions) about.

WHAT THE DICKENS
The dickens in this exclamation is a euphemism for the devil. Used for centuries, it was meant to disguise the actual name of the devil in case the call upon him was answered.

WHITE ELEPHANT
An ancient Siamese tradition was that a white (albino) elephant, because of its rarity did not work and became the property of the king. To show displeasure with a courtier the king would give him one of the elephants. The huge appetite of the animal would eventually financially ruin the courtier. The expression has thus come to mean something which is useless and expensive.

WOWSER
This term is widely used to refer to somebody who is a prudish teetotaller and kill-joy. It is attributed to John Norton, founder of the Sydney *Truth*, who coined the acronym in the 1890s from the slogan We Only Want Social Evils Remedied. He used the term wowser to describe a pious political opponent.

H.V.

Sources:
Brasch, R. *How Did it Begin? Customs and Superstitions and their Romantic Origins.* Fontana/Collins, Sydney, 1985.
Brasch, R. *Mistakes, Misnomers and Misconceptions.* Fontana/Collins, Sydney, 1983.
Brasch, R. *There's a Reason for Everything: More Customs and Superstitions and How They All Began.* Fontana/Collins, Sydney, 1982.
Hall, T. *How Did Things Start?* Collins, Sydney, 1979.
Rusden, J. et. al. *The Book of the Year.* Oxford University Press, Melbourne, 1984.

Morse Code

Alphabet
A	._	N	_.
B	_...	O	___
C	_._.	P	._ _.
D	_..	Q	_ _._
E	.	R	._.
F	.._.	S	...
G	_ _.	T	_
H	....	U	.._
I	..	V	..._
J	._ _ _	W	._ _
K	_._	X	_.._
L	._..	Y	_._ _
M	_ _	Z	_ _..

Figures
1 ._ _ _ _
2 .._ _ _
3 ..._ _
4 ...._
5 .....
6 _....
7 _ _...
8 _ _ _..
9 _ _ _ _.
0 _ _ _ _ _

Punctuation
. ...
, ._._._
; _._._.
: _ _ _...
? .._ _..
! _ _.._ _

Army Signalling Code
1	._	6	_....
2	.._	7	_ _...
3	..._ _	8	_ _ _..
4	...._	9	_ _..
5	.	0	_

Braille Alphabet

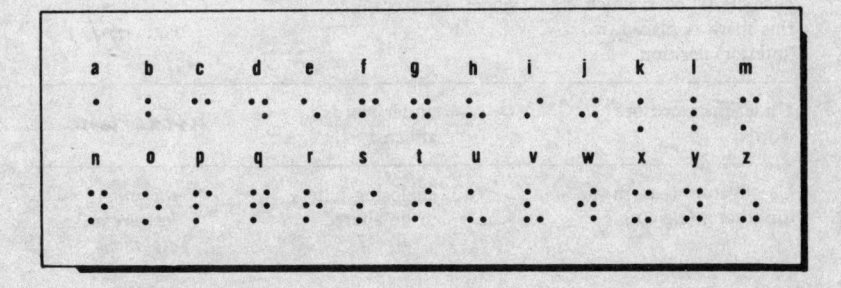

PROOFREADER'S MARKS

Instruction	Textual mark	Marginal mark
GENERAL TEXT INSTRUCTIONS		
Correction is concluded	None	/
Insert in text the matter indicated in margin	⋏	New matter followed by /
Delete	Strike through characters to be deleted	♂
Delete and close up	⌒ above and ⌣ below letters to be taken out	♂̂
Leave as printed	. . . . under characters to remain	*stet*
Substitute or insert character(s) under which this mark is placed, in 'superior' position	/ through character or ⋏ where required	⏻ under character (e.g. ⌇)
Substitute or insert character(s) over which this mark is placed, in 'inferior' position	/ through character or ⋏ where required	⋎ over character (e.g. ⌇)
Underline word or words	——— under words affected	*underline*
Use ligature (e.g. ffi) or diphthong (e.g. œ)	⌣ enclosing letters to be altered	⌢ enclosing ligature or diphthong required
Substitute separate letters for ligature or diphthong	/ through ligature or diphthong to be altered	*write out separate letters followed by* /
Indent one em	⌐	□
Indent two ems	⊏	□□
Move matter to right	[at left or right side of group to be moved	[

PROOFREADER'S MARKS • 329

Instruction	Textual mark	Marginal mark
Move matter to left	⎬ at right or left side of group to be moved	⎬
Move matter to position indicated	[ ] at limits of required position	move
Take over character(s) or line to next line, column or page	⌐	take over
Take back character(s) or line to previous line, column or page	⌐	take back
Raise lines*	⎯⎯⏉⎯⎯ over lines to be moved ⎯⎯⎣⎯⎦⎯⎯ under lines to be moved	raise
Lower lines*	⎯⎤⎯⎡⎯⎯ over lines to be moved ⎯⎯↓⎯⎯ under lines to be moved	lower
Correct the vertical alignment	‖	‖
Straighten lines	═══ through lines to be straightened	═══
Push down space	Encircle space affected	⊥
Begin a new paragraph	⌐ before first word of new paragraph	n.p.
No fresh paragraph here	⌒ between paragraphs	run on
Spell out abbreviation or figure in full	Encircle words or figures to be altered	spell out
Insert omitted portion of copy	∧	out - see copy
Refer to appropriate authority anything of doubtful accuracy	Encircle words etc., affected	ⓘ
Transpose	⌐⎯⌐ between characters or words	trs

* Amount of space may be indicated.

330 • FACTS AND FIGURES

Instruction	Textual mark	Marginal mark
Place in centre of line	Indicate position with ⌈ ⌉	centre

LETTERING STYLE

Instruction	Textual mark	Marginal mark
Change to italic	——— under characters to be altered	ital
Change to even small capitals	══ under characters to be altered	s.c.
Change to capital letters	══ under characters to be altered	caps
Use capital letters for initial letters and small capitals for rest of words	══ under initial letters and ══ under the rest of the words	c. & s.c.
Change to bold type	~~~ under characters to be altered	bold
Change to lower case	Encircle characters to be altered	l.c.
Change to roman type	Encircle characters to be altered	rom.
Wrong font. Replace by letter of correct font	Encircle character to be altered	w.f.
Invert type	Encircle character to be altered	⊙
Change damaged character(s)	Encircle character(s) to be altered	×

LETTERING SPACE

Instruction	Textual mark	Marginal mark
Close up – delete space between characters	⌒ linking characters	⌒
Insert space*	⋏	#
Insert space between lines or paragraphs*	> between lines to be spaced	#

* Amount of space may be indicated.

Instruction	Textual mark	Marginal mark
Reduce space between lines*	( ) connecting lines to be closed up	less # or close up
Make space appear equal between words	| between words	eq. #
Reduce space between words*	| between words	less #
Add space between letters*	|||| between tops of letters requiring space	letter #

PUNCTUATION MARKS

Instruction	Textual mark	Marginal mark
Substitute or insert comma	/ through character or ∧ where required	,/
Substitute or insert semicolon	/ through character or ∧ where required	;/
Substitute or insert full stop	/ through character or ∧ where required	⊙
Substitute or insert colon	/ through character or ∧ where required	⊙
Substitute or insert question mark	/ through character or ∧ where required	?/
Substitute or insert exclamation mark	/ through character or ∧ where required	!/
Insert parentheses	∧ or ∧∧	(/)/
Insert brackets	∧ or ∧∧	[/]/
Insert hyphen	∧	|-|
Insert en (half-em) rule	∧	⊢en⊣
Insert one-em rule	∧	⊢em⊣
Insert two-em rule	∧	⊢2em⊣
Insert apostrophe	∧	'/

* Amount of space may be indicated.

Instruction	Textual mark	Marginal mark
Insert single quotation marks	⋏ or ⋏⋏	⁋ ⁋
Insert double quotation marks	⋏ or ⋏⋏	" "
Insert ellipsis	⋏	... /
Insert leader	⋏	⊙
Insert diagonal stroke	⋏	/

* Amount of space may be indicated.

KEEPING COOL
FOOD PRESERVATION IN AUSTRALIA BEFORE THE DOMESTIC ELECTRIC REFRIGERATOR

FOOD SAFE
One of the earliest methods used by rural settlers for keeping meat and other perishable food was a bag suspended under a verandah or tree. The circulation of air would cool water, usually stored in a canvas bag, and help preserve meat which was kept in a sugar bag. The method was refined into the food safe, a wooden box with timber shelves, sides and a hinged door of fine wire or zinc mesh. The wire prevented insects and flies from contaminating the contents and allowed air to circulate.

COOLGARDIE SAFE
The Coolgardie Safe, often known by its abbreviated form as cool safe, was a tall stand which supported a water tank on top and wooden shelves inside the framework. The outside was covered in fine wire mesh. Draped around the outside of the mesh was a hessian curtain kept clear of the wooden frame by wires. Wicks ran from the top to the curtain, wetting it. The evaporating water from the curtain reduced the temperature of the air inside the frame thus preserving food stored on the shelves. The stronger and hotter the breezes, the faster was the evaporation and so greater the cooling effect. The curtain hem rested on a drip tray at the bottom of the safe to collect any water which did not evaporate. This water could then be recirculated. Later, more elaborate cool safes used limestone-slab sides.

COOL ROOM
Sometimes a separate small mud-brick structure was built near to the home. It had mud walls sixty centimetres or more thick as insulation against the heat outside. The roof was made of iron, but the heat passing through was reduced by layers of bark. Any openings or windows were covered with fine wire mesh or muslin. Perishables were then stored inside.

STORES OVER WATER TANKS AND WELLS
Food could be successfully stored on shelves constructed inside household water tanks or wells. Small openings at the top allowed the air to circulate and its contact with the water reduced the temperature in the internal space between the water level and the roof or cover.

ICE CHEST

Ice chests, which became popular in the 1850s, were simple wooden cabinets which had been lined with cork or sawdust for insulation. The internal compartment was further lined with zinc sheeting and contained perforated or wire shelves. At the top of the chest was a separate section for a large block of ice. A water pipe connected this section to a drip tray at the bottom to drain the melted ice.

When first introduced, the expense of the ice, which had to be imported from America, precluded all but the wealthy from purchasing a chest. A report from the 1850s states that the chest used 50 pounds (22.7 kilograms) of ice per week at a cost of £4 10s. When ice was locally produced the cost went down and so the chest became a feature of most kitchens.

KEROSENE REFRIGERATOR

Although refrigeration as a process has been used in Australia since the 1880s to transport beef and mutton to England, domestic refrigerators did not come onto the market until 1923. In that year Edward Hallstrom started making refrigerators powered by kerosene. The fridges were large cabinets with a top-opening lid, rather like modern upright freezers in appearance. The kerosene was stored in a large round tank above the cabinet. Later models had a flat rectangular tank which slid under the bottom of the fridge. This type of tank held about 1 gallon (4.5 litres) of kerosene, which lasted for approximately three to four days. These refrigerators were quite efficient and were still widely used in the 1950s especially in rural homesteads where electricity was not connected.

H.V.

Sources:

Smith, R. and Johnson, A. *Pioneer Australia*. Curry O'Neil, Melbourne, 1981.

Symons, M. *One Continuous Picnic: A History of Eating in Australia*. Duck Press, Adelaide, 1982.

Unstead, R. J. and Henderson, W. F. *Pioneer Home Life in Australia*. A. & C. Black, London, 1971.

HOW THE AUSTRALIAN ECONOMY WORKS

THE ECONOMIC PROBLEM

The *economic problem* is that resources are limited whilst wants are not. There are several dimensions to this problem. For example, consumer wants for food, clothing, housing, and entertainment cannot be fully satisfied because incomes are constrained. Thus consumers must aim to satisfy those wants which are most pressing. Also, in choosing to increase income by working longer hours, workers are forgoing leisure time in which to enjoy consumption. It is not possible to maximise both income and leisure simultaneously, so a choice must be made between work and leisure activities. The need to choose among alternatives illustrates the nature of the economic problem and is fundamental to economics.

Markets resolve the problem of the scarcity of resources relative to wants. They achieve this by establishing prices which indicate the value of goods and services, thereby facilitating choice among alternatives. *Prices* are determined by the market forces of supply and demand. In the labour market, the most productive workers will be in greatest demand and command the highest wages (e.g. one astute decision by an investment adviser may save a client millions of dollars). Similarly, wages will be highest for labour which is skilled and in relatively short supply (e.g. surgeons). Wages are a signal to both workers and firms of the value of labour services. Thus workers will be influenced by wages in choosing between work and leisure. Higher wages should ultimately increase the size of the labour force by encouraging more women to take up work. They may also reduce the demand for labour by inducing firms to substitute machinery for labour in production.

In capitalist economies where resources are owned by individuals, the fundamental problems of what, how and for whom to produce are resolved through the exchange of goods and services in markets. With potential buyers and sellers responding to prices, markets will clear where supply equals demand and with all mutually advantageous trades accomplished. Modern money-using markets for commodities and labour services facilitate *specialisation*. By enabling firms to concentrate on the production of particular commodities and permitting labour to be employed where it is most productive, specialisation improves efficiency and promotes faster economic growth. This is borne out by the experience of the Industrial Revolution in eighteenth century Europe, when the emergence of sophisticated commodity and labour markets promoted significant advances in productivity through economies of large scale production.

THE CIRCULAR FLOW OF INCOME

Households and firms, the main consumption and production units of any economy, exchange goods and services on commodity markets and labour services on labour markets. Since output and labour services are exchanged for money, this gives rise to what economists call the *circular flow of income*. There are two types of flow between households and firms. First there are the real or physical flows of labour services (from households to firms) and of goods and services (from firms to households). However, the real flows generate equivalent money flows in the reverse direction (e.g. firms pay incomes to households and households pay firms for goods and services). These money flows are depicted in Figure 1 by the symbols Y for income and C for consumption.

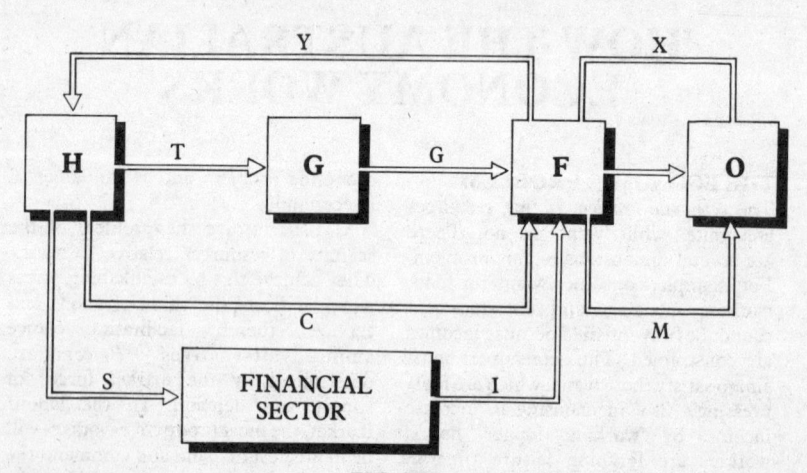

FIGURE 1
Sectors are shown by symbols to denote households (H), firms (F), government (G) and overseas (O). Similarly, money flows are income (Y), consumers' expenditure (C), savings (S), investment (I), taxes (T), government expenditures (G), exports (X) and imports (M). The arrows into a sector represent receipts whilst the arrows out are payments.

THE ROLE OF FINANCE

The household sector relies extensively on finance. For example, households save by purchasing securities such as interest-bearing deposits issued by banks, building societies, credit unions etc. or shares and debentures issued by firms. Financial institutions in turn grant loans or extend credit to households and firms. By creating a market in securities, the financial sector of the economy increases opportunities for exchange. For example, households can make choices such as decreasing present consumption in return for more consumption later by using financial assets as a store of potential future consumption. Indeed, it is common for the same household to save and dissave at different stages of its life cycle, thereby maintaining fairly steady consumption over time. Some economists believe that higher interest rates provide a strong incentive to save by inducing individuals to defer consumption.

Financial markets also enhance efficiency in the firm sector of the economy by giving firms more options for financing the purchase of capital goods such as buildings and equipment. By issuing shares and debentures, firms can borrow from households and financial institutions. These financial flows are depicted in Figure 2. From the viewpoint of households, shares and debentures are a claim on the real assets or capital goods of firms. Thus, ultimately, capital goods are owned by households. Without financial markets, investment expenditure would largely have to be financed out of retained earnings and through direct financing. Access to external finance, particularly at a time of low profits, facilitates greater investment within the economy.

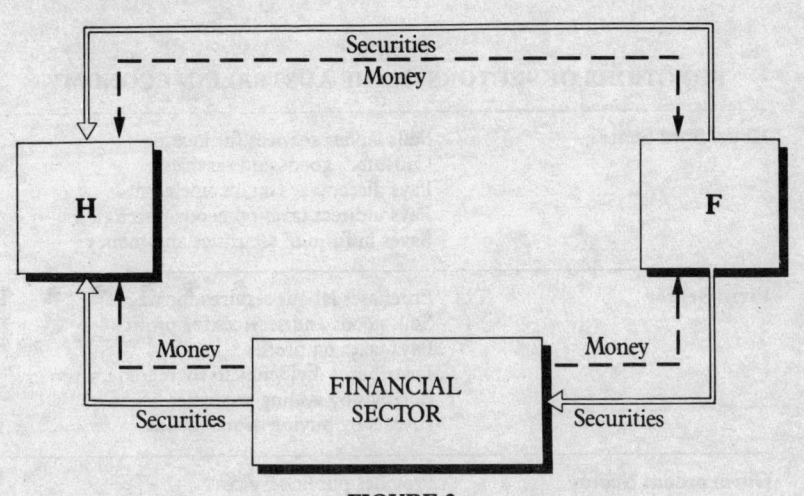

FIGURE 2

Saving is depicted as money flows between the household, financial and firm sectors. The financial flows associated with the government and overseas sectors are ignored in Figure 2.

From the overview of the functions of the major sectors of the Australian economy (provided in Table 1), it can be seen that the government and overseas sectors also rely extensively on financial markets. Governments borrow to finance budget deficits (i.e. an excess of spending over revenues) by issuing treasury notes and bonds. Similarly, overseas borrowing, or trade in financial securities, enables the spending of a country to diverge temporarily from its income. It is the function of foreign exchange markets to facilitate the swapping of the currencies of different countries so that domestic and overseas residents can exchange both commodities and financial assets. Significantly, the growth of international commodity and financial markets has encouraged countries to specialise in the production of goods and services in which they have a comparative advantage. This has contributed significantly to growth in the world economy.

The financial sector of the economy is unique because of its intermediary function. Financial institutions such as banks, money market corporations and finance companies, specialise in borrowing and lending. By accepting deposits and granting loans, funds flow between the various sectors of the economy and enhance the efficiency of commodity markets. It is difficult to envisage commodity markets operating as effectively without credit or transactions between money and financial assets. In essence, financial institutions issue securities to sectors which have surplus funds available for lending. By definition, surplus sectors save more than they invest. In turn they purchase securities issued by sectors which are short of funds and need to borrow. The result is a flow of funds from surplus to deficit sectors matched by a flow of securities in the reverse direction, with flows being channelled through financial intermediaries.

TABLE 1
FUNCTIONS OF SECTORS IN THE AUSTRALIAN ECONOMY

Household Sector	Sells labour services for income Consumes goods and services Pays direct taxes on income earnt Pays indirect taxes on goods purchased Saves in form of securities and money
Firm Sector	Purchases labour services for wages Sells goods and services for profit Pays taxes on profits Distributes dividends to shareholders Borrows by issuing securities Invests by buying capital goods
Government Sector	Provides public services Levies taxes on incomes and goods Redistributes income via transfers Borrows by issuing securities Borrows by issuing money
Overseas Sector	Buys and sells goods and services Buys and sells securities
Financial Sector	Borrows by issuing securities Lends by purchasing securities

The sectoral balances and associated borrowing and lending by each sector of the Australian economy are illustrated in Table 2. Typically, the household sector has surplus funds for lending, saving more than it invests in dwellings. Conversely the firm sector is usually a deficit sector because it invests more than it saves in the form of retained profits. Private sector saving (column 1), or saving by households and firms, provides the funds to finance government deficits (column 2) and investment (column 6). The government sector has been a substantial net borrower with deficits increasing relative to gross domestic product until 1985–86, but subsequently decreasing. In Australia, national saving (column 3), or saving by the private sector net of government sector dissaving, has always been insufficient to finance investment.

This shortfall has been made up by overseas borrowing (column 4), which has increased steadily as a proportion of gross domestic product (GDP) throughout the 1980s.

It can be appreciated that imbalances between income and expenditure flows (or their counterpart of saving and investment flows) may exist for each sector of the economy. Such imbalances can only be financed by borrowers incurring liabilities (i.e. issuing financial securities) and lenders acquiring claims (i.e. purchasing financial securities). For the economy as a whole, it is the sale of securities to the rest of the world which has enabled Australians to consume more goods and services than they produce. Borrowing from overseas finances current account deficits on the balance of payments.

TABLE 2
SAVING AND PRIVATE INVESTMENT
(Per Cent of GDP)

		Saving				Investment
Year	Private	Govt	National	Overseas	Total	
Average— 1974-75 to 1979-80	19.6	-4.5	15.1	2.0	17.1	16.2
Year— 1980-81	18.8	-3.7	15.1	3.6	18.7	18.5
1981-82	17.2	-3.9	13.3	5.8	19.1	19.1
1982-83	16.2	-6.3	9.9	4.5	14.4	16.2
1983-84	19.7	-7.3	12.4	3.7	16.1	15.1
1984-85	19.1	-6.9	12.2	5.0	17.2	15.6
1985-86	18.3	-6.9	11.4	5.8	17.2	15.9

Source: 1986–87 Budget Paper No. 1, p. 42.

MEASURING THE PERFORMANCE OF THE ECONOMY

A necessary first step in explaining the behaviour of the economy is to measure its performance. There are several indicators of performance including unemployment, inflation, and the balance of payments, but the most fundamental is *gross domestic product* or the total production of goods and services. This can be measured in nominal and real terms. *Nominal GDP* is the dollar value of goods and services that an economy produces during a given period. The contribution of each firm is simply the difference between its *revenue* from sales of output and the cost of *intermediate goods*, such as raw materials. This is called its value added in production. Market prices are used to assign values to output, although government services which are not marketed (e.g. defence services) are valued at their dollar cost of production. Only current production (e.g. new houses) is counted whilst sales of second-hand goods are excluded from GDP.

A difficulty with changes in nominal GDP as a measure of *economic growth* is that underlying movements in physical output may not be apparent when prices change. To overcome this problem associated with changing prices, output is valued in constant prices (i.e. in terms of the prices of goods and services prevailing in a base year). Economists refer to GDP in constant prices as *real GDP*. For Australia in 1987, real GDP measured in 1979-80 prices was $153 billion. Using the same prices to measure GDP for 1986, we can calculate that real output grew by 4.4 per cent in 1987. Growth of real GDP is a much better indicator of how an economy is performing. However, it is difficult to make valid comparisons of real GDP over a large number of years because the market share of each good in production changes gradually over time due to changes in demand patterns and the emergence of new commodities. Ultimately such changes necessitate the designation of a new base year so that valid comparisons can be drawn.

Real GDP per capita is widely used by economists as a measure of a nation's *standard of living*, or its potential consumption. However, it is an imperfect measure because it says nothing about the *distribution of income* across households. Leisure time and a variety of non-market services performed in the home are excluded from GDP but these too are relevant to the standard of living. Also transactions, both legal and illegal, in the underground economy are not counted. This is why economists look at a multitude of measures of economic performance, including the breakdown of domestic production into purchases of goods by consumers, investors, the government and residents of other economies. Each of the major expenditure types are influenced by different factors, including monetary and fiscal policies.

THE COMPONENTS OF DEMAND

Of the major expenditure items, *private consumption*, or purchases of goods and services by households for their own use, comprised 57.5 per cent of real GDP in Australia in 1987. Consumption includes goods such as non-durables (e.g. food and clothing), services (e.g. tourism) and consumer durables (e.g. washing machines and motor cars) which yield a flow of services over many periods. Typically, households are reluctant to reduce consumption unless incomes fall permanently.

Gross *private investment* comprises purchases of new capital goods such as machinery, the construction of factories and the net change in inventories of goods held by firms. Purchases of new dwellings by households are also included in investment. Capital goods are analogous to consumer durables because they can be used by firms to produce goods and services over many years. Total investment by households and firms (excluding purchases of consumer durables which are not officially treated as investment) accounted for approximately 16 per cent of real GDP in 1987. Unlike consumption expenditure, investment is volatile and fluctuates over time. Many economists regard investment expenditure as primarily responsible for cyclical fluctuations in the economy.

A third category of expenditure, *government purchases* of goods and services, comprises consumption and investment expenditures by Commonwealth, state and local governments. Government expenditure accounted for 24.5 per cent of Australia's real GDP in 1987. The government also makes transfer payments (e.g. pensions, unemployment benefits, subsidies), whose function is to redistribute income.

Governments may stimulate consumption and investment by cutting taxes and increasing transfer payments.

The expenditures of the private and government sectors of the economy are aggregated to compute GDP as depicted below:

$$GDP = C + I + G + (X - M)$$

The overseas sector is incorporated by adding exports and subtracting imports. *Exports* (X), or overseas purchases of domestic goods and services, largely comprise rural products, metal ores, mineral fuels and tourism. *Imports* (M), or overseas output which is consumed domestically, is dominated by machinery, equipment and manufactured products. Exports and imports accounted for approximately 20 per cent and 18 per cent respectively of Australia's GDP in 1987. Imports are subtracted because there is a significant import component in each of consumption (C), investment (I) and government expenditure (G). The resulting measure tells us that GDP is total expenditure on domestic output from domestic and overseas sources.

SOME IMPORTANT PRICE INDICATORS

Gross domestic product relates to the quantity of goods and services produced in a given year but economic performance is also measured in terms of the prices that relate to these quantities. For example, the dollar prices of goods and services are of great significance to consumers because they determine the purchasing power of household incomes. This is why real rather than nominal GDP is the better measure of the standard of living. The price level is also important for the competitiveness of Australian industry. Ultimately the prices of Australian goods relative to those of our major competitors determine whether export and import-competing industries can compete on world markets. Economists are particularly interested in the general price level and its rate of change, the *inflation rate*.

The price level for the economy as a whole is measured by an index whose rate of change approximates the inflation rate. The major price index used in Australia is the *consumer price index* (CPI). It is compiled by averaging commodity prices with each commodity weighted in terms of its market share. The CPI is not comprehensive, being based on a representative sample of goods purchased by a typical household. Other significant prices include *wage rates* (i.e. the price of labour services), *interest rates* (i.e. the cost of borrowing and the reward for lending) and *exchange rates* (i.e. the price of exchange between the currencies of different countries). These prices are determined in labour markets, financial markets and foreign exchange markets respectively and play a very important role in determining the level of real output within the economy.

THE BALANCE OF PAYMENTS

The *balance of payments* accounts summarise market transactions between Australian residents and foreigners. They comprise a current account for transactions in goods and services, and a capital account where purchases and sales of securities are recorded. By convention, a balance of payments surplus or deficit refers to the sum of the current and capital accounts. Australia usually spends more than its income, running current account deficits. Such deficits are financed by foreign borrowing, sometimes referred to as net foreign investment, which results in the rest of the world acquiring financial claims on Australia. Thus the current account deficit indicates the rate at which the nation is adding to its *foreign debt*, both private and official.

Australia's current account deficit of $12.3 billion in 1987 comprised exports minus imports (-$0.7 billion), net services (-$3.3 billion), and net income and transfers overseas (-$8.4 billion). The *balance of trade*, or exports minus imports, was particularly large in 1985 and 1986. Typically *net services*, which comprise shipping, insurance etc., are in deficit. Recently, *net income and transfers overseas* have increased sharply, exacerbating a weak current account. This was largely due to the escalation of debt interest payments.

EXCHANGE RATES AND INTEREST RATES

From 1945 to the early 1970s, most countries maintained fixed exchange rates by pegging their currencies to the US dollar. Under this system, the Reserve Bank's role was to maintain a stock of foreign currencies and interest-bearing assets which could be readily converted into US dollars. Such assets would be bought or sold to clear the foreign exchange market at the fixed rate of exchange. For example, when there was a deficit in the balance of payments, more US dollars would be demanded by Australians to pay for foreign goods and assets than were currently being earnt from exports. Consequently the Reserve Bank would sell US dollars for Australian dollars at the fixed rate of exchange.

Since the floating of the Australian dollar in 1983, Australia has generally allowed its exchange rate to vary in order to clear the market for foreign exchange. On occasions, when the Australian dollar came under severe pressure, the Reserve Bank intervened to steady the market. For example, it sold approximately US $1.2 million in mid-1986 to minimise the fall in the Australian dollar, whilst it purchased substantial amounts of foreign currencies later in 1986, when the exchange rate was under strong upward pressure. Reserve Bank intervention in the foreign exchange market, or 'dirty' floating, has implications for the liquidity of the financial system as was the case under fixed exchange rates. The Reserve Bank claims that its intervention is even-handed over time. This means that in the long run, the exchange rate is determined by market forces, as under a free float, whilst in the short run, the Reserve Bank intervenes in an attempt to minimise volatility.

Exchange rates are determined by the interaction of the supply of and demand for Australian dollars on foreign exchange markets. These are influenced by both real and monetary factors such as the level of GDP, the rate of inflation, interest rates and market sentiment or psychology. GDP exerts its influence through the current account. For example, higher domestic income increases the demand for imports, exerting downward pressure on exchange rates, whilst higher income overseas stimulates exports, leading to a currency appreciation. During the years 1983–85, Australia experienced a faster growth rate than the rest of the world. This contributed to imports rising faster than exports, the deterioration in the balance of trade and the depreciation of the Australian dollar from 1985 onwards. The balance of payments acts as a constraint on growth, ultimately forcing governments to introduce measures to slow down growth and take pressure off the currency.

Relative inflation rates are an important determinant of the competitiveness of Australian firms on world markets. Throughout the 1980s, Australia experienced higher inflation rates than most of the OECD economies, resulting in a declining share of world trade and contributing to our current account deficit. As a general rule, the higher the inflation rate of a country, the greater the depreciation of that country's currency.

Interest rates primarily affect the demand for domestic and overseas financial assets thereby influencing exchange rates through capital flows. Characterised by a rapid dissemination of information, international financial markets provide a good example of a relatively perfect market, especially where there are no capital controls. With investors seeking to maximise their returns, funds will flow to countries where interest rates are highest. A country wishing to defend its currency may choose to tighten domestic credit and raise interest rates above world levels, thereby attracting capital inflow and improving the capital account. To the extent that interest rates reflect the inflation rate, high inflation countries will also experience equally high interest rates. High inflation may lead to the expectation of currency depreciation, necessitating higher nominal interest rates on domestic financial assets to compensate for the risk of capital losses associated with depreciation.

AUSTRALIA'S OVERSEAS DEBT CRISIS

In the mid-1980s Australia experienced a rapid deterioration in the current account of the balance of payments. There were several explanations, including strong domestic demand coupled with slow growth in the world economy and a decline in the international competitiveness of Australian industry due to relatively high domestic wage and price inflation. The resources boom of the early 1980s, which at first offered the promise of higher incomes, encouraged substantial overseas borrowing. This led to an appreciation of the Australian dollar which exacerbated the lack of competitiveness of export and import competing industries.

However, a decline in the *terms of trade* (i.e. the prices of tradeable goods and services produced domestically relative to those produced in the rest of the world) was the most significant factor underlying the adverse current account balance. Unfortunately Australia specialises in the production of such tradeables as primary products and minerals, prices of which fell due to depressed world markets. A deterioration in the terms of trade largely affects production and exports, with only minimal effects on consumption and demand. Unless imports fall along with exports, a current account deficit is inevitable. It should be remembered that current account deficits are due to spending by a nation in excess of its income. Thus the problem for policy makers is to induce consumers to accept a reduction in the standard of living or for the nation to increase its saving.

Currency depreciation was the response of the foreign exchange market to Australia's balance of payments problems. The Australian dollar depreciated sharply in 1985 and 1986, but the decline in the current account deficit was slow to arrest. Economists describe this sluggish response as the 'J curve'. With import prices in Australian dollar terms rising by the amount of the depreciation, the Australian experience was that the value of imports rose initially. The problem was that the current account could only improve when export and import volumes had time to adjust. Ultimately these adjustments did take place as demand responded to new prices and as domestic industry acquired the capacity for import replacement and production of more exports.

Australia's overseas debt/GDP ratio has continued to escalate despite improvements in the balance of payments. With much of our debt denominated in US dollars, the currency depreciation increased the value of the debt. This is referred to as a valuation effect. However, high real interest rates, attributable in part to a greater risk premium on overseas borrowings, have made it more difficult to service the debt. The statistics in Table 3 reveal that the net income and transfers deficit, which largely comprises interest on debt, has enlarged the current account deficit. Large deficits today have implications for the current account deficit in the future because the servicing payments on external liabilities appear in the current account in future years. Thus currency depreciation and high interest rates have been jointly responsible for a compounding of Australia's overseas debt crisis.

The first step in the approach of the government to the overseas debt crisis involved a change in policy. The aim was to reduce the reliance on overseas saving by increasing the saving of the domestic economy. This was to be achieved by a series of smaller budget deficits and even surpluses in order to reduce government borrowing and interest rates. Ultimately this should stimulate additional investment and enable the restructuring of industry. Clearly a cut in the government deficit may not be sufficient to improve the current account deficit. For instance, if additional private spending takes the place of a reduced government deficit, then the total overspending of the economy will be unchanged. In order to improve the current account the

TABLE 3
CURRENT ACCOUNT DEFICITS AND NET OVERSEAS DEBT

Year	Balance of Trade Deficit	Transfers Deficit	Current A/C Deficit	Overseas Debt
1959–60 to 1979–80	0.3	2.1	2.4	6.0
1980–81	2.0	2.1	4.1	
1981–82	3.8	2.2	6.0	14.0
1982–83	2.3	1.7	4.0	
1983–84	1.4	2.4	3.8	
1984–85	2.3	2.9	5.2	28.0
1985–86	3.1	2.8	5.9	

Source: EPAC, Council Paper No. 22, October 1986.

overspending of both the private and government sectors must be reduced. This is why current policy is attempting to achieve lower consumption as well as lower government spending.

The second aspect of policy has been to capitalise on the depreciation of the Australian dollar and maintain improved international competitiveness. The objective was to ensure that export demand increases and import replacement continues in the long run. The problem is that depreciation is inflationary because it raises import prices which are reflected in the consumer price index. In Australia, where wages are traditionally indexed to prices, there is the additional problem that currency depreciation may lead to a second round of wage and price increases, exacerbating inflation. In order to prevent this, the government has attempted to break the nexus between wages and prices by arguing for wage increases below the rate of inflation at national wage hearings.

Industry policies and micro-economic reforms have also been implemented with the long term objective of restructuring the Australian economy. It is argued that manufacturing must be fostered in order to reduce our dependence on rural commodities and minerals which are vulnerable to fluctuations in world commodity prices. Industry plans for motor vehicles, textiles, footwear and clothing have been implemented. These involve the introduction of new technology, the retraining of labour and the reduction of tariffs and import quotas. Industry plans are being implemented to facilitate the adjustment process as resources are reallocated to the production of manufactures.

FISCAL POLICY AND GOVERNMENT DEBT

Fiscal policy comprises changes in government expenditures, tax rates and transfer payments as implemented through the budget. Government purchases of goods and services are used to provide public services which would be under-provided or not produced at all by the private sector. There is a range of methods of provision. For example, services such as defence, law and order and public works are publicly produced and provided free of charge whilst other public services, such as those of Qantas and the Commonwealth Bank are marketed like private goods. Depending upon the nature of the product, the private sector can react to the provision of government services by increasing or decreasing output. For example, the private sector will produce more when public services such as ports, railways and roads are provided because productivity is enhanced. Conversely, more provision by government of services such as health and education, which are produced both privately and publicly in Australia, means less private provision.

Transfer payments and taxes influence private behaviour by changing prices or the signals provided by markets to producers and consumers. For example, services such as the arts are privately produced with the assistance of subsidies to ensure that they are available in sufficient quantities. Taxes influence decisions in private markets by changing incentives. For example, lower income tax rates may encourage additional work effort, lower taxes on company profits may increase the amount of investment by firms and changes in taxes on goods and services will influence the pattern of consumer demand. High taxes on interest income also reduce saving by lowering after-tax income.

There have been substantial changes to the Australian tax system since 1985. A flatter rate scale has been introduced for personal income tax with a rate of 49 cents in the dollar for the highest incomes. Reductions in *marginal rates of income tax* at all income levels were made possible because of the additional revenue raised by the introduction of capital gains and fringe benefits taxes. These new taxes are part of a move towards a broadly based income tax. The reforms were designed to reduce widespread tax avoidance induced by high marginal tax rates on middle and upper income groups and further reductions are planned for 1989. As well, taxes and transfers such as social security programs influence the distribution of income within the community and the reforms have aimed to increase the equity of the tax system.

Economists see governments as performing a management role, believing the private sector to be unstable and slow to adjust to market signals. For an economy experiencing excess capacity, a general fall in prices is necessary to clear markets. However, prices and wages are sticky. The inability of prices for goods and labour to fall instantaneously across the economy provides scope for the government to stimulate demand and output by increasing its expenditures and transfers and lowering taxes. Moreover, fiscal policies will be quite effective because the expansion of demand will exert multiplied effects on output.

The *budget deficit* refers to the excess of government expenditures over receipts. Expenditures include outlays on goods, services and debt interest

TABLE 4
BUDGET DEFICITS AND NET GOVERNMENT DEBT
(per cent of GDP)

Year	Primary PSBR	Interest Payments	PSBR	Net Public Sector Debt
1980–81	1.1	2.0	3.1	24.0
1981–82	1.4	2.2	3.6	24.2
1982–83	3.7	2.5	6.2	26.8
1983–84	4.2	3.0	7.2	30.3
1984–85	2.3	3.4	5.7	33.5
1985–86	0.9	3.7	4.6	33.9

Source: EPAC, Council Paper No. 16, March 1986.

payments, while receipts comprise both tax and non-tax revenue. From Table 4, which aggregates the deficits of all levels of government to obtain the public sector borrowing requirement (PSBR), it can be seen that the interest component of deficits has increased substantially in recent years. This has been caused by a build-up of debt following a series of large deficits in the 1970s and early 1980s. High interest rates engendered by the balance of payments crisis have also contributed to government interest payments.

The components of the deficit and its financing may be summarised as follows:-

Outlays – Receipts + Debt Interest = Money Finance + Debt Finance

To finance its total deficit (including the servicing of the debt), the government issues bonds to the non-bank private sector. This is known as *bond finance* and has no effect on the money supply. However, bond finance will tend to raise interest rates and crowd out private expenditures thus reducing the multiplier effects of the budget. Another less desirable method of financing is *money finance*. It involves the Reserve Bank printing money which the government puts into circulation through its budget program. It is possible for a series of large deficits to cause inflation when deficits are money-financed. The Commonwealth government pursues an explicit policy of bond financing, thus ensuring that budgets do not increase the money supply.

Deficits have cyclical and structural components which reflect the two sets of forces at play determining their size. Due to the progressive rate structure of the tax-welfare system, tax revenues decline and transfer payments to the unemployed rise during recessions. Budget deficits automatically become larger because of this cyclical effect. Generally deficits are largest during periods of recession and when interest rates are high. Deficits also rise when more expansionary fiscal policies such as tax cuts and expenditure increases are adopted. Economists describe policy induced increases as the structural component of the deficit and are concerned to avoid large structural deficits because of their ongoing nature. If structural deficits are too large, competition between the government and corporate sectors for funds to finance their respective borrowings will be intense, making it difficult to sustain expansion of activity within the private sector of the economy.

Australian fiscal policy has been markedly contractionary since mid-1985. The government's strategy was to reduce demand, lowering imports and thereby rectifying current account imbalances. It also wanted to relieve pressure on interest rates in the hope that investment would pick up as well as to check the expansion of government debt and interest payments. The fear was that with large and sustained budget deficits, the interest component would cause the deficit to blow-out, as the government would need to borrow more to finance larger deficits and this would increase interest rates. Budgetary flexibility was under threat because the increase in taxes or the cut in outlays necessary to stabilise the debt/GDP ratio becomes progressively larger as deficits are allowed to continue. To stabilise the government/GDP ratio and restore fiscal balance, the government committed itself to no increase in tax revenue and expenditures relative to GDP for the term of one parliament.

Countries such as Japan, Germany and the United Kingdom were among the first to tackle and reduce budget balances in the early 1980s. Unfortunately at this time, the United States under Reagan adopted expansionary fiscal policies, and asymmetries in fiscal balances began to emerge. With the continued demand for savings by countries with significant government deficits, such as the United States, there was upward pressure on world interest rates, with adverse consequences for investment worldwide. Due to international linkages through capital markets, large government deficits in the United States have had their counterpart in large external surpluses elsewhere. Despite conservative fiscal strategies, domestic investment in Europe and Japan has failed to grow as quickly as anticipated because of the incentive to invest abroad. Asymmetries in fiscal balances pose a threat to the continuing stability of the world economy in the late 1980s, with their rectification requiring expansion in the surplus countries and contraction in the deficit countries.

MONETARY POLICY IN AUSTRALIA

The nature of monetary policy in Australia has changed markedly with the *floating of the exchange rate* and *deregulation* of the financial system. A feature of deregulation has been the granting of new bank licences and the removal of Reserve Bank controls over bank lending and interest rates. Competition between banks and non-bank intermediaries such as building societies, credit cooperatives, money market corporations and finance companies has been enhanced with lending now determined by market interest rates.

The Reserve Bank adjusts the supply of money when it chooses to intervene in the domestic money or foreign exchange markets. Money market operations, which involve transactions in government securities, are now the prime instrument of monetary policy in Australia. When the Reserve Bank purchases Commonwealth government bonds or treasury notes (in this case called *rediscounting*), additional money is put into circulation. Changes in the Reserve Bank's portfolio of government securities is referred to as domestic credit. The Reserve Bank also extends credit to the government by financing its deficits and invoking repurchase agreements with authorised money market dealers. Under these agreements, bonds are sold and bought back (or vice versa) at an agreed price, the objective being to smooth seasonal fluctuations in liquidity. Reserve Bank loans to banks and money market dealers will also increase the money supply. Such loans only occur on an irregular basis and at a penal rate of interest to make it unprofitable for the banks to borrow from the Reserve Bank. A *prime assets ratio* (PAR) requirement forces the banks to hold 12 per cent of total Australian dollar assets in liquid assets such as government securities and is used largely for prudential reasons.

Changes in *net foreign assets*, the official foreign reserve holdings of the Reserve Bank, signify intervention in the foreign exchange market. Such intervention is designed to support the exchange rate. When the Reserve Bank buys foreign currencies, this puts more Australian dollars into circulation. However the monetary effects of intervention can be neutralised by Reserve Bank sales of government securities. Such sales withdraw money from circulation and require the Reserve Bank to intervene in the domestic money market.

Reserve Bank intervention in domestic money and foreign exchange markets (i.e. purchases of government securities or foreign currencies) enables the private banks to acquire excess reserves and increase their lending to the public. Bank deposits expand by some multiple of the increase in liquidity generated by the Reserve Bank. However, the banks are limited in their ability to create new deposits and money by their own reserve requirements and by the demand of the public for currency. Ultimately the banks are constrained by the excess reserves made available to them by Reserve Bank actions in money markets.

As a result of financial innovation and deregulation, traditional relationships between monetary aggregates and indicators of economic performance have been distorted. In 1985, the Reserve Bank abandoned its previous policy of targeting the monetary aggregate M3 (comprising currency held by the non-bank public and bank deposits of trading and saving banks). Currently, it monitors a 'check list' of financial and economic indicators (e.g. interest rates, exchange rates, money aggregates, inflation and unemployment) to determine whether monetary policies should be changed.

Money plays a significant role in ensuring a smoothly operating economy. It is used to buy or sell goods, labour services and financial assets and as such is demanded as a medium of exchange. It is also a store of wealth. One of the Reserve Bank's tasks is to predict the demand for money by the community and to ensure its supply is adequate. If the money supply is too great, this will result in excess demand for real output and, subsequently, inflation. The problem with inflation is that it erodes the real value of money holdings, making them less attractive relative to other assets. When inflation rises, money cannot offer a competitive yield (e.g. the currency component of money offers no interest at all) and people will substitute interest-bearing financial assets or other inflation hedges such as precious metals and jewellery.

Economists tend to view inflation, or chronic rises in the general price level, as associated with too much money. Thus the prime responsibility of the monetary authorities is to ensure financial stability. Monetary policy is potentially a powerful tool which, if mismanaged, may lead to real disturbances and cyclical fluctuations in the economy. With prices slow to adjust to clear all markets, and with incomplete information about prices in various markets, an erratic monetary policy will result in booms and recessions in real activity. It is for this reason that many economists advocate monetary targeting to ensure a steady expansion of the money supply in line with the real demand for money in a growing economy.

WAGES POLICY IN AUSTRALIA

The wage determination system in Australia is based on minimum wages or awards established by the Australian Conciliation and Arbitration Commission and state wage tribunals. At a tripartite conference in March 1983, government, unions and business groups reached the Accord Mark I which endorsed a return to the earlier centralised wage system along with the principle of full wage indexation to prices. The aim was to ensure that money wage increases continued to fall in line with inflation.

With the deterioration in the terms of trade and the threat of a depreciation induced price-wage spiral, the government attempted to use its influence over wage determination as a tool of macro-economic management. When the Accord Mark II was negotiated in September 1985, the principle of indexation was modified, with the Arbitration Commission required to consider the state of the economy. Accordingly, at subsequent national wage cases, the commission acceded to government and business arguments for discounting the effects of price movements induced by the depreciation of the Australian dollar.

The Accord Mark III, a two-tier wage determination process involving both centralised and decentralised negotiations, was established in 1987. The first tier has taken the form of flat rate national wage increases. The second tier involves percentage increases up to a ceiling of 4 per cent. These increases are negotiated on an industry-by-industry basis and are ratified when improvements in productivity are agreed upon.

Economists refer to a set of wage principles designed to modify economic performance as a *wages or incomes policy*. Since 1983, the wages policy pursued in Australia has been remarkably successful in taking pressure off the other policy arms of the government. With wages rising more slowly than prices, a fall in real wages has been achieved, with the loss in real incomes moderated by reductions in income taxes in 1986 and 1987. The fall in real wages has reduced consumer demand and insulated domestic prices from overseas influences. Both results were consistent with the government's overall strategy of restructuring the domestic economy and diversifying its manufacturing base. The flexibility of labour markets has also been enhanced by incentives for productivity improvements and by the partial decentralisation of wage negotiations.

CONCLUSIONS
Australia faces a crucial period in its economic history. There have been declines in living standards for the first time since the war and policies have been implemented to revitalise the economy so that sustained growth is possible. There is to be a shift in the structure of the economy from primary industries to manufacturing and services but successful restructuring requires community acceptance of falling real wages and smaller government deficits in the short term. Unless Australia rises to the challenge and succeeds in its endeavours to diversify its manufacturing base, it may go the way of those prophets of doom who have predicted a decline into 'banana republic' status.

T. W.

AUSTRALIAN CURRENCY

EIGHTEENTH CENTURY
When the colony of New South Wales was first established as a penal settlement, no consideration had been given to the issue of currency. Convicts received no wages and civil and military personnel were to be provided for by the British government. As a consequence, a variety of forms of exchange existed. Foreign and British coins brought by the settlers and mariners were used with store receipts, promissory notes and bills on the British Treasury but barter in rum, tea, sugar, flour and other produce was by far the greatest form of exchange. Insufficient currency, especially a shortage of coins, together with an over-reliance on privately issued notes were major problems until the mid-nineteenth century.

NINETEENTH CENTURY
The Holey Dollar:
An attempt to issue an 'Australian' coinage was made by Governor Macquarie when ten thousand pounds worth of Spanish dollars arrived in the colony in 1812. Macquarie decreed the centre of the coin be punched out, making two coins: the outer ring being the 'holey dollar' worth five shillings, and the 'dump' worth fifteen pence. Both the holey dollar and the dump were overstruck with the words 'New South Wales 1813'.

1826 Legislation:
The Spanish dollar was beginning to emerge as the standard form of currency. The Bank of New South Wales, first established in 1817, had little effect on the currency shortage and although it began to issue notes in Spanish dollars these just added to the plethora of paper notes already in use. In 1826 the British government decreed that British sterling pounds, shillings and pence were to be the official money used in the colony. Spanish dollars passed out of use by 1830.

Economic Expansion:
Rapid economic growth coupled with the effects of the goldrushes exacerbated the shortage of coins. Store receipts, promissory notes, private banknotes and tradesmen's tokens abounded in lieu of coins. In some states attempts were made to issue a distinct coinage. Victoria's so-called 'Kangaroo Office' set up by a syndicate of English businessmen hoping to cash in on low gold prices, produced a small number of gold pieces before the venture failed. In South Australia the government produced the 'Adelaide Office Pound' or 'Sovereign' in 1852 but had ceased minting the coin by 1853.

The Establishment of Mints:
A branch of the British Royal Mint was opened in Sydney in 1855 for the purpose of creating coins with some of the gold then readily available as a result of the gold rushes. The first Australian coins to be minted were gold sovereigns and half sovereigns bearing the inscription 'Australia, Sydney Mint'. Further branches were opened in Melbourne in 1872 and

Perth in 1899. After 1871, coins issued bore the same design as British coins with the addition of the letter 'S' if minted in Sydney, 'M' for Melbourne and later, 'P' for those struck in Perth.

TWENTIETH CENTURY

At Federation, currency in use in Australia comprised British silver and bronze coins, Australian-minted sovereigns and half sovereigns, private banknotes and Queensland Government Treasury notes. Silver coins were struck in 1910, followed by bronze pennies and halfpennies in 1911. Coinciding with the introduction of this new Australian minted coinage was the 1910 Bank Notes Act which gave the Commonwealth government the sole right to issue notes. Existing private and Queensland government notes were overprinted with the words 'Australian Note' until the Treasury issued a new set of Commonwealth notes in 1913. The function of issuing notes was transferred to the Commonwealth Bank in 1920. New sets of notes were issued in 1920, 1933 and on the accession of King George VI and Queen Elizabeth II. Similarly, new coins were issued with each change in the monarchy.

1966 Decimal Currency:

On 14 February 1966 dollars and cents replaced pounds, shillings and pence as legal tender. During the period of transition both currencies were used while the pounds, shillings and pence were gradually withdrawn.

The coins issued at that time, the 1c (bronze), 2c (bronze), 5c (cupro-nickel), 10c (cupro-nickel), 20c (cupro-nickel) and 50c (silver), were designed by Stuart Devlin. The reverse of the coins featured native Australian animals, the obverse had a portrait of Queen Elizabeth II designed by Arnold Machin. The high cost of silver led to the withdrawal of the 50c piece in 1969 and its replacement with a twelve-sided cupro-nickel coin. Three new coins, $1, $2, and $200 have been introduced since: the $1 in 1984; the $2 in 1988; and the 22 carat gold $200, designed by Stuart Devlin, in 1980. Coins minted since 1985 show a new portrait of the Queen by Raphael Maklouf, the third such portrait of the Queen to be issued on Australian coins during her reign.

Special issue coins have been minted from time to time to commemorate a specific event like the XII Commonwealth Games in Brisbane (1982) and the International Year of Peace (1986). They have a design appropriate to the occasion substitued for the illustration of the native animal. The $10 Bicentennial Commemorative Issue silver coin, designed by Stuart Devlin, shows the sailing ships of the First Fleet with a landing party in the foreground rowing ashore. Only a limited number were minted and sold for $40 when released in April 1988.

The original note denominations issued in 1966 and designed by Gordon Andrews were the $1, $2, $10 and $20 notes. The $5 and $50 notes were introduced in 1967 and 1973 respectively, also designed by Gordon Andrews. The notes, except the $1 which showed Aboriginal art, featured portraits of prominent Australians. The $100 note came into circulation in 1984 and continued the famous Australians motif, while in the same year the $1 note was phased out of circulation.

H.V.

Sources:

The Australian Encyclopaedia. Grolier, Sydney, 1983.

Robertson, P. *Guiness Book of Australian Firsts.* Collins, Australia, 1987.

Rusden, J. *et. al. The Book of the Year.* Oxford University Press, Melbourne, 1984.

VOLUME OF MONEY

(*Source:* Reserve Bank of Australia)
($ million)

Average of weekly figures for month of–	Notes and coin in hands of public	Deposits of public with all trading banks(a) Current	Fixed	Certificates of deposit	Deposits with all savings banks(b)	Total Original	Seasonally adjusted
1986							
October	9,043	15,469	33,314	3,654	44,041	105,521	105,489
November	9,162	15,333	33,349	3,145	44,274	105,263	105,841
December(c)	9,538	16,409	34,118	2,556	45,054	107,675	106,645
1987							
January	9,349	16,451	34,501	2,583	45,690	108,573	108,197
February	9,305	16,325	34,934	2,731	45,806	109,101	108,767
March	9,350	16,998	34,996	2,598	46,808	110,750	110,641
April	9,525	17,018	35,214	2,393	48,352	112,502	112,321
May	9,481	16,988	34,588	2,483	49,823	113,363	114,474
June	9,598	17,046	34,493	2,544	51,563	115,244	115,766
July	9,739	17,534	34,607	2,568	53,075	117,522	117,081
August	9,811	17,391	33,911	2,616	53,956	117,685	118,120
September	9,944	18,387	33,645	2,681	54,643	119,301	119,106
October	10,101	19,498	33,823	2,607	55,189	121,219	121,077
November	10,280	19,672	34,887	2,639	55,669	123,147	123,706
December	10,841	20,377	34,787	2,471	56,754	125,229	123,946

(a) *Excludes* Government and inter-bank deposits, but *includes* deposits of the public with the Reserve Bank. (b) Interpolated 'weekly average' based on end of month figures. (c) *Excludes* one Wednesday.

Source: Banking Australia December 1987. ABS Cat. no. 5605.0.

INDUSTRY SECTORS

	Males	Females	Persons	Prop %
Australian Government	335,080	166,327	501,407	7.7
State Government	562,491	461,379	1,023,870	15.7
Local Government	107,653	35,956	143,609	2.2
Private Sector	2,872,362	1,836,532	4,708,894	72.3
Not Stated	74,318	61,417	135,735	2.1
Total	**3,951,904**	**2,561,611**	**6,513,515**	**100.0**

Source: ABS 1986 Census of Population and Housing.

COST OF LIVING

1928
Food (average prices)
Bread (2 lb loaf) .... 6.0 pence
Milk (1 quart) .... 9.1 pence
Eggs (1 dozen) .... 2 shillings 3.5 pence
Tea (1 lb) .... 2 shillings 2.8 pence
Beef—sirloin (1 lb) .... 9.2 pence

Basic Wage
Sydney .... 4 pounds 5 shillings
Melbourne 4 pounds 7 shillings 6 pence
Brisbane .... 4 pounds 5 shillings
Adelaide .. 4 pounds 5 shillings 6 pence
Perth .... 4 pounds 5 shillings
Hobart ... 4 pounds 2 shillings 6 pence

Real Estate
Marrickville, NSW: Family residence—1,150 pounds.
Moonee Ponds, Vic.: Double front brick villa with six rooms—1,200 pounds.
Sandringham, Vic.: Modern, tiled villa with all conveniences—750 pounds.
Kew, Vic.: 'Super Stylish' brick bungalow with six rooms—1,450 pounds
Essendon, Vic.: Double front, weatherboard villa, five large rooms, garage—1,450 pounds.
Mt Lawley, WA: Four-bedroom brick, tiled roof home, sewered, spacious verandah—1,450 pounds.
Claremont, WA: Four-bedroom home, dining room, drawing room, smoke room, laundry, garage, tennis court—2,100 pounds.
Inglewood, WA: Modern, new tiled roof brick residence, five very large rooms, bathroom, washhouse—1,400 pounds.
Kingswood, SA: Seven large rooms, large bathroom, cellar, pantry, kitchen, garage—2,000 pounds.
Kensington Park, SA: Brick bungalow, four rooms, large entrance hall, garden—860 pounds.
Norwood, SA: Four-room bungalow and sleep-out—985 pounds.
Indooroopilly, Qld: New bungalow, three bedrooms—550 pounds.
Sandgate, Qld: New, modern, four-roomed cottage, bathroom, garage—320 pounds.
Greenslopes, Qld: 'Pretty, new bungalow', two bedrooms, large living room, enamel bath—685 pounds.
The Tivoli Theatre in Castlereagh Street, Sydney, was sold for 90,000 pounds.
Premium office space in Sydney's central business district cost 6-7 shillings per square foot.

Travel
From Sydney to London via Melbourne, Adelaide, Fremantle, Colombo, Port Said and Malta—38-45 pounds or 65 pounds Deck Cabin Class, one way.

1948

Food *(average prices)*
Bread *(2 lb loaf)* ....6.9 pence
Milk *(1 quart)* ....8.7 pence
Eggs *(1 dozen)* ...2 shillings 10.5 pence
Tea *(1 lb)* ....2 shillings 9 pence
Beef—sirloin *(1 lb)* 1 shilling 3.5 pence

Basic Wage
Sydney ....6 pounds 1 shilling
Melbourne ....6 pounds
Brisbane 5 pounds 7 shillings 6 pence
Adelaide ....5 pounds 8 shillings
Perth ....5 pounds 8 shillings
Hobart ....5 pounds 9 shillings

Real Estate
Marrickville, NSW: Family residence, three bedrooms—2,400 pounds.
Paddington, NSW: Brick terrace house, three bedrooms—1,650 pounds.
Killara, NSW: Residential blocks of land sold at auction for 1,800 pounds.
Kew, Vic.: Modern brick villa, seven rooms, garage—3,000 pounds.
Sandringham, Vic.: Concrete veneer, five-room house—2,600 pounds.
Essendon, Vic.: Weatherboard and brick house, eight rooms—8,000 pounds.
Kalamunda, WA: Six acres of land with excellent views—150 pounds.
Mt Lawley, WA: Brick home, tiled roof, seven rooms, garage, workshop—2,165 pounds.
Surfers Paradise, Qld: Modern brick and tiled roof villa, two bedrooms—2,300 pounds.
Caloundra, Qld: 'Ultra-modern home, tastefully furnished', electrically fitted throughout—2,100 pounds.
Sandgate, Qld: New home, handy to beach, new furniture—2,000 pounds.

Travel
Flight from Sydney to Perth—27 pounds 7 shillings and 6 pence.
Flight from Sydney to Melbourne—5 pounds 10 shillings and 6 pence.
Flight from Sydney to London—325 pounds.
Passenger embarkations (internal airline services)—1,207,839.
Passengers on international services—41,124.

1968

Food *(average prices)*
Bread *(2 lb loaf)* ....19.1 cents
Milk *(1 quart)*..............22 cents
Eggs *(1 dozen)*.............61.7 cents
Tea *(1 lb)*.................61.6 cents

Basic Wage
Sydney $45.21
Melbourne $44.59
Brisbane $45.54
Adelaide $43.78
Perth $45.04
Hobart......................$45.26

Real Estate
Marrickville, NSW: Brick and tiled roof three-bedroom house—$12,000.
Paddington, NSW: Three-bedroom brick terrace—$16,600.
St Ives, NSW: residential block of land sold at auction for $7,500.
Kew, Vic.: 'Gracious' two-storey white brick, four-bedroom house, double garage—$55,000.
Essendon, Vic.: Three-bedroom brick house, triple carport—$20,000.
Mt Lawley, WA: 'Grand old brick home', three bedrooms, separate lounge, separate dining room—$12,500.
Inglewood, WA: Three-bedroom weatherboard home in very good condition, 66 ft frontage and 170 ft depth—$13,000.
Kalamunda, WA: Three-bedroom home, built partly from natural stone, large verandah, double garage—$18,000.
Greenslopes, Qld: Three-bedroom family home, wall-to-wall carpets, views—$10,000.
Surfers Paradise, Qld: Absolute waterfrontage, brick veneer, fully furnished, wall-to-wall carpet, three bedrooms, rumpus room—$46,000.
Indooroopilly, Qld: 'Executive home in superb brick veneer', tiled roof, three bedrooms, separate lounge and dining—$28,000.
Sandgate, Qld: Four bedroom, renovated, high position home—$5,900.

Travel
All inclusive 14-day 'Oriental Tour' to Singapore and Hong Kong—$695.00.
Ocean voyage from Sydney to Southampton—$325.00.
Sydney to London by air—$975.10.
Sydney to Melbourne by air—$28.40.
Sydney to Perth by air—$133.50.
Passenger embarkations, internal flights—5,184,828.
Passengers flying to Australia—452,714.
Passengers flying from Australia—401,293.

1987-88

Food *(average prices)*
Bread *(680 g loaf)* $1.13

Milk *(2 x 600 ml bottles)* 0.96
    (1 litre carton) 0.83
Eggs *(1 dozen, 55 g)* $1.59
Tea *(250 g)* $1.43
Beef—rump *(1 kilogram)* $8.71

Minimum Wage
Sydney ......$187.37 (as at Feb. 1988)
Melbourne advised that no single figure was appropriate
Brisbane $217.50
Adelaide $188.40 (forms part of adult wage clause in about one-third of SA awards)
Perth ......$222.90 (as at 5 Feb. 1988)
Hobart.....................$214.70
Federal Award $181.37 (as at 10 March 1987)
Note: What was known as the basic wage is now subsumed by a myriad of wage awards and allowances. Each of the relevant state departments advised that the figure quoted was subject to interpretation of conditions outlined in clauses of particular awards, and whether federal awards apply in a particular case.

Real Estate
Marrickville, NSW: Three-bedroom brick cottage—$135,000.
Paddington, NSW: Two-bedroom security apartment—$235,000.
Killara, NSW: 'Spacious', four bedroom, two-storey residence—$660,000.
Essendon, Vic.: 'Edwardian family home', four double-size bedrooms, two bathrooms—$190,000.
Kew, Vic.: 'Victorian' brick home in need of renovation—$250,000.
Mt Lawley, WA: 'Immaculately presented' brick and tile, two-bedroom home, thirty years old, in original condition—$76,850.
Claremont, WA: 'Quality' three-bedroom unit—$300,000.
Inglewood, WA: 'Refurbished, character home', brick/iron, two bedrooms, front and side verandah—$70,000.
Kalamunda, WA: Large house, four bedrooms, two bathrooms, pool—$205,000.
Kingswood, SA: Two-bedroom brick home, formal dining room, study, renovated kitchen—$90,000.
Kensington Gardens, SA: 'Character style bungalow, ideally suited for the handyman', two large bedrooms, open fireplaces—$80,000.
Caloundra, Qld: Three-bedroom duplex, close to beach—$53,000.
Indooroopilly, Qld: Attractive four-bedroom family home, saltwater pool—$102,000.
Greenslopes, Qld: Two-bedroom unit—$54,000.

Travel
Sydney to London return flight—$1,490 *(as at April 1988)*.
Sydney to Melbourne flight—$171.00 *(as at April 1988)*.
Sydney to Perth flight—$444.00 *(as at April 1988)*.
Passengers flying to Australia—3,593,500 *(ABS tentative)*.
Passengers flying from Australia—3,425,900 *(ABS tentative)*.

AUSTRALIA'S TOP 100 COMPANIES

Rank '88	'87	'86	Company	Revenue ($'000)	Pre-Tax Profit ($'000)	Total Assets ($'000)
1	1	4	Coles Myer	11,369,529	413,867	3,861,607
2	4	2	Elders IXL	10,560,327	396,777	9,794,727
3	2	1	BHP	9,372,483	1,459,761	17,519,694
4	3	3	Westpac	9,187,900	848,500	70,333,504
5	5	5	ANZ	8,083,546	965,755	65,310,024

Rank '88	Rank '87	Rank '86	Company	Revenue ($'000)	Pre-Tax Profit ($'000)	Total Assets ($'000)
6	15	20	National Mutual	7,805,447	6,507,361	19,517,170
7	6	10	AMP	6,600,000	2,600,000	25,000,000
8	8	8	Telecom	6,047,500	443,300	14,466,000
9	9	11	Nat Aust Bank	5,983,700	605,300	46,971,500
10	24	24	Brierley Investments	5,892,762	557,323	9,734,429
11	7	7	Woolworths	5,780,258?	6,690	1,469,723
12	11	12	Commonwealth Bank	5,452,424	378,056	43,886,852
13	13	21	News Corp	5,317,876	455,528	12,646,199
14	10	9	CRA	5,030,050	570,612	8,255,324
15	12	6	Shell	4,950,036	301,732	4,236,904
16	16	18	Fletcher Challenge	4,795,641	419,241	6,638,154
17	14	14	BP	4,056,700	103,100	2,898,500
18	19	25	Reserve Bank	4,047,764	2,676,101	26,073,010
19	20	28	Mitsui	3,291,506	10,971	367,075
20	18	17	Mobil	3,230,621*	-29,193	961,310
21	22	19	Pioneer Concrete	3,112,860	261,964	2,439,959
22	23	27	TNT	3,087,614	171,163	2,508,715
23	46	63	IEL	2,917,065	306,502	5,964,597
24	27	33	Pacific Dunlop	2,715,911	236,973	1,770,935
25	28	35	Amcor	2,596,112	145,228	1,861,274
26	37	41	Qantas	2,562,523	114,674	2,021,782
27	25	82	Bell Resources	2,537,700*	343,400	4,158,700
28	17	16	Wheat Board	2,510,654	na	2,363,564
29	32	117	Bond Corp	2,488,801	140,823	4,115,617
30	33	26	ACI	2,473,100	190,700	2,281,000
31	35	34	ICI	2,461,700	242,600	2,034,800
32	21	29	CSR	2,417,957	225,956	3,972,050
33	38	44	Boral	2,398,350	331,530	2,326,408
34	30	22	Caltex	2,366,980	31,054	930,332
35	26	23	Mitsubishi Aust	2,238,141	6,127	99,969
36	+	+	Davids Holdings	2,200,000E	na	na
37	36	32	Elcom NSW	2,187,068	-4,805	6,569,392
38	34	13	Esso Exploration	2,171,000*	659,696	2,875,650
39	40	39	Amatil	2,102,993	144,772	1,299,431

Rank '88	Rank '87	Rank '86	Company	Revenue ($'000)	Pre-Tax Profit ($'000)	Total Assets ($'000)
40	41	30	Ford Motor	2,029,182	74,607	1,108,206
41	43	43	SEC Vic.	2,021,260	139,965	8,288,466
42	53	51	Colonial Mutual	1,970,000	513,372	5,304,095
43	42	37	Comalco	1,965,300	268,200	2,610,600
44	44	48	TAB NSW	1,936,052	69,029	120,828
45	75	74	Bell Group	1,935,700	125,100	3,047,500
46	58	79	State Bank Vic.	1,874,716	116,515	16,329,400
47	49	62	Ansett	1,846,705	155,087	2,277,514
48	52	53	AGC	1,802,300	213,600	8,485,100
49	48	38	Dalgety Farm	1,798,080	21,654	215,855
50	51	65	Mayne Nickless	1,760,000	95,626	944,142
51	47	45	Ampol	1,749,943	50,281	1,092,041
52	76	31	Dalgety Inv.	1,685,186	19,011	346,234
53	45	47	C Itoh	1,674,836	3,654	364,147
54	57	—	Franklins	1,653,072	31,597	na
55	63	75	State Super NSW	1,626,639	871,140	5,143,720
56	81	42	NZI	1,622,816	129,953	5,008,360
57	56	59	Marubeni	1,553,118	2,147	208,682
58	50	50	James Hardie	1,512,897	90,322	1,488,057
59	59	58	Aust Post	1,505,099	54,890	716,947
60	79	87	Rothmans	1,496,689	128,258	544,493
61	125	174	Goodman Fielder	1,496,645	128,471	2,215,693
62	61	66	ANI	1,458,152	100,733	792,833
63	55	54	MIM	1,449,702	81,359	3,704,085
64	107	164	BTR Nylex	1,444,306	209,354	1,485,912
65	54	46	State Rail NSW	1,426,192	78	4,824,576
66	72	64	Alcoa	1,400,853	308,292	2,397,757
67	62	68	TAB Vic.	1,376,842	166,631	167,719
68	66	76	Leighton	1,327,853	12,542	549,892
69	+	+	JGL Investments	1,300,000E	na	na
70	91	106	Lend Lease	1,293,510	132,511	1,438,573
71	67	84	State Bank NSW	1,285,842	52,216	10,210,988
72	69	107	Brambles	1,279,463	165,922	1,386,391
73	64	55	Burns Philp	1,259,699	68,459	1,058,950

TOP COMPANIES • 355

'88	Rank '87	'86	Company	Revenue ($'000)	Pre-Tax Profit ($'000)	Total Assets ($'000)
74	65	60	Qld Sugar	1,252,300	-576	396,566
75	130	133	Cons Press	1,197,694	63,074	2,149,272
76	77	615	Ariadne	1,192,310	156,258	1,648,422
77	88	77	North BH	1,155,726	117,144	1,430,597
78	386	708	Weeks Petroleum	1,137,884	131,496	1,278,202
79	74	73	IBM	1,129,370	83,049	788,797
80	98	95	Metal Manufact	1,069,326	94,421	658,560
81	85	89	SEC WA	1,067,311	261	4,055,244
82	73	81	Sumitomo	1,056,000	-123	41,305
83	84	88	David Jones	1,040,899	189,367	1,800,745
84	90	91	Nissho Iwai	1,025,490	323	148,067
85	87	94	Wesfarmers	1,021,692	47,248	460,817
86	83	80	Qld Bail	1,003,043	102,789	na
87	+	+	American Express	1,000,000E	na	na
88	+	+	Smorgon	1,000,000E	na	na
89	89	93	NZ Forest	994,090	82,486	1,901,196
90	71	70	Wormald	986,114	40,149	885,308
91	82	78	Tubemakers	977,740	59,384	666,622
92	129	194	Capita	969,661	709,656	2,132,160
93	103	206	FAI	960,796	150,801	2,162,169
94	92	99	Aust Airlines	947,732	42,650	1,338,611
95	143	349	Wool Corp	940,360	178,895	1,406,652
96	184	+	Composite Buyers	937,000	-2,124	182,387
97	96	96	John Fairfax	927,373	80,883	1,833,191
98	160	143	Super Fund Inv	926,019	918,609	4,358,572
99	118	109	Hooker Corp	914,366	85,858	1,028,068
100	112	144	State Bank SA	899,266	52,081	7,893,767

Source: IBIS Business Information and *Australian Business.*

FAMILY STATUS AND WHETHER IN THE LABOUR FORCE, CIVILIAN POPULATION, DURING THE YEAR ENDING FEBRUARY 1986
('000)

Family status	Worked at some time Males	Worked at some time Females	Looked for work at some time Males	Looked for work at some time Females	In the labour force at some time Males	In the labour force at some time Females	Out of the labour force at some time Males	Out of the labour force at some time Females	Total Persons
Member of a family	3,795.5	2,601.1	600.2	542.3	3,997.6	2,834.0	1,738.3	3,394.1	10,010.8
Husband or wife	2,824.7	1,791.5	275.8	258.6	2,906.1	1,910.7	1,102.7	2,453.0	7,171.8
With children aged 0-14 present	1,594.9	943.3	169.8	170.6	1643.3	1,029.1	245.2	1,159.0	3,338.3
Without children aged 0-14 present	1,229.8	848.2	106.0	88.0	1,262.8	881.6	857.5	1,293.9	3,833.5
Not-married family head	69.0	179.2	13.4	56.7	73.4	211.3	48.4	350.4	577.5
With children aged 0-14 present	24.7	99.7	7.2	42.4	27.8	123.5	10.3	175.9	265.2
Without children aged 0-14 present	44.2	79.5	6.2	14.3	45.6	87.9	38.1	174.5	312.3
Child of family head	841.0	598.7	287.2	216.5	948.5	675.0	533.8	472.0	2,012.9
Other relative of family head	60.7	31.7	23.7	10.6	69.7	37.0	53.4	118.8	248.6
Not a member of a family	570.8	391.9	114.7	86.6	601.5	411.4	280.7	590.3	1,668.4
Living alone	264.6	168.4	42.4	25.0	279.0	176.0	189.1	496.1	1,053.3
Not living alone	306.2	223.5	72.4	61.6	322.5	235.4	91.6	94.2	615.1
Not family coded	153.7	126.0	42.2	37.7	166.3	140.3	78.7	137.5	421.9
Total	4,520.0	3,119.1	757.1	666.6	4,765.5	3,385.6	2,097.8	4,121.9	12,101.1

Source: Labour Force Experience Australia during the year ending February 1986. *ABS Cat. no. 6206.0.*

EDUCATIONAL ATTAINMENT AND WHETHER IN THE LABOUR FORCE, CIVILIAN POPULATION, DURING THE YEAR ENDING FEBRUARY 1986
('000)

Educational attainment	Worked at some time Males	Worked at some time Females	Looked for work at some time Males	Looked for work at some time Females	In the labour force at some time Males	In the labour force at some time Females	Out of the labour force at some time Males	Out of the labour force at some time Females	Total Persons
With post-school qualifications	2,095.9	1,243.4	222.6	201.8	2,143.0	1,312.3	640.5	960.4	4,213.4
Degree	473.3	273.7	37.6	33.1	484.7	281.5	109.9	156.3	864.8
Trade; technical or other certificate	1,574.1	917.8	173.1	155.3	1,606.9	972.2	516.0	750.3	3,201.3
Other	48.5	51.9	12.0	13.5	51.5	58.7	14.6	53.8	147.3
Without post-school qualifications	2,348.4	1,788.0	495.9	424.9	2,519.8	1,960.5	1,223.9	2,933.6	7,389.9
Attended highest level of secondary school available	552.4	418.5	117.9	101.8	594.7	456.6	255.1	415.5	1,374.8
Did not attend highest level of secondary school available	1,790.2	1,365.0	376.9	321.1	1,918.6	1,498.1	957.6	2,491.1	5,966.9
Left school at age—									
16 years and over	642.9	549.1	139.4	138.0	679.3	598.0	197.2	585.0	1,724.5
15 years and under	1,147.3	815.9	237.5	183.1	1,239.3	900.1	760.4	1,906.1	4,242.4
Never attended school	5.8	4.6	*	*	6.4	5.8	11.3	27.0	48.2
Still at school	75.7	87.7	38.5	39.9	102.7	112.9	233.3	228.0	497.8
Total	4,520.0	3,119.1	757.1	666.6	4,765.5	3,385.6	2,097.8	4,121.9	12,101.1

Source: Labour Force Experience Australia during the year ending February 1986. ABS Cat. no. 6206.0.

LABOUR FORCE AND AGE 1976 TO 1986
PROPORTION WHO PARTICIPATED AT SOME TIME DURING THE REFERENCE PERIOD

Age group at the time of the survey

Survey conducted in February—	15-19	20-24	25-34	35-44	45-54	55-59	60-64	65 and over	Total
Males									
1976	65.4	95.0	98.6	98.6	96.6	91.6	77.2	23.9	**84.8**
1977	65.0	95.1	98.5	98.1	96.5	90.0	74.1	22.5	**84.2**
1979	67.2	95.2	98.6	97.4	94.5	88.1	68.4	17.0	**82.7**
1980	67.3	95.1	98.3	97.8	93.6	86.1	61.3	17.5	**82.1**
1981	78.4	97.2	98.4	97.3	93.3	85.6	59.8	15.7	**83.2**
1982	76.8	98.0	98.2	97.5	93.2	87.9	56.7	13.6	**82.8**
1983	75.8	97.6	98.4	97.1	94.0	84.1	59.4	12.9	**82.4**
1984	73.8	96.3	98.1	97.7	94.3	83.5	54.6	13.3	**81.8**
1985	72.3	95.9	97.6	96.9	92.7	82.1	53.4	12.3	**80.8**
1986	73.8	96.6	97.2	96.6	92.2	82.3	50.7	10.7	**80.0**
Married Females									
1976	70.5	68.2	53.7	59.4	51.7	33.9	17.3	4.4	**49.1**
1977	70.8	69.0	54.2	59.6	54.7	32.9	14.4	4.1	**49.4**
1979	70.1	69.8	56.6	62.3	50.1	35.2	15.8	4.0	**49.5**
1980	72.0	70.2	59.1	65.0	53.5	33.9	14.7	4.2	**50.9**

1981	68.1	70.3	61.6	64.9	52.6	33.1	16.8	4.9	51.3
1982	68.8	70.1	61.1	66.8	57.3	31.9	12.4	3.9	51.8
1983	73.4	69.6	63.2	67.0	53.7	34.2	15.8	4.4	52.2
1984	67.9	70.1	61.2	65.9	53.9	32.4	15.1	3.9	51.2
1985	69.7	70.5	63.8	68.2	56.8	30.9	13.9	3.3	52.5
1986	71.6	72.7	66.6	71.6	56.9	33.5	14.6	3.8	54.0

All Females

1976	61.6	76.3	57.4	61.0	53.6	36.1	20.9	5.1	49.9
1977	61.6	77.6	58.0	61.0	55.7	36.0	17.9	4.9	50.3
1979	65.8	79.2	59.7	62.8	52.0	36.4	16.4	3.5	50.5
1980	64.3	80.6	62.8	66.3	54.3	35.0	16.6	3.3	51.8
1981	73.5	81.8	65.9	65.8	54.0	34.0	17.7	3.8	53.6
1982	73.7	81.8	65.5	67.9	58.1	34.7	14.8	3.6	54.1
1983	72.4	81.7	66.8	67.7	54.7	36.0	16.7	3.8	54.3
1984	71.1	82.2	65.9	66.7	55.9	34.7	15.9	3.1	53.9
1985	72.0	82.4	68.4	69.3	57.9	33.6	15.6	2.8	54.5
1986	72.6	84.1	70.9	71.6	58.3	36.1	15.8	3.0	55.1

Persons

1976	63.5	85.7	78.4	80.1	75.5	63.3	48.0	13.1	67.2
1977	63.3	86.4	78.5	79.9	76.4	62.6	45.0	12.4	67.1
1979	66.5	87.2	79.2	80.5	73.7	62.1	41.3	9.3	66.4
1980	65.8	87.9	80.5	82.4	74.4	60.4	38.1	9.4	66.7

Age group at the time of the survey

Survey conducted in February—	15-19	20-24	25-34	35-44	45-54	55-59	60-64	65 and over	Total
1981	76.0	89.6	82.1	81.9	74.1	59.7	38.1	9.0	**68.2**
1982	75.3	89.9	81.7	83.0	76.0	61.4	35.2	7.9	**68.3**
1983	74.1	89.7	82.5	82.7	74.9	59.9	37.2	7.8	**68.2**
1984	72.5	89.2	82.0	82.0	75.7	59.3	34.4	7.7	**67.7**
1985	72.1	89.2	83.0	83.3	75.6	58.0	34.0	6.9	**67.5**
1986	73.2	90.3	84.0	84.3	75.6	59.4	32.8	6.2	**67.4**

Adapted from: Labour Force Experience Australia during the year ending February 1986. ABS Cat. no. 6206.0.

PERSONS OUT OF THE LABOUR FORCE AT SOME TIME DURING THE YEAR ENDING FEBRUARY 1986 AGE AND TIME OUT OF THE LABOUR FORCE
('000)

Time out of the labour force (weeks)

Age group	1 and under 4	4 and under 13	13 and under 26	26 and under 39	39 and under 49	49 and under 52	52	Total
Married Males								
15-19	*	*	*	*	*	*	*	*
20-24	7.2	*	*	*	*	*	*	16.3
25-34	48.3	35.5	8.9	6.0	5.1	*	14.9	120.4
35-44	52.1	38.9	7.4	4.5	*	*	22.9	129.8
45-54	31.7	28.8	8.6	*	4.7	4.7	40.6	118.4
55-59	11.0	10.1	*	6.9	*	*	48.0	83.6
60-64	6.5	8.6	8.0	5.4	6.3	*	141.2	174.7
65 and over	*	8.8	6.6	4.5	6.3	*	457.3	483.9
Total	**158.9**	**135.0**	**45.0**	**32.1**	**22.3**	**7.5**	**726.4**	**1,127.2**
All Males								
15-19	16.2	24.4	28.6	35.4	109.0	38.0	177.7	429.2
20-24	38.5	37.9	16.3	17.3	25.1	4.9	22.5	162.5

Time out of the labour force (weeks)

Age group	1 and under 4	4 and under 13	13 and under 26	26 and under 39	39 and under 49	49 and under 52	52	Total
25-34	70.1	56.9	19.1	13.2	13.3	4.8	36.5	212.9
35-44	59.3	48.7	11.9	6.8	5.6	4.8	38.5	171.9
45-54	34.0	34.0	9.9	5.9	5.1	*	62.1	152.1
55-59	12.9	12.2	4.8	8.5	*	*	67.3	110.0
60-64	9.2	9.6	9.7	6.6	4.5	*	169.6	210.9
65 and over	*	9.7	8.1	4.9	5.1	5.1	618.1	648.3
Total	**242.7**	**233.5**	**108.4**	**98.6**	**168.5**	**53.9**	**1,192.1**	**2,097.8**
Married Females								
15-19	*	*	*	*	*	*	6.2	11.1
20-24	10.6	17.5	12.7	15.5	16.1	4.5	67.5	144.4
25-34	46.8	67.8	45.8	61.0	58.8	33.1	320.4	633.8
35-44	51.8	77.0	34.5	46.1	45.7	24.1	260.9	540.1
45-54	22.5	37.0	16.9	17.4	17.2	8.4	264.6	384.0
55-59	5.9	6.7	6.2	5.3	4.6	*	189.4	220.4
60-64	5.3	5.3	5.3	5.3	*	*	210.8	224.0
65 and over	*	*	*	*	*	*	375.5	380.7
Total	**141.8**	**210.9**	**120.8**	**149.4**	**146.6**	**73.9**	**1,695.3**	**2,538.6**
All Females								
15-19	18.1	31.7	34.4	52.8	94.8	27.9	178.1	437.8

20-24	28.6	42.8	27.2	28.8	34.7	9.5	104.4	275.9
25-34	61.7	88.8	61.8	72.8	70.3	40.0	372.7	768.2
35-44	58.3	86.1	41.5	54.2	50.9	26.8	312.5	630.2
45-54	28.2	44.3	18.6	21.1	21.3	10.9	317.8	462.2
55-59	7.1	9.1	8.7	7.0	6.5	*	238.3	280.0
60-64	5.1	5.2	5.9	6.0	4.5	*	304.0	327.3
65 and over	5.1	*	5.9	6.0	*	*	929.9	940.4
Total	**207.1**	**310.7**	**198.1**	**242.7**	**284.8**	**120.8**	**2,757.8**	**4,121.9**
All Persons								
15-19	34.3	56.0	62.9	88.2	203.8	65.9	355.8	867.0
20-24	67.1	80.7	43.5	46.1	59.7	14.4	126.8	438.4
25-34	131.8	145.8	80.9	86.0	83.6	43.8	409.2	981.1
35-44	117.6	134.8	53.4	61.0	56.5	27.8	351.0	802.1
45-54	62.2	78.3	28.5	27.0	26.4	12.1	379.9	614.3
55-59	20.0	21.4	13.5	15.6	9.3	4.6	305.7	390.1
60-64	12.5	14.8	13.8	10.9	9.0	6.1	473.5	538.2
65 and over	*	12.4	9.9	6.6	4.9	6.1	1,548.0	1,588.6
Total	**449.8**	**544.2**	**306.5**	**341.4**	**453.3**	**174.7**	**3,949.9**	**6,219.7**

Source: Labour Force Experience Australia during the year ending February 1986. *ABS Cat. no. 6206.0.*

OCCUPATIONS

	Males	Females	Persons	Prop %
Managers & Administrators:				
Legislators & Govt Appointed	1,681	174	1,855	0.0
General Managers	30,726	2,962	33,688	0.5
Specialist Managers	154,838	28,562	183,400	2.8
Farmers & Farm Managers	173,552	78,589	252,141	3.9
Managerial Supervisors (Sales & Service)	124,815	65,872	190,687	2.9
Managerial Supervisors (Other)	77,101	11,940	89,041	1.4
Total*	571,798	190,157	761,955	11.7
Professionals:				
Natural Scientists	23,551	7,669	31,220	0.5
Building Professionals & Engineers	84,265	2,378	86,643	1.3
Health Diagnosis & Treatment Practitioners	46,318	28,416	74,734	1.1
School Teachers	75,193	142,540	217,733	3.3
Other Teachers & Instructors	40,069	31,893	71,962	1.1
Social Professionals	32,835	13,647	46,482	0.7
Business Professionals	107,532	38,352	145,884	2.2
Artists & Related Professionals	30,463	17,673	48,136	0.7
Miscellaneous Professionals	17,302	22,050	39,352	0.6
Total*	462,223	307,476	769,699	11.8

Para-professionals:

Medical & Science Technicians	9,432	8,535	17,967	0.3
Engineers & Building Associates & Technicians	83,337	6,690	90,027	1.4
Air & Sea Transport Technical Workrs	15,608	515	16,123	0.2
Nurses	10,658	127,563	138,221	2.1
Police Officers	30,691	3,190	33,881	0.5
Miscellaneous Para-professionals	84,880	33,260	118,140	1.8
Total*	**241,198**	**180,446**	**421,644**	**6.5**

Tradespersons:

Metal Fitting & Machining	108,672	882	109,554	1.7
Other Metal Tradepersons	95,013	1,742	96,755	1.5
Electrical & Electronic	148,189	2,439	150,628	2.3
Building Tradespersons	204,907	3,149	208,056	3.2
Printing Tradespersons	29,472	6,389	35,861	0.6
Vehicle Tradespersons	114,194	1,107	115,301	1.8
Food Tradespersons	68,407	27,134	95,541	1.5
Amenity Horticultural	36,486	4,759	41,245	0.6
Miscellaneous Tradespersons	79,161	48,459	127,620	2.0
Total*	**900,470**	**96,340**	**996,810**	**15.3**

	Males	Females	Persons	Prop %
Clerks:				
Stenographers & Typists	4,690	247,634	252,324	3.9
Data Processors & Business Machine Operators	14,203	58,538	72,741	1.1
Numerical Clerks	81,908	183,444	265,352	4.1
Filing, Sorting & Copying	15,848	29,566	45,414	0.7
Material Recording & Despatch	56,147	24,571	80,718	1.2
Reception, Telephonist, Messenger	17,959	120,653	138,612	2.1
Miscellaneous Clerks	31,135	52,119	83,254	1.3
Total*	293,344	819,435	1,112,779	17.1
Sales & Personal Services:				
Investment, Insurance & Real Estate	45,182	11,680	56,862	0.9
Sales Representatives	62,238	14,885	77,123	1.2
Sales Assistants	121,246	210,853	332,099	5.1
Tellers, Cashiers, Ticket	19,591	91,643	111,234	1.7
Miscellaneous Salespersons	46,195	72,279	118,474	1.8
Personal Service Workers	11,460	86,560	98,020	1.5
Total*	317,621	491,305	808,926	12.4
Plant & Machine Operators:				
Road & Rail Transport Drivers	190,592	12,168	202,760	3.1
Mobile Plant Operators	91,268	1,274	92,542	1.4

Stationary Plant Operators	54,663	743	55,406	0.9
Machine Operators	57,210	58,266	115,476	1.8
Total*	**449,502**	**85,517**	**535,019**	**8.2**
Labourers & Related Workers:				
Trade Assistants & Factory Labourers	146,994	81,991	228,985	3.5
Agricultural Labourers & Related	59,041	17,845	76,886	1.2
Cleaners & Laundry Workers	60,303	99,803	160,106	2.5
Construction & Mining Labourers	92,058	2,440	94,498	1.5
Miscellaneous Labourers & Related	208,098	119,346	327,444	5.0
Total*	**606,908**	**329,112**	**936,020**	**14.4**
Inadequately described	68,073	29,638	97,711	1.5
Not stated	40,767	32,185	72,952	1.1
Total	3,951,904	2,561,611	6,513,515	100.00

* including no further description

Adapted from: ABS 1986 Census of Population and Housing.

INCOME (ANNUAL)

	Males	Individual Females	Persons	Prop %	Families	Prop %	Household	Prop %
NIL	349,032	977,820	1,326,852	11.1	29,506	0.7	42,644	0.8
$1-$2,000	88,326	435,046	523,372	4.4	13,962	0.3	18,243	0.3
$2,001-$4,000	159,324	313,602	472,926	4.0	9,008	0.2	29,047	0.6
$4,001-$6,000	756,534	1,136,771	1,893,305	15.8	65,123	1.6	358,016	6.8
$6,001-$9,000	433,005	733,146	1,166,151	9.7	139,509	3.4	243,557	4.6
$9,001-$12,000	457,136	533,197	990,333	8.3	422,734	10.2	477,626	9.1
$12,001-$15,000	528,943	439,756	968,699	8.1	299,819	7.2	368,278	7.0
$15,001-$18,000	718,446	406,246	1,124,692	9.4	256,801	6.2	343,244	6.5
$18,001-$22,000	720,912	293,670	1,014,582	8.5	385,528	9.3	475,528	9.0
$22,001-$26,000	447,646	150,574	598,220	5.0	294,182	7.1	356,935	6.8
$26,001-$32,000	444,149	110,498	554,647	4.6	485,293	11.7	553,249	10.5
$32,001-$40,000	251,277	38,451	289,728	2.4	489,655	11.8	546,079	10.4
$40,001-$50,000	109,893	12,203	122,096	1.0	356,706	8.6	402,860	7.7
$50,001-and over	98,312	12,261	110,573	0.9	390,209	9.4	464,923	8.8
Not stated	341,357	467,778	809,135	6.8	417,952	10.1	483,069	9.2
Spouse(s) temporarily absent	N	N	N	0.0	102,024	2.5	101,218	1.9
Total	5,904,292	6,061,019	11,965,311	100.0	4,158,011	100.0	5,264,516	100.0

Source: ABS 1986 Census of Population and Housing.

INDUSTRIAL DISPUTES IN PROGRESS DURING EACH YEAR 1985 AND 1986

WORKING DAYS LOST PER THOUSAND EMPLOYEES, STATE

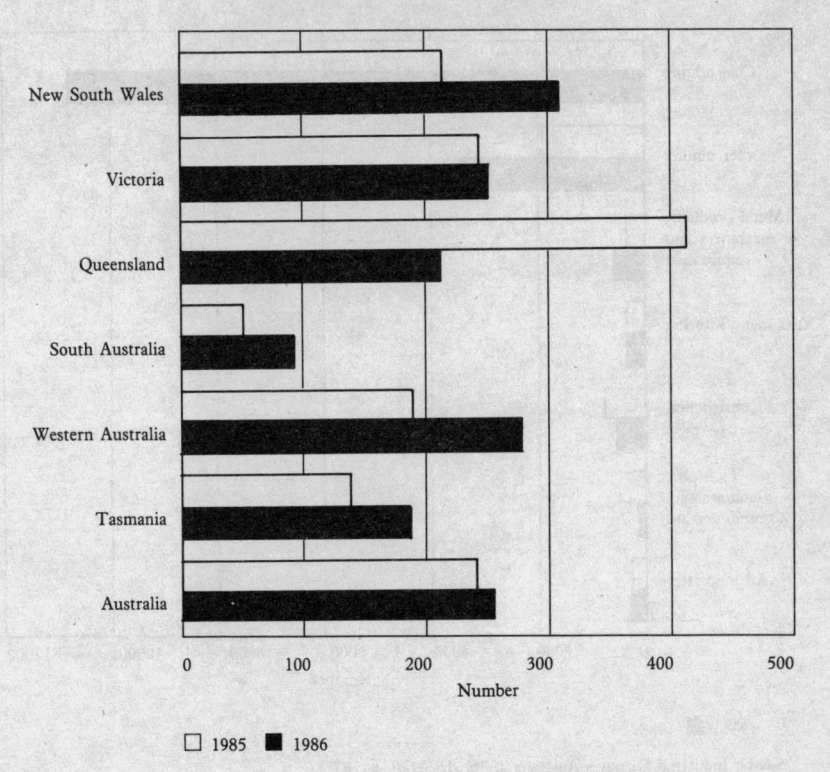

☐ 1985 ■ 1986

Source: Industrial Disputes Australia 1986. *ABS Cat. no. 6322.0.*

INDUSTRIAL DISPUTES IN PROGRESS DURING EACH YEAR 1985 AND 1986
WORKING DAYS LOST PER THOUSAND EMPLOYEES, INDUSTRY

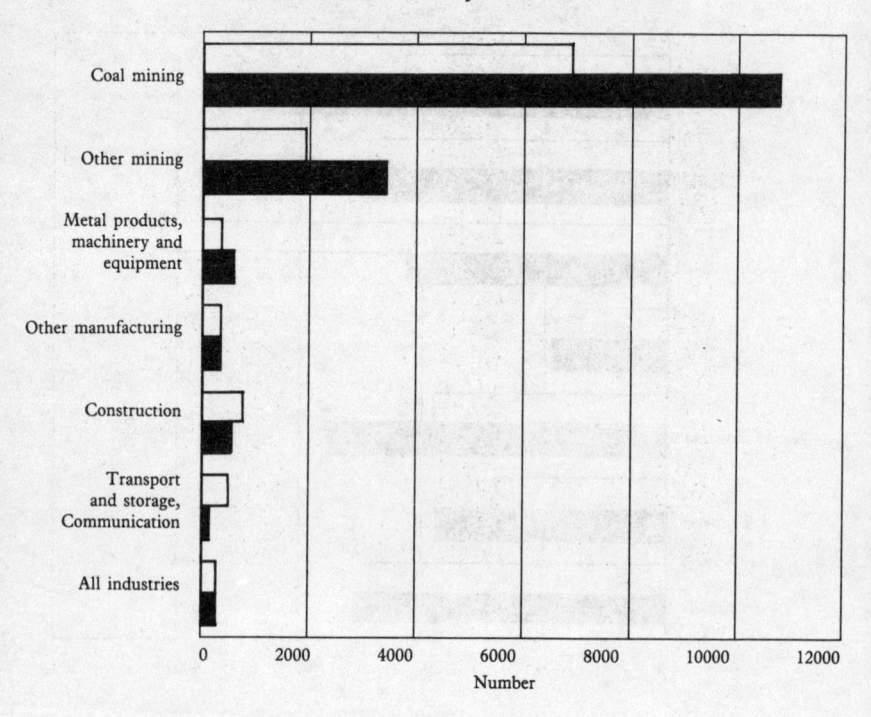

☐ 1985 ■ 1986

Source: Industrial Disputes Australia 1986. *ABS Cat. no. 6322.0.*

INDUSTRIAL DISPUTES ENDING DURING 1986
DURATION OF DISPUTE

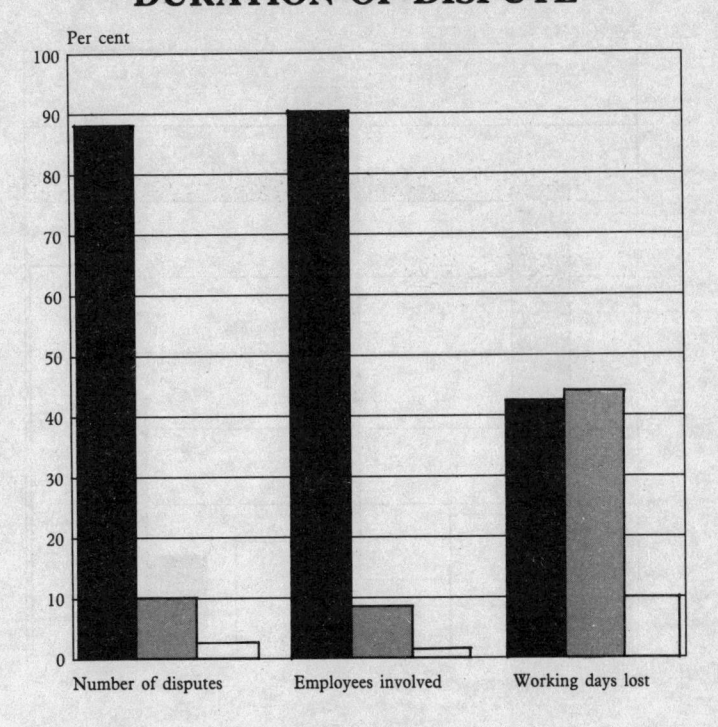

■ Less than five days ▨ 5 and less than 20 days ☐ 20 days and over

Source: Industrial Disputes Australia 1986. *ABS Cat. no. 6322.0.*

INDUSTRIAL DISPUTES ENDING DURING 1986
METHOD OF SETTLEMENT

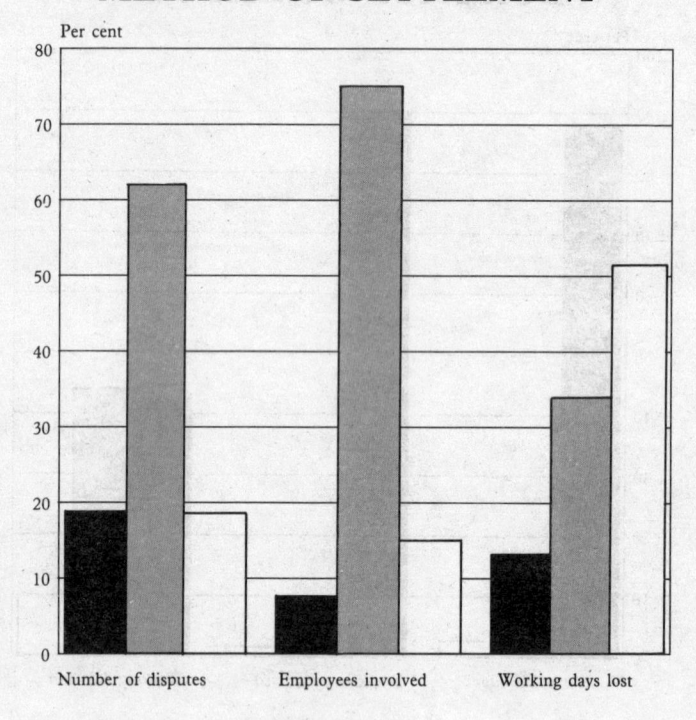

■ Negotiation ■ Resumption without negotiation □ Other

Source: Industrial Disputes Australia 1986. *ABS Cat. no. 6322.0.*

AVERAGE WEEKLY EARNINGS
ALL EMPLOYEES, STATES AND TERRITORIES, NOVEMBER 1986
($)

State or Territory	Full-time employees Adults Males	Full-time employees Adults Females	Full-time employees Adults Persons	Full-time employees Juniors Males	Full-time employees Juniors Females	Full-time employees Juniors Persons	All employees Males	All employees Females	All employees Persons
New South Wales	499.00	384.20	461.00	223.00	212.60	218.20	454.10	294.10	386.50
Victoria	488.30	388.60	457.10	220.90	220.60	220.80	446.70	301.00	388.50
Queensland	465.40	361.80	434.90	221.30	206.00	213.50	421.50	263.90	357.00
South Australia	456.40	367.80	430.60	209.20	216.90	212.30	415.50	266.60	352.70
Western Australia	499.40	381.20	465.60	222.10	216.20	218.50	468.30	270.30	385.20
Tasmania	472.00	369.10	443.50	225.90	216.20	221.40	435.00	263.90	363.90
Northern Territory	540.80	426.50	501.40	256.70	221.00	240.10	499.60	351.30	440.00
Australian Capital Territory	559.50	415.10	504.80	226.30	220.90	223.20	507.60	337.80	431.90
Australia	**488.60**	**382.00**	**455.20**	**220.90**	**214.50**	**217.90**	**446.30**	**287.60**	**380.60**

Source: Average Earnings and Hours of Employees Australia November 1986. ABS Cat. no. 6304. 0.

AVERAGE WEEKLY EARNINGS
ALL EMPLOYEES, INDUSTRIES, AUSTRALIA, NOVEMBER 1986
($)

Industry	Full-time employees Adults Males	Adults Females	Adults Persons	Juniors Males	Juniors Females	Juniors Persons	All employees Males	All employees Females	All employees Persons
Mining	689.30	426.80	669.60	388.60	260.70	351.50	676.60	386.10	650.20
Manufacturing									
Food, beverages and tobacco	463.70	337.70	435.30	217.80	202.10	213.30	441.40	299.20	404.30
Textiles; clothing and footwear	456.90	353.90	433.90	242.40	210.90	231.40	432.60	295.80	394.80
Paper, paper products, printing and publishing	438.90	304.50	370.40	238.60	189.70	207.60	418.70	275.50	340.10
Chemical, petroleum and coal products	502.60	353.60	458.80	220.50	217.40	219.20	464.30	297.30	405.80
Metal products, machinery and equipment—Basic metal products	555.20	379.60	505.60	256.60	*	*	544.50	351.10	484.10
Fabricated metal products; other machinery and equipment	524.60	394.40	515.20	260.20	244.80	258.50	511.50	355.40	498.20
Transport equipment	452.50	332.00	430.50	214.50	197.30	211.40	433.80	299.00	405.10
	446.40	343.30	435.00	231.60	228.40	231.40	431.30	321.70	418.60
Total metal products, etc.	**465.30**	**340.20**	**447.50**	**226.90**	**207.30**	**224.20**	**448.40**	**308.50**	**425.40**
Other manufacturing	421.50	326.90	403.30	185.60	196.20	187.50	394.10	296.10	373.20
Electricity, gas and water	511.00	386.90	500.70	271.10	236.50	262.70	497.10	345.10	481.70

Construction	498.70	343.10	482.50	236.60	203.60	232.70	476.00	271.10	443.30
Wholesale trade	470.20	363.10	442.10	225.80	222.00	224.80	438.50	307.10	398.10
Retail trade	384.20	318.80	361.40	194.20	194.30	194.20	297.90	189.40	240.60
Transport and storage	496.00	394.10	482.40	231.70	220.00	227.60	474.90	344.80	454.10
Communication	457.60	391.70	443.40	308.10	242.20	289.40	451.10	362.20	430.10
Finance, property and business services	517.00	376.10	456.50	229.40	225.40	226.60	458.90	285.20	367.60
Public administration and defence	473.40	396.70	449.40	236.10	230.90	232.90	460.60	334.80	414.10
Community services	544.60	422.20	476.50	244.40	236.90	238.30	491.20	327.00	384.20
Recreation, personal and other services	427.10	346.10	396.00	188.30	199.80	196.20	318.40	208.40	255.70
Total all industries	**488.60**	**382.00**	**455.20**	**220.90**	**214.50**	**217.90**	**446.30**	**287.60**	**380.60**

Source: Average Earnings of Hours and Employees Australia November 1986. ABS Cat. no. 6304.0.

IMPORTS, AUSTRALIA

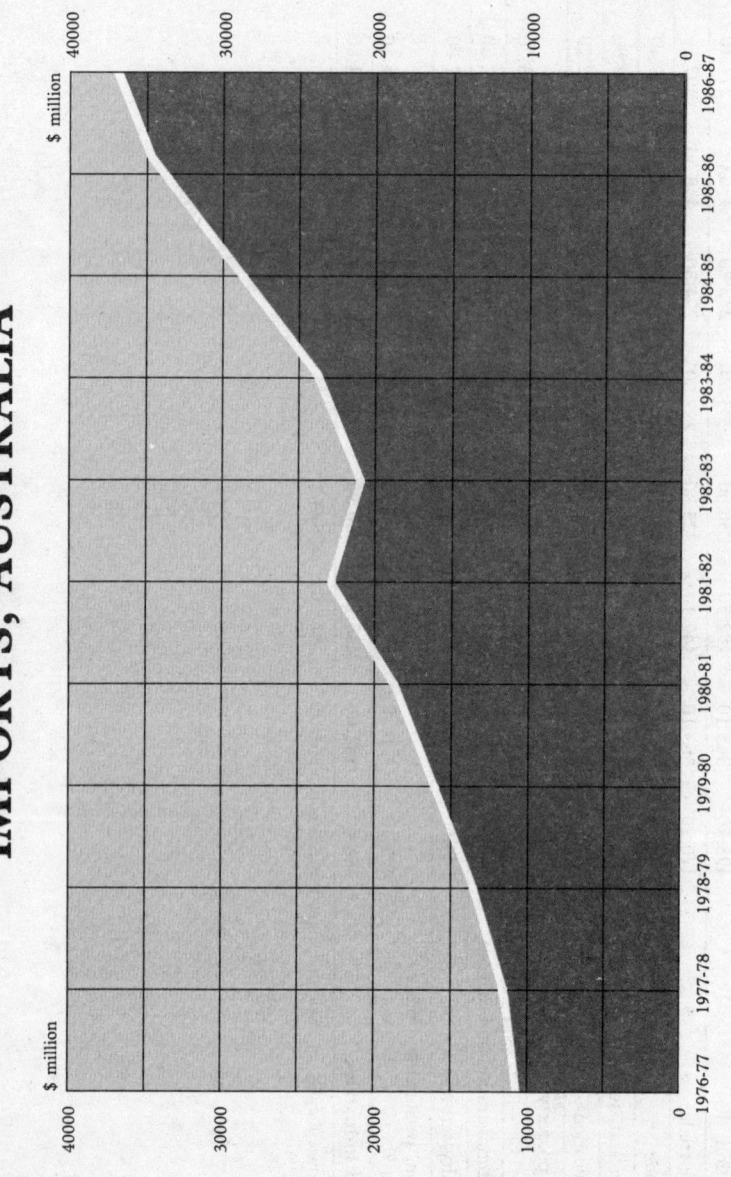

Source: Imports, Australia Annual Summary Tables 1986-87. ABS Cat. no. 5426.0.

IMPORTS BY STATE
$'000

State	1984-85	1985-86	1986-87
New South Wales	12,487,436	15,129,910	16,131,220
Victoria	10,084,483	12,408,781	13,743,043
Queensland	2,271,024	2,649,953	2,503,854
South Australia	1,593,380	1,736,757	1,501,827
Western Australia	2,032,788	2,063,074	2,545,141
Tasmania	252,702	299,398	289,374
Northern Territory	304,952	354,509	265,773
Australian Capital Territory	31,680	48,814	41,677
Total Imports	**29,049,445**	**34,691,197**	**37,021,910**

Source: Imports, Australia Annual Summary Tables 1986-87. *ABS Cat. no. 5426.0.*

DISTRIBUTION OF IMPORTS FROM MAJOR COUNTRIES AND COUNTRY GROUPS
YEAR ENDED JUNE 1987
Total imports $37,021.9m

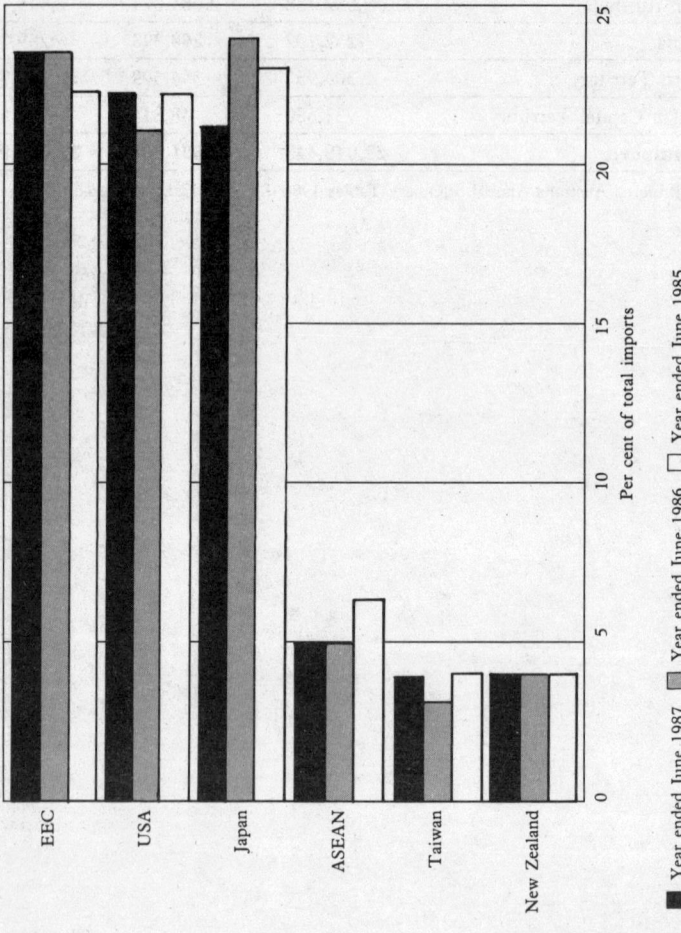

■ Year ended June 1987   ▨ Year ended June 1986   □ Year ended June 1985

Source: Imports, Australia Annual Summary Tables 1986–87. ABS Cat. no. 5426.0.

DISTRIBUTION OF IMPORTS BY MAJOR COMMODITIES
YEAR ENDED JUNE 1987
Total imports $37,021.9m

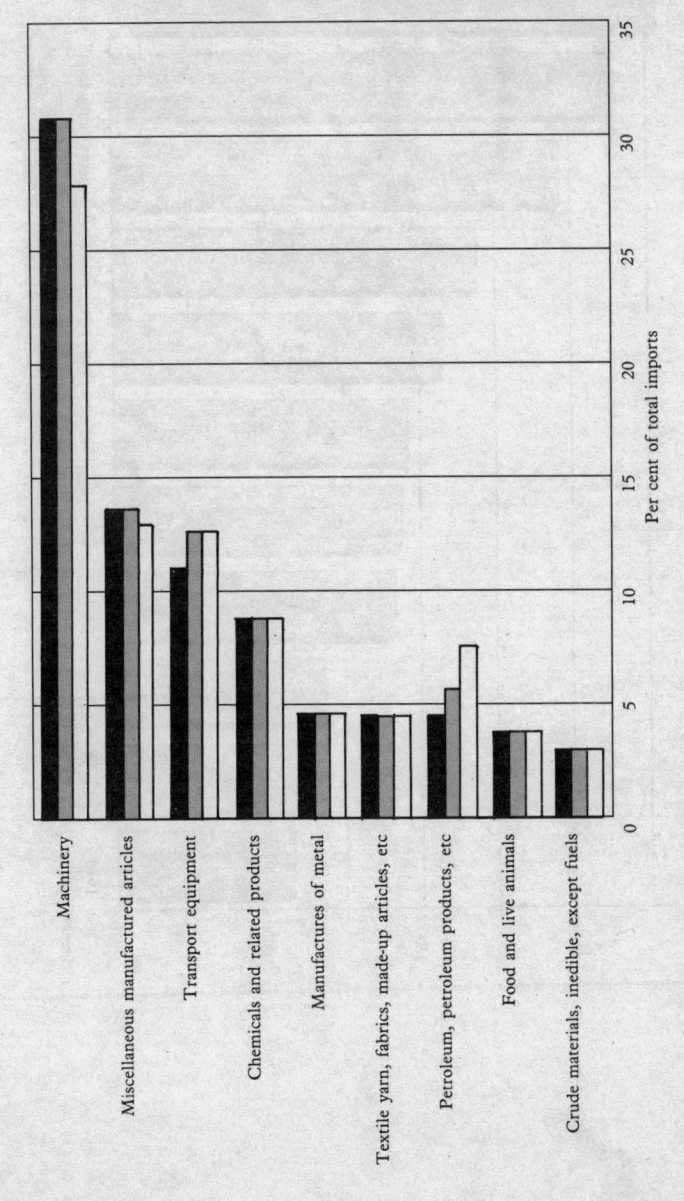

■ Year ended June 1987 ▨ Year ended June 1986 ☐ Year ended June 1985

Adapted from: Imports, Australia Annual Summary Tables 1986–87. ABS Cat. no. 5426.0.

EXPORTS

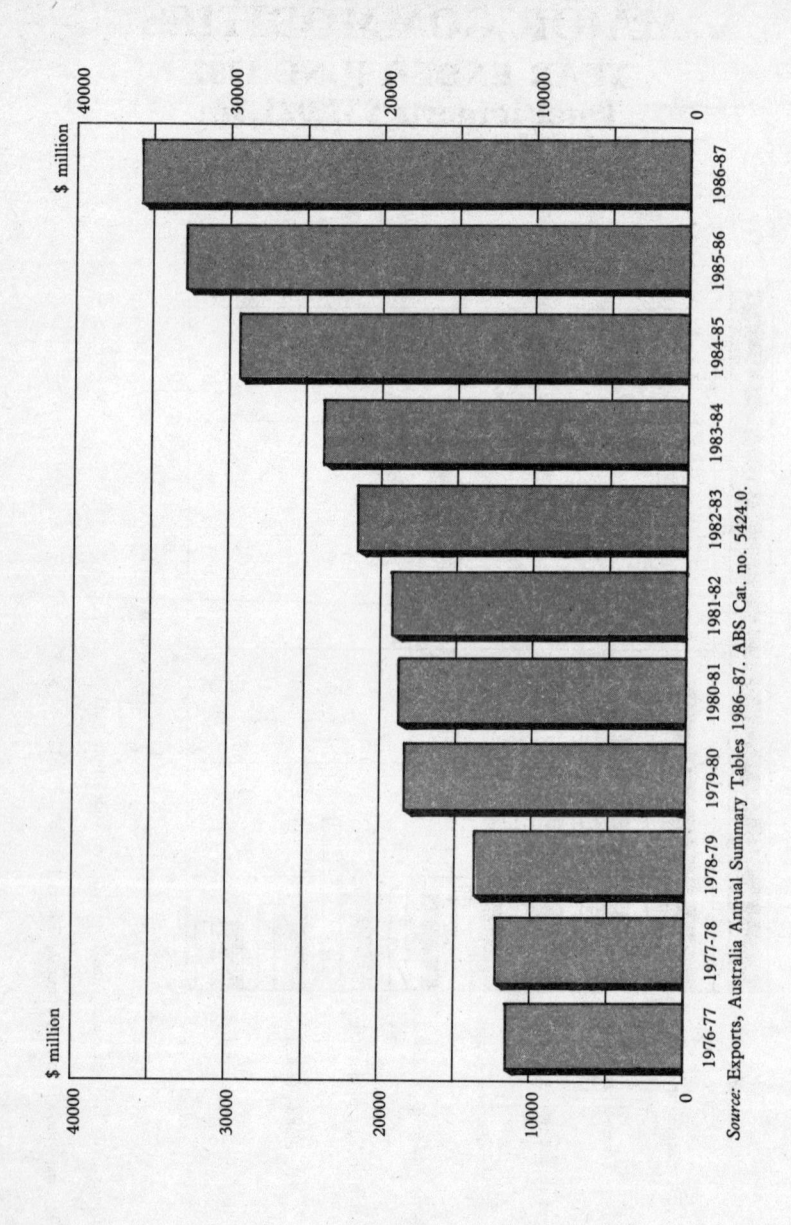

Source: Exports, Australia Annual Summary Tables 1986-87. ABS Cat. no. 5424.0.

DISTRIBUTION OF EXPORTS BY MAJOR COMMODITIES
YEAR ENDED JUNE 1987
Total exports $35,782.6m

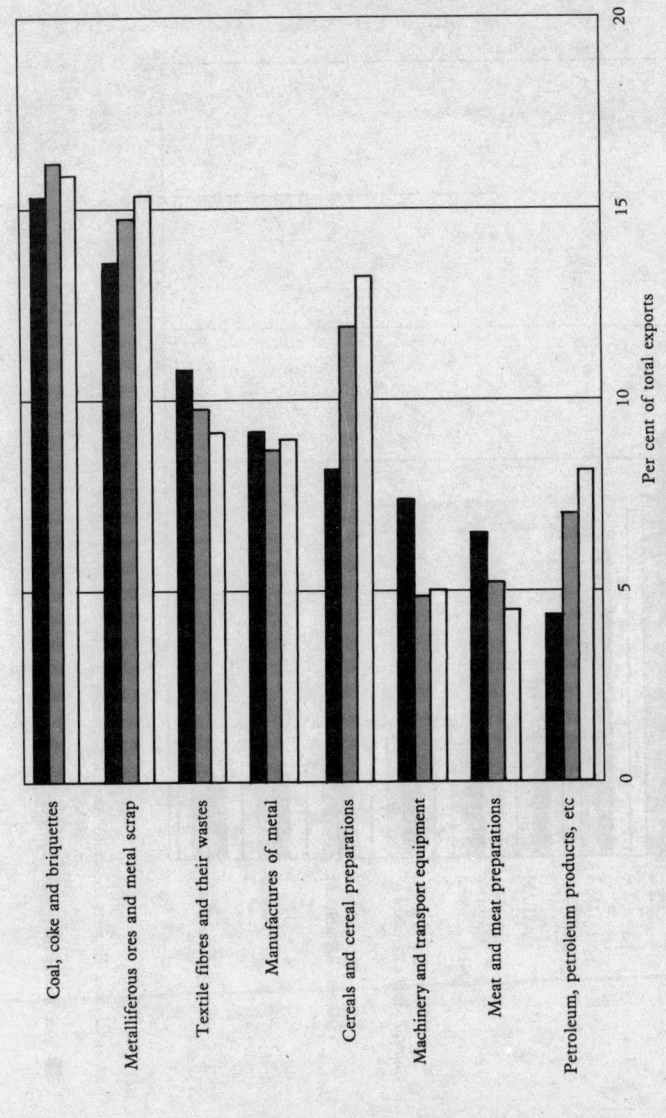

Adapted from: Exports, Australia Annual Summary Tables 1986–87. ABS Cat. no. 5424.0.

■ Year ended June 1987   ▩ Year ended June 1986   □ Year ended June 1985

DISTRIBUTION OF EXPORTS TO MAJOR COUNTRIES AND COUNTRY GROUPS
YEAR ENDED JUNE 1987
Total exports $35,782.6m

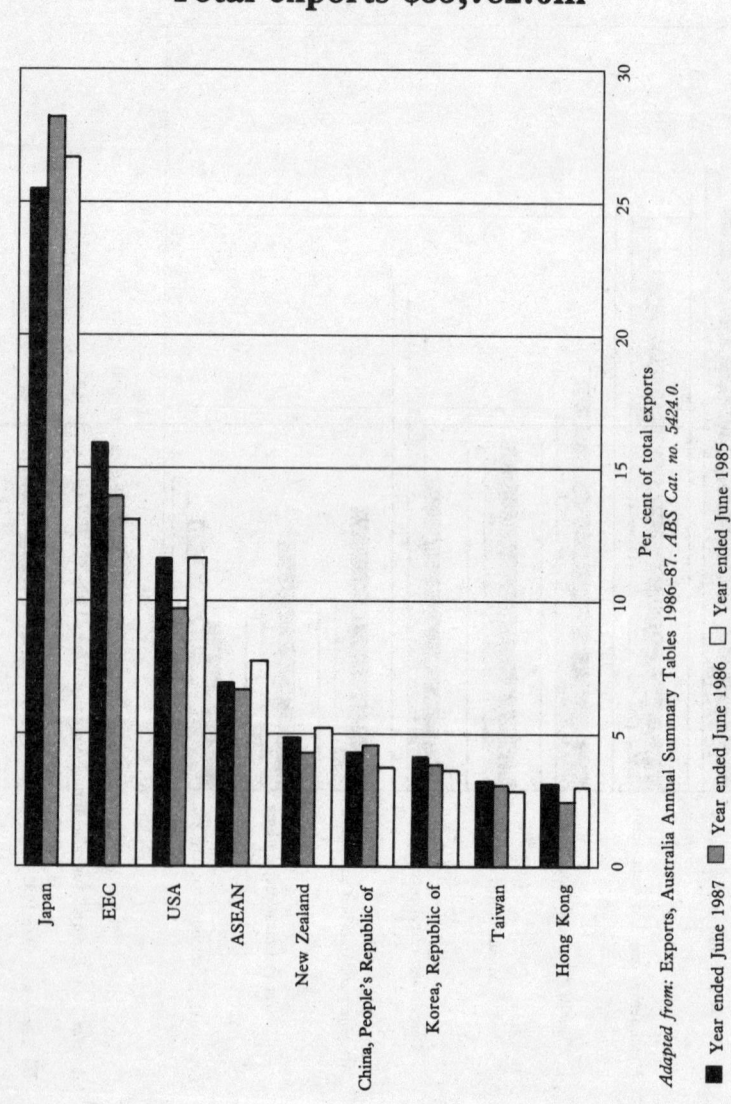

Adapted from: Exports, Australia Annual Summary Tables 1986–87. ABS Cat. no. 5424.0.

■ Year ended June 1987 ▨ Year ended June 1986 ☐ Year ended June 1985

EXPORTS BY STATE
$'000

State	1984-85	1985-86	1986-87
Australian produce			
New South Wales	6,674,013	7,363,192	8,355,789
Victoria	6,382,286	6,819,345	7,398,045
Queensland	6,488,019	7,587,782	7,734,635
South Australia	1,916,234	1,987,297	2,047,147
Western Australia	5,993,128	6,512,113	6,667,949
Tasmania	843,314	902,269	1,094,664
Northern Territory	550,902	603,927	750,318
Australian Capital Territory	862	3,803	924
State not available for publication	123,608	121,212	121,009
Total	**28,972,366**	**31,900,940**	**34,170,480**
Re-exports	735,747	894,067	1,612,104
Total exports	**29,708,113**	**32,795,007**	**35,782,583**

Australian produce is recorded on a State of origin basis. Re-export data are not available on a comparable basis.

Adapted from: Exports, Australia Annual Summary Tables 1986–87. *ABS Cat. no. 5426.0.*

WINE SALES

Major Category Type	Dec '86	Dec '87	Year to Date Jan '86 to Dec '86	Jan '87 to Dec '87
Fortified				
Sherry - Dry	1.0%	0.9%	1.0%	0.9%
- Medium	1.1%	1.0%	1.2%	1.2%
- Sweet	2.6%	2.3%	3.1%	2.7%
Port	4.4%	4.5%	5.1%	5.1%
Muscat	0.6%	0.5%	0.8%	0.7%
Other	.0%	.0%	.0%	0.1%
Total Fortified Wine	9.7%	9.2%	11.2%	10.6%
Table				
White	61.7%	58.4%	64.3%	62.8%
Red	9.1%	10.3%	11.6%	13.0%
Rose	2.1%	2.1%	2.1%	2.2%
Total Table Wine	72.8%	70.8%	78.1%	78.1%
Sparkling				
Bottle Fermentation	11.7%	14.7%	6.0%	6.9%
Bulk Fermentation	3.4%	3.3%	2.8%	2.3%
Total Sparkling Wine	15.2%	18.0%	8.8%	9.2%
Carbonated Wine	0.5%	0.5%	0.4%	0.4%
Flavoured Wine	0.8%	0.8%	0.7%	0.9%
Vermouth				
Dry	0.4%	0.3%	0.4%	0.4%
Sweet	0.6%	0.4%	0.5%	0.4%
Total Vermouth	1.0%	0.8%	0.9%	0.8%

Source: Australian Wine and Brandy Producers' Association Incorporated.

EXPORTS OF TABLE WINE

December 1987

Country	Bottled Quantity (Litres)	Bottled Value ($A)	Bulk Quantity (Litres)	Bulk Value ($A)	Total Quantity (Litres)	Total Value ($A)
Bahrain	2,694	2,814	-	-	2,694	2,814
Barbados	180	579	-	-	180	579
Canada	18,936	61,787	-	-	18,936	61,787
Denmark	32,679	114,930	60,120	47,214	92,799	162,144
Fiji	10,878	19,923	-	-	10,878	19,923
French Polynesia	17,475	20,150	-	-	17,475	20,150
Germany Federal Rep.	9,482	53,703	-	-	9,482	53,703
Hong Kong	28,937	112,087	-	-	28,937	112,087
Indonesia	28,264	36,623	15,600	17,028	43,864	53,651
Japan	61,555	165,313	-	-	61,555	165,313
Korea Dem. P. Rep.	2,007	8,424	-	-	2,007	8,424
Korea Rep.	2,250	10,634	-	-	2,250	10,634
Malaysia	2,257	10,036	900	804	3,157	10,840
Netherlands	20,178	53,278	19,038	11,423	39,216	64,701
New Zealand	164,605	534,498	-	-	164,605	534,498
Norfolk Island	1,368	8,341	-	-	1,368	8,341

Country	Bottled Quantity (Litres)	Bottled Value ($A)	Bulk Quantity (Litres)	Bulk Value ($A)	Total Quantity (Litres)	Total Value ($A)
Oman	12,000	12,000	-	-	12,000	12,000
Pakistan	1,420	3,615	-	-	1,420	3,615
Papua New Guinea	42,496	144,336	-	-	42,496	144,336
Philippines	261	1,052	-	-	261	1,052
Singapore	40,529	90,582	4,000	14,980	44,529	105,562
Solomon Islands	844	1,187	-	-	844	1,187
South Africa	18	1,000	-	-	18	1,000
Sri Lanka	945	1,135	-	-	945	1,135
Sweden	38,260	105,595	722,500	582,864	760,760	688,459
Switzerland	594	1,815	-	-	594	1,815
Thailand	13,815	29,461	-	-	13,815	29,461
Tonga	426	804	-	-	426	804
Trust Terr. of Pacific Is.	290	614	-	-	290	614
United Arab Emirates	22,148	29,959	-	-	22,148	29,959
United Kingdom	245,930	931,401	178,323	268,423	424,253	1,199,824
USA	234,544	1,137,881	-	-	234,544	1,137,881
Vanuatu	23,468	26,984	16,800	17,472	40,268	44,456
Western Samoa	273	1,387	-	-	273	1,387

Zimbabwe	1,620	6,554	-	-	1,620	6,554
Ships' and Aircraft Stores	180	530	2,209	2,054	2,389	2,584
December 1987	1,083,806	3,741,012	1,019,490	962,262	2,103,296	4,703,274
December 1986	656,319	1,919,174	445,002	351,378	1,131,321	2,270,552
% change	57.9	94.9	129.1	173.9	85.9	107.1
Financial Year to Date						
July 1987—Dec 1987	10,891,822	35,152,381	5,000,250	4,912,626	15,892,072	40,065,007
July 1986—Dec 1986	4,878,448	13,385,037	2,809,902	2,025,965	7,688,350	15,411,002
% change	123.3	162.6	78.0	142.5	106.7	160.0

Source: Australian Wine and Brandy Producers' Association Incorporated.

WHO OWNS WHAT

The level of foreign investment in Australia has risen steadily since World War II. Australian governments have generally encouraged this participation and today the flow of foreign funds into Australian enterprises is an essential component of the country's industry. An establishment is considered to be a foreign-controlled company when 25 per cent or more of the voting shares are owned by a foreign country or person and there is no equal or greater share held by an Australian.

The food, beverages and tobacco industry and the base metal industry are the two fields which attract the most money from foreign investment. As part of a move to more Australian participation, foreign investment in the mining industry has been waning since the 1970s and so in 1982–83 Australia owned 49.6 per cent of the value added to this industry. In approximately 92 per cent of manufacturing enterprises the degree of foreign investment is less than 25 per cent and in only 5.8 per cent is it greater than 50 per cent. So which companies dominate the Australian market and who owns them?

Let's begin in the lanes of the supermarket. One of the most common ingredients of all food products on the shelves has to be sugar. Sugar production is one of Australia's most unusual industries in that legislation provides for the Queensland government to buy all raw sugar milled in Australia. The resulting income is distributed according to local awards from the common industry funds to the growers and millers. Approximately half of the sugar mills are owned by Australian proprietary companies and the other half by cooperatives of canegrowers. There are fifteen cooperatives and they account for 43 per cent of raw sugar produced in Australia. CSR holds 36 per cent of the remaining sixteen mills, Bundaberg Sugar Company Ltd 12 per cent and Howard Smith Industries Pty Ltd 5 per cent. Our penchant for sugar earnt this industry nearly $1 billion annual revenue in 1987.

The Australian wine industry produces more than 320 million litres of wine per annum. Penfolds holds about 40 per cent of this market with its Kaiser Stuhl, Penfolds, Seaview, Tulloch and Wynn labels. Lindemans is owned by the American company, Philip Morris, and with its labels—Leo Buring, Lindemans and Rouge Homme—claims about 20 per cent of the wine sales. Orlando, which is British owned, takes 10 per cent and the remainder is shared, amongst others, by Hardys, McWilliams, Mildara, Seppelts, Wyndham Estate and Yalumba.

Beer manufacturers produce 1.8 billion litres per year with an annual turnover of $3 billion. Elders IXL and Bond Corporation are the names behind more than 90 per cent of sales. One of Australia's top five companies, Elders IXL has about 350 branches in Australia and offices in the United Kingdom, the United States and throughout Asia. Amongst its variety of activities it also owns Carlton United Breweries which produces Fosters, Victorian Bitter, Carlton Draught, Reschs and LA 2.1. Bond Brewing, owned by Bond Corporation, produces the Swan, Tooheys and XXXX beers. There are three other major beer producers in the Australian market: South Australian Brewing Company Ltd (West End and Southwark), Cooper and Sons Ltd (Coopers) and Tasmanian Breweries Ltd (Cascade and Boags).

British-owned Bushells market 53 per cent of our tea and Australian-owned Arnotts makes 75 per cent of our biscuits. Arnotts Ltd began as a family business in 1865 and later merged with other manufacturers including Brockhoff, Guest, Mills and Ware, Swallow and Peak Frean. It is also a significant force in snack foods, especially potato crisps, and controls a range of flour milling, stock feed and card and plastic packaging companies.

Australia's largest breadmaker is George Weston which has an annual revenue of about $27 million. The multinational company, Nestle, holds 59 per cent of an Australian coffee market worth $318 million, followed by Bushells with 15 per cent.

Kelloggs and Nabisco are American-owned companies which command about 43 per cent and 22 per cent of the Australian breakfast cereal market respectively. Another 21 per cent is claimed by Sanitarium, founded and owned by the Seventh Day Adventist religious organisation in Australia. Fast foods is another area dominated by American interests. The big names are familiar to us all: Kentucky Fried Chicken, McDonalds and Pizza Hut.

Every year clear cleaning our teeth earns the toothpaste industry $60 million. Colgate Palmolive, based in the United States, cleans up 55 per cent of the market; Unilever, owned by Lever and Kitchen (UK), is second largest, claiming 22 per cent and Beecham, also based in the United Kingdom, comes third.

Unilever and Colgate Palmolive are also washing most of our laundry. They are followed by the Australian-owned company R. & M. Gow, and one of Australia's leading manufacturers and distributors of foods, wines, toiletries and household cleansers, the British-based Reckitt and Colman Australia Ltd. Reckitt and Colman brands include Keens, Holbrooks, Enavite, Planters, Nugget, Meltonian, Brasso, Pine-O-Clean, Trix, Mr Sheen, Mortein, Fabulon, Preen, Harpic, Steradent, Dettol, Disprin, Loxene, Decoré and Gossamer.

There are more than twenty internationally recognised brands competing in Australia's cosmetic market. Health and beauty products earn $1011.5 million per annum and $390 million is generated by fragrances and cosmetics. The Anglo-Dutch company Rexona leads the toiletries market while other major health and beauty market shares are held by Fabergé and Shiseido. Fabergé is half owned by Australian shareholders and half by Rapid-American Corporation of the United States. Shiseido is an expanding Japanese manufacturer. The Canadian-owned company Estee Lauder Pty Ltd has managed to secure the major share of the Australian cosmetics market and French-based Clarins is another major player.

There are three major competitors in the tobacco market. Amatil Ltd is Australia's largest manufacturer and distributor of tobacco products. W. D. & H. O. Wills Australia Ltd is their principal subsidiary whose own list of subsidiaries includes Benson and Hedges, Kool, Country Life, Escort, Hallmark and Ardath. Incidentally, Associated Products and Distribution Pty Ltd is another of Amatil's major subsidiaries marketing, instead of a smoke, Smiths crisps, Cheezels, Twisties, Shelleys, Kirks soft drinks, Coca-Cola, Mynor drinks and Nobbys Nuts. Amatil also has interests in Steggles (frozen poultry), Courage Breweries, the meat industry, pastoral companies and engineering.

Rothmans of Pall Mall (Aust.) Pty Ltd is a major competitor in the tobacco market and holds a 3 per cent edge in tobacco sales, mainly due to the successful Winfield brand. Their other brand names are Dunhill and Peter Stuyvesant. Rothmans is 50 per cent Australian and 50 per cent British owned. The third company is Philip Morris Aust. Ltd which is totally American owned and includes Alpine, Marlboro and the increasingly popular Peter Jackson.

British publishing houses continue to dominate Australian book publishers and distributors. Penguin and William Collins account for half of general book sales and Collins Australia, a subsidiary of William Collins, is the leading publisher in Australia. One of its major brands is Fontana paperbacks. Angus and Robertson is the largest Australian publisher and distributor in a booksellers' market worth $800 million.

The textile industry is largely Australian owned. Bonds Coats Patons Ltd are cotton and wool spinners, manufacturers of knitting yarns (including Sirdar and Villawool), sewing thread, underwear, fashionwear, nightwear, babywear, nappies and towels (including Dri-Glo and Dickies). No longer based in the United Kingdom, they are owned by Pacific Dunlop Ltd which commands nearly $1 billion in annual sales of textiles, footwear and clothing. Their clothing and household textiles brands also include Rio, Holeproof, Sheridan, Dreamspun, Berlei, Hestia, and Brandella; footwear includes Dunlop, Slazenger, Grosby, Footworks, Hollandia, Paragini, Jiffies, Adidas, Candy and more. Names such as Bradmill, Speedo, King Gee and Formfit all belong to the Linter Group Ltd which is Australian owned. Linter's subsidiaries also include Australian Consolidated Hosiery, Kortex, Jacquard, Pelaco Australia, and Exacto.

The 1980s has seen a growing Japanese influence in the expanding Australian automotive industry which was largely dominated by American manufacturers during the preceding decade. Car sales slumped in 1987 when only 140,208 vehicles were registered during the year ending in April. There are five major companies of which the two American giants Ford and Holden drive off with about 44 per cent of the overall market and also dominate the passenger car sector. The commercial sector is dominated by the Japanese producers. Toyota, Mitsubishi and Nissan claim 42 per cent of overall vehicle sales and the other Japanese manufacturers, Honda, Mazda, Daihatsu, Suzuki and Subaru, make up all but 1 per cent of the market. Honda is a leading motorcycle manufacturer.

Oil in Australia is a $12 billion industry of which 60 per cent is paid in state and federal taxes. Caltex (75 per cent American, 25 per cent Australian), Shell (60 per cent Dutch, 40 per cent British), BP (British), Mobil (American), Ampol (Australian), and Esso (American) comprise, in that order, the major oil-refining companies in Australia. Ampol, the only wholly Australian-owned producer, claims 13 per cent of the market.

Dunlop Pacific and Goodyear entered a joint venture in 1987 forming South Pacific Tyres, and lay claim to 41 per cent of the rubber tyre market. Bridgestone, 60 per cent of which is owned by the Bridgestone Corporation based in Tokyo, claims another 20 per cent, and the rest is supplied by importers.

ICI Australia Ltd is owned by Imperial Chemical Industries PLC, UK and is a clear leader in the Australian chemical market. It manufactures a whole range of fertilisers and agricultural chemicals, pharmaceuticals and animal health products, plastics, paints, explosives, inks, soap and cosmetics. The other main contenders for the $2.3 billion in chemicals are Dow Chemical (American), Hoechst (West German), Monsanto (American), and Shell Chemical (Dutch).

Computer companies are chiefly American and Japanese owned. IBM has overall the largest range of products and the largest market share but Apple is the leader in personal computer sales. Hewlett Packard Australia Ltd and Burrows are the next major American-owned companies and Fujitsu is the major Japanese supplier. Brisbane-based Computer Corp of Australia (CCA) is the largest Australian personal computer manufacturer and IBM is the largest manufacturer of PCs in Australia.

Building materials is predominantly a locally owned industry. There is around $720 million in cement each year. Forty per cent of this market is held by Blue Circle Southern Cement which is owned by the Australian company, Boral Ltd. CSR-Pioneer Concrete is the next major cement mixer followed by Adelaide Brighton Cement Holdings Ltd of which Boral also holds 10 per cent. Boral, Pioneer-Concrete and CSR also lead in ready-made mixed concrete which is a $900 million industry, with about a quarter of the market supplied by each company.

Through its subsidiaries, Softwood Holdings Ltd and Formica Australia, CSR is Australia's biggest producer of particle board. Boral, PGH (ACI), and CSR comprise over 60 per cent of the $630 million in bricks. Monier Redland

Ltd, owned by the British group Redland PLC, has about 65 per cent of the Australian roofing market.

Local steelmakers supply between 75-85 per cent of Australian steel production needs. The Broken Hill Proprietary Company Ltd (BHP) was formed in 1885 to mine at Broken Hill and is now the largest industrial company in Australia. Its interests are organised into four divisions: steel, minerals, oils and gas, as well as subsidiaries and investments. It fulfils 70 per cent of the country's steel requirements with an annual revenue in excess of $4 billion. BHP has substantial interests in offshore petroleum exploration, a 50 per cent share in Bass Strait petroleum fields and a styrene monomer plant at Footscray, Victoria. It has a major interest in a number of manufacturing companies including Rheem Australia, Australia Wire Industries, Blue Circle Southern Cement, John Lysaght (sheet steel) and Australian Industrial Refractories (bricks). Smorgon Consolidated Industries (Australian) has a small share of the steel market and Comsteel, based at Newcastle, New South Wales, produces rolled steel worth $25 million a year.

Flat glass is produced only by Pilkington-ACI Operations Ltd, a British and Australian company. It commands $294 million in sales to processors such as O'Brien Glass Industries Ltd and T. & K. Glass (Aust.), a division of ACI International. The food and beverage glass market is supplied by two major companies: Australian Glass Manufacturers, a subsidiary of ACI International Ltd, which is predominantly Australian owned with a small New Zealand interest; and the wholly Australian-owned Smorgon Consolidated Industries.

The paper and packaging industry is wrapped up by three major companies. These are Associated Pulp and Paper Mills (APPM), owned by North Broken Hill Holdings, making fine paper and printing paper; Australian Newsprint Mills (ANM), a division of Amcor, making two-thirds of Australia's paper and paper board used by the packaging industry; and Australian Paper Manufacturers (APM), a subsidiary of Australian Newsprint Holdings Ltd, supplying 40 per cent of Australian newsprint. Other major companies involved in this industry are Smorgon Consolidated Industries, Kimberley-Clark Australia Pty Ltd (50 per cent Australian and 50 per cent American owned) and Bowater Scott Ltd (British owned).

Electronics create a $2.2 billion market, 15 per cent of which is claimed by Amalgamated Wireless (Australasia) Ltd (AWA) and 12 per cent by Standard Telephones and Cables (STC), a subsidiary of the large American organisation, ITT Corporation. STC is also the principle telecommunications supplier in the Australian market. Philips (Dutch), Plessey (British), L. M. Ericsson (Swedish), Siemans (West German) and NEC (Japanese) are other large contenders in the electronics market. Japanese manufacturers including Sanyo, Sharp, Mitsubishi and NEC dominate television sales.

Australian National Industries Ltd is 100 per cent Australian and through its Comeng subsidiary, supplies 70 per cent of Australia's rolling stock. It is the largest engineering-based company. Commonwealth Industrial Gases Ltd (CIG), British owned with 41 per cent Australian shareholders, produces the most welding products. Hawker de Havilland Ltd is also British based, owned by the Hawker Siddeley Group, and is the largest aerospace company in Australia. The subsidiary of the British based The General Electric Company, GEC Australia Ltd, is the largest electrical engineering company.

L.K.

COMPUTERS AND THE LAW

Computer technology changes everything bit by bit. The law is no exception. In some areas the law is changed in order to cope with problems which arise because of the introduction of computers. Such is the case with the law of data protection, copyright and crime. These are areas where the introduction of computers has created problems which do not seem to fit comfortably within the pre-computer legal structure.

In other areas, the law is changing as a direct result of the application of computer technology. The introduction of large-scale data information retrieval systems has meant that lawyers can find more information easier and faster than ever before. In some jurisdictions, this has led to calls that the information presented in court should be restricted in some way so as to avoid an 'information overload' in litigation.

Although it is too soon to know for certain, the most exciting changes in the law may be from the application of artificial intelligence to legal problems. Particularly in the form of expert systems, this technology holds the promise of providing better and cheaper legal services, especially in areas where the user of the legal service is disadvantaged under the present legal system.

'Computers and the Law' is not, then, a single well-developed topic. It is a collection of changes which are occurring in the legal system as a result of the widespread and rapid growth in the use of computers. It is not possible, then, to discuss all of the changes here, but the following topics are representative.

DATA PROTECTION

We are all 'data subjects', as the Commonwealth government's ill-fated Australia Card Bill (1986) described us. We are the subject matter (if not the subjects) of dozens of computerised databases that record our characteristics, history and transactions from cradle to grave. What rights do we have in relation to these record systems that potentially have such power over our lives?

Data protection, sometimes called *information privacy*, refers to laws that regulate information about individuals. *Privacy* is a broader term, since it also includes protection against physical intrusions and visual surveillance.

Data Protection in Australia

Data protection law in Australia is underdeveloped compared with Europe and North America, despite the fact that Australia has promised to adhere to the Organisation for Economic Co-Operation and Development's 1980 Guidelines on the Protection of Privacy and Transborder Flows of Personal Data. Australia has no constitutional protection of privacy; the common law courts have not developed any general tort law of privacy protection and only an incomplete law of confidential information. Since the courts have been unable or unwilling to develop such law, it is over to the legislature to act. Unfortunately, there has been very little parliamentary action with the result that there is very little data protection law in Australia.

The Commonwealth and Victorian Freedom of Information Acts give individuals a right to obtain access to records concerning them, along with access to records of other Commonwealth and Victorian government agencies. They may also force agencies to amend records concerning their 'personal affairs' if those records are inaccurate, incomplete, out-of-date or misleading. No such rights exist in other states, although the Liberal-Country government elected in New South Wales in 1988 has promised to introduce such legislation.

State Agencies

Two states have established types of 'data protection agencies', based on the ombudsman model, that is, an independent body with powers to hear complaints and to make recommendations. The New South Wales Privacy Committee is an independent statutory body established by the *Privacy Committee Act* 1975. It was the only permanent data protection agency in Australia until Queensland established a similar committee in 1985.

The New South Wales committee consists of twelve part-time members and a small permanent staff of research and complaints officers. Its functions are to investigate complaints, conduct research and make reports on matters relating to 'the privacy of persons'. Privacy is not defined in the act, and there are no judicial decisions interpreting the act. It makes no distinction between the public and private sectors, and does not exempt anyone from investigation. The committee, may, therefore, investigate any type of violation of privacy by any person, business or agency. The committee has no powers to compel the adoption of its recommendations and although it has no powers of direct compulsion, the committee can require any person to give any statement of information or produce any document, and it has the powers and immunities of a Royal Commission.

The committee makes an annual report to parliament which is protected by parliamentary privilege. In recent years, it has formally 'named' organisations and persons in its annual report which it considers have invaded privacy unjustifiably. Bodies and persons so named have included the Hibernian Credit Union Limited, the New South Wales Department of Education, *60 Minutes*, the television program, Waltons Credits Limited, and Denallen Investigations Pty Ltd. In three of these cases companies were named because of the way in which they had misused the Credit Reference Association of Australia (CRAA). Being named in the committee's annual report usually results in considerable publicity in the press.

The committee investigates about 300 complaints per year, the breakdown of which in its 1986 annual report was as follows:

25% credit related
12% employment
10% data systems
10% medical
5% debt collection methods
5% unsolicited mail
5% retail store—bag searches
5% confidentiality
5% police methods/criminal records
5% media
3% others

(The figures given in the report only account for 90 per cent of all cases. The reason is not known.)

Commonwealth activities

The Commonwealth government introduced a Privacy Bill in 1986 as part of a 'package deal' with the Australia Card legislation; as one cartoonist commented, they would protect our privacy after taking it away. With the demise of the Australia Card, the Privacy Bill has been referred to a Senate committee. It is now twelve years since the Australian Law Reform Commission was asked to investigate privacy protection and it seems we are no closer to any useful Commonwealth legislation. Meanwhile, data surveillance marches on. A Commonwealth interdepartmental committee recommended in 1987 that all Commonwealth agencies routinely swap information about their 'clientele' except where this was illegal, and that laws should be changed so that it would not be illegal. Such expansion of 'data matching' may serve many of the same functions as the ID card would have.

Private sector

With regard to the private sector, three states have credit reporting legislation: the *Invasion of Privacy Act* 1970 (Qld), the *Fair Credit Reports Act* 1974 (SA) and the *Credit Reporting Act* 1978 (Vic.). These acts are similar in form and were drafted during the 1970s when credit reporting in Australia was mainly conducted by local credit bureaus using manual, paper based, record systems. The legislation is quite inappropriate to the 1980s when one Australia-wide computerised credit bureau, the CRAA, completely dominates consumer credit reporting and is moving to dominate commercial credit reporting as well.

CRAA holds files on over five million consumers, and issues over five million reports per year. In practice, it ignores the procedural aspects of the existing state legislation and instead implements Australia-wide a set of data protection principles based on a Voluntary Agreement between the credit industry and the New South Wales Privacy Committee. The Voluntary Agreement gives people a right to obtain access to their credit bureau files, and to obtain correction of inaccurate and incomplete information. It is used in this way by over 20,000 consumers per year. CRAA deletes all information after five years, except bankruptcies which are kept for seven years. The Voluntary Agreement does not, however, place any controls on who can have access to credit records, and already the insurance industry, real estate agencies and some government departments have access. CRAA is becoming the 'Australia Card register' of the private sector, the hub of a multipurpose data surveillance system. Nor is there any right of damages for negligent or malicious misuse of records. It is apparent that legislation is needed.

Property rights in programs and databases

The Australian computer software industry has a production value of $590 million per year, employs 8000 people and, has an annual growth rate of 25.3 per cent. The industry, one of the fastest growing in Australia, believes that it cannot survive without the protection of the law of copyright. The effect that the sale and distribution of unauthorised copies of software has on this lucrative market is difficult to assess, but was enough to prompt the Federation Against Software Theft (FAST) to announce in March 1988 that its sixteen software distributor members had each contributed $10,000 to a fund to campaign against pirates.

The legal foundation of FAST's campaign is the federal *Copyright Amendment Act* 1984 which was intended to provide copyright protection to software after a decision by the Federal Court in a case involving Apple computers cast doubt on whether copyright law at that time was adequate.

The Apple case

In the case of *Apple v Computer Edge*, Apple had produced the source code originally in writing of a number of computer programs. *Source code* refers to the notation in which programmers write programs. Other programs are then used to convert that source code into *object code*, the form of a program which causes a computer to perform operations. Apple had also produced ROMs (Read-Only Memory chips), a form of computer storage, for inclusion in Apple II computers, and these ROMs embodied the same programs in object code. Computer Edge sold Wombat computers, the manufacturer of which had copied the Apple ROMs to produce its own ROMs, and in doing so had copied the programs in the form in which they existed in the Apple ROMs. Apple claimed that the Wombat manufacturer, in copying the ROMs, had either reproduced or adapted either the source code or the object code in the Apple programs. The judge held that Apple had failed to establish copyright but, on appeal, a two to one majority of the Full Bench of the Federal Court upheld Apple's claim. The situation was uncertain enough, however, for the software industry to mount a campaign calling for urgent action by the federal government.

The Copyright Amendment Act

The *Copyright Amendment Act* 1984 attempted to extend protection to programs by:
1 defining *literary work* to include a computer program;
2 defining *computer program* so that it includes both source code and object code;
3 defining *adaptation* in relation to a

computer program so as to include a version of the work, whether or not in the original language code or notation of the work;

4 defining *material form*, in relation to any work or adaptation of a work to include 'any form (whether visible or not) of storage from which the work or adaptation, or a substantial part of the work or adaptation, can be reproduced'.

The problem is that the 1984 amendments predate the final 1986 decision of the High Court in the Apple Case (*Computer Edge P/L v. Apple Computer Inc.* (1986) 60 ALJR 313), and it turns out that the amendments are based on assumptions on which the High Court has now cast doubt. Although the High Court's decision was made under the pre-1984 law, the then Chief Justice Sir Harry Gibbs commented in passing that he was not sure that the 1984 amendments were free from doubt. He implied that it was arguable that even the amendments only dealt with written computer programs, and did not cover the case of an infringer who only 'looks at the circuitry and copies that'.

Problems with the Amendment

The majority of the High Court held that, although the written source code was copyright as a literary work, the object code in the form in which it existed in the ROMs was not. Nor was object code in that form a reproduction or an adaptation of the source code. In general terms, the majority insisted that any material form of a literary work must express that work in a visible form, irrespective of whether it claims to represent the substance of the original work, an adaptation of it, or a reproduction of it. The 1984 amendments do not address this requirement directly.

The court decided that the object code in either the Apple or Wombat ROMs was not an adaptation of the source code, or a 'translation' of the source code. The court maintained that the term 'translation' referrred to languages and that the object code embodied in the ROMs was 'clearly not a language', because the essential purpose of language is to convey thought. The court decided to describe the electrical charges stored in the ROM not as a 'machine readable language' because this would confuse metaphor with reality. This reasoning causes two problems with the 1984 amendments.

One of the elements of the 1984 definition of a computer program is 'an expression, in any language, code or notation, of a set of instructions'. On the reasoning of the majority in the Apple decision, the object code which is stored in a ROM cannot be an expression in a 'language' since it is not in written form. Indeed, it is merely a collection of 'electrical charges' which can be interpreted by a computer. And if it is not a 'language', then even less is it 'an expression' in a language. The second problem is that the 1984 definition of 'adaptation' as 'a version of the work (whether or not in the language, code or notation in which the work was originally expressed)' implies that the version must be in some 'language code or notation'. This gives rise to the same problems of interpretation. The terms of the act are certainly ambiguous. In such a situation, the rules of statutory interpretation allow the court to use extrinsic materials, particularly Parliamentary Explanatory Memoranda, as an aid to clarification. The Explanatory Memorandum for the amendment clearly supports a broad meaning of 'computer program', but there must inevitably be some remaining doubt about the final interpretation of the terms should the matter again come before a court.

An infringing copy of a program must be either an adaptation of the program or a reproduction in a material form. In considering whether the Wombat ROMs were a reproduction of the source code, the court considered that the necessary element of 'resemblance' was absent. 'The ROMs and EPROM (Eraseable Programmable Read Only Memory, a special kind of ROM) embody the idea, and logical structure, of the source programs, but do not reproduce the expression of the idea and of the logical thought which is to be found in the source programs.' The source code was seen as instructions to construct a ROM with certain functional attributes, 'like a recipe for rabbit pie' and although there is copyright in the written recipe there is no copyright in the pie! The 1984 amendments contain no definition of 'reproduction', and therefore do not directly address these problems.

Application to text

Perhaps the most serious failing of the 1984 amendments in the light of the Apple case concerns textual works. We would think of letters in a word processor, lists of customers in a bank's computer system, and bibliographies, books or cases on a multi-user database, as all being literary works if they were in print. While held in computer storage media, such texts have the same problems as programs in satisfying the Apple requirements in the Apple case for a literary work. The 1984 amendments do not address this problem. Database operators, or manufacturers of CD-ROMs (Compact Disk Read Only Memory), could claim unjustified discrimination against the creators of texts in electronic form in comparison with creators using conventional paper-based media.

Infringement by users

Despite these problems with the 1984 amendments, users of a pirate program might infringe copyright when they make its contents visible on screen. This will not in itself satisfy the copyright owner who wants a remedy against the pirate, not his customers. But it could be argued that the pirate has, by the sale of the pirated item, authorised the purchaser to commit such infringements if the purchaser is to make any use of it, and this 'authorising' is an infringement of copyright itself. This approach would provide copyright protection for programs which normally produce screen displays or printouts, but not all computer programs do this. Some programs are concerned only with the internal workings of the computer; others are for the purposes of controlling a machine or a process. The proper form of protection for such programs may well be patent law.

COMPUTER CRIME

It is difficult to commit computer crime in Australia. Under the existing criminal law, activities such as breaching computer system security to obtain confidential information or free computer time will not give rise to criminal liability. Similarly, the copying, modification or destruction of computerised data will not amount to criminal conduct. Only the Northern Territory, the Australian Capital Territory and Victoria have moved to adopt specific computer crime legislation to alter this position.

Incidence

The incidence of computer-related abuse is difficult to assess. It is suspected that much abuse goes undetected or unreported. In the United States, it has been estimated that fewer than 1 per cent of cases are reported.

Of the cases which have been reported, those which would appear to be most serious can be broadly classified as computer-related fraud. One of the few cases which has been considered by an Australian court concerned a bank's computer system manager who reprogrammed the bank's computer to inflate customers' accounts. The excess amounts were then transferred to his own account.

In another Australian case, an accountant placed a 'logic bomb' in a business's computer-based records system. The 'bomb' consisted of a number of changes in the programs underlying the system which would cause records to be destroyed at a later time. After moving interstate, the accountant telephoned his previous employers, demanding money in exchange for information about the 'bomb'.

The introduction of automatic teller machines (ATM) has provided another avenue for computer abuse. In the first half of 1984, some 3386 instances of ATM abuse were reported to police in New South Wales. In the period January to September 1985, 9403 instances were reported in Victoria.

The Law

With a few exceptions, most instances of computer-related abuse must be dealt with according to general criminal law provisions and principles. Where a computer is used simply as a tool in the commission of a crime, or as a physical target of crime, no new problems are raised. For example, where changes to computerised records are used to effect the deception of a human being, or where a computer itself is physically stolen or damaged, the existing law will apply.

Where, on the other hand, the alleged conduct relates only to such actions as the unauthorised copying, abstraction or alteration of data, no crime will have been committed in most cases.

The reasons for this are various. Conventional offences such as larceny and malicious injury to property will only apply to physical property and not to information or records stored in a computer. In respect to larceny, there are also problems with the requirements of asportation or 'carrying off' and intention to permanently deprive.

In the High Court case of *Kennison v Daire*, the defendant was charged with larceny following unauthorised withdrawals from an automatic teller machine. It was argued by the defendant that the bank had consented to the withdrawals by programming the ATM to dispense money when a card was inserted and a personal identification number entered. This argument was rejected by the court holding that the bank's action in merely making possible the withdrawal did not indicate consent.

It is generally not possible to deceive a machine. Offences such as obtaining by deception, obtaining by false pretences and fraudulent personation, will generally not apply. It also is unlikely that tampering with computer records would be caught by the forgery provisions, since in order to commit forgery it is necessary that an 'instrument' or document be forged. It is unlikely that computer records would fall within these categories.

The Australian Capital Territory has altered its Crimes Act to expressly provide that the forgery provisions will apply to alterations of computer records. The definition of 'instrument' has been expanded to include various forms of computerised storage. Where a machine responds to an instrument as if it were genuine, such as an unauthorised plastic card in an automatic teller machine, this will provide sufficient deception for forgery purposes. The Northern Territory has enacted similar legislation.

The unauthorised use of computer time will generally not constitute a criminal offence. It is possible that this may fall within the 'larceny of electricity provisions' which are present in most of the Crimes Acts, but this has not been tested.

Again the Australian Capital Territory has altered its legislation in this respect. Where a person dishonestly uses a computer or machine with the intent to produce a gain for themselves or a loss to another person, that person will be liable for an offence carrying a maximum of ten years' imprisonment. The definition of 'machine' includes any machine designed to be operated by means of a coin, banknote, token, disk, tape or any identifying card or article. It has been pointed out that this makes the application of the section very wide producing anomalous results such as the apparent criminalisation of infringement of copyright through use of coin-operated photostat machines but not through use of non-coin-operated machines. Unauthorised use of a motor vehicle (being a machine operated by a key) would also seem caught by this section!

Recent Developments

In July 1986 the Law Reform Commission of Tasmania published a report examining the state of Australian criminal law on 'computer misuse'. The report called for a legislative response to computer misuse by all Australian jurisdictions. The Standing Committee of Attorneys General met in March 1987 and decided that uniform national legislation on computer crime was not necessary and that the matter was to be left to the States.

In September 1987 the Victorian

government introduced the Crimes (Computers) Bill 1987. The bill makes it clear that certain existing offences are to be extended to include the fraudulent manipulation of computer data. Deception which is facilitated by the manipulation of computer data will now clearly fall within the offence of 'obtaining by deception' and the alteration of computer records will be 'forgery' within the meaning of the new definitions.

At the time of writing, there has been no other legislative response from either the Commonwealth or the other states.

Conclusion

Many overseas jurisdictions have had some form of computer crime legislation for a considerable time. It would seem that Australia is moving in a similar direction. From a policy perspective this shift may not be wholly desirable.

It is arguable that even with such legislation the problems of detection and lack of reporting will render it inoperative. The United States has had widespread adoption of computer crime provisions in most state codes since about 1980. Until July 1986, there were fewer than 100 prosecuted cases.

It should also be remembered that the targets of computer abuse will generally be large corporations, financial institutions and government departments. Arguably, such bodies should be able to take care of themselves in maintaining the security of their computer systems. Without large scale and costly re-equipment and retraining within law enforcement agencies, it is unlikely that such agencies will be able to carry any new laws into effect.

EXPERT SYSTEMS

An *expert system* is a computer program intended to perform a task, which would otherwise be performed by a human expert. Increasingly, expert systems technologies are being applied to the law. It differs from a conventional computer program in several significant respects. An expert system is knowledge based—it embodies knowledge relevant to some specific field of expertise or problem domain, and it is a distinct and quite separate part of the program. Another part of the program—the inference engine—is responsible for applying the knowledge. Expert systems generally operate heuristically rather than procedurally. This means that inexact rules of inference, deduction and induction are applied, so-called heuristics or rules of thumb. As human experts can be wrong, expert systems can also make mistakes.

Legal Expert Systems

Expert systems may be applied to legal problems in a variety of ways. Advisory systems may be constructed which will provide lawyer-like advice to the user. Intelligent document generation systems are intended to assist the lawyer in the problems of drafting long and complex legal documents. Expert systems may also provide 'smart' monitoring systems which will, for example, remind the lawyer of critical deadlines which must be observed and which may produce the necessary legal documentation to assist in the meeting of those deadlines.

The solution to any legal problem may involve a number of disparate forms of reasoning. These can include fairly procedural deductive analysis, the application of legal precedents, reasoning by analogy, and the balancing of discretionary factors. A legal expert system must duplicate all of these approaches if it is to be successful.

Another feature of the operation of the law that is significant is the importance of argument. Whereas the explanation facility in most expert systems is used merely to give the user confidence in the system's conclusions, the explanation is the major product of the legal expert system. Without explanation of the legal argument which justifies the conclusion reached, legal advice is of little or no value.

Legal expert systems may be targeted at lawyers themselves or at lay persons. To the lawyer, these systems can assist with the reasoning process, ensuring that issues are covered in a systematic way and that nothing is left out. They may also serve to allow non-qualified but legally trained persons—para-legals—to handle a greater range of matters.

To the legal lay person, legal expert systems can offer advice where otherwise this may not have been possible. Some areas of the law, such as bankruptcy, social security, tenancy and immigration are particularly suitable as target domains for such systems since, almost by definition, the people most in need of such advice are the least able to pay high legal costs.

Existing Systems

At the present time, there are very few commercial legal expert systems which are used in legal offices or elsewhere in the community. Most are still in the developmental phase and include:

Social Security Enquiry System (SSES)
This system is being developed by David Mead and Peter Johnston of Canberra College of Advanced Education. It advises which social security benefit entitlements may be available to the user. Since accepting some benefits may preclude the availability of others, the system is designed to advise the user of the optimum combination of benefits. It also considers special needs of the individual user such as the need to obtain benefits quickly versus the desire to obtain the greatest possible benefits.

The Datalex Research Project
The Datalex Research Project is a joint research project which is managed by Graham Greenleaf, Andrew Mowbray and Alan Tyree. Its purpose is to devise tools for the creation of legal expert systems and then to develop expert systems. Several systems are operational.

INTEST is an expert system which determines the distribution of assets when a person dies without leaving a valid will. These matters are governed entirely by the *Wills, Probate and Administration Act* 1898. INTEST was developed using the Legal Expert System Generator (LES) expert system shell which was developed as part of the Datalex Project.

The problem of case law and its use in legal reasoning is one which seems unique to legal systems. The Datalex Project has developed a method of dealing with case law reasoning which is exemplified in the FINDER expert system. FINDER advises on the law-related disputes which arise when a chattel is found by one person and is claimed by another who may or may not be the original owner of the chattel. The area is legally interesting because it is governed entirely by case law.

The techniques of case law and statute law are brought together in COPYRITA. It advises the user on problems of copyright which fall within the *Copyright Act* 1968. Although the act is the primary source of law for the solution of copyright problems, it must be read subject to case law which has interpreted its terms.

Overseas systems

There is a significant amount of overseas research into the application of artificial intelligence to legal problems. *Artificial Intelligence* (AI) is the general study of methods which can be used to make machines exhibit behaviour which we ordinarily consider to be manifestations of intelligence. AI is thus the general field of study of which expert systems forms a part. The First International Conference on Artificial Intelligence and the Law was held at Northeastern University, Boston, USA in May of 1987. The conference attracted participants from more than a dozen countries; the proceedings of the conference are an excellent introduction to the work which was being done.

There are several well-known systems which have been developed by the Rand Corporation. LDS (Legal Decision-making System) was one of the first legal expert systems. It assesses product liability claims and advises on appropriate levels of settlement. The knowledge base includes both formal legal information as well as heuristic principles and strategies.

The history of LDS is interesting and points to another, unusual, use of expert systems. The builders of LDS originally wished to study the operation of the legal system which is outside the court structure. Were it not for the fact that the vast majority of cases are settled by negotiation between the parties, the entire legal system would collapse from the overload. The researchers found, however, that the details of the actual cases which had been settled were not available, being considered as confidential by the parties involved. LDS was originally built as a very clever 'simulator' which could provide information which was not available in the 'real' world.

The experience gained in building LDS has been applied to build a system which will assist the parties to come to a settlement figure. SAL (System for Asbestos Litigation) is similar in design to LDS and assists in the evaluation of damages in asbestos-related personal injuries claims.

G. G., A. M., A. T.

Sources:
Bequai, A. *Computer Crime*. Lexington, Lexington, Massachusetts 1978.
Brown, R. A. 'Computer-Related Crime Under Commonwealth Law and the Draft Federal Criminal Code'. *Criminal Law Journal*, December 1986, vol. 10 no. 6,376.
Crimes Act 1900 (NSW in its application to ACT) s. 93, s. 115
Criminal Code 1983 (NT) s. 276
Kennison v. Daire (1986) 60 ALJR 249
Kennison v. Daire (1985) 38 SASR 404
Law Reform Commission of Tasmania. Report on Computer Misuse, no. 47
The Queen v. Evenett (1987) 24 ACR 330
The Queen v. Bernard Wayne Hollingsworth (Supreme Court of Tasmania, 1983).
Sullivan, C. 'Unauthorised Automatic Teller Machine Transactions—Consequences for Customers of Financial Institutions'.
Australian Business Law Review, June 1987.

ABORIGINAL SACRED SITES AND LAND CLAIMS

HISTORICAL BACKGROUND

In 1788 the first European settlement was officially established in New South Wales. The version of history endorsed by the recent Bicentennial celebrations judges this to be the moment when the Australian nation was born. Governor Phillip formally took office when the Union Jack was raised at Sydney Cove to the tunes of a military band and the words of a declaration of possession. According to Mr Justice Blackburn, delivering his judgement on the Yirrkala land case in 1971, this action assisted in ensuring that 'every square inch of territory in the colony became the property of the Crown'.

The Yirrkala land case was an important turning point in the history of Aboriginal land rights in Australia. It arose because a group of Aborigines in the Northern Territory objected to a government lease granted to the mining company Nabalco. Counsel for the plaintiffs argued that the land in question was the property of the Aboriginal people who had occupied it and inherited it through many generations, and that Aboriginal ownership had not been affected by Phillip's declaration. In this way Aboriginal people were challenging the official idea that before 1788 Australia had been *terra nullius*, a country without sovereignty and without any recognisable form of indigenous land tenure. But Justice Blackburn judged to the contrary. After patiently assessing much evidence on the nature of local Aboriginal land tenure, he concluded that Yirrkala Aborigines did not have a proprietary interest in land according to Australian law. Implicitly endorsing a popular conception of Aborigines and their relationship to land, he stated that it seemed appropriate to say that the Yirrkala people belonged to their land, but that their land did not belong to them—that the people belonged to their country, but that they did not *own* it.

Justice Blackburn reached his judgement only after a good deal of soul searching. He noted that 'There are great and difficult moral issues involved in the colonisation by a more advanced people of a country inhabited by a less advanced people', but he thought it beyond his brief to consider such issues in detail. However, his judgement prompted many moral reactions and helped to intensify the already growing land rights movement among Aborigines and their supporters.

In response to this intensification, the federal Labor Party made the granting of Aboriginal land rights part of its electoral platform in 1972. In 1973 the newly elected Labor government set up an inquiry, headed by Mr Justice Woodward, to look at 'appropriate means to recognise and establish the traditional rights and interests of the Aborigines in relation to land'. Justice Woodward submitted two reports in 1973 and 1974, which helped to shape the *Aboriginal Land Rights (Northern Territory) Act* 1976, originally introduced as a bill by the newly elected Liberal-Country Party government.

The land rights movement which quickened in the 1970s, and is still operative today, is not entirely new. Aborigines had been organising against their dispossession from the start, and the current land rights movement has to be understood as part of a continuing historical process. Calls for land rights peaked many times in the nineteenth and early twentieth centuries, with varying degrees of success. The recent wave of calls had its beginnings in the 1960s, prompted by actions like that of the Gurindji people who withdrew their labour from Wave Hill cattle station in 1967 in response to what they saw as exploitation forced upon them on their own land. What *is* new about the current situation, however, is the shape given to land rights by the notion of 'tradition' which is embodied in the Northern

Territory Land Rights Act of 1976. For while the act was not the first legislation to grant some form of land rights to Aboriginal people, it was the first to introduce the idea of 'traditional ownership' as a basis for making claims. If granted, it would result in Aborigines holding inalienable freehold title to their lands.

If Northern Territory Aborigines seek to have their traditional ownership of land recognised in Australian law, they usually have to establish first that the land is either unalienated crown land—'in which no person [other than the Crown] has an estate or interest'—or alienated crown land—'in which all estates and interests not held by the Crown are held by, or on behalf of, Aboriginals'. This means that Aborigines cannot claim all their traditional lands in the Northern Territory and is tantamount to saying that the only land claimable is that which has already been leased to them or land in which white Australians have not yet shown a strong economic interest.

Establishing that their traditional land is claimable is only the first step in a long process of research and judicial inquiry. Anthropological, historical and legal documentation has to be amassed and written up into claim reports by Aboriginal land councils. These reports then have to be substantiated and defended in court hearings before the Aboriginal Land Commissioner, who also investigates objections to the claim. In the end, largely (though not exclusively) on the basis of findings presented by the commissioner, the federal government decides either to grant or withhold the land.

The Northern Territory Aboriginal Land Rights Act defines *traditional Aboriginal owners* as 'a local descent group of Aboriginals who—(a) have common spiritual affiliations to a site on the land, being affiliations that place the group under a primary spiritual responsibility for that site and for the land; and (b) are entitled by Aboriginal tradition to forage as of right over the land'. A *sacred site* is 'a site that is sacred to Aboriginals or is otherwise of significance according to Aboriginal tradition'. *Tradition* is defined as 'the body of traditions, observances, customs and beliefs of Aboriginals or of a community or group of Aboriginals, and includes those traditions, observances, customs and beliefs as applied in relation to particular persons, sites, areas of land, things or relationships'. The definitions are thus broad, but it is necessary for Northern Territory Aborigines to satisfy all these requirements before land can be granted to them through the judicial procedures of a claim.

THE SOCIAL AND RELIGIOUS BASES OF NORTHERN TERRITORY CLAIMS

The Northern Territory land rights legislation is remarkable for the way in which it defines land ownership partly in terms of religious traditions. Before the Woodward inquiry it was well known that Aborigines had a religious orientation towards their land, but the judgement of Justice Blackburn in the Yirrkala land case stated that this was not true ownership. Aboriginal people, he said, had a spiritual connection with the land, but this connection was not one which could be translated into legal concepts of property. The Northern Territory Land Rights Act sought to rectify this situation by making the legal basis of claims commensurate with the way in which Aboriginal people themselves construe land ownership. While the legal framework of the act has been much debated and criticised, it is nevertheless possible to summarise the religious and social dimensions of Aboriginal land tenure as a system which the act was designed to reflect.

Aborigines subscribe to a religious view of the world, a view which has long been popularised in Australia as 'the Dreaming' or 'the Dreamtime'. But what white Australians know as the Dreaming, Aborigines are more likely to call 'the Law'. In the popular imagination, the Dreaming consists mainly of myths telling of fantastic events occurring in the distant past, though it may also conjure up images of exotic songs and dances—

corroborees. But the Aboriginal term, 'Law', stresses other facets of the Dreaming as well, since for Aborigines myths and rituals are part of a wider framework of society embracing kinship obligations, marriage rules and duties towards the maintenance of land (most often referred to in English as 'country'). All these are connected to Aboriginal life as a system of law and order. The Dreaming is not a mere set of stories about the past: it is the legal foundation of a social order which Aborigines seek to maintain from the past to the present and into the future. As Aboriginal people themselves say, their first duty is to 'follow the Dreaming'—to maintain and obey 'the Law'.

Aboriginal religion belongs to a general type sometimes known as 'totemism'. *Totemism* is found in many parts of the world and can be briefly defined as a religious attitude which links people with natural phenomena, typically animals and plants, but also natural elements, such as fire and water, and heavenly bodies, such as the sun and the moon. In Aboriginal Australia, totemism is also remarkable for the way in which it links people to country through a network of sacred sites connected with Dreaming stories. The totemic nexus of people, places and natural phenomena varies a great deal throughout the continent, but many principles of organisation are general. The broad definition of traditional ownership in the Northern Territory Land Rights Act was calculated to mirror these principles.

The best known and most widespread totemic relationship is the one which links a clan with one or more natural species and a territory. The clan is normally defined in terms of patrilineal descent, with membership being passed on from fathers to their children, and usually adopts a totemic species as its emblem or name, so that it may be known as, say, the kangaroo or fire or fish clan. In this way, totems act as signifiers of group identity, with the differences between species being used to affirm differences between social groups. For example, in saying 'I am a kangaroo', an Aboriginal man uses a shorthand phrase to indicate his sense of belonging to a particular social group as opposed to all others. This is similar to a Sydney Rugby League player saying 'I am an eel' to indicate that he plays for Parramatta and that he is not, for example, a Balmain tiger.

The football analogy is apt, because Aboriginal clans, like Sydney Rugby League teams, are localised, each having a territory which its members regard as their home. When, for example, an Aboriginal man says that he is a kangaroo, he is not only saying that he belongs to a particular clan, but also that he belongs to a particular clan estate— his 'country'. He and his fellow clan members regard this country as their very own and they have a special duty to take care of it. The Northern Territory Land Rights Act defines this 'local descent group's' care of country as 'primary spiritual responsibility' to the land.

Membership of descent groups is, however, more complex than this, since patrilineal descent is not the only mode of inheritance. Neither is patrilineal descent itself uniform. An Aboriginal man will say, for example, that he belongs to the clan and territory of his father and paternal grandfather, but this does not preclude him from belonging to other groups and territories through different descent lines. For Aborigines, matrilineal descent—inheritance through one's mother—is also an important way of belonging to social groups and land, so that any particular person is never affiliated to a single place. Apart from belonging to the clan and territory of his paternal grandfather, an Aboriginal person also usually belongs to those of his maternal grandfather, his maternal grandmother and his paternal grandmother. In other words, a person inherits totems and countries through both his father and his mother, and he also inherits rights through their mothers and fathers (his four grandparents). Through a mixture of patrilineal and matrilineal ties spanning three generations, an Aboriginal person normally belongs to at least four

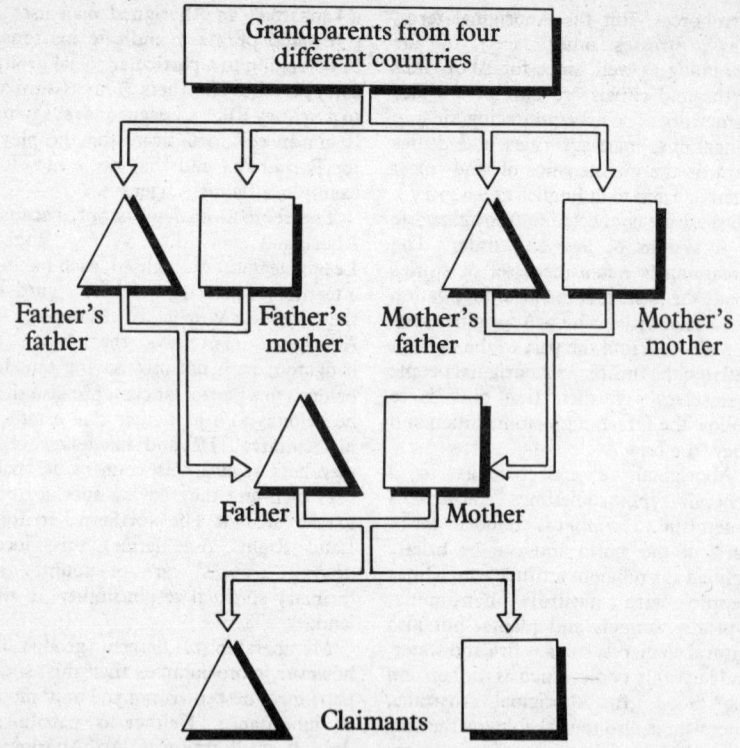

Fig. 1: Aboriginal descent linkages

different social groups, territories and their associated totems.

Connections to country are complicated further by various kinds of non-descent links. These are numerous and include factors such as conception, birth and death. An Aboriginal person might claim to belong to the country where he was conceived, the country where he was born, or the country where a relative died and was buried, and in this way he will regard himself as being affiliated to the local groups of those countries through non-descent ties. All in all, it is thus possible for an Aboriginal person to belong to many different countries at the same time and this makes the process of documenting a local descent group a lengthy and difficult procedure. In addition, links to country that are forged by means other than descent are sometimes difficult to argue for within the legal framework of the act because, on the face of it, the act does not recognise them. Nevertheless, in Aboriginal terms, such links may be very real and can have a great bearing on the question of who has 'primary spiritual responsibility' for any particular area of land under claim.

Aboriginal totems are symbols of identity. They define who one is and where one belongs, and within the totemic framework it is possible for a person to be a member of several different groups and to belong to several different places—just as it would, for example, be theoretically possible for a man to play Rugby League for Parramatta and VFL for Sydney, thus making him both an eel and a swan at the same time. However, the different facets of identity are not necessarily the same in each case. Aboriginal people have different duties towards people and places according to the ways in which they are linked to them, though these duties always carry some element of spirituality defined by totemism and the Dreaming.

Aboriginal territories are marked by sacred sites which were created by totemic ancestors. Sacred myths tell how the ancestors, human in form, but magically associated with natural phenomena, journey across the landscape creating all of its features—flora, fauna, creeks, hills, heavenly bodies, and so on. Wherever a totemic ancestor breaks a journey, he or she creates the surrounding environment, and the places from which this creativity emanated are regarded as sacred sites, embodying the ancestor's totemic essence.

A totemic ancestor does not literally manufacture and construct the environment, so much as make it significant through mental and artistic operations. For example, the ancestor may dream a vision of part of the world and then project it outwards onto the landscape. The projected vision is usually accompanied by the singing out of a name, and this name becomes attached to the creation, thus carrying the ancestor's identity with it. This process is called 'marking' and the imagery is that of artistic expression, analogous to the way in which an artist puts a signature on a work. The sum total of an ancestor's names represents the whole of his or her journey encapsulated in a single song cycle. As well as music, other modes of expression, such as dancing and painting, may also be emphasised as being part of the ancestor's creative potential. Above all else, such expressive activity represents the very process of claiming land. When an ancestor sings the country, he or she is at the same time claiming it as a personal possession. Having created it through artistic endeavour, the country remains a fundamental part of the ancestor's existence.

Mythical creativity did not only happen in the past, since in order to keep the Dreaming alive, it has to be acted out with every generation of living people. The songs which the ancestors first sang still exist and it is the duty of those who know them to ensure their continuity by passing them on to younger generations. This occurs in the context of rituals which are dramatic re-enactments of ancestral dancing, painting and singing. But while the rituals are repetitions of actions performed by ancestors, they are not mere duplicates. When a man performs a dance for others to see and learn, he actually assumes a totemic identity, and when he dances and sings he uses precisely the same creative powers as the original ancestors did. In other words, he himself is taking direct responsibility for the creation of his country in this generation, just as his ancestors did in theirs. His ritual actions thus demonstrate his claims to land and he asserts his authoritative ownership of country at the same time that he is making sure that his juniors will be able to do so at a later date. Such action is what Aborigines call 'looking after' the land—expressing both ownership and the guarantee of inheritance. It is also what the Northern Territory Land Rights Act means by 'spiritual responsibility'.

Ritual sequences and song cycles are transmitted according to the Law through the lines of inheritance outlined earlier—patrilineality, matrilineality, conception, birth and so on. Within this framework people may receive different types of rights in ritual property. For example, a person's link to his paternal grandfather's land usually allows him to play the part of the clan's totemic ancestor in ritual in the same way that his father, grandfather and more distant patrilineal ancestors did before him. On the other hand, his ritual role in relation to his maternal grandfather's country is different. There he may play the part of 'manager' in ritual, decorating the actors and supervising the correct procedures for the performance of song cycles and ritual dramas. The roles of performer and manager are thus complementary, with both being necessary for any expression of ownership of land. Other links to country may involve people playing different or similar roles in ritual performances. It is largely through the documentation of Northern Territory land claims that the full range of these rights have come to be understood.

Knowledge of sacred performances is not necessarily automatically transmitted just because a man stands in the correct relationship to receive it. Because such knowledge is so important for the maintenance of the Law, it has to be earned by people who show themselves responsible enough to use it. Older people who hold sacred knowledge carefully watch the behaviour of juniors and select from them the most mature as potential future ritual leaders or 'bosses'. While all people gain some knowledge and, therefore, ownership of country, this knowledge is graded in terms of secrecy, with some men and women gaining a great deal and others lesser amounts. The transmission of the Law therefore takes place within a context of political negotiation. Those deemed most responsible become important, powerful owners or managers of land and find themselves in positions where they can capitalise on their different links to country. Others may have to be content with less power and authority and with fewer ownership rights.

Aboriginal myths can thus be much more than mere stories, just as rituals are much more than simple dramatic acts. In the context of land rights, they are *possessions which are inherited and politically negotiated*. Myths, songs, sacred objects, paintings, and so on are, in effect, title deeds to land. When one asks an Aboriginal man to 'prove' his ownership of land, his response will be, if he deems the context to be one of trust, to show sacred objects associated with his country and to sing the appropriate songs, since these are his proofs of title. But because Aboriginal title deeds are secret, spiritual possessions, people are extremely careful and circumspect in proving their ownership of land. This has sometimes made the establishment of traditional ownership problematic in land claim hearings.

The use of title deeds is rather more than a simple declaration of ownership. It is also to take responsibility for the spiritual creation of the country through a process of identification. In singing his country, a man imbues it with his ancestral identity, creating both a bond of sentiment between the country and himself, and a similar tie between the country and his heirs, who recognise him to be a part of the country long after his death. It was these sentimental bonds which prompted Justice Blackburn to say that Aborigines did not so much possess land as see themselves possessed by it. It is indeed true that Aborigines are beholden to the land, and to their ancestors embodied there, but it is wrong to suggest that this precludes them owning that land. What in fact is the case is that Aboriginal land ownership involves human identification with sacred sites and obeying the Law of older generations who have become symbolised *by* those sites. In effect, Aborigines pass on ownership of land through the control of copyright. People create songs, paintings and dances pertaining to sacred sites and are careful to pass on the rights to reproduce these in every generation. In this way, the living definitively own the country that has been passed on to them at the same time that the country possesses them, since they follow the ancestors who have become embodied there. They are also, in demonstrating their ownership and care of country, on the way to becoming ancestors themselves. In short, ownership entails identification with the land and a sense of mutual possession.

When the Northern Territory Land Rights Act was framed, it did not take directly into account all of the complex dimensions of Aboriginal land ownership. It specified, for example, that traditional owners had to be part of 'a local descent group', when in fact ownership may sometimes be transmitted by means other than descent. In addition, when the first land claims were lodged in the mid- and late 1970s, anthropologists and lawyers tended to work with a rather narrow definition of descent, restricting it only to patrilineal affiliation to a clan estate. As time passes, however, the framework of the act is being interpreted more widely to include owners affiliated to land by other means. This has proved relatively easy and successful in the case of traditional owners associated with country through maternal and grandmaternal ties, but the problem of including people as owners through birth, conception or other non-descent means remains a difficult one, even though such claims may be supported by other Aboriginal claimants. The act is thus not a perfect mirror of the complexities of Aboriginal land tenure in the Northern Territory, but it has certainly been the most comprehensive effort to date to try to embody Aboriginal legal concepts of land tenure within the framework of Australian law.

Land that has been granted to Aborigines through the Northern Territory Land Rights Act has given many Aborigines a security of tenure which they have never before had under Australian law. A little less than half of the Northern Territory (generally its poorest land) is potentially claimable under the act, and something like one-half of this has already been granted. This land is held by trusts with exclusively Aboriginal membership, though this may include Aborigines who are not traditional owners, since a trust only holds land on their behalf. In turn, each land trust is administered by one of three Aboriginal land councils, whose members are elected by Aboriginal communities. So although Northern Territory land rights are firmly based on social and religious principles of traditional ownership, they involve many new administrative procedures which are quite novel and bureaucratic but nevertheless Aboriginal.

THE WIDER CONTEXT OF LAND RIGHTS

The principles of the Dreaming underpinning the network of sacred sites in Aboriginal Australia are not completely religious. While religious doctrines always lie behind the negotiation of land ownership, title to land gives Aborigines the right to include and exclude others from the country's benefits, and people who wish to use land owned by others must always consult and gain permission from the rightful owners. Aboriginal landowners regard their countries as their homes, and the degree to which they feel at home in any particular place is a function of their identification with it. Aboriginal countries are thus the same as any other homes or 'homelands'—places which people belong to, and which belong to people. Anybody who ignores or fails to respect this mutual identification is, in Aboriginal terms, guilty of trespass.

The new bureaucratic structure in which Aborigines find themselves in the Northern Territory is a transformation of the pre-contact mode of land ownership—in which local groups had complete autonomy—into a situation where local countries are embedded in a wider, centralised framework of control. The Dreaming could not remain the same after the incursion of white Australians into Aboriginal homelands and the current situation has to be understood in terms of Aborigines assuming political and economic means appropriate for dealing with novel problems on a pan-Aboriginal level. Northern Territory Aborigines still maintain local knowledge of their sacred sites, but local homelands are now part of a broader Aboriginal nation encompassing not only the Northern Territory, but the whole of Australia. Countries that were small and relatively independent before the arrival of whites are thus becoming parts of a larger Aboriginal country, and local autonomy is to some extent being surrendered in the name of broader political conflicts and allegiances.

When Governor Phillip took office in 1788, the whole of Australia was crisscrossed by Dreaming paths, sacred sites and autonomous local group areas. Though Phillip did not realise it, in 'marking' Sydney Cove with the Union Jack, the music of a military band and the words of a declaration of possession, he was explicitly challenging a similar way of claiming land already in operation. That challenge was to be repeated time and time again throughout the continent, though it came to be masked by the official doctrine of *terra nullius*, which allowed white Australians to act as if there had been no prior occupation. Aborigines, of course, always found this doctrine profoundly offensive, invasive and destructive, and in view of what is now known about Aboriginal land tenure, the doctrine cannot be said to be accurate, even though it has found its way into the machinery of Australian law.

The land rights movement is spread throughout Australia, its adherents coming from many different backgrounds. The common theme which runs through the movement is pan-Aboriginality, whose political force owes its existence to the sentiments of Aboriginal people formed in relation to a common history of dispossession. Aborigines today are not alike in every respect, but everywhere they have experienced the (for them) largely destructive encounter with white Australia. All Aborigines are descended from ancestors who adhered to the Dreaming, and all of them see the Dreaming, and the way in which it underpinned their rights in land, as vital aspects of their heritage. So while some contemporary Aborigines do not maintain countries in the 'traditional' manner (as defined by the Northern Territory Land Rights Act), they are nevertheless likely to be deeply concerned about their culture and the transformations it has undergone during the last 200 years. Two key aspects of that concern are the demands for national land rights legislation and recognition of Aboriginal sovereignty.

Grants of land rights and the protection of Aboriginal sacred sites have so far been undertaken only on a piecemeal basis. All states (including the Northern Territory) have legislation to protect Aboriginal heritage. There is also federal legislation to this effect. The implementation of these laws usually involves consultations with local Aboriginal people, though none of the protection agencies are exclusively Aboriginal controlled. Only the Northern Territory and New South Wales have state-wide land rights legislation, although the amount of land open to claim in New South Wales is much less than that available in the Northern Territory. South Australia, Victoria, Queensland, Western Australia, Tasmania and the Australian Capital Territory all have land set aside for Aboriginal benefit, but the amount and conditions of use vary greatly. South Australia is notable for its granting of freehold title to two very large areas of desert to Aboriginal people in 1981 and 1984, while Western Australia and Queensland have extensive areas of land either leased to Aborigines or as reserves for Aboriginal use. Only tiny portions of Victoria, Tasmania and the Australian Capital Territory are held by or for Aboriginal people.

The current land rights situation is very much in a state of flux. Claims are being lodged in the Northern Territory and New South Wales, but decisions on them take a good deal of time. In 1984 Paul Seaman, Commissioner for the Aboriginal Land Inquiry in Western Australia, submitted his report, but efforts to legislate for land rights in 1985 were defeated in the Legislative Council. Promises of land rights by the Victorian Labor government have yet to be realised, while recent plans by the federal Labor government to introduce national land rights legislation have been shelved. In the remaining states, land rights moves have been slight. The political climate in Australia as a whole is not particularly sympathetic to Aboriginal land rights at the present time. The current Liberal–Country government of New South Wales, for example, was recently elected with a promise to dismantle land rights legislation in that state.

Aboriginal land rights and sacred site protection are complicated by the fact that they are not uniform throughout Australia. Many Aborigines would like to see them simplified by the introduction of national legislation, particularly in the land rights area, where

ABORIGINAL LAND TENURE AND POPULATION 1986

	% of population Aboriginal*	Aboriginal freehold land (sq km and as % of total area)		Leasehold land (sq km and as % of total area)		Reserves and Missions (sq km and as % of total area)	
N.S.W. & A.C.T.	1.04	190	(0.02)	475	(0.06)	—	—
Victoria	0.31	31	(0.01)	—	—	—	—
Queensland	2.37	5	(0.00)	15,659	(0.91)	18,925	(1.10)
S. Australia	1.06	184,738	(18.77)	520	(0.05)	—	—
W. Australia	2.69	36	(0.00)	42,886	(1.70)	189,263	(7.50)
Tasmania	1.54	2	(0.00)	—	—	—	—
N. Territory	22.44	458,280	(34.04)	29,447	(2.19)	42	(0.00)
Australia	**1.43**	**643,282**	**(8.37)**	**88,987**	**(1.16)**	**208,230**	**(2.71)**

* According to 1986 Census
Source: Department of Aboriginal Affairs, *Aboriginal Statistics 1986* Australian Government Publishing Service, Canberra, 1987

state and territory laws are markedly divergent. For example, the Northern Territory legislation privileges those Aborigines whose traditional lands are claimable, while leaving others, whose needs are just as great, in a lesser position. This is in contrast to New South Wales, where claims are based as much on need as traditional entitlement. The Northern Territory also differs greatly from South Australia, where traditional ownership is defined in much broader and inclusive terms. On the whole, the social justice and compensation arguments which lie behind the land rights movement tend to favour claims being made in relation to need, because this would potentially include more Aboriginal people in claims. According to one argument, tradition would in any case underlie all needs claims, since Aborigines everywhere in Australia share a fundamental ancestral heritage—an historical link with the land and the Dreaming and its having been adversely affected by the coming of Europeans.

Underlying the call for national land rights legislation is the fundamental issue of sovereignty. Aborigines never formally ceded their land to European Australians, because the latter never recognised that the land was Aboriginal in the first place. Britain, and other European colonial powers, negotiated treaties with native peoples in many other parts of the world, including New Zealand, and many Aboriginal people would now like to see some similar formal recognition of their original title to Australia. Immediately prior to the Bicentennial, Prime Minister Hawke made tentative moves in this direction with the offer of a treaty or 'compact' between Aborigines and the Australian state. That offer was cautiously welcomed by Aboriginal organisations, but it is difficult to tell what the eventual outcome of the offer will be.

Before Europeans arrived in Australia, Aborigines recognised their lands to be part of a sacred endowment handed down to them by innumerable generations of ancestors. The land as a whole was sacred and an inalienable part of their cultural identity. Sacred sites embodied ancestral power in its most potent form at particular locations, but the whole of the country was created by totemic beings and no part of it remained untouched by the Dreaming. Consequently, every part of the country was identified with the people who owned it: in a sense, the whole of Australia was a sacred site.

The Dreaming is no less alive today than it was then, though it has undergone innumerable transformations due to contact with Europeans. As the Dreaming has been reworked in response to practical problems raised by living with white Australians, Aborigines have come to see it in a new light. Amongst other things, Aborigines *as a whole* now claim the Dreaming and its embodiment in the country as the definitive marks of a distinctive culture which has, for the best part of 200 years, been placed squarely on the defensive in the face of white invasion. Thus, for Aborigines, Australia remains a genuinely sacred place.

It can be argued, however, that Australia has become no less a sacred place to a great many other people as well. Certainly, the recent Bicentenary celebrations show that many white Australians, be they religiously minded or not, are thoroughly committed to and identify with, their country. Part of this identification has entailed a widespread recognition of Aboriginal life and culture. Aboriginal art, dance and theatre, for example, are areas in which white Australians have displayed tremendous interest in recent times. Even the latest version of the great Australian outback hero, 'Crocodile' Dundee, is a man who claims to have been brought up by Aborigines and to have a unique appreciation of Aboriginal ways.

On the whole, Aborigines do not object to such a national consciousness, even in its appropriation of Aboriginal heritage in order to give the country its own uniquely *Australian* history. They are keen, however, to capture a place within that history which gives them dignity and self-respect, and for them this requires that recompense be made for times past in which Aboriginal life and livelihood were viewed as things to be transformed, trampled upon, or even exterminated. Thus if Aborigines are now expected to share something of their heritage with their fellow Australians, it is not surprising that they are demanding first of all that the heritage be recognised as being rightfully and originally their own. Their desire is that their ancestral tracks not be wiped from the face of the earth, but reinstated in the landscape. Such would be the effect of a successfully negotiated treaty giving full recognition to Aboriginal sovereignty and land rights.

J. M.

Sources:

Edwards, R. (ed.) *The Preservation of Australia's Aboriginal Heritage*. Australian Institute of Aboriginal Studies, Canberra, 1975.

Harris, S. *'It's Coming Yet . . .': An Aboriginal treaty within Australia between Australians*. The Aboriginal Treaty Committee, Canberra, 1979.

Levi-Strauss, C. *Totemism*. Penguin, Melbourne, 1973.

Maddock, K. *Our Land is Your Land*. Penguin, Melbourne, 1983.

Munn, N. D. 'The Transformation of Subjects into Objects in Walbiri and Pitjantjatjara Myth'. In M. Charlesworth, H. Morphy, D. Bell and K. Maddock (eds), *Religion in Aboriginal Australia: An Anthology*. University of Queensland Press, Brisbane, 1984.

Peterson, N. *Aboriginal Land Rights: A Handbook*. Australian Institute of Aboriginal Studies, Canberra, 1981.

Peterson, N. *Australian Territorial Organization*. University of Sydney, Sydney, 1986.

Peterson, N. and Langton, M. (eds). *Aborigines, Land and Land Rights*. Australian Institute of Aboriginal Studies, Canberra, 1983.

Reynolds, H. *The Law of the Land*. Penguin, Melbourne, 1987.

Toyne, P. and Vachon, D. *Growing up the Country: The Pitjantjatjara Struggle for their Land*. Penguin, Melbourne, 1984.

Williams, N. M. *The Yolngu and their Land*. Australian Institute of Aboriginal Studies, Canberra, 1986.

POISONOUS PLANTS

* May cause mild illness if large enough quantity eaten
** May cause symptoms but no danger to life
*** Serious illness possible

Aconite: (Monkshood): As for Delphinium.
African Violet: Not poisonous.
Agapanthus: Not poisonous.
Anemone: As for Delphinium.
Angel's Trumpet *(Datura arborea)****: This is a small tree with softy hairy leaves. The trumpet-shaped flower is approximately 20 cm long and is white nerved with green. Induce vomiting immediately if more than half a leaf or a couple of seeds eaten. Symptoms begin within three hours and typically are dry throat, thirstiness, palpitations and flushed dry skin. Contact your local Poisons Information Centre or general practitioner.
Apricot, Cherry, Plum, Peach kernels*: If uncooked they contain small quantities of hydrocyanic acid. Ten to twenty kernels have caused symptoms in children. Induce vomiting if more than 10 have been eaten, otherwise no treatment is necessary.
Ardisia: Not poisonous.
Arum Lily**: All parts of these common white lilies will cause a burning pain in the mouth if eaten, due to the presence of quite high concentrations of oxalic acid. Children typically come running for help, crying and screaming, due to the intense pain and for this reason only small quantities are ever eaten and there is no chance of serious illness.

Give milk and ice-cream to cool the burning pain. The calcium in these foods will inactivate the oxalate causing the trouble. Skin dermatitis has also been reported.
Asparagus Fern berries: Not poisonous.
Aspidistra: Not poisonous.
Atropa belladonna: See Deadly Nightshade.
Azalea: The leaves and stems contain a cardiac glycoside but poisoning will occur only after eating a large quantity.
Begonia: Not poisonous.
Belladonna Lily*: As for Arum Lily.

Bird of Paradise (Strelitzia): Not poisonous.
Brunfelsia: Not poisonous.
Buddleia: Not poisonous.
Bulbs*: Bulbs of any plant should not be eaten, but generally they taste so awful that only one or two bites could possibly be swallowed. If you suspect that a lot has been eaten, induce vomiting immediately, observe the child for two hours and call your local Poisons Information Centre or GP if worried.
Buttercup*: May cause skin irritation or dermatitis and when eaten causes a burning sensation in the mouth. This would irritate the stomach and intestines too, causing both vomiting and diarrhoea, but these symptoms have only ever been observed in stock. Give large quantities of milk to dilute the poison.
Cactus plants: Not poisonous.
Calendula: See Marigold.
Camellia: Not poisonous.
Candelabra Cactus*: See Poinsettia.
Cape Lilac: See White Cedar.
Capsicum*: See Chilli.
Cassia*: This is a very commonly eaten plant and is not poisonous although eating very large numbers of pods or eating a few pods daily for a week or so have caused diarrhoea and vomiting.
Castor Oil beans***: A very common plant on waste land, the Castor Oil plant grows up to four and a half metres high with large leaves, greenish-white to rust-coloured flowers and spiny seed capsules containing three seeds. It is only chewed seeds that are dangerous but two to three of these are sufficient to cause serious illness.

Symptoms may be delayed up to 36 hours after ingestion but more commonly begin after a couple of hours. The most obvious symptom is bloody diarrhoea. If the child is even suspected of eating any beans, vomiting must be induced immediately and the child taken straight to hospital.
Celery: Not poisonous but vast quantities of green leaves have caused gastritis in cows.
Cherry kernels*: See Apricot kernels.

Chilli*: The offending plant is most commonly the attractive ornamental chilli whose fruits cause immediate severe burning pain in the mouth. Rub the child's mouth with olive oil or butter and give plenty of ice-cream or cold milk and soon all symptoms will have gone.

Christmas Rose* (Hellebore): As for Buttercup.

Chrysanthemum: Not poisonous but causes a mild stinging sensation in the mouth. It has also caused dermatitis in sensitive people. Give cold milk to stop the burning.

Clivia* (Kaffir Lily): Same mild problems as for Daffodil.

Colocasia** (Taro): As for Arum Lily.

Convolvulus (Morning Glory): The seeds of one US species contain an hallucinogenic ingredient but the common garden morning glory is not this species. Not poisonous.

Cornflower: Not poisonous.

Cotoneaster: Not poisonous but eating the berries should be discouraged.

Crataegus: Berries are frequently eaten but are not poisonous.

Crown of Thorns*: See Poinsettia.

Cunjevoi**: As for Arum Lily.

Cyclamen: The tuber is poisonous but because it has an acrid, bitter taste, poisoning is rare. If more than half a tuber has been eaten, medical attention is advised.

Daffodil*: Both the stems and bulbs contain active principles likely to cause vomiting and diarrhoea, but unless the equivalent of one plant is eaten, symptoms are unlikely. When mistaken for onions has caused gastritis.

Dahlia: Not poisonous.

Daisy: All varieties may cause the same mild problems as chrysanthemums. See Chrysanthemum.

Dandelion: Not poisonous.

Daphne**: All parts are poisonous, especially the berries, but children rarely eat this plant. It causes severe gastroenteritis with vomiting and diarrhoea beginning after a couple of hours. Skin allergies occur occasionally too. If more than one to two leaves or berries are eaten, induce vomiting immediately and give large quantities of milk. Contact your local Poisons Information Centre or doctor if worried.

Deadly Nightshade*** (*Atropa belladonna*): A perennial about 1 metre high with pointed oval leaves about 15 cm long. The single flowers emerging from the joint of the leaf and stem are blue-purple or dull red bells about 2.5 cm long. The berry is round, about 1.2 cm wide and is purple to shiny black when ripe.

Poisoning is extremely rare even in countries where the plant grows wild, but if you have this plant growing, it would be wise to pull it out. For symptoms and treatment see Angel's Trumpet.

Delphinium*: This species of plant has been shown to be a problem with cattle and sheep who like eating it in large quantities, but human poisoning has never been reported. The amount likely to be eaten casually by a child would cause no harm — at worst some mild diarrhoea. Give milk and food to dilute. Sensitive skin may show allergy to these plants.

Dieffenbachia**: As for Arum Lily.

Dumb Cane** (Dieffenbachia): As for Arum Lily.

Elder: The berries may cause nausea if uncooked but once cooked are no problem.

Elephant's Ears**: As for Arum Lily.

Forget-me-not: Not poisonous.

Foxglove***: Although this common garden plant is the source of the much used drug digitalis, reports of poisoning of children are very rare. One case reported was a mild intoxication which resulted from a two-year-old drinking the water from a vase which had contained these flowers. The only other case on record reports a child chewing many seeds. If you have this plant in your garden and your child does eat everything he touches, it may be wise to take it out just for a year or two till he grows out of this habit. If you discover or suspect that any has been eaten, induce vomiting immediately and observe closely for three to six hours for vomiting, diarrhoea, abdominal pain, headache or any distinct change in condition. Go straight to hospital if any of these symptoms appear.

Frangipani: Not poisonous, but give milk to get rid of the objectionable taste.

Freesia: Not poisonous, but the bulbs may cause mild stinging in the mouth if they are chewed. Give milk to wash the mouth clean.

Fuchsia: Not poisonous.

Gardenia: Not poisonous.

Geranium: Not poisonous, but may cause skin allergy in sensitive people.

Gladioli: Not poisonous, but may cause a burning sensation in the mouth. Give milk to wash mouth clean.

Gloxinia: Not poisonous.

Gum trees: Not poisonous in quantities likely to be eaten by children, but a couple of species have caused problems with cattle in times of drought. Give milk.

Hawthorn (Crataegus): The bright orange berries attract children but are not poisonous.

Hellebore*: See Christmas Rose.

Hibiscus: Not poisonous.

Holly*: Said to cause vomiting and diarrhoea if more than 20 berries eaten but the prickles on the leaf make it unlikely that this would occur. If worried induce vomiting immediately.

Hyacinth*: Ten bulbs eaten by a two-year-old may cause violent diarrhoea. Skin allergy from just touching the plant has also been reported. If bulbs are eaten, induce vomiting to prevent purging.

Hydrangea: Mild gastroenteritis and nausea occurred in one family when the children added hydrangea buds to a tossed salad, but under normal circumstances the symptoms would not seem severe enough to warrant treatment other than a drink of milk.

Iris: The bulb is extremely unpalatable and unlikely to be eaten, but like the rest of the plant may cause mild gastroenteritis. Serious poisoning is unknown. Give milk to minimise irritation. Skin irritations after handling the plant have been reported.

Ivy*: A few cases of mild poisoning in children when 'very considerable' numbers of the berries were reported to have caused diarrhoea. If only a couple of berries eaten just give milk, but for 10 to 20 berries, induce vomiting immediately. Dermatitis resulting from handling the plant has been reported.

Jacaranda: Not poisonous.

Jade Plant: Not poisonous.

Jonquil*: See Daffodil.

Kaffir Lily: See Clivia.

Laburnum**: This is not a common tree in Australia but there are many English reports of children eating one to two pods. All vomited within minutes and other observed symptoms include drowsiness, weakness and palpitation.

Give large quantities of milk and contact your local Poisons Information Centre or medical practitioner.

Lantana***: There are several reports of quite serious poisoning in children as a result of eating green lantana berries. Symptoms, beginning two to six hours after ingestion, include weakness, vomiting, dilated pupils and slow deep breathing.

It is most important to induce vomiting immediately, then no symptoms will develop. Immediately upon discovery of the ingestion take the child to hospital.

Larkspur*: See Delphinium.

Lilac: Not poisonous.

Lilli Pilli: Not poisonous.

Lilies*: There are a vast number of varieties. A few are poisonous but most only cause a local sting in the mouth and, if sufficient has been eaten, diarrhoea and vomiting. A glass of cold milk or some ice-cream is usually the best treatment. Check under the specific name of the lily.

Lily of the Valley**: Supposed to be poisonous, but there have been no specific cases reported. To play safe, if your child eats a couple of leaves or a stem of flowers induce vomiting immediately and observe carefully for the next 24 hours for vomiting, diarrhoea, weakness and headache.

Lobelia**: All parts of this plant are poisonous, but severe symptoms in children have not been reported. Should much of it be eaten, vomiting will occur within half an hour followed by sweating and a rapid pulse. It would be a wise precaution to induce vomiting immediately the ingestion occurs to avoid symptoms developing, if possible.

Lupin*: There is massive evidence of stock poisoning but no human ingestions have been reported. The new green shoots and the pods and their seeds are the most poisonous parts so if your child eats much immediate induction of vomiting would be a good idea.

Marigold: Not poisonous but may cause a stinging sensation in mouth. Give milk to wash it off the tongue and cheeks and to dilute it.

Monkshood*: As for Delphinium.

Monstera: The leaves may cause a mild burning sensation in the mouth if they are

chewed. Rinse the mouth well and give cold milk to ease the stinging.
Moreton Bay Fig: Not poisonous.
Morning Glory: See Convolvulus.
Mother-in-Law Plant**: See Arum Lily.
Nasturtium: Not poisonous.
Oak: Acorns and leaves are poisonous to stock, but it would be impossible for children to eat them in quantities large enough to cause a problem.
Ochna: The berries are frequently eaten by children but are not poisonous.
Oleander***: Although this is a very common garden shrub poisonings by it are extremely rare. Human deaths have been reported, but such cases are poorly described. The taste of the sap is very bitter indeed and it is almost impossible to imagine a child persevering long enough to eat a lethal amount. Symptoms would begin with vomiting and diarrhoea.

If your child has eaten any part of the tree, immediately induce vomiting just to be safe and observe for six hours for vomiting or any change in condition. Contact your local Poisons Information Centre or doctor.

Skin allergies to oleander are common.
Orchids: Not poisonous.
Ornamental Chilli*: See Chilli.
Pansy: Not poisonous.
Peach kernels: See Apricot kernels.
Pencil Tree*: See Poinsettia.
Pepper Tree*: The fruit is irritant when eaten and may cause a burning sensation in the mouth and mild gastroenteritis. Wash mouth out well and give cold milk to drink.
Philodendron*: Some species may cause a mild stinging in the mouth. Rub olive oil or butter in the mouth and give cold milk or ice-cream. Loose bowel motions may be observed, but this should be short lived. Skin allergies have been occasionally reported.
Pigface: Not poisonous, in the quantity likely to be eaten by children.
Plum kernels: See Apricot kernels.
Poinsettia* and other Euphorbias (Crown of Thorns, Snow on the Mountain, Pencil Tree, Candelabra Cactus): The milky sap from all of these plants will cause blistering on the skin and so if sucked by a child will cause an immediate stinging pain in the mouth. This also makes ingestion of more than one mouthful extremely unlikely.

Dilution of the acrid principle with milk and food and oils should be sufficient to stop the symptoms and prevent diarrhoea and vomiting occurring.

If the sap gets into the eyes immediately flood for five minutes with warm water. If the eye remains sore and swollen for more than 12 hours see a doctor.
Poison Ivy**: See Rhus.
Poppy: Not poisonous.
Potato: The vines, sprouts and sun-spoiled green potatoes have caused stock poisoning, but so long as all the green is pared from the potato and it is cooked there is no danger of poisoning.
Primrose: Not poisonous, but has caused dermatitis in sensitive people.
Privet: The berries in very large numbers would probably cause vomiting and diarrhoea, but cases of poisoning in children are virtually unknown. A drink of milk and some food should be adequate to prevent irritation of the stomach.
Prunus: See Apricot kernels.
Rhododendron: See Azalea.
Rhubarb**: The leaf (not the leaf stalk) contains large amounts of oxalic acid and is therefore potentially dangerous and should not be eaten raw or cooked. Several whole leaves would need to be eaten before the poisoning became severe. Symptoms of excessive salivation, vomiting and diarrhoea would be expected after one to two hours.

Give large quantities of milk as this will inactivate the oxalic acid before any damage can be done. If a large quantity has been eaten, immediate induction of vomiting is essential.
Rhus**: Dermatitis may be caused by touching broken parts of the plant or handling animals, clothing or implements which have touched broken stems. There is no evidence that unbroken stems or leaves give off any poisonous exudate. The plant is toxic all year round. The dermatitis is manifested by reddened and itchy skin in mild cases and blisters which exude serum in severe cases, when infection is a real danger.

Eating of the leaves or fruit by a sensitive person is very dangerous; the dermatitis-like reaction also takes place in the mouth, stomach and intestines causing serious gastric upset. About half the population is estimated to be sensitive to the plant, and those who are not sensitive do not develop any symptoms whatever. It is not possible to get a reaction without actually touching the plant or a carrier (shoes, clothing, garden tools, pets).

Should contact occur wash the area immediately. This will not prevent the reaction occurring, just prevent transmission. Seek medical advice if blisters develop.

The smoke from burning Rhus is also allergenic.

Rose: Not poisonous.
Rubber Tree Plant: Not poisonous.
Saxifrage: As for Hydrangea.
Snow on the Mountain*: See Poinsettia.
Strawberries, wild: Not poisonous.
Strelitzia: Not poisonous.
Sweet-pea: Continuous eating of the seeds has caused poisoning in stock, but this has not been reported with children. All the same, do not allow your child to get a taste for the seeds, just in case.
Taro**: See Arum Lily.
Toadstools**: No one has died from eating these in Australia but there are a few varieties which cause symptoms. Symptoms begin within a couple of hours and may be severe vomiting and diarrhoea, or hilarity or hallucinations. They are easily controlled in hospital. The toadstool species which cause adverse effects rarely look like the edible mushrooms. The round puff-balls that spring up in abundance after rain are non-poisonous, as are the small spindly pale-coloured toadstools that accompany them in everyone's backyard after a good storm.

If you have picked what you think are field mushrooms and you're in doubt, don't use them—they could be one of the non-edible varieties. There is no easy way to distinguish the safe from the unsafe.

Tomato*: The leaves of the tomato taste most unpleasant and ingestion is therefore unlikely. If quite a large quantity is eaten, gastritis should be expected.
Violet: Not poisonous.
Violet, African: Not poisonous.
Virginia Creeper: There is some suspicion, but no evidence, that the berries may be poisonous, causing vomiting and diarrhoea. If many (say, 10) have been eaten, induce vomiting immediately just to be on the safe side.
Wandering Jew: Not poisonous, but causes skin allergies in some people.
Wattle: Not poisonous in quantities likely to be taken by children.
White Cedar or Cape Lilac**: Fruits have caused severe dehydration because of vomiting and diarrhoea but these symptoms can be controlled in hospital. The berries have a foul odour and taste, so poisonings are rare.
Wistaria: Not poisonous.
Yew*: Very rarely eaten, but a large quantity of the leaves and seeds will cause gastritis.

Source: McCaughey, H. *Is It Poisonous?* Angus & Robertson, Sydney, 1980.

AUSTRALIAN REGULATIONS CONTROLLING TRADE IN ENDANGERED SPECIES

Since 1976 Australia has been a signatory to the Convention on International Trade in Endangered Species of Wild Fauna and Flora (CITES). This international convention was established in an attempt to control and monitor trade in endangered species.

No commercial trade is permitted in the most-endangered species which includes the burrowing and brush-tailed bettongs, the peregrine falcon, the orange-bellied parrot and all sea turtles. Species which might become endangered if the trade in them was not controlled and monitored require special permits which must be issued by the government authority in the exporting country before trade is permitted. Some Australian species in this category are the mountain pygmy possum, the plains wanderer, the red-tailed black cockatoo, the oenpelli python, the Australian lungfish, some birdwing butterflies and all orchids.

CITES is implemented in Australia by the *Wildlife Protection (Regulation of Exports & Imports) Act* 1982. Under this act, export controls apply to all Australian native animals and plants except those listed on its Schedule 4 (mainly marine fish, barramundi, fruits, timber and the like).

Species on the official list of Australian endangered vertebrate fauna are given an equivalent level of protection as the most-endangered species—all these species are listed on Schedule 1 of the act. Export trade in Schedule 1 species is only permitted to approved zoos or for scientific purposes. Those listed on Schedule 2 of the act can be exported for zoological or scientific purposes, and for commercial purposes if the animals or plants are taken in accordance with a management program approved by the federal government. All other native Australian animals and plants (except the exclusions mentioned above) are subject to similar export controls. The act also controls the importation of wildlife.

In addition to controls on overseas trade each state and territory has its own legislation aimed at controlling and monitoring inter- and intra-state trade. These place conditions and restrictions on the buying, selling, keeping, interstate trading and taking from the wild of many plants and animals. Permits are necessary for all these actions, and authorities have the discretion not to issue them if they consider it would be detrimental to the species. Many states have more stringent requirements and greater penalties for breaches of wildlife laws relating to endangered species. There seems to be a recent positive trend with states and territories moving to amend their legislation towards stricter controls over trade in endangered species. Laws are still far from uniform, however, and different states and territories vary widely in both their recognition of endangered species and the ways in which they control and monitor trade in them.

Source: D. Callister, TRAFFIC (Oceania)

IMPORTED PESTS

Every day of the year airline passengers landing in Australia are obliged to remain aboard their aircraft whilst Customs officers fumigate the aircraft cabin. The fumigation is intended to catch unwanted foreign insects, hitchhikers bringing disease or having the potential of becoming a pest. These unwanted air passengers are just some in a long line of plants, animals and insects accidentally or deliberately imported into Australia since the First Fleet. The animals, plants and insects covered in this article are a representative sample of the estimated 1500 plant species, thirty types of mammal (compared with approximately 230 native species) and an unknown number of insects.

Most of these imported species have been harmless, such as ornamental shrubs and flowers, or have been of commercial value, such as grains, cattle, and sheep. Some, like the rabbit, have been, or are, a threat to the economy and ecology of the country. Less well known, but equally important, is the effect of feral animals and other imported species on the nation's ecological infrastructure. Feral animals spread disease and destroy native flora and fauna. Plants and insects take over from native species. Many of these species were deliberately introduced, the animals for hunting, the plants for decorating gardens, the insects for biological control. Other species, particularly insects, came in by accident.

Honours for the first non-Australian species ashore probably goes to the cockroach, closely followed by the rat, and then the house mouse. All three may have landed with the First Fleet. cockroaches are supreme scavengers and undoubtedly one of the most disliked of all insects but despite their association with dirt they are not, in fact, a significant source of disease. Worldwide, there are 3500 species of cockroach, of which about 400 are Australian. Only about six of these have any interest in human beings and three of them are imported: the American, the German and the Oriental.

Rats, also heartily disliked, come in two varieties: the roof rat, also often known as the ship rat or black rat, and the Norway rat or common or sewer rat. They are a source of disease and one of the most destructive pests of stored food, especially cereals.

Their cousin, the common house mouse is not just an inhabitant of domestic kitchens. Mouse plagues in Australia have been far worse than rat plagues. In favourable conditions a female mouse can produce a litter every four weeks, with between six and nine per litter. In plague quantities mice chew and eat anything soft enough for their teeth to penetrate, from the farmer's grain store to the wiring on televisions and fridges. Photographs exist from early this century of 'mousers' standing beside piles of dead mice several feet high. The 1979-80 mouse plague in Victoria is estimated to have cost the community $15 to $20 million.

Another early arrival was probably the European house fly, which may not be as numerous or as irritating as the native bush fly but is more likely to spread disease. The early settlers often carried cages of European house flies, which they released into the bush believing they would displace the bush fly.

The European green blowfly was another unwanted introduction. It lays its eggs in the flesh of sheep and when the eggs hatch the maggots emerge and cause the sheep stress and infection which can kill if untreated. Blowfly is estimated to cost the grazing industry $150 million a year.

The dog was also an early immigrant. Some went wild and, contrary to accepted opinion, some bred with the dingo to produce a wild dog crossbreed. Probably about three-quarters of dingoes now are crossbreeds. Wild dogs are partial to sheep, though they do not do as much damage as is often thought. It has been suggested, however, that if wild dogs are not controlled Australia may eventually develop its own native wolf.

Not all imports were accidental. Our nineteenth century ancestors, with the best of intentions and unaware of the dangers, formed acclimatisation societies to promote the introduction of animals, birds, fish and plants. These societies were primarily responsible for spoiling Australia's bird life. They imported about forty species, about fifteen of which became well established. Among those introduced are the curassow, a type of South American turkey, which has died out, skylarks, thrushes, robins, nightingales, and chaffinches. The Victorian Acclimatisation Society was particularly active and released, among others, the English house sparrow, the starling and the Indian myna bird. They were originally brought out to eat caterpillars and made market gardening almost impossible. They ate the caterpillars and a good deal else, including crops and orchard fruit.

At present starlings are found in all states but Western Australia. Their advance there has been stopped by the Nullarbor Plain desert and lack of water. Whenever starlings do manage to survive these deprivations, as well as the mobbings of native magpies, they are hunted with nets and guns by the Agriculture Protection Board in Western Australia because it is feared that they spread disease. Armed agriculture officials spent five days in April 1988 searching for an Asiatic tree sparrow which was spotted after arriving on a foreign ship. It was finally found and shot.

Trout and salmon were unsuccessfully imported in 1841, then again in 1861. Trout were particularly successful in Tasmania but salmon failed. European carp were also introduced, and damaged rivers and ponds by stirring the bottom whilst feeding and spawning. Carp were declared a noxious fish in 1962 in Victoria and an energetic effort was made to destroy them, until it was discovered the La Trobe River was infested with them and the effort was abandoned.

Imported animals include monkeys; the agouti, a particularly vicious rodent from South America; donkeys; camels; horses; elands from South Africa; alpacas and llamas from South America; and South African Zebu cattle, which were the source of the cattle tick. The cattle tick, which transmits tick fever and is currently confined to the north, is the most serious external parasite of cattle in Australia.

While no one knows whose pet dog was the first to run wild, Private Brumby's horses are credited with founding Australia's wild horse population in 1804. Now half a million strong, with about 300,000 in the Northern Territory, they compete with commercial stock for water and feed. Horses were also let loose because mechanisation made them redundant as work animals, as was the case with camels and donkeys. Camels, used by a number of explorers, were found in Victoria as early as 1845. They now number about 35,000 and run wild in Western Australia, South Australia, Queensland and the Northern Territory. They cause considerable damage to fencing and, most importantly, their disgusting watering habits foul waterholes. Donkeys, used as pack animals, were brought to Australia in 1866. Now there are over 1.5 million roaming wild in the bush where they damage vegetation and compete with commercial stock for feed.

Domestic cattle run wild in Australia, but are not as prolific as other wild animals, mainly because there is usually a profit in catching them for market. Zebu cattle were plentiful in the Northern Territory until the 1950s and until the advent of helicopters they were hunted from horseback and shot, as in the nineteenth century, with large-calibre revolvers.

Australia's Top End now supports more than half the world's free ranging Asian water buffalo. They were imported from Indonesia in the 1820s and 1830s to settlements at Raffles Bay and Port Essington on the Coburg Peninsula, and Escape Cliffs at the mouth of the Adelaide River. By 1849 the settlements had been abandoned and so had the buffalo. They are the subject of a sizeable industry—a source of hides and dog food—but wild buffalo carry brucellosis and tuberculosis. They are also a source of soil erosion and damage to vegetation and have caused considerable damage to Kakadu National Park.

Pigs came on the *Endeavour* in 1770, escaped and flourished; they are omnivorous and there is nothing they will not eat, including each other. There are now an estimated three million feral pigs in New South Wales alone and four million more in Queensland. Pigs kill sheep, especially lambs, damage crops and generally tear up the ground and vegetation. They are poisoned with the controversial 10-80, and are open game for shooters, yet still their numbers grow. A sow can produce two litters per year, with between three to twelve young per litter.

Approximately 350,000 wild goats are found in Western Australia, South Australia and the western half of New South Wales. Goats were a source of meat and milk in the nineteenth century for farmers and other workers and abandoned angora and cashmere goats, the consequence of failed commercial ventures, have added to their numbers. Goats destroy vegetation, especially small plants and have been known to eject rock wallabies from caves; the wallabies then suffer from heat exposure.

A number of animals were introduced for the purposes of sport, namely deer, hares, rabbits and the fox. Deer appeared in 1860 in Victoria. They threatened grazing pasture but, essentially docile in nature, they proved susceptible to poisoning and hunting. They are also without the enormous breeding capacity of other feral animals.

The red fox, found throughout most of the world, is often regarded as a rogue, clever and appealing. The fox was imported to Victoria in 1864 for hunting purposes, although some foxes may have been introduced as early as 1845. Later importations in 1870 and 1871 guaranteed their survival and by 1916 foxes were found at Esperance in Western Australia. A bounty introduced in 1929 saw 893,000 foxes killed over the ensuing thirty years in Western Australia alone. Payment was discontinued in 1960 due to controversy over its effectiveness. Foxes have done little damage commercially, though they are known to attack lambs and poultry. Their main damage has been to wildlife.

Hares were present before 1862 but in that year they were imported and probably successfully established by William Lyall in Victoria. By 1873 hare coursing was legal in Victoria. The hare, though a nuisance and unprotected, never reached the virulent plague levels of the rabbit.

No other species holds such pride of place in the folklore of Australia as the rabbit. As an example of interference with the balance of nature it is almost unparalleled. The rabbit, despised and seen only on the dining tables of the very poor or the gastronomically adventurous, was once considered a dish fit for a gentleman. Some of the convicts were deported to Australia for hunting rabbits, which were protected in England by the game laws. Here, where they bred in their millions, and with the introduction of myxomatosis the public was put off rabbit flesh. At the height of their fecundity rabbits constituted the greatest animal plague and commercial threat to the grazing industry in the history of settled Australia. Eight to ten rabbits will eat as much grazing as one sheep, and fifty will eat as much as a cow. At one time they bred and died in their millions—paddocks could yield thousands—and, despite myxomatosis, they continue to thrive and could still prove a major menace if allowed to get out of control.

The First Fleet carried rabbits for eating, and they were soon running wild in New South Wales. Later, they were released in other states and on islands off the Australian coast. In the first half of the nineteenth century comments were made on the number of rabbits, but never that they constituted a major pest. Probably the only reason the Victorian Acclimatisation Society and others did not import the rabbit is because there were plenty already in Australia.

The right circumstances did not arise for unrestricted breeding until the 1860s. By then the timber, which rabbits dislike, had been cleared and most of the native cats, wild dogs, hawks, eagles and goannas that were the rabbit's enemies had been shot, poisoned or trapped.

Thomas Austin of Barwon Park, Winchelsea, near Geelong, Victoria, is commonly acknowledged as the culprit for the problem when he released twenty-four wild rabbits in 1859. He hoped they would breed and could be used for hunting: by 1865 he had allegedly killed 20,000 of the beasts on his property. Austin was not the only person to release rabbits, merely the most public about it, and by the time the danger had become evident it was too late. By 1869 William Robertson of Glen Alvie, Victoria, reckoned he had spent 10,000 pounds and killed 2,033,000 rabbits. In 1887 in the first eight months of the year ten million rabbits were reported destroyed in New South Wales.

Everything and anything was tried in an effort to control rabbits: digging out; poisoning (which killed numerous other animals and birds); ferrets; cats; mongooses; shooting and fencing. It was all ineffectual.

In 1919 the rabbit disease myxomatosis, native to Brazil, was first noticed by the Commonwealth Institute of Science and Industry. No action was taken, in part because of the valuable trade in rabbit meat. Nevertheless, after considerable delay research into the efficacy of myxomatosis did commence in 1933. The first trials in 1936 were not successful, principally because it was not yet realised that myxomatosis was carried between rabbits by parasites, usually fleas. The CSIRO lost interest and research ceased in 1943.

Further trials were begun by the CSIRO in 1950, but were not thought a success and a statement was issued to that effect. Local graziers near the test property thought otherwise and arrived to take away infected rabbits in the boots of their cars. The disease spread and the animals died in their millions. By 1953 most of Australia was free of rabbits and the wool clip suddenly increased by 31,800,000 kilograms. But attempts at eradication were inadequate so the rabbit survived, and by 1967 numbers were about one-fifth of the total rabbit population in 1953.

The rabbit is fighting back. While myxomatosis can still be effective, the number of myxomatosis-resistant rabbits is increasing. A plague of rabbits which threatened Victorian farmers in 1987 was likened to the worst of the 1950s.

Potentially the most dangerous feral animal in terms of permanent damage to the wildlife of Australia is the domestic cat. Cats, despite their lazy mien, are natural hunters and breed almost as rapidly as rabbits. They are thought to have been introduced to Australia on the north coast by visiting Malay fishing boats and, ironically, the New South Wales government released thousands of cats into the bush in the 1880s in an attempt to control the rabbit plague. The dumping of unwanted cats also significantly adds to their number.

There are probably several million feral cats living in the Australian bush and they have virtually wiped out several species of small ground marsupials; numbats (banded anteaters), bilbies (rabbit-eared bandicoots) and bettongs (rat-kangaroos). Another two million stray cats are estimated living in Australia's cities. On average a cat, domestic or feral, kills at least one living thing a day.

Malaysian fishermen may also have introduced some of the first foreign plants into the country when they camped on Australia's northern beaches. Tamarind seeds were included in their rations, and this tree is now found on some beaches. Joseph Banks sent to England for, among others, olives, lemon grass, carrib, mulberries, hops, ginger, pears, peaches, apples and chestnuts. Dr Richard Groves of the CSIRO Division of Plant Industry estimates that for every 100 species introduced, only about ten colonise successfully, of which only about five naturalise (spread over a wide area); and only one or two of these five become weeds. One such, the blackberry, was introduced to Tasmania around 1843 and subsequently overran the state. It was brought to the mainland in the 1860s and remained a nuisance until the development of hormone sprays. Though it appears an unknown person has illegally imported blackberry rust from France and released it in New South Wales the removal of blackberry is still expensive and time consuming.

The prickly pear is the plant equivalent of the rabbit. A cactus of American origin, there are several genera present in Australia, the most common being the common prickly pear and the spiny prickly pear. The weed was such a problem that in 1920 the Commonwealth Prickly Pear Board was created (ceased 1939). By 1925 prickly pear had infested about sixty million acres of land—approximately 80 per cent in Queensland and the rest in New South Wales—about half of which was useless.

Several genera of prickly pear were introduced during the 1880s for cochineal breeding, stock feed, or as garden plants. A bill was moved in 1882 in the New South Wales parliament calling for the plant's eradication. As early as 1889 the biological control of prickly pear was advocated in Queensland and in 1903 *Dactylopius ceylonicus* was introduced from Ceylon but failed to establish itself. It was introduced again in 1914 by the Queensland Prickly-Pear Travelling Commission, which had investigated natural enemies of the prickly pear in several countries. This time *D. ceylonicus* was more successful but it only attacked drooping prickly pear.

Prickly pear continued to thrive until the introduction of *Cactoblastis cactorum* in 1926 by the Commonwealth Prickly Pear Board. The moth's larvae bores through the plant, which is 90 per cent water, and it literally collapses and new growth springs up from the land it once occupied. Currently, prickly pear, though no longer a major problem, still warrants the attention of such bodies as the Prickly Pear Destruction Commission in New South Wales.

The South African bitou bush (often known as boneseed, jungle weed, jungle flower, South African Star Bush or Higgins' curse) was hailed twenty years ago as the answer to the stabilisation of shifting sand dunes. It still is but it also destroys all other flora in the process and even pushes people out; it is so dense it can block access to beaches. Probably introduced as a garden shrub in Victoria in 1850 it was used in the late 1940s in New South Wales as a sand binder. The bitou bush symbolises the danger imported plants pose to native and there is no telling how many ecological niches it has destroyed. It is now found along 60 per cent of the New South Wales coastline, and is the dominant vegetation of 21 per cent of the coastline. Research is under way in South Africa to find a natural enemy.

The number of weeds which make life difficult for farmers and graziers are too numerous to mention. Noogoora burr is, at present, perhaps the most serious. It was introduced with cotton seed from the Mississippi delta of North America and first discovered at Noogoora Station in Queensland in the 1860s. It occurs in all Australian states, particularly New South Wales and Queensland. Noogoora burr is poisonous to stock, displaces pasture and when it sticks to sheep, reduces the value of fleeces. Research into the biological control of Noogoora burr was started in the United States in 1929 and extended to India in 1939-40. Several insect species were imported under quarantine between 1930-40 but only one, *Euaresta aequalis*, was released. It only succeeded around Brisbane. Research continues.

Patterson's Curse, which often covers whole paddocks with its brilliant purple flowers, appears to have been originally introduced as an ornamental flower. It spread independently from separate points: Gladstone in South Australia; Albany in New South Wales; and a location in Western Australia. In South Australia the plant was not regarded as a pest and is called Salvation Jane because in dry spells it is one of the few plants to survive and provide animal feed.

Insects were not deliberately imported in any number until the beginning of biological control. They lacked glamour and commercial worth, and most came in by accident. The first dung beetles, brought in for research purposes in 1966, were found to be sheltering unwanted mites under their wing casings. The New South Wales Acclimatisation Society tried to breed the cochineal insect, which was parasitic to the prickly pear, but unlike the prickly pear it did not fare well.

Some of the introduced insect species, like the animals and plants, are famous throughout Australia. The Argentine ant is familiar to most school children, who have often been asked to assist in its eradication. Ants can damage plants and seedlings, are a general nuisance around the house and spread disease.

The dung beetle lives in cattle dung, of which there are millions of pats produced each day in Australia. Dung smothers pasture while the grass which grows up around it is unpalatable to cattle. It is also a breeding ground for flies, in particular the buffalo fly which can so irritate cattle that they lose weight and give poor milk.

Dung beetles derive nourishment from dung and also use it as a breeding ground. They cause the dung to break up before it becomes a threat to pasture or a breeding ground for flies. Small mites attached to the dung beetle attack fly larvae which the dung beetle ignores. Best known of the dung beetles are the ball rollers but there are several other common varieties in Australia such as the *Sisyphus rubrus* from South Africa, which was introduced to Queensland by the CSIRO in 1973.

The European wasp is regarded as an import of technology: nests are often found near seaports and airports where hibernating queens have been released from shipments of goods. At least one hibernating queen was delivered to New Zealand in 1945 in a shipment of aircraft parts and nests in Australia were first reported in 1959. It is now widely spread throughout Tasmania, New South Wales and Victoria, and will inevitably spread through the rest of the country as it has no natural enemies in Australia. It preys on native insects and is an economic threat to berry and grape growers and beekeepers. People allergic to its sting can fall extremely ill, and inquisitive wasps have ruined more than one outdoor barbecue. Current efforts to control its spread centre on a parasitic ichneumonid wasp—*Sphecophaga vesparum*.

The red-back spider, long regarded as a native, may well be an impostor who stowed away last century on a ship bound for Queensland from Asia, Africa or the Americas. The red-back was first described at Rockhampton in 1870, more than eighty years after white settlement and more than 200 years after other spider species had been reported. Before an antivenene was discovered in 1956 at least thirteen Australians were killed by red-back bites and these days an estimated 200 people a year are treated for extremely painful bites. Only the female red-back is big enough to bite humans effectively. It is a highly venomous spider, capable of killing snakes, lizards and mice. Although not normally aggressive they bite if they are trapped or squeezed. It is a strong coloniser and produces hundreds of eggs. The red-back prefers to live near humans in suburban gardens and homes rather than natural bushland.

METHOD OF CONTROL

Controlling animal, plant and insect pests is not simple because humans and the environment are interrelated. The rabbit did not become a menace until forests were cleared and predators removed. Perversely, the spread of feral cats was aided by man releasing cats into the wild under the mistaken impression they would kill rabbits. Significantly, insects seldom attain pest proportions in uncultivated land. Cultivated crops, specially selected, neutered and bred, offer an insect pest a large number of healthy plants to breed on, and chemical spraying has often wiped out the natural predators of insects which man wishes to control.

That Australia has not been invaded by many other species is probably due to luck, and possibly the presence of some native plant, insect or disease with which an import cannot compete. Bluetongue, a virulent sheep disease, has probably failed to establish itself in Australia because a milder version of the disease already exists. Still, there are no guarantees.

Australia is presently free of foot-and-mouth disease, Rift Valley fever, swine fever, and rabies. An outbreak of any of these diseases could cost the rural sector as much as $4 billion in the first year, and lead to the slaughter of up to a quarter of the nation's livestock. If a disease was spread by feral animals it could take years to eradicate. Feral pigs, for example, will most likely be the ones to spread foot-and-mouth disease if it ever reaches these shores.

The most effective method in the long term of protecting a species from its enemies is to make it more resistant, to breed healthier animals and plants. But this takes time and is by no means guaranteed. Quarantine, which aims at keeping pests out altogether, is the next best method of control. Strict quarantine regulations apply in various parts of the country to protect crops, especially fruit and vegetables, from plant diseases and insects. While quarantine of Australia's ports and airports is difficult enough, the country's north is wide open to everything from drug, bird, pornography and illegal immigrant smuggling. Aerial surveillance is in the hands of a commercial organisation but coastal patrolling and radar coverage are inadequate. Quarantine officers are few and far between.

A major area of weakness is the Torres Strait Islands, which lie between Papua New Guinea and Australia. Travel in the area is easy in small boats and is frequent among the local islanders who have traded with each other for centuries. It is possible to see Australian territory, Thursday Island, with the naked eye from foreign territory. While the chances of insects such as the Old World screwworm fly, which could devastate the northern cattle industry, making the journey by flying or being carried by the wind is low, the danger comes from inadvertent delivery during inter-island trading.

The Lindsay Report on quarantine, compiled by Professor David Lindsay, Dean of the Faculty of Agriculture at the University of Western Australia, examines the problems of quarantine for Australia as a whole. The report, however, is worth only as much as the federal government's commitment which, at present, is low.

Methods of control vary for those pests already in Australia. In addition to using myxomatosis, rabbits can be hunted and sold for profit. Most animals can be culled by shooting and their flesh and hides sold. Shooting from helicopters is the best method for large animals and, involving commercial interests, has the advantage that it does not cost the community. A culling program is under way to reduce the water buffalo population to 45,000 and restrict it to southern Arnhem Land. In Western Australia 27,000 donkeys were shot from the air in 1985-86 and an equal number from the ground. Unfortunately, the population is capable of recovery within four years. While the shooting of water buffalo has not aroused much protest, the shooting of horses in central Australia has encountered considerable opposition. Sooner or later, however, some sort of national program of culling feral animals will have to be introduced.

Feral cats are not so easily shot, nor trapped because they tend to favour bush and timbered country. A possible solution would be the introduction of a cat-specific disease, a sort of cat myxomatosis, which would probably require cat owners to have their pets vaccinated.

Whereas hunting and trapping can take care of most animals, biological control is the best way of controlling plants and insects. Biological control, like health food, is free of artificial additives. It is 'natural', using nature to defeat nature. Disease, myxomatosis being the classic example, is a form of biological control, but the disadvantage is that species gradually acquire resistance to the disease. Biological control through insects or plants seldom involves eradication, rather it aims to achieve an acceptable balance; prickly pear was devastated but not eradicated.

Modern biological control commenced with the successful control of cottony-cushion scale, which devastated the Californian citrus industry in 1887. Ironically, the cushion scale originated in Australia, and the United States government imported from Australia a natural enemy of the cottony-cushion scale, a ladybird, in late 1889. Fifteen months later, at a cost of $US1500, the project was a success. Later, chemical spraying reduced the ladybird population and this led to a renewed outbreak of cottony-cushion scale. The remedy this time cost many millions of dollars.

Australian interest in biological control was prompted by American entomologists who came to Australia in search of parasites and predators to combat Californian and Hawaiian pests. Western Australia was the first state to take action and in 1896 a coccinellid was apparently the first insect to be introduced into Australia. Biological control was popular in Australia in the first quarter of this century, but it was time consuming and failures outnumbered successes.

Chemical spraying, which seemed to offer a ready solution, was adopted enthusiastically but it has ultimately caused more problems than it has solved. It gives with one hand but often takes with the other. Herbicides and pesticides have damaging side effects, such as killing animals and birds and being harmful to humans. In addition, as pests develop resistance to chemicals, new and sometimes more lethal chemicals are used. In combating one species of pest chemicals often destroy other, benign species. An example in Australia is the spraying in the early 1970s of apples and other fruit for fungus; this also killed the natural enemies of the two-spotted spider and the European red spider mite which attack the leaves, resulting in a weaker tree and reduced fruit production. The CSIRO fortunately found a predatory mite, a strain of *Typlodromus occidentalis*, which is resistant to most chemical sprays. It was introduced in 1975-76 and was widely used by 1982. A second spray-resistant mite had to be introduced in 1977 when it was found the first was partial only to the two-spotted mite.

Given such circumstances and the recent widespread concern about the effects of chemicals on humans, biological control is back in favour but extreme care has to be taken. Witness the experience of the Queensland cane toad which is poisonous to animals, eats native insects and isn't much good to anyone. It was introduced into Queensland from Hawaii in 1935 in an attempt to control sugar cane pests but the sugar cane pests could fly, whereas the cane toad could not. Furthermore, the cane toad found food abundant and natural predators non-existent and it has since been advancing through Australia at a rate of about twenty-seven kilometres a year. They are moving down into New South Wales and have been caught hitchhiking in boxes of fruit bound for Western Australia.

A recent success has been the destruction of *Salvinia molesta*, a rapid-growing South American water weed which suffocates bodies of water by deoxygenation. It was introduced into Australia probably as an ornamental plant for ponds and the like, and was first identified in dire need of biological control in 1975 when 10,000 hectares of clogged waterways were reported. It is now prevalent in nearly every river system in the Northern Territory. In 1980 the CSIRO introduced a weevil, *Cyrtobagous* spp., into Lake Moondarra at Mt Isa, then Australia's largest infestation of Salvinia. By May 1981 400 hectares of Salvinia had been cleared and the destruction continues.

Apart from the direct import of disease, biological control of insect and plant species has expanded into a number of other areas, some promising. Microbial pesticides are not true pesticides but tiny organisms, sometimes numbering billions and usually mixed with water to form a spray. Nematodes, tiny worms, have been used to control the Sirex wood wasp, which threatened Australia's pine plantations. More than 2000 million can be held in a person's cupped hands. They are non-toxic but require considerable care in their use. Also, the rotting corpses of the target pest may consequently contain an unwelcome additive for the crop in question.

Repellants can include amplified sounds, such as bat calls to drive moths away from orchards. Attractants have been more fully developed, and sex attractants have been particularly successful; attractively baited traps laced with insecticide or the broadcast of mating calls.

Pheromones is the term for chemicals released by animals, especially insects. They are extremely important in determining the behaviour of the insect population. When a person receives a bee sting the bee also lays a pheromone which attracts other bees. Research into pheromones is relatively new and there are potential advantages for the future. Natural or artificial pheromones are used to manipulate insect behaviour by luring them into traps or into areas to be treated with pesticides, or by inhibiting breeding habits. They are used to control the oriental fruit moth, which is partial to Australian peaches.

Genetic control involves chemical or X-ray sterilisation of male or female insects which are then released to mate with their wild counterparts. This method has been used successfully to control the screw-worm fly in America as well as flies along the Mexican border. Total eradication is seldom possible, however, and after seven years of success in America changes in the factory-bred sterilised screw-worm fly led to a reduction in effectiveness and a return of the screw-worm.

Another form of genetic control is the introduction of genetically incompatible insects of the same species. The blowfly has been the subject of research since 1911, when a sarcophagid parasite was brought into Australia from Japan. A variety of other imported and natural parasites have been tried since then but none has ever had any marked effect on the blowfly population. In 1960 a CSIRO publication stated that 'the biological control of sheep blowfly is almost an impossibility'. In the early 1980s, however, the CSIRO introduced genetically mutated male flies on Flinders Island, off Tasmania. The male flies passed on a genetic mutation that bred blind female flies which quickly fell prey to predators and starvation, and the blowfly population fell to barely detectable levels—until the money ran out. In 1988 the program, dependent on a grant from the Australian Wool Corporation, was set to begin again.

Disruption involves methods like excessive irrigation to flush insects off plants and disrupt their breeding cycle. Similiarly, ploughing can disrupt breeding cycles, as can the destruction of crop residues after harvesting, strip farming and crop rotation, sowing and harvest dates and practices and the planting of non-crop plants (though little is known about this idea as yet).

Australia, cut off from the rest of the world for millions of years, has a unique ecology, much of it still undiscovered; it is estimated that only about one-third of the country's insects have been identified. Many may never be discovered because a new ecosystem is emerging. It will not resemble the Australia the first European settlers encountered or even that of fifty years ago.

A useful measure which could be taken is the establishment of genetic 'banks', possibly on remote islands off the Australian coast. These 'banks' would be repositories of native flora and fauna with access barred to all but a few scientists. In the years to come they might be all that is left of the Australia we know.

T. R.

THE HISTORY OF AVIATION IN AUSTRALIA

THE PIONEER YEARS

The history of aviation in Australia begins in 1851 when an ex-convict, Doctor William Bland (1789-1868), proposed a Sydney to London air service using a five tonne steam-powered airship of his own design. He believed that his 'Atomic Ship' would cut to five days the journey which then took up to three months by sea. His plans, alas, proved impracticable and the airship was never built.

The first person to actually leave the ground in Australia was William Dean, who flew at Melbourne on 1 February 1858 in a gas-filled balloon. Other balloonists soon followed, and as gas and hot-air balloons became more common, inventors began to concentrate on the goal of heavier-than-air flight.

Lawrence Hargrave (1850-1915), whose portrait appears on the Australian twenty dollar note, built several model aircraft which flew under their own power, and experimented with his own designs of box kites. On 12 November 1894 he became the first person in Australia to fly by means of a heavier-than-air aircraft when he was lifted five metres into the air by four of his box kites at Stanwell Park, New South Wales. Although his kites were tethered to the ground and his flight was short and not controllable, his designs and discoveries contributed a great deal to the eventual mastery of the air.

In 1903, the American Wilbur Wright became the first person in the world to truly fly a powered aircraft, and although several Australian attempts were made in the 1900s, it was to be another American, the escapologist Harry Houdini, who made the first powered, controlled flight in Australia when he flew a French-built Voisin aircraft on 18 March 1910 at Diggers Rest near Melbourne.

The first Australian to fly a powered aircraft followed soon after. John Duigan (1882-1951) took off on 16 July 1910 at Mia Mia, Victoria, in an aircraft he had designed and built himself. This historic machine is now exhibited in the Melbourne Science Museum.

Although flight had been achieved in Australia and it was to become increasingly more common in the next four years, the aircraft used were low-powered, unreliable and generally at the mercy of the weather as it was dangerous to attempt to fly in wind speeds of more than a few knots. It was therefore a significant milestone when the Frenchman Maurice Gillaux carried the first airmail in Australia from Melbourne to Sydney in just over two days, arriving on 18 July 1914.

World War I brought to a close this pioneering era in flying. When peace came in 1918, aeroplanes were far more powerful and reliable and capable of carrying much greater loads for longer distances – the result of intensive experimentation and development during the war.

Because of this development, South Australian-born Ross Smith (1892-1922) and his brother Keith (1890-1953) were able to make the long distance link between England and Australia that Doctor Bland had dreamed of in 1851. Their flight in a war-surplus Vickers Vimy bomber took twenty-seven days and they landed at Darwin on 10 December 1919, winning a £10,000 prize from the Australian government. The Smith brothers were knighted for their achievement and the twin-engined biplane they used has been preserved and is displayed at Adelaide Airport.

Many Austalians who had learned to fly during the war returned home and attempted to earn a living by giving demonstration flights and joy-rides up and down the country. Others had grander plans and established Australia's earliest airlines, the first being Norman Brearley (b.1890) who began Western Australian Airways which flew its first scheduled flights on 5 December 1921. After a faltering start, the airline prospered and operated until 1936 when it was taken over by Australian National Airways.

The oldest Australian airline still operating was set up by Hudson Fysh (1895-1974) as Queensland and Northern Territory Aerial Service Ltd (later abbreviated to QANTAS), which began its first service on 2 November 1922. The airline was then based at Longreach in Queensland, and within a few years was regularly flying passengers, mail and freight, throughout the state. It has become the second oldest airline still operating in the world.

Other airlines were not so lucky and were forced to close down. Using war surplus aircraft that were not designed for the carriage of passengers or freight, they found it impossible to attract enough customers prepared to pay the high fares they had to charge to cover their costs. The airlines that survived did so mainly due to the government subsidies paid to carry mail to and from remote areas of Australia.

THE TRAIL BLAZERS

During the 1920s and early 1930s when airlines and small air-charter operators were fighting for their survival, other Australian pilots were becoming world famous for their long-distance flights. They were popular heroes and did much to popularise the idea of flying. The public eagerly followed news of their exploits in newspapers and on the radio, and a sign of the enthusiasm of the times is the fact that in 1928, a crowd of 30,000 greeted Kingsford Smith on his arrival from New Zealand at two o'clock in the morning.

It should be remembered that these pilots were true pioneers, taking enormous risks over virtually unmapped routes, with very few properly constructed aerodromes — most landings were made on makeshift strips such as racecourses and beaches. An additional hazard facing the England to Australia pilots was the long stretch over the water from Timor to Darwin — 800 kilometres over the Arafura Sea — where an engine failure meant almost certain death.

Some of the most famous pilots of this era were:

Sir Charles Kingsford Smith (1897-1935)

A fighter pilot in World War I, 'Smithy' became one of Australia's first airline pilots, flying with Western Australian Airways. A brilliant pilot, he held numerous air records and was the first to fly over many of today's major world air-routes. Among his most important flights were:

1928 first flight across the Pacific — America to Australia
1928 first non-stop Melbourne-Perth flight (2870 kilometres in 23 hours)
1928 first Australia-New Zealand flight
1930 first London-New York flight
1930 first pilot to fly round the world with crossings of the equator
1935 first Australia-America flight (11,750 kilometres in 57.5 hours).

Many of his long-distance flights were achieved in a three-engined Fokker aircraft named the 'Southern Cross' which is now on display at Brisbane Airport. He disappeared over the Bay of Bengal in November 1935 whilst attempting to break the speed record from England to Australia. As Australia's most famous airman, his portrait appears on the twenty dollar note.

Bert Hinkler (1892-1933)

Queensland-born Hinkler learnt to fly during the war and later became a test pilot in England. After several record long-distance flights in Europe, he made the first solo flight to Australia in a single-engined Avro Avian in February 1928. He took just under sixteen days to cover the distance, almost halving the record time, which was still held by the Smith brothers. He made several more record flights but was killed in a crash in Italy whilst on his way to Australia in 1933.

Lores Bonney (b.1897)

Having been inspired by her cousin, Bert Hinkler, Lores Bonney learnt to fly in 1931. Over the next few years she created several records by her long-distance flights:

1931 longest distance covered in one day in Australia, Brisbane to Wangaratta (1524 kilometres). This record was gained just over one month after passing her flying licence tests and was her first solo cross-country flight.
1932 first woman to circumnavigate Australia by air.
1933 first woman to fly from Australia to England.
1937 first person to fly from Australia to South Africa.

In 1934 she was awarded the MBE for her exceptional services to aviation.

Ray Parer (1894-1967)

Known to the press as 'Battling Parer', he

is chiefly remembered for coming spectacularly last in the two air races from England to Australia. With John McIntosh, he took 237 days (eight days actual flying time) to reach Australia in 1921, having overcome incredible hardships, not least of which was the dilapidated condition of their aircraft. In the 1934 race, again plagued with mechanical troubles, he took 116 days to make the same journey. Parer was also involved in pioneering flying in New Guinea, running his own passenger and freight airline.

Freda Thompson (1906–80)
In 1930, Freda Thompson became the twentieth woman to gain a pilot's licence in Australia. She flew solo from England to Australia in 1935, taking just over a month to do so. Earlier that year, she had become the first woman in Australia to gain an instructor's rating (meaning she was qualified to teach others to fly). During World War II she helped form the Victorian Branch of the Women's Air Training Corps. Freda was an active member of the Royal Victorian Aero Club for over forty years, and in 1948 she became the first woman to be elected its president. She was awarded the OBE in 1972 for her services to flying and an annual air race named in her honour and commemorating her achievements began in 1974.

Harry Hawker (1889–1921)
Born at Moorabbin, Victoria, Hawker gained his flying licence in England in 1912, and seven weeks later beat the British endurance record by staying airborne continuously for almost eight and a half hours. He became a test pilot for the Sopwith Aircraft Company and gained several altitude and speed records. After a flying demonstration tour of Australia in early 1914, he returned to England and continued his test pilot duties during the war. He made an unsuccessful attempt to fly the Atlantic in 1919, being forced down into the sea. Hawker was killed in an aircraft accident in 1921 and the Sopwith Aircraft Company was renamed Hawker Engineering in his honour.

Sir Patrick Gordon Taylor (1896–1966)
A World War I pilot, Taylor accompanied Kingsford Smith as navigator and co-pilot on several of his record-breaking flights. He was awarded the George Cross for bravery in 1935 when he repeatedly climbed out onto the wing struts to transfer oil from an engine which had failed to another which threatened to stop during a flight in the 'Southern Cross' from Australia to New Zealand. Taylor was a superb navigator – he made the first flight over the Indian Ocean from Australia to Africa in 1939, and in 1951 pioneered the South Pacific route to and from South America. He was knighted in 1954.

THE FIRST GREAT AIRLIFT
Whilst air-routes were being pioneered in Australia and around the world, a remarkable development was taking place in New Guinea (which had become an Australian dependency after World War I). Aircraft had been used there for exploration in the early 1920s, but it was the rich gold strike made in the Bulolo Valley in 1925 that began the world's first great airlift. Because of the lack of roads and the mountainous jungle terrain, it took ten days to travel overland from the coast to the goldfields, with equipment and food being limited to what could be carried by native bearers. One of the mining companies – Guinea Gold – decided that aerial transport would be easier, quicker and cheaper, and in 1927 their pilot 'Pard' Mustar, landed the first aeroplane at Wau airstrip close to the goldfields.

The idea was instantly successful and in the first six months of operation the aircraft carried 40,000 kilograms of supplies and 150 passengers. Other operators soon followed, but the original company (now operating as Guinea Airways) still led the way. By the end of 1932, with the aid of two specially adapted Junkers freight aircraft (each capable of lifting over 3000 kilograms at a time), Guinea Airways had flown over one and a half million kilometres, carried over 12,000 passengers and 7,000 tonnes of freight. Amongst the freight were the components for two complete gold dredges and the hydroelectric generating plant to run them – together weighing over 2200 tonnes. Air transport was the only way this equipment could have been put in place, and during the early 1930s more freight was carried by air in New Guinea than in all other countries in the world. After this amazing start, the aeroplane has continued to play a major part in the development of New Guinea and is today still the only effective transport link with remote inland villages.

AIRLINE DEVELOPMENT

The 1934 England to Australia air race demonstrated the rapid development of passenger aircraft. Although won by Scott and Black in their specially built de Havilland Comet racer, the aircraft that gained a very close second place was a Dutch airline DC-2, carrying fare-paying passengers and a large amount of mail. The twin-engined, all metal DC-2 and its development, the DC-3, became the mainstay of Australia's airlines in the late 1930s, linking capital cities with regular, reliable services.

The first regular airmail run between Europe and Australia began in 1934, and by 1938 a thrice-weekly passenger service was being flown from Australia to England by Qantas, using large flying boats.

With the coming of World War II, the airline services continued to expand, carrying mainly service personnel and war materials. When Singapore fell to the Japanese, Australia's air link to Britain was cut. To transport official documents, mail and the occasional VIP, Qantas began operating Catalina flying boats from Perth to Ceylon (now Sri Lanka) in 1943. At over 5600 kilometres, it was the longest scheduled non-stop airline service in the world and took twenty-seven hours. Since this time, Qantas has concentrated more on overseas flights and now no longer flies passengers on Australian internal routes.

After the war, the Labor government attempted to nationalise Australia's airlines. Although this move was defeated in a referendum, the government decided to form its own airline and in 1946 Trans Australia Airlines (TAA) was established. In 1986 its name was changed to Australian Airlines. Competition on interstate routes came from two other airlines: Australian National Airways (ANA) and Ansett Airlines, both of which had begun operations in the mid 1930s and had prospered during the war years. They amalgamated in 1957 to form Ansett-ANA (later Ansett Airlines of Australia) which bought out many smaller airlines in the 1950s and 1960s to create a large network of services throughout Australia and New Guinea.

Since the merger, passenger traffic has been almost equally divided between Ansett and TAA which now operate fleets of modern jet aircraft. Because of the government's two airline policy, no others have been allowed to compete on an Australia-wide basis. This policy is currently under review, however, and it is possible that the situation will change in the near future.

In the late 1960s, the two major airlines discontinued services to many country towns because they were unable to attract enough passengers to make the operation of large aircraft profitable on these routes. New regional airlines (known as 'third level airlines') were founded to fill this gap. By 1986 about fifty of these companies were operating, flying over a million passengers a year in relatively small propeller-driven aircraft.

GENERAL AVIATION

Side by side with the development of airlines has been the development of aviation for business and private use. In 1939, there were about 300 civil aircraft in Australia, today there are 7500, only about 320 of which are used for regular public transport services. Most of the others are privately owned (about 4300) and the rest are used commercially for aerial work. Their tasks are many and varied, including fighting bushfires, sowing rice, rounding up cattle and transporting live crayfish to market. In fact, the aeroplane has become an indispensable part of everyday life, perhaps more so in Australia than in other countries because of the vast size of our island continent.

DEPARTMENT OF AVIATION

Overall control of civil aviation in Australia is vested in the Department of Aviation. This body, which has existed in various forms and under several names, was founded in 1920 as part of the Department of Defence to regulate and control air navigation.

Its beginning coincided with the first expansion of civil aviation and it was soon busy holding examinations for the licensing of pilots and engineers and surveying landing grounds. Since that beginning, it has expanded until, in 1986, it had a staff of about 9500. The department develops and implements aviation policies and advises the government on aviation matters. It has established and operates most of the major airports throughout Australia and provides air traffic control services which handle over two million aircraft movements a year. The department also operates a flying unit, utilising a fleet of fifteen aircraft to maintain a continuous check on the accuracy of the nationwide network of navigation and landing aids.

One of the department's primary tasks is to promote safety in aviation, and to that end it is still the licensing body for all aircrew and aircraft engineers, also operating a crash investigation service to ascertain the cause of every aircraft accident. The department's vigilance in these matters contributes a great deal to the extremely low accident rate that Australia enjoys.

THE ROYAL FLYING DOCTOR SERVICE

One of the major difficulties of life in outback Australia has always been isolation from medical services for the victims of accident or disease. When the Reverend John Flynn (1880–1951) began work as an outback missionary in 1912 he quickly recognised the size of the problem, as at that time there were only two doctors serving an area of almost two million square kilometres in the Northern Territory and Western Australia.

In the 1920s he began to seek support for what he called 'a mantle of safety' provided by aircraft bringing doctors to remote areas. A reliable means of communication also had to be found because most of the patients were removed from telephones or the telegraph. With the development by Alfred Traeger of a portable two-way radio set powered by a foot-operated generator—the famous 'pedal wireless'—the Aerial Medical Service (as it was first called) became a reality.

A base was set up at Cloncurry, Queensland, and the first official medical flight was made on 17 May 1928, using an aircraft chartered from Qantas. As the success of the service became obvious, more bases were established in other states, and specially equipped aircraft were purchased to replace those originally hired from airlines.

The name was changed to the Flying Doctor Service in 1941 and the prefix 'Royal' granted in 1955 after a visit by the Queen to the Broken Hill Base. The RFDS today has fourteen bases from which its doctors serve the inhabitants of three-quarters of Australia. Thirty-three aircraft are in use, flying a total of more than eight million kilometres a year, bringing medical attention to over 100,000 patients of whom more than 9000 are transported to hospital. Routine monthly visits are made to isolated communities, and advice by radio is given in hundreds of cases in which illness is not serious enough to warrant a flight.

In addition to the RFDS, most states operate an aerial ambulance service. Doctors are not usually carried on these flights, which are used to bring emergency patients to larger hospitals in the capital cities, saving hours of travelling time by road.

AIRCRAFT PRODUCTION IN AUSTRALIA

As already noted, the first Australian-built aircraft was the Duigan biplane of 1910. Other privately constructed aircraft soon followed, both of local and overseas designs. However it was not until October 1919 that the first company was formed to build aircraft commercially in Australia. This was the Australian Aircraft and Engineering Company in Sydney which assembled and later part-manufactured English-designed Avro 504s. A similar operation was carried out in Melbourne by the Larkin Aircraft Supply Company, which manufactured Gypsy Moths in the 1920s.

Qantas and West Australian Airways also produced aircraft under licence for their own use, and the English de Havilland Aircraft Company set up a branch in Australia in 1929 to part-manufacture and assemble their products. Several Australian designs were also produced in small numbers, the most successful being the Genairco, of which about twenty were built.

All of these companies operated on quite a small scale, however, and the total production between the two world wars barely reached 200 aircraft. Even then, the engines and many metal parts were imported in most cases.

This was to change drastically with the

founding of the Commonwealth Aircraft Corporation in 1936 (which was, despite the name, a private company), set up to produce aircraft and engines for the expanding RAAF. Its first product was the Wirraway, built in 1939. A modified version of an American design, 755 were eventually built for the RAAF during World War II. The Wirraway was soon followed by the Australian-designed Wackett trainer (202 built) and the Boomerang fighter (250 built).

The de Havilland Aircraft Company in Sydney also continued to produce aircraft during the war, building over 1000 Tiger Moths as well as a number of other designs.

The Commonwealth government itself entered aircraft production in 1941, forming the Beaufort Division of the Department of Aircraft Production (later named the Government Aircraft Factories) which manufactured Beaufort bombers and Beaufighter fighter-bombers.

By the end of the war, Australian aircraft factories had delivered to the RAAF over 3500 aircraft of eleven different types, and almost 3000 engines had also been made in Australia by Australian workmen and largely from Australian materials.

Postwar, production was scaled down as contracts were cancelled, but manufacture of aircraft did continue, and most of the RAAF's front-line aircraft of the last forty years have been built (although not designed) in Australia. These include Lincoln and Canberra bombers, Vampire, Sabre and Mirage fighters, Macchi trainers, and currently, FA-18 Hornet fighter-bombers.

Production of civil aircraft in Australia has not fared so well, but four types—all designed in Australia—have been produced in some numbers. They are the de Havilland Drover transport, the Victa Airtourer light aircraft (165 of which were built by the Victa lawn-mower company), the Transavia Airtruk agricultural aircraft and the GAF Nomad transport. Only the Airtruk is still being produced, but major subassemblies are being built for United States and European airliners by the Australian industry.

The main problems facing the Australian aircraft industry have always been twofold—the lack of any continuing government support and the small local market for aircraft. Although the industry has demonstrated time and again that it has the capability to build quality products, it has never been able to surmount these problems.

Mention must also be made of the increasing popularity of home-built aircraft, over 300 of which have been constructed by private individuals over the last twenty years.

AUSTRALIAN MILITARY AVIATION
The Royal Australian Air Force

The Australian Flying Corps (AFC) was formed by the army in October 1912, but the first military aircraft was not flown in Australia until 1 March 1914, when a Bristol Boxkite, piloted by Lieutenant E. Harrison flew at Point Cook, Victoria, the AFC's only aerodrome. Flying training commenced there in August 1914, shortly after the outbreak of war.

The first Australian-trained military airmen left Melbourne in April 1915, bound for Mesopotamia. By the end of the war, four Australian squadrons were serving on the principal fronts, with a training wing of four more squadrons based in England to provide reinforcements. Many other Australian pilots also served with the British Royal Flying Corps squadrons.

The Australians distinguished themselves in the air during World War I—over sixty of them each shot down more than five enemy aircraft, top scorers being Captain Robert Little (47), Major R. S. Dallas (39) and Captain A. H. Cobby (32). In 1917, Lieutenant F. H. McNamara became the first Australian pilot to be awarded the Victoria Cross. He gained this high honour for the exceptional bravery he displayed in landing behind the Turkish lines to pick up another pilot who had been forced down.

After the war, the AFC was demobilised and it was not until 1920 that an Australian Air Corps was again created to run the Point Cook Flying School. In 1921 this corps was formed into the Royal Australian Air Force (RAAF), a completely separate service from the army which up to then had controlled military flying.

During the inter-war years, the RAAF gradually expanded from its initial establishment of twenty-one officers and 130 other ranks. Exploratory flights were undertaken, and Wing Commander Goble and Flight Lieutenant McIntyre made the first round-Australia flight in 1924, covering almost 14,000 kilometres. In 1926, Group Captain Williams made a survey flight along the east coast of Australia and to the Solomon Islands – the first overseas flight of the RAAF.

At the beginning of World War II, the RAAF had 246 aircraft, ten operational squadrons and a strength of 310 officers and 3179 other ranks. The war brought massive expansion, with peak strength being attained in 1944 of 164,000 officers and men. These airmen served in all theatres of war, from bomber raids on Berlin to fighter combat over the jungles of New Guinea. Almost 700 aircraft were lost in combat, and 10,562 members of the RAAF were killed.

With the surrender of Germany and Japan in 1945, the RAAF became the fourth largest air force in the world, but the coming of peace meant a rapid reduction in size. The lowest point was reached in 1948 when the total strength fell to just over 8000.

The RAAF was again involved in combat shortly after the outbreak of the Korean War in 1950. During the three years of the war, No. 77 Squadron flew almost 5000 combat missions. They operated initially with Mustang aircraft, but later converted to Meteors, the RAAF's first jet aircraft to see action. They also participated in the Malayan emergency, and for ten years from 1950 flew bombing missions against communist terrorists in the Malayan jungles.

In 1964 the RAAF entered the Vietnam War, eventually operating three squadrons there until 1972 when Australian involvement ceased. No. 35 Squadron operating Caribou transport aircraft was the first unit to serve in Vietnam, followed by No. 9 Squadron with Iroquois helicopters and No. 2 Squadron with Canberra low-level bombers. A total of 4443 RAAF personnel served in Vietnam.

The RAAF today is a small (about 22,000) but highly trained force, with fifteen front-line squadrons operating modern aircraft. The FA-18 Hornet fighter is rapidly replacing the Mirage, and along with two squadrons the F-111 bombers, provides a potent strike force. Long-range maritime surveillance is carried out by P3C Orions, whilst Hercules and Caribou aircraft are engaged in transport duties along with Chinook and Iroquois helicopters.

Apart from its defence role, the RAAF carries out humanitarian operations in times of disaster such as cyclones, fires and floods. It also flies search-and-rescue missions and has been called on many times to provide overseas aid by the United Nations.

Royal Australian Navy Fleet Air Arm

After successful experimentation with aircraft launched from cruisers in 1917, it was decided that the Royal Australian Navy (RAN) should have an air arm, but it was not until 1929 that the seaplane-carrier HMAS *Albatross* was commissioned. Its aircraft had to be lowered over the side by crane and took off and landed on the sea, being hoisted back on board after each flight. They were flown by both naval officers and RAAF pilots until HMAS *Albatross* was taken out of service in 1933 because of lack of finance.

In 1947 the Fleet Air Arm was reinstated, and HMAS *Sydney* became its first real aircraft carrier in 1948, providing anti-submarine and fighter protection for the fleet. A shore base was established at Nowra, New South Wales, to train personnel for the new service. In 1951, HMAS *Sydney* was deployed to the Korean war zone and her aircraft, flying mainly ground-attack missions against North Korean bases and transport, performed valuable service for the allies.

A second aircraft carrier, HMAS *Melbourne*, entered service in 1956, operating new jet and turboprop aircraft. As these aircraft could not operate from HMAS *Sydney*, she was soon retired and became a fast troop transport. HMAS *Melbourne* continued to operate as an aircraft carrier and flagship of the Royal Australian Navy until the early 1980s. The Fleet Air Arm's fixed-wing aircraft were retired with her and today all FAA front-line units operate only helicopters for antisubmarine and transport work, flying from flight decks installed on the larger RAN ships.

Army Aviation

As has already been mentioned, Australian military aviation was under the control of the Army until 1921 when the RAAF was formed as a separate service. The army again became involved in aviation in 1951 when artillery officers began training as pilots for observation duties. In 1960, an Army Light Aircraft Squadron was formed at Amberley, Queensland, and all army flying concentrated in this unit, operating both helicopters and light aircraft. The Australian Army Aviation Corps was formed on 1 July 1968, and the army rapidly took over all facets of the operation, including servicing and overhaul of aircraft which had previously been the responsibility of the RAAF.

Army pilots served as forward air controllers in Korea and Vietnam, and today, in addition to providing support for the army within Australia, the air corps is also used extensively for survey work and humanitarian aid to neighbouring countries. The main base is at Oakey, Queensland, with major units at Sydney and Townsville. About fifty helicopters are operated as well as thirty fixed-wing aircraft.

R.W.

AIRCRAFT MOVEMENTS, 1986–87
CONTROLLED AERODROMES

The term 'Controlled Aerodrome' relates to those airports having Air Traffic Control facilities.

Airport	Movements
Adelaide	96,006
Albury	38,083
Alice Springs	42,371
Archerfield	254,896
Avalon	30,992
Bankstown	355,891
Brisbane	105,422
Cairns	74,026
Camden	98,172
Canberra	136,199
Coffs Harbor	33,665
Coolangatta	69,263
Darwin	74,138
Essendon	71,152
Hamilton Island	4,690
Hobart/Cambridge	39,729
Jandakot	228,083
Karratha	23,708
Launceston	40,534
Mackay	42,239
Maroochydore	46,200
Melbourne	107,013
Moorabbin	283,971
Mount Isa	27,627
Parafield	194,179
Perth	78,026
Port Hedland	24,800
Proserpine	4,378
Rockhampton	37,590
Sydney	203,590
Tamworth	33,324
Townsville	78,186
Wagga Wagga	31,088

Source: Department of Aviation.

AUSTRALIAN AIR DISTANCES

All distances are expressed in kilometres and calculated by means of the Great Circle Distance formula. A Great Circle Distance is the shortest distance between any two points on the globe, over the earth's surface.

Adelaide-Alice Springs	1,316
Adelaide-Auckland	3,258
Adelaide-Ayers Rock	1,306
Adelaide-Birdsville	1,009
Adelaide-Brisbane	1,617
Adelaide-Broken Hill	426
Adelaide-Canberra	972
Adelaide-Cooma	957
Adelaide-Darwin	2,619
Adelaide-Hobart	1,172
Adelaide-Melbourne	643
Adelaide-Nullarbor	812
Adelaide-Perth	2,120
Adelaide-Sydney	1,166
Adelaide-Wagga Wagga	815
Brisbane-Bundaberg	290
Brisbane-Cairns	1,392
Brisbane-Canberra	951
Brisbane-Coolangatta	92
Brisbane-Darwin	2,852
Brisbane-Gladstone	437
Brisbane-Great Keppel Island	518
Brisbane-Gympie	132
Brisbane-Lord Howe Island	739
Brisbane-Melbourne	1,376
Brisbane-Mount Isa	1,572
Brisbane-Oakey	133
Brisbane-Perth	3,611
Brisbane-Rockhampton	520
Brisbane-Sydney	747
Brisbane-Taree	500
Brisbane-Townsville	1,114
Canberra-Cooma	112
Canberra-Darwin	3,141
Canberra-Hobart	850
Canberra-Melbourne	470
Canberra-Perth	3,091
Canberra-Sydney	237
Canberra-Wagga Wagga	158
Darwin-Denpasar	1,766
Darwin-Frankfurt	13,359
Darwin-Gove	647
Darwin-Hong Kong	4,263
Darwin-Jakarta	2,720
Darwin-Kuala Lumpur	3,674
Darwin-London	13,888
Darwin-Mount Isa	1,297
Darwin-Perth	2,651
Darwin-Rockhampton	2,403
Darwin-Singapore	3,350
Darwin-Sydney	3,154
Hobart-Melbourne	617
Hobart-Mildura	1,067
Hobart-Sydney	1,040
Hobart-Townsville	2,622
Hobart-Wynyard	253
Melbourne-Mildura	457
Melbourne-Muscat	11,302
Melbourne-Nadi	3,871
Melbourne-New York	16,711
Melbourne-Noumea	2,689
Melbourne-Pago Pago	3,640
Melbourne-Papeete	6,706
Melbourne-Paris	16,771
Melbourne-Perth	2,707
Melbourne-Rome	15,971
Melbourne-San Francisco	12,657
Melbourne-Singapore	6,040
Melbourne-Skopie	15,241
Melbourne-Sydney	707
Melbourne-Taree	951
Melbourne-Tel Aviv	13,750
Melbourne-Tokyo	8,148
Melbourne-Vancouver	13,204
Melbourne-Vienna	15,744
Melbourne-Wellington	2,595
Melbourne-Zurich	16,355
Perth-Port Hedland	1,312
Perth-Rome	13,342
Perth-Rottnest Island	41
Perth-Singapore	3,909
Perth-Sydney	3,284
Perth-Townsville	3,384
Sydney-Oakey	728
Sydney-Tel Aviv	14,177
Sydney-Tokyo	7,807
Sydney-Toronto	15,567
Sydney-Townsville	1,689
Sydney-Vancouver	12,504
Sydney-Wagga Wagga	367
Sydney-Wellington	2,233
Sydney-Zurich	16,595

Source: Department of Aviation.
Australian Air Distances. Canberra, 1985.

VISITORS TO AUSTRALIA 1986

MAIN PURPOSE OF VISIT

	Visitors	%
Holiday	694,572	48.6
Visiting Relatives	326,045	22.8
Business	169,645	11.9
In Transit	99,388	7.0
Employment	19,676	1.4
Education	24,230	1.7
Convention	26,487	1.9
Accompanying Business Visitor	14,955	1.0
Other Reasons	54,378	3.8
Total Visitors	**1,429,376**	**100.0**

MONTH OF VISIT

	Holiday	Visiting Relatives	Business	In Transit	Other/ Not Stated	Total Visitors	%
January	45,690	21,385	10,099	8,061	12,782	98,017	6.9
February	57,290	22,333	16,513	8,293	13,576	118,006	8.3
March	60,701	33,390	15,367	9,197	10,816	129,470	9.1
April	54,094	19,394	15,949	8,226	12,944	110,608	7.7
May	41,534	18,087	13,548	7,496	11,076	91,741	6.4
June	42,846	22,707	13,260	6,806	9,203	94,823	6.6
July	51,610	25,661	12,485	7,751	12,013	109,521	7.7
August	47,867	22,014	13,447	9,471	12,288	105,086	7.4
September	43,963	18,388	13,681	7,123	11,816	94,971	6.6
October	67,851	26,118	16,628	7,903	11,774	130,273	9.1
November	82,989	32,825	18,832	9,513	12,582	156,741	11.0
December	98,138	63,744	9,835	9,548	8,855	190,119	13.3
Total Visitors	**694,572**	**326,045**	**169,645**	**99,388**	**139,726**	**1,429,376**	**100.0**
% of Total	**48.6**	**22.8**	**11.9**	**7.0**	**9.8**	**100.0**	

MODE OF TRANSPORT

	1981	1982	1983	1984	1985	1986
Air	932,108	950,172	938,196	1,008,534	1,132,689	1,417,219
% of Total	99.5	99.5	99.4	99.4	99.1	99.1
Sea	4,619	4,502	5,686	6,540	9,872	12,157
% of Total	0.5	0.5	0.6	0.6	0.9	0.9
Total Visitors	**936,727**	**954,674**	**943,882**	**1,015,074**	**1,142,561**	**1,429,376**

VISITOR ARRIVALS BY MONTH OF VISIT 1986

Country of Residence	Jan	Feb	Mar	Apr	May
South Africa	851	941	1,280	1,041	946
Other Africa	601	488	711	600	502
Total Africa	**1,453**	**1,429**	**1,991**	**1,641**	**1,448**
United States	17,591	21,242	20,537	26,109	13,760
Canada	4,796	4,964	3,953	4,118	2,211
Total North America	22,387	26,206	24,490	30,227	15,971
Other America	605	444	473	609	642
Total Americas	**22,992**	**26,649**	**24,963**	**30,837**	**16,613**
Japan	**8,770**	**13,907**	**15,305**	**15,238**	**8,547**
Arab Gulf States	496	497	615	297	312
Hong Kong	1,944	5,349	3,074	1,800	1,609
India	546	464	590	479	779
Indonesia	1,510	1,357	1,355	1,141	958
Malaysia	2,309	4,722	3,149	3,510	2,105
Philippines	668	655	923	1,016	994
Singapore	1,883	4,149	3,536	2,465	2,600
Thailand	377	647	758	1,089	573
Taiwan	447	1,811	1,292	1,345	556
Other Asia	1,914	2,054	2,129	1,998	1,858
Total Asia	**12,094**	**21,705**	**17,421**	**15,141**	**12,345**
United Kingdom	**13,968**	**15,833**	**25,098**	**10,594**	**7,609**
Austria	403	418	286	260	231
Belgium	212	271	212	151	110
France	1,033	973	1,054	782	850
Germany*	3,098	4,897	4,684	2,145	1,688
Greece	562	610	477	357	295
Italy	1,110	1,475	1,005	843	744
Netherlands	2,288	1,623	1,436	873	664
Scandinavia	2,476	2,623	2,028	1,432	912
Switzerland	1,814	1,495	1,482	1,008	872
Yugoslavia	609	690	875	283	286
Other Europe	757	1,009	853	877	468
Total Europe	**14,362**	**16,084**	**14,392**	**9,011**	**7,120**
New Zealand	15,506	15,867	23,824	22,505	32,851

Jun	Jul	Aug	Sep	Oct	Nov	Dec	Total Visitors
680	1,059	1,000	907	1,076	1,261	1,453	12,495
358	386	672	429	547	630	1,172	7,107
1,048	1,445	1,672	1,337	1,623	1,890	2,625	19,602
13,388	16,939	15,534	16,031	26,315	32,641	26,911	246,999
1,704	2,835	2,847	2,488	4,146	6,592	6,302	46,956
15,092	19,774	18,381	18,519	30,461	39,233	33,213	293,955
478	682	563	765	914	644	899	7,717
15,570	20,455	18,945	19,283	31,375	39,878	34,112	301,672
8,577	8,327	9,988	9,799	12,718	17,089	17,334	145,608
630	487	660	295	334	405	410	5,434
1,561	3,669	3,419	1,703	2,193	2,516	4,683	33,519
440	344	511	524	807	633	735	6,853
2,314	1,369	1,221	1,127	1,136	1,190	3,052	17,731
1,994	2,329	2,601	2,271	2,955	5,549	5,151	38,647
867	881	945	745	1,156	1,203	1,122	11,175
4,289	1,955	2,613	3,316	3,260	5,546	9,362	44,974
378	381	536	641	1,011	782	870	8,042
328	265	362	519	1,283	1,946	1,802	11,956
1,500	1,983	1,978	1,880	2,325	2,920	3,027	25,569
14,301	13,663	14,846	13,020	16,460	22,690	30,214	203,900
7,886	10,113	9,166	8,960	16,179	19,927	30,699	183,382
258	414	281	229	620	694	1,010	5,104
126	321	224	141	217	257	281	2,524
908	1,348	1,471	1,091	1,248	1,429	1,680	13,867
1,544	2,839	3,043	2,341	3,934	4,744	6,913	41,869
510	485	243	348	502	790	1,225	6,404
799	1,252	1,840	805	1,436	2,136	3,847	17,292
732	1,069	1,149	976	1,463	1,560	2,072	15,907
1,365	1,154	1,112	2,097	3,105	3,646	4,793	26,742
763	1,092	778	995	1,565	2,164	2,852	16,880
461	316	373	185	358	783	1,153	6,371
601	756	1,036	855	1,120	1,369	1,439	11,140
8,067	11,046	11,550	10,063	15,568	19,572	27,265	164,100
33,723	38,341	32,806	26,616	29,228	28,778	36,697	336,741

Country of Residence	Jan	Feb	Mar	Apr	May
Fiji	1,225	1,052	1,194	918	927
Papua New Guinea	4,016	1,895	2,039	2,360	1,904
New Caledonia	1,856	1,400	911	545	782
Other Oceania	946	1,191	1,042	961	993
Total Oceania	**23,549**	**21,405**	**29,010**	**27,289**	**37,457**
Not Stated	317	355	427	346	339
Total Visitors	**98,017**	**118,006**	**129,470**	**110,608**	**91,741**

*Includes both Federal and Democratic Republics

Jun	Jul	Aug	Sep	Oct	Nov	Dec	Total Visitors
851	779	1,005	758	811	1,169	2,596	13,285
2,497	2,541	2,152	2,826	2,833	2,452	4,427	31,943
489	612	842	652	692	1,044	1,272	11,095
923	999	1,097	929	1,206	1,220	1,577	13,086
38,483	43,272	37,902	31,781	34,770	34,663	46,569	406,150
445	582	513	406	381	441	399	4,962
94,823	109,521	105,086	94,971	130,273	156,741	190,119	1,429,376

OVERSEAS TRAVEL BY AUSTRALIANS

Country of Main Destination	1981	1982	1983	1984	1985	1986	Total Market Share (%)	Regional Market Share (%)
South Africa	7,871	8,342	7,031	7,781	7,720	5,576	0.4	35.0
Other Africa	8,656	7,554	7,303	8,936	9,771	10,376	0.7	65.0
Total Africa	**16,527**	**15,896**	**14,334**	**16,717**	**17,490**	**15,952**	**1.0**	**100.0**
United States	143,454	160,288	142,973	150,069	145,239	154,197	10.0	83.1
Canada	13,902	14,184	14,278	15,779	17,029	21,018	1.4	11.3
Total North America	157,356	174,472	157,251	165,848	162,268	175,215	11.4	94.4
Other America	8,188	7,412	6,567	8,122	9,284	10,396	0.7	5.6
Total Americas	**165,544**	**181,884**	**163,818**	**173,970**	**171,552**	**185,611**	**12.1**	**100.0**
Japan	**19,211**	**24,047**	**24,252**	**26,331**	**31,324**	**26,540**	**1.7**	**100.0**
Hong Kong	65,401	73,349	78,921	96,137	99,151	119,320	7.8	24.2
India	11,123	11,810	12,812	14,383	15,337	17,267	1.1	3.5
Indonesia	83,083	80,481	80,195	87,843	100,354	104,376	6.8	21.1
Malaysia	35,749	36,708	38,878	38,670	41,351	41,607	2.7	8.4
Philippines	27,013	30,282	26,184	26,703	27,348	29,970	1.9	6.1
Singapore	69,220	71,108	54,864	61,333	61,551	80,812	5.2	16.4
Thailand	13,033	16,325	16,899	19,829	24,912	34,558	2.2	7.0
Other Asia	38,510	42,313	45,379	54,109	65,229	65,742	4.3	13.3
Total Asia	**343,132**	**362,376**	**354,133**	**399,088**	**435,233**	**493,652**	**32.1**	**100.0**
United Kingdom	**155,697**	**155,168**	**165,472**	**200,515**	**218,478**	**210,425**	**13.7**	**100.0**
France	9,173	10,857	9,709	12,967	14,012	14,306	0.9	7.7

Germany*	18,129	20,716	18,683	23,255	24,839	25,286	1.6	13.6
Greece	27,127	27,385	25,002	28,531	32,482	31,648	2.1	17.0
Italy	33,545	35,374	35,565	39,486	43,875	39,348	2.6	21.1
Netherlands	11,221	11,978	11,208	12,214	13,474	13,335	0.9	7.2
Scandinavia	5,032	5,376	6,063	6,474	7,293	7,721	0.5	4.1
Switzerland	4,762	5,212	5,614	6,614	7,485	7,508	0.5	4.0
Yugoslavia	14,731	14,557	13,507	15,378	17,015	17,299	1.1	9.3
Other Europe	22,291	25,342	23,454	29,850	31,274	29,804	1.9	16.0
Total Europe	**146,008**	**156,798**	**148,805**	**174,768**	**191,749**	**186,256**	**12.1**	**100.0**
New Zealand	212,371	213,514	211,678	237,181	279,165	256,233	16.6	61.7
Fiji	74,940	90,253	79,095	88,750	82,101	77,256	5.0	18.6
New Caledonia	21,395	21,145	19,892	24,146	5,041	10,042	0.7	2.4
Papua New Guinea	24,792	25,095	25,467	26,332	25,761	25,798	1.7	6.2
Vanuatu	4,510	12,491	15,448	16,217	11,061	8,744	0.6	2.1
Other Oceania	23,162	23,647	25,821	29,806	36,199	37,290	2.4	9.0
Total Oceania	**361,170**	**386,145**	**377,402**	**422,432**	**439,328**	**415,363**	**27.0**	**100.0**
At Sea/Not Stated	10,009	4,594	4,745	4,686	6,874	5,755	0.4	
Total Departures	**1,217,299**	**1,286,908**	**1,252,961**	**1,418,508**	**1,512,028**	**1,539,555**	**100.0**	

*Includes both Federal and Democratic Republics

MAIN DESTINATION BY PURPOSE OF VISIT

Country of Destination	Holiday	Visiting Relatives	Business	Convention	Other	Total Departures
South Africa	1,579	2,933	534	90	440	5576
Other Africa	5,291	2,884	1,013	103	1,085	10,376
Total Africa	**6,870**	**5,817**	**1,547**	**193**	**1,525**	**15,952**
United States	83,158	17,498	33,169	6,847	13,525	154,197
Canada	9,515	5,873	2,432	830	2,368	21,018
Total North America	92,673	23,371	35,601	7,677	15,893	175,215
Other America	4,391	3,722	1,191	210	882	10,396
Total Americas	**97,064**	**27,094**	**36,792**	**7,886**	**16,775**	**185,611**
Japan	**9,429**	**1,892**	**9,987**	**1,140**	**4,093**	**26,540**
Hong Kong	86,562	8,854	15,631	1,854	6,419	119,320
India	10,131	3,853	1,624	335	1,303	17,267
Indonesia	90,026	2,898	5,396	1,119	4,937	104,376
Malaysia	22,646	8,215	5,548	972	4,225	41,607
Philippines	17,554	6,398	3,562	400	2,057	29,970
Singapore	55,884	4,469	11,082	3,566	5,811	80,812
Thailand	25,294	1,845	3,930	1,528	1,962	34,558
Other Asia	33,628	12,902	11,294	1,090	6,828	65,742
Total Asia	**341,725**	**49,434**	**58,068**	**10,884**	**33,541**	**493,652**
United Kingdom	107,591	67,268	19,029	2,440	14,097	210,425
France	7,579	2,543	2,451	222	1,512	14,306
Germany*	7,318	9,392	6,129	423	2,024	25,286
Greece	17,772	11,083	702	121	1,970	31,648
Italy	16,097	17,074	3,462	389	2,326	39,348
Netherlands	3,486	7,559	1,206	218	866	13,335
Scandinavia	2,249	2,669	1,623	290	890	7,721
Switzerland	3,001	1,819	1,497	357	833	7,508
Yugoslavia	6,518	9,404	119	87	1,171	17,299
Other Europe	13,390	11,596	2,246	555	2,017	29,804
Total Europe	**77,410**	**73,141**	**19,435**	**2,661**	**13,609**	**186,256**
New Zealand	122,396	72,393	36,980	4,628	19,836	256,233
Fiji	62,343	3,416	4,571	2,451	4,474	77,256
New Caledonia	8,246	554	580	80	591	100,042
Papua New Guinea	5,979	3,362	7,975	121	8,360	25,798

Country of Destination	Holiday	Visiting Relatives	Business	Convention	Other	Total Departures
Vanuatu	6,787	261	773	305	618	8,744
Other Oceania	26,978	2,601	3,453	783	3,475	37,290
Total Oceania	232,729	82,578	54,333	8,369	37,354	415,363
At Sea/Not Stated	2,587	1,259	485	44	1,381	5,755
Total Departures	875,405	308,482	199,676	33,617	122,375	1,539,555
% of Total	56.9	20.0	13.0	2.2	7.9	100.0

*Includes both Federal and Democratic Republics.

MAIN PURPOSE OF DEPARTURE

	Departures	%
Holiday	875,405	56.9
Visiting Relatives	308,482	20.0
Business	199,676	13.0
Convention	33,617	2.2
Accompanying Business Visitor	23,110	1.5
Employment	26,612	1.7
Education	12,571	0.8
Other Reasons	60,081	3.9
Total Departures	**1,539,555**	**100.0**

MODE OF TRANSPORT

	1981	1982	1983	1984	1985	1986
Air	1,210,291	1,280,811	1,245,171	1,412,857	1,505,123	1,535,107
% of Total	99.4	99.5	99.4	99.6	99.5	99.7
Sea	7,008	6,097	7,790	5,651	6,905	4,448
% of Total	0.6	0.5	0.6	0.4	0.5	0.3
Total Departures	1,217,299	1,286,908	1,252,961	1,418,508	1,512,028	1,539,555

METHOD OF TRAVEL TO WORK

	Males	Females	Persons
Train	216,584	169,784	386,368
Bus	161,162	174,560	335,722
Ferry/Tram	32,994	35,119	68,113
Taxi	20,898	15,488	36,386
Car as driver	2,431,584	1,203,418	3,635,002
Car as passenger	274,720	299,245	573,965
Motor bike	79,225	4,509	83,734
Bicycle	73,157	19,532	92,689
Walked only	202,617	137,980	340,597
Worked at home	175,418	194,575	369,993
Did not go to work	295,222	324,241	619,463
Not stated	106,278	82,168	188,466

Total not supplied as question allowed multiple answers

Source: ABS 1986 Census of Population and Housing.

RETENTION RATES OF SECONDARY SCHOOL STUDENTS IN AUSTRALIA

Percentage of students staying on to Year 10

1 *Australia wide*

	per cent
Government schools	92.0
Non-government schools	
Anglican	109.0
Catholic	96.3
Other	106.7
Total	**99.9**
All schools	94.1

2 *By gender*

Male	93.2
Female	95.1

Percentage of students staying on to Years 11 and 12

1	Australia wide	Year 11	Year 12
	Government schools	63.2	42.3
	Non-government schools		
	Anglican	107.0	94.3
	Catholic	73.3	57.4
	Other	101.0	89.2
	Total	**82.4**	**67.4**
	All schools	68.3	48.7

2	By gender	Year 11	Year 12
	Male	65.7	45.6
	Female	70.9	52.1

3	By state or territory (Year 12 only)	Government schools	Non-government schools	Total
	New South Wales	39.1	60.0	44.4
	Victoria	37.5	69.5	46.8
	Queensland	51.1	75.1	57.5
	South Australia	47.8	84.0	54.8
	Western Australia	45.4	65.9	50.3
	Tasmania	27.1	44.5	30.3
	Northern Territory	33.4	38.0	34.1
	Australian Capital Territory	81.2	70.9	77.7

Source: National Schools Statistics Collection. Australian Bureau of Statistics, Canberra, 1986.

TYPE OF EDUCATIONAL INSTITUTION BEING ATTENDED

		Males	Females	Persons	Prop %
Pre-School		105,189	98,332	203,521	5.5
Infant/Primary:	Govt	555,859	520,109	1,075,968	29.3
	Non Govt	174,008	169,286	343,294	9.3
Total		**729,867**	**689,395**	**1,419,262**	**38.6**
Secondary:	Govt	402,849	392,893	795,742	21.7
	Non Govt	172,072	175,181	347,253	9.5
Total		**574,921**	**568,074**	**1,142,995**	**31.1**
TAFE College:	Full Time	25,916	26,406	52,322	1.4
	Part Time	146,690	101,280	247,970	6.8
Total		**172,606**	**127,686**	**300,292**	**8.2**
CAE:	Full Time	26,016	38,490	64,506	1.8
	Part Time	35,655	32,477	68,132	1.9
Total		**61,671**	**70,967**	**132,638**	**3.6**
University:	Full Time	61,632	50,469	112,101	3.1
	Part Time	37,038	34,242	71,280	1.9
Total		**98,670**	**84,711**	**183,381**	**5.0**

Other:	Full Time	15,513	18,360	33,873	0.9
	Part Time	21,226	20,539	41,765	1.1
	Total	36,739	38,899	75,638	2.1
Not Stated		108,137	107,372	215,509	5.9
Total		1,887,800	1,785,436	3,673,236	100.0

AGE LEFT SCHOOL

	Males	Females	Persons	Prop %
Under 15 years of age	1,185,268	1,259,515	2,444,783	20.4
15	1,298,149	1,465,049	2,763,198	23.1
16	1,164,918	1,222,120	2,387,038	19.9
17	851,571	878,963	1,730,534	14.5
18	533,917	437,628	971,545	8.1
19	84,632	52,601	137,233	1.1
20	40,773	28,581	69,354	0.6
21 years and over	92,672	52,691	145,363	1.2
Still at school	283,635	279,809	563,444	4.7
Did not go to school	42,578	54,365	96,943	0.8
Not stated	326,179	329,697	655,876	5.5
Total	5,904,292	6,061,019	11,965,311	100.00

QUALIFICATION

Field	Degree	Diploma	Level Trade	Other	Not Qualified	Total*	Total Males	Total Females
Management	60,803	61,335	0	334,539	N	456,677	175,507	281,170
Natural & Math Sciences	89,693	11,188	0	22,225	N	123,106	83,467	39,639
Engineering & Technology	55,823	28,500	0	84,312	N	168,635	162,940	5,695
Architecture & Building	13,410	9,467	282,805	20,438	N	326,120	317,769	8,351
Social Sciences	111,342	16,978	0	18,558	N	146,878	75,001	71,877
Humanities	61,957	885	0	431	N	63,273	24,719	38,554
Religion	3,616	8,739	0	457	N	12,812	10,374	2,438
Education	99,163	214,964	0	3,830	N	317,957	88,170	229,787
Medical	70,919	33,410	3,996	303,745	N	412,070	81,462	330,608
Veterinary	4,289	0	0	1,423	N	5,712	3,558	2,154
Arts	10,438	19,402	0	25,858	N	55,698	21,422	34,276
Agriculture	10,558	9,325	13,979	32,326	N	66,188	56,273	9,915
Manufacturing	0	0	695,840	74,554	N	770,394	724,614	45,780
Services	1,009	485	172,528	31,026	N	205,048	124,400	80,648
Military	273	4,019	0	786	N	5,078	4,930	148

Other	10,156	955	3,546	459,821	N	474,478	252,036	222,442
Not Qualified	N	N	N	N	7,200,776	7,200,776	3,171,036	4,029,740
Total*	603,449	419,652	1,172,694	1,414,329	7,200,776	11,965,311	5,904,292	6,061,019
Total Males	369,844	189,507	1,054,483	592,808	3,171,036	5,904,292	N	N
Total Females	233,605	230,145	118,211	821,521	4,029,740	6,061,019	N	N

* including not stated

Source: ABS 1986 Census of Population and Housing.

GOVERNMENT

THIRD HAWKE MINISTRY (August 1988)

Hon. Robert (Bob) J. L. Hawke AC, MP (Member for Wills, Vic.)	*Prime Minister.
Hon. Lionel Bowen MP (Member for Kingsford-Smith, NSW)	*Deputy Prime Minister, Attorney-General, Minister Assisting the Prime Minister for Commonwealth–State Relations
Senator the Hon. Michael Tate (Senator for Tas.)	Minister for Justice
Senator the Hon. Nick Bolkus (Senator for SA)	Minister for Consumer Affairs, Minister Assisting the Treasurer for Prices
Senator the Hon. John Button (Senator for Vic.)	*Leader of the Government in the Senate, Minister for Industry, Technology and Commerce.
Hon. Barry O. Jones, MP (Member for Lalor, Vic.)	Minister for Science, Customs and Small Business
Senator the Hon. Gareth Evans, QC (Senator for Vic.)	*Deputy Leader of the Government and the Manager of Government Business in the Senate, Minister for Foreign Affairs and Trade
Hon. Peter Morris, MP (Member for Shortland, NSW)	Minister for Transport and Communications Support, Minister Assisting the Prime Minister, Minister Assisting the Treasurer
Hon. Paul J. Keating, MP (Member for Blaxland, NSW)	*Treasurer
Senator the Hon. Peter Walsh (Member for WA)	*Minister for Finance
Hon. Robert J. Brown, MP (Member for Charlton, NSW)	Minister Assisting the Minister for Transport and Communications
Hon. Michael Duffy, MP (Member for Holt, Vic.)	*Minister for Trade Negotiations, Minister Assisting the Minister for Industry, Technology and Commerce, Minister Assisting the Minister for Primary Industries and Energy
Hon. Ralph Willis, MP (Member for Gellibrand, Vic.)	*Minister for Industrial Relations, Minister Assisting the Prime Minister in Public Service Matters
Hon. John S. Dawkins, MP (Member for Fremantle, WA)	*Minister for Employment, Education and Training
Hon. Peter Duncan, MP (Member for Makin, SA)	Minister for Employment and Education Services

FEDERAL GOVERNMENT • 451

Hon. Gerard (Gerry) L. Hand, MP (Member for Melbourne, Vic.)	Minister for Aboriginal Affairs
Hon. Kim C. Beazley, MP (Member for Swan, WA)	*Minister for Defence, Vice-President of the Executive Council, Leader of the House
Hon. Roslyn (Ros) Kelly, MP (Member for Canberra, ACT)	Minister for Defence Science and Personnel
Hon. John C. Kerin, MP (Member for Werriwa, NSW)	*Minister for Primary Industries and Energy
Senator the Hon. Peter Cook (Senator for WA)	Minister for Resources
Hon. Brian Howe, MP (Member for Batman, Vic.)	*Minister for Social Security
Hon. Stewart West, MP (Member for Cunningham, NSW)	*Minister for Administrative Services
Senator the Hon. Robert Ray (Senator for Vic.)	*Minister for Immigration, Local Government and Ethnic Affairs, Minister Assisting the Minister for Transport and Communications, Deputy Manager of Government Business in the Senate
Hon. Neal Blewett, MP (Member for Bonython, SA)	*Minister for Community Services and Health
Hon. Peter Staples, MP (Member for Jagajaga, Vic.)	Minister for Housing and Aged Care
Hon. Benjamin (Ben) Humphreys, MP (Member for Griffith, Qld)	Minister for Veterans' Affairs
Senator the Hon. Graham Richardson (Senator for NSW)	*Minister for the Arts, Sport, the Environment and Territories
Hon. Gary Punch, MP (Member for Barton, NSW)	Minister for Transport and Communications Support
Hon. A. Clyde Holding, MP (Member for Melbourne Ports, Vic.)	*Minister for the Arts and Territories, Minister Assisting the Prime Minister for Multicultural Affairs
Senator the Hon. Margaret Reynolds (Senator for Qld)	Minister for Local Government, Minister Assisting the Prime Minister for the Status of Women

* Denotes Minister in the Cabinet.

FEDERAL LIBERAL SHADOW MINISTRY (August 1988)

Hon. John Howard, MP (Member for Bennelong, NSW)	* Leader of the Opposition
Rt Hon. Ian Sinclair, MP (NP) (Member for New England, NSW)	* Leader of the National Party, Shadow Minister for Trade and Resources
Hon. Andrew Peacock, MP (Member for Kooyong, Vic.)	* Deputy Leader of the Opposition, Shadow Treasurer
Mr Bruce Lloyd, MP (NP) (Member for Murray, Vic.)	* Deputy Leader of the National Party, Shadow Minister for Primary Industry
Senator the Hon. F. M. Chaney (Senator for WA)	* Leader of the Opposition in the Senate, Shadow Minister for Industry, Technology and Commerce
Senator Austin Lewis (Senator for Vic.)	* Deputy Leader of the Opposition in the Senate, Shadow Minister for Industry, Technology and Commerce
Mr John Spender, QC, MP (Member for North Sydney, NSW)	*Shadow Minister for Foreign Affairs
Hon. John Moore, MP (Member for Ryan, Qld)	*Shadow Minister for Business and Consumer Affairs
Hon J. J. Carlton, MP (Member for Mackellar, NSW)	*Shadow Minister for Education
Senator John Stone (NP) (Senator for Qld)	*Shadow Minister for Finance
Mr Wilson Tuckey, MP (Member for O'Connor, WA)	*Shadow Minister for Health
Senator the Hon. Tony Messner (Senator for SA)	*Shadow Minister for Communications
Mr Julian Beale, MP (Member for Deakin, Vic.)	Shadow Minister for Transport and Aviation
Mr Charles Blunt, MP (NP) (Member for Richmond, NSW)	* Shadow Minister for Community Services, Shadow Minister Assisting the Leader of the National Party
Hon. W. C. Fife, MP (Member for Hume, NSW)	*Shadow Minister for Administrative Services, Leader of Opposition Business in the House
Senator Chris Puplick (Senator for NSW)	* Shadow Minister for Environment and the Arts.
Mr Peter White, MC, MP (Member for McPherson, Qld)	Shadow Minister for Defence

FEDERAL GOVERNMENT • 453

Mr David M. Connolly, MP (Member for Bradfield, NSW)	Shadow Minister for Social Security
Mr Ray A. Braithwaite, MP (NP) (Member for Dawson, Qld)	Shadow Minister for Northern Australia and External Territories
Mr Peter K. Reith, MP (Member for Flinders, Vic.)	Shadow Attorney-General
Mr Peter Shack, MP (Member for Tangney, WA)	*Shadow Minister for Employment, Training and Youth Affairs
Mr Tim Fischer, MP (NP) (Member for Farrer, NSW)	Shadow Minister for Veterans' Affairs
Mr Alan Cadman, MP (Member for Mitchell, NSW)	Shadow Minister for Immigration and Ethnic Affairs
Mr James Porter, MP (Member for Barker, SA)	Shadow Minister for Housing and Public Administration
Mr John R. Sharp, MP (NP) (Member for Gilmore, NSW)	Shadow Minister for Tourism and Sport
Mr Chris Miles, MP (Member for Braddon, Tas.)	Shadow Minister for Aboriginal Affairs
Mr Warwick Smith, MP (Member for Bass, Tas.)	Shadow Minister for Science and Energy
Senator Jim Short (Senator for Vic.)	Shadow Minister for Home Affairs
Senator Amanda Vanstone (Senator for SA)	Shadow Special Minister of State and Status of Women with responsibility for the ACT
Mr Ian M. D. Cameron, MP (NP) (Member for Maranoa, Qld)	Shadow Minister for Local Government

* Denotes Member of Shadow Cabinet.

AUSTRALIAN DEMOCRATS SHADOW MINISTRY (August 1988)

Senator Janine Haines (Senator for SA)	Federal Parliamentary Leader, Shadow Prime Minister and Cabinet, Shadow Minister for Finance and Treasury
Senator Michael Macklin (Senator for Qld)	Deputy Leader, Shadow Minister for Foreign Affairs and Trade, Shadow Attorney-General, Shadow Minister for Employment, Education and Training, Shadow Minister for Electoral and Constitutional Matters

Senator Norm Sanders (Senator for Tas.)	Shadow Minister for Defence, Shadow Minister for Transport, Shadow Minister for Environment, Shadow Minister for Energy and Resources
Senator Janet Powell (Senator for Vic.)	Shadow Minister for Social Security, Shadow Minister for Administrative Services, Shadow Minister for Local Government, Shadow Minister for Consumer Affairs, Shadow Minister for Primary Industry, Shadow Minister for Communications
Senator Paul McLean (Senator for NSW)	Shadow Minister for Veterans' Affairs, Shadow Minister for Industrial Relations, Shadow Minister for Small Business
Senator Jean Jenkins (Senator for WA)	Shadow Minister for Immigration and Ethnic Affairs, Shadow Minister for Arts, Sport, Tourism and Territories
Senator John Coulter (Senator for SA)	Shadow Minister for Community Services and Health, Shadow Minister for Industry, Commerce and Technology

STATE MINISTRIES

NEW SOUTH WALES

Greiner Ministry (August 1988)

The Hon. N. F. Greiner, MP	Premier, Treasurer, Minister for Ethnic Affairs
The Hon. W. T. J. Murray, MP	Deputy Premier, Minister for Public Works, Minister for State Development
The Hon. P. E. J. Collins, MP	Minister for Health, Minister for the Arts
The Hon. I. M. Armstrong, MP	Minister for Agriculture and Rural Affairs
The Hon. J. R. A. Dowd, MP	Attorney-General
The Hon. J. J. Schipp, MP	Minister for Housing
The Hon. T. J. Moore, MP	Minister for Environment, Assistant Minister for Transport
The Hon. G. B. West, MP	Minister for Tourism, Chief Secretary
The Hon. E. P. Pickering, MLC	Minister for Police and Emergency Services, Vice-President of the Executive Council

The Hon. R. Rowland Smith, MLC	Minister for Sport, Recreation and Racing
The Hon. V. Chadwick, MLC	Minister for Family and Community Services
The Hon. T. A. Metherell, MP	Minister for Education and Youth Affairs
The Hon. B. G. Baird, MP	Minister for Transport
The Hon. M. Singleton, MP	Minister for Administrative Services, Assistant Minister for Transport
The Hon. G. B. P. Peacocke, MP	Minister for Business and Consumer Affairs
The Hon. N. E. W. Pickard, MP	Minister for Energy, Minister for Mineral Resources
The Hon. J. J. Fahey, MP	Minister for Employment and Industrial Relations
The Hon. I. R. Causley, MP	Minister for Natural Resources
The Hon. D. A. Hay, MP	Minister for Local Government, Minister for Planning
The Hon. M. R. Yabsley, MP	Minister for Corrective Services

NORTHERN TERRITORY

Hatton Ministry (August 1988)

The Hon. Steve Hatton, MLA	Chief Minister, Minister for Fire and Emergency Services, Minister for Police, Minister Responsible for the Public Service, Minister for Constitutional Development, Auditor-General, Ombudsman, Women's Affairs and Women's Advisory Council
The Hon. Ray Hanrahan, MLA	Deputy Chief Minister, Minister for Lands and Housing, Minister for Conservation and Tourism
The Hon. Barry Coulter, MLA	Treasurer, Minister for Local Government, Minister for Mines and Energy
The Hon. Marshall Perron, MLA	Minister for Industries and Development
The Hon. Daryl Manzie, MLA	Attorney-General, Minister for Education
The Hon. Don Dale, MLA	Minister for Health and Community Services
The Hon. Terence McCarthy, MLA	Minister for Labour and Administrative Services
The Hon. Fred Finch, MLA	Minister for Transport and Works

QUEENSLAND
Ahern Ministry (August 1988)

The Hon. Michael Ahern, MLA	Premier, Treasurer, Minister for the Arts
The Hon. William Angus Manson Gunn, MLA	Deputy Premier, Minister for Public Works, Main Roads, Minister for Police
The Hon. James Randell, MLA	Minister for Local Government and Racing
The Hon. Ivan James Gibbs, MLA	Minister for Transport
The Hon. Mrs Leisha Harvey, MLA	Minister for Health
The Hon. William Hamline Glasson, MLA	Minister for Land Management
The Hon. Brian Douglas Austin, MLA	Minister for Finance, Minister Assisting the Premier
The Hon. Brian Littleproud, MLA	Minister for Education
The Hon. Vincent Patrick Lester, MLA	Minister for Employment, Training and Industrial Affairs
The Hon. Martin James Tenni, MLA	Minister for Mines and Energy
The Hon. Neville John Harper, MLA	Minister for Primary Industries
The Hon. Geoffrey Hugh Muntz, MLA	Minister for Tourism, Conservation, Environment
The Hon. Peter Richard McKechnie, MLA	Minister for Family Services and Housing Welfare
The Hon. Robert Carl Katter, MLA	Minister for Northern Development, Community Services and Ethnic Affairs
The Hon. Theo Cooper, MLA	Minister for Administrative Services and Corrective Services
The Hon. Donald McConnell Neal, MLA	Minister for Water Resources and Maritime Services
The Hon. Paul John Clauson, MLA	Minister for Justice, Attorney-General
The Hon. Robert Borbridge, MLA	Minister for Industry, Small Business, Communications and Technology

SOUTH AUSTRALIA
Bannon Ministry (August 1988)

The Hon. John Charles Bannon, MP	Premier, Treasurer, Minister for the Arts

The Hon. (Dr) Donald Jack Hopgood, MP	Deputy Premier, Minister for Environment and Planning, Minister of Emergency Services, Chief Secretary, Minister of Water Resources
The Hon. Christopher John Sumner, MLC	Attorney-General, Minister of Consumer Affairs, Minister of Corporate Affairs, Minister of Ethnic Affairs
The Hon. Roy Kitto Abbott, MP	Minister of Lands, Marine, Forests, Repatriation
The Hon. (Dr) John Robert Cornwall, MLC	Minister of Health and Community Welfare
The Hon. Lynn Maurice Ferguson Arnold, MP	Minister of Employment and Further Education, Minister of State Development and Technology
The Hon. Gavin Francis Keneally, MP	Minister of Transport
The Hon. Ronald George Payne, MP	Minister of Mines and Energy
The Hon. Gregory John Crafter, MP	Minister of Education and Children's Services, Minister of Aboriginal Affairs
The Hon. Terence Henry Hemmings, MP	Minister of Housing and Construction, Minister of Public Works
The Hon. Frank Trevor Blevins, MP	Minister of Labour, Minister of Correctional Services, Minister Assisting the Treasurer
The Hon. Barbara Jean Wiese, MLC	Minister of Tourism, Minister of Local Government, Minister of Youth Affairs, Minister Assisting the Minister for the Arts
The Hon. Kym Mayes, MP	Minister of Recreation and Sport, Minister of Agriculture and Fisheries

TASMANIA

Gray Ministry (August 1988)

The Hon. Robin Trevor Gray, MHA	Premier, Treasurer, Minister for State Development, Minister for Small Business, Energy
The Hon. Geoffrey Allan Pearsall, MHA	Deputy Premier, Minister for Tourism, Minister for Police and Emergency Services, Licensing, Road Safety, Gaming

The Hon. Richard John Beswick, MHA	Minister for Employment and Training, Minister for Housing, Minister for Labour and Industry, Minister for Consumer Affairs
The Hon. Ian Maxwell Braid, MHA	Minister for Main Roads, Minister for Water Resources, Minister for Local Government, Minister for Racing
The Hon. Francis Roger Groom, MHA	Minister for Health, Community Welfare and Elderly, Minister for Ethnic Affairs
The Hon. John Bennett, MHA	Attorney-General, Minister of Lands, National Parks, Sport and Recreation
The Hon. Nick Evers, MHA	Minister for Public Administration, Minister of Primary Industry, Minister of Transport
The Hon. Ray Groom, MHA	Minister for Forests, Mines, Sea Fisheries, Minister Assisting the Premier
The Hon. Peter Hodgman, MHA	Minister of Construction, Administrative Services, Environment, Inland Fisheries
The Hon. Peter Rae, MHA	Minister of Education and the Arts, Industrial Relations, Deregulation and Technology

VICTORIA
Cain Ministry (August 1988)

The Hon. John Cain, MP	Premier, Minister Responsible for Women's Affairs
The Hon. Robert Clive Fordham, MP	Deputy Premier, Leader of the House, Minister for Industry, Technology and Resources
The Hon. Evan Herbert Walker, MLC	Leader of Government in Legislative Council, Minister for Agriculture and Rural Affairs
The Hon. David Ronald White, MLC	Deputy Leader in Legislative Council, Minister for Health
The Hon. Steven Marshall Crabb, MP	Minister for Labour, Police and Emergency Services
The Hon. Robert Allen Jolly, MP	Treasurer
The Hon. Ian Robert Cathie, MP	Minister for the Arts, Assistant Minister for Education
The Hon. Thomas William Roper, MP	Minister for Planning and Environment

The Hon. James Harley Kennan, MLC	Minister for Transport
The Hon. Caroline Hogg, MLC	Minister for Education
The Hon. Frank Noel Wilkes, MP	Minister for Water Resources, Minister for Tourism
The Hon. Charles Race Thorson Mathews, MP	Minister for Community Services
The Hon. James Lionel Simmonds, MP	Minister for Local Government
The Hon. Ronald William Walsh, MP	Minister for Housing and Construction
The Hon. Neil Benjamin Trezise, MP	Minister for Sport and Recreation
The Hon. (Mrs) Joan Elizabeth Kirner, MLC	Minister for Conservation, Forests and Lands
The Hon. Peter Cornelius Spyker, MP	Minister for Property and Services, Youth Affairs, Prices, Minister for Ethnic Affairs, Assistant Minister for Labour
The Hon. Andrew McCutcheon, MP	Attorney-General
Dr K. A. Coghill, MP	Parliamentary Secretary of the Cabinet

WESTERN AUSTRALIA
Burke Ministry (August 1988)

The Hon. Brian Thomas Burke, MLA	Premier, Tresurer, Minister for Public Sector Management, Minister for Women's Interests
The Hon. Malcolm John Bryce, MLA	Deputy Premier, Minister for Industry and Technology, Defence Liaison, Communications, Parliamentary and Electoral Reforming
The Hon. Joseph Max Berinson, MLC	Attorney-General, Minister for Budget Management, Minister for Prisons
The Hon. Gordon Leslie Hill, MLA	Minister for Police and Emergency Services, Minister for Multi-cultural and Ethnic Affairs
The Hon. Jeffrey Phillip Carr, MLA	Minister for Local Government and Regional Development
The Hon. Robert John Pearce, MLA	Minister for Education, Planning, and Intergovernment Relations, Leader of the House in the Legislative Assembly

The Hon. Barry James Hodge, MLA	Minister for Conservation and Land Management, Environment
The Hon. David Charles Parker, MLA	Minister for Minerals and Energy, the Arts, Economic Development
The Hon. Julian Fletcher Grill, MLA	Minister for Agriculture, the South-West, Fisheries
The Hon. Keith James Wilson, MLA	Minister for Housing, Minister for Lands
The Hon. Peter M'Callum Dowding, MLA	Minister for Labour, Productivity and Employment, Minister for Works and Services, Minister Assisting the Minister for Public Sector Management, Minister Assisting the Treasurer
The Hon. Ian Frederick Taylor, MLA	Minister for Health, Minister of Consumer Affairs, Minister Assisting the Minister for Economic Development
The Hon. (Mrs) Pamela Anne Beggs, MLA	Minister for Tourism, Racing and Gaming
The Hon. (Mrs) Elsie Kay Hallahan, MLC	Minister for Community Services, the Family, Youth, Minister Assisting the Minister for Women's Interests, Minister for the Aged
The Hon. Gavan John Troy, MLA	Minister for Transport, Small Business
The Hon. Ernest Francis Bridge, MLA	Minister for Water Resources, the North-West, Minister for Aboriginal Affairs
The Hon. Graham Edwards, MLC	Minister for Sport and Recreation, Parliamentary Secretary to the Cabinet

FEDERAL ELECTION POLLING DATES

All are for both houses unless indicated

Year	Date
1901	29–30 March
1903	16 December
1906	12 December
1910	13 April
1913	31 May

Year	Date	
1914	5 September	simultaneous dissolution
1917	5 May	
1919	13 December	
1922	16 December	
1925	14 November	
1928	17 November	
1929	12 October	House of Representatives
1931	19 December	
1934	15 September	
1937	23 October	
1940	21 September	
1943	21 August	
1946	28 September	
1949	10 December	
1951	28 April	simultaneous dissolution
1953	9 May	Senate
1954	29 May	House of Representatives
1955	10 December	
1958	22 November	
1961	9 December	
1963	30 November	House of Representatives
1964	5 December	Senate
1966	26 November	House of Representatives

Year	Date	
1967	25 November	Senate
1969	25 October	House of Representatives
1970	21 November	Senate
1972	2 December	House of Representatives
1974	18 May	simultaneous dissolution
1975	13 December	simultaneous dissolution
1977	10 December	
1980	18 October	
1983	5 March	simultaneous dissolution
1984	1 December	
1987	11 July	

DEFUNCT POLITICAL PARTIES

Until the 1890s fluid political groupings rather than cohesive parties functioned in Australian politics but with Federation, more permanent groups were established. The two-party system of government, Labor and non-Labor, dates from the end of the first decade of federal government. Since then hundreds of parties have been formed, some very significant but with little electoral success, like the Communist Party of Australia; others coming into being over a single issue like the Nuclear Disarmament Party in the mid-1980s, and others being established around a person. The following is a list of some of the major political organisations that no longer survive but which played a significant part in Australia's political life.

ALL FOR AUSTRALIA LEAGUE
The All for Australia League was formed in 1931 and worked closely with the Nationalist Party. Joe Lyons was approached by the league when he left the Scullin Labor government over the economic policies being pursued by it to deal with the Great Depression. Orthodox economic policies were favoured by Lyons with the emphasis on responsibility in government and the rectitude of meeting overseas debts. The league merged with the Nationalists in May 1931 to form the United Australia Party (qv).

AUSTRALIA PARTY
In 1966 the Liberal Reform Group was set up by Sydney businessman Gordon Barton. This was a group of Liberal Party dissidents opposed to the party's support for Australia's involvement in the Vietnam War. In the 1966 election the group polled about 5 per cent of the vote and developed a broader spectrum

of policies. In 1967 the name was changed to the Australian Reform Movement and in 1969 to the Australia Party. The issues now included quality of life, social welfare and environmental concerns. The peak period of the party was 1969-72. No member was ever elected to parliament although the independent senator for Tasmania, Reginald Turnbull, briefly switched to the party in 1969-70. The preferences of party voters generally went to the ALP. After the defeat of the Whitlam government and the polarisation of the major parties, the Australia Party disintegrated and by 1977 much of its ground was taken by the Australian Democrats.

DEMOCRATIC LABOR PARTY (DLP)

In 1955 the ALP split, with a right wing section leaving to form the DLP. Since 1945 anti-communist Industrial Groups had worked to destroy the communist strength in the trade unions, often working with the Catholic Movement. Dr Evatt, ALP leader, attacked the activities of the Groupers and the party executive finally moved to disband them. Seven expelled Victorian federal MPs formed the Anti-Communist Labor Party, later renamed the DLP. In Queensland the group which split from the party was called the Queensland Labor Party, which was allied with the DLP until 1962 when they finally merged.

With a strong anti-communist platform, the DLP played a significant role in maintaining the Liberal-Country Party Coalition in government and in keeping the ALP out of office. Its strength was in the Senate. The base of the party was in Victoria and a close ally was the National Civic Council (the name for the Catholic Movement after 1957). Senator George Cole from Tasmania was leader from 1956 to 1965. In 1962 Gair's Queensland party joined and Gair was leader from 1965 to 1973. The party dissolved in 1977, weakened by its ageing leadership, changing issues and Gair's defection when he accepted the Whitlam government's offer to be Ambassador to Ireland in 1974.

DOUGLAS SOCIAL CREDIT MOVEMENT

The Douglas Social Credit Movement arose out of the 1930s depression. Started by Major Clifford Hugh Douglas, an English social economist, it was a popularist campaign, offering a simple remedy to the Depression crisis by suggesting banks supply money to create credit. Douglas visited Australia in 1934 and the movement spread through the country. The party unsuccessfully contested the federal elections in 1934 and waned as the Depression lifted.

FAMILY ACTION MOVEMENT

The Family Action Movement was the electoral arm of the Festival of Light established in New South Wales before the 1974 elections. Three Senate candidates were fielded including Reverend Fred Nile. The movement outpolled the Australia Party. In 1977 their name was changed to Call to Australia.

FREE TRADE PARTY

In the nineteenth century the colonies developed their own tariff policies, imposing customs duties on goods imported from each other. Victoria was protectionist with high tariffs to protect local industry, New South Wales was free trade with the others following a middle course. Sir Henry Parkes was the free trade leader and the group survived into the Commonwealth parliament under Sir George Reid. With the uniform Commonwealth tariff in 1908, the cause was lost and in 1909 the Free Trade Party merged with Deakin's Protectionist Party to form the Fusion (Liberal) Party.

FUSION PARTY

After the uniform tariff was implemented in 1908, prior divisions between the Free Traders (conservatives) and Protectionists (Deakinite liberals) were removed. When Labor removed its support from Deakin in 1908, Deakin formed a new Fusion Party in 1909 by merging with Joseph Cook's Free Traders. A Fusion government was led by Deakin (1909-10) and the party was led by him until his retirement in 1913 when it became known as the Liberal Party. The two-party system in Australian politics dates from this 1909 fusion of non-Labor groups into one party.

LANG LABOR

Jack Lang, controversial New South Wales Premier, and his supporters caused a split in the ALP when he refused to implement the economic measures adopted by the Scullin government to deal with the Depression. In March 1931 the East Sydney by-election was won by Eddie Ward: six New South Wales members led by John Beasley withdrew from the ALP caucus after the caucus refused to admit Ward because he supported the platform of the New South Wales branch rather than the federal party. Lang's New South Wales branch was expelled from the party in March 1931. In the 1931 elections, in New South Wales Lang Labor polled better than the ALP. The Lang Labor group combined with the United Australia Party (qv) in November 1931 to defeat the Scullin government on a confidence motion.

Lang was dismissed as Premier by Governor Game in 1932. The divisions in New South Wales Labor continued until 1936 when the Lang group was readmitted into the party, recognising the federal constitution of the party. By 1940 Lang's hegemony over the New South Wales party was broken.

LIBERAL MOVEMENT

In 1972 a ginger group led by Steele Hall (Premier 1968-70) formed within the South Australian Liberal Country League. In 1973 the movement split away. Hall rejected any amalgamation with the Australia Party in 1975 and in 1976 re-entered the South Australian Liberal Party. A minority under Robin Millhouse formed a New Liberal Movement, which moved into the Australian Democrats in 1977. Hall held a Senate seat for the Liberal Movement from 1974 to 1977.

NATIONAL LABOR PARTY

This was a group of Labor supporters of Billy Hughes who left the Labor Party in 1916 after their failure to introduce conscription for overseas service. They briefly formed a National Labor Party before merging with the Liberal Party to form the Nationalist Party (qv).

NATIONALIST PARTY

When the ALP split in 1916 over conscription, Billy Hughes left the party to form the National Labor Party. In January 1917 Hughes joined with the Liberal Party, led by Joseph Cook, to form the Nationalist Party. In 1917 the party won government with a majority in both houses. In 1922 the Country Party under Earle Page held the balance of power. Page refused to work with Hughes and Hughes was forced to resign in favour of Bruce who then formed a coalition government with Page. In 1929 Hughes was expelled after supporting a Labor censure motion against the government. Bruce lost his seat in the election and J. G. Latham became leader of the party. The Nationalist Party was a loose organisation of various interest groups and it was replaced by the United Australia Party in 1931.

PROTECTIONIST PARTY

Before Federation there were disagreements between the colonies over tariff policy. Each had its own customs duties on the goods they imported from each other. Victoria was the key protectionist state with high duties to protect local industry and Deakin was the main leader of the group. Deakin called the three main groupings in the Commonwealth's first decade of parliament the 'three elevens': the Protectionists, the Free Traders and the Labor Party. National development favoured protection and they were the strongest group in the new federal parliament where Sir Edmund Barton formed the first government. The pioneer measures in political and social economy of Barton's successor, Deakin, were known as 'New Protection'. In 1909 after the uniform Commonwealth tariff was introduced, the Protectionists merged with the Free Traders to form the Fusion Party.

UNITED AUSTRALIA PARTY (UAP)

The UAP was the main non-Labor party

from 1931 until 1944 when the Liberal Party was formed. It grew out of the All for Australia League which brought together right wing Laborites, led by Joe Lyons, and the Nationalists and was committed to solving the economic problems of the time by using orthodox deflationary measures. Financial backing for the new party came from the National Union in Victoria and the Consultative Council of New South Wales. From 1931 to 1934 the party ruled in its own right and from 1934 in coalition with the Country Party. After Lyons' death in 1939, the party declined, troubled with personality clashes and factional fights. Its poor performance in 1943 led to its reconstitution under Menzies as the Liberal Party.

WORKERS' PARTY
The Workers' Party was formed by John Singleton in 1975 in all states except Victoria. It was influenced by the thinking of Ayn Rand and propounded a return to the free enterprise system of laissez-faire capitalism, wanting less government intervention and being antisocialist in tone. In 1977 it changed its name to the Progress Party.

J. B.

PRIME MINISTERS

BARTON, Sir Edmund

b. 18 January 1849 Glebe, Sydney
d. 7 January 1920

Term of office:
1.1.1901–24.9.1903
Protectionist PM, Minister for External Affairs

Barton was educated at Fort Street Model School, Sydney Grammar School, and the University of Sydney, graduating as a BA in 1868 and MA in 1870. In 1871 he was admitted to the Bar (taking silk in 1889). On 28 December 1877 he married Jane (Jean) Ross.

In 1879 Barton was elected to the New South Wales Legislative Assembly for the University of Sydney seat and subsequently held the seats of Wellington (1880–81), East Sydney (1882–87) and Hastings-Macleay (1898–99). He was Speaker of the New South Wales Legislative Assembly from 1883 to 1887 and Attorney-General from October 1891 to December 1893 in Dibbs' Protectionist Ministry. He moved twice to the Legislative Council, from 1887 to 1891 and 1897 to 1898, and resigned from the New South Wales parliament in February 1900.

A convert to the federation cause, Barton was successor to Parkes as leader of the movement and a principal advocate in the 1890s. He was prominent in the Federal Conventions and the drafting of the Constitution and in 1900 led a delegation to London to see through the passage of the Commonwealth Bill. After the Hopetoun blunder, in which the Governor-General Lord Hopetoun invited anti-federationist New South Wales Premier Sir William Lyne to form the first ministry, Barton was commissioned to be Australia's first Prime Minister. Lyne was unable to form a government as prominent federationists refused to serve. Barton was elected for the seat of Hunter in the March elections of 1901. The achievements of his government were the establishment of the machinery of government for the new Commonwealth, and the implementation of national immigration (the White Australia Policy) and tariff policies.

In 1902 Barton attended the coronation of Edward VII. He resigned office on 23 September 1903 to become a judge on the new High Court, where he sat for seventeen years. He was appointed Privy Counsellor in 1901 and received the GCMG in 1902. He was a Fellow of the University of Sydney

Senate from 1880 to 1889 and from 1892 to 1920. He is best known for his speech 'For the first time in history, we have a nation for a continent and a continent for a nation'.

DEAKIN, Alfred

b. 3 August 1856 Collingwood, Melbourne
d. 7 October 1919

Terms of office:
24.9.1903-27.4.1904
Protectionist PM, Minister for External Affairs

5.7.1905-13.11.1908
Protectionist PM, Minister for External Affairs

2.6.1909-29.4.1910
Fusion PM

Deakin was educated at Melbourne Grammar School and studied law at the University of Melbourne. In 1877 he went to the Bar but with little initial success, worked as a journalist for David Syme on the *Age* and the *Leader* until 1883. He married Elizabeth (Pattie) Browne on 3 April 1882.

In February 1879 Deakin was elected to the Victorian parliament as Liberal member for West Bourke. He resigned almost immediately because of doubts over the administration of the poll and subsequently lost the by-election. In July 1880 he regained the seat and from 1883 to 1890 he held office in the Liberal-conservative coalition governments as Commissioner of Public Works (1883-86), Commissioner of Water Supply (1883-84 and 1886-90), Chief Secretary (1886-90) and Solicitor-General (1883-86) and 1890). His main measures were the pioneer Factories and Shops Act of 1885 and the Irrigation Act of 1886. As a backbencher in the 1890s (from 1889 for the seat of Essendon and Flemington), he returned to the law whilst pursuing his main interest—federation. As a prominent federationist and leader of the cause in Victoria, he went to London in 1900 for the passing of the Commonwealth Bill.

In the Barton Protectionist ministry, Deakin was Attorney-General, responsible for the drafting of the foundation legislation of the Commonwealth. He held the federal seat of Ballarat until he retired. Deakin succeeded Barton in 1903 and was Prime Minister three times in the first decade of the Commonwealth. It was in his second ministry that, with Labor support, the bulk of his achievements occurred, including the fixing of the national capital site, the implementation of conciliation and arbitration legislation, the introduction of old age pensions, the passing of the first protective federal tariff and the taking of full control over British New Guinea.

Whilst a federal parliamentarian, Deakin also pursued a journalistic career writing an anonymous weekly column for London's *Morning Post* (1901-13) and articles for London's *National Review* (1904-5).

Out of office through the withdrawal of Labor support, Deakin's liberal Protectionists fused with the Free Traders and Sir John Forrest's Corner group. This was the end of the 'three elevens' as Deakin had called the three main parliamentary groupings—the Protectionists, Free Traders and Labor—and the start of the two-party system. Deakin won a third term in 1909 only to be ousted in 1910. With failing health and his memory faltering, he retired in 1913. He was chairman of the 1914 Royal Commission to investigate wartime food supplies and prices. With his health further deteriorating Deakin became, after 1916, a recluse. He found during his career that his progressive liberalism was overtaken by more radical Labor policies.

WATSON, John Christian

b. 9 April 1867 Valparaiso, Chile
d. 18 November 1941

Term of office:
27.4.1904-17.8.1904
Labor PM, Treasurer

Educated in New Zealand, Watson left school early and worked as a compositor before emigrating to Sydney in 1886. Active in the Typographical Union, he became president of the Sydney Trades and Labor Council. Watson married Ada Lowe in 1889 and Antonia Lane in 1925.

In 1894 Watson won the New South Wales Legislative Assembly seat of Young for the new Labor Party, transferring to federal parliament in 1901 when he won the seat of Bland (later South Sydney). The Labor Party supported Barton and the Protectionists in the early years of the Commonwealth but Watson became the first Labor Prime Minister in 1904 when support was withdrawn from the Deakin governmnent over its arbitration legislation. A minority administration, Watson's government fell after four months when the opposition parties combined to defeat it, again over arbitration legislation. Watson's government was important in giving Labor experience in power and demonstrating that ordinary working men could handle administration.

Watson was leader of the party until October 1907, remaining in parliament until 1910. He was expelled from the Labor Party as an advocate of conscription in 1916. After his retirement he was the director of a number of companies and chairman of the National Roads and Motorists' Association of New South Wales.

REID, Sir George Houston

b. 25 February 1845 Johnstone, Renfrewshire, Scotland
d. 12 September 1918 London

Term of office:
18.8.1904–5.7.1905
Free Trade/Protectionist PM, Minister for External Affairs

Reid came to Australia with his family in 1852, initially to Melbourne and then to Sydney in 1858. He left school at thirteen to work as a clerk in a merchant's office from 1856 to 1864. Reid worked in the New South Wales Public Service in the Colonial Treasury (until 1878) and then as secretary to the Crown Law offices until 1880. After studying law part-time, he was admitted to the Bar in 1879 and in 1891 he married Flora Bromby.

In 1880 Reid won the seat of East Sydney and in 1883 he was briefly Minister for Public Instruction before being unseated on a technicality. He regained the seat in 1886. Reid became leader of the Free Traders on Parkes' resignation. He was New South Wales Premier and Treasurer (1894–99) in government with the support of the Labor Party. An uncertain supporter of federation, he was known as 'Yes-No' Reid.

Reid led the Free Traders at the 1901 federal election and became leader of the opposition. In 1904 after Watson resigned, Reid formed a government in coalition with McLean, leader of the Protectionists. With no secure majority, the Liberals combined with Labor to defeat him. Reid stayed in parliament until 1908 and in 1910 became Australia's first High Comissioner in London. He entered the House of Commons after completing his term in 1916. He was awarded the KCMG in 1909, the GCMG in 1911 and GCB in 1916.

FISHER, Andrew

b. 29 August 1862 Crosshouse, Ayrshire, Scotland
d. 22 October 1928 London

Terms of office:
13.11.1908–2.6.1909
Labor PM, Treasurer

29.4.1910–24.6.1913
Labor PM, Treasurer

17.9.1914–27.10.1915
Labor PM, Treasurer

Fisher left school at the age of ten to work in the coalmines. In 1885 he emigrated to Queensland settling in Gympie. Working on the coalfields there, he was active in union affairs and the new political labour movement. He married Margaret Irvine in 1901.

In 1893 he won one of the Gympie seats for the newly established Labor Party. He lost the seat in 1896 until 1899 during which period he helped establish the Gympie *Truth*. In 1899 he was Minister for Railways and Public Works in the six-day Dawson ministry.

A pro-federationist, Fisher won the seat of Wide Bay in 1901 for the new federal Labor Party. In the 1904 Watson government he was Minister for Trade and Customs. Fisher became deputy leader in 1905 and Labor leader in 1907. In 1908 the party withdrew its support for Deakin and Fisher became Prime Minister with a minority government. He was soon defeated in parliament by Deakin's new Fusion Party.

Fisher's second term was the most important, being a period of reform unmatched until the 1940s. Amongst his government's achievements were the start to the national capital, the foundation of the Commonwealth Bank, the building of the transcontinental railway from Kalgoorlie to Port Augusta, the introduction of maternity allowances and the liberalisation of pensions. In the 1914 election campaign, Fisher made his famous promise that Australia would help the empire to her 'last man and last shilling' but he was not a conscriptionist. In his third term in office, the pressures of the war and the conscription issue within the Labor Party led to his resignation in October 1915. Fisher was High Commissioner in London until 1921, succeeding Reid. Until 1988 when his record was overtaken by Hawke, Fisher was the longest serving Labor Prime Minister.

COOK, Sir Joseph

b. 7 December 1860 Silverdale, Staffordshire, England
d. 30 July 1947

Term of office:
24.6.1913-17.9.1914
Liberal PM, Minister for Home Affairs

Cook worked in the coalmines from the age of nine. An active unionist and lay preacher for the Primitive Methodists, he emigrated to New South Wales at the age of twenty-five, shortly after his marriage to Mary Turner in 1885. He worked in Lithgow as a miner and was involved in his local trade union and the new Labor Electoral League.

In 1891 Cook won the seat of Hartley as a Labor candidate. He was leader of the New South Wales parliamentary Labor Party in 1893 but broke with them when he refused to take the 'pledge' to accept caucus direction. He served in the Reid government as Postmaster-General (1894-98) and then Secretary for Mines and Agriculture (1898-99).

With Federation Cook entered federal parliament as the member for Parramatta, serving on the opposition benches under Reid. In 1905 he was deputy leader of the Free Traders, becoming leader in 1908. He was one of the architects of the new Fusion Party and served in Deakin's third ministry as Minister for Defence (1901-10). After Deakin's resignation in 1913, Cook became leader of the Liberal Party, the name by which the fusion group became known. Cook was Prime Minister in 1913-14 but with a slim majority and a Labor-controlled Senate, little could be achieved and a double dissolution brought a new election.

Cook served under Hughes as Minister for the Navy (1917-20) and Treasurer (1920-21). He represented Australia at the Versailles Peace Conference in 1919 and replaced Fisher as High Commissioner in London in 1921, serving until 1927. He received his GCMG in 1918. In 1928-29 he was chairman of the Royal Commission into the finances of South Australia.

A self-made man, Cook believed in the virtues of self-improvement and duty and was an efficient deputy to Reid, Deakin and Hughes. He moved from being a free trader to protectionist and from Labor to conservative during his career.

HUGHES, William Morris

b. 25 September 1862 Pimlico, London, England
d. 28 October 1952

Terms of office:
27.10.1915-14.11.1916
Labor PM, Attorney-General
14.11.1916-17.2.1917
National Labor PM, Attorney-General
17.2.1917-9.2.1923
Nationalist PM, Attorney-General (until 1921); Minister for External Affairs (from 1922).

Raised in Wales by an aunt, Hughes became a schoolteacher. In 1884 he was an assisted migrant to Queensland where he worked in a variety of jobs. In 1886 he moved to Sydney and in 1890 settled in Balmain, opening a shop. In 1886 he married Elizabeth Cutts (d. 1906) and in 1911 Mary Campbell (who became a Dame in 1922).

Active in the Labour Electoral League, in 1894 Hughes was elected to the New South Wales Legislative Assembly for the seat of Lang. As well as being a parliamentarian, he was secretary of the Sydney Wharf Labourers from 1899 to 1916 and president of the Waterside Workers' Federation from 1902 to 1916. He was member for the federal seat of West Sydney from 1901 to 1916. In the short-lived Watson government, Hughes was Minister for External Affairs. He was chairman of the Royal Commission into navigation (1904-07) and wrote a weekly column for the *Daily Telegraph* (1907-11). In the three Fisher ministries, he was Attorney-General (Hughes went to the Bar in 1903) and was elected leader when Fisher resigned.

Hughes's support for conscription brought a split in the ALP and his expulsion from the party. He formed the National Labour Party before joining Cook's Liberals to form the Nationalist Party in 1917. In 1917 Hughes changed his seat to Bendigo, Victoria. In 1918 he went to London and represented Australia at the Versailles Peace Conference, having successfully argued for a separate presence and voice for Australia. He returned a hero in 1919 and became known as 'the Little Digger'. In 1923 Hughes was removed as leader of his party in favour of Bruce when Page, leader of the Country Party, refused to work with him. In 1925 Hughes was expelled from the Nationalists for his criticism of the government and in 1929 he was instrumental in bringing down the Bruce government.

Hughes joined Lyons' new United Australia Party and served as Minister for Health and Repatriation (1934-37), Minister for External Affairs (1937-39), Attorney-General (1938-41), Minister for Industry (1939-40) and Minister for the Navy (1940-41). He then joined Menzies' postwar Liberal Party and was in parliament for the seat of North Sydney (1922-49) and Bradfield (1949-52) until his death.

Slightly built and severely deaf, Hughes was a controversial figure arousing extremes of like and dislike.

BRUCE, Stanley Melbourne Viscount Bruce

b. 15 April 1883 St Kilda, Melbourne
d. 25 August 1967 London

Term of office:
9.2.1923-22.10.1929
Nationalist/CP PM, Minister for External Affairs

Bruce was educated at Melbourne Grammar and Cambridge University, studying law and gaining his BA in 1905. He worked as a barrister in London but his main occupation was managing the English side of his family's importing business Paterson Laing & Bruce. He married Ethel Anderson in 1913. In World War I Bruce joined the Inns of Court regiment and was twice wounded in the Gallipoli campaign.

Returning to Australia in 1917, Bruce won the federal seat of Flinders at a 1918 by-election as a Nationalist. In 1921 he was the Australian delegate to the League of Nations. From 1922 to 1923 he was Treasurer and when Page refused to support Hughes, Bruce formed a coalition government with Page's Country Party. Under his government a firmer control of the economy was achieved and an extension of federal activities into finance, roads, railways and police occurred. In 1929 Nationalist dissidents led by Hughes defeated the government on a proposal to give the states sole responsibility for arbitration. Bruce lost his seat in the October 1929 election.

In 1931 he rewon Flinders and was briefly assistant Treasurer under Lyons in 1932 before going to London to represent the government as minister without portfolio. He was High Commissioner from 1933 to 1945 and represented Australia at the League of Nations from 1932 to 1939. Bruce was an influential figure in London and a confidant of Baldwin in the abdication crisis. From 1946 to 1951 he was chairman of the World Food Council and in 1947 he was created Viscount Bruce of Melbourne. From 1947 to 1957 he was chairman of the British Finance Corporation for Industry and, although living in London, was the first chancellor of the Australian National University (1951-61).

A patrician figure, caricatured by his spats, he was seen as an Englishman who happened to be born in Australia.

SCULLIN, James Henry

b. 18 September 1876 Trawalla, Victoria
d. 28 January 1953

Term of office:
22.10.1929-6.1.1932
Labor PM, Minister for External Affairs, Minister for Industry

Leaving school early, Scullin worked as a goldminer before opening a grocery store in Ballarat. In 1903 he was a founding member of the local Labor Party branch and became organiser for the Australian Workers' Union. In 1907 he married Marie McNamara.

In 1910 Scullin won the seat of Corangamite and after losing it in 1913 he worked as editor for the Ballarat *Evening Echo*. Scullin played a prominent part in the expulsion of the conscriptionists from the party in 1916-17. In 1922 he won the seat of Yarra, which he held to his retirement. In 1927 he became deputy leader of the Labor Party and leader in 1928. Winning government in 1929, his term coincided with the worst of the Great Depression and he was faced with a hostile Senate and internal party differences on the economic policies to be pursued. In 1931 the Lyons group left the party as did E. J. Ward and the Lang Labor group and Scullin's government was defeated when the Lang group moved against it. He remained leader until 1935 and was a close adviser to his successor, Curtin, during World War II. He left politics in 1949.

Scullin was the first Australian-born Labor Prime Minister and the first Roman Catholic Prime Minister.

LYONS, Joseph Aloysius

b. 15 September 1879 Stanley, Tasmania
d. 7 April 1939 in office

Term of office:
6.1.1932-9.11.1934
UAP PM, Treasurer

9.11.1934-7.4.1939
UAP/CP PM, Treasurer (to October 1935)

Lyons worked as a schoolteacher from 1895, going to the Hobart Teachers' Training College in 1907. He formed the first local branch of the Workers' Political League. In 1915 he married Enid Burnell, later Dame Enid, the first woman member of the House of Representatives and member of Menzies' postwar government.

In 1909 Lyons won the seat of Wilmot

for Labor in the Tasmanian House of Assembly. He served in John Earle's Labor government of 1914-16 as Treasurer, Minister for Education and Minister for Railways. In 1916 Lyons, an anti-conscriptionist, replaced Earle as leader of the party and of the opposition, after Earle's expulsion. In 1923 he became Premier and Treasurer, in office until 1928. He was also Minister for Mines (1925-27).

In 1929 Lyons won the federal seat of Wilmot and served in the Scullin government as Postmaster-General and Minister for Works and Railways. A defender of orthodox economic policies, Lyons was in conflict with Labor's financial policy over the Depression. He was approached by 'the Group', a group of powerful Melbourne businessmen and non-Labor leaders, to form a new party. In February 1931 Lyons left the Labor Party and in April formed the United Australia Party. He won office in 1932, and from 1934 had a coalition government with Earle Page of the Country Party. With the Depression lifting, external circumstances were more favourable to his government than Scullin experienced.

His government was cautious rather than innovative and Lyons, with his simplicity of manner, had great appeal to the electorate. He died in office.

PAGE, Sir Earle Christmas Grafton

b. 8 August 1880 Grafton, New South Wales
d. 20 December 1961

Term of office:
7-26.4.1939
UAP/CP PM, Minister for Commerce

Page was educated at Grafton High School, Sydney High and the University of Sydney, where he studied medicine. He practised in Grafton and later also had farming and grazing interests. Page served in World War I with the Army Medical Corps in Egypt and France. He launched the Northern New State Movement on his return and in 1919 was a Farmers' and Settlers' Association candidate for the seat of Cowper. He married Ethel Blunt in 1906 (d. 1958) and in 1960 Jean Thomas.

Page joined the newly formed Country Party, becoming its leader in April 1921. After 1922 the party held the balance of power and from 1923 to 1929 Page served in the coalition government with Bruce and from 1934 to 1939 with Lyons. Page was Treasurer (1923-29), Minister for Commerce (1934-39) and Minister for Health (1938). On Lyons' death Page served briefly as Prime Minister until the UAP elected Menzies as leader. Page made a bitter personal attack on Menzies in parliament and resigned from the leadership of the Country Party in September 1939, refusing to work with Menzies. His attitude later changed and he served as Minister for Commerce (1940-41) and in Menzies' postwar governments as Minister for Health (1949-56). He was responsible for the introduction of a comprehensive health scheme.

In 1961 Page was defeated in his seat but died before knowing. He was knighted in 1938.

MENZIES, Sir Robert Gordon (1)

b. 20 December 1894 Jeparit, Victoria
d. 15 May 1978

Terms of office:
26.4.1939-14.3.1940
UAP PM, Treasurer, Minister for Defence Coordination (from November 1939)

14.3.1940-29.8.1941
UAP/CP PM, Minister for Defence Coordination, Minister for Information (to December 1940), Minister for Munitions (from June 1940)

Menzies served a third term 1949-66

Menzies was educated at state schools, Wesley College and the University of Melbourne, where he graduated in law in 1916 with first-class honours. He went to the Bar in 1918. He was the first pupil of Sir Owen Dixon and achieved great success in the Engineers' case of 1920. In 1920 he married Pattie Leckie. He took silk in 1929.

In 1928 Menzies entered the Victorian Legislative Council and formed the Young Nationalists and in 1929 he moved to the Legislative Assembly for the seat of Nunawading. He served in the Argyle coalition government as Attorney-General and Minister for Railways (1932-34).

In 1934 Menzies changed to federal parliament winning the seat of Kooyong. He was Attorney-General and Minister for Industry (1934-38). In March 1938 he resigned from Cabinet over the deferral of the National Insurance Act. After Lyons' death he became leader of the UAP and Prime Minister. The UAP was racked with factional disputes and personality clashes and the Menzies government was accused of not doing enough to prepare for war. After the 1940 election two independents held the balance of power in the House and Menzies was forced to resign in August 1941 when the party moved against him. In contrast to Menzies' later postwar success, his first two years as Prime Minister were a failure. He had no broad popularity and the transformation in his period in opposition before pulling the anti-Labor movement together into a new party is one of the success stories in Australian politics.

FADDEN, Sir Arthur William

b. 13 April 1895 Ingham, Queensland
d. 21 April 1973

Term of office:
29.8.1941-7.10.1941
CP/UAP   PM, Treasurer

Leaving school at fifteen, Fadden first worked for a sugar mill before becoming assistant town clerk in Mackay in 1913. He studied accounting and in 1918 became town clerk before moving to Townsville to work as a public accountant. In 1916 he married Irma Thornber.

In 1932 Fadden was elected to the Legislative Assembly for the Country Party but lost the seat in a redistribution. In 1936 he won the federal seat of Darling Downs. In 1940 he was Minister assisting both the Treasurer and the Minister for Supply and Development. After the air crash which killed three UAP ministers in August 1940, he became Minister for Air and Civil Aviation and then Treasurer (1940-41). In March 1941 he became leader of the Country Party after Page's resignation over Menzies. After Menzies was forced to resign as Prime Minister, Fadden became Prime Minister for 'forty days and forty nights'. Parliament was in the hands of two independents who combined with Labor to reject the budget. Fadden was leader of the opposition until 1943 when Menzies resumed leadership of the UAP.

Fadden worked with Menzies in his postwar governments as deputy Prime Minister and Treasurer from 1949 to 1958. He was leader of the Country Party until his retirement in 1958. In his career he had been Prime Minister for forty days and acting Prime Minister for 692 days.

CURTIN, John Joseph

b. 8 January 1885 Creswick, Victoria
d. 5 July 1945 in office

Term of office:
7.10.1941-5.7.1945
Labor   PM, Minister for Defence Coordination (to April 1942); Minister for Defence (from April 1942)

Educated at state schools, Curtin left at thirteen to work for a Melbourne printing office and became a journalist. He was state secretary of the Timberworkers' Union from 1911 to 1915. In 1916 Curtin was secretary of the Victorian campaign against conscription, and was briefly gaoled for failing to comply with his conscription call-up. In 1917 he went to Western Australia as editor of the *Westralian*

Worker. He married Elsie Needham in 1917.

In 1928 Curtin won the federal seat of Fremantle. After losing it in 1931 he worked as a freelance journalist until regaining the seat in 1934. He became Labor Party leader in 1935 and worked to reunify the party after the New South Wales schism with the Lang group. He almost lost his seat again in the 1940 election but was saved by a parcel of votes from AIF constituents in the Middle East. Curtin became Prime Minister when the two independents controlling the parliament voted with Labor to defeat Fadden.

Curtin was a great wartime Prime Minister. In his famous New Year message of 1942, he appealed to the United States for help when Australia seemed threatened with invasion by the Japanese: 'Without inhibitions of any kind, I make it quite clear that Australia looks to America, free of any pangs as to our traditional links or kinship with the United Kingdom.' Curtin allowed General Douglas MacArthur to assume control of all allied troops in the South-West Pacific and clashed with Churchill when he insisted in bringing the troops back from the Middle East. Ironically for a man of his beliefs, Curtin introduced limited overseas conscription. Curtin died in office, worn out by the great strains of wartime leadership.

FORDE, Francis Michael

b. 18 July 1890 Mitchell, Queensland
d. 18 January 1983

Term of office:
6-13.7.1945
Labor PM, Minister for the Army

Forde was educated at the Christian Brothers College, Toowoomba, and worked as a teacher and then electrical engineer for the PMG in Rockhampton. He joined the Labor Party and was an anti-conscriptionist in World War I. In 1917 he won a by-election for the Queensland Legislative Assembly and moved to federal parliament in 1922 winning the seat of Capricornia, which he held for twenty-four years. He married Veronica O'Reilly in 1925.

Forde served in the Scullin government as Minister for Trade (1931-32). He was deputy leader of the party from 1932 but lost the leadership vote to Curtin in 1935. A loyal deputy, he served in Curtin's government as Minister for the Army from 1941 to 1945. He became caretaker Prime Minister after Curtin's death until the party elected Chifley leader and then he served as Minister for the Army until 1946 when he lost his seat. He went to Ottawa as High Commissioner to Canada in 1946 until 1953 and briefly re-entered the Queensland Legislative Assembly in 1955 as member for Flinders, losing office in 1957.

CHIFLEY, Joseph Benedict

b. 22 September 1885 Bathurst, New South Wales
d. 13 June 1951

Term of office:
13.7.1945-19.12.1949
Labor PM, Treasurer

Chifley left school at fifteen and after various jobs he joined the railways in 1903, becoming a driver in 1914. He married Elizabeth McKenzie in 1914. Prominent in the 1917 railway strike, he was victimised because of his actions and demoted.

In 1928 Chifley won the federal seat of Macquarie. He served as Minister for Defence under Scullin in 1931 before losing his seat and spent the rest of the 1930s working to defeat the influence of the Lang group in New South Wales Labor. Twice he unsuccessfully contested Macquarie. He was prominent in local Bathurst affairs, being a shire councillor for fifteen years. In 1936-37 he sat on the Royal Commission on the Australian monetary banking systems. In 1940 he was director of labour supply and regulation in the new Department of Munitions before retiring to contest and win the seat of Macquarie in 1940.

Chifley served as Treasurer under Curtin from 1941 to 1945 and was Minister for Postwar Reconstruction from 1943 to 1945. Under him uniform taxation and PAYE were introduced. He has the reputation as one of the great Treasurers in Australian history. Chifley became Prime Minister after Curtin's death and amongst his government's achievements are improvements to social services; the setting up of TAA in 1946; the nationalisation of Qantas; the establishment of the Snowy Mountains hydro-electric scheme in 1949; the beginning of the massive postwar immigration program; and the replacement of first-past-the-post voting in the Senate by proportional representation. He was defeated in 1949 over the issue of the nationalisation of private banks and the overlong continuance of petrol rationing.

MENZIES, Sir Robert Gordon (2)

b. 20 December 1894 Jeparit, Victoria
d. 15 May 1978

Term of office:
19.12.1949–26.1.1966
Lib/CP PM, Minister for External Affairs 1960–61

Menzies served two previous terms 1939–41

After his defeat in 1941, Menzies made a remarkable recovery during eight years in opposition to become Prime Minister and hold office for sixteen unbroken years. He brought together the anti-Labor groups and the UAP to form the new Liberal Party in 1945 and while the Country Party retained its separate identity his governments were in coalition with it. His term in office was assisted by the split in the ALP in 1955.

There was great animosity between Menzies and the ALP leader, Dr Evatt. In 1951 Menzies' attempt to ban the Communist Party failed after the bill was defeated in the High Court and on a referendum. In 1961 the ALP were nearly victorious with Menzies' government winning by only one seat.

Menzies was a great speaker and dominated his party. Two main achievements of his government were the growth of Canberra and its consolidation as the nation's capital and his education reforms, for universities and secondary schools, with a major extension of Commonwealth responsibility into this traditional state sphere. Also Australia's defence links with the United States were embodied in ANZUS in 1951 and SEATO in 1955.

His long period in office has led to the years 1950 to 1966 being called the Menzies era and it is seen as a time of great economic prosperity. During his office, Australia's commitment to Vietnam began. Menzies was a staunch advocate of the Commonwealth and had a great esteem for the monarchy. He received several ancient imperial honours amongst them being made Warden of the Cinque Ports in 1965. He retired on 20 January 1966 aged seventy-one. Menzies is Australia's longest serving Prime Minister, holding office for a record 6740 days over three terms.

HOLT, Harold Edward

b. 5 August 1908 Sydney, New South Wales
d. 17 December 1967 in office

Term of office:
26.1.1966–19.12.1967
Lib/CP PM

Holt was educated at Wesley College, Melbourne, and the University of Melbourne, where he studied law. He worked as a solicitor from 1933 and was secretary of the Victorian Cinematograph Exhibitors' Association. He married Zara Fell (nee Dickens) in 1946.

Holt was a member of Menzies' Young Nationalists. In 1935 he won the seat of Fawkner at a by-election and held it until his death. He was a protégé of Menzies and served in 1939–40 as minister without portfolio. He enlisted as a gunner in the AIF in 1940 but was recalled to take up a ministerial position.

Holt was Minister for Labour and National Service (1940-41).

In Menzies' postwar governments, Holt served as Minister for Labour and National Service (1949-58), Minister for Immigration (1949-56), and Treasurer (1958-66) on Fadden's retirement. He was deputy leader of the party from 1956 and Menzies' heir apparent. He became leader and Prime Minister on Menzies' retirement in 1966. During his term in office, Australia's commitment to the Vietnam war grew as did hostility to it. His slogan 'All the way with LBJ' symbolised the increased commitment. During his office, President L. B. Johnson visited in 1966 as did Marshal Ky, Vice-President of South Vietnam. On 17 December 1967 Holt disappeared while surfing at Portsea.

McEWEN, Sir John (Jack)

b. 29 March 1900 Chiltern, Victoria
d. 20 November 1980

Term of office:
19.12.1967-10.1.1968
Lib/CP   PM, Minister for Trade and Industry

Raised by his grandmother, McEwen left school at thirteen. In 1918 he enlisted in the AIF and became a soldier settler after the war, acquiring a dairying block in the Goulburn Valley, Victoria, where he became a successful dairy farmer. McEwen married Annie McLeod in 1921 (d. 1927) and Mary Byrne in 1968.

McEwen joined the Victorian Farmers' Union and in 1934 won the seat of Echuca for the Country Party. He was Minister for the Interior in the Lyons government from 1936 to 1939 and served Menzies as Minister for External Affairs in 1940 and Minister for Air and Civil Aviation from 1940 to 1941. In Menzies' postwar governments, McEwen was Minister for Commerce and Agriculture from 1949 to 1956 and Minister for Trade from 1956 until his retirement in 1971. He was seen as a good administrator and the strong man of non-Labor politics.

On Holt's death, McEwen advised the Governor-General Lord Casey that he would not have McMahon as Prime Minister. McEwen was installed as temporary Prime Minister until the Liberals elected Gorton as leader. He was deputy Prime Minister (1958-71), deputy leader of the Country Party (1943-58) and its leader (1958-71). In 1971 he received the GCMG. He was member for Echuca (1934-37), for Indi (1937-49) and Murray (1949-71).

GORTON, Sir John Grey

b. 9 September 1911 Melbourne

Term of office:
10.1.1968-10.3.1971
Lib/CP   PM

Gorton was educated at Geelong Grammar and Oxford University. On the death of his father, he managed the family property near Kerang, Victoria, and joined the Country Party. He married Bettina Brown in 1935. In World War II he was a fighter pilot and was seriously injured in air operations. Gorton was elected to the Kerang Shire Council (1947-52) and was shire president (1949-50). He joined the Liberal-Country Party and won a Victorian Senate place in 1949.

Gorton was chairman of the Joint Committee on Foreign Affairs from 1952 to 1956. He served Menzies as Minister for the Navy (1958-63), Minister for the Interior (1963-64), Minister for Works (1963-67), Minister for Education and Science (1966-68) and leader of the government in the Senate (1967-68). He was elected leader on 9 January 1968 after Holt's death. In February he was elected to the House of Representatives for the seat of Higgins, Holt's old seat. Within the party there was growing criticism of him as well as rumblings about Gorton's style of leadership. McEwen removed his veto on McMahon being Prime Minister and the way was clear for a challenge. On 10 March 1971 in a party vote of confidence—the vote was 33-33—Gorton cast his own vote against himself.

Gorton was Minister for Defence for five months in 1975 before McMahon dismissed him after a series of critical newspaper articles titled 'I did it my way'. In 1975 Gorton unsuccessfully stood as an independent Senate candidate for the Australian Capital Territory. He received the GCMG in 1977.

McMAHON, Sir William

b. 23 February 1908 Sydney
d. 31 March 1988

Term of office:
10.3.1971–5.12.1972
Lib/CP PM, Minister for Foreign Affairs (to March 1971)

McMahon was educated at Sydney Grammar and the University of Sydney, where he studied law. He worked as a solicitor before serving in the AIF in World War II. After the war he took his economics degree and in 1949 entered federal parliament for the seat of Lowe. He married Sonia Hopkins in 1965.

McMahon served in the Menzies governments as Minister for the Navy (1951–56), Minister for Air (1951–54), Minister for Social Services (1954–56), Minister for Primary Industries (1956–58), Minister for Labour and National Service (1958–66), Treasurer (1966–69) and Minister for Foreign Affairs (1969–71). Because McMahon had been a severe critic of McEwen's economic policies, McEwen vetoed him as Prime Minister after Holt's death. McEwen later removed the veto and when Gorton voted himself out of office, McMahon became Prime Minister.

McMahon's term was plagued on several fronts; his own gaffes in parliament; the domination by Whitlam as opposition leader; and criticism of him within his own party, particularly by Gorton. He lost the election in 1972, retired in 1982 and was knighted in 1977. McMahon was the first non-Labor Prime Minister to lose office at an election since Bruce in 1929.

WHITLAM, (Edward) Gough

b. 11 July 1916 Melbourne

Term of office:
5.12.1972–11.11.1975
Labor PM, Minister for Foreign Affairs (to November 1973)

Whitlam was educated at Knox Grammar, Canberra Grammar and the University of Sydney, where he graduated as a BA in 1938. He was in the air force during World War II and after studying law went to the Bar in 1947. He became a QC in 1962. Whitlam married Margaret Dovey in 1942 and joined the ALP in 1945.

Whitlam, a brilliant parliamentarian and academic lawyer, entered parliament for the seat of Werriwa in 1951. He was deputy leader of the party from 1960 to 1967 and on succeeding Calwell as leader in 1967, extensive reform of the internal machinery of the ALP took place with the rewriting of policies and the broadening of the party's electoral appeal. Whitlam had a parliamentary ascendance over Holt, Gorton and McMahon and his election victory in 1972 to the slogan of 'It's time' ended Labor's twenty-three years in the wilderness.

Whitlam and his deputy, Lance Barnard, served as a duumvirate for the first two weeks in office sharing all the portfolios until the election results were finalised. A great reform program was undertaken by the Whitlam government including the recognition of the People's Republic of China, the ending of Australia's involvement in Vietnam, the setting of Papua New Guinea's date of independence as 1975, and numerous social welfare measures ranging from urban improvement and universal health insurance to the establishment of the Family Court. Whitlam's period in office coincided with the economic downturn of the 1973 oil crisis and recession. His government was racked by a series of crises, the most serious being the unorthodox loan negotiations of Rex Connor, Minister for Minerals and Energy, in 1975. In November 1975 the opposition used its Senate majority to block supply and on 11 November the Governor-General Sir John Kerr dismissed the Whitlam government, provoking a constitutional crisis.

Whitlam was soundly defeated at the 1975 and 1977 elections and retired in 1978. In 1983 he was appointed Australian Ambassador to UNESCO in Paris.

FRASER, (John) Malcolm

b. 21 May 1930 Melbourne

Term of office:
11.11.1975–11.3.1983
Lib/CP PM

Fraser was educated at Melbourne Grammar and Oxford University. He managed his family's grazing property, Nareen, in western Victoria, and entered parliament in 1955 for the local seat of Wannon. In 1956 he married Tamara Beggs.

After ten years on the backbench, Fraser served as Minister for the Army (1966–68), Minister for Education and Science (1968–69), Minister for Defence (1969–71) and Minister for Education and Science (1971–72). He replaced Billy Snedden as leader of the Liberal Party in March 1975 and engineered the collapse of the Whitlam Labor government by blocking supply in October 1975. When the Governor-General Sir John Kerr sacked Whitlam on 11 November, Fraser served as caretaker Prime Minister until he won the December election with a record majority.

In office the Fraser government sought to rein in the deficit but there was a recession by 1982 and by 1983 unemployment was rising and business activity declining. Fraser lost office to the Hawke Labor government in 1983.

In 1985 Fraser was appointed by the Hawke government as the Australian representative on the international committee on apartheid in South Africa. Fraser is the second longest serving Prime Minister after Menzies, holding office continuously for seven years and four months. He was often caricatured as 'the prefect' because of his stern manner.

HAWKE, Robert James Lee (Bob)

b. 9 December 1929 Bordertown, South Australia

Term of office:
11.3.1983–
Labor PM

Educated at Perth Modern School and the University of Western Australia, where he studied law and economics, Hawke went to Oxford University as a Rhodes Scholar in 1952. He received his Bachelor of Letters in 1955 and in 1956 took up a research scholarship at the Australian National University in Canberra. He married Hazel Masterson in 1956.

In 1958 he joined the Australian Council of Trade Unions (ACTU) first as researcher and then as union advocate. He was president from 1970 to 1980 as well as president of the ALP from 1973 to 1978.

In 1980 he resigned from the ACTU to enter parliament for the seat of Wills. There was continuous speculation as to his leadership ambitions and a bid narrowly failed in July 1982. In February 1983 he ousted Bill Hayden on the same day that Fraser called an early election and Hawke won office in a landslide ALP victory.

His government's catchphrase was 'national consensus' and a National Economic Summit in mid-1983 led to the Prices and Incomes Accord. A charismatic figure with high personal popularity, Hawke won the next two elections in December 1984 and July 1987 leading Australia into its Bicentennial year. He is the longest serving Labor Prime Minister, overtaking in 1988 Fisher's previous record, and the third longest serving Prime Minister after Menzies and Fraser.

J. B.

WOMEN IN AUSTRALIAN PARLIAMENTS

FEDERAL PARLIAMENT

ACT **Kelly, Roslyn**
b. 25.1.1948
ALP MLA Canberra .... SEP 1974–79
     MHR Canberra .... OCT 1980–

Reid, Margaret
b. 28.5.1935
LIB SEN .... MAY 1981–

Ryan, Susan
b. 10.10.1942
ALP MLA Canberra .... SEP 1974–NOV 1975
     SEN .... DEC 1975–DEC 1987

NSW **Bishop, Bronwyn**
LIB SEN .... JUL 1987–

McHugh, Jeannette
ALP MHR Phillip .... MAR 1983–

West, Suzanne
ALP SEN .... FEB 1987–JUN 1987

Qld **Bjelke-Petersen, Lady Florence**
b. 11.8.1920
NPA SEN .... MAR 1981–

Crawford, Mary
ALP MHR Forde .... JUL 1987–

Darling, Elaine
b. 6.6.1936
ALP MHR Lilley .... OCT 1980–

Martin, Kathryn (later Sullivan qv)
b. 8.3.1942
LIB SEN .... MAY 1974–NOV 1984

Rankin, Dame Annabelle
b. 28.7.1908
LIB SEN .... JUL 1947–MAY 1971

Reynolds, Margaret
b. 19.7.1941
ALP SEN .... MAR 1983–

Sullivan, Kathryn (nee Martin qv)
b. 8.3.1942
LIB MHR Moncrieff .... DEC 1984–

SA **Brownbill, Kay**
b. 21.7.1914
LIB MHR Kingston .... NOV 1966–OCT 1969

WOMEN IN PARLIAMENT • 479

Buttfield, Dame Nancy
b. 12.11.1912
LIB   SEN ....OCT 1955–JUN 1965
                                                            JUL 1968–APR 1974

Crowley, Rosemary
b. 30.7.1938
ALP   SEN ....MAR 1983–

Haines, Janine
b. 8.5.1945
AD   SEN ....DEC 1977–JUN 1978
                                                                  JUL 1981–

Harvey, Elizabeth
ALP   MHR   Hawker...JULY 1987–

Vanstone, Amanda
LIB   SEN ....FEB 1985–

Tas.   **Hearn, Jean**
b. 30.3.1921
ALP   SEN ....OCT 1980–JUN 1985

Lyons, Dame Enid
b. 9.7.1897 d. 2.9.1981
UAP: LIB (from 1944)   MHR   Darwin..........AUG 1943–MAR 1951

Newman, Jocelyn
LIB   SEN ....JUL 1987–

Walters, Shirley
b. 31.8.1925
LIB   SEN ....DEC 1975–

Vic.   **Blackburn, Doris**
b. 18.9.1889 d. 12.12.1970
IND   LAB   MHR   Bourke ....SEP 1946–DEC 1949

Breen, Dame Marie
b. 3.11.1902
LIB   SEN..JUL 1962–JUN 1968

Child, Joan
ALP   MHR   Henty....................................MAY 1974–DEC 1975
                                                                  OCT 1980 –

Guilfoyle, Dame Margaret
b. 15.5.1926
LIB   SEN...JUL 1971–JUN 1987

Mayer, Helen
b. 7.9.1932
ALP   MHR   Chisholm............................MAR 1983–JUN 1987

Melzer, Jean
b. 7.2.1926
ALP   SEN..MAY 1974–JUN 1981

Patterson, Kay
LIB   SEN ....JUL 1987–

Powell, Janet
AD   SEN ....JUL 1987–

Wedgwood, Dame Ivy
d. 24.7.1975
LIB   SEN ....FEB 1950–JUN 1971

Zakharov, Olive
b. 19.3.1929
ALP   SEN ....MAR 1983–

WA   Coleman, Ruth
b. 27.9.1931
ALP   SEN ....MAY 1974–JUN 1987

Fatin, Wendy
b. 10.4.1941
ALP   MHR   Canning ....MAR 1983–

Giles, Patricia
b. 16.11.1928
ALP   SEN ....JUL 1981–

Jakobsen, Carolyn
b. 11.9.1947
ALP   MHR   Cowan ....DEC 1984–

Jenkins, Jean
AD   SEN ....JUL 1987–

Knowles, Susan
LIB   SEN ....FEB 1985–

Robertson, Agnes
b. 31.7.1882 d. 29.1.1968
LIB;   CP (from 1955)   SEN ....FEB 1950–JUN 1962

Tangney, Dame Dorothy
b. 13.3.1911 d. 1.6.1985
ALP   SEN ....AUG 1943–JUN 1968

Vallentine, Josephine
b. 30.5.1946
NDP;   IND   SEN ....JULY 1985–

STATE PARLIAMENT
ACT   Cains, Beverley
b. 25.2.1938
FAM   MHA   Canberra ....JUN 1979–

Craven, Susan
b. 3.2.1951
ALP   MHA   Fraser 1982–

Grant, Elizabeth Mary
b. 23.2.1930
LIB   MHA   Canberra ....JUN 1979–82

Hocking, Betty
b. 13.3.1928
FAM   MHA   Fraser 1982–

Horder, Maureen
b. 23.11.1950
ALP   MHA   Canberra..JUN 1979–

Taggart, Joan
b. 2.4.1917
ALP   MHA   Canberra...1982–

Walmsley, Robyn
b. 23.1.1947
ALP   MHA   Canberra..JUN 1979–

Worsley, Maureen
b. 13.9.1937
AP;   IND (from 1977)   MHA   Canberra...................SEP 1974–79

NSW **Allan, Pam**
ALP   MLA   Wentworthville....................................MAR 1988–

Anderson, Kathleen
b. 19.5.1921
ALP   MLC..APR 1973–AUG 1981

Arena, Franca
b. 23.8.1937
ALP   MLC...SEP 1981–

Barron, Evelyn
b. 24.10.1898
ALP   MLC...APR 1964–APR 1976

Bignold, Marie
IND   MLC...DEC 1984–

Chadwick, Virginia
b. 19.12.1944
LIB   MLC ....OCT 1978–

Cohen, Anne
LIB   MLA   Minchinbury..MAR 1988–

Crosio, Janice
b. 3.1.1939
ALP   MLA   Fairfield ....SEP 1981–

Davis, Margaret
b. 23.9.1933
LIB   MLC ....APR 1967–OCT 1978

Evans, Beryl Alice
LIB   MLC..APR 1984–

Fisher, Marie
ALP   MLC ....OCT 1978–MAR 1988

Foot, Rosemary
b. 2.4.1936
LIB   MLA   Vaucluse................................OCT 1978–FEB 1986

Fowler, Lilian
b. 7.6.1886 d. 11.5.1954
LANG   LAB   MLA   Newtown ....MAY 1944–MAY 1950

Fraser, Dawn
IND   MLA   Balmain .... MAR 1988–

Furley, Mabel
b. 13.3.1904
LIB   MLC .... NOV 1962–APR 1976

Goldsmith, Marlene
LIB   MLC .... MAR 1988–

Green, Catherine
b. 1.8.1881 d. 25.1.1965
ALP   MLC .... NOV 1931–SEP 1932

Grusovin, Deirdre
ALP   MLC .... OCT 1978–

Isaksen, Dorothy
b. 13.4.1930
ALP   MLC .... OCT 1978–FEB 1988

Jakins, Judith
b. 8.2.1940
NPA   MLC .... APR 1984–

Kirkby, Elisabeth
b. 26.1.1921
AD   MLC .... SEP 1981–

Kite, Delcia
ALP   MLC .... MAY 1976–

Lloyd, Violet
b. 17.5.1923
LIB   MLC .... APR 1973–AUG 1981

Machin, Wendy
NPA   MLA   Gloucester .... OCT 1985–

Meillon, Mary
b. 4.10.1919 d. 9.6.1980
LIB   MLA   Murray .... OCT 1973–JUN 1980

Melville, Gertrude
b. 7.10.1884 d. 21.8.1959
ALP   MLC .... SEP 1952–AUG 1959

Moore, Clover
IND   MLA   Bligh .... MAR 1988–

Nile, Elaine
CTA   MLC .... MAR 1988–

Nori, Sandra
ALP   MLA   McKell .... MAR 1988–

Press, Anne
b. 25.8.1903
LAB (to Nov 1959); IND   LAB;
LIB (from 1967);   MLC .... OCT 1959–OCT 1978

Preston-Stanley, Millicent
b. 9.9.1883 d. 23.6.1955
NAT   MLA .... MAY 1925–SEP 1927

WOMEN IN PARLIAMENT • 483

Quirk, Mary
b. 7.12.1881 d. 4.3.1952
LAB; IND LAB MLA Balmain..............JAN 1939–MAY 1950

Roper, Edna
21.7.1913
ALP MLC .... APR 1958–NOV 1978

Rygate, Amelia
b. 27.1.1898
IND LAB; LAB (from 1966); MLC............SEP 1961–OCT 1978

Sham-Ho, Helen
b. 9.9.1943
LIB MLC..MAR 1988–

Symonds, Elizabeth
b. 12.7.1939
ALP MLC...SEP 1982–

Walker, Judith
ALP MLC..DEC 1984–

Webster, Ellen
b. 1881 d. 20.10.1965
ALP MLC ....NOV 1931–APR 1934

NT

Andrew, Elizabeth
CLP MLA Sanderson ....OCT 1974–AUG 1977

Berlowitz, Lynda
IND MLC..1960–62

D'Rozario, June
b. 19.6.1949
ALP MLA Sanderson..AUG 1977–

Lawrie, Dawn
IND MLC..OCT 1971–OCT 1974
MLA Nightcliff..OCT 1974–

O'Neil, Pamela
b. 20.9.1945
ALP MLA Fannie Bay ....AUG 1977–1983

Padgham-Purich, (Cecilia) Noel
CLP MLA Tiwi..AUG 1977–

QLD

Chapman, Yvonne
NPA MLA Pine Rivers...OCT 1983–

Harvey, Leisha
NPA MLA Greenslopes..OCT 1983–

Jordan, Violet
b. 29.6.1913 d. 7.5.1982
ALP MLA Ipswich West ....MAY 1966–DEC 1974

Kippin, Victoria
b. 7.9.1942
NPA MLA Mourilyan..............................DEC 1974–NOV 1980

Kyburz, Rosemary
b. 16.4.1944
LIB MLA Salisbury .... DEC 1974–OCT 1983

Longman, Irene
b. 24.4.1877 d. 29.7.1964
CPN MLA Bulimba .... MAY 1929–JUN 1932

McCauley, Diane
NPA MLA Callide .... OCT 1986–

Nelson, Beryce
b. 10.1.1947
LIB MLA Aspley .... NOV 1980–OCT 1983

Warner, Anne Marie
ALP MLA Kurilpa .... OCT 1983–

SA **Adamson, Jennifer**
b. 5.12.1937
LIB MLA Coles .... SEP 1977–

Appleby, June
b. 2.6.1941
ALP MLA Brighton .... NOV 1982–

Byrne, Molly
ALP MLA Barossa .... MAR 1965–79

Cooper, Jessie
LCL MLC .... MAR 1959–79

Gayler, Dianne
ALP MLA .... DEC 1985–

Laidlaw, Diana
b. 2.9.1951
LIB MLC .... NOV 1982–

Lenehan, Susan
ALP MLA .... NOV 1982–

Levy, Judith Anne
b. 29.9.1934
ALP MLC .... JUL 1975–

Pickles, Carolyn
ALP MLC .... DEC 1985–

Southcott, Heather
AD MLA Mitcham .... MAY 1982–NOV 1982

Steele, Joyce
b. 29.5.1909
LCL MLA Burnside .... MAR 1959–72

Wiese, Barbara
b. 14.1.1950
ALP MLC .... SEP 1979–

Tas. **Benjamin, Phyllis**
b. 30.8.1907
ALP MLC .... MAY 1952–MAY 1976

Best, Amelia
b. 29.4.1900 d. 10.11.1979
LIB MHA Wilmot ....FEB 1955–OCT 1956
NOV 1958–MAY 1959

Bladel, Frances
ALP MLA Franklin ....FEB 1986–

Grounds, Lucy
b. 10.9.1908
ALP MLC ....SEP 1951–MAY 1958

Heaven, Lynda
b. 12.4.1902
ALP MHA Franklin..MAR 1962–64

Holmes, Carmel
LIB MLA Denison 1984–FEB 1986

Jackson, Judith
ALP MLA Denison ....FEB 1986–

James, Gillian
b. 6.12.1934
ALP MHA Bass ....DEC 1976–

McIntyre, Margaret
b. 28.11.1886 d. 2.9.1948
IND MLC...MAY–SEP 1948

Miller, Dame Mabel
b. 30.11.1906 d. 30.12.1978
LIB MHA Franklin ....FEB 1955–MAY 1964

Venn, Kathleen
b. 12.11.1926
ALP MLC ....MAY 1976–80

Willey, Mary
b. 5.6.1941
ALP; IND (from 1981?) MHA Bass ....JUL 1979–82

Vic. **Baylor, Gracia**
b. 8.10.1929
LIB MLC...MAY 1979–FEB 1985

Brownbill, Fanny
b. 28.4.1890 d. 10.10.1948
ALP MLA Geelong ....JUN 1938–OCT 1948

Callister, Valerie
b. 16.6.1950
ALP MLA Morwell...JUN 1981–

Chambers, Joan
b. 18.3.1930
LIB MLA Ballarat South..........................MAY 1979–FEB 1982

Coxsedge, Joan
ALP MLC ....JUL 1979–

Dixon, Judith
b. 28.4.1945
ALP   MLC .... JUN 1982–

Gleeson, Elizabeth
ALP   MLA   Thomastown .... MAR 1985–

Goble, Dorothy
b. 11.3.1910
LIB   MLA   Mitcham .... APR 1967–FEB 1976

Hill, Jane
b. 1.7.1936
ALP   MLA   Frankston .... APR 1982–

Hirsh, Carolyn
ALP   MLA   Wantirna .... MAR 1985–

Hogg, Caroline
b. 1942
ALP   MLC .... JUN 1982–

Kirner, Joan
b. 20.6.1938
ALP   MLC .... JUN 1982–

Lyster, Maureen
ALP   MLC .... MAR 1985–

McLean, Jean
ALP   MLC .... MAR 1985–

Patrick, Jeannette
b. 2.11.1929
LIB   MLA   Brighton .... MAR 1976–FEB 1985

Peacock, Lady Millie
b. 3.8.1870 d. 7.2.1948
UAP   MLA   Allandale .... NOV 1933–FEB 1935

Ray, Margaret
b. 15.7.1933
ALP   MLA   Box Hill .... APR 1982–

Setches, Kay
b. 28.11.1944
ALP   MLA   Ringwood .... APR 1982–

Sibree, Prudence
b. 7.8.1946
LIB   MLA   Kew .... AUG 1981–

Toner, Pauline
b. 16.3.1935
ALP   MLA   Greensborough .... NOV 1977–

Weber, Ivy
b. 7.6.1892 d. 6.3.1976
IND   MLA   Nunawading .... OCT 1937–JUL 1943

Wilson, Janet
ALP   MLA   Dandenong North .... MAR 1985–

WA **Beggs, Pamela**
ALP   MLA   Whitford ....FEB 1983–

Buchanan, Pamela
ALP   MLA   Pilbara ....FEB 1983–

Cardell-Oliver, Dame Annie
d. 12.1.1965
NAT; LIB   MLA   Subiaco ....FEB 1936–FEB 1953

Cowan, Edith
b. 2.8.1861 d. 9.6.1932
NAT   MLA   West Perth ....MAR 1921–MAR 1924

Craig, Margaret
b. 8.12.1930
LIB   MLA   Wellington ....MAR 1974–FEB 1983

Elliott, Lyla
b. 2.7.1934
ALP   MLC ....MAY 1971–1986

Hallahan, Elsie Kay
b. 4.11.1941
ALP   MLC ....MAY 1983–

Henderson, Yvonne
b. 16.5.1948
ALP   MLA   Gosnells ....FEB 1983–

Holman, Mary
b. 18.7.1893 d. 20.3.1939
ALP   MLA   Forrest ....APR 1925–MAR 1939

Hutchison, Ruby
b. 15.2.1892 d. 17.12.1974
ALP   MLC ....MAY 1954–MAY 1971

Jones, Beryl
ALP   MLC ....FEB 1986–

Lawrence, Dr Carmen
ALP   MLA   Subiaco ....FEB 1986–

McAleer, Margaret
b. 16.2.1930
LIB   MLC .... MAR 1974–

Piesse, Winifred
b. 12.6.1923
NCP   MLC ....FEB 1977–MAY 1983

Vaughan, Grace
b. 1.4.1922
ALP   MLC ....MAR 1974–MAY 1980

Watkins, Jacqueline
ALP   MLA   Joondalup ....FEB 1983–

Watson, Dr Judyth
ALP   MLA   Canning ....FEB 1986–

ABBREVIATIONS

Houses
MHA	Member of House of Assembly
MHR	Member of House of Representatives
MLA	Member of Legislative Assembly
SEN	Senator

Parties
AD	Australian Democrats
ALP	Australian Labor Party
AP	Australia Party
CLP	Country Liberal Party
CP	Country Party
CPN	Country Progressive Nationalist
CTA	Call to Australia
FAM	Family Team
IND	Independent
IND LAB	Independent Labor
LANG LAB	Lang Labor (NSW Labor)
LCL	Liberal Country League
LIB	Liberal Party
NAT	Nationalist Party
NCP	National Country Party
NDP	Nuclear Disarmament Party
NPA	National Party of Australia (ex-Country Party)

Source: Goot, M. and Henwood, B. *Biographical Register of Women in Australian Parliaments* (forthcoming).

TOP 100 GROSSING FILMS IN AUSTRALIA

at 31 December 1987

No.	Film Title	Year of Release	Billings
1	**Crocodile Dundee**	1986	19,769,153
2	E.T.	1983	11,362,994
3	**Man From Snowy River**	1982	7,818,462
4	Star Wars	1977	6,410,093
5	Ghostbusters	1984	5,768,430
6	Grease	1978	5,312,952
7	Raiders of the Lost Ark	1981	4,855,181
8	Jaws	1975	4,773,283
9	Return of the Jedi	1983	4,548,834
10	Back to the Future	1985	4,547,647
11	Sound of Music	1965	4,544,440
12	Tootsie	1983	4,502,707
13	The Sting	1974	4,423,706
14	Out of Africa	1986	4,290,072
15	Gone With the Wind	1940	4,266,055
16	Indiana Jones & the Temple of Doom	1984	4,238,783
17	**Gallipoli**	1981	4,109,173
18	Beverly Hills Cop	1985	4,093,850
19	Towering Inferno	1975	3,940,198
20	**Max Max II**	1982	3,769.395
21	**Phar Lap**	1983	3,761,568
22	Top Gun	1986	3,756,909
23	Gremlins	1985	3,635,225
24	Superman	1979	3,527,884
25	Rocky IV	1985	3,471,353
26	Empire Strikes Back	1980	3,458,252
27	Flying High	1980	3,457,686
28	Gandhi	1983	3,440,268
29	Beverly Hills Cop 2	1987	3,259,201
30	Monty Python's Life of Brian	1980	3,175,079
31	Kramer vs Kramer	1980	3,095,961

No.	Film Title	Year of Release	Billings
32	Rambo—First Blood Part II	1985	2,986,761
33	Police Academy	1984	2,918,840
34	Jewel of the Nile	1986	2,909,520
35	Superman II	1982	2,879,219
36	For Your Eyes Only	1981	2,866,957
37	Platoon	1987	2,686,308
38	Porkys	1982	2,682,474
39	Flashdance	1983	2,672,915
40	Doctor Zhivago	1966	2,660,960
41	Saturday Night Fever	1978	2,644,903
42	Rocky III	1982	2,628,571
43	Officer and a Gentleman	1983	2,556,580
44	Poseidon Adventure	1973	2,526,877
45	Arthur	1982	2,465,355
46	Lethal Weapon	1987	2,389,955
47	Earthquake	1974	2,330,790
48	Close Encounters of the Third Kind	1978	2,306,805
49	Amadeus	1985	2,291,577
50	**Mad Max, Beyond Thunderdome**	**1985**	**2,289,712**
51	The Exorcist	1974	2,241,466
52	Terms of Endearment	1984	2,172,456
53	Chariots of Fire	1981	2,159,113
54	Octopussy	1983	2,152,445
55	Moonraker	1979	2,151,769
56	The Spy Who Loved Me	1978	2,124,648
57	Golden Child	1986	2,124,324
58	Ryan's Daughter	1971	2,109,256
59	My Fair Lady	1965	2,098,000
60	Aliens	1986	2,093,095
61	Rocky	1977	2,067,565
62	Can't Stop the Music	1980	2,054,733
63	Three Amigos	1986	2,040,892
64	Police Academy II	1985	2,032,136
65	First Blood	1983	2,027,380
66	American Werewolf in London	1981	2,024,341

No.	Film Title	Year of Release	Billings
67	The Gods Must Be Crazy	1984	2,022,561
68	The Godfather	1972	2,009,396
69	Never-Ending Story	1985	1,994,789
70	Jaws 2	1978	1,989,160
71	The Muppet Movie	1980	1,983,738
72	Smokey and the Bandit	1977	1,977,584
73	**Max Max**	**1979**	**1,962,535**
74	The Rose	1980	1,886,842
75	Nightshift	1983	1,868,501
76	Karate Kid Part II	1986	1,854,752
77	On Golden Pond	1982	1,851,353
78	Blazing Saddles	1974	1,841,755
79	A View to a Kill	1985	1,814,060
80	Those Magnificent Men in Flying Machines	1965	1,812,642
81	**Picnic at Hanging Rock**	**1980**	**1,791,824**
82	Greystoke	1984	1,789,512
83	**Alvin Purple**	**1974**	**1,772,827**
84	Elephant Man	1981	1,766,962
85	Apocalypse Now	1980	1,707,649
86	Footloose	1984	1,700,673
87	What's Up Doc	1972	1,697,133
88	Superman III	1984	1,693,863
89	Fiddler on the Roof	1972	1,691,907
90	Papillon	1974	1,687,482
91	Poltergeist	1982	1,675,280
92	Never Say Never Again	1983	1,670,299
93	Witches of Eastwick	1987	1,664,323
94	Rocky II	1979	1,658,895
95	**Breaker Morant**	**1980**	**1,657,363**
96	La Bamba	1987	1,649,687
97	South Pacific	1958	1,639,959
98	King Kong	1977	1,630,388
99	Every Which Way But Loose	1979	1,618,581
100	Alien	1979	1,610,761

Source: Motion Picture Distributors Association of Australia.

VIDEOS
Top 50 Renting Titles

1 December 1986 to 1 December 1987

No.	Title	Company
1.	Top Gun	(CIC-Taft)
2.	Soul Man	(Roadshow)
3.	Heartbreak Ridge	(Warner)
4.	Big Trouble in Little China	(CBS/Fox)
5.	Working Class Man	(CIC-Taft)
6.	Karate Kid II	(RCA/Columbia/Hoyts)
7.	The Morning After	(Roadshow)
8.	Wild Cats	(Warner)
9.	The Boy Who Could Fly	(Warner)
10.	The Color Purple	(Warner)
11.	Out of Africa	(CIC-Taft)
12.	Back to School	(RCA/Columbia/Hoyts)
13.	Short Circuit	(Roadshow)
14.	Ferris Beuller's Day Off	(CIC-Taft)
15.	The Three Amigos	(RCA/Columbia/Hoyts)
16.	The Hitcher Highlander The Gods Must Be Crazy	(Cannon)* (Cannon)* (CBS/Fox)*
17.	The Mosquito Coast	(CBS/Fox)
18.	8 Million Ways to Die Armed & Dangerous	(CBS/Fox)* (RCA/Columbia/Hoyts)*
19.	Young Blood	(Warner)
20.	Raw Deal	(RCA/Columbia/Hoyts)
21.	Back to the Future	(CIC-Taft)
22.	Extremities	(Filmpac/Vestron)
23.	Labyrinth Murphy's Law	(CEL)* (RCA/Columbia/Hoyts)*
24.	Instant Justice	(Warner)
25.	Crossroads	(RCA/Columbia/Hoyts)
26.	Cobra	(Warner)
27.	Legal Eagles Better Off Dead Enemy Mine	(CIC-Taft)* (CBS/Fox)* (CBS/Fox)*

No.	Title	Company
28.	Police Academy 3	(Warner)
29.	Down & Out in Beverley Hills	(Touchstone)
30.	Poltergeist 2 Haunted Honeymoon Deadly Friend A Chorus Line	(CEL)* (RCA/Columbia/Hoyts)* (Warner)* (CEL)*
31.	Space Camp	(Roadshow)
32.	Spies Like Us	(Warner)
33.	Bikini Shop	(Seven Keys)
34.	Indiana Jones & The Temple of Doom	(CIC-Taft)
35.	Running Scared	(CEL)
36.	Ruthless People Kiss of the Spider Woman	(Touchstone)* (CBS/Fox)*
37.	Jewel of the Nile	(CBS/Fox)
38.	Eye of the Tiger	(Roadshow)
39.	One Crazy Summer	(Warner)
40.	Club Paradise	(Warner)
41.	Critical Condition	(CIC-Taft)
42.	Recruits	(CBS/Fox)
43.	Jake Speed	(Premiere)
44.	Critters	(RCA/Columbia/Hoyts)
45.	Target Off Beat	(CBS/Fox)* (Touchstone)*
46.	They Still Call Me Bruce American Anthem	(Macro)* (Roadshow)*
47.	Young Sherlock Holmes & the Pyramid of Fear Howard—A New Breed of Hero	(CIC-Taft)* (CIC-Taft)*
48.	Salvador Light of Day	(CEL)* (Roadshow)*
49.	American Flyers Touch & Go	(Warner)* (Seven Keys)*
50.	Jagged Edge	(RCA/Columbia/Hoyts)

* Tied
Source: Video Business.

PAPERBACK BESTSELLERS

The following lists contain paperback bestsellers for the period 1 December 1986 to 30 November 1987. The titles have been divided into Adult Fiction; Adult Non-Fiction; and Children's Fiction and Non-Fiction. Only books which have sold in excess of 25,000 copies have been included in the adult fiction and non-fiction categories. The children's fiction and non-fiction categories contain books that sold more than 15,000 copies.

All three lists include not only titles published for the first time during the period covered, but backlist titles and titles that were reissued for specific reasons such as film or TV tie-ins. The notation after each title indicates whether it is new (N), re-issued (R), backlisted (B), Australian (A) or imported (O). An Australian title is defined as one written by an Australian citizen, whether resident or not, as well as one written by authors currently residing in Australia.

ADULT FICTION

Position	Title	Author	Publisher	Price	Release	Code
Sales over 170,000 copies						
1.	*Footrot Flats 12*	Murray Ball	Orin Books	$3.95	September 1987	O/N
Sales over 160,000 copies						
2.	*Power of the Sword*	Wilbur Smith	Pan	$9.95	October 1987	O/N
Sales over 130,000 copies						
3.	*Hollywood Husbands*	Jackie Collins	Pan	$10.95	September 1987	O/N
Sales over 120,000 copies						
4.	*Dark Angel*	Virginia Andrews	Fontana	$9.95	June 1987	O/N
5.	*Lucky*	Jackie Collins	Pan	$9.95	December 1986	O/N
6.	*Act of Will*	Barbara Taylor Bradford	Grafton	$10.95	April 1987	O/N
Sales over 100,000 copies						
7.	*It*	Stephen King	NEL	$12.95	December 1987	O/N

Sales over 80,000 copies

8.	Matter of Honour	Jeffrey Archer	Coronet	$10.95	August 1987	O/N
9.	Bourne Supremacy	Robert Ludlum	Grafton	$10.95	January 1987	O/N

Sales over 60,000 copies

10.	I'll Take Manhattan	Judith Krantz	Bantam	$8.95	April 1987	O/N

Sales over 50,000 copies

11.	Darkness at Sethanon	Raymond E. Feist	Grafton	$9.95	September 1987	O/N
12.	A Perfect Spy	John Le Carre	Coronet	$10.95	July 1987	O/N
13.	Shan	Eric von Lustbader	Grafton	$9.95	November 1987	O/N
14.	Mirror of Her Dreams	Stephen Donaldson	Fontana	$9.95	October 1987	O/N
15.	The Harp in the South	Ruth Park	Penguin	$8.95	April 1987	A/R
16.	London Match	Len Deighton	Grafton	$8.95	December 1986	O/N

Sales over 40,000 copies

17.	Night of the Fox	Jack Higgins	Pan	$9.95	August 1987	O/N
18.	Wanderlust	Danielle Steel	Sphere	$9.95	November 1987	O/N
19.	Hold the Dream	Barbara Taylor Bradford	Grafton	$10.95	April 1986	O/B
20.	Love and War	John Jakes	Fontana	$10.95	June 1987	O/R
21.	Golden Cup	Belva Plain	Fontana	$9.95	November 1987	O/N
22.	Stallion Gate	Martin Cruz Smith	Pan	$8.95	November 1987	O/N
23.	Lonely Sea	Alistair Maclean	Fontana	$8.95	December 1986	O/N

ADULT FICTION

Position	Title	Author	Publisher	Price	Release	Code
24.	*The Moth*	Catherine Cookson	Corgi	$8.95	November 1987	O/N
25.	*Sword of Honour*	Nelson De Mille	Grafton	$9.95	July 1987	O/N
Sales over 35,000 copies						
26.	*Paradise Postponed*	John Mortimer	Penguin	$8.95	February 1987	O/N
27.	*The Bachman Books*	Stephen King	NEL	$12.95	October 1987	O/N
28.	*Dragon Riders*	Christie Dickason	Coronet	$11.95	December 1987	O/N
29.	*If Tomorrow Comes*	Sidney Sheldon	Pan	$9.95	February 1987	O/R
30.	*Voice of the Heart*	Barbara Taylor Bradford	Grafton	$10.95	May 1984	O/B
31.	*Magic Cottage*	James Herbert	NEL	$9.95	September 1987	O/N
Sales over 30,000 copies						
32.	*Woman of Substance*	Barbara Taylor Bradford	Grafton	$10.95	May 1984	O/B
33.	*Emerald Decision*	Craig Thomas	Fontana	$8.95	August 1987	O/N
34.	*Flowers in the Attic*	Virginia Andrews	Fontana	$9.95	August 1980	O/B
35.	*Secrets*	Danielle Steel	Sphere	$8.95	January 1987	O/N
36.	*Secret of Hanging Rock*	Joan Lindsay	Angus & Robertson	$7.95	January 1987	A/N
Sales over 25,000 copies						
37.	*Whirlwind*	James Clavell	Coronet	$14.95	November 1987	O/N
38.	*Name of the Rose*	Umberto Eco	Pan	$14.95	February 1987	O/R
39.	*Golden Lion*	Pamela Haines	Fontana	$9.95	October 1987	O/N
40.	*Cover Story*	Colin Forbes	Pan	$9.95	March 1987	O/N

41.	The Mosquito Coast	Paul Theroux	Penguin	$8.95	December 1986	O/R
42.	Contact	Carl Sagan	Arrow	$9.95	February 1987	O/N
43.	Red Crystal	Clare Francis	Pan	$9.95	February 1987	O/N
44.	Fortunes	Vera Cowie	Fontana	$9.95	July 1987	O/N
45.	Private Affairs	Judith Michael	Sphere	$9.95	October 1987	O/N
46.	Heaven	Virginia Andrews	Fontana	$9.95	October 1987	O/B
47.	Endless Game	Brian Forbes	Fontana	$9.95	May 1987	O/N
48.	Fourth Protocol	Frederick Forsyth	Corgi	$8.95	May 1987	O/R
49.	Her Father's Daughter	William J. Coughlin	Pan	$8.95	April 1987	O/N
50.	Chances	Jackie Collins	Pan	$10.95	July 1983	O/B
51.	Lie Down With Lions	Ken Follett	Corgi	$8.95	March 1987	O/N
52.	To Kill a Mocking Bird	Harper Lee	Pan	$8.95	June 1974	O/B
53.	Adam's Empire	Evan Green	Futura	$10.95	November 1987	O/N
54.	Through a Glass Darkly	Karleen Koen	Futura	$10.95	October 1987	O/N
55.	In Love & Friendship	Hilary Norman	Coronet	$10.95	November 1987	O/N

ADULT NON-FICTION

Sales over 60,000 copies

1.	Taste of Life From the Microwave	Julie Stafford	Greenhouse	$14.95	August 1987	Health A/N

Sales over 40,000 copies

2.	King Wally	A. McGregor	UQP	$9.95	May 1987	Biography A/N
3.	Gabriel Gaté's Family Food	Gabriel Gaté	Anne O'Donovan Pty Ltd	$14.95	August 1987	Cooking A/N
4.	Yates All Colour Garden Guide	Yates	Collins Australia	$12.95	November 1987	Gardening A/N
5.	Taste of Life	Julie Stafford	Greenhouse	$14.95	November 1983	Health A/B

Sales over 35,000 copies

6.	Pat Cash	Brian Matthews	Penguin	$9.95	October 1987	Biography A/N

Sales over 30,000 copies

7.	BP Touring Atlas of Australia 1987		Viking O'Neil	$11.95	July 1987	Reference/Leisure A/N
8.	Fit for Life	M. & H. Diamond	Angus & Robertson	$9.95	August 1987	Health O/N
9.	Making Rubik's Magic	Albie Fiore	Puffin	$4.95	January 1987	Hobbies/Leisure O/N

Sales over 25,000 copies

10.	James Herriot's Dog Stories	James Herriot	Pan	$10.95	May 1987	Autobiography/Animals O/N

11.	*The Age Good Food Guide 1987*	Claude Forell	Anne O'Donovan Pty Ltd	$10.95	September 1987	Reference A/N
12.	*A Fortunate Life*	A. B. Facey	Penguin	$9.95	April 1985	Autobiography A/B
13.	*Everywoman*	Derek Llewellyn-Jones	Faber	$10.95	June 1986	Reference A/B
14.	*Yeager*	Chuck Yeager	Arrow	$8.95	November 1986	Autobiography O/N

CHILDREN'S FICTION AND NON-FICTION

Sales over 110,000 copies

1.	*Garfield—A Weekend Away*	Jim Davis	Budget Books Pty Ltd	$7.95	April 1987	Fiction O/N

Sales over 90,000 copies

2.	*Lettering Book Companion*	Noelene Morris	Ashton Scholastic	$4.95	March 1987	Non-Fiction A/N

Sales over 80,000 copies

3.	*Lettering Book*	Noelene Morris	Ashton Scholastic	$6.95	February 1987	Non-Fiction A/R
4.	*Garfield Stepping Out*	Jim Davis	Budget Books Pty Ltd	$2.95	February 1987	Fiction O/N

Sales over 60,000 copies

5.	*Doggone Joke Book*	Bob Stine	Scholastic UK	$3.50	May 1987	Fiction O/N
6.	*Anne of Avonlea*	L. M. Montgomery	Angus & Robertson	$6.95	April 1987	Fiction O/R

Sales over 50,000 copies

7.	*The Hobbit*	J. R. R. Tolkien	Unwin Paperbacks	$7.95	July 1987	Fiction O/R
8.	*Garfield Kool Cat*	Jim Davis	Budget Books Pty Ltd	$2.95	June 1987	Fiction O/N

CHILDREN'S FICTION AND NON-FICTION

Position	Title	Author	Publisher	Price	Release	Code
9.	Garfield—This Is Your Life	Jim Davis	Budget Books	$4.95	April 1987	Fiction O/N
Sales over 40,000 copies						
10.	Clifford's Good Deeds	Norman Bridwell	Scholastic	$3.95	July 1987	Fiction O/R
11.	Anne of Green Gables	L. M. Montgomery	Angus & Robertson	$6.95	April 1987	Fiction O/R
12.	How to Draw Cartoons	Syd Hoff	Scholastic	$3.95	July 1987	Non-fiction O/R
Sales over 35,000 copies						
13.	Haunted Castle	J. McKeller and J. Bullough	Hippo Books (Scholastic)	$4.50	February 1987	Fiction O/N
14.	Miami Mice	Bob Stine	Scholastic	$3.95	June 1987	Fiction O/N
15.	Clifford Gets a Job	Norman Bridwell	Scholastic	$3.95	November 1986	Fiction O/R
16.	A Book About Your Skeleton	Ruth Belov Gross	Scholastic	$3.95	June 1987	Non-Fiction O/R
17.	Unreal, Banana Peel	June Factor	OUP	$10.95	November 1986	Fiction A/B
Sales over 30,000 copies						
18.	Ghosts Who Went to School	J. Spearing	Scholastic	$3.95	February 1987	Fiction O/R
19.	Advanced Paper Aircraft —Vol 3	Campbell Morris	Angus & Robertson	$4.95	April 1987	Non-Fiction A/N
20.	Really Ridiculous Rabbit Riddles	Jeanne & Margaret Wallace	Scholastic	$3.50	September 1987	Fiction O/N
21.	Playing Beatie Bow	Ruth Park	Puffin	$6.95	January 1982	Fiction A/B
22.	Big Bunny and the Magic Show	Steven Kroll	Scholastic	$3.95	March 1987	Fiction O/N
23.	Twelve Days of Christmas	June Williams & John McIntosh	Akers & Dorrington	$5.95	October 1985	Fiction A/B

Sales over 25,000 copies

24.	Animals of the Sea	Millicent Selsam	Scholastic	$3.95	March 1987	Non-Fiction O/R
25.	Paperbag Princess	Robert Munsch	Hippo Books (Scholastic)	$3.95	February 1987	Fiction O/R
26.	Molly and the Slow Teeth	Pat Ross	Scholastic	$3.95	February 1987	Fiction O/R
27.	Sixth Grade Can Really Kill You	B. De Clements	Scholastic	$3.95	February 1987	Fiction O/N
28.	Roald Dahl's Revolting Rhymes	Roald Dahl	Puffin	$6.95	June 1984	Fiction O/B

Sales over 20,000 copies

29.	Anne of the Island	L. M. Montgomery	Angus & Robertson	$6.95	April 1987	Fiction O/R
30.	Far Out, Brussel Sprout	June Factor	OUP	$10.95	September 1983	Fiction A/B
31.	All Right, Vegemite	June Factor	OUP	$10.95	November 1985	Fiction A/B
32.	Halfway Across the Galaxy and Turn Left	Robin Klein	Puffin	$6.95	December 1986	Fiction A/N
33.	Bears Magic and Other Stories	Carla Stevens	Scholastic	$3.95	March 1987	Fiction O/R
34.	The BFG	Roald Dahl	Puffin	$6.95	March 1985	Fiction O/B
35.	There's a Dragon in my Closet	John F. Green	Scholastic	$3.95	May 1987	Fiction O/N
36.	Bridge to Terabithia	Katherine Paterson	Puffin	$5.95	December 1982	Fiction A/B
37.	Where's Spot	Eric Hill	Puffin	$8.95	November 1985	Fiction O/B
38.	Chronicles of Avonlea	L. M. Montgomery	Angus & Robertson	$6.95	April 1987	Fiction O/R
39.	The Twits	Roald Dahl	Puffin	$5.95	July 1982	Fiction O/B
40.	Outsiders	S. E. Hinton	Fontana Lions	$5.95	January 1987	Fiction O/B

CHILDREN'S FICTION AND NON-FICTION

Position	Title	Author	Publisher	Price	Release	Code
41.	The Witches	Roald Dahl	Puffin	$6.95	October 1985	Fiction O/B
42.	Space Demons	Gillian Rubenstein	Omnibus	$6.95	March 1987	Fiction A/N
43.	Tilly's Rescue	Faith Jacques	Pan	$5.95	December	Fiction O/B
44.	Mike's Birthday Bulldozer	Nan Bosworth	Ashton Scholastic	$4.50	May 1987	Fiction A/R
45.	Franklin in the Dark	Paulette Bourgeois	Ashton Scholastic	$4.95	July 1987	Fiction A/N

Sales over 15,000 copies

Position	Title	Author	Publisher	Price	Release	Code
46.	Hating Alison Ashley	Robin Klein	Puffin	$6.95	May 1984	Fiction A/B
47.	A Horse Named Doodlebug	Irene Brady	Scholastic	$3.95	May 1987	Fiction O/R
48.	All About Anna	Libby Hathorn	Methuen Australia	$5.95	March 1987	Fiction A/R
49.	Secret Tree House	Ruth Chew	Scholastic	$3.95	March 1987	Fiction O/B
50.	Sail Away	Mem Fox	Ashton Scholastic	$5.50	February 1987	Fiction A/N
51.	Charlie & the Chocolate Factory	Roald Dahl	Puffin	$6.95	October 1985	Fiction O/B
52.	Boss of the Pool	Robin Klein	Omnibus	$5.95	March 1987	Fiction A/N
53.	Z for Zachariah	Robert O'Brien	Fontana Lions	$5.95	June 1975	Fiction O/B
54.	Anne of Windy Willows	L. M. Montgomery	Angus & Robertson	$6.95	July 1987	Fiction O/B
55.	First Look at Animals With Backbone	Millicent Selsam & Joyce Hunt	Scholastic	$3.95	May 1987	Non-Fiction O/R
56.	Spot's First Walk	Eric Hill	Puffin	$8.95	November 1985	Fiction O/B
57.	Country Bunny Little Gold Shoes	Du Bose Heyward	Scholastic	$4.50	March 1987	Fiction O/R
58.	Boy	Roald Dahl	Puffin	$6.95	July 1986	Fiction O/B

59.	Unreal	Paul Jennings	Puffin	$6.95	December 1985	Fiction A/B
60.	George's Marvellous Medicine	Roald Dahl	Puffin	$5.95	March 1983	Fiction O/B
61.	Spot Goes to School	Eric Hill	Puffin	$9.95	January 1987	Fiction O/N
62.	Dirty Beasts	Roald Dahl	Puffin	$6.95	July 1986	Fiction O/B
63.	What Do You Do With a Kangaroo	Mercer Mayer	Scholastic	$4.50	November 1986	Fiction O/R
64.	Australian Oxford Mini Dictionary	Editors: Evelyn Forbes, Anne Knight, George Turner, Joyce Hawkins	OUP	$5.95	January 1987	Non-Fiction A/N
65.	Anne's House of Dreams	L. M. Montgomery	Angus & Robertson	$6.95	July 1987	Fiction O/R
66.	Anne of Ingleside	L. M. Montgomery	Angus & Robertson	$6.95	July 1987	Fiction O/R
67.	James & the Giant Peach	Roald Dahl	Puffin	$5.95	December 1973	Fiction O/B
68.	The Bend in the River	Lynne Taylor	Greenhouse Publications Pty Ltd	$6.95	October 1987	Fiction A/N
69.	Rainbow Valley	L. M. Montgomery	Angus & Robertson	$6.95	July 1987	Fiction O/R
70.	Australian 123 Dictionary	Editors: Rosemary Sansome and Angela Ridsdale	OUP	$6.95	August 1985	Non-Fiction A/B
71.	Advanced Paper Aircraft — Vol 1	Campbell Morris	Angus & Robertson	$4.95	January 1987	Non-Fiction A/R
72.	The Very Hungry Caterpillar	Eric Carle	Puffin	$5.95	October 1975	Fiction O/B
73.	Further Chronicles of Avonlea	L. M. Montgomery	Angus & Robertson	$6.95	July 1987	Fiction O/R
74.	Emily Climbs	L. M. Montgomery	Angus & Robertson	$6.95	April 1987	Fiction O/R
75.	Dear Zoo	Rod Campbell	Puffin	$8.95	November 1986	Fiction O/B

CHILDREN'S FICTION AND NON-FICTION

Position	Title	Author	Publisher	Price	Release	Code
76.	Spot's Birthday Party	Eric Hill	Puffin	$8.95	November 1985	Fiction O/B
77.	Pollyanna	Eleanor H. Porter	Angus & Robertson	$6.95	April 1987	Fiction O/R
78.	Australian Schoolmate Dictionary	George Turner	OUP	$5.50	October 1984	Non-Fiction A/B
79.	Rilla of Ingleside	L. M. Montgomery	Angus & Robertson	$6.95	July 1987	Fiction O/R
80.	Unbelievable!	Paul Jennings	Puffin	$6.95	November 1986	Fiction A/B
81.	Is Anyone Hungry	Peter Pavey	Greenhouse Publications Pty Ltd	$5.95	June 1987	Fiction A/N

Source: Australian Book Publishers Association.

NEWSPAPER AND MAGAZINE CIRCULATION FIGURES

NATIONAL NEWSPAPERS

The Australian	Sydney	129,393
Australian Financial Review	Sydney	67,485

MAJOR METROPOLITAN NEWSPAPERS

Weekday

The Sun News-Pictorial	Melbourne	570,000
The West Australian	Perth	327,645
The Daily Telegraph	Sydney	299,797
The Daily Mirror	Sydney	273,248
Sydney Morning Herald	Sydney	258,700
The Age	Melbourne	230,487
The Herald	Melbourne	217,284
The Courier Mail	Brisbane	214,000
The Advertiser	Adelaide	212,770
Truth	Melbourne	171,568
The News	Adelaide	170,000
The Daily Sun	Brisbane	125,778
The Daily News	Perth	98,158
Canberra Chronicle	Canberra	77,500
The Mercury	Hobart	56,000
The Canberra Times	Canberra	43,330
Northern Territory News	Darwin	17,398

Sunday

Sunday Telegraph	Sydney	637,534
The Sun Herald	Sydney	568,287
The Sunday Sun	Brisbane	364,326
The Sunday Mail	Brisbane	319,861
The Sunday Times	Perth	290,000
The Sunday Mail	Adelaide	245,000
The Sunday Press	Melbourne	166,000
The Sunday Observer	Melbourne	110,553
The Sunday Tasmanian	Hobart	40,000
Sunday Territorian	Darwin	18,256

MULTICULTURAL PRESS

Arabic

Al Bairak	Sydney	32,000
El Telegraph	Sydney	21,000
Sada Loubnan	Sydney	20,000
Saout-El-Moughttareb	Sydney	18,000
Al Dalil	Sydney	15,000
Al Watan	Sydney	10,000
An Nahda	Sydney	10,000
An-Nahar	Sydney	8,000
Free Pakistan	Canberra	4,000
Tareeq Aj-Jaliah	Sydney	2,000
Al Masry	Sydney	1,000

Argentinian

Noticias y Deportes	Sydney	10,000
Treinta Dias	Sydney	4,500

Chinese

Sing Tao Jih Pao	Sydney	10,000
Chinese Herald	Sydney	10,000
Australian Chinese Daily	Sydney	8,000
Action China	Nathan, Qld	3,000
Australia China Review	Melbourne	2,500
Victorian Bulletin of the Aust. China Friendship Society	Melbourne	2,500
Aust. Chinese Community Assoc. News	Sydney	2,000
Qiad Sheng News	Sydney	1,500
Australian Chinese Forum Newsletter	Sydney	500

Croatian

Hrvatska Tjednik	Melbourne	8,500
Hrvatska Vhiesnik	Melbourne	6,000
Spremnost Croatian Weekly	Sydney	5,000
Hrvatska Slobodo	Melbourne	3,000

Czechoslovakian

Hlasy	Sydney	1,500

Dutch

Dutch Courier	Melbourne	12,000
Dutch Australian Weekly	Sydney	7,000

Het Kompas	Parramatta	600
Estonian		
Meie Kodu	Sydney	4,000
Filipino		
Sandigan	Sydney	3,000
Finnish		
Finlandia News	Brisbane	2,600
Suomi	Melbourne	1,200
French		
Le Courier Australien	Sydney	7,000
German		
Die Woche in Australien	Sydney	8,500
Neue Heimat und Welt	Melbourne	8,000
Australien Kurier	Sydney	3,500
Greek		
Neos Kosmos	Sydney	25,000
Nea Patrida	Sydney	25,696
Ellinikos Kirikos	Sydney	22,928
Acropolis	Sydney	20,000
Nea Ellada	Melbourne	15,000
O Kosmos	Sydney	14,000
To Vema	Sydney	14,000
Ellinis	Sydney	10,000
Nea Poreia	Sydney	8,000
Pirsos	Melbourne	7,000
Omoyenia	Melbourne	5,000
Athletic Echo	Melbourne	5,000
Ellinika Nea	Adelaide	1,000
Hungarian		
Magyar Elet	Melbourne	11,000
Perthi Magyar Hirek	Perth	300
Indian/Pakistani		
The Indian Down Under	Sydney	3,000
Musa Waat	Sydney	3,000
Ghalib	Sydney	2,000
Iranian		
Arash	Sydney	1,000

Irish

The Irish Voice	Sydney	8,000

Italian

Pronto Guide	Sydney	60,000
Settimanale Italiano	Melbourne	40,000
Australian Tempo Libero	Melbourne	35,000
Il Globo	Melbourne	32,100
Extra Informativo	Sydney	24,000
La Fiamma	Sydney	17,000
Nuovo Paese	Sydney	8,000
Il Campanile	Melbourne	7,000
Ieri Oggie E Domani	Sydney	5,000
Il Messaggero	Melbourne	4,000
Il Progresso Italo-Australiano	Melbourne	2,000

Japanese

Nichigo Press and Meatpie	Sydney	10,000

Jewish

Australian Jewish News	Melbourne	8,500
Australian Jewish Times	Sydney	6,029
Australian Israel Review	Melbourne	3,500

Kampuchean

Phnom-Penh Themi	Melbourne	3,000
Smaradey Khmer	Sydney	3,000

Korean

Han Ho Times	Sydney	4,500
Hoju Soshik	Sydney	4,000
Daehan Shinbo	Sydney	4,000

Latvian

Australian Latvian News	Melbourne	2,500

Lithuanian

Musu Pastoge	Sydney	1,200

Macedonian

Macedonia Weekly Herald	Melbourne	5,000
Macedonia Weekly	Melbourne	3,500

Maltese

The Malta Cross	Sydney	6,200
The Maltese Herald	Sydney	5,760

Mauritian

Voice of Mauritius	Canberra	3,500

Polish

Tygodnik Polski	Melbourne	6,500
Wiadomoski Polski	Sydney	5,000
Nowa Epoka	Adelaide	800

Portuguese

O Portuguese na Australia	Sydney	8,000
Correigo Portuguese	Sydney	3,000

Russian

Edinele	Sydney	4,300
Pravda	Sydney	1,000

Scandinavian

Scandinavian Herald	Sydney	1,500

Slovenian

Vestnik	Melbourne	700

Spanish

Heraldo Spanol	Sydney	15,000
El Espanol en Australia	Sydney	8,500
Version	Sydney	1,300

Turkish

Dunya	Sydney	6,200
Tele Haber	Sydney	5,500
Kaynak	Melbourne	5,250
Yorum	Sydney	4,800
Emek	Melbourne	4,000
Yeni Vatan	Sydney	3,500
Kuzey Kibrisin Sesi	Sydney	2,500
Turk Sesi	Melbourne	2,000
Turk Dayanisma	Sydney	1,000

Ukranian

Wilna Dumpka	Sydney	1,500

Vietnamese

Chieu Duong	Sydney	70,000–100,000
Chuong Saigon	Sydney	15,000
Tivi Tuan-San	Melbourne	15,000
Viet Luan	Sydney	10,000

Hoa Nien Magazine	Melbourne	2,000
Yugoslav		
Novo Doba	Sydney	10,300
Novosti	Sydney	5,992

MAGAZINES
Art and Craft

Craft Art Magazine	Sydney	20,000
Handmade Australia	Sydney	16,588
Australian Artist	Sydney	15,000
Art and Australia	Sydney	12,000
Craft and Australia	Sydney	10,000
Astrology		
Horoscope	Sydney	10,000
Astrological Monthly Review	Sydney	6,530
Aviation		
QANTAS Airways Inflight	Melbourne	490,000
The Australian Way	Sydney	70,000
Daily Commercial News	Sydney	8,500
Books and Literary		
Australian Bookseller and Publisher	Melbourne	8,000
Australian Book Review	Melbourne	4,000
Meanjin	Melbourne	2,600
Business and Finance		
Personal Investment	Melbourne	70,461
Business Review Weekly	Melbourne	61,881
Australian Business	Sydney	54,000
Personal Success	Melbourne	35,000
The Business Bulletin	Sydney	16,117
Computers		
Computing Australia	Sydney	28,581
Australian Personal Computer	Sydney	27,848
Your Computer	Sydney	20,000
Consumer Affairs		
Choice	Sydney	190,000
Entertainment		
Artswest	Sydney	447,441

On the Street	Sydney	21,860
The Entertainer Newspaper	Charm Haven, NSW	15,000
Dance Australia	Melbourne	10,000
Xpress	Sydney	6,000
Capital News	Tamworth	6,000

Family Life

Family Circle	Sydney	400,920
Parents and Children Magazine	Sydney	36,166

Farm and Rural

The Weekly Times	Melbourne	101,602
The Land	North Richmond	72,000
Farmer and Grazier	Toowoomba	44,000
National Farmer	Melbourne	37,670
Queensland Country Life	Brisbane	32,587
Farm	Melbourne	23,025
Stock Journal	Adelaide	22,880
Stock and Land	Melbourne	22,555
Town and Country Farmer	Melbourne	18,200
The Country Woman	Sydney	14,999
Elders Weekly	Perth	14,488

Fashion

Hero	Sydney	100,000
Vogue Australia	Sydney	64,920
Studio Collections	Sydney	60,000
Mode	Sydney	57,200
Follow Me—Gentlemen	Sydney	40,000
Follow Me	Sydney	35,000
Stileto	Sydney	32,000

Film, Television and Video

TV Week	Melbourne	758,176
What's On Video and Cinema	Melbourne	174,162
TV Radio Extra	Adelaide	88,094
Movie 88	Sydney	60,000
Variety	Sydney	36,000
Cinema Papers	Melbourne	15,000

Food

Signature	Sydney	160,000

Australian Gourmet	Sydney	68,000
Wine and Spirit Magazine	Sydney	25,000
Winestate	Adelaide	20,000
Epicurean	Melbourne	14,452

General

Reader's Digest	Sydney	450,000
People	Sydney	230,601
Australasian Post	Melbourne	213,271
The Bulletin with Newsweek	Sydney	118,000
Time Australia	Melbourne	107,000
Billy Blue	Sydney	30,000

Geography

Australian Geographic	Sydney	120,000
Geo	Sydney	55,000

Health and Fitness

Healthy Life News	Sydney	200,000
Prevention	Sydney	60,000
Australian Slimming	Sydney	48,000
Nature and Health	Sydney	30,000
Australian Wellbeing	Sydney	30,000

Hobbies and Games

Australian Hi-Fi Magazine	Sydney	25,000
CB Action	Melbourne	24,000
Australian Natural History	Sydney	21,000
Stamp News	Dubbo, NSW	14,000
Australian Bridge	Melbourne	2,500
Chess in Australia	Sydney	1,800

Homes and Gardens

Better Homes and Gardens	Sydney	240,695
Australian Home Beautiful	Melbourne	94,018
Australian House and Garden	Sydney	92,400
Your Garden	Melbourne	83,617
Good Housekeeping	Sydney	82,472
Vogue Living	Sydney	46,070
Homes and Living	Perth	35,100

Lifestyle

Belle	Sydney	52,000

Simply Living	Sydney	30,000

Men

Australian Penthouse Magazine	Sydney	118,837
Australian Playboy	Sydney	40,533

Motoring

The Open Road	Sydney	1,463,000
Royal Auto	Melbourne	880,841
Road Patrol	Perth	308,000
Street Machine	Sydney	113,900
Performance Street Car	Sydney	58,725
Wheels	Sydney	48,500
Modern Motor	Sydney	46,200
Car Australia	Melbourne	45,650
Superstreet	Sydney	32,230
Australian Auto Action	Melbourne	23,335
Bushdriver	Sydney	22,000
4x4 Australia	Melbourne	20,800
Racing Car News	Sydney	20,000

Music

Smash Hits	Melbourne	73,515
Countdown Magazine	Sydney	55,685
24 Hours	Sydney	31,000
RAM	Sydney	27,000
Juke	Melbourne	26,000
Opera Australia	Sydney	2,367

Pensioners

Australian Senior Citizens	Toukley, NSW	56,000
The Over 50's Travel and Leisure Guide	Sydney	35,000
Pensioner's Voice	Sydney	20,000

Political and Social Issues

IPA Review	Melbourne	20,113
New Internationalist	Melbourne	11,000
Australian Society	Melbourne	8,000
Quadrant Magazine	Sydney	6,000
Australian Quarterly	Sydney	2,000

Religion

The Catholic Weekly	Sydney	21,433

The Advocate	Melbourne	19,000
On Being	Melbourne	12,000

Sport

Basketball

The Australian Basketballer	Melbourne	13,300

Bikes

Ozbike	Sydney	29,000
Two Wheels	Sydney	21,200
Australian Motorcycle News	Melbourne	18,960
Australasian Dirt Bike	Sydney	18,150
Australian Trail and Track	Melbourne	17,000
Revs Motorcycle News	Sydney	15,800

Boating

Club Marine Magazine	Melbourne	39,218
Australian Nautical News	Melbourne	13,000

Bowls

Bowls in Victoria	Melbourne	60,000

Cricket

ABC Cricket Book	Sydney	43,000
Australian Cricket	Sydney	15,000

Fishing

Modern Fishing	Sydney	21,800
Australian Angler's Fishing World	Sydney	18,435
Australian Oyster	Sydney	600

Football

VFL The Football Record	Melbourne	90,000
Rugby League Week	Sydney	53,900

Golf

Australian Golf Digest	Sydney	24,000

Horses

Horse News	Rouse Hill, NSW	18,600
Hoofs and Horns	Sydney	15,000

Netball

Australian Netball News	Parramatta	30,000

Racing

Racetrack	Sydney	22,000

Running
Fun Runner	Sydney	17,500

Sailing
Sailwind Quarterly	Sydney	20,000

Shooting
Australasian Sporting Shooter	Sydney	21,786
Guns Australia	Sydney	12,454

Swimming and Surfing
Tracks	Sydney	35,500
Australian Waves	Sydney	15,000
The International Swimmer	Sydney	4,000

Tennis
Tennis	Melbourne	23,000

Women
The Australian Women's Weekly	Sydney	1,105,000
New Idea	Melbourne	929,115
Woman's Day	Sydney	625,000
Cleo	Sydney	255,000
Cosmopolitan	Sydney	200,000
Mode for Brides	Sydney	30,000
Bride to Be	Sydney	22,300

Source: Media People, March 1988.

AUSTRALIAN NATIONAL TOP TEN BEST-SELLING ALBUMS, SINGLES AND CD'S 1987

1987 Albums

1.	Whispering Jack	John Farnham
2.	Crowded House	Crowded House
3.	Slippery When Wet	Bon Jovi
4.	Graceland	Paul Simon
5.	The Joshua Tree	U2
6.	Tango in the Night	Fleetwood Mac
7.	Revenge	Eurythmics
8.	Men and Women	Simply Red
9.	Whitney	Whitney Houston
10.	Different Light	The Bangles

1987 Singles

1.	Locomotion	Kylie Minogue
2.	La Bamba	Los Lobos
3.	Old Time Rock and Roll	Bob Seger
4.	Slice of Heaven	Dave Dobbyn with Herbs
5.	Respectable	Mel & Kim
6.	You Keep Me Hangin' On	Kim Wilde
7.	Walk Like an Egyptian	The Bangles
8.	Electric Blue	Icehouse
9.	Boom Boom (Let's Go Back To My Room)	Paul Lekakis
10.	The Final Countdown	Europe

1987 Compact Discs

1.	Whispering Jack	John Farnham
2.	Graceland	Paul Simon
3.	Crowded House	Crowded House
4.	Tango in the Night	Fleetwood Mac
5.	Men and Women	Simply Red
6.	The Joshua Tree	U2
7.	Revenge	Eurythmics

8.	La Bamba	Motion Picture Soundtrack
9.	Man of Colours	Icehouse
10.	Whitney	Whitney Houston

Reprinted from the Australian Music Report with permission.

OZ ROCK

Australian music in 1987 was at a crossroads, a state-of-play that was symbolised by the 'Australia-Made' series of concerts early in 1988. Intended as a celebration of the past, present and future of Australian rock at a time when it had finally achieved full acceptance overseas, Australia-Made gave rise to as many questions as cheers.

Born of the rough and tumble atmosphere of pubs, 'Oz rock' and the industry that supports it, has matured sufficiently for it to find real international success. Having caught up with the rest of the world, it now faces the task of staying abreast and there are signs that this may be an uphill battle.

The pub rock tradition has instilled some regressive attitudes and, in the face of watchful foreign ownership, the major record companies lack initiative. The range of independent labels, if they are willing, have the freedom and imagination to encourage development, but are hamstrung by a lack of money—and it takes money to make competitive records in this day and age.

The Australia-Made series of concerts around the country featured not only some of the biggest bands in the land but also others more off-centre, from **InXS**, **Jimmy Barnes**, the **Divinyls** and the **Models** to **I'm Talking**, the **Saints**, the **Triffids** and **Mental As Anything**.

In the wake of the smashing international success of *Crocodile Dundee* and the America's Cup defence and in anticipation of the nation's Bicentenary, it was an event that could only claim to be capitalising on a rush of nationalistic fervour.

An event it was. As all the hype kept reminding us: 'You'll think all your summers have come at once.' The publicity was well-orchestrated from the outset, and with seven shows in seven capital cities in four weeks it was a massive undertaking.

In one respect conceived as a rebuttal to the fact that **Dire Straits** was able to tour Australia, playing to quarter of a million people in Sydney alone and grossing $35m, nearly all of which left the country, Australia-Made attracted disappointing crowds (39,000 altogether)—making enough to cover costs. Perhaps the crowds were disappointing because it was a cosmetic, unconvincing concept and at worst it smacked of self-congratulation.

Predictably, Australia-Made gushed that it represented a coming of age for Australian music but it was more like a full stop on the end of the paragraph in which Australian music came of age. The shouting after the game was over.

It's been taken for granted for some time now, that any band that wants to really make a go of it in Australia has to keep one eye on the international market. Australia is too small to sustain a band: it needs not only to maximise its potential audience but to set itself inspiring challenges. Otherwise, it has to be prepared to play eleven months a year on the pub circuit just to stay alive.

The mechanics required to straddle markets in Australia and overseas are established now and Australia is an active participant in the dialogue of selling music around the world. Oddly enough, the cultural cringe suffered by

Australia has never stopped her from trying to sell herself overseas. A chip on your shoulder like that only makes you more determined, if a little unbalanced.

By the early seventies, the major record companies—five out of six of them foreign owned—were sufficiently entrenched in the local scene to start looking for talent that might work overseas. Unfortunately, however, the majors were only intent on finding Australian music that would appease their superiors overseas—that sounded like music they'd already heard.

Still, it's hard to criticise people like Olivia Newton-John or Rick Springfield, two early Australian exports who sustained their careers overseas. If they sold out, they sold out personally, when they moved lock, stock and barrel to LA. Australian exports before this, like the **Easybeats**, were largely one-hit wonders.

The **Little River Band** was probably the first Australian act that chose to maintain an Australian base: recording here whilst working the American market. They found significant success but it's ironic that it was with a sound that could just as well have been that of an American band. What **LRB** did prove, however, was that there was no reason why the world market wouldn't—consistently—buy records made in Australia. After a swag of notable failures like **Skyhooks**, **Cold Chisel**, **Split Enz**, and the **Angels**, it took punk to prove that Australian records, placed on the international market, didn't have to be merely echoes of international precedents. By the late seventies, with the electronic communications revolution having linked it directly to the rest of the world, Australia was no longer the isolated backwater it once was.

It is ironic that the **Saints** should be on the Australia-Made bill when they most definitely did not have a high profile down-under. It was the **Saints** who helped usher the punk revolution on the world stage with their self-made debut single '(I'm) Stranded', but at the time the unimaginative Australian music industry was afraid of punk, seeing it as a threat. It took a directive from a London record company head office to get the band signed by its Australian branch. The **Saints** survived thanks mainly to their popularity in Europe.

Part of the punk ethos was, of course, DIY (do it yourself). Both around the world and in Australia independent labels sprang up to release records the out-of-touch majors wouldn't, and the generation reared on imported and local culture saw no great disparity between the two. It is ten years since the initial explosion of punk in 1977 and Australian 'underground' bands have proved they can translate to a similar status overseas. The mechanism is available for almost any band to open channels to the international marketplace and Australian bands no longer have any reason to assume they are inferior, or to fear condescension. It's like leaving on the blinkers, in fact, for a band to believe its appeal must end at the Australian coastline: it's part of an international musical exchange and the Australian well will quickly dry up anyway.

Like the **Saints** before them, a band like Sydney speed-metal merchants the **Hard-Ons**, who obviously have a limited appeal, are only able to survive because they sell records internationally and can tour the world. They benefit from the network of independent record labels that criss-cross the globe and interact.

Naturally the majors aren't about to try to fry such small fish and although they've learnt some lessons in the last decade, they still have a tendency to look for acts with a homogenised, 'mid-Pacific' sound, if for no other reason than they can be very successful. Thus we have acts like **Noiseworks**, the **Venetians**, **John Farnham** and **Mark Edwards**, although **Geisha**, the blandest of the record company creations, seems to have disappeared.

It could be said that acts like these wouldn't have qualified for Australia-Made anyway, as there's so little of Australia in them. But there are other acts that certainly would have fitted— the **Hoodoo Gurus**, **Pseudo Echo**, **Icehouse**, the **Celibate Rifles**, the **Go Betweens**, **Hunters & Collectors**,

Crowded House, Nick Cave and the Bad Seeds, Paul Kelly and the Coloured Girls, and Midnight Oil.

Some of the biggest Australian hitmakers in 1987, however, would by no means have qualified for the Australia-Made bill, because of their parochial appeal. The biggest single of the year, according to the Australian Music Report, was a remake of 'Locomotion' by Kylie Minogue, the star of Australia's favourite soapie *Neighbours*. One of the next biggest singles, 'Suddenly' by Angry Anderson, was also tied in to *Neighbours*, and a large part of its success was probably also due to that fact.

In the year's Top 50 singles, five out of sixteen Australian entries (not including 'Locomotion' were cover versions—the Party Boys' 'He's Gonna Step On You Again', the Angels' 'We Gotta Get Out Of This Place', Pseudo Echo's 'Funkytown', Jimmy Barnes' and Michael Hutchence's Australia-Made anthem 'Good Times' (an Easybeats' oldie) and the Chantoozies' 'Witch Queen'—local equivalents of a worldwide trend which saw covers like Los Lobos' 'La Bamba' and Club Neuvauo's 'Lean On Me' topping charts.

'Funkytown' was probably the only one that cut it overseas because it was the only one that really sounded like an update: it proffered inherent values rather than relying solely on personality appeal.

The synthesised pomp-pop sound of Icehouse hit a peak during 1987 with the album *Man Of Colours* and the several singles lifted off it: they crossed the Pacific and finally broke through in America as well. The two biggest selling albums of 1987 were John Farnham's *Whispering Jack* and Crowded House's eponymously titled debut, both of which grew out of a series of hit singles from the previous year.

Both Midnight Oil and old Australian Crawler James Reyne returned to vinyl after absences, making the albums *Diesel and Dust* and *James Reyne* respectively—both were as satisfying as they were successful.

Soloist Jenny Morris released the album *Body & Soul*, recorded with a large cast (including members of InXS), and it deservedly won the ARIA (Australian Record Industry Association) Best Female Artist award.

Naturally though, the full gamut of Australian music isn't contained exclusively in the mainstream charts. Often enough, a record successful in the independent outlets sells sufficient numbers to qualify for the mainstream charts, but is overlooked because they obtain their information from mainstream outlets only. The indy charts are dominated by revivalist garage bands and Gothic poseurs, from the Lime Spiders and the Screaming Tribesmen to the Wreckery, but the success of the indy single, 'All Set To Go' by the Hard-Ons, is indicative that this specialist audience is by no means necessarily hipper or more tasteful (as it likes to think it is) than the mainstream.

Names synonymous with exciting music in 1987, regardless of their chart placements, were the Black Sorrows, the Go Betweens, Ed Kuepper, Not Drowning Waving, Weddings Parties Anything, Steve Kilbey (on leave from the Church), Big Pig, the Rockmelons, Hunters & Collectors, Louis Tillet, the Died Pretty, the Hoodoo Gurus, Stephen Cummings, and Peter Blakeley. Australia even produced two of the finest country records made anywhere in the world last year in the Flying Emus' *This Town* and Anne Kirkpatrick's *Come Back Again*.

The Australia-Made bill, then, encompassed only a fraction of the variety in Australian music. If there was a common thread running through it, it was that with the exception of I'm Talking all its acts could only be called 'rock'—and rock shaped by the Australian pub rock tradition.

It is, of course, this quality in Australian rock that makes it unique and attractive to audiences overseas. At the same time it's a concept that's fast becoming redundant. The reason InXS have streaked ahead of the bunch, and Jimmy Barnes, say, has been left behind, is because they've moved on, accepted new techniques and attitudes and adapted them, whilst not forgetting the crucial lesson learnt in Australian pubs—how to kick arse.

Will Australia be known as the last outpost of an outmoded cultural tradition? It's a cute idea given Australia's image and reality as a frontier, but sooner or later you've got to grow up, admit some subtlety and sophistication. Unless it adapts, exported Australian music will only sound quaint, like the earliest rock'n'roll or mono recordings do now.

Despite all the flagwaving—Australia Made included—this country hasn't yet grown out of its colonial origins. Some have overcome the cultural cringe but Australia may never escape its unofficial position as a colony of the USA. Like the rest of the world, we learnt rock'n'roll from the Americans but Australia adapted it and, largely thanks to the pub rock tradition, eventually emerged with a distinctive form of its own. It still—as Australia-Made did prove—has some life left in it.

Ultimately, Australia-Made was probably a gratuitous gesture as there is no longer any need to wave the flag. That Australia can produce corporate rock, for instance (an Australian tradition itself initiated by **Rick Springfield** and the **Little River Band**), with the best, and the worst, of them is surely a sign of increasing confidence and maturity.

It's an equally encouraging sign that an act like **Crowded House**, say, who haven't submitted to the corporative imperative, haven't waved the flag vociferously either. Their nationality is inherent in their individuality.

Still, it's no small irony that **Crowded House** bypassed Australian record companies altogether in their quick trip to the top: they went directly to America and signed a worldwide deal with Capitol Records. If Australian music can transcend its established origins will the Australian record companies keep up?

The path **Crowded House** took was paved by songwriter **Neil Finn**'s reputation as a former member of **Split Enz** but that can't account for what's happened to **Peter Blakeley**. Blakeley is just about the finest singer this country has ever produced, and while he was slowly acquiring a reputation here, his progress (without thanks to any record company) wasn't commensurate with his potential. Next thing you know, Capitol Records in the USA (again) sent a rep out to Australia to sign Blakeley to the sort of deal he deserves.

Blakeley's potential is obvious to anyone with ears—so how come no major Australian record company seemed to be able to hear it? Or if they could, why didn't they act? Why did it take a foreigner to come in and get the job done?

Twenty years ago, in Melbourne, pubs had only just begun to enjoy late-night, 10 o'clock closing. At the end of 1981, another of Melbourne's antiquated liquor laws was changed, opening pubs up to live entertainment, viz. rock'n'roll.

It was these welcome changes, coupled with the fact that Melbourne was at the time the undisputed centre of the Australian music industry, that gave rise to what was probably the first true, distinctly Australian rock genre— 'pub rock'.

The pubs were rough-and-tumble places where the punters demanded their rock'n'roll loud, tough and fast. Armed with massive stacks of amps which had by then become the order of the day, bands like **Billy Thorpe and the Aztecs** and other 'high-energy heavy-metal boogie' merchants were equal to the task.

By the mid seventies, a band called **AC/DC** had pushed the **Aztecs** off their throne, and a few years later would become one of the first Australian bands to make a real success overseas without selling out.

By this time, the emphasis in Australian music was swinging back to Sydney. Pub venues had taken root, and immediately provided a home to bands like **Cold Chisel** (fronted by **Jimmy Barnes**), **Rose Tattoo** (**Angry Anderson**) and the **Angels**. Even the punk revolution was based in the pub tradition: perhaps not the **Saints** because they came from Brisbane where there never was a pub circuit (although they soon found their niche in the pubs), but certainly in Sydney and Melbourne punk cut its teeth in pubs. Bands like **InXS**, the **Divinyls**, **Midnight Oil** and **Mental as Anything** grew out of Sydney pubs after the first punk explosion.

Punk was, of course, essentially a white, middle-class movement, so it was suited to Australian youth. But consider the major innovations in pop since then: disco died off as punk started; after punk came garage electronic music like the **Human League**; then, in Britain, the ska revival, and the re-emergence of the songwriter (as in the likes of **Elvis Costello**); after that, new romanticism started what the new pop finished (in a figure like **Boy George**) and from there it's flowered to culminate in a contemporary figure like **George Michael**. In the early eighties, the innovative emphasis swung back to American music, black as well as white—hip-hop, the jagged dance music of alienated black kids, and hardcore, the faster, harder logical extension of punk rock. Both emerged out of ghettos, although it was all too uncompromising to crossover. The sixties revival, even though it's probably had more impact on the indy scene than anything in the early-to-mid-eighties, was surely doomed to a creative impasse.

The real seminal figure of the time was probably **Madonna**, as she was the one who first, or at least most successfully, fused a new pop front with hip-hop dance beats and mixes which is now the state-of-the-art.

Garage electronic music, like punk, suited Australian youth. The ska revival here was all affectation and the songwriter didn't re-emerge because in the form of the likes of **Paul Kelly** he never went away. New romanticism was destined never to really stick in Australia as Australians distrust anything so seemingly foppish. Hip-hop, of course, is totally alien to Australian youth, while hardcore could only ever have a minority appeal.

The new pop, from **Boy George** to **Madonna** and **George Michael**, has of course caught on in Australia, but only in the hearts of young girls. Musicians and technicians have spurned it, as they do hip-hop and did disco which can only then make you wonder, how well-equipped Australia is to make records for the future.

Australia still has to import talent to get truly competitive records made. The hardware's here—the Australian company Fairlight, for instance, is one of the world's leaders in the field of music computers, and Australian recording studios may be as advanced as any in the world—but there's a dearth of creative nuts, producers and engineers, to put in the driver's seat.

Soon after the completion of Australia-Made, the acts that didn't break-up—unlike the **Models** and **I'm Talking**—all disappeared from view for most of the year, either to record overseas or in Australia with imported producers, or to tour overseas, or both.

InXS ensconced themselves in Rhinoceros Studios in Woolloomooloo, Sydney, with English producer Chris Thomas, and emerged just before 1987 was out with *Kick*. Without doubt their finest and certainly most successful album to date, it is an exciting collection of almost flawless songs set to the band's crackling melange of rock and hard funk.

Mental As Anything also recorded in Australia, with American producer Richard Gottherer, but the reason that album *Mouth To Mouth* was unsuccessful was that it showed that the **Mentals** seem to be losing their commitment.

The **Divinyls** went to New York to record *Temperamental*, which wasn't released until early 1988. The **Saints** made their first foray to America, touring there to good response, and recording the album *Prodigal Son* in New York and London and also released early in 1988.

Jimmy Barnes made *Freight-Train Heart* somewhere between Australia and America with personnel half-and-half as well. Even if his vision hadn't been so old-guard the album would have failed to really cut it because it was too full of this compromise. Predictably, his loyal Australian following bought the album in truckloads but the Americans refused to succumb.

The **Triffids** returned to their home base in London to record the lushly-produced *Calenture*. Released early in 1988, it may yet provide them with a breakthrough.

The only thing that's certain in the selection of a producer and a studio is that neither provides any guarantees. **James Reyne**, for instance, recorded his eponymously titled debut solo album in LA and it wasn't even released in America; while **Icehouse**, **Midnight Oil**, **Pseudo Echo** and the **Hoodoo Gurus** all recorded in Australia, with Australian personnel, and found varying degrees of success overseas.

There are just as many acts, though, who've suffered for totally local control over their recordings. **Jenny Morris**'s *Body & Soul* was an enticing set of ballads and upbeat numbers which was let down only by thin, patchy production. A record will rarely make it overseas or within Australia, without optimum production.

Paul Kelly and the Coloured Girls are another band who've suffered from underproduction. The album *Under The Sun*, the follow-up to the double set *Gossip*, was another excellent collection of songs from the pen of one of Australia's finest songwriters, performed by one of the most versatile bands but its effectiveness fell short due again, to thin, patchy production.

The **Coloured Girls** are a band that have made their reputation and following in the pubs. Despite the shortcomings of their records, there's good reason why they are beginning to make inroads overseas unlike other bands big on the pub circuit like the **Angels**, the **Cockroaches**, the **Party Boys** and **Spy V. Spy**.

The reason is simple—songs. The success of albums like *The Cockroaches*, *AO Mod. TV Vers.* (**Spy V. Spy**) and *Howling* (the **Angels**) is that they are a facsimile of the bands' live personae. These bands are all products of the pub tradition and they survive by virtue of the intensity and accessibility of their performances rather than the strength of their songs. The hit single the **Angels** had was a cover version, and the **Party Boys** play almost entirely covers.

The **Choirboys** made a return to the live arena in 1987, and their comeback was as successful as it was because not only did they make a superior transition to vinyl (produced by American Brian McGee, who also produced the **Saints**) but also because they 'had songs'. 'Run To Paradise' was very deservedly a huge hit.

Outside Sydney, the capital of music in Australia at the moment, the pub circuit also breeds regional heroes. Even bands that are big in Melbourne, like **Painters & Dockers**, **Blue Ruin** and the **Wreckery** can't connect in Sydney. In a smaller city like Adelaide, the status of outfits like the **Exploding White Mice**, **Mad Turks from Istanbul**, the **Screaming Believers**, the **Lizard Train** and **King Snake Roost** is serviced by a single indy label, Greasy Pop Records.

Bands like **Spy V. Spy** or the **Choirboys** deviate little from the prerequisites imposed upon them by the pub tradition but there are other acts, notably less successful however, who do try to do something original: the literate, tensile rock of **Ed Kuepper**; the alternatively eccentric/romantic pop of the **Go Betweens**; **Weddings Parties Anything**'s blend of bush band and pub-rocking; the ambient experimentalism of **Not Drowning Waving**; the rootsiness of the **Black Sorrows**; **Big Pig**'s tribal gospel-disco; the **Rockmelons**' dance groove; the late night urbanity of **Stephen Cummings**; the striding bluesy and jazzy inclinations of **Louis Tillett**; the mature hard-rock assault of the **New Christs**; the provocative speed-metal of the **Hard-Ons** and **Mass Appeal**; the wilfully offensive experimentalism of the Black-Eye Records collective, from **Thug** to **Lubricated Goat**; the power-trio classicism of **Tall Tales & True**; the ethereal harmonies of the **Crystal Set**; the acoustic angst of **White Cross**; the urgent, socially-aware thrash of the **Celibate Rifles**; **Died Pretty**'s dark rock epics; the power-pop of the **Happy Hate-Me-Nots**; and the brilliant blue-eyed soul of **Peter Blakeley**.

It's perhaps predictable that most of

these acts record for independent labels and that they haven't (yet) achieved broader success. Apart from refusing to conform to lowest-common-denominator demands, they often can't boast (because they can't afford) the production commercial radio demands—and that's what makes hit records in Australia. Still, they can and do venture overseas where they can come in at a similar level as in Australia and then move forward from there.

If it wasn't for the independents, we would never enjoy the sort of out-of-the-blue gems that may or may not be one-offs for their makers—in 1987 singles like the **Mothers'** 'Drives Me Wild', **God**'s 'My Pal' and the **Hummingbirds'** 'Everything You Said'.

A single like 'Locomotion' was as big a hit as it was because it appealed to a huge, across-the-board audience—the people who watch *Neighbours*. The next biggest Australian single, **Dave Dobbyn**'s 'Slice Of Heaven', which was also a tie-in to the movie *Footrot Flats*, was no doubt successful for the same reason. It's a fact that it's still teenagers who put records in the charts. The children of the baby boom generation are still buying records as they get older but they're more likely to buy albums, CDs or independents. The teenagers who make hits, reared on high technology, may never go to pubs to see bands but are more likely to go to discos; they may buy nothing but 12" singles (now large department stores like David Jones stock *only* 12" records). Clearly this is an audience with a different set of standards from that which supported the rise of the pub rock tradition.

The propensity of cover versions in the charts—and there were more that didn't make the charts, like **Mental As Anything**'s 'Love Me Tender', **Cattletruck**'s 'Resurrection Shuffle', the **Huxton Creepers**' 'Pretty Flamingo', **X**'s 'Dream Baby' and **Dragon**'s 'Celebrate'—is surely an indication that rock'n'roll is running out of ideas. Just as fast as it's running out of currency.

The omnipresence of rock'n'roll in advertising is sapping its potency. **Jimmy Barnes** and **Michael Hutchence** revived the **Easybeats**' 'Good Times' for Australia-Made; after that, it turned up in the movie *The Lost Boys*, and then in a commercial for Bundaberg Rum. It's hard to take a song seriously after that.

The music of the Australian pub rock tradition in many ways hasn't yet surpassed the basic tenets established in the sixties. Of course, the sixties themselves were revived a few years back, when bands wearing pudding-bowl haircuts and paisley shirts enjoyed a brief moment in vogue, but by now they've been well and truly left behind. Whither, then, the **Stems**, **Ups & Downs**, the **Huxton Creepers**, the **Pony**?

After the sixties revival came, predictably, the seventies revival, which we're still in the throes of now. The various genres have been resurrected and none as slavishly as heavy metal. **Led Zeppelin** sell as many records now as ever, and in 1987 a neo-metal-pop band like **Bon Jovi** was able to tour Australia to rapturous response, not to mention **Zeppelin** clones the **Cult**. Here there is also a whole heap of home-grown neo-metallurgists, like **Mortal Sin** and **Escape**.

Given the safety of distance, it's now also possible to revel in the absolute kitsch of the seventies and so in Sydney, especially, there is a bank of what might be termed art cabaret bands, from **Hot Property** to the **Diddy Dimwits** wearing flares, platform shoes and playing awful songs like 'The Night Chicago Died' and 'Computer Games'. We can only hope this won't soon spawn more cover version hits.

Even New Age/ambient music, which is becoming increasingly popular, could be traced back to the seventies. Early art-rockers from the seventies, from **Tangerine Dream** to **Brian Eno**, initially adapted ambient intentions to a rock audience, and in fact it's very likely the same audience, only older, is into the New Age. Then you get an album like *Walk*, by a solo **Chris Abrahams**, the brilliant keyboardist who's played with the **Benders** and the **Sparklers**, and while it's certainly ambient, it's also a lot more.

A more important rediscovery is the black dance music—hard funk—of the early seventies. If the 'rare groove' evenings that fill clubs with yuppies and teenagers alike could be said to be merely another exercise in nostalgia—although that's unlikely, as this was music that was terribly under-exposed in its time, especially in Australia,—it's still the rare groove imperative that's integral to what is surely the most innovative development in music of late—hip-hop-house.

Of course, it's standard practice in pop, just as the **Rolling Stones** drew from **Muddy Waters**, that white boys discover the ghettoised black music of a previous generation and update it. But the exchange between black and white is more equitable now. This, after all, is a music that was invented by DJs who would scratch-mix together several tracks to make one new one. In the post-modern era, this is the perfect new form. Any source is fair game; so black DJs would scratch together, on top of the groove, metal guitar licks (which are very white of course, **Led Zeppelin** and **AC/DC**), or snippets of, say, **Kraftwerk**.

I'm Talking drew on seventies disco more than anything else, but they eventually broke-up after being unable to break through and to *convince* overseas. Indeed, other Australian practitioners of dance music, like **Flotsam Jetsam**, have suffered from a similar limpness, no doubt due in no small part to their lack of heritage.

Naturally it would be false for Australians—or anyone—to hope to match, say, 'Pump Up The Volume', the epochal house (the latest trend in English and American dance music) hit. The crews of Australian rappers that are beginning to emerge now are obviously awe-struck by their antecedents.

The **Rockmelons** have been heading in the right direction, sticking to their guns, but still they're running on good ideas rather than execution. If the **Rockmelons** are more akin to a 'production team', that is to say songwriters and *executive* producers, then they still need the talent, the personnel to follow it through.

At the other end of the scale, the return in this high-tech age to low-tech roots, to acoustic instrumentation and the classical values of songs, is understandable and may even be a little necessary. But if the return to country music, for example, is only to amount to the reactionary traditionalism of bands like the **Danglin' Brothers**, or the **Slaughtermen**, it's a waste of time (although worse are the campy country cabaret bands, of which there also seems to be a glut at the moment). The **Flying Emus** and **Anne Kirkpatrick**, who are moving from authentic country towards pop/rock are ironically more satisfying because they're unperturbed by notions of purity.

The house revolution is simply an experiment in new ways of making records. If live rock'n'roll is dying out, Australia is still, after all, producing vital music out of that tradition. But music is changing; the audience is changing, already there's an audience that only relates to music through disco sound-systems and on video, and clearly as this audience pushes through it will become more powerful.

Australian music shouldn't be a relic of the past; at the same time, neither should it trade in its heritage.

There's a lesson in every hit record, from **Madonna** to **Crowded House**, **Suzanne Vega** to **InXS**, and the industry in Australia has to be open enough to accept them. Just as it has to be able to see why **Spy V. Spy** wouldn't make it outside Australia.

A good song will always succeed: **Crowded House** could have recorded in a barn and they probably still would have had a hit. Their self-titled debut album was more effective because they put a priority on simply getting the songs across by the best means available, and in doing that, if to a slightly lesser extent than someone like **Suzanne Vega**, they proved it was possible to make a record that had a contemporary immediacy as well as 'warm', 'human' acoustic sounds.

To make *Kick* InXS used whatever techniques were most suitable, and the techniques available now are broad and broadening all the time. In the process they made what is undoubtedly their best record, and for their trouble it climbed to No. 1 in America in early 1988.

There may even be a lesson to be learnt from the **Hard-Ons**. If they are Luddites, then at least these Luddites have found a way to sell themselves all over the world. The lesson to be learnt from **Noiseworks** is the question nobody asked all year: whatever did happen to **Geisha**?

C. W.

AUSTRALIAN FOLK MUSIC

The story of Australian folk music is one of adoption and adaptation. Unlike the music of 'tin-pan alley', which is produced to meet a certain market demand, folk music springs from the community and spreads throughout that community orally, as a by-product of daily life. Of course, it first requires someone to sit down and compose the words and music, but in true folk tradition these become almost incidental. A song becomes its own vehicle, being passed on from one person to another.

Singers have always played a role as storytellers. They are basic to the oral tradition of every society. In Elizabethan England commercial printers actually employed songwriters to sit in the Old Bailey and compose ballads relating the grisly facts of current scandals. Within days these 'broadsides' would be selling on the streets of London, just like newspapers.

The 'broadside ballads', as they became known, sold in staggeringly large numbers. Poor families, unable to afford books, often used them to learn to read and write. The broadsides also served the purpose of warning the population not to get into mischief, otherwise 'you too could end up in Van Diemen's Land'.

In Australia the tradition was continued—there were many broadsides from the early days of colonial transportation, including 'Henry's Downfall', 'The Poacher's Fate' and 'Van Diemen's Land'.

It was, and still is, common for new words to be set to popular old tunes. The British broadside printers nearly always suggested tunes, usually well-known ones, for their new ballads. The ballad banner would proclaim something like: 'A bold new song on the dreadful murder of Maria Marten who was so cruelly murdered behind the red barn in Suffolk County, to be sung to the tune of the Old Oak Tree.' At a time when singing was one of the main forms of social entertainment, it was likely that one in every ten people would have known a tune such as the 'Old Oak Tree'.

Contemporary songwriters in Australia still sometimes use old tunes to carry new words. It is easy to see how the 1970s Sydney green bans song 'Across the Western Suburbs' grew out of the much older sea song 'Across the Western Ocean'. This new song includes the line 'Before we knew it, we were living in Mount Druitt', referring to how inner-city dwellers were being forced to move to far western suburbs. Graffiti watchers may remember that this very same line appeared on several inner-city hoardings.

In many ways all folk songs are political songs. There is not a great deal of difference between a convict writing a song to express his anger at the system, a shearer writing to protest at his working conditions or a contemporary writer protesting at the demolition of inner-city housing. Such songs become traditional when they are passed on orally and are still with us after many years. The green ban songs are remembered orally (they were not written down) and most people singing them do not know who composed them. Any folk song written today, however, would find it harder to enter into the tradition, mainly because of our changing entertainment patterns. In many ways singing has become a thing of the past!.

Perhaps this is why folk songs are as highly considered as they are—they are a part of our history, part of a declining tradition. Even the term 'folk song' is a relatively recent one, originating from German. In the old days songs were songs, and singing was the primary social entertainment,

One of Australia's earliest and best-known traditional songs is 'Moreton Bay' a powerful indictment of the cruel convict system dramatically written in the first person. The song is a litany of complaints, in particular against one Captain Logan, the commander of the Brisbane penal settlement:

*For three long years I was beastly treated,
And heavy irons on my legs I wore,
My back with flogging was lacerated,
And oft-times painted with my crimson gore.
And many a man from down-right starvation
Lies mouldering now underneath the clay:
And Captain Logan he had us mangled
All on the triangles of Moreton Bay.*

The song also describes the downfall of Logan as a warning, as well as presenting an interesting historical picture. There is strong evidence presented by folklorist John Meredith to indicate that the author of the ballad was the convict poet Frank MacNamara, who is also believed to have written 'A Convict's Tour to Hell' and 'The Plains of Emu'.

'Moreton Bay' would have had great appeal among the convict population. Not only did it tell their story, but, as a bonus, the villain of the story gets his just return:

*Like the Egyptians and ancient Hebrews,
We were oppressed under Logan's yoke,
Till a native black lying there in ambush
Did deal this tyrant his mortal stroke.
My fellow prisoners be exhilarated
That all such monsters such a death may find,
And when from bondage we are liberated
Our former sufferings will fade from mind.*

Songs like 'Moreton Bay' and the equally popular 'Bold Jack Donahue' were often regarded by the authorities as 'treason' songs and men caught singing or whistling them risked a severe lashing as punishment. For men whose only comeback at the system was to sing these anti-establishment songs such a threat was, in reality, a challenge. As they were transferred from penal farm to road gang, or from military detention to other colonies, the songs would go with them. It is said that Ned Kelly often sang both 'Moreton Bay' and 'Bold Jack Donahue'.

As Australia moved from penal settlement to the 'Land of Golden Opportunity', so the songs changed. The early songs of the transportation era are dark and full of anger as they relate the harsh life of the convict and the reality of being cast many thousands of miles from homeland and loved ones. But the keynote of the early colonial era, of the songs of the freed-men, ticket-of-leavers and the settlers tended to be one of despair for this huge inhospitable new land. The song 'Immigrant's Lament' seems to sum up the attitude of the majority:

*Illawarra, Mittagong, Parramatta, Wollongong,
If you want to become an orangutan,
Well, go to the bush of Australia!*

After the discovery of gold in the 1850s the image of Australia changed dramatically as would-be fortune hunters rushed to explore the very latest goldfields. They moved across the country, forcing it to 'open up' with their roadways, water services, newspapers and, of course, food and entertainment. The songs from the golden years are many and various. There are the songs of the frustrated gold-diggers, who seemed to complain about nearly everything from the blazing heat to the licence-hunting troopers. The most popular included the song of Irish hopeful, 'Denis O'Reilly', who travelled

'With his swag all on his shoulders and a black billy in his hand', the song 'The Miner', which was sometimes coupled with the American popular ballad 'Don't Go Down the Mine'—even though the majority of our miners were working river gold and didn't go down the mine, and the songs penned by the songwriter and entertainer, Charles Thatcher.

Known across the goldfields of Australia and New Zealand as the 'Colonial Minstrel', Charles Thatcher (1831-82) was a major contributor to our national repertoire of goldrush songs. His songs, among the few by a known writer, slipped easily into the popular tradition, and many are still being sung today. His most popular songs included 'Look Out Below', 'Coming Down the Flat', 'Poll the Grogseller' and 'Where's Your Licence?'

Meanwhile, as the gold-diggers were unearthing the precious metal another class of hopeful Australians was on the lookout for a quick fortune. The bushrangers of Australia hold a special place in our folklore, similar in some ways to England's Robin Hood. It was widely believed that any man who could escape the system and manage to actually survive in the wild Australian bush was brave indeed. If they could manage to 'make a living', all the better! In line with this sympathetic attitude the songs and ballads dealing with the likes of Ben Hall, Frank Gardiner, Ned Kelly and all the other 'Wild Colonial Boys' are full of admiration. Not one song takes the 'boys' to task for robbing public monies. The titles give an indication of the sentiments of songwriters and singers alike: 'Poor Ned Kelly', 'Ned Kelly Was Born in a Ramshackle Hut', and song lines such as the following, from the haunting 'My Name is Edward Kelly', leave absolutely no doubt as to the feelings of the general populace:

> I never would surrender to any coat of blue,
> Or any man that wears the crown belonging to that crew.
> They're game, there's no doubt of it, when they are on their beat,
> But it took ten traps to take Ben Hall, when he was fast asleep.

As the goldrushes declined and rural development took hold, the activities of wheat farming, sheep raising and cattle droving changed the nature of the folk songs. Australia had indeed become the 'new promised land' and for the first time its people started to feel separate from the British. By this time 'Australian-born' was considered desirable and it was a case of colonial versus Sterling. This emerging nationalism can be clearly seen in songs like 'Australia's on the Wallaby':

> *Our fathers came in search of gold,*
> *The claims had proved a duffer;*
> *The syndicates and banks went broke*
> *And so we had to suffer.*
> *They fought for freedom for themselves*
> *Themselves and mates of toil,*
> *Australia's sons are weary and*
> *The billy's on the boil.*
>
> *Chorus*
> *Australia's on the wallaby*
> *Just listen to the cooee;*
> *The kangaroo he rolls his swag*
> *And the emu shoulders bluey.*
> *The boomerangs are whizzing round*
> *The dingo scratches gravel,*
> *The possum, bear and bandicoot*
> *Are all out on their travels.*

From the early 1890s onwards Australia proved itself a money earner, sending mountains of wool back to England. At the same time the working class began to feel that it was they who had been shorn! Trouble was brewing in the shearing sheds and the cattle camps as the workers began to demand better conditions. Bitter battles erupted all over the country and just as the shearers' union was formed the country dipped into the first economic depression it had ever experienced.

Bitter times produce bitter songs and many of them from this period tell of the struggles faced by the working class, in particular the shearers. Certain poems printed in the *Bulletin*, like Banjo Paterson's 'A Bushman's Song', were quickly seized upon by the shearers, who just as quickly put tunes to the words. 'A Bushman's Song', better known as 'Travelling Down the Castlereagh', became a sort of anthem against scab labour:

> I asked a cove for shearing once along the Marthaguy:
> 'We shear non-union here', says he. 'I call it scab', says I.
> I looked along the shearin' floor before I turned to go—
> There were eight or ten non-union men a shearin' in a row.
>
> It was shift, boys, shift, for there wasn't the slightest doubt
> That I had to make a shift with the leprosy about,
> So I saddled up my horses and I whistled up my dog,
> And left his scabby station at the old jig jog.

Andrew Barton Paterson was Australia's first collector of authentic, i.e. anonymous, folk songs and we owe him an immense debt of gratitude. He undoubtedly 'saved' many of the old songs from disappearing by including them in his 'Old Bush Songs' collection, which was published by Angus and Robertson. Paterson, better known as 'The Banjo', was a regular contributor to the *Bulletin* magazine and through its pages he appealed for contributions from the readers. Songs and poems flowed into the *Bulletin*'s office and Paterson selected those he considered to be the most authentic. The *Bulletin* had a large readership and was widely known as the 'bushman's Bible'.

Henry Lawson collected in a different style, taking the old bush yarns and myths and then writing stories, poems and songs that reintroduced the familiar material to his readers. Both Paterson and Lawson wrote in a style that appealed to the average Australian. Here at last were Australians writing about Australia in an Australian style.

The process by which the authentic folk songs collected by Paterson and Lawson would have entered into a community's oral tradition might have worked something like this: Dad and Dave lived in the bush and their nearest neighbours, Mabel and Bert, lived fifty miles away. Every second month Dad and Dave would head off to the nearest town to 'kick up their heels' at the local dance. The woolshed dances were extremely popular and during the course of the evening several people would get a chance to take the floor for a song or poem. The people of yesterdays' Australia were not subjected to the vast amounts of information that the electronic media bring to modern, urbanised Australians. So they tended to really listen to songs and poetry in order to remember them.

After the dance finished Dad and Dave would hop onto the horse-drawn sulky and commence their five-hour ride home. Having no car radio, they might entertain each other by singing—quite probably one of the songs that they had heard during the evening. If they had forgotten the words they would simply improvise—knowing the story and the tune was sufficient. They would also whistle and sing the same song during their work on the farm and by the end of the week, when Mabel and Bert came over for the evening, they would sing their new song. It had changed, but it was basically the same song, and it had already 'passed into the tradition' in the space of a week.

The same process might start again with Bert and Mabel, who would also take the elements of the song with them. And so it went on until the song had indeed 'travelled the bush'. It is a process that helps us understand how one folk song can have variants and, for example, the character in the 'Wild Colonial Boy' can be John Doolin, John Dowling, Jack Dooley or Donahue, depending on the version of the song.

In the process of oral transmission the folk song is personalised by the singer, who might unconsciously twist the tune to suit his or her style. The words of course tend to be changed simply by the transition of time and lapses in memory. As far as the singer is concerned these traditional songs are part of a personal repertoire, something the singer 'owns' and for which he or she has responsibility. It is not uncommon to find singers so emotionally involved with their songs that they cry, laugh or make comments as they sing. Noted Australian traditional singer Sally Sloan always made an emotional plea for Ben Hall's innocence when she performed her ballad of Ben Hall's death. This type of intimate involvement further distinguishes the folk song from the music of 'tin-pan alley'.

The singers are the real personalities of folk songs. It is they who give the songs life. In earlier times we were more inclined to sing and to build a repertoire of 'party pieces'. It is part of our image of past family life—as they shared all the household tasks, like churning the butter, making fat soap, wallpapering the walls with newspaper or simply cleaning up after a meal—all accompanied by singing. Many of the songs would have been songs that Mother and Father brought out from the old country. Others would be the newer songs, the Australian songs.

As the twentieth century unfolded, so the songs changed with the times. We wrote songs about the railways that were snaking across Australia, we wrote songs about the then young mining industry, we wrote songs about the bushlife that was already disappearing as the population drifted towards the cities. We wrote songs about the brash new cities, too.

The music halls played an important role in the dissemination of folk songs. Old songs were once again called upon to lend their tunes for parodies on everything from the Sydney saveloy sellers to the winding tramways of Melbourne. A typical music hall program would include popular sentimental ballads like 'The Luggage Van Ahead' or the equally tragic 'Don't Sell My Mother's Picture in the Sale' through to the latest crop of new songs such as 'Take Me up the Harbour' and 'Melbourne, Marvellous Melbourne'. Black and white ministrel shows were also popular. Many of the Stephen Forster songs gained popularity in the bush, with some, like 'Gentle Annie', becoming Australianised in the process. The true traditional singer does not differentiate between popular and folk songs. A song is a song, be it a music hall ditty, a grand old ballad or a popular sentimental ballad.

Hardship always leads to a more 'frustrated' type of folk song and the songs from Australia's participation in World War I and II are a good example, as are the songs from the Great Depression of the 1930s. It is during these times of trouble that the more decorative songs are abandoned, and the tendency is more towards throwaway ditties and parodies like this one:

I'm spending my nights in the doss-house
I'm spending my days on the street,
I'm looking for work, but I find none.
I wish I had something to eat.

Chorus
Soup, soup, soup, soup,
They gave me a big plate of soup,
Soup, soup, soup, soup,
They gave me a big plate of soup.

I went out to fight for my country,
I went out to blooming well die,
I went out to fight for my country,
And this was my country's reply:

(Chorus)

After World War II Australia found itself part of an ever-changing world where new technologies were being announced daily, especially in the field of communication. This included the popularisation of the wireless, the gramophone and later television. The record industry, which played such a major role in bringing music to world audiences, had already seen the commercialisation of the 'old songs' followed by the promotion of country music, blues, jazz and then rock'n'roll. In many ways the entertainment revolution rang the death knell for the singer of traditional songs. Almost overnight our entertainment patterns changed from being a nation of people that entertained each other to a nation of people who got entertained.

But folk music is not dead. The tradition has merely changed. Contemporary folk songs tend to be written by songwriters or poets and their work distributed by modern means. Take, for example, the works of popular folk poet Eric Bogle, whose songs such as the epic 'And the Band Played Waltzing Matilda' are distributed throughout Australia. Although these contemporary songs are created in the style of folk songs they are not usually passed into the tradition orally for they are learnt from songbooks and sound recordings. We tend to label these songs as contemporary folk songs to distinguish them from traditional folk songs and from standard music industry creations. The most popular contemporary folk composers in Australia are Bernard Bolan, Ted Egan, Judy Small, John Williamson, John Schumann and, of course, Eric Bogle.

The folk songs of Australia, of which there are well over 2000, tend to be 'rough and tumble' creations that reflect the pioneering nature of our history. They are songs that carry the Australian myths of mateship, hard yakka and independence from England. They lack the musical and lyrical embellishments of Irish and British folk music, tending towards straightforward tunes and words that 'call a spade a spade'. This is not to say that the Australian songs lack beauty and musicality. They reflect different cultural experiences, as seen by average Australians. They are an unofficial history of the Australian people.

European culture is relatively young in Australia. We cannot lay claim to ancient myths and legends. We have no direct tradition of dragon-slaying knights, no epic histories of grand battles. However, this did not stop us making stories that celebrated our community behaviour.

For many years folklore scholars tended to compare our folklore with that of Britain and Ireland, but they should have been looking at the folklore of the United States, where the historic backgrounds were similar. Both Australia and the United States saw ancient indigenous peoples invaded by European settlers, who viewed the territories as newly discovered land. Both saw conflict with the native landowners. Both experienced pioneering development, and, finally, both share common frustrations and aspirations. These common elements are even more obvious in our mutual folk song catalogues, where you will find many tall tales, inflated heroes, boasting and comic attitudes.

Human beings everywhere seem to have an in-built need to sing. It is this that will keep folk music alive. Even if the average Australian would be hard pressed to remember all the words of 'Waltzing Matilda' or 'Click Go the Shears', the old songs should not be considered as archive or library items, for they are very much part of a living tradition. As an expression of our cultural creativity, they will survive.

A thriving national network of folk music organisations exists to coordinate the various folk clubs and festivals, and the Australia Council now funds the Australian folk trust, the central body covering research and performance.

W. F.

HISTORY OF THE PACIFIC

PREHISTORY OF POLYNESIA
Polynesia refers to the grouping of islands scattered across a vast triangular area of the eastern Pacific Ocean, bounded by the Hawaiian Islands, New Zealand and Easter Island. It comprises the groups of Samoa, Cook Islands, Tahiti and the other Society Islands, the Marquesas and Tubuai Islands, the Tuamotu Archipelago, the islands of Niue, Tokelau, Tuvalu, Tonga, Wallis and Futuna, the Hawaiian Islands and Pitcairn Island.

The first settlers of Polynesia seem to have arrived in the Tongan islands shortly after 1500 BC, obviously bringing with them seaworthy vessels and a knowledge of navigation. The single outrigger canoe with a dug-out or carvel-built hull has been found almost everywhere in Oceania. It was most highly developed by the Micronesians and featured deep V-section hulls to reduce leeward drift and triangular sails which enabled great manoeuvrability. The standard vessel for Polynesian voyaging, however, was the great double canoe with its equal-sized, symmetrical hulls and towering sterns. These vessels were up to 30 metres in length and had a seating capacity for up to 144 paddlers. In 1774 James Cook witnessed war preparations in the Society Islands involving a fleet of 160 double war canoes together with 170 smaller craft, carrying an estimated total force of 7760 men. The spectacle left Cook deeply impressed.

The question of how the Polynesians transported large numbers of people over huge stretches of ocean has generated more debate than any other aspect of Polynesian history. We know that Polynesia was certainly not settled from afar by successive waves of drifting peoples because the direction of prevailing winds and currents in the area are from east to west apart from intermittent westerlies during summer periods. Shorter drift voyages from Tonga to Fiji, Samoa to Tuvalu, Pitcairn to Mangareva, and from Rapa to the Australs and Southern Cooks are a distinct possibility and in fact have been shown to be feasible by Thor Heyerdahl. At the time of European contact the Society and Tuamotu islanders were in contact with one another, as were the Fijians, the Tongans, and the Samoans. Groups living in New Zealand, Hawaii and Easter Islands apparently were not, which suggests that the Polynesians were not undertaking long exploratory voyages at that time.

Computer simulations have shown that Polynesia cannot be reached from the Americas, unless the voyage was to commence some 500 kilometres offshore, and, therefore, that the settlers of Polynesia could not have come from the east. In fact it is virtually impossible to drift into the Polynesian area from any outside landmass, and it is also impossible to drift along courses which the Polynesians are known to have made, for example from Fiji to Tonga, from Samoa to the Society Islands, and from central Polynesia to Hawaii, Easter Island and New Zealand.

While it will probably never be known how the initial settlement of Polynesia took place, it is clear that as soon as adequate geographical knowledge of the area was gained, two-way voyages between islands became common practice. Such voyages made use of particular seasons of the year for sailing; courses which were aligned with horizon stars, backsights on natural or artificial landmarks; careful observations of wave directions; sunrise and sunset positions; reef positions; homing birds at dusk; cloud formations; and a range of other natural phenomena. The success of such techniques, however, was limited to localised areas and it is doubtful that they could have been effective for voyages from one end of Oceania to the other.

A multiplicity of often confusing and competing theories regarding the origins of the Polynesians has developed over the last two centuries. While the Polynesians themselves must have had oral traditions about their origins, no systematic recording of these was carried out until the mid-nineteenth century. By this time Polynesian geographical knowledge had been so altered by the impact of European contact that the traditions, while retaining much historical validity, could not provide a reliable and incorporative view of Polynesian prehistory. No real progress was made until the advent of archaeological research in the area in the 1950s. It was the unearthing of Lapita sites in both Melanesia and western Polynesia that located the origins of the Polynesian people firmly within eastern Melanesia.

Perhaps the most cryptic puzzle of prehistoric Polynesia is presented by Easter Island, which lies nearly 2000 kilometres from Pitcairn Island, and approximately 4000 kilometres from the South American coast. It has the most dramatic stone monuments and statues in all of Oceania yet by the time of the first European visits its traditional culture had all but disappeared. The once-inhabited Polynesian island of Pitcairn was settled by the Bounty mutineers in 1790.

The prevailing view is that Easter Island was first settled by people from the Marquesas and we know that the settlers cultivated sweet potatoes, yams, taro, bananas, sugar cane and the paper mulberry tree. Heyerdahl has argued that these plants are evidence of contact between Easter Island and South America although their antiquity seems to predate that of human occupation and they could, therefore, have been introduced naturally.

By the time of the first European visit to Easter Island in 1722 there had been serious environmental degradation, and pollen analyses indicate that the island had once been quite heavily forested. On La Perouse's visit to the island in 1786, noteworthy at least for the excellent illustrations and descriptions he recorded, the population was estimated at about 2000. In 1862 1000 islanders were forcibly removed to be sold as slaves in Peru and over 900 of these people died. After an international outcry a remaining fifteen islanders were returned to their home, all with smallpox. By 1877 there were a mere 110 people left on Easter Island who had survived the spread of the disease.

There are some 600 large stone statues on Easter Island, as well as about 150 unfinished works remaining in the quarries located around the rim of the Rano Raraku volcano. Each statue was carved into the rockface and removed only when modelling was almost complete, then they were lowered by ropes to the foot of the slopes below. Each statue was moved to its final location by huge sleds and painstakingly erected with levers and ramps. The largest erect statue is 11.5 metres in height, weighs nearly 100 tonnes and it is estimated to have taken thirty men one year to carve and ninety men three months to erect. Another, unfinished work has been cut into a horizontal rockface and is over 20 metres long, bearing testimony to the incredible strength, determination and skill of the Easter Island craftsmen. Statue carving seems to have started around 1200 AD, abruptly ceasing at approximately 1500, probably due to the lack of timber necessary for construction.

The question of South American contact with Easter Island has achieved prominence largely through the work of Thor Heyerdahl, whose famous expedition attempted to demonstrate the settlement of peoples there from southern Peru and Bolivia. However, the linguistic affiliation of Easter Island with Polynesia, skeletal remains on the island which are all Polynesian, and the fact that all artefacts discovered there are of clear Polynesian type must be taken into account. Furthermore, the coastal cultures of South America best placed strategically for possible colonising expeditions had no discernible maritime traditions. All this is not to suggest that a visit to the island by South American Indians never took place, but that the evidence makes the possibilitiy of a substantial American influence on Easter Island remote.

PREHISTORY OF NEW ZEALAND

New Zealand probably has a more detailed archaeological record than any other area in the Pacific. Archaeologists have estimated that its early Polynesian settlers arrived at some point between 750 and 1000 AD and that at the time of James Cook's first landing in 1769, there was a Maori population in the order of 100,000 to 150,000 people. It is evident that at this time the people had retained the character of their Polynesian ancestry in language and social organisation.

The traditional views about the origin of the Maoris largely revolve around the arrival of ancestors in great canoes and, from genealogical evidence surviving to the nineteenth century, it appears that the main period of settlement was around the fourteenth century. By the end of the nineteenth century European scholars had more or less settled on an interpretation of the Maori traditions, which had it that the discovery of New Zealand was by a man named Kupe or Bgahne and that he was followed by the group of Polynesians led by Toi and Whatonga in about 1125 AD. This group was in turn overrun by the original Maoris who arrived in a fleet of seven or so great canoes in about 1350.

For present-day archaeology, however, the Kupe-Toi fleet sequence of arrivals from beyond New Zealand has little credibility. The contemporary prevailing view is that New Zealand was settled once and that, for the most part, its cultural development was an indigenous process. Its early prehistory is represented by a variety of archaeological remains which are paralleled very closely by artefacts found in the Society Islands and in the Marquesas, all of which date to the centuries around and before 1000 AD. There is little doubt that the first Maoris came from an area bounded by the Marquesas, Society, Cook and Austral Islands.

The early period of settlement was characterised by an economy based on fishing, gathering and the hunting of moas, huge flightless birds that became extinct in the seventh century, as well as some rudimentary horticultural activity. After the thirteenth century it seems the development of the North and South Islands diverged. Those living on the South Island continued fishing and gathering and living in seasonal, undefended camps, while those in the North Island developed fortified settlements capable of sustaining large communities, cultivated the sweet potato or *kumara*, which was of enormous ritual and social significance, as well as developing a highly elaborate material culture.

Perhaps the most intriguing aspect of New Zealand's prehistory is that while it displays economic and cultural changes of a far more dramatic order than elsewhere in Polynesia, there are no signs that these changes were stimulated by contacts with people from the outside world.

PREHISTORY OF MICRONESIA

Micronesia comprises the Mariana, Palauan, Caroline, Marshall and Gilbert Island groups and the island of Nauru, in the south-western Pacific. While the greater part of Micronesia remains archaeologically unexplored, relics of material culture and linguistic evidence show that western Micronesia, comprising the largely volcanic Palauan and Marianas Islands, was settled directly from Indonesia or the Philippines shortly after 1500 BC. It is thought that eastern or Nuclear Micronesia, consisting mostly of atolls, was settled from a region of eastern Melanesia at about the same time.

The Marianas, a chain of fifteen volcanic and raised coral islands, have yielded evidence of a people who made a distinctive pottery called 'Mariana Red'—characteristically thin, red-slipped and plain, and closely related to Philippine wares. Examples of some of the most remarkable stone architecture in Oceania are also to be found here. Parallel rows of upright coral or rock pillars up to 5 metres in height, topped with large bowl-shaped stones, were erected to support structures called *latte*, the name also given to the culture of this period. These formations date from about 900 AD. Each village had one or several *latte* and they would seem to be not unlike the raised pile houses found throughout islands in South-East Asia.

A similar form of stone architecture is found on the island of Yap where archaeological evidence indicates settlement at least 1000 years ago. It is unlikely, however, that the island remained uninhabited until this time. Little has yet been revealed about the origins of settlement in the Palauan group and archaeological interest has focused on its huge terraced hills and large stone anthropomorphic carvings.

Sufficient data for constructing the prehistory of eastern Micronesia has not yet been collected. The ruins of Ponape in the Carolines, however, have fascinated Europeans since they were first reported in 1835. Known as Nan Madol, they comprise some ninety-two platforms up to 8.5 metres in height and constructed from crushed coral and basalt. They cover an area of 70 hectares and once supported temples and royal dwellings for the leaders of the long vanquished Sau Dynasty which rose to prominence several centuries before European contact.

The prehistoric sequence of events for Micronesia has been determined from the archaeology of the Marianas which suggests the arrival of settlers in western Micronesia from the central Philippines approximately 3500 years ago. Historical hypotheses concerning the origins and development of settlement in eastern Micronesia can only be built on the linguistic and cultural evidence which points to contact with eastern Melanesia, particularly Lapita culture, at the same time.

PREHISTORY OF MELANESIA

Melanesia is an ethno-geographic grouping of south-western Pacific Islands incorporating the island of New Guinea, the Admiralty Islands, the Bismarck and Louisade archipelagoes, the Solomon Islands, New Caledonia, the Santa Cruz Islands, Norfolk Island, the Loyalty Islands, Vanuatu, Fiji and several smaller islands. As a geographical entity Melanesia is divided from Polynesia by the Andesite Line of volcanic and seismic activity, by the Equator which lies to the north, and is bounded by Australia to the south.

The major archaeological clues to Melanesia's past are hafted axe-adzes. Some, 26,000 years old, have been found in the Papuan highlands (similar finds of the same antiquity have been discovered in Australia's Arnhem Land). There is then a gap in the archaeological record until stone tools dating to about 15,000 years ago were found in rock shelters in the New Guinea highlands. Axe-adzes, pig bones and marine shells appeared at least 5000 years ago, indicating quite clearly that from 3000 BC the highlands were not isolated from developments taking place in islands such as Timor to the west.

Indications from pollen analyses of forest clearance provide substantial evidence for the existence of cultivation in the highlands from the fourth millenium BC. Although the circumstances surrounding the commencement of agriculture in New Guinea are still matters of speculation, many archaeologists believe that a rudimentary form of cultivation existed there prior to the arrival of Austronesian groups some 5000 years ago. This view is based on evidence of the prior existence of dense populations of Papuan speakers which would have, in all likelihood, prevented the outright Austronesian colonisation of New Guinea.

There is no archaeological information regarding the Austronesian expansion into Melanesia but there is little doubt that this marked the introduction of pottery to the region. The most significant pottery in this respect was that of the Lapita Culture, borne by maritime explorers who rapidly settled throughout Melanesia around 1500 BC. It is now accepted in archaeological circles that the makers of Lapita pottery came from eastern Indonesia or the Philippines.

Examples of Lapita pottery, distinguished by a highly standardised decoration of dentate or toothlike stamping, have been found from northern New Guinea to Samoa, in the Bismarcks, the Solomons, the Santa Cruz islands, Vanuatu, and New

Caledonia; and range in age from 3500 to 2000 years. Evidence suggests that the Lapita potters—sometimes called the vikings of the Pacific—were efficient colonisers as well as competent ocean voyagers, having initiated settlements in Fiji, Tonga and Samoa. The Polynesians, who settled the Tongan islands at around 1300 BC and the Samoan islands at around 1000 BC are regarded as the direct descendents of those who shared the Lapita Culture.

A more recent period of penetration from Indonesia or the Philippines into western Melanesia seems to have taken place from about 1000 years ago. The evidence for this is the sudden appearance of comb-incised pottery which gradually replaced the Lapita-derived wares over a period of about 500 years. However, there is no evidence of any major movements in population associated with the spread of the comb-incising technique.

One of the most significant archaeological discoveries in the Pacific relates to the arrival of a group of matrilineal, high-caste individuals in Vanuatu just prior to the cataclysmic eruption of a nearby volcanic island in about 1400 AD. The people of Efate in central Vanuatu maintain the tradition of the arrival of these people, one of whom, Roy Mata, was buried with his followers who voluntarily sacrificed their lives. Excavations have revealed that over forty people were killed or buried alive in what seems to be Mata's grave, dating to approximately 1265 AD. Three further sites, dating to about 1400 AD have been found on the island of Tongoa and each contains the relics of sacrificial victims.

The prehistory of Melanesia continues to be the subject of painstaking investigation and scholarly debate. The essential division in this prehistory would be the period of the Papuans, who lived in Melanesia for over 30,000 years, and that of the Austronesians, who began entering the area approximately 5000 years ago. Two separate groups of Austronesians appear to be involved: an early group which left no ceramic remains, and a later one which produced Lapita ware.

EUROPEAN EXPLORATION OF THE PACIFIC

Direct European involvement in the Pacific dates from the early sixteenth century when initial exploration was prompted by the desire to open up commercial routes linking Europe with the spice islands of the Far East. The success of the early voyages established a precedent for scientific explorations and stimulated interest in voyages of discovery, particularly that of a great southern continent, Terra Australis.

The Spanish

The first European to see the Pacific Ocean was the Spanish conquistador and explorer Vasco Nunez de Balboa. After settling in Hispaniola (Haiti) in around 1500, Balboa joined an expedition to Uraba in what is now Colombia, and later founded the important settlement of Santa Maria de la Antigua on the isthmus of Panama. Informed by local Indians that a sea and a province infinitely rich in gold lay to the south (a reference probably to the Pacific Ocean and to Inca Peru), Balboa sailed on 1 September 1513 from Santa Maria to Acla, the narrowest part of the isthmus. With some 200 Spaniards and a party of hundreds more Indian carriers he traversed the isthmus and climbed the Cordillera mountain range. On 25 or 27 September 1513, standing 'silent, upon a peak in Darien' (Panama) Balboa saw the Pacific. He later took possession of the Mar del Sur (South Sea) and the adjacent territory in the name of the King of Castile. Balboa met an untimely end when, accused of treason by the jealous Governor of Darien, Pedrarias, he was judicially beheaded in 1519.

The most famous navigator of the Pacific who sailed under the Spanish flag was the Portuguese-born Fernao de Magalhaes, known to the Spanish as Fernando de Magallanes and to the English as Ferdinand Magellan. Having renounced his nationality, the accomplished navigator and explorer offered his services to King Charles I of Spain in 1517. In 1518 Magellan and Rui Faleiro were ordered to lead an expedition to locate a route to the Moluccas by sailing continuously westward, thereby avoiding the Cape of Good Hope which at the time was controlled by the Portuguese. While an attack of insanity stopped Faleiro from sailing, Magellan departed from Salucar de Barrameda on 20 September 1519 on the flagship *Trinidad*, with consorts *San Antonio*, *Concepcion*, *Vittoria* and *Santiago*.

The fleet reached Port St Julian in what is now southern Argentina on 31 March where the Spanish revolted against their Portuguese commander. The mutiny was ruthlessly quelled by Magellan who then continued on to the Cape of Virgins and entered the channel which now bears his name on 21 October. After thirty-eight days of sailing through the treacherous 523 kilometre passage *Trinidad*, *Vittoria* and *Concepcion* emerged into the great 'Sea of the South', subsequently named by Magellan the 'Pacific'. A tortuous voyage followed, the crewmen suffering the ravages of hunger, thirst, and scurvy until, driven by Magellan's determination, the fleet reached Guam in the Marianas on 6 March 1521. Here the sailors ate fresh food for the first time in ninety-nine days. On 9 March Magellan sailed west-south-west to islands now known as the Philippines where he secured the first Pacific treaty for Spain. Shortly afterwards he was killed in a local quarrel and only the 85 ton *Vittoria* managed the return trip to Spain with proof that the earth was round.

Magellan was thus the first navigator to traverse the Pacific Ocean from east to west and in so doing demonstrated that Columbus *had* discovered a New World rather than the route to China; and dispelled the prevailing notion that the 'East Indies' were situated in proximity to the 'West Indies'.

The Spanish traders, once established on the west coast of Central and South America, crossed and recrossed the Pacific to the Philippines, often without landing anywhere in between. Some did, however, attempt to locate the great southern continent.

The Portuguese

The Portuguese were aided in their quests for exploration by an established maritime tradition; rapid developments in technology which permitted the construction of hardy ocean-going vessels; and their geographical location in south-western Europe which enabled them to easily harness the wind and currents of the Atlantic Ocean. After having found the sea route to India, the Portuguese made moves to achieve access to the rest of Asia. Learning much about Asia from Islamic rulers with whom they had established alliances in Africa, Arabia and India, the Portuguese sent expeditions further east until by 1520 they had set up trading posts in the Moluccas, Ambon and Banda Islands.

In 1568 the viceroy of Peru sent Álvaro de Mendaña to explore the commercial possibilities of the Pacific. Mendaña named the islands he discovered to the east of New Guinea the Solomons in reference to the riches he hoped they would yield. However, he found 'no specimens of spices, not of gold and silver, nor of merchandise, nor of any other source of profit, and all the people were naked savages'. Believing the archipelago he had found to be a spur of a greater southern continent, Mendaña sailed once more from Callao (near modern Lima) in April 1595 with Pedro de Quiros. The party reached the Santa Cruz Islands where Mendaña perished and Quiros continued on to Manila. Quiros set out again in 1606, discovering the island he named Austrialia del Espiritu Santo (Vanuatu) where he intended to found the 'New Jerusalem'. His attempts to settle the island failed, however, due to Melanesian hostility. He returned to Acapulco while his second in command, Luis de Torres, sailed to the southern shore of the island of New Guinea and onwards to the Philippines, unaware that the great southern continent lay only to the left of the strait that now bears his name.

The Dutch

From the beginning of the seventeenth century, Pacific exploration was dominated by the Dutch. In 1615 the Dutch entered Melanesia when the navigator Jacques Le Maire reached the Bismarck Archipelago, New Ireland and New Hanover. More significantly, however, in 1602 the governing body of the Dutch Provinces granted the Dutch East India Company a monopoly of the nation's trade in the vast area between the Cape of Good Hope and the Strait of Magellan. By 1615 captains of vessels owned by the Dutch East India Company were steering fixed routes to the spice islands—due east from the Cape of Good Hope for approximately 5,300 kilometres, until they were in the longitude of the Sunda Strait when they turned north to Batavia. In this way it was not long before Dutch captains were striking and charting the Australian coast.

The first was Dirck Hartog who reached the west coast in October 1616 in the *Eendracht*. He was followed by Ciaeszoon van Hillegom in the *Zeewold* in May 1618, Jaconszoon in the *Mauritius* in July 1618, Houtman and Dedel in the *Dordrecht* and *Amsterdam* in 1619 and the captain of the *Leeuwin* in 1622. In 1627 Pieter Nuyts in the *Gulden Zeepard* sailed 1500 kilometres of the southern coastline and in June 1629 the *Batavia* was wrecked on Houtman Abrolhos.

Because these sightings aroused interest in the size and economic potential of the southern landmass, in 1636 Anthonie van Diemen, the governor-general at Batavia, sent two small craft to investigate the northern and north-western coasts. In 1642 he sent Abel Tasman to explore the southern Indian Ocean. Tasman navigated and charted parts of the coasts of New Zealand and Tasmania, sailed north to Tonga and the islands of Fiji, around New Caledonia and back to Batavia. He carried out further explorations of the north coast of Australia from Cape York to North West Cape in 1644.

In 1722 the Dutch explorer Jacob Roggeveen traversed the Pacific from east to west, discovering Easter Island, much of the Tuamotu Archipelago, the northern islands of the Society chain and parts of Samoa.

The British

British exploration of the Pacific which flourished in the 1760s had its origins in 1540 when Roger Barlow argued for the search and discovery of Terra Australis. In 1574 Richard Grenville sought approval from Elizabeth I for 'the discouerie, traffique and enioyenge for the Quenes Majestie and her subiectes of all or anie landes, islandes and countries southewardes beyonde the aequinoctial, or where the Pole Antartik hathe anie elevation about the Horison'.

In 1577 Sir Francis Drake was chosen to lead an expedition to find the entrance of the Strait of Anian, thought to lie south-westwards across America from the vicinity of Hudsons Bay. Sailing on the 100 ton *The Golden Hind* and with four other small ships, Drake reached the Brazilian coast in early 1578. He abandoned two of his supply ships, taking their cargo of provisions on board the remaining three, and on 21 August 1578 entered the Strait of Magellan. After sixteen days he sighted the Pacific but his flagship became separated from the others during a violent storm and he proceeded north along the South American coast alone, plundering Spanish positions along the way. He sailed as far as 48 degrees north unsuccessfully seeking a north-west passage back to the Atlantic and becoming the first European to sight the west coast of what is now Canada.

In July 1579 Drake sailed across the Pacific and after sixty-eight days sighted what was probably the Palauan island group. From there he proceeded to the Philippines and the Moluccas where he concluded a trading treaty with a local Islamic leader. *The Golden Hind*, loaded with bars of gold and silver and Spanish coinage and spices from the Moluccas, arrived back in Plymouth harbour on 26 September 1580. Drake was the first Englishman to traverse the Pacific Ocean and the first captain to sail his ship around the world, Magellan having died before completing his attempt at circumnavigation sixty years earlier.

In 1677 William Dampier recommended searching for a north-west passage from the Pacific and the following year he stated that Terra Australis was most deserving of investigation by the Admiralty. Interest in the area increased in the early decades of the eighteenth century with the formation of the South Sea Company in 1711 and in 1740 George Aston sailed around Cape Horn, attacking Spanish settlements along the west coasts of America.

John Byron, after surveying the Falkland Islands in 1764, proceeded into the Pacific through the Straits of Magellan. His intention was 'to make a NW Course til we get the true Trade wind, and then shape a Course to the Wtward in hopes of falling in with Solomons Islands if there are such, or else to make some new Discovery'. Byron, however, ventured into the ocean too far to the north and sighted no land in the central Pacific, nor did he find the Solomons before sailing home via Batavia.

Spurred on by the Spanish claiming exclusive rights to navigate the Pacific Ocean, Britain hastened its attempts to locate Terra Australis. In 1766 Samuel Wallis in the *Dolphin* and Philip Carteret in the *Swallow* were ordered to sail directly west from the Strait of Magellan and locate the southern continent which was thought to lie between Cape Horn and New Zealand, and to 'take Possession of convenient Situations in the Country' if it was inhabited. If not, they were to take possession 'for his Majesty . . . as first Discoverers and Possessors'.

Wallis and Carteret entered the Strait of Magellan in December 1766, emerging separately some four months later. Forced to sail northwards by prevailing westerly winds, Wallis's course took him through the Tuamotus and on 19 June 1767 the crew of the *Dolphin* were the first Europeans to gaze upon Tahiti. Contrary to his instructions, Wallis claimed Tahiti for the King and ignored his orders to seek the southern continent, setting sail instead for the Ladrones and then England which he reached in May 1768.

Meanwhile, Carteret traversed the Pacific alone, having been abandoned by Wallis in the Strait of Magellan. He discovered Pitcairn Island, rediscovered Santa Cruz and the Solomons but was unable to replenish his supplies because of hostility from the Melanesians. He eventually struggled back to England via New Britain and Mindanao, arriving in May 1769. Also at this time the French navigator Bougainville was completing his own circumnavigation and had found Tahiti, rediscovered Austrialia del Espiritu Santo and the Solomons and sailed around New Guinea.

It was on Wallis's advice that the British Admiralty decided to prepare a voyage to Tahiti for the Royal Society to observe the transit of Venus occurring on 3 June 1769. Lieutenant James Cook was given charge of the 368 ton HMS *Endeavour* to carry out this task and, in addition, was secretly ordered to search for the great southern continent which European philosophers still believed must exist in order to balance the landmasses of the northern hemisphere. Accompanied by the botanist Joseph Banks, Cook set off from Plymouth in August 1768 and arrived in the Pacific in January 1769. After making astronomical observations in Tahiti he sailed south and south-west, circumnavigating and charting both islands of New Zealand. He then traversed the Tasman Sea reaching the hitherto undiscovered east coast of New Holland at Point Hicks on 19 April 1770 where he made his first landfall. On 29 April he arrived at Botany Bay, spending a week collecting botanical specimens and recording his observations of the area before sailing northwards chartering the coast. The ship was grounded on the perilous coral reefs and two months were spent repairing the damage at Endeavour River. Sailing north once more Cook hoisted the British flag on Possession Island on 22 August 1770, and in the knowledge that 'The Eastern Coast from the Latitude of 38 degrees South down to this place . . . was never seen or viseted by any European before us', claimed it was 'New South Wales' for King George III.

The *Endeavour* proceeded to Batavia, where thirty of Cook's men died from fever and dysentery contracted while on land. Until this time, Cook's insistence on appropriate diet and hygiene meant that his crew had suffered none of the debilitating effects which usually afflicted sailors on long ocean voyages in the eighteenth century. Scurvy often appeared among crewmen through a lack of fresh provisions and from the consumption of salt used in preserving meat which quickly depleted the body's store of vitamins. The measures which Cook took in maintaining the health of his sailors subsequently made his name a byword in British naval circles.

The coastline of the southern continent was, by now, substantially charted but it was not until 1799 that the island of Tasmania was circumnavigated by George Bass and Matthew Flinders, and it was 1803 before the southern coastline was completely charted by Flinders.

Cook's second voyage, on the *Resolution*, took place between 1772 and 1775. This expedition travelled beyond latitude 70 degrees south in the waters of the Antarctic, and to Tonga and Easter Island. It also led to the European discovery of Norfolk Island and what is now New Caledonia, Cook naming it after his native Scotland (the ancient name was Caledonia), and proved that there were no great landmasses beyond the ice-free southern hemisphere. A third voyage, again on the *Resolution*, commenced in July 1776 and was an attempt to locate a north-west passage between the Atlantic and Pacific oceans around the North American continent, or a north-east passage around Siberia. Cook's search was unsuccessful but in 1778 he landed on the Hawaiian Islands, naming them the Sandwich Islands after the Earl of Sandwich. This voyage, in fact, did much to define the geography of the northern Pacific. It led, however, to his death on 14 February 1779 at Kealakekua in Hawaii, after a quarrel with Polynesians. The voyages of James Cook largely completed the charting of the Australian continent's perimeters and, with his journeys throughout the Pacific, he probably changed European maps of the world more than any other explorer.

Impact of Pacific Exploration on Europe

The Pacific Ocean was the last great ocean opened to European exploration and this was at a time when knowledge of much of the earth's continental landmasses was scant. The scientific voyages, largely following the precedent of Cook's expeditions, played a crucial role in the development of botany, geology, and meteorology. The English naturalist Charles Darwin sailed through the Pacific on HMS *Beagle* in the first half of the nineteenth century and it was largely from his observations in the Pacific, together with those of another Pacific naturalist, Thomas Henry Huxley, that organic evolution emerged as a scientific explanation for the development of life on earth. The exploration of the Pacific thus had an impact on how Europeans regarded the world of nature as a whole and challenged the neo-classical values which had characterised European cosmological theory for centuries.

M. N.

Sources:

Beaglehole, J. C. *The Exploration of the Pacific*, A. & C. Black, London, 1934.

Bellwood, Peter. *Man's Conquest of the Pacific*. Collins, Sydney, 1978.

Encyclopaedia Britannica. Chicago, 1985.

Frost, Alan, 'Towards Australia: The Coming of the Europeans 1400 to 1788' in D. J. Mulvaney and J. Peter White (eds) *Australia to 1788*. Fairfax, Syme and Weldon Associates, Sydney, 1987.

Goldman, Irving. *Ancient Polynesian Society*. Chicago University Press, Chicago, 1970.

Smith, Bernard. *European Vision and the South Pacific*. Harper and Row, Sydney, 1985.

LANGUAGES OF THE PACIFIC

The languages of the Pacific fall into two main linguistic groupings, the eastern Austronesian or Oceanic group, which is part of the larger Austronesian family extending from Easter Island to Madagascar, and the Papuan group, which comprises languages spoken in most of New Guinea and adjacent parts of Melanesia.

The Oceanic group includes the languages of Melanesia, Polynesia and much of Micronesia. Melanesia contains more than 300 of the total 400 to 500 Oceanic languages, a linguistic diversity which reflects the long-term influence of borrowings from Polynesia as well as the highly localised nature of communication networks in the region. Perhaps the politically most important Melanesian language is Bauan Fijian, differentiated into two major dialects—eastern and western. It is spoken by about 260,000 people and widely used in media and administration in the Fiji island group.

The Polynesian languages are comparatively homogeneous and readily form their own subgroup within the Oceanic branch of the Austronesian family. These languages are spoken within the region bounded by Hawaii, Easter Island and New Zealand. The major languages are Samoan, spoken by about 200,000 people in Western and American Samoa and in the large migrant communities of New Zealand and the United States; Tongan, with about 100,000 speakers; and Tahitian, Maori and Hawaiian.

In Micronesia another subgroup, Nuclear Micronesian, comprises the languages spoken on the Marshall Islands, Gilbert Islands, Hall Islands, Truk, Mortlock Islands, Ponape, Ngatik, Pingelap, Yap, Nauru, Kosrae Island and the Carolines. Of these there are approximately 160,000 speakers in all. Palauan and Chamorro are two Western Austronesian languages, connected remotely with the Philippines and north-eastern Indonesia, spoken by about 80,000 people in western Micronesia. On the tiny atolls south of Truk and Ponape some 2000 people speak the Polynesian Nukuoro and Kapingamarangi languages.

The Papuan languages are spoken by approximately 2.7 million people in an area of western Melanesia centred on the island of New Guinea. Examples are found also in Timor, Halmahera, Alor and Pantar to the west, and in New Britain, New Ireland, Bougainville, the Louisade Archipelago and the Solomon Islands to the east. Each of the languages in this group is spoken by only a few hundred to a few thousand people, although Enga, which is numerically the largest, has more than 150,000 speakers in the Enga Province of Papua New Guinea. Oceanic languages are also found in New Guinea but these are generally restricted to districts along the northern and south-eastern coastal areas and on neighbouring islands.

Languages of the Pacific region which are not part of the Oceanic or Papuan groups are those of Aboriginal Australia, of which there are some 260 spanning the continent, and Tasmania. It is believed at present that ancestral Aboriginal languages were introduced by peoples probably arriving via New Guinea at least 50,000 years ago.

While the Indianised kingdoms of Austronesian South-East Asia were literate from about 500 AD, pre-European systems of writing have not been recorded from anywhere within the adjacent region of Oceania, unless it can one day be proved that the enigmatic script of Easter Island predated the arrival of the Dutch navigator Jacob Roggeveen in 1722. However, the languages of the Pacific incorporate vast and richly detailed oral traditions which flourished throughout the enormous depth of Pacific prehistory. Linguists believe that the Oceanic languages of Melanesia, Polynesia and Nuclear Micronesia are descended from a single major proto-form language; however, the people who speak these languages today clearly do not share a single physical ancestry.

M. N.

THE AUSTRALIAN ANTARCTIC PROGRAM

Antarctica has a special place in world history. It is the only piece of land on earth where disputation over national sovereignty has taken a back seat behind international cooperation. An international treaty between nations involved with Antarctica has demonstrated what is possible if countries agree to work together.

Antarctica has been called a continent for science, and the extent of cooperative effort between countries working there is quite remarkable — even when the countries concerned are elsewhere at loggerheads. Military activity is banned on the continent (although the military is often employed there for peaceful purposes). Nations have agreed that Antarctica should be used only for peaceful purposes, and that scientific research has a prominent place in activity there.

For over fifty years Australia has laid claim to 42 per cent of Antarctica. Other countries — Argentina, Britain, Chile, France, New Zealand and Norway — also lay claim to slices of the continent.

Yet since 1959, when the Antarctic Treaty was signed, all these countries have agreed to set aside any disputation over territorial claims and work with others which do not recognise their sovereignty, most notably the United States and the Soviet Union.

A PART OF OUR HISTORY

Antarctica is very much a part of the Australian heritage. The historical associations of the two continents go back to Australia's own early history — to James Cook's great southern voyage of 172-75.

Cook's was the first of many pioneering Southern Ocean journeys in search of knowledge or wealth, a lot of which were out of Australian ports. Most of the early Antarctic explorers sought to exploit the region's vast animal resources and were mainly after oil from whales and seals. However, for a number of expeditions around the turn of the twentieth century, scientific endeavour was a primary motive.

The real success of the Australasian expedition to the Antarctic coast south of Australia in 1911 was that it established that Australia could make a valuable contribution to international Antarctic science. Adelaide geologist Douglas Mawson planned and led the Australian Antarctic Expedition (AAE), and his successes spurred on a combined British, Australian and New Zealand expedition under his leadership in the late 1920s. During this journey along the Indian Ocean sector of the Antarctic coast Mawson laid claim for his country to the parts of Antarctica mapped and explored, and to the ice-covered land beyond to the South Pole. His claims were formalised in 1936 with the establishment in Australian law of the vast Australian Antarctic Territory.

Since World War II Australia has played a major role in the exploration and study of Antarctica. Inspired by Mawson's achievements, Australian scientific expeditions quickly won international recognition for their contributions to knowledge of the Antarctic region. In 1947-48 the first of the Australian National Antarctic Research Expeditions (ANARE) set up research stations on Heard and Macquarie Islands. The latter remains Australia's oldest permanently occupied Antarctic station.

In 1948 the Antarctic Division of the Department of External Affairs was established under the leadership of Phillip Law, a Melbourne physicist. In the remarkably short time of a decade Australia was to confirm its position as a leader in Antarctic science.

Within six years Australia became the first country to establish a permanent continental station south of the Antarctic Circle. Mawson was built on an isolated rock outcrop next to a beautiful natural harbour, in a remote part of East Antarctica south-west of Australia. Three years later Davis, in the Vestfold Hills 630 kilometres to the east, became Australia's second and southernmost continental station.

By the end of the decade Australia had acquired a third Antarctic station when the United States handed over its Wilkes Base, nearly 1400 kilometres further east. In 1969 encroaching snow forced the closure of Wilkes, and a new station, Casey, was established a short distance away.

IN THE NATIONAL INTEREST

Since World War II, Australia has pursued a continuous scientific program. Through its Antarctic science, Australia seeks to secure the knowledge needed to effectively manage Antarctica's resources, to protect the nation's long-term economic and strategic interests and to increase its international credibility and influence in Antarctic matters.

In support of these objectives it sends about 400 expeditioners each year to Antarctic and subantarctic stations. In recent years the shipping program has involved a total of eight voyages annually by two vessels.

By 1989 Australia will have an Australian-built icebreaking research ship purpose-designed to serve the needs of Antarctic science. In particular, the ship will put Australia in a better position than ever before to meet its international marine science obligations.

Australia's year-round scientific program today is centred on the four permanent stations at Mawson, Davis, Casey and Macquarie Island, staffed over winter by about 120 people. Over the short summer season the number of Australians visiting Antarctica is around 500. Summer programs are operated from both the permanent stations and smaller bases elsewhere, including Cape Denison (Commonwealth Bay Base), Bunger Hills (Edgeworth David Base), Larsemann Hills (Law Base), Scullin Monolith and subantarctic Heard Island.

THE CURRENCY OF CREDIBILITY

Science has been called 'the currency of credibility' in the international administration of Antarctica. The Antarctic Treaty gives science a uniquely important function and to become a consultative party under the treaty, a nation must establish a significant science program.

A major role for science in Antarctica has obvious benefits to the world. It remains the least known, least explored of all earth's landmasses and science not only brings knowledge of Antarctica, but a greater understanding of the dynamics and ecosystems of the whole world.

In giving science a prominent role in Antarctic exploration, Australia's Antarctic pioneers helped to put their country in a position of great influence when, in the late 1950s, the idea of establishing an international Antarctic treaty was first discussed. Australia was one of twelve original signatories to the Antarctic Treaty, which today is attracting the attention of a growing number of nations. Twenty-five countries have joined the treaty system since the original signing, and there is a strong interest among many more countries in having a stake in the continent's future.

Australia has kept its place in the Antarctic Treaty system with a scientific program covering a wide range of disciplines. In the 1980s it has maintained a program incorporating studies of the upper atmosphere and outer space, the movement and structure of the ice sheet and the unique life forms of the continent and its surrounding oceans.

A GROWING ANTARCTIC COMMITMENT

Scientific work in the early years of ANARE concentrated on physical sciences—meteorology, glaciology, geology and physics. The permanent laboratories and observation stations which Australia established in Antarctica during this time placed it in the forefront of Antarctic physical science.

One area of research to which Australia has made a big contribution is meteorology. Our knowledge of weather patterns in our region and throughout the southern hemisphere has increased enormously because of meteorological research over forty years in Antarctica and the Southern Ocean.

Today, Australia's Antarctic-based research into the atmosphere and beyond has international significance. Its cosmic ray physics facilities at Mawson are an important part of a world observation network—the only underground observatory in the southern hemisphere. Upper atmosphere studies have helped us understand more fully the interaction between the upper and lower atmospheres and its influence on weather patterns.

Australian studies over many years of Antarctica's vast ice sheet have proved of similar importance. Extensive ice sheet traverses involving deep drilling and seismic surveying have established patterns of growth and contraction in the ice sheet over millions of years, greatly improving our understanding of global climatic changes.

In the 1980s biology has become one of the key elements in national Antarctic science programs. Australia hosts the permanent secretariat of the Commission for the Conservation of Antarctic Marine Living Resources, and now plays a major part in continuing international research to investigate the ecology and abundance of Antarctic marine life with the aim of properly conserving this all-important resource for the future.

Source: Australian Antarctic Division.

CRUX AUSTRALIS
THE SOUTHERN CROSS

The Southern Cross is the smallest constellation in the entire sky, but probably the best-known to Australians. The five brightest stars in the constellation join the Federation Star and the Union Flag to form the Australian flag and the second verse of the national anthem begins 'Beneath the radiant Southern Cross . . .'. The four brightest stars appear on the New Zealand flag, again accompanied by the Union Flag. The five brightest were used on early postage stamps of Brazil, surrounded by a ring of stars representing the states. An engraved map of South America, made in 1508, gave the name for the continent 'Terra Sancte Crucis'. The Southern Cross has appeared on other postage stamps, sometimes as a background, as in an issue to mark the hundredth anniversary of the Royal Society of New Zealand and sometimes as the subject of a design, as in the 'Night Sky' issue of Botswana.

Ptolemy (c. 120–180) included the Cross in his constellation Centaurus and its designation as a separate constellation is usually attributed to Royer, writing in 1679. There are, however, many earlier references. In 1516 the navigator Corsali wrote: '*Above these [the Magellanic Clouds] appeareth a marvelyous crosse in the myddest of fyve notable starres which compasse it abowt (as doth Charles Wayne the northe pole) with other starres whiche move with them abowt .xxx. degrees distant from the pole, and make their course in .xxiiii. houres. This crosse is so fayre and beutiful, that none other hevenly sygne may be compared to it as may appear by this fygure.*'

Pigafetta, who travelled with Magellan, noted it as 'El Crucero' in 1520, and other explorers and navigators used similar names. Mollineux, in England, included the 'Cross of the South' in his celestial globe in 1592.

It was also referred to as the 'Southern Celestial Clock'; in the words of von Humboldt: '*The two great stars, which mark the summit and the foot of the Cross, having nearly the same right ascension, it follows that the constellation is almost perpendicular at the moment when it passes the meridian. This circumstance is known to the people of every nation situated beyond the Tropics or in the southern hemisphere.*

'*It has been observed at what hour of the night, in different seasons, the Cross is erect or inclined.*

'*It is a time piece, which advances very regularly nearly four minutes a day, and no other group of stars affords to the naked eye an observation of time so easily made.*'

The sketch shows the principal features of the constellation. The brightest star, α, is magnitude 0.83 and bluish-white in colour. Its name, Acrux, was probably invented by Burritt (showing little imagination!). In 1685 α Cru was found to be a double star and a third component of the system was discovered later. The two brighter components are 5″ apart and the third is 60″ distant.

Next in brightness at magnitude 1.28 is β Cru, also bluish-white, and having the charming but seldom-used name Mimosa. The third, γ, is a red giant of magnitude 1.69 and the difference in colour between this and the two brighter stars is easily seen. The points of the Cross are completed by δ Cru, another blue star of magnitude 2.8; ε Cru is magnitude 3.6 and yellowish in colour.

The well-known open cluster NGC 4755 surrounds the 6th magnitude reddish star κ Cru. The many stars of various colours led to the popular name for this cluster 'The Jewel Box'.

Another feature in Crux is the Coal Sack, a dark nebula. This is an example of a non-luminous cloud of dust-like material, which is probably similar to the interstellar dust but more dense. Dark nebulae are not totally opaque and some stars can be seen through them.

According to Maegraith, Aborigines of the Aranda and Luritja tribes join γ and δ Crucis with γ and δ Centauri to form a constellation Iritjinga, the Eagle-

Hawk, while α and β Cru are seen as the Luritja parents of a boy represented by α Cen, one of our 'Pointers'.

The following legend of the Southern Cross was collected by Ethel Hassell at Jarramungup, Western Australia, in the 1880s and is quoted in her book *My Dusky Friends* : 'A long, long, time ago, there was no cross in the sky. The stars all clustered together like in the milky way, and there were wide open spaces between. Sometimes one cluster of stars visit one another, but now and then they get lost and we can see them falling to the earth; other times they take a long time to get back to their own country, and if we watch the heavens carefully we can see them travelling to and fro, but the Southern Cross is different to all other stars, they never travel, because they are women. These women belong to a tribe that lived near the sea, where the earth and the water touch the sky. The tribe had been travelling a long distance, and at dusk had to camp at a place where the wood and the water were some distance apart. After a little discussion it was decided to build the mias nearer to the wood than to the water, this was accordingly done, after supper they all went down to the water and had a drink, and then came back to the camp but the little children were too tired to go to the water hole, so several of the girls were given big pieces of bark, and told to get some water, and bring it back to the camp for the children. These girls instead of coming straight back, began to play. They ran about, and scooping it up with their pieces of bark splashing themselves with the water, and wasted it. As they were away such a long time, and the night was getting dark, the men got anxious and went to look for them. When they found them playing, they were so angry that they took out their hunting spears and gave them each a prod in the calves of their legs. The girls held the pieces of bark down over their legs to protect themselves, and ran as fast as they could, the men following them with their spears. As they ran a big wind sprang up, and blew them up into the sky. The men threw their spears up after them, and they scattered out to avoid them, that is why they are not clustered up like other stars. They stayed up there because they were afraid if they came down, the men would be so angry with them for running away that they would kill them, and they are a lesson to other girls not to play on the way, for as they are so far apart from each other, they can never find a man, and they therefore can never be married.'

Source: Hassell, Ethel. *My Dusky Friends*. C. W. Hassell, Perth, 1975.

THE SOLAR SYSTEM—PLANETS

(with the Sun for comparison)

Name	Mean Distance from Sun Millions of km	Astronomical Units	Mass (Earth=1)	kg	Equatorial radius km	(Earth=1)	Sidereal period Tropical years
Mercury	57.9	0.387	0.056	3.35×10^{23}	2,439	0.382	0.24085
Venus	108.2	0.723	0.815	4.870×10^{24}	6,050	0.949	0.61521
Earth	149.6	1.000	1.000	5.976×10^{24}	6,378	1.000	1.00004
Mars	227.9	1.524	0.107	6.40×10^{23}	3,398	0.532	1.88089
Minor Planets - see below							
Jupiter	778.3	5.203	317.89	1.90×10^{27}	71,900	11.27	11.86223
Saturn	1,427.	9.539	95.15	5.69×10^{26}	60,000	9.44	29.4577
Uranus	2,870.	19.18	14.54	8.69×10^{25}	25,400	4.10	84.0139
Neptune	4,497.	30.06	17.23	1.03×10^{26}	24,750	3.88	164.793
Pluto	5,900.	39.44	(0.002)	(1.20×10^{22})	(1,500)	(0.24)	247.7
Sun	-	-	332,946.	1.99×10^{30}	696,000	109.	-

There may be 40,000 or more minor planets, or asteroids, mostly in the gap between Mars and Jupiter. Many of them are just small, irregular lumps of rock, so the 'radius' is almost meaningless. Masses are very uncertain. The eight largest minor planets are given below.

Vesta	353.	2.36	2.4×10^{20}	270	0.04	3.630
Ceres	410.	2.74	1.17×10^{21}	500	0.08	4.061
Pallas	413.	2.76	2.6×10^{20}	305	0.05	4.607
Interamnia	458.	3.06		175	0.03	5.345
Hygeia	471.	3.15	6.0×10^{19}	225	0.04	5.593
Euphrosyne	471.	3.15		185	0.03	5.606
Davida	477.	3.19	3.09×10^{19}	162	0.03	5.700
Cybele	512.	3.42		155	0.02	6.333

THE SOLAR SYSTEM—
THE SATELLITES

(in order of distance from primary)

No. Name	Mean distance from primary Thousands of km	Mean radius km	Mass (Primary=1)	Mass (Moon=1)
Mercury - none				
Venus - none				
Earth				
1 Moon	384.390	1,738	0.0123	1.000
Mars				
1 Phobos	9.38	24		
2 Deimos	23.50	13		
Jupiter				
Rings				
1 Metis	128.2	(20)		
2 Adrastea	128.5	(15)		
3 Amalthea	181.3	120		
4 Thebe	223.0	(40)		
5 Io	421.6	1,830	4.696×10^{-5}	1.213
6 Europa	670.9	1,525	2.565×10^{-5}	0.663
7 Ganymede	1,070.0	2,635	7.845×10^{-5}	2.027
8 Callisto	1,883.0	2,500	5.603×10^{-5}	1.448
9 Leda	11,110.	4		
10 Himalia	11,470.	85		
11 Lysithea	11,710.	10		
12 Elara	11,743.	40		
13 Ananke	20,700.	8		
14 Carme	22,350.	12		
15 Pasiphae	23,300.	13		
16 Sinope	23,700.	10		
Saturn				
Rings	12.6–76.45			
1 Atlas				
2 Prometheus				
3 Pandora				
4 Janus	169.0	150		
5 Epimetheus				

No. Name	Mean distance from primary Thousands of km	Mean radius km	Mass (Primary=1)	Mass (Moon=1)
6 Mimas	186.0	200	6.6×10^{-8}	0.00051
7 Enceladus	238.0	275	1.5×10^{-7}	0.001
8 Tethys	295.0	600	1.10×10^{-6}	0.0085
9 Telesto				
10 Calypso				
11 Dione	378.00	575	2.04×10^{-6}	0.0158
12 Dione B				
13 Rhea	528.0	725	$(3. \times 10^{-6})$	(0.025)
14 Titan	1,223.	2,900	2.46×10^{-4}	1.905
15 Hyperion	1,484.	150	$(2. \times 10^{-7})$	(0.0015)
16 Iapetus	3,562.	900	$(4. \times 10^{-6})$	(0.02)
17 Phoebe	12,960.	100		
Uranus Rings				
1 1986U7				
2 1986U8				
3 1986U9				
4 1986U3				
5 1986U6				
7 1986U2				
8 1986U4				
9 1986U5				
10 1985U1				
11 Miranda	130.0	120	$1. \times 10^{-6}$	0.001
12 Ariel	192.0	350	1.5×10^{-5}	0.018
13 Umbriel	267.0	250	$6. \times 10^{-6}$	0.007
14 Titania	438.0	500	5.0×10^{-5}	0.059
15 Oberon	586.0	450	2.9×10^{-5}	0.034
Neptune 1 Triton	355.0	1,900	1.3×10^{-3}	1.8
2 Nereid	5,562.	120		
Pluto 1 Charon	19.70	(750)	2.5×10^{-3}	.021

THE CONSTELLATIONS

Name	Abbreviation	Meaning	Area, square degrees	Right Ascension h m	Furthest extent h m	Declination o '	o '
						(to nearest minute)	
Andromeda	And	Andromeda (daughter of Cepheus)	272	22 49	02 31	+52 30	+21 00
Antlia	Ant	The Airpump	239	09 22	11 00	−24 00	−39 45
Apus	Aps	The Bird of Paradise	206	13 40	18 00	−67 30	−82 30
Aquarius	Aqr	The Water Bearer	980	20 32	23 50	+02 45	−25 30
Aquila	Aql	The Eagle	652	18 35	20 32	+19 30	−12 02
Ara	Ara	The Altar	237	16 25	18 00	−45 30	−67 30
Aries	Ari	The Ram	441	01 40	03 22	+30 40	+09 55
Auriga	Aur	The Charioteer	657	04 30	07 22	+56 00	+28 30
Bootes	Boo	The Ox-driver	907	13 30	15 45	+55 30	+08 00
Caelum	Cae	The Burin (or Graving Tool)	125	04 16	05 00	−27 15	−49 00
Camelopardus	Cam	The Giraffe	757	03 06	14 30	+86 30	+52 30
Cancer	Cnc	The Crab	506	07 48	09 15	+33 30	+07 00
Canes Venatici	CVn	The Hunting Dogs	465	12 00	14 02	+53 00	+28 30
Canis Major	CMa	The Great Dog	380	06 07	07 22	−11 00	−33 00
Canis Minor	CMi	The Little Dog	183	07 01	08 05	+13 30	00 00

Capricornus	Cap	The Sea-goat	414	20 00	21 52	-09 00	-28 00
Carina	Car	The Keel	494	06 16	11 05	-50 45	-75 00
Cassiopeia	Cas	Cassiopeia (mother of Andromeda)	598	22 52	03 25	+77 00	+46 00
Centaurus	Cen	The Centaur	1,060	11 00	14 55	-29 30	-64 00
Cepheus	Cep	Cepheus (King of Ethiopia)	588	20 32	08 00	+88 00	+52 45
Cetus	Cet	The Sea-monster (or Whale)	1,232	23 50	03 17	+09 55	-25 30
Chamaeleon	Cha	The Chamaeleon	132	07 40	13 40	-75 00	-82 30
Circinus	Cir	The Pair of Compasses	93	13 30	15 20	-55 00	-70 00
Columba	Col	The Dove	270	05 00	06 35	-27 15	-43 00
Coma Berenices	Com	Berenice's Hair	386	11 52	13 30	+34 00	+14 00
Corona Australis	CrA	The Southern Crown	128	17 50	19 10	-37 00	-45 30
Corona Borealis	CrB	The Northern Crown	179	15 11	16 20	+40 00	+26 00
Corvus	Crv	The Crow (or Raven)	184	11 50	12 50	-11 00	-24 30
Crater	Crt	The Cup	282	10 45	11 50	-06 00	-24 30
Crux Australis	Cru	The Southern Cross	68	11 50	12 50	-55 00	-64 00
Cygnus	Cyg	The Swan	804	19 05	21 58	+59 30	+29 00
Delphinus	Del	The Dolphin	189	20 08	21 03	+20 30	+02 00
Dorado	Dor	The Swordfish	179	03 50	06 35	-49 00	-70 00
Draco	Dra	The Dragon	1,083	09 01	20 36	+86 00	+47 30
Equuleus	Equ	The Foal	72	20 52	21 20	+12 30	+02 00
Eridanus	Eri	The River	1,138	01 20	05 05	00 00	-58 30

Name	Abbreviation	Meaning	Area, square degrees	Right Ascension h m h m	Furthest extent Declination o' o' (to nearest minute)
Fornax	For	The Furnace	398	01 40 03 45	-24 23 -40 00
Gemini	Gem	The Twins	514	05 53 08 00	+35 30 +12 00
Grus	Gru	The Crane	366	21 20 23 20	-37 00 -57 00
Hercules	Her	Hercules (the Hero)	1,225	15 45 18 52	+51 30 +04 00
Horologium	Hor	The Clock	249	02 10 04 16	-40 00 -67 30
Hydra	Hya	The Water Serpent	1,303	09 35 14 55	+07 00 -35 00
Hydrus	Hyi	The Water Snake	243	23 50 04 35	-58 30 -82 30
Indus	Ind	The Indian	294	20 20 23 20	-45 30 -75 00
Lacerta	Lac	The Lizard	201	21 54 22 52	+56 15 +35 00
Leo	Leo	The Lion	947	09 15 11 52	+33 30 -06 00
Leo Minor	LMi	The Little Lion	232	09 15 11 00	+42 00 +23 30
Lepus	Lep	The Hare	290	04 50 06 07	-11 00 -27 15
Libra	Lib	The Balance (or Scales)	538	14 15 15 55	00 00 -29 30
Lupus	Lup	The Wolf	334	14 10 16 00	-29 30 -55 00
Lynx	Lyn	The Lynx	545	06 06 09 35	+60 00 +33 30
Lyra	Lyr	The Lyre	286	18 10 19 24	+47 30 +25 30
Mensa	Men	The Table	153	03 30 07 40	-70 00 -85 00

Microscopium	Mic	The Microscope	210	20 20	21 20	-28 00	-45 30
Monoceros	Mon	The Unicorn	482	05 50	08 05	+12 00	-11 00
Musca	Mus	The Fly	138	11 05	13 40	-64 00	-75 00
Norma	Nor	The Level	165	15 20	16 26	-42 00	-60 00
Octans	Oct	The Octant	291	Circumpolar		-75 00	-90 00
Ophiuchus	Oph	Ophiuchus, the Serpent-bearer	948	15 55	18 40	+14 20	-30 00
Orion	Ori	Orion, the Hunter	594	04 37	06 18	+22 50	-11 00
Pavo	Pav	The Peacock	378	17 30	21 20	-57 00	-75 00
Pegasus	Peg	The Winged Horse	1,121	21 03	00 08	+36 00	+01 45
Perseus	Per	Perseus (son of Zeus)	615	01 22	04 42	+58 30	+30 40
Phoenix	Phe	the Phoenix	469	23 20	02 20	-40 00	-58 30
Pictor	Pic	The Painter's Easel	247	04 30	06 50	-43 00	-64 00
Pisces	Psc	The Fishes	889	22 45	02 00	+33 00	-07 00
Piscis Australis	PsA	The Southern Fish	245	21 20	23 00	-25 30	-37 00
Puppis	Pup	The Poop	673	06 00	08 22	-11 00	-50 45
Pyxis	Pyx	The Mariner's Compass	221	08 22	09 22	-17 00	-36 45
Reticulum	Ret	The Net	114	03 17	04 35	-53 45	-67 30
Sagitta	Sge	The Arrow	80	18 52	20 15	+21 15	+15 45
Sagittarius	Sgr	The Archer	867	17 36	20 20	-12 02	-45 30
Scorpius	Sco	The Scorpion	497	15 40	17 50	-08 00	-30 00
Sculptor	Scl	The Sculptor's Workshop	475	23 00	01 40	-25 30	-40 00

Name	Abbreviation	Meaning	Area, square degrees	Right Ascension h m	Furthest extent h m	Declination o ' (to nearest minute) o '
Scutum	Sct	The Shield	109	18 15	18 52	-04 00 -16 00
Serpens (Caput) (Cauda)	Ser	The Serpent (Head) (Tail)	637	15 05 17 10	16 05 18 52	+26 00 -03 15 +06 15 -16 00
Sextans	Sex	The Sextant	314	09 35	10 45	+07 00 -11 00
Taurus	Tau	The Bull	797	03 17	05 53	+30 40 -01 45
Telescopium	Tel	The Telescope	252	18 00	20 20	-45 30 -57 00
Triangulum	Tri	The Triangle	132	01 24	02 43	+36 45 +25 00
Triangulum Australe	TrA	The Southern Triangle	110	14 45	17 00	-60 00 -70 00
Tucana	Tuc	The Toucan	295	22 00	01 20	-57 00 -76 00
Ursa Major	UMa	The Great Bear	1,280	07 58	14 25	+73 30 +29 00
Ursa Minor	UMi	The Little Bear	256	Circumpolar		+90 00 +66 00
Vela	Vel	The Sails	500	08 00	11 00	-36 45 -56 30
Virgo	Vir	The Virgin	1,294	11 31	15 05	+15 00 -22 00
Volans	Vol	The Flying Fish	141	06 35	09 02	-64 00 -75 00
Vulpecula	Vul	The Fox	268	18 52	21 20	+29 00 +19 10

Notes:
1. The constellation boundaries are for the equinox 1875 and are taken from Delporte ('Delimitation Scientifique des Constellations', 1930). It should be noted that the constellation areas are irregular; the figures given here are the outer limits, west, east, north and south, but the area is that within the actual constellation boundaries.
2. Serpens is one constellation in two completely separate areas, known as Caput, the Head, and Cauda, the Tail. Limits are given for each area, but one area only is given which includes both parts.
3. When quoting constellation designations for stars in full, the genitive of the constellation name is used; e.g. the brightest star in the constellation Gemini is α Geminorum, i.e., 'α of the Twins'. Any elementary Latin grammar will give the correct genitive.

STARS OF MAGNITUDE 2.5 OR BRIGHTER

* indicates visible from most or all of Australia

	Const. name		Name	Visual magnitude	Right Ascension (2000) h m	Declination ° ′	Spectral type	Approx. distance Light yrs
	α	And	Alpheratz	2.02	00 08.4	+29 05	B9P	90
	β	Cas	Chaph	2.25	00 09.2	+59 05	F2	45
*	α	Phe	Ankaa	2.39	00 26.3	−42 18	K0	93
	α	Cas	Shadar	2.24	00 40.5	+56 32	K0	150
*	β	Cet	Deneb Kaitos; Diphda	2.04	00 43.6	−17 59	K1	57
	β	And	Mirach	2.03	01 09.7	+35 37	M0	76
*	α	Eri	Achernar	0.47	01 37.7	−57 15	B5	118
	γ¹	And	Almaak	2.28	02 03.9	+42 20	K3	260
*	α	Ari	Hamal	2.00	02 07.2	+23 27	K2	76
*#	ο	Cet	Mira	1.7max	02 19.3	−02 59	M6	103
	α	UMi	Polaris	2.0v	02 31.2	+89 15	F8	680
	α	Per	Mirfak	1.79	03 24.3	+49 51	F5	570
*	α	Tau	Aldebaran	0.86	04 35.9	+16 30	K5	68
*	β	Ori	Rigel	0.08	05 14.5	−08 12	B8	900
	α	Aur	Capella	0.09	05 16.7	+46 00	G8+F	45

*	γ	Ori	Bellatrix	1.64	05 25.1	+06 21	B2	470
	β	Tau	Al Nath	1.65	05 26.3	+28 36	B7	300
*	δ	Ori	Mintaka	2.20	05 32.0	-00 18	O9.5	1,500
*	ε	Ori	Alnilam	1.70	05 36.2	-01 12	B0	1,600
*	ζ	Ori	Alnitak	2.05	05 40.8	-01 57	O9.5	1,600
*	κ	Ori	Saiph	2.04	05 47.8	-09 40	B0.5	2,100
*	α	Ori	Betelgeuse	0.80	05 55.2	+07 24	M2	520
	β	Aur	Menkalina	1.90	05 59.5	+44 57	A2	88
*	β	CMa	Murzim	1.98	06 22.7	-17 57	B1	750
*	α	Car	Canopus	-0.73	06 23.9	-52 41	F0	650
	γ	Gem	Alhena	1.93	06 37.7	+16 24	A0	105
*	α	CMa	Sirius	-1.47	06 45.1	-16 43	A1	9
*	ε	CMa	Adhara	1.50	06 58.6	-28 58	B2	680
*	δ	CMa	Wezen (Al Wazn)	1.84	07 08.4	-26 24	F8	2,100
*	η	CMa	Aludra	2.40	07 24.1	-29 18	B5	2,700
	α¹	Gem	Castor	1.99	07 34.6	+31 53	A1	45
*	α	CMi	Procyon	0.34	07 39.3	+05 14	F5	11
	β	Gem	Pollux	1.15	07 45.3	+28 01	K0	35
*	ζ	Pup	Suhail Hadar	2.25	08 03.6	-40 00	O5	2,400
*	γ²	Vel	Al Suhail al Muhlif	1.82	08 09.5	-47 21	WC7	520

	Const. name	Name	Visual magnitude	Right Ascension (2000) h m	Declination ° '	Spectral type	Approx. distance Light yrs
* ε	Car	Avior	1.85	08 22.5	−59 30	K0+B	340
* δ	Vel	Koo She	1.95	08 44.7	−54 43	A0	76
* λ	Vel	Al Suhail al Wazn	2.25	09 08.0	−43 26	K5	750
* β	Car	Miaplacidus	1.67	09 13.2	−69 43	A1	86
* ι	Car	Tureis	2.24	09 17.1	−59 16	F0	750
* κ	Vel	Markeb	2.49	09 22.1	−55 01	B2	470
* α	Hya	Alphard	1.99	09 27.6	−08 40	K4	94
* α	Leo	Regulus	1.36	10 08.4	+11 58	B7	84
	Leo	Algieba	2.0cmb	10 20.0	+19 51	K0+G7	90
	β UMa	Merak	2.36	11 01.8	+56 23	A1	78
	α UMa	Dubhe	1.79	11 03.7	+61 45	K0	105
* β	Leo	Denebola	2.14	11 49.1	+14 34	A3	43
	γ UMa	Phad	2.44	11 53.8	+53 42	A0	90
* α	Cru	Acrux	0.83cmb	12 26.6	−63 06	B1+B1	370
	γ Cru		1.62	12 31.2	−57 07	M3	220
* γ	Cen	Menkent	2.16	12 41.5	−48 58	A0	160
* β	Cru	Mimosa	1.24	12 47.7	−59 42	B0.5	490
	ε UMa	Alioth	1.76	12 54.0	+55 57	A0p	68

		Name					
ζ	UMa	Mizar	2.09cmb	13 23.9	+54 56	A2+A	88
* α	Vir	Spica	0.96	13 25.2	-11 09	B1	220
* ε	Cen		2.30	13 39.9	-53 28	B1	570
η	UMa	Alkaid	1.86	13 47.5	+49 19	B3	210
* β	Cen	Agena	0.59	14 03.8	-60 22	B1	490
* θ	Cen		2.05	14 06.7	-36 23	K0	55
* α	Boo	Arcturus	0.06	14 15.7	+19 11	K2	36
* η	Cen		2.35	14 35.5	-42 09	B1.5p	390
* α	Cen	Al Rijil	-0.27cmb	14 39.6	-60 50	G2+K1	4.3
* α	Lup	Men	2.30	14 41.9	-47 24	B2	430
ε	Boo	Izar	2.4cmb	14 45.0	+27 05	K0+A2	103
β	UMi	Kochab	2.08	14 50.7	+74 09	K4	105
α	CrB	Alphekka	2.23	15 34.7	+26 43	A0	76
* δ	Sco	Dschubba	2.32	16 00.3	-22 37	B0	590
* α	Sco	Antares	0.9v	16 29.4	-26 26	M1+A3	520
* α	TrA	Atria	1.91	16 48.7	-69 02	K4	82
* ε	Sco	Wei	2.28	16 50.2	-34 18	K2	65
* η	Oph	Sabik	2.44	17 10.4	-15 43	A2.5	69
* λ	Sco	Shaula	1.62	17 33.6	-37 06	B1	610
* α	Oph	Ras alhague	2.08	17 34.9	+12 34	A5	58
* θ	Sco	Sargas	1.88	17 37.3	-43 00	F0	650

560 • FACTS AND FIGURES

	Const. name	Name	Visual magnitude	Right Ascension (2000) h m	Declination ° '	Spectral type	Approx. distance Light yrs
*	κ Sco	Girtab	2.41	17 42.5	-39 02	B2	470
	γ Dra	Eltanin	2.22	17 56.6	+51 29	K5	117
*	ε Sgr	Kaus Australis	1.84	18 24.2	-34 23	B9	124
	α Lyr	Vega	0.04	18 36.9	+38 47	A0	26.5
*	σ Sgr	Nunki	2.10	18 55.3	-26 18	B2	300
*	α Aql	Altair	0.77	19 50.8	+08 52	A7	16
	γ Cyg	Sadr	2.24	20. 22.2	+40 15	F8	750
*	α Pav		1.93	20 25.6	-56 44	B3	310
	α Cyg	Deneb	1.26	20 41.4	+45 16	A2	1,600
	ε Cyg	Gienah	2.45	20 46.2	+33 58	K0	74
	α Cep	Alderamin	2.41	21 18.6	+62 35	A7	52
*	ε Peg	Enif	2.42	21 44.2	+09 53	K2	780
*	α Gru	Alnair	1.73	22 08.2	-46 58	B5	64
*	β Gru		2.1v	22 42.7	-46 53	M3	280
*	α PsA	Fomalhaut	1.16	22 57.6	-29 37	A3	22.5
*	α Peg	Markab	2.49	23 04.8	+15 12	B9.5	100

\# The variable Mira reaches the maximum brightness mag. 1.7 only occasionally; it is generally much fainter.
v Variable magnitude
cmb Combined magnitude of two close components

VISIBILITY OF STARS FROM THE SOUTHERN HEMISPHERE

The declination range of visible stars is determined by the latitude of the observer. For Sydney, with a latitude of about -34°, the northern limit of declination is +56° (90 - 34 = 56). This limit, however, is theoretical rather than practical, unless the observer is spending a 'Night on a Bare Mountain', with a clear view of the horizon, no man-made light and first-class conditions. The practical limit is about 20° south of the theoretical limit for ordinary purposes and at least 5° further south for astronomical work. At latitude -34° stars south of -56° are circumpolar, i.e. always above the horizon. The table below gives the limits mentioned for major centres.

	Latitude	*North Declination limits* *Theoretical Practical* *(to nearest degree)*	*Circumpolar* *S. of Declination*
Australia:			
Adelaide	-35	+55 +35	-55
Alice Springs	-23	+67 +47	-67
Brisbane	-27	+63 +43	-63
Canberra	-35	+55 +35	-55
Darwin	-12	+78 +58	-78
Hobart	-43	+47 +27	-47
Melbourne	-37	+53 +33	-53
Perth	-32	+58 +38	-58
Sydney	-34	+56 +36	-56
New Zealand			
Auckland	-37	+53 +33	-53
Wellington	-41	+49 +29	-49
Papua New Guinea			
Port Moresby	-09	+81 +61	-81

Source: Pamela Morris-Kennedy, Mt. Stromlo & Siding Spring Observatories.

Part Four
International

AFGHANISTAN

De Afghanistan Demokrateek Jamhuriat
Jomhuri-ye Demowkratik-e Afghanestan
DEMOCRATIC REPUBLIC OF AFGHANISTAN

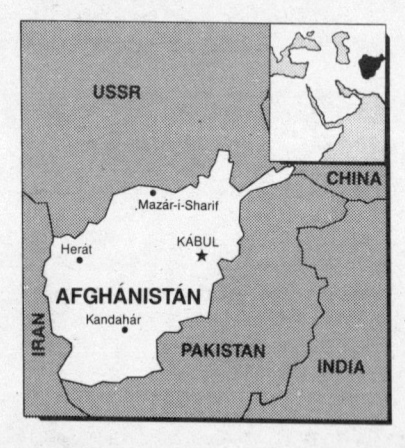

CAPITAL: Kabul

AREA AND POPULATION: 652,090 km^2, 6% cultivated land. Population: 15,056,000 (1986 est.). Population density: 26/km^2. Population growth (1977-84): 2.5%. Ethnic composition: Pathan, 55%; Tajik 30%; Uzbek; Hazara; Baluchi; Turkoman.

CLIMATE AND GEOGRAPHY: The climate is dry with extremes of temperature (−2.8°C to +24.4°C in Kabul). Winters are severe with considerable snowfall. The country is bounded to the north by the USSR, east and south by Pakistan, and west by Iran. Landlocked and mountainous, Afghanistan has fertile plains, lowlands and valleys which support agriculture.

CURRENCY: Afghani (Afg) of 100 puls.

DEFENCE: Military service lasts for 4 years (conscripts only). Total armed forces (1986/87): 50,000. Army 45,000 (mostly conscripts); Air Force 5,000. Defections from the Afghan Army are common. Paramilitary forces: 42,000 − gendarmerie, secret police and 'Defence of the Revolution' forces. Opposition forces: perhaps 130,000 guerillas (possibly 30,000 intermittently active), supported by 37 exile political groups (7 official).

GOVERNMENT: One-party (People's Democratic Party of Afghanistan, PDPA), pro-communist state, divided into 29 provinces. Since the putsch of 27 April 1978, the constitution has been abrogated and replaced by 'Revolutionary Duty Guidelines'. The Supreme Council and National Fatherland Front was created in July 1981. Ruling body: Revolutionary Council. Head of State: President Najibullah. Prime Minister: Mohammad Hassan Sharg. Foreign Minister: Shah M. Dost.

LANGUAGE: Pushtu and Dari (Persian) (both official).

NATIONAL ANTHEM: So che da mezaka asman wee (So long as there is the Earth and the heavens).

RELIGION: Sunni Moslem, 80%; Shiite Moslem, 20%.

TOURIST INFORMATION: Passport and visa required by Australian citizens. Visas may be obtained from representatives of Afghanistan in People's Republic of China, Czechoslovakia, Egypt, France, FRG, India, Indonesia, Iran, Iraq, Italy, Japan, Pakistan, Saudi Arabia, Turkey, UK, USA, USSR and Yugoslavia. Tourists are advised to report upon arrival to the Tourist Bureau, Press Department, in Kabul. Permission in writing to take still photographs or movie film should be obtained from the Tourist Bureau. Airlines flying to Afghanistan: Ariana Afghan Airlines, Aeroflot, Indian Airlines. An airport tax of Afg 200 is levied at the airport of departure. Malaria prophylaxis is recommended.

ALBANIA

Republika Popullore Socialiste e Shqipërisë
PEOPLE'S SOCIALIST REPUBLIC OF ALBANIA

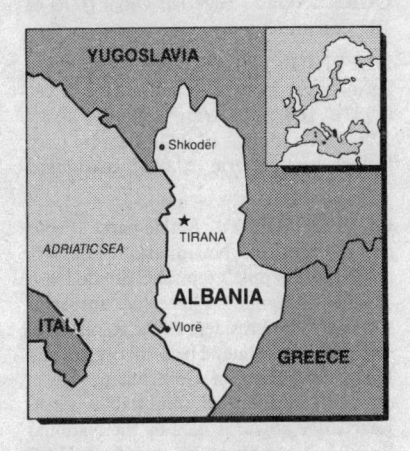

CAPITAL: Tirana (Tiranë)

AREA AND POPULATION: 28,748 km², 43% cultivated land. Population: 3,020,000 (1986 est.). Population density: 103/km². Population growth (1970-82): 2.5%. Ethnic composition: Albanian (Tosk and Gheg) 96%; Yugoslav 1%; Greek 2.5%.

CLIMATE AND GEOGRAPHY:
Albania has a Mediterranean climate. Frequent cyclones make the weather unstable in winter. In the north-east of the country the average temperature is 14°C, and in the south-west 18°C. Annual rainfall: 1353 mm (Tirana). In the highlands the winters can be very severe and heavy snowfalls are often recorded. The country is bordered by Yugoslavia to the north and east, Greece to the south, and the Adriatic and Ionian seas to the west. Most of the country consists of hills and mountains, with a narrow coastal plain.

CURRENCY: Lek of 100 qintars.

DEFENCE: Military service is for 2 years. Total armed forces (1986/87): 40,400 (20,000 conscripts). Army 30,000; Air Force 7,200 (under the jurisdiction of the Army); Navy 3,200. Para-military forces: internal security forces 5,000; frontier forces 7,500. Most of Albania's defence equipment was supplied by China before relations were suspended.

GOVERNMENT: Socialist people's republic divided into 26 districts. The single-chamber legislative body (People's Assembly) of 250 deputies meets bi-annually. Daily functions are delegated to the Presidium—a chairman, 3 deputy chairmen, a secretary and 10 members. Elections are held every 4 years. All candidates are members of the Albanian Democratic Front. The last election in Albania was held in November 1987. There was 1 candidate per constituency. The Executive body of Albania is the Council of Ministers. The Prime Minister is the Chairman of the Council which consists of 3 deputy prime ministers, 15 ministers and the chairman of the State Planning Commission. There is universal suffrage. Minimum voting age: 18. Head of State and Chairman of the Presidium: Ramiz Alia. Prime Minister and Chairman of the Council of Ministers: Adil Carcani. Foreign Minister: Reiz Malile.

LANGUAGE: Albanian, with 2 principal dialects—Gheg and Tosk.

NATIONAL ANTHEM: Hymni i Flamurit (Hymn to the Flag).

RELIGION: Constitutionally an atheist state. Before 1945 the population was over 60% Sunni Moslem; Orthodox 160,000; Roman Catholic 124,000; Jewish 300.

TOURIST INFORMATION: Passport and visa required by Australian citizens. Visas are issued only to businessmen and groups of at least 10 persons. Entry is refused to visitors who do not comply with existing clothing and general appearance requirements. Prohibited are: miniskirts, maxiskirts and 'extravagant' trousers. All aspects of tourism are handled by the state tourist department, Albturist. International flights leave from Rinas Airport (Tirana). There is a weekly flight by Olympic Airways to Athens and regular flights to Belgrade, Bucharest, Budapest and East Berlin. No regular internal service exists. Visas may be obtained from representatives of Albania in Algeria, Austria, Bulgaria, People's Republic of China, Cuba, Czechoslovakia, Egypt, France, GDR, Hungary, Italy, North Korea, Poland, Romania, Sweden, Switzerland, Turkey, Vietnam, Yugoslavia and the UN in the USA. Exit permits are required by all persons leaving Albania and there is an airport tax of Lek 30. Vaccinations for cholera and yellow fever are required.

ALGERIA

Al-Jumhuriya al-Jazairiya ad-Dimuqratiya ash-Shabiya
DEMOCRATIC AND POPULAR REPUBLIC OF ALGERIA

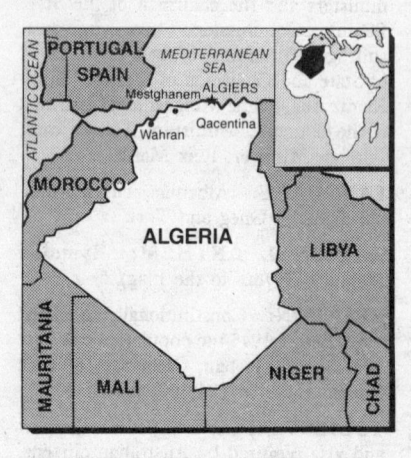

CAPITAL: Algiers (Al-Jazair)

AREA AND POPULATION: 2,381,741 km^2, 13% cultivated land. Population: 22,817,000 (1986 est.). Population density: 9.3/km^2, less than 1/km^2 in the south. Population growth (1970-82): 3.1%. Ethnic composition: Arab 75%; Berber 25%. Approx. 2,300,000 Algerians work abroad.

CLIMATE AND GEOGRAPHY: The climate is warm-temperate on the coast and arid inland. Winters are mild and summers hot and dry. Average annual rainfall: 432 mm. The country is bounded to the north by the Mediterranean Sea, to the south-east by Niger, to the south-west by Mauritania and Mali, to the east by Libya and Tunisia and to the west by Western Sahara and Morocco. The coast comprises fertile plains. Two major chains of the Atlas mountains (running east-west) enclose a dry plateau. The Sahara lies to the south.

CURRENCY: Algerian Dinar (DA) of 100 centimes.

DEFENCE: Military service is for a period of 6 months. Total armed forces (1987): 168,500. Army 150,000; Navy 7,000; Air Force 12,000. Para-military forces: gendarmerie 30,000; coastguard 550.

GOVERNMENT: Single-party (Front de Libération Nationale), Islamic, democratic people's republic, divided into 31 departments. There is universal suffrage. The President of the Republic is also Head of State, Head of the Armed Forces and Head of Government. He is elected for a 5-year (renewable) term. Legislative power is held by the National People's Assembly of 261 members. Head of State: Bendjedid Chadli. Prime Minister: Abdelhamid Brahimi. Foreign Minister: Ahmed Taleb Ibrahimi.

LANGUAGE: Arabic (official), French (commercial), Berber dialects.

NATIONAL ANTHEM: Qassaman.

RELIGION: Sunni Moslem 99%; Roman Catholic 150,000; Jewish, approx. 1,000; small Protestant groups.

TOURIST INFORMATION: Passport and visa required by Australian citizens. Visas may be obtained from representatives of Algeria in Argentina, Belgium, Brazil, Bulgaria, Canada, People's Republic of China, Cuba, Czechoslovakia, France, Gabon, FRG, Ghana, Guinea, Indonesia, India Iraq, Italy, Ivory Coast, Japan, Jordan, Kuwait, Lebanon, Libya, Mali, Netherlands, Pakistan, Panama, Saudi Arabia, Senegal, Spain, Sweden, Switzerland, Syria, Tanzania, Tunisia, UK, USA, USSR, Yemen and Yugoslavia. National airline: Air Algérie. There is no departure tax. With the exception of gold coins, any amount of foreign currency may be taken into Algeria, but must be declared upon arrival. This declaration must be produced whenever foreign currency is exchanged for dinars, and must be surrendered to customs officials upon departure. Customs officials may ask to see the unspent balance of foreign currency. Care should be taken not to change too much foreign currency into dinars as it may be difficult to reconvert later. It is considered impolite to smoke in public during Ramadan. Vaccination against yellow fever is required and malaria prophylaxis is advisable.

ANDORRA

Principat d'Andorra
PRINCIPALITY OF ANDORRA

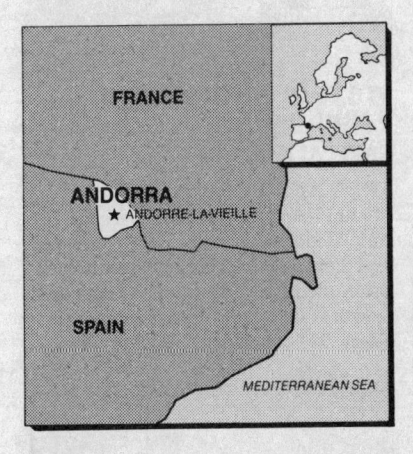

CAPITAL: Andorre-la-Vieille/Andorra la Vella

AREA AND POPULATION: 465 km^2, 4% cultivated land. Population: 49,000 (1986 est.). Population density: 98.5/km^2. Ethnic composition: Spanish, 55%; Andorran 27%; French 7%.

CLIMATE AND GEOGRAPHY: The climate is cool in summer and snowfalls are frequent in winter. Andorra is situated in the eastern Pyrenees, on the Franco-Spanish border. The country consists of gorges and narrow valleys surrounded by mountains.

CURRENCY: Spanish Peseta and French Franc.

DEFENCE: No defence forces are maintained.

GOVERNMENT: Co-principality (sovereignty exercised by the President of the French Republic and the Bishop of Urgel). Each co-prince heads a Permanent Delegation for Andorran Affairs. Delegations consist of 28 members elected for 4 years. Only native-born Andorrans have the right to vote. Head of Government: Josep Pintat Solans.

LANGUAGE: Catalan (official), Spanish, French.

NATIONAL ANTHEM: El Gran Carlemany (Great Charlemagne).

RELIGION: Roman Catholic; Jewish minority.

TOURIST INFORMATION: Passport but no visa required by Australian citizens. Entry is from France or Spain. Andorra itself is duty free. Nearest airports: Barcelona and Perpignan.

ANGOLA

República Popular de Angola
PEOPLE'S REPUBLIC OF ANGOLA

CAPITAL: Luanda

AREA AND POPULATION:
1,246,700 km^2, 1.4% cultivated land. Population: 8,164,000 (1986 est.). Population density: 7.1/km^2. Population growth (1970-82): 2.5%. Ethnic composition: Ovimbundu 38%; Kimbundu 23%; European 1%, Mesticos 2%.

CLIMATE AND GEOGRAPHY: The climate is tropical, with low rainfall in the west increasing inland. The average temperature in Luanda is 23.1°C. Average annual rainfall: 338 mm. The country is bounded to the north by Congo and Zaïre, to the south by South West Africa/Namibia, to the east by Zambia and to the west by the Atlantic Ocean. Most of Angola consists of a plateau, rising from a narrow coastal strip.

CURRENCY: Kwanza (Kz) of 100 lwei.

DEFENCE: Military service lasts for 2 years. Total armed forces (1987): 50,500 (? 24,000 conscripts). Army 36,000; Navy 1,250; Air Force 2,000. Para-military forces: militia 50,000; 11+ infantry battalions; border guard 7,000; South West African People's Organisation (SWAPO) 8,900; 'Popular Vigilance Brigades'. About 27,000 Cuban and 500 East German military personnel operate aircraft and heavy equipment. Assistance is also received from Portuguese volunteers and some 950 Soviet advisers and technicians. Opposition forces: UNITA 26,000 'regulars', 34,000 support militia; National Front for the Liberation of Angola, 5,000 claimed.

GOVERNMENT: One-party (Movimento Popular de Libertação de Angola – Partido do Trabalho), socialist people's republic divided into 18 provinces. The new constitution of November 1975 is based on Marxist principles. The Revolutionary Council and National People's Assembly of 203 members is elected for 3 years (extended for further 3 years in 1986). There is universal suffrage. President and Foreign Minister: José Eduardo dos Santos.

LANGUAGE: Portuguese (official), various Bantu dialects.

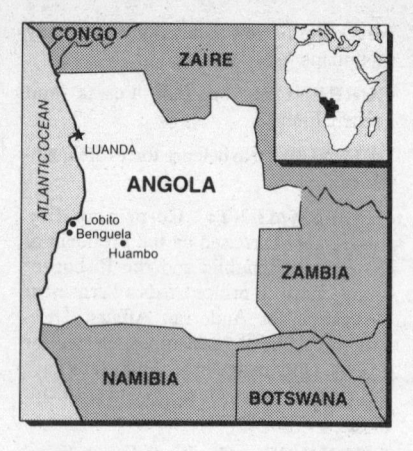

RELIGION: Roman Catholic 46%; Protestant 12%; Animist 42%.

TOURIST INFORMATION: Passport and visa required by Australian citizens. An exit permit must be obtained immediately after arrival in Angola. National airline: TAAG (Linhas Aereas de Angola). There is no departure tax. The import of alcohol is permitted, provided that the bottles (3) are of different contents. A minimum foreign-currency equivalent of Kz 500 for each day of stay must be converted into local currency. Vaccination against cholera and yellow fever is required and malaria prophylaxis recommended.

ANTIGUA AND BARBUDA

STATE OF ANTIGUA AND BARBUDA

CAPITAL: St John's

AREA AND POPULATION: 443 km^2 (Antigua 280 km^2, Barbuda 161 km^2, Redonda 2 km^2), 54% cultivated land. Population: 82,000 (1986 est.). Population density: 185.1/km^2. Population growth (1980): 1.1%. Ethnic composition: Negro 92%; mulatto 3.5%; European.

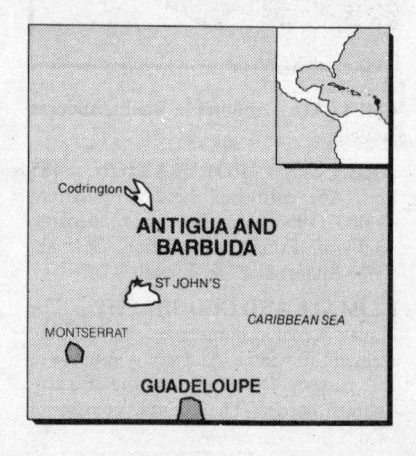

CLIMATE AND GEOGRAPHY: The climate is tropical, with a hot season of high rainfall from May to November. Average annual rainfall: 1,000 mm. The country consists of 3 islands of the Lesser Antilles group, situated in the Eastern Caribbean. Redonda is uninhabited.

CURRENCY: East Caribbean Dollar (EC$) of 100 cents.

DEFENCE: The defence force has a strength of approximately 700.

GOVERNMENT: Parliamentary democratic monarchy. The Antigua Parliament consists of a Senate (17 members) and House of Representatives (17 elected members). Barbuda has partial autonomy with its own Barbuda Council. Head of State: Queen Elizabeth II, represented by Governor-General Sir Wilfred Ebenezer Jacobs, KCVO, OBE, QC. Prime Minister: Vere Cornwall Bird. Foreign Minister: Lester Bryant Bird.

LANGUAGE: English (official), Creole.

NATIONAL ANTHEM: Fair Antigua and Barbuda.

RELIGION: Predominantly Anglican.

TOURIST INFORMATION: Passport but no visa required by Australian citizens. Departure tax: EC$10-15.

ARGENTINA

República Argentina
ARGENTINE REPUBLIC

CAPITAL: Buenos Aires

AREA AND POPULATION: 2,776,889 km^2, 11% cultivated land. Population: 31,186,000 (1986 est.). Population density: 10.7/km^2. Population growth (1970-82): 1.4%. Ethnic composition: European (Spanish and Italian background), 98%; Mestizo 0.76%; European (German background) 3.3%; Indian 0.2%.

CLIMATE AND GEOGRAPHY: The country can be divided into 5 major physical regions: Andes (cool, winter sports area in south); Chaco (dry, barely fertile, sparsely-populated); Mesopotamia (sub-tropical plains and forests, cattle-grazing area); Pampas (fertile central grasslands supporting cattle, sheep and grain crops) and Patagonia (semi-arid, sometimes snow-bound, southern third of country, given over to sheep-grazing). Situated in the tapering southern cone of South America east of the Andes, Argentina shares borders with Chile in the west, Bolivia, Paraguay and Brazil in the north and north-east, and with Uruguay in the east. The country extends approx. 3,700 km from its sub-tropical north to the sub-antarctic southern extremity of Tierra del Fuego. Argentina also claims part of Antarctica and the Falkland (Malvinas) Islands as national territory. The Antarctic claim is disputed by Britain and Chile, and the Falklands claim by Britain alone.

CURRENCY: Austral ($a) of 100 centavos.

DEFENCE: Military service lasts for 6-12 months in the Army, 1 year in the Air Force, and 14 months in the Navy. Total armed forces (1987): 79,000 (38,000 conscripts). Army 40,000 (25,000 conscripts); Navy 24,000 (8,000 conscripts); Air Force 15,000 (5,000 conscripts). Para-military forces: gendarmerie 13,000; coastguard 9,000.

GOVERNMENT: The Argentine constitution provides for a federal and republican system of government, modelled on that of the United States. In November 1985 a general election was held for the Federal Chamber of Deputies. The Radical Citizens Union obtained 130 seats and the Justice Party (Peronist) 103. Other minor parties obtained 21 seats. President of the Republic: Dr Raúl Alfonsín. Vice-President: Dr Victor Martínez. Foreign Minister: Dante Caputto.

LANGUAGE: Spanish (official), Indian languages, English, Italian, German, French.

NATIONAL ANTHEM: Oid; mortales! El grito sagrado, libertad, libertad (Hear, oh mortals, the sacred cry, freedom, freedom).

RELIGION: Roman Catholic 92%; Protestant 1.5%; Jewish 500,000; Islamic minority groups.

TOURIST INFORMATION: Passport and visa required by Australian citizens. Malaria prophylaxis is recommended if travelling in the northern provinces of Salta and Jujuy. Medical and hospital expenses are extremely high for non-Argentinians. Full medical and hospital insurance coverage is recommended. The Australian Embassy can provide addresses of English-speaking doctors and dentists, and of the British Hospital in Buenos Aires. There is no direct commercial air service between Australia and Argentina. Customs regulations are detailed and strictly enforced. Visitors planning to bring scientific goods or professional equipment into Argentina should check the regulations before leaving Australia. Ezeiza, the international airport serving Buenos Aires, is situated 32 km from the city. A departure tax of $a6 is levied on passengers departing for destinations within Argentina; $a20 for destinations in Uruguay and $a50 for destinations abroad.

AUSTRALIA

COMMONWEALTH OF AUSTRALIA

CAPITAL: Canberra

AREA AND POPULATION:
7,682,300 km^2, 64% commercially utilised land (mainly wheat). Population: 16,000,000 (1987 est.). Population density: 2/km^2. Population growth (1970-81): 1.4%. Ethnic composition: British background, approx. 75%; other European, approx. 20%; Asian and African, approx. 3.5%; Aborigines and Torres Strait Islanders (including mixed race), 1.5%.

CLIMATE AND GEOGRAPHY:
The climate ranges from tropical monsoon to cool temperate, with large areas of arid desert. Central and southern Queensland are tropical, north and central New South Wales are warm temperate, as are parts of Victoria, Western Australia and Tasmania, where most rain falls in winter. Four seasons are recognisable across most of the continent. However, there are only 2 seasons in northern Australia. The wet lasts from November to March. Rainfall diminishes markedly from the coast to the interior. Average annual rainfall (mm): Sydney, 1,215; Melbourne, 659; Brisbane, 1,153; Adelaide, 528; Perth, 873; Hobart, 629; Darwin, 1,536; Canberra, 629.

Average daily hours of sunshine: Sydney, 6.7; Melbourne, 5.7; Brisbane, 7.5; Adelaide, 6.9; Perth, 7.9; Hobart, 5.8; Darwin, 8.5; Canberra, 7.2. Average temperature range (January) in °C: Sydney, 18.4-25.5; Melbourne, 14-25.8; Brisbane, 20.7-29.4; Adelaide, 16.4-29.5; Perth, 17.7-29.6; Hobart, 11.6-21.4; Darwin, 24.7-31.7; Canberra, 13.1-27.6. Average temperature range (July): Sydney, 7.9-15.9; Melbourne, 5.7-13.3; Brisbane, 9.5-20.4; Adelaide, 7.3-15; Perth, 9-17.3; Hobart, 4.4-11.5; Darwin, 19.2-30.3; Canberra, −0.3-11.1.

The area of Australia is almost as great as that of the United States of America (excluding Alaska), about 50% greater than Europe (excluding USSR), and 32 times greater than the United Kingdom. The land lies between latitudes 10°41'S (Cape York, Qld) and 43°39'S (South Cape, Tas.) and between longitudes 113°09'E (Steep Point, WA) and 153°39'E (Cape Byron, NSW). The most southerly point of the mainland is South Point (Wilson's Promontory, Vic.), 39°08'S. The latitudinal distance between Cape York and South Point, Wilson's Promontory (South East Cape, Tas.) is about 3,180 km (3,680 km) respectively and the longitudinal distance between Steep Point and Cape Byron is about 4,000 km. The average altitude of the surface of the Australian land mass is only about 300 m. Approximately 87% of the total land mass is less than 500 m and 99.5% is less than 1,000 m. The highest point is Mt Kosciusko (2,228 m) and the lowest point is Lake Eyre (−15 m).

Australia has 3 major landform features: the western plateau, the interior lowlands and the eastern uplands. The western half of the continent consists of a great plateau of altitude 300 to 600 m. The interior lowlands include the channel country of south-west Queensland (drainage to Lake Eyre) and the Murray-Darling system to the south. The eastern uplands consist of a broad belt of varied width, extending from north Queensland to Tasmania and consisting largely of tablelands, ranges and ridges with only limited mountain areas above 1,000 m. *Australian External Territories:* Australian Antarctic Territory (all islands and territories other than Adelie Land situated south of latitude 60°S and lying between longitudes 160°E and 45°E); Cocos (Keeling) Islands (a group of 27 small coral islands in 2 separate atolls in the Indian Ocean 2,768 km north-west of Perth); Christmas Island (an isolated peak in the Indian Ocean in latitude 10°24'S and longitude 105°40'E); Coral Sea Islands Territory (scattered reefs and islands spread over a sea area of 1,035,995 km^2 of which only a few km^2 is land area. The territory lies between the Great Barrier Reef and longitude 157°10'E and between latitudes 12° and 24°S); Norfolk Island (situated in latitude 29°02'S and longitude 167°57'E. The island covers an area of approx. 3,455 ha, and is about 8 km long and 5 km wide. It is 1,676 km from Sydney and 1,063 km from Auckland. The island served as a penal station from 1788 to 1813 and from 1825 to 1855. In 1856, 194 descendants of the *Bounty* mutineers were transferred there from Pitcairn Island); Heard and McDonald Islands (situated approx. 4,100 km south-west of Fremantle, these islands were transferred from the United Kingdom to Australia on 26 December 1947); Territory of Ashmore and Cartier Islands (situated in the Indian Ocean, 320 km off the north-west coast of Western Australia, and placed under the authority of the Commonwealth on 23 July 1931).

CURRENCY: $A of 100 cents.

DEFENCE: Military service is voluntary. Total armed forces (1986/87): 70,456. Army 32,116; Navy 15,553 (including Fleet Air Arm); Air Force 22,787. Paramilitary force: Bureau of Customs.

GOVERNMENT: Parliamentary-democratic monarchy and independent member of the Commonwealth of Nations. Bicameral parliament: House of Representatives and Senate. There is universal adult suffrage. The states have their own parliaments, executive councils and governors. Head of State: Queen Elizabeth II, represented by Governor-General Sir Ninian Stephen. Head of Government: Prime Minister Bob Hawke. Foreign Minister: Gareth Evans.

LANGUAGE: English (official), Aboriginal languages.

NATIONAL ANTHEM: Advance Australia Fair.

RELIGION: Anglican 36.1%; Roman Catholic 33%; Uniting Church 4.9%; Orthodox 2.9%; Lutheran 1.4%; Baptist 1.3%; Moslem 76,000; Jewish 62,000; Buddhist 35,000; Animist.

AUSTRIA

Republik Österreich
REPUBLIC OF AUSTRIA
CAPITAL: Vienna (Wien)

AREA AND POPULATION: 83,855 km², 20% cultivated land. Population: 7,546,000 (1986 est.). Population density: 90/km². Population growth (1970-82): 0.1%. Ethnic composition: German 96%; Slovene and Croatian.

CLIMATE AND GEOGRAPHY: The climate ranges from cool temperate to mountain type, according to situation. Summers are warm but winters are cold, with considerable snowfall. Wettest months: May to August. Rainfall figures show a marked increase from east to west, which also coincides with rising height above sea-level. The annual temperature variation is not high – the average in the Vienna Basin is −2°C in January and 19.5°C in July. The country is bordered to the west by Switzerland and Liechtenstein, to the north by the Federal Republic of Germany and Czechoslovakia, to the east by Hungary and to the south by Yugoslavia and Italy.

CURRENCY: Schilling (S) of 100 Groschen.

DEFENCE: Compulsory military service entails 6 months recruit training plus 60 days refresher training over a period of 15 years, with an additional 30-90 days for specialists. Total armed forces (1986/87): 54,700 (27,300 conscripts) with approx. 70,000 reservists undergoing refresher training. Army 50,000 (25,000 conscripts); Air Force 4,700 (2,300 conscripts).

GOVERNMENT: Parliamentary democracy. The Head of State is the Federal President, who holds office for 6 years. Voting in presidential elections is compulsory. The President appoints the Chancellor and federal ministers. There is a bicameral parliament: *Nationalrat* and *Bundesrat* (National Council and Federal Council). Suffrage is universal and the minimum voting age 19. Nine federal provinces are each administered by a provincial government headed by a provincial governor, elected by the provincial parliament. Head of State: Kurt Waldheim. Chancellor: Franz Vranitzky. Foreign Minister: Alois Mock.

LANGUAGE: German (official), Slovene.

NATIONAL ANTHEM: Land der Berge, Land am Strome (Land of mountains and of streams).

RELIGION: Roman Catholic 84.3%; Protestant 5.6%; Moslem 1%; Jewish 7,000.

TOURIST INFORMATION: Passport but no visa required by Australian citizens. It is not permitted to wear military or other uniforms in Austria without special permission obtained from a diplomatic representative. The international airport at Schwechat is situated 18 km from Vienna.

BAHAMAS

COMMONWEALTH OF THE BAHAMAS

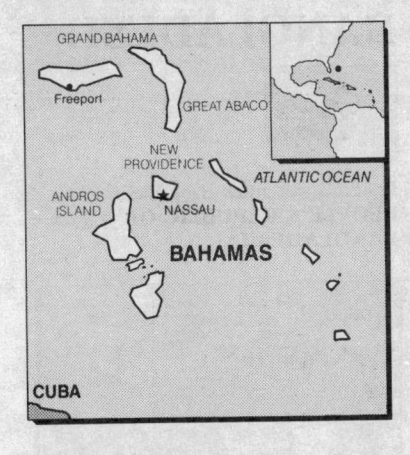

CAPITAL: Nassau

AREA AND POPULATION: 13,935 km^2, 2% arable land. Population: 235,000 (1986 est.). Population density: 16.9/km^2. Population growth (1979): 3.6%. Ethnic composition: Negro and mulatto 85%; mestizo and white 15%.

CLIMATE AND GEOGRAPHY: The Bahamas experiences mild winters and warm summers. The rainy season runs from May to June and September to October. Average annual rainfall: 1,180 mm. Average annual temperature: 24°C. The country consists of about 700 islands and 1,000 cays situated off the south-east coast of Florida.

CURRENCY: Bahamian dollar (B$) of 100 cents.

DEFENCE: A para-military marine force of 496 volunteers is maintained.

GOVERNMENT: Bicameral parliamentary democracy. The House of Assembly consists of 43 members elected by universal suffrage. The 16 members of the Senate are appointed by the Governor-General on the advice of the parliamentary leaders. There are 18 administrative districts. Head of State: Queen Elizabeth II, represented since 1973 by Governor-General Sir Gerald C. Cash. Head of Government: Prime Minister Sir Lynden Oscar Pindling. Foreign Minister: Clement T. Maynard.

LANGUAGE: English.

NATIONAL ANTHEM: March on, Bahamaland!

RELIGION: Baptist 29%; Anglican 23%; Roman Catholic 23%; Methodist 7%; Jewish minority; remainder African Animist.

TOURIST INFORMATION: Passport but no visa required by Australian citizens. Nassau International Airport is located on New Providence, approx. 14 km from Nassau. There are frequent flights to the Bahamas from US, Canadian and European cities. National airline: Bahamasair. A departure tax of B$5 is levied on all passengers leaving the Bahamas. A yellow fever vaccination is required.

BAHRAIN

Dawlat al-Bahrayn
STATE OF BAHRAIN

CAPITAL: Manama

AREA AND POPULATION: 668 km^2, 5% cultivated land. Population: 442,000 (1986 est.). Population density: 662/km^2. Population growth (1975-81): 3.6%. Ethnic composition: Arab 73%; Iranian 9%; Indian and Pakistani 5%; European minority.

CLIMATE AND GEOGRAPHY: The climate varies from warm (December to March) to hot and humid (June to September). Average temperature: 27.5°C. Average annual rainfall: 130 mm. Bahrain consists of a group of about 35 islands lying in the Arabian Gulf, 29 km from the coast of Saudi Arabia. The largest and most important island is Bahrain.

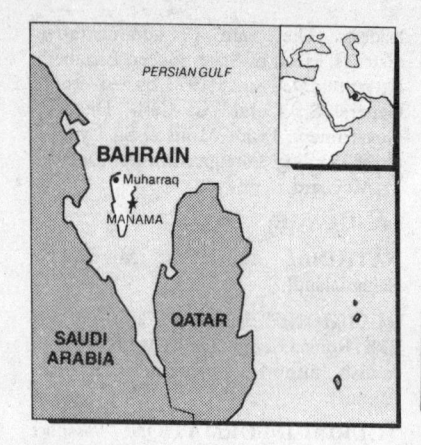

CURRENCY: Bahrain dinar (BD) of 1,000 fils.

DEFENCE: Total armed forces (1986/87): 2,800. Army 2,300; Navy 300; Air Force 200. Para-military forces: police 2,000; coastguard 250.

GOVERNMENT: Sheikhdom — an absolute monarchy with an oligarchic structure. There are 10 administrative regions. Women do not have the right to vote. Parliament was dissolved in 1975, the constitution revoked and political parties declared illegal. Head of State and Head of Government: HH Sheikh Isa bin Sulman al-Khalifa. Prime Minister: Sheikh Khalifa bin Sulman al-Khalifa. Foreign Minister: Sheikh Mohammed bin Mubarak al-Khalifa.

LANGUAGE: Arabic (official), English.

RELIGION: Shiite Moslem 55%; Sunni Moslem 40%; Christian; Hindu.

TOURIST INFORMATION: Passport and visa required by Australian citizens intending to stay longer than 72 hours in Bahrain. It is possible to leave the airport after paying a fee of BD4 for a transit visa which can be extended in town for a further BD8. A weekly total of 14 north and south-bound Qantas flights pass through Bahrain. There is some risk of disease in Bahrain, although Europeans generally are susceptible only to occasional bouts of mild enteritis and prickly heat. Sporadic outbreaks of cholera and typhoid can occur in summer, when hands and food should be washed meticulously. Tipping of taxi-drivers is unnecessary. Airport porters expect 200-300 fils for each piece of luggage, hotel and restaurant staff a maximum of 10% of the bill. National airline: Gulf Air.

BANGLADESH

Praja Gamatrantick Bangladesh
PEOPLE'S REPUBLIC OF BANGLADESH

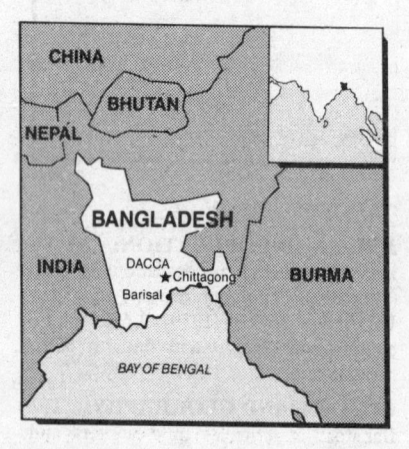

CAPITAL: Dacca (Dhaka)

AREA AND POPULATION: 143,998 km^2, 65.7% cultivated land. Population: 104,204,000 (1986 est.). Population density: 723.6/km^2. Population growth (1970-82): 2.6%. Ethnic composition: Bengali 98%; tribal peoples.

CLIMATE AND GEOGRAPHY: The climate is tropical and monsoon — hot and very humid during summer but dry and mild during winter. Rainfall is heavy, especially during the monsoon season from June to September. Average temperature: winter 19°C; summer 28°C. Average annual rainfall (Dacca): 2,025 mm. Bangladesh is bounded to the north, east and west by India, to the south-east by

Burma and to the south by the Bay of Bengal. The south-east of the country is hilly, inhabited by tribal peoples similar to their neighbours in north-east India and Burma. The western part is a vast alluvial plain.

CURRENCY: Taka (Tk) of 100 poisha.

DEFENCE: Military service is voluntary. Total armed forces (1986/87): 92,300. Army 81,800; Navy 7,500 (spares are in short supply and some equipment is unserviceable); Air Force 3,000. Para-military forces: Bangladesh Rifles 30,000; Bangladesh Ansans (security guards) 20,000; armed police reserve 5,000.

GOVERNMENT: People's republic divided into 20 administrative districts. Parliament has one chamber of 300 members, elected every 5 years by citizens over the age of 18. Thirty seats are reserved for women members elected by the Parliament. Head of State Lieut.-Gen. Hossain Mohammad Ershad. Prime Minister: Mizanur Rahman Chowdhury. Foreign Minister: H. R. Chowdhury.

LANGUAGE: Bengali (official), English.

NATIONAL ANTHEM: Amar Sonar Bangla, ami tomay bhalobashi (My golden Bengal, I love you).

RELIGION: Moslem 85.9%; Hindu 12.7%; Buddhist 0.6%; Christian 0.5%; tribal religionist 0.1%.

TOURIST INFORMATION: Passport but no visa required by Australian citizens provided that the period of stay does not exceed 15 days and that a return or onward ticket is held. A fee of Tk 200 (payable at the airport of departure) is levied on passengers embarking on international flights, and Tk 10 for domestic flights. National airline: Bangladesh Biman. The importation of US$150 (or equivalent) is permitted. Higher amounts must be declared. Malaria prophylaxis is recommended for visitors leaving Dacca city. Reconversion of local currency into foreign currencies is possible up to Tk 500 or 25% of the amount imported, whichever is the lower.

BARBADOS

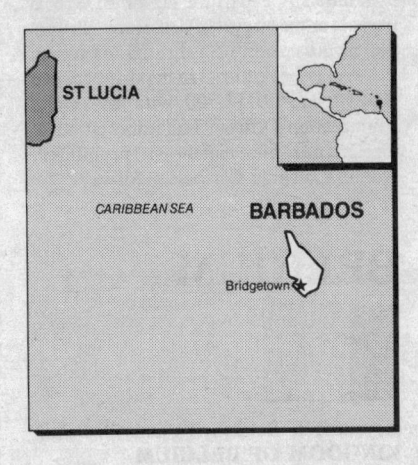

CAPITAL: Bridgetown

AREA AND POPULATION: 430 km², 76% cultivated land. Population: 253,000 (1986 est.). Population density: 588.4/km². Population growth (1979): 0.9%. Ethnic composition: Negro and mulatto, over 90%; Caucasian 4%.

CLIMATE AND GEOGRAPHY: The climate is equable, with a wet season from June to November. Average temperature: 25.5°C. Average annual rainfall: 1,275 mm. The country is situated in the Caribbean Sea, to the east of the Windward Islands.

CURRENCY: Barbados dollar (BD$) of 100 cents.

DEFENCE: A small para-military marine force is maintained.

GOVERNMENT: Bicameral parliamentary democracy. Head of State: Queen Elizabeth II, represented by Governor-General Sir Hugh Springer. Prime Minister Erskine Sandiford. Foreign Minister: Cameron Tudor.

LANGUAGE: English (official), French.

RELIGION: Anglican 70%; Methodist, 9%; Roman Catholic 4%; Moravian and Jewish minorities.

TOURIST INFORMATION: Passport but no visa required by Australian citizens, provided the period of stay does not exceed 3 months. A departure tax of BD$16 is payable at the airport of departure. Visitors not in possession of a through or return ticket may be required to deposit between BD$96 and BD$1,500 with the Chief Immigration Officer. The importation of foreign rum and matches is prohibited. National airline: Caribbean Airways.

BELGIUM

Royaume de Belgique/Koninkrijk België
KINGDOM OF BELGIUM

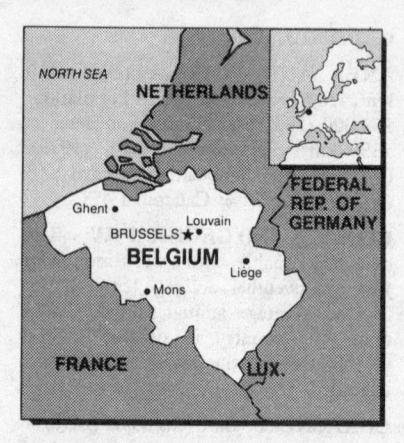

CAPITAL: Brussels

AREA AND POPULATION: 30,519 km², 28% cultivated land. Population: 9,868,000 (1986 est.). Population density: 323.3/km². Population growth (1970-82): 0.2%. Ethnic composition: Flemish (Dutch-speaking) 58%; Walloon (French-speaking) 41%; remainder of mixed French and Dutch, and of German origin.

CLIMATE AND GEOGRAPHY:
Belgium has a moderate European climate. Average temperature (Brussels) is 2.2°C in January and 17.8°C in July. Average annual rainfall (Brussels): 825 mm. The country is situated along the North Sea coast between France and the Netherlands, and extends inland to Luxembourg and the Federal Republic of Germany. Although mostly flat, the land becomes hilly and forested in the south-east (Ardennes) region. Belgium's only natural geographic frontier, the coastline, is 67 km long and the greatest distance between any two points (Ostend and Arlon) is 290 km.

CURRENCY: Belgian franc (FB) of 100 centimes.

DEFENCE: Military service lasts for 8 or 10 months (8 months if conscripts are posted to Germany and 10 months if serving in Belgium). Total armed forces (1987): 91,900 (3,600 women, 30,300 conscripts). Army 67,400; Navy 4,500; Air Force 20,000. Para-military force: gendarmerie 15,900.

GOVERNMENT: Constitutional monarchy. Bicameral parliament—Senate and House of Representatives. Senators must be at least 40 years of age, and members of the House of Representatives at least 25. There is universal suffrage. The electoral system of proportional representation usually results in coalition governments. There have been 31 coalition governments since WW II. Head of State: King Baudouin. Head of Government: Prime Minister Dr Wilfried Martens. Foreign Minister: Léo Tindemans.

LANGUAGES: French, Dutch and German (all official).

NATIONAL ANTHEM: La Brabançonne.

RELIGION: Roman Catholic 96%; Protestant 100,000; Jewish 35,000.

TOURIST INFORMATION: Passport but no visa required by Australian citizens. There is no departure tax. The international airport at Zaventem is located 11 km from Brussels. National airline: SABENA.

BELIZE

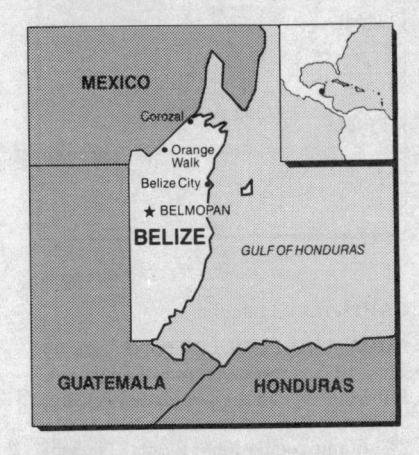

CAPITAL: Belmopan

AREA AND POPULATION: 22,963 km², 4% cultivated land. Population: 168,400 (1986 est.). Population density: 7.2/km². Population growth (1981): 3.6%. Ethnic composition: Negro and mulatto 52%; mestizo 22%; Mayan and Indian 13%; Carib 6%; Chinese and Indian 5%; European 2%.

CLIMATE AND GEOGRAPHY: The climate is tropical, with high rainfall. Average temperature: 25°C. Average annual rainfall: 1,890 mm. Belize is located in Central America, bounded to the north by Mexico, to the west by Guatemala and to the east and south by the Caribbean Sea. The coastal strip is low and swampy, with many salt and freshwater lagoons. The southern and western regions contain heavily forested mountain ranges.

CURRENCY: Belize dollar ($B) of 100 cents.

DEFENCE: Military service is voluntary. Total armed forces (1987): 600. Army 545; Navy 40; Air Force 15.

GOVERNMENT: Constitutional monarchy and parliamentary democracy. The bicameral parliament consists of the Senate and the House of Representatives. There is universal suffrage. Head of State: Queen Elizabeth II, represented by Governor-General Dame Elmira Minita Gordon. Prime Minister: Manuel Amadeo Esquivel. Foreign Minister: Dean Barrow.

LANGUAGE: English (official), Spanish, creole, Carib, Mayan.

RELIGION: Roman Catholic 66%; Protestant 30%; Jewish, Buddhist, Moslem and Hindu minorities.

TOURIST INFORMATION: Passport but no visa required by Australian citizens. Malaria prophylaxis is recommended. Belize International Airport is 15 km from the city. There is a departure tax of $B20.

BENIN

République Populaire du Bénin
PEOPLE'S REPUBLIC OF BENIN

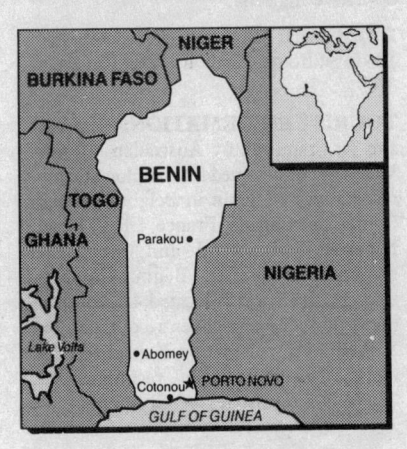

CAPITAL: Porto Novo

AREA AND POPULATION: 112,622 km², 11% cultivated land. Population: 4,141,000 (1986 est.). Population density: 36.8/km². Population growth (1970-82): 2.7%. Ethnic composition: Fon 47%; Adja 12%; Bariba 10%; Yoruba 9%; Somba 5%; Aizo 5%.

CLIMATE AND GEOGRAPHY: The climate is equatorial, with a long rainy season from March to July and a short rainy season in October and November. Average temperature: 26°C. Average annual rainfall: 1,325 mm. The country is bounded to the north by Niger and Burkina Faso, to the south by the Gulf of Guinea, to the east by Nigeria and to the west by Togo. Most of Benin is flat and covered with dense vegetation.

CURRENCY: Franc CFA.

DEFENCE: Military service is by selective conscription for a period of 18 months. Total armed forces (1987): 3,450. Army 3,200; Navy 150; Air Force 100. Para-military force: gendarmerie 2,000.

GOVERNMENT: Marxist-Leninist single-party (Parti de la Révolution Populaire du Bénin) system. The 196 members of the National Revolutionary Assembly are elected by universal adult suffrage. Head of State: President Brig.-Gen. Ahmed Kerekou. Foreign Minister: Guy Laudry Hazoume.

LANGUAGE: French (official); about 60 native dialects.

RELIGION: Animist 70%; Moslem 10-15%; Roman Catholic 12%; Protestant 3%.

TOURIST INFORMATION: Passport and visa required by Australian citizens. Visas may be obtained from diplomatic representatives of Benin in Belgium, Brazil, Cameroon, Canada, France, FRG, Israel, Nigeria, Switzerland and the USA. National airline: Air Bénin. Cotonou-Cadjehoun airport is located 4.7 km from the major commercial centre of Cotonou. Yellow fever vaccination is required and malaria prophylaxis is recommended. There is a tourist tax of CFA 2.50.

BHUTAN

Druk-yul
KINGDOM OF BHUTAN

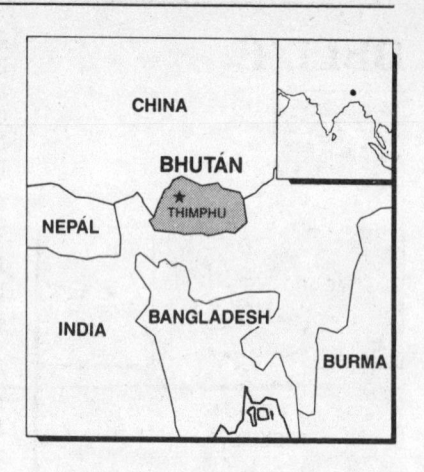

CAPITAL: Thimphu

AREA AND POPULATION: 47,600 km^2, 12% cultivated land. Population: 1,446,000 (1986 est.). Population density: 30.8/km^2. Population growth (1970-82): 2%. Ethnic composition: Bhotia (Tibetan) 60%; Nepalese 25%; Lepcha; Indian.

CLIMATE AND GEOGRAPHY: The climate is cold in the north, moderating through the centre to sub-tropical in the south. Annual rainfall ranges from 1,000 mm to 5,000 mm depending upon altitude. Bhutan is situated in the eastern Himalayas, bordered to the north and east by Tibet and India, to the south by India and to the west by Sikkim. The southern region contains thick forests, the centre fertile valleys and the northern region very high mountains.

CURRENCY: Ngultrum (Nu) of 100 chetrum. Indian currency is also legal tender.

DEFENCE: An army of about 4,000 men is maintained.

GOVERNMENT: Constitutional monarchy. There are 18 administrative districts, each with its own governor appointed by the King. The National Assembly consists of 151 members elected for a 3-year term. Head of State: (Dragon) King Jigme Singye Wangchuk. Foreign Minister: Lyonpo Dawa Tsering.

LANGUAGE: Dzongkha (official), Nepali, English.

RELIGION: Buddhist 75%; Hindu 25%.

TOURIST INFORMATION: Passport and visa required by Australian citizens. Visa applications should reach the Department of Tourism in Bhutan at least 2 1/2 months before the intended visit. Select groups of 6 to 20 tourists may be issued with 10-day visas. People wishing to visit the country for mountaineering, publicity or research will not be admitted. National airline: Druk Air. The airport is located at Paro, near Thimphu. Vaccination is recommended against yellow fever and malaria prophylaxis is recommended.

BOLIVIA

República de Bolivia
REPUBLIC OF BOLIVIA

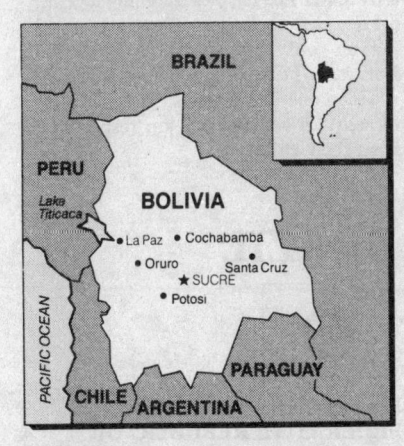

CAPITAL: Sucre

AREA AND POPULATION:
1,098,581 km², 3% cultivated land. Population: 6,200,000 (1986 est.). Population density: 5.6/km². Population growth (1970-82): 2.6%. Ethnic composition: Quechua 30%; Aymara 25% mixed 30%; European 14%.

CLIMATE AND GEOGRAPHY: The climate is hot, with heavy rainfall in the tropical eastern lowlands, while the altiplano is generally drier and cooler. Average annual rainfall in La Paz: 574 mm. Bolivia is bordered by Brazil to the north and east, by Argentina and Paraguay to the south and by Chile and Peru to the west. Two regions are distinguished: the tropical eastern lowlands, partly jungle and partly open cattle ranges and pastures, and the high plateau (alti-plano), occupying the western part of the country, much of it 4,000 m above sea-level. The seat of government is La Paz.

CURRENCY: Boliviano (BOB).

DEFENCE: Military service is selective for a period of 12 months. Total armed forces (1987): 28,000. Army 20,000; Navy 4,000 (including 600 marines); Air Force 4,000.

GOVERNMENT: Presidential republic. The bicameral legislature—Senate and Chamber of Deputies—is elected by universal suffrage. Head of State and Head of Government: President Victor Paz Estenssoro. Foreign Minister: Guillermo Bedregal.

LANGUAGE: Spanish (official), Quechua (34.4% of Indians), Aymara (25.5% of Indians).

NATIONAL ANTHEM: Bolivianos, el hado propicio (Oh Bolivians, our long felt desires).

RELIGION: Roman Catholic 95%; Protestant 45,000; Jewish 2,000.

TOURIST INFORMATION: Passport and visa required by Australian citizens. Malaria prophylaxis and vaccination against yellow fever are recommended for tourists venturing outside main cities. Travellers arriving in La Paz should rest for half a day in order to adapt progressively to the altitude. National airline: Lloyd Aereo Boliviana. There is a departure tax of US$10 (international flights) and $BOB1.50 (internal flights).

BOTSWANA

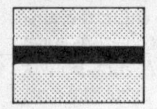

REPUBLIC OF BOTSWANA
CAPITAL: Gaborone

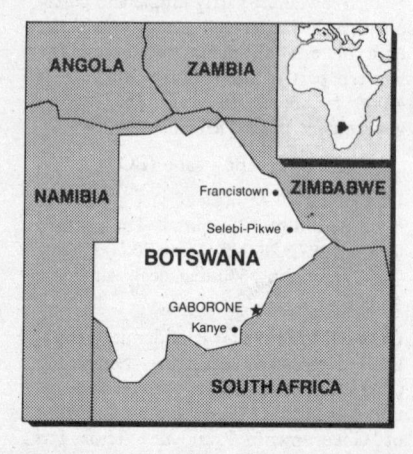

AREA AND POPULATION:
600,372/km², 5% cultivated land. Population: 1,104,000 (1986 est.). Population density: 1.8/km². Population growth (1978): 2.7%. Ethnic composition: Tswana 94%; Bushman 5%; European 1%.

CLIMATE AND GEOGRAPHY: The climate is semi-arid continental. Temperatures vary according to season and region, ranging from 38°C in summer (October to February) to below freezing in winter (May to August). Average annual rainfall: 538 mm. The country is situated in the centre of the Southern African Plateau at a mean altitude of 1,000 m. It is bordered to the north and west by South West Africa (Namibia), to the south by South Africa and to the north-east by Zimbabwe. There are swamplands and farming areas in the north. The Kalahari Desert spreads over the south-west.

CURRENCY: Pula (P) of 100 thebe.

DEFENCE: Military service is voluntary. Total armed forces (1987): 3,000 (all services form part of the army). Army 2,850; Air Force 150. Para-military force: police 1,000.

GOVERNMENT: Parliamentary democratic republic. The constitution provides for general elections to be held every 5 years for a unicameral legislature (National Assembly), which has 39 members plus the President. There is a House of Chiefs which advises the government in matters of traditional law and custom. Head of State and President of the Republic: Dr Quett Ketumile Joni Masire. Foreign Minister: Dr G. K. T. Chiepe.

LANGUAGE: English (official), Setswana (national).

NATIONAL ANTHEM: Fatshe la rona (Blessed be this noble land).

RELIGION: Animist majority; Christian 15%.

TOURIST INFORMATION: Passport but no visa required by Australian citizens for stays of up to 30 days. Malaria prophylaxis is recommended, as are precautions against tsetse flies. Rabies is endemic in Botswana. Foreign currency, cameras and films must be declared upon arrival. Married couples travelling together are entitled to import allowances for 1 person only. National airline: Air Botswana. There are international airports at Gaborone and Francistown. They are located 2.5 km and 6.5 km respectively from their cities.

BRAZIL

República Federativa do Brasil
FEDERATIVE REPUBLIC OF BRAZIL

CAPITAL: Brasilia

AREA AND POPULATION:
8,511,965 km², 5% cultivated land. Population: 143,277,000 (1986 est. excluding forest Indians). Population density: 16.8/km². Population growth (1970-82): 2.4%. Ethnic composition:

European (of Portuguese, Italian and Spanish origin) 54.7%; mulatto 39.1%; Caboclo (Euro-Indian) 5.9%; Negro and Cafuso (Negro-Indian); Indian; Japanese; German.

CLIMATE AND GEOGRAPHY: The climate is predominantly tropical, with altitude, prevailing winds and proximity to the sea affecting temperatures. Average annual rainfall: 1,082 mm to 2,438 mm, depending on the area, with flooding common to the Amazon Basin. Brazil is bounded on the east by the Atlantic Ocean and on its north-west and southern borders by all South American countries except Chile and Ecuador. The country can be divided into 3 main areas: Amazon lowlands — vast, tropical rainforests and 'selvas' (plains); central highlands and plains; Atlantic coastlands — a narrow lowland between the highland escarpment and the sea.

CURRENCY: Cruzado (Cr$) of 1,000 cruzeiros.

DEFENCE: Military service is compulsory for 12 months. Total armed forces (1987): 283,885 (137,700 conscripts). Army 182,900; Navy 50,285; Air Force 50,700. Para-military forces: 240,000 public security forces in state militias.

GOVERNMENT: Presidential federal republic. Voting is compulsory between 18 and 65 years of age and optional for persons over 65. Enlisted men do not have the vote. Head of State and President of the Republic: José Sarney. Foreign Minister: Roberto Abreu Sodré.

LANGUAGE: Portuguese (official), English.

NATIONAL ANTHEM: Ouviram do Ipirangas margens placidas (From peaceful Ypiranga's banks).

RELIGION: Roman Catholic 89%; Protestant 5-6%; Jewish 160,000; Animist; Orthodox; Buddhist.

TOURIST INFORMATION: Passport and visa required by Australian citizens. Passengers with members or limbs in plaster must hold x-ray plates or medical attestation. Vaccination against yellow fever is advisable for persons visiting rural areas. Malaria prophylaxis is recommended. National airline: VARIG. A departure tax of US$9.05 or US$8.18 is payable on international flights (amount depends on airport used), or Cr$48/Cr$42 on internal flights. The export of local currency is prohibited.

BRUNEI

Negara Brunei Darussalam
(State of Brunei, Home of Peace)
SULTANATE OF BRUNEI

CAPITAL: Bandar Seri Begawan

AREA AND POPULATION: 5,765 km^2, 2% cultivated land. Population: 240,000 (1986 est). Population density: 41.6/km^2. Population growth (1975-78): 3.3%. Ethnic composition: Malay 65%; Chinese 26%; indigenous groups, Indian, Indonesian, Thai and European, 17%.

CLIMATE AND GEOGRAPHY: The climate is tropical, with little variation throughout the year. The temperature ranges from 25°C to 32°C, with high humidity. Average annual rainfall: 3,750 mm. Brunei is situated on the north-west coast of Borneo, bounded on its landward sides by Sarawak. The landscape is mainly equatorial jungle.

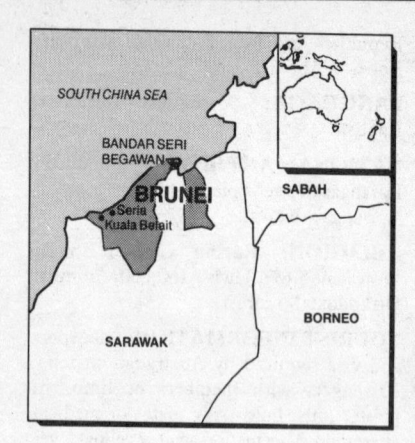

CURRENCY: Brunei dollar (BR$) of 100 cents.

DEFENCE: Military service is voluntary. Total armed forces (1987): 4,050. Army 3,380; Navy 450; Air Force 200. Para-military forces: Royal Brunei Police 1,750; Gurkha reserve unit: 900.

GOVERNMENT: Independent sultanate. The Council of Ministers is presided over by the Sultan. Head of State: (Duli Yang Maha Mulia Paduka Seri Baginda Sultan and Yang di-Pertuan Negeri Brunei) Sir Muda Hassanal Bolkiah Mu'izzaddin Waddaulah (ibni Duli Yang Teremat Mulia Paduka Seri Begawan Sultan Sir Muda Omar Ali Saifuddin Sa'adul Khairi Waddin). Foreign Minister: Pengiran Muda Mohamed Bolkiah.

LANGUAGE: Malay (official), Chinese, English.

NATIONAL ANTHEM: Ya Allah lanjutkan lah usia duli tuanku (Oh God, long live our majesty the Sultan).

RELIGION: Moslem 64% (Islam is the official religion); Buddhist 14%; Christian 10%; Confucianist minorities.

TOURIST INFORMATION: Passport and visa required by Australian citizens. There is an export restriction on articles of an antique or historical nature made or discovered in Brunei. National airline: Royal Brunei Airlines. Bandar Seri Begawan airport is located 10 km from the city.

BULGARIA

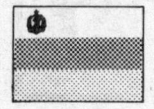

Narodna Republika Bulgaria
PEOPLE'S REPUBLIC OF BULGARIA
CAPITAL: Sofia

AREA AND POPULATION: 110,912 km^2, 39% cultivated land. Population: 8,990,000 (1986 est.) Population density: 81/km^2. Population growth (1970-82): 0.4%. Ethnic composition: Bulgarian 85%; Turkish 8%; Gypsy 2.5%.

CLIMATE AND GEOGRAPHY: The climate is temperate continental. Average temperature (Sofia): -2.2°C in January and 20.6°C in July. Annual rainfall varies from 500 mm on the coast to 1,905 mm in the mountains. The country is situated in the eastern Balkan Peninsula, bounded to the north by Romania, to the south by Turkey and Greece, to the east by the Black Sea and to the west by Yugoslavia. One-third of the country is mountainous, with an average height above sea-level of 470 m. The Balkan mountains are the longest chain in Bulgaria, running parallel to the Danube from Yugoslavia to the Black Sea.

CURRENCY: Lev of 100 stotinki.

DEFENCE: Military service is compulsory for 2 years (Army and Air

Force) or 3 years (Navy). Total armed forces (1987): 148,500. Army 105,000; Navy 8,500; Air Force 35,000. Paramilitary forces: People's Territorial Militia 150,000; Ministry of Interior border guards 15,000; security police 7,500; voluntary Organisation for Cooperation in National Defence (numbers not known).

GOVERNMENT: People's republic with a unicameral parliament (Narodno Subranie). Voting is compulsory for all citizens over the age of 18. The highest policy-making and executive body is the Politburo, consisting of 11 full and 6 candidate members elected by and from the Central Committee of the Communist Party. Head of State and Chairman of the State Council: Todor Zhivkov. Head of Government and Premier: Georgy Atanasov. Foreign Minister: Petur Mladenov.

LANGUAGE: Bulgarian.

NATIONAL ANTHEM: Gorda stara planeena (Proudly rise the Balkan peaks).

RELIGION: Orthodox Christian 85%; Moslem 13%;, Roman Catholic 55,000; Protestant 22,000; Jewish 700 (these figures relate only to the 40% of the population who profess religious beliefs).

TOURIST INFORMATION: Passport and visa required by Australian citizens. Travellers are advised to hold 2 passport photographs for any contingencies. Visas are available from Bulgarian embassies or consulates or at the Bulgarian border. Prices vary, with border prices being highest. Business visas may be obtained only from embassies or consulates; they are valid for 1 entry only but for no set period. All accommodation arrangements should be made through Balkan-Tourist. National airline: BALKAN.

BURKINA FASO

République démocratique et populaire de Burkina Faso
(Burkina Faso = Land of incorruptible men)
DEMOCRATIC PEOPLE'S REPUBLIC OF BURKINA FASO

CAPITAL: Ouagadougou

AREA AND POPULATION: 274,200 km^2, 10-20% cultivated land. Population: 7,084,000 (1986 est.). Population density: 25.8/km^2. Population growth (1970-82): 2%. Ethnic composition: Voltaic groups, about 50%; Bobo 16%; Fulbe 10%; Haussa; Tuareg; European (mostly French).

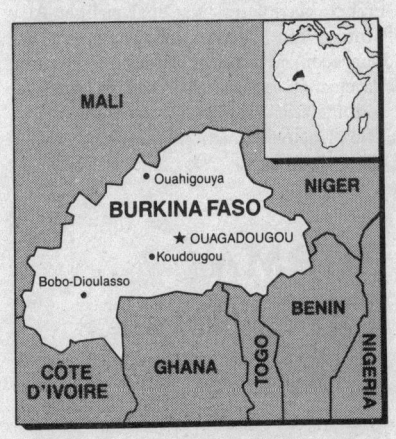

CLIMATE AND GEOGRAPHY: The climate is hot and mainly dry. Average annual temperature: 26.3°C. There is a rainy season from May to November. Average annual rainfall: 894 mm. The country is a landlocked state in the savannah region of West Africa. To the north and west it is bordered by Mali, and to the east by Niger. Benin, Togo, Ghana and Côte D'Ivoire are to the south.

CURRENCY: Franc CFA of 100 centimes.

DEFENCE: Military service is voluntary. All services, including the gendarmerie, form part of the Army. Total armed forces (1987): 4,000. Army 3,900; Air Force 100. Para-military forces: people's militia 40,000; gendarmerie 650; security company 250.

GOVERNMENT: Military government: the 12-member National Revolutionary Council headed by the President. Head of State: President Captain Thomas Sankara. Foreign Minister: Bazombué Léandre Bassolet.

LANGUAGE: French (official), More, Sudanic tribal.

RELIGION: Animist 65%; Moslem 25%; Christian 10%.

TOURIST INFORMATION: Passport and visa required by Australian citizens. Visas may be obtained from representatives of Burkina Faso in Belgium, Canada, France, FRG, Ghana, Israel, Côte D'Ivoire Japan, Liberia, Mali, UK and USA or French consulates. National airline: Air Volta. The international airport at Ouagadougou is located 8 km from the city. Vaccination against yellow fever is required and malaria prophylaxis recommended. The principal attraction for tourists is big-game hunting.

BURMA

Pyidaungsu Socialist Thammada Myanma Naingngandaw
SOCIALIST REPUBLIC OF THE UNION OF BURMA

CAPITAL: Rangoon

AREA AND POPULATION: 678,000 km², 15% cultivated land. Population: 37,641,000 (1986 est.). Population density: 55.5/km². Population growth (1970-82): 2.2%. Ethnic composition: Burman 68%; Shan 9%; Karen 7%; Rakhine 4%; Indian; Chinese.

CLIMATE AND GEOGRAPHY: The climate is equatorial on the coast, tropical monsoon over most of the interior and humid temperate in the north. Average temperature (Rangoon): 26°C. Average annual rainfall (Rangoon): 2,616 mm. Burma is the largest country in the South-East Asian mainland. It is bordered to the north by China, to the south by the Andaman Sea, to the east by China, Laos and Thailand, and to the west by India, Bangladesh and the Bay of Bengal. Dense forests cover much of the country.

CURRENCY: Kyat (K) of 100 pyas.

DEFENCE: Military service is voluntary. Total armed forces (1987): 186,000. Army 170,000; Navy 7,000 (spares are in short supply and some equipment is unserviceable); Air Force 9,000. Para-military forces: people's police 38,000; people's militia 35,000; Fishery Dept. Opposition: Burmese Communist Party 12,000 regulars, 8,000 militia; Kachin Independence Army 5,000; Karen National Liberation Army 5,000; Shan State Army 3,500; Shan United Army 3,000; Shan United Revolutionary Army 900-1,200; Mon State Army 700; Karenni Army 600; Palaung State Liberation Army 500; Pa-O National Army 500; Wa National Army 300; Kayan New Land Party 100; Kawthoolei Muslim Liberation Front (numbers not known).

GOVERNMENT: Socialist republic. The unicameral parliament (People's Congress) has 475 members. Head of State: President General U San Yu. Prime Minister: Dr U Maung Maung Kha. Foreign Minister: U Ye Goung.

LANGUAGE: Burmese (official), English.

NATIONAL ANTHEM: Gba majay Bma (We shall love Burma).

RELIGION: Buddhist 85%; Moslem 2-3%; Hindu 2%; Christian 2%; Jewish 200.

TOURIST INFORMATION: Passport and visa required by Australian citizens. Entry is permitted only by air or sea and an exit permit is required. A departure tax of K15 is payable at Rangoon airport or at the carrier's office in Rangoon. National airline: Burma Airways Corporation. Rangoon-Mingaladon airport is located 19 km from the city. Malaria prophylaxis is recommended. Imported currency and travellers' cheques should be declared on the Foreign Exchange Control form, which must be produced for any transactions. A minimum of US$100 has to be changed into local currency on arrival. American Express cards (only) can be used in the larger hotels but must also be declared upon arrival. Visitors should declare cameras, jewellery, watches and any electronic equipment and should be able to produce these items for Customs inspection on leaving Burma. Tipping, though officially discouraged in hotels, is quite common. It is considered impolite to wear revealing or 'slovenly' clothing.

BURUNDI

Republika y'Uburundi/
République du Burundi
REPUBLIC OF BURUNDI

CAPITAL: Bujumbura

AREA AND POPULATION: 27,834 km², 50% cultivated land. Population: 4,807,000 (1986 est.). Population density: 172.7/km². Population growth (1970-82): 2.2%. Ethnic composition: Hutu, 85%; Tutsi 14%; Twa 1%; European (mostly Belgian) and Asian (mostly Indian) minorities.

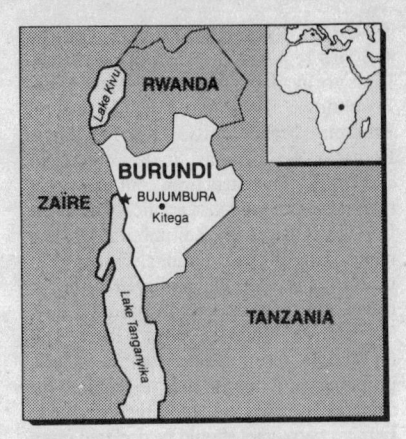

CLIMATE AND GEOGRAPHY: The climate is equatorial, modified by altitude. The wet seasons last from March to May and September to December. Average temperature: 22.8°C. Average annual rainfall: 825 mm. Burundi is situated on the northern shore of Lake Tanganyika in central Africa, just south of the equator. It is bordered to the north by Rwanda, to the east by Tanzania and to the west by Zaïre. Much of the country is grassy highland.

CURRENCY: Burundi franc (FBu) of 100 centimes.

DEFENCE: Military service is voluntary. Total armed forces (1987): 7,200. Army 5,500; Navy 50; Air Force 150. Para-military force: gendarmerie 1,500 (forms part of Army).

GOVERNMENT: Republic, governed by the (only) political party: National Union for Progress and Unity (UPRONA). Ultimate power is vested in the Central Committee which consists of the President and 48 other members. A cabinet of 18 ministers is appointed by and responsible to the President. Head of State: President Colonel Jean-Baptiste Bagaza. Foreign Minister: Egide Nkuriyingoma.

LANGUAGE: French and Kirundi (both official), Kiswahili (commercial).

NATIONAL ANTHEM: Uburundi bwacu (Beloved Burundi).

RELIGION: Roman Catholic 62%; Pentecostal 3%; Anglican 1%; Moslem 1%; Animist.

TOURIST INFORMATION: Passport and visa required by Australian citizens. Visas are available from representatives of Burundi in Belgium, Canada, Egypt, Ethiopia, France, FRG, Kenya, Libya, Romania, Saudi Arabia, Switzerland, USA and USSR. Travellers from countries other than these can send visa applications to the Foreign Office in Bujumbura, stating name, date of birth, nationality, passport number and date of validity, reason for travel and references in Burundi, if any. Vaccination against yellow fever and typhoid is recommended, as is malaria prophylaxis. A deposit may be required for cameras, typewriters, tape recorders etc. Foreign currencies should be declared upon arrival. National airline: Air Burundi. Bujumbura airport is located 11 km from the city.

CAMEROON

République du Cameroun
REPUBLIC OF CAMEROON

CAPITAL: Yaoundé

AREA AND POPULATION: 480,621 km^2, 16% cultivated land. Population: 10,008,000 (1986 est.). Population density: 20.8/km^2. Population growth (1970-82): 3%. Ethnic composition: Bantu 40%; semi-Bantu and Sudanese tribes 20%; Pygmy and European (mostly French) minorities; refugees from Chad: 150,000.

CLIMATE AND GEOGRAPHY: In the rainforests to the west and south the climate is tropical, with high temperatures and high humidity. The heaviest rain falls between March and November. Average temperature in Yaoundé: 23.6°C. The north has a drier climate with more extreme temperatures, ranging from 6°C at night in January to 43°C by day in July. In the mountainous area to the west it is considerably cooler, with the temperature varying according to altitude. Annual rainfall varies from 1,555 mm to 4,026 mm. The country is situated at the junction of West and Central Africa. Triangular in shape, it is bordered by the Congo, Gabon and Equatorial Guinea to the south, by Chad to the east and by Nigeria and the Gulf of Guinea to the west. The north of the country is semi-desert, the south and west savannah uplands, and the east dense forest.

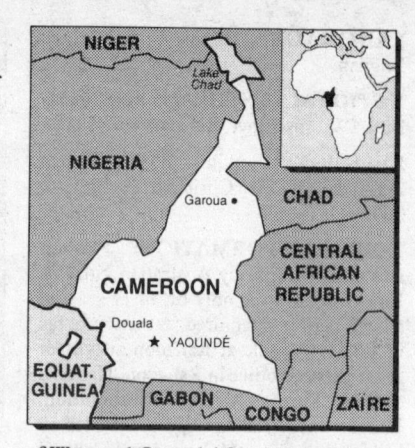

CURRENCY: Franc CFA of 100 centimes.

DEFENCE: Military service is voluntary but pre-military training is compulsory. Total armed forces (1987): 7,300. Army 6,600; Navy 350; Air Force 350. Para-military force: gendarmerie 4,000.

GOVERNMENT: Presidential republic. The President is elected for a 5-year term and is eligible for re-election. Legislative power rests with the President and the National Assembly which is composed of 120 members and is elected for a 5-year period by universal suffrage. There is only 1 political party, the Union Nationale Camerounaise. Head of State: President Paul Biya. Foreign Minister: Philippe Mataga.

LANGUAGES: French and English (both official), Bantu, semi-Bantu and Sudanese dialects.

NATIONAL ANTHEM: O Cameroun, berceau de nos ancêtres (Oh Cameroon, cradle of our ancestors).

RELIGION: Roman Catholic, 35%; Animist 25%; Moslem 22%; Protestant 18%.

CANADA

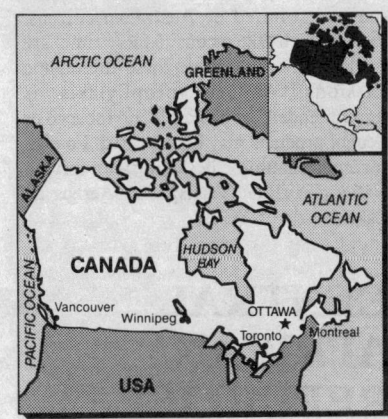

TOURIST INFORMATION: Passport and visa required by Australian citizens. Visas may be obtained from representatives of Cameroon in Algiers, Belgium, Canada, Central African Republic, People's Republic of China, Congo, Denmark, Egypt, Ethiopia, Fernando Po, France, FRG, Italy, Liberia, Netherlands, Saudi Arabia, Spain, Switzerland, Tunisia, UK, USA, USSR, Zaire and the UN in New York. Yellow fever vaccination is compulsory and malaria prophylaxis is recommended. National airline: Cameroon Airlines. The international airports of Douala and Yaoundé are located 4.8 km and 4 km from their respective cities.

CAPITAL: Ottawa

AREA AND POPULATION: 9,976,139 km^2, 5% cultivated land. Population: 25,625,000 (1986 est.). Population density: 2.6/km^2. Population growth (1970-82): 1.2%. Ethnic composition: Canadians of British background 40%; French background 27%; other European 23%; Indian and Eskimo minorities.

CLIMATE AND GEOGRAPHY: The climate ranges from polar in the north to cool temperate in the south. Winters are predominantly very severe, with average temperatures in January from −19.3°C in Winnipeg, to 2.2°C in Vancouver. Summers can be hot inland, with average temperatures in July from 19.6°C in Winnipeg, to 17.8°C in Vancouver. Average annual rainfall: 539 mm (Winnipeg); 1,458 mm (Vancouver). Canada is the second largest country in the world. It is bordered to the south by the United States of America. The mainland coastline (approx. 58,160 km) is very broken and irregular. Large bays and peninsulas alternate and there are numerous coastal islands. The largest islands off the east coast are Newfoundland, Cape Breton, Prince Edward and Anticosti, while Vancouver, Queen Charlotte and Southampton Islands are the largest off the west coast. Canada contains more lakes (32 plus the Great Lakes on the US border) and inland waters than any other country.

CURRENCY: Canadian dollar (C$) of 100 cents.

DEFENCE: Military service is voluntary. Total armed forces (1986/87): 83,000. Army 21,000; Navy 5,500; Air Force 15,300. The Canadian Armed Forces were unified in 1968. Of the total strength, some 41,200 are not identified by service. Para-military forces: coastguard 6,561; Canadian Rangers 1,220.

GOVERNMENT: Constitutional monarchy with a bicameral legislature. Executive authority is vested in the Governor-General and the Privy Council. The legislature consists of the House of Commons and the Senate. Appointment of the 104 Senators is along regional lines and is made by the Governor-General, acting on the advice of the Prime Minister. The House of Commons has 282 elected members who represent the provinces and territories according to population. The 10 provincial governments all have unicameral legislatures. Election of governments both at federal and provincial levels is by simple majority. The Northwest Territories and the Yukon are evolving towards eventual self-government. Governor General: Jeanne Sauvé. Prime Minister: Brian Mulroney.

Foreign Minister: Charles Joseph Clark.

LANGUAGES: French and English (both official).

NATIONAL ANTHEM: Oh Canada.

RELIGION: Roman Catholic 46.2%; United Church 17.5%; Episcopalian (Anglican) 11.8%; Presbyterian 4%; Lutheran 4%; Baptist 3.3%.

TOURIST INFORMATION: Passport but no visa required by Australian citizens. No vaccinations are required. National airlines: Air Canada, Canadian Pacific Airlines, Wardair.

CAPE VERDE

República de Cabo Verde
REPUBLIC OF CAPE VERDE

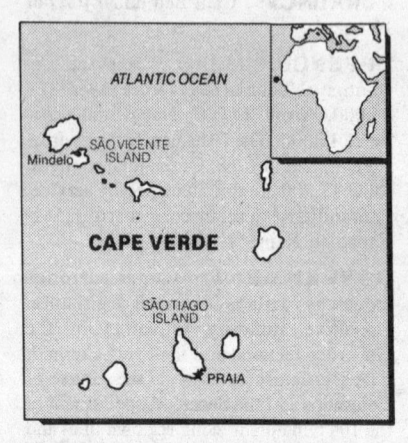

CAPITAL: Praia

AREA AND POPULATION: 4,033 km^2, 9% cultivated land. Population: 319,000 (1986 est.). Population density: 79.1/km^2. Population growth (1975-78): 1.9%. Ethnic composition: creole (mulatto) 71%; Negro 28%; European 1%. Approx. 600,000 Cape Verde citizens work abroad.

CLIMATE AND GEOGRAPHY: The climate is arid, with a cool season from December to June. There are periodic severe droughts. Annual rainfall varies from 127 mm in the northern islands to 304 mm in the southern islands. The country is situated in the Atlantic Ocean, 620 km WNW of Senegal and consists of 10 islands and 5 islets.

CURRENCY: Escudo Caboverdianos of 100 centavos.

DEFENCE: Military service is by selective conscription. Total armed forces (1987): 1,170. Army 1,000; Navy 120; Air Force 50.

GOVERNMENT: Republic. There is only 1 political party, the Partido Africano da Independencia de Cabo Verde. The 83-seat legislature is elected for 5 years by universal suffrage. Head of State: President Aristides Maria Pereira. Prime Minister: General Pedro Pires. Foreign Minister: Silvino Manuel da Luz.

LANGUAGE: Portuguese (official), Crioulu (African/Portuguese creole).

RELIGION: Roman Catholic over 98%; Animist.

TOURIST INFORMATION: Passport and visa required by Australian citizens. Visas (which take a considerable time) are available through Portuguese diplomatic missions. Malaria prophylaxis is recommended. In principle, no tobacco or alcohol products may be imported. Foreign currency should be declared upon arrival. National airline: Transportes Aereos do Cabo Verde (TACV).

CENTRAL AFRICAN REPUBLIC

République centrafricaine/
Be ti Kodro ti Africa

CAPITAL: Bangui

AREA AND POPULATION: 622,984 km^2, 5% cultivated land. Population:

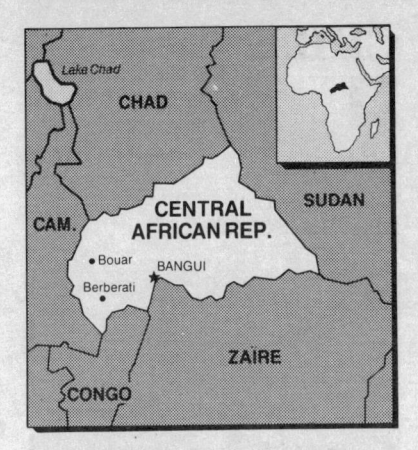

2,744,000 (1986 est.). Population density: 4.4/km². Population growth (1970-81): 2.3%. Ethnic composition: Banda 27%; Baya 34%; Mandja 21%; Sara 10%; several thousand Europeans (mostly French).

CLIMATE AND GEOGRAPHY: The climate is tropical. The wet seasons May-June to October-November. Average annual rainfall: 1,471 mm. Average temperature (Bangui): 25.5°C. The CAR is bounded to the north by Chad, to the south by Zaïre and Congo, to the east by Sudan and to the west by Cameroon. Most of the country is rolling or flat plateau. There is a dense tropical rainforest in the southwest.

CURRENCY: Franc CFA of 100 centimes.

DEFENCE: There is selective national service for a period of 2 years. Total armed forces (1987): 2,385. Army 2,000; Air Force 300; Navy 85. Para-military forces: gendarmerie 700; Republican Guard 700; Presidential Guard 500; regional legions; National Young Pioneers (boys and girls 14-18).

GOVERNMENT: Presidential republic. All legislative and executive power has been in the hands of the Military Committee for National Recovery (CMRN) since the military coup of September 1981 (constitution of 1.2.81 suspended). Head of State, Head of Government, Minister of Defence and Veterans' Affairs and Chairman of the CMRN: General André Kolingba. Foreign Minister and Minister for International Co-operation: Second Lieut. Clément Michel N'Gai Voueto.

LANGUAGE: French (official), Sangho (national).

NATIONAL ANTHEM: La Renaissance.

RELIGION: Roman Catholic 25%; Protestant 25%; Moslem 8%; Animist 57%.

TOURIST INFORMATION: Passport and visa required by Australian citizens. French consulates act for the CAR in countries where the CAR has no representation of its own. Vaccination against yellow fever is required (transit passengers included). Malaria prophylaxis is recommended. A Tourist Development Tax (Departure Tax) of Francs CFA 2,000 is levied on all passengers departing on international flights. National airline: the CAR is a shareholder in Air Afrique. Bangui-M'Poko airport is located 8 km from the city.

CHAD

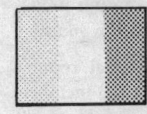

République du Tchad
REPUBLIC OF CHAD

CAPITAL: N'djaména

AREA AND POPULATION: 1,284,000 km², 3% cultivated land. Population: 5,231,000 (1986 est.). Population density: 4.1/km². Population growth (1970-82): 2%. Ethnic composition: Sudanese Arab 30%; Sudanic tribes 25%; European (mainly French) 4,000; Nilotic, Saharan tribes.

CLIMATE AND GEOGRAPHY: The climate is tropical, with desert conditions in the north. Average temperature: 26°C. Average annual rainfall: 744 mm. Chad is situated in central northern Africa, bounded to the north by Libya, to the south by the Central African Republic, to the east by Sudan and to the west by Cameroon, Nigeria and Niger. The topography ranges from equatorial forests to mid-Saharan desert towards the north.

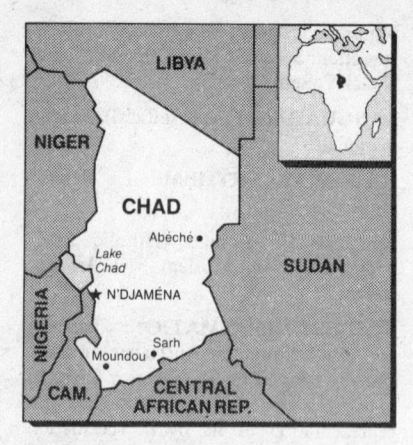

CURRENCY: Franc CFA of 100 centimes.

DEFENCE: Military service is by conscription for a period of 3 years. Total armed forces (1987): 14,200. Army 14,200; Air Force 200. Para-military forces: National and Nomad Guards 3,900; village militias 3,900; gendarmerie 1,800; security companies 1,000; police 800. Opposition: 10,000 (Libyan-backed Arab groups in the north and African groups in the south).

GOVERNMENT: Presidential republic. There is a single-chamber, 33-member parliament. Head of State and Head of Government: President Hissène Habré. Foreign Minister: Gouara Lassou.

LANGUAGE: French (official), Arabic.

RELIGION: Moslem 44%; Christian 33%; Animist 23%.

TOURIST INFORMATION: Passport and visa required by Australian citizens. French consulates act for Chad in countries where Chad has no representative of its own. A special permit, issued by the Ministère de l'Intérieur, is required for all destinations in Chad except N'djaména. This permit is only obtainable upon arrival and may take a considerable time. Vaccination against yellow fever is recommended, as is malaria prophylaxis. Foreign currencies should be declared upon arrival. There is a tourist tax of CFA 2,000 payable on departure. National airline: Air Chad.

CHILE

República de Chile
REPUBLIC OF CHILE

CAPITAL: Santiago

AREA AND POPULATION: 756,945 km^2, 8% cultivated land. Population: 12,261,000 (1986 est.). Population density: 16.2/km^2. Population growth (1970-82): 1.7%. Ethnic composition: mestizo 66%; Spanish 25%; Araucanian Indian 1.5%; other Indian 3.5%.

CLIMATE AND GEOGRAPHY: The climate ranges from hot and dry in the north to temperate in the centre, with little rain in summer. Winters are severe and summers cold in the windy southern regions. Average annual rainfall (Santiago): 375 mm. Chile forms a long narrow strip of land on the west coast of the South American continent, stretching about 4,300 km from 17°30'S to 26°30'S, with an average breadth of 180 km. It is situated on a major geophysical fault, suffering frequent earth tremors and intermittent serious earthquakes. The country is bordered to the north by Peru, to the east by Bolivia and Argentina and to the west by the Pacific Ocean.

CURRENCY: Chilean Peso of 1,000 escudos.

DEFENCE: Military service for 1 year (Army and Air Force), or 2 years (Navy) is compulsory for males at age 19. Total armed forces (1987): 101,000. Army 57,000; Navy 29,000; Air Force 15,000. Para-military forces: Carabineros 27,000; coastguard.

GOVERNMENT: Four-man military dictatorship. The new constitution, approved by plebiscite on 11 September 1980, provides for elections for a Congress to be held in 1989. The President, backed by the military junta is to remain in power until then, with provision for his re-nomination for a further 8-year term. Head of State: President General Augusto Pinochet Ugarte. Foreign Minister: Jaime del Valle Alliende.

LANGUAGE: Spanish.

NATIONAL ANTHEM: Dulce patria, recibe los votos (Fair fatherland, accept our devotion).

RELIGION: Roman Catholic 79%; Protestant 6%; Jewish 30,000.

TOURIST INFORMATION: Passport but no visa required by Australian citizens provided the period of stay does not exceed 90 days. No vaccinations are required but typhoid inoculation is advisable. Tuberculosis, hepatitis, meningitis and typhoid are more common than in Australia. Lettuce, unpeeled vegetables and shellfish (especially oysters) should be avoided. National airline: Lan-Chile. Pudahuel airport is situated 20 km from Santiago de Chile. A departure tax of US$12.5 or its equivalent in pesos is levied on all passengers leaving from Pudahuel.

CHINA

Zhonghua Renmin Gonghe Guo
PEOPLE'S REPUBLIC OF CHINA

CAPITAL: Beijing (Peking)

AREA AND POPULATION:
9,572,900 km², 11% cultivated land. Population: 1,045,537,000 (1986 est.). Population density: 109.2/km². Population growth (1970-81): 1.5%, 1983: 1.4%. Ethnic composition: Chinese 94%; Thai; Mongol; Tibetan; Manchu; 55 minority groups.

CLIMATE AND GEOGRAPHY:
From November to April, China's climate is dominated by the Asian or Mongolian anti-cyclone. North-westerly, northerly and north-easterly winds are associated with the movement of cold, dry polar continental air masses across China. In July-August, the climate is dominated by the warm, moist airstreams of the summer monsoon from the south and south-east. The Qinlin range, running west-east, presents a barrier to the cold winds from the north in winter and the rain-bearing winds from the south in summer. In general, rainfall and rainfall reliability decrease from south to north and east to west. Average temperature (Beijing): −4.4°C (January); 26°C (July). Average annual rainfall (Beijing): 623 mm. Rainfall occurs mainly from May to October. China has a varied and complex land surface. In the west, the Qinghai-Tibet plateau, at an average height of over 4,000 m, is rimmed by major mountain ranges, including the Himalayas and the 8,800-m peak of Everest on the southern rim. To the north of Tibet there is a series of inland drainage areas at various levels. Further to the north, the Dzungarian Basin contains some streams flowing via the Siberian rivers to the Arctic. East of the Tibetan plateau and ranges, from which rise most of the major rivers of south and south-east Asia as well as China's Yangtze River, the limestone plateau has produced the famous karst formation of Guilin – a popular subject with Chinese landscape painters and poets. To the north of these areas and east of the inland basins, the desert and plateau areas of Shaanxi and Shanxi extend to the agriculturally important coastal alluvial plains. Between the southern limestone plateau and the northern loess plateau, the Sichuan basin possesses a climate moderated by sheltering mountains and this, with Sichuan's rich soils, has made it a major agricultural area. The Bohai, Yellow, East China and South China seas border the eastern coast. There are

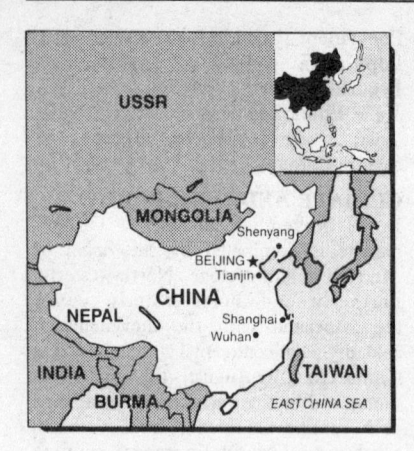

thousands of scattered islands, the biggest and most productive being Hainan. In the north-east corner, the valleys of the Liao and Sungari rivers form the Manchurian plains.

CURRENCY: Yuan of 10 jiao, divided into 10 fen.

DEFENCE: Selective military service is compulsory for 3 years (Army) or 4 years (Air Force) and 5 years (Navy). Total armed forces (1987): 2,898,000. Army 2,110,000 (25% reduction under way); Navy 248,000; Air Force 490,000. The term 'People's Liberation Army' covers all services; the Ground, Naval and Air components have been listed separately here for purposes of comparison. Para-military forces: ordinary militia 6,000,000; basic militia 4,300,000; People's Armed Police Force (Ministry of Security) 1,700,000 (includes border security, patrol and internal security forces).

GOVERNMENT: One-party people's republic. The highest organ of state is the National People's Congress (NPC). It is elected every 5 years and holds 1 session per year in normal circumstances. The seventh NPC, which met in April 1987, numbered 2,719 deputies from People's Congresses of the provinces, autonomous regions and municipalities. The composition of the NPC is as follows: workers and peasants 26.6%; revolutionary cadres 21.4%; intellectuals 28.5; 'patriotic personages' 18.2%; soldiers 9%; returned overseas Chinese 1.3%. The President of the People's Republic of China is the Head of State. Both the President and the Vice-President are elected by the NPC. Their duties are largely of a protocol nature, taking the load off the Premier of the State Council. The State Council is the most important administrative organ of the Central Government. It is composed of a Premier and 4 Vice-Premiers, 10 State Councillors, Ministers, the Auditor-General and the Secretary-General. Head of State: Chairman Yang Shangkun. Head of Government Premier Li Peng. Head of Communist Party: General Secretary Zhao Ziyang. Foreign Minister: Qian Qichon.

LANGUAGE: Mandarin Chinese (official), other Chinese dialects, Tibetan, Turkic. Since 1979, the Pinyin phonetic alphabet has been adopted (officially) for the transcription of Chinese characters.

NATIONAL ANTHEM: March of the Volunteers.

RELIGION: Officially atheist; Confucianism; Buddhism; Taoism; and Islam are traditional; 'Patriotic' Catholicism (not recognized by the Vatican); Protestantism.

TOURIST INFORMATION: Passport and visa required by Australian citizens. All passengers leaving the country require an exit visa, the regulations stated on which must be strictly adhered to. National airline: CAAC. Beijing airport is situated 26 km from the city. There is a departure tax of 15 yuan. Foreign currencies should be declared upon arrival. Stomach upsets may result from dietary changes but they can be treated in China. Serious illness may involve evacuation to Japan or Hong Kong. Boiled water is provided in hotel rooms and hot water is available in flasks. Accommodation is almost always warm, but warm overcoats and good boots are needed in winter (November to March), anywhere from the Changjiang (Yangtze) Valley northward. Malaria prophylaxis is recommended. If a long-term stay is anticipated, Japanese encephalitis type B vaccinations may also be advisable.

COLOMBIA

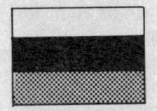

República de Colombia
REPUBLIC OF COLOMBIA

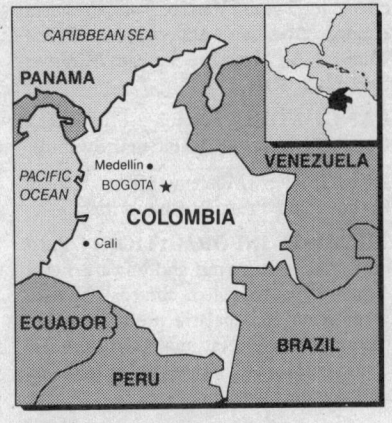

CAPITAL: Bogotá

AREA AND POPULATION:
1,138,914 km², 9% cultivated land. Population: 29,956,000 (1986 est.). Population density: 26.3/km². Population growth (1970-82): 1.9%. Ethnic composition: mestizo 60%; European (mostly of Spanish background) 20%; Negro 5%; Indian 7%; mulatto.

CLIMATE AND GEOGRAPHY: The climate varies from tropical to temperate, according to altitude. Average annual rainfall (Bogotá): 1,052 mm. Average temperature (Bogotá): 14.2°C. Colombia is the only country in South America to have coastlines on both the Atlantic and Pacific Oceans. It is bounded to the north-east by Venezuela, to the south-east by Brazil, to the south by Peru and Ecuador and to the north-west by Panama. Three major cordilleras of the Andes run through Colombia, from north to south. These form a geographic region of their own, where nearly all the population lives. Eleven of the country's 14 main cities are found here, including the capital, Bogotá.

CURRENCY: Colombian Peso of 100 centavos.

DEFENCE: Selective military service is for 2 years. Total armed forces (1987): 66,900. Army 53,000; Navy 9,700; Air Force 4,200. Para-military forces: national police force 50,000; coastguard. Opposition: Revolutionary Workers' Party; Colombian Revolutionary Armed Forces (FARC).

GOVERNMENT: Presidential republic. The bicameral parliament consists of a Senate (112 members) and a House of Representatives (199 members). There is universal suffrage, women having been granted the vote on 25. 8.54. Head of State: President Virgilio Barco Vargas. Foreign Minister: Julio Londoño Paredes.

LANGUAGE: Spanish.

NATIONAL ANTHEM: Oh! Gloria inmarcesible (Oh undiminishing glory).

RELIGION: Roman Catholic 95%; Protestant 100,000; Jewish 12,000.

TOURIST INFORMATION: Passport and visa required by Australian citizens. Visitors holding a 'Visa Temporal' (temporary visa) or 'Visa Ordinaria' (normal visa) must report within 48 hours, with their papers and 5 passport photos, to the Bureau of Foreigners of the Departmento de Seguridad in Bogotá or to the Mayor's office in other cities. Vaccination against yellow fever and malaria prophylaxis are recommended. Few parts of Colombia are unhealthy, and the sanitary conditions of the major cities are good. Hepatitis is common in some areas, so care should be taken with food and drink. Gamma globulin injections before travel are advisable. Travel by road within Colombia can be tedious and flying is preferable. National airline: Avianca. Bogotá-Eldorado airport is located 13 km from the city. There is a departure tax of US$15 or the equivalent in pesos.

COMOROS

République fédérale islamique des Comores
Jumhuriyat al-Qumur al-Ittiadiyah al-Islamiyah
FEDERAL ISLAMIC REPUBLIC OF THE COMORES

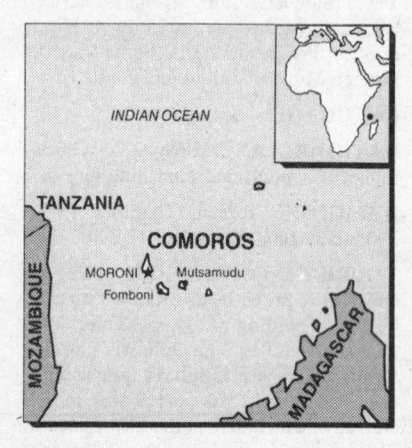

CAPITAL: Moroni

AREA AND POPULATION: 1,860 km^2, 50% cultivated land. Population: 420,000 (1986 est.). Population density: 193.5/km^2. Population growth (1981): 2.2%. Ethnic composition: Arab; Malgache; Bantu; Indian; several hundred Europeans (mostly French).

CLIMATE AND GEOGRAPHY: The climate is tropical with monsoon winds. The wet season lasts from November to April. The average annual rainfall is 2,825 mm. The country consists of 3 islands (Njazidja, Mwali, Nzwani) in the Indian Ocean, between the African mainland and Madagascar. The islands are of volcanic origin with an active volcano on Njazidja.

CURRENCY: Franc CFA of 100 centimes.

DEFENCE: Total armed forces (1987): approx. 1,000. Army 700; Navy and Air Arm approx. 300.

GOVERNMENT: Federal Islamic Republic. Under the constitution, the nearby island of Mayotte has the right to join the Republic when it so chooses. The President is elected for a 6-year (renewable) term. He appoints the Prime Minister and up to 9 other Ministers to form the Council of Government. The 39-member unicameral Federal Assembly is directly elected for 5 years. Head of State: President Ahmed Abdallah Abderemane. Prime Minister: Ali Mroudjae. Foreign Minister: Saïd Madi Kafe.

LANGUAGE: French (official); Comoran (blend of Arabic and Swahili).

RELIGION: Moslem 95%; Roman Catholic and Protestant minorities.

TOURIST INFORMATION: Passport, visa, exit permit and onward ticket required by Australian citizens. Cholera vaccination and malaria prophylaxis are recommended. National airline: Air Comores. Moroni-Hayaha airport is located 20 km from the city.

CONGO

République populaire du Congo
PEOPLE'S REPUBLIC OF THE CONGO

CAPITAL: Brazzaville

AREA AND POPULATION: 342,000 km^2, 2% cultivated land. Population: 1,853,000 (1986 est.). Population density: 5.4/km^2. Population growth (1970-82): 3%. Ethnic composition: Bakongo 45%; Bateke 20%; Sanga 15%; Pygmy 0.7%; European (mostly French) 0.7%.

CLIMATE AND GEOGRAPHY: The climate is equatorial with moderate rainfall. The Congo Basin is more humid and rainfall there approaches 2,500 mm. Average annual rainfall (Brazzaville): 1,473 mm. Average temperature (Brazzaville): 24.2°C. Congo is bounded to the north by Cameroon and the Central African

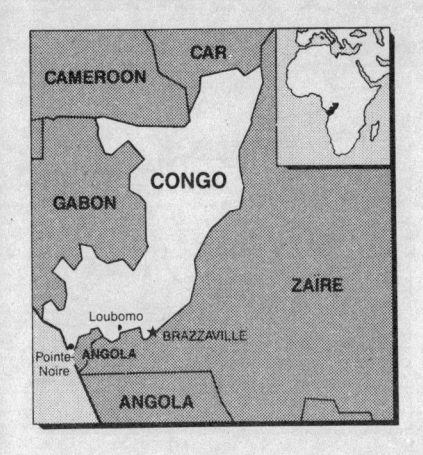

Republic, to the south and east by Zaïre, by Angola and the Atlantic Ocean to the south-west and by Gabon to the west. Much of the country is covered by thick forests. The centre is a plateau. The Congo river basin consists of flood plains, with savannah in the upper portion.

CURRENCY: Franc CFA of 100 centimes.

DEFENCE: Military service is voluntary for 2 years. Total armed forces (1987): 8,750. Army 8,000; Navy 250; Air Force 500. Para-military forces: people's militia 4,700; gendarmerie 1,400.

GOVERNMENT: People's republic. The National Congress of the sole political party (Parti congolais du travail) elects the President for a 5-year term. The PCT also elects a Central Committee and a Political Bureau to administer it, and nominates all 153 members of the People's National Assembly. Head of State: President Colonel Denis Sassou-Nguesso. Prime Minister: Ange-Edouard Poungui. Foreign Minister: Antoine Ndinga Oba.

LANGUAGE: French (official), Lingala, Kikongo.

RELIGION: Roman Catholic 40%; Protestant 10-12%; Moslem 2%; Animist 47%.

TOURIST INFORMATION: Passport, visa and onward ticket required by Australian citizens. Tourists must also present evidence of a prior hotel reservation. Businesspeople must present documents proving their profession or an invitation from business contacts in Congo. An exit permit must be obtained 48 hours prior to departure on proof of payment of hotel bill. Vaccination against cholera and yellow fever is required and malaria prophylaxis is recommended. Departure tax (domestic flights): Francs CFA 500. National airline: Lina Congo. Brazzaville-Maya Maya airport is located 4 km from the city.

COSTA RICA

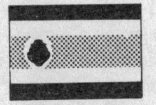

República de Costa Rica
REPUBLIC OF COSTA RICA

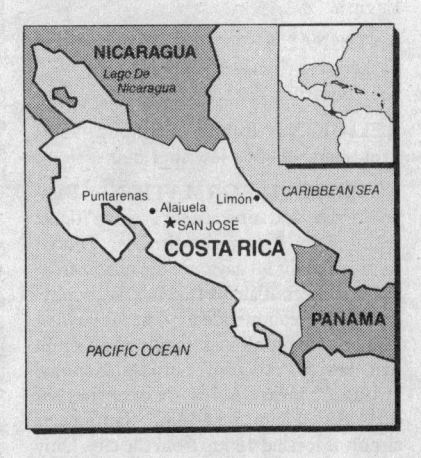

CAPITAL: San José

AREA AND POPULATION: 50,700 km², 10% cultivated land. Population: 2,714,000 (1986 est.). Population density: 53.5/km². Population growth (1970-82): 2.5%. Ethnic composition: European (mostly of Spanish background), over 75%; Negro and mulatto 2%; Indian 0.2%; foreign refugees approx. 200,000.

CLIMATE AND GEOGRAPHY: The climate is tropical with abundant rainfall. The dry season lasts from December to April. Average temperature: 19.7°C. Average annual rainfall: 1,793 mm. Costa

Rica is bounded to the north by Nicaragua, to the south and west by the Pacific Ocean, to the south-east by Panama and to the east by the Caribbean Sea. There are lowlands on both coastlines, mainly swampy on the Caribbean coast, and an interior plateau with an altitude of about 1,200 m.

CURRENCY: Colone of 100 centimos.

DEFENCE: No compulsory military service or training. Total security forces (1987): 9,600. Civil Guard 6,000; Navy 100; Rural Guard 3,500. There are numerous private armies.

GOVERNMENT: Presidential republic. The unicameral parliament is elected by universal suffrage for a 4-year term. Head of State: President Dr Oscar Arias Sanchez. Foreign Minister: Rodrigo Madrigal Nieto.

LANGUAGE: Spanish (official), English.

NATIONAL ANTHEM: Noble patria, tu hermosa bandera (Noble fatherland, your beautiful flag).

RELIGION: Roman Catholic 95%; Protestant 40,000; Jewish 1,500.

TOURIST INFORMATION: Passport, visa and onward or return ticket required by Australian citizens. Tourist cards, valid for 90 days, are obtainable from airline offices at airports. Malaria prophylaxis is recommended. The following fashions are prohibited: long and unkempt hair, beards, 'indecent' clothing. National airline: Lineas Aereas Costarricenses (LACSA). San José-Juan Santamaria airport is located 18 km from the city. Only US dollars are accepted for exchange.

CÔTE D'IVOIRE

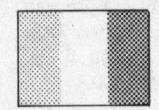

IVORY COAST

CAPITAL: Abidjan

AREA AND POPULATION: 322,463 km², 12% cultivated land. Population: 10,500,000 (1986 est.). Population density: 32.6/km². Population growth (1970-82): 4.9%. Ethnic composition (mainly Sudanese tribes): Baule 23%; Bete 18%; Senufo 15%; Malinke 11%; Lebanese and Syrians 1.2%; French 0.6%; foreign workers from Burkina Faso.

CLIMATE AND GEOGRAPHY: The climate is tropical, with wet seasons affected by proximity to the sea. Average temperature (Abidjan): 27°C (January), 24°C (July). Average annual rainfall: 2,100 mm. The Republic is situated on the Gulf of Guinea, bordered to the north by Mali and Burkina Faso, with Ghana to the east and Guinea and Liberia to the west. The western part of the country is covered by forests, and an inland plain leads to low mountains in the north-west. The Atlantic coastline is 600 km long and mostly fringed with sandy beaches.

CURRENCY: Franc CFA of 100 centimes.

DEFENCE: Military service is by selective conscription for a period of 6 months. Total armed forces (1987): 13,230. Army 6,100; Navy 700; Air Force 930. Para-military force: 7,800.

GOVERNMENT: Presidential republic. The unicameral Parliament of 175 members is elected for a 5-year term by universal suffrage. Single legal political party: Parti démocratique de la Côte d'Ivoire. Head of State: President Félix Houphouët-Boigny. Foreign Minister: Simeon Ake.

LANGUAGE: French (official), tribal languages.

NATIONAL ANTHEM: Salut o terre d'espérance; pays de l'hospitalité (We salute you, oh land of hope, country of hospitality).

RELIGION: Indigenous (animist) 63%; Christian (mainly Roman Catholic) 12%.

TOURIST INFORMATION: Passport and visa required by Australian citizens. Visas are available from Ivory Coast diplomatic missions in Belgium, Canada, France, FRG, Ghana, Italy, Liberia, Netherlands, Switzerland, Tanzania, UK, USA and from French representations acting for the Ivory Coast. Vaccination against yellow fever is required and malaria prophylaxis is recommended. National airline: Air Ivoire. Abidjan-Port Bouet airport is located 16 km from the city.

CUBA

República de Cuba
REPUBLIC OF CUBA

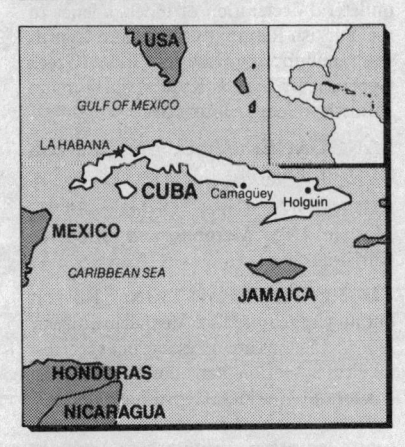

CAPITAL: Havana (La Habana)

AREA AND POPULATION: 114,524 km^2, 28% cultivated land. Population: 10,221,000 (1986 est.). Population density: 89.2/km^2. Population growth (1970-82): 1.1%. Ethnic composition: European (Spanish background), 70%; mestizo and mulatto 15-17%; Negro 12%; Chinese 0.5%.

CLIMATE AND GEOGRAPHY: The climate is subtropical, warm and humid. The rainy season lasts from May to October. Average temperature: 25°C. Average annual rainfall: 1,224 mm. Cuba forms an archipelago composed of the Isla de Cuba (Island of Cuba), Isla de la Juventud (Island of Youth) and about 1,600 neighbouring cays. It is located in the Caribbean Sea, between North and South America, bounded to the east by Haiti, to the west by the Yucatan Peninsula, to the north by Florida and to the south by Jamaica. Most of the country consists of low hills and fertile valleys.

CURRENCY: Cuban Peso (CUB$) of 100 centavos.

DEFENCE: Military service is compulsory for 3 years for all men; women may volunteer for 2 years. Total armed forces (1987): 158,000. Army 130,000; Navy 12,000; Air Force 16,000. Paramilitary forces: territorial militia 1,200,000; civil defence force 100,000; Ministry of Defence Youth Labour Army 100,000; Ministry of the Interior state security forces 15,000; frontier guards 3,500.

GOVERNMENT: Socialist Republic divided into 14 provinces. The new constitution of 1976 is based on Marxist-Leninist principles. The government consists of bodies of People's Power (highest representatives of state power at municipal, provincial and national leadership levels). The supreme body is the National Assembly. Head of State and First Secretary of Communist Party of Cuba (approx. 450,000 members): Fidel Castro Ruz. Foreign Minister: Isidoro Malmierca Peoli.

LANGUAGE: Spanish (official), English.

NATIONAL ANTHEM: Al combate corred Bayameses (To battle, men of Bayamo).

RELIGION: Roman Catholic 42%; no religion 49%.

TOURIST INFORMATION: Passport and visa or tourist card required by

Australian citizens. Travellers must hold tickets and documentation for return or onward journey. National airline: Cubana. Havana-José Marti airport is located 10 km from the city. Tipping is forbidden.

CYPRUS

Kypriaki Dimokratia
Kibris Cumhuriyeti
REPUBLIC OF CYPRUS

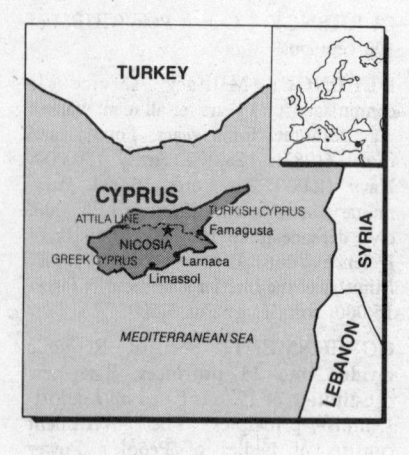

CAPITAL: Nicosia

AREA AND POPULATION: 9,251 km², 46% cultivated land. Population: 673,000 (1986 est.). Population density: 72.7/km². Population growth (1975-78): −0.1%. Ethnic composition: Greek Cypriot 80%; Turkish Cypriot 18.7%; Maronite, Armenian and other minorities.

CLIMATE AND GEOGRAPHY: The climate is Mediterranean, with hot dry summers and mild damp winters. Average temperature (Nicosia): 10°C (January), 28.3°C (July). Average annual rainfall (Nicosia): 371 mm. Cyprus is the third-largest island in the Mediterranean, situated at its north-eastern end, 64 km south of Turkey, 97 km west of Syria and 384 km north of Egypt. Although small in area, Cyprus has a striking variety of landscape. It is dominated by 2 mountain ranges: the narrow and barren Kyrenia Range in the north and the forest-covered Troodos Range in the south-west, culminating in the peak of Mt Olympus at an altitude of 1,950 m. Between these ranges lies the broad plain of Messaoria to the east and the more fertile Morphou basin to the west.

CURRENCY: Cyprus pound of 100 cents.

DEFENCE: (a) Republic of Cyprus: Military service is compulsory for a period of 26 months. Total armed forces (1987): 13,000 (National Guard). Para-military force: police 3,000. (b) Turkish—Cypriot Security Forces: 25,000 Turkish mainland troops; 5,000 Turkish Cypriots.

GOVERNMENT: Presidential republic according to the 1960 constitution, which provided for a House of Representatives consisting of 56 Greek Cypriot members and 24 Turkish Cypriot. Turkish Cypriot members ceased to attend sittings of the House from December 1963. On 13 February 1975 the Turkish Cypriot leader, Rauf Denktash, announced the formation of a Turkish Cypriot state within a federal republic. On 15 November 1983 the unilateral declaration of independence of the Turkish Republic of Northern Cyprus was announced. Head of State (Greek Cypriot): Dr Spyros Kyprianou. Foreign Minister: George Iacovou.

LANGUAGE: Greek and Turkish (official), English.

RELIGION: Greek Orthodox 77%; Moslem 18%; Maronite and Armenian Christian 3%.

TOURIST INFORMATION: Passport but no visa required by Australian citizens. No vaccinations are necessary but specialist medical attention may not be available. Visitors to 'Turkish Cyprus' are not permitted to enter Government-of-Cyprus-controlled areas. Visitors may apply 48 hours in advance to the check-point at the Ledra Palace Hotel to seek permission to enter the TRNC on a visit. Permission will not be granted to Australians of Greek or Greek Cypriot origin. Before arrival in Cyprus, visitors should acquaint themselves with the extent of the Greek and Turkish areas in order to avoid the possibility of the object of their visit being inaccessible, on the other side of the island. Turkish Lira and Cyprus Pounds circulate in the Turkish area but the Turkish Lira is expected to become the official currency in the near future. Foreign currency should be declared upon arrival. National airline: Cyprus Airways. Larnaca airport is located 47 km from Nicosia.

CZECHO-SLOVAKIA

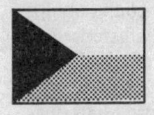

Československá Socialistická Republika
CZECHOSLOVAK SOCIALIST REPUBLIC

CAPITAL: Prague (Praha)

AREA AND POPULATION: 127,903 km^2, 42% cultivated land. Population: 15,542,000 (1986 est.). Population density: 121.5/km^2. Population growth (1970-82): 0.6%. Ethnic composition: Czech 63%; Slovak 31%; Hungarian 4%; Polish, German, Ukrainian, Russian and Gipsy minorities.

CLIMATE AND GEOGRAPHY: The climate is humid continental, with long cold winters and short but warm summers. Average temperature (Prague): −1.5°C (January), 19.4°C (July). Average annual rainfall: 483 mm. Czechoslovakia is a landlocked country, bordered to the north and north-east by Poland and the German Democratic Republic, to the south by Austria and Hungary, to the west by the Federal Republic of Germany and to the east by the USSR. The country is divided into 3 main areas: the Bohemian plateau to the west, the central Moravian lowlands, and the eastern Slovakia mountains to the east.

CURRENCY: Koruna (Kčs) of 100 haler.

DEFENCE: Military service is compulsory for a period of 2 years (Army) or 3 years (Air Force). Total armed forces (1987): 201,000. Army 145,000; Air Force 56,000. Para-military forces: people's militia 120,000; border troops 11,000; Association for Cooperation with the Army.

GOVERNMENT: Federal socialist republic consisting of the Czech Socialist Republic and the Slovak Socialist Republic. Each republic is governed by a National Council (Czech−200 members, Slovak−150). The Federal Assembly has 75 Czech and 75 Slovak delegates elected by their respective National Councils and the Chamber of the People, which has 200 deputies elected by national suffrage. Head of State and General Secretary of the Communist Party of Czechoslovakia: President Dr Gustáv Husák. Prime Minister: Lubomir Štrougal. Foreign Minister: Bohuslav Chňoupek.

LANGUAGE: Czech and Slovak (both official).

NATIONAL ANTHEM: Kde domov můj (Where is my motherland).

RELIGION: Roman Catholic, 65%; Protestant 8%; Greek Orthodox; Jewish.

TOURIST INFORMATION: Passport and visa required by Australian citizens. It is essential that visitors leave Czechoslovakia before the expiration of the visa, if an extension has not been granted. Australians of Czechoslovak origin should carefully check the status of their

Czechoslovak citizenship before travelling to Czechoslovakia. Those considered to be Czechoslovak citizens by the authorities may have trouble leaving the country — Australian citizenship is often disregarded in these circumstances. All visitors are required to register with the local police within 24 hours of arrival and on each change of address. Registration is carried out automatically for visitors staying at a hotel or official camping site. Tourists are required to exchange the equivalent of about US$12 per person for every day they are in Czechoslovakia unless they are in a tourist group, the members of which have paid the whole sum for the tour in advance. Holders of certain credit cards are also exempt. It is prohibited to take in material expounding ideas which do not correspond to the interests of a socialist country. National airline: JAT.

DENMARK

Kongeriget Danmark
KINGDOM OF DENMARK

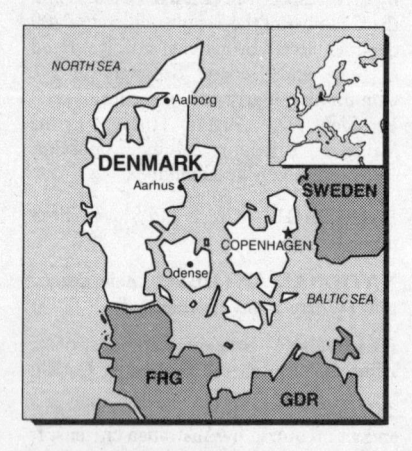

CAPITAL: Copenhagen

AREA AND POPULATION: 43,075 km^2, 63% cultivated land. Population: 5,097,000 (1986 est.). Population density: 118.3/km^2. Population growth (1970-82): 0.3%. Ethnic composition: Danish 96.5%; German 1.7%; Swedish 0.4%.

CLIMATE AND GEOGRAPHY: The climate is modified by marine influences and the effect of the Gulf Stream, producing cold winters and warm, cloudy summers. Windy conditions are common. Average temperature: −0.5°C (winter), 16°C (summer). Average annual rainfall (Copenhagen): 571 mm. Denmark may best be described as an archipelago. It is one of the most fragmented land masses in Europe. While the land frontier with Germany is only 67.7 km long, the coastline, taking into account the many islands, exceeds 7,300 km. The country is low-lying, with the highest point only 173 m above sea-level. It is characterised by undulating plains, gently rolling hills and many lakes. There are numerous inlets which form good natural harbours. External territories: Greenland, Faeroe Islands.

CURRENCY: Krone (Kr) of 100 øre.

DEFENCE: Selective military service is for a period of 9-18 months. Total armed forces (1987): 76,300. Army 58,000; Navy 8,800; Air Force 9,500.

GOVERNMENT: Constitutional monarchy. The unicameral parliament (*Folketing*) is elected for a 4-year term by universal suffrage. Greenland and the Faeroe Islands are both self-governing and are represented by 2 members each in the *Folketing*. Legislative power lies with the queen (who must be a member of the Evangelical-Lutheran Church) and the *Folketing* jointly, the authority being exercised through her ministers. There are 179 Members of Parliament, 135 elected by proportional representation. The remaining seats are divided among the parties unable to obtain sufficient returns at the general election. Head of State: Queen Margrethe II. Prime Minister: Poul Schlüter. Foreign Minister: Uffe Ellemann-Jensen.

LANGUAGE: Danish (official). German is used as the language of instruction in some schools in Nord Slesvig.

NATIONAL ANTHEMS: Kong Kristian stod ved højen mast (King Christian stood at the high mast) and Der er et yndigt land (There is a beautiful country).

RELIGION: Lutheran 97%; Roman Catholic 27,000; Jewish 6,500.

TOURIST INFORMATION: Passport but no visa required for Australian citizens. An onward or return ticket is required and at least US$20 for each day of intended stay. No vaccinations required. Kastrup International Airport is situated 10 km from the centre of Copenhagen. An embarkation tax of Kr200 is levied when leaving the Faeroe Islands. Import regulations to Greenland are very strict.

DJIBOUTI

Jumhouriyya Djibouti
REPUBLIC OF DJIBOUTI

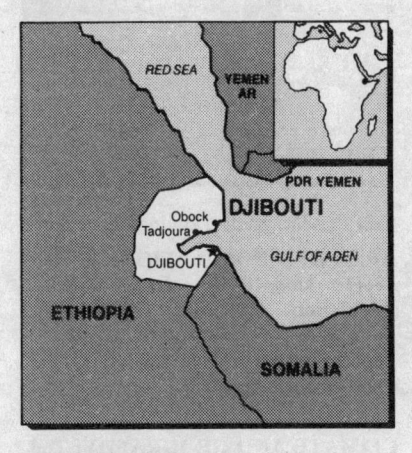

CAPITAL: Djibouti

AREA AND POPULATION: 22,000 km², negligible cultivated land. Population: 304,000 (1986 est.). Population density: 13.8/km². Population growth (1975-78): 2.2%. Ethnic composition: Issa (North Somali) 47%; Afar 37%; European (mainly French) 8%; Arabs 6%.

CLIMATE AND GEOGRAPHY: The climate is hot and dry. Average temperature (Djibouti): 31°C. Average annual rainfall: 130 mm. Djibouti is bounded to the north-east by the Gulf of Aden, south-east by Somalia and on all other sides by Ethiopia. Much of the coastline consists of white sandy beaches. The inland is semi-desert.

CURRENCY: Djibouti Franc (FD) of 100 centimes.

DEFENCE: Military service is voluntary. Total armed forces (1987): 4,500. Army 2,870; Navy 40; Air Force 90. All services form part of the Army. Paramilitary force: gendarmerie 1,500.

GOVERNMENT: Presidential republic. The unicameral parliament has 65 members, 26 of whom are Somali, 23 Afar and 16 Arab. Since October 1981, only 1 political party, 'Rassemblement Populaire pour le Progres' (Popular Assembly for Progress), has been permitted. Head of State: Hassan Gouled Aptidon. Head of Government: Barkat Gourat Hamadou. Foreign Minister: Moumin Bahdon Farah.

LANGUAGE: French (official), Arabic, Somali, Saho-Afar.

RELIGION: Sunni Moslem 94%; Christian 24,000 (mainly Roman Catholic).

TOURIST INFORMATION: Passport and visa issued by the Embassy of the Republic of Djibouti in Paris or by representatives of France abroad required by Australian citizens. Malaria prophylaxis is recommended. French banknotes and all foreign currencies may be negotiated, but traveller's cheques issued in French Francs or Pounds Sterling are not accepted unless endorsed 'pour compte étranger' (external account). A return or onward ticket is required as is an exit permit. National airline: Air Djibouti. Djibouti-d'Ambouli airport is located 6 km from the city.

DOMINICA

COMMONWEALTH OF DOMINICA

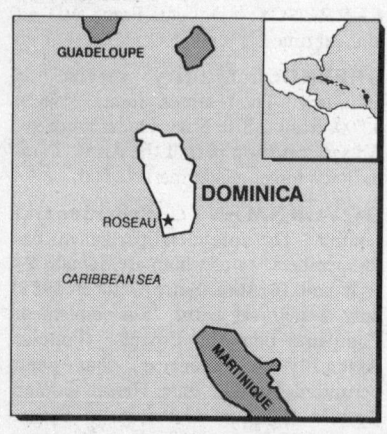

CAPITAL: Roseau

AREA AND POPULATION: 751 km², 9% cultivated land. Population: 74,000 (1986 est.). Population density: 98.5/km². Population growth (1975-78): 2.7%. Ethnic composition: Negro, over 66%; mulatto 0.7%; Carib; small European minority.

CLIMATE AND GEOGRAPHY: The climate is tropical, with a rainy season from June to October. Rainfall is heavy, averaging from 1,750 mm to 6,250 mm per annum. Dominica is the largest island in the Windward group of the West Indies.

CURRENCY: East Caribbean dollar (EC$) of 100 cents.

DEFENCE: No defence force is maintained.

GOVERNMENT: Republic. The unicameral parliament, the House of Assembly, has 21 elected and 9 nominated members. There is universal suffrage. Head of State: Clarence A. Seignoret. Head of Government and Foreign Minister: Mary Eugenia Charles.

LANGUAGE: English (official), French creole.

RELIGION: Roman Catholic 80%; Methodist and Anglican minorities.

TOURIST INFORMATION: At the time of going to press no reliable information could be obtained for Dominica. Canefield airport (for small aircraft only) is located 4 km from Roseau.

DOMINICAN REPUBLIC

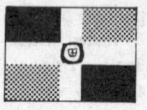

República Dominicana

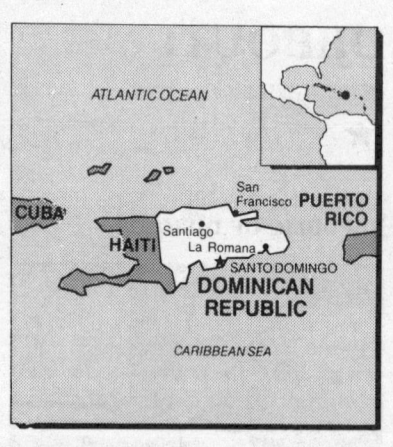

CAPITAL: Santo Domingo

AREA AND POPULATION: 48,734 km², 25% cultivated land. Population: 6,785,000 (1986 est.). Population density: 139.2/km². Population growth (1970-82): 3%. Ethnic composition: mulatto 75%; European 15%; Negro 10%.

CLIMATE AND GEOGRAPHY: The climate is tropical maritime, with a rainy season from May to November. Hurricanes may occur from June to November. Average temperature: 25.5°C. Average annual rainfall: 1,400 mm. The Republic is situated in the Caribbean Sea, occupying the eastern two-thirds of the island of Hispaniola and adjoining the Republic of

Haiti. The country is fertile, well-watered and mountainous, about 80% of its area being covered by a series of massive ranges extending from north-west to south-east.

CURRENCY: Peso Oro (RD$) of 100 centavos.

DEFENCE: Military service is voluntary. Total armed forces (1987): 21,300. Army 13,000; Navy 4,000. Air Force 4,300. Para-military force: national police special operations unit 1,000.

GOVERNMENT: Presidential republic. The bicameral parliament (Chamber of Deputies of 120 members and Senate of 27 members) is elected for 4 years by universal suffrage. Head of State: President Jaoquin Balaguer. Foreign Minister: Dr Donald Reid Cabral.

LANGUAGE: Spanish (official), French creole, English.

NATIONAL ANTHEM: Quisqueyanos valientes, alzemos (Brave men of Quisqueyana, let us raise our song).

RELIGION: Roman Catholic 93%; Protestant and Jewish, 2%.

TOURIST INFORMATION: Passport and Tourist Card required by Australian citizens. Entry will be refused to members of the Hare Krishna religion. Persons with long hair, beard, moustache or 'highly informal' clothing may be subjected to a body search. Possession of drugs will result in fines or imprisonment. Malaria prophylaxis is recommended. An airport tax of US$10 is levied on all passengers embarking in the Dominican Republic. National airline: Dominicana. Santo Domingo-Las Americas airport is located 30 km from the city.

ECUADOR

República del Ecuador
REPUBLIC OF ECUADOR

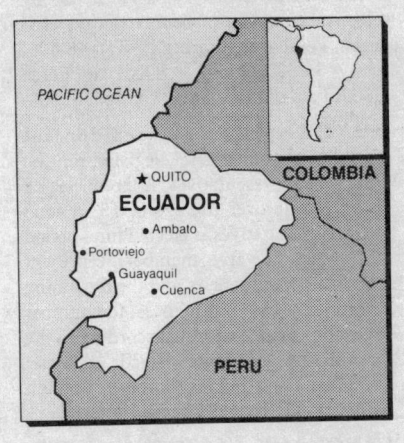

CAPITAL: Quito

AREA AND POPULATION: 283,561 km², 15% cultivated land. Population: 9,647,000 (1986 est.). Population density: 34/km². Population growth (1970-82): 2.6%. Ethnic composition: mestizo 55%; Indian 25%; European 10%; Negro and mulatto, 10%.

CLIMATE AND GEOGRAPHY: The climate ranges from equatorial, through warm temperate, to mountain conditions, according to altitude. While there is little temperature variation in the Sierra, the coastal plains have a hot and wet season from January to April, and a dry and cooler season from May to December. Ecuador is bordered to the north by Colombia and to the south and east by Peru. Two mountain ranges, part of the Andean chain, form the geographic backbone of Ecuador and serve as the natural boundaries of the country's 3 major geographic zones: the lush rainforests east of the Eastern Cordillera, known as the Oriente; the high Sierra between the Eastern and Western Cordilleras, and the fertile swampy plains of the 'costa', which descend from the Western Cordillera to the Pacific Ocean.

The Galapagos Islands, famous for their unique wildlife, lie in the Pacific off the west coast and form an integral part of Ecuador. The government has declared the islands a national park, with a view to preserving the wildlife heritage.

CURRENCY: Sucre of 100 centavos.

DEFENCE: Military service is by selective conscription, for a period of 2 years. Total armed forces (1987): 48,600. Army 35,000; Navy 3,800; Air Force 4,800. Para-military force: coastguard 200.

GOVERNMENT: Presidential republic. A unicameral legislature, the House of Representatives, is freely elected by all people over the age of 18. A total of 69 representatives is elected for a period of 5 years. Twelve members represent 'national' constituencies and the remaining 57 represent the 20 provinces, the number for each province varying according to the size of the electorate. Head of State: President Léon Febres Cordero. Foreign Minister: Dr Rafael Garcia Velasco.

LANGUAGE: Spanish (official), Quechuan, Jivaroan.

RELIGION: Roman Catholic 90%; Protestant 20,000; Jewish 1,000; Animist.

TOURIST INFORMATION: Passport and onward or return ticket required by Australian citizens. A visa is unnecessary unless the stay in Ecuador exceeds 90 days. Passports, however, should be endorsed by Ecuadorian Consulates prior to departure with 'temporary stay'. Vaccination against yellow fever and malaria prophylaxis are recommended for visits outside the main cities. Passengers departing on international flights must pay the Civil Aviation Tax of US$20. National airline: Ecuatoriana. Guayaquil-Simon Bolivar airport is located 8 km from the city.

EGYPT

Al-Jumhuriyat Misr al-Arabiya
ARAB REPUBLIC OF EGYPT

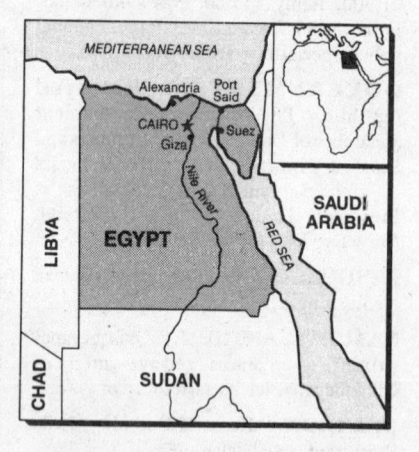

CAPITAL: Cairo

AREA AND POPULATION: 1,001,449 km^2, 3% cultivated land. Population: 50,525,000 (1986 est.). Population density: 50.5/km^2. Population growth (1970-82): 2.5%. Ethnic composition: Arabicised Hamite 90%; Bedouin, Nubian, Greek and Italian minorities. Over 2,000,000 Egyptians work in other Arabic countries.

CLIMATE AND GEOGRAPHY: The climate is dry, with low and erratic rainfall. Daytime temperatures are very high in summer and moderate in winter. Average annual rainfall (Cairo): 28 mm. Egypt is bordered to the south by Sudan and to the west by Libya. Most of the country is sandy and rocky desert. A chain of mountains runs along the Red Sea Coast, the edge of its eastern plateau forming a cliff along part of the perimeter of Cairo. The Western Desert does not have the same ruggedness as that of the east, its main feature being a scattering of oases such as Dakhla, Faiyum, Kharga and Siwa. For the most part, inhabited Egypt consists only of a thin strip between vast deserts to east and west, fanning out north of Cairo into a lush flat delta.

CURRENCY: Egyptian Pound of 100 piastres or 1,000 milliemes.

DEFENCE: Military service is by conscription for a period of 3 years for males between the ages of 20 and 35. Total armed forces (1987): 365,000. Army 320,000; Navy 20,000; Air Force 25,000. Para-military forces: National Guard 60,000; Defence and Security Force 60,000; Frontier Corps 12,000; coastguard 7,000.

GOVERNMENT: Presidential republic. The President is elected by plebiscite for a 6-year term and his election must be ratified by at least two-thirds of the members of the People's Assembly. He can appoint his cabinet as he chooses. The People's Assembly contains 458 members elected under a system of proportional representation. Up to another 10 can be appointed by the President. Under the constitution, at least 50% of Assembly members must be workers or farmers. Head of State: President Hosni Mubarak. Prime Minister: Atef Sedki. Foreign Minister: Ahmed Esmat Abdel Meguit.

LANGUAGE: Arabic (official), English, French.

RELIGION: Moslem (almost all Sunnis) 90%; Coptic Christian 7%; Roman Catholic and Greek Orthodox, 50,000; Protestant 15,000; Jewish 400.

TOURIST INFORMATION: Passport and visa required by Australian citizens. Cholera, smallpox, typhoid, tetanus and polio inoculations are advisable. Malaria prophylaxis is recommended. Doctors and dentists are fairly easily contacted and medical services generally are adequate for most minor disorders. Visitors arriving for a short stay must register at the Office of Foreigners and Nationality within 7 days of arrival. Normally hotels will attend to this. Tipping is an expected practice and is especially expected of foreigners. Foreign currency should be declared upon arrival. All foreign visitors staying in Egypt longer than 48 hours must exchange the equivalent of 12.80 pounds. Egyptian pounds purchased can, in theory, be reconverted into foreign currency upon departure provided that the receipt for the original transaction is produced and a minimum of 20 pounds per day has been used. National airline: EgyptAir. Cairo airport is located 23 km from the centre of the city.

EL SALVADOR

República de El Salvador
REPUBLIC OF EL SALVADOR

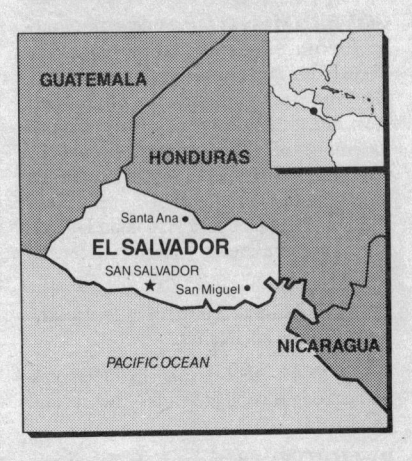

CAPITAL: San Salvador

AREA AND POPULATION: 21,393 km^2, 34% cultivated land. Population: 5,105,000 (1986 est.). Population density: 358.6/km^2. Population growth (1970-82): 3.0%. Ethnic composition: mestizo 89%; Indian 10%; European (mostly of Spanish background) 1%.

CLIMATE AND GEOGRAPHY: The climate is warm, with cool nights inland. Rainfall is usually heavy, except during the dry season from November to April. Average temperature (San Salvador): 22.8°C. Average annual rainfall: 1,775 mm. El Salvador is the smallest of the Central American states. It is bordered to the north by Honduras, to the south by the Pacific Ocean and to the west by Guatemala. With the exception of low plains along the Pacific coast, which represent 12% of the territory, the rest of the country is formed by mountains, volcanoes and high plains.

CURRENCY: Colon (C) of 100 centavos.

DEFENCE: Military service is by selective conscription for a period of 2 years. Total armed forces (1987): 41,650. Army 38,650; Navy 300; Air Force 2,700. Para-military forces: territorial civil defence police 7,000(?); national police 6,000; National Guard 3,600; Treasury police 2,000. Opposition: Dirección Revolucionaria Unificada (DRU) perhaps 10,000 combatants.

GOVERNMENT: Presidential republic. Executive power is vested in a president elected for a non-renewable term of 5 years. He appoints ministers and under-secretaries. Legislative power lies with an Assembly of 60 members elected by universal suffrage and proportional representation for a term of 3 years. Head of State: President José Napoleon Duarte. Foreign Minister: Ricardo Acevedo Peralta.

LANGUAGE: Spanish (official), English, Mayan, Nahua.

NATIONAL ANTHEM: Saludemos la patria orgullosos (Salute the proud fatherland).

RELIGION: Roman Catholic 85%; Protestant 75,000; Jewish 300.

TOURIST INFORMATION: Passport and visa required by Australian citizens. Also needed is a telex authorisation from the Minister of Interior written in the passport by an embassy or consulate of El Salvador. Vaccination against yellow fever and malaria prophylaxis are recommended. A permit must be obtained from the Ministry of Defence before firearms or ammunition can be imported into El Salvador. San Salvador-Ilopango airport is located 13 km from the city. A departure tax of C20 is levied on passengers embarking on international flights.

EQUATORIAL GUINEA

República de Guinea Ecuatorial
REPUBLIC OF EQUATORIAL GUINEA

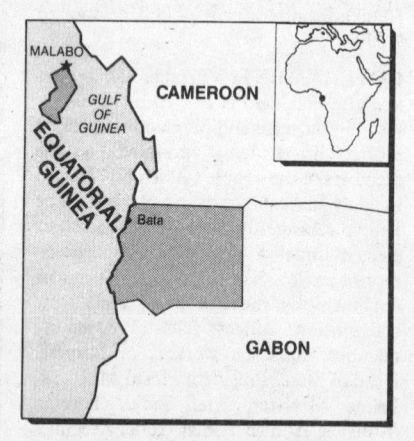

CAPITAL: Malabo

AREA AND POPULATION: 28,051 km^2, 8% cultivated land. Population: 359,000 (1986 est.) Population density: 12.8/km^2. Population growth (1975-78): 2.3%. Ethnic composition: Bantu (Fang) 80%; Bubi 15%; Fernandino (mixed race) and European (mainly Spanish) minorities.

CLIMATE AND GEOGRAPHY: The climate is equatorial, with a wet season from December to February. The country consists of a section of the west African mainland, bordered to the north by Cameroon and to the south and east by Gabon. It includes 5 islands in the Gulf of Guinea. The mainland consists of a coastal plain and low hills beyond.

CURRENCY: Franc CFA of 100 centimes.

DEFENCE: Military service is voluntary. Total armed forces (1987): 2,300. Army 2,000; Navy 150; Air Force 150. Para-military force: Guardia Nacional 2,000.

GOVERNMENT: Presidential republic. An 11-member cabinet and a 41-member National Assembly are under the control of a military junta. At a referendum held in August 1982, 95% of electors chose to retain military rule until 1989. Head of State: President Lieutenant-Colonel Teodoro Obiang Nguema Mbasogo. Foreign Minister: Marcelino Nguema Onguene.

LANGUAGE: Spanish (official), Bubi, Fang, Portuguese creole, English.

RELIGION: Roman Catholic 83%; Protestant minorities; Animist.

TOURIST INFORMATION: Passport and visa required by Australian citizens. It is advisable to apply for a visa at least 2 months in advance from, for example, the Equatorial Guinean Embassy in Madrid or in Yaoundé, Cameroon. Two passport photos are needed for police control. Vaccination against cholera and yellow fever, and malaria prophylaxis are recommended. Malabo airport is located 7 km from the city.

ETHIOPIA

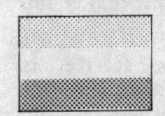

Hebretesebawit Ityopia
PEOPLE'S REPUBLIC OF ETHIOPIA

CAPITAL: Addis Ababa

AREA AND POPULATION: 1,221,900 km², 12% cultivated land. Population: 43,882,000 (1986 est.). Population density: 35.9/km². Population growth (1970-82): 2%. Ethnic composition: Oromo 40%; Amhara 25%; Tigre 12%; Sidama 9%; Dankali; Somali; Nilotic and Italian minorities.

CLIMATE AND GEOGRAPHY: The climate is temperate on the plateau and hot in the lowlands. The main rainy season lasts from June to August. Drought is common. Average maximum temperature (Addis Ababa and Harar): 17°C. Average minimum temperature: 16°C. Average annual rainfall Addis Ababa: 1,237 mm. Ethiopia is situated on the north-east coast of Africa, between latitudes 3° and 17° North and longitudes 33° and 45° East. It forms the Horn of Africa, together with Djibouti and the Somali Republic, which lie on Ethiopia's eastern and south-eastern boundaries. Ethiopia is bounded to the north by the Red Sea, to the south by Kenya and to the west by the Sudan. A high central plateau descends to plains on both the west and south-east. In the north the terrain is very rugged, while to the south the landscape is generally flatter and more suited to agriculture.

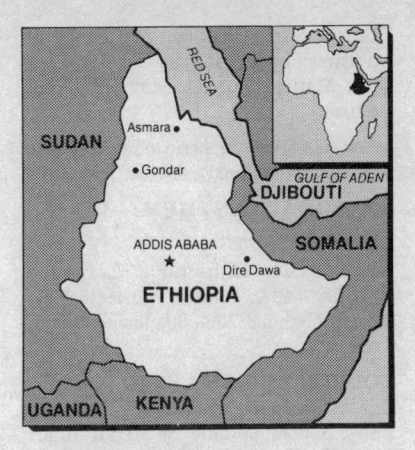

CURRENCY: Birr of 100 cents.

DEFENCE: Military service is by selective conscription for a period of 30 months. Total armed forces (1987): 225,500. Army 220,000; Navy 15,000; Air Force 4,000. Para-military forces: 169,000. Opposition: Eritrean People's Liberation Front 13,000; Eritrean Liberation Front 6,500; Eritrean Liberation Front/People's Liberation Forces 5,000; People's Liberation Front Revolutionary Guard 5,000; Tigre People's Liberation Front 5,000; Western Somali Liberation Front (numbers not known).

GOVERNMENT: One-party state with socialism as the state ideology. The Provisional Military Administration Council (Derg) is supported by a Council of Ministers. The composition and size of the Derg is unknown, there being no published list of members, but is thought to be about 30. Chairman of the Derg,

Head of State, Chairman of Council of Ministers: Lieutenant-Colonel Mengistu Haile Mariam. Foreign Minister: Bayeh Berhanu.

LANGUAGE: Amharic (official), Tigre, Afar, Galla (regional), Arabic.

NATIONAL ANTHEM: Ityopya, Ityopya Kidemi.

RELIGION: Ethiopian Orthodox Christian 40%; Sunni Moslem 40%; Roman Catholic 200,000; Jewish 8,000; Animist 10,000.

TOURIST INFORMATION: Passport and visa required by Australian citizens. Entry is possible only by air via Addis Ababa International Airport. Passengers must hold return or onward tickets and US$50 or equivalent per day of stay. Visitors to lowland areas are advised to take precautions against malaria. Vaccination against yellow fever is recommended if visiting areas outside the main cities. Viral hepatitis is a particular problem and a course of gamma globulin is strongly recommended. An exit permit is required for visitors who have stayed longer than 30 days. National airline: Ethiopian Airlines. Addis Ababa-Bole airport is located 8 km from the city.

FIJI

Matanitu Ko Fiti
REPUBLIC OF FIJI

CAPITAL: Suva

AREA AND POPULATION: 18,275 km^2, 9% cultivated land. Population: 715,000 (1986 est.). Population density: 39.1/km^2. Population growth (1978): 1.8%. Ethnic composition: Indian 50%; Fijian (Melanesian) 45%; Rotuma 2.2%; European-Fijian 1.7%; Chinese and European minorities.

CLIMATE AND GEOGRAPHY: The climate is tropical, tempered by south-east trade winds. The hotter months are from December to April, when humidity is high. Average temperature: 24.7°C. Average annual rainfall: 2,974 mm. Fiji is a group of over 300 islands, plus many more coral atolls and cays, situated in the south-west Pacific Ocean 1,770 km south of the Equator. About 100 islands are permanently inhabited. The mountainous areas are generally covered with dense forests but the lowlands are more lightly timbered and the soil is generally deep, easily worked and rich.

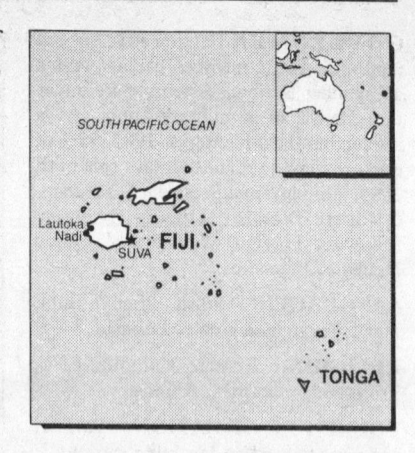

CURRENCY: Fiji Dollar (F$) of 100 cents.

DEFENCE: Military service is voluntary. Total armed forces (1986/87): 2,670. Army 2,500; Navy 170.

GOVERNMENT: A republic under an interim government. The bicameral parliament consists of the Senate of 22 members and the House of Representatives of 52 members. Voting in elections is not compulsory. Head of State: Ratu Penaia K. Ganilau. Prime Minister: Ratu Kamisese Mara.

LANGUAGES: English and Fijian (both official), Hindustani.

NATIONAL ANTHEM: Hail to Fiji.

RELIGION: Christian 51%; Hindu 40%; Moslem 9%.

TOURIST INFORMATION: Passport and onward or return ticket required by Australian citizens, plus sufficient funds for maintenance whilst in Fiji. Passports must be valid for at least 3 months from the date of entry, and for 4 months if staying 1 month. National airline: Air Pacific. Qantas has 6 flights a week to Nadi from Melbourne or Sydney. A departure tax of F$10 is payable by passengers leaving on international flights. Nadi airport is located 200 km from Suva, and Suva-Nausori airport 22 km from the city.

FINLAND

Suomen Tasavalta/
Republiken Finland
REPUBLIC OF FINLAND

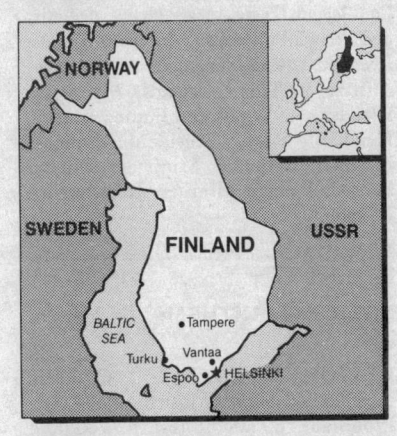

CAPITAL: Helsinki

AREA AND POPULATION: 337,008 km², 8% cultivated land. Population: 4,931,000 (1986 est.). Population density: 14.6/km². Population growth (1970-82): 0.4%. Ethnic composition: Finnish 94%; Swedish 6%; small Lappish minority. Some 5% of the population live abroad.

CLIMATE AND GEOGRAPHY: The climate is severe in the 6 months of winter, with milder temperatures in the southern regions. Snow cover lasts for over 6 months in the far north. The warmest month is July. Average temperature (Helsinki): −6°C (January), 16.5°C (July). Average annual rainfall: 618 mm. Finland occupies the greater part of the plain and plateau area to the north-east of the Baltic Basin. It is bounded to the north by Norway, to the south by the Baltic Sea, to the west by Sweden and to the east by the USSR. One-tenth of the area of Finland is covered by about 60,000 lakes. The coast has an almost continuous fringe of islands.

CURRENCY: Markka (plural Markkaa) of 100 pennia.

DEFENCE: Military service is compulsory for 8 to 11 months (11 months for officers and NCOs). Total armed forces (1986/87): 40,500. Army 34,900; Navy 2,500; Air Force 2,900. Para-military forces: Ministry of Interior frontier guards 5,500; coastguard 600.

GOVERNMENT: Parliamentary-democratic republic. A unicameral parliament of 200 members is elected by proportional representation for a period of 4 years. Head of State: President Dr Mauno Koivisto. Prime Minister: Harri Holkeri. Foreign Minister: Paavo Väyrynen.

LANGUAGES: Finnish and Swedish (both official).

NATIONAL ANTHEM: Maamme laulu (Song of our country).

RELIGION: Lutheran 91.5%; Greek Orthodox 1.3%; Roman Catholic 3,000; Jewish 1,300; Moslem 1,000.

TOURIST INFORMATION: Passport and return or onward tickets required by Australian citizens. No vaccinations are required. Helsinki International Airport is situated 19 km from the centre of the city.

FRANCE

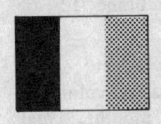

République Française
FRENCH REPUBLIC

CAPITAL: Paris

AREA AND POPULATION: 543,965 km², 32% cultivated land. Population: 55,239,000 (1986 est.). Population density: 101/km². Population growth (1970-82): 0.5%. Ethnic composition: French; other

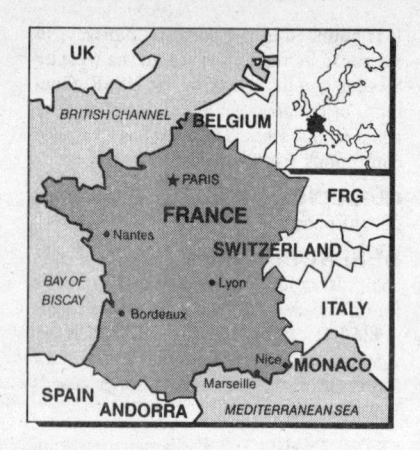

European; African; Asian; refugees (European and South-East Asian).

CLIMATE AND GEOGRAPHY: Four regional climatic variations predominate: continental (north and centre); Atlantic (most of the western coastline), with mild winters and cool, rainy summers; Mediterranean (southern coast), with mild winters and hot summers; alpine (in the south-east), with long, cold winters and rainy summers. Average temperature (Paris): 3°C (January), 18°C (July). Annual rainfall (Paris): 573 mm. France is bordered to the north by Belgium, to the south by Spain, to the west by the Atlantic Ocean and the English Channel, and to the east by the FRG, Switzerland, Luxembourg and Italy. The country has wide, fertile plains in the north, alpine regions in the south-east and long coastlines in the south and west.

CURRENCY: French Franc (FF) of 100 centimes.

DEFENCE: Military service is compulsory for 12 months and voluntary for a period of 16 to 24 months. Total armed forces (1987): 566,148. Strategic Nuclear Forces 18,820 (Army 2,499; Navy 5,053; Air Force 9,957; gendarmerie 747); Army 296,480; Navy 75,000; Air Force 95,978; Inter-service central staff 4,517; Service de Santé 8,465. Forces abroad: Germany 50,000; Overseas Dependencies 21,000; other overseas forces 11,000. Paramilitary force: gendarmerie 89,816.

GOVERNMENT: Presidential republic. The bicameral Parliament (Senate of 319 members and National Assembly of 577 members), is elected by universal suffrage for 9 or 5 years. The country is divided into 22 regions for national development work, planning and budgetary policy purposes. There are 96 Départements within the regions. France has 5 overseas Départements: Guadeloupe, Martinique, Guiana, St Pierre et Miquelon, La Réunion; a 'Collectivité territoriale' Mayotte, which the French Government is prepared to cede to the Federal Islamic Republic of the Comoros should the population so wish; and 4 Overseas Territories: Southern and Antarctic Territories (Kerguelen Islands, Crozet Islands, Amsterdam Island, Saint-Paul Island, Terre Adèle); New Caledonia; and French Polynesia (Windward Islands, Leeward Islands, Tuamotu Archipelago, Austral or Tubuai Islands, Marquesas Islands); and Wallis and Futuna Islands. Head of State: President François Mitterand. Prime Minister: Michel Rocard. Foreign Minister: Jean-Bernard Raimond.

LANGUAGE: French (official), regional languages.

NATIONAL ANTHEM: La Marseillaise.

RELIGION: Roman Catholic 45,500,000; Sunni Moslem 2,400,000; Protestant 800,000; Jewish 700,000; Armenian Orthodox 180,000.

TOURIST INFORMATION: Passport and visa required by Australian citizens. National airline: Air France. The 2 international airports, Charles de Gaulle and Orly, are situated 23 km and 14 km respectively from the centre of Paris.

GABON

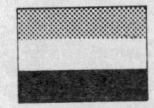

République Gabonaise
GABONESE REPUBLIC
CAPITAL: Libreville

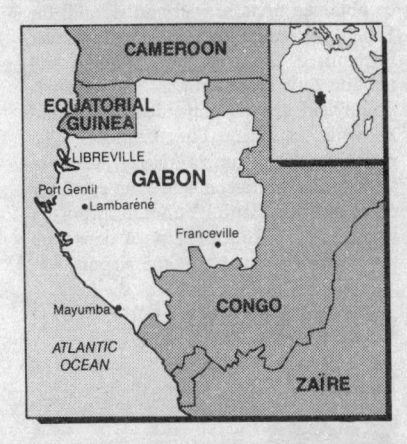

AREA AND POPULATION: 267,667 km^2, 1.2% cultivated land. Population: 1,017,000 (1986 est.). Population density: 3.8/km^2. Population growth (1975-78): 0.9%. Ethnic composition: Bantu (Fang) 25%; Eshira 25%; Adouma 17%; other Bantu tribes; Pygmy 1%; French minority.

CLIMATE AND GEOGRAPHY: The climate is equatorial, with high temperatures and heavy rainfall. Average temperature: 25.3°C. Average annual rainfall: 2,510 mm. Gabon is bounded to the north by Cameroon and Equatorial Guinea, to the south and east by Congo and to the west by the Atlantic Ocean. The country is heavily forested. There is a sandy coastal strip with a series of palm-fringed bays, lagoons and estuaries. There are mountains in the north, south-east and centre.

CURRENCY: Franc CFA of 100 centimes.

DEFENCE: Military service is voluntary. Total armed forces (1987): 2,850. Army 1,900; Navy 350; Air Force 600. Para-military forces: coastguard 2,800; gendarmerie 2,000; Republican Guard; Rapid Intervention Force.

GOVERNMENT: Presidential republic. The unicameral Parliament (National Assembly) of 111 members is elected for a 5-year term. There is only 1 legal political party — Parti démocratique gabonais. Head of State: President El-Haj Omar Albert-Bernard Bongo. Prime Minister: Léon Mébiame. Foreign Minister: Martin Bongo.

LANGUAGE: French (official), Bantu languages.

RELIGION: Roman Catholic 65%; Protestant 15%; Moslem 10,000; Animist.

TOURIST INFORMATION: Passport, visa, return or onward tickets and confirmed hotel reservation required by Australian citizens. Foreign currencies should be declared. It is necessary to report to the local police authorities within 48 hours of arrival. Vaccination against yellow fever is required and malaria prophylaxis is recommended. National airline: Air Gabon International. Libreville-Leon M'Ba airport is located 12 km from the city.

THE GAMBIA

REPUBLIC OF THE GAMBIA
CAPITAL: Banjul

AREA AND POPULATION: 11,295 km^2, 25-55% cultivated land. Population: 774,000 (1986 est.). Population density: 68.5/km^2. Population growth (1975-78): 1.1%. Ethnic composition: Mandingo 36%; Fula 17%; Woloff 14%; Senegalese 3.2%; European minority.

CLIMATE AND GEOGRAPHY: The climate is tropical, with a hot, rainy season from June to October and a cool, dry season from November to May. Temperatures range from 19°C to 44°C on the coast. Average annual rainfall: 1,295 mm. The Gambia is bordered on the western side by the Atlantic Ocean and is completely surrounded on the remaining three sides by the Republic of Senegal. Essentially the valley of one of the finest waterways in Africa, Gambia River, the country reaches 328 km inland, varying in width from 22 km to 55 km. It is fairly flat, the highest point being 35 m, in the interior. Near the river estuary, the country is characterised by mangrove swamps. Further inland freshwater marshes are found, followed by woodland with fallow bush and a sandstone plateau where most of the crops are grown.

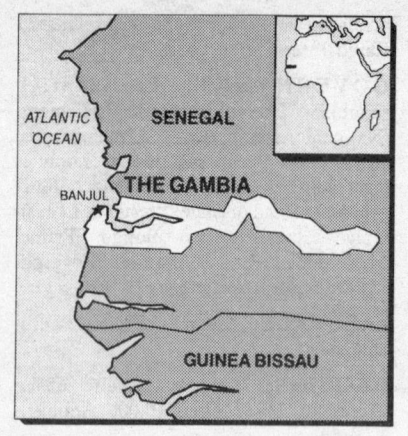

CURRENCY: Dalasi (D) of 100 bututs.

DEFENCE: Military service is voluntary. Total armed forces (1986/87): 600; gendarmerie 400; Army 125; Navy 50; Air Force 25.

GOVERNMENT: Parliamentary democracy based on the republican form. The President is the Head of State and commander-in-chief of the armed forces. He is elected by direct universal suffrage and personally appoints the Vice-President, who is leader of government in the House of Representatives, and other Cabinet Members from Members of the House. Legislative power is held by the House of Representatives which is composed of 35 members, elected by direct universal suffrage every 5 years, 4 chiefs and 5 nominated members. Head of State: President Sir Dawda Kairiba Jawara. Foreign Minister: Alhaji Lamine Kiti Jabang.

LANGUAGE: English (official), Mandingo, Woloff, Fula, Arabic.

NATIONAL ANTHEM: For The Gambia, our homeland, we strive and work and pray.

RELIGION: Sunni Moslem 95%; Protestant 35,000; Roman Catholic 10,000.

TOURIST INFORMATION: Passport but no visa required by Australian citizens. Visitors must hold documents for return or onward journey. A Visitor's Pass may be obtained upon arrival and is valid for 1 month. Vaccination against yellow fever is required, while tetanus, typhoid and poliomyelitis vaccinations and malaria prophylaxis are recommended. Rabies and hepatitis exist in The Gambia. The national airline, Gambia Airways, does not operate any aircraft, it acts as an agent for other airlines. Banjul-Yundum airport is located 29 km from the city. A departure tax of D35 is payable at the airport.

GERMANY, EAST

Deutsche Demokratische Republik
GERMAN DEMOCRATIC REPUBLIC

CAPITAL: Berlin (East)

AREA AND POPULATION: 108,333 km², 46% cultivated land. Population:

16,692,000 (1986 est.). Population density: 154.1/km². Population growth (1970-82): 0.2%. Ethnic composition: German; small Slavic Sorb minority.

CLIMATE AND GEOGRAPHY: The climate is moderate continental. Average temperature (Berlin): −0.5°C (January), 19°C (July). Average annual rainfall (Berlin): 563 mm. The Republic is bounded to the north by the Baltic Sea, to the south-east by Czechoslovakia, to the east by Poland and to the west by the Federal Republic of Germany. The chief rivers are the Elbe and the Oder, with a total navigable length of 1,830 km. Much of the country lies in the Great North German Plain which is made up of light, sandy soil with a high water table and many lakes.

CURRENCY: Mark of the DDR (M) of 100 Pfennige.

DEFENCE: Military service is compulsory for 18 months (Army) and 24 months (Air Force and Navy, sea-going). Total regular forces (1986/87): 179,000. Army 123,000; Navy 15,500; Air Force 40,000. Para-military forces: Society for Sport and Technology (youth aged 16-18) 450,000 (75% active); Ministry of Defence frontier troops 49,000; Ministry of the Interior People's Police Alert Units 13,000; Ministry for State Security guard regiment 7,000; workers' militia 3,000.

GOVERNMENT: Socialist state with a unicameral Parliament (Volkskammer) of 500 members, elected for a 4-year term. Parliament elects the Chairman and members of the Council of State and the Chairman (Prime Minister) and members of the Council of Ministers. Real power, however, lies with the 2,000,000-strong Socialist Unity Party of Germany (SED). Head of State and Secretary-General of the SED: Erich Honecker. Prime Minister: Willi Stoph. Foreign Minister: Oskar Fischer.

LANGUAGE: German.

NATIONAL ANTHEM: Auferstanden aus Ruinen (Risen from ruins).

RELIGION: Protestant 7,700,000; Lutheran 1,500,000 Roman Catholic 1,200,000; Jewish 700.

TOURIST INFORMATION: Passport and visa required by Australian citizens. The equivalent of M25 in hard currency must be exchanged for each day of stay. Re-exchange is not possible. Foreign currency should be declared upon arrival. No vaccinations are required.

GERMANY, WEST

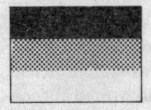

Bundesrepublik Deutschland
FEDERAL REPUBLIC OF GERMANY

CAPITAL: Bonn

AREA AND POPULATION: 248,706 km², 31% cultivated land. Population: 60,734,000 (1986 est.). Population density: 244.2/km². Population growth (1970-82): 0.1%. Ethnic composition: German 90%; foreign workers 7.3%; Danish and Sinti (Gipsy) minorities.

CLIMATE AND GEOGRAPHY: The climate is temperate but changeable. Westerly winds and oceanic and Gulf Stream influences prevail in the north-west. The east and south-east are continental. Rainfall occurs throughout the year, varying from 500 mm in the lowlands to 2,000 mm in the Alps. The FRG is bordered to the north by Denmark, to the south by Switzerland, Liechtenstein and Austria, to the east by the German Democratic Republic and Czechoslovakia, and to the west by the Netherlands, Belgium, Luxembourg and France. There are 3 main topographical regions: the North German Plain, the Central German uplands, and the Alpine foothills and Alps. The country's most significant rivers are the Rhine, Elbe, Main, Mosel and Danube.

CURRENCY: Deutsche Mark (DM) of 100 Pfennige.

DEFENCE: Military service is compulsory for 15 months, either in the Bundeswehr or in some form of Zivildienst (community service). Total armed forces (1986/87): 488,000. Army 340,800; Navy 36,500; Air Force 108,700. Para-military forces: border police 20,000; coast guard.

GOVERNMENT: Federal republic. The bicameral Parliament consists of the 41-member Upper House (Bundesrat) representing the Länder (states), and the Lower House (Bundestag) of 496 members elected for a 4-year term. One-half of the Bundestag members are elected to represent electoral districts on a first-past-the-post basis. The remaining half are chosen by the political parties from lists, so that the total representation of the parties in the Bundestag corresponds to the proportion of the popular vote they received. To prevent a multiplicity of minor parties, a party must obtain 5 per cent of the vote in order to be represented in Parliament. Each voter votes twice, once for the local member and once for a party list. Head of State: Federal President Dr Richard von Weizsäcker. Chancellor: Dr Helmut Kohl. Foreign Minister: Hans-Dietrich Genscher.

LANGUAGE: German (official), English widely spoken.

NATIONAL ANTHEM: Einigkeit und Recht und Freiheit (Unity, right and liberty).

RELIGION: Roman Catholic 45%; Protestant 44%; Jewish 27,701; Moslem; Greek Orthodox.

TOURIST INFORMATION: Passport required by Australian citizens. No vaccinations are needed. Accommodation, especially in the summer months, should be booked in advance. Information on accommodation can also be obtained from Tourist Information Offices located at most airports and main railway stations. The FRG has 4 international airports: Tegel, 10 km from Berlin; Frankfurt, 10 km from Frankfurt; Fuhlsbüttel, 12 km from Hamburg and München-Riem, 10 km from Munich (München). National airline: Lufthansa.

GHANA

REPUBLIC OF GHANA
CAPITAL: Accra

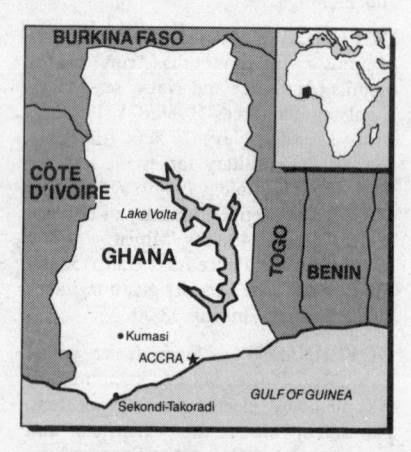

AREA AND POPULATION: 238,305 km², 12% cultivated land. Population: 13,004,000 (1985 est.). Population density: 56.9/km². Population growth (1970-82): 3.0%. Ethnic composition: Akan 44%; Moshi-Dagomba 16%; Ewe 13%; Ga 8%.

CLIMATE AND GEOGRAPHY: The climate is tropical, hot and humid. Average temperatures range between 24.4°C and 27.8°C, and the humidity from 75% to 90%. The humidity drops only during the 'harmattan', a hot and dusty wind blowing from the Sahara from December to February/March. The rainy season lasts from May to August. Average annual rainfall: 1,083 mm. Ghana is bordered to the north by Burkina Faso, to the south by the Gulf of Guinea, to the east by Togo and to the west by Côte D'Ivoire. The country is dominated by the vast Lake Volta which covers one-fifth of the total area. The south-east section of the country is a coastal plain covered with grass and scrub. The central section is heavily forested, while the northern section is inland savanna.

CURRENCY: Cedi (C) of 100 pesewas.

DEFENCE: Military service is voluntary. Total armed forces (1987): 11,200. Army 9,000; Navy 1,200; Air Force 1,000. Para-military forces: people's militia; Committees for the Defence of the Revolution.

GOVERNMENT: Presidential republic. Since the military coup of 31.12.1982, the country has been ruled by the 10-member Provisional National Defence Council headed by Flight-Lieutenant Jerry Rawlings. Foreign Minister: Dr Obed Asomoah.

LANGUAGE: English (official), Twi, Fanti, Ga Ewe, Dagbani and Hausa.

NATIONAL ANTHEM: Hail the name of Ghana.

RELIGION: Christian 52%; Moslem 13%; Animist 30%.

TOURIST INFORMATION: Passport, visa and return or onward ticket required by Australian citizens. On arrival all passengers must obtain a 'Particulars of aliens' registration card. Two passport photographs are needed. Vaccination against yellow fever is required, while vaccination against cholera and malaria prophylaxis are advisable. Foreign currencies must be declared. A basic medical kit should be carried. National airline: Ghana Airways. Accra-Kotoka airport is located 10 km from the city.

GREECE

Elliniki Dimokratia
HELLENIC REPUBLIC

CAPITAL: Athens

AREA AND POPULATION: 131,957 km^2, 29% cultivated land. Population: 9,954,000 (1986 est.). About 3,000,000 Greeks live abroad. Population density: 75.4/km^2. Population growth (1970-82): 1.0%. Ethnic composition: Greek 98.5%; Turkish 0.9%; Bulgarian 0.3%; Armenian 0.2%.

CLIMATE AND GEOGRAPHY: The climate is Mediterranean in coastal regions and islands, with mild winters and hot, dry summers. The northern, mountainous areas have a continental climate, with severe, snowy winters and hot summers. Average temperature (Athens): 8.6°C (January), 28.2°C (July). Average annual rainfall: 415 mm. Much of the mainland is mountainous, unsuitable for agriculture or close settlement. The combination of mountain ranges and heavily indented coastlines constitutes a barrier to easy communications between regions and has contributed to the historical development of Greece as a country of small, independent and feuding city-states. In the north, Greece shares a land frontier with Albania, Yugoslavia, Bulgaria and Turkey.

CURRENCY: Drachma (Dr) of 100 lepta.

DEFENCE: Military service is compulsory for 22 months (Army), 26 months (Navy) and 24 months (Air Force). Total armed forces (1987): 209,000. Army 165,500; Navy 19,500; Air Force 24,000. Para-military forces: gendarmerie 25,000; coastguard and customs 4,000.

GOVERNMENT: Parliamentary-democratic republic. There is universal suffrage. Head of State: President Christos Sartzetakis. Prime Minister: Andreas Papandreou. Foreign Minister: Karolos Papoulias.

LANGUAGE: Greek – katheravousa (official and in newspapers) and demotiki (spoken language).

NATIONAL ANTHEM: Imnos eis tin eleftherian (Hymn to freedom).

RELIGION: Greek Orthodox 97%; Moslem 1%; Protestant and Roman Catholic 35,000; Jewish 6,500.

TOURIST INFORMATION: Passport and return or onward ticket required by Australian citizens. Admission is refused to holders of passports bearing any visa, stamp or other indication that they intend to visit or have visited the Turkish area of Cyprus. Visitors who propose arriving between May and September should ensure that any hotel reservations are made well in advance. Specialist medical attention is available in Athens but private hospitals and dental facilities are expensive. Pollution is an increasing problem, particularly in down-town Athens where fumes from motor vehicles and factories are often in excess of normally acceptable levels. National airline: Olympic Airways.

GRENADA

STATE OF GRENADA
CAPITAL: St George's
AREA AND POPULATION: 344 km², 47% cultivated land. Population: 86,000 (1986 est.). Population density: 250/km². Population growth (1975-78): 2.8%. Ethnic composition: Afro-american 52%; Mulatto 42%; Indian 5%; European 1%.

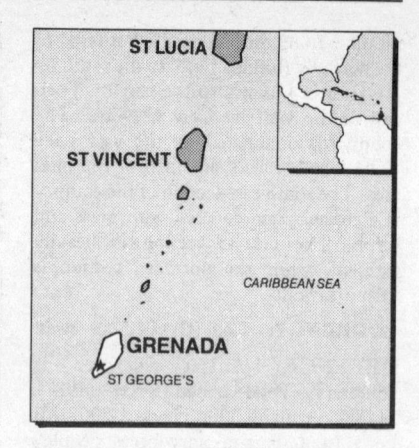

CLIMATE AND GEOGRAPHY: The climate is tropical, with a dry season from January to May. Average annual rainfall: 1,500 mm on the coast and 4,500 mm in the mountains. Grenada is the southernmost of the Windward Islands and is situated off the coast of Venezuela in the Caribbean Sea. The island is divided by a central mountain range.

CURRENCY: Eastern Caribbean Dollar (EC$) of 100 cents.

DEFENCE: A People's Revolutionary Army of about 6,500 persons, founded in 1979, was disbanded in 1983. No other forces are maintained.

GOVERNMENT: Constitutional monarchy. The bicameral Parliament consists of a Senate of 15 members and a House of Representatives. There is universal suffrage but no obligation to vote. Head of State: Queen Elizabeth II, represented by Governor-General Sir Paul Scoon. Prime Minister: Herbert Blaize. Foreign Minister: Ben Jones.

LANGUAGE: English (official), French and English creoles.

RELIGION: Roman Catholic 64%; Anglican 22%.

TOURIST INFORMATION: Passport and return or onward ticket required by

Australian citizens. No vaccinations are needed. A Passenger Service Charge of EC$5 is levied on all passengers leaving Grenada. National airline: Grenada is a shareholder in LIAT. Pearls airport is located 19 km from the capital.

GUATEMALA

República de Guatemala
REPUBLIC OF GUATEMALA

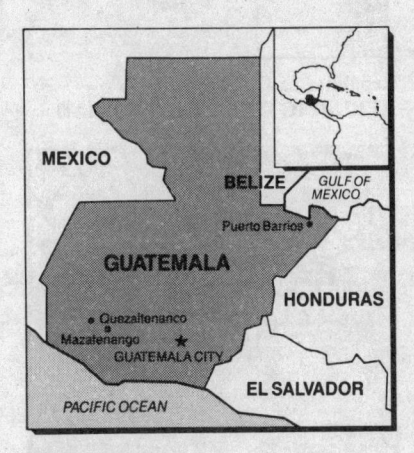

CAPITAL: Guatemala City

AREA AND POPULATION: 108,889 km², 17% cultivated land. Population: 8,600,000 (1986 est.). Population density: 79/km². Population growth (1970-82): 3.1%. Ethnic composition: Indian (Maya-Quiche) 55%; Mestizo 40%; European (mostly of Spanish background) 5%; Mulatto.

CLIMATE AND GEOGRAPHY: The climate is tropical, with a wet season from May to October. Average temperature (Guatemala City): 17.2°C (January), 20.6°C (July). Average annual rainfall: 1,316 mm. Guatemala is bounded to the north and west by Mexico, to the south by the Pacific Ocean and to the east by El Salvador, Honduras, the Caribbean Sea and Belize. The landscape is predominantly mountainous and heavily forested. There are numerous volcanoes in the south.

CURRENCY: Quetzal (Q) of 100 centavos.

DEFENCE: Military service is compulsory for 24 to 30 months. Total armed forces (1987): 32,000. Army 30,300; Navy 1,000; Air Force 700. Para-military forces: territorial militia 900,000; national police 9,500; Treasury police 2,100. Opposition 2,000.

GOVERNMENT: Presidential republic. The constitution and political activity were suspended after the coup of 23 March 1982. Another coup on 8 August 1983 led to elections to the National Constituent Assembly on 1 July 1984 and a return from military to civilian rule in 1985. Head of State: President Marco Vinicio Cerezo Arévalo. Foreign Minister: Mario Quinoñes Amezquita.

LANGUAGE: Spanish (official), 23 Maya-Quiche dialects.

NATIONAL ANTHEM: ¡Guatemala! Feliz (Guatemala be praised).

RELIGION: Roman Catholic 96%; Protestant 100,000; Jewish 1,900.

TOURIST INFORMATION: Passport and visa required by Australian citizens. Malaria prophylaxis is recommended. A departure tax of Q20 is levied on international passengers leaving Guatemala. National airline: Empresa Guatemalteca de Aviacion (Aviateca). Guatemala City-La Aurora airport is located 6 km from the city.

GUINEA

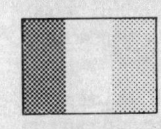

République de Guinée
REPUBLIC OF GUINEA

CAPITAL: Conakry

AREA AND POPULATION: 245,857 km², 19% cultivated land. Population: 5,736,000 (1986 est.). Population density: 23.2/km². Population growth (1970-82):

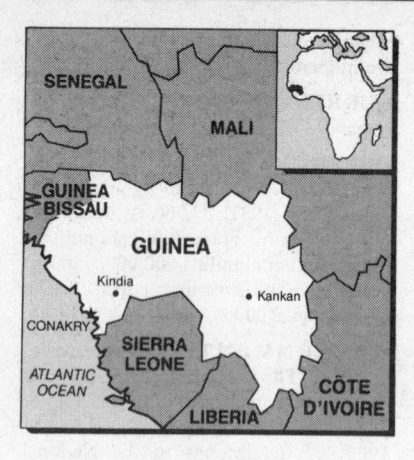

2%. Ethnic composition: Fulani 40.3%; Mandingo 25.8%; Susu 11%; Kissi 6.5%; other tribal groups.

CLIMATE AND GEOGRAPHY: The climate is tropical, with a wet season from May to October. Average temperature (Conakry): 26.7°C (January), 25°C (July). Average annual rainfall: 4,293 mm. Guinea is situated in west Africa, bordered to the north by Guinea-Bissau, Senegal and Mali, to the south by Sierra Leone and Liberia, to the east by Côte d'Ivoire and to the west by the Atlantic Ocean. The country is hilly and many of the rivers which rise there supply water to much of southern Africa. The coastal plain is made up of mangrove swamps. To the south are the Guinea Highlands.

CURRENCY: Guinea Franc (GF).

DEFENCE: Military service is compulsory for a period of 2 years. Total armed forces (1986/87): 9,900. Army 8,500; Navy 600; Air Force 800. Paramilitary forces: people's militia 7,000; Republican Guard 1,600; gendarmerie 1,000.

GOVERNMENT: Presidential 'socialist' republic. The unicameral Parliament of 210 deputies is elected by universal suffrage for a 7-year term. Head of State and President: Brigadier General Lansana Conté. Foreign Minister: Fanciné Touré.

LANGUAGE: French and 8 African languages (all official).

RELIGION: Sunni Moslem 85%; Christian 10%; Animist.

TOURIST INFORMATION: Passport and visa required by Australian citizens. Vaccination against cholera is required and yellow fever and malaria prophylaxis are recommended. There is a departure tax ranging from GF100 to GF200 depending on destination. National airline: Air Guinée. Conakry airport is located 13 km from the city.

GUINEA-BISSAU

República da Guiné-Bissau
REPUBLIC OF GUINEA-BISSAU

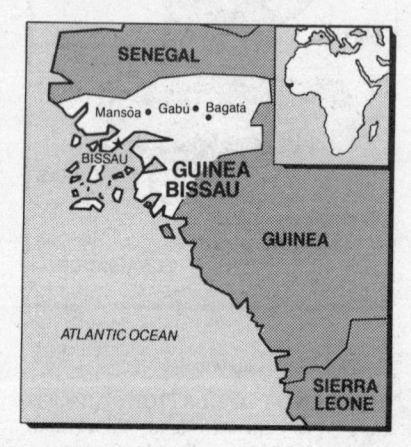

CAPITAL: Bissau

AREA AND POPULATION: 36,125 km², 8% cultivated land. Population: 858,000 (1986 est.). Population density: 23.8/km². Population growth (1975-78): 1.7%. Ethnic composition: Balanta 30%; Fulani 20%; Mandjako 14%; Malinke 13%; Pepel 7%; other tribal groups.

CLIMATE AND GEOGRAPHY: The climate is tropical, with a wet season from June to November. The 'harmattan' (Saharan hot and dusty wind) blows from December to May. Average temperature (Bissau): 24.4°C (January), 26.7°C (July). Average annual rainfall: 1,950 mm.

Guinea-Bissau is situated in West Africa, bordered to the north by Senegal, to the south and east by Guinea and to the west by the Atlantic Ocean. Most of the country is covered by a swampy plain. There is a low savannah region to the east.

CURRENCY: Guinea Peso (PG) of 100 centavos.

DEFENCE: Military service is thought to be by selective conscription. Total armed forces (1987): 8,525. Army 6,200; Navy 250; Air Force 75. Para-military force: gendarmerie 2,000.

GOVERNMENT: Republic. A new National People's Assembly, established in April 1984, replaced the Revolutionary Council which had ruled since the 1980 coup. Head of State: President General João Bernardo Vieira. Foreign Minister: Júlio Semedo.

LANGUAGE: Portuguese (official), Sudanese languages, Crioulo.

RELIGION: Traditional 65%; Moslem 30%; Roman Catholic 4%.

TOURIST INFORMATION: Passport and visa required by Australian citizens. Vaccination against yellow fever and malaria prophylaxis are recommended. Foreign currency should be declared upon arrival. A departure tax of US$8 or US$12 applies, depending on destination. National airline: Linhas Aereas da Guiné-Bissau. Bissau-Craveiro Lopes airport is located 11 km from the city.

GUYANA

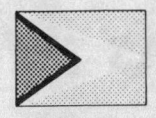

COOPERATIVE REPUBLIC OF GUYANA

CAPITAL: Georgetown

AREA AND POPULATION: 214,969 km², 29% cultivated land. Population: 771,000 (1986 est.). Population density: 3.6/km². Population growth (1975-78): 1.7%. Ethnic composition: Indian 48-52%; Negro 32%; native Indian 4%; European 2%; Chinese 0.7%.

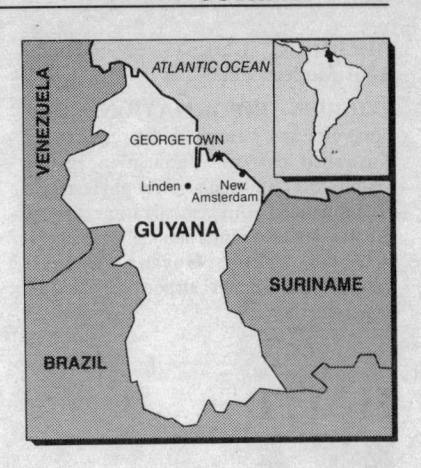

CLIMATE AND GEOGRAPHY: The climate is tropical, with high humidity moderated by sea breezes. Average temperature (Georgetown): 26.1°C (January), 27.2°C (July). Average annual rainfall: 2,175 mm. Guyana is situated on the north-east coast of South America with Brazil to the south, Suriname to the east and Venezuela to the west. Dense tropical forests cover much of the country. There is a fertile flat coastal area where 90% of the population lives.

CURRENCY: Guyana Dollar (G$) of 100 cents.

DEFENCE: Military service is voluntary. Total armed forces (1987): 5,330 (all services form part of the Army). Army 5,000; Navy 150; Air Force 180. Para-military forces: 5,000.

GOVERNMENT: Independent cooperative republic. The unicameral Parliament of 65 members is elected under a single-list system of proportional representation, with the entire country forming 1 electoral region and each elector voting for a party list of candidates. Head of State: President H. Desmond Hotle. Foreign Minister: Rashleigh E. Jackson.

LANGUAGE: English (official), Hindi, Negro patois.

NATIONAL ANTHEM: Dear land of Guyana, of rivers and plains.

RELIGION: Christian 57%; Hindu 34%; Moslem 9%.

TOURIST INFORMATION: Passport, visa and onward ticket required by Australian citizens. Vaccination against yellow fever and malaria prophylaxis are recommended. An embarkation tax of G$50 is levied on international passengers. National airline: Guyana Airways. Georgetown-Timehri airport is located 40 km from the city.

HAITI

République d'Haiti
REPUBLIC OF HAITI

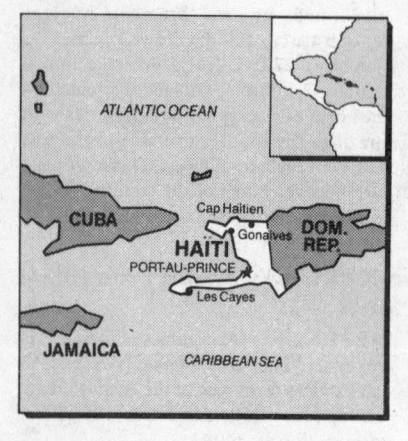

CAPITAL: Port-au-Prince

AREA AND POPULATION: 27,750 km², 32% cultivated land. Population: 5,762,000 (1986 est.). Population density: 211.3/km². Population growth (1970-82): 1.7%. Ethnic composition: Negro, over 80%; Mulatto 15-20%; European minority.

CLIMATE AND GEOGRAPHY: The climate is tropical maritime, with wet seasons from April to June and August to November. Average temperature (Port-au-Prince): 24.4°C (January), 28.9°C (July). Average annual rainfall: 1,321 mm. Haiti occupies the western third of the island of Hispaniola in the West Indies. Much of the country is mountainous and forested. The coastline is dotted with magnificent beaches.

CURRENCY: Gourde (Gde) of 100 centimes.

DEFENCE: Military service is voluntary. Total armed forces (1987): 7,425. Army 6,900; Navy 325 (coastguard); Air Force 200.

GOVERNMENT: Presidential. On 9 February 1986 a 6-man military/civilian commission, the National Council of Government, ousted former President Jean-Claude ('Baby Doc') Duvalier and assumed control of the country. A new draft Constitution was approved in March 1987. The unicameral National Assembly comprises 59 deputies elected for 6-year terms by universal suffrage. Head of State: General Henri Namphy. Foreign Minister: Colonel Hérard Abraham.

LANGUAGE: French, Creole (official).

NATIONAL ANTHEM: La Dessalinienne.

RELIGION: Roman Catholic 80%; Protestant 10%; Voodoo cultist.

TOURIST INFORMATION: Passport, visa and return or onward ticket are required by Australian citizens. Vaccination against yellow fever and malaria prophylaxis are recommended. US dollars are accepted and exchanged everywhere. An airport tax of US$15 or Gde75 is levied on departing passengers. National airline: Haiti Air Inter. Port-au-Prince airport is located 13 km from the city.

HONDURAS

República de Honduras
REPUBLIC OF HONDURAS

CAPITAL: Tegucigalpa

AREA AND POPULATION: 112,088 km², 16% cultivated land. Population:

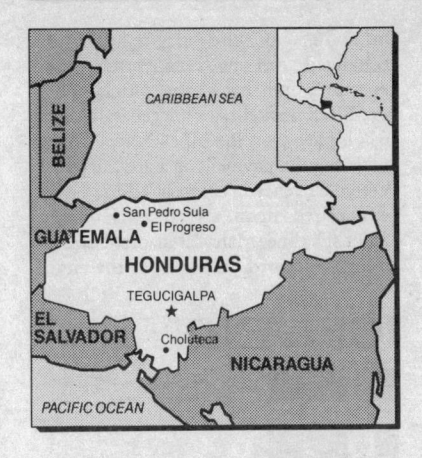

4,648,000 (1986 est.). Population density: 41.5/km². Population growth (1970-82): 3.4%. Ethnic composition: Mestizo 80%; Indian 10%; European 5%; Negro; Mulatto; Sambo; Miskito Indian refugees from Nicaragua, 15,000.

CLIMATE AND GEOGRAPHY: The climate is tropical, with 2 wet seasons in the upland areas. The Carribean coast has most rain and higher temperatures. Average temperature (Tegucigalpa): 19°C (January), 23.3°C (July). Average annual rainfall: 1,621 mm. Honduras is bounded to the north by the Caribbean Sea, to the south by the Pacific Ocean, to the east and south-east by Nicaragua, to the south-west by El Salvador and to the west by Guatemala.

CURRENCY: Lempira (L) of 100 centavos.

DEFENCE: Military service is compulsory for a period of approximately 12 months. Total armed forces (1987): 18,800. Army 17,000; Navy 700; Air Force 1,100. Para-military force: Public Security Force (national police) 5,000.

GOVERNMENT: Presidential republic. The unicameral Parliament (Congress of Deputies) of 134 deputies is elected by universal suffrage. Head of State: President José Azcona Hoyo. Foreign Minister: Carlos Lopez-Contreras.

LANGUAGE: Spanish (official), English, Indian dialects.

NATIONAL ANTHEM: Tu bandera es un lampo de cielo (Your flag is a heavenly light).

RELIGION: Roman Catholic 86%; Protestant 36,000; Jewish 200.

TOURIST INFORMATION: Passport and visa required by Australian citizens. Persons staying in Honduras longer than 48 hours for commercial or touristic purposes must report to the Department of Public Security within that time. Malaria prophylaxis is recommended. An airport tax of US$10 is levied on international passengers. National airlines: TAN (Transportes Aereos Nacionales); SAHSA (Servicio Aereo de Honduras SA); LANSA (Lineas Aereas Nacionales SA); ANHAS (Aereovias Nacionales SA). Tegucigalpa-Toncontin airport is located 5 km from the city.

HUNGARY

Magyar Népköztársaság
HUNGARIAN PEOPLE'S REPUBLIC

CAPITAL: Budapest

AREA AND POPULATION: 93,032 km², 60% cultivated land. Population: 10,624,000 (1986 est.). Population density:

114.4/km². Population growth (1970-82): 0.3%. Ethnic composition: Magyar 92%; German 2.5%; Slovak, Croatian, Serbian, Romanian and Gypsy minorities.

CLIMATE AND GEOGRAPHY: The climate is humid continental, with warm summers and cold winters. Average temperature (Budapest): 0°C (January), 21.5° (July). Average annual rainfall: 625 mm. Hungary is situated in western Europe, bordered to the north by Czechoslovakia, to the north-east by the USSR, to the east by Romania, to the south by Yugoslavia and to the west by Austria. The eastern half of the country is mainly a large fertile plain, while the west and north are hilly.

CURRENCY: Forint (Ft) of 100 filler (rare—Ft1 coin is the smallest in common circulation).

DEFENCE: Military service is compulsory for 18 months (Army, Navy and Border Guards) and 24 months (Air Force). Total regular forces (1987): 105,500. Army 83,000 (including the Danube Flotilla); Air Force 22,000; Navy 500. Para-military forces: part-time workers' militia 60,000; border guards 15,000; Sport Association for National Defence (numbers not known).

GOVERNMENT: Communist people's republic. There is a unicameral Parliament (Orszaggyules) and universal suffrage. Head of State and Chairman of Presidential Council: Karoly Nemeth. Prime Minister: Karoly Grosz. Foreign Minister: Péter Várkonyi.

LANGUAGE: Hungarian (official), German. Ethnic minorities have the right to be educated in their own tongue.

NATIONAL ANTHEM: Isten áldd meg a magyart (God bless the Hungarians).

RELIGION: Roman Catholic 67%; Calvinist 20%; Lutheran 5%; Jewish 80,000-100,000; Orthodox 40,000.

TOURIST INFORMATION: Passport and visa required by Australian citizens. Travellers should be careful not to exchange too much hard currency into Forints upon arrival. Hungary is not an expensive country by Australian standards. Only 50% of the original amount exchanged can be reconverted upon departure, and that at the 'official' (low) rate. Black-market rates are generally some 70% higher than the official rates. Major hotels expect payment in hard currency. Foreign currency in excess of US$200 must be declared upon arrival in Hungary. National airline: Malev. Budapest-Ferihegy airport is located 16 km from the city.

ICELAND

Lydveldio Island
REPUBLIC OF ICELAND

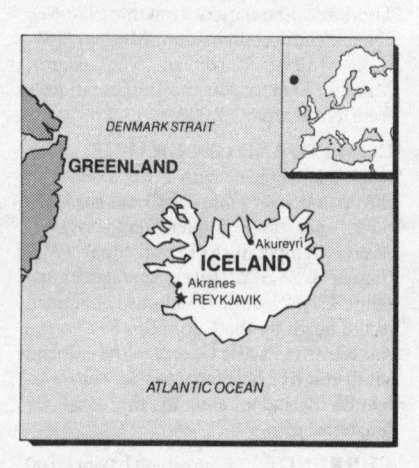

CAPITAL: Reykjavik

AREA AND POPULATION: 103,000 km², 1% cultivated land. Population: 244,000 (1986 est.). Population density: 2.4/km². Population growth (1984): 1.3%. Ethnic composition: Icelanders, almost 100%.

CLIMATE AND GEOGRAPHY: The climate is cool temperate oceanic, affected by the Gulf Stream and prevailing southwest winds. Precipitation is mainly in the form of snow. Average temperature (Reykjavik): 1°C (January), 11°C (July). Iceland is a large island of recent volcanic origin close to the Arctic Circle in the

North Atlantic. The landscape is wild and rugged.

CURRENCY: Icelandic Krona (Kr) of 100 aurar.

DEFENCE: No defence forces are maintained. Under the North Atlantic Treaty, US forces are stationed on Iceland as the Iceland Defence Force. Para-military force: coastguard 120.

GOVERNMENT: Parliamentary democratic republic. The 60-member Parliament has an Upper and a Lower House. There is universal suffrage, with elections being held every 4 years. Head of State: President Mrs Vigdis Finnbogadottir. Prime Minister: Steingrimur Hermannsson. Foreign Minister: Mathias A. Mathiesen.

LANGUAGE: Icelandic.

NATIONAL ANTHEM: O Gud vors lands.

RELIGION: Evangelical Lutheran 97%, Roman Catholic 1,000.

TOURIST INFORMATION: Passport but no visa required by Australian citizens for stays not exceeding 3 months. There are regular flights to Reykjavik from the UK, Scandinavia, some European countries and the USA.

INDIA

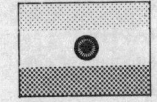

Bharat
REPUBLIC OF INDIA

CAPITAL: New Delhi

AREA AND POPULATION: 3,280,481 km^2, 57% cultivated land. Population: 783,940,000 (1986 est.). Population density: 239/km^2. Population growth (1970-82): 2.3%. Ethnic composition: Indo-Aryan 72%; Dravidian 25%; Mongoloid 3%. Between 4 and 5 million Indians live abroad.

CLIMATE AND GEOGRAPHY: The climate is cool from December to March; hot from April to May; rainy from June to September; dry from October to November. Average temperature (New Delhi): 13.9°C (January), 31.1°C (July). Average annual rainfall: 640 mm. India is bordered to the north by China, Nepal and Bhutan, to the south by the Indian Ocean, to the east by Bangladesh, Burma and the Bay of Bengal, and to the west by Pakistan and the Arabian Sea. There are 3 major geographical regions: the Himalayan Mountain region which extends along the entire northern border; the Peninsula to the south, including the Deccan Plateau; and, in between, the great plains of the Indus and Ganges Basins.

CURRENCY: Rupee (Rs) of 100 paise.

DEFENCE: Military service is voluntary. Total armed forces (1986/87): 1,160,000. Army 1,100,000; Navy 47,000; Air Force 13,000. Para-military forces: border security force 85,000; national security force 112,000; coastguard 2,000.

GOVERNMENT: Democratic parliamentary republic. Bicameral parliament (Council of States of up to 250 members, and House of the People of 544 members). The country is divided into 24 states (Andhra Pradesh, Arunachal Pradesh, Assam, Bihar, Gujarat, Haryana, Himachal Pradesh, Jammu and Kashmir, Karnataka, Kerala, Madhya Pradesh, Maharashtra, Manipur, Meghalaya, Mizoram, Nagaland, Orissa, Punjab,

Rajasthan, Sikkim, Tamil Nadu, Tripura, Uttar Pradesh, West Bengal) and 9 Union Territories (Andoman and Nicobar Islands, Chandigarh, Dadra and Nagar Haveli, Goa, Daman and Diu, Lakshadweep, Pondicherry). Head of State: President Ramaswamy Venkataraman. Prime Minister: Rajiv Gandhi. Foreign Minister: P. V. Narasimha Rao.

LANGUAGE: Hindi (official), English (associate official), 15 other main and regional languages, 24 secondary languages, and over 720 dialects.

NATIONAL ANTHEM: Jana-ganamana (Thou art the ruler of the minds of all people).

RELIGION: Hindu 82.7%; Moslem 11.2% (Sunni:Shiite 3:1); Christian 2.6%; Sikh 1.9%; Buddhist 0.7%; Jain 0.47%.

TOURIST INFORMATION: Passport and visa required by Australian citizens. Even transit passengers are advised to obtain a visa in case their flight is delayed and they have to leave the airport. Visas should be applied for well before departure. Electrical and high-technology articles should be declared upon arrival. It may be necessary to lodge a bond with Indian Customs, the amount being refundable upon re-export of the items. Vaccination against cholera and typhoid, gamma globulin injections against hepatitis and malaria prophylaxis are recommended. It is unwise to drink unboiled water. Specialist medical and dental attention is available in most cities. Public hospital facilities are not always adequate, but there are satisfactory private hospitals. National airline: Air India. Bombay-Santa Cruz airport is located 29 km from the city.

INDONESIA

Republik Indonesia
REPUBLIC OF INDONESIA

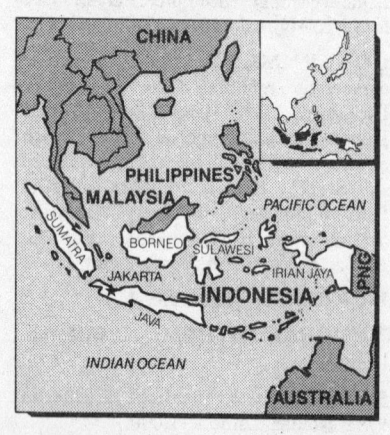

CAPITAL: Jakarta

AREA AND POPULATION: 1,919,400 km^2, 9% cultivated land. Population: 176,764,000 (1986 est.). Population density: 92.1/km^2. Population growth (1970-82): 2.3%. Ethnic composition: Aceh, Batak, Minangkabau (Sumatra); Javanese, Sundanese (Java); Madurese (Madura); Balinese (Bali); Sasak (Lombok); Menadonese, Minaha, Toraja, Buginese (Sulawesi); Dayak (Kalimantan); Irianese (Irian Jaya); Ambonese (Molucca); Timorese (Timor).

CLIMATE AND GEOGRAPHY: The climate is tropical monsoon, with a dry season from June to September and a wet season from October to April. Average temperature (Jakarta): 25.6°C. Average annual rainfall: 1,775 mm. Humidity is high throughout the year. Indonesia consists of over 13,000 islands, of which less than half are inhabited. The principal islands are Java, Sumatra, Kalimantan (Borneo), Sulawesi (Celebes) and Irian Jaya (western part of the island of New Guinea). The country is seismically active, and has about 60 active volcanoes.

CURRENCY: Rupiah (Rp) of 100 sen.

DEFENCE: Military service is by selective conscription for a period of 2 years. Total armed forces (1987): 278,800. Army 216,000; Navy 35,800; Air Force 27,000. Para-military forces: militia 70,000; police mobile brigade 12,000; coastguard; Civil Defence Force; Maritime Security Agency.

GOVERNMENT: Centralist republic. The unicameral Parliament (House of People's Representatives) consists of 364 elected and 96 presidentially appointed members. Head of State: President General Suharto. Foreign Minister: Dr Mochtar Kusumaatmadja.

LANGUAGE: Bahasa Indonesia (official), approx. 250 regional languages.

NATIONAL ANTHEM: Indonesia raya (Great Indonesia).

RELIGION: Moslem 90%; Protestant 3-4%; Roman Catholic 2%; Hindu 1.5-3% (Bali); Animist 1%; Buddhist and Confucian 0.4%.

TOURIST INFORMATION: Passport required by Australian citizens. A visa is required for journalists and for a stay of more than 2 months. Vaccination against cholera and malaria prophylaxis are recommended. An airport tax of Rp9,000 (international flights) or Rp2,000 (domestic flights) is levied on passengers departing from Jakarta and Denpasar. National airline: Garuda. Denpasar-Ngurah Rai airport is located 13 km from the city.

IRAN

Jomhori-e-Islami-e-Iran
ISLAMIC REPUBLIC OF IRAN

CAPITAL: Tehran

AREA AND POPULATION:
1,648,000 km², 10% cultivated land. Population: 49,764,874 (1986 census). Population density: 30.2/km². Population growth (1970-82): 3.1%. Ethnic composition: Persian 63%; Turkoman and Baluchi, 19%; Arab 4%; Kurd 3%.

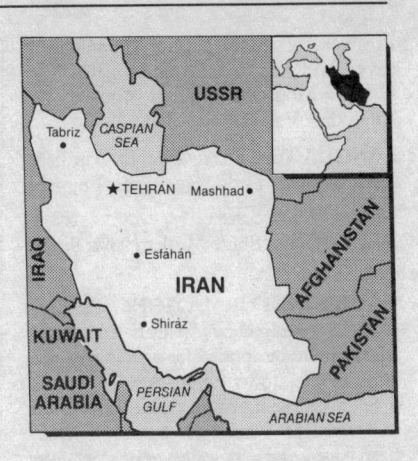

CLIMATE AND GEOGRAPHY: The climate ranges from desert, to temperate near the Caspian Sea. Average temperature (Tehran): 2.2°C (January), 29.4°C (July). Average annual rainfall: 246 mm. Iran is bounded to the north by the USSR and the Caspian Sea, to the south by the Gulf of Oman and the Persian Gulf, to the east by Afghanistan and Pakistan and to the west by Iraq and Turkey. The interior highlands and plains are surrounded by high mountains. Large salt deserts cover much of the country but there are also many oases and forests. Most of the population inhabits the north and north-east.

CURRENCY: Rial (Rl) of 100 dinars.

DEFENCE: Military service is compulsory for 24 months. Total armed forces (1987): 710,000 regulars, 350,000 reserves. Army 305,000; Navy 20,000; Air Force 35,000; Revolutionary Guard Corps 350,000 (still independent of the Army). Para-military forces: Popular Mobilization Army volunteers, mostly youths; gendarmerie 70,000; border tribe militia; Sevama secret police.

GOVERNMENT: Islamic republic. Supreme authority is vested in the hands of a religious leader (wali faqih), elected by the Moslem clergy and entitled to hold the position for life. Legislative power is held by a 270-seat Islamic Consultative Assembly (Majlis) directed by a 12-member Council of Guardians. Head of State and

President of the Republic: Hojatolislam Sayed Ali Khamenei. Prime Minister: Mir Hussein Moussavi. Foreign Minister: Dr Ali Akbar Velayati.

LANGUAGE: Farsi (official), Kurdish, Luri, Baluchi, Turkic languages, English, French.

RELIGION: Shiite Moslem 93%; Sunni Moslem 5%.

TOURIST INFORMATION: Passport and visa required by Australian citizens. Visas should be applied for well in advance and can take up to 2 months to be issued. The government of Iran refuses admission and transit to women not wearing Islamic head cover, scarf, long sleeves or stockings. It is necessary to report to police headquarters in Tehran or the main police office in other Iranian cities within 8 days of arrival in order to obtain a Residential Permit. It is advisable to have several passport photos and photocopies of the page of passport containing personal dates on hand as owners of hotels etc. must inform authorities of visitors. Yellow fever vaccination is required and malaria prophylaxis is recommended. National airline: Iran Air. Abadan airport is located 12 km from Tehran.

IRAQ

★ ★ ★

Al-Jumhouriya al-'Iraqia
REPUBLIC OF IRAQ

CAPITAL: Baghdad

AREA AND POPULATION: 434,924 km^2, 12% cultivated land. Population: 16,019,000 (1986 est.). Population density: 36.8/km^2. Population growth (1970-82): 3.5%. Ethnic composition: Arab 75%; Kurd 15%; Turk 2%; Assyrian; Turkoman; Chaldean; Armenian.

CLIMATE AND GEOGRAPHY: The climate is arid, with hot summers and cold winters. Average temperature (Baghdad): 10°C (January), 35°C (July). Average annual rainfall: 140 mm. Iraq is bordered to the north by Turkey, to the south by Kuwait and Saudi Arabia, to the east by Iran and to the west by Jordan and Syria. The country is largely in the form of a basin, lying between the Western Desert and the Zagros Mountains (Kurdistan) along the Iranian frontier to the north. The land descends from the mountains to the desert in a series of hills and steppes, with winter rain and melted snow being carried south by the Tigris and Euphrates rivers.

CURRENCY: Iraqi Dinar (ID) of 1,000 fils.

DEFENCE: Military service lasting 24 months is compulsory for all men at 18 years of age. This period is extended during war. Total armed forces (1986/87): 843,000. Army 800,000 (losses and the resupply system make estimates tentative); Navy 3,000; Air Force 40,000. Paramilitary forces: People's Army 650,000; security troops 4,800.

GOVERNMENT: Presidential republic. The supreme legislative and decision-making body in the Iraqi government structure is the Revolutionary Command Council whose Chairman is both Head of State and Supreme Commander of the Armed Forces. The President appoints a Council of Ministers. Head of State: Saddam Hussein at-Takriti. Foreign Minister: Tariq Aziz Isa.

LANGUAGE: Arabic (official), Kurdish, others.

RELIGION: Shiite Moslem 55%; Sunni Moslem 40%; Christian 5%; Yazidi 30,000; Mandai 12,000; Jewish 500.

TOURIST INFORMATION: Passport and visa required by Australian citizens. The government of Iraq refuses admission to Jewish passengers if their Jewish religion is mentioned in their passports. Passengers must contact the Residence Office within 14 days of arrival to obtain an 'Arrival Notice' for which they will need 2 passport photos. Vaccination against yellow fever and malaria prophylaxis are recommended. All passengers intending to stay more than 5 days must report for an AIDS test. A medical certificate issued outside Iraq will not be accepted. Hotel bills must be settled in hard currency at the nearest Rafidain Bank. There is a departure tax of ID2.000. National airline: Iraqi Airways. Baghdad-Saddam airport is located 20 km from the city.

IRELAND

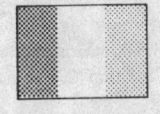

Poblacht Na h'Eireann
IRISH REPUBLIC

CAPITAL: Dublin (Baile Atha Cliath)

AREA AND POPULATION: 70,285 km^2, 14% cultivated land. Population: 3,588,000 (1985 est.). Population density: 51.1/km^2. Population growth (1970-82): 1.5%. Ethnic composition: Irish.

CLIMATE AND GEOGRAPHY: The climate is equable, affected by the Gulf Stream. Rainfall is well distributed. The coldest months are January and February. Average temperature (Dublin): 5°C (January), 15°C (July). Average annual rainfall: 750 mm. Ireland consists of a large undulating central lowland of limestone, with a discontinuous border of coastal mountains. The central plain contains extensive areas of bog and numerous lakes. The impact of 2 glaciations on the topography is evident. No part of the country is more than 110 km from the sea. The Republic is bordered to the north by Northern Ireland.

CURRENCY: Irish Pound (Punt) of 100 pence.

DEFENCE: Military service is voluntary. Total armed forces (1987): 17,243. Army 12,282; Navy 943 (to be increased to about 1,500); Air Force 800.

GOVERNMENT: Parliamentary democracy with a bicameral legislature. The President is elected for not more than 2 7-year terms by direct vote if there is more than 1 nomination. The Dail (Lower House of Parliament) consists of 166 deputies elected by a system of proportional representation. The Senate consists of 60 members. Head of State: Dr Padraig Ohlrighile (Patrick J. Hillery). Prime Minister: Charles Haughey. Foreign Minister: Brian Lenihan.

LANGUAGE: Irish and English.

NATIONAL ANTHEM: The Soldier's Song.

RELIGION: Roman Catholic 94%; Anglican (Church of Ireland) 3.2%; Jewish 0.8%; Presbyterian 0.5%.

TOURIST INFORMATION: Passport but no visa required by Australian citizens. Britain and Ireland form a 'common travel area' and an entry permit issued in either country allows the holder to visit the other. It is advisable to have return or onward tickets. National airline: Aer Lingus.

ISRAEL

Medinat Israel
STATE OF ISRAEL

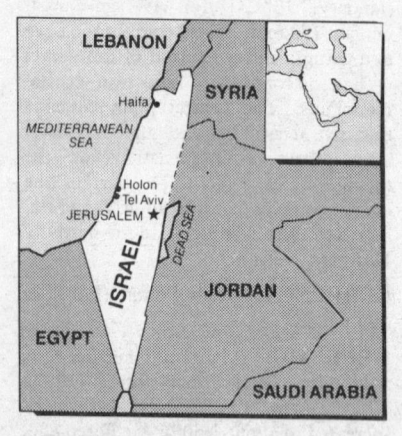

CAPITAL: Jerusalem

AREA AND POPULATION: 20,770 km², 20% cultivated land. Population: 4,208,000 (1986 est.). Population density: 202.6/km². Population growth (1970-82): 2.5%. Ethnic composition (1982): European and American 1,350,400; African 766,300; Asian 745,200; Israelis of European and American fathers 569,200; of Israeli fathers 494,600; of Asian fathers 451,800; of African fathers 434,200; Arab 689,000.

CLIMATE AND GEOGRAPHY: The climate is Mediterranean, with hot, rainless summers and mild winters. Average temperature (Jerusalem): 9°C (January), 23°C (July). Average annual rainfall: 528 mm. Israel is bordered to the north by the Mediterranean Sea, to the north-east by Lebanon and Syria, to the east and south by Jordan and to the west by Egypt. There are 4 distinct geographic zones: the coastal strip; the Galilee area containing the country's most fertile land; the mountain range stretching 322 km from Lebanon to the Sinai; and the Negev Desert.

CURRENCY: Israeli Shekel (IS) of 100 new agorot.

DEFENCE: Military service is compulsory, lasting 36 months for men and 24 months for women (Jews and Druze only; Christians and Arabs may volunteer). Annual training is given thereafter for reservists up to age 54 for men and 34 (or marriage) for women. Total armed forces (1987): 146,600. Army 112,000; Navy 6,600; Air Force 28,000. Para-military forces: border guards 4,500; Arab militia; coastguard; Gadna (youth volunteers aged 15-18).

GOVERNMENT: Parliamentary republic. There is no formal Constitution. The unicameral Parliament (Knesset) of 120 members is elected by universal suffrage under a proportional representation system. The President is elected by the Knesset for a 5-year term which may be extended by a further term. Head of State: President Chaim Herzog. Prime Minister: Itzhak Shamir. Foreign Minister: Shimon Peres.

LANGUAGE: Hebrew and Arabic (both official).

NATIONAL ANTHEM: Hatikvah (The Hope).

RELIGION: Jewish 83.5%; Moslem (mostly Sunni) 12.9%; Christian 2.4%; Druze 1.4%.

TOURIST INFORMATION: Passport but no visa required by Australian citizens provided the period of stay does not exceed 3 months. A departure tax of US$8 (destinations in Egypt) or US$10 (all other countries) is payable at Ben Gurion airport. National airline: El Al. Tel Aviv-Ben Gurion airport is located 20 km from the city centre.

ITALY

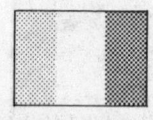

Repubblica Italiana
ITALIAN REPUBLIC

CAPITAL: Rome (Roma)

AREA AND POPULATION: 301,268 km², 50% cultivated land. Population:

57,226,000 (1986 est.). Population density: 190/km². Population growth (1970-82): 0.4%. Ethnic composition: Italian 95%; Sardinian 2.6%; Germanic 0.5%; French 0.4%; Rhaeto-romanic 0.4%; Greek 0.3%; Albanian 0.2%; Slovene 0.2%. Almost 30 million Italians live abroad.

CLIMATE AND GEOGRAPHY: The climate ranges from continental in the north, with high rainfall, to Mediterranean in the peninsula and islands, with low rainfall. Average temperature (Rome): 7°C (January), 25°C (July). Average annual rainfall: 657 mm. Italy is bordered to the north by Switzerland and Austria, to the east by Yugoslavia and to the west by France. Mainland Italy occupies a long narrow peninsula (350 km at its widest part) which stretches 1,200 km from the Italian Alps to the Mediterrranean Sea. Its island territories include Sicily, Sardinia and another 70 smaller islands. Four-fifths of the country consists of hills and mountains.

CURRENCY: Lira (Lit) of 100 centesimi.

DEFENCE: Military service is compulsory for 12 months (Army and Air Force) and 18 months (Navy). Total armed forces (1986/87): 385,100. Army 270,000; Navy 44,500; Air Force 70,600. Paramilitary forces: carabinieri 90,000; Ministry of Interior public security guards 67,927; Treasury Department finance guards 48,691.

GOVERNMENT: Parliamentary democratic republic. The bicameral Parliament consists of a Chamber of Deputies of 630 members and Senate of 315 members. The Chamber of Deputies is elected by universal and direct suffrage for a period of 5 years. The Senate is also elected for 5 years, but on a regional basis, each Region having at least 7 Senators. Head of State: Francesco Cossiga. Prime Minister: Ciriaco de Mita. Foreign Minister: Giulio Andreotti.

LANGUAGE: Italian (official), German (South Tyrol), French (Val d'Aosta), Ladin (South Tyrol), Slovenian (Trieste and Gorizia).

NATIONAL ANTHEM: Fratelli d'Italia (Brothers of Italy).

RELIGION: Roman Catholic 99%; Protestant 180,000; Jewish 35,000.

TOURIST INFORMATION: Passport but no visa required by Australian citizens. Health insurance is recommended as medical and dental costs in Italy are very high. Public hospital facilities are not always adequate but there are satisfactory private hospitals. National airline: Alitalia.

JAMAICA

CAPITAL: Kingston

AREA AND POPULATION: 10,961 km², 24% cultivated land. Population: 2,288,000 (1986 est.). Population density: 208.7/km². Population growth (1970-82): 1.5%. Ethnic composition: Negro 76%; Mulatto 15%; European, Indian and Chinese minorities.

CLIMATE AND GEOGRAPHY: The climate is tropical, with coastal sea breezes and less humid conditions in upland areas. Rainfall is plentiful and the country is hurricane affected. Average temperature (Kingston): 24°C (January), 27°C (July). Average annual rainfall: 800 mm. The island of Jamaica is situated in the Caribbean Sea to the south of Cuba and west of Haiti. It is crossed by a range of mountains, high in the east (about 2,000 m) and descending towards the west. The island's vegetation varies from tropical to subtropical.

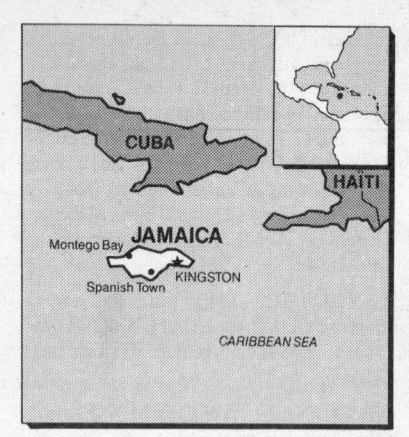

CURRENCY: Jamaican Dollar (J$) of 100 cents.

DEFENCE: Military service is voluntary. Total armed forces (1987): 2,100 (all services form part of the Army). Army 1,780; Navy 150; Air Force 170. Paramilitary force: mobile reserve 1,030.

GOVERNMENT: Parliamentary democratic monarchy. The bicameral Parliament consists of the House of Representatives of 60 members, elected by universal adult suffrage for a period of 5 years, and the Senate of 21 appointed members. Head of State: Queen Elizabeth II, represented by Governor-General Florizel Augustus Glasspole. Prime Minister: Edward Seaga. Foreign Minister: Hugh Shearer.

LANGUAGE: English (official), creole.

RELIGION: Protestant 70%; Roman Catholic 8%; Jewish 600; Hindu; Moslem.

TOURIST INFORMATION: Passport, onward or return ticket but no visa required by Australian citizens. Foreign currencies should be declared upon arrival. An airport tax of J$40 is levied on all passengers embarking in Jamaica. National airline: Air Jamaica. Kingston-Norman Manley airport is located 17 km from the city.

JAPAN

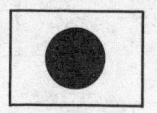

Nippon

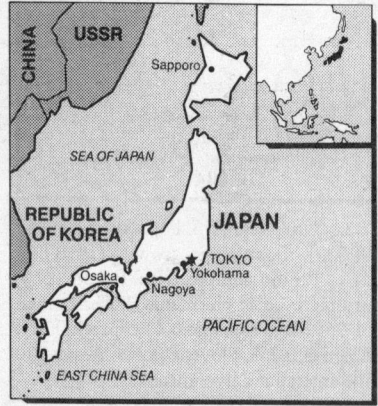

CAPITAL: Tokyo

AREA AND POPULATION: 377,767 km², 13% cultivated land. Population: 121,402,000 (1986 est). Population density: 321.4/km². Population growth (1970-82): 1.1%. Ethnic composition: Japanese, 99.4%; Korean 0.5%, Chinese and Ainu minorities. In October 1984, 478,168 Japanese were living abroad.

CLIMATE AND GEOGRAPHY: The climate is generally mild, with warm, humid summers. The rainy season occurs in June and July. In winter snowfall is considerable in Hokkaido and in the northeastern part of Honshu. Typhoons are frequent from August to October. Average temperature (Tokyo): 4.7°C (January), 25.2°C (July). Average annual rainfall: 1,460 mm. Japan is an island group in the North Pacific, consisting of 4 major islands and about 4,000 minor islands. Major Islands: Hokkaido (83,000 km²), Honshu (231,000 km²), Shikoku (19,000 km²), Kyushu (42,000 km²). About four-fifths of the country is hilly and mountainous. The Japanese Alps run north-south through central Honshu. Lowlands and plains are small and are found mostly along the coast, which is deeply indented with natural harbours.

CURRENCY: Yen of 100 sen.

DEFENCE: Military service is voluntary. Total armed forces (1987): 244,600. Army 155,000; Navy 45,600; Air Force 44,000. Para-military force: coastguard 12,000.

GOVERNMENT: Parliamentary democratic monarchy. Legislative power rests with the Diet, consisting of the House of Representatives (512 members) and the House of Councillors (252 members). Head of State: Emperor Hirohito. Prime Minister: Noboru Takeshito. Foreign Minister: Sosuke Uno.

LANGUAGE: Japanese—3 character systems in use (katakana, hiragana, kanji).

NATIONAL ANTHEM: Kimi ga yo wa (May 1,000 years of happy reign be Yours).

RELIGIONS: Shinto 112,107,000; Buddhist 89,965,000; Confucianist 14,000,000; Christian 1,656,000; New Religionist.

TOURIST INFORMATION: Passport and visa required by Australian citizens. There are no particular health precautions that need to be taken in Japan but people with respiratory complaints may be troubled by the smog-laden atmosphere of Tokyo. Medical and dental treatment is expensive. Direct tipping is rare and is discouraged. A 'Passenger Service Facility Charge' of 2,000 yen is levied on passengers leaving Narita Airport on international flights. National airline: Japan Airlines. Tokyo-Narita airport is located 65 km from the city.

JORDAN

Al-Mamlaka al-Urduniya al-Hashemiyah
HASHEMITE KINGDOM OF JORDAN

CAPITAL: Amman

AREA AND POPULATION: 97,740 km², 14% cultivated land. Population: 2,756,000 (1986 est.). Population density: 28.2/km². Population growth (1970-82): 2.5%. Ethnic composition: Jordanian Arab and Palestinian, over 99%; Circassian 0.2%; Armenian and Kurd, 0.1%.

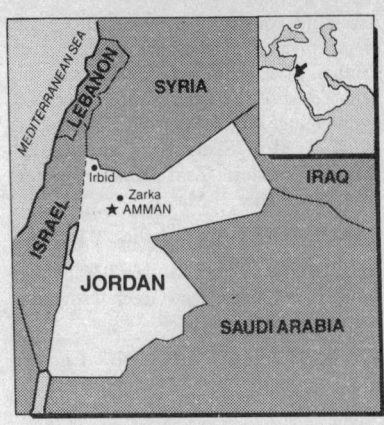

CLIMATE AND GEOGRAPHY: The climate is Mediterranean, with hot dry summers and cool wet winters. Average temperature (Amman): 7.5°C (January), 25°C (July). Average annual rainfall: 290 mm. Jordan is bounded to the north by Syria, to the south by Saudi Arabia, to the east by Iraq and to the west by Israel. Aqaba, at the northern end of the Red Sea, is the country's only port. Running north-south through the country is the Jordan Rift Valley which forms the depressions of the Jordan River, Lake Tiberias and the Dead Sea (360 m below sea level).

CURRENCY: Jordan Dinar (JD) of 1,000 fils.

DEFENCE: Military service is voluntary. Service in the People's Army (militia, forming) is compulsory for a period of 2 years. Total armed forces (1987): 70,700. Army 62,750; Navy (coastguard) 300; Air Force 7,200. Para-military forces: public security force 3,500; civil militia 2,500; Palestine Liberation Army 1,500.

GOVERNMENT: Constitutional monarchy. The King appoints the Prime Minister, and other ministers are appointed by the King on the recommendation of the Prime Minister. The King's younger brother, Crown Prince Hassan, is the legal successor to the throne. There is a National

Assembly consisting of a Senate of 30 members and a National Consultative Council of 60 members. Members of the Senate and of the Council are appointed by the King. Women were enfranchised in 1984. Head of State: King Hussein II. Prime Minister: Zaid Rifai. Foreign Minister: Taher al-Masri.

LANGUAGE: Arabic (official), English.

RELIGION: Sunni Moslem 93%; Shiite Moslem 3%; Christian (Greek Orthodox, Armenian Orthodox) 5%.

TOURIST INFORMATION: Passport and visa required by Australian citizens. A temporary visa can be obtained at Amman airport. It is not considered advisable to drink the tap water and foods such as salads should be avoided in summer. National airline: Alia, Royal Jordanian Airlines. Amman-Queen Alia airport is located 28 km from the city.

KAMPUCHEA

DEMOCRATIC KAMPUCHEA

Since April 1975, the military situation in Kampuchea has made it impossible to obtain reliable statistical and other data.

CAPITAL: Phnom Penh

AREA AND POPULATION: 181,035 km^2, 17% cultivated land. Population: 6,388,000 (1986 est.). Pop. density: 35.3/km^2. Pop. growth (1983): 1.9%. Ethnic composition: Khmer 93%; Vietnamese 3%; Chinese, 4%; Khmer Loeu; Cham-Malay; Thai; Laotian.

CLIMATE AND GEOGRAPHY: The climate is very hot and humid, although the heat is moderated by heavy rains. The rainy season lasts from April to October. Average temperature (Phnom Penh): 25.6°C (January), 28.9°C (July). Average annual rainfall: 1,308 mm. Kampuchea is bordered to the north-east by Laos, to the north-west by Thailand, to the south and east by Vietnam and to the south-west by the Gulf of Thailand. The central area of the country is level, while the south-east contains hills and mountains. About 75% of the area is forested.

CURRENCY: Riel of 100 sen.

DEFENCE: Military service is by conscription for 18 months minimum. Total armed forces (1986/87): 42,000. Army 35,000, Navy 7,000. Para-military forces: militia; regional armed forces/self-defence forces; people's police force. Opposition: Coalition of Democratic Kampuchea (Khmer Rouge 35,000; Kampuchean People's National Liberation Front 15,000; Armée Nationale Sihanoukienne 9,000). Though informally merged, the three forces operate independently for the most part.

GOVERNMENT: People's republic. The former US-backed Lon Nol government fell as Royal Government of National Union forces finally captured Phnom Penh on 17 April 1975. A new leftist government, headed by Khieu Samphan, was installed. Pol Pot, the secretary of the Communist Party of Kampuchea, became Prime Minister. On 25 December 1978 Vietnam invaded Kampuchea (then Cambodia) and on 10 January 1979 set up a government in Phnom Penh with Heng Samrin, a former Khmer Rouge division commander, as its titular head. After much urging by ASEAN, the Coalition Government of Democratic Kampuchea was formed in Kuala Lumpur on 22 June 1982. The Government, headed by Prince Norodom

Sihanouk, controls little of the country, but is recognised by the United Nations and most of the non-communist countries, as well as by China. Head of State: Heng Samrin. Prime Minister: Hun Sen.

LANGUAGE: Khmer (official), French, Vietnamese.

RELIGION: Buddhist 90%; Sunni Moslem 50,000.

TOURIST INFORMATION: Passport and visa required by Australian citizens. Visas are not issued for tourist purposes. Prospective travellers should make enquiries well in advance at Kampuchean diplomatic missions in Hanoi, Havana, Moscow, New Delhi, Ulan Bator or Vientiane. Airline serving: Hang Khong Vietnam. Phnom Penh airport is located 8 km from the city.

KENYA

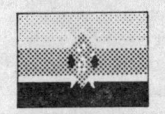

Jamhuri ya Kenya
REPUBLIC OF KENYA

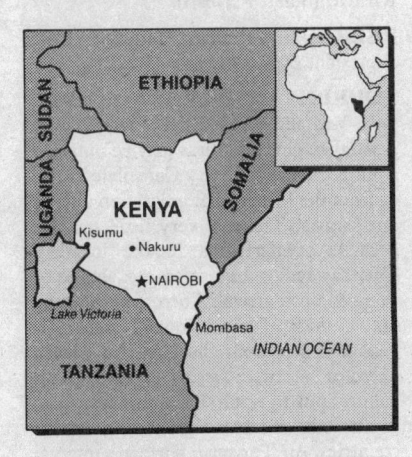

CAPITAL: Nairobi

AREA AND POPULATION: 582,646 km², 4% cultivated land. Population: 21,044,000 (1986 est.). Population density: 36.1/km². Population growth (1970-82): 4%. Ethnic composition: Bantu 60%; Nilotic 14%; Hamitic and Nilohamitic tribes; Arab, Indian and European minorities.

CLIMATE AND GEOGRAPHY: The climate is tropical, affected by monsoons. Differences in altitude make for varied conditions between the hot, coastal lowlands and the plateau. The wet season, from March to May, is known as the 'long rains'. Average temperature (Nairobi): 18°C (January), 16°C (July). Average annual rainfall: 958 mm. Kenya is located on the Indian Ocean coast of Africa, bordered to the north by Sudan, Ethiopia and Somalia, to the south by Tanzania and to the west by Uganda. The coastal portion of the country stretches some 608 km from the Somali border to Tanzania. From the hot, humid coast the land rises gradually inland through dry bush country, the Nyika, to the savanna grasslands and highlands. A prominent feature is the sector of the Great Rift Valley which, in places, is up to 60 km wide and runs through the country between 610 and 914 m below the land on both sides. Along the floor of the Valley is a series of lakes, stretching from Lake Turkana in the north to Lake Magadi in the south.

CURRENCY: Kenya Shilling (KS) of 100 cents.

DEFENCE: Military service is voluntary. Total armed forces (1986/87): 13,350. Army 13,000; Navy 350. Paramilitary force: police 1,800.

GOVERNMENT: Presidential republic. The unicameral Parliament (National Assembly) consists of 158 elected representatives, 12 nominated members, the Speaker and the Attorney-General. Head of State: President Daniel Arap Moi. Foreign Minister: Elijah Mwagale.

LANGUAGE: Kiswahili (official), English.

RELIGION: Protestant 38%; Roman Catholic 28%; Moslem 6%; Jewish 200; Hindu; Animist.

TOURIST INFORMATION: Passport and visa required by Australian citizens. A deposit may be required on arrival if return or onward tickets are not held. Typhoid, para-typhoid and yellow fever vaccinations and malaria prophylaxis are recommended. Qantas flies to Harare (Zimbabwe), where connecting flights to Kenya may be met. There is a departure tax of US$10 (to be paid only in freely convertible foreign currency). National airline: Kenya Airways. Nairobi-Jomo Kenyatta airport is located 17 km from the city.

KIRIBATI

Ribaberikin Kiribati
REPUBLIC OF KIRIBATI

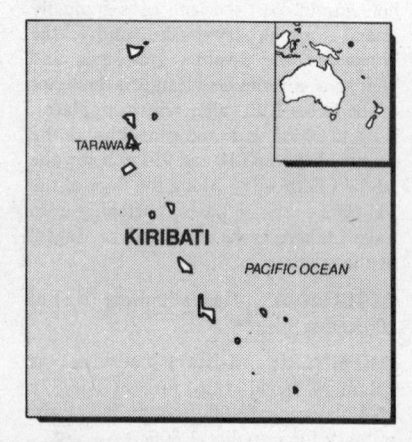

CAPITAL: Tarawa

AREA AND POPULATION: 717 km^2. Population: 63,000 (1986 est.). Population density: 87.9/km^2. Population growth (1975-78): 2.2%. Ethnic composition: Micronesian 80%; Polynesian; Chinese; European.

CLIMATE AND GEOGRAPHY: The climate is maritime equatorial (Central Gilberts, Phoenix Islands and Banaba) and tropical (northern and southern islands). Average temperature (Tarawa): 28°C. Average annual rainfall: 1,977 mm. Rains and gales usually occur from October to March. Kiribati comprises 33 atolls in the mid-Pacific Ocean. They form 3 major groups: Gilberts (17), Phoenix (8) and Line (8), scattered over an ocean area of about 5,000,000 km^2. From east to west they extend 3,870 km, and from north to south 2,050 km. With the exception of Banaba Island, which is a coral formation rising to 81 m, the islands are low-lying coral atolls with coastal lagoons. There is no luxuriant vegetation but coconut palms and pandanus trees grow on most islands.

CURRENCY Australian Dollar of 100 cents.

DEFENCE No defence force is maintained.

GOVERNMENT Sovereign democratic republic. The President (Beretitenti), presides over the Cabinet. The Parliament of Kiribati is the House of Assembly (Maneaba ni Maungatabu), a unicameral body of 36 elected members. Head of State, Head of Government and Foreign Minister: President Ieremia T. Tabai. There are no political parties, only clan groupings.

LANGUAGE: English (official), Kiribati (Gilbertese). The alphabet used has only 13 letters. 'S' is not among them, hence the spelling 'Kiribati' is used to render 'Gilberts', and is pronounced 'Kiribass'.

NATIONAL ANTHEM: Teirake kain Kiribati (Stand Kiribati).

RELIGION: Roman Catholic 50%; Protestant 50%.

TOURIST INFORMATION: Passport, visa and onward ticket required by Australian citizens. Visas may be obtained from Kiribati Honorary Consulate Office or from the Principal Immigration Officer on Tarawa. There is very little tourism because of Kiribati's remote location. Cameras, radios, binoculars etc. should be declared upon arrival. There is a departure tax of A$5. Tarawa-Bonriki airport is located 5 km from the city. Air Nauru operates a twice-weekly service with connections to Australia, south-east Asia, north Asia and to neighbouring Pacific countries. Air Tungaru, Kiribati's internal airline, operates services to most of the outer islands in the group. It also operates a fortnightly service to Honolulu via Christmas Island.

KOREA, NORTH

Chosun Minchu-chui Inmin Konghwa-guk
DEMOCRATIC PEOPLE'S REPUBLIC OF KOREA

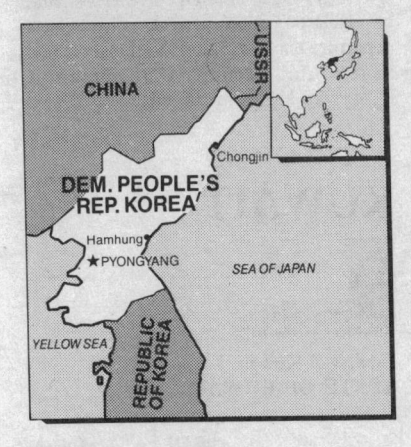

CAPITAL: Pyongyang

AREA AND POPULATION: 120,538 km², 23% cultivated land. Population: 20,543,000 (1986 est.). Population density: 170.4/km². Population growth (1970-82): 2.5%. Ethnic composition: almost exclusively Korean.

CLIMATE AND GEOGRAPHY: The climate is warm temperate, with cold winters in the north. Most rain falls in the summer. Average temperature (Pyongyang): −7°C (January), 24°C (July). Average annual rainfall: 920 mm. The People's Republic is bordered to the north by China and the USSR, to the south by the Republic of Korea, to the east by the Sea of Japan, and to the west by the Yellow Sea. Mountains and hills cover nearly all the country.

CURRENCY: Won of 100 chon.

DEFENCE: Military service is compulsory for 5 years (Army and Navy) and 3 to 4 years (Air Force). Total armed forces (1987): 836,000. Army 750,000; Navy 31,000; Air Force 55,000. Paramilitary forces: Workers'-Farmers' Red Guard (militia) 3,000,000; ranger commando force 100,000.

GOVERNMENT: Communist people's republic. The Supreme People's Assembly of 655 members is elected by universal adult suffrage every 4 years. The government consists of the Administration Council, directed by the Central People's Committee. Head of State: Kim Il Sung. Foreign Minister: Kim Yong Nam.

LANGUAGE: Korean (official), Russian, Chinese.

NATIONAL ANTHEM: A chi mun bin na ra i gang san (Shine bright, o dawn, on this land so fair).

RELIGION: Buddhist; Confucianist; Chondoist; Christian.

TOURIST INFORMATION: Passport and visa required by Australian citizens. Visas applications may be made at Korean DPR diplomatic missions in Berlin (East), Prague (Czechoslovakia) and Moscow (USSR), among others, and take about 1 month. No vaccinations are required. National airline: Chosominhang. Pyongyang-Sunan airport is located 30 km from the city.

KOREA, SOUTH

Taehan-min'guk
REPUBLIC OF KOREA

CAPITAL: Seoul

AREA AND POPULATION: 98,484 km², 23% cultivated land. Population: 43,284,000 (1986 est.). Population density: 439.5/km². Population growth (1970–82): 1.7%. Ethnic composition: almost exclusively Korean. About 1,200,000 Koreans live abroad.

CLIMATE AND GEOGRAPHY: The extreme south has a humid warm temperate climate, while the remainder of the country is continental temperate. Winters are very cold. Most rain falls between April and September. Average temperature (Seoul): −5°C (January), 25°C (July). Average

LANGUAGE: Korean.

RELIGION: Buddhist 27%; Protestant 19%; Confucianist 13%; Roman Catholic 3%.

TOURIST INFORMATION: Passport but no visa required by Australian citizens provided that the period of stay does not exceed 15 days and that they hold onward or return tickets. Foreign currencies should be declared upon arrival. There is a departure tax of W5,000. National airline: Korean Air. Seoul-Kim Po airport is located 25 km from the city.

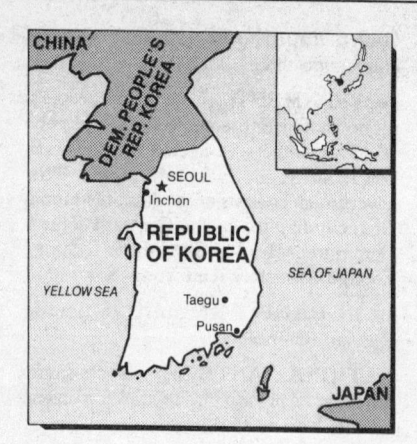

annual rainfall: 1,250 mm. The Republic is bordered to the north by the demilitarised zone and North Korea, to the south by the Korea Strait, to the east by the Sea of Japan and to the west by the Yellow Sea. The principal geographic feature is the mountainous backbone running southwards down the east coast and bearing to the west near the southern tip of the peninsula. The eastern coast is steep and rugged. The western slopes, however, are gentle, ending in a network of estuaries and tidal flats. A great number of islands, some of them volcanic, lie off the south-western coast.

CURRENCY: The Won (W).

DEFENCE: Military service is compulsory for 30 months in the Army and 3 years in the Navy and Air Force. Total armed forces (1987): 607,000. Army 520,000; Navy 29,000; Marines 25,000; Air Force 33,000. Para-military forces: Civilian Defence Corps (to age 50) 3,500,000; Student Homeland Defence Corps (schools) 600,000; coastguard; Hydrographic Service.

GOVERNMENT: Presidential republic. The president is elected by the Electoral College of 5,271 directly elected members for a 7-year term. There is a State Council of Ministers appointed by the President and a National Assembly of 299 members directly elected for 4 years. Head of State: President Roh Tae-woo. Prime Minister: Lee Hyun Jae. Foreign Minister: Choi Kwang soo.

KUWAIT

Dowlat al-Kuwait
STATE OF KUWAIT

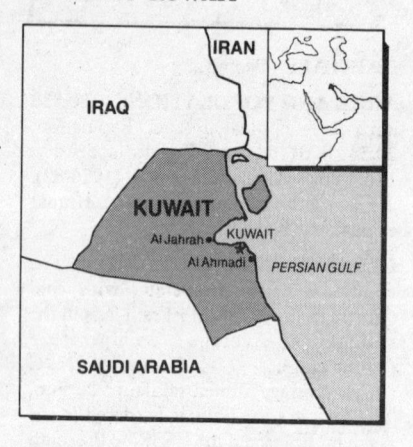

CAPITAL: Kuwait

AREA AND POPULATION: 17,818 km^2, 0.1% cultivated land. Population: 1,771,000 (1986 est.). Population density: 99.4/km^2. Population growth (1970-82): 6.3%. Ethnic composition: Kuwaiti Arab 42%; Palestinian 20%; Egyptian 6%; Iraqi 5%; Persian 4%; Indian 3%; Pakistani 2%; Bedouin.

CLIMATE AND GEOGRAPHY: The climate is hot and dry, with a long summer and a short winter. Average temperature (Kuwait): 13°C (January), 37°C (July). Average annual rainfall 125 mm. Kuwait is situated at the north-west end of the Persian Gulf, bordered to the north by Iraq and to the south and west by Saudi Arabia. The terrain is flat sandy desert, rising slightly towards the west. The Partitioned Zone separates Kuwait and Saudi Arabia in the extreme south.

CURRENCY: Kuwait Dinar (KD) of 1,000 fils.

DEFENCE: Military service is compulsory for 18 months. Total armed forces (1987): 13,100. Army 10,000; Navy 1,100; Air Force 2,000. Para-military forces: National Guard; palace guard; border guard.

GOVERNMENT: Constitutional monarchy. The National Assembly of 50 members is elected by adult males for a 4-year term. Head of State: Shaikh Jabir al-Ahmad al-Jabir Al-Sabah, 13th Amir of Kuwait. Prime Minister: Shaikh Saad Al-Abdullah al-Salem Al-Sabah. Foreign Minister: Shaikh Sabah al-Ahmad al-Jabir al-Sabah.

LANGUAGE: Arabic (official), English.

RELIGION: Sunni and Shiite Moslem 93% (70:30); Christian (mostly Roman Catholic) 60,000.

TOURIST INFORMATION: Passport and visa required by Australian citizens. Entry will be refused to visitors whose passports contain evidence of earlier or intended entry to Israel. Standards of hygiene in leading hotels are good but stomach upsets are not uncommon. Tap water should be avoided. National airline: Kuwait Airways. Kuwait airport is located 16 km from the city.

LAOS

Sāthālamalid Pasāthu'paait Pasāsim Lāo
LAO PEOPLE'S DEMOCRATIC REPUBLIC

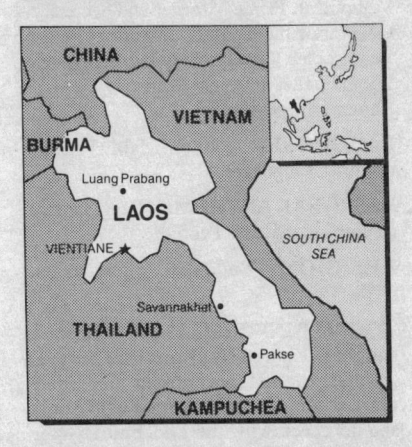

CAPITAL: Vientiane

AREA AND POPULATION: 236,800 km^2, 4% cultivated land. Population: 3,679,000 (1986 est.). Population density: 15.5/km^2. Population growth (1970-82): 2%. Ethnic composition: Lao-Lum (Valley Lao) 56%; Lao-Theung (Mountain Lao) 34%; Lao-Soung (Highland Lao) 9%; about 70 other minor ethnic groupings.

CLIMATE AND GEOGRAPHY: The climate is tropical monsoon, with very heavy rains from May to October. Average temperature (Vientiane): 21°C (January), 27°C (July). Average annual rainfall: 1,700 mm. Laos is bordered to the north by China, to the south by Kampuchea, to the east by Vietnam and to the west by Burma and Thailand. The country is mostly mountainous and densely forested. The Mekong River forms much of the border with Thailand and is a major communications route.

CURRENCY: Kip (K) of 100 att.

DEFENCE: Military service is compulsory for 18 months. Total armed forces (1987): 53,700. Army 50,000; Navy

1,700; Air Force 2,000. Para-military forces: militia; self-defence forces.

GOVERNMENT: Democratic people's republic based on Marxist-Leninist principles. The legislative body is the Supreme People's Council of 45 members nominated by the Congress of People's Representatives for an indefinite period. Head of State: President Phoumi Vongvichit. Prime Minister and Secretary-General of the Central Committee of the Lao People's Revolutionary Party: Kaysone Phomvihane. Foreign Minister: General Phoune Sipaseuth.

LANGUAGE: Lao (official), French, minority languages.

NATIONAL ANTHEM: Peng Sat Lao (Hymn of the Lao People).

RELIGION: Buddhists 58%; tribal 34%.

TOURIST INFORMATION: Passport and visa required by Australian citizens. Tourism is not encouraged but some tourists are admitted. Intending visitors should check with the Lao Embassy for details of the latest regulations. Officially, people entering the country are not required to provide valid International Health Certificates showing vaccination against smallpox and cholera, but these are advisable as cards may be checked anyway. Inoculations against typhoid, tetanus, tuberculosis and polio are also advisable. Malaria prophylaxis is recommended. Vaccinations against rabies and hepatitis are wise precautions. There is a departure tax of US$5. National airline: Lao Aviation. Vientiane-Vattay airport is located 4 km from the city.

LEBANON

Al-Jumhouriya al-Lubnaniya
REPUBLIC OF LEBANON

CAPITAL: Beirut

AREA AND POPULATION: 10,400 km^2, 34% cultivated land. Population: 2,674,000 (1986 est.). Population density: 257.1/km^2. Population growth (1970-82): 0.5%. Ethnic composition: Lebanese 82%; Armenian 5%; Palestinian 9%.

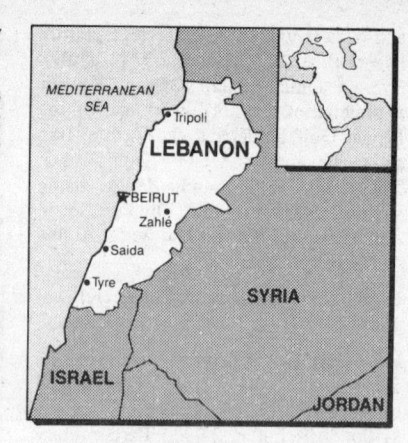

CLIMATE AND GEOGRAPHY: The climate is Mediterranean, with short warm winters and long hot summers. Rainfall can be torrential. Average temperature (Beirut): 13°C (January), 27°C (July). Average annual rainfall (Beirut): 893 mm. Lebanon is bordered to the north and east by Syria, to the south by Israel and to the west by the Mediterranean Sea. The country is mountainous. The fertile Bekaa Valley lies between the Lebanon and Anti-Lebanon Ranges.

CURRENCY: Lebanese Pound (LEL) of 100 piastres.

DEFENCE: Military service was made compulsory in 1975 but is not universally applied. The duration of service is 18 months. Total armed forces (1987): perhaps 16,000. Army 15,000 (all units below strength); Navy 450; Air Force 1,100. Para-military forces: gendarmerie 5,000; internal security force 8,000; border guard—forming, to be 4,500; Customs officials. Private militias (strengths are estimates only): Lebanese Forces Militia (Phalange) 4,500; MARADA Brigade; Maronite Christian 1,000; National Guard (forming); South Lebanon Army 1,000; al-Tanzin extremist militia. Druze: Progressive Socialist Party (Jumblatt) 5,000. Sunni: Islamic Unity Movement 1,000; Mourabitoun militia (underground) 400; Jundullah. Shiite: Amal (orthodox) 6,000; Hizbollah (fundamentalists) 1,000; al-Amal al-Islam 600; Islamic Resistance Movement. Other: Lebanese Arab Army (Lebanese Army deserters); Lebanese National Resistance Front (anti-Israeli forces in South Yemen). All data should be regarded as estimates.

GOVERNMENT: Republic with unicameral Parliament of 99 members. According to constitutional convention, the President must be a Maronite Christian, the Prime Minister a Sunni Moslem and the Speaker of the Chamber Deputies a Shiite Moslem. Head of State: President Amin Gemayel. Prime Minister and Foreign Minister: Rashid Karami.

LANGUAGE: Arabic (official), French, English.

NATIONAL ANTHEM: Kulluna lil watan lil 'ula lil 'alam (We all belong to the homeland and to the world).

RELIGION: Moslem 60%; Maronite Christian 25%; Greek Orthodox 7%; Druze 7%.

TOURIST INFORMATION: Passport and visa required by Australian citizens. Entry will be refused to visitors whose passports contain evidence of earlier or intended visits to Israel. There is a departure tax of LEL 150-250. National airline: Middle East Airlines (MEA). Beirut airport is located 16 km from the city.

LESOTHO

'Muso oa Lesotho
KINGDOM OF LESOTHO

CAPITAL: Maseru

AREA AND POPULATION: 30,355 km^2, 15% cultivated land. Population: 1,552,000 (1986 est.). Population density: 51.1/km^2. Population growth (1970-82): 2.4%. Ethnic composition: almost exclusively Basuto; European and Indian minorities.

CLIMATE AND GEOGRAPHY: The climate is pleasant, temperatures ranging from 32°C in summer to −6°C in winter. Most rain falls in summer, from October to April. Average annual rainfall: 725 mm. Lesotho is situated within the Republic of South Africa, bounded to the north by the Orange Free State and Natal, to the south by Cape Province, to the east by Natal and East Griqualand and to the west by the Orange Free State. The terrain is mountainous, descending westwards to a lowland belt where two-thirds of the population live.

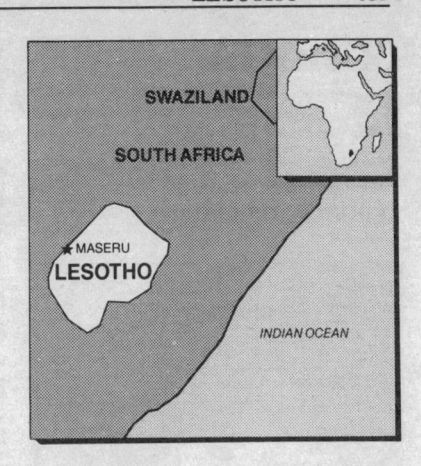

CURRENCY: Loti (M—pl. Maloti) of 100 lisente.

DEFENCE: No defence force is maintained. Para-military force: police mobile unit.

GOVERNMENT: Monarchy with a bicameral Parliament consisting of a Senate of 11 appointed members and 22 principal chiefs and a National Assembly of 60 members elected by universal adult suffrage. Head of State: King Moshoeshoe II. Following the military coup of 25 January 1986, Prime Minister Chief Leabua Jonathon was ousted and replaced by Major-General Justin Lekhanya.

LANGUAGE: Sesotho and English (both official).

RELIGION: Roman Catholic 43%; Protestant 49%; Moslem; Animist.

TOURIST INFORMATION: Passport but no visa required by Australian citizens. A departure tax of M10 is levied on all passengers boarding international flights. National airline: Air Lesotho Corporation.

LIBERIA

REPUBLIC OF LIBERIA

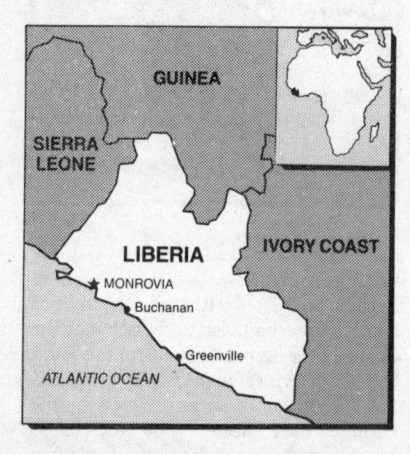

CAPITAL: Monrovia

AREA AND POPULATION: 112,600 km², 4% cultivated land. Population: 2,307,000 (1986 est.). Population density: 20.5/km². Population growth (1970-82): 3.5%. Ethnic composition: Kpelle and Bassa, 33%; Kru; Mandingo; Gio; Vai; Gola; 13 other minor tribes; descendants of black immigrants from America who founded Liberia 5%; Lebanese, American, European, several thousand each.

CLIMATE AND GEOGRAPHY: The climate is equatorial, with high temperatures, humidity and rainfall. Temperatures are moderated on the coast by sea breezes. There are distinct wet and dry seasons. Humidity is affected by the 'harmattan' (hot Saharan) wind from December to March. Average temperature (Monrovia): 26°C (January), 24°C (July). Average annual rainfall: 5,138 mm. Liberia is bordered to the north by Sierra Leone and Guinea, to the south and west by the Atlantic Ocean and to the east by Côte D'Ivoire. The country can be divided into 3 belts lying parallel to the coast: a low coastal belt with tidal creeks, shallow lagoons and mangrove marshes; a relatively elevated forest area 180-360 m high; and a mountainous area with peaks up to 1,750 m.

CURRENCY: Liberian Dollar (L$) of 100 cents, pegged to the US$.

DEFENCE: Military service is voluntary. Total armed forces (1987): 7,000. Army 6,300; Navy (coastguard) 450; Air Force 250. Para-military force: national police 2,000.

GOVERNMENT: Presidential republic with a bicameral (Senate and House of Representatives) Parliament. Head of State: Samuel K. Doe. Foreign Minister: Ernest Eastman.

LANGUAGE: English (official), over 20 tribal languages.

NATIONAL ANTHEM: All hail, Liberia, hail!

RELIGION: Animist majority; Moslem 15%; Roman Catholic 24,000; Protestant 20,000.

TOURIST INFORMATION: Passport and visa required by Australian citizens. Malaria prophylaxis is essential. Yellow fever, cholera, tetanus, typhoid and poliomyelitis vaccinations are strongly recommended. Rabies and hepatitis exist in Liberia. A departure tax of L$10 is levied on international passengers. National airline: Air Liberia. Monrovia-Roberts airport is located 60 km from the city.

LIBYA

Al-Jamahiriyah al-Arabiya al-Libya al-Shabiya al-Ishtirakiya
SOCIALIST PEOPLE'S LIBYAN ARAB JAMAHIRIYA (The Masses)

CAPITAL: Tripoli

AREA AND POPULATION: 1,759,540 km², 1% cultivated land. Population: 3,876,000 (1986 est.). Population density: 2.2/km². Population growth (1970-82): 4.1%. Ethnic composition: Arab-Berber 80%; Tuareg, Kulughli, Negro and Berber minorities.

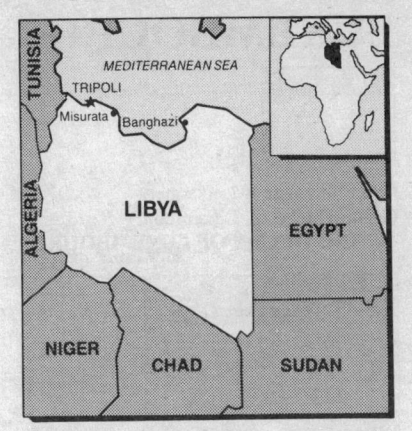

CLIMATE AND GEOGRAPHY: The climate is predominantly arid, but is warm temperate on the coast. Average temperature (Tripoli): 11°C (January), 27°C (July). Average annual rainfall (Tripoli): 400 mm. Libya is situated in North Africa, bordered to the north by the Mediterranean Sea, to the south by Niger, Chad and the Sudan, to the east by Egypt and to the west by Tunisia and Algeria. Desert and semi-desert regions cover about 90% of the country. A low coastal plain extends along the majority of the country's Mediterranean coastline. There are low mountains in the north and higher mountains in the south.

CURRENCY: Libyan Dinar (LD) of 1,000 millimes.

DEFENCE: Military service is by selective conscription for 18 months. Total armed forces (1987): 67,500. Army 55,000; Navy 4,000; Air Force 8,500. Para-military forces: Islamic Pan-African Legion 7,000; Customs/coastguard; Muslim Youth; People's Cavalry Force parade unit.

GOVERNMENT: Republic under military control. The country is divided into 25 municipalities and 126 Basic People's Congresses. The General People's Congress, as the national legislature, comprises 3 delegates from each of the Basic People's Congresses. It is assisted by a 5-member General People's Secretariat. Head of State and Secretary of the General People's Congress: Omar Montasser. Leader of the Revolution: Muammar Qadhafi.

LANGUAGE: Arabic (official), Berber dialects, English.

RELIGION: Moslem 97%; Christian minority.

TOURIST INFORMATION: Passport and visa required by Australian citizens. Entry will be refused to visitors whose passports contain valid or expired visas for Israel and/or South Africa. Visitors must have US$500 or its equivalent in freely convertible currency with them upon arrival. This amount should be registered in the passport and must be changed into local currency. Re-exchange is possible minus US$50 per actual day of stay. The following are prohibited imports: alcoholic beverages, pork and pork products, obscene literature, goods of Israeli origin, Coca Cola, other articles produced by companies which trade with Israel. Malaria prophylaxis is recommended. National airline: Libyan Arab Airlines. Tripoli airport is located 34 km from the city.

LIECHTEN-STEIN

Fürstentum Liechtenstein
PRINCIPALITY OF LIECHTENSTEIN

CAPITAL: Vaduz

AREA AND POPULATION: 160 km², 24.3% cultivated land. Population: 28,000 (1986 est.). Population density: 175/km². Population growth (1978-83): 0.9%. Ethnic composition: Alemmanic 95%; other migrant worker minorities.

CLIMATE AND GEOGRAPHY: The climate varies according to altitude. Summers can be warm with considerable rainfall. Winters are fine, with clear, cold air and cloudless skies. Liechtenstein is situated on the Upper Rhine in Central

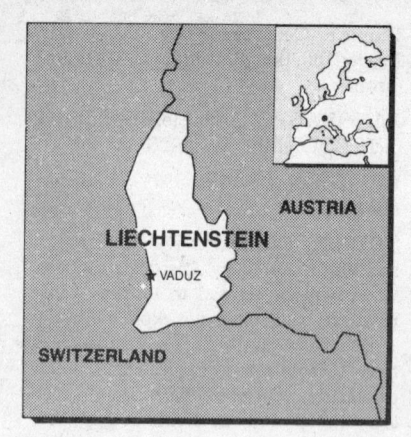

Europe, with Austria to the east and Switzerland to the west. The Rhine valley occupies one-third of the country; the Alps cover the rest.

CURRENCY: Swiss Franc (SFr) of 100 rappen.

DEFENCE: No defence force is maintained.

GOVERNMENT: Constitutional monarchy ruled by hereditary princes. The current ruler is Prince Franz Josef II of Liechtenstein. The unicameral Parliament of 15 members is elected for 4 years by universal adult male suffrage. Women are allowed to vote in the Communes of Vaduz and Gamprin. Prime Minister: Hans Brunhart.

LANGUAGE: German (official), local Alemmanic dialect.

NATIONAL ANTHEM: Oben am jungen Rhein (High on the Rhine)

RELIGION: Roman Catholic 86%; Protestant 8%.

TOURIST INFORMATION: Passport but no visa required by Australian citizens.

LUXEMBOURG

Grousherzogdem Letzebuerg
Grand-Duché de Luxembourg
GRAND DUCHY OF LUXEMBOURG

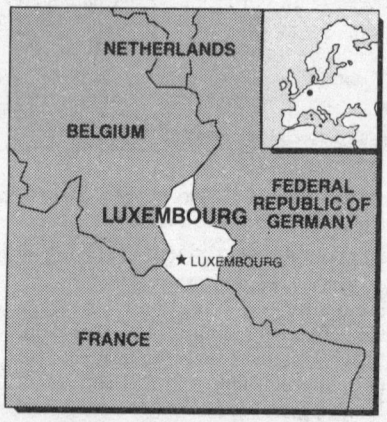

CAPITAL: Luxembourg

AREA AND POPULATION: 2,586 km^2, 25% cultivated land. Population: 367,000 (1986). Population density: 141.9/km^2. Population growth (1982): 0.04%. Ethnic composition: predominantly French and German mixture; foreigners 26.2%.

CLIMATE AND GEOGRAPHY: The climate is temperate, with very cold winters in upland areas. Rainfall is evenly distributed throughout the year. Average temperature: 0.5°C (January), 18°C (July). Average annual rainfall: 740 mm. Luxembourg is bounded to the south by France, to the west by Belgium and to the east by the FRG. The north of the country (Ardennes) is covered by heavy forests, the south is a low, open plateau. The southeast is the rich wine-growing valley of Moselle.

CURRENCY: Luxembourg Franc (FrLux) of 100 centimes, fixed at par value with the Belgian Franc.

DEFENCE: Military service is voluntary for a minimum of 3 years. Total armed forces (1986/87): 690. Army 690; Air Force: Luxembourg has no air force of its own but for legal purposes all NATO's airborne early-warning aircraft have Luxembourg registration. Para-military force: gendarmerie 470.

GOVERNMENT: Constitutional monarchy. The unicameral Parliament (Chamber of Deputies) is elected by universal adult suffrage for a 5-year term. Head of State: Grand-Duke Jean. Head of Government and Finance Minister: Jacques Santer. Foreign Minister: Jacques Poos.

LANGUAGE: Luxembourgian (national), French, German, English.

NATIONAL ANTHEM: Ons Hemecht (Our homeland).

RELIGION: Roman Catholic 95%; Protestant 3,900; Jewish 1,000.

TOURIST INFORMATION: Passport but no visa required by Australian citizens.

MADAGASCAR

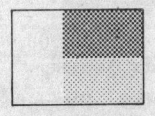

Repoblika Demokratika n'i Madagascar
DEMOCRATIC REPUBLIC OF MADAGASCAR

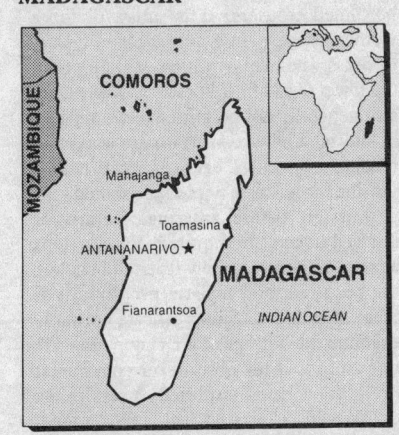

CAPITAL: Antananarivo
AREA AND POPULATION: 587,041 km², 5% cultivated land. Population: 10,294,000 (1986 est.). Population density: 17.3/km². Population growth (1985): 2.8%. Ethnic composition: Indonesian and African mixture 99%; Indian, French, Chinese, Comorian and Arab minorities.

CLIMATE AND GEOGRAPHY: The climate is tropical, with mountains affecting rainfall distribution. The trade wind blows continuously and is particularly violent between May and September. As well, the country lies in the path of the south-western cyclones from the Indian Ocean. Average temperature (Antananarivo): 21°C (January), 15°C (July). Average annual rainfall (Antananarivo): 1,350 mm. Madagascar is situated in the Indian Ocean about 400 km from the south-east coast of Africa. The island of Madagascar itself is the fourth largest in the world. There are 3 distinct geographic zones: the central plateau, which forms a permanent obstacle to the winds; a narrow littoral strip to the east; and a low plateau and vast plains to the west.

CURRENCY: Madagascar Franc (FMG) of 100 centimes.

DEFENCE: Military service is compulsory for a period of 18 months. Total armed forces (1987): 21,100. Army 20,000; Navy 600; Air Force 500. Para-military force: gendarmerie 8,000.

GOVERNMENT: Presidential republic. The Charter of the Revolution establishes the Supreme Council of the Revolution (CSR) as the highest political institution. Headed by the President, it has 22 members. The Cabinet, consisting of 21 ministers, is appointed by and is responsible to the President. Head of State: Didier Ratsiraka. Prime Minister: Désiré Rakotoarijaona. Foreign Minister: Jean Bemananjara.

LANGUAGE: Malagasy (of Malayo-Polynesian origin–official), French, English.

NATIONAL ANTHEM: Ry tanindrazanay malala ô (Oh our beloved fatherland).

RELIGION: Roman Catholic 28%; Protestant 22%; Moslem 3%; Animist 47%.

MALAWI

Mfuko La Malawi
REPUBLIC OF MALAWI

CAPITAL: Lilongwe

AREA AND POPULATION: 118,484 km^2, 34% cultivated land. Population: 7,292,000 (1986 est.). Population density: 77.2/km^2. Population growth (1985): 3.3%. Ethnic composition: mainly Bantu; European (mostly British), Asian and mixed race minorities. Some 280,000 Malawi citizens live abroad, mostly in the RSA.

CLIMATE AND GEOGRAPHY: The climate is sub-tropical, with a dry season from May to October. Average temperature (Lilongwe): 23°C (January), 16°C (July). Average annual rainfall (Lilongwe): 900 mm. Malawi is a landlocked country in Africa, bordered to the north-east by Tanzania, to the south and west by Mozambique and to the east by Zambia. The country is divided essentially into the hot lowlands of the Shire River and the shores of Lake Malawi on the one hand, and the cooler plateaux, ranging in elevation from 1,000 to 3,000 m, on the other.

CURRENCY: Malawi Kwacha (MK) of 100 tambala.

DEFENCE: Military service is voluntary for a period of 7 years. Total armed forces (1987): 5,280 (all services form part of the Army). Army 5,000; Navy 130; Air Force 150. Para-military forces: police 1,000; border patrol.

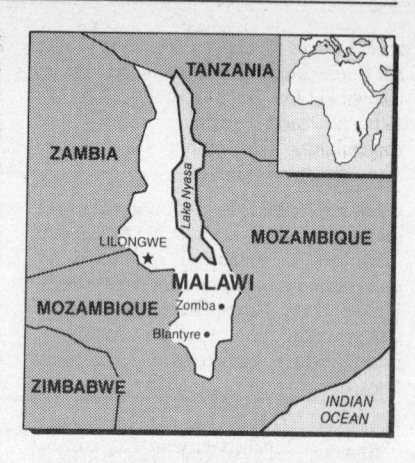

GOVERNMENT: Presidential republic with a unicameral Parliament (National Assembly), all members of which belong to the only legal political party, the Malawi Congress Party. Head of State (elected in 1971 for life): Dr Hastings Banda.

LANGUAGE: English and Chichewa (both official).

NATIONAL ANTHEM: O God bless our land of Malawi.

RELIGION: Moslem 500,000; Christian 1,793,500; Hindu; Animist.

TOURIST INFORMATION: Passport but no visa required by Australian citizens. Under Malawian law it is an offence for men to have long hair or to wear bell-bottomed trousers. It is unlawful for a woman to wear, in a public place, a skirt or dress, the hem of which is higher than the lower level of her kneecaps. Women are also generally not permitted to wear slacks or shorts. These regulations are waived in recognised tourist resorts. Journalists visiting for business or pleasure should seek permission before entering. Return or onward tickets are required. Vaccinations against smallpox, yellow fever and cholera are required, and malaria prophylaxis is recommended. Customs officers normally examine the luggage of arriving passengers to ensure that no 'obscene' or communist literature is being imported. A service tax of MK20 is levied on international passengers. National airline: Air Malawi. Lilongwe-Kamuzu airport is located 28 km from the city.

MALAYSIA

Persekutuan Tanah Malaysia
FEDERATION OF MALAYSIA

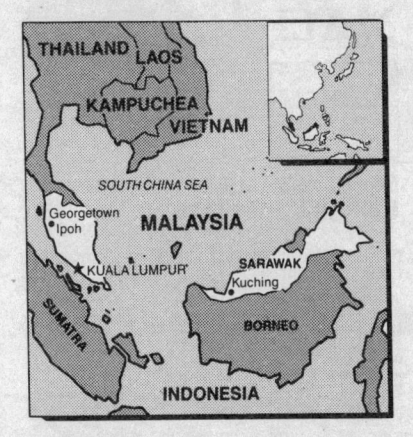

CAPITAL: Kuala Lumpur

AREA AND POPULATION: 329,752 km^2, 13% cultivated land. Population: 16,109,000 (1986 est.). Population density: 48.6/km^2. Population growth (1985): 2.3%. Ethnic composition: Malay 59%; Chinese 32%; Indian 12%; indigenous groups in Sabah and Sarawak, 3%.

CLIMATE AND GEOGRAPHY: The climate is equatorial, with uniform high temperatures throughout the year, high rainfall and humidity. Seasons are marked by the incidence of rainfall brought by monsoons. Average temperature (Kuala Lumpur): 27.2°C. Average annual rainfall: 2,600 mm. Peninsular Malaysia is bordered to the north by Thailand, to the south, across the Straits of Malacca, by Indonesia, to the east by the South China Sea and to the west by the Andaman Sea. The states of Sarawak and Sabah are located along the northern coast of the island of Borneo. Malaysia has a wide swampy coastal plain, with interior jungles and mountains running from north to south.

CURRENCY: Malaysian Ringgit (M$) of 100 sen.

DEFENCE: Military service is voluntary. Total armed forces (1987): 110,000. Army 90,000; Navy 9,000; Air Force 11,000. Para-military forces: People's Volunteer Corps, over 350,000; police field force 18,000; area security units (home guard) 3,100; border scouts (in Sabah and Sarawak) 1,200.

GOVERNMENT: Federal parliamentary democracy with a constitutional monarch. The Head of State, the Yang di-Pertuan Agong, is elected every 5 years by the 9 Malay rulers from amongst themselves. There is a bicameral system of government: a House of Representatives of 177 members and a Senate of up to 68 members, 26 of them nominated by the State Governments and 32 appointed by the Yang di-Pertuan Agong on the advice of the Prime Minister. The Parliament has a life of 5 years. Head of State: Sultan Mahmood Iskandar ibni Al-Marhum Sultan Ismail. Prime Minister: Datuk Seri Dr Mahathir bin Mohamad. Foreign Minister: Datuk Rais Yatim.

LANGUAGE: Malay (official), English, Chinese, Indian languages.

RELIGION: Sunni Moslem 50%; Hindu and Buddhist, 7%; Roman Catholic 3%; Jewish 800; Protestant; Animist.

TOURIST INFORMATION: Passport but no visa required by Australian citizens. Malaria prophylaxis is recommended. There is a departure tax of M$3 (internal flights), M$5 (flights to Brunei and Singapore) or M$15 (international). National airline: Malaysian Airline System (MAS). Kuala Lumpur-Subang airport is located 22 km from the city. Penalties for drug possession are high.

MALDIVES

Divehi Jumhuriya
REPUBLIC OF THE MALDIVES

CAPITAL: Malé

AREA AND POPULATION: 298 km^2, 10% cultivated land. Population:

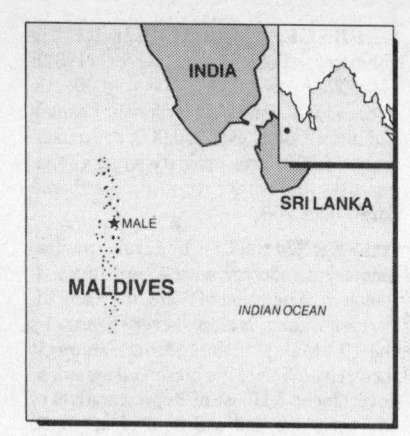

181,453 (1985 est.). Population density: 600/km². Population growth (1975-78): 2.4%. Ethnic composition: Arab/Malay/Sinhalese mixture.

CLIMATE AND GEOGRAPHY: The climate is equatorial, with minor temperature variations. Rainfall is heavy but usually of short duration. The Maldives are situated in the Indian Ocean, 640 km to the south-west of Sri Lanka. The Republic consists of some 1,200 low-lying coral islands, only 220 of which are inhabited.

CURRENCY: Rufiyaa (Rf) of 100 laari.

DEFENCE: No defence force is maintained.

GOVERNMENT: Presidential republic. The President is elected for a 5-year term by universal adult suffrage. The unicameral Parliament (Majlis) has 48 members, 8 nominated by the President, 2 elected from Malé and 2 elected from each of 19 atoll groups. Head of State: President Maumoon Abdul Gayoom. Foreign Minister: Fathulla Jameel. There are no political parties.

LANGUAGE: Divehi (official – similar to Elu or old Sinhalese), English.

NATIONAL ANTHEM: Gavmii mi ekuverikan matii tibegen kuriime salaam (We salute you in this national unity).

RELIGION: Sunni Moslem.

TOURIST INFORMATION: Passport and visa required by Australian citizens. Tourist visas are issued at no cost upon arrival. Malaria prophylaxis is recommended. The importation of alcoholic beverages is prohibited, as are goods of Israeli origin. A departure tax of US$7 is levied on foreigners. National airline: Maldives International Airlines. Hululé airport is located on the island adjacent to Malé.

MALI

République du Mali
REPUBLIC OF MALI

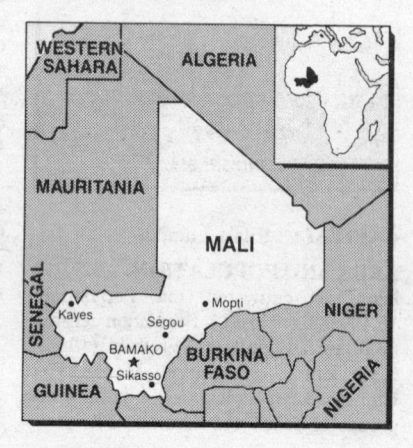

CAPITAL: Bamako

AREA AND POPULATION:
1,240,142 km², 2% cultivated land. Population: 8,303,000 (1986 est.). Population density: 6.6/km². Population growth (1985): 2.7%. Ethnic composition: Mande 50%; Peul 17%; Voltaic 12%; Songhai; Tuareg; Moorish.

CLIMATE AND GEOGRAPHY: The climate is tropical, with drier conditions in the north and east. Average temperature (Bamako): 24°C (January), 27°C (July). Average annual rainfall: 695 mm. Mali is a landlocked country in north-west Africa, bordered to the north by Algeria, to the south by Burkina Faso, Côte D'Ivoire and Guinea, to the west by Mauritania and Senegal and to the east by Niger. A grassy plain in the upper basin of the Senegal and Niger Rivers extends north into the Sahara.

CURRENCY: Franc CFA of 100 centimes.

DEFENCE: Military service is selective for a period of 2 years. Total armed forces (1987): 5,000. Army 4,600; Air Force 400. Para-military forces: militia 3,000; Republican Guard 2,000; Civilian Defence Organisation 1,500; gendarmerie 1,200.

GOVERNMENT: Presidential republic. The unicameral Parliament (National Assembly) of 82 members is elected by universal adult suffrage for a period of 3 years. The sole political party is the Union démocratique du peuple malien, governed by a 19-member Central Executive Bureau responsible to a 137-member National Council which nominates all candidates for election. Head of State: President General Moussa Traoré. Foreign Minister: Modibo Keita.

LANGUAGE: French (official), Arabic, Mande languages.

RELIGION: Sunni Moslem 90%; Animist 9%; Christian 1%.

TOURIST INFORMATION: Passport and visa required by Australian citizens. Return or onward ticket also required. Yellow fever vaccination and malaria prophylaxis are recommended. Foreign currency should be declared upon arrival. There is a departure tax of CFA500 for internal flights; CFA1250 for flights within Africa; and CFA2500 for international flights. National airline: Air Mali. Bamako-Sénou airport is located 15 km from the city.

MALTA

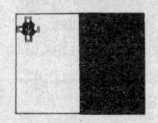

Repubblika Ta'Malta
REPUBLIC OF MALTA

CAPITAL: Valletta

AREA AND POPULATION: 315.6 km², 43% cultivated land. Population: 354,000 (1986 est.). Population density: 1,063.7/km². Population growth (1985): 0.7%. Ethnic composition: mostly Maltese of Italian and Arabic background; British minority.

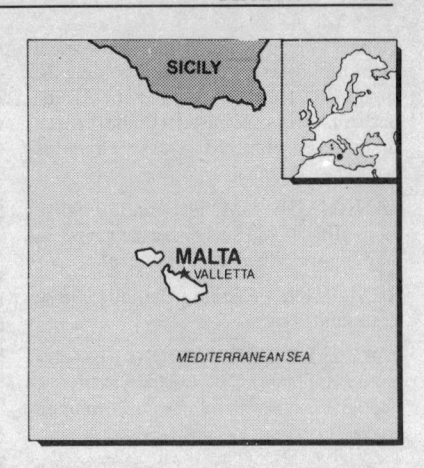

CLIMATE AND GEOGRAPHY: The climate is Mediterranean, with summer drought and mild, wet winters. Relatively high humidity and strong winds prevail throughout the year. Average temperature (Valletta): 13°C (January), 26°C (July). Average annual rainfall varies from 250 mm to 1,000 mm. The Republic is a small archipelago in the Mediterranean Sea, consisting of the islands of Malta, Gozo and Comino, and 3 very small uninhabited islands. It lies 93 km south of Sicily, 352 km north of Tripoli and about 288 km east of Tunis. Malta itself is a rocky plateau, the highest point of which is about 250 m above sea level. It is serrated by a number of valleys which are terraced into small fields enclosed by dry stone walls. The island lacks natural resources except fine harbours. The soil is not fertile and there are neither rivers nor woods.

CURRENCY: Maltese Pound of 100 cents.

DEFENCE: Military service is voluntary. Total armed forces (1986/87): 775. Task Force 500; Armed Forces of Malta 275. Para-military forces: reserves (Id Dejma) 900.

GOVERNMENT: Republic. Parliament consists of a President, a House of Representatives of elected members and a

Cabinet formed by the Prime Minister and such numbers of ministers as may be appointed. Head of State: Mrs Agatha Barbara. Prime Minister: Eddie Fenech Adami. Foreign Minister: Dr Alex Sceberras Trigona.

LANGUAGE: Maltese and English (both official) and such other languages as may be prescribed by Parliament.

RELIGION: Roman Catholic 98%; Protestant; Jewish.

TOURIST INFORMATION: Passport but no visa required by Australian citizens. Foreign currency should be declared upon arrival.

MAURITANIA

Al-Jumhuriya al-Islamiya al-Muritaniya
Republique Islamique de Mauritanie
ISLAMIC REPUBLIC OF MAURITANIA

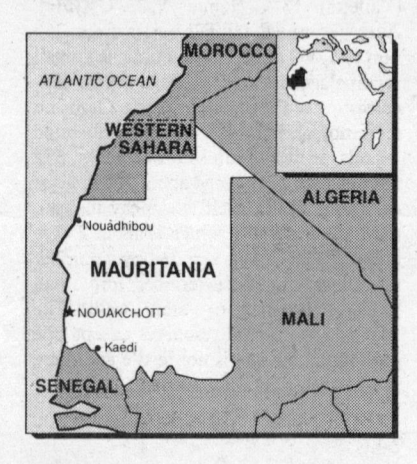

CAPITAL: Nouakchott

AREA AND POPULATION: 1,030,700 km², 1% cultivated land. Population: 1,691,500 (1986 est.). Population density: 1.6/km². Population growth (1985): 2.1%. Ethnic composition: Moorish (Arab/Berber mixture), 80%; Negro.

CLIMATE AND GEOGRAPHY: The climate ranges from arid to tropical. The rainy season lasts from July to September. Average temperature (Nouakchott): 22°C (January), 28°C (July). Average annual rainfall: 158 mm. Mauritania is situated in north-west Africa, bordered to the north by Western Sahara, to the north-east by Algeria, to the south by Senegal, to the east and south-east by Mali and to the west by the Atlantic Ocean. The north is arid and extends into the Sahara. The central region is a plateau rising some 500 m. The northern bank of the Senegal River is the only area with permanent vegetation.

CURRENCY: Ouguiya (UM) of 5 khoums.

DEFENCE: Military service is voluntary. Total armed forces (1987): 8,450. Army 8,000; Navy 300; Air Force 150. Para-military forces: gendarmerie 2,500; National Guard 1,400; border guard 100.

GOVERNMENT: Presidential republic currently ruled by a military council, the Military Committee for National Salvation (CMSN), of 24 members. Head of State, Prime Minister, Minister of Defence and Secretary-General of the CMSN: President Moaouia Ould Sidi Mohamed Taya. Foreign Minister: Major Ahmed Ould Minnih.

LANGUAGE: French and Arabic (both official).

RELIGION: Almost 100% Moslem of the Qadiriyah sect.

TOURIST INFORMATION: Passport and visa required by Australian citizens. Vaccination against yellow fever (compulsory if staying more than 2 weeks) and malaria prophylaxis are recommended. Foreign currency should be declared upon arrival. A departure tax of UM560 is levied on international passengers. National airline: Air Mauritanie. Nouakchott airport is located 4 km from the city.

MAURITIUS

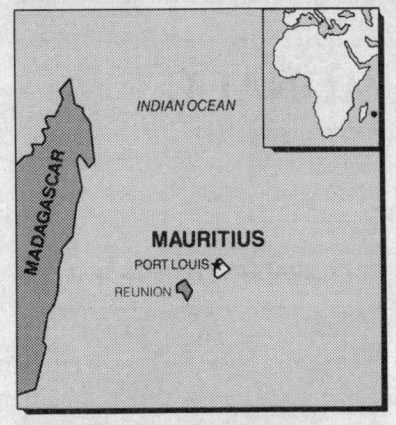

CAPITAL: Port Louis

AREA AND POPULATION: 2,045 km^2, 58% cultivated land. Population: 1,024,900 (1985 est.). Population density: 505.1/km^2. Population growth (1985): 1.4%. Ethnic composition: Indian 68%; Creole 27%; Chinese 3%; European 14,000.

CLIMATE AND GEOGRAPHY: Subtropical climate, with relatively high humidity throughout the year. The heaviest rains occur between January and May. Rainfall varies from 1,016 mm along the western coast to 5,000 mm on the windward side of plateau. The islands are cyclone affected. Average temperature (Port Louis): 23°C (January), 27°C (July). Mauritius is situated in the south-west Indian Ocean about 800 km east of Madagascar and 2,000 km off the African coast. An extensive plateau in the centre of the island rises to a level of 580 m. Bordering it are 3 mountain ranges with fantastically shaped masses of basalt which testify to the island's volcanic origin.

CURRENCY: Mauritius Rupee (Rs) of 100 cents.

DEFENCE: No defence force is maintained. Para-military force: police 4,082.

GOVERNMENT: Parliamentary republic. The Legislative Assembly of 62 members is elected every 5 years by universal adult suffrage. Head of State: Queen Elizabeth II, represented by Governor-General Sir Veerasamy Ringadoo. Prime Minister: Aneerood Jugnauth. Foreign Minister: Madun Dulloo.

LANGUAGE: English (official), French, Creole.

NATIONAL ANTHEM: Glory to thee, motherland, O motherland of mine.

RELIGION: Hindu 50%; Roman Catholic 26%; Moslem 16%; Protestant 3%; Buddhist 0.6%.

TOURIST INFORMATION: Passport but no visa required by Australian citizens. Return or onward tickets are required. Malaria prophylaxis is recommended. Drinking water should be boiled and filtered. Good doctors and hospitals are available. A tax of Rs100 is levied on all passengers embarking in Mauritius. National airline: Air Mauritius. Plaisance airport is located 50 km from Port Louis.

MEXICO

Estados Unidos Mexicanos
UNITED MEXICAN STATES

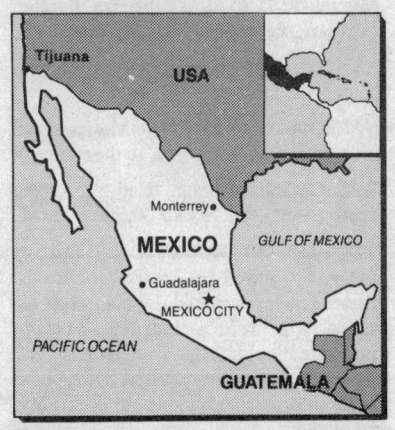

CAPITAL: Mexico City

AREA AND POPULATION:
1,958,201 km², 12% cultivated land. Population: 81,709,000 (1986 est.). Population density: 40.9/km². Population growth (1987): 2.3%. Ethnic composition: Mestizo 55%; European (mostly of Spanish descent) 10-15%; Indian 29%; foreigners 2%.

CLIMATE AND GEOGRAPHY: The climate is tropical in the southern lowlands, temperate to cool in the central plateau and highlands, and dry in northern areas. Summer, from June to October, is the wet season. Average temperature (Mexico City): 13°C (January), 16°C (July). Average annual rainfall: 747 mm. Mexico is bordered to the north by the USA and to the south by Guatemala and Belize. The terrain varies widely but is mainly a plateau, flanked by eastern and western mountain ranges which lie inland from the coasts and roughly parallel to them.

CURRENCY: Peso of 100 centavos.

DEFENCE: Military service is voluntary. There is a part-time conscript militia. Total armed forces (1987): 138,950. Army 105,000; Navy 27,450; Air Force 6,500.

GOVERNMENT: Presidential republic. The bicameral Parliament (Congreso de la Union) consists of a Chamber of Senators (64 members) and a Chamber of Deputies (400 members). All citizens over the age of 18 (or 16 if married) have the vote. Head of State: President Miguel de la Madrid Hurtado; Foreign Minister: Bernado Sepúlveda Amor.

LANGUAGE: Spanish (official), Indian languages.

NATIONAL ANTHEM: Mexicanos, al grito de guerra (Mexicans, to the war cry).

RELIGION: Roman Catholic 98%; Protestant 1.8%; Jewish 37,500.

TOURIST INFORMATION: Passport and visa required by Australian citizens. Passengers are required to hold tickets for onward or return journey. Foreign currency should be declared upon arrival. No vaccinations are required but typhoid vaccination is advisable and malaria prophylaxis is also recommended. Visitors to Mexico City will probably experience some breathlessness and general lassitude because of the altitude. Respiratory problems are also likely as a result of the smog and heavily polluted air. There is a departure tax of US$10. National airlines: Mexicana, Aeromexico. Mexico City-Benito Juarez airport is located 13 km from the city.

MONACO

Principauté de Monaco
PRINCIPALITY OF MONACO

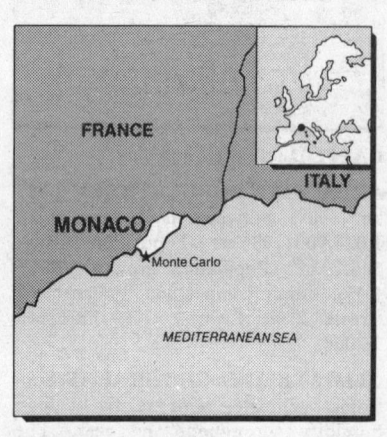

CAPITAL: Monaco

AREA AND POPULATION: 1.9 km². Population: 28,000 (1986 est.). Population density: 14,736.8/km². Population growth (1985): −.3%. Ethnic composition: French 47%; Monegasque 16%; Italian 16%.

CLIMATE AND GEOGRAPHY: Mediterranean climate with mild winters and warm to hot summers. Monaco is situated in southern France close to the Franco-Italian border at Menton.

CURRENCY: French Franc (FF) of 100 centimes. Monaco has its own coins.

DEFENCE: No defence force is maintained.

GOVERNMENT: Hereditary monarchy. The National Council of 18 members is elected every 5 years and the Communal Council of 15 members every four years. Head of State: Prince Rainier III. Minister of State: Jean Ausseil.

LANGUAGE: French (official), Monegasque.

RELIGION: Roman Catholic 90%; Anglican; Jewish.

TOURIST INFORMATION: Passport and visa required by Australian citizens.

MONGOLIA

Bügd Nayramdakh Mongol Ard Uls
MONGOLIAN PEOPLE'S REPUBLIC

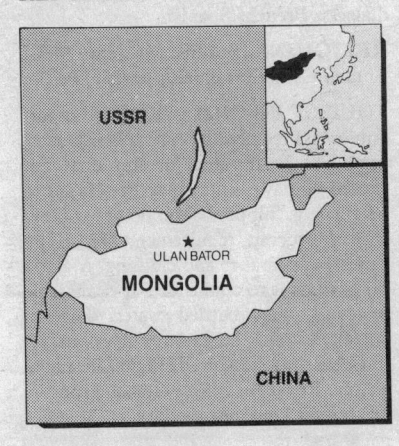

CAPITAL: Ulan Bator

AREA AND POPULATION: 1,565,000 km², 1% cultivated land. Population: 1,942,000 (1986 est.). Population density: 1.2/km². Population growth (1985): 2.5%. Ethnic composition: Mongolian 83%; Turkic Kazakh 5.2%; Russian; Chinese.

CLIMATE AND GEOGRAPHY: Extreme continental climate with long cold winters and short hot summers. The country is earthquake-affected. Average annual rainfall: 208 mm. Average temperature (Ulan Bator): −26°C (January), 16°C (July). Mongolia is bordered by the USSR to the north and by China to the south. Most of the country lies between 1,000 m and 2,000 m above sea level, with mountain ranges in the west and north-west. To the south and south-east are the arid and infertile wastelands of the Gobi Desert, where sparse grasslands and open sands have defied the cultivation of crops. To the east the country is characterised by ravines extending northward to the Soviet border.

CURRENCY: Tugrik of 100 möngö.

DEFENCE: Military service is compulsory for 3 years. Total armed forces (1986/87): 25,500. Army 22,000; Air Force 3,500 (100 pilots). Para-military forces: Ministry of Public Security forces 15,000; militia (police); internal security troops; frontier guards.

GOVERNMENT: Communist people's republic. The unicameral Parliament (Great People's Khural) of 370 members is elected by universal adult suffrage for a 5-year period. It elects from its ranks 9 members of the Presidium which conducts current state affairs. Real power lies in the hands of the Mongolian People's Revolutionary Party. Head of State: Chairman Zhambyn Batmunkh. Head of Government: Dumaagiyn Sodnom. Foreign Minister: Mangalyn Dugersuren.

LANGUAGE: Mongolian.

RELIGION: Tibetan Buddhist Lamaism.

TOURIST INFORMATION: Passport and visa required by Australian citizens. Visa applications should be made well in advance. Taking photos without permission is generally considered impolite. National airline: Air Mongol. Ulan Bator-Buyant Uhaa airport is located 15 km from the city.

MOROCCO

Al-Mamlaka al-Maghrebia
KINGDOM OF MOROCCO

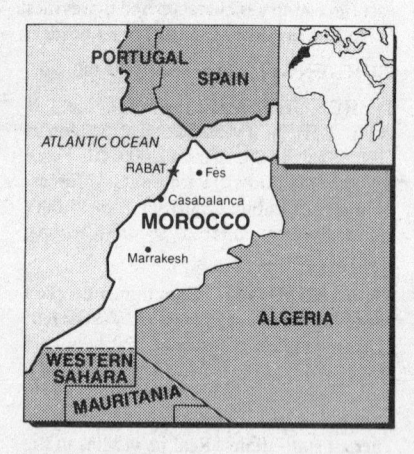

CAPITAL: Rabat

AREA AND POPULATION: 458,730 km², 18% cultivated land. Population: 23,667,000 (1986 est.). Population density: 48.7/km². Population growth (1985): 3.2%. Ethnic composition: Berber 40%; Arab 20%; Arab-Berber; Negro; foreigners (French, Tunisian, Spanish), over 100,000.

CLIMATE AND GEOGRAPHY: The climate ranges from semi-arid in the south to warm temperate Mediterranean conditions in the north. Cooler temperatures occur in the mountains. Average temperature (Rabat): 12.9°C (January), 22.2°C (July). Average annual rainfall (Rabat): 564 mm. Morocco is bordered to the east by Algeria and to the south by Western Sahara. The Atlas Mountains rise from the Atlantic lowland in the north and extend to the Sahara in the south. The scenery changes dramatically, with the northern slopes covered by forests and shrubs while the southern slopes are bare and sunbleached.

CURRENCY: Dirham (DH) of 100 centimes.

DEFENCE: Military service is compulsory for a period of 18 months. Total armed forces (1987): 202,000. Army 150,000; Navy 4,000; Air Force 13,000. Para-military forces: 35,000 (including the Gendarmerie Royale, Force Auxiliaire and Mobile Intervention Corps).

GOVERNMENT: Constitutional monarchy. The unicameral legislature of 264 deputies is elected for a 4-year term. Two-thirds of the members are elected by universal adult suffrage, while the remaining one-third is indirectly elected through an electoral college composed of representatives from town councils, regional assemblies, the chamber of commerce, industry and agriculture, and the trade unions. Head of State: King Hassan II. Prime Minister: Mohamed Karim Lamrani. Foreign Minister: Abdellatif Filali.

LANGUAGE: Arabic (official), Berber dialects, French, Spanish.

RELIGION: Sunni Moslem 98%; Roman Catholic 110,000; Jewish 20,000.

TOURIST INFORMATION: Passport but no visa required by Australian citizens, provided the duration of stay does not exceed 90 days. Entry may be refused to people (e.g. 'hippies') who do not comply with Moroccan requirements regarding general appearance and clothing. Malaria prophylaxis is recommended. It is advisable to drink only bottled water. Foreign currencies must be declared upon arrival if the amount exceeds DH15,000. National airline: Royal Air Maroc. Rabat airport is located 10 km from the city.

MOZAMBIQUE

República Popular de Moçambique
PEOPLE'S REPUBLIC OF MOZAMBIQUE

CAPITAL: Maputo

AREA AND POPULATION: 799,380 km², 4% cultivated land. Population:

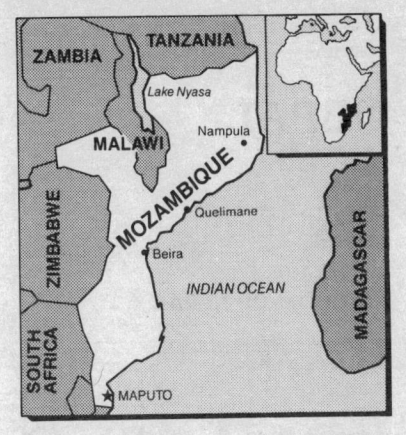

14,022,000 (1986 est.). Population density: 17.8/km². Population growth (1985): 2.7%. Ethnic composition: Bantu, over 90%; foreign minority. About 120,000 Mozambique nationals work abroad.

CLIMATE AND GEOGRAPHY: Except in the high plateau zone and in the mountains, the climate varies from tropical to sub-tropical. The wet season lasts from November to April but rainfall is irregular and the southern districts especially are subject to droughts and floods. The average temperature in Maputo is 18°C in the dry season and 26°C in the wet season. Mozambique is bordered to the north by Tanzania, to the south by Swaziland and the RSA, to the east by the Indian Ocean and to the west by Malawi, Zambia and Zimbabwe. From the broad coastal plain/lowlands area, the land rises to a high plateau zone 540–900 m high. There is also a mountainous region on the western margin. The country has a large number of rivers, including the Zambezi and the Limpopo.

CURRENCY: Metical (MT) of 100 centavos.

DEFENCE: Military service is by selective conscription for a period of 2 years (men and women). Total armed forces (1987): 29,800; Army 28,000; Navy 800; Air Force 1,000. Para-military forces: border guard 9,500; provincial people's militias; local militias (village self-defence forces). Opposition: National Resistance Movement of Mozambique, 18,000 reported, perhaps 10,000 trained.

GOVERNMENT: Socialist people's republic. The President is also the President of FRELIMO, the only legal political party. He has executive power and governs with an appointed Council of Ministers. There is a National People's Assembly elected by members of Provincial People's Assemblies. The party leadership comprises a Central Committee of 130 members and a Political Bureau of 12 members. Head of State: President Joaquim Alberto Chissano.

LANGUAGE: Portuguese (official), Bantu languages.

RELIGION: Animist 60%; Christian 18%; Moslem 16%.

TOURIST INFORMATION: Passport and visa required by Australian citizens. Although available, in theory, from Mozambican diplomatic missions, visas must usually be obtained by a contact in Maputo. The importation of 'dangerous' alcoholic beverages and drugs is forbidden. Malaria prophylaxis is recommended. Foreign currency must be declared upon arrival. There is an airport tax of MT1000 for international flights and MT500 for domestic. National airline: Linhas Aereas de Moçambique. Maputo-Mavalane airport is located 8 km from the city.

NAURU

Naoero
REPUBLIC OF NAURU

CAPITAL: Yaren

AREA AND POPULATION: 21.3 km². Population: 8,000 (1986 est.). Population density: 429.3/km². Population growth (1985): 1.9%. Ethnic composition: Nauruans (mixed—Polynesian, Micronesian, Melanesian) 57%; foreign workers 26%; Chinese/Vietnamese 8%; European 8%.

CLIMATE AND GEOGRAPHY: The temperature ranges from 23°C at night to 33°C during the day. The average humidity is about 80%. Average annual rainfall: 1,862 mm. The humidity and temperature vary little during the year, except during the wet season (November to February), when storms and winds bring a slight fall in temperature. Situated in western Pacific Ocean just south of the Equator, the island is oval in shape and is surrounded by a coral reef. Rich tropical vegetation covers much of the coastal belt and the area that has not been mined. There has been rejuvenation of secondary growth in the older mined-out areas. Pandanus and coconut palms are found on the coast. The only other arable land surrounds the Bauda Lagoon which is located in a depression in the central plateau.

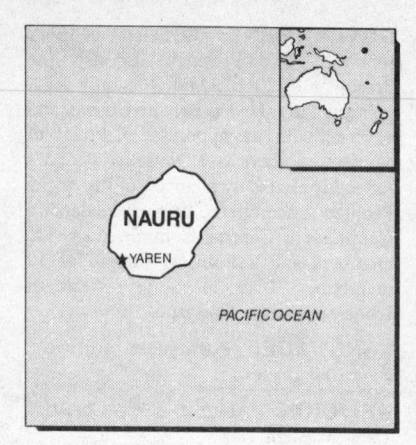

CURRENCY: Australian dollar of 100 cents.

DEFENCE: No defence force is maintained.

GOVERNMENT: Parliamentary republic. The Legislative Council has 18 members elected on a 3-yearly basis by universal adult suffrage. Head of State and Minister for Foreign Affairs: Hammer DeRoburt. There are no political parties.

LANGUAGE: English, Nauruan.

RELIGION: Protestant 70%; Roman Catholic 30%.

TOURIST INFORMATION: Passport and visa required by Australian citizens. It is necessary to produce an onward or return ticket in order to obtain a visa. There is an airport tax of $10. National airline: Air Nauru.

NEPAL

Sri Nepala Sarkar
KINGDOM OF NEPAL

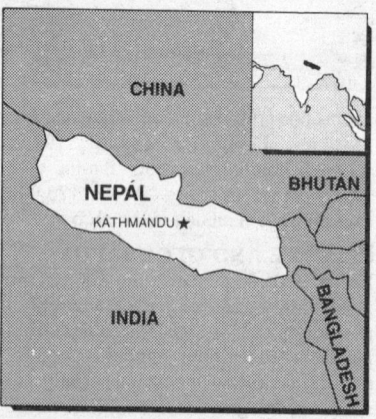

CAPITAL: Kathmandu

AREA AND POPULATION: 147,181 km^2, 17% cultivated land. Population: 17,422,000 (1986 est.). Population density: 114.3/km^2. Population growth (1985): 2.5%. Ethnic composition: Indo-Mongolian (Pahari, Newar and Tharu); Tibetan (Tamang, Rai, Limbu and Magar); Indian; Gurkha; Sherpa.

CLIMATE AND GEOGRAPHY: Moderate climate with high rainfall, especially from May to September, and a dry season from November to January. Average temperature (Kathmandu): 10°C (January), 24.4°C (July). Nepal is bordered to the north by China and to the south by India. The country is predominantly mountainous, containing the world's highest mountains, 6 of which rise to over 8,000 m. At the same time, there are also tropical jungles which are no more than 180 m above sea level.

CURRENCY: Nepalese Rupee (Rs) of 100 paisa.

DEFENCE: Military service is voluntary. Total armed forces (1987): 30,000. Army 30,000. Para-military force: police force 25,000.

GOVERNMENT: Constitutional monarchy. The National Legislature consists of 140 members, 112 elected and 28 appointed by the King. The Cabinet is also appointed by the King who has the power of veto over decisions taken by the Government. Political parties are officially banned. Head of State: Maharajadhiraja Birendra Bir Bikram Shah Dev. Prime Minister: Marich Man Singh Shrestha. Foreign Minister: Shilendra Kumar Upadhayay.

LANGUAGE: Nepali (official), Newari, Maithili, Tibetan dialects.

NATIONAL ANTHEM: May glory crown our illustrious Sovereign.

RELIGION: Mahayana Buddhist; Hindu; Moslem.

TOURIST INFORMATION: Passport and visa required by Australian citizens. A 7-day tourist visa may be obtained upon arrival. There is a departure tax of Rs200. Malaria prophylaxis is recommended. Special permits are necessary for trekking and applications must be made at the Central Immigration Office in Kathmandu. National airline: Royal Nepal Airlines. Kathmandu-Tribhuvan airport is located 6 km from the city.

THE NETHERLANDS

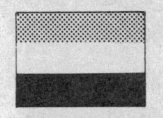

Koninkrijk der Nederlanden
KINGDOM OF THE NETHERLANDS

CAPITAL: Amsterdam

AREA AND POPULATION: 41,548 km², 70% cultivated land. Population: 14,536,000 (1986 est.). Population density: 429.3/km². Population growth (1985): 4%. Ethnic composition: Dutch; Northern European; Surinamese; Netherlands Antillean; Indonesian; Turkish; Moroccan; German; Belgian; Spanish.

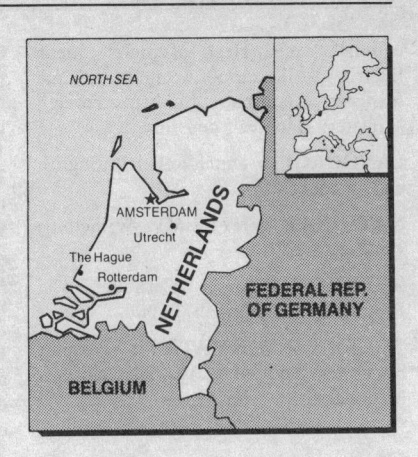

CLIMATE AND GEOGRAPHY: The climate is cool temperate maritime. Wet, cold and windy weather may be expected at almost any time of the year. The average winter temperature varies between 1°C and 3°C. Summer can be warm and sunny. Average annual rainfall: 800 mm. The country is bordered to the south by Belgium and to the west by the Federal Republic of Germany. With the exception of the south-east corner, most of the country is flat. About one-third of the land is below sea level. The whole is well-watered and crossed by numerous rivers, canals and lakes. Two major European rivers, the Rhine and the Maas, flow into the sea near Rotterdam.

CURRENCY: Guilder (Fl) of 100 cents.

DEFENCE: Military service is partly compulsory and partly voluntary. Total armed forces (1987): 110,116 (including Royal Military Constabulary). Army 71,400; Navy 16,850; Air Force 17,957. Para-military forces: Royal Military Constabulary 3,909; Civil Defence Corps 22,000 on mobilisation under Army command.

GOVERNMENT: Constitutional monarchy with a Parliament elected by universal suffrage. General elections, using a system of proportional representation, are held every 4 years. There are 3 systems of government: at local, provincial and national levels. Head of State: Queen Beatrix Wilhelmina Armgard. Prime Minister: Rudolphus Lubbers. Foreign Minister: Hans van den Broek.

LANGUAGE: Dutch (official), English widely spoken.

NATIONAL ANTHEM: Wilhelmus van Nassoue.

RELIGION: Roman Catholic 36%; Protestant 31%; Jewish 30,000.

TOURIST INFORMATION: Passport but no visa required by Australian citizens. National airline: KLM.

NEW ZEALAND

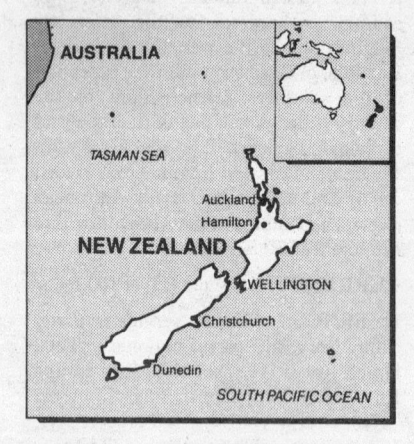

CAPITAL: Wellington

AREA AND POPULATION: 268,704 km², 13% cultivated land. Population: 3,305,000 (1986 est.). Population density: 12.4/km². Population growth (1982): 8%. Ethnic composition: European of English, Scottish and Irish background, 85.4%; Maori 8.6%; Chinese and Indian minorities.

CLIMATE AND GEOGRAPHY: Temperate climate with comfortable extremes of temperature and rainfall. Average temperatures decrease southwards from 15°C in the far north to 9°C in the south. Rainfall generally is high and for most of the country is spread evenly throughout the year. A large part of the country has at least 2,000 hours of bright sunlight annually. Because of the topography, there are marked regional climatic differences. Situated in the south-west Pacific Ocean, New Zealand lies along a south-westerly and north-easterly axis, parallel to the direction of the mountain chains. Less than one-quarter of the land surface area is below 200 m. The Southern Alps dominate the length of the South Island, reaching their greatest height in Mt Cook (3,764 m). Much of the North Island is mountainous, particularly in the southern, central and eastern areas. The tallest peaks (Mts Egmont, Ruapehu, Ngauruhoe and Tongariro) are volcanic. There are many natural lakes, of which the largest is Lake Taupo in the centre of the North Island. The South Island has a series of glacial lakes. Minor islands: Kermadec Islands, Three Kings Islands, Auckland Islands, Campbell Island, Antipodes Islands, Bounty Islands, Snares Islands, Solander Island. Territories overseas: Tokelau, Ross Dependency. Self-governing territories overseas: Cook Islands, Niue.

CURRENCY: New Zealand Dollar (NZ$) of 100 cents.

DEFENCE: Military service is voluntary, supplemented by Territorial Army service: 7 weeks basic training, 20 days per year. Total armed forces (1986-87): 12,750. Army 5,814; Navy 2,760; Air Force 4,176.

GOVERNMENT: Constitutional monarchy with a system of cabinet goverment based on the British model. There is no single, written constitution, it being contained instead in statute, convention and decisions of the superior courts. New Zealand has only 1 legislative chamber, the House of Representatives, elected by universal adult suffrage and secret ballot. All people over the age of 18 are eligible to vote and must register, although voting is not compulsory. Head of State: Queen Elizabeth II, represented by Governor-General Sir Paul Reeves. Prime Minister and Foreign Minister: David Lange.

LANGUAGE: English (official), Maori.

NATIONAL ANTHEMS: God Save the Queen, and God Defend New Zealand.

RELIGION: Protestant 70%; Roman Catholic 495,300; Maori religions (35,781 Ratana and 6,117 Ringatu); Jewish 3,360.

TOURIST INFORMATION: Neither passport nor visa required by Australian citizens when entering New Zealand. A passport is required, however, to re-enter Australia from New Zealand. Australian visitors may drive in New Zealand on a current Australian licence. National airline: Air New Zealand. Auckland airport is located 22 km from the city.

NICARAGUA

República de Nicaragua
REPUBLIC OF NICARAGUA

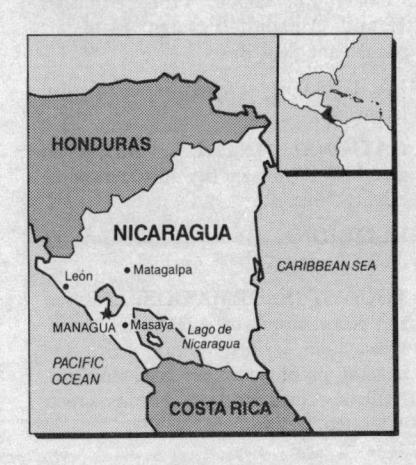

CAPITAL: Managua

AREA AND POPULATION: 139,000 km², 7% cultivated land. Population: 3,342,000 (1986 est.). Population density: 26.1/km². Population growth (1985): 3.5%. Ethnic compositon: Mestizo 60-70%; European 17%; Negro 10-15%; Indian 4-6%; Mulatto; Zambo.

CLIMATE AND GEOGRAPHY: The climate is tropical, with a wet season from May to January. Average temperature (Managua): 26°C (January), 30°C (July). Average annual rainfall: 1,140 mm. Nicaragua is bordered to the north by Honduras, to the south by Costa Rica, to the east by the Caribbean Sea and to the west by the Pacific Ocean. The Cordillera Mountains run north-west to south-east through the middle of the country. In the south-west is Lake Nicaragua, 148 km long and 55 km at its widest.

CURRENCY: Córdoba (C$) of 100 centavos.

DEFENCE: Military service is by conscription (introduced in 1983) for 2 years, for men between 17 and 22 years of age. Total armed forces (1987): 75,000. Army 72,000; Navy 600; Air Force 2,000. Para-military forces: civilian militia 50,000(?); border guard 5,000; Ministry of Interior troops 2,000. Opposition: United Nicaraguan Opposition (UNO) 24,000 reported, 12,000-15,000 active; Union Democratica Nicaraguense (UDN)/Fuerzas Revolucionarias Nicaraguenses (FARN) 3,500(?); Democratic Revolutionary Alliance (ARDE) 1,000(?) active; Frente Revolucionario Sandino (FRS).

GOVERNMENT: Republic. The National Assembly has 96 members but the real power is in the hands of the 9-man Junta of the Government of National Reconstruction. Head of State: Daniel Ortega Saavedra. Foreign Minister: Father Miguel d'Escoto Brockmann.

LANGUAGE: Spanish (official), English, Indian Chibcha.

NATIONAL ANTHEM: Salve a ti Nicaragua (Hail to you Nicaragua).

RELIGION: Roman Catholic 95%; Protestant 3%; Jewish 200.

TOURIST INFORMATION: Passport and visa required by Australian citizens. Onward or return tickets are required. All visitors staying in Nicaragua longer than 24 hours must exchange US$60 into C$.

There is a departure tax of US$10. Visitors must carry their passports with them at all times, especially in Managua, where immigration police on the street frequently ask to see them. Border officials do not like army-type clothing on travellers and will confiscate green or khaki rucksacks, boots, parkas and canteens. The luggage inspection on entering and leaving the country is very thorough and customs formalities can take up to 3 hours. No photographs should be taken of military personnel or installations. Malaria prophylaxis is recommended. Airlines serving: Aeroflot, Aeronica, Copa, Cubana, Iberia, Sahsa, Taca International Panam, Lanica. Managua-Augusto Cesar Sandino airport is located 11 km from the city.

NIGER

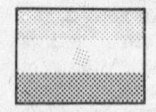

République du Niger
REPUBLIC OF NIGER

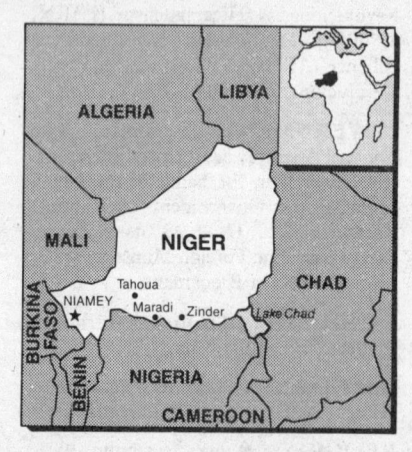

CAPITAL: Niamey

AREA AND POPULATION:
1,186,408 km², 3% cultivated land. Population: 6,715,000 (1986 est.). Population density: 5.4/km². Population growth (1985) 2.8%. Ethnic composition: Hausa 56%; Songhai and Djerma, 22%; Fulani 8%; Beriberi-Manga 9%; Tuareg 8%.

CLIMATE AND GEOGRAPHY: The country lacks water with the exception of the south-western districts, which are well-watered by the Niger River and its tributaries, and the southern zone where there are wells. Average temperature (Niamey): 35°C. Average annual rainfall: 560 mm in the south and 180 mm in the Sahara zone. Niger is bordered to the north by Algeria and Libya, to the south by Nigeria and Benin, to the east by Chad and to the west by Mali and Burkina Faso.

CURRENCY: Franc CFA of 100 centimes.

DEFENCE: Military service is by selective conscription for a period of 2 years. Total armed forces (1987): 2,270. Army 2,150; Air Force 120. Para-military forces: Republican Guard 1,500(?); gendarmerie 850(?); Presidential Guard 200(?); nomad patrol groups.

GOVERNMENT: Presidential republic. The country is administered by a Supreme Military Council of 12 officers led by the President, who appoints a Council of Ministers. Acting Head of State: Colonel Ali Saibou. Prime Minister: Hamid Algabid. Foreign Minister: Mahamané Sani Bako.

LANGUAGE: French (official), tribal languages.

NATIONAL ANTHEM: Auprès du grand Niger puissant (By the waters of the mighty Niger).

RELIGION: Moslem 97%; Christian 0.5%; Animist.

TOURIST INFORMATION: Passport and visa required by Australian citizens. Vaccination against yellow fever and malaria prophylaxis are recommended. National airline: Air Niger. Niamey airport is located 12 km from the city.

NIGERIA

FEDERAL REPUBLIC OF NIGERIA

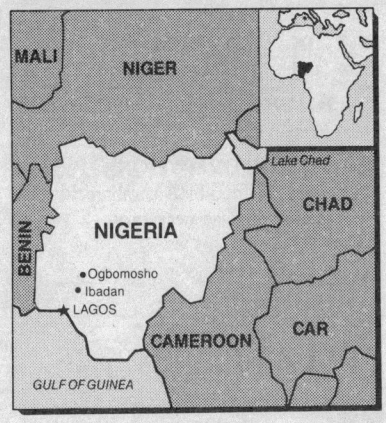

CAPITAL: Lagos

AREA AND POPULATION: 923,773 km^2, 34% cultivated land. Population: 105,448,000 (1986 est.). Population density: 106.2/km^2. Population growth (1985): 2.8%. Ethnic composition: Yoruba 20%; Ibo 17%; Hausa; Fulani; Tuareg; European minority.

CLIMATE AND GEOGRAPHY: Tropical climate, hot and extremely humid. There are 2 seasons: the rainy and the dry. The Lagos area usually receives its rains between May and July or August. There follows a period of relatively pleasant weather, broken in October by occasional thunderstorms, until the advent of the dry season from November to April. Average temperature (Lagos): 27.2°C (January), 25.6°C (July). Average annual rainfall (Lagos): 1,836 mm. Nigeria is bounded to the north by Niger, to the south by the Gulf of Guinea, to the east by Chad and Cameroon and to the west by Benin. There are 4 main geographic zones: the flat, humid coastal plain; gently rolling hills covered by tropical rain forest; open savanna with a few low ranges; and a vast undulating plateau on the edge of the Sahara, rising in the east-central region to 2,040 m.

CURRENCY: Naira (N) of 100 kobo.

DEFENCE: Military service is voluntary. Total armed forces (1987): 94,000. Army 80,000; Navy 5,000; Air Force 9,000. Para-military forces: port security police 12,000; Security and Civil Defence Corp; police; coastguard.

GOVERNMENT: Presidential republic. After a bloodless military coup on 27 August 1985, Major-General Ibrahim Babangida was appointed President and Commander of the Armed Forces. A 28-member Armed Forces Ruling Council was formed. Foreign Minister: Dr Bolaji Akinyemi.

LANGUAGE: English (official), Hausa, Igbo, Yoruba.

RELIGION: Moslem 48%; Christian 34%; Animist.

TOURIST INFORMATION: Passport and visa required by Australian citizens. Vaccination against yellow fever is required and malaria prophylaxis is recommended. Foreign currency should be declared upon arrival. National airline: Nigeria Airways. Lagos-Murtala Mohammed airport is located 22 km from the city.

NORWAY

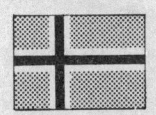

Kongeriket Norge
KINGDOM OF NORWAY

CAPITAL: Oslo

AREA AND POPULATION: 323,895 km^2, 3% cultivated land. Population: 4,165,000 (1986 est.). Population density: 12.8/km^2. Population growth (1985): 0.2%. Ethnic composition: Germanic (Nordic, Alpine, Baltic); Sameh (Lapps) and Finnish (Kwänen) minorities.

CLIMATE AND GEOGRAPHY: The climate is determined to a great extent by the Gulf Stream which carries warm water from the tropics to Norwegian coastal waters, keeping most harbours free from ice during winter. Mean temperatures in coastal districts are considerably higher than would be expected at such high latitudes. The greatest differences between summer and winter temperatures are found in the inland valleys in the south-east. Average temperature (Oslo): −3.9°C (January), 17.3°C (July). Average annual rainfall (Oslo): 683 mm. Norway is bordered to the east by Sweden, Finland and the USSR. It is a rugged country, four-fifths of it being more than 150 m above sea level (average 500 m). Despite this, Norway is not an alpine country but consists instead of unwooded highland plateaux, dotted by many lakes. The land slopes gradually towards the east and drops steeply to the sea in the west.

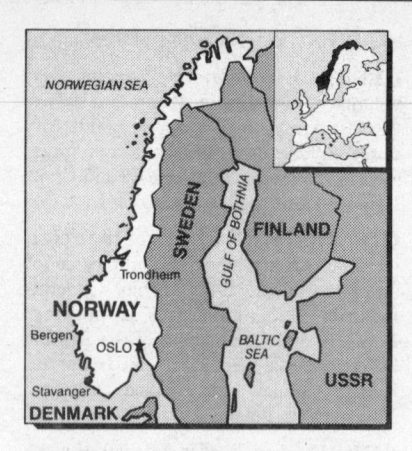

CURRENCY: Norwegian Krone (NKr) of 100 ore.

DEFENCE: Military service is universal and compulsory for 12 months (Army) or 15 months (Navy and Air Force). Total armed forces (1987): 37,000. Army 20,000; Navy 7,600; Air Force 9,400. Para-military forces: home guard 79,700; civil defence force; coastguard.

GOVERNMENT: Constitutional monarchy. The bicameral Parliament (Storting) consists of 155 members elected for 4 years by universal adult suffrage. Bills on legislation, constitutional budgetary control and government appointments are dealt with by the Odelsting (116 members). The 39 other members form the Lagting, whose consent is required to the decisions of the Odelsting. Thus, Norway has, in effect, a modified single-house system.

Head of State: King Olav V. Prime Minister: Gro Harlem Brundtland. Foreign Minister: position vacant.

LANGUAGE: Bokmål (derived from Danish and preferred by the majority of the population) and Nynorsk (an artificial language amalgamated from various Norwegian dialects).

NATIONAL ANTHEM: Ja, vi elsker dette landet (Yes, we love this country).

RELIGION: Evangelical Lutheran 94%; Roman Catholic 11,000; Jewish 900.

TOURIST INFORMATION: Passport but no visa required by Australian citizens. No vaccinations are necessary.

OMAN

SULTANATE OF OMAN

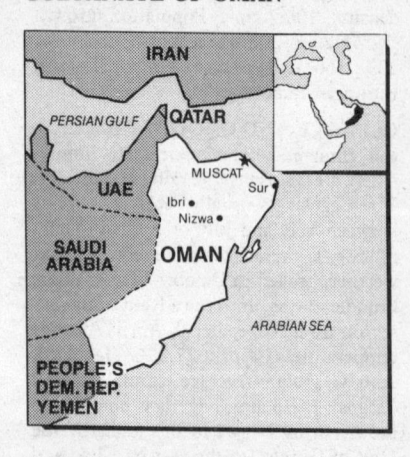

CAPITAL: Muscat

AREA AND POPULATION: 212,457 km², 0.2% cultivated land. Population: 1,271,000 (1986 est.). Population density: 3.7/km². Population growth (1970-82): 4.3%. Ethnic composition: Arab 88%; Baluchi 4%; Indian and Pakistani 2-3%; Persian 3%; Negro 2%.

CLIMATE AND GEOGRAPHY: A desert climate prevails, with an exceptionally hot and humid period from April to October. Light monsoon rains fall in the south from June to September. Average temperature (Muscat): 22.2°C (January), 33.3°C (July). Average annual rainfall: 99.1 mm. The largest of the Gulf States, Oman is situated at the eastern corner of Arabia and has some 1,600 km of coastline, stretching from the Musandam Peninsula to Ras Darbat Ali, where the province of Dhofar borders the People's Democratic Republic of Yemen.

CURRENCY: Rial Omani (RO) of 1,000 baiza.

DEFENCE: Military service is voluntary. Total armed forces (1987): 21,900. Army 16,500; Navy 2,400; Air Force 3,000. Para-military forces: tribal home guard (Firqat) 5,000; police coastguard; Musandam security force.

GOVERNMENT: Absolute monarchy with no formal constitution. The Sultan legislates by decree and appoints a Cabinet to assist him. Head of State, Prime Minister and Foreign Minister: Sultan Qaboos bin Sa'id.

LANGUAGE: Arabic (official), Persian, Urdu.

NATIONAL ANTHEM: Ya rabbana fahfadh lana Sultanana Sa'id (God save our Sultan Sa'id).

RELIGION: Ibadhi Moslem 70%; Sunni Moslem 25%; Shiite Moslem.

TOURIST INFORMATION: Passport and visa required by Australian citizens entering Oman on business. A 'No Objection Certificate' must be submitted before a visa is granted. No tourist visas will be issued. A visa will be denied if there is any evidence in the passport that the holder has visited or intends to visit Israel. Alcoholic beverages cannot be taken into Oman. Malaria prophylaxis is recommended. National airline: Gulf Air. Muscat-Seeb airport is located 40 km from the city.

PAKISTAN

Islami Jamhuriya-e-Pakistan
ISLAMIC REPUBLIC OF PAKISTAN

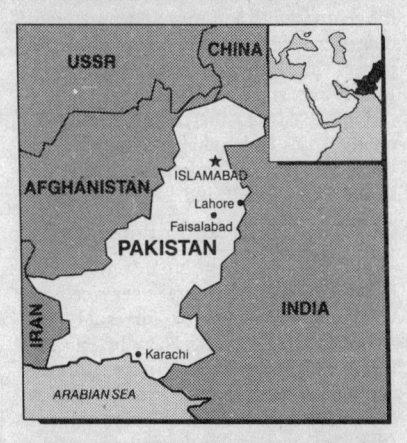

CAPITAL: Islamabad

AREA AND POPULATION: 803,943 km², 26% cultivated land. Population: 101,855,000 (1986). Population density: 129/km². Population growth (1985): 2.6%. Ethnic composition: Punjabi 66%; Sindhi 13%; Urdu 8%; Baluchi 3%; Afghan refugees, about 2.6 million.

CLIMATE AND GEOGRAPHY:
Other than in the mountain areas, summers are very hot. Karachi is warm all year round, the most pleasant months being December, January and February. In Quetta, the winters are cold, but are pleasantly cool in Islamabad and Lahore. From April to September a region of intense low pressure develops to the north of the Indian sub-continent and the resultant monsoon winds bring heavy rain to much of Pakistan. Average temperature (Islamabad): 10°C (January), 32.3°C (July). Average annual rainfall (Islamabad): 900 mm. Pakistan is bounded to the east by India, to the north and north-west by Afghanistan, to the west by Iran and to the south by the Arabian Sea. China has a common border with the Pakistan-controlled part of Kashmir known as Azad

Kashmir. This territory is disputed by India. The Soviet Union is separated from Pakistan by a strip of Afghan territory which, at its narrowest, is only a few kilometres wide. Both the boundary with China and the points near the Soviet Union are in mountainous terrain and until recently were virtually impassable. The country is largely desert or semi-desert in the centre, south and west. The mountain ranges and their foothills to the north are part of the Himalayan chain. But for the Indus River and its tributaries which flow through Pakistan, the country would be totally arid. The Indus system provides water for the massive irrigation complex of the Punjab and Sind.

CURRENCY: Pakistan Rupee (Rs) of 100 paisas.

DEFENCE: Military service is voluntary. Total armed forces (1987): 481,850. Army 450,000; Navy 14,250; Air Force 17,600. Para-military forces: National Guard 75,000; Frontier Corps 65,000; Pakistan Rangers 15,000; Northern Light Infantry 7,000; coastguard 2,000.

GOVERNMENT: The 1973 constitution was restored on 10 March 1985, and a number of amendment bills to it have been approved by the National Assembly, giving President Zia almost unlimited power. On 30 December 1985 Zia lifted martial law, 8 years after he had imposed it. Until his death in August 1988 General M. Zia-ul-Haq was Head of State, President and Chief Martial Law Administrator, Chairman of the Planning Commission, Science and Technology, States and Frontier Regions and Establishment. An election is pending.

LANGUAGE: Urdu (official) and Punjabi are the most common. English is the language of business and central government. Provincial languages include Punjabi, Sindhi, Pushtu, Baluchi and Brahvi.

RELIGION: Sunni Moslem 97.2%; Hindu 1.4%; Christian 1.4%. Islam is the State religion.

TOURIST INFORMATION: Passport and visa required by Australian citizens. The importation of alcoholic beverages is strictly prohibited. Malaria prophylaxis is recommended. Drinking water should be boiled. Dysentery is common. Precautions should be taken against cholera. There are good doctors in Karachi and Islamabad but hospital facilities outside Karachi are variable. Although summers are very hot, men do not wear shorts. Throughout the year women should be conscious of the social and religious attitudes towards what, by Pakistani standards, would be immodest dress. Scarves and long-sleeved shirts may deflect unwelcome attention. Tipping or 'bakhshish' is widespread for services in hotels and restaurants. A departure tax of Rs100 is levied on international passengers. National airline: Pakistan International Airlines. Karachi civil airport is located 15 km from the city.

PANAMA

República de Panamá
REPUBLIC OF PANAMA

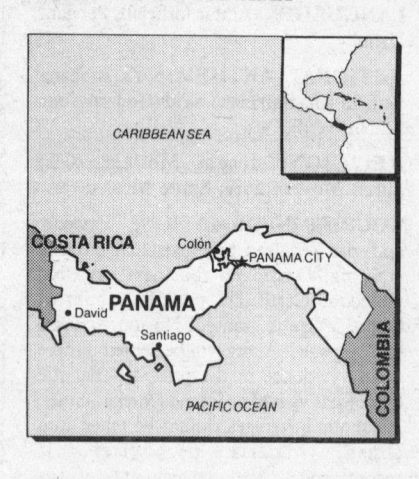

CAPITAL: Panama City

AREA AND POPULATION: 78,046 km², 8% cultivated land. Population: 2,227,000 (1986 est.). Population density: 29/km². Population growth (1985): 2.1%. Ethnic composition: Mestizo 50-60%;

Negro and Mulatto, 15-20%; European 10-15%; Indian 5-10%; Asian 2%.

CLIMATE AND GEOGRAPHY: Panama has a tropical climate, with high temperatures and a short, dry season from January to April. Average temperature (Panama City): 26.1°C (January), 27.2°C (July). Average annual rainfall (Panama City): 1,770 mm. Panama is bounded to the north by the Caribbean Sea, to the south by the Pacific Ocean, to the east by Colombia and to the west by Costa Rica. The landscape is mountainous, with lowlands along both coastlines.

CURRENCY: Balboa of 100 centesimos. The only paper currency is that of the USA. US coinage is also legal tender.

DEFENCE: Military service is voluntary. Total armed forces (1987): 12,250 (all services form part of the Army). Army (National Guard) 11,500; Navy 550; Air Force 200.

GOVERNMENT: Presidential republic. The Legislative Council consists of 67 members. The President and Vice-President are elected directly by universal adult suffrage. Head of State: Acting President Solis Palma. Foreign Minister: Jorge Abadia Arias.

LANGUAGE: Spanish (official), English.

NATIONAL ANTHEM: Alcanzamos por fin la victoria (Victory is ours at last).

RELIGION: Roman Catholic 93%; Protestant 6%; Jewish 2,000.

TOURIST INFORMATION: Passport and Tourist Card required by Australian citizens. All visitors must hold return or through tickets. Malaria prophylaxis is recommended as is yellow fever vaccination for visitors travelling outside the main cities. A departure tax of 15 balboas is levied on all passengers departing from Panama. National airline: Air Panama International. Panama City-General Omar Torrijos Herrera airport is located 26 km from the city.

PAPUA NEW GUINEA

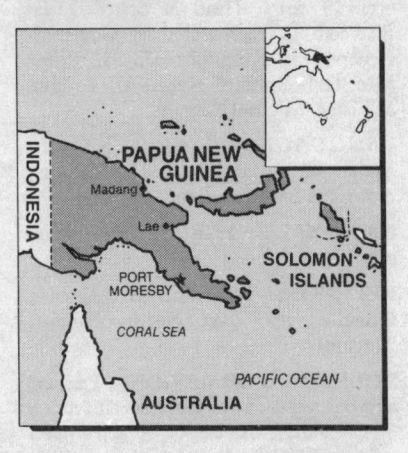

CAPITAL: Port Moresby

AREA AND POPULATION: 462,840 km², 1% cultivated land. Population: 3,395,000 (1986 est.). Population density: 7.3/km². Population growth (1985): 3.1%. Ethnic composition: Papuan (about 750 different tribes); Melanesian; Indonesian; Chinese; Polynesian; European minority.

CLIMATE AND GEOGRAPHY: The country lies wholly within the tropics, the coastal areas experiencing high temperatures and high humidity. Temperatures vary little throughout the year, ranging from 27.8°C (January) to 25.6°C (July) in Port Moresby. Average annual rainfall: 1,011 mm. A central core of mountains has peaks rising to over 4,000 m. The interior of the mainland contains a series of well-watered valleys stretching from the headwaters of the Markham River to the Irian Jaya border, and on both sides of the divide. Adjacent to the big rivers permanent inland swamps cover large areas of land, while mangrove swamps occur all along the mainland coast, especially in the south-western districts.

CURRENCY: Kina (K) of 100 toea.

DEFENCE: Military service is voluntary. Total armed forces (1987): 3,232 (all services form part of the Army). Army 2,846; Navy 300; Air Force 86. Paramilitary force: police 4,600.

GOVERNMENT: Constitutional monarchy. The National Parliament of 109 members is elected by universal suffrage every 5 years. Head of State: Queen Elizabeth II, represented by Governor-General Sir Kingsford Dibela. Prime Minister: Rabbie Namaliu. Foreign Minister: Michael Somare.

LANGUAGE: English (official), Melanesian Pidgin (lingua franca), numerous local languages.

NATIONAL ANTHEM: Arise all you sons.

RELIGION: Protestant 63%; Roman Catholic 31%; cargo cultist; Animist; Totemist.

TOURIST INFORMATION: Passport and visa required by Australian citizens. A 30-day tourist visa can be obtained upon entry to PNG (at Jackson's airport only). Malaria prophylaxis is recommended. Tipping is not a custom and is frowned upon. There is a departure tax of K10 per adult. National airline: Air Niugini. Port Moresby-Jackson's airport is located 8 km from the city.

PARAGUAY

República del Paraguay
REPUBLIC OF PARAGUAY

CAPITAL: Asunción

AREA AND POPULATION: 406,752 km², 3% cultivated land. Population: 4,119,000 (1986). Population density: 8.1/km². Population growth (1985): 2.8%. Ethnic composition: Mestizo 95%; European 3%; Indian (Guarani) 2%; Japanese and Korean minorities. Between 500,000 and 800,000 Paraguayans live abroad.

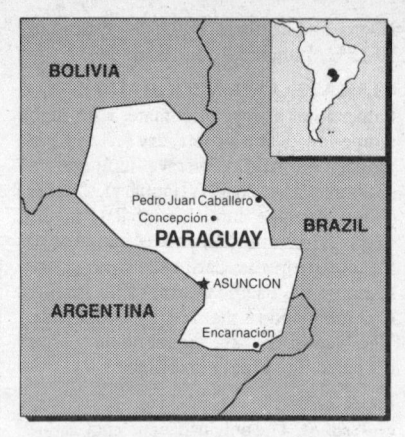

CLIMATE AND GEOGRAPHY: Paraguay has a tropical climate, with abundant rainfall and only a short dry season from July to September. Average temperature (Asunción): 27.2°C (January), 17.8°C (July). Average annual rainfall: 1,316 mm. The Republic is bordered to the north by Bolivia, to the south by Argentina and to the east by Brazil. There are 2 geographical zones: the Chaco, a vast stretch of scrub forest, growing drier towards the west and supporting few inhabitants, but serving as an important beef and cattle area; Paraguay proper, the Parana Plateau rainforest and the undulating and extremely fertile central plain, where the population is concentrated.

CURRENCY: Guarani (G) of 100 centimos.

DEFENCE: Military service is compulsory for 18 months (Army and Air Force) and two years (Navy). Total armed forces (1987): 15,970. Army 12,500; Navy 2,500; Air Force 970. Para-military forces: special police service 6,000; capital police force.

GOVERNMENT: Republic with an elected Parliament. Under the Constitution of 1967, the President holds office for 5 years and can be re-elected. The bicameral Parliament consists of a Senate of 30 members and a Chamber of Deputies of 60 members. Voting is secret and compulsory for all citizens over 18 years of age. Women were allowed the vote for the first time in 1963. Head of State: President General

Alfredo Stroessner. Foreign Minister: Dr Carlos Augusto Saldivar.

LANGUAGE: Spanish and Guarani— most Paraguayans are bilingual.

NATIONAL ANTHEM: ¡Paraguayos, república o muerte! (Paraguayans, the Republic or death).

RELIGION: Roman Catholic 97%; Protestant 2%; Mennonite 13,000; 1,200 Jewish.

TOURIST INFORMATION: Passport and visa required by Australian citizens. Visitors should be vaccinated against smallpox and inoculated against tetanus, typhoid and para-typhoid, and be cautious of salads and drinking water. Malaria prophylaxis is also recommended. Medical, hospital and dental facilities are adequate but fees are high. A departure tax of G3,500 is levied on passengers embarking for abroad. National airline: Lineas Aereas Paraguayas. Asunción-Presidente General Stroessner/Campo Grande airport is located 15 km from the city.

PERU

República del Perú
REPUBLIC OF PERU

CAPITAL: Lima

AREA AND POPULATION:
1,285,216 km², 3% cultivated land. Population: 20,207,000 (1986 est.). Population density: 15.4/km². Population growth (1985): 2.5%. Ethnic composition: Indian 45%; Mestizo 37%; European (mostly of Spanish background), 15%; Mulatto, Negro, Japanese and Chinese— about 10,000 in each group.

CLIMATE AND GEOGRAPHY: The climate ranges from equatorial to desert, with permanent snow in the high mountains. Temperatures vary little in coastal areas, daily or annually, but the daily range is considerable in the Sierra. Desert conditions prevail in the extreme south, where the climate is uniformly dry, with a few heavy showers falling between January and March. Average temperature (Lima): 23.3°C (January), 16.7°C (July). Average annual rainfall (Lima): 48 mm. Peru is bounded to the north by Ecuador and Colombia, to the south by Chile, to the east by Brazil and Bolivia and to the west by the Pacific Ocean. The country is divided into 3 distinct geographical zones: the coastal plain (Costa); the Andean highlands (Sierra); and the eastern mountain slopes and jungle plains (Selva). The latter is drained by the melting snows of the Sierra to form the Amazon River.

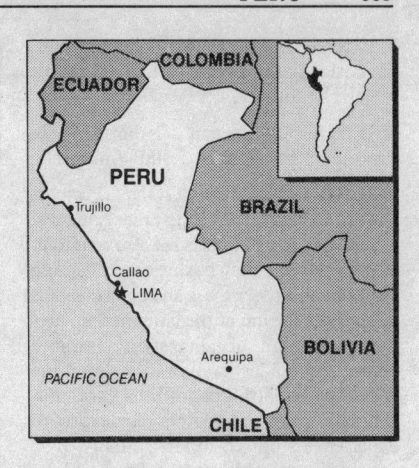

CURRENCY: Inti of 1000 soles.

DEFENCE: Military service is by selective conscription for a period of 2 years. Total armed forces (1987): 122,100. Army 85,000; Navy 21,100; Air Force 16,000. Para-military forces: Guardia Civil 36,000; Republican Guard 15,000; coastguard 600.

GOVERNMENT: Presidential republic. The bicameral Parliament (Chamber of Deputies and Senate) is elected for a 5-year term. There is universal suffrage. Head of State: President Alan García Perez. Prime Minister: Louis Alva Castro. Foreign Minister: Allan Wagner Dizon.

LANGUAGE: Spanish (official), many Andean Indians still use Quechua or Aymara as their principal, and sometimes only, means of communication.

NATIONAL ANTHEM: Somos libres, seamoslo siempre (We are free, let us remain so forever).

RELIGION: Roman Catholic 95%; Protestant 1%; Jewish 5,300; Animist.

TOURIST INFORMATION: Passport and visa required by Australian citizens. Onward or return tickets are also required. It is important that businessmen visiting Peru obtain a tourist visa and *not* a business visa, as possession of the latter necessitates the production of a taxation clearance before the holder is allowed to leave the country. Health conditions are not generally good and visitors may expect to experience stomach upsets initially. The humid climate of Lima is unfavourable to people suffering from respiratory or allergy problems, and those with cardiac conditions would be unwise to visit the Sierra. Immunisation is recommended against tuberculosis, typhoid, tetanus, poliomyelitis and, if intending to visit the jungle, yellow fever. There is a departure tax of US$10. National airline: Aeroperu. Lima-Jorge Chavez airport is located 15 km from the city.

PHILIPPINES

República de Filipinas
Republika ng Pilipinas
REPUBLIC OF THE PHILIPPINES

CAPITAL: Manila

AREA AND POPULATION: 300,000 km^2, 34% cultivated land. Population: 58,091,000 (1986 est.). Population density: 186.5/km^2. Population growth (1985): 2.4%. Ethnic composition: mainly Malay; Chinese 1-2%; Negrito and North American minorities.

CLIMATE AND GEOGRAPHY: The climate throughout the lowlands of Luzon is uniformly hot, with April and May the hottest months. In Manila, the average temperature is 26°C; during May it often rises above 38°C. The average humidity varies from 69% in April to 86% in September; however humidity of 96% or higher occurs after tropical downpours. Heavy rainfall is normally associated with typhoons, which occur frequently from June to November. The Philippines is an archipelago situated off the south-east coast of Asia. Its nearest neighbours are Malaysia, Indonesia and Taiwan. The main and most densely populated island is Luzon, while the large southern islands of Mindanao and Palawan are relatively sparsely populated. Some 7,100 other islands make up the rest of the group.

CURRENCY: Peso (P) of 100 centavos.

DEFENCE: Military service is voluntary. Total armed forces (1987): 113,000. Army 70,000; Navy 26,000; Air Force 17,000. Para-military forces: Philippine Constabulary 50,000; Ministry of Defence forces 42,000; coastguard 2,000. Opposition: New People's Army 16,500; Bangsa Moro Army 11,000; Cordillera People's Liberation Army, a few hundred. Figures should be used with caution.

GOVERNMENT: Presidential republic. The Congress consists of 2 chambers: the Senate and the House of Representatives. There is universal suffrage. Head of State: President Corazon Aquino. Vice President: Salvador Laurel.

LANGUAGE: Pilipino (official – based on the Malayan dialect Tagalog), English, Spanish.

NATIONAL ANTHEM: Bayang Magiliw (Land of the morning).

RELIGION: Roman Catholic 83%; Protestant 9%; Moslem; Buddhist.

TOURIST INFORMATION: Passport and visa required by Australian citizens. Malaria prophylaxis is recommended for visitors to the southern islands. There is a high incidence of tuberculosis in the Philippines. Drinking water is provided in thermos jugs in Manila hotels and is satisfactory, although some discomfort may occur because hotel water supplies are usually artesian. There is a departure tax of P200 for international flights and P10 for domestic flights. National airline: Philippine Airlines. Manila airport is located 12 km from the city.

POLAND

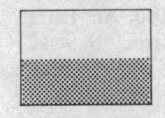

Polska Rzeczpospolita Ludowa
POLISH PEOPLE'S REPUBLIC

CAPITAL: Warsaw

AREA AND POPULATION: 312,683 km^2, 49% cultivated land. Population: 37,546,000 (1986 est.). Population density: 119.7/km^2. Population growth (1985): 0.9%. Ethnic composition: Polish 98-99%; German; Ukrainian; Byelorussian; Slovakian; Russian; Gypsy; Lithuanian; Greek and Macedonian; Czechoslovakian. Some 9,500,000 Poles live abroad, 6,500,000 in the USA, 750,000 in France and 450,000 in Brazil.

CLIMATE AND GEOGRAPHY: Poland has a temperate climate, influenced by moist air from the Atlantic and Baltic, and by cold dry air movements from Asia. Spring, summer and autumn are mild but winter can be severe. Average temperature (Warsaw): $-3.9°C$ (January), $18.9°C$ (July). Average annual rainfall (Warsaw): 553 mm. Poland is bounded to the north by the Baltic Sea and the Russian Soviet Federal Socialist Republic, to the south by Czechoslovakia, to the east by Lithuania, White Russia and the Ukraine, and to the west by the German Democratic Republic. The country is generally flat, with minor undulations. The northern area is glaciated and contains innumerable lakes.

CURRENCY: Zloty (Zl) of 100 groszy.

DEFENCE: Military service is compulsory for 2 years (Army, internal security forces, Air Force) and 3 years (Navy and special services). Total regular forces (1987): 402,000. Army 295,000; Navy 19,000; Air Force 88,000. Paramilitary forces: citizen's militia 200,000; Ministry of Defence internal defence troops 65,500; police anti-riot units 28,000; Ministry of Interior troops and border guard 24,000.

GOVERNMENT: Socialist people's republic. The unicameral Parliament of 460 members is elected by universal adult suffrage for a 4-year term. It elects a Council of State, composed of a Chairman, Secretary and 15 members, and a Council of Ministers. Head of State: Woyciech Jaruzelski. Prime Minister: Zbiegniew Meissner. Foreign Minister: Marian Orzechowski.

LANGUAGE: Polish.

NATIONAL ANTHEM: Jeszcze Polska nie zginela (Poland has not yet been destroyed).

RELIGION: Roman Catholic 90%; Polish Orthodox 2%; Protestant 1%; Old Catholic Mariavite 30,000; Jewish 12,000.

TOURIST INFORMATION: Passport and visa required by Australian citizens. A compulsory currency exchange of US$15 or its equivalent in another freely convertible currency must be made upon arrival for each day to be spent in Poland. Visitors planning to stay longer than 30 days must register immediately with the police authorities. Foreign currencies should be declared upon arrival. The export of zlotys is forbidden. National airline: Lot.

PORTUGAL

República Portuguesa
REPUBLIC OF PORTUGAL

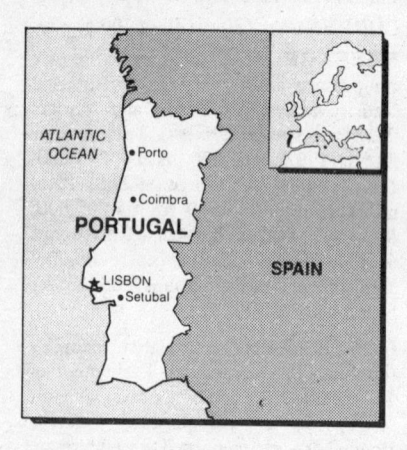

CAPITAL: Lisbon

AREA AND POPULATION: 91,985 km^2, 39% cultivated land. Population: 10,095,000 (1986 est.). Population density: 102/km^2. Population growth (1985): 0.4%. Ethnic composition: almost exclusively Portuguese; small African minority.

CLIMATE AND GEOGRAPHY: The climate ranges from the cool damp Atlantic type in the north, to a warm dry Mediterranean climate in the south. July and August are virtually rainless everywhere. Inland areas in the north have greater temperature variation, with continental winds blowing from the interior. Average temperature (Lisbon): 11°C (January), 22°C (July). Average annual rainfall (Lisbon): 686 mm. Portugal is bordered to the north and east by Spain, and to the south and west by the Atlantic Ocean. The north is mountainous, the highest mountains being snow-covered in winter. To the south of the Tagus River lie the hot dry plains of the Alentejo, and the hills and littoral of the Algarve on the southern coast. In addition to the mainland, Portugal includes the archipelagos of Madeira and the Azores, and the Territory of Macau.

CURRENCY: Escudo (Esc) of 100 centavos.

DEFENCE: Military service is compulsory for 16 months (Army), 24 months (Navy) and 21 to 24 months (Air Force). Total armed forces (1987): 67,800. Army 40,000; Navy 14,000; Air Force 13,800. Para-military forces: National Republican Guard 15,510; public security police 13,000; border security guard 8,853.

GOVERNMENT: Parliamentary democratic republic embodying elements of both the Westminster and the Presidential systems. Powers are divided between an elected president, a unicameral legislature and an independent judiciary. The influence of the armed forces in government has diminished but is still latent. Head of State: President Dr Mario Alberto Nobre Lopes Soares. Prime Minister: Professor Anibal Cavaco Silva. Foreign Minister: P. Peres de Miranda.

LANGUAGE: Portuguese.

NATIONAL ANTHEM: A Portuguesa.

RELIGION: Almost exclusively Roman Catholic; Protestant 40,000; Jewish 6,000.

TOURIST INFORMATION: Passport but no visa required by Australian citizens. All visitors other than nationals of Portugal must have funds of at least Esc5,000 plus Esc500 per day of stay. Portuguese banks do not offer exchange facilities for Australian dollars. National airline: Air Portugal.

QATAR

Dawlat al-Qatar
STATE OF QATAR

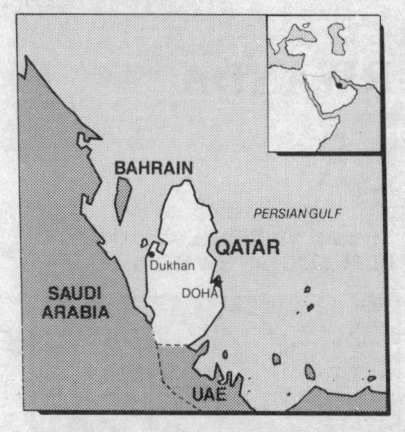

CAPITAL: Doha

AREA AND POPULATION: 11,437 km², 2.9% cultivated land. Population: 305,000 (1986 est.). Population density: 27.4/km². Population growth (1975-78): 5.7%. Ethnic composition: Arab 40%; Persian 10%; Pakistani 18%.

CLIMATE AND GEOGRAPHY: The climate is hot and arid but periods of cold weather may occur in January and February, with the temperature dropping to as low as 7°C. Rainfall varies between 50 mm and 70 mm a year and falls between November and March, usually in sudden and heavy showers. The period from June to September can be very hot, with temperatures reaching 49°C. The heat is sometimes made unpleasant by high humidity, at times in excess of 95%. Average temperature (Doha): 16.7°C (January), 36.7°C (July). Average annual rainfall (Doha): 62 mm. Qatar is situated on the Persian Gulf, bordered to the south by the United Arab Emirates and to the west by Saudi Arabia. Mostly a flat desert, there is some vegetation in the north.

CURRENCY: Qatar Riyal of 100 dirhams.

DEFENCE: Military service is voluntary. Total armed forces (1987): 6,000. Army 5,000; Navy 700 (including Marine Police); Air Force 300. Paramilitary force: police.

GOVERNMENT: Sheikhdom. There is no parliament but ministers are assisted by a 30-man nominated Consultative Council. Head of State: Amir Sheikh Khalifa Bin-Hamad al-Thani. Foreign Minister: Sheikh Ahmad bin Saif al-Thani.

LANGUAGE: Arabic (official); Persian, English.

RELIGION: Sunni Moslem 98%.

TOURIST INFORMATION: Passport and visa required by Australian citizens. The importation of alcoholic beverages is strictly forbidden. Medical treatment is free for residents and visitors. National airline: Gulf Air. Doha airport is located 6.5 km from the city.

ROMANIA

Republica Socialistă România
SOCIALIST REPUBLIC OF ROMANIA

CAPITAL: Bucharest

AREA AND POPULATION: 237,500 km², 45% cultivated land. Population:

22,830,000 (1986 est.). Population density: 95.8/km². Population growth (1985): 0.5%. Ethnic composition: Romanian 88.1%; Hungarian 7.9%; German 1.67%; Ukrainian, Serbian, Russian, Croatian, Tartar, Turkish and Bulgarian minorities.

CLIMATE AND GEOGRAPHY:
Continental climate with long, hot summers. Temperatures in summer range from 21°C to 32°C. Winters, which last from November to March, are cold, with considerable ice and snow. Average temperature (Bucharest): −2.7°C (January), 23.5°C (July). Average rainfall (Bucharest): 579 mm. Romania is bordered to the north and east by Moldavia and the Ukraine, to the south by Bulgaria and to the west by Hungary and Yugoslavia. The greater part of the country is hilly, with the Carpathian Mountains stretching down its centre from north to south. Along the whole of the coastline and in the south stretches the large, flat and fertile Danubian plain.

CURRENCY: Leu (pl. Lei) of 100 bani.

DEFENCE: Military service is compulsory for 16 months (Army and Air Force) and 24 months (Navy). Total regular forces (1987): 189,700. Army 150,000; Navy 7,700; Air Force 32,000. Paramilitary forces: local defence forces 900,000; Youth Homeland Defence Force 650,000; Ministry of Defence security troops 20,000; border guards 17,000; Patriotic Guard 12,000(?); Voluntary Sports Association.

GOVERNMENT: Socialist republic. The unicameral Parliament (Marea Adunare Nationala) of 369 members is elected by all workers over the age of 18, for a period of 5 years. Head of State: President Nicolae Ceaușescu. Chairman of the Council of Ministers (Prime Minister): Constantin Dăscălescu. Foreign Minister: Ioan Totu.

LANGUAGE: Romanian.

NATIONAL ANTHEM: Trei culori (Three colours).

RELIGION: Romanian Orthodox 80%; Roman Catholic 6%; Protestant 5%; Jewish 26,000; small Moslem minority.

TOURIST INORMATION: Passport and visa required by Australian citizens. It is compulsory to exchange US$10 (or equivalent in another freely convertible currency) per person per day of stay in Romania. National airline: TAROM. Bucharest-Otopeni airport is located 20 km from the city.

RWANDA

Republika y'u Rwanda
REPUBLIC OF RWANDA

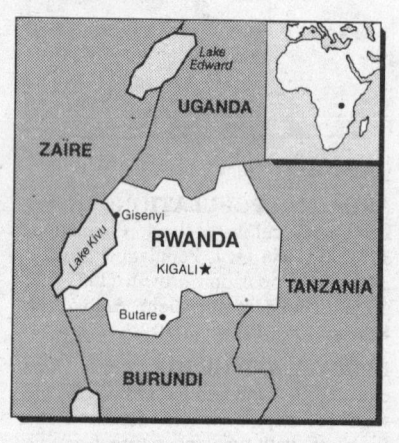

CAPITAL: Kigali

AREA AND POPULATION: 26,338 km², 48% cultivated land. Population: 6,489,000 (1986 est.). Population density: 255.6/km². Population growth (1985): 3.8%. Ethnic composition: Bantu tribes, 90%; Hamitic-Nilotic Watusi or Tutsi, 9%; Pygmy; European (mostly Belgian); Indian; Asian.

CLIMATE AND GEOGRAPHY:
Highland tropical climate with wet seasons from October to December and March to May. Average temperature (Kigali): 19.4°C (January), 21.1°C (July). Average annual rainfall: 1,000 mm. Rwanda is bordered to the north by Uganda, to the south by Burundi, to the east by Tanzania

and to the west by Zaïre. Grassy uplands and hills cover most of the country. There is a chain of volcanoes in the north-west. The source of the Nile has been located in the headwaters of the Kagera River, south-west of Kigali.

CURRENCY: Rwanda franc (F.Rw.) of 100 centimes.

DEFENCE: Military service is voluntary. Total armed forces (1987): 5,150 (all services form part of the Army). Army 5,000; Air Force 150. Para-military forces: gendarmerie 1,200.

GOVERNMENT: Presidential republic. Executive power rests with the President, who is elected for a 5-year term by universal suffrage. He presides over a Council of Ministers whom he appoints. Head of State: President Major-General Junéval Habyarimana. Foreign Minister: François Ngarukiyintwari.

LANGUAGES: French and Kinyarwanda (both official), Kiswahili.

NATIONAL ANTHEM: Rwanda rwacu, Rwanda gihugu cyambyaye (My Rwanda, land that gave me birth).

RELIGION: Roman Catholic 56%; Protestant 7%; Moslem 9%; Animist.

TOURIST INFORMATION: Passport and visa required by Australian citizens. Vaccination against yellow fever is required, and malaria prophylaxis is recommended. A departure tax of F.Rw.800 is levied on international and F.Rw.250 on domestic passengers. National airline: Air Rwanda. Kigali-Kanombe airport is located 12 km from the city.

ST CHRISTOPHER AND NEVIS

FEDERATION OF
ST CHRISTOPHER AND NEVIS

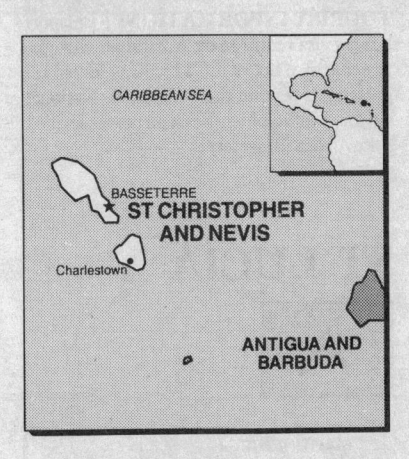

CAPITAL: Basseterre

AREA AND POPULATION: 261 km² (St Christopher 168 km², Nevis 93 km²). Population: 40,000 (1986 est.). Population density: 179.4/km². Population growth (1980): 1.5%. Ethnic composition: Negro and Mulatto, 95%; Indian; Chinese; European.

CLIMATE AND GEOGRAPHY:
Pleasant climate with cool breezes thoughout the year. Humidity is low and there is no particular rainy season. Average annual rainfall: 1,375 mm. The islands form part of the Lesser Antilles in the eastern Caribbean Sea.

CURRENCY: Eastern Caribbean Dollar (EC$) of 100 cents.

DEFENCE: Great Britain is responsible for the Federation's defence.

GOVERNMENT: 'Sovereign democratic federal state', according to the 1983 Constitution. The unicameral Parliament has 11 elected members and 3 appointed senators. Head of State: Queen Elizabeth II, represented by Governor-General Sir Clement Athelston Arrindell. Prime Minister and Foreign Minister: Dr Kennedy Alphonse Simmonds.

LANGUAGE: English.

NATIONAL ANTHEM: O land of beauty.

RELIGION: Anglican; Methodist; Roman Catholic.

TOURIST INFORMATION: Passport but no visa required by Australian citizens. A departure tax of EC$13.50 is levied on passengers leaving the Federation. National airline: Liat. Golden Rock airport is located 3 km from Basseterre.

ST LUCIA

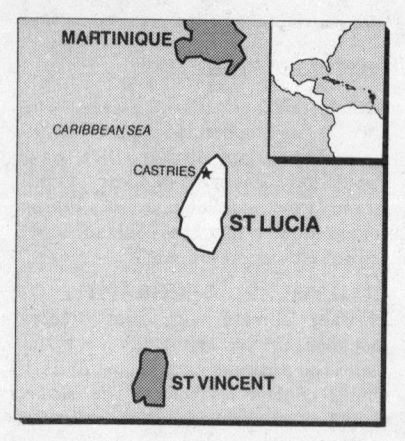

CAPITAL: Castries

AREA AND POPULATION: 616 km^2, 50% cultivated land. Population: 123,000 (1986 est.). Population density: 225.9/km^2. Ethnic composition: Negro 66%; Indian 4%; European 1%; Mulatto.

CLIMATE AND GEOGRAPHY: The climate is tropical, with a dry season from January to April and a rainy season from May to August. Average temperature: 26.7°C. Average annual rainfall: 2,500 mm. St Lucia is a small island of the Lesser Antilles situated in the eastern Caribbean. Mountainous and volcanic in origin, the country is covered by rich tropical vegetation.

CURRENCY: Eastern Caribbean Dollar (EC$) of 100 cents.

DEFENCE: No defence force is maintained.

GOVERNMENT: Constitutional monarchy. The bicameral Parliament consists of a Senate of 11 members appointed by the Governor-General and a House of Assembly of 17 members elected for 5 years. Head of State: Queen Elizabeth II, represented by Governor-General Sir Allen Lewis. Prime Minister: John George Melvin Compton.

LANGUAGE: English (official), French creole.

NATIONAL ANTHEM: Sons and daughters of St Lucia, love the land that gave us birth.

RELIGION: Roman Catholic 90%; Protestant minority.

TOURIST INFORMATION: Passport but no visa required by Australian citizens. Visitors may be required to deposit an amount equal to their return passage. Those travelling on business are required to pay EC$150. A 'Passenger Service Charge' of EC$12 is levied on all passengers embarking for international, and EC$6 for inter-Caribbean destinations. National airline: St Lucia Airways. Hewanorra airport is located 60 km from Castries.

ST VINCENT AND THE GRENADINES

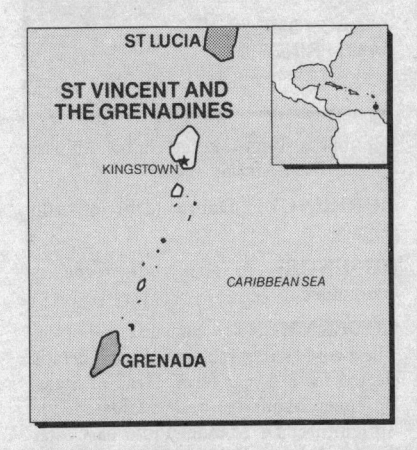

CAPITAL: Kingstown

AREA AND POPULATION: 388 km², 50% cultivated land. Population: 103,000 (1986 est.). Population density: 284.9/km². Population growth (1985): 2.3%. Ethnic composition: Negro 66%; Indian 4%; Mulatto.

CLIMATE AND GEOGRAPHY: Tropical marine climate, with north-east Trade Winds predominating. The rainy season lasts from June to December. The average annual rainfall ranges from 3,750 mm in the mountains to 1,500 mm on the south-east coast. The country forms part of the Windward chain of islands in the eastern Caribbean. St Vincent, like all of the Windwards, is volcanic and mountainous (Mt Soufriere rises 1,220 m), and is covered with luxurious flora.

CURRENCY: Eastern Caribbean Dollar (EC$) of 100 cents.

DEFENCE: A small para-military marine force is maintained.

GOVERNMENT: Constitutional monarchy. The unicameral Parliament consists of 13 elected members and 6 senators chosen by the Governor-General. Head of State: Queen Elizabeth II, represented by Governor-General Joseph Lambert Eustace. Prime Minister and Foreign Minister: James Mitchell.

LANGUAGE: English (official), Creole.

NATIONAL ANTHEM: St Vincent! Land so beautiful.

RELIGION: Protestant majority, Roman Catholic minority.

TOURIST INFORMATION: Passport but no visa required by Australian citizens. There is a departure tax of EC$10. National airline: Liat.

SAN MARINO

Repubblica di San Marino
REPUBLIC OF SAN MARINO

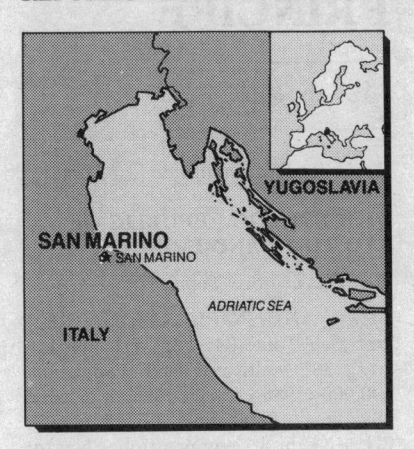

CAPITAL: San Marino

AREA AND POPULATION: 61.19 km², 17% cultivated land. Population: 23,000 (1986 est.). Population density: 369.1/km². Ethnic composition: Sanmarinese; Italian. Some 20,000 citizens live abroad.

CLIMATE AND GEOGRAPHY: The climate is that of north-central Italy. San Marino is a land-locked state in central Italy some 20 km from the Adriatic coast, lying on the slopes of Mt Titano. The landscape is, for the most part, green rolling hills.

CURRENCY: Italian and Vatican City currencies are used.

DEFENCE: Militia, consisting, in case of necessity, of all able-bodied men between the ages of 16 and 55 (teachers, students etc. excepted).

GOVERNMENT: Republic. The Parliament of 60 members is elected for 5 years by universal adult suffrage.

LANGUAGE: Italian.

RELIGION: Roman Catholic.

TOURIST INFORMATION: Passport but no visa required by Australian citizens. There is no border control between Italy and San Marino.

SÃO TOMÉ E PRÍNCIPE

República Democrática de São Tomé e Príncipe
DEMOCRATIC REPUBLIC OF SAO TOME AND PRINCIPE

CAPITAL: Sao Tomé

AREA AND POPULATION: 1,001 km^2 (Sao Tome 845 km^2, Principe 128 km^2), 38% cultivated land. Population: 108,000 (1986 est.). Population density: 109.7/km^2. Population growth (1985): 2.1%. Ethnic composition: Negro; Mulatto; Portuguese.

CLIMATE AND GEOGRAPHY: The climate is tropical, modified by altitude and the effect of the cool Benguela current. The wet season extends from October to May. Average temperature (Sao Tomé): 25°C. Average annual rainfall: 951 mm. The Republic is situated in the Gulf of Guinea, off the West African coast.

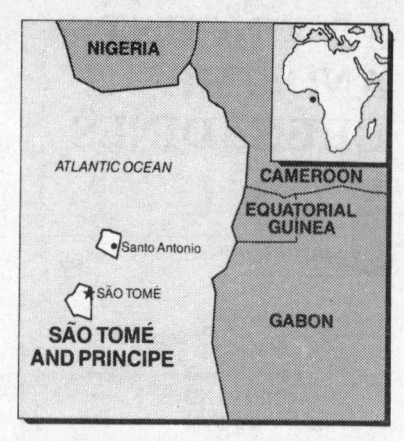

CURRENCY: Dobra (Db) of 100 centavos.

DEFENCE: A small air force is maintained.

GOVERNMENT: Socialist republic. The People's Assembly of 40 members is elected for a 4-year term. Head of State, Defence Minister and Minister for Agriculture: Dr Manuel Pinto da Costa. Foreign Minister: Maria do Nascimento da Graça Amorim.

LANGUAGE: Portuguese (official), Portuguese creole, Bantu languages.

RELIGION: Roman Catholic 90%; Animist.

TOURIST INFORMATION: Passport and visa required by Australian citizens. Vaccination against yellow fever is recommended as is malaria prophylaxis. National airline: Transportes Aéreos de São Tomé.

SAUDI ARABIA

Al-Mamlaka al-'Arabiya as-Sa'udiya
KINGDOM OF SAUDI ARABIA

CAPITAL: Riyadh

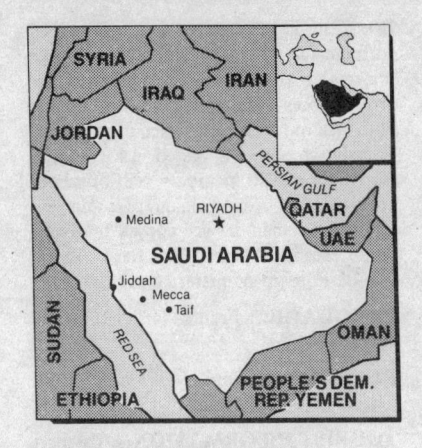

AREA AND POPULATION:
2,149,690 km², 0.5% cultivated land. Population: 11,519,000 (1986 est.). Population density: 5.0/km². Population growth (1985): 3.1%. Ethnic composition: Arab (Saudi, Egyptian, Palestinian, Jordanian, Syrian, Yemeni); Persian; Negro; Asian (Pakistani and Indian).

CLIMATE AND GEOGRAPHY:
Desert climate—intense heat and little rain. Coastal areas, especially the Red Sea coast, experience high humidity throughout the year. Average temperature (Riyadh): 14.4°C (January), 33.3°C (July). Rainfall averages between 50 mm and 100 mm per year. Saudi Arabia is bordered to the north by Iraq and Jordan, to the south by Oman, North and South Yemen, to the west by the Red Sea and to the east by the United Arab Emirates, Qatar, Kuwait and the Persian Gulf. Most of the surface area is desert plateau from 500 m to 2,000 m high, with lava beds in the west-central portion and sand and gravel constituting the remainder.

CURRENCY:
Saudi Riyal of 100 halalas.

DEFENCE:
Military service is compulsory for males aged between 18 and 35. Total armed forces (1987): 67,800. Army 40,000; Navy 4,200; Air Force 14,000. Para-military forces: National Guard 25,000; foreign contract military personnel 10,000; frontier force and coastguard 8,500; Ministry of Interior counter-terrorist unit; general Civil Defence Administration units.

GOVERNMENT:
Monarchy with no formal constitution apart from the Koran and the Sharia. Since 1953 an appointed Council of Ministers has assisted the King in the task of government and is now the effective legislature and executive body within the Kingdom. There are no political parties and no popular representation. Head of State: King Fahd ibn Abdel Aziz. Prime Minister: Crown Prince Abdullah ibn Abdul Aziz. Foreign Minister: Prince Saud al Faisal.

LANGUAGE:
Arabic.

RELIGION:
Sunni Moslem 85%; Shiite Moslem 15%.

TOURIST INFORMATION:
Passport and visa required by Australian citizens. Entry will be refused to visitors whose passports are, will be or have been valid for entry to Israel; Jewish passengers whose religion is mentioned in their passports; visitors arriving in an apparently intoxicated state; visitors who do not comply with Saudi Arabian general appearance and behaviour taboos such as women exposing legs or arms or wearing too thin or tight clothing, men wearing shorts, men and women displaying affection in public in any manner. The importation of alcoholic beverages is prohibited, even for transit passengers. Nothing can be imported free of duty except clothes and strictly personal effects. Customs charges apply to such items as cameras and typewriters. If these articles are re-exported within 90 days, customs charges may be refunded. It is not advisable to put a film in a camera. Malaria prophylaxis is recommended. National airline: Saudia. Jeddah-King Abdul Aziz airport is located 25 km from the city.

SENEGAL

République du Sénégal
REPUBLIC OF SENEGAL
CAPITAL: Dakar

President is elected by direct universal suffrage for a 5-year term and is eligible for re-election. He is commander of the armed forces and nominates his ministers, with whom he exercises executive power. Legislative power is vested in a National Assembly of 120 members, half of whom are elected by proportional representation, while the remainder are chosen by direct vote. Head of State: President Abdou Diouf. Foreign Minister: Ibrahima Fall.

LANGUAGE: French (official), tribal languages.

RELIGION: Sunni Moslem 75-90%; Christian 4-6%; Animist.

TOURIST INFORMATION: Passport and visa required by Australian citizens. Malaria prophylaxis and vaccination against typhoid, tetanus and poliomyelitis are recommended. Yellow fever and cholera vaccinations are required. Visitors arriving without a return ticket must pay a deposit equivalent to the cheapest fare between their place of origin and Senegal. This sum is refundable from the local Treasury before leaving Senegal. National airline: Air Senegal. Dakar-Yoff airport is located 17 km from the city.

AREA AND POPULATION: 196,192 km^2, 27% cultivated land. Population: 6,980,000 (1986 est.). Population density: 34.4/km^2. Population growth (1985): 2.6%. Ethnic composition: Wolof 36%; Serer 13%; Fulbe 13%; Toucouleur 9%; other Sudanese tribes; European, Lebanese and Syrian minorities.

CLIMATE AND GEOGRAPHY: Tropical climate. On the coast, however, it is surprisingly cool and breezy. The rainy season extends from July to September. Average temperature (Dakar): 22.2°C (January), 27.8°C (July). Average annual rainfall: 541 mm. Senegal is bordered to the north by Mauritania, to the south by Guinea and Guinea-Bissau, to the east by Mali and to the west by the Atlantic Ocean. Apart from the high ground along the eastern and south-eastern borders, the country consists of plains covered by savanna. The Senegal River forms the northern border. The coast between there and Dakar is comprised of a large body of sand dunes. The Cap Vert peninsula, which lies in the path of the prevailing winds, is, by contrast, green and luxuriant.

CURRENCY: Franc CFA of 100 centimes.

DEFENCE: Military service is by selective conscription. Total armed forces (1987): 9,450. Army 8,500; Navy 450; Air Force 500. Para-military forces: gendarmerie; Customs.

GOVERNMENT: Parliamentary democracy based on the republican form. The

SEYCHELLES

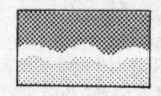

REPUBLIC OF SEYCHELLES
CAPITAL: Victoria

AREA AND POPULATION: 453 km^2, 54% cultivated land. Population: 67,000 (1986 est.). Population density: 145.6/km^2. Population growth (1985): 1.8%. Ethnic composition: Negro; Mulatto; French Creole; Indian, Chinese and Malayan minorities.

CLIMATE AND GEOGRAPHY: The climate is tropical. There are 2 seasons: hot from December to May and cooler from June to November. Rainfall varies over the group but the greater part falls in the hot months during the north-west Trades.

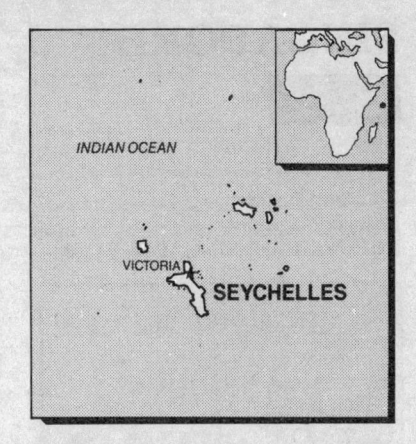

provided an onward or return ticket is held. There is no malaria in the Seychelles. National airline: Air Seychelles. Seychelles International Airport is located 10 km from Victoria.

SIERRA LEONE

REPUBLIC OF SIERRA LEONE

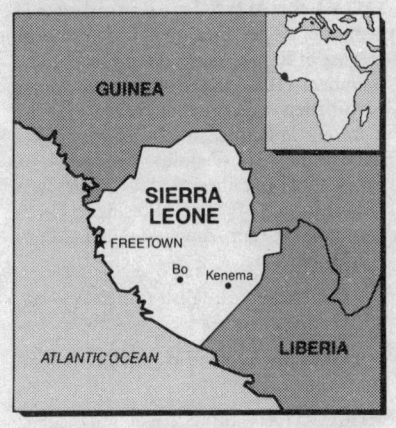

Relative humidity exceeds 75% throughout the year and average temperatures are 24°C (minimum) and 30°C (maximum). The Seychelles are situated in the Indian Ocean 1,800 km east of Mombasa, Kenya, and 3,300 km south-west of Bombay, India. The group is an archipelago of 37 granite and 52 coralline islands, plus numerous rocks and small bays. The granite islands rise fairly steeply from the sea, with the highest reaching 912 m. The coral islands are reefs in various stages of formation, rising only a few metres above sea level. Vegetation on the granite islands is lush and tropical.

CURRENCY: Seychelles Rupee (SRs).

DEFENCE: Military service is by conscription for a period of 2 years. Total armed forces (1987): 1,200 (all services form part of the Army). Army 1,000; Navy 100; Air Force 100. Para-military force: people's militia 900.

GOVERNMENT: Republic with unicameral Parliament (National Assembly) of 25 members, 23 elected by universal adult suffrage and 2 appointed by the President to represent the Inner and Outer Islands. Head of State: President France-Albert René. Foreign Minister: Maxime Ferrari.

LANGUAGE: Creole (official), English, French.

RELIGION: Roman Catholic 91%; Anglican 7.5%.

TOURIST INFORMATION: Passport but no visa required by Australian citizens

CAPITAL: Freetown

AREA AND POPULATION: 73,326 km², 25% cultivated land. Population: 3,987,000 (1986 est.). Population density: 51.7/km². Population growth (1985): 2.7%. Ethnic composition: Mende 29%; Temne 30%; Negro 2%; other Sudanese tribes; European (mostly British) and Lebanese minorities.

CLIMATE AND GEOGRAPHY: Wet tropical climate. The wet season lasts from May to October and the dry season from November to April. Early morning fog and the 'harmattan' (a hot, dry, dust-laden wind from the Sahara) are common in the north during the 'dry'. Temperature and humidity are consistently high throughout the year. Average temperature (Freetown): 26.2°C. The Republic is bordered to the north and east by Guinea, to the south by Liberia and to the west by the Atlantic Ocean. Apart from the mountainous peninsula on which Freetown is located, the land rises in a series of irregular steps from the coastal swamplands of the south-west, via a broad coastal plain, to interior mountains and plateaux. There are many small river systems and the deep-water anchorage off Freetown is 1 of the 3 largest natural harbours in the world.

CURRENCY: Leone (Le) of 100 cents.

DEFENCE: Military service is voluntary. Total armed forces (1987): 3,280. Army 3,100; Navy 150 (coastguard); Air Force 30. Para-military force: State Security Division 800.

GOVERNMENT: Presidential republic. The unicameral Parliament (House of Representatives) consists of 124 members—105 elected members whose nomination must be approved by the Central Committee of the sole political party, the All People's Congress, 7 presidential nominees and 12 paramount chiefs. Head of State: President Saidu Momoh. Foreign Minister: Alhaji Abdul Karim Koroma.

LANGUAGE: English (official), Krio, Mende and Temne.

NATIONAL ANTHEM: High we exalt thee, realm of the free.

RELIGION: Sunni Moslem 39%; Protestant 70,000; Roman Catholic 58,500; Animist.

TOURIST INFORMATION: Passport and visa required by Australian citizens. Malaria prophylaxis is essential. Yellow fever and cholera vaccinations are required and inoculations against tetanus, typhoid and poliomyelitis are strongly recommended. Rabies and hepatitis exist in Sierra Leone. National airline: Sierra Leone Airlines. Freetown-Lungi airport is separated from Freetown by the mouth of the Sierra Leone River. Because this body of water must be crossed using a slow and infrequent ferry, it usually takes between 2 and 3 hours to travel to the centre of town. A departure tax of US$10 is levied on international passengers.

SINGAPORE

Xinjiapo Gonghegno
Majulah Singapura
REPUBLIC OF SINGAPORE

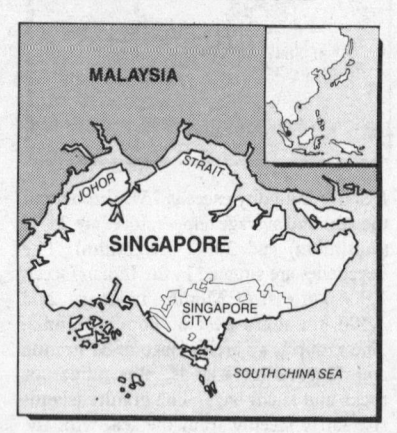

CAPITAL: Singapore

AREA AND POPULATION: 620.2 km^2, 12% cultivated land. Population: 2,584,000 (1986 est.). Population density: 4,179.2/km^2. Population growth (1985): 1.0%. Ethnic composition: Chinese 70.0%; Malay 15%; Indian and Pakistani 6.3%; European minority.

CLIMATE AND GEOGRAPHY:
Equatorial climate—hot and humid. The average minimum daily temperature is 24°C and the average maximum, usually in the afternoon, is 31°C. November to January are the cooler months. Relative humidity is highest at night and in the early hours of the morning, just before sunrise, when it often exceeds 90%. Average annual rainfall: 2,367 mm. Singapore is an island off the tip of the Malayan Peninsula, in South-East Asia. It is low-lying, the highest hill, Bukit Timah, standing 177 m above sea level. There are a number of saline rivers on the island, the longest of which is Sungei Seletar. The city of Singapore and the main port lie at the centre of the southern coastline. Substantial areas of land are reclaimed from the sea each year.

CURRENCY: Singapore Dollar (S$) of 100 cents.

DEFENCE: Military service is compulsory for 24 months (30 months for NCOs). Total armed forces (1986/87): 54,500. Army 45,000; Navy 3,500; Air Force 6,000. Para-military forces: police/marine police 7,500; Gurkha guard units; People's Defence Force.

GOVERNMENT: Republic with a unicameral legislature (Parliament) of 79 members elected for a 5-year term by universal adult suffrage. Parliament appoints the President, who is titular Head of State, for a term of 4 years. Head of State: President Wee Kim Wee. Prime Minister: Lee Kuan Yew. Foreign Minister: Suppiah Dhanabalan.

LANGUAGE: Malay, Chinese, Tamil and English (all official). English is the language of administration.

RELIGION: Confucianist; Taoist; Buddhist; Moslem; Hindu; Christian.

TOURIST INFORMATION: Passport but no visa required by Australian citizens. A return or onward ticket is required. Entry may be refused to visitors whose dress and general appearance do not conform to local standards, e.g. 'hippies' and males with hair reaching below the collar and/or covering the ears and/or falling across the forehead to eyebrow level. The penalty for trafficking illegal drugs is death. There is a passenger service charge of S$12 for international destinations and S$5 for internal. National airline: Singapore Airlines. Singapore-Changi airport is located 20 km from the city.

SOLOMON ISLANDS

CAPITAL: Honiara

AREA AND POPULATION: 27,556 km², 2% cultivated land. Population: 283,000 (1986 est.). Population density: 10/km². Population growth (1985): 3.7%. Ethnic composition: Melanesian 93%; Polynesian 4%; Micronesian, Chinese and European minorities.

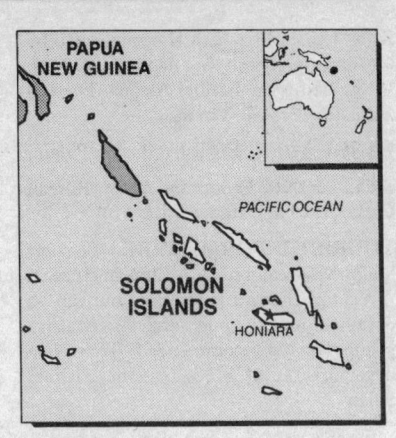

CLIMATE AND GEOGRAPHY: Equatorial climate with minor seasonal variations. The noon temperature in Honiara is usually around 30°C, accompanied by high humidity. Evenings are cool, with temperatures dropping to as low as 19°C during the night, accompanied by a refreshing breeze from the mountains. The average annual rainfall in Honiara is 2,300 mm – abnormally low compared with other parts of the country, where it often exceeds 7,500 mm. The Solomons are a scattered archipelago of mountainous islands and hundreds of coral atolls stretching over 1,500 km south-east of Bougainville, New Guinea, to the Santa Cruz Islands. Ninety per cent of the land is dense tropical forest, the main islands having deep narrow valleys, rivers that are subject to sudden and heavy flooding and are rarely navigable for any length, coastal swamps and extensive coral reefs and lagoons.

CURRENCY: Solomon Island Dollar (SI$) of 100 cents.

DEFENCE: No defence force is maintained.

GOVERNMENT: Constitutional monarchy. The unicameral National Parliament is composed of not less than 30 and not more than 50 members elected every 4 years by universal adult suffrage. Head of

State: Queen Elizabeth II, represented by Governor-General Sir Baddeley Devisi. Prime Minister: Ezekiel Alebua. Foreign Minister: Paul J. Tovua.

LANGUAGE: English (official), Pidgin.

RELIGION: Protestant 76%; Roman Catholic 19%; cargo cultist.

TOURIST INFORMATION: Passport but no visa required by Australian citizens. A Visitor's Permit is required but can be obtained only upon arrival. Malaria prophylaxis is recommended. There is a departure tax of SI$5. National airline: Solair.

SOMALIA

Jamhuriyadda Dimugradiga Somaliya
SOMALI DEMOCRATIC REPUBLIC

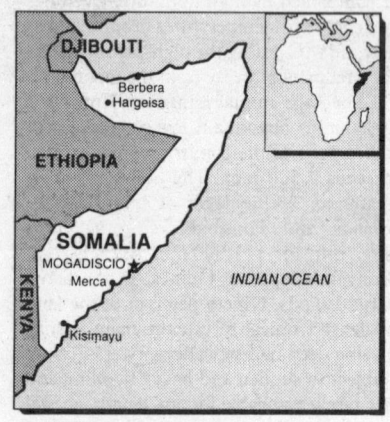

CAPITAL: Mogadiscio

AREA AND POPULATION: 637,657 km^2, 2% cultivated land. Population: 7,825,000 (1986 est.). Population density: 9.7/km^2. Population growth (1985): 3%. Ethnic composition: Hamitic 95%; Bantu 1.6%; Arab, Italian, British, Indian and Pakistani minorities. Over 40% of the population is nomadic.

CLIMATE AND GEOGRAPHY: The climate is hot, though pleasant on high ground and along the coast during June to September. Average rainfall (Mogadiscio): 429 mm. Average temperature (Mogadiscio): 25.8°C. Somalia is situated in the extreme north-eastern corner of the 'Horn' of Africa, jutting out into the Indian Ocean and facing Arabia. To the north-west, it is bounded by Djibouti and to the west and south by Ethiopia and Kenya. The dominant features of the topography are the dry savanna plains, with a high mountain escarpment in the north, facing the coast.

CURRENCY: Somali Shilling of 100 cents.

DEFENCE: Military service is by selective conscription for a period of 2 years. Total armed forces (1987): 42,700. Army 40,000; Navy 700; Air Force 2,000. Para-military forces: people's militia 20,000; police 8,000; border guards 1,500.

GOVERNMENT: Socialist republic. The Government is composed of the Politburo and Central Committee of the Somali Revolutionary Socialist Party, and the Council of Ministers. The People's Assembly is the legislative body and consists of 171 elected deputies and 6 presidential nominees. The normal duration of the Assembly is 6 years. Head of State: President Major-General Mohammed Siyad Barre. Foreign Minister: Dr Abdurrahman Jama Barre.

LANGUAGE: Somali (in Roman script) and Arabic (both official), Italian, English.

RELIGION: Sunni Moslem 99%; Roman Catholic 2,300.

TOURIST INFORMATION: Passport and visa required by Australian citizens. The possibility of travel is severely limited due to poor access, a lack of transport, and continuing security problems in most parts of the country. Vaccination against smallpox, cholera and yellow fever is required and malaria prophylaxis and precautions against viral hepatitis are advisable. Medical facilities are very poor. There is no public transport. There is a departure tax of 150 shillings. National airline: Somali Airlines. Mogadiscio airport is located 6 km from the city.

SOUTH AFRICA

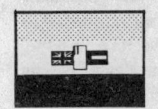

REPUBLIEK VAN SUID-AFRIKA
REPUBLIC OF SOUTH AFRICA

CAPITAL: Pretoria

AREA AND POPULATION:
1,123,226 km² (without the 'independent' Homelands of Transkei, Bophuthatswana, Ciskei, Venda and Kwa Ndebele), 12% cultivated land. Population: 23,241,000 (1986 est.). Population density: 25.1/km². Population growth (1985): 2.3%. Ethnic composition: black (mostly Bantu) 68%; white (mostly European) 18.2%; mixed race ('coloureds') 10.5%; Asian 3.2%.

CLIMATE AND GEOGRAPHY: The south-western corner of the country, including Cape Town, has a Mediterranean climate, with winter rainfall. In the north-east (Natal), the climate is sub-tropical. Elsewhere, including the highveld, it is temperate. Average temperature (Pretoria): 21.1°C (January), 11.1°C (July). Average annual rainfall (Pretoria): 785 mm. The RSA is bordered to the north by Namibia, Botswana, Zimbabwe, Mozambique and Swaziland and completely surrounds Lesotho. Around the southern and eastern coasts is a narrow mountain belt with an average height above sea level of 150-180 m. From this chain an inland plateau (highveld) extends westwards, ranging from 1,200 to 1,800 m in height and sloping down to the west coast.

CURRENCY: Rand (R) of 100 cents.

DEFENCE: Military service is compulsory for 2 years for every white male citizen aged between 18 and 65. Total armed forces (1986/87): 106,400. Army 75,050; Navy 7,650; Air Force 13,000; South West Africa Territory Force 21,000. Para-military forces: commandos 130,000; police 35,500; police reserves 20,000; coastguard—being formed.

GOVERNMENT: Federal republic. The 3-chamber Parliament consists of the House of Assembly with 178 members elected by white voters; the House of Representatives with 85 members elected by coloured voters; and the House of Delegates with 45 members elected by Indian voters. These Houses choose respectively 50 white, 25 coloured and 13 Indian members of an electoral college which elects the President. Each House discusses separately legislation on the affairs of its own community. Head of State and Prime Minister: President Pieter Willem Botha. Foreign Minister: Dr Roelof Frederic (Pik) Botha.

LANGUAGE: Afrikaans and English (both official), Bantu languages.

NATIONAL ANTHEM: Die Stem van Suid Afrika (The Call of South Africa).

RELIGION: Whites: 1,693,640 Dutch Reformed Church, 456,020 Anglican, 414,080 Methodist, 393,640 Roman Catholic, 119,220 Jewish. Blacks: 11,554,280 Methodist, 4,954,000 black independent churches, 1,103,560 Dutch Reformed Church, 1,676,680 Roman Catholic, 797,040 Anglican. Coloureds and Asians: 678,380 Dutch Reformed Church, 512,360 Hindu, 360,380 Anglican, 318,000 Moslem, 285,980 Roman Catholic.

TOURIST INFORMATION: Passport and visa required by Australian citizens. If a visitor applies for and obtains a multiple re-entry visa, it will simplify re-entering South Africa after visiting an adjoining country such as Swaziland. Health standards in South Africa are high, however bilharzia and malaria persist. Bilharzia, a debilitating abdominal disease, may be contracted from contact with water in rivers and lakes, particularly in Natal and the Transvaal. Malaria is endemic in the lowveld (the eastern coastal plain) in which is located the Kruger National Park. Milk obtained in rural areas is often not pasteurised. National airline: South African Airways. Johannesburg-Jan Smuts airport is located 30 km from the city.

SPAIN

España

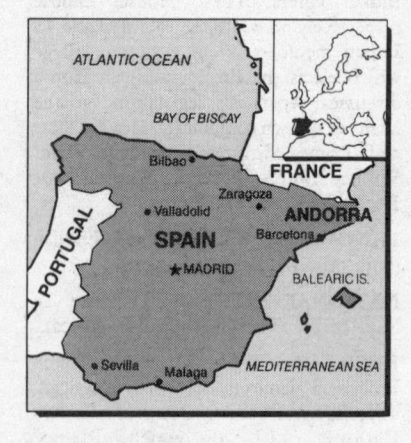

CAPITAL: Madrid

AREA AND POPULATION: 504,750 km^2, 41% cultivated land. Population: 38,829,000 (1985 est.). Population density: 76.8/km^2. Population growth (1986): 1.3%. Ethnic composition: Castilian Spanish 73%; Catalan 16%; Basque 2.4%; Gipsy minority. Some 3,000,000 Spaniards live abroad.

CLIMATE AND GEOGRAPHY: Most of the country has a Mediterranean climate, with mild moist winters and hot dry summers. The northern coastal region has a moist climate, with rainfall well-distributed throughout the year, mild winters and warm summers. Average temperature (Madrid): 5°C (January), 25°C (July). Average annual rainfall: 419 mm. Spain is situated in western Europe, bounded to the north by the Bay of Biscay and the Pyrenees (which form the border with France and Andorra), to the south and east by the Mediterranean and the Straits of Gibraltar, and to the west by Portugal and the Atlantic Ocean. The north is mountainous and covered by lush vegetation. The south has lowlands, and the interior is a high plateau broken by mountain ranges and river valleys. Island territories: Canary Islands; Balearic Islands. Overseas territories: Alhucemas, Ceuta, Chafarinas, Melilla, Peñon de Velez.

CURRENCY: Peseta (Pta) of 100 centimos.

DEFENCE: Military service is compulsory for a period of 12 months. Total armed forces (1987): 417,700 (to be reduced between 1986 and 1990). Army 230,000 (to be reduced); Navy 64,700; Air Force 33,000 (to be reduced). Para-military forces: *Guardia Civil* 63,500; *Policia Nacional* 47,000; maritime surveillance force.

GOVERNMENT: Constitutional monarchy. The bicameral Parliament (Cortes) consists of the Congress of Deputies (350 members) and the Senate (250 members). Senators and Deputies are elected by universal, but not compulsory, adult suffrage for a 4-year term. Head of State: King Juan Carlos I de Borbón y Borbón. President of the Government (Prime Minister): Felipe González Márquez. Foreign Minister: Francisco Fernandez Ordoñez.

LANGUAGE: Castilian Spanish (official), Catalan, Galician, Basque.

RELIGION: Almost exclusively Roman Catholic; Protestant 32,000; Jewish 13,000; Moslem 1,000.

TOURIST INFORMATION: Passport but no visa required by Australian citizens staying up to 1 month. No vaccinations are required. National airline: Iberia.

SRI LANKA

Sri Lanka Prajatantrika Samajawadi Janarajaya
DEMOCRATIC SOCIALIST REPUBLIC OF SRI LANKA

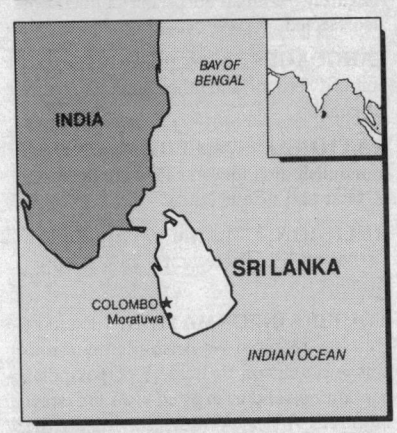

CAPITAL: Colombo

AREA AND POPULATION: 65,610 km^2, 34% cultivated land. Population: 16,638,000 (1986 est.). Population density: 244.8/km^2. Population growth (1985): 2.1%. Ethnic composition: Sinhalese 74%; Sri Lankan Tamil 12.6%; Indian Tamil 5.6%; Moors 7.12%; Burgher (mixed Sri Lankan and European); Malay.

CLIMATE AND GEOGRAPHY: The climate is tropical throughout the year, with low annual temperature variations. It is affected by the north-east monsoon (December to February) and the south-west monsoon (May to September). Average temperature (Colombo): 26°C (January), 27°C (July). Average annual rainfall: 2,527 mm. Sri Lanka is a pear-shaped island about 19 km south-east of the southern extremity of India, from which it is separated by a strip of shallow water known as Palk Strait. The central area is hilly and mountainous, while the coast and the northern area are flat.

CURRENCY: Sri Lanka Rupee (Rs) of 100 cents.

DEFENCE: Military service is voluntary. Total armed forces (1987): 36,900 (including active reservists). Army 30,000; Navy 4,400; Air Force 2,500. Paramilitary forces: police 28,000; volunteer force 500; home guard. Opposition: Eelam National Liberation Front; People's Liberation Organisation of Tamil Eelam.

GOVERNMENT: Democratic socialist republic. The unicameral Parliament (National Assembly) of 168 members is elected by universal adult suffrage for 6 years. Head of State: President Junius Richard Jayawardene. Prime Minister: Ranasinghe Premadasa. Foreign Minister: A. C. S. Hameed.

LANGUAGE: Sinhala (official), English, Tamil.

RELIGION: Buddhist 69%; Hindu 15%; Christian 7%; Moslem 7%.

TOURIST INFORMATION: Passport but no visa required by Australian citizens, however passports must be valid for at least 2 months beyond the intended length of stay. Foreign currency, including traveller's cheques, must be declared upon arrival. Visitors may be required to deposit a sum not exceeding Rs 500 with immigration authorities. This deposit is refundable on departure, less any expenditure incurred on their behalf by the Sri Lankan Government. Malaria prophylaxis is recommended. There is a departure tax of Rs200. Tap water is not drinkable unless boiled and filtered. Medical services are cheap, reasonable and readily available. National airline: Air Lanka. Colombo airport is located 30 km from the city. Visitors should exercise caution during the current unrest.

SUDAN

Al-Jamhuryat es-Sudan
REPUBLIC OF THE SUDAN
CAPITAL: Khartoum

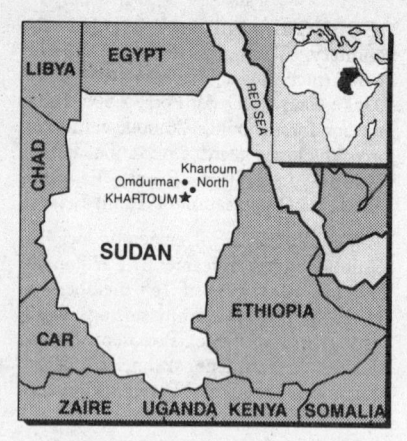

AREA AND POPULATION:
2,505,813 km², 5% cultivated land. Population: 22,932,000 (1986 est.). Population density: 9.7/km². Population growth (1985): 2.8%. Ethnic composition: Arab 40-50%; Nilo-Hamitic and Nilotic (in the south), 30%; Hamitic Nubian 10%; European; refugees from Ethiopia, Uganda, Zaîre and Chad, about 700,000.

CLIMATE AND GEOGRAPHY:
Continental climate, with only the Red Sea coast experiencing maritime influences. Temperatures are generally high throughout the year. Winters are virtually cloudless and night temperatures are consequently cool. Average temperature (Khartoum): 23.3°C (January), 31.7°C (July). Average annual rainfall: 157 mm. The Sudan is bordered to the north by Egypt and Libya, to the south by Uganda, Zaîre and Kenya, to the east by Ethiopia and the Red Sea, and to the west by Chad and the Central African Republic. The north consists of the Libyan Desert in the west and the Nubian Desert in the east. Central Sudan is fertile, with fields and forests. The south has rich soil with abundant rain.

CURRENCY:
Sudanese Pound of 100 piastres and 1,000 milliemes.

DEFENCE:
Military service is voluntary. Total armed forces (1986/87): 56,750. Army 53,000; Navy 750; Air Force 3,000. Para-military forces: border guard 2,500; National Guard 500. Opposition: Sudanese People's Liberation Movement 12,500.

GOVERNMENT:
Republic. On 6 April 1985 General Swareddahab staged a successful coup against former President Nimeiri, while the latter was on a visit to the United States. Upon assuming power, General Swareddahab dismissed the entire Presidential Council. Elections held in April 1986 resulted in the establishment of the first democratic parliament in the Sudan in 17 years, the 301-seat National Assembly. A 5-man Surpreme Council was also elected.

LANGUAGE:
Arabic (official), English, Hamitic, Nilotic and other Sudanese tribal languages.

NATIONAL ANTHEM:
Nahnu djundullah djundulwatan (We are the army of God and of our land).

RELIGION:
Moslem 73%; Roman Catholic 4-5%; Protestant 0.25%; Coptic; Animist.

TOURIST INFORMATION:
Passport and visa required by Australian citizens. Entry is refused to holders of passports containing valid or expired visas for Israel or South Africa. Visitors staying in the Sudan longer than 3 days must report to the police. Vaccination against yellow fever and malaria prophylaxis are recommended. The importation of alcoholic beverages, goods of Israeli or South African origin and blank pro-forma invoices is forbidden. Foreign currencies should be declared upon arrival. The departure tax ranges from 15 to 40 pounds. National airline: Sudan Airways. Khartoum airport is located 4.5 km from the city.

SURINAME

Republiek van Suriname
REPUBLIC OF SURINAME

CAPITAL: Paramaribo

AREA AND POPULATION:
163,820 km², 1% cultivated land. Population: 381,000 (1986 est.). Population density: 2.3/km². Population growth (1985): 2.1%.

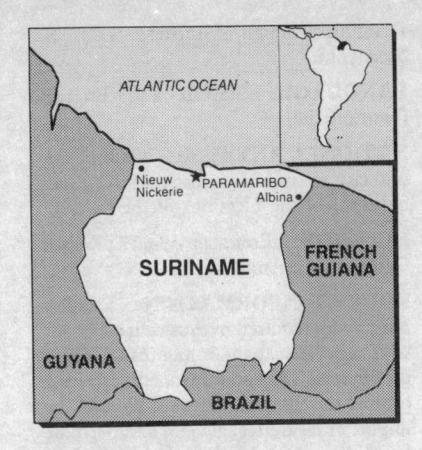

Ethnic composition: Hindustani (East Indian) 37%; Creole (African mixed) 31%; Javanese 15%; Negro 10%; Indian 3%; Chinese 2%; European 1%.

CLIMATE AND GEOGRAPHY:
Tropical, with 2 rainy seasons: April to July and December/January. The most pleasant times of the year are the brief dry season between February and April and the extremely dry months of September and October. Temperatures are high throughout the year (21–32°C), with very little seasonal change. The humidity varies between 75% and 87%. Suriname lies outside the hurricane zone and thus escapes serious wind and flood damage. The country is located in South America to the north of Brazil and between Guyana and French Guiana. The coastal plain consists of vast swamps on clay originating from the Amazon River. The rest of the country is covered with dense tropical forests, except for some small stretches of savanna and rice fields. Huge rivers, continuously fed by creeks and small streams, flow over many rapids in the hilly interior, but cross the coastal plain through large and deep estuaries, with muddy shallow bars at their mouths.

CURRENCY: Suriname Guilder (Sfl) of 100 cents.

DEFENCE: Military service is voluntary. Total armed forces (1987): 2,535 (all services form part of the Army). Army 2,350; Navy 125; Air Force 60. Paramilitary force: national militia 900.

GOVERNMENT: Following the military coup of 25 February 1980 Suriname was ruled by an 8-member National Military Council. In March 1984 a new government was appointed, consisting of representatives of the military, the labour unions and the private sector. In December 1984 a plan for a return to democracy was announced, involving the establishment of a 31-member National Assembly with the responsibility of drafting a new constitution. Elections were held in November 1987. Head of State: President Ramsewak Shankar.

LANGUAGE: Dutch and English (both official), Hindi, Javanese, Chinese, Sranan Tongo (Surinamese).

RELIGION: Christian 37%; Hindi 33%; Moslem 22%.

TOURIST INFORMATION: Passport and visa required by Australian citizens. Yellow fever vaccination and malaria prophylaxis are recommended. Non-residents arriving at Zanderij airport must exchange the equivalent of Sf500 in freely convertible currency. Those arriving via the Nieuw Nickerie or Albina border points must exchange the equivalent of Sfl 200. National airline: Suriname Airways. Paramaribo-Zanderij airport is located 45 km from the city.

SWAZILAND

Umbuso we Swatini
KINGDOM OF SWAZILAND

CAPITAL: Mbabane

AREA AND POPULATION: 17,364 km², 19% cultivated land. Population: 692,000 (1986 est.). Population density: 38.6/km². Population growth (1985): 3%. Ethnic composition: Swazi 90%; Zulu; European; other African.

CLIMATE AND GEOGRAPHY:
Temperate climate, with 2 main seasons. The rainy season extends from November to March, with temperatures ranging from

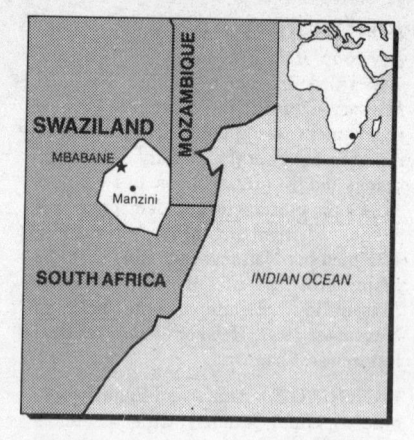

mild to hot. Thunderstorms are frequent. During the dry season, from May to September, the weather is cool, with bright sunny days. Average annual rainfall: 1,402 mm. The Kingdom is situated in south-eastern Africa, separated from the Indian Ocean by Mozambique. It is bounded to the north, west and south by South Africa. The country is divided into 4 regions: the Highveld, Middleveld, Lowveld and the Lubombo plateau, running from north to south. The Highveld rises to over 1,800 m, the Middleveld to 900 m and the Lowveld to 300 m.

CURRENCY: Lilangeni (pl. emalangeni) of 100 cents.

DEFENCE: An army of 5,000 men and an Army Air Wing with 2 aircraft are maintained.

GOVERNMENT: Monarchy, the Constitution of 1967 having been suspended by King Sobhuza II in 1973, and political parties forbidden. Until the successor to King Sobhuza II (d. 21.8.82) came of age (June 1986), executive authority rested with the Queen Regent Ntombi, who was advised by senior councillors. The Electoral College elected 40 members of the National Assembly and 10 members of the Senate, the Queen appointing another 10 to each house. The traditional Swazi National Council of Elders was even more powerful than the formal government. In September 1987 the parliament was dissolved and elections were called for November. Head of State: King Mswati III. Prime Minister: Sotja E. Dlamini. Foreign Minister: S. J. S. Sibanyoni.

LANGUAGE: SiSwati and English (both official).

NATIONAL ANTHEM: Nkulunkulu, mnikati wetibusiso temaSwati (O God, bestower of the blessings of the Swazi).

RELIGION: Protestant 55-60%; Roman Catholic 8%; Animist.

TOURIST INFORMATION: Passport but no visa required by Australian citizens who stay less than 2 months. Malaria prophylaxis is recommended. Married couples travelling together are allowed free import of cigarettes, alcohol and perfume for 1 person only. Permission to take photographs at the Incwala and Umhlanga ceremonies must first be obtained from the Government Information Service in Mbabane. National airline: Royal Swazi National Airways. Manzini-Matsapha airport is located 37 km from Mbabane.

SWEDEN

Konungariket Sverige
KINGDOM OF SWEDEN

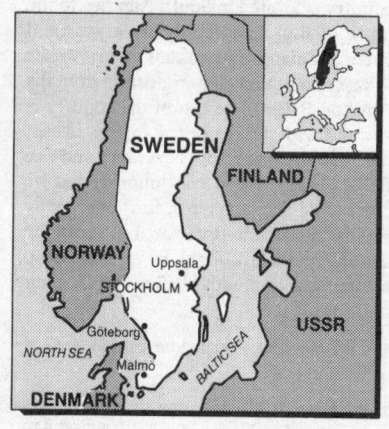

CAPITAL: Stockholm

AREA AND POPULATION: 449,964 km², 7% cultivated land. Population:

8,357,000 (1986 est.). Population density: 20/km². Population growth (1985): 0%. Ethnic composition: almost exclusively Swedish (of Germanic origin); Finnish, Sameh (Lapps) and European minorities.

CLIMATE AND GEOGRAPHY: The warm Gulf Stream in the Atlantic makes Sweden's climate slightly milder than its northern latitude would suggest. However, it is often snow-bound in winter (November to March) and winter temperatures are well below freezing for long periods. Summer (June to August) is usually warm and dry, spring (April to May) is mild and dry, and autumn (September to October) is rainy. Average temperature (Stockholm): −4.2°C (January), 15.5°C (July). Average annual rainfall: 632 mm. Sweden occupies the eastern half of the Scandinavian peninsula. Along the coasts are archipelagos, where ancient mountain ranges lie submerged beneath the sea. There are 24,000 islands in the Stockholm archipelago. Forests, mainly of pine and birch, cover more than half of the country's land area.

CURRENCY: Swedish Krone (skr) of 100 öre.

DEFENCE: Military service is compulsory for 7 1/2 to 15 months (Army and Navy) and 8 to 15 months (Air Force). Total armed forces (1987): 64,700. Army 47,000; Navy 9,700; Air Force 8,000. Paramilitary force: coastguard 570.

GOVERNMENT: Parliamentary democratic hereditary monarchy. The unicameral Parliament (Riksdag) of 349 members is elected for a 3-year term by proportional representation. The ministers who constitute the Government are usually, although not always, drawn from the Riksdag. Head of State: King Carl XVI Gustaf. Prime Minister: Ingvar Carlsson. Foreign Minister: Lena Hjelm-Wallen.

LANGUAGE: Swedish.

NATIONAL ANTHEM: Du gamla, du fria, du fjallhoga nord (You ancient, you beautiful, you mountainous north).

RELIGION: Almost exclusively Evangelical Lutheran; Roman Catholic 118,646; Jewish 13,000.

TOURIST INFORMATION: Passport but no visa required by Australian citizens. National airline: Scandinavian Airlines System (SAS).

SWITZERLAND

Schweiz/Suisse/Svizzera/Svizzra
Confoederatio Helvetica
SWISS CONFEDERATION

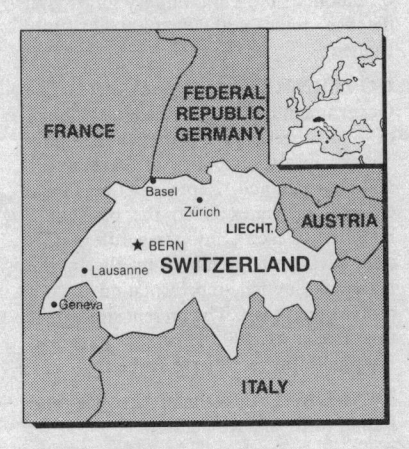

CAPITAL: Bern

AREA AND POPULATION: 41,293 km², 10% cultivated land. Population: 6,466,000 (1986 est.). Population density: 158.7/km². Population growth (1985): 0.2%. Ethnic composition: mixed European – predominantly French, German and Italian.

CLIMATE AND GEOGRAPHY: The climate is affected by relief and altitude, ranging from continental to mountainous. Winters are long and summers short. Summers can be quite hot and humid but extreme temperatures are rarely reached. Winters are usually fine, clear and cold. Average temperature (Bern): 0°C (January), 18.5°C (July). Switzerland is a small country located in the centre of Europe, bordered by France, Germany, Austria, Italy and Liechtenstein. No part of Switzerland is less than 200 m above sea level and many of its mountains are over 4,000 m. About three-fifths of the area is taken up by the Alpine region, stretching right across the country and reaching its summit in Monte Rosa.

CURRENCY: Swiss Franc (sfr) of 100 Rappen.

DEFENCE: Military service is compulsory, consisting of 17 weeks recruit training followed by varying periods of reservist refresher training. Total armed forces (1987): about 1,500 regulars and 18,500 recruits. Army war establishment: 580,000 on mobilisation. Air Force: 45,000 on mobilisation. Para-military force: civil defence force 480,000 (300,000 fully trained).

GOVERNMENT: Federal State. The Government comprises a Federal Council of 7 members and a National Assembly divided into the Council of States and a National Council. Representation in the Council of States is on the basis of 2 members to each Canton, regardless of its size, giving 46 members in all. In the National Council, representation is on a proportional basis. The present strength of this House is 200. Head of State and Foreign Minister: Pierre Aubert.

LANGUAGE: German, French and Italian (official), Romantsch.

NATIONAL ANTHEM: Trittst im Morgenrot daher (A walk in the morning light).

RELIGION: Roman Catholic 49%; Protestant 48%; Jewish; Old Catholic.

TOURIST INFORMATION: Passport but no visa required by Australian citizens. National airline: Swissair. Basel-Mulhouse airport is located on French territory and arriving passengers have the choice of entering France or Switzerland.

SYRIA

Al-Jamhouriya al-Arabiya as-Souriya
SYRIAN ARAB REPUBLIC

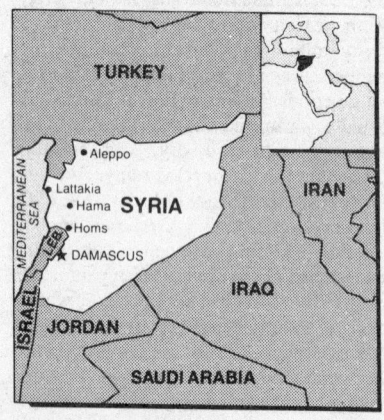

CAPITAL: Damascus

AREA AND POPULATION: 185,180 km^2, 48% cultivated land. Population: 10,931,000 (1986 est.). Population density: 57.1/km^2. Population growth (1985): 3.8%. Ethnic composition: Arab 90%; Kurd, Turk, Armenian, Assyrian and Circassian minorities.

CLIMATE AND GEOGRAPHY:
There are 4 distinct seasons: winter (December to March) is cold and wet; spring (April to May) is mild but can be spoilt by strong, dust-bearing winds and showers; summer (June to September) is hot; and autumn (October to November) is clear and warm during the day, with cool nights. Average temperature (Damascus): 7°C (January), 27°C (July). Syria is situated at the eastern end of the Mediterranean Sea, bordered to the north by Turkey, to the south by Israel and Jordan, to the east by Iraq and to the west by the Mediterranean Sea and Lebanon. The west of the country consists of a narrow coastal plain backed by mountain and hill country. Eastward the land gradually becomes steppe country, broken occasionally by low residual mountain ranges.

CURRENCY: Syrian Pound of 100 piastres.

DEFENCE: Military service is compulsory for a period of 30 months. Total armed forces (1987): 392,500. Army 320,000; Navy 2,500; Air Force 70,000. Para-military forces: gendarmerie 8,000; Palestine Liberation Army 4,500; frontier force 1,800; Ba'ath Party Workers' Militia.

GOVERNMENT: Presidential republic. Power is concentrated in the hands of the President (President Assad) and a number of associates, most of whom are simultaneously members of the Executive, the Ba'ath Party and the military. Under the Constitution of 1973, which dictates that the President must be a Moslem, there is an Executive-President, elected for a 6-year term, and a unicameral People's Council which may pass legislation, subject to presidential ratification. There is also a Council of Ministers headed by a Prime Minister, an independent judiciary and a French-style civil service. Prime Minister: Dr Abdul Rauf al-Kasm. Foreign Minister: Abdul Halim Khaddam.

LANGUAGE: Arabic.

RELIGION: Sunni, Shiite and Ismaili Moslem, over 85%; Alawite 7%; Druze 2%; Christian 600,000; Jewish 4,000.

TOURIST INFORMATION: Passport and visa required by Australian citizens. Visas may be obtained upon arrival at airport or border. There are no serious health problems except in summer, when cholera outbreaks often occur in the north. Malaria prophylaxis is recommended. Visitors intending to stay in Syria more than 15 days must report to the 'Direction de l'immigration des passeports et de la nationalité' within 15 days. Journalists must report to the Ministry of Information within 24 hours of arrival. All visitors must exchange US$100 or eqivalent in hard currency into Syrian Pounds upon arrival. There is a departure tax of 10 pounds for destinations outside the Arab League. National airline: Syrian Arab Airlines. Damascus airport is located 30 km from the city.

TAIWAN

Ta Chung-Hwa Min-Kwo
REPUBLIC OF CHINA

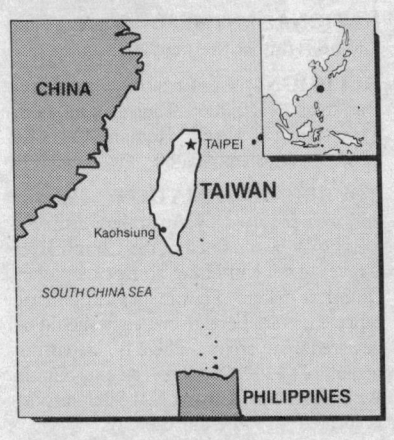

CAPITAL: Taipei

AREA AND POPULATION: 36,188 km^2, 25% cultivated land. Population: 19,601,000 (1986 est.). Population density: 539/km^2. Population growth (1985): 1.4%. Ethnic composition: Primarily mainland Han Chinese; Malayo-Polynesian aboriginals, 200,000.

CLIMATE AND GEOGRAPHY: Sub-tropical climate, with cool winters and hot humid summers. Taiwan is an island situated between the East and South China seas, about 160 km from the coast of Fujian province, mainland China. The country is mountainous, with a central chain running from north to south. The west is flat and fertile; the east is steep and craggy.

CURRENCY: New Taiwanese Dollar (NT$) of 100 cents.

DEFENCE: Military service is compulsory for 2 years. Total armed forces (1987): 424,000. Army 270,000; Navy 38,000; Air Force 77,000. Para-military forces: Taiwan Garrison Command 25,000; Customs Service.

GOVERNMENT: Republic, controlled by former members of the Nationalist

Chinese Government. The National Assembly of 976 members operates through 5 yuans (councils), elected by universal suffrage. Head of State: President Lee Teng-hui. Prime Minister: Yu Kuo-hua. Foreign Minister: Chu Fu-sung.

LANGUAGE: Chinese (Mandarin) (official), Taiwan and Hakka dialects.

NATIONAL ANTHEM: San Min Chu I (The rights of the people).

RELIGION: Confucianist majority; Buddhist 7,500,000; Taoist 3,300,000; Protestant 400,000; Roman Catholic 278,000; Moslem 42,000.

TOURIST INFORMATION: Passport and visa required by Australian citizens. Visas may be obtained at the Chung Hwa Travel Service in Hong Kong or in other countries where Taiwan has diplomatic representation. Foreign currency should be declared upon arrival. There is a departure tax of NT$300. National airline: China Airlines. Taipei-Chiang Kai Shek airport is located 40 km from the city.

TANZANIA

Jamhuriya Mwungano wa Tanzania.
UNITED REPUBLIC OF TANZANIA

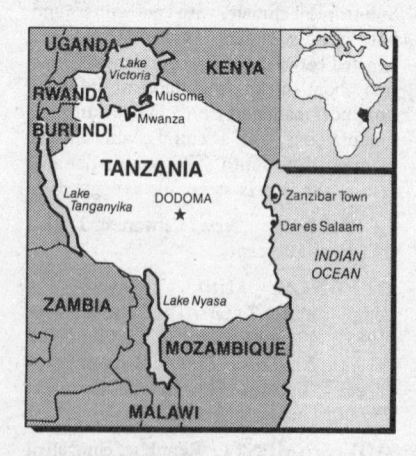

CAPITAL: Dodoma

AREA AND POPULATION: 945,050 km^2, 15% cultivated land. Population: 21,415,000 (1986 est.). Population density: 24.3/km^2. Population growth (1985): 3.4%. Ethnic composition: Predominantly Bantu—over 120 different tribes.

CLIMATE AND GEOGRAPHY: The climate varies with altitude. It is hot and humid in coastal areas, drier on the central plateau and semi-temperate in the mountains. Average temperature (Dodoma): 23.9°C (January), 19.4°C (July). Average annual rainfall: 572 mm. Tanzania is bordered to the north by Lake Victoria and Uganda, to the north-east by Kenya, to the north-west by Rwanda and Burundi, to the south by Mozambique, south-west by Zambia and Malawi, and to the west by Lake Tanganyika. The coastal plains have lush, tropical vegetation; the southern area of the country is a high plateau; and the north is the Masai Steppe (213 m—1,067 m).

CURRENCY: Tanzanian Shilling (Sh) of 100 senti.

DEFENCE: Military service is compulsory for 2 years. Total armed forces (1987): 40,200. Army 38,500; Navy 700; Air Force 1,000. Para-military forces: citizen's militia 100,000; police field force 1,400; police marine unit 100.

GOVERNMENT: Presidential republic. The President is the Executive Head of State, subject to election by universal suffrage. He is also chief of the armed forces and president of Tanzania's sole political party, the Chama Cha Mapinduzi (CCM), (Revolutionary Party). The legislative powers for the mainland are vested in the National Assembly. Internal matters in Zanzibar are within the exclusive jurisdiction of the Zanzibar Executive and the Revolutionary Council of Zanzibar. Members of Parliament are elected for 5 years. Head of State: President Ndugu Ali Hassan Mwinyi. Prime Minister: Joseph Warioba. Foreign Minister: Benjamin Mkapa.

LANGUAGE: Swahili and English (both official), Bantu languages.

NATIONAL ANTHEM: Mungu ibiriki Africa (God bless Africa).

RELIGION: Moslem 35%; Roman Catholic 20%; Protestant 10%; Hindu; Animist.

TOURIST INFORMATION: Passport but no visa required by Australian citizens. All visitors are required to obtain a Visitor's Pass on arrival and there is a compulsory currency exchange of US$50. Typhoid and paratyphoid fever and yellow fever inoculations are required. Malaria prophylaxis is recommended. Medical and dental facilities, except for minor ailments, are inadequate locally. There is a departure tax of US$10. National airline: Air Tanzania. Dar es Salaam airport is located 13 km from the city.

THAILAND

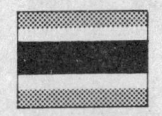

Prates Thai
KINGDOM OF THAILAND

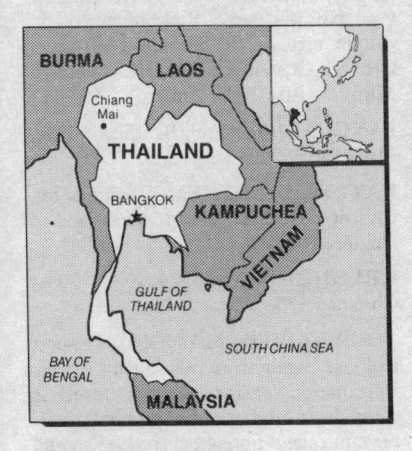

CAPITAL: Bangkok

AREA AND POPULATION: 513,115 km², 24% cultivated land. Population: 52,438,000 (1986 est.). Population density: 102.3/km². Population growth (1985): 2.4%. Ethnic composition: Thai 85%; Chinese 14%; Malay 3%; Indo-Chinese refugees, about 300,000.

CLIMATE AND GEOGRAPHY: Tropical climate, hot and humid. There are 3 seasons: rainy (June to October), cool (November to February) and hot (March to May). Average temperature (Bangkok): 25.6°C (January), 28.3°C (July). Average annual rainfall: 1,400 mm. Thailand is bordered to the north by Burma and Laos, to the south by Malaysia, to the east by Laos and Cambodia and to the west by Burma. There are 4 natural geographic zones: the northern mountains, which are an extension of the Himalayas; the rich alluvial central plains; the high plateau country to the east; and the alternatively hilly and flat peninsular area to the south.

CURRENCY: Baht (B) of 100 satangs.

DEFENCE: Military service is compulsory for 2 years. Total armed forces (1987): 246,200. Army 166,000; Navy 32,200; Air Force 48,000. Para-military forces: volunteer defence corps 33,000; border patrol police 20,000; rangers 13,000; special action force 3,800; marine police 1,700; police aviation force 500; village scouts; National Defence Volunteers. Opposition: Communist Party of Malaya 1,500; Communist Party of Thailand 500; Thai People's Revolutionary Movement 250.

GOVERNMENT: Constitutional monarchy. The Parliament comprises an elected House of Representatives (347 members) and an appointed Senate (244 members). The Prime Minister is appointed by the King on the advice of the Parliament. Head of State: King Bhumibol Adulyadej. Prime Minister: General Prem Tinsulanonda. Foreign Minister: Air Chief Marshall Siddhi Savetsila.

LANGUAGE: Thai (official), English, Jawi.

RELIGION: Theravada Buddhist 95%; Moslem 4%; Christian 0.6%.

TOURIST INFORMATION: Passport and visa required by Australian citizens. The government of Thailand may refuse entry to visitors of 'hippy' appearance, with long, untidy and dirty-looking hair, dressed in an 'offensive' manner, e.g. only singlet or waistcoat, shorts or silk pants, with slippers or rubber/wooden sandals, unless these form part of a national costume.

Vaccination against cholera and malaria prophylaxis are recommended. Gastro-intestinal diseases and heat rashes are the main discomforts experienced. Care should be exercised with dogs as rabies is common and is also transmitted by mammals such as cats and gibbons. Medical and dental standards are high in Bangkok. There is a departure tax of B150. National airline: Thai International. Bangkok-Don Muang airport is located 25 km from the city.

TOGO

République Togolaise
REPUBLIC OF TOGO

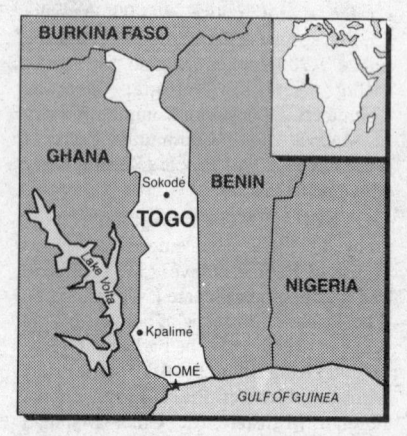

CAPITAL: Lomé

AREA AND POPULATION: 56,785 km², 26% cultivated land. Population: 3,118,000 (1988 est.). Population density: 54.1/km². Population growth (1985): 3.1%. Ethnic composition: Ewe 47%; some 40 other tribal groups; European (mostly French) minority.

CLIMATE AND GEOGRAPHY: The climate is sub-equatorial in the south, with a long dry season from mid-November to March, a major rainy season from April to July and a short rainy season from October to mid-November. In the north, the climate is of the Sudanese type, with a rainy season from April to October and a dry season from November to March. Average temperature (Lome): 27.2°C (January), 24.4°C (July). Average annual rainfall: 875 mm. Togo is located on the southern coast of West Africa, facing the Gulf of Guinea. It is bordered to the north by Burkina Faso, to the east by Benin and to the west by Ghana. In the south, a sandy coastal strip leads to a clay-based region varying in altitude from 60 m to 200 m. This in turn gives way to the rocky basin of the Mono River. In the north-west, a dry savanna stretches to the frontier of Burkina Faso.

CURRENCY: Franc CFA of 100 centimes.

DEFENCE: Military service is by selective conscription for a period of 2 years. Total armed forces (1987): 4,365 (all services form part of the Army). Army 4,000; Navy 105; Air Force 260. Para-military forces: Presidential Guard 800; gendarmerie 750.

GOVERNMENT: Presidential republic. The unicameral Parliament (National Assembly) of 77 Deputies is elected by universal suffrage for a 5-year term. Sole legal political party: Rassemblement du peuple togolais (RPT). Head of State: General Gnassingbe Eyadema. Foreign Minister: Atsu-Koffi Amega.

LANGUAGES: French (official), Ewe, Mina and Voltaic languages.

NATIONAL ANTHEM: Salut a toi, pays de nos aieux! (Hail to thee, land of our forefathers!).

RELIGION: Animist, over 50%; Christian 37%; Moslem 7%.

TOURIST INFORMATION: Passport and visa required by Australian citizens. Vaccination against yellow fever is compulsory and malaria prophylaxis is recommended. Foreign currencies should be declared upon arrival. A refundable deposit which is the equivalent of the return air fare must be paid on arrival. National airline: Air Togo. Lomé airport is located 9 km from the city.

TONGA

KINGDOM OF TONGA

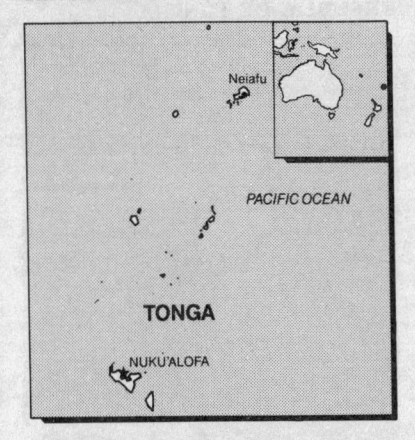

CAPITAL: Nuku'alofa

AREA AND POPULATION: 748 km², 77% cultivated land. Population: 104,000 (1986 est.). Population density: 136.3/km². Population growth (1985): −0.2%. Ethnic composition: Polynesian 99%; European.

CLIMATE AND GEOGRAPHY: The climate varies from hot and humid in the north to cool and dry in the south. The Niuatoputapu group of islands has an average rainfall of 2,500 mm and Vava'u 2,750 mm, while Tongatapu and Ha'apai each have 1,500 mm. The average temperature ranges from 23.5°C on Vava'u to 21°C on Tongatapu. The average humidity is about 77%. Hurricanes occur from time to time, but are more frequent in the northern islands. The Kingdom is a group of about 150 volcanic and coral islands (36 inhabited), located in the Pacific Ocean between the Fiji and Cook Islands.

CURRENCY: Pa'anga (T$) of 100 seniti.

DEFENCE: Total armed forces (1984): about 208. Army 158; Navy 50.

GOVERNMENT: Constitutional monarchy. The Legislative Assembly is composed of 9 nobles, 9 elected representatives and 8 Privy Councillors. Elections are held every 3 years. There is universal suffrage. Head of State: King Taufu'ahau Tupou IV. Prime Minister: Prince Fatafehi Tu'ipelehake. Foreign Minister: Prince Tupouto'a.

LANGUAGE: Tongan (official), English

RELIGION: Methodist 77%; Roman Catholic 14%.

TOURIST INFORMATION: Passport but no visa required by Australian citizens. An onward or return ticket is required. Tonga is served by 5 overseas airlines: Air Pacific, Polynesian Airlines, Air New Zealand, Air Nauru and South Pacific Island Airways. Fua'amotu International Airport is situated on Tongatapu. There is a departure tax of T$5.

TRINIDAD AND TOBAGO

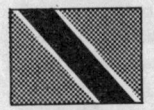

REPUBLIC OF TRINIDAD AND TOBAGO

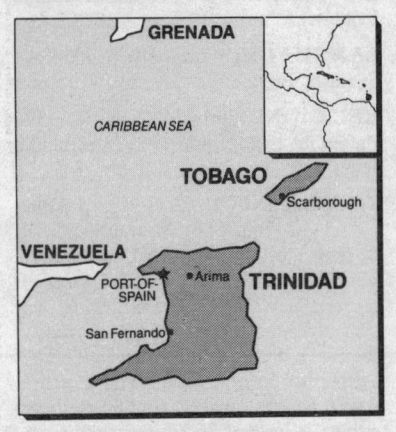

CAPITAL: Port-of-Spain

AREA AND POPULATION: 5,128 km², 30% cultivated land. Population: 1,204,000 (1986 est.). Population density:

234.4/km². Population growth (1985): 2%. Ethnic composition: Negro 41%; East Indian 40%; Mulatto 14%; European 2%; Chinese 1%.

CLIMATE AND GEOGRAPHY: The climate is tropical, with a dry season from January to June and a wet season for the remainder of the year. Average temperature (Port-of-Spain): 26°C. Average annual rainfall: 1,631 mm. Most southerly of the West Indian islands, those of the republic are situated about 32 km off the coast of Venezuela. The Northern Range of mountains runs along the north of Trinidad. The west coast is low and central Trinidad is flat and fertile. Tobago has magnificent tropical flora and fauna.

CURRENCY: Trinidad and Tobago Dollar (TT$) of 100 cents.

DEFENCE: Military service is voluntary. Total armed forces (1987): 2,130 (all services form part of the Army). Army 1,500; Navy (coastguard) 590; Air Force 50. Para-military force: police 400.

GOVERNMENT: Presidential republic. The bicameral legislature consists of a Senate of 31 members and a House of Representatives of 36 members (34 for Trinidad and 2 for Tobago). Tobago has internal autonomy. Head of State: President Noor Hassanali. Prime Minister: A. N. Robinson. Foreign Minister: Basdeo Panday.

LANGUAGE: English (official), Spanish, French.

RELIGION: Roman Catholic 33%; Protestant 15%; Hindu 24%; Moslem 6%; Jewish 300.

TOURIST INFORMATION: Passport but no visa required by Australian citizens. A return or onward ticket is required. Vaccination against yellow fever is recommended for visitors venturing away from the main cities. Foreign currencies should be declared upon arrival. There is a departure tax of TT$20. National airline: BWIA International. Port-of-Spain-Piarco airport is located 25 km from the city.

TUNISIA

Al-Djoumhouria Attunusia
REPUBLIC OF TUNISIA

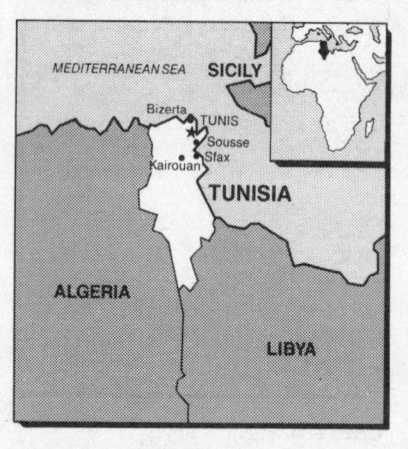

CAPITAL: Tunis

AREA AND POPULATION: 154,530 km², 32% cultivated land. Population: 7,424,000 (1986 est.). Population density: 47.1/km². Population growth (1985): 2.4%. Ethnic composition: Arab 98%; French, Italian and Maltese minorities.

CLIMATE AND GEOGRAPHY: The climate is warm temperate in the north, with mild wet winters and hot dry summers. The south is desert. Average temperature (Tunis): 8.9°C (January), 25.6°C (July). Average annual rainfall: 400 mm. Tunisia is situated on the north coast of Africa, bordered to the north and east by the Mediterranean Sea, to the south by Libya and to the west by Algeria. The coastline is dotted with small islands. The central coastal plains are grassy; the north is wooded and fertile; and the south is arid.

CURRENCY: Dinar of 1,000 millimes.

DEFENCE: Military service is by selective conscription for a period of 12 months. Total armed forces (1987): 36,100. Army 30,000; Navy 2,600; Air Force 3,500. Para-military forces: National Guard 7,000; gendarmerie 3,300.

GOVERNMENT: Presidential republic. The unicameral Parliament consists of the National Assembly of 125 seats. The President and the members of the National Assembly are elected by direct universal suffrage for a period of 5 years. The President cannot be re-elected more than 3 times but a proclamation of the National Assembly on 18 March 1975 declared President Bourgiba 'President for Life'. Head of State: President Habib Ben Ali Bourgiba. Prime Minister: Rachid Sfar. Foreign Minister: Beji Caied Essebsi.

LANGUAGE: Arabic (official), French.

RELIGION: Sunni Moslem 99%; Roman Catholic 20,000; Jewish 9,000; small Protestant minority.

TOURIST INFORMATION: Passport and visa required by Australian citizens. All alien non-residents must be in possession of return or onward tickets. A departure tax of 45 dinars is payable at airline offices, travel agencies or banking offices. Re-exchange of local into foreign currency upon departure is possible up to 30% of the total amount imported and exchanged (max. 100 dinars), upon presentation of bank exchange receipts. Valuable articles should be declared upon arrival to ensure re-export. National airline: Tunis Air. Tunis-Carthage airport is located 8 km from the city.

TURKEY

Türkiye Cumhuriyeti
REPUBLIC OF TURKEY

CAPITAL: Ankara

AREA AND POPULATION: 779,452 km², 34% cultivated land. Population: 51,819,000 (1986 est.). Population density: 60/km². Population growth (1985): 2.4%. Ethnic composition: Turkish 85%; Kurdish 12%; Circassian; Greek; Armenian; Georgian; Laze.

CLIMATE AND GEOGRAPHY: The climate is generally temperate but with marked variations within the country. The coastal region in the south and south-west has a Mediterranean climate, with hot dry summers and mild wet winters. The average temperature in January is 10°C and in July, 28°C. The Black Sea has a sultry summer and a cool winter. In central Anatolia summers are hot and winters cold, with frequent snowfalls. South-eastern Anatolia experiences hot dry summers and less severe winters. Turkey is bounded to the north by Bulgaria and the Black Sea, to the south by Iraq, Syria and the Mediterranean, to the east by the USSR and Iran, and to the west by the Aegean Sea and Greece. Two east-west mountain ranges enclose the Central Anatolian Plateau, but join up in a vast mountainous region in the far east of the country. Fertile coastal plains characterise the south and west.

CURRENCY: Turkish Lira (TL) of 100 kurus.

DEFENCE: Military service is compulsory for 18 months. Total armed forces (1987): 653,275. Army 542,000; Navy 53,900; Air Force 57,375. Paramilitary forces: gendarmerie 125,000; coastguard 1,000.

GOVERNMENT: Republic. Parliament (Turkish Grand National Assembly) was dissolved in 1980 and its functions and powers taken over by the National Security Council (NSC). From 1981 until 6 November 1983, when elections were again held, a Consultative Assembly acted as the lower house and the NSC as the upper house. Head of State: President Kenan Evren. Prime Minister: Turgut Özal. Foreign Minister: Vahit Halefoğlu.

LANGUAGE: Turkish.

NATIONAL ANTHEM: Korkma! Sonmez bu safaklarda yuzen al sancak (Fear not! Be not dismayed).

RELIGION: Sunni Moslem 98%; Christian 160,000; Jewish 38,000.

TOURIST INFORMATION: Passport but no visa required by Australian citizens provided the duration of stay does not exceed 3 months. Malaria prophylaxis is recommended. Foreign currencies should be specified in travellers' passports upon arrival in order to avoid difficulties on departure. National airline: Turkish Airlines. Istanbul-Yesilkoy airport is located 24 km from the city.

TUVALU

(Tuvalu = eight standing together)

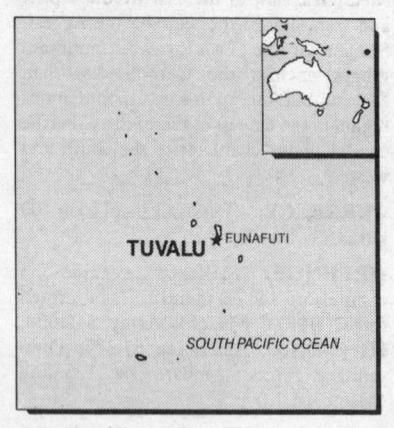

CAPITAL: Funafuti

AREA AND POPULATION: 24.6 km². Population: 8,580 (1986 est.). Population density: 342/km². Population growth (1985): 6.1%. Ethnic composition: Polynesians 96%; Melanesians.

CLIMATE AND GEOGRAPHY: The climate is tropical, with no marked wet and dry or hot and cold periods, the heat being moderated by north-easterly Trade Winds from March to October. Average temperature: 29°C. Average annual rainfall: 3,500 mm. Tuvalu consists of 9 atolls extending 560 km north-south in the south-west Pacific. Nearest neighbours: Fiji (south), Kiribati (north), Solomon Islands (west). None of the Tuvaluan atolls is more than 5 m above sea level. Vegetation consists mainly of coconut palms.

CURRENCY: Tuvaluan coins up to T$1 are in circulation but the common unit of currency is the Australian dollar.

DEFENCE: No defence force is maintained.

GOVERNMENT: Independent constitutional monarchy. The 12-member Parliament is elected by universal suffrage for 4 years. There is a Town Council on Funafuti; the other islands each have an Island Council of 6 elected members. Tuvalu has no political parties in the European sense — they are replaced by clan groupings. Head of State: Queen Elizabeth II. Governor-General: Tupua Leupena. Prime Minister and Foreign Minister: Dr Tomasi Puapua.

LANGUAGE: Tuvaluan, a Polynesian language closely related to Samoan. The Gilbertese dialect is spoken on Nui.

NATIONAL ANTHEM: Tuvalu mo te Atua (Tuvalu for the Almighty).

RELIGION: Church of Tuvalu (Congregationalist) 97%.

TOURIST INFORMATION: Australian visitors must have a passport and possess tickets for onward travel. No visa is required. There is 1 small hotel on Funafuti. Air fares in area are amongst the highest per route mile in the world. Items such as cameras, binoculars and portable radios may be brought into Tuvalu duty-free but must be declared upon arrival. There is a departure tax of A$10. National airline: Air Tungaru.

UGANDA

REPUBLIC OF UGANDA

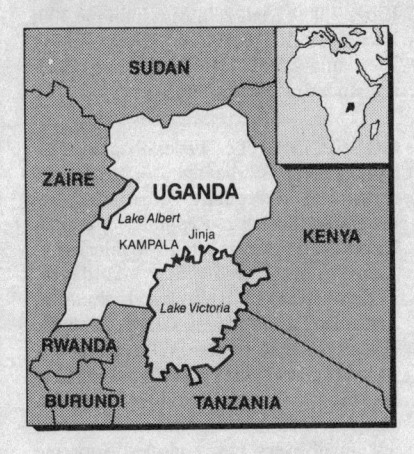

CAPITAL: Kampala

AREA AND POPULATION: 236,860 km², 29% cultivated land. Population: 15,158,000 (1986 est.). Population density: 70.6/km². Population growth (1985): 3.1%. Ethnic composition: Bugandan 20%; Nilotic 13%; Hamitic 13%; Sudanese 5%; European and Arabic minorities.

CLIMATE AND GEOGRAPHY: The temperature varies little throughout the year (18.3°C to 29°C), giving the country an equatorial climate modified by altitude. Except in the Karamoja area, rainfall is generally good and is greatest bordering Lake Victoria and in the mountains, where some areas have up to 2,000 mm per year. Uganda is situated at the Equator, on the East African Plateau, 1,000 km from the Indian Ocean. The Republic is bordered to the north by Sudan, to the south by Tanzania and Rwanda, to the east by Kenya and to the west by Zaïre.

CURRENCY: Uganda Shilling of 100 cents.

DEFENCE: Military service is voluntary. Total armed forces (1986/87): The current strength is unknown – it was 6,000. The regular forces are believed to be absorbing elements of other (irregular) groups. Opposition: The attitudes of former opposition groups – the Uganda National Rescue Front and the Uganda Freedom Movement – to the present government are unclear.

GOVERNMENT: On 28 January 1986 an offensive by the National Resistance Army, led by Yoweri Museveni, overthrew the military government of Major-General Tito Okello. The Military Council was also dissolved.

LANGUAGE: English (official), Kiswahili, Luganda.

RELIGION: Christian 62-3%; Moslem 5-10%; Animist.

TOURIST INFORMATION: Passport but no visa required for Australian citizens. Yellow fever vaccination is compulsory and malaria prophylaxis is recommended. Foreign currencies should be declared upon arrival. A departure tax of US$10 is payable upon departure at Entebbe airport. Visitors should keep the Ugandan Ministry of Foreign Affairs informed of their general whereabouts in order to avoid any security difficulties that might arise. National airline: Uganda Airlines. Dr Obote airport is located 30 km from Kampala.

UNION OF SOVIET SOCIALIST REPUBLICS

Soyuz Sovyetskikh Sotsialisticheskikh Respublik

CAPITAL: Moscow

AREA AND POPULATION: 22,274,900 km², 11% cultivated land. Population: 279,904,000 (1986 est.). Population density: 12.6/km². Population growth (1985): 0.8%. Ethnic composition (most numerous nationalities at 1979 census): Russian 52.4%; Ukrainian 16.1%; Uzbek 4.8%; Byelorussian; Kazakh; Tatar; Azerbaijanian.

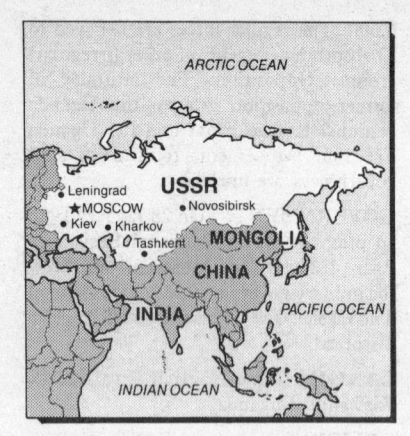

CLIMATE AND GEOGRAPHY: The USSR contains several different climatic zones, ranging from polar conditions in the north, through sub-arctic and humid continental, to sub-tropical and semi-arid in the south. Rainfall is greatest in areas bordering the Baltic Sea, Black Sea, Caspian Sea and the eastern coasts of Asiatic Russia. Average temperature (Moscow): −9.4°C (January), 18.3°C (July). Average annual rainfall (Moscow): 630 mm. The largest country in the world, the USSR extends across the northern Eurasian land mass, from the Baltic Sea to the Bering Strait. It is bordered to the west by Finland, Poland, Czechoslovakia, Hungary and Romania, and to the south by Turkey, Iran, Afghanistan, China, Mongolia, and North Korea. The country is an immense plain framed by mountains and scattered with plateaux and large water systems. Tundra covers the extreme north.

CURRENCY: Rouble of 100 kopeks.

DEFENCE: Military service is compulsory for 2 years (Army and Air Force) and 3 years (Navy and border guards). Total armed forces (1986/87): 5,130,000. Ground forces (Army): 1,991,000; Navy 500,000; Air Force 453,000. Para-military forces: KGB 230,000; MVD 340,000; part-time military training organization (DOSAAF) − claims active membership of 80,000,000 (of whom 5,000,000 are instructors and activists); Young Pioneers. **Forces abroad:** Afghanistan 118,000 (about 10,000 MVD and KGB); Mongolia 65,000; Vietnam 7,000(?). **Advisers, technicians etc:** Algeria 1,000; Angola 1,500; Congo 100; Cuba 8,000; Ethiopia 1,500; India 200; Iraq 600; Kampuchea 200; Laos 500; Libya 2,000; Mali 200; Mozambique 300; Nicaragua 50; Peru 160; Syria 4,000; Vietnam 2,500; North Yemen 500; remainder of Africa, 900.

GOVERNMENT: Federal union with a bicameral Parliament. The USSR consists of 15 republics (Russian Soviet Federated Socialist Republic, Ukraine, Uzbekistan, Kazakhstan, Byelorussia, Azerbaijan, Georgia, Moldavia, Tadzhikistan, Kirghizia, Lithuania, Armenia, Turkmenistan, Latvia, Estonia). Under the new Constitution ratified on 7 October 1977, the Council of Ministers of the USSR (the country's highest executive body) is appointed at the first session of every newly elected Supreme Soviet (about every 4 years). Appointments to the Council of Ministers, which become necessary at times when the Supreme Soviet is not in session, are made by the Presidium of the Supreme Soviet. The Council of Ministers is a collegial organ consisting of a Chairman, who is the head of Government (or Premier), First Vice-Chairman, Vice-Chairmen (57 at present), Chairmen of State Committees of the Council of Ministers, the Chairman of the Committee of the Council of Ministers, the Chairman of the Committee of People's Control, the heads of some central administrative organs and the Heads of Government of each of the Republics, who are *ex-officio* members of the USSR Government. The Communist Party, whose leading role in the Soviet state is explicitly affirmed in the Soviet Constitution, has a monopoly of political power. Chairman of the Presidium of the Supreme Soviet of the USSR: A. A. Gromyko. First Vice-Chairman: P. N. Demichev. Secretary of the Presidium: Tengiz Menteshashvili. Chairman of the Council of Ministers of the USSR: N. I. Ryzhkov. Foreign Minister: Eduard Shevardnadze.

LANGUAGE: Russian (official). School instruction is given in over 100 languages.

RELIGION: Moslem 43,000,000; Christian 40,000,000; Russian Orthodox 30,000,000; Armenian Orthodox; Jewish; Buddhist.

TOURIST INFORMATION: Passport and visa required by Australian citizens. All arrangements for private visits to the USSR, except external air travel, are made through the government tourist organisation, 'Intourist'. Intourist runs the main tourist hotels and arranges guides, rail travel, internal air travel and theatre. There is an Intourist service bureau in all the main hotels. An important feature of booking a journey to or through the Soviet Union is a requirement that all travel reservations be made and confirmed before a visa is issued by Soviet diplomatic missions. It is not possible to travel to the USSR on an 'open-date' ticket. As a rule, visitors will not know the name of the hotel in which they will be staying until they are met by Intourist representatives at the point of arrival. All holdings of foreign currency must be declared upon arrival. Photographing, filming or sketching any kind of military facility, seaports, large hydro-technical structures, railroad junctions, tunnels, railway and highway bridges, industrial enterprises, research institutes, power stations, radio towers and stations, telegraph and telephone stations, is prohibited. National airline: Aeroflot.

UNITED ARAB EMIRATES

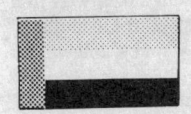

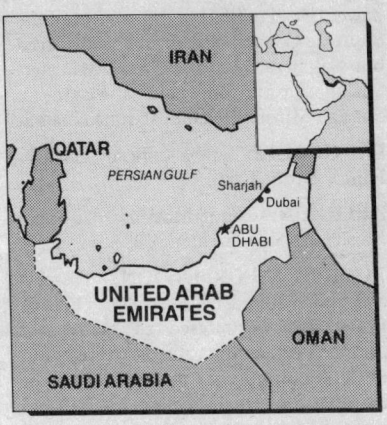

Al-Imarat al-'Arabiya al-Muttahida

CAPITAL: Abu Dhabi

AREA AND POPULATION: 83,657 km², 1% cultivated land. Population: 1,326,000 (1986 est.). Population density: 16.9/km². Population growth (1970-82): 15.5%. Ethnic composition: Arab 70%, Persian, Indian and Pakistani minorities.

CLIMATE AND GEOGRAPHY: Desert conditions prevail, with limited and erratic rainfall. The period from May to November is usually rainless, while the wettest months are February and March. Temperatures are very high in summer. Average temperature (Dubai): 23.4°C (January), 42.3°C (July). Average annual rainfall: 60 mm. Situated on the Persian Gulf, the UAE are bordered to the north by the Gulf, to the north-west by Qatar, to the south and west by Saudi Arabia and to the east by Oman. A flat coastal plain gives way to uninhabited sand dunes in the south. The Hajar Mountains are in the east.

CURRENCY: UAE Dirham (DH) of 10 dinar and 1,000 fils.

DEFENCE: Military service is voluntary. Total armed forces (1987): 43,000 (the Union Defence Force and the armed forces of the United Arab Emirates were formally merged in 1976; Abu Dhabi and Dubai still maintain a degree of independence. Perhaps a third of the force is drawn from non-nationals.) Army 40,000; Navy 1,200; Air Force 1,500. Para-military force: coastguard.

GOVERNMENT: The UAE is a federation of 7 autonomous Emirates, headed by a Supreme Council composed of the 7 rulers who, in turn, appoint a Council of Ministers. There is a National Council of 40 members which may propose amendments but which has no executive power. Head of State and President of the Supreme Council of Rulers: Shaikh Zayed bin Sultan al-Nahyan. Prime Minister: Shaikh Rashid bin Said al-Maktoum. Foreign Minster: Rashid Abdulla Nuaimi.

LANGUAGE: Arabic (official), English, Hindi, Urdu, Farsi.

RELIGION: Sunni Moslem 67%; Shiite Moslem 30%; Christian 1.3%..

TOURIST INFORMATION: Passport and visa required by Australian citizens. Entry will be refused to holders of passports containing valid or expired visas for Israel. Entry visas to the UAE can be issued at Abu Dhabi, Dubai, Sharjah and Ras al-Khaimah airports. A 30-day visa will be issued at Dubai airport to groups of bona fide tourists of at least 10 persons. Malaria prophylaxis is recommended. The quantity of alcoholic beverages which may be imported varies among Emirates. National airline: Gulf Air. Abu Dhabi airport is located 19 km from the city.

UNITED KINGDOM OF GREAT BRITAIN AND NORTHERN IRELAND

CAPITAL: London

AREA AND POPULATION: 244,046 km², 30% cultivated land (80% including pastures). England: 130,357 km²; Scotland: 78,762 km²; Wales: 20,761 km²; Northern Ireland: 13,482 km². Population: 56,458,000 (1986 est.). Population density (without Northern Ireland): 232/km². Population growth (1985): .01%. Ethnic composition: English 81.5%; Scottish 9.6%; Irish 2.4%; Welsh 1.9%; Northern Irish 1.8%; West Indian, Indian and Pakistani, over 2%.

CLIMATE AND GEOGRAPHY: Cool temperate oceanic climate, with mild conditions and rainfall evenly distributed throughout the year. The weather is very changeable because of cyclonic influences. In general, temperatures are higher in the west and lower in the east in winter, and the reverse in summer. Rainfall is greatest in the west, where most of the high ground occurs. Average temperature (London): 4.5°C (January), 18°C (July). Average annual rainfall (London): 600 mm. The UK is situated off the north-west of Europe, separated from it by the Straits of Dover, the English Channel and the North Sea. England is mostly rolling land, rising to the uplands of southern Scotland. Scotland has lowlands in the centre and granite highlands in the north. The coast is heavily indented, especially on the western side. Practically all of Wales lies within the highland zone of Britain: the Cambrian mountains, lying north-west to south-east, occupy most of the country. Northern Ireland has a rocky and wild northern coastline, with several deep indentations. To the north-east lie the basalt uplands of County Antrim, while granite mountains in the south-east gradually give way to the central lowlands of the Lough Erne basin. British Dependent Territories: Channel Islands, South Georgia, South Sandwich Islands, Bermuda, British Indian Ocean Territory,

Gibraltar, Canton and Enderbury (joint control with the United States), Hong Kong, Pitcairn Islands, St Helena, Ascension, Tristan da Cunha, Turks and Caicos Islands, Virgin Islands.

CURRENCY: Pound Sterling of 100 new pence.

DEFENCE: Military service is voluntary. Total armed forces (1986/87): 323,800. Army 162,100; Navy 68,300; Air Force 93,400. **Forces abroad:** Army 70,641; Navy/Marines 5,321; Air Force 17,202.

GOVERNMENT: Parliamentary democratic monarchy. There is no formal (written) consitution. The bicameral Parliament consists of the House of Commons of 635 members elected for 5 years and House of Lords of 1,177 members. Head of State: Queen Elizabeth II. Prime Minister: Margaret Thatcher. Foreign Minister: Sir Geoffrey Howe.

LANGUAGE: English (official), Welsh, Gaelic, Manx, Cornish.

NATIONAL ANTHEM: God Save the Queen.

RELIGION: Predominantly Protestant; Roman Catholic 4,269,019; Moslem 1,000,000; Jewish 390,000.

TOURIST INFORMATION: Passport but no visa required by Australian citizens. National airline: British Airways. London-Heathrow airport is located 24 km from the city.

UNITED STATES OF AMERICA

CAPITAL: Washington, DC.

AREA AND POPULATION:
9,363,123 km^2, 21% cultivated land. Population: 240,856,000 (1986 est.). Population density: 25.5/km^2. Population growth (1985): .6%. Ethnic composition: White American 83.2%; Negro and Mulatto 11.7%; Indian, Japanese and Chinese 5.1%.

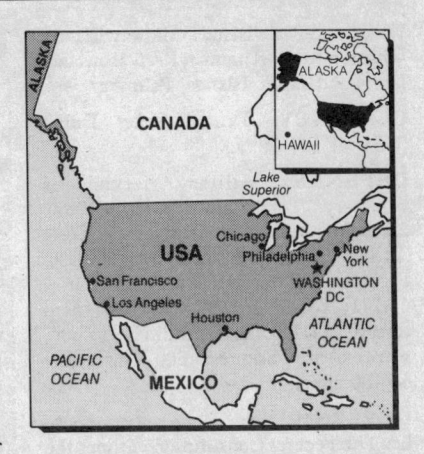

CLIMATE AND GEOGRAPHY: The climate is mostly temperate. The northern half receives snow, while the south-western region experiences dry, sub-tropical weather and is largely desert. All of the eastern side of the country receives 750-1,250 mm of rain or snow, and this provides the basis for a flourishing agriculture. Westward across the prairies, the rainfall drops to 450 mm. The north Pacific coast is temperate and humid; southern California is Mediterranean. The south-eastern states are sub-tropical and humid, with frequent rain and occasional hurricanes. The central and northern states of the east have a humid continental climate. Representative January and July average temperatures (in °C) are: Minneapolis −11.1 to 21.7; Miami 19.4 to 27.8; San Francisco 10 to 15; Washington, DC 1.1 to 25. Continental United States stretches 4,500 km from the Atlantic Ocean on the east to the Pacific Ocean on the west. It borders Canada on the north and reaches south to Mexico and the Gulf of Mexico. Alaska borders north-western Canada, while Hawaii lies in the Pacific Ocean, 3,200 km from the mainland. Outlying US areas: Commonwealth of Puerto Rica, Guam, Virgin Islands of the United States, Panama Canal Zone, American Samoa, Marianas, Carolines and Marshalls, Wake,

URUGUAY

República Oriental del Uruguay
ORIENTAL REPUBLIC OF URUGUAY

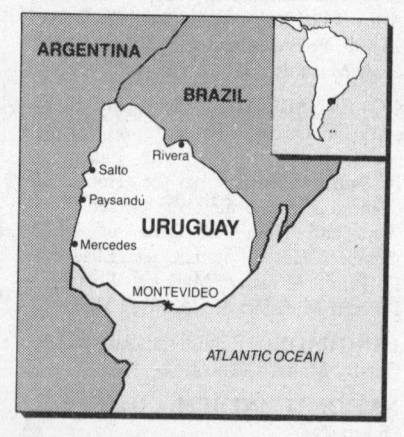

Wilkes and Peale Islands, Midway Islands, Johnston Atoll, Kingman Reef, Howland, Jarvis and Baker Islands, Palmyra.

CURRENCY: United States Dollar (US$) of 100 cents.

DEFENCE: Military service is voluntary. Total armed forces (1987): 2,169,709. Army 770,904; Navy 592,700; Air Force 605,805; Marine Corps 200,300. Para-military forces: Civil Air Patrol 65,771; coastguard 37,860; coastguard reserve 24,400; state militias 11,500. **Forces abroad**: 525,600, including 64,400 afloat.

GOVERNMENT: Presidential republic. The Federal Constitution outlines the structure of the national government, its powers and activities. Residual functions are performed by the individual states, which have their own constitutions and laws. Within each state are counties, cities and townships, each of which has its own elected government. The United States was the first nation to adopt a written constitution and to separate the powers of the government into 3 branches: the Executive, headed by the President; the Legislature, which includes both houses of Congress (Senate and House of Representatives), and the Judiciary, headed by the Supreme Court. Head of State: President Ronald Reagan, Foreign Minister: George P. Shultz.

LANGUAGE: American English.

NATIONAL ANTHEM: The Star-spangled Banner.

RELIGION: Protestant 78,702,000; Roman Catholic 52,286,000; Jewish 5,817,000; members of Eastern Churches 4,052,000; Old Catholic, Polish National Catholic and Armenian, 921,085; Buddhist 100,000.

TOURIST INFORMATION: Passport and visa required by Australian citizens.

CAPITAL: Montevideo

AREA AND POPULATION: 186,926 km², 12% cultivated land. Population: 2,947,000 (1986 est.). Population density: 17.4/km². Population growth (1985): 0.8%. Ethnic composition: Uruguayan (of Spanish and Italian background) 89%; Mestizo 5-10%; Mulatto 3%. Some 700,000 Uruguayans live abroad.

CLIMATE AND GEOGRAPHY: The climate is warm temperate, with mild winters and warm summers. There is no completely dry season but the wettest months extend from March to June. Average temperature (Montevideo): 22.2°C (January), 10°C (July). Average annual rainfall: 950 mm. Uruguay is situated on the east coast of South America, bordered to the north by Brazil and to the west by Argentina. In many respects, the country forms a transitional zone between the pampas of Argentina and the hilly uplands of Brazil. Apart from small areas of coastal plains and alluvial flood plains, the geography is extremely uniform, consisting of undulated hills with virtually no forest areas.

CURRENCY: Nuevo Peso of 100 centésimos.

DEFENCE: Military service is voluntary for 1 to 2 years. Total armed forces (1987): 32,430. Army 22,300; Navy 6,630; Air Force 3,500. Para-military forces: Metropolitan Guard 650; Republican Guard 520; coastguard 1,500.

GOVERNMENT: Presidential republic. The principal institutions of government are the President and his Cabinet, the Council of State, and the National Security Council which combines some Cabinet members and senior military officers. The main function of the Council is to make senior governmental appointments, including that of the President. It is also heavily involved in policy making. Head of State: President Dr Julio Sanguinetti. Foreign Minister: Enrique Iglesias.

LANGUAGE: Spanish.

NATIONAL ANTHEM: Orientales, la patria o la tumba (Uruguayans, the fatherland or death).

RELIGION: Predominantly Roman Catholic; Protestant 75,000; Jewish 50,000.

TOURIST INFORMATION: Passport and visa required by Australian citizens. There are no major health problems. There is a departure tax of US$4.50. National airline: Pluna. Montevideo-Carrasco airport is located 19 km from the city.

VANUATU

(Vanu'atu = The Land That Rises From The Sea)
Ripablik Blang Vanuatu
REPUBLIC OF VANUATU

CAPITAL: Vila

AREA AND POPULATION: 14,763 km², 5% cultivated land. Population: 136,000 (1986 est.). Population density: 8.9 km². Population growth (1981): 3.1%. Ethnic composition: Melanesian 91%; Polynesian or Micronesian, 3%; French and British minorities.

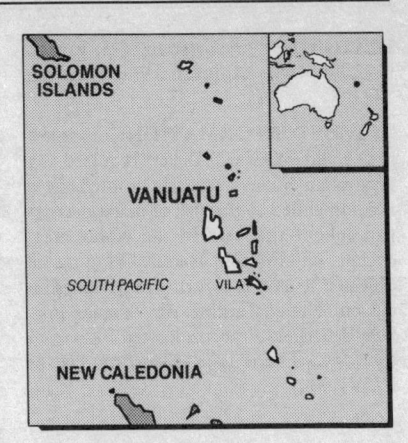

CLIMATE AND GEOGRAPHY: The climate varies from tropical in the north to sub-tropical in the south. Average annual rainfall: 3,062 mm. Between December and April, all islands may experience cyclones. The country forms an archipelago stretching from south of Solomon Islands to Hunter and Mathew Islands, east of New Caledonia. Principal islands: Vanua Lava, Gaua, Espiritu Santo, Maewo, Pentecost, Malakula, Ambrym, Epi, Efate, Erromango, Tanna and Anatom. There are active volcanoes on several islands. The islands themselves range in size from 1.2 km² to 3,900 km². The majority have rugged interiors and narrow coastal strips where most of the population lives.

CURRENCY: Vatu (VUV) and Australian dollar.

DEFENCE: No defence force is maintained.

GOVERNMENT: Democratic and independent republic. The President is elected by the Parliament for a 5-year term. There is universal suffrage, and parliamentary elections are held every 4 years. Head of Government, Prime Minister Father Walter Hadye Lini. Foreign Minister: Donald Kalpokas.

LANGUAGE: Bislama (national), French and English (both official).

NATIONAL ANTHEM: Yumi, yumi ... (We the people of Vanuatu with united voice).

RELIGION: Presbyterian 40%; Roman Catholic 16%; Animist 15%; Anglican 14%.

TOURIST INFORMATION: Passport and valid outward ticket required by Australian citizens. Malaria prophylaxis is recommended as the risk of malaria exists throughout the year in the whole area, except on Futuna Island. Tipping is objected to as it is contrary to Melanesian custom. National airline: Air Vanuatu. Port Vila-Bauerfield airport is located 5 km from the city. There is a departure tax of VUV1,000.

VATICAN

Stato della Città del Vaticano
VATICAN CITY STATE

AREA AND POPULATION: 0.44 km^2. Population: 1,000 (1986); 3,700 employees from Italy; 80 Swiss guards; over 180 diplomatic representatives abroad.

CLIMATE AND GEOGRAPHY: As for Rome.

CURRENCY: Vatican Lira (parity with Italian Lira) of 100 centesimi.

DEFENCE: No conventional defence force is maintained.

GOVERNMENT: Sovereign state. The Pope exercises sovereignty and has absolute legislative, executive and judicial powers. He is elected by the College of Cardinals, meeting in secret enclave. The election is by scrutiny and requires a two-thirds majority. Head of State: Pope John Paul II. Secretary of State: Cardinal Agostino Casaroli.

LANGUAGE: Latin and Italian.

TOURIST INFORMATION: As for Italy—passport but no visa required by Australian citizens.

VENEZUELA

República de Venezuela
REPUBLIC OF VENEZUELA

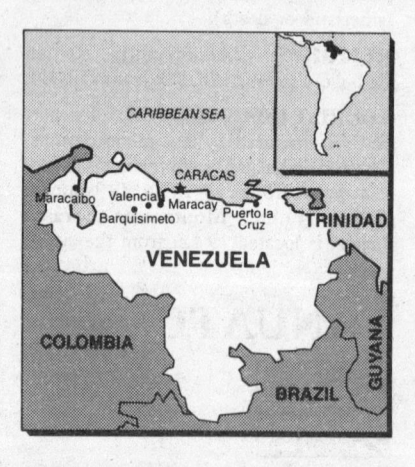

CAPITAL: Caracas

AREA AND POPULATION: 912,050 km^2, 4% cultivated land. Population: 17,791,000 (1986 est.). Population density: 19.3/km^2. Population growth (1985): 2.6%. Ethnic composition: Mestizo and Mulatto, over 69%; European (mostly of Spanish and Italian background) 20%; Negro 8-9%; Indian 1-2%; Colombian (illegal immigrants), over 1,000,000.

CLIMATE AND GEOGRAPHY: The climate ranges from warm temperate to tropical. Temperatures vary little throughout the year and rainfall is plentiful. Average temperature (Caracas): 18.3°C (January), 20.6°C (July). Average annual rainfall: 833 mm. Venezuela is bounded to the north by the Caribbean Sea, to the south by Brazil, to the south-west and west by Colombia and to the east by Guyana. In the south-east rise the Guyana Highlands, a sandstone plateau covering almost half of the country. Plains, called 'Llanos', extend between the highlands and the Andes. The basins of the Orinoco and Apure Rivers are flooded for 6 months of the year and largely drought-stricken for the remainder.

CURRENCY: Bolivar (Bs) of 100 centimos.

DEFENCE: Military service is by selective conscription for a period of 2 years. Total armed forces (1987): 49,000. Army 34,000; Navy 10,500; Air Force 4,500. Para-military force: Fuerzas Armadas de Cooperación 20,000.

GOVERNMENT: Presidential federative republic. The bicameral Parliament consists of a Senate of 52 members and a Chamber of Deputies of 208 members. Voting is compulsory for men and women over the age of 18. Owing to the high illiteracy rate, voting is by coloured ballot cards. Head of State: President Dr Jaime Lusinchi. Foreign Minister: Simón Alberto Consalvi.

LANGUAGE: Spanish (official), Indian dialects.

NATIONAL ANTHEM: Gloria al bravo pueblo (Glory to the brave people).

RELIGION: Roman Catholic 96%; Protestant 2%; Jewish 15,000.

TOURIST INFORMATION: Passport and Tourist Card (tarjeta de ingreso) required by Australian citizens. Vaccination against yellow fever and malaria prophylaxis are recommended. There are arrival and departure taxes. National airline: Viasa. Caracas-Simon Bolivar airport is located 21 km from the city.

REPUBLIC OF VIETNAM

Công Hòa Xã Hôi Chu Nghĩa Viêt Nam
SOCIALIST REPUBLIC OF VIETNAM

CAPITAL: Hanoi

AREA AND POPULATION: 329,556 km², 23% cultivated land. Population: 61,994,000 (1986 est.). Population density: 184.6/km². Population growth (1985): 2.5%. Ethnic composition: Vietnamese (Kinh) 84%; Chinese 2-3%; Muong, Thai, Meo, Khmer, Man, Cham minorities.

CLIMATE AND GEOGRAPHY: The climate is mainly tropical, with high humidity on the coastal plains. In the north, a hot and rainy season prevails during the summer monsoon from May to September. The average temperature in Hanoi is about 30°C during this period. A cool season prevails from December to March, with the average temperature less than 20°C. Average annual rainfall is 1,500 mm in the plains and over 2,000 mm in the mountain regions. The south has a monsoon climate, with an average temperature of 27°C in Ho Chi Minh City. The cooler season lasts from December to February, while the rainy season lasts from about May to November, with the hottest and most humid weather in July and August. Average annual rainfall is about 2,000 mm. The central coastal region has a different weather pattern, with the bulk of the rain occurring from October to March. Vietnam is bordered to the north by China and by Laos and Kampuchea to the west. The country may be divided geographically into 4 distinct major areas: the Red River Delta (and surrounding mountains); the Mekong Delta; a narrow coastal plain; and the Central Highlands. Forests account for approximately 50% of the total area. Alluvial deposits arising from the decomposition of basalt have made the arable soil of Vietnam rich and fertile.

CURRENCY: Dong (D) of 10 Hào and 100 Xu.

DEFENCE: Military service is compulsory for 2 years (some ethnic minorities), 3 years (Kinh conscripts) and 4 years (specialists). Total armed forces (1987): 1,152,000. Army 1,000,000; Navy 40,000; Air Force 12,000. Para-military forces: People's Self Defence Force 1,000,000; People's Regional Force (militia) 500,000; Border Defence Forces 60,000. Forces abroad: 180,000.

GOVERNMENT: Proletarian dictatorship based on Marxist-Leninist principles. The unicameral Parliament (National Assembly) of 496 members is elected by universal suffrage. Head of State and Chairman of the State Council: Vo Chi Cong. Chairman of the National Assembly: Nguyen Huu Tho. Chairman of the Council of Ministers: Do Muoi. Foreign Minister: Nguyen Co Thach.

LANGUAGE: Vietnamese (official), French, Russian, English.

NATIONAL ANTHEM: Tien quan ca (The troops are advancing).

RELIGION: Buddhist, Taoist, Caodaist, Roman Catholic.

TOURIST INFORMATION: Passport and visa required by Australian citizens. Visas may take a considerable time to be granted. Malaria prophylaxis is recommended. There is an airport tax of US$5. National airline: Hang Khong Vietnam. Hanoi-Noi Bai airport is located 45 km from the city.

WESTERN SAMOA

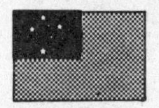

Malotuto'atasi o Samoa i Sisifo
INDEPENDENT STATE OF WESTERN SAMOA

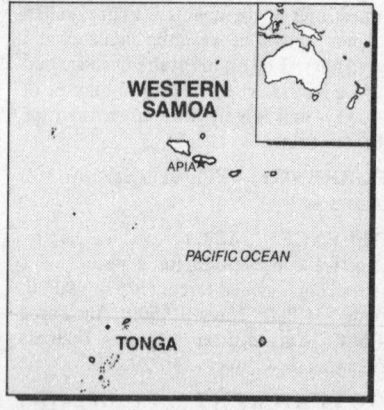

CAPITAL: Apia

AREA AND POPULATION: 2,831 km², 43% cultivated land. Population: 165,000 (1986 est.), 72% on Upolu and 28% on Savai'i. Population density: 56/km². Population growth (1985): 3%. Ethnic composition: Samoan (Polynesian) 88%; Euronesian 10%; European minority.

CLIMATE AND GEOGRAPHY: Tropical marine climate, with a marked dry season from May to August. The southern and south-east windward sides of the islands receive higher rainfall than the leeward sides. Average temperature (Apia): 26.7°C (January), 25.6°C (July). Western Samoa's closest neighbours are American Samoa, Tonga, Wallis Island and Tokelau. Western Samoa itself comprises 2 main islands and 7 smaller islands, 5 of which are uninhabited. The islands are volcanic, with little flat land except along the coasts.

CURRENCY: Tala (dollar) of 100 sene.

DEFENCE: Western Samoa does not maintain any military forces. Military aircraft from any nation are usually granted diplomatic clearance to use the airport if necessary.

GOVERNMENT: Mixture of traditional and parliamentary systems. The Legislative Assembly (*Fono*) consists of 47 members, 45 of whom are elected by *Matai* (native Western Samoans) suffrage. The remaining 2 are elected by universal suffrage from the individual voters' roll (about 1,600). This latter roll is open to people of European blood who are not members of a *matai* family. Elections are held every 3 years. Head of State: HH Malietoa Tanumafili II. Head of Government: Prime Minister and Foreign Minister Vaai Kolone.

LANGUAGE: Samoan (a Polynesian language), with English as the language of commerce.

NATIONAL ANTHEM: The Banner of Freedom.

RELIGION: Protestant 70%; Roman Catholic 22%.

TOURIST INFORMATION: Visitors must hold a valid passport or similar identity document. No entry permit is required if the length of stay does not exceed 30 days. There is an airport departure tax of 20 tala for non-residents, plus a hotel room tax. Visitors are advised not to walk through villages unescorted. The concept of Sunday as the Sabbath is taken very seriously by the local population. National airline: Polynesian Airlines. Apia-Faleolo airport is located 35 km from the city.

YEMEN, NORTH

Al-Jamhuriya al-Arabiya al-Yamaniya
YEMEN ARAB REPUBLIC
CAPITAL: San'a
AREA AND POPULATION: 195,000 km², 14% cultivated land. Population: 6,339,000 (1986 est.). Population density: 51.7/km². Population growth (1985): 3.4%. Ethnic composition: Arab majority; Negro.

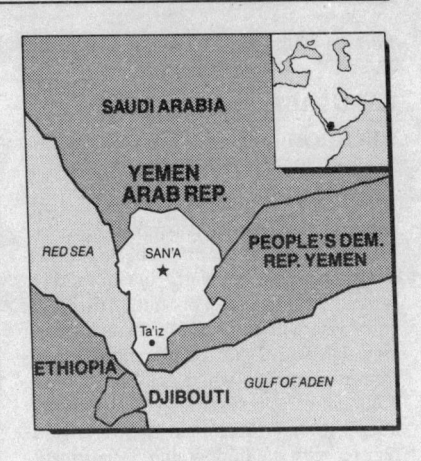

CLIMATE AND GEOGRAPHY:
Very hot and humid along the coast. Winds blowing north-west in summer and south-west in winter bring severe sandstorms but little rain. The mountainous regions have a temperate climate, with cool winters. Average temperature (San'a): 13.9°C (January), 21.7°C (July). Average annual rainfall: 508 mm. The Republic is bordered to the north by Saudi Arabia and to the south and east by the People's Democratic Republic of Yemen (South Yemen). With the exception of the semi-desert coastal plain, which runs the entire length of the territory, the country is composed of fertile highland plateaux. These are broken by wadis and river valleys that are dry in summer.

CURRENCY: Yemen Riyal (Rl) of 100 fils.

DEFENCE: Military service is compulsory for a period of 3 years. Total armed forces (1986-87): 36,550. Army 35,000; Navy 660; Air Force 1,000. Paramilitary forces: Tribal levies 20,000; Ministry of National Security force 5,000.

GOVERNMENT: Islamic Arab sovereign republic. Only men can vote. The 99-man People's Constituent Assembly was established in 1978 and the 1,000-man General People's Congress in 1982. Head of State: President Lieutenant-Colonel Ali Abdullah Saleh. Prime Minister: Maj. Abdul Aziz Abdel Ghani.

Foreign Minister: Dr Abdul Karim al-Iranyi.

LANGUAGE: Arabic.

RELIGION: Shiite Moslem 59%; Sunni Moslem 39%; Jewish 2,000.

TOURIST INFORMATION: Passport and visa required by Australian citizens. Admission to the country will be refused to visitors whose passports contain valid or expired visas for Israel or South Africa. An entry visa will be issued at the airport of arrival provided that the passenger arrives from a country in which the YAR has no diplomatic representation. Visitors who intend to stay more than 3 days should register with the Immigration Department within 3 days of their arrival. There is a compulsory currency exchange of US$50. Malaria prophylaxis is recommended. The departure tax for international flights is R175. National airline: Yemenia. San'a-El Rahaba airport is located 13 km from the city.

YEMEN, SOUTH

Al-Jumhurijah al-Yemen al-Dimuqratiyah al-Sha'abijah
PEOPLE'S DEMOCRATIC REPUBLIC OF YEMEN

CAPITAL: Aden

AREA AND POPULATION: 287,682 km², 0.6% cultivated land. Population: 2,275,000 (1986 est.). Population density: 6.9/km². Population growth (1985): 2.8%. Ethnic composition: Arab 75%; Indian; Somali; Nomad, Pakistani and European minorities.

CLIMATE AND GEOGRAPHY: A desert climate prevails, modified in part by altitude. Average temperature (Aden): 24°C (January), 32°C (July). Average annual rainfall: 46 mm. The PDRY is bordered to the north by Saudi Arabia, to the south by the Gulf of Aden, to the east by Oman and to the west by the Yemen Arab Republic. A sandy coast rises to a high central mountain range, which gives way to desert sands.

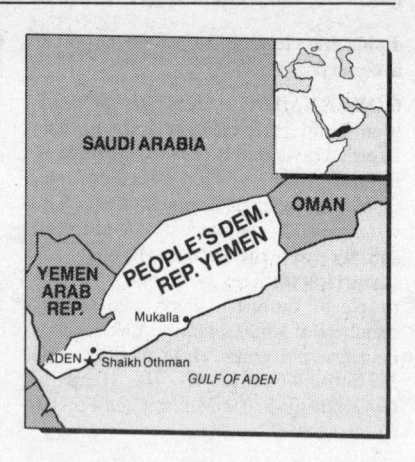

CURRENCY: South Yemen Dinar (YD) of 1,000 fils.

DEFENCE: Military service is compulsory for a period of 2 years. Total armed forces (1987): 27,500. Army 24,000; Navy 1,000; Air Force 2,500. Para-military forces: public security force 30,000 (increasing); people's militia 15,000.

GOVERNMENT: People's republic. The unicameral legislature (Supreme People's Council) has 111 members. Head of State: (President) Haider Abubaker al-Attas.

LANGUAGE: Arabic.

RELIGION: Sunni Moslem 91%; Christian 4%; Hindu 3.5%.

TOURIST INFORMATION: Passport and visa required by Australian citizens. Holders of passports containing current or expired visas for Israel, South Africa or Rhodesia (not Zimbabwean) will be refused entry. Return or onward tickets are required. There is a departure tax. Malaria prophylaxis is recommended. Foreign currencies should be declared upon arrival. National airline: Alyemda. Aden-Khormaksar airport is located 10 km from the city.

YUGOSLAVIA

Socijalistička Federativna
Republika Jugoslavija
SOCIALIST FEDERAL REPUBLIC OF YUGOSLAVIA

CAPITAL: Belgrade (Beograd)

AREA AND POPULATION: 255,804 km^2, 33% cultivated land. Population: 23,284,000 (1986 est.). Population density: 90.3/km^2. Population growth (1985): 0.9%. Ethnic composition: Serbian 36.3%; Croatian 19.7%; Slovene 8%; Macedonian 6%; Montenegrin 2.6%; Albanian, Bulgarian, Czech, Hungarian, Italian, Romanian, Ruthenian, Slovakian, Turkish Ukrainian minorities (total 11.2%).

CLIMATE AND GEOGRAPHY: Most parts experience a typical central-European climate, with cold winters and hot summers, while the coastal area has a Mediterranean climate, with mild wet winters and sunny summers. Average temperature (Belgrade): −1.5°C (January), 22°C (July). Average annual rainfall: 610 mm. Yugoslavia is bounded to the north by Austria and Hungary, to the north-east by Romania, to the south by Greece, to the east by Bulgaria and to the west by Albania, the Adriatic Sea and Italy. The Dinaric Alps run parallel to the Adriatic coast, and plains stretch across the north and east river basins.

CURRENCY: Yugoslav Dinar of 100 para.

DEFENCE: Military service is compulsory for a period of 15 months. Total armed forces (1987): 210,600. Army 161,500; Navy 13,100; Air Force 36,000. Para-military force: frontier guards 15,000.

GOVERNMENT: Federally based people's republic. There are 6 republics: Serbia, Croatia, Slovenia, Bosnia and Herzegovina, Macedonia and Montenegro. The bicameral legislature consists of the Federal Chamber (220 delegates) and the Chamber of Republics and Provinces (88 delegates). There is universal suffrage for all citizens over the age of 18 (or 16, if employed). The State Presidency of 9 members (8 from the Republics and Provinces plus the President of the Presidium of the League of Communists) is elected every 5 years. The annual President is Head of State. President of the Federal Executive Council (Prime Minister): Branko Mikulic. Foreign Minister: Raif Dizdarevič.

LANGUAGE: Serbo-Croatian serves as the lingua franca, the Consitution laying down that 'The languages of the nations and nationalities and their alphabets shall be equal throughout the territory of Yugoslavia.'

NATIONAL ANTHEM: Hej, Slaveni, jošte živi reč naših dedova (O Slavs, our ancestors' words still live).

RELIGION: Serbian Orthodox 41.5%; Roman Catholic 31.8%; Moslem 12.4%; Protestant 150,000; Jewish 7,000.

TOURIST INFORMATION: Passport and visa required by Australian citizens. Return or onward tickets and visible means of support sufficient for stay are required. The re-exchange of dinars into foreign currencies is not possible except for holders of so-called Dinar Tourist Cheques obtained during the first transaction. There are departure taxes. National airline: JAT.

ZAÏRE

République du Zaîre
REPUBLIC OF ZAÏRE

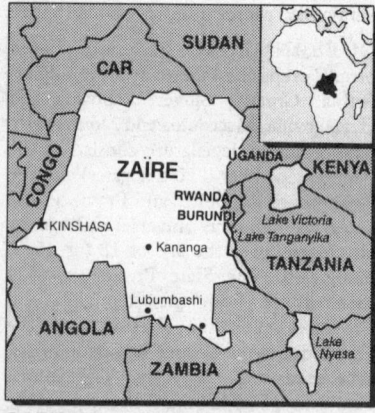

CAPITAL: Kinshasa

AREA AND POPULATION: 2,344,885 km², 5% cultivated land. Population: 31,333,000 (1986 est.). Population density: 13/km². Population growth (1985): 2.9%. Ethnic composition: Bantu 80%; Sudanese, Nilotic, Hamitic and Pygmy tribes; European (mostly Belgian) minority.

CLIMATE AND GEOGRAPHY: Equatorial climate, especially in the central region. The average daily temperature in the coastal and basin areas is 27°C and in the mountainous regions, 18°C. Humidity is generally high. In the north, the northern hemisphere winter brings the dry season but in the south the dry season occurs during the southern hemisphere winter. The climate is favourable for agriculture (particularly forestry) but it also has other less fortunate effects—there are vast stretches of land where the soil has been leached of its soluble elements by heavy rainfall and, in addition, the carriers of malaria, sleeping sickness, bilharzia and other tropical diseases flourish in such a warm, rainy climate. Zaîre is bordered to the north by the Central African Republic and Sudan, to the south by Zambia, to the west by Angola and Congo and to the east by Uganda, Burundi and Rwanda. The country has a wide variety of geographical features, ranging from the equatorial rain forests, which cover over 40% of the country, to the mountains, volcanoes and lakes of Kivu Province in the east. Much of the remainder of the country is made up of vast stretches of savanna and sparse forest lands.

CURRENCY: Zaîre (Z) of 100 makuta.

DEFENCE: Military service is voluntary. Total armed forces (1986/87): 51,000 (incl. gendarmerie). Army 22,000; Navy 1,500; Air force 2,500. Para-military force: gendarmerie 25,000.

GOVERNMENT: Presidential republic. The President is elected for a 7-year term by direct universal suffrage. The unicameral legislature of 244 members is elected for a 5-year term, also by direct universal suffrage. Head of State: President Marshall Mobutu Sésé Séko Kuku Ngbendu wa Zabanga. Prime Minister: Mabi Mulumba. Foreign Minister: Ekila Liyonda.

LANGUAGE: French (official), Kiswahili, Kikongo, Lingala.

NATIONAL ANTHEM: Zaîrois, dans la paix retrouvée (Zaîrians, in refound peace).

RELIGION: Roman Catholic 30-45%; Protestant 20%; Moslem 1%; Jewish 1,500; Animist.

TOURIST INFORMATION: Passport and visa required by Australian citizens. Visitors should not attempt to enter Zaîre on the assumption that entry papers will be issued on arrival. Inoculations for cholera and yellow fever are required and malaria prophylaxis and vaccination against typhoid are recommended. Although tap water is drinkable in most places, it is considered desirable to boil and filter it. There are hospitals, private practitioners, dentists and pharmacies in all major towns. As standards vary, however, and costs are always high, it is wise to avoid visiting Zaîre if there is the possibility that urgent and specialised medical attention may be required. Accommodation and entertainment in Zaîre are very expensive. The standard rate of tipping is 10%. Tipping is applied to services of all kinds and is used to obtain assistance in many dealings. National airline: Air Zaîre. Kinshasa-N'djili airport is located 25 km from the city.

ZAMBIA

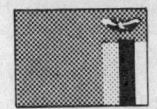

REPUBLIC OF ZAMBIA

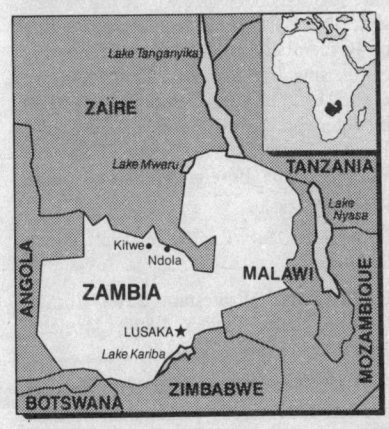

CAPITAL: Lusaka

AREA AND POPULATION: 752,614 km², 7% cultivated land. Population: 7,054,000 (1986 est.). Population density: 9.3/km². Population growth (1985): 3.2%. Ethnic composition: Bantu tribes (Bemba, Tonga, Ngoni, Lozi), over 90%; Indian, Zimbabwean and European minorities.

CLIMATE AND GEOGRAPHY: Tropical climate with 3 seasons: cool, dry (May to August), hot, dry (September to November) and wet (December to April). Frosts may occur in some areas during the cool season. Average temperature (Lusaka): 21.1°C (January), 16.1°C (July). Average annual rainfall (Lusaka): 836 mm. Zambia is bordered to the north by Tanzania and Zaîre, to the south by Botswana, Zimbabwe, South West Africa (Namibia) and Mozambique, to the east by Malawi and to the west by Angola. The country is mostly a high plateau covered with thick forests.

CURRENCY: Kwacha (K) of 100 ngwee.

DEFENCE: Military service is voluntary. Total armed forces (1987); 16,200. Army 15,000; Air Force 1,200. Para-military forces: police mobile unit 700; police para-military unit 500.

GOVERNMENT: Presidential republic. Parliament consists of the National Assembly (125 members) and House of Chiefs (27 members). There is only 1 political party – the United National Independence Party. Head of State: President Dr Kenneth David Kaunda. Prime Minister: Keby Musokotwanae. Foreign Minister: L. K. H. Goma.

LANGUAGE: English (official), Bantu languages.

NATIONAL ANTHEM: Stand and sing of Zambia, proud and free.

RELIGION: Roman Catholic 20%; Protestant 10%; Moslem; Hindu; Jewish; Animist.

TOURIST INFORMATION: Passport but no visa required by Australian citizens. Payment of accommodation in hotels or lodges is to be made in foreign currency. Payment in Kwacha is accepted only where proof is shown of the exchange of foreign currency into Kwacha. Malaria prophylaxis is recommended. There is an airport tax of US$10. National airline: Zambia Airways. Lusaka airport is located 25 km from the city.

ZIMBABWE

REPUBLIC OF ZIMBABWE

CAPITAL: Harare.

AREA AND POPULATION: 390,308 km², 7% cultivated land. Population: 8,984,000 (1986 est.). Population density: 22.4/km². Population growth (1985): 4%. Ethnic composition: Shona 80%; Ndebele 19%; European 3.7%; coloured and Asian minorities.

CURRENCY: Zimbabwe Dollar (Z$) of 100 cents.

DEFENCE: Military service is voluntary. Total armed forces (1987): 43,000. Army 42,000; Air Force 1,000. Para-military forces: police force 15,000; national militia 20,000; police support unit 3,000.

GOVERNMENT: Parliamentary democracy. The President is the Head of State and the Commander-in-Chief of the Defence Forces. He is elected by Members of Parliament, holds office for 6 years and can be elected for a second term. Zimbabwe's Parliament consists of a Senate of 40 members and a House of Assembly comprising 100 members, 80 of whom are elected by voters on a common roll and 20 by voters on the white roll. President and Head of State: Canaan Banana. President: R. G. Mugabe. Foreign Minister: Nathan Shamuyarira.

LANGUAGE: English (official), Bantu languages.

RELIGION: Protestant 23%; Roman Catholic 10%; Jewish 4,800; Moslem; Animist.

TOURIST INFORMATION: Passport but no visa required by Australian citizens. There are few health problems in Harare or other major urban areas but precautions must be taken when staying in rural areas. Malaria prophylaxis is recommended. Visitors are advised not to swim in lakes and rivers as bilharzia could be contracted. There is a regular Qantas flight to Harare via Perth. Foreign currencies should be declared on arrival. There is a departure tax of US$10. National airline: Air Zimbabwe. Harare airport is located 12 km from the city.

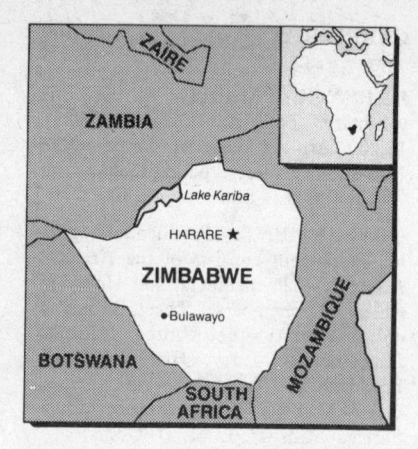

CLIMATE AND GEOGRAPHY:
Although Zimbabwe lies within the tropics, the high elevation of the country means that the climate is generally not tropical. Average temperature (Harare): 20.6°C (January), 13.9°C (July). Average annual rainfall (Harare): 828 mm. Zimbabwe is a land-locked country in south-central Africa, between the Limpopo and Zambezi Rivers. It is bordered to the north by Zambia, to the south by South Africa, to the east by Mozambique and to the west by Botswana. There are 4 main relief regions. The central plateau of high veld, 1,200 m to 1,500 m above sea level, traverses the country from south-west to north-east and occupies about 25% of the land area. It is flanked on either side by the middle veld, the altitude of which is between 760 m and 1,200 m, covering 40% of the area. The low veld region, below 600 m, comprises the narrow basin of the Zambezi river in the south and south-east. The fourth region, known as the Eastern Highlands, is very mountainous, rising to 2,594 m at the summit of Mount Inyangani.

EXTERNAL TERRITORIES

AUSTRALIA

ASHMORE AND CARTIER ISLANDS, TERRITORY OF

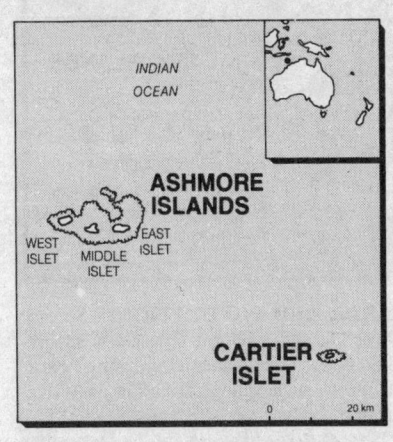

AREA AND POPULATION: 5 km². Uninhabited. Indonesian fishing boats visit the area as does the RAN and RAAF.

CLIMATE AND GEOGRAPHY: The territory is in the Indian Ocean, 320 km off the north-west coast of Australia. Ashmore (Middle, East and West) Islands are 48 km north-west of Cartier Island. The islands, of coral and sand, are small and low lying.

GOVERNMENT: The territory was annexed to form part of the Northern Territory. With Northern Territory self-government, the territory is now a direct responsibility of the Commonwealth government.

AUSTRALIAN ANTARCTIC TERRITORY

AREA AND POPULATION: 6,199,846 km². The territory comprises almost 50% of the Antarctic continent. Population consists of scientific personnel.

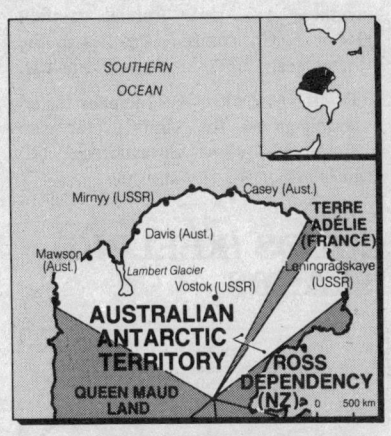

CLIMATE AND GEOGRAPHY: All the islands and territories other than Adelie Land situated south of 60°S latitude and lying between 160°E longitude and 45°E longitude. The chief stations are Mawson station on MacRobertson Land; Davis station on Princess Elizabeth Land; and Casey station on Wilkes Land.

GOVERNMENT: Australian Capital Territory laws apply where they are applicable. The territory is administered by the Minister for Science.

CHRISTMAS ISLAND

AREA AND POPULATION: 135 km². Population (1983): 3,000.

CLIMATE AND GEOGRAPHY: A pleasant climate, with a temperature range of 23°-26°C. The wet season is from November to April. Annual rainfall: 2,040 mm. Christmas Island lies in the Indian Ocean, 2,623 km from Fremantle.

GOVERNMENT: A 9 member Island Assembly advises the Administrator, who is appointed by the Governor-General. Administrator: F. T. Paterson.

COCOS (KEELING) ISLANDS

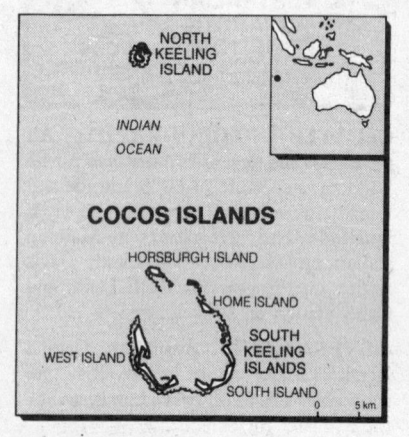

AREA AND POPULATION: 14.2 km^2. Population (1984): 584. Most of the European community live on West Island (208) with the Cocos Malays on Home Island (376).

CLIMATE AND GEOGRAPHY: Pleasant climate, affected much of the year by trade winds. Temperature range: 20°-31°C. Average rainfall: 2,000 mm. The territory, in the Indian Ocean 3,685 km west of Darwin, consists of 2 atolls of 27 small coral islands.

GOVERNMENT: An administrator appointed by the Governor-General. The Cocos (Keeling) Islands Council is the elected body of the Cocos Malay community, which advises the Administrator. Administrator: E. H. Hanfield.

CORAL SEA ISLANDS, TERRITORY OF

AREA AND POPULATION: Spread over 780,000 km^2 but only a few square kilometres of land area. Uninhabited apart from the meteorological station on Willis Island.

CLIMATE AND GEOGRAPHY The territory, east of Queensland, consists of scattered reefs and islands over a large area. The better known islands are Cato island, Chilcott islet and the Willis group.

GOVERNMENT: The laws of the Australian Capital Territory apply. There is no administration on the islands.

HEARD AND McDONALD ISLANDS

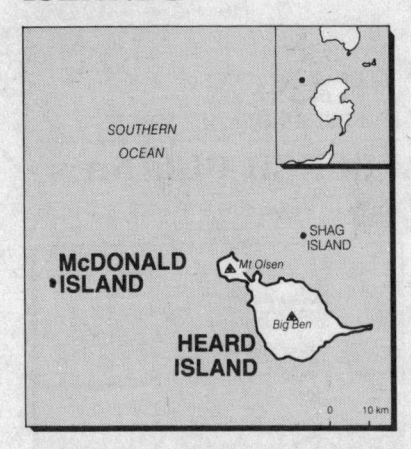

AREA AND POPULATION: 412 km². Uninhabited.

CLIMATE AND GEOGRAPHY: The islands lie over 4,000 km south-west of Fremantle. The McDonald Islands are 42 km west of Heard Island. Visits are made by scientific expeditions.

GOVERNMENT: The islands are administered by the Department of Science.

NORFOLK ISLAND

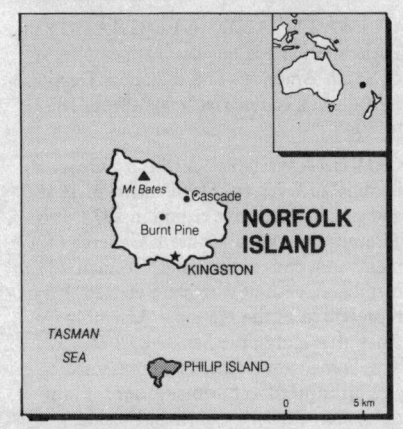

CAPITAL: Kingston.

AREA AND POPULATION: 34.5 km². Population (1986): 2,367.

CLIMATE AND GEOGRAPHY: Mild subtropical climate with 16°-28°C the average daily maximum temperature. Average annual rainfall: 1,350 mm. Norfolk Island lies 1,676 km north-east of Sydney.

GOVERNMENT: Responsible government with a Legislative Assembly (9 members) and Executive Council. Administrator: Commodore J. A. Matthew.

LANGUAGE: Descendents of the *Bounty* families, known as the Islanders, speak a mixture of West Country English and Tahitian.

DENMARK
FAEROE ISLANDS
Faerøerne/ Føroyar

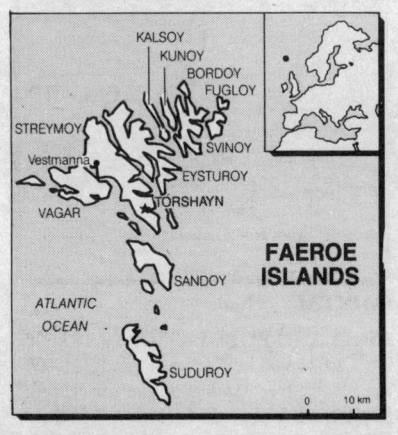

CAPITAL: Torshavn

AREA AND POPULATION: 1,399 km². Only 2% is cultivated. Population (1985 est.): 45,728 on 17 inhabited islands.

CLIMATE AND GEOGRAPHY: Situated in the North Atlantic, the archipelago lies due north of Scotland. The islands are mountainous and volcanic. The main islands are Streymoy, Eysturoy, Vágar, Suouroy, Sandoy and Bordoy.

CURRENCY: Faeroese krone of 100 øre interchangeable with the Danish krone.

GOVERNMENT: The Islands are a self-governing region of the Kingdom of

Denmark. The parliament (Lagting) comprises 32 elected members. Parliament elects the administration (Landsstyre) of 4 to 6 members. Denmark is represented by an appointed commissioner (Rigsombudmand) who administers other matters. The Faeroes have 2 members in the Danish parliament (the Folketing). Chief Minister (Lagmand): Atli P. Dam.

LANGUAGE: Faeroese.

RELIGION: Evangelical Lutherans 75%; Plymouth Brethren 20%.

GREENLAND
Kalaallit Nunaat

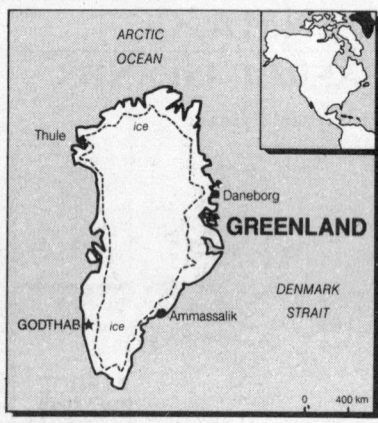

CAPITAL: Nuuk

AREA AND POPULATION: 2,175,600 km². 1,833,900 km² is icecap and 341,700 km² is ice-free land. Population (1986): 53,406. Ethnic composition: mainly Eskimo.

CLIMATE AND GEOGRAPHY: Greenland is a huge island lying between the North Atlantic and the Polar sea. Most of the island is a high plateau.

GOVERNMENT: Home rule was introduced in 1979 and full self-government attained in 1981. There is a democratically elected council (Landsrad). The parliament (Landsting) has 26 members and the administration (the Landsstyre), 6 members. Two representatives are sent to the Danish parliament (the Folketing). Premier: Jonathan Motzfeldt.

LANGUAGE: Greenlandic.

RELIGION: Evangelical Lutherans about 98%.

FRANCE
OVERSEAS DEPARTMENTS

FRENCH GUIANA
Guyane Française

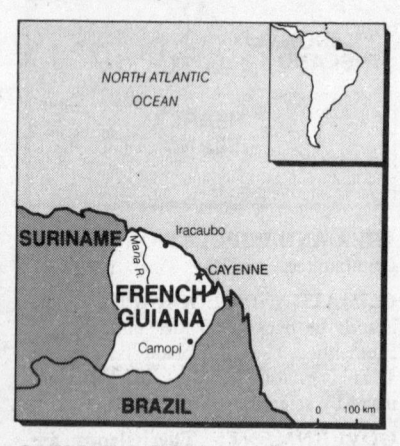

CAPITAL: Cayenne

AREA AND POPULATION: 83,533 km². Only 10,436 hectares under cultivation. Population (1986 est.): 85,800.

CLIMATE AND GEOGRAPHY: French Guiana is on the north-east coast of South America. The infamous Devil's Island was a convict settlement from 1852 to 1945.

GOVERNMENT: French Guiana became an Overseas Department in 1946 and an administrative region in 1974. It is administered by a Conseil General (19 members) and a Regional Council (31 members), both of which are elected. It is represented in the National Assembly by 2 deputies and in the Senate by 1 senator. The French government is represented by an appointed commissioner. Commissioner: Bernard Courtois. President of the Conseil General: Elie Castor. President of the Regional Council: Georges Othily.

RELIGION: Roman Catholic.

TOURIST INFORMATION: Passport, visa and onward or return ticket required by Australian citizens. An authorisation from the Prefect of French Guiana must be obtained before arrival if visiting Indian villages, 'Haut Maroni' or 'Haut-Oyapoc'. Vaccination required against yellow fever. Malaria prophylaxis is recommended.

GUADELOUPE

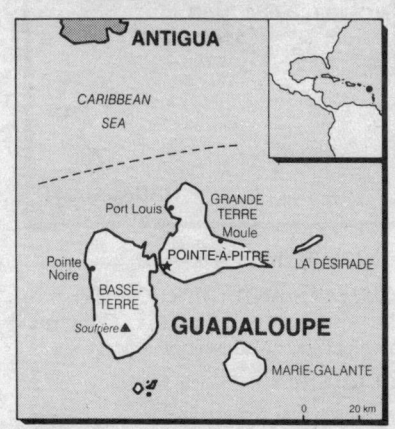

CAPITAL: Basse-Terre

AREA AND POPULATION: 1702 km^2. Population (1986 est.): 330,600. Ethnic composition: mainly Negro and mulatto.

CLIMATE AND GEOGRAPHY: Guadeloupe consists of a group of islands in the Lesser Antilles in the Caribbean. The two main islands are Basse-Terre and Grande-Terre.

GOVERNMENT: Guadeloupe became an Overseas Department in 1946 and an administrative region in 1974. It is administered by a Conseil General (42 members) and a Regional Council (39 members), both of which are elected. It is represented in the National Assembly by 4 deputies and in the Senate by 2 senators. The French government is represented by an appointed commissioner. Commissioner: Maurice Saborin. President of the Conseil General: Dominique Larifla. President of the Regional Council: Felix Proto.

LANGUAGE: French (official); a creole dialect is spoken by the vast majority.

RELIGION: Roman Catholic.

TOURIST INFORMATION: Passport, visa and return or onward ticket required by Australian citizens, also sufficient funds for lodging and duration of stay.

MARTINIQUE

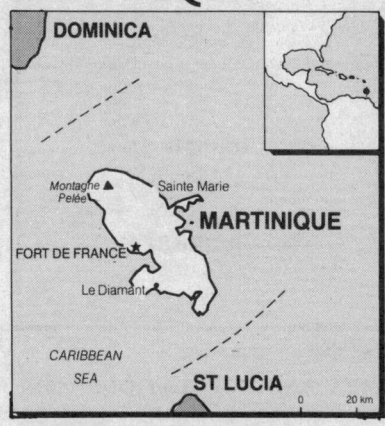

CAPITAL: Fort-de-France

AREA AND POPULATION: 1079 km^2. Population (1986 est.): 328,000.

CLIMATE AND GEOGRAPHY: The island is one of the Windward Islands in the Lesser Antilles, between Dominica and St Lucia.

GOVERNMENT: Martinique became an Overseas Department in 1946 and an administrative region in 1974. It is administered by a Conseil General (44 members) and a Regional Council (41 members), both of which are elected. The French government is represented by an appointed commissioner. Martinique is represented in the National Assembly by 4 deputies and in the Senate by 2 senators. Commissioner: Edouard Lacroix. President of the Conseil General: Emile Maurice. President of the Regional Council: Aime Cesaire.

LANGUAGE: French (official); a creole dialect is spoken by the majority.

RELIGION: Roman Catholic.

TOURIST INFORMATION: Passport, visa and return or onward ticket required

REUNION
Réunion

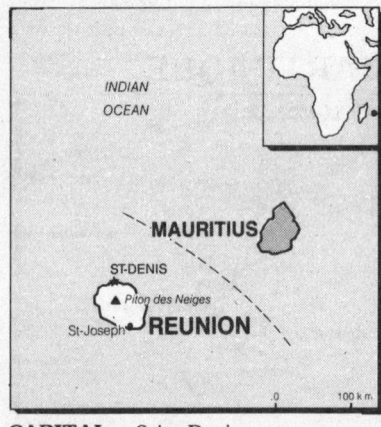

CAPITAL: Saint-Denis

AREA AND POPULATION: 2,512 km². Population (1986 est.): 552,500.

CLIMATE AND GEOGRAPHY: The climate is subtropical maritime, free from extremes of weather. There is no well-defined dry season. Average temperature: 26.7°C (January), 21.1°C (July). Annual rainfall: 1,400 mm. The island of Reunion is in the Indian Ocean, about 640 km east of Madagascar. Reunion administers five small uninhabited islands: Juan de Nova, Europa, Bassas da India, Iles Glorieuses and Tromelin.

GOVERNMENT: Reunion became an Overseas Department in 1946 and an administrative region in 1974. The island is administered by a Conseil General (36 members) and a Regional Council (45), both of which are elected. Reunion is represented in the National Assembly by 5 deputies and in the Senate by 2 members. The French government is represented by an appointed commissioner. Commissioner: Jean Anciaux. President of the Conseil General: Auguste Legros. President of the Regional Council: Pierre Lagourgue.

LANGUAGE: French (official); creole; Gujurati.

RELIGION: Majority Roman Catholic.

TERRITORIAL COLLECTIVITIES

MAYOTTE

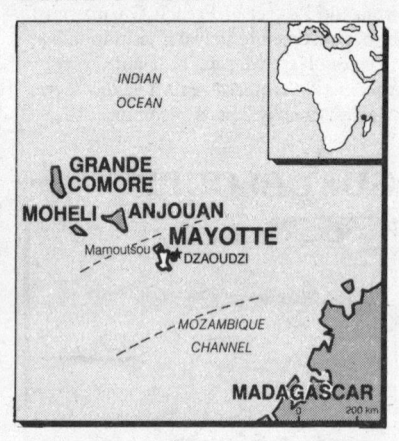

CHIEF TOWN: Dzaoudzi

CLIMATE AND GEOGRAPHY: Mayotte is part of the Comoros archipelago, north-west of Madagascar.

CURRENCY: French franc.

GOVERNMENT: A territorial collectivity. The island is administered by a Conseil General (17 elected members). The French government is represented by an appointed commissioner. Mayotte is represented in the National Assembly by 1 deputy and in the Senate by 1 member. Commissioner: Christian Pellerin. President of the Conseil General: Younoussa Bamana.

LANGUAGE: French (official); Mahorian.

RELIGION: Sunni moslem 97%; Christian (mainly Roman Catholic) minority.

ST PIERRE AND MIQUELON
Îles Saint-Pierre et Miquelon

CAPITAL: St Pierre

AREA AND POPULATION: 242 km². Population (1986 est.) 6,300.

CLIMATE AND GEOGRAPHY: The archipelago of 8 small islands lies off the south-west coast of Newfoundland.

NEW CALEDONIA • 719

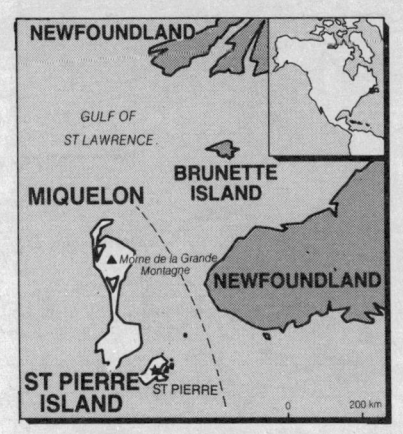

GOVERNMENT: A territorial collectivity. The islands are administered by a Conseil General (14 elected members). They are represented in the National Assembly by 1 deputy and in the Senate by 1 senator. The French government is represented by an appointed commissioner. Commissioner: Bernard Leurquin. President of the Conseil General: Marc Plantegenest.

RELIGION: Roman Catholic.

OVERSEAS TERRITORIES

FRENCH POLYNESIA
Territoire de la Polynésie Francaise

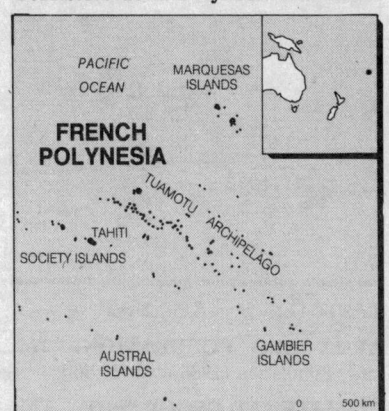

CAPITAL: Papeete, Tahiti

AREA AND POPULATION: 3,521 km². Population (1986 est.): 180,000.

CLIMATE AND GEOGRAPHY: Average temperature (Papeete): 27.1°C (January), 24°C (July). Annual rainfall: 2,106 mm. The territory consists of 5 archipelagoes with over 100 islands scattered over a wide area in the South Pacific: the Windward Islands including Tahiti; the Leeward Islands; the Tuamotu archipelago including the Gambier Islands; the Austral or Tubuai Islands and the Marquesas Islands.

CURRENCY: French Pacific franc (CFP).

GOVERNMENT: Overseas territory. The territory is administered by a Council of Ministers and a Territorial Assembly (41 elected members). French Polynesia is represented in the National Assembly by 2 deputies and in the Senate by 1 senator. High Commissioner: Pierre Angeli. President: Gaston Flosse.

LANGUAGE: French (official); Tahitian.

RELIGION: Protestants 46.5%; Roman Catholics 39.4%; Mormon 5.1%.

TOURIST INFORMATION: Passport, visa and onward or return ticket required by Australian citizens.

NEW CALEDONIA
Nouvelle Calédonie et Dépendances

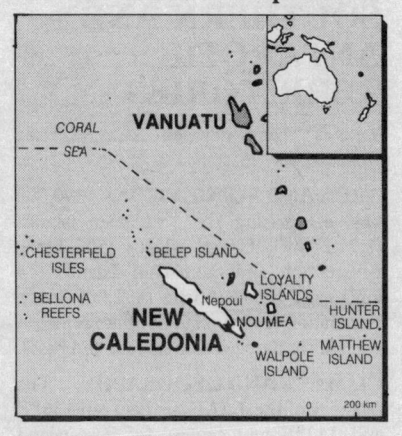

CAPITAL: Noumea

AREA AND POPULATION: 18,576 km². Population (1986 est.): 151,400.

Ethnic composition: Europeans 37%; Melanesians 43%; Vietnamese and Indonesians 5%; Polynesians 4%; Wallisians 8%.

CLIMATE AND GEOGRAPHY: Situated in the Pacific Ocean, east of Queensland, the territory consists of the island of New Caledonia and various outlying islands—the Loyalty Islands, the Isle of Pines, the Belep archipelago and other small islands.

CURRENCY: French Pacific franc (CFP).

GOVERNMENT: An overseas territory. The territory is administered by an Executive Council (5 members) and a Territorial Congress (46 members). The Council consists of the President of the Congress and the 4 Regional Council presidents. In France New Caledonia is represented by 2 deputies and 1 senator. High Commissioner: Jean Montpezat. President: Dick Ukeiwe.

RELIGION: Roman Catholic 72%; Protestant 16%; Moslem 4%.

TOURIST INFORMATION: Passport and onward or return ticket required by Australian citizens. To stay longer than 3 months necessitates a visa. Vaccination against typhoid and paratyphoid fevers is recommended.

SOUTHERN AND ANTARCTIC TERRITORIES

Terres Australes et Antarctiques Françaises

AREA AND POPULATION: 390,000 km^2 comprising the Kerguelen islands (7,215 km^2), Crozet islands (505 km^2), Amsterdam and Saint-Paul Islands (54 km^2), and Terre Adelie (432,000 km^2). Population (1985): 210. Staff are replaced annually at the scientific stations and bases.

CLIMATE AND GEOGRAPHY: The territory of the TAAF lies between 136°E and 142°E and consists of four island groups in the Indian Ocean—the Kerguelen and Crozet archipelagoes, the islands of Saint Paul and Amsterdam—and Terre Adelie, an ice-covered plateau on the Antarctic continent.

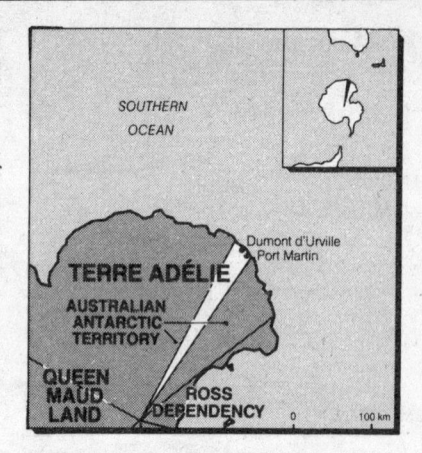

GOVERNMENT: The Administrator is assisted by a consultative council (7 members) meeting twice yearly in Paris. Administrateur superieur: Vice-Admiral Claude Pieri.

WALLIS AND FUTUNA

CAPITAL: Mata Utu, Uvea

AREA AND POPULATION: 274 km^2. Population (1986 est.): 13,500.

CLIMATE AND GEOGRAPHY: The territory consists of two groups of islands in the central Pacific. These are the Iles de Hoorn, 240 km north-east of Fiji, comprising the islands of Futuna and Alofi (uninhabited) and the Wallis archipelago, 160 km further north-east, consisting of one main island, Uvea, with a surrounding coral reef.

CURRENCY: French Pacific Franc (CFP).

GOVERNMENT: An overseas territory. The senior administrator is assisted by a Territorial Assembly (20 members). The islands are represented in the National Assembly by 1 deputy and in the Senate by 1 senator. Administrateur superieur: Robert Thil. President of the Territorial Assembly: Falakiko Gata.

LANGUAGE: French (official); Wallisian; Futunian.

RELIGION: Roman Catholic.

TOURIST INFORMATION: As for New Caledonia.

NETHERLANDS ARUBA

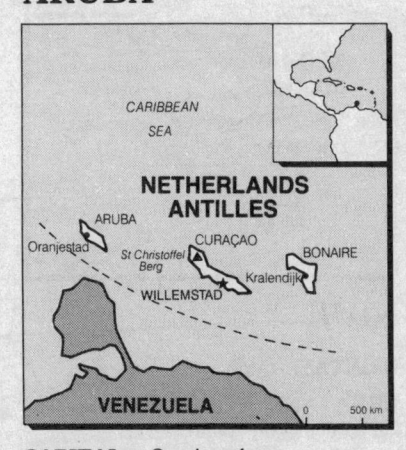

CAPITAL: Oranjestad

AREA AND POPULATION: 193 km². Population (1987 est.): 65,800.

CLIMATE AND GEOGRAPHY: Tropical maritime climate. Average temperature: 26°C (January), 29°C (July). Annual rainfall: 432 mm. Aruba is part of the Netherlands Antilles in the south Caribbean.

CURRENCY: Aruban guilder.

GOVERNMENT: An autonomous part of the Kingdom of the Netherlands. Full independence is expected in 1996. The Governor is appointed by the monarch. A Council of Ministers advises the Governor and the unicameral legislature (Staten) has 21 members. Governor: Felipe Tromp. Prime Minister: J. H. A. Eman.

LANGUAGE: Dutch (official); Papiamento.

RELIGION: Roman Catholic over 90%.

NETHERLANDS ANTILLES
De Nederlandse Antillen

CAPITAL: Willemstad

AREA AND POPULATION: 800 km² Population (1987 est.): 189,960.

CLIMATE AND GEOGRAPHY: Tropical maritime climate. Average temperature: 26.1°C (January), 27.8°C (July). Annual rainfall: 582 mm. The Netherlands Antilles, in the eastern Caribbean, comprises two groups of islands: Curacao and Bonaire of the Leeward Islands and Sint Maarten, Sint Eustatius and Saba of the Windward Islands.

CURRENCY: Netherlands Antilles guilder.

GOVERNMENT: Internally autonomous part of the Kingdom of the Netherlands. Executive power rests with the Governor and Council of Ministers. The legislature comprises a unicameral Staten of 22 members. Each island has its own Council. Governor: Dr Rene Romer. Prime Minister: Domenico Felip Martina.

LANGUAGE: Dutch (official); Papiamento is spoken in the Leeward Islands and English in the Windwards.

RELIGION: Roman Catholic 85%.

TOURIST INFORMATION: Passport, sufficient means of support and a return or through ticket are required by Australian citizens. The Certificate of Admission is issued on arrival for a temporary stay between 14 and 30 days. There is a departure tax of 10 guilders.

NEW ZEALAND
COOK ISLANDS

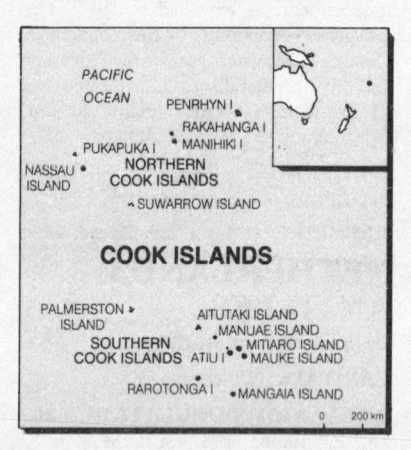

CAPITAL: Avarua, Rarotonga

AREA AND POPULATION: 240 km² of land area over 2,200,000 km² of ocean. Population (1981): 17,754. More than half the population live on Rarotonga.

CLIMATE AND GEOGRAPHY: Equable climate. Mean annual temperature: 24°C. Average rainfall: 2,030 mm. The Cook Islands are two groups of 15 scattered islands known as the Northern group and the Lower group, situated midway between Samoa and Tahiti.

CURRENCY: Cook Island and New Zealand dollars.

GOVERNMENT: A self-governing territory in free association with New Zealand. They have common citizenship of New Zealand and a common head of state, the Queen. There is a ministerial system of government with a Cabinet (7 members) and a Legislative Assembly (24 members). New Zealand is responsible for their defence and external affairs and has a Representative in the Cook Islands. A House of Arikis (Chiefs) advises the government. Prime Minister: Sir Thomas Davis.

TOURIST INFORMATION: Passport not required for nationals of Australia if their stay does not exceed 31 days. They will require a passport for re-entry to New Zealand. There is a departure tax of NZ$20.

KERMEDEC ISLANDS

AREA AND POPULATION: 33 km². Population: 10 at Raoul Island Meteorological Station.

CLIMATE AND GEOGRAPHY: Mild climate. Mean annual temperature: 19°C. Annual rainfall: 1,450 mm. Situated 965 km north of Auckland. The volcanic islands consist of Raoul Island, Macauley Island, the Herald group, Curtis Island and L'Esperance.

GOVERNMENT: Administered by the New Zealand Land and Survey Department.

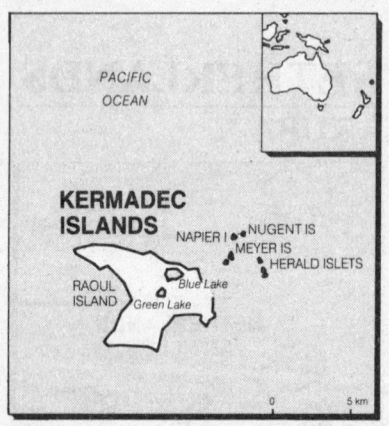

NIUE

CAPITAL: Alofi

AREA AND POPULATION: 258 km². Population (1986): 2,531.

CLIMATE AND GEOGRAPHY: Lying 2,148 km from Auckland, Niue is the largest and most western of the Cook Islands.

GOVERNMENT: Self-governing state in free association with New Zealand. The Legislative Assembly has 20 members. New Zealand is responsible for defence and external affairs. Premier: Robert Rex.

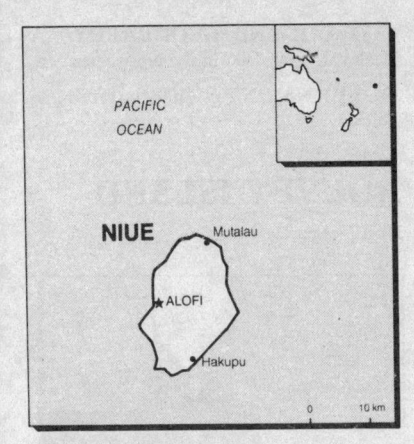

LANGUAGE: English; indigenous Polynesian language.

RELIGION: Ekalesia Niue (related to London Missionary Society) 75%.

TOURIST INFORMATION: Passport, sufficient funds for maintenance and confirmed return or onward tickets are required by Australian citizens for a stay of less than 30 days. A departure tax of NZ$10 is levied on all passengers leaving Niue.

ROSS DEPENDENCY

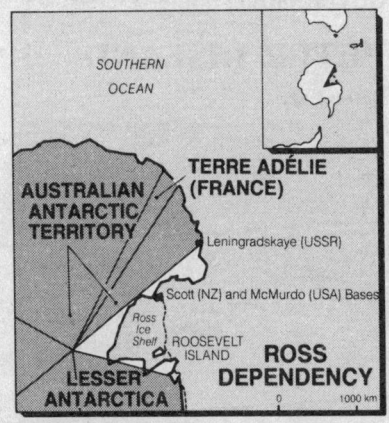

MAIN BASE: Scott Base, Ross Island

AREA AND POPULATION: 400,000 –450,000 km² (est.). Mostly ice-covered. Scott Base is inhabited throughout the year but has only about 12 people in winter. Vanda station is occupied every summer.

CLIMATE AND GEOGRAPHY: The territory lies between 160°E longitude and 150°W longitude and south of 60°S latitude.

GOVERNMENT: Governed according to regulations promulgated by the New Zealand Governor-General.

TOKELAU

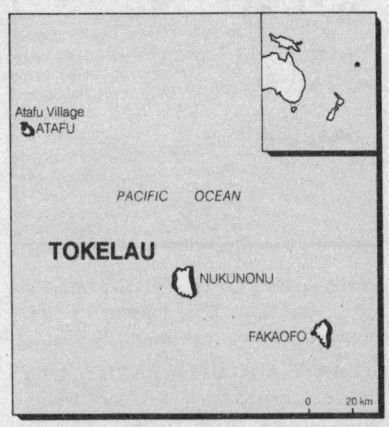

AREA AND POPULATION: 12 km². Population (1986): 1,703. Between 1965 and 1975 the population agreed to resettle in New Zealand because of a restricted economic future. After 528 migrated permanently, the scheme was suspended.

CLIMATE AND GEOGRAPHY: Tokelau, a scattered group of three small atolls, lies 480 km north of Western Samoa. The three islands are Afafu, Nukunonu and Fakaofo.

GOVERNMENT: Legislative powers are vested in the Governor-General in Council and the Administrator is the Secretary of Foreign Affairs. Certain powers are delegated to the district officer in Apia, Western Samoa. Each atoll has a Council of Elders (Taupulega).

LANGUAGE: Tokelauan; English.

RELIGION: Atagu (Congregational Church of Samoa); Nukunonu (Roman Catholic); Fakaofo (both).

NORWAY
SVALBARD

AREA AND POPULATION: 62,000 km². Population: 3,800 (approx.) Ethnic composition: Norwegians and Russians.

CLIMATE AND GEOGRAPHY: Arctic climate tempered by mild Atlantic winds. An archipelago in the Arctic Ocean, the main island is Spitzbergen.

GOVERNMENT: Incorporated in Norway. Governor: Leif Eldring.

JAN MAYEN

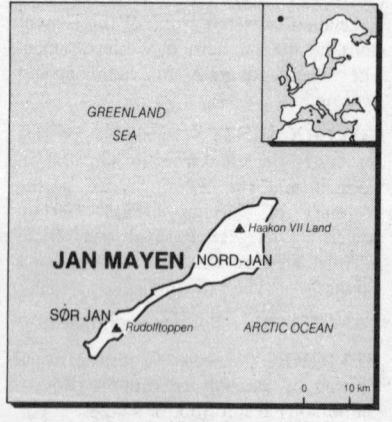

AREA AND POPULATION: 373 km². Uninhabited except for a meteorological station.

CLIMATE AND GEOGRAPHY: A bleak volcanic island in the Norwegian Sea.

GOVERNMENT: Incorporated in Norway.

BOUVET ISLAND
Bouvetøya

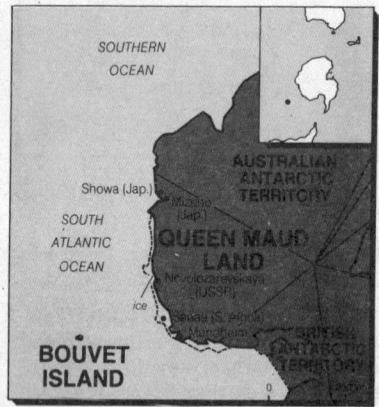

AREA AND POPULATION: 50 km² Uninhabited.

CLIMATE AND GEOGRAPHY: A glacier-covered island in the South Atlantic.

GOVERNMENT: A dependency.

PETER I ISLAND
Peter I Øy

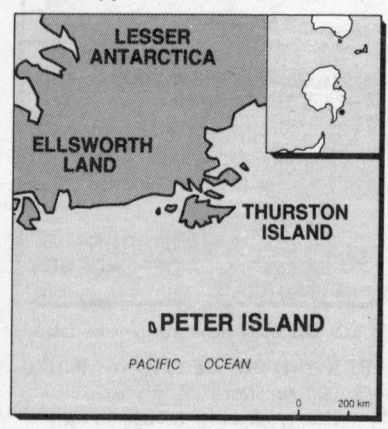

AREA AND POPULATION: 180 km². Uninhabited.

CLIMATE AND GEOGRAPHY: Peter I Island is in the Bellingshausen Sea off Antarctica.

GOVERNMENT: A dependency.

QUEEN MAUD LAND
Dronning Maud Land

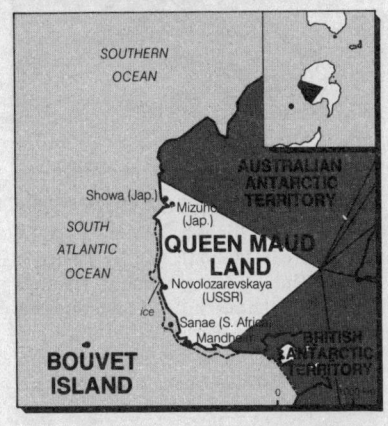

CLIMATE AND GEOGRAPHY: Queen Maud Land is in the Antarctic territory between 20°W and 45°E.

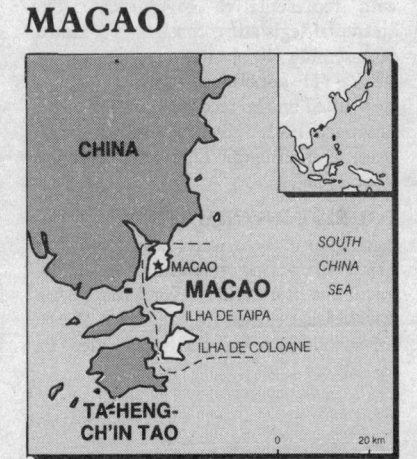

PORTUGAL
MACAO

AREA AND POPULATION: 16.92 km². Population (1985 est.) 400,000.

CLIMATE AND GEOGRAPHY: Tropical climate. Macao comprises a peninsula and two small islets – Taipa and Coloane – in the mouth of the Canton River.

CURRENCY: Pataca of 100 avos.

GOVERNMENT: A Chinese territory under Portuguese administration, Macao is to be handed over to China in 1999. Internal legislative authority consists of a Legislative Assembly (17 deputies). The Governor is appointed by the Portuguese president. Governor: Rear Admiral Vasco Almeida e Costa.

LANGUAGE: Portuguese (official); Cantonese; English.

TOURIST INFORMATION: Passport required by Australian citizens.

UNITED KINGDOM
ANGUILLA

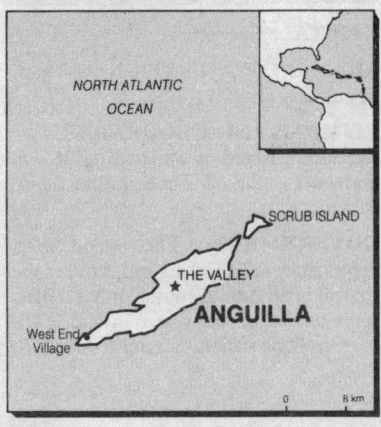

CAPITAL: The Valley

AREA AND POPULATION: 155 km². Population (1984 est.): 7,019.

CLIMATE AND GEOGRAPHY: Anguilla is one of the most northern of the Leeward Islands in the Caribbean Sea. It includes the island of Sombrero.

CURRENCY: Eastern Caribbean dollar.

GOVERNMENT: Anguilla seceded from St Christopher. Executive power rests with the Governor and the legislature comprises an Executive Council (6 members) and a House of Assembly (17 elected, 2 nominated and 2 official). Governor: A. T. Baillie. Chief Minister: Emile Gumbs.

ASCENSION ISLAND

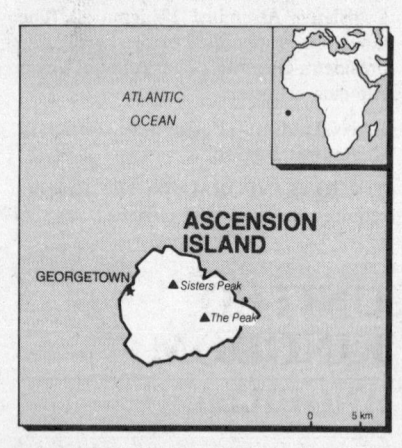

CAPITAL: Georgetown

AREA AND POPULATION: 88 km². Population (1985): 1,708.

CLIMATE AND GEOGRAPHY: Ascension Island is situated 1,126 km north-west of St Helena in the South Atlantic.

GOVERNMENT: The island is a dependency of St Helena and is under the control of an Administrator. It has a BBC communications relay station and a US space tracking station. Administrator: T. S. Blick.

BERMUDA

CAPITAL: Hamilton

AREA AND POPULATION: 53.3 km². 6 km² are leased to the USA for naval and air bases until 2040. There are 244 hectares under cultivation. Population (1985 est.): 57,145.

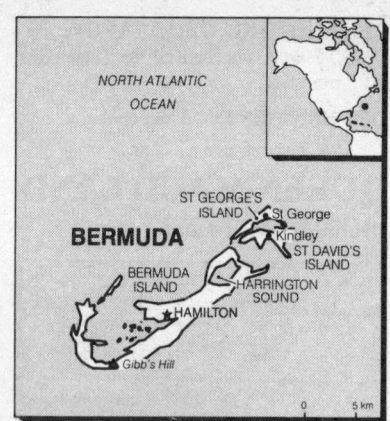

CLIMATE AND GEOGRAPHY: The climate is warm and humid. Average temperature (Hamilton): 17.2°C (January), 26.1°C (July). Average annual rainfall (throughout the year): 1,463 mm. Situated in the western Atlantic, 1,104 km from New York, Bermuda consists of a group of 150 small islands, about 20 of which are inhabited.

CURRENCY: Bermuda dollar of 100 cents.

DEFENCE: Bermuda Regiment of 734 men and women (1987); British and American military, naval and air force personnel are based in Bermuda.

GOVERNMENT: Bermuda is a colony with representative government. The bicameral legislature consists of a House of Assembly (40 elected members), and a Senate (11 appointed), with a Cabinet (appointed on the recommendation of the Premier). Full universal adult suffrage. Governor: Viscount Dunrossil. Premier: John Swan.

TOURIST INFORMATION: Australian citizens must hold onward or return tickets. Documents must be valid for travel to a destination beyond the USA if the USA is the next intended port of call. An airport tax of B$10 is levied on passengers.

BRITISH ANTARCTIC TERRITORY

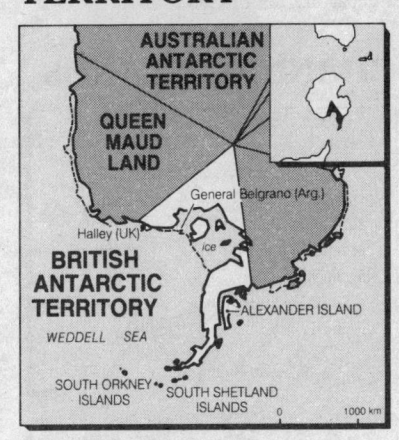

AREA AND POPULATION: 1,812,992 km². No permanent residents. Itinerant scientific and logistics staff of about 300.

CLIMATE AND GEOGRAPHY: The main areas are South Orkney and South Shetland Islands, the Antarctic peninsula (Palmer Land and Graham Land) and Coats Land.

GOVERNMENT: The territory is administered by a High Commissioner resident in Port Stanley. Designated personnel exercise certain legal and administrative functions. High Commissioner: Gordon Jewkes.

BRITISH INDIAN OCEAN TERRITORY

AREA AND POPULATION: 60 km². No permanent population.

CLIMATE AND GEOGRAPHY: The territory comprises the Chagos Archipelago, lying 1,899 km north-east of Mauritius. It consists of 5 coral atolls: Diego Garcia, Peros Banhos, Salomon, Eagle and Egmont.

DEFENCE: The territory was established to meet British and American defence requirements in the Indian Ocean. A US navy support facility is on Diego Garcia.

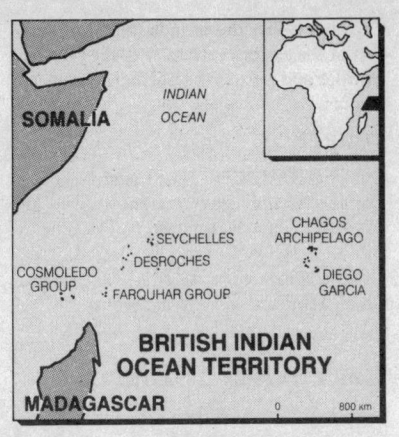

GOVERNMENT: Commissioner: W. Marsden. Administrator: T.C.S. Stitt. Both are non-residents.

BRITISH VIRGIN ISLANDS

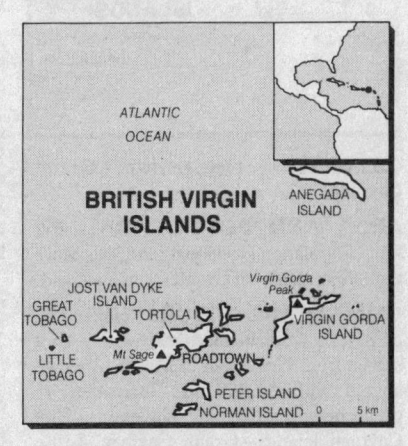

CAPITAL: Road Town, Tortola

AREA AND POPULATION: 130 km². Population (1980): 12,034. Fifteen of the islands are inhabited, with the largest being Tortola (9,322), Virgin Gorda (1,443), Anegada (169) and Jost Van Dyke (136).

CLIMATE AND GEOGRAPHY: A sub-tropical climate. Average annual rainfall: 1,250 mm. Situated in the

Caribbean Sea, the islands (about 40) are part of the eastern extremity of the Greater Antilles and part of the northern Leeward Islands.

CURRENCY: United States dollar.

GOVERNMENT: The islands have representative government with an Executive Council (4 ministers, 1 ex officio) and Legislative Council (9 elected, 1 ex officio). Governor: J. Mark Herdman. Chief Minister: H. Lavity Stoutt.

CAYMAN ISLANDS

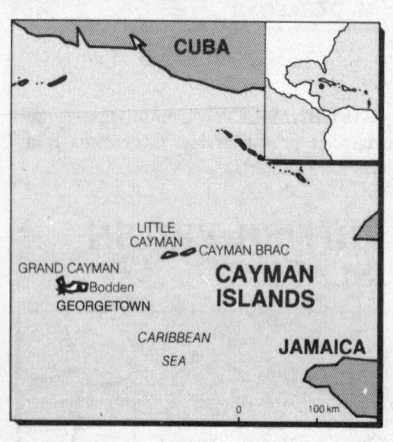

CAPITAL: Georgetown, Grand Cayman

AREA AND POPULATION: 260 km². Population (1985 est.): 20,300. More than 90% reside on Grand Cayman island.

CLIMATE AND GEOGRAPHY: The climate is tropical maritime, with a cool season from November to March. Average annual rainfall: 1,400 mm. Hurricanes can occur between July and November. The Cayman Islands—Grand Cayman, Little Cayman and Cayman Brac—are in the Caribbean Sea, 322 km north-west of Jamaica.

CURRENCY: Cayman Island dollar of 100 cents.

GOVERNMENT: The Cayman Islands are a crown colony, under a Governor. There is a Legislative Assembly (12 elected, 3 official) and an Executive Council (3 official, 4 elected). Governor: A. J. Scott.

LANGUAGE: English.

TOURIST INFORMATION: Passport required by Australian citizens. There is a departure tax of C$6.

CHANNEL ISLANDS

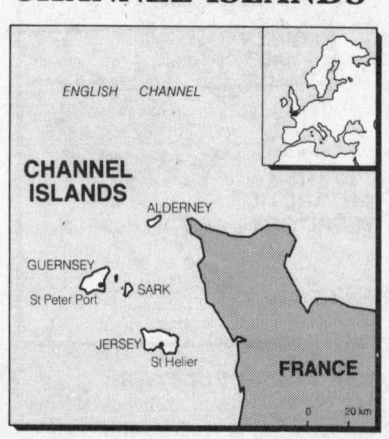

CAPITAL: St Helier, Jersey; St Peter Port, Guernsey.

AREA AND POPULATION: 194 km². Population: Jersey 80,212; 55,482 (1986); Alderney 2,086 (1981 est.); Sark 420 (1984 est.).

CLIMATE AND GEOGRAPHY: The climate is mild. Average rainfall: Jersey 797.1 mm; Guernsey 761.9 mm. Temperature range: (Jersey) lowest −9.3°C, highest 30.1°C; (Guernsey) lowest −4.7°C, highest 26.4°C. Situated off the north-west coast of France in the English Channel, the Channel Islands consist of Jersey and Guernsey, and the dependencies of Guernsey—Alderney, Brechou, Great Sark, Little Sark, Herm, Jethou and Lihou.

GOVERNMENT: The Lieutenant-Governors of Jersey and Guernsey are appointed by the Crown, as are the Bailiffs. The legislature of Jersey—the States of Jersey—consists of 12 senators, 12 constables and 29 deputies, all elected on universal suffrage. The parliament of Guernsey—the States of Deliberation—comprises the Bailiff, 12 Counseillers, the 2 Law Officers of the Crown, 33 People's Deputies, 10 Douzaine Representatives and 2 representatives of the States of Alderney.

Alderney has its own elected President and States (12 members). Sark is a mixture of feudal and popular government with its Chief Pleas (parliament) of 40 tenants and 12 elected deputies, presided over by the Seneschal. Heads of government: Jersey—Lieutenant-Governor: Admiral Sir William Pillar; Bailiff and President of the States: Peter Crill. Guernsey—Lieutenant-Governor: Sir Alexander Boswell; Bailiff and President of the States: Sir Charles Frossard. Alderney—President of the States: J Kay-Mouat. Sark—Seigneur: J. M. Beaumont; Seneschal: L. P. de Carteret.

LANGUAGE: French; English; Norman French dialect.

FALKLAND ISLANDS

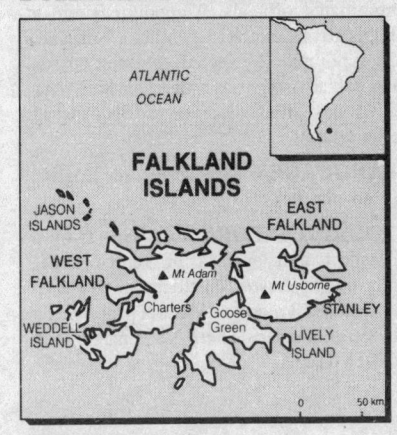

CAPITAL: Stanley

AREA AND POPULATION: 12,173 km^2. Population (1986): 1,919. Ethnic composition: nearly all of British descent with about 80% born in the islands.

CLIMATE AND GEOGRAPHY: A cool temperate climate with strong winds, especially in spring. Average temperature (Stanley): 9.4°C (January), 1.7°C (July). Average annual rainfall: 681 mm. The islands are in the South Atlantic Ocean, about 768 km north-east of Cape Horn. Most of the colony is divided into sheep runs.

CURRENCY: Falkland pound.

DEFENCE: On 2 April 1982, the islands were invaded by Argentina. Britain regained possession on 14 and 15 June after the Argentine surrender. A large garrison of British servicemen is stationed near Stanley.

GOVERNMENT: A crown colony, executive power is vested in the Governor. An Executive Council (3 elected and 2 ex officio) and a Legislative Council (8 elected, 2 ex officio) comprise the legislature. Governor: G. W. Jewkes. Chief Executive: D. G. P. Taylor.

GIBRALTAR

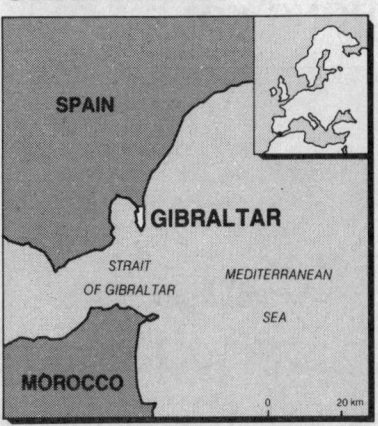

AREA AND POPULATION: 6.5 km^2. Population (1985 est.): 28,843. Ethnic composition: British Gibraltarian 69.4%; other British 18.8%. The population is mostly of Genoese, Portuguese, Maltese and Spanish descent.

CLIMATE AND GEOGRAPHY: The climate is warm temperate, with winter westerlies bringing rain. Average temperature: 12.8°C (January), 23.9°C (July). Average annual rainfall: 772 mm. Gibraltar is a rocky promontory on the southern coast of Spain, at the entrance to the Mediterranean.

CURRENCY: Gibraltar government notes and UK coins.

DEFENCE: The Gibraltar Regiment is a part-time infantry battalion with a small regular cadre. A British army battalion is also resident.

GOVERNMENT: A crown colony, executive authority is exercised by the

Governor. A House of Assembly (15 elected, 2 ex officio and Speaker) and a Council (4 ex officio, 5 appointed Assembly members) comprise the legislature. A Council of Ministers is presided over by the Chief Minister. A Mayor is elected from the Assembly. Governor: Air Chief Marshal Sir Peter Terry. Chief Minister: Sir Joshua Hassan.

RELIGION: Roman Catholic.

TOURIST INFORMATION: Passport required by Australian citizens.

HONG KONG

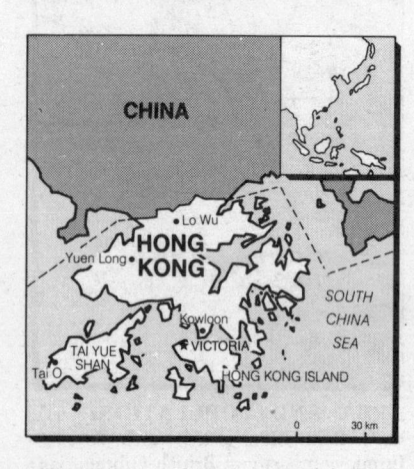

CAPITAL: Victoria

AREA AND POPULATION: 1,069 km² comprising Hong Kong island (79.21 km²), the New Territories (about 975 km²) and the Kowloon peninsula (11.31 km²). A large part is steep and unproductive hillside, with only 9% suitable for crop farming. Population (1986): 5,431,200. About 59% of the population was born in Hong Kong.

CLIMATE AND GEOGRAPHY: The warm subtropical climate is much affected by monsoons. The winter is cool and dry and the summer, hot and humid. Average temperature: 15.6°C (January), 28.3°C (July). Average annual rainfall: 2,162 mm. The territory is east of the mouth of the Pearl River. Hong Kong island is separated from the mainland by a natural harbour. The New Territories are the area immediately adjacent on the mainland and the numerous islands nearby. 2,154 hectares have been reclaimed since 1945.

CURRENCY: Hong Kong dollar.

DEFENCE: The Hong Kong garrison is under the Commander of the British Forces. The army constitutes the bulk of the garrison. The naval base is at HMS *Tamar* and the RAF at Shek Kong. The local auxiliary defence units consist of the Royal Hong Kong Regiment (The Volunteers): 950; and the Royal Hong Kong Auxiliary Air Force: 131.

GOVERNMENT: A crown colony, Hong Kong is under British administration, leased from China until 1997. The Governor is assisted by an Executive Council (4 ex officio, 3 nominated officials, 9 appointed) and a Legislative Council (3 ex officio, 7 official, 22 appointed, 24 elected). District boards have an advisory role. Governor: Sir David Wilson. Chief Secretary: Sir David Akers-Jones.

LANGUAGES: Chinese and English (both official).

TOURIST INFORMATION: Only a passport and onward or return ticket required by Australian citizens if visit does not exceed 3 months. Malaria prophylaxis is recommended. There is a departure tax of HK$120.

ISLE OF MAN

CAPITAL: Douglas

AREA AND POPULATION: 572 km². Population (1986): 64,282.

CLIMATE AND GEOGRAPHY: The Isle of Man is in the Irish Sea, 32 km from Scotland.

GOVERNMENT: The Isle of Man is self-governing, with a Governor appointed by the Crown. The legislature, the Tynwald, consists of the Legislative Council (10 members) and the House of Keys (24 elected members). The island has its own laws. An Executive Council (9 members) advises the Governor. Lieutenant-Governor: Major-General Laurence New.

MONTSERRAT

CAPITAL: Plymouth

AREA AND POPULATION: 106 km². Population (1985): 11,852.

CLIMATE AND GEOGRAPHY: A tropical climate with no well-defined rainy season. Average annual rainfall: 1,628 mm. Average temperature: 24.4°C (January), 27.2°C (July). Montserrat is in the Caribbean Sea in the Leeward Island group, 40 km south-west of Antigua.

CURRENCY: Eastern Caribbean dollar of 100 cents.

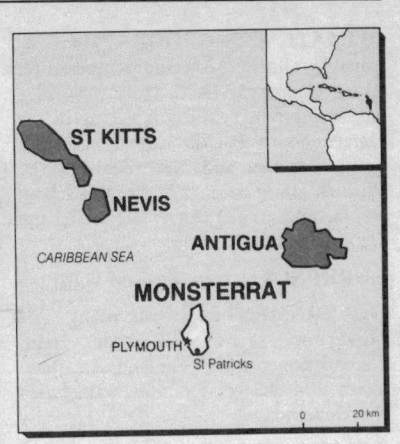

GOVERNMENT: Part of the Leeward Islands until 1956, Montserrat is a crown colony. An Executive Council (4 elected ministers, 2 officials) and Legislative Council (7 elected, 2 officials, 2 nominated) comprise the legislature. Governor: A. C. Watson. Chief Minister: J. A. Osborne.

TOURIST INFORMATION: No passport or visa required for Australian citizens except for a valid return or onward ticket and sufficient funds for intended stay. There is an airport service fee of US$5.

PITCAIRN ISLANDS

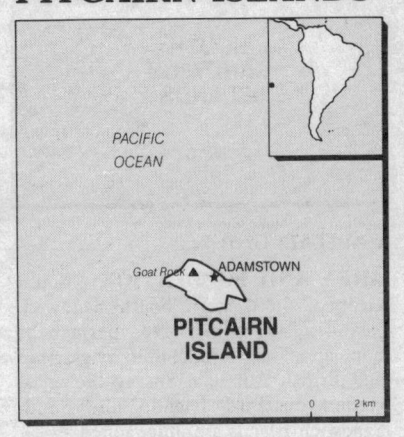

CAPITAL: Adamstown

AREA AND POPULATION: 4.53 km². Population (1986): 64. Only Pitcairn Island is inhabited. It was settled by the mutineers of HMS *Bounty*.

CLIMATE AND GEOGRAPHY:
Equable climate. Average temperature: 24°C (January), 19°C (July). Average annual rainfall: 2,000 mm. Lying in the eastern South Pacific halfway between South America and New Zealand, the Pitcairn group consists of Pitcairn Island and the uninhabited Ducie, Henderson and Oeno Islands.

CURRENCY: New Zealand dollar.

GOVERNMENT: British colony. The Governor is the British High Commissioner to New Zealand. An Island Council (4 elected, 5 nominated) advises the Governor.

RELIGION: Seventh Day Adventist.

SOUTH GEORGIA AND SOUTH SANDWICH ISLANDS

CAPITAL: Grytviken

AREA AND POPULATION: South Georgia: 3,592 km². South Sandwich Islands: 337 km². No permanent population: only a small military garrison and British Antarctic Survey biological station on Bird Island. The South Sandwich Islands are uninhabited.

CLIMATE AND GEOGRAPHY:
With little seasonal variation, the climate is wet and cold with strong winds. South Georgia Island is 1,287 km south-east of the Falkland Islands, and the South Sandwich Islands 752 km south-east of South Georgia Island.

DEFENCE: Argentina invaded South Georgia on 3 April 1982; a British naval task force recovered the island on 25 April. There is a small military garrison.

GOVERNMENT: Until 1985 the territories were dependencies of the Falkland Islands. Executive power rests with a Commissioner who at present also administers the Falklands. Commissioner: G. W. Jewkes.

ST HELENA

CAPITAL: Jamestown

AREA AND POPULATION: 122 km². Population (1985 est.): 6,258.

CLIMATE AND GEOGRAPHY:
Mild climate. Temperature range: 24°C–29°C (summer), 18°–24°C (winter). Annual rainfall: 325–925 mm according to altitude. Situated in the South Atlantic, St Helena lies 1,920 km off the west coast of Africa.

GOVERNMENT: Colony. Executive power rests with a Governor and the legislature comprises an Executive Council and Legislative Council (2 ex officio, 12 elected). Governor: F. E. Baker.

THE TURKS AND CAICOS ISLANDS

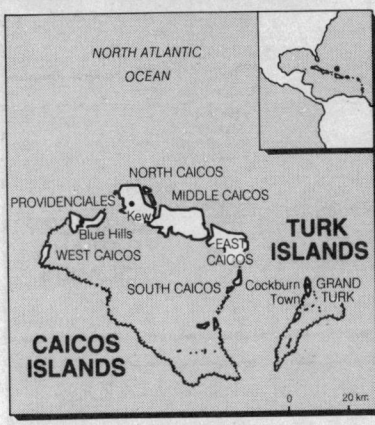

CAPITAL: Grand Turk

AREA AND POPULATION: 430 km². Population (1980): 7,436. Only 6 islands are inhabited: Grand Caicos, South Caicos, Middle Caicos, North Caicos, Providenciales and Salt Cay.

CLIMATE AND GEOGRAPHY: An equable climate with regular trade winds though sometimes hurricanes occur. Average temperature: 24.4°C (January), 28.3°C (July). Average annual rainfall: 725 mm. Situated in the West Indies, the islands form part of the south-eastern archipelago of the Bahamas. There are upwards of 30 small cays.

CURRENCY: United States dollar.

GOVERNMENT: A crown colony. The legislature comprises an Executive Council (8 members) and a Legislative Council (Speaker, 3 officials, 11 elected, 2 appointed). Chief Minister: Nathaniel Francis.

TRISTAN DA CUNHA

CAPITAL: Edinburgh

AREA AND POPULATION: 104 km². Population (1985): 313 – all in Edinburgh.

CLIMATE AND GEOGRAPHY: A group of islands of volcanic origin situated in the South Atlantic halfway between the Cape of Good Hope and South America, 2,124 km south-west of St Helena. The islands are Tristan da Cunha, Inaccessible Island, the three Nightingale Islands and Gough Island.

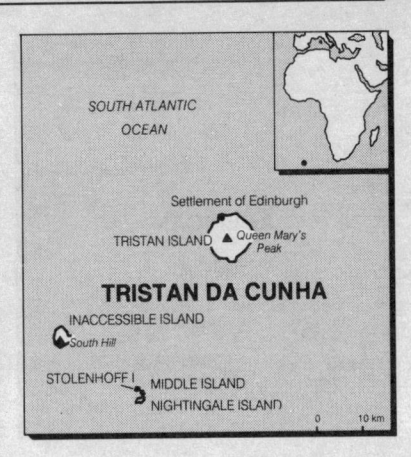

GOVERNMENT: The Tristan da Cunha islands are dependencies of St Helena and are under the control of an Administrator. An Island Council (3 nominated, 7 elected) advises the Administrator. Administrator: R. Perry.

UNITED STATES OF AMERICA
AMERICAN SAMOA

CAPITAL: Pago Pago, Tutuila

AREA AND POPULATION: 197 km². Population (1985): 34,500. Nearly all the population are of Polynesian descent.

CLIMATE AND GEOGRAPHY: Tropical maritime, with a high rainfall. Average temperature (Pago Pago): 21°C–32°C. Average annual rainfall: 4,850 mm. American Samoa lies 3,700 km south-west of Honolulu and consists of 6 small islands: Tutuila, Aunu'u, Ta'u, Olosega, Ofu and Rose (uninhabited). Swain's Island, 336 km to the north-west, is a part of the territory.

CURRENCY: United States dollar.

GOVERNMENT: An unincorporated territory. A bicameral legislature has limited legislative authority and consists of a House of Representatives (20 elected and 1 non-voting member for Swain's Island) and a Senate (18 elected in meetings of the chiefs). A Governor is elected and the territory has a member in the US Congress. Governor: A.P. Lutali.

LANGUAGE: Samoan and English.

RELIGION: Congregational Church over 50%; Roman Catholic about 23%.

TOURIST INFORMATION: Passport only is required by Australian citizens if their stay does not exceed 30 days.

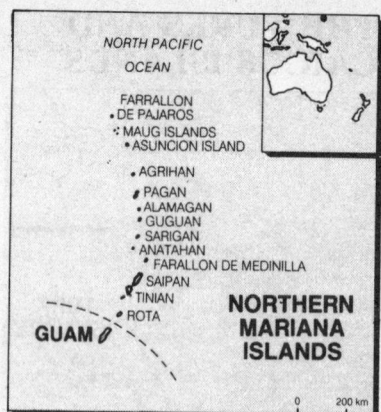

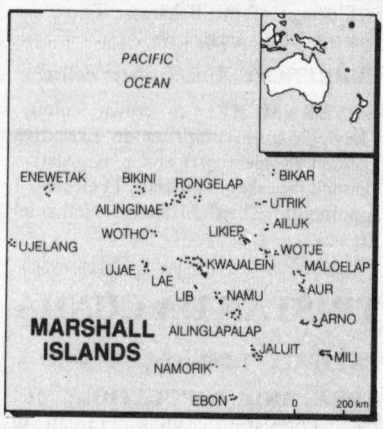

FREELY ASSOCIATED STATES:

COMMONWEALTH OF THE NORTHERN MARIANA ISLANDS, FEDERATED STATES OF MICRONESIA, MARSHALL ISLANDS

CAPITAL: Saipan, Mariana Islands; Kolonia, Pohnpei, FSM; Majuro, Marshall Islands

AREA AND POPULATION: 1,352 km^2: Northern Marianas 479 km^2; FSM 692 km^2; Marshall Islands 181 km^2. Population (1984 est.): 142,933.

CLIMATE AND GEOGRAPHY: High temperatures and rainfall. Average temperature (Jaluit, Marshall Islands): 27.2°C (January), 27.8°C (July). Average annual rainfall: 4,045 mm. The area is generally known as Micronesia and it consists of 3 major archipelagos, with over 2,000 islands and atolls: the Caroline islands, the Marianas and the Marshall Islands. The Marianas comprise an archipelago of 16 islands. The Federated States of Micronesia extends across the Caroline archipelago and comprises four states: Yap, Kosrae, Truk and Pohnpei. The Marshall Islands comprise 29 atolls and 5 coral islands.

GOVERNMENT: The freely associated states, previously part of the United Nations Trust Territory of the Pacific Islands, have full self-government. Free association with the United States gives the United States authority over military and defence in return for assistance to the autonomous governments. The Northern Marianas is a commonwealth with an elected Governor and Lieutenant-Governor and bicameral parliament of Senate (9 members) and House of Representatives (15 members). The Federated States of Micronesia has a federal Congress with a federal President and Vice-President. Each state is self-governing. The Congress has one 4-year senator from each state and ten 2-year senators. The Marshall Islands is a republic with an elected Assembly (33 members) and a President.

TOURIST INFORMATION: Entry requirements are as for the United States.

GUAM

CAPITAL: Agana

AREA AND POPULATION: 541 km². Population (1985): 120,977. Ethnic composition: mostly Chamorro (Micronesian) descent.

CLIMATE AND GEOGRAPHY: Tropical maritime with copious rainfall, the greatest falls from July to October. Average temperature (Agana): 27.2°C (January), 27.2°C (July). Average annual rainfall: 2,325 mm. Guam is the largest, most southern island of the Marianas archipelago, almost 6,000 km west of Hawaii.

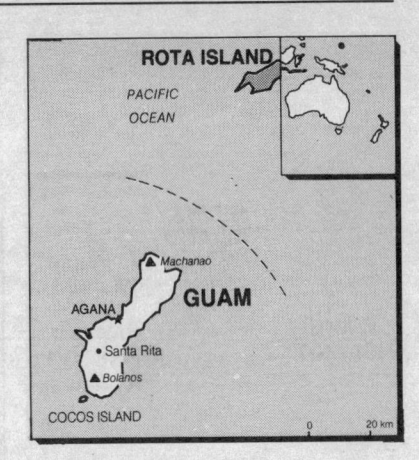

GOVERNMENT: An unincorporated territory. A Governor holds executive power and there is a unicameral legislature (21 members). Guam is represented by one non-voting delegate to the House of Representatives: it does not vote in the US presidential elections. Governor: Ricardo Bordallo.

LANGUAGE: English (official); Chamorro.

RELIGION: Roman Catholic about 98%.

TOURIST INFORMATION: Passport and visa required by Australian citizens.

PACIFIC TERRITORIES

JOHNSTON ATOLL

Two small islands, Johnston Atoll and Sand Island, 1,150 km south-west of Hawaii. 1.3 km². Population (1980): 327. Sand Island is uninhabited. Administered by the US air force.

MIDWAY ISLANDS

Two small islands, Sand and Eastern, at the western end of the Hawaiin chain in the North Pacific; 1,840 km north-west of Hawaii. 5.2 km². Population (1980): 453. Administered by the US navy.

WAKE ISLAND

Three small islands—Wake, Wilkes and Peale—lying 3,700 km west of Hawaii. 7.8

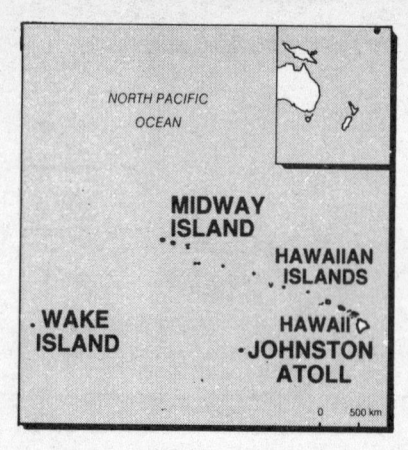

KINGMAN REEF

1,480 km south of Honolulu. Uninhabited. Administered by the US navy.

PALAU

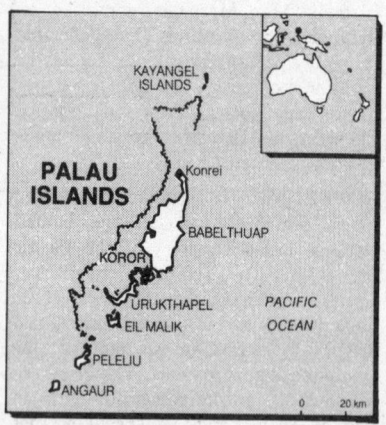

km². Population (1980): 302. Administered by the US air force.

TOURIST INFORMATION: Entry requirements are as for the United States.

HOWLAND, JARVIS AND BAKER ISLANDS

2400–2640 km south-west of Hawaii. 7.77 km². Uninhabited. Administered by the Department of the Interior.

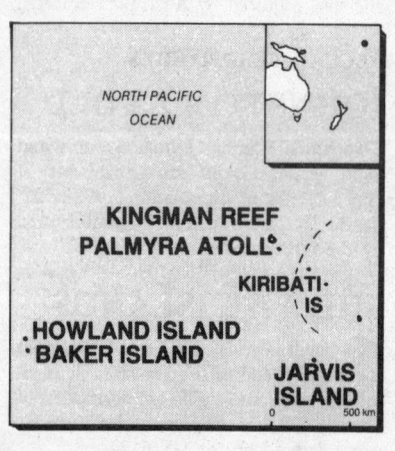

PALMYRA ISLAND

An atoll approximately 1,600 km south of Hawaii. 10.4 km². Uninhabited.

CAPITAL: Koror

AREA AND POPULATION: 460 km². Population (1984 est.): 13,000.

CLIMATE AND GEOGRAPHY: The average year-round temperature is 26°C. Average annual rainfall: 3,810 mm. Situated west of the Federated States of Micronesia, Palau consists of 26 larger islands and over 300 islets in the Caroline chain. The largest is Babelthuap.

GOVERNMENT: Republic. Palau is the only one of the former Trust Territory of Pacific entities to remain under the United Nations Trusteeship Agreement. The elected bicameral parliament consists of a Senate (18 members) and House of Delegates (16 members). The United States is represented by a High Commissioner. A Council of Chiefs advises the President on traditional law and custom.

LANGUAGE: Palauan.

TOURIST INFORMATION: As for the United States.

PUERTO RICO, COMMONWEALTH OF

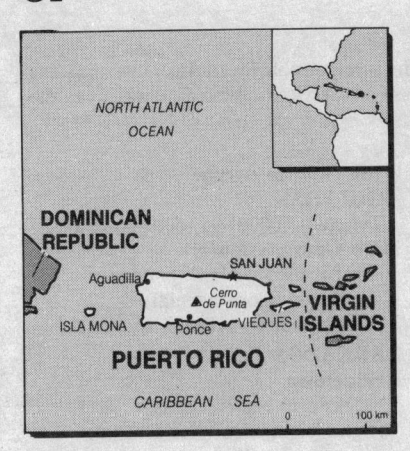

CAPITAL: San Juan

AREA AND POPULATION: 8,897 km^2. Population (1985): 3,279,231. Ethnic composition (1980): Hispanic (99.9%).

CLIMATE AND GEOGRAPHY: Mild with an average temperature of 25°C. The island of Puerto Rico is the most easterly of the Greater Antilles, lying between the Dominican Republic and the US Virgin Islands in the Caribbean Sea.

GOVERNMENT: Self-governing. Executive power resides in an elected Governor. An advisory council, the Council of Secretaries, is comprised of the 14 heads of departments. The legislature is a Senate (27 members) and House of Representatives (51 members). Puerto Rico elects a Resident Commissioner to the Congress but they have no vote. The island does not have a vote in the US presidential elections. Governor: Rafael Hernandez Colon.

LANGUAGE: Spanish; English.

TOURIST INFORMATION: Passport and visa required for Australian citizens.

VIRGIN ISLANDS

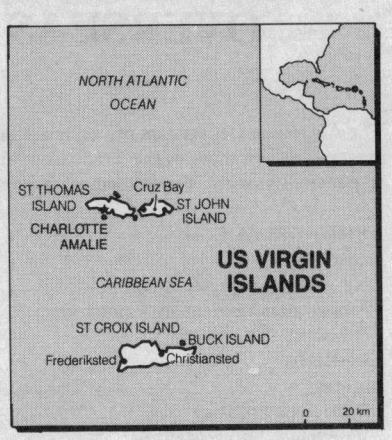

CAPITAL: Charlotte Amalie, St Thomas

AREA AND POPULATION: 344 km^2. Population (1984): 107,500. Ethnic composition: native born 20–25%; other Caribbean 35–40%; American 10%; European 5%.

CLIMATE AND GEOGRAPHY: Subtropical with gentle trade winds. Average temperature: 25°C–27.8°C. Average annual rainfall: 1,143 mm. The islands lie 65 km east of Puerto Rico in the south and west of the Virgin Islands group. The islands are St Thomas, St Croix, St John and about 50 small cays (mostly uninhabited).

CURRENCY: United States dollar.

GOVERNMENT: The islands are administered by the US Department of Interior. A unicameral legislature (15 senators) has limited powers. A Governor is elected. The islands do not participate in the US presidential elections and have a non-voting representative in Congress. Governor: Alexander Farrelly.

LANGUAGE: English; Spanish.

TOURIST INFORMATION: Passport and visa required for Australian citizens.

AUSTRALIAN MISSIONS OVERSEAS (April 1988)

The Australian Department of Foreign Affairs is responsible for all Australian missions overseas, except those of the Trade Commissioner Service (indicated *), which are the responsibility of the Department of Trade.

AFGHANISTAN
Kabul
 No resident representative
 Ambassador resident in Islamabad, Pakistan
ALGERIA
Algiers
 Australian Embassy
 12 Avenue Emile Marquis
 Djenane-el-Malik
 Hydra
 ALGIERS
 Tel: 602846, 601965, 609321
 (Weekly public holidays – Thursday and Friday)
Ambassador:
 His Excellency Mr C. G. O'Hanlon
ARGENTINA
Buenos Aires
 Australian Embassy
 Avenida Santa Fe 846 Piso 80
 (Swissair Building)
 BUENOS AIRES
 Tel: (01) 31-26841/48, 3125155
Ambassador:
 His Excellency Mr K. R. Douglas-Scott
AUSTRIA
Vienna
 Australian Embassy
 Mattiellistrasse 2-4
 A-1040 VIENNA
 Tel: (0222) 528580, 529710
Ambassador:
 His Excellency Mr M. J. Wilson
BAHAMAS
Nassau
 No resident representative
 High Commissioner resident in Kingston, Jamaica
Counsellor (Commercial):
 (Resident in Caracas, Venezuela)
BANGLADESH
Dhaka
 Australian High Commission
 184 Gulshan Avenue
 GULSHAN
 Tel: (02) 600091-95, 600456, 603775
High Commissioner:
 His Excellency Mr S. J. Boyd
Counsellor (Commercial):
 (Resident in New Delhi, India)
BARBADOS
Bridgetown
 No resident representative
 High Commissioner resident in Kingston, Jamaica
Counsellor (Commercial):
 (Resident in Caracas, Venezuela)
BELGIUM
Brussels
 Australian Embassy
 52 Avenue des Arts
 1040 BRUSSELS
 Tel: (02) 5113997, 5134146
Ambassador:
 His Excellency Mr P. C. J. Curtis
Counsellor (Financial):
 (Resident in Bonn, FRG)
Counsellor (Immigration):
 (Resident in The Hague, The Netherlands)
BOLIVIA
La Paz
 No resident representative
 Ambassador resident in Santiago, Chile
Counsellor (Commercial):
 (Resident in Caracas, Venezuela)
BOTSWANA
 No resident representative
 High Commissioner resident in Harare, Zimbabwe
BRAZIL
Brasilia
 Australian Embassy
 SHIS QI 19
 CONJUNTO 16
 CASA 1

DIPLOMATIC MISSIONS • 739

BRASILIA D.F.
Tel: (061) 286-7922
Ambassador:
His Excellency Mr W. Pearson

BRITAIN
London
Australian High Commission
Australia House
The Strand
LONDON WC 2 B 4LA
Tel: 01-379-4334 (b.h.).
Teleg: AUSTCOM LDN
Telex: 27565
High Commissioner:
His Excellency the Hon. D. McClelland, AC (Personal mail to visitors to the UK should be sent to State Agents-General or to the UK offices of Australian banks)
Edinburgh
Australian Consulate
Hobart House
80 Hanover Street
EDINBURGH EH2 2DL
Tel: (031) 2266271, 226623
Manchester
Australian Consulate
Chatsworth House
Lever Street
MANCHESTER M1 2DL
Tel: (061) 228 1344

BRUNEI
Bandar Seri Begawan
Australian High Commission
4th Floor
Teck Guan Plaza
Cnr Jalan Sultan and Jalan McArthur
Bandar Seri Begawan
NEGARA BRUNEI DARUSSALAM
Tel: (02) 29435/6
High Commissioner:
His Excellency Mr J. M. Starey

BULGARIA
Sofia
No resident representative
Ambassador resident in Belgrade, Yugoslavia
Counsellor (Commercial):
(Resident in Belgrade, Yugoslavia)

BURMA
Rangoon
Australian Embassy
88 Strand Road
Rangoon

Tel: (01) 80711, 80076, 80965
Ambassador:
His Excellency Mr C. L. Lamb
Defence Attaché:
(Resident in Bangkok, Thailand)
Counsellor (Commercial):
(Resident in Bangkok, Thailand)

CANADA
Ottawa
Australian High Commission
The National Building (13th Floor)
130 Slater Street
Ottawa K1P 5H6
ONTARIO
Tel: (613) 236-0841
High Commissioner:
His Excellency Mr R. S. Laurie
Minister (Economic):
(Resident in Washington, USA)
Counsellor (Legal):
(Resident in Washington, USA)
Defence Adviser:
(Resident in Washington, USA)
Naval Adviser:
(Resident in Washington, USA)
Army Adviser:
(Resident in Washington, USA)
Air Adviser:
(Resident in Washington, USA)
Toronto*
Australian Consulate-General
Suite 2324
Commerce Court West
Cnr King and Bay Streets
Toronto, ONTARIO M5L 1B9
Tel: (416) 367-0783
Vancouver*
Australian Consulate-General
800 Oceanic Plaza
1066 West Hastings Street
Vancouver, BC V6E 3X1
Tel: (604) 684-1177/8, 684-2191

CHILE
Santiago
Australian Embassy
420 Gertrudis Echenique
Las Condes
SANTIAGO DE CHILE
Tel: (02) 2285065
Ambassador:
His Excellency Mr M. J. Dan
Counsellor (Commercial):
(Resident in Buenos Aires, Argentina)

CHINA
Beijing
Australian Embassy
15 Donzhimenwai Street
San Li Tun
BEIJING
Tel: 522331-6
Ambassador:
His Excellency Mr D. M. Sadleir
Shanghai
Australian Consul-General
17 Fuxing Road West
SHANGHAI
Tel: 374580
Consul-General:
Mr A. M. McLean
COLOMBIA
Bogota
No resident representative
Ambassador resident in Caracas,
Venezuela
Counsellor (Commercial):
(Resident in Caracas, Venezuela)
COSTA RICA
San Jose
No resident representative
Ambassador resident in Mexico City,
Mexico
Counsellor (Commercial):
(Resident in Mexico City, Mexico)
CYPRUS
Nicosia
Australian High Commission
4 Annis Komminis Street
(Cnr Strassinos Avenue)
NICOSIA
Tel: (02) 473001
High Commissioner:
His Excellency Mr D. B. Wadham
CZECHOSLOVAKIA
Prague
No resident representative
Ambassador resident in Warsaw,
Poland
Second Secretary (Consular Affairs):
(Resident in Warsaw, Poland)
Counsellor (Commercial):
(Resident in Vienna, Austria)
DENMARK
Copenhagen
Australian Embassy
Kristianagade 21
2100 COPENHAGEN
Tel: (01) 262244, 262934, 262719

Ambassador:
His Excellency Mr J. Benson
Counsellor (Commercial):
(Resident in Stockholm, Sweden)
ECUADOR
Quito
No resident representative
Ambassador resident in Caracas,
Venezuela
Counsellor (Commercial):
(Resident in Caracas, Venezuela)
EGYPT
Cairo
Australian Embassy
5th Floor
Cairo Plaza South
Corniche-el-Nil
Boulac
CAIRO
Tel: (02) 777900, 777994, 777116
Ambassador:
His Excellency Mr I. Hutchens
EUROPEAN COMMUNITIES
Brussels
Australian Mission
52 Avenue des Arts
1040 BRUSSELS
Tel: (02) 5113997, 5134146
Ambassador:
His Excellency Mr P. C. J. Curtis
FIJI
Suva
Australian High Commission
7th and 8th Floors
Dominion House
Thomson Street
SUVA
Tel: 312844
High Commissioner:
His Excellency Mr R. L. C. Cotton
FINLAND
Helsinki
No resident representative
Ambassador resident in Stockholm,
Sweden
FRANCE
Paris
Australian Embassy
4 Rue Jean Rey
75724 PARIS CEDEX 15
Tel: (1)* 45756200 (b.h.), 45756233 (a.h.)
*Within France trunk access is 16.
Dial 16, await further dial tone, then dial area code and number.

Ambassador:
His Excellency Mr E. R. Pocock
GABON
Libreville
No resident representative
Ambassador resident in Lagos,
Nigeria
GERMAN DEMOCRATIC REPUBLIC
Berlin
No resident representative
Ambassador resident in Warsaw,
Poland
GERMANY, FEDERAL REPUBLIC OF
Bonn
  Australian Embassy
  Godesberger Allee 107
  5300, BONN 2
  Tel: (0228) 81030
Ambassador:
His Excellency Mr R. J. Greet
West Berlin
Office of the Australian Military Mission
Europa Centre
12th Floor
1 BERLIN 30
Tel: (030) 2618030
Head and Deputy Head: (Both resident in Bonn, FRG)
GREECE
Athens
  Australian Embassy
  15 Messogeion Street
  Ambelokipi 11526
  ATHENS
  Tel: (01) 775-7650/4
Ambassador:
His Excellency Mr K. I. Gates
Minister (Commercial):
(Resident in Rome, Italy)
GRENADA
St George's
No resident representative
High Commissioner resident in
Kingston, Jamaica
GUATEMALA
Guatemala City
No resident representative
Ambassador resident in Mexico City,
Mexico
GUYANA
Georgetown
No resident representative

High Commissioner resident in
Kingston, Jamaica
HOLY SEE
(Rome)
Office of the Australian Embassy to
the Holy See
Corso Trieste 27
00198 ROME
Tel: (06) 852792
Ambassador:
(Resident in Dublin, Ireland)
His Excellency Mr F. W. S. Milne, MBE
HONG KONG
Australian Consulate-General
23rd and 24th Floors
Harbour Centre
25 Harbour Road
WANCHAI
Tel: (5) 731881
Consul-General:
Ms P. A. Wensley
HUNGARY
Budapest
  Australian Embassy
  Forum Hotel
  V, Apaczai Csere Ju 12-14
  BUDAPEST
  Tel: (1) 188100, 188346, 188087
Ambassador:
His Excellency Mr O. J. Cordell
Counsellor (Commercial):
(Resident in Vienna, Austria)
ICELAND
Reykjavik
No resident representative
Ambassador resident in Copenhagen,
Denmark
INDIA
New Delhi
  Australian High Commission
  Australian Compound
  No 1/50-G Shantipath
  Chanakyapuri
  NEW DELHI 21
  Tel: (011) 601336-601339, 601400
High Commissioner:
His Excellency Mr G. B. Feakes, AO
Bombay
  Australian Consulate-General
  16th Floor
  Maker Towers, E Block
  Cuffe Parade
  Colaba
  BOMBAY
  Tel: (022) 211071/2, 217366

Consul-General:
Mr G. M. Bromilow

INDONESIA
Jakarta
Australian Embassy
Jalan Thamrin 15
Gambir
JAKARTA
Tel: (021) 323109, 350511
Ambassador:
His Excellency Mr W. L. Morrison
Bali
Australian Consulate
Jalan Raya Sanur 146
Tanjung Bungkak
DEN PASAR
Tel: (0361) 25997, 25998
Consul:
Mr K. McMahon

IRAN
Tehran
Australian Embassy
123 Shahid Khalid Al-Islambuli Avenue
Abassabad
TEHRAN
Tel: (021) 626202, 626223, 626236, 627906 (a.h.)
Ambassador:
His Excellency Mr M. A. S. Landale
Defence Attaché:
(Resident in Islamabad, Pakistan)

IRAQ
Baghdad
Australian Embassy
Masbah 39B/35
BAGHDAD
Tel: (01) 7193256, 7193430, 7193434, 7193435
Ambassador:
His Excellency Mr W. R. M. Steele

IRELAND
Dublin
Australian Embassy
Fitzwilton House
Wilton Terrace
DUBLIN 2
Tel: (01) 761517/9
Ambassador:
His Excellency F. W. S. Milne, MBE
Minister (Commercial):
(Resident in London, UK)

ISRAEL
Tel Aviv
Australian Embassy
185 Hayarkon Street
TEL AVIV
Tel: (03) 243152
Ambassador:
His Excellency Mr J. B. Campbell

ITALY
Rome
Australian Embassy
Via Alessandria 215
ROME 00198
Tel: (06) 841241
Ambassador:
His Excellency Mr D. Campbell
Milan*
Australian Consulate-General
Via Turati 40
MILAN 20121
Tel: (02) 659 8727/9
Consul-General:
Mr A. Karas

JAMAICA
Kingston
Australian High Commission
4th Floor
National Life Building
64 Knutsford Boulevard
KINGSTON 5
Tel: (92) 62550, 63551/2
High Commissioner:
His Excellency Mr D. I. Wille
Counsellor (Commercial):
(Resident in Caracas, Venezuela)

JAPAN
Tokyo
Australian Embassy
No 1-14 Mita 2 Chome
Minato-Ku
TOKYO
Tel: (03) 4530251/9
Ambassador:
His Excellency Mr W. G. T. Miller
Sankaido Building
7th Floor
9-13 Akasaka 1-Chome
Minato-Ku
TOKYO 107
Tel: (03) 5827231/9
Osaka*
Australian Consulate-General
23rd Floor
Osaka International Building
Azuchimachi 2-Chome
Higashi-ku
OSAKA
Tel: (06) 271-7071/6

Consul-General:
Mr A. K. Hogg
JORDAN
Amman
Australian Embassy
Between 4th and 5th Circles
Wadi Sir Road
Jabel Amman
AMMAN
Tel: (06) 613246/7
Ambassador:
His Excellency Mr T. J. Goggin
Counsellor (Commercial):
(Resident in Baghdad, Iraq)
KENYA
Nairobi
Australian High Commission
Development House
Moi Avenue
NAIROBI
Tel: (02) 334666/72
High Commissioner:
His Excellency Mr D. S. Campbell
KIRIBATI
Tarawa
Australian High Commission
Bairiki
TARAWA
Tel: 21184, 21192
High Commissioner:
His Excellency Mr P. G. Bassett
KOREA, REPUBLIC OF
Seoul
Australian Embassy
5th Floor
Kukdong-Shell Building
58-1 Shinmoonro 1-Ka
Chongro-Ku
SEOUL
Tel: (02) 730-6491/5
Ambassador:
His Excellency Mr R. Broinowski
Minister (Financial):
(Resident in Tokyo, Japan)
Counsellor (Energy, Science and Technology):
(Resident in Tokyo, Japan)
Counsellor (Customs):
(Resident in Tokyo, Japan)
Counsellor (Information):
(Resident in Tokyo, Japan)
KUWAIT
Kuwait
Australian Embassy
7th Floor, Al-Rashed Building
Fahd Al-Salem Street
KUWAIT
Tel: 433560, 437321, 2415880, 2415844
Ambassador:
(Resident in Jeddah, Saudi Arabia)
LAOS
Vientiane
Australian Embassy
Rue J. Nehru
Quartier Phone Xay
VIENTIANE
Tel: 2477, 4278
Ambassador:
His Excellency Mr P. A. Jackson
Counsellor (Commercial):
(Resident in Bangkok, Thailand)
LEBANON
Beirut
Australian Embassy
Farra Building
463 Bliss Street
RAS BEIRUT
Tel: 803340/3, 803439
(Embassy temporarily closed)
Ambassador:
(Resident in Damascus, Syria)
Counsellor (Commercial):
(Resident in Baghdad, Iraq)
LESOTHO
No resident representative
High Commissioner resident in Pretoria, South Africa
LUXEMBOURG
No resident representative
Ambassador resident in Brussels, Belgium
MADAGASCAR
Antananarivo
No resident representative
Ambassador resident in Dar es Salaam, Tanzania
MALAYSIA
Kuala Lumpur
Australian High Commission
6 Jalan Yap Kwan Seng
KUALA LUMPUR
Tel: (03) 2423122, 2423458, 2423942
High Commissioner:
His Excellency Mr C. O. F. Hogue
MALDIVES, REPUBLIC OF
Male
No resident representative
Ambassador resident in Colombo, Sri Lanka

MALTA
Sliema
Australian High Commission
6th Floor
Airways House
Gaiety Lane
SLIEMA
Tel: 338201
High Commissioner:
His Excellency Mr G. E. C. Gibson
Minister (Commercial):
(Resident in Rome, Italy)

MAURITIUS
Port Louis
Australian High Commission
Rogers House
5 President John Kennedy Street
PORT LOUIS
Tel: 081701, 081702
High Commissioner:
His Excellency Mr I. L. James
Counsellor (Commercial):
(Resident in Nairobi, Kenya)

MEXICO
Mexico City
Australian Embassy
Plaza Polanco Torre B
10° Piso
Jaime Balmes II
Col. Los Morales
MEXICO D.F. 11510,
Tel: (5) 5663055
Ambassador:
His Excellency Mr W. Farmer

MONGOLIA
Ulan Bator
No resident representative
Ambassador resident in Moscow, USSR

MOROCCO
Rabat
No resident representative
Ambassador resident in Paris, France

MOZAMBIQUE
No resident representative
Ambassador resident in Harare, Zimbabwe

NAURU
Australian High Commission
Civic Centre
NAURU
Tel: 5230/1
High Commissioner:
Her Excellency Ms B. L. Gwinne

NEPAL
Kathmandu
Australian Embassy
Bhat Bhateni
KATHMANDU
Tel: 411578, 411579, 411304
Ambassador:
Ms D. K. Johnstone
Counsellor (Commercial):
(Resident in New Delhi, India)

THE NETHERLANDS
The Hague
Australian Embassy
Koninginnegracht 23
2514 AB THE HAGUE
Tel: (070) 630983
Ambassador:
His Excellency Dr D. Grimes

NEW CALEDONIA
Noumea
Australian Consulate-General
8th Floor
18 Rue de Maréchal Foch
NOUMEA
Tel: 272414
Consul-General:
Mr D. O'Leary
Consul (Commercial):
(Resident in Suva, Fiji)

NEW ZEALAND
Wellington
Australian High Commission
72-78 Hobson Street
Thorndon
WELLINGTON
Tel: (04) 736411/2, 736412 (after hours)
High Commissioner:
His Excellency Mr W. A. McKinnon, CBE
Auckland*
Australian Consulate-General
7th and 8th Floors
Union House
32-38 Quay Street
AUCKLAND 1
Tel: (09) 32429, 795-725
Consul-General:
Mr T. N. Cronin

NIGERIA
Lagos
Australian High Commission
16 Adeola Hopewell Street
LAGOS
Tel: (01) 618875, 618910

High Commissioner:
Mr R. H. Wyndham
Counsellor (Commercial):
(Resident in Nairobi, Kenya)
NORWAY
Oslo
No resident representative
Ambassador resident in Stockholm, Sweden
OMAN
No resident representative
Ambassador resident in Riyadh, Saudi Arabia
Counsellor (Commercial):
(Resident in Abu Dhabi, United Arab Emirates)
OECD
FRANCE
Paris
Australian Delegation
4 Rue Jean Rey
75015 PARIS CEDEX 15
Tel: (1) 45756200, 45756233 (a.h.)
Ambassador:
His Excellency Mr E. R. Pocock
PAKISTAN
Islamabad
Australian Embassy
Plot 17, Sector G4/4
Diplomatic Enclave No. 2
ISLAMABAD
Tel: (051) 822111/5
Ambassador:
His Excellency Mr G. Price, MBE
Counsellor (Commercial):
(Resident in Kuwait)
PANAMA
Panama City
No resident representative
Ambassador resident in Mexico City, Mexico
PAPUA NEW GUINEA
Port Moresby
Australian High Commission
Waigani
HOHOLA
Tel: 259333
High Commissioner:
His Excellency Mr L. L. Joseph
PARAGUAY
Asuncion
No resident representative
Ambassador resident in Buenos Aires, Argentina

PERU
Lima
No resident representative
Ambassador resident in Brazilia, Brazil
PHILIPPINES
Manila
Australian Embassy
China Banking Corporation Building
3rd Floor
Paseo de Roxas, Makati
Tel. (02) 874961, 882671/2
MANILA
Ambassador:
His Excellency Mr J. S. Holloway
POLAND
Warsaw
Australian Embassy
Estonska 3/5
Saska Kepa
WARSAW
Tel: (022) 176081/6
Ambassador:
His Excellency Mr L. Herron
Counsellor (Commercial):
(Resident in Vienna, Austria)
PORTUGAL
Lisbon
Australian Embassy
Avenida de Liberdade 244-40
LISBON 1200
Tel: (01) 523350, 523421, 523066, 523137, 523208
Ambassador:
His Excellency Mr B. W. Woodberry
Counsellor (Commercial):
(Resident in Madrid, Spain)
QATAR
No resident representative
Ambassador resident in Riyadh, Saudi Arabia
Counsellor (Commercial):
(Resident in Bahrain)
ROMANIA
Bucharest
No resident representative
Ambassador resident in Belgrade, Yugoslavia
Counsellor (Commercial):
(Resident in Belgrade, Yugoslavia)
SAUDI ARABIA
Riyadh
Australian Embassy
Opposite Riyadh Palace Hotel
Murabaa District

RIYADH
Tel: (01) 4012171, 4012145, 4012645
Ambassador:
His Excellency Mr A. J. McGoldrick
Jeddah
Australian Consulate-General
59 Amir Abdullah Al-Faysal Street
Al Hamra's District 5
Jeddah
Tel: (02) 6651303, 6652329, 6671107
SEYCHELLES
Mahe
No resident representative
High Commissioner resident in
Nairobi, Kenya
SINGAPORE
Australian High Commission
25 Napier Road
SINGAPORE 10
Tel: 7379311, 7379144
High Commissioner:
Her Excellency Ms M. R. McGovern
SOLOMON ISLANDS
Honiara
Australian High Commission
Mendana Avenue
HONIARA
Tel: 21561
High Commissioner:
His Excellency Mr M. J. Gaylard
SOUTH AFRICA
Pretoria
Australian Embassy
Mutual and Federal Building
4th Floor
220 Vermeulen Street
PRETORIA 0001
Tel: (012) 325-4315/24
Ambassador:
His Excellency Mr R. N. Birch
Capetown
Australian Embassy (Visa Office)
10th Floor
1001 Colonial Mutual Building
106 Adderley Street
CAPETOWN
Tel: (021) 232160
SPAIN
Madrid
Australian Embassy
Paseo de la Castellano 143
28046 MADRID
Tel: (1) 2798504/03/02/01
Ambassador:
His Excellency Mr C. Mott

SRI LANKA
Colombo
Australian High Commission
3 Cambridge Place
COLOMBO
Tel: (01) 598767/8/9
High Commissioner:
Vacant
Counsellor (Commercial):
(Resident in New Delhi, India)
SUDAN
Khartoum
No resident representative
Ambassador resident in Cairo, Egypt
SWAZILAND
No resident representative
High Commissioner resident in
Pretoria, South Africa
SWEDEN
Stockholm
Australian Embassy
Sergels Torg 12
STOCKHOLM C
Tel: (08) 244660
Ambassador:
His Excellency Mr I. E. Nicholson
SWITZERLAND
Bern
Australian Embassy
29 Alpenstrasse
BERN
Tel: (031) 430143/7
Ambassador:
His Excellency Mr D. A. Townsend
Minister (Commercial):
(Resident in Bonn, FRG)
First Secretary (Information):
(Resident in Bonn, FRG)
**Defence Attaché and Assistant
Defence and Air Attaché:**
(Both resident in Paris, France)
Geneva
Australian Consulate
56-58 Rue de Moillebeau
Petit Saconnex
1211 GENEVA 19
Tel: (022) 346200
Consul:
Mr M. J. Blackburn
SYRIA
Damascus
Australian Embassy
128A Farabi Street
Mezzeh

DAMASCUS
Tel: (011) 664317, 662603, 660238
Ambassador:
His Excellency Mr R. J. Spurr
Counsellor (Commercial):
(Resident in Baghdad, Iraq)
THAILAND
Bangkok
Australian Embassy
37 South Sathorn Road
BANGKOK 12
Tel: (02) 2860411
Ambassador:
His Excellency Mr R. J. Smith
TONGA
Nuku'alofa
Australian High Commission
Salote Road
NUKU'ALOFA
Tel: 21244/5
High Commissioner:
His Excellency Dr R. C. Hills
Counsellor (Commercial):
(Resident in Suva, Fiji)
TRINIDAD AND TOBAGO
Port of Spain
No resident representative
High Commissioner resident in Kingston, Jamaica
TUNISIA
Tunis
No resident representative
Ambassador resident in Algiers, Algeria
TURKEY
Ankara
Australian Embassy
83 Nenehatun Caddesi
Gazi Osman Pasa
ANKARA
Tel: (041) 286715
Ambassador:
His Excellency Dr D. W. Witheford
Counsellor (Commercial):
(Resident in Tel Aviv, Israel)
TUVALU
Funafuti
No resident representative
Commissioner resident in Suva, Fiji
UGANDA
Kampala
No resident representative
High Commissioner:
Resident in Nairobi, Kenya

UNION OF SOVIET SOCIALIST REPUBLICS
Moscow
Australian Embassy
13 Kropotkinsky Pereulok
MOSCOW
Tel: (095)* 2465011/6
* Within the USSR the area code is 95
Ambassador:
His Excellency Mr C. R. Ashwin, AO
UNITED ARAB EMIRATES
Australian Embassy
Sayed Mahamed Glass Tower Building
11th Floor
Tourist Club Area near Tourist Club Gates
ABU DHABI
Tel: (02) 821800
Ambassador:
Resident in Riyadh, Saudi Arabia
UNITED NATIONS
New York
Australian Mission to the United Nations
885 Second Avenue
NEW YORK, NY 10017
Tel: (212) 4216910
Ambassador and Permanent Representative:
His Excellency Mr R. A. Woolcott, AO
Geneva
Australian Permanent Mission to the Office of the United Nations
56 Rue de Moillebeau
Petit Saconnex
1211 GENEVA 19
Tel: (022) 346200
Ambassador and Permanent Representative:
His Excellency Mr R. H. Robertson
Paris
Australian Permanent Delegation to the United Nations Educational, Scientific and Cultural Organisation
4 Rue Jean Rey
75724 PARIS CEDEX 15
Tel: (1) 5756200, 5756233 (a.h.)
Vienna
United National Industrial Development Organisation
Mattiellistrasse 2-4
A-1040 VIENNA
Tel: (0222) 528580

Resident Representative:
Mr J. R. Kelso
UNITED STATES OF AMERICA
Washington
  Australian Embassy
  1601 Massachusetts Avenue, NW
  Washington, DC 20036
  Tel: (202) 7973000
Ambassador:
His Excellency Mr F. R. Dalrymple, AO
Los Angeles
  Australian Consulate-General
  611 North Larchmont Blvd
  Los Angeles, CA 900004
  Tel: (213) 380-0980/2
Consul-General:
Mr B. J. Teasey
Chicago
  Australian Consulate-General
  321 North Clark Street
  Suite 2930
  Chicago, Ill. 60601
  Tel: (312) 645 9440
Consul-General:
Mr T. B. McCarthy
Honolulu
  Australian Consulate-General
  1000 Bishop Street
  Honolulu, HAWAII 96813
  Tel: (808) 5245050
Consul-General:
Mr R. C. Smith
New York
  Australian Consulate-General
  International Building
  636 Fifth Avenue
  New York, NY 10111
  Tel: (212) 2454000
Consul-General:
The Hon. C. J. Hurford
San Francisco
  Australian Consulate-General
  Qantas Building
  360 Post Street
  San Francisco 8, CA 94108
  Tel: (415) 3626160
Consul-General:
Mr D. C. Rutter
Houston
  Australian Consulate-General
  1990 South Post Oak Boulevard
  Suite 800
  Houston, TEXAS 77056-9998
  Tel: (713) 629-9131

Consul-General:
Mr R. C. Whitty
URUGUAY
Montevideo
  No resident representative
  Ambassador resident in Buenos Aires, Argentina
VANUATU
Vila
  Australian High Commission
  Melitco House
  VILA
  Tel: 2777
High Commissioner:
His Excellency Mr G. L. Urwin
VENEZUELA
Caracas
  Australian Embassy
  Centro Plaza, Torre C, piso 20
  1st Transversal
  Los Palos Grandes
  CARACAS
  Tel: (02) 283-3487, 283-3488, 283-3490, 283-3090, 283-3110
Ambassador:
His Excellency Mr A. F. Dingle
VIETNAM
Hanoi
  Australian Embassy
  66 Ly Thyong Kiet
  HANOI
  Tel: 52763, 54468
Ambassador:
His Excellency Mr G. Alliband
Counsellor (Commercial):
(Resident in Bangkok, Thailand)
WESTERN SAMOA
Apia
  Australian High Commission
  Fea Gai Ma Leata Building
  Beach Road
  Tamaligi
  APIA
  Tel: 23411/2
High Commissioner:
His Excellency Mr A. P. Godfrey-Smith
YEMEN ARAB REPUBLIC
Sana'a
  No resident representative
  Ambassador resident in Riyadh, Saudi Arabia
YUGOSLAVIA
Belgrade
  Australian Embassy

13 Cika Ljubina
BELGRADE
Tel: (011) 624655, 632261
Ambassador:
His Excellency Mr J. H. A. Hoyle
ZAMBIA
Lusaka
Australian High Commission
3rd Floor, Memaco House
Sapele Road, (off South End, Cairo Road)
LUSAKA
Tel: (01) 219001/3
High Commissioner:
His Excellency Mr E. J. L. Ride, AM
Counsellor (Commercial):
(Resident in Nairobi, Kenya)

ZIMBABWE
Harare
Australian High Commission
3rd Floor
Throgmorton House
Cnr Samora Machel Ave and Julius Nyerere Way
HARARE
Tel: (0)* 794591/4
* Within Zimbabwe the area code is 10
High Commissioner:
His Excellency Mr P. F. Peters
Counsellor (Commercial):
(Resident in Nairobi, Kenya)

Source: Department of Foreign Affairs, Canberra.

CLIMATES AROUND THE WORLD

Average daily highs for the month are shown in Celsius and in Fahrenheit temperatures; average monthly precipitation is shown in rainfall millimetres; and average daily humidity is shown in percentages.

Place	Temperature (C/F)	Rainfall (mm)	Humidity (%)
JANUARY			
Adelaide	30/86	20	42
Alice Springs	36/97	50	31
Athens	18/64	62	77
Auckland	26/79	76	71
Boston	14/57	102	72
Brisbane	25/77	165	66
Cairns	32/90	430	74
Cairo	23/74	5	69
Canberra	28/82	61	61
Cape Town	25/78	5	72
Chicago	0/32	51	80
Darwin	32/90	391	82
Dublin	8/46	67	88
Florence	9/48	63	83
Frankfurt	3/37	58	86

Place	Temperature (C/F)	Rainfall (mm)	Humidity (%)
Hobart	21/70	48	59
Hong Kong	18/64	25	77
Honolulu	24/76	102	75
London	6/43	54	86
Los Angeles	18/65	76	67
Madrid	9/48	39	86
Melbourne	26/79	48	61
Mexico City	19/66	12	79
Moscow	-9/16	39	82
New York	3/37	102	72
Paris	6/43	56	88
Peking	1/33	5	68
Perth	29/85	5	51
Rio de Janeiro	29/84	127	82
Rome	11/52	71	85
San Francisco	13/55	127	85
Sydney	26/79	102	67
Tel Aviv	18/65	178	66
Tokyo	8/47	51	73
Toronto	-1/30	76	78
Venice	6/43	37	86
Vienna	1/34	39	81
Washington DC	5/42	76	73
Wellington	20/69	76	73
Zurich	2/36	74	88

FEBRUARY

Place	Temperature (C/F)	Rainfall (mm)	Humidity (%)
Adelaide	29/84	21	44
Alice Springs	35/95	25	34
Athens	19/66	37	74
Auckland	26/79	102	72
Boston	12/54	76	71
Brisbane	29/84	164	69
Cairns	31/89	406	76
Cairo	28/81	5	64
Canberra	27/81	61	67

CLIMATES • 751

Place	Temperature (C/F)	Rainfall (mm)	Humidity (%)
Cape Town	26/79	5	91
Chicago	1/34	51	79
Darwin	31/88	330	84
Dublin	8/46	55	86
Florence	11/52	65	84
Frankfurt	5/41	44	86
Hobart	22/72	41	63
Hong Kong	17/63	51	82
Honolulu	24/76	76	75
London	7/45	40	85
Los Angeles	19/66	76	74
Madrid	11/52	34	83
Melbourne	26/79	49	63
Mexico City	20/69	5	72
Moscow	-6/21	38	82
New York	3/38	102	70
Paris	7/45	46	87
Peking	4/39	5	67
Perth	29/85	5	53
Rio de Janeiro	29/85	127	84
Rome	13/55	62	86
San Francisco	15/59	102	84
Sydney	25/79	115	70
Tel Aviv	19/67	102	65
Tokyo	9/48	76	71
Toronto	-1/30	51	78
Venice	8/46	48	80
Vienna	3/37	44	80
Washington DC	6/44	76	71
Wellington	20/69	76	75
Zurich	5/41	69	88
MARCH Adelaide	27/81	24	48
Alice Springs	32/90	25	36
Athens	22/72	37	71

Place	Temperature (C/F)	Rainfall (mm)	Humidity (%)
Auckland	25/77	76	74
Boston	18/65	102	70
Brisbane	28/82	145	71
Cairns	30/87	457	78
Cairo	33/91	5	63
Canberra	24/75	53	69
Cape Town	20/69	5	93
Chicago	6/43	76	77
Darwin	32/90	260	84
Dublin	10/50	51	82
Florence	14/57	61	85
Frankfurt	11/52	38	84
Hobart	20/68	47	65
Hong Kong	19/67	76	84
Honolulu	25/77	76	73
London	10/50	37	81
Los Angeles	19/67	76	77
Madrid	15/59	43	80
Melbourne	24/75	53	66
Mexico City	24/75	5	68
Moscow	0/32	36	82
New York	7/45	102	70
Paris	12/54	35	85
Peking	11/52	5	69
Perth	27/81	25	58
Rio de Janeiro	28/83	127	87
Rome	15/59	57	83
San Francisco	16/61	76	83
Sydney	24/75	133	74
Tel Aviv	21/71	51	62
Tokyo	12/54	102	75
Toronto	3/37	76	76
Venice	12/54	61	86
Vienna	8/46	44	78
Washington DC	11/53	102	72

Place	Temperature (C/F)	Rainfall (mm)	Humidity (%)
Wellington	19/67	76	76
Zurich	16/61	64	86 |//
APRIL			
Adelaide	23/73	44	57
Alice Springs	27/81	5	40
Athens	26/79	23	65
Auckland	22/73	102	78
Boston	26/80	102	69
Brisbane	26/79	86	70
Cairns	29/85	279	78
Cairo	38/100	5	55
Canberra	20/68	48	75
Cape Town	19/66	25	93
Chicago	13/55	76	74
Darwin	33/91	103	76
Dublin	13/55	45	76
Florence	19/66	61	87
Frankfurt	16/61	44	79
Hobart	17/63	54	70
Hong Kong	24/75	127	87
Honolulu	25/78	51	69
London	13/55	37	71
Los Angeles	21/70	25	82
Madrid	18/64	48	74
Melbourne	20/68	58	72
Mexico City	25/77	20	66
Moscow	10/50	37	73
New York	14/57	76	68
Paris	16/61	42	82
Peking	20/68	12	63
Perth	24/76	51	61
Rio de Janeiro	27/80	102	87
Rome	19/66	51	83
San Francisco	16/62	40	83
Sydney	22/72	123	74

Place	Temperature (C/F)	Rainfall (mm)	Humidity (%)
Tel Aviv	25/77	25	60
Tokyo	17/63	127	81
Toronto	10/50	76	74
Venice	17/63	78	86
Vienna	15/59	45	72
Washington DC	18/64	76	68
Wellington	17/63	102	79
Zurich	15/59	76	81

MAY

Place	Temperature (C/F)	Rainfall (mm)	Humidity (%)
Adelaide	19/66	68	67
Alice Springs	23/73	25	47
Athens	31/88	23	60
Auckland	19/67	127	80
Boston	30/87	76	70
Brisbane	23/73	71	71
Cairns	27/81	102	77
Cairo	40/104	5	50
Canberra	15/59	49	84
Cape Town	18/64	25	90
Chicago	18/65	76	73
Darwin	32/90	14	68
Dublin	15/59	60	75
Florence	23/73	70	87
Frankfurt	20/68	55	78
Hobart	14/57	49	75
Hong Kong	28/82	305	87
Honolulu	27/80	25	69
London	17/63	46	70
Los Angeles	22/72	5	86
Madrid	21/70	47	72
Melbourne	17/63	58	78
Mexico City	25/78	51	69
Moscow	19/66	53	58
New York	20/68	76	70
Paris	20/68	57	83

Place	Temperature (C/F)	Rainfall (mm)	Humidity (%)
Peking	26/80	25	69
Perth	20/69	127	72
Rio de Janeiro	25/77	76	87
Rome	23/73	46	77
San Francisco	17/63	25	85
Sydney	19/66	122	75
Tel Aviv	28/83	5	62
Tokyo	21/71	152	85
Toronto	17/63	76	78
Venice	21/70	65	85
Vienna	19/66	70	74
Washington DC	24/75	102	72
Wellington	14/58	127	80
Zurich	19/66	101	80

JUNE

Place	Temperature (C/F)	Rainfall (mm)	Humidity (%)
Adelaide	16/61	72	75
Alice Springs	19/67	12	54
Athens	36/97	14	50
Auckland	17/63	127	83
Boston	34/93	76	72
Brisbane	21/70	68	72
Cairns	26/79	76	77
Cairo	41/106	0	55
Canberra	12/54	39	85
Cape Town	16/62	51	88
Chicago	24/75	102	76
Darwin	30/86	3	64
Dublin	18/64	57	76
Florence	27/81	56	85
Frankfurt	23/73	73	78
Hobart	12/54	58	78
Hong Kong	29/85	406	86
Honolulu	27/81	25	69
London	20/68	45	70
Los Angeles	24/76	0	87

Place	Temperature (C/F)	Rainfall (mm)	Humidity (%)
Madrid	27/81	27	66
Melbourne	14/57	50	83
Mexico City	24/76	127	82
Moscow	21/70	58	62
New York	25/78	76	73
Paris	23/73	54	83
Peking	31/89	51	77
Perth	18/64	178	76
Rio de Janeiro	24/76	51	86
Rome	28/82	37	74
San Francisco	19/66	-	88
Sydney	17/63	133	75
Tel Aviv	29/85	0	67
Tokyo	24/76	178	89
Toronto	22/73	76	78
Venice	25/77	69	83
Vienna	22/72	67	74
Washington DC	28/83	102	75
Wellington	13/55	127	81
Zurich	23/73	129	80

JULY

Place	Temperature (C/F)	Rainfall (mm)	Humidity (%)
Adelaide	15/59	66	76
Alice Springs	19/67	5	49
Athens	39/102	6	47
Auckland	16/62	152	84
Boston	35/95	76	71
Brisbane	20/68	56	70
Cairns	25/78	51	74
Cairo	39/102	0	65
Canberra	11/52	38	84
Cape Town	15/60	51	89
Chicago	27/81	76	75
Darwin	30/86	1	64
Dublin	20/68	70	78
Florence	36/86	35	82

Place	Temperature (C/F)	Rainfall (mm)	Humidity (%)
Frankfurt	25/77	70	81
Hobart	12/54	53	78
Hong Kong	30/87	381	87
Honolulu	28/82	25	70
London	22/72	57	71
Los Angeles	27/81	0	88
Madrid	31/88	11	58
Melbourne	13/55	48	81
Mexico City	23/73	178	84
Moscow	23/73	88	68
New York	28/82	102	77
Paris	25/77	59	83
Peking	32/90	178	88
Perth	17/63	178	76
Rio de Janeiro	24/75	51	86
Rome	30/86	15	70
San Francisco	18/65	0	91
Sydney	16/61	102	74
Tel Aviv	31/88	0	70
Tokyo	28/83	152	91
Toronto	26/79	76	79
Venice	27/81	52	82
Vienna	25/77	84	74
Washington DC	30/87	102	79
Wellington	11/53	127	81
Zurich	25/77	136	81
AUGUST Adelaide	16/61	61	70
Alice Springs	23/73	8	39
Athens	38/100	7	48
Auckland	17/63	127	80
Boston	34/93	102	76
Brisbane	22/72	46	66
Cairns	26/80	51	72
Cairo	38/101	0	69

Place	Temperature (C/F)	Rainfall (mm)	Humidity (%)
Canberra	13/55	45	80
Cape Town	16/61	25	89
Chicago	26/79	76	79
Darwin	31/88	2	69
Dublin	19/66	74	80
Florence	30/86	47	85
Frankfurt	24/75	76	85
Hobart	13/55	52	73
Hong Kong	30/87	376	87
Honolulu	28/83	25	71
London	21/70	59	76
Los Angeles	28/82	0	87
Madrid	30/86	15	62
Melbourne	15/59	51	75
Mexico City	23/73	152	85
Moscow	22/72	71	74
New York	26/80	102	79
Paris	24/75	64	87
Peking	30/87	152	88
Perth	18/64	152	73
Rio de Janeiro	24/76	51	84
Rome	30/86	21	73
San Francisco	18/65	0	92
Sydney	18/64	78	68
Tel Aviv	32/90	0	70
Tokyo	30/86	152	92
Toronto	25/77	76	83
Venice	27/81	69	84
Vienna	24/75	72	78
Washington DC	29/84	102	80
Wellington	12/54	127	80
Zurich	24/75	124	85

SEPTEMBER

Place	Temperature (C/F)	Rainfall (mm)	Humidity (%)
Adelaide	19/66	51	61
Alice Springs	28/81	8	31

Place	Temperature (C/F)	Rainfall (mm)	Humidity (%)
Athens	34/93	15	58
Auckland	18/65	102	76
Boston	31/89	76	77
Brisbane	24/75	47	62
Cairns	28/83	51	69
Cairo	36/97	0	68
Canberra	16/61	52	72
Cape Town	17/63	25	92
Chicago	23/73	76	80
Darwin	32/90	13	71
Dublin	17/63	72	83
Florence	26/79	70	88
Frankfurt	21/70	57	89
Hobart	15/59	52	66
Hong Kong	29/85	250	83
Honolulu	28/83	25	71
London	19/66	49	80
Los Angeles	27/81	5	82
Madrid	25/77	32	72
Melbourne	17/63	58	68
Mexico City	23/74	127	86
Moscow	16/61	58	78
New York	26/79	76	79
Paris	21/70	55	90
Peking	26/79	51	82
Perth	19/67	76	67
Rio de Janeiro	24/75	76	84
Rome	26/79	63	83
San Francisco	20/69	8	88
Sydney	20/68	68	66
Tel Aviv	31/88	2	67
Tokyo	26/79	229	91
Toronto	20/69	76	87
Venice	24/75	59	87
Vienna	20/68	42	83

Place	Temperature (C/F)	Rainfall (mm)	Humidity (%)
Washington DC	25/78	102	81
Wellington	14/57	102	76
Zurich	20/68	102	90

OCTOBER

Place	Temperature (C/F)	Rainfall (mm)	Humidity (%)
Adelaide	22/72	44	52
Alice Springs	31/88	25	27
Athens	30/86	51	76
Auckland	20/68	102	74
Boston	28/82	76	75
Brisbane	26/79	75	60
Cairns	30/86	51	67
Cairo	35/96	-	67
Canberra	20/68	69	65
Cape Town	18/65	8	88
Chicago	16/61	76	78
Darwin	33/91	50	71
Dublin	14/57	70	85
Florence	20/68	94	87
Frankfurt	14/57	52	91
Hobart	17/63	63	62
Hong Kong	23/74	127	75
Honolulu	28/82	51	73
London	14/57	57	85
Los Angeles	24/76	10	75
Madrid	19/66	53	81
Melbourne	20/68	68	63
Mexico City	21/70	51	83
Moscow	9/48	45	81
New York	20/69	102	76
Paris	17/63	50	91
Peking	20/68	25	73
Perth	21/70	51	60
Rio de Janeiro	25/77	76	83
Rome	22/72	99	86
San Francisco	20/68	25	85

Place	Temperature (C/F)	Rainfall (mm)	Humidity (%)
Sydney	22/72	77	62
Tel Aviv	29/85	25	66
Tokyo	20/69	203	88
Toronto	13/56	51	87
Venice	19/66	77	88
Vienna	14/57	56	86
Washington DC	19/67	76	81
Wellington	15/60	102	75
Zurich	14/57	77	92

NOVEMBER

Place	Temperature (C/F)	Rainfall (mm)	Humidity (%)
Adelaide	25/77	31	45
Alice Springs	34/93	25	27
Athens	24/75	56	78
Auckland	23/73	80	71
Boston	21/71	102	73
Brisbane	28/82	99	60
Cairns	31/88	102	68
Cairo	31/89	0	68
Canberra	22/72	62	61
Cape Town	19/67	5	90
Chicago	8/47	51	79
Darwin	33/91	126	73
Dublin	10/50	67	88
Florence	14/57	110	89
Frankfurt	8/46	55	89
Hobart	19/66	56	59
Hong Kong	23/74	51	73
Honolulu	26/80	76	74
London	10/50	64	88
Los Angeles	23/73	25	62
Madrid	13/55	47	84
Melbourne	22/72	60	61
Mexico City	20/68	20	82
Moscow	2/36	47	87
New York	10/51	76	75

Place	Temperature (C/F)	Rainfall (mm)	Humidity (%)
Paris	10/50	51	91
Peking	9/49	5	69
Perth	24/76	25	54
Rio de Janeiro	26/79	102	82
Rome	13/55	93	85
San Francisco	17/63	76	83
Sydney	24/75	79	61
Tel Aviv	25/78	102	61
Tokyo	15/60	102	83
Toronto	6/43	76	82
Venice	12/54	94	88
Vienna	7/45	52	84
Washington DC	13/55	76	77
Wellington	17/63	102	74
Zurich	7/45	73	90

DECEMBER

Place	Temperature (C/F)	Rainfall (mm)	Humidity (%)
Adelaide	28/82	26	42
Alice Springs	35/96	21	29
Athens	20/68	71	78
Auckland	24/76	76	70
Boston	13/56	76	74
Brisbane	30/86	130	62
Cairns	32/90	229	69
Cairo	26/79	5	70
Canberra	26/79	52	59
Cape Town	20/69	8	90
Chicago	2/36	51	80
Darwin	30/86	243	77
Dublin	8/46	74	88
Florence	11/52	93	88
Frankfurt	4/39	54	88
Hobart	20/68	56	58
Hong Kong	20/68	25	74
Honolulu	25/78	102	75
London	7/45	48	87

Place	Temperature (C/F)	Rainfall (mm)	Humidity (%)
Los Angeles	19/67	76	60
Madrid	9/48	48	86
Melbourne	24/75	58	60
Mexico City	19/66	8	81
Moscow	-5/23	54	85
New York	5/41	102	73
Paris	6/43	50	90
Peking	2/36	5	65
Perth	27/81	12	50
Rio de Janeiro	28/82	127	82
Rome	13/55	93	85
San Francisco	14/57	102	83
Sydney	25/77	78	64
Tel Aviv	20/68	178	66
Tokyo	11/52	51	77
Toronto	0/33	76	80
Venice	8/46	61	88
Vienna	3/37	45	84
Washington DC	7/45	76	74
Wellington	19/67	102	74
Zurich	3/37	64	89

INDEX

Abbott, Hon. Roy Kitto 457
ABC *see* Australian Broadcasting Corporation
Abeles, Sir Peter 10
Abercrombie, J. 161
Abidjan 596
Abonyi, Atti 184
Aboriginal Land Rights Act 296, 401
Aborigines 4, 6, 7, 16, 288, 293, 295, 296
    Anglican priest exorcises gaol 5
    Bicentennial protest 16, 17
    first Aborigine to die on British soil 17
    first cricket team to tour England 84
    float in Gay Mardi Gras parade 18
    inquiry into deaths in custody 10, 11
    languages 540
    Myall Creek massacre 290
    racial conflict 3, 11
    sacred sites and land claims 9, 297, 401-10
    Southern Cross legend 545
    Tasmanian 290
    treaty 409-10
Abrahams, Chris 523
Abu (circus elephant) 12
Abu Dhabi 699
AC/DC 520, 524
Accra 614
Ackhurst, Daphne 207
Acquired Immunodeficiency Syndrome (AIDS) *see* AIDS
acupuncture 321
Adamstown 731
Addis Ababa 607
Adelaide 290, 321
Adelaide Cup (horse race) 122-3
Aden 708
Admiral's Cup (yacht race) 180
Admiralty Islands 534
Advance Australia Fair 287, 571
aerodromes 433
Afghanistan 26, 29, 47, 564, 738
Agana 735
Agar, Alex 68
Age 291, 505
Ahearn, Jack 138
Ahern, David 298
Ahern, Hon. Michael 15, 456
AIDS 6
    cumulative analysis of cases in Australia 280-1
    death rate 15
    immigrants to US tested for 30
    as an insurance risk 284
    reported in 102 countries 27
    USSR tests citizens and foreigners for 34
Ainsworth, Patricia 310
air distances, Australian 434
air travel 435
aircraft movements 433
Ajax (racehorse) 120, 122
AJC Derby (horse race) 130
Albania 565-6
Albert, Frank 157
Albert, Prince 303

Aldenhoven, Alan 75
Alderton, Laurie 138
Alexandra of Kent, Princess 304, 306, 307
Alfred, Prince 303
Algeria 27, 31, 566-7, 738
Algiers 566
All for Australia League 462
Allan, Pam 481
Allan, Trevor 172
Allen, Don 95
Allen, Peter 310
Allen, Terry 228
Alley, Rewi 298
Alofi 722
Alor 540
Alston, Adrian 184
Alvin Purple (film) 491
Amazon Basin rainforests 33
American Eagle (yacht) 177
American Samoa 540, 733-4
America's Cup (yacht race) 180, 225, 226
    Australia wins 297
Ames, Jennifer 310
Amman 631
Amos, Simon 7
Amsterdam 655
Amsterdam Island 720
Anderson, Angry 310, 519, 520
Anderson, Geordie 139
Anderson, James O. 198
Anderson, John 155
Anderson, Judith 310
Anderson, Thomas 155
Andesite Line 534
Andorra 567
Andorre-la-Vieille 567
Andrews, Gordon 348
Angelo, C. 222
Angels 518, 519, 520, 522
Anglican Church
    and first Aborigine to die on British soil 17
    ordination of women in 5, 11, 13
Angola 44 47 567-8
Anguilla 725
Ankara 695
Anna Kristina (sailing ship) 11
Anne, Princess, royal visits 305-8
Annetts, James 7
Ansett Airlines of Australia 294, 354, 429
Ansett Transport Industries 10
    end of the two-airline agreement 13
Antananarivo 643
Antarctica 47, 541-3, 713
    Treaty 541, 542
Antigua 568-9
Antonie, Peter 160
Anzac Day 6, 321
Anzacs 293
ANZUS alliance 30, 295
Apia 706
Apkwini 8
Apple 390, 394

Appleby, June 484
Arafura Sea 288
Archdale, Betty 91
Archer (racehorse) 111, 112, 113, 224, 291
Archibald, J. F. 292
area, of Australia 570
Arena, Franca 481
Argentina 27, 37, 46, 569-70, 738
Argentine ant 422
Armstrong, Hon. I. M. 454
Armstrong, Jim 222
Armstrong 500 (motor race) 146
Arnold, Hon. Lyn Maurice Ferguson 457
Arnold, Montague 172
Arnold, Reg 95
Arnold, Richard 172
Arthur, Frank 188
Arthur, Lieutenant-Governor George 290
Aruba 721
Ascension Island 726
Ashbury, James 180
Ashes, The 292
Ashmore Island 571, 713
Aston, George 537
Asuncion 664
Athens 615
athletics see track and field
Atkins, Frank 94
Atkins, Fred 223
Auchterlonie, Dorothy 310
Aussat 1 297
Aussat 3 12
Austin, Hon. Brian Douglas 456
Austin, Lawrence 73
Austin, Lillian 18
Austin, Lou 221
Austin, Thomas 291, 420
Austral Island 531, 533
Australia 570-2
 average weekly earnings 373
 defence pact with Papua New Guinea 47
 European exploration of the Pacific 535-9
 events during 1987 3-16
 events during 1988 16-19
 external territories 571, 713-15
 important dates in history 288-97
 imports 376
 industrial disputes 369
 map of 239
 milestones in sport 223-6
 missions overseas (April 1988) 738-49
 named 289
 population growth 261
 resident population 262-3, 265
Australia (yacht) 180
Australia Card 12, 393
 abandoned 13
Australia Day 16, 321
Australia del Espiritu Santo 536, 538
 see also Vanuatu
Australia II (yacht) 180, 226, 297
Australia III (yacht) 180
Australia Party 462
Australian Airlines 297, 355, 429
 end of the two-airline agreement 13

Australian Antarctic Territory 713
 see also Antarctica
Australian Ballet Company 295
Australian Broadcasting Corporation (ABC)
 established as Commission 294
 Four Corners journalists charged with criminal defamation 12
 Jack High 136
 last episode of *Countdown* 10
 proposed amalgamation with SBS 5
 Robert Somerville as chairman of 7
 Sports Award 52-3, 225
Australian Broadcasting Tribunal 3, 12
Australian Capital Territory
 average weekly earnings 373
 exports 383
 extreme maximum temperatures 278
 extreme minimum temperatures 277
 imports 377
 map of Australia 239
 population growth 261
 public holidays 1989 237
 resident population 262-3, 265
 retention rates of secondary school students 445
 school terms 1989 238
 women in parliament 478, 480
 see also Canberra
Australian Democrats, shadow ministry 453-4
Australian Drivers Championship 145
Australian football 53-67, 224
Australian Grand Prix (motorcycles) 137
Australian Grand Prix (motor racing) 14, 139, 142-4
Australian Inland Mission Aerial Service 294
Australian Institute of Sport 19
Australian Jockey Club 111
 see also AJC Derby
Australian Labor Party (ALP) 17, 296, 450-2
 Aboriginal land rights 401
 founded 292
Australian Masters (golf) 100
Australian National Airways (ANA) 294, 426, 429
Australian National University 295
Australian of the Year 301
 young 302
Australian Open (golf) 97, 98
Australian PGA Championship (golf) 101
Australian Privacy Foundation 12
Australian Rally Championship 148
Australian Rules Football
 see Australian football
Australian Soccer Federation 183
Australian Sports Car Championship 148
Australian Touring Car Championship 144-5
Australian Women's Weekly 294
Australians (yacht) 176
Austria 27, 49, 572, 738
automatic teller machines (ATM) 8, 396
automotive industry 390
Avarua 722
average weekly earnings 373, 374-5
aviation 426-35
 end of the two-airline agreement 13
 military 431-3
Ayers Rock see Uluru

Baartz, Ray 184
Baby Bonus 293
Bacon, Kevin 96
Badger, Harold 120
Badgery 310
Baghdad 626
Bagot, R. C. 92
Bahamas 573, 738
Bahrain 573-4
Bailey, Les 137
Bainbridge, O. 93
Baird, Hon. B. G. 455
Baker, Reginald 'Snowy' 76, 77
Baker-Finch, Ian 100, 227
Baker Island 736
balance of payments 339
balance of trade 339
Balandra (yacht) 181
Balboa, Vasco Nunez 535
Bamako 646
Banda Island 536
Bandar Seri Begawan 581
Bandido bike gang 8
Bangkok 691
Bangladesh 42, 44, 50, 574-5, 738
Bangui 588
Banjul 611
Bank of New South Wales 347
Bankcard 296
Banks, Joseph 288, 420, 538
Bannerman, Charles 84
Bannon, Hon. John Charles 456
Bannon Ministry 456-7
bantamweight 321
Barb, The (racehorse) 112, 113
Barbados 30, 575-6, 738
Barber, Tony 74, 76
Barbie, Klaus 28, 32
Barbuda 568-9
Barker, E. 95
Barker, Miss 136
Barker, Nigel 209
Barnes, Eric 74
Barnes, George 74
Barnes, Jimmy 517, 519, 520, 521, 523
Barnes, Keith 167
Barnett, Walter 111
barracking 321
Barry, Keith 157
Barry, Margaret 310
barter 347
Bartlett, Kevin 56, 140
Barton, Sir Edmund 293, 464, 465-6
Barton, Gordon 462
basic wage 350-2
basketball 67-8, 514
Bass, George 289, 539
Bass Strait 288
Basse-Terre 717
Basseterre 671
Batavia 537, 538
Batavia (ship) 537
Batchelor, Warner 76
Bathurst 290
Bathurst Gaol 14

Bayley, J. M. 204
Beach, William 159
Beagle, HMS (ship) 539
Beale, Julian 452
Beane, Douglas 9
Bear, Bullen 310
Beasley, John 464
Beazley, Hon. Kim C. 451
Beckley, Sarah 314
Beecham 389
beer manufacturers 388
Beetson, Arthur 165
Beggs, Hon. Mrs Pamela Anne 460, 486
Beijing 591
Beirut 638
Belgium 24, 48, 576, 738
Belgrade 709
Belize 577
Bell, Derek 140
Bell, Frank and Charlie 193
bell-bottom trousers 321
Bellof, Stefan 140
Belmopan 577
Benaud, Richie 86
Bender, Ann 196
Benders 523
Benectin (drug) 32
Benin 577-8
Bennett, Hon. John 458
Berg, Charles Josef 298
Berger, Gerhard 14
Berinson, Hon. Joseph Max 459
Berlin (East) 612
Bermuda 726
Bern 687
Berringer, John 68
Berry, Kevin 155
Bertrand, John 180, 226
Berwick, Harry 229
Best Sun (greyhound) 108
Beswick, Hon. Richard John 458
bettongs 420
 brush-tailed 416
 burrowing 416
Bhutan 578-9
Bicentenary
 Aboriginal perspective of European settlement 18
 birthday cake 10
 Britain gives *Young Endeavour* 14
 China loans two giant pandas 19
 Commemorative Issue silver coin 348
 Dirck Hartog's plate 16
 First Fleet Re-enactment 7, 10, 17
 Mount Everest expedition 18
 rental values on Australia Day 16
 Tall Ships 15, 17
Big Pig 519, 522
Bignold, Marie 481
bikini 321
bilbies 420
billycan 321
bionic ear 9
birds, introduced 291, 418
birdwing butterfly 416

birth rates
  crude 242
  live births 240-1
  nuptial and ex-nuptial 243
  multiple births 243
biscuits 388
Bishop, Bronwyn 478
Bishop, Jack 188
Bishop, Steele 94
Bismarck Archipelago 534, 536
Bissau 618
bitou bush, South African 421
Bjelke-Petersen, Lady Florence 478
Bjelke-Petersen, Sir Joh 5, 8, 10, 11, 15
  announces New National Party 6
  campaigns to become Prime Minister 5
  opposes condom vending machines 12
Black Sorrows 519, 522
blackberry 421
Blackburn, Mr Justice 401
Blackburn, Sir Richard 298
Blackmore, Elizabeth 103
Bladel, Frances 485
Blake, Peter 177
Blakley, Peter 519, 520, 522
Bland, Dr William 426
Blaxland, Gregory 289
Blevins, Hon. Frank Trevor 457
Blewett, Hon. Neal 451
Bligh, Governor 289
Bligh, Ivo 292
Bliss, Johnny 197
Blue Mountains 289
Blue Ruin 522
Bluebird (powerboat) 142, 158
Blunt, Charles 452
Boardman, Leslie 154
Bodyline Series (cricket) 85
Boer War 292
Boggo Road Gaol, riot 15
Bogle, Eric 530
Bogota 593
Bolan, Bernard 530
Bolger, Glen 97
Bolger, James 138
Bolivia 33, 579, 738
Bolkus, Hon. Nick 450
Bon Jovi 516
Bond, Alan 180, 297
Bond Corporation 5, 353, 388
Boney, Lloyd 11
Bonn 613
Bonney, Lores 427
Borbridge, Hon. Robert 456
Border, Alan 226
Borthwick, Pat 102
Botany Bay 288, 538
Both, Edward 298
Botham, Ian 226
Botswana 580, 738
Bougainville 540
Bounty, HMS (ship) 571, 715, 731
  mutineers 532
Bourke, Governor 290
Bourke, Kevin 97
Boustead, Kerry 165

Bouvet Island 724
Bowen, Cliff 74
Bowen, Jim 74
Bowen, Hon. Lionel 450
box office 321
boxing 18, 68-81, 71-2, 77-81, 224
  bantamweight 321
Boy George 521
Boyd, Esme 207
Brabham, Geoffrey 141, 227
Brabham, Sir Jack 140, 143, 151, 190, 225, 301
Brackenregg, H. L. 161
Bradfield, Alan 298
Bradman, Sir Donald 86, 225
Braid, Hon. Ian Maxwell 458
Braille alphabet 327
Braithwaite, Ray A. 453
Brand, Mona 310
Brasilia 580
Brass, John 166, 172
Brazil 40, 48, 544, 580-1, 738
Brazzaville 594
Breaker Morant (film) 491
breakfast cereal 389
Brearley, Norman 426
Brearly, Reg 142
Breasley, Arthur 'Scobie' 120, 121, 134
Brereton, Laurie 5, 15
Breton, Ken le 188
Brett, Arthur 176
Bridge, Hon. Ernest Francis 460
Bridgetown 575
Briers, Louise 103
Bright, Ray 90
Brisbane, Sir Thomas 109, 110
Brisbane Cup (horse race) 123-5
Briscoe, Billy 122
British Antarctic territory 727
British Indian Ocean territory 727
British Open Golf Championship 104-7
British Royal Mint 347
British Virgin Islands 727
Britt, Edgar 121
Broad, Mike 142
broadcasting 293, 295
Broadway, Elizabeth 315
Brodie, Jim 172
Broken Hill Proprietary Company Ltd (BHP) 292, 352, 391
  jobs cut from Port Kembla Steelworks 13
Bromwich, John 198, 204, 225
Brookes, Norman E. 198, 204, 224
Brooks, Neil 156
Brown, D. 161
Brown, Dave 166
Brown, Hilary 188
Brown, J. G. 195
Brown, Jamieson 310
Brown, John 7, 16
Brown, Hon. Robert J. 450
Brown, Tom 172
Brown, Wally 196
Browne, Ian 155
Browne, Vic 94
Brownlow, Charles 55
Brownlow Medal 55, 59-60, 224

Bruce, Stanley Melbourne 464, 469-70
brucellosis 419
Brumby, Private 418
Brunei 581-2, 739
Brunner, Alois 40
Brussels 576, 740
Brusso, Noah 69
Bryce, Hon. Malcolm John 459
bubonic plague 292
Buchanan, Pamela 486
Bucharest 669
Budapest 621
Budge, Donald 201
budget deficit 343-4
Buenos Aires 569
Builders Labourers' Federation 13, 296
building materials 390
Bujumbura 585
Bulgaria 582-3, 739
Bulletin 292, 528
Bundaberg Sugar Company 388
Bungey, E. 136
bunkum 321
Bunton Jnr, Haydn 56, 62
Bunton Snr, Haydn 55, 56, 59, 62
Burdon, Alex 161, 162
Burgess, T. 135
Burke, Hon. Brian Thomas 18, 459
Burke Ministry 459-60
Burkina Faso 40, 583-4
Burma 35, 36, 49, 584-5, 739
Burnet, Sir Macfarlane 301
Burns, Frank 74
Burns, Tommy 69, 70, 75, 79, 224
Burnum Burnum 16
Burrell, Sir Henry Mackay 298
Burrow, Kathleen Mary 298
Burrows 390
Burundi 36, 585-6
Business Daily (newspaper) 11
buskers, attempt to eradicate 3
Butchard, Greg 176
Butler, Harry 301
Button, Hon. John 450
Buxton, Douglas 182
Byrne, Gary 184
Byrnes, Tracey 121
Byron, John 538

Cadman, Alan 453
Caicos Islands 733
Cain, Hon. Robert Clive 458
Cain Ministry 458-9
Cains, Beverley 480
Caird, Maureen 155, 209
Cairo 604
Calder, A. 92
calendar
 70 year 232-3
 1988 234
 1989 235
 1990 236
 public holidays 237
 school terms 1989 238
Californian condor 27
Callister, Valerie 485

Cambria (schooner) 180
camels 418
Cameron, Ian M. D. 453
Cameroon 586-7
Camille (yacht) 180
Campbell, Bonnie 55
Campbell, Colin 298
Campbell, Donald 142, 158
Campbell, Keith 137
Campbell, Sir Walter 15
Campbell-Craig, Lorayne 298
Campbellfield 137
Canada 24, 38, 40, 43, 45, 587-8, 739
Canberra 239, 293, 294, 322, 570
Candlish, A. 159
cane toad 424
Cann, Rod 173
Cann, W. A. 161
Cape Verde 588
capital gains tax 343
Caprice of Huon (yacht) 180, 181
Caracas 704
Carbine (racehorse) 112, 122
Cardigan, Bert Wolfe 122
Cardigan Bay (racehorse) 217
Cardy, Alan 172
Carey, Alex 298
Carlos, Max 76
Carlton, Hon. J. J. 452
Carlton, Jimmy 209
Caroline Islands 533, 540
Carr, Bob 7
Carr, Hon. Jeffrey Phillip 459
Carr, Paul 158
Carr, Val 158
Carr, Wally 73
Carruthers, Jimmy 69, 70, 76, 225
Carruthers, Kel 137, 138
Carslake, Bernard 'Brownie' 121
Carteret, Philip 538
Cartier Island 571, 713
Casey, Fred 74, 76
Casey, Lord 301
Casey, William 23, 30
Cash, Pat 9, 14, 226
 annual earnings 227
 haunted by a ghost 13
Cassidy, Stan 121
cassowary, 'killer' 19
Castle Hill uprising 289
Castries 672
cat, feral 420, 423
Cathie, Hon. Ian Robert 458
cattle tick 418
Cattletruck 523
Caulfield Cup (horse race) 125-6
Causley, Hon. I. R. 455
Cavalier, Rod 7
Cawley (nee Goolagong), Evonne 301
Cayenne 716
Cayman Islands 728
Celibate Rifles 518, 522
cement 390
census 292
Central African Republic 31, 588-9
Chad 21, 37, 38, 589-90

Chadwick, Hon. V. 455
Chadwick, Virginia 481
Chaffey, Bill 298
Chamberlain, Azaria 297
Chamberlain, Lindy 8, 12, 297
Chambers, Robert 159
Champion, Malcolm 154
Chaney, Hon. F. M. 452
Channel Islands 728
Chantoozies 519
Chapman, Yvonne 483
Chappell, Greg 87, 90
Chappell, Ian 90
Charles, Prince of Wales
    royal visits 305-8
    survives avalanche 49
Charleston (yacht) 177
Charlotte Amalie 737
Charlton, Andrew 'Boy' 155
chauvinism 322
Cheadle, F. B. 161
chemical spraying 424
Chernobyl nuclear accident 12, 32, 39, 40, 46
Chester, Gavin 97
Chifley, Joseph Benedict 473-4
child endowment 294
Chile 25, 26, 590-1, 739
China 22, 24, 29, 33, 38, 40, 46, 49, 50, 591-2, 740
    exports from 382
    incursions into Vietnam 21
    loans pandas 19
    Macao to be transferred to 21
    The Shiralee (mini-series) sold to 15
chlorofluorocarbons 38
Choirboys 522
Christensen, Ernie 170
Christmas cards 322
Christmas Island 571, 713-14
    Assembly sacked 14
Chrystal Set 522
Cilento, Lady Phyllis 298
Circular Quay 3
Clancy, Pat 298
Clarins 389
Clark, Danny 94, 95, 227
Clark, Professor Manning 301
Clarke, Ron 210
Clauson, Hon. Paul John 456
Clay, Norm 189
Clayton, Derek 210
Clean Air Act 7
Cleary, Michael 166, 172
climate 4, 277-9, 570-1
    around the world 749-63
Clyne, Peter 298
coalminers, strike 17
Coates, Colin 154
Cobby, Captain A. H. 431
Cobby, Anita 8
Cobley, James 136
Cobley, John 136
cockatoo, red-tailed black 416
Cockroaches 522
cocky 322
Cocos (Keeling) Islands 571, 714
Coe, Hannah Maria 315

Coghill, Dr K. A. 459
Cohen, Janice 481
Cold Chisel 518, 520
Cole, Senator George 463
Coles, Phil 196
Collins, Don 136
Collins, Hon. P. E. J. 454
Colombia 46, 50, 593, 740
Colombo 683
Colossus of Rhodes 9
Comanchero bike gang 8
Comeng 391
Commonwealth Games 82-3, 225, 348
    boxing 76
    cycling 93
    lawn bowls 136
    rowing and sculling 160
    track and field 210
    wrestling 222
Commonwealth Heads of Government Meeting
    (CHOGM) 40
Communist Party 294, 295
Comoros 594
companies
    Australia's top 100, 352-5
    foreign investment 388-91
computers 392
    companies 390
    expert systems 398
    magazines 510
    music 521
Conakry 617
Conciliation and Arbitration Commission 293, 346
    introduces two-tier wage system 5
condom vending machine 12
condoms to prevent the spread of AIDS
    Bathurst Gaol 14
    demonstrators distribute to women at US navy ball 12
    Queensland opposes vending machines 12
Coneeley, Robert 195
Congo 594-5
Connolly, David M. 453
Connolly, Maureen 201
Connor, Dennis 180
Conolly, Phillip 289
conscription 293, 294, 296
Constellation, USS 12
constellations 550-5
    Southern Cross 544-5
Constitution, Commonwealth of Australia 292
consumer price index 339
contraceptive pill 36, 295
Cook, Bill 121
Cook, George 160
Cook, Captain James 288, 531, 533, 538-9, 541
Cook, Sir Joseph 463, 464, 468
Cook, Kenneth 298
Cook, Hon. Peter 451
Cook Islands 21, 531, 533, 722
cool room 332
Coolgardie safe 332
Cooper, Brad 155
Cooper, Hon. Theo 456
Cooper and Sons Ltd 388
Copenhagen 600
copyright, computer software 394-6

COPYRITA 399
Coral Sea Islands Territory 571, 714
Cordaly, C. 136
Cornelsen, Greg 173
Cornett, Renato 77
Cornforth, Professor John W. 301
Cornwall, Hon. (Dr) John Robert 457
Cornwall and York, Duke and Duchess of 303
Corrigan, Tommy 121
cosmetic market 389
cost of living 350-2
Costa Rica 595-6, 740
Costello, Elvis 521
Cote D'Ivoire 21, 596-7
Cotton, Henry 229
Coulter, Hon. Barry 455
Coulter, John 453
Countdown (television program) 10
Court (nee Smith), Margaret 198, 201, 204, 225, 226
Courtney, E. 161
Coventry, Gordon 56
Coventry, Syd 59
Cowan, Andrew 142
Cowley, Gene 187
Cowper, Sir Norman 298
Cox, Lionel 95, 155
Cox, Miss 136
Coyle, Brian 142
Coyne, Thelma 204
Crabb, Hon. Steven Marshall 458
Craddock, Crash 310
Craftner, Hon. Gregory John 457
Crago, Brian 95
Crampton, Bruce 99, 101, 227
Cranley, R. 136
Crapp, Lorraine 155
Craven, J. H. 139
Craven, Susan 480
Crawford, Jack 199
Crawford, Sir John 301
Crawford, Mary 478
credit reporting 393-4
Creighton, Guy 97
Creswell, Toby 310
Crew, Ellis 136
cricket 83-92, 224
  Ashes created 292
  Australia wins World Cup 14
  first intercolonial 291
  first match 223
  first Test 224
  first Test between England and Australia 292
  hat trick 322
  magazines 514
  records 87-9
  World Series 90
crimes
  computer 396
  dog's jacket stolen 7
  explosives stolen 16
  failure to pay Harbour Bridge toll 18
  handbag theft 4
  Mafia leaders convicted in US 21
  offensive behaviour in Darwin 4
  Trimbole's body returns to Australia 7

Crocodile Dundee (film) 489
crocodiles
  Adelaide's suburban West Lakes 18
  attacks 6, 10
  freshwater, served in Adelaide restaurants 13
  orders to remove 10
Croker, Norma 155, 209
Cronin, Michael 166, 167
Crooke, J. R. 113
Crosio, Janice 481
Crowded House 516, 519, 520, 524
Crowley, Rosemary 479
Crozet islands 720
Cuba 597-8
Cullen, Dave 74
Cummings, Bart 112, 113, 227
Cummings, Stephen 519, 522
Cuneo, John 155
currency, Australian 347-8, 571
  decimal 296, 348
  exchange rates 339
  floating the dollar 340
  Holey Dollar 347
  see also money
Curtin, Prime Minister 294
Cusack, Tom 211
Cuthbert, Betty 154, 155, 208, 209, 225, 226
Cutts, John 111, 112, 113, 224
cycling 15, 92-5
Cyclone Tracy 296
Cyprus 48, 598-9, 740
Czechoslovakia 44-5, 599-600, 740

Dacca 574
Dagg, Fred 310
Daihatsu 390
Dakar 675
Dale, Dick 310
Dale, Hon. Don 455
Dallas, Major R. S. 431
d'Alpuget, L. 161
Dalton, D. 137
Damascus 688
Dame Pattie (yacht) 180
Dampier, William 288, 537
Danglin' Brothers 524
Danielson, Larry Burton 18
Dankbaar, Ann 9
Danvers, Jack 310
Darcy, Les 69, 74, 224
Dark, Eric 298
Darling, Elaine 478
Darling, Sir Ralph 110
Darwin 4, 293, 322
  Japanese bombers attack 294
Darwin, Charles 539
data protection 392-6
Datalex Research Project, The 399
Date, Reg 184
Datsun, Charlie 188
Dauth, John 3, 4
David, Mary Edgeworth 298
Davidson, Alan 86
Davidson, Owen 201
Davies, Charles 177
Davies, Jim 189

Davis, Abraham (Alby) 68
Davis, Dwight F. 205
Davis, Greg 173
Davis, Ian 90
Davis, Rodger 101, 227
Davis Cup 198, 205-7, 224, 225
Davison, Lex 139, 141
Dawkins, Hon. John S. 450
Day, Sydney 139
de Castella, Robert 210, 227, 301
de Groot, Francis Edward 294
De Luca's fruit shop 10
De Mestre, Etienne 111, 112
Deakin, Alfred 463, 464, 466
Dean, Paddy 188
Dean, Sonia 310
Dean, William 426
Deas-Thompson, George 172
death rates 255-8
   AIDS 15
   Europe's worst winter 22
   infant deaths 260
   principal causes of death 259
   as a result of climbing Uluru (Ayer's Rock) 12
Debendox 16, 17
decimal currency see currency, decimal
Deegan, Allan Thomas 298
deer 419
Deloitte, Quarton Levitt 159
demand 338-9
Democratic Labor Party (DLP) 295, 463
Deng Xiaoping 40
Denison, Sir Hugh 113
Denman, Lady 293
Denmark 37, 43, 600-1, 715-16, 740
Dennis, Clare 155
depression see economy
Devereaux, J. 161
Devitt, John 155
Devlin, Bruce 99, 100
Devlin, Stuart 348
Devlin, Wayne 77
Diamonde, Dick 310
Dibnah, Corinne 103
Diddy Dimwits 523
Died Pretty 519, 522
Dinan, John 214
dingo 417
Dingo Principle, The (television show) 7
Dire Straits 517
disasters
   cross-channel ferry capsizes 24
   Granville train 3
   radiation accident in Brazil 40
   students die in school bus 4
disease
   deaths caused by 255-8
   introduced 423
   see also AIDS
Divinyls 517, 521
divorce
   age-specific 253
   duration of marriage 254
   Family Law Act 296
   uniform laws 295
Dixon, Judith 485

Djibouti 601
Djibouti (city) 601
Dobbie, John 136
Dobbins, R. 136
Dobbs, A. 161
Dobbyn, Dave 523
Dodoma 690
dog 417
Doha 669
Dolphin (ship) 538
Dominica 602
Dominican Republic 602-3
Donaldson, Jack 214
donkeys 418, 423
Donohoe, Fran 221
Donohoe, Jon 196
Doubell, Ralph 155, 208
Dougharty, J. D. 113
Douglas 731
Douglas, Shane 310
Douglas Social Credit Movement 463
Dowd, Hon. J. R. A. 454
Dowding, Hon. Peter M'Callum 18, 460
Downes, Harold 214
Dragon 523
Drake, Charlie 310
Drake, Sir Francis 537
Drake, Frank 167
Dreaming, the 402-3
Drover transport (plane) 431
D'Rozario, June 483
Druitt, Montague John 39
Drury, Michael 18
Dublin 627
Duckett, Frank 188
Duffy, Hon. Michael 450
Dufty, Kevin 298
Duggan, Ray 189
Duggan, Vic 188
Duigan, John 426
Duke of Edinburgh Award Scheme 305, 306
Dulhunty, Roger 175
'dump' 347
Duncan, Billy 121
Duncan, Hon. Peter 450
dung beetle 422
Dunhill Cup (golf) 101
Dunk, Billy 101
Dunlop, A. W. 198
Dunlop, Sir Edward 301
Dunn, Bill 182
Durack, Sarah 'Fanny' 154, 224
Dusty, Slim 310
Dutch East India Company 536
Dwyer, Con 92
Dwyer, Hughie 73
Dzaoudzi 718

earthquakes 17, 24, 38
East Germany see Germany, East
East-West Airlines 9, 10
Easter bunny 322
Easter Island 532, 537, 539, 540
Easton, Sheena 310
Easybeats 518, 523

Ebert, Russell 55
Eccles, Sir John 301
echidnas, hibernating 17
economy 333-47
 depression during 1890s 292
 invalid and old age pensions introduced 293
 sectors in the Australian 336
 slump during the 1840s 290
Ecuador 24, 603-4, 740
Edelsten, Geoffrey 7, 12, 15-16
Edelsten, Leanne 7
Edgar, George 215
Edge, Selwyn 141
Edinburgh (Tristan da Cunha) 733
Edmondson, Mark 207
Edmonson, Bill 214
education
 age of leaving school 447
 institutions being attended 446
 qualification 447-9
 retention rates of secondary school students 444-5
Edward, Prince of Wales 21, 303
Edwards, A. 92
Edwards, Hon. Graham 460
Edwards, Mark 518
Edwards, Ross 90
Egan, Ted 530
Egypt 26, 45, 48, 604-5, 740
El Salvador 25, 605-6
elands 418
Elders IXL 14, 352, 388
electronics 391
elephant juice *see* etorphine
Elizabeth, The Queen Mother 304, 305
Elizabeth II
 portrait on coins 348
 royal visits 304-8
 signed the *Proclamation of Australia Act* 297
Ella, Mark 173, 302
Elliot, Albert 142
Elliot, John 14
Elliott, Herb 155, 208, 210
Ellis, Lester 69, 77
Ellis, William Webb 172
Emerson, Roy 204
Emmerton, Bill 214
Empire Games *see* Commonwealth Games
endangered species, controlling trade in 416
Endeavour (ship) 288, 538
Endeavour River 538
engineering 391
English Derby 133-5
Eno, Brian 523
Epsom Derby 133
Equatorial Guinea 606-7
equestrian 95-7
Equestrian Federation of Australia 95, 96
Ericsson L. M. 391
Escape 523
Esta, Estella 13
Ethiopia 607-8
etorphine 4, 15
Eureka flag 309
Eureka Stockade uprising 291
Eurell, Greg 96, 97
Eurell, Laurie 96

Evans, Beryl Alice 481
Evans, Hon. Gareth J. 450
Evans, George 289
Evans, Peter 156
Evatt, Herbert V. 294
Eve, Richmond 'Dick' 155
Everidge, Dame Edna 310
Evers, Hon. Nick 458
Evil Angels (film) 12
exchange rates 339, 340-1, 346
 floating of the 345
Exploding White Mice 522
exports 339, 380
 by state 383
 major commodities 381
 major countries 382
 wine 385-7
eyeteeth 322

Fadden, Sir Arthur William 472
Faeroe Islands 715
Fahey, Hon. J. J. 455
Fair, John 138
Fairfax, John 290
Fairfax, Sir Warwick 13, 19, 298
Faleiro, Rui 535
Falkland Islands 538, 729
Famechon, Johnny 69, 70, 226
Family Action Movement 463
Family Law Act 296
family status 356
Fanning, Fred 56
Farmer, Graham 62
Farmer, Ken 55, 56
Farnan, Bill 69
Farnham, John 301, 516, 518, 519
Farrelly, Bernard 'Midge' 195, 226
fast foods 389
Fatal Shore, The (book) 4
Father's Day 322
Father's Day massacre 8
Fatin, Wendy 480
fauna
 endangered 416
 imported pests 417-25
 unknown species discovered 10
Favell, Les 86, 228
federal election 7, 460-2
Fenech, Jeff 18, 69, 70, 76, 77, 78, 226
Fenton, L. 181
feral animals 417
Ferguson, Adair 160
Ferguson, James 12
Ferreri, Paul 70, 73, 78
Ferrier, Jim 99, 100, 104, 225
Ferris, John 85
Fife, Hon. W. C. 452
Fiji 26, 29, 36, 38, 39, 44, 534, 535, 537, 608-9, 740
films
 magazines 511
 'R' (restricted) classification 296
 top 100 grossing 489-91
Finch, Hon. Fred 455
Finch, James 18
FINDER 399
Finey, George 298

Finland 47, 609, 740
Finlay, J. 92
Finn, Neil 520
First Fleet 288
First Fleet Re-enactment 17
  Aboriginal supporters demonstrate 7
  leaves Portsmouth 7
  Norwegian seaman drowned 11
  vessels arrive in Rio de Janeiro 10
firsts, in Australian history
  Aboriginal cricket team in England 84
  airmail delivery 426
  airmail service between Australia and Britain 294
  arrival tax 16
  Australian coins to be minted 347
  Australian Football match 54
  in aviation 426-8
  bank 289
  betting tickets 121
  birth certificate to transsexual woman 13
  in boxing 68-70
  broadcasts 293
  census 292
  corporate child care centre 15
  drivers' licences carrying photographs 4
  earliest known convict industrial site uncovered at Newcastle 10
  federal parliament 293
  film of the Melbourne Cup 111
  flight from Britain to Australia 293
  gas lighting in Sydney 290
  heart transplant operation 296
  hibernating echidnas 17
  Holden 295
  important dates in history 288
  income tax 292
  liver transplant 6
  Melbourne Cup 111
  Melbourne elects woman Lord Mayor 11
  merino wool shipped to England 289
  milestones in Australian sport 223-6
  New South Wales woman appointed to Supreme Court Bench 9
  non-members admitted to Sydney Cricket Ground Members Stand 14
  novel 290
  official horserace 289
  ordination of women favoured by Anglican Church 5
  overseas flight 294
  overseas telegram 291
  overseas telephone call 294
  paid sick leave and long-service leave 295
  pavement artist arrested 3
  performance of *Waltzing Matilda* 292
  post office opens 289
  postage stamp to honour a racehorse 217
  Queensland afternoon newspaper, the *Sun* 17
  rabbits introduced 291
  restaurants in Adelaide serving freshwater crocodile 13
  scholarship to NASA's international student program 12
  sex education in Queensland 16
  smoking banned on domestic airlines 15
  supernova star identified 5
  Sydney monorail columns erected 4

Sydney Morning Herald 290
Tall Ships reach Australia 15
telegraph between Melbourne and Williamstown 291
telephone exchange 292
television broadcasts 295
train service between Sydney and Melbourne 292
$2 coin 12
use of mobile barrier 217
woman appointed to the High Court 297
women elected to federal parliament 294
fiscal policy 342
Fischer, Tim 453
Fisher, Andrew 467-8
Fisher, Hurtle 110
Fitzgerald, Robert D. 298
Fitzsimmons, Bob 68
Flack, Albert 208
Flack, Edwin H. 153, 154, 204, 208, 209, 224
flags 309, 544
Flagstaff Gardens (golf) 97
flat out, to be 325
Fleet, Snowy 310
Fletcher, Ken 201
Flinders, Matthew 289, 539
Flood, Trevor 138
floods 10, 14
flora
  endangered 416
  poisonous plants 411-15
  unknown species discovered 10
Flotsam Jetsam 524
flying boats 429
flying doctor service 294, 430
Flying Emus 519, 524
Flying Pieman, The 208
Flynn, Reverend John 430
Foley, Bob 214
Foley, Larry 68
food preservation 332
food prices 350-2
food safe 332
foot-and-mouth disease 423
football *see* Australian Football
  see also Rugby League; Rugby Union; Soccer
footrace, Sydney to Melbourne 6
Forbes, David 155
Ford, Florrie 310
Ford, Michelle 156
Ford Motor 354 390
Forde, Francis Michael 473
Fordham, Hon. Robert Clive 458
Foreman, George 80
Forrest, W. H. 198
Fort-de-France 717
Foster, George 227
Foster, Reginald Tingey 298
Foundation 41 16, 17
fox 419
France 23, 28, 32, 35, 37, 38, 43, 609-10, 740
  ambassador expelled from Vanuatu 39
  bans Australian wine 18
  escapees from the island of Reunion 3
  Mururoa Atoll 41
  naval base in Fiji 36
  New Caledonia 3, 4, 35, 37

newspaper story on Aborigines 6
nuclear testing in the South Pacific 29
overseas departments 716-18
overseas territories 719-21
state of emergency in Tahiti 40
territorial collectivities 718-19
Fraser, Dawn 153, 154, 155, 225, 301, 481
Fraser, (John) Malcolm 477
Free Trade Party 463, 466, 467
Freedom of Information Acts 392
Freeman, Henry 159
Freeman, Sir Ralph 294
Freetown 677
French, Bob 181
French, Graeme 94
French Guiana 12, 716
French Polynesia 719
Freya (yacht) 177, 180
fringe benefits tax 343
Frost, Margaret 221
Frost, Vic 221
Fry, E. 161
Funafuti 696
Fusion Party 463 464
Futuna 531, 720
Fysh, W. Hudson 293, 426

Gabb, Ken 16
Gabon 611, 741
Gaborone 580
Gaddafi, Colonel 31
Gall, Stephen 138
Gallipoli 293
Galloway, Billy 188
Gambia, The 611-12
Gardner, Corrie H. 153
Gardner, Wayne 13, 137, 138, 227
Garrard, Dick 222, 223
Garrard, Richard 222
Garrett, Peter, opposes Australia Card 12
gas lighting 290
Gath, Brian 217
Gattellari, Fortunato ('Lucky') 74, 75
Gattellari, Rocky 70, 74, 76
Gaudron, Solicitor-General Mary 297
Gavin, Marty 302
Gay Mardi Gras 18
Gayler, Dianne 484
Geisha 518, 525
Geisler, Louis 138
General Practitioners, Royal Australian College of 7
Gentzen, Wilf 76
geography, of Australia 282, 570-1
George, Prince 303
Georgetown (Ascension Island) 726
Georgetown (Cayman Islands) 728
Georgetown (Guyana) 619
Germany, East 35, 612-13, 741
Germany, West 22, 25, 33, 41, 613-14, 741
Gerulaitis, Vitas 207
Ghana 614-15
Gibb, Barry 310
Gibbs, Sir Harry 4, 395
Gibbs, Hon. Ivan James 456
Gibbs, May 5
Gibraltar 49, 729

Gibson, Justin 103
Gilbert, Lachlan 176
Gilbert, Stuart 176
Gilbert Islands 533, 540
Giles, Patricia 480
Gill, Jenny 195
Gill, Michael 11
Gillaux, Maurice 426
Gilmour, Gary 90
Gilroy, Cardinal Sir Norman 301
Giltinan, James J. 161, 162, 182
Gladesville Bridge 304
Glanville, H. 161
Glass, Charles 35
Glasson, Hon. William Hamline 456
Gleeson, Elizabeth 485
Glennon, Pat 121, 134
Gloucester, Duke and Duchess of 305, 307
Go, Hirimi 8
Go Betweens 518-9, 522
goats, wild 419
Goble, Wing Commander 432
God 523
Goggin, Lindy 103
Gold, William 10
Golden Hind, The (ship) 537
Golden Slipper Stakes (horse race) 126-7
goldrushes 290
Goldsmith, Marlene 482
golf 97-107, 224, 225, 514
Goolagong, Evonne 204
Goondiwindi 3
Gordon, Ian 75
Gorrick, Izaac 'Bungaree' 68
Gorton, Sir John Grey 475-6
Gough, George 56
Gough, Les 190
Goulburn Gaol, riot at 4
Gould, John 11
Gould, Shane 154, 155, 301
Goullet, Alfred 93, 95
government 571
federal ministry 450-4
first federal parliament 293
Queensland abolishes the Upper House 293
state ministries 454-60
Gow, Keith 298
Grace, W. G. 83, 85
Graham, David 99, 100, 101, 226, 227
Graham, Hon. James 97
Grand Cayman 728
Grand Flaneur (racehorse) 111, 120
Grand Slam (tennis) 201
Grand Turk 733
Granny Smith apples 322
Grant, Alan 298
Graves, R. 161
Gray, Edgar L. 'Dunc' 93, 155, 225
Gray, Miss 136
Gray, Hon. Robin Trevor 457
Gray Ministry 457-8
Great Barrier Reef 5
Great Britain 21, 23, 26, 29, 31, 33, 35, 37, 39, 42, 45, 47, 49, 700-1, 739
Bicentennial gift to Australia 14
exploration of the Pacific 537-9

Queensland boy refused entry visa 15
    see also United Kingdom
Greece 25, 615-16, 741
Green, Dennis 154, 196
Green, Dick 159
Green, Jack 137
Green, Jackie 73, 74
Green, Teddy 74
Green Ban 296
greenhouse effect 38
Greenland 25, 716
Greenleaf, Graham 399
Greenpeace 9
Greeves, Edward Goodrich 'Cargie' 55, 59, 224
Greig, Keith 55
Greiner, Hon. N. F. 19, 454
Greiner Ministry 454-5
Grenada 616-17, 741
Grenadines, The 673
Grenda, Michael 156
Gretel (yacht) 180, 225
Gretel II (yacht) 180
Grey, Ian 19, 50
Greyhound Coursing Association 108
greyhound racing 107-9
Griffiths, Albert (Young Griffo) 68, 69, 70, 224
Griffiths, Ernest 157
Grill, Hon. Julian Fletcher 460
Grim Reaper television advertisement 6
Grime, Billy 73
Groom, Hon. Francis Roger 458
Groom, Hon. Ray 458
gross domestic product 337-8
Grosskreutz, Max 188
Grout, Wally 86
Grusovin, Deirdre 482
Grytviken 732
Guadeloupe 717
Guam 735
Guatemala 34, 617, 741
Guatemala City 617
Guildford, Syd 57
Guinea 617-18
    see also Equatorial Guinea
Guinea Airways 428
Guinea-Bissau 618-19
Gulf of Carpentaria 288
gun amnesty 17
Gunn, Hon. William Angus Manson 6, 456
Gunston, Norman 310
Gunsynd (racehorse) 120, 122
Gurindji people 401
Guyana 619-20, 741

Hackenschmidt, George 223
Haines, Senator Janine 12, 453
    opposes Australia Card 12
Haiti 42, 46, 620
halfpennies 348
Hall, John Farnsworth 298
Hall, Steele 464
Hall Islands 540
Hallahan, Hon. Mrs Elsie Kay 460, 487
Halliday, Sir George 298
Halloway, A. 161
Hallstrom, Edward 333

Halmahera 540
Halpin, Jerry 93
Halvorsen, Trygve and Magnus 177
ham actor 322
Hamill, H. C. 161
Hamilton 726
Hammersley, W. J. 54
Hand, Hon. Gerard (Gerry) 16, 451
Hanlan, Edward 159
Hanrahan, Hon. Ray 455
Happy-Hate-Me-Nots 522
Harare 45, 711
Hard-Ons 518, 519, 522, 525
Hardie-Ferodo 1000 (motor race) 146
Hardwick, Harold 74, 76, 154
Hardy, Bobby 310
Hardys 388
hare 419
Hargrave, Lawrence 426
Hargraves, Luke 176
Harkness, Don 139
Harmonic Convergence 11
Harold Park 215, 216
Harper, Hon. Neville John 456
Harper, R. 207
Harris, Bert 222
Harrison, Lieutenant E. 431
Harrison, Henry Colden 53
Hart, Gary 28
Hartnett, Richard Hayes 176
Hartog, Dirk 16, 288, 537
Harvey, Elizabeth 479
Harvey, Hon. Mrs Leisha 456, 483
Hassell, Ethel 545
hat trick 322
Hattersley, Harry 104
Hatton, Hon. Steve 5, 455
Hatton Ministry 455
Havana 597
Hawaiian Islands 531, 539, 540
Hawke, Hon. Robert (Bob) J. L. 9, 13, 16, 450, 477, 571
    Aboriginal treaty and 409-10
    arranges emigration of Jewish families 15
    election date 7
    and nuclear waste industry 18
Hawker, Harry 428
Hawthorne, Phil 166, 172
Hay, Hon. D. A. 455
Hay, Louey 9
Hayden, Bill 571
Hayes, Colin 121
Haynes, John 292
Hayworth, Rita, death of 28
Hazelton, Ross 196
Healy, Cecil 154
Healy, Brother John Dominic 298
Heard Island 541, 542, 571, 715
Hearns, Thomas 227
heart transplant, first operation 296
Heath, Hon. Edward 177
Heath, Rodney 197
Heather, Reg 121
Hede, Jack 187
Hedley, C. 161
Hefford, Audrey 137

Heinz, Henry John II 298
Heinze, Sir Bernard 301
Helpmann, Max 299
Helpmann, Sir Robert 301
Helsinki 609
Hemmings, Fred 195
Hemmings, Hon. Terence Henry 457
Henderson, Yvonne 487
Henneberry, Fred 75
Hennessy, A. S. 161
Henricks, John 155
Henry, Prince 303, 304
Herald and Weekly Times 3, 4
Hess, Rudolf 35
Hewlett Packard Australia Ltd 390
Heyerdahl, Thor 531, 532
Hickin, Abe 68
Hicks, Lt Zachary 288
Hickson, A. J. 172
Higgins, Mat 211
Higgin's curse 421
High Court, Canberra 307
Highett, F. 197
Hill, Edward Fowler 299
Hill, Hon. Gordon Leslie 459
Hill, Jane 486
Hill, Peter 302
Hinch, Derryn 13
Hindmarsh, Jim 172
Hinkler, Bert 427
Hinton, Harry 138
Hinze, Russ 6
Hirsh, Carolyn 486
Hoad, Lew 204
Hobart Cup (horse race) 129–30
Hocking, Betty 480
Hodge, Hon. Barry James 460
Hodgman, Hon. Peter 458
Hoffey, Frank 299
Hogan, Paul 301
Hogarth, Kevin 76
Hogg, Hon. Caroline 459, 486
Holden 295, 390
Holding, Hon. A. Clyde 451
Holes, Pat 91
Holey Dollar 347
Hollis, Charlie 299
Holmes, Bob 182
Holmes Snr, Freeman 216, 217
Holt, Harold Edward 305, 474–5
Holy See 741
homosexuality 296
Honan, Bob 166, 172
Honduras 31, 620–1
Hong Kong 22, 730, 741
   exports from 382
Honiara 679
Hoobin, Jack 94
Hoodoo Gurus 518, 519, 522
Hookes, David 90
Hopgood, Hon. (Dr) Donald Jack 457
Hopper, N. C. 93
Horder, Maureen 480
Horner, Sally 96
horses, wild 418
horseracing 109–35
   etorphine detected 15

   first 223–4
   first official 289
   George Way jnr disqualified 4
   magazines 514–15
Hoskins, John S. 187, 188, 228
Hot Property 523
Houdini, Harry 426
Hougoumont (ship) 291
housing 276
Houtman Abrolhos 537
Howard, Bruce 214
Howard, Hon. John 452
Howard, Trevor, death of 45
Howe, Hon. Brian 451
Howe, George 289
Howland Island 736
Hoyle, H. 162
Hubble, Garry 75
Hudson, Peter 55
Huessner, Dennis 196
Hughes, Kim 7
Hughes, Robert 4
Hughes, William Morris 'Billy' 293, 464, 469
Hulme, Dennis 141
Human League 521
humidity, average relative 279
Hummingbird 523
Humphreys, Hon. Benjamin (Ben) 451
Hungary 25, 50, 621–2, 741
Hunters & Collectors 519
Hunting, A. J. 187, 188
Hutchence, Michael 519, 523
Hutchings, Brian 196
Huxley, Thomas Henry 539
Huxley, Vic 188
Huxton Creepers 523
Hyde, Greg 176
Hyde Park 109
Hynes, Patrick 228

ice chest 333
iceberg 47
Icehouse 516, 517, 518, 519, 522
Iceland 622–3, 741
Illingworth, Captain John 177, 225
I'm Talking 517, 519, 521
Impetuous (yacht) 181
imports 339, 376
   costs 4
   major commodities 379
   major countries 378
   by state 377
in-vitro quads 7
income
   annual 368
   average weekly earnings 373, 374–5
   circular flow of 334
income tax 292, 343
indexation 346
India 21, 23, 31, 32, 46–7, 623–4, 741
   Union Carbide gas leak 43
Indianapolis 500 149–51
Indonesia 3, 27, 29, 40, 45, 46, 47, 49, 624–5, 742
   Australian Embassy staff investigated 3

industrial disputes
  duration 371
  method of settlement 372
  working days lost 369, 370
  see also strikes
industry
  average weekly earnings 374-5
  sectors 350
  who owns what 388-91
  working days lost in disputes 370
inflation rate 339, 340, 346
Inglis, Andrew 97
insurance
  disability income insurance 283-4
  life expectancy 283
Inter-Dominion Pacing Championship 218-19, 225
interest rates 339, 340-1, 346
INTEST 399
Investigator (ship) 289
investment 337-8, 388
InXs 517, 519, 521, 524
Iran 21, 23, 25, 33, 39, 43, 625-6, 742
  Australian diplomats asked to leave Tehran 7
  deaths during violent rioting in Mecca 33
  France breaks off diplomatic relations with 32
  Persian Gulf war 36, 40
Iran-Contra arms scandal 22, 23, 24, 30, 32, 35, 41, 49
Iraq 21, 23, 46, 626-7, 742
  Persian Gulf war 36
  US frigate hit by Exocet missile 29
Ireland 23, 627, 742
Ireland, Northern 700-1
Irish Republican Army (IRA) 29, 49
Iron Man competition 196
Irvine, Ken 167
Irving, Professor M. H. 158
Isaacs, Simon 299
Islamabad 661
Isle of Man 731
Isle of Man Tourist Trophy 137
Israel 25, 42, 44, 45, 48, 50, 628, 742
Italy 24, 26, 28, 30, 37, 42, 628-9
Ivshenko, Paul 176

Jack, Gary 167
Jack the Ripper 39
jackpot 323
Jackson, Judith 485
Jackson, Marjorie 155, 208, 209, 211
Jackson, Neville 310
Jackson, Peter 69
Jackson, Rex 11
Jacobs, B. 95
Jakarta 624
Jakins, Judith 482
Jakobsen, Carolyn 480
Jamaica 37, 629-30, 742
James, Harry 142
James, Harvey 310
James Hardie 1000 (motor race) 145-6, 147
Jameson, Geoffrey 222
Jamestown 732
Jan Mayen 724
Jane, Bob 226
Janssen, Brian 75, 77
Janssen, Mark 75
Jansz, Willem 288
Japan 21, 27, 28, 36, 41, 630-1, 742
  Australian Embassy in Tokyo 18-19
  exports from 382
  honeymooners to Australia 8
  imports from 378
  introduction of the Aussie meat pie 3
  proposal for technology city 13, 18
Jardine, Douglas 85
Jarvis Island 736
Jeffkins, Rupert 141
Jenkins, Jean 453, 480
Jerome, Jerry 73
Jerusalem 628
John, Elton 3
John Fairfax Ltd 13, 355
John Paul, Pope 25, 26, 297
Johns, Greg 176
Johns, Les 167
Johnson, Athol 136
Johnson, Gordon 94
Johnson, Jim 112
Johnson, Louise 10
Johnson, Noel 188
Johnson, Rev. 288
Johnson, Ron 188
Johnston, Craig 227
Johnston, Malcolm 121
Johnston, Peter 399
Johnston Atoll 735
Johnstone, Rae 'Togo' 121
Jolly, Hon. Robert Allen 458
Jones, Alan 140, 141, 152, 226, 227
Jones, Hon. Barry 450
Jones, Beryl 487
Jones, Irvine 188
Jones, Linda 121
Jones, Tommy 73
Jones, Tony 70
Jordan 631-2, 743
Joynton Smith, Sir James 162
Julius, Sir George 216
jungle flower 421
jungle weed 421

Kable, Young 68
Kabul 564
Kahanamoku, Duke 193, 194
Kamahl 310
Kampala 697
Kampuchea 43, 632-3
Kanak Socialist National Liberation Front (FLNKS) 4, 36
Kangaroos Rugby Team 162
Kathmandu 654
Katter, Hon. Robert Carl 456
Kavanagh, Ken 137
Kearney, Ken 166, 172
Kearns, Billy 299
Keating, Hon. Paul J. 297, 450
  May mini-budget 8
  presents a balanced budget 12
  $2 coin struck 12
Kelevitz, Zsigmond 222
Kellow, Charles 142

Kelly, Geoff 136
Kelly, Greg 175
Kelly, James 68
Kelly, Most Reverend John Anthony 299
Kelly, Ned 68
  hanged 292
  photograph auctioned 14
Kelly, Hon. Roslyn (Ros) 451, 478
Kelly, Shelley 97
Kelly (Paul) and the Coloured Girls 519, 521, 522
Kemp, Charles 290
Keneally, Hon. Gavin Francis 457
Kenna, Peter 299
Kennan, Hon. James Harley 459
Kennedy, Edwina 103
Kennedy, Kenneth 154, 225
Kennett, Jeff 5
Kennison v Daire 397
Kenny, Grant 196
Kenny, Hayden 196
Kenny, Michael John Butler 'Jack' 299
Kenny, Sir Patrick 299
Kenny, Sarah 175
Kent, Duke of 305, 308
Kent, William 289
Kentucky Fried Chicken 389
Kenya 633-4, 743
Kerguelen Islands 23, 720
Kerin, Hon. John C. 451
Kermedec Islands 722
kerosene refrigerator 333
Kerr, Bernard 299
Kerr, Sir John 14
Kerry, Mark 156
Khartoum 683
Kialoa (yacht) 177
Kigali 670
Kilbey, Steve 519
Kilroy, J. B. 177
Kinder, T. 136
King, Jack 93
King, Mick 70
King, R. 136
King Snake Roost 522
Kingman Reef 736
Kings Cross Wax Works 10
King's Cup (rowing) 160, 224
Kingsford Smith, Sir Charles 112, 427, 428
Kingston (Jamaica) 629
Kingston (Norfolk Island) 715
Kingston Town (racehorse) 120, 122, 217
Kingstown 673
Kinshasa 710
Kiribati 634, 743
Kirkby, Elisabeth 482
Kirkpatrick, Anne 519, 524
Kirkwood, Joe 100, 104
Kirner, Hon. Joan Elizabeth 459, 486
Kismet (yacht) 182
Kite, Delcia 482
Kline, Lindsay 84, 87
Knight, Jack 222
Knight, Julian 11
Knight, L. 136
Knight, Stephen 166, 172

knock off work 323
Knowles, Susan 480
Knox, David 173
Knox, Sir William 17
Konrads, John 155
Kookaburra (yacht) 180
Korea, North 45-6, 635
Korea, South 22, 27, 29, 31, 32, 35, 42, 44, 46, 50, 635-6, 743
  exports from 382
Korean War 432
Koror 736
Kosmina, John 184
Kosrae Island 540
Kouros, Yiannos 6
Kraftwerk 524
Krilich, Max 165
Krisps, Henry 299
Ku Klux Klan 28
Kuala Lumpur 645
Kuepper, Ed 519, 522
Kuwait 45, 636-7, 743
Kuwait (city) 636
Kyle, Sir Wallace 299

labour force 334
  age and 358-60
  educational attainment 357
  eight-hour working day introduced 291
  family status 356
  forty-hour working week 295
  persons out of, during 1986 361-3
  proportion of workers covered by superannuation 286
Lachlan River 289
Lagos 659
Laidlaw, Diana 484
Lake Eyre 282, 571
Lake Gairdner 282
Lake Torrens 282
Lalor, Peter 291
Lamont, Billy 188
land rights 297, 401-10
Landy, John 209
Lane, Freddy C. V. 153
Lane, Geoff 120
Lang, Bill 70
Lang, Jack 294, 464
Lang, John 165
Lang Labor Party 464
Langbecker, Kerry 97
Langlands, Graeme 166, 167
languages
  Aboriginal 540
  of the Pacific 540
lantana 413
Laos 637-8, 743
Lapita Culture 534, 535
Lappin, Billy 121
Larra, James 109
Latta, James 215
Laver, Rod 201, 207, 225
Lavis, Neale 96, 155
law
  Aboriginal 403
  computer technology 392

land rights legislation 401-10
  regulations controlling trade in endangered
    species 416
Law, Phillip 541
Lawford, Peter 194
lawn bowls 135-7
  magazines 514
Lawn Tennis Association of Australasia 198
Lawn Tennis Federation of Australia 198
Lawrence, Dr Carmen 487
Lawrence, Peter 299
Lawson, Aub 188
Lawson, Henry 528
Lawson, Jimmy 68
Lawson, William 289
Le Figaro (newspaper) 6
Le Maire, Jacques 536
Leach, Geordie 310
Lebanon 21, 28, 30, 35, 38, 46, 638-9, 743
Led Zeppelin 523
Lee, Bing 299
Leech, Faith 155
legal expert systems 398-400
Legionnaire's disease 8
Legislative Council, established 289
Leglise, Pat 77
Leisk, Les 138
Lemonthyme and Southern Forest, Tas. 18
Lend Lease Corporation 15
Lendl, Ivan 227
Lenehan, Susan 484
Lennon, John 47
Lesotho 639, 743
Lester, Hon. Vincent Patrick 456
Letham, Isabel 194
Leves, Melinda 6
Levy, Judith Anne 484
Lewis, Austin 452
Lewis, Bobby 112, 113
Lewis, Chris 217
Lewis, Wally 165, 167, 172
Lexcen, Ben 12, 180, 297
Liberace, death of 23
Liberal Movement 464
Liberal Party 4, 19, 295, 452-3
  coalition reformed 11
  introduce 'incentivation' 4
  John Elliot elected president of 14
Liberia 640
Liberty (yacht) 180
Libreville 611
Libya 640-1
Liechtenstein 641-2
life expectancy 283
Lifton, Charles 68
Light, Colonel William 321
Lightning Stakes 217
Lillee, Dennis 87, 90, 226
Lilongwe 644
Lima 665
Lime Spiders 519
Lindsay, Professor David 423
Lingiari, Vincent 299
Lisbon 668
Lisle, Jim 166, 172
lithographs, auction of John Gould's 11

Litten, Jack 217
Little, Captain Robert 431
Little River Band 518, 520
Littleproud, Hon. Brian 456
live hare coursing 107-8
liver transplant 6
Livingstone, Margaret 310
Lizard Train 522
llamas 418
Lloyd, Bruce 452
Lock, Jane 103
Locke, Bobby 98, 99, 229
Lome 692
Londish, Sid 10
London 700-1
London-Sydney Marathon Rallies 142
Londos, Jim 223
Long, Gerry 310
Long, Grant 175, 176
loo, origin of word 323
Lorita Marie (yacht) 180
lottery prize, late claim 11
Lough, Fitz 197
Louisade Archipelago 534, 540
Loyalty Islands 534
Luanda 567
Lubricated Goat 522
Lucky Creed (racehorse) 217, 221
Luedecke, Tom 176
Lukin, Dean 156
lungfish, Australian 416
Lusaka 711
Luscombe, Fred 135
Lutge, Dinny 162
Luxembourg 642-3, 743
Luxembourg (city) 642
Lyall, William 419
Lycett, R. 197
Lynagh, Michael 173
Lyons, Enid 294
Lyons, Joseph Aloysius 462, 465, 470-1
Lyster, Maureen 486

Mable, R. 161
McAleer, Margaret 487
McAllister, 'Snowy' 194
Macao 21, 725
McArthur, General Douglas 294
Macarthur, John 289
McBride, Dr William 16, 17
McCarten, Jack 120
McCarthy, Dudley 299
McCarthy, Hon. Terence 455
McCauley, Diane 484
McCaw, Sandra 102
McClements, Lynne 155
McCosker, Rick 90
McCusker, Neal 299
McCutcheon, Hon. Andrew 459
McDonald, Colin 86
McDonald, John 167
McDonald Island 571, 715
McDonnell, Holly 9
McEvoy, F. J. 154
McEwan, Brian 299
McEwen, Sir John (Jack) 475

McFarland, Floyd 93
McFarlane, Robert 30
McGinness, P. J. 293
McGlede, Stephen 94
McGowan, Jack 73
McGregor, Ken 201
Machin, Arnold 348
Machin, Wendy 482
McHugh, Jeannette 478
McInnes, Laurie 8
McIntosh, Hugh D. 92
McIntosh, John 428
McIntyre, Briget 96
McIntyre, Deahnne 302
Mackaness, John 110
McKay, Keith 188
Mackay, Ken 86
McKechnie, Hon. Peter Richard 456
McKelvey, Steve 193
McKenzie, C. B. 97, 102
McKenzie, E. 197
Mackenzie, Stuart 160
Mackerras, Neil 299
McKibbin, Miss 136
Macklin, Michael 453
McKnight, Allan Duncan 299
McLachlan, Bill (jockey) 121
McLachlan, Bill (powerboat driver) 158
McLachlan, W. H. 'Midge' 112
Maclean, Alistair 23
McLean, Jean 486
McLean, John 172
McLean, Paul 173, 453
McLeod, Mona 102
MacMahon, Ted 299
McMahon, Sir William 476
McManus, Paul 15
McNamara, Lieutenant F. H. 431
McNamara, Reg 95
McNeill, C. H. 136
McNeill, Sir James 299
McNeilly, George 299
McNicol, Sir Alan Wedel Ramsay 299
MacPherson, Billy 208, 209
Macquarie, Lachlan 289
Macquarie Island 541, 542
Macquarie River 289
McVean, Jeff 97
McVilly, Cecil 159
Mad Max (film) 491
Mad Max II (film) 489
Mad Max, Beyond Thunderdome (film) 490
Mad Turks from Istanbul 522
Madagascar 643-4, 743
Maddock, Russell 121
Madigan, Tony 76
Madonna 521
Madrid 25, 682
magazine circulation figures 505-10
Magellan, Ferdinand 535
Maguire, Dennis 196
Maklouf, Raphael 348
Malabo 606
Malawi 644
Malaysia 27, 40, 645, 743
Maldives 645-6, 743

Male 645
Mali 646-7
Malkin, Colin 142
Malone, Mick 90
Malone, Moses 227
Malta 23, 29, 647-8, 744
Man from Snowy River (film) 489
Managua 657
Manama 573
Mandela, Nelson 41
Mangareva 531
Manila 666
Manson, Hon. William Angus 456
Manzie, Hon. Daryl 455
Maoris 533, 540
Maputo 652
Marchant, Tony 155
Marcos, President Ferdinand 22
Marcos, Imelda 22
Margaret, Princess 305, 306
Margarey, W. A. 64
Margarey Medal 55, 64-6
Mariana Islands 533
Marina, Princess 304
markets 333, 335
Maroubra Speedway 138
Marquesas 531, 533
marriages
  category of celebrant, states and territories 247-8
  month of celebration of marriage 249
  previous marital status 245-6
  registered in states and territories 244
  relative ages of bridegroom and bride 250-2
Marsh, Graham 100, 101
Marsh, Rodney 87, 90
Marshall Islands 533, 540, 734
Martin, A. C. 214
Martin, Lisa 210
Martinique 717
Marvin, Lee, death of 35
Maseru 639
Mason, Peter 299
Mass Appeal 522
Masters, Margaret 102, 103
Mathews, Hon. Charles Race Thorson 459
Mathews, Justice Jane Hamilton 9
Matthews, Greg 84
Mattioli, Rocky 69, 75
Mauritania 648
Mauritius 649, 744
Mawson, Douglas 541
mayday 323
Mayes, Hon. Kym 457
Mayfield-Smith, Brian 227
Mayotte 718
Mbabane 685
Mbeki, Govan 41
Mead, David 399
Meadows, Ginger 6
Meaney, Frank 299
meat pie, exported to Japan 3
Meckiff, Ian 84, 86
medical
  bionic ear 9
  boy dies from rabies 15

Debendox 16, 17
genetic probe to determine the sex of a baby 31
mental hospitals sold 12
new pregnancy test 8
sexual abuse charges 9
shortage of doctors 16
surprise pregnancy 6
transplants 6, 14
Mehegan, Hughie 72
Melanesia 534-5, 540
Melba, Dame Nellie 10, 311, 323
Melba toast 323
Melbourne 10, 290, 323
Olympic Games in 153
Melbourne, HMAS (aircraft carrier) 432
Melbourne Cup 224, 225
first 111, 291
Phar Lap wins 294
second and third placegetters 116-19
winners 113-16
Melbourne Motordrome 138, 187
Meldrum, Molly 10
Mellor, Fleur 155, 209
Melrose, Tony 172
Mendana, Alvaro de 536
Meninga, Mal 167
Mental as Anything 517, 521, 523
Menzies, Sir Robert Gordon 295, 296, 306, 471-2, 474
Mercedes II (yacht) 181
Meredith, Geoff 188
merino sheep 289
Messenger, Herbert Henry 'Dally' 161, 162
Messner, Hon. Tony 452
Metcalfe, Jack 210
meteorology 542
Meteors (jet) 432
Metherell, Hon. T. A. 455
Mexico 33, 42, 649-50, 744
Mexico City 649
Michael, Barry 69
Michael, George 521
Michael of Kent, Prince and Princess 307
Michaelis, Kevin William 299
Micronesia 533-4, 540
Micronesia, Federated States of 734
Middlesborough General Hospital 9
Middleton, A. C. (Albert) 93
Middleton, Doreen 93
Midnight Oil 519, 521, 522
Midway Islands 735
Midwinter, William (Billy) 85
migration
birthplace of parents of Australian-born persons 270-1
Chinese restricted 291
by country of birth 268-9
language other than English spoken at home 272-3
population growth 261
Mildara 388
Mildren, Alec 139
Miles, Chris 453
Millard, W. J. 211
Miller, Tony (boxer) 77
Miller, Tony (footballer) 174, 229

Miller, 'Professor' William 221
Mills, George 110
Mills, Martin 311
Millsom, Gus 216
Milson, James 176
Milton, W. V. 172
minerals 391
Minogue, Kylie 516, 519
Miquelon 718
Miracle Mile 217, 220
missions overseas, Australian 738-49
Mitchell, Professor Charles 4
Mitrevski, Peter 78
Mo 311
Mockridge, Carol 299
Mockridge, Russell 95, 155
Models 517, 521
Mogadiscio 680
Moir, P. 161
Moluccas 536, 537
Molyneux, Jan 92
Mombasa, Reg 311
Monaco 650-1
Monaco (city) 650
money
executive salary levels 18
floating the dollar 297
role in economy 346
volume of 349
see also currency, Australian; economy; wages
Mongolia 651
monorail 4, 8
Monrovia 640
Monsanto 390
Montevideo 702
Montserrat 731
Moore, Alan 75
Moore, C. D. 110
Moore, Clover 482
Moore, George 120, 121, 134
Moore, Hon. John 452
Moore, Kevin 299
Moore, Paul 75
Moore, Hon. T. J. 454
Moore, W. H. 110
Moran, Dr H. 173
Moreton Bay 290, 291
Morgan, Lawrence 96, 155
Morgan, Sandra 155
Moriarty, John 216
Morning Cloud (yacht) 177
Morocco 652, 744
Moroni 594
Morris, Jenny 519
Morris, Hon. Peter 450
Morris, Rod 165
Morris, Ruth 311
Morris T. H. 222
Morrison, Don 196
Morse code 323, 327
Mortal Sin 523
Mortlock Islands 540
Morton, Tex 311
Moscow 697
Moses, Sir Charles 299
Moss, Stirling 139, 140

Mossop, Rex 166, 172
Mothering Sunday 323
Mothers 523
Mother's Day 323
Moto-Cross 138
motor racing 139-52
  Australian Grand Prix 14, 297
  see also motorcycling; speedway racing
motorcycling 137-9
  Gardner wins Brazilian Grand Prix 13
  magazines 514
motoring magazines 513
Mt Everest, Bicentennial expedition 18
Mt Kosciusko 282, 571
Mt Panorama, Bathurst 137, 146, 225
Movizio, Samuel 6
Mowbray, Andrew 399
Mozambique 33, 50, 652-3, 744
  Australian missionary arrested 14, 19
mud in your eye 323
Muirhead Royal Commission 11
Mulholland, Billy 75
Mulholland, Wayne 70, 75, 78
Mulley, George 120, 122
Mullins, Peter 97
Mulock, Ron 4
multicultural press 506-10
Mundey, Jack 296
Mundine, Tony 70, 73
Munro, Darby 112
Munro, Jack 108
Muntz, Hon. Geoffrey Hugh 456
murders
  Anita Cobby 8
  Clifton Hill 11
  death rates 258
  Father's Day Massacre 8
  Myall Creek massacre 290
  Queen Street Massacre 15
Murdoch, Rupert 10
Murdoch, William 84, 85
Murphy, Justice Lionel 5
Murphy, 'Torpedo' Billy 69
Murray, A. 136
Murray, Alan 100
Murray, H. F. 136
Murray, Iain 180, 182
Murray, Jan 6
Murray, Kevin 56
Murray, Hon. W. T. J. 454
Murray-Darling river system 282
Mururoa Atoll 23 ,29, 41
Muscat 660
Musgrove, Eric 97
music
  Australian folk 525-30
  magazines 513
  Oz rock 517
  top ten best-selling albums and singles 516
Mustar, Pard 428
Myall Creek massacre 290
Mytton, Devereaux 182
myxomatosis 419, 420, 423

Nabalco 401
Nagle, Kel 99, 100, 101, 103, 106

Nairobi 633
names
  derivation of 321-6
  most popular 312-14
  pseudonyms 310-11
Namibia 48
Narvo, Herb 75
Nassau 573
National Advisory Committee on AIDS (NACAIDS) 6
National Aeronautics and Space Administration (NASA) 37
National Coursing Association 108
National Gallery, Canberra 307
National Institute for Dramatic Art (NIDA) 295
National Labor Party 464
National Party 11
National Service 296
National Soccer League 183
National Tennis Stadium 201
Nationalist Party 464
Naughton, John 121
Nauru 48, 533, 540, 653-4, 744
Nawi 8
N'djamena 589
Neal, Hon. Donald McConnell 456
Neall, Gail 155
Nepal 49, 654-5, 744
Ness, Miss 136
Nestle 389
netball 152-3
  magazines 514
Netherlands, The 655-6, 744
  exploration of the Pacific 536-7
  external territories 721
Netherlands Antilles 721
Neville, Ray 112
Nevis 671-2
New Britain 540
New Caledonia 4, 35, 37, 40, 45, 48, 534, 537, 539, 719, 744
  Australia supports independence 3
  Australian Consul-General ordered to leave 3
  economic reforms in 38
New Christs 522
New Delhi 23, 623
New Guinea 534, 538, 540
  Australia separates from 288
  see also Papua New Guinea
New Hanover 536
New Ireland 536, 540
New South Wales
  average weekly earnings 373
  exports 383
  extreme maximum temperatures 277
  extreme minimum temperatures 277
  flag 309
  Greiner Ministry 454-5
  highest daily rainfall 278
  imports 377
  industrial disputes 369
  introduces compulsory state schooling 292
  map of Australia 239
  named 538
  paid sick leave and long-service leave 295
  population growth 261
  public holidays 1989 237

representative government 290
resident population 262-3, 265
retention rates of secondary school students 445
school terms 1989 238
transportation of convicts ends 290
women in parliament 478, 481
NSW Bowling Association 135
New South Wales Corps 289
NSW Greyhound Breeders', Owners' and Trainers' Association 108
New South Wales Institute of Technology 13
New South Wales Teachers' Federation 18
NSW Trotting Authority 221
NSW Trotting Club 108, 215
New Zealand 22, 24, 30, 35, 47, 537, 656-7, 744
  bans US nuclear warships 22
  Cook in 538
  exports from 382
  external territories 722-3
  flag 544
  imports from 378
  languages of 540
  Nuclear Free Zone, Disarmament and Arms Control Bill 30
  prehistory of 532-3
New Zealand (yacht) 177
Newbiggen, Bob 196
Newcastle
  convict site 10
Newcastle State Dockyard 5
Newcombe, John 201, 207
Newman, Jocelyn 479
Newman, Kevin 221
News Corporation 10, 353
newspaper circulation figures 505-10
Newton, Albert 136
Newton-John, Olivia 518
Ngatik 540
Niamey 658
Nicaragua 22, 42, 44, 50, 657-8
Nicholls, Arthur 159
Nichols, Kevin 156
Nicholson, John 94
Nick Cave and the Bad Seeds 519
Nicklaus, Jack 97, 99
Nicoll, H. F. (Harry) 216
Nicosia 598
Niger 658
Nigeria 31, 32, 659, 744
Nile, Elaine 482
Nile, Reverend Fred 463
Nissen, Henry 74
Nitani, Yurie 8
Niue 531, 722
Noble, Trisha 311
Noiseworks 518, 525
None, Fred 193
Noogoora burr 421
Norfolk (ship) 289
Norfolk Island 534, 539, 571, 715
Nori, Sandra 482
Norman, Decima 210
Norman, Greg 100, 101, 107, 227
North, Lieutenant-Colonel Oliver 30, 32, 49
North Broken Hill Holdings 355, 391
North Korea *see* Korea, North

Northam, Bill 154, 155, 182
Northern Mariana Islands 734
Northern Territory
  average weekly earnings 373
  exports 383
  extreme maximum temperatures 278
  extreme minimum temperatures 277
  granted self-government 297
  Hatton Ministry 455
  highest daily rainfall 279
  imports 377
  map of Australia 239
  population 262-3, 265
  public holidays 1989 237
  retention rates of secondary school students 445
  school terms 1989 238
  women in parliament 483
Norton, John 326
Norway 40, 659-60, 745
  external territories 724-5
Not Drowning Waving 519, 522
Notting, Fred 193
Nouakchott 648
Noumea 719
  Australian Consul-General ordered to leave 3
nuclear missiles 23
nuclear waste industry 18
Nuku'alofa 693
numbats 420
Nunn, Glynis 156, 209
Nutcote 5
Nuuk 716
Nuyts, Pieter 537

obituaries 298-300
  sporting 228-9
O'Brien, Ian 155
occupations 364-7
O'Connor, Michael 166, 167, 172
O'Connor, Ossie 142
O'Connor, William Paul 299
O'Donnell, Peter 155, 182
O'Donnell, Phyllis 195
O'Donoghue, Lois 301
O'Farrell, Henry James 303
offsider 323
Ogilvy, Hon. Angus 306, 307
O'Hagan, Jack Francis 299
O'Halloran, Kevin 155
oil strike 8
O'Keeffe, Kerry 90
Oldfield, Bert 86
Oleander 414
Oliphant, Greg 165
Olympia Speedway 138, 187
Olympic Games 153-7, 224
  boxing 76
  cancelled 154
  cycling 93, 95
  equestrian 95-6
  gold medals 154-6
  medal tally 156
  in Melbourne 225, 295
  1988 27, 44
  North Korea withdraws 46
  rowing and sculling 159

soccer 183, 185
tennis 204
track and field 208-10
Winter Olympics 154, 156-7, 225
wrestling 222
yachting 181-2
Olympic Speedway 187
Olympics, International Youth Skill 18
Oman 660-1, 745
One Best-Seller (book) 10
O'Neill, Norman 86
O'Neill, Pam 121
Oodgerooo Noonuccal 16
Opperman, Sir Hubert 93, 94
Oranjestad 721
Ord, Lecki 11
oriental fruit moth 425
Orlando 388
Osborne, H. 93
Oslo 659
Otama, HMAS 10
Ottawa 587
Ouagadougou 583
overseas debt 339, 341-5
ozone layer 38

Pacific islanders 291
Pacific Ocean 323
European exploration of 535-9
history of 531-9
languages of 540
pacing see trotting and pacing
Packer, Frank 294
Packer, Kerry 90
Padgham-Purich, (Cecilia) Noel 483
Page, Sir Earle Christmas Grafton 464, 471
Pago Pago 733
Painters & Dockers 522
Paisley, Una 92
Pakistan 23, 26, 33, 661-2, 745
Palau 34, 736
Palauan Islands 533, 537
Paleface Adios (racehorse) 217, 221
Palestinian Liberation Organisation (PLO) 27, 45, 46
Palestinians 44, 45, 46, 48, 50
Palisade (film) 8
Palm, Bert 136
Palmer, Ambrose 73
Palmer, Arnold 97, 99
Palmyra Island 736
Panama 32, 48, 49, 662-3, 745
Panama City 662
pancreas 14
Pantar 540
Papeete 719
paper and packaging industry 391
paperback bestsellers 494-504
Papua New Guinea 32, 34, 36, 41, 44, 46, 47, 663-4, 745
becomes self-governing 296
call to end French rule in New Caledonia 37
parachuting record 12
Paraguay 26, 48, 664-5, 745
Paramaribo 684

Parella, R. 136
Parer, Ray 427
Paris 609
Parish, Don 167
Parker, Hon. David Charles 460
Parker, H. A. 198
Parkes, Sir Henry 463
Parkinson, J. 55
Parliament House (new) 308
flagpole problems 3
Parr, George 83
parrot, orange-bellied 416
Parsons (nee Hickey), Marea 103
particle board 390
Party Boys 519, 522
Pascoe, Len 90
Paterson, Banjo 292, 325, 527
Paterson, C. D. 193
Patrick, Vic 75
Patterson, Gerald L. 198
Patterson, Kay 479
Patterson, Sid 93, 94, 95
Paul, Lyn 311
Payne, Hon. Ronald George 457
Peace March, Palm Sunday 6
Peach Melba 323
Peacock, Hon. Andrew 5, 452
Peacocke, Hon. G. B. P. 455
Pearce, Frank 188
Pearce, H. R. 'Bobby' 155, 159, 160
Pearce, Harry 160
Pearce, Hon. Robert John 459
Pearce, S. 161
Pearsall, Hon. Geoffrey Allan 457
Pearson, Bill 55
pedal wireless 430
Peden, Margaret 91
Peel, Harry 138
Peel, Steve 77
Peking 591
Pele 186
Penman, Dr David 13
pennies 348
Pennington, Professor David 6
pensions 293
Perdon, George 214
peregrine falcon 416
Performing Arts Complex, Brisbane 308
Perkins, Charles 11
Perron, Hon. Marshall 455
Persian Gulf 29, 33, 34, 36, 39, 40, 44
see also Iran; Iraq
Perth 10, 324
Peru 38, 665-6, 745
pests, imported 417-25
Peter I Island 724
Peter Pan (racehorse) 112, 122
Peterson, George 299
Pethybridge, Horace 93
Pettingell, Sir William 299
Phar Lap (film) 489
Phar Lap (racehorse) 113, 225
dies in USA 122
wins Melbourne cup 294
pheromones 425
Philip, Prince, royal visits 304-8

Philippines 21, 23, 24, 28, 33-4, 37, 42, 44, 47, 50, 537, 666-7, 745
Phillip, Captain Arthur 288
Phillips, Frank 104
Phillips, Captain Mark 306, 307, 308
Phillips, Rex 197
Phillis, Tom 137
Phnom Penh 632
Pickard, Hon. N. E. W. 455
Pickering, Hon. E. P. 454
Pickles, Carolyn 484
Pickworth, Ossie 98, 99
picnic 324
Picnic at Hanging Rock (film) 491
Pidding, Noel 167
Pignolet, Josephine 300
pigs, feral 419
Pike, Jim 113, 225
pin money 324
Pine Gap American military base 14
Pingelap 540
Pioneer Motor Cycle Club 137
Pironi, Didier 228
Pitcairn Island 531, 538, 731
Pitt, Bill 139
Plain, Josephine 311
plains wanderer 416
planets 546-7
plants
    endangered 416
    poisonous 411-15
Player, Gary 98, 99
Plaza, Martin 311
Plessey 391
plimsoll line 324
plonk 324
Plymouth 731
Poidevin, Simon 173
Poindexter, Rear Admiral John 30, 32, 49
Point Cook Flying School 431
Point Hicks 538
poisonous plants *see* plants, poisonous
Poland 29, 38, 46, 667-8, 745
Police Car (yacht) 181
political parties
    abbreviations 488
    defunct 462-5
Pollard, Snub 311
polling dates, Federal 460-2
Pollock, Bob 217
Polynesia 531-2, 540
Ponape 540
Pons, Bernard 4
Pony 523
Poole, Keith 136
Popular Alm (racehorse) 217, 220
population 570
    Aboriginal 409
    by age groups, states and territories 265-7
    of capital and major cities 264
    educational attainment and whether in the labour force 357
    family status and whether in the labour force 356
    first census 292
    growth rates 261
    labour force by age 358-60
    resident 262-3, 265
    by states 262-3
    see also birth rates
Port-au-Prince 620
Port Kembla Steelworks 13
Port Louis 649
Port Moresby 663
Port-of-Spain 693
Porter, James 453
Porto Novo 577
Portugal 668, 745
    exploration of the Pacific 536
    external territories 725
Poseidon (racehorse) 113, 122, 224
Possession Island 288, 538
possum, mountain-pygmy 416
postal rates, standard 293
postcodes 296
Postle, Arthur 214
Powell, Adrian 154
Powell, George 70
Powell, Janet 453, 479
Power, Clarice 137
powerboating 157-8
Prague 599
Praia 588
Pratt, Bob 55
pregnancy test 8
Prell, Sue 104
Presley, Elvis 6
Preston, Richard 311
Pretoria 681
Price, Don 172
Price, Ray 166, 172
prickly pear 421, 423
Priestley, Bill 112
prime ministers 465-77
Prior, Sid 76
privacy 392-4
proofreader's marks 328-32
Prost, Alain 140, 143, 144, 226, 227
Protectionist Party 464
Prouse, Geoff 121, 226
Pseudo Echo 518, 519, 522
pseudonyms 310-11
public holidays, 1989 237
Public Service 285
publishing 389
    newspaper and magazine circulation figures 505-15
    paperback bestsellers 494-504
Puerto Rico, Commonwealth of 21, 736-7
Pugh, 'Digger' 188
pull the leg, to 325
Pulz, Penny 102, 103
Punch, Hon. Gary 451
Puplick, Chris 452
Purcell, Ted 222
Purchase, Roy 222
Purtell, Jack 112
Pyongyang 635
python, oenpelli 416

Qantas 293, 353, 426, 427, 429, 430
    bought by the Australian Government 295

first overseas flight 294
flies to Britain via USA and Europe 295
Qatar 669, 745
quarantine 423
Queen Maud Land 725
Queensland
  Ahern Ministry 456
  average weekly earnings 373
  exports 383
  extreme maximum temperatures 278
  extreme minimum temperatures 277
  flag 309
  highest daily rainfall 278
  imports 377
  industrial disputes 369
  map of Australia 239
  opposes condom vending machines 11
  population growth 261
  public holidays 1989 237
  resident population 262-3, 265
  responsible government 291
  retention rates of secondary school students 445
  school terms 1989 238
  sex education to be taught 16
  women in parliament 478, 483
Queensland and Northern Territory Aerial Services Ltd *see* Qantas
Queensland Labor Party 463
Quinlan, John 311
Quintus Servinton (novel) 290
Quiros, Pedro de 536
Quist, Adrian 198, 204, 225
Quito 603

Rabat 652
rabbits 417, 419
  Akubra imports skins from Europe 6
  first introduced 291
  plague 419
rabies 15
racing *see* cycling
  see also greyhound racing; horseracing; motor racing; motorcycling; sidecar racing; speedcar racing; speedway racing; sprint car racing; trotting and pacing
radioactive food, seized 12
Radley, Paul 302
Rae, Dawn 92
Rae, Hon. Peter 458
Rafferty, Chips 311
Rafferty, Tony 214
Rafferty's rules 324
Ragamuffin (yacht) 181
Rain Lover (racehorse) 112, 122
rainfall, highest daily 278
raining cats and dogs 324
Randell, Hon. James 456
random breath-testing 297
Rangoon 584
Rani (yacht) 177, 225
Rapa 531
Raper, Ted 172
Rarotonga 722
Rasic, Rale 226
rat 417
Ravelomanantsoa, Jean-Louis 211, 226

Ray, Margaret 486
Ray, Hon. Robert 451
Read, Peter 76
real estate prices 350-2
Reckett and Coleman Australia Ltd 389
red-back spider 422
red herring 324
red tape 324
Reddiex, Jim 142
Reddy, Rod 165
Redex Trial 141
Redpath, Ian 90
refrigerator, kerosene 333
Reid, Alex 97
Reid, Sir George Houston 463, 467
Reid, Margaret 478
Reith, Peter K. 453
religion 274-5, 572
  Aboriginal 403-7
Rene, Roy *see* Mo
Renouf, Sir Frank and Lady Susan 15
Renshaw, Hon. John Brophy 'Jack' 300
Renwick, Steve 75
Repco Reliability Trial 141
rescue and resuscitation 196
rescues 7, 15
  'Black Sunday' Bondi Beach 197
Reserve Bank 340, 345, 353
Resolution (ship) 539
Returned Services League 3
Reubner, George 172
Reunion 718
Revell, Ray 190
Rexona 389
Reykjavik 622
Reyne, James 519, 522
Reynolds, Dick 55, 59
Reynolds, Jack 193
Reynolds, Hon. Margaret 451, 478
Rheuben, Peter 136, 137
Ribot, John 167
Rice, Jim 227
Richards, Ron 73, 75
Richardson, Geoff 166, 172
Richardson, Hon. Graham 451
Richardson, Henry Handel 311
Richardson, Colonel J. S. 292
Richmond, Joan 141
Richmond Report 12
Riddell, Miss 197
Riddell, W. J. C. 197
Risdon Cove 289
Rising Fast (racehorse) 112, 122
Rixon, Annie 311
Riyadh 674
Road Town 727
Roberts, T. L. 214
Robertson, Austin 214
Robertson, Austin (Jnr) 57
Robertson, Don 142
Robinson, A. F. 197
Robinson, Most Reverend Donald 13
Robinson, Edie 208
Robinson, Richie 90
Roche, Tony 201
Rockmelons 519, 522, 524

rodeo 324
Rodgers, Barry 196
Roe, Raigh 301
Rogers, Bill 97
Rogerson, Roger 13, 18
Roggeveen, Jacob 537, 540
Romania 42, 669-70, 745
Romano, A. O. 122
Rome 628
Rooney, Jim 184
Roper, Hon. Thomas William 458
Ropis, Frank 75
Ropis, Matt 74
Rosberg, Keke 140, 226, 297
Rose, Lionel 69, 70, 226, 301
Rose, Murray 154, 155
Rose Tattoo 520
Roseau 602
Rosenberg, A. 161
Rosewall, Ken 204, 207
Ross, Lloyd 300
Ross, Miss 197
Ross Dependency 723
Rossiter, Sir John Frederick 300
Rothmans Medal (Rugby League) 170-1, 171
Rothmans Medal (soccer) 184
Rothwell, Geoffrey 300
Rouse, James 111
rowing and sculling 158-60
Rowley, Stanley 153, 209
Royal Australian Air Force 293, 431-2
Royal Flying Doctor Service 294, 430
Royal National Park 292
Royal Sydney Yacht Squadron 176
royal visits 303-8
Roycroft, Barry 96
Roycroft, Bill 96, 154, 155
Roycroft, Bill (Jnr) 96
Roycroft, Clarke 96
Roycroft, Vicki 97
Roycroft, Wayne 96
rubber tyre market 390
Rude, Rodney 311
Rugby League 161-71, 224
   Australia v. Great Britain Test statistics 163-4
   Brisbane clubs 169
   Brisbane Premiership 169-70
   Manly defeats Canberra 13
   NSW clubs 168
   player of the year 170, 171
   Sydney Premiership 168-9
   Test matches 167
Rugby Union 172-5, 224
   Test matches 174, 175
Rum Rebellion 289
Rumley, Trevor 185
run amok, to 325
Rush, Gary 191
Rush, Michael 159
Russell, Dave 75, 77
Russell, Julian 300
Russell, Keightly 'Blue' 194
Russell, Wal 177
Ruxton, Bruce 3
Rwanda 670-1
Ryan, Dinny 55
Ryan, Kevin 166, 172

Ryan, Noel 196
Ryan, Ronald 296
Ryan, Senator Susan 16, 478

sack, to get the 325
sacred sites 401-10
Sadler, Joseph 159
Safe Sex Campaign 6
Saffron, Abe 5, 14
sailboarding 175-6
sailing and yachting 19, 176-82, 515
Sailor's Guide (racehorse) 120, 122
St Albans, Peter 112
St Christopher 671-2
Saint-Denis 718
St George, F. 207
St George, Stewart 188
St George's 616
St Helena 732
St Helier 728
St John's 568
St Lucia 672
Saint-Paul Island 720
St Peter Port 728
St Pierre 718
St Thomas 737
St Vincent 673
Saints 517, 520, 521
Salisbury, Charles 300
Sam, Doug 77
Samoa 531, 535, 537
   see also American Samoa; Western Samoa
San Andreas Fault 39
San Jose 595
San Juan 737
San Marino 673-4
San Marino (city) 673
San Salvador 605
San'a 707
Sandercock, Alf 136
Sanders, Billy 188
Sanders, Jon 19
Sanders, Norm 454
Sandover Medal 55, 61-3
Sands, Alfie 74, 76
Sands, Clem 76
Sands, Dave 73, 74, 76
Sands, Ritchie 76
Sands, Russell 74, 75, 76
Sands, Snowy 76
Sandwich Islands 539
Saniga, Bob 158
Santa Cruz Islands 534, 538
Santiago 590
Santo Domingo 602
Sao Tome 674
Sao Tome Principe 674
Sarazen, Gene 97, 99, 106
Sargeant, James 155, 182
satellites 297
   Aussat 3 launched 12
   'space junk' burns over NSW 14
satellites, of the planets 548-8
Saudi Arabia 33, 674-5, 745
Sayers, W. E. 136
Scarf, Eddie 222

Scaysbrook, Jim 138
Schaefer, Manfred 184
Schenke, Betty 137
Schipp, Hon. J. J. 454
Schlam, Sig 188
Schuback, I. 137
Schumann, John 530
Schuppan, Vern 141, 226, 227
Scotland 700-1
Scott, Bon 311
Scott, Gordon 300
Scott, John 181
Scott, Hon. Michael 97, 98, 224
Scott, O. R. 311
Screaming Believers 522
Screaming Tribesmen 519
Scullin, James Henry 294, 470
Scullin Monolith 542
sculling *see* rowing and sculling
scurvy 538
sea turtle 416
Seaman, Paul 408
Searle, Henry 160
seat belts 296
Second Fleet 289
secret ballot 291
Sedgman, Frank 201, 225
Seekers, The 301
Segovia, Andre, death of 30
Sellwood, Neville 121, 122
semaphore alphabet 320
Senegal 675-6
Seoul 635
Sestier, Walter 111
Setches, Kay 486
Seychelles 676-7, 746
Seymour, Peter 300
Shack, Peter 453
Sham-Ho, Helen 483
Shanahan, Albert 112
shark, world record 2 tonne 14
Sharp, B. 136
Sharp, John R. 453
Shaw, Albert Edward 300
Shaw, John 155
Shaw, Thomas 135
Shaw, Victoria 311
Shearer, Dale 167
Sheedy, J. H. 135
Sheehy, Dan 176
Sheffield Shield 90-1, 224, 292
Shehadie, Sir Nicholas 5
Shepherd, Dave 172
Sherman, D. 136
Sherrin, Les 137
Shiseido 389
Short, Jim 453
Short, Russell 19
shout (a drink), to 325
Shute, Nevil 311
Sibree, Prudence 486
sidecar racing 189-90
Sieben, Jon 156, 302
Sierra Leone 25, 677-8
Siever, Robert 121
Simmonds, Hon. James Lionel 459

Simms, Eric 166
Sinclair, Rt Hon. Ian 452
Sinclair, Marion 300
Singapore 25, 678-9, 746
  plan for Australian studies program 12
Singapore (city) 678
Singleton, Hon. M. 455
Sirius, HMS (ship) 4
Skilton, Bob 55, 59
Skinner, Edward S. 211
Skyhooks 518
Slack, Andrew 173
Slaughtermen 524
Slavin, Frank 68
sleepers 324
Sloan, Sally 529
slouch hat 325
Small, Judy 530
Smith, Alan 165
Smith, Dave 73
Smith, Dick 301
Smith, Greedy 311
Smith, Jonathon 68
Smith, Norman 'Wizard' 142
Smith, Pat 137
Smith, Peter 188
Smith, Phil 172
Smith, Hon. R. Rowland 455
Smith, Ross and Keith 293, 426
Smith, Tommy 227
Smith, Warwick 453
smoking
  advertising banned 13, 43
  banned on domestic airlines 15
  new warning labels 9
  tobacco markets 389
Snead, J. C. (Jerry) 97, 99
Sneddon, Rt Hon. Sir Billy Mackie 300
Snell, J. 136
Snowdon, Lord 305
Snowy Mountains Authority 295
soccer 182-6
  first recorded game 224
  World Cup Finals 226
Sochacki, Julie 302
Social Security Enquiry System (SSES) 399
Society Islands 531, 533, 537
Sofia 582
Solar Car Race 14
solar cooker 4
solar system 546-9
Solomon Islands 534, 536, 538, 540, 679-80, 746
  call to end French rule in New Caledonia 37
Somalia 680
Somerville, Robert 7
son of a gun 325
Soutar, D. G. (Dan) 101
South Africa 22, 26-7, 28-9, 35, 39, 41, 44, 50, 681-2, 746
  Archbishop Tutu in Australia 3
  Pat Cash plays in 14
South Australia
  average weekly earnings 373
  Bannon Ministry 456-7
  becomes an independent colony 290
  exports 383

extreme maximum temperatures 278
extreme minimum temperatures 277
flag 309
highest daily rainfall 278
imports 377
industrial disputes 369
map of Australia 239
population growth 261
public holidays 1989 237
resident population 262-3, 265
responsible government 291
retention rates of secondary school students 445
school terms 1989 238
women in parliament 478-9
South-East Asia Treaty Organisation (SEATO) 295
South Georgia Island 732
South Korea *see* Korea, South
South Sandwich Island 732
South Sea Company 537
Southern and Antarctic Territories 720
Southern Cross 544-5
Southern Cross (plane) 427, 428
Southern Cross (yacht) 180
sovereigns 348
Spain 30, 39, 682, 746
  exploration of the Pacific 535-6
Sparkes, Bill 68
Sparklers 524
Spears, Bob 93, 94, 224
Special Broadcasting Service (SBS) 5
speedcar racing 190
speedway racing 186-93
  Australian championship winners 189
  see also motor racing; motorcycling
Speerin, Peter 189
Speight, Julie 93
Spender, John 452
Spinks, Charlie 188
Spirit of Australia (powerboat) 157, 226
Split Enz 518, 520
sport 7, 51-229
Spratly Islands 49
Springfield, Rick 518, 520
sprint car racing 191
Spy V. Spy 522, 524
Spycatcher (book) 5
Spyker, Hon. Peter Cornelius 459
Squires, Bill 69, 70, 224
Sri Lanka 22, 23, 27, 30, 34, 40, 41, 683, 746
  Australian missionary killed 12
Stampede II (hydroplane) 158
Stanley 729
Staples, Hon. Peter 451
Star Bush, South African 421
Starr, Bongo 311
stars 556-60
  Southern Cross 544-5
  visibility from the Southern Hemisphere 561
Stars and Stripes (yacht) 180
State of Origin Rugby League matches 165
Stawell Gift (athletics) 211-14, 224, 226
Stems 523
Stephen, Sir Ninian 12, 571
Stephen, Septimus 172
Stephenson, Jan 102, 227
Sterns, Niels 300

Stevens, Brian 158
Stevens, John Cox 180
Stewart, C. 136
Stewart, Ian 55, 59
Stirling, Captain James 290
stock car racing 191
stock market crash 14, 39
Stockholm 686
Stone, John 452
stowaway 14
Stratton, J. P. (James) 216
Strickland, Shirley 153-4, 155, 209, 210
strikes 292
  derivation of 325
  see also industrial disputes
Stuart, Barry 196
Stuntz, J. 161
Sturrock, Jock 181, 182, 301
Style Manual 12
Sucre 579
Sudan 683-4, 746
Sudan War 292
sugar industry 388
suicide 258
Sullivan, Bob 172
Sullivan, Kathryn 478
Sulman, Tom 141
Summons, Arthur 166, 172
Sumner, Hon. Christopher John 457
Sun (Sydney newspaper), closed 19
Sunraycer (solar car) 14
Super-Cross 138
superannuation 285-6
supernova 5, 25
surf boats 196
surf lifesaving 195-7, 323
surfing 193-5
  magazines 515
Suriname 684-5
Sutherland, Dame Joan 17, 301
Sutton, Gary 94
Suva 608
Svalbard 724
Swan River Colony 290
Swaziland 685-6, 746
Sweden 39, 686-7, 746
Swinbourne, Bert 182
Swindell, Judge Frederick 108
Switzerland 42, 49, 687-8, 746
Sydney 14, 325
  City Council sacked 6
  Clean Air Act 7
  midget submarines enter harbour 294
Sydney, HMAS (aircraft carrier) 432
Sydney Airport
  bomb scare 5
  flooded 17
Sydney Citizens Against the Monorail (SCAM) 8
Sydney Cove 288
Sydney Cove Redevelopment Authority 10
Sydney Cricket Ground 14
  last Rugby League Grand Final 13
Sydney Cup (horse race) 128-9
Sydney Football Stadium 13
Sydney Gazette and New South Wales Advertiser
  (newspaper) 289

Sydney Harbour Bridge 8, 18, 294
Sydney Harbour Tunnel 8
Sydney Morning Herald (newspaper) 290, 505
Sydney to Hobart Ocean Race 177, 178-9
Sydney Tower, protestors ascend 9
Syme, David and Ebenezer 291
Symonds, Elizabeth 483
Syria 40-1, 688-9, 746
System for Asbestos Litigation (SAL) 400

Taggart, Joan 481
Tahiti 40, 531, 538, 540, 719
Taipei 689
Taiwan 46, 689-90
    exports from 382
    imports from 378
Talbot, Michael 7
Tall Ships 15, 17
Tall Tales & True 522
Tamil civil war 22, 23, 27, 30, 34, 40
Tangerine Dream 523
Tangney, Dorothy 294
Tanner, Roscoe 207
Tanzania 690-1
Tarawa 634
Taree (yacht) 182
Taronga Park Zoo 3
Tarrant, Captain Harley 139, 141
Tasker, Rolly 181
Tasman, Abel 288, 537
Tasman Bridge 305
Tasmania 537
    average weekly earnings 373
    circumnavigated 539
    exports 383
    extreme maximum temperatures 278
    extreme minimum temperatures 277
    first settlement 289
    flag 309
    Gray Ministry 457-8
    highest daily rainfall 279
    imports 377
    industrial disputes 369
    land bridge 288
    map of Australia 239
    officially renamed 291
    population growth 261
    public holidays 1989 237
    resident population 262-3, 265
    responsible government 291
    retention rates of secondary school students 445
    school terms 1989 238
    women in parliament 479, 484-5
Tatchell, T. 197
Tate, Hon. Michael 450
Tauntau, Vic 194
taxation
    arrival tax 16, 17
    fringe benefits tax 343
    income tax 292, 343
    problem solving unit set up 18
    protester pays with trees 17
    tax avoidance 343
    see also income tax
Taylor, Hon. Ian Frederick 460
Taylor, Jim 32

Taylor, John 121
Taylor, Major 93
Taylor, Ollie 76
Taylor, Sir Patrick Gordon 428
Tayshus, Austen 311
tea ladies 19
Tegucigalpa 620
Tehran 625
Telecom 15, 353
telegraph
    overland 291
    overseas cable 291
telephone 292, 294
television 15, 295, 296, 297
temperatures 277-8
Tennant, Kylie 300
Tenni, Hon. Martin James 546
tennis 197-207
    Australian Open Championship 201-4
    first recorded game 224
    magazines 515
    Pat Cash plays in South Africa 14
    Pat Cash wins at Wimbledon 9
Terra Australis 535, 537, 538
Terre Adelie 720
textile industry 389
Thailand 24, 36, 43, 48, 691-2, 747
Thalidomide 16
Thatcher, Charles 527
Thatcher, Margaret 31
Theile, David 155
Theodore, E. G. 294
Therry, John 289
Thimphu 578
Think Big (racehorse) 112, 122
Third Fleet 289
Thomas, Bill 121
Thomas, Diana 103
Thomas, Kevin 221
Thomas, R. V. 204
Thompson, Freda 428
Thompson, Hector 70
Thompson, J. N. 54
Thompson, Jack (jockey) 112
Thompson, Joe 112
Thompson, Junior 74, 78
Thompson, Mickey 229
Thompson, Patricia 300
Thompson, W. 96
Thompson, William 68
Thomson, Jeff 90
Thomson, Peter 99, 100, 101, 103, 106, 225
Thorn, Frank 73
Thornett, Dick 166, 172
Thornett, Ken 167
Thorp, Roland 300
Thorpe (Billy) and the Aztecs 520
Tibet 33, 38
Tillet, Louis 519, 522
Times on Sunday (newspaper), closed 19
Timor 540
tips 325
Tirana 565
Titus, Jack 56
TNT Ltd 10, 353
To the Ends of the Earth (book) 7

INDEX • 791

tobacco *see* smoking
Tobago 693-4, 747
Tobin, Les 137
Todd, John 56
Todd, Rod 56
Todd, Ron 55
Togo 692
Tokelau 531, 723
Tokyo 630
Tonelli, Mark 156
Toner, Pauline 486
Tonga 39, 531, 535, 537, 539, 540, 693, 747
Toogood, John 103
Toogood, Peter 103
Toohey, Jack 121
Toombs, Ron 138
Torrens system 291
Torres, Luis Vaez de 288, 536
Torres Strait 288
Torshavn 715
Tortola 727
totemism 403
touch and go 325
Tour de France (bicycle race) 93, 95
tourism 435, 436-9
  growth 18
  overseas travel by Australians 440-3
Townsend, William Edwin 300
  visitors to Australia 435
Toyer, John 158
Toyota 390
track and field 208-14
Trade Unions, Australian Council of 293
Trade Unions, Congress of International Confederation of Free 19
Trans-Australian Airlines (TAA) 295, 297, 429
transplants 6, 14
travel
  by Australians, overseas 440-3
  prices 350-2
  visitor arrivals by month of visit 436-9
  visitors to Australia 435
  to work 444
  see also tourism
Trench, C. 197
Trevaskis, Tom 222
Trezise, Hon. Neil Benjamin 459
Trickett, Edward 159
Triffids 517, 522
Trigg, Frank Elliott 'Sam' 300
Trimble, Robert 300
Trimbole, Robert 300
Trinidad 693-4, 747
Tripoli 640
Tristan da Cunha 733
Trott, Albert 85
trotting and pacing 215-21
trout 418
Troy, Hon. Gavin John 460
Truk 540
Trumper, Victor 161, 162
Truth 326
Tuamotu Archipelago 531, 537, 538
tuberculosis 419
Tubman, Ken 142
Tubuai Islands 531
Tucker, Kenrick 95

Tuckey, Wilson 452
Tulloch (racehorse) 120, 122
Tunis 694
Tunisia 25, 41, 694-5, 747
Turkey 25, 36-7, 43, 695-6, 747
Turks, The 733
Turnbull, A. D. (Tony) 216
Turnbull, Don 204
Turnbull, Reginald 463
Turnbull, Wendy 227
Turner, R. 177
Turner, William 135
Turtur, Michael 156
Tutner, A. V. 142
Tutu, Archbishop Desmond 3
Tuvalu 531, 696, 747
Tyree, Alan 399
Tyson, Mike
  annual earnings 227

Uganda 39, 697, 747
Ulan Bator 651
Uluru (Ayer's Rock) 12
unemployment rates 19, 294, 346
  see also labour force
Unilever 389
Union Flag 309
Union Jack 309
Union of Soviet Socialist Republics 22, 23, 24, 26, 29-30, 32, 34-5, 41, 44, 46, 48-9, 697-9
  Jewish families emigrate from 15
  nuclear agreement with United States 37, 42, 43
  Soviet spies in US embassy 24
  United States President to visit 49
United Arab Emirates 699-700, 747
United Australia Party (UAP) 462, 464
United Kingdom 700-1
  external territories 725-33
  see also Great Britain
United Nations 747
United States of America 21-2, 23, 24, 27, 28, 30, 31-2, 35, 37-9, 41, 43, 45, 47, 49, 701-2, 748
  appeals to Poland 38
  exports from 382
  external territories 733-4
  freely associated states 734-5
  imports from 378
  nuclear agreement with USSR 42, 43
  nuclear ships in Palau 34
  Pacific territories 735-7
  pilot shot down over Nicaragua 44
universal male suffrage 291
University of Sydney founded 290
University of Technology, Sydney 13
unleaded petrol 297
Unwin, Ben 188
Ups & Downs 523
Uren, Tommy 73
Uruguay 702-3, 748
Utjesenovic, Doug 184

Vaduz 641
Vails, Nelson 95
Vallentine, Josephine 14, 480
Valletta 647
Valley, The 725

INDEX

van Diemen, Anthonie 537
Van Diemen's Land 288
   convict women 314-20
   transportation ends 291
Van Praag, Lionel 188, 192, 225, 228
Van Praagh, Peggy 296
Vanda, Harry 311
Vanderfield, Dr Roger 174
Vanstone, Amanda 453, 479
Vanuatu 39, 43, 534, 535, 536, 703-4, 748
   call to end French rule in New Caledonia 37
   see also Australia del Espiritu Santo
Varey, Frank 229
Vatican 24, 25, 704, 741
Vegemite 293
Venetians 518
Venezuela 704-5, 748
Vetri, Victoria 311
Victoria
   average weekly earnings 373
   becomes a separate colony 291
   Cain Ministry 458-9
   exports 383
   extreme maximum temperatures 278
   extreme minimum temperatures 277
   flag 309
   highest daily rainfall 278
   imports 377
   industrial disputes 369
   map of Australia 239
   population growth 261
   public holidays 1989 237
   resident population 262-3, 265
   responsible government 291
   retention rates of secondary school students 445
   school terms 1989 238
   women in parliament 479, 485
Victoria (city) 676
Victoria (Hong Kong) 730
Victorian Football Association (VFA) 54, 56
Victorian Football League (VFL) 54, 56
   clubs 57-8
   Premiership winners 58-9
Victorian Rules 54
videos
   magazines 511
   top 50 renting titles 492-3
Vidler, Ken 196
Vienna 572
Vientiane 637
Vietnam, Republic of 21, 23-4, 31, 49, 296, 705-6, 748
Vietnam War 9, 432
   Australian veterans march in a 'welcome home' parade 13
Vila 703
Vinnicombe, Martin 94
Virgin Islands 737
   see also British Virgin Islands
visitors to Australia 435, 436-9
Vivian, Brian 100
Vizents, Allan 300
Voitre, Keith 121
Von Nida, Norman 99, 101
voting
   compulsory 293
   at eighteen 296
   federal franchise 293
   preferential 292
   secret ballot 291
   universal male suffrage 291
   for women 292
VRC Derby (horse race) 131-2

Wade, Sir Charles 173
wages 333-4, 339, 346
   see also money
Wainer, Bertram 300
Waite, Captain Arthur 139, 141, 142, 225
Waite, Terry 21
Wake Island 735
Waldheim, Dr Kurt 27, 49
Waldock, Michael 302
Wales 700-1
Walker, Bill 55
Walker, Hon. Evan Herbert 458
Walker, Grace 158
Walker, Johnnie 300
Walker, Judith 483
Walker, Kath 16
Walker, Max 90
Walker, Murray 94
Wallace, Sir Gordon 300
Wallaroo Club 172
Wallis 531, 720
Wallis, Samuel 538
Walmsley, Robyn 481
Walsh, Senator Peter 19, 450
Walsh, Hon. Ronald William 459
Walters, Doug 90
Walters, Shirley 479
Waltzing Matilda 292, 325
Warby, Ken 157, 226
Ward, Eddie 464
Wardell, Robert 110
Warne-Smith, Ivor 55, 59
Warner, Anne Marie 484
Warnock, R. 92
Warren, John 184
Warsaw 667
Warwick, John 311
Washington, DC 701
water buffalo, Asian 418, 423
Waterhouse, Bill 12
Waterhouse, Henry 289
Waters, Dean 75, 77
Waters, Guy 75, 77
Waters, Troy 75
Watkins, Jacqueline 487
Watson, A. 93
Watson, John Christian 466-7
Watson, Dr Judyth 487
Watson, Tom 97
Watson, W. 107
Watts, J. D. (Jack) 217
Watts, Tom 158
Wave Hill cattle station 401
Way Jnr, George 4
Wearne, Phillip 300
Weddings Parties Anything 519, 522
Weise, Hon. Barbara Jean 457, 484
Welinski, Andre 142

Wellington 656
Wenden, Michael 155
Wentworth, William Charles 110, 289
West, Claude 194
West, Hon. G. B. 454
West, Hon. Stewart 451
West Australian Airways 426, 430
West Germany see Germany, West
Western Australia
  average weekly earnings 373
  Burke Ministry 459-60
  exports 383
  extreme maximum temperatures 278
  extreme minimum temperatures 277
  flag 309
  highest daily rainfall 278
  imports 377
  industrial disputes 369
  map of Australia 239
  population growth 261
  public holidays 1989 237
  referendum to secede 294
  resident population 262-3, 265
  responsible government 291
  retention rates of secondary school students 445
  school terms 1989 238
  transportation of convicts ends 291
  women in parliament 480
Western Samoa 540, 706-7, 748
Weston, George 389
Weston, Robert 300
Westpac 8, 352
what the dickens, meaning 326
Whatmore, Charles 139
White, C. 136
White, Hon. David Ronald 458
White, Graham 196
White, Harold 300
White, Harry 112
White, Hon. James 112
White, Jeff 73, 75
White, Patrick 296, 301
White, Peter 140, 452
White, Vic 74
White Cross 522
white elephant 326
Whitfield, Beverley 155
Whitlam, Gough 14, 296, 476-7
  CIA involved in dismissal of 17
Whitton, Ivo 98
Whyte, L. A. 97
Whyte, Lew 194
Wickham, Alick 193
Wicks, Debbie 221
Wilding, Anthony 198
Wilkes, Hon. Frank Noel 459
Wilkinson, Arthur, 'Bluey' 188, 192
Wilkinson, Jim 185
Willard, James 204
Willemstad 721
Williams, Sir Edward 301
Williams, Harry Llewellyn 103
Williams, Ken 174
Williams, Miss 136
Williams, Tom 70
Williamson, Bill 121

Williamson, John 530
Willis, Bill 191
Willis, Hon. Ralph 450
Wills, Miss 93
Wills, Thomas Wentworth 53
Wilmot, Robert 176
Wilson, A. 'Toch' 112
Wilson, Betty Rebecca 91
Wilson, Janet 486
Wilson, Hon. Keith James 460
Wilson, Peter 184, 185
Wimbledon Championship 9, 199
Winchester, J. 95
Windbag (racehorse) 112, 122
Windever, Sir Victor 300
Windle, Bob 155
Windsor, Harry 300
windsurfing see sailboarding
wine 388
  exports 385-7
  sales 384
Winser, Legh 103, 104
Winter, A. W. 'Nick' 155, 208, 209
Winter, John 155, 208
Winter Olympics 154, 156-7, 225
Wirraway 431
Wisdom, Elsie 141
Wollongong (NSW) 8, 13
women
  in Australian parliaments 478-9
  convicts 314-20
  cricket 91-2
  cycling 93
  elected to federal parliament 294
  enfranchised 292
  equal employment and advancement 17
  equestrian 96
  first appointed to the High Court 297
  first university to admit 290
  golf 102
  jockeys 121
  in the labour force, by age 359
  lawn bowls 136
  magazines 515
  ordination of 5, 11, 13
  out of the labour force 362-3
  sailboarding 175
  tennis 197, 207
  track and field 209
  trotting and pacing 221
Wood, Bill 55
Wood, David 95
Wood, Mervyn 155, 160
Wood, Patrick O'Hara 198, 204
Woodcock, Tommy 113
Woods, Dean 156
Woods, Samuel (Sammy) 85
Woodward, Mr Justice 401
Woomera 9, 11
Wootton, Frank 121
workforce see labour force
working days lost 370
World Boxing Association (WBA) 77, 79
World Boxing Council (WBC) 77, 79
World Championship Formula One Grand Prix 140
World Cup (golf) 100

World Cup (soccer) 185, 186
World Drivers Championship 151-2
World Jamboree 16
World Series (Rugby League) 163
World Series Cricket 90
World War I 293, 431
World War II 294, 295, 432
Worrell, Eric 300
wowser 326
Wran, Neville 5, 18
Wray, Leonora 103
Wreckery 519, 522
Wren, John 216
wrestling 221-3
Wright, Ken 172
Wright, Peter 5
Wright, Wilbur 426
Wright, Wild 68
Wrigley, Henry 300
Wylde, Wilbur 311
Wylie, Arthur 140
Wylie, Bruce 176
Wynne, Nancye 204

X 523

Yabsley, Hon. M. R. 455

yachting *see* sailing and yachting
Yahoo II (yacht) 177
Yakich, Nick 197
Yalumba 388
Yaounde 586
Yap 540
Yaren 653
Yemen, North 707-8, 748
Yemen, South 708
Yemmerrawanyea Kebbarah 17
Yirrkala land case 401
Young, Cliff 214
Young, Sir Guilford Clyde 300
Young, Jack 188, 192, 225, 228
Young, Mick 17, 19
Young, Simone 302
Young, Steve 227
Young Endeavour (ship) 14
Yugoslavia 709, 748
Yunupingu, Galarrwuy 301

Zaire 710-11
Zakharov, Olive 480
Zambia 47, 711, 749
Zep, Jo Jo 311
Zimbabwe 711-12, 749